UNIVERSITY DEGREE COURSE OFFERS

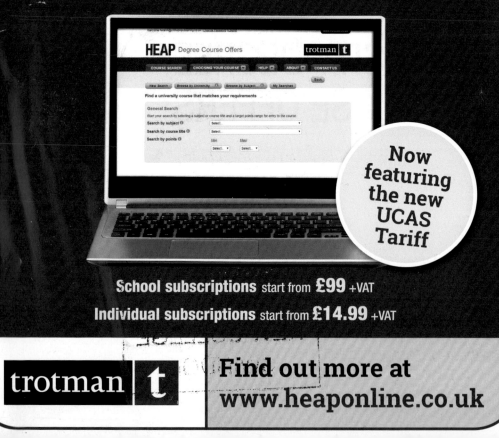

M|P|W

Mander Portman Woodward

HEAP 2017

UNIVERSITY DEGREE COURSE OFFERS

The essential guide to winning
your place at university

Brian Heap

47th edition
with the new UCAS Tariff

HEAP 2017: UNIVERSITY DEGREE COURSE OFFERS

In order to ensure that *Heap 2017: University Degree Course Offers* retains its reputation as the definitive guide for students wishing to study at UK universities and other higher education institutions, hundreds of questionnaires are distributed, months of research and analysis are undertaken, and painstaking data checking and proofing are carried out.

Every effort has been made to maintain absolute accuracy in providing course information and to ensure that the entire book is as up to date as possible. However, changes are constantly taking place in higher education so it is important for readers to check carefully with prospectuses and websites before submitting their applications. The author, compilers and publishers cannot be held responsible for any inaccuracies in information supplied to them by third parties or contained in resources and websites listed in the book.

We hope you find this 47th edition useful, and would welcome your feedback as to how we can ensure the 48th edition is even better.

Author Brian Heap
Advertising Sales Crimson Publishing Services
Contact Simon Connor on 020 8445 4464 or email simonc@crimsonpublishingservices.co.uk

This 47th edition published in 2016 by Trotman Publishing an imprint of Crimson Publishing Ltd, 19–21c Charles Street, Bath BA1 1HX
www.trotman.co.uk

© Brian Heap 2016

A CIP record for this book is available from the British Library

ISBN 978 1 909319 88 2

Typeset by IDSUK (DataConnection) Ltd
Printed and bound in Spain by GraphyCems

M|P|W

Mander Portman Woodward

Founded in 1973, **Mander Portman Woodward (MPW)** is one of the UK's best known groups of independent sixth-form colleges with centres in London, Birmingham and Cambridge. It offers over 40 subjects at A level with no restrictions on subject combinations and a maximum class size of eight.

MPW has one of the highest numbers of university placements each year of any independent school in the country. It has developed considerable expertise over the years in the field of applications strategy and is frequently consulted by students facing some of the more daunting challenges that may arise in areas such as getting into Oxbridge, Medicine or Law. This expertise is available to a wider audience in the form of **Getting Into** guides on higher education and the seminars that are run for sixth-formers at its London centre. We are grateful to Trotman for publishing the Guides and hope that this latest edition of **University Degree Course Offers** will prove as popular and useful as ever.

If you would like to know more about MPW Courses or Getting Into guides, please telephone us on 020 7835 1355 or visit our website, www.mpw.ac.uk.

'Our first stop for students sourcing university information and the courses they are interested in.'
Lorraine Durrands, Careers Co-ordinator, Kesteven & Grantham Girls' School, 2016

'The students find it an invaluable resource.'
Rebecca Mockridge, Sixth Form Administrator, Queen's College Taunton, 2016

'It's a really quick way of getting an overview of the standard offer for a particular course or course type ... and is helpful in terms of advising both on offer conditions, but also when choosing A-level subjects for particular interests.'
Etta Searle, Careers Co-ordinator, Wyke 6th Form College, 2016

'The definitive guide to university degree course offers ... clearly laid out and remarkably easy to navigate ... should be stocked in every sixth form library.'
Teach Secondary, October 2015

'Degree Course Offers is probably the UK's longest running and best known reference work on the subject.'
Education Advisers Limited, 2015

'HEAP University Degree Course Offers is simply "The Bible" for careers advisors and students alike.'
Stephen King, MA (Lib), School Librarian and Careers Coordinator, The Duke of York's Royal Military School, 2015

'We buy this book every year and use it all the time, it offers essential careers and higher education advice.'
Dr Beth Linklater, Director of Student Support, Queen Mary's College, 2015

'A fantastic and invaluable resource for UCAS advisers, university applicants and their parents.'
Mark Collins, Head of Economics/Business & Careers, St Teresa's School, 2015

'An invaluable guide to UK degree entry requirements. My "go to" handbook when kick-starting the UCAS process.'
Susan Gower, Head of Year 9 and Careers, Croydon High School, 2015

'I've been a UCAS adviser for most of the past 25 years and I've come to rely on HEAP for clear guidance and up to date info.'
Gabe Crisp, Aspire Co-ordinator, Worthing College, 2015

'An excellent one-stop shop for finding out information on different universities and courses.'
Oswestry School, 2013

'Degree Course Offers is my bible and I couldn't be without it ... it gives students focus and saves them time.'
South Thames College, 2013

'Degree Course Offers remains an essential component of our careers library, providing a quick reference to entry requirements and course specific tips for university applications.'
Mid Kent College, 2013

'Degree Course Offers ... will keep aspirations realistic.'
www.newteachers.tes.co.uk, 2011

'An extremely useful guide ....'
Woodhouse Grove School, 2010

'Look out for Brian Heap's excellent books on choosing higher education courses.'
Carre's Grammar School, 2010

'Degree Course Offers *by Brian Heap – not to be missed. Invaluable.'*
Maidstone Grammar School, 2010

'Degree Course Offers ... *a really good resource.'*
www.positive-parents.com, 2009

'The guru of university choice.'
The Times, 2007

'For those of you going through Clearing, an absolute must is the Degree Course Offers *book. This guide operates subject by subject and gives you each university's requirements, standard offers and, most importantly, "course features".'*
The Independent, August 2007

'Brian Heap, the guru of university admissions.'
The Independent, September 2007

'I would like to take this opportunity to congratulate you in maintaining the quality and currency of the information in your guide. We are aware of its wide range and its reputation for impartiality.'
University Senior Assistant Registrar, 2007

'This guide contains useful, practical information for all university applicants and those advising them. I heartily recommend it.'
Dr John Dunford, General Secretary, Association of School and College Leaders, 2005

'An invaluable guide to helping students and their advisers find their way through the maze of degree courses currently on offer.'
Kath Wright, President, Association for Careers Education and Guidance, 2005

'No one is better informed or more experienced than Brian Heap in mediating this range of information to university and college applicants.'
Careers Education and Guidance, October 2005

'The course-listings bible.'
The Guardian, June 2005

CONTENTS

AUTHOR'S ACKNOWLEDGEMENTS

This book and the website www.heaponline.co.uk are a team effort, in which I, my editor Della Oliver, with Miranda Lim and Emily Kendall and a supporting team at Trotman Publishing, make every effort each year to check the contents for accuracy, including all offers from official sources, up to the publication deadline in March. My team's effort throughout the months of preparation therefore deserves my gratitude and praise. In respect of the offers however, the reader should recognise that offers are constantly changing depending on the range and abilities of candidates and therefore are shown as 'typical' or target offers.

In the ever-changing world of higher education, research must be on-going and each year many individuals are involved in providing additional up-to-date information. These include Caroline Russell at UCAS, Sarah Hannaford at the Cambridge Admissions Office, Helen Charlesworth at the University of Oxford Public Relations Office, Lisa Murphy, OT, at Cheltenham General Hospital and my daughter Jane Heap (Head of Careers) at Putney High School. In addition, my appreciation goes to HEIST for information on graduate destinations, the many universities and colleges which annually update information, and individual admissions staff who return our requests for information, along with the many teachers and students who furnish me with information on their experiences. To all, I add my grateful thanks.

Finally, I should also add my appreciation to my wife Rita for her 'on the spot' administrative help (and patience!) through 47 years of publication!

Brian Heap BA, DA (Manc), ATD
May 2016

ABOUT THIS BOOK

Heap 2017: University Degree Course Offers for 47 years has been a first-stop reference for university and college applicants choosing their courses in higher education by providing information from official sources about how to choose courses and how admissions tutors select students. **Brand new content for this year's edition includes points offers listed under the new UCAS Tariff in Chapter 7 and Appendix 1, and new university admission details in Chapter 3.**

For 2017/18 higher education applicants, this edition of *Heap 2017: University Degree Course Offers* again aims to provide the latest possible information from universities to help equip them to obtain a degree course place in a fiercely competitive applications process. This level of competition will make it essential for every applicant to research carefully courses and institutions.

There are many students who restrict their applications to a small number of well-known universities. They must realise that in doing so they are very likely to receive rejections from all of them. Applicants must spread their choices across a wide range of institutions.

How do applicants decide on a strategy to find a place on a degree course? There are more than 1200 separate degree subjects and over 50,000 Joint and Combined Honours courses so how can applicants choose a course that is right for their futures? What can applicants do to find a course place and a university or college that is right for them?

Heap 2017: University Degree Course Offers is intended to help applicants find their way through these problems by providing the latest possible information about university course offers from official sources, and by giving guidance and information about:

- **Degree courses** – what Honours level courses involve, the range and differences between them, and what applicants need to consider when choosing and deciding on subjects and courses
- **Universities and higher education colleges** – the range and differences between universities and colleges, and the questions applicants might ask when deciding where to study
- **Admissions information** for every university (listed in **Chapter 3**)
- **Target A-level grades/UCAS points offers** (listed in points order in the subject tables in **Chapter 7**) for 2017 entry to Honours degree courses in universities and colleges, with additional Appendix data for applicants with Scottish Highers/Advanced Highers, the Advanced Welsh Baccalaureate – Skills Challenge Certificate, the International Baccalaureate Diploma, BTEC, the Extended Project, Music examinations and Art and Design Foundation Studies qualifications
- **The UCAS applications process** – what to do, when to do it and how to prepare the personal statement in the UCAS application
- **Universities' and colleges' admissions policies** – how admissions tutors select students
- **Which universities, colleges and courses use admissions tests for entry**
- **Finance, fees and sources of help**
- **Graduate destinations data for each subject area**
- **Action after results day** – and what to do if your grades don't match your offer
- **Entry to UK universities and higher education colleges for international students**

Heap 2017: University Degree Course Offers provides essential information for all students preparing to go into higher education in 2017, covering all stages of researching, planning, deciding and applying to courses and universities. To provide the latest possible information the book is compiled each year between October and March for publication in May and includes important data from the many universities and colleges responding to questionnaires each year.

Every effort is made to ensure the book is as up to date as possible. Nevertheless, the increased demand for places is expected to lead to offers changes during 2017/18, and after prospectuses have been published. Some institutions may also discontinue courses as a result of government cuts and the changes in tuition fees. It will be essential for applicants to check institutions' websites **frequently** to find out any changes in offers, course availability and requirements. If you have any queries, contact admissions staff without delay to find out the latest information as institutions, for many courses, will be looking for a very close, if not precise, match between their requirements and what you offer in your application, qualifications and grades.

Heap 2017: University Degree Course Offers is your starting point for moving on into higher education and planning ahead. Used in conjunction with *Choosing Your Degree Course & University* (see **Appendix 4**) it will take you through all the stages in choosing the course and place of study that is right for you.

Brian Heap
May 2016

Every effort has been made to maintain absolute accuracy in providing course information and to ensure that the entire book is as up to date as possible. However, changes are constantly taking place in higher education so it is important for readers to check carefully with prospectuses and websites before submitting their applications.

You and 600,000 other students, including 100,000 from EU and overseas countries, will be applying for university this year with a choice of over 1200 degree subjects and 50,000 course variations in over 150 universities and colleges in the UK. The scale of such an exercise may seem enormous but there are ways and means of simplifying the exercise and making the important decisions, starting with the choice of possible degree courses.

Choosing your A-levels (or equivalent qualifications) is often done on the basis of selecting your best subjects or those you find the most interesting, and of course those which are required for a chosen career. All subjects tend to fall into one of three categories: academic, vocational and practical, with the competitive universities usually preferring the challenging academic subjects, eg English, history, mathematics and the sciences (see **Chapter 4** under 'Applications to the Russell Group'). As a rule, you would be advised to include at least two such subjects in your choice. Non-academic subjects would normally include communication and media studies, leisure studies and performing arts (see **Chapter 3** under London (LSE)), etc although some of these subjects, including art, dance and drama are also relevant when choosing these degree courses, with selection for the last three being based on portfolio work and auditions.

Most courses in higher education lead to a degree or a diploma and for either you will have to make a subject choice. You have two main options:

A Choosing a course that is either similar to, or the same as, one (or more) of your school subjects, or related to an interest outside the school curriculum, such as Anthropology, American Studies, Archaeology. See **Section A** below.

B Choosing a course in preparation for a future career, for example Medicine, Architecture, Engineering. See **Section B** below and also **Appendix 3**.

SECTION A
Choosing your course by school subjects
Before making the choice of school subjects there is an important point to consider about university degree courses. A degree course is not always a training path for a career; its purpose is also to teach you how to learn through self-directed study, decision making and research when much of your time will be spent working on your own, so that when you have graduated you can easily adapt to any task whatever the career. Thus it is not unusual, for example, to find students who have degrees in history or languages going on to train as accountants and lawyers and many other non-scientific careers. From one university a recently qualified dentist went on to train as an airline pilot!

Some school subjects you are taking, however, are closely linked to a number of possible degree courses and the following list will provide you with a good starting point to your research.

Accounting Accountancy, Accounting, Actuarial Mathematics, Banking and Finance, Business Studies (Finance), Economics, Finance Investment and Risk, Financial Mathematics, Financial Software Engineering, Management Sciences, Mathematics. See also **Section B**.

Ancient history Archaeology, Biblical Studies, Classical Greek, Classics and Classical Civilisation, Latin, Middle and Near Eastern Studies.

Arabic Arabic. See also **Languages** below.

Archaeology Ancient History, Anthropology, Archaeological Sciences, Archaeology, Bioarchaeology, Classical Civilisation, Conservation of Objects in Museums and Archaeology, Egyptology, Geology, History, Marine Archaeology, Viking Studies. See also **Section B**.

Art and design Art, Fine Art, Furniture Design, Graphic Design, Photography, Textile Design, Theatre Design, Three-Dimensional Design, Typography and Graphic Communication. See also **Section B**.

Bengali Bengali. See also **Languages** below.

Biblical Hebrew Hebrew, Religious Studies, Theology.

Biology Agricultural Sciences, Animal Behaviour, Audiology, Bioinformatics, Biological Sciences, Biology, Biomedical Sciences, Biotechnology, Dental Hygiene, Ecology and Conservation, Environmental Sciences, Genetics, Human Embryology, Infection and Immunity, Life Sciences, Medicine, Microbiology, Molecular Sciences, Natural Sciences, Physiology, Plant Biology, Plant Science, Veterinary Science, Zoology. See also **Section B**.

Business Accounting, Banking, Business Management, Business Statistics, Computing, Economics, Entrepreneurship, Finance, Hospitality Management, Human Resource Management, Information Systems, Logistics, Management Sciences, Marketing, Mathematics, Publishing, Retail Management, Transport Management, Web Design and Development. See also **Section B**.

Chemistry Biochemistry, Cancer Biology, Chemical Engineering, Chemical Physics, Chemistry, Dentistry, Environmental Sciences, Fire Engineering, Forensic Sciences, Medicinal Chemistry, Medicine, Microbiology, Natural Sciences, Nutritional Biochemistry, Pharmacology, Pharmacy, Veterinary Science, Virology and Immunology. See also **Section B**.

Chinese Chinese. See also **Languages** below.

Classics and classical civilisation Ancient History, Archaeology, Classical Studies, Classics, Greek (Classical), Latin.

Communication studies Advertising, Communication Studies, Drama, Education, English Language, Information and Library Studies, Journalism, Languages, Linguistics, Media and Communications, Psychology, Public Relations, Publishing, Speech Sciences. See also **Section B**.

Computing Artificial Intelligence, Business Information Systems, Computer Engineering, Computer Science, Computing, Cybernetics, E-Commerce, Electronic Engineering, Games Technology, Intelligent Product Design, Multimedia Systems Engineering, Network Management and Security, Robotics, Software Engineering. See also **Section B**.

Critical thinking (Check acceptability with universities and colleges: subject may not be included in offers.)

Dance Arts Management, Ballet Education, Choreography, Dance, Drama, Education, Music, Musical Theatre, Performance Management, Performing Arts, Sport and Exercise, Street Arts, Theatre and Performance, Theatre Arts, Writing Directing and Performance. See also **Section B**.

Design technology Food Technology, Manufacturing Engineering, Product Design, Sport Equipment Design, Systems and Control. See also **Section B**.

Drama and theatre studies Acting, Community Drama, Costume Production, Creative Writing, Dance, Drama, Education Studies, English Comedy: Writing and Performance, International Theatre, Music, Performing Arts, Scenic Arts, Scriptwriting, Set Design, Stage Management, Theatre Arts, Theatre Practice. See also **Section B**.

Dutch Dutch. See also **Languages** below.

Economics Accountancy, Banking, Business Administration, Business Economics, Business Studies, Development Studies, Economics, Estate Management, Finance, Management Science, Mathematics, Political Economy, Politics, Quantity Surveying, Sociology, Statistics.

Electronics Computing, Electronics, Engineering (Aeronautical, Aerospace, Communication, Computer, Software, Systems), Mechatronics, Medical Electronics, Multimedia Technology, Technology. See also **Section B**.

English language and literature Communication Studies, Comparative Literature, Creative Writing, Drama, Education, English Language, English Literature, Information and Library Studies/Management, Journalism, Linguistics, Media Writing, Philosophy, Publishing, Scottish Literature, Scriptwriting, Theatre Studies.

Environmental sciences Biological Sciences, Biology, Earth Sciences, Ecology, Environment and Planning, Environmental Management, Environmental Sciences, Forestry, Geography, Geology, Land Management, Marine Biology, Meteorology, Oceanography, Outdoor Education, Plant Sciences, Sustainable Development, Wastes Management, Water Science, Wildlife Biology, Wildlife Conservation, Zoology.

French French, International Business Studies, International Hospitality Management, Law with French Law. See also **Languages** below.

General studies (Check acceptability with universities and colleges: subject may not be included in offers.)

Geography Development Studies, Earth Sciences, Environmental Policy, Environmental Sciences, Estate Management, Forestry, Geographical Information Science, Geography, Geology, Land Economy, Meteorology, Oceanography, Surveying, Town and Country Planning, Urban Studies, Water Science.

Geology Earth Sciences, Geography, Geology, Geophysical Sciences, Geosciences, Meteorology, Mining Engineering, Natural Sciences, Oceanography, Palaeontology and Evolution, Planetary Sciences, Water and Environmental Management. See also **Section B**.

German German, International Business Studies, International Hospitality Management, Law with German Law. See also **Languages** below.

Government/Politics Development Studies, Economics, Global Politics, Government, History, Human Rights, Industrial Relations, International Politics, Law, Peace Studies, Politics, Public Administration, Social and Political Science, Social Policy, Sociology, Strategic Studies, War Studies.

Gujarati Gujarati. See also **Languages** below.

Health and social care Early Childhood Studies, Environmental Health, Health and Social Care, Health Promotion, Health Psychology, Health Sciences, Health Studies, Nursing, Nutrition, Public Health, Social Sciences, Social Work, Sport and Health, Working with Children and Young People, Youth and Community Work. See also **Section B**.

History African Studies, American Studies, Ancient History, Archaeology, Art History, Classical Civilisations, Classical Studies, Education, Egyptology, Fashion and Dress History, History, International Relations, Law, Literature, Medieval Studies, Museum and Heritage Studies, Philosophy, Politics, Russian Studies, Scandinavian Studies, Scottish History, Social and Economic History, Theology and Religious Studies, Victorian Studies.

Home economics Culinary Arts Management, Design and Technology Education, Food and Consumer Management, Food Science, Home Economics (Food Design and Technology), Hospitality Management, Nutrition.

Information and communication technology Business Information Systems, Communications Systems Design, Communications Technology, Digital Communications, Electrical and Electronic Engineering, Geographic Information Science, Information and Library Studies, Information Management, Information Sciences, Information Systems, Internet Engineering, Mobile Computing, Multimedia Computing, Telecommunications Engineering. See also **Section B**.

Italian Italian. See also **Languages** below.

Japanese Japanese. See also **Languages** below.

Languages Languages, Modern Languages, Translating and Interpreting. **NB** Apart from French and German – and Spanish for some universities – it is not usually necessary to have completed an A-level language course before studying the many languages (over 60) offered at degree level. Many universities provide opportunities to study a language in a wide range of degree courses. See also **The Erasmus+ Programme** details in **Chapter 4**.

Law Criminal Justice, Criminology, European Business Law, Human Rights, International Business, International Relations, Law, Legal Studies, Police Sciences, Social Sciences, Sociology, Youth Justice. See also **Section B**.

Leisure studies Adventure Tourism Management, Countryside Recreation and Tourism, Equine Business Management, Events Management, Fitness and Health, Health and Leisure Studies, Hospitality and Leisure Management, Leisure Marketing, Outdoor Leadership, Personal Fitness Training, Sport and Leisure Management, Sport Leisure and Culture, Sports Education, Tourism Management, Tourism Marketing.

Mathematics Accountancy, Actuarial Mathematics, Aeronautical Engineering, Astrophysics, Business Management, Chemical Engineering, Civil Engineering, Computational Science, Computer Systems Engineering, Control Systems Engineering, Cybernetics, Economics, Engineering Science, Ergonomics, Financial Mathematics, Further and Additional Mathematics, Geophysics, Management Science, Materials Science and Technology, Mechanical Engineering, Meteorology, Naval Architecture, Physics, Quantity Surveying, Statistics, Systems Analysis, Telecommunications.

Media studies Advertising, Animation, Broadcasting, Communication Studies, Creative Writing, English, Film and Television Studies, Journalism, Mass Communication, Media courses, Media Culture and Society, Media Production, Media Technology, Multimedia, Photography, Publishing, Radio Production and Communication, Society Culture and Media, Translation Media and French/Spanish, Web and Broadcasting. See also **Section B**.

Modern Greek Greek. See also **Languages** above.

Modern Hebrew Hebrew. See also **Languages** above.

Music Audio and Music Production, Creative Music Technology, Education, Music, Music Broadcasting, Music Informatics, Music Management, Music Systems Engineering, Musical Theatre, Musician, Performance Arts, Popular and World Musics, Sonic Arts. See also **Section B**.

Persian Persian. See also **Languages** above.

Philosophy Classical Studies, Cultural Studies, Divinity, Educational Studies, Ethics, History of Ideas, History of Science, Law, Mathematics, Natural Sciences, Philosophy, Politics Philosophy and Economics, Psychology, Religious Studies, Social Sciences, Theology.

Physics Aeronautical Engineering, Architecture, Astronomy, Astrophysics, Automotive Engineering, Biomedical Engineering, Biophysics, Chemical Physics, Civil Engineering, Communications Engineering, Computer Science, Cybernetics, Education, Electrical/Electronic Engineering, Engineering Science, Ergonomics, Geophysics, Materials Science and Technology, Mechanical Engineering, Medical Physics, Meteorology, Nanotechnology, Naval Architecture, Oceanography, Optometry, Photonics, Planetary Science, Quantum Informatics, Radiography, Renewable Energy, Telecommunications Engineering.

Polish Polish. See also **Languages** above.

Portuguese Portuguese. See also **Languages** above.

Psychology Advertising, Animal Behaviour, Anthropology, Artificial Intelligence, Behavioural Science, Childhood Strudies, Cognitive Science, Counselling Studies, Criminology, Education, Human Resource Management, Marketing, Neuroscience, Nursing, Politics, Psychology, Social Sciences, Sociology, Speech and Language Therapy. See also **Section B**.

Punjabi Punjabi. See also **Languages** above.

Religious studies Abrahamic Religions (Christianity, Islam and Judaism), Anthropology, Archaeology, Biblical Studies, Christian Youth Work, Comparative Religion, Divinity, Education, Ethics, History of Art, International Relations, Islamic Studies, Jewish Studies, Philosophy, Psychology, Religious Studies, Social Policy, Theology.

Russian Russian. See also **Languages** above.

Sport and physical education Chiropractic, Coaching Science, Community Sport Development, Dance Studies, Exercise and Health, Exercise Science, Fitness Science, Football Studies, Golf Studies, Osteopathy,

Outdoor Pursuits, Physical Education, Physiotherapy, Sport and Exercise Science, Sport and Health, Sport Coaching, Sport Equipment Design, Sport Management, Sport Marketing, Teaching (Primary) (Secondary).

Statistics Actuarial Studies, Business Analysis, Business Studies, Informatics, Management Sciences, Statistics. See also **Mathematics** above and **Section B** Mathematics-related careers.

Travel and tourism See **Section B**.

Turkish Turkish. See also **Languages** above.

Urdu Urdu. See also **Languages** above.

SECTION B
Choosing your course by career interests
An alternative strategy for deciding on the subject of your degree or diploma course is to relate it to your career interests. Choose a career interest below and check the range of degree courses open to you.

Accountancy Accountancy, Accounting, Actuarial Science, Banking, Business Studies, Economics, Finance and Business, Finance and Investment, Financial Services, Management Science, Real Estate Management, Risk Management.

Actuarial work Actuarial Mathematics, Actuarial Science, Actuarial Studies, Financial Mathematics, Risk Analysis and Insurance.

Agricultural careers Agri-Business, Agricultural Engineering, Agriculture, Animal Sciences, Aquaculture and Fishery Sciences, Conservation and Habitat Management, Countryside Management, Crop Science, Ecology, Environmental Science, Estate Management, Forestry, Horticulture, Landscape Management, Plant Sciences, Rural Resource Management, Soil Science, Wildlife Management.

Animal careers Agricultural Sciences, Animal Behaviour and Welfare, Biological Sciences, Bioveterinary Science, Equine Management/Science/Studies, Veterinary Nursing, Veterinary Practice Management, Veterinary Science, Zoology.

Archaeology Ancient History, Anthropology, Archaeology, Bioarchaeology, Classical Civilisation and Classics, Egyptology, Geography, History, History of Art and Architecture, Viking Studies.

Architecture Architectural Design, Architectural Technology, Architecture, Building, Building Conservation, City and Regional Planning, Civil Engineering, Conservation and Restoration, Construction Engineering and Management, Interior Architecture, Stained Glass Restoration and Conservation, Structural Engineering.

Art and Design careers Advertising, Animation, Architecture, Art, Design, Digital Media Design, Education (Art), Fashion and Textiles, Fine Art, Games Art and Design, Glassware, Graphic Design, Illustration, Industrial Design, Jewellery, Landscape Architecture, Photography, Stained Glass, Three-Dimensional Design.

Astronomy Astronomy, Astrophysics, Mathematics, Natural Sciences, Planetary Geology, Physics, Quantum and Cosmological Physics, Space Science, Space Technology and Planetary Exploration.

Audiology Audiology, Education of the Deaf, Human Communication, Nursing, Speech and Language Therapy.

Banking/Insurance Accountancy, Actuarial Sciences, Banking, Business Studies, Economics, Financial Services, Insurance, Real Estate Management, Risk Management.

Biology-related careers Agricultural Sciences, Animal Sciences, Biochemistry, Biological Sciences, Biology, Biomedical Sciences, Biotechnology, Cell Biology, Ecology, Education, Environmental Biology, Environmental Sciences, Freshwater Science, Genetics, Immunology, Life Sciences, Marine Biology, Medical Biochemistry, Medicine, Microbiology, Molecular Biology, Natural Sciences, Oceanography, Pharmacy, Plant Science, Physiology, Wildlife Conservation, Zoology.

Book Publishing Advertising, Business Studies, Communications, Creative Writing, Illustration, Journalism, Media Communication, Photography, Printing, Publishing, Science Communication, Web and Multimedia.

Brewing and Distilling Biochemistry, Brewing and Distilling, Chemistry, Food Science and Technology, Viticulture and Oenology.

Broadcasting Audio Video and Digital Broadcast Engineering, Broadcast Documentary, Broadcast Media, Broadcast Technology and Production, Digital Media, Electronic Engineering (Broadcast Systems), Film and TV Broadcasting, Media and Communications Studies, Media Production, Multimedia, Music Broadcasting, Outside Broadcast Technology, Radio Journalism, Television Studio Production, TV Production, Video and Broadcasting.

Building Architecture, Building Conservation, Building Services Engineering, Building Studies, Building Surveying, Civil Engineering, Estate Management, General Practice Surveying, Land Surveying, Quantity Surveying.

Business Accountancy, Advertising, Banking, Business Administration, Business Analysis, Business Studies, Business Systems, E-Commerce, Economics, Estate Management, European Business, Hospitality Management, Housing Management, Human Resource Management, Industrial Relations, Insurance, Logistics, Management Sciences, Marketing, Property Development, Public Relations, Publishing, Supply Chain Management, Transport Management, Tourism.

Cartography Geographic Information Systems, Geographical Information Science, Geography, Land Surveying.

Catering Consumer Studies, Culinary Arts Management, Dietetics, Food Science, Hospitality Management, International and Hospitality Business Management, Nutrition.

Chemistry-related careers Agricultural Science, Biochemistry, Botany, Ceramics, Chemical Engineering, Chemistry, Colour Chemistry, Education, Environmental Sciences, Geochemistry, Materials Science and Technology, Medical Chemistry, Nanotechnology, Natural Sciences, Pharmacology, Pharmacy, Physiology, Technologies (for example Food, Plastics).

Computing Artificial Intelligence, Bioinformatics, Business Computing, Business Studies, Computer Engineering, Computer Games Development, Computer Science, Computers, Electronics and Communications, Digital Forensics and System Security, Electronic Engineering, Games Design, Information and Communication Technology, Internet Computing, Mathematics, Multimedia Computing, Physics, Software Systems, Telecommunications, Virtual Reality Design.

Construction Architectural Technology, Architecture, Building, Building Services Engineering, Civil Engineering, Construction Management, Fire Risk Engineering, Landscape Architecture, Quantity Surveying, Surveying, Town and Country Planning.

Dance Ballet Education, Choreography, Dance, Drama, Movement Studies, Performance/Performing Arts, Physical Education, Theatre Studies.

Dentistry Biochemistry, Dental Materials, Dental Technician, Dentistry, Equine Dentistry, Medicine, Nursing, Oral Health Sciences, Pharmacy.

Drama Dance, Drama, Education, Movement Studies, Musical Theatre, Scenic Arts, Teaching, Theatre Management.

Education Ballet Education, British Sign Language, Childhood Studies, Coach Education, Deaf Studies, Early Years Education, Education Studies, Education with QTS, Education without QTS, Music Education, Physical Education, Primary Education, Psychology, Secondary Education, Social Work, Special Educational Needs, Speech and Language Therapy, Sport and Exercise, Teaching, Technology for Teaching and Learning, Youth Studies.

Electronics Automotive Electronics, Avionics, Computer Systems, Computer Technology, Computing, Digital Electronics, Digital Media Technology, Electronic Design, Electronic Engineering, Electronics, Information Systems, Internet Engineering, Mechatronics, Medical Electronics, Motorsport Electronic Systems, Multimedia Computing, Software Development, Sound Engineering.

Engineering Engineering (including Aeronautical, Aerospace, Chemical, Civil, Computing, Control, Electrical, Electronic, Energy, Environmental, Food Process, Manufacturing, Mechanical, Motorsport, Nuclear, Product Design, Software, Telecommunications), Geology and Geotechnics, Horology, Mathematics, Physics.

Estate Management Architecture, Building, Civil Engineering, Economics, Estate Management, Forestry, Housing Studies, Landscape Architecture, Property Development, Real Estate Management, Town and Country Planning.

Food Science and Technology Biochemistry, Brewing and Distilling, Chemistry, Culinary Arts, Dietetics, Food and Consumer Studies, Food Safety Management, Food Science and Technology, Food Supply Chain Management, Fresh Produce Management, Hospitality and Food Management, Nutrition, Public Health Nutrition, Viticulture and Oenology.

Forestry Arboriculture, Biological Sciences, Countryside Management, Ecology, Environmental Science, Forestry, Horticulture, Plant Sciences, Rural Resource Management, Tropical Forestry, Urban Forestry.

Furniture Design Furniture Design, Furniture Production, History of Art and Design, Three-Dimensional Design, Timber Technology.

Geology-related careers Chemistry, Earth Sciences, Engineering (Civil, Minerals), Environmental Sciences, Geochemistry, Geography, Geology, Land Surveying, Oceanography, Soil Science.

Graphic Design Advertising, Graphic Design, Photography, Printing, Web Design.

Health and Safety careers Biomedical Informatics, Biomedical Sciences, Community and Health Studies, Environmental Health, Exercise and Health Science, Fire Science Engineering, Health and Social Care, Health Management, Health Promotion, Health Psychology, Health Sciences, Holistic Therapy, Nursing, Occupational Safety and Health, Paramedic Science, Public Health, Public Services Management. (See also **Medical careers**.)

Horticulture Agriculture, Crop Science, Horticulture, Landscape Architecture, Plant Science, Soil Science.

Hospitality Management Business and Management, Culinary Arts Management, Events and Facilities Management, Food Science, Food Technology, Heritage Management, Hospitality Management, Human Resource Management, International Hospitality Management, Leisure Services Management, Licensed Retail Management, Spa Management, Travel and Tourism Management.

Housing Architecture, Estate Management, General Practice Surveying, Housing, Social Administration, Town and Country Planning.

Law Business Law, Commercial Law, Consumer Law, Criminal Justice, Criminology, European Law, Government and Politics, International History, Land Management, Law, Legal Studies, Politics, Sociology.

Leisure and Recreation Adventure Tourism, Airline and Airport Management, Business Travel and Tourism, Community Arts, Countryside Management, Dance, Drama, Event Management, Fitness Science, Hospitality Management, International Tourism Management, Leisure Management, Movement Studies, Music, Physical Education, Sport and Leisure Management, Sport Development, Sports Management, Theatre Studies, Travel and Tourism.

Library and Information Management Administration, Business Information Systems, Digital Media, Education Studies, Information and Communication Studies, Information and Library Studies, Information Management, Information Sciences and Technology, Management and Marketing, Media and Cultural Studies, Media Communications, Museum and Galleries Studies, Publishing.

Marketing Advertising, Business Studies, Consumer Science, E-Marketing, Health Promotion, International Business, Marketing, Psychology, Public Relations, Retail Management, Sports Development, Travel and Tourism.

Materials Science/Metallurgy Automotive Materials, Chemistry, Engineering, Glass Science and Technology, Materials Science and Technology, Mineral Surveying, Physics, Polymer Science, Sports Materials, Textile Science.

Mathematics-related careers Accountancy, Actuarial Science, Astronomy, Banking, Business Decision Mathematics, Business Studies, Computer Studies, Economics, Education, Engineering, Financial Mathematics, Mathematical Physics, Mathematics, Physics, Quantity Surveying, Statistics.

Media careers Advertising, Broadcasting, Communications, Computer Graphics, Creative Writing, Film/Video Production, Journalism, Media, Multimedia, Photography, Public Relations, Psychology, Visual Communication.

Medical careers Anatomy, Biochemistry, Biological Sciences, Biomedical Sciences, Chiropractic, Dentistry, Genetics, Human Physiology, Immunology, Medical Engineering, Medical Sciences/Medicine, Nursing, Occupational Therapy, Orthoptics, Osteopathy, Pathology and Microbiology, Pharmacology, Pharmacy, Physiotherapy, Psychology, Radiography, Speech and Language Therapy, Sports Biomedicine, Virology.

Music Commercial Music, Creative Music Technology, Digital Music, Drama, Folk and Traditional Music, Music, Music Composition, Music Education, Music Industry Management, Music Performance, Music Production, Music Studies, Musical Theatre, Performance/Performing Arts, Popular Music, Sonic Arts, Sound and Multimedia Technology, Theatre Studies.

Nautical careers Marine Engineering, Marine Studies, Nautical Studies, Naval Architecture, Oceanography, Offshore Engineering, Ship Science.

Naval Architecture Boat Design, Marine Engineering, Marine Studies, Naval Architecture, Offshore Engineering, Ship Science, Yacht and Powercraft Design, Yacht Production.

Nursing Anatomy, Applied Biology, Biochemistry, Biological Sciences, Biology, Dentistry, Education, Environmental Health and Community Studies, Health Studies, Human Biology, Medicine, Midwifery, Nursing, Occupational Therapy, Orthoptics, Physiotherapy, Podiatry, Psychology, Radiography, Social Administration, Speech and Language Therapy, Veterinary Nursing. (See also **Medical careers**.)

Nutrition Dietetics, Food Science and Technology, Health Promotion, Human Nutrition, Nursing, Nutrition, Sport and Fitness.

Occupational Therapy Art, General and Mental Nursing, Occupational Therapy, Orthoptics, Physiotherapy, Psychology, Social Sciences, Speech and Language Therapy.

Optometry Applied Physics, Optometry, Orthoptics, Physics.

Photography/Film/TV Animation, Communication Studies (some courses), Digital Video Design, Documentary Communications, Film and Media, Graphic Art, Media Studies, Moving Image, Multimedia, Photography.

Physics-related careers Applied Physics, Astronomy, Astrophysics, Avionics and Space Systems, Education, Electronics, Engineering (Civil, Electrical, Mechanical), Laser Physics, Mathematical Physics, Medical Instrumentation, Molecular Physics, Nanotechnology, Natural Sciences, Optometry, Physics, Planetary and Space Physics, Quantum and Cosmological Physics, Theoretical Physics.

Physiotherapy Chiropractic, Exercise Science, Nursing, Orthoptics, Osteopathy, Physical Education, Physiotherapy, Sport and Exercise, Sports Rehabilitation.

Production Technology Engineering (Manufacturing, Mechanical), Materials Science.

Property and Valuation Management Architecture, Building Surveying, Estate Agency, Property Investment and Finance, Property Management and Valuation, Quantity Surveying, Real Estate Management, Residential Property, Urban Land Economics.

Psychology Advertising, Animal Sciences, Anthropology, Applied Social Studies, Behavioural Science, Business, Cognitive Science, Criminology, Early Childhood Studies, Education, Human Resource Management, Human Sciences, Linguistics, Marketing, Neuroscience, Occupational Therapy, Psychology (Clinical, Developmental, Educational, Experimental, Forensic, Health, Occupational, Social, Sports), Psychosocial Sciences, Public Relations, Social Sciences, Sociology.

Public Administration Applied Social Studies, Business Studies, Public Administration, Public Policy Investment and Management, Public Services, Social Administration, Social Policy, Youth Studies.

Quantity Surveying Architecture, Building, Civil Engineering, Construction and Commercial Management, Environmental Construction Surveying, Surveying (Building, Land and Valuation), Surveying Technology.

Radiography Anatomy, Audiology, Biological Sciences, Clinical Photography, Diagnostic Imaging, Diagnostic Radiography, Digital Imaging, Imaging Science and Technology, Medical Imaging, Moving Image, Nursing, Orthoptics, Photography, Physics, Physiology, Physiotherapy, Radiography, Radiotherapy, Therapeutic Radiography.

Silversmithing/Jewellery Design Silversmithing and Jewellery, Silversmithing Goldsmithing and Jewellery, Silversmithing Metalwork and Jewellery, Three-Dimensional Design.

Social Work Abuse Studies, Applied Social Science, Community Work, Counselling Studies, Early Childhood Studies, Education, Health and Social Care, Human Rights, Journalism, Law, Nursing, Playwork, Politics and Government, Psychology, Public Administration, Religious Studies, Social Administration, Social Policy, Social Work, Sociology, Town and Country Planning, Youth Studies.

Speech and Language Therapy Audiology, Education (Special Education), Linguistics, Nursing, Occupational Therapy, Psychology, Radiography, Speech and Language Therapy.

Sport and Physical Education Coaching Sciences, Exercise Sciences, Fitness Science, Health and Fitness Management, Leisure and Recreation Management, Physical Education, Sport and Recreational Studies, Sport Journalism, Sports Psychology, Sports Science, Sports Studies.

Statistics Business Studies, Economics, Informatics, Mathematics, Operational Research, Population Sciences, Statistics.

Surveying Building Surveying, General Practice Surveying, Property Development, Quantity Surveying, Real Estate Management.

Technology Audio Technology, Dental Technology, Design Technology, Food Science and Technology, Football Technology, Logistics Technology, Medical Technology, Music Studio Technology, Paper Science, Polymer Science, Product Design Technology, Sports Technology, Technology for Teaching and Learning, Timber Technology.

Textile Design Applied Art and Design, Art, Clothing Studies, Fashion Design, Interior Design, Textile Design (Embroidery, Constructive Textiles, Printed Textiles), Textile Management.

Theatre Design Drama, Interior Design, Leisure and Recreational Studies, Theatre Design, Theatre Management, Theatre Studies.

Three-Dimensional Design Architecture, Industrial Design, Interior Design, Theatre Design, Three-Dimensional Design.

Town and Regional Planning Architecture, Architecture and Planning, City and Regional Planning, Environmental Planning, Estate Management, Geography, Housing, Land Economy, Planning and Development, Population Sciences, Property Planning and Development, Spatial Planning, Statistics, Sustainable Development, Town and Regional Planning, Transport Management, Urban and Regional Planning.

Transport Air Transport Engineering, Air Transport Operations, Air Transport with Pilot Training, Business Studies, Civil and Transportation Engineering, Cruise Operations Management, Industrial Design (Transport), Logistics, Planning with Transport, Supply Chain Management, Sustainable Transport Design, Town and Regional Planning, Urban Planning Design and Management.

Typography and Graphic Communication Design (Graphic and Typographic Design), Digital Graphics, Fine Art (Print and Digital Media), Graphic Communication and Typography, Graphic Design, Illustration, Illustration and Print, Printmaking, Publication Design, Publishing, Visual Communication.

Veterinary careers Agricultural Sciences, Agriculture, Anatomical Science, Animal Behaviour and Welfare, Animal Sciences, Bioveterinary Sciences, Equine Dentistry, Equine Science, Medicine, Pharmacology, Pharmacy, Veterinary Medicine, Veterinary Nursing, Veterinary Practice Management, Zoology.

COURSE TYPES AND DIFFERENCES

You will then need to decide on the type of course you want to follow. The way in which Honours degree courses are arranged differs between institutions. For example, a subject might be offered as a single subject course (a Single Honours degree), or as a two-subject course (a Joint Honours degree), or as one of two, three or four subjects (a Combined Honours degree) or a major/minor degree (75% and 25% of each subject respectively). **Chapter 3 University and College Course and Admissions Profiles** gives more information about the different types of courses and provides for each university a resumé of the ways their courses are structured and their admissions policies.

Courses in the same subject at different universities and colleges can have different subject requirements so it is important to check the acceptability of your GCE A-levels/AS and GCSE subjects (or equivalent) for all your preferred courses. Specific GCE A-levels/AS, and in some cases, GCSE subjects, may be stipulated. (See also **Chapter 6** and **Appendix 1** for information on Scottish Highers/Advanced Highers, the Advanced Welsh Baccalaureate – Skills Challenge Certificate, the International Baccalaureate Diploma, BTEC, the Extended Project, Music examinations and Art and Design Foundation Studies, and **Appendix 2** for international qualifications.)

SANDWICH COURSES AND PROFESSIONAL PLACEMENTS

One variation on Single Honours courses is that of the sandwich course, in which students will spend part of their degree course on professional, industrial or commercial placements. Media coverage on student debt and the introduction of higher tuition fees (see **Chapter 2**) highlights the importance of sandwich courses. Many sandwich and placement courses are on offer, in which industrial, commercial and public sector placements take place, usually, in the third year of a four-year degree course. There is also a Work-Based Learning (WBL) programme, which Chester University established several years ago, with some other institutions following suit, in which students take a WBL module in the second year of their degree course. This involves a placement lasting a few weeks when students can have the opportunity to try out possible careers. Other universities and colleges may offer longer placements of periods of six months with different employers for students taking vocational courses.

However, the most structured arrangements are known as 'professional placements' which a number of universities offer and which are very advantageous to students (see the subject tables in **Chapter 7** and university/college websites and prospectuses). Although placements in some fields such as health, social care, and education may be unpaid, in most cases a salary is paid. Where a placement is unpaid the placement period is shorter – 30 weeks – to allow students time to undertake paid work. It is important to note that during the placement year students' tuition fees will be reduced, however the amount payable for tuition fees will vary from university to university. Students studying in England and Wales participating in the one-year Erasmus+ programme (see **Chapter 4**) will pay up to 15% of the full-time fees charged by their home university, with a percentage payable for students in Scotland and Northern Ireland.

The advantages of sandwich courses are quite considerable although students should be aware that in periods of economic uncertainty safeguards are necessary when selecting courses and universities. While students can arrange their own placement, with the approval of their Head of Department, it is more usual for university staff to make contacts with firms and to recommend students. With the present cutbacks, however, some firms may be less likely to take on students or to pay them during their placement. This is an important issue to raise with admissions tutors before applying and it is important also to find out how your studies would continue if placements are not possible. To help you to consider the advantages of sandwich courses, included below are views of some students, employers and university staff. They could well help you decide whether a four-year sandwich course is, for you, preferable to a three-year full-time degree.

Students report ...
'I was able to earn £15,000 during my year out and £4000 during my three-month vacation with the same firm.' (**Bath** Engineering)

'There's really no other better way to find out what you want to do for your future career than having tried it for a year.' (**Aston** Human Resources Management)

'It was a welcome break in formal university education: I met some great people including students from other universities.' (**Kingston** Biochemistry)

'Having experienced a year in a working environment, I am more confident and more employable than students without this experience.' (**Aston** Business Studies)

'At Sanolfi in Toulouse, I learned to think on my feet – no two days were the same.' (**Aston** European Studies)

'I have seen how an organisation works at first-hand, learned how academic skills may be applied in a working environment, become proficient in the use of various software, acquired new skills in interpersonal relationships and communications and used my period away to realign my career perspectives.' (**Aston** European Studies)

'I was working alongside graduate employees and the firm offered me a job when I graduated.' (**Bath** Mathematics)

Employers, too, gain from having students ...
'We meet a lot of enthusiastic potential recruits who bring new ideas into the firm, and we can offer them commercially sponsored help for their final year project.'

'The quality of this student has remained high throughout the year. He will do well for his next employer, whoever that may be. However, I sincerely hope that it will be with us.'

University staff advise ...
'We refer to sandwich courses as professional placements, not "work experience" which is a phrase we reserve for short non-professional experiences, for example summer or pre-university jobs. The opportunity is available to all students but their success in gaining a good placement depends on academic ability.' (**Bath**)

'Where a placement year is optional, those who opt for it are more likely to be awarded a First or an Upper Second compared to those who don't, not because they are given more marks for doing it, but because they always seem to have added context and motivation for their final year.' (**Aston**)

When choosing your sandwich course, check with the university (a) that the institution will guarantee a list of employers, (b) whether placement experience counts towards the final degree result, (c) that placements are paid and (d) that placements are validated by professional bodies. Finally, once you start on the course, remember that your first-year academic performance will be taken into account by potential employers. Now read on!

What do employers require when considering students?
Aston (Biol) Successful second year undergraduates; (Bus) Number of UCAS points, degree programme, any prior experience; (Eng) UCAS points scores and expected degree classification; (Mech Eng) Students interviewed and selected by the company according to student ability, what they are studying and specific needs of the job. **Bath** (Chem) 'Good students': Upper Second or above and non-international students (those without work visas). Students with strong vivisection views rejected; (Mech Elec Eng) Subject-based, eg electronics, aerospace, computing and electrical engineering; (Mech Eng) Good communication, IT and social skills; (Maths) Interest in positions of responsibility, teamwork, integrity, self-motivation, analytical ability, communication, recent work experience, knowledge of the company, desire to work for the company; GCSE maths/English A, AL 144 UCAS points minimum (excluding general studies and critical thinking), predicted 2.1; (Phys) Many organisations have cut-offs regarding students' first-year performance (eg must be heading for a 2.1 although some require better than this), some need students to be particularly good in some areas (eg lab work, computer programming), many require UK nationality with minimum residency condition. **Brunel** Requirements not usually specified except for IT jobs since they need technical skills. **Cardiff Met (UWIC)** (Clsrm Asst) Disclosure and Barring Service (DBS) checks. **Kingston** (Bus Law) Theoretical knowledge and a stated interest in certain areas (eg finance, human resources, marketing, sales, IT), excellent communication skills, teamwork, ability to prioritise, time management and a professional attitude; (Sci) Grades are rarely mentioned: it's usually a specific module or course requirement undertaken by the students that they are looking for, as well as a good attitude, motivation, initiative: a good all-rounder. **Loughborough** (Civ Eng) Target specific courses.

What are the advantages of placements to the students?

Aston (Biol) Many take jobs with their placement employers (eg NHS), gaining valuable research and clinical experience; (Bus) Graduate job offers, sponsorship through the final year of the course, gym membership, staff discounts; (Eng) Some students are fast-tracked into full-time employment and, in some cases, have been given higher starting salaries as a result of the placement with the company; (Mech Eng) Offers of full-time employment on graduation, bursaries for their final year of study, final year projects following placements, better class of degree. **Bath** (Chem) Sponsorships for final year project work, offers of full-time employment, PhD offers and work-to-study courses, industrial references, establishment of prizes; (Maths) Sponsorship in the second year, graduate employment, bonuses during placement, travel abroad during placement, sponsorship during final year; (Phys) Job offers on graduation, sponsored final year, improved study skills for final year, job market awareness, career decisions. **Brunel** Higher percentage of students get Firsts, many students get a job offer from the placement provider, higher salaries often paid to sandwich course students, some students get exemptions from professional exams, eg ACCA, ACA and IMechE. **Cardiff Met (UWIC)** (Clsrm Asst) Good experience in team work, classroom experience, coaching, mentoring: decisions made whether or not to follow a teaching career. **Kingston** (Bus Law) Sponsorships fewer these days but students return with more confidence and maturity and better able to complete their final year; 60% receive job offers on completion of a successful placement; (Sci) Full-time employment on graduation and occasionally part-time work in the final year; many students are encouraged to write their final year dissertation whilst on placement and benefit from the company's support, subject matter and validation. **Loughborough** (Civ Eng) Most students are sponsored by their firms and perform better in their final examinations; (Prod Des) Final year bursary for some students, offer of employment by the sponsor and a final year design project for the sponsor.

MATURE APPLICANTS

There are a great many mature students following first degree courses in UK universities and colleges. The following is a list of key points a group of mature students found useful in exploring and deciding on a university course.

- Check with your nearest university or college to find out about the courses they can offer, for example degrees, diplomas, full-time, part-time.
- Some institutions will require examination passes in some subjects, others may not.
- An age limit may apply for some vocational courses, for example Medicine, Dentistry and Teaching.
- If entry requirements are an obstacle, prospective students should approach their local colleges for information on Access or Open College courses. These courses are fast-growing in number and popularity, offering adults an alternative route into higher education other than A-levels. They are usually developed jointly by colleges of further education and the local higher education institution.
- Demands of the course – how much time will be required for study? What are the assignments and the deadlines to be met? How is your work assessed – unseen examinations, continuous assessment, practicals?
- The demands on finance – cost of the course – loan needed – loss of earnings – drop in income if changing to another career – travel requirements – accommodation – need to work part-time for income?
- The availability and suitability of the course – geographical location – competition for places – where it will lead – student support services, for example childcare, library.
- What benefits will you derive? Fulfilment, transferable skills, social contacts, sense of achievement, enjoyment, self-esteem, career enhancement?
- Why would employers want to recruit you? Ability to adapt to the work scene, realistic and balanced approach, mature attitude to work?
- Why would employers not want to recruit you? Salary expectations, inability to fit in with younger colleagues, limited mobility? However, some employers particularly welcome older graduates: civil service, local authorities, health service, religious, charitable and voluntary organisations, teaching, social/probation work, careers work, housing.

MODULAR COURSES AND CREDIT ACCUMULATION AND TRANSFER SCHEMES (CATS)

Courses can also differ considerably not only in their content but in how they are organised. Many universities and colleges of higher education have modularised their courses which means you can choose modules of different subjects, and 'build' your course within specified 'pathways' with the help and approval of your course tutor. It also means that you are likely to be assessed after completing each module, rather than in your last year for all your previous years' learning. In almost every course the options and modules offered include some which reflect the research interests of individual members of staff. In some courses subsidiary subjects are available as minor courses alongside a Single Honours course. In an increasing number of courses these additional subjects include a foreign language, and the importance of this cannot be over-emphasised, as language skills are increasingly in demand by employers, and studying a language may also open up opportunities for further study abroad. A popular option is the Erasmus+ programme (see **Chapter 4**) which enables university students to apply for courses in Europe for periods of up to a year, with some of the courses being taught in English. Many institutions have introduced Credit Accumulation and Transfer Schemes (CATS). These allow students to be awarded credits for modules or units of study they have successfully completed which are accumulated towards a certificate, diploma or degree. They can also put their completed modules towards higher education study in other universities or colleges. Students wanting to transfer their credits should talk to the admissions office of the university they want to enter as there may be additional special subjects or module requirements for the degree they want to study.

FOUNDATION DEGREES AND FOUNDATION COURSES

Foundation courses, not be confused with Foundation degrees, normally require two years' full-time study, or longer for part-time study. They are also often taught in local colleges and may be taken part-time to allow students to continue to work. In comparison a Foundation degree can lead into the second or final year of related Honours degree courses when offered by the university validating the Foundation degree. Two-year Higher National Diplomas will also qualify for entry into the second or final year of degree courses. These, too, are often offered at universities as well as colleges of further education and partnership colleges linked to universities.

Part-time degrees and lifelong learning or distance learning courses are also often available and details of these can be found on university websites and in prospectuses. Some universities publish separate prospectuses for part-time courses.

NEXT STEPS

When choosing your course remember that one course is not better than another – it is just different. The best course for you is the one which best suits you. To give some indication of the differences between courses, see **Chapter 3** and also *Choosing Your Degree Course & University*, the companion book to *Heap 2017: University Degree Course Offers* (see **Appendix 4**). After provisionally choosing your courses, read the prospectuses again carefully to be sure that you understand what is included in the three, four or more years of study. Each institution differs in its course content even though the course titles may be the same and courses differ in other ways, for example:

- methods of assessment (eg unseen examinations, continuous assessment, project work, dissertations)
- contact time with tutors
- how they are taught (for example, frequency and size of lectures, seminars)
- practicals; field work requirements
- library, computing, laboratory and studio facilities
- amount of free study time available.

These are useful points of comparison between courses in different institutions when you are on an Open Day visit or making final course choices. Other important factors to consider when comparing courses include the availability of opportunities for studying and working abroad during your course, professional body accreditation of courses leading to certain professional careers (see **Appendix 3**), and the career destinations of previous graduates.

Once you have chosen your course subject(s) and the type of course you want to follow, the next step is to find out about the universities and colleges offering courses in your subject area, how much a higher education course will cost you and what financial help is available. The next chapter, **University Choice and Finance** provides information to help you do this.

TAKING A GAP YEAR

Choosing your course is the first decision you need to make, the second is choosing your university and then, for an increasing number, the third is deciding whether or not to take a Gap Year. But there lies the problem. Because of the very large number of things to do and places to go, you'll find that you almost need a Gap Year to choose the right one (although a read through *Your Gap Year* by Susan Griffith (see **Appendix 4**) is a good place to start)!

Planning ahead is important but, in the end, bear in mind that you might be overtaken by events, not least in failing to get the grades you need for a place on the course or at the university you were counting on. This could mean repeating A-levels and re-applying, which in turn could mean waiting for interviews and offers and deferring the start of your 'gap'.

Once you have decided to go, however, it's a question of whether you will go under your own steam or through a Gap Year agency. Unless you are streetwise, or preferably 'world wise', then an agency offers several advantages. Some agencies may cover a broad field of opportunities whilst others will focus on a specific region and activity, such as the African Conservation Experience, offering animal and plant conservation work in game and nature reserves in southern Africa.

When making the choice, some students will always prefer a 'do-it-yourself' arrangement. However, there are many advantages to going through specialist agencies. Not only can they offer a choice of destinations and opportunities but also they can provide a lot of essential and helpful advice before your departure on issues such as health precautions and insurance. Support is also available in the case of accidents or illnesses when a link can be established between the agency and parents.

Finally, in order to enhance your next university or college application, applying for a job for the year could be an even better option than spending a year travelling. Not only will it provide you with some financial security but it will also introduce you to the world of work, which could be more challenging than the Inca Trail!

CHOOSING YOUR UNIVERSITY OR COLLEGE
Location, reputation and Open Days

For many applicants the choice of university or college is probably the main priority, with location being a key factor. However, many students have little or no knowledge of regional geography and have no concept of where universities are located: one student thought that Bangor University (situated in North Wales) was located at Bognor on England's south coast!

Some institutions – probably those nearest home or those farthest away – will be rejected quickly. In addition to the region, location and immediate surroundings of a university or college, applicants have their own individual priorities – perhaps a hectic city life or, alternatively, a quiet life in the country! But university isn't all about studying, so it's not a bad idea to link your leisure interests with what the university or college can offer or with the opportunities available in the locality. Many applicants have theatrical, musical or artistic interests while others have sporting interests and achievements ranging from basketball, cricket and football to riding, rowing, sailing, mountaineering, and even fishing for England!

Some other decisions about your choice of university or college, however, could be made for the wrong reasons. Many students, for example, talk about 'reputation' or base their decisions on league tables. Reputations are fairly clear-cut in the case of some institutions. Oxford and Cambridge are both top world-class universities in which all courses have been established for many years and are supported by first class facilities. In other universities certain subjects are predominant, such as the social sciences at the London School of Economics, and the sciences and technologies at Imperial London.

Many other leading universities in the UK are also very strong in some subjects but not necessarily in all. This is why it is wrong to conclude that a 'university has a good reputation' – most universities are not necessarily good at everything! In seeking advice, you should also be a little wary of school staff who will usually always claim that their own university or college has a 'good reputation'. Teachers obviously can provide good advice on the courses and the general atmosphere of their own institution, but they are not in a good position to make comparisons with other universities.

The best way to find out about universities and colleges and the courses that interest you is to visit your preferred institutions. Open Days provide the opportunity to talk to staff and students although, with thousands of students wandering round campuses, it may be difficult to meet and talk to the right people. Also, many institutions hold Open Days during vacations when many students are away which means that you may only hear talks from the staff, and not have any opportunity to meet students. However, it is often possible to visit a university or college in your own time and simply 'walk in'. Alternatively, a letter to the Head of Department requesting a visit could enable you to get a closer look at the subject facilities. But failing this, you will be invited automatically to visit when you receive an offer and then you can meet the students in the department.

ACTION POINTS
Before deciding on your preferred universities and courses, check out the following points.

Teaching staff
How do the students react to their tutors? Do staff have a flair and enthusiasm for their subject? Are they approachable? Do they mark your work regularly and is the feedback helpful, or are you left to get on with your own work with very little direction? What are the research interests of the staff?

Teaching styles

How will you be taught, for example, lectures, seminars, tutorials? Are lectures popular? If not, why not? How much online learning will you have? How much time will you be expected to work on your own? If there are field courses, how often are they arranged and are they compulsory? How much will they cost?

Facilities

Are the facilities of a high standard and easily available? Is the laboratory equipment 'state of the art' or just adequate? Are the libraries well-stocked with software packages, books and journals? What are the computing facilities? Is there plenty of space to study or do rooms and workspaces become overcrowded? Do students have to pay for any materials?

New students

Are there induction courses for new students? What student services and facilities are available? Is it possible to buy second-hand copies of set books?

Work placements

Are work placements an optional or compulsory part of the course? Who arranges them? Are the placements popular? Do they count towards your degree? Are work placements paid? How long are they?

Transferable skills

Transferable skills are now regarded as important by all future employers. Does the department provide training in communication skills, teamwork, time-management and information technology as part of the degree course?

Accommodation

How easy is it to find accommodation? Where are the halls of residence? Are they conveniently located for libraries and lecture theatres? Are they self-catering? Alternatively, what is the cost of meals in the university refectory? Which types of student accommodation are the most popular? What is the annual cost of accommodation? If there is more than one campus, is a shuttle-bus service provided?

Costs

Find out the costs of materials, accommodation and travel in addition to tuition fees (see below) and your own personal needs. What are the opportunities for earning money, on or off campus? Does the department or faculty have any rules about part-time employment?

FINANCE: WHAT WILL IT COST AND WHAT HELP IS THERE?

Tuition fees and other costs

Tuition fees are charged for degree courses in England, Wales and Northern Ireland. The level of tuition fees for courses has in the past been decided annually and has varied between institutions.

Specific details of the charges to be made by individual universities for each course will be available on websites, but depending on the popularity of universities and certain courses the maximum charge will be £9000, although some institutions will charge a lower level of fees of up to £6000.

You may also have additional charges, depending on your course of study. For example, studio fees for Art courses could reach £400 per year, while for other courses, such as Architecture, Science and Engineering, there could be charges for equipment. There could also be charges for fieldwork trips, study abroad and vacation courses. To find out your likely yearly course costs, in addition to your tuition fees, check with your subject department.

Also, check your fee status if you are planning a sandwich course involving either unpaid or paid placements. You can receive a salary of between £13,000 and £15,000 doing a one-year placement but if you earn more than this you'll need to check your fee status carefully with your finance officer and consult the relevant websites listed below.

Loans Tuition fee loans are available to all students from England, Wales, Scotland and Northern Ireland to help pay their fees. Loan repayments are made only after graduation and, currently, when annual earnings are more than £21,000 a year. Scottish students are eligible to have their fees paid by the Scottish government if they choose to study in Scotland. Students from Wales are currently able to apply for a non-repayable tuition fee grant if their tuition fees exceed £3,900, in addition to receiving a tuition fee loan.

University scholarships These are usually merit-based and are often competitive although some universities offer valuable scholarships to any new entrant who has achieved top grades at A-level. Scholarships vary considerably and are often subject-specific, offered through faculties or departments, so check the availability of any awards with the subject departmental head. Additionally, there are often music, choral and organ awards, and scholarships and bursaries for sporting achievement. Entry scholarships are offered by several universities which normally stipulate that the applicant must place the university as their first choice and achieve the specified high grades. Changes in bursaries and scholarships take place every year so it is important to check university and college websites.

University bursaries These are usually paid in cases of financial need: all universities charging course fees are obliged to offer some bursaries to students from lower-income families. The term 'bursary' is usually used to denote an award to students requiring financial assistance or who are disadvantaged in various ways. Universities are committed to fair access to all students from lower income backgrounds and individual universities and colleges have bursaries, trust funds and sponsorships for those students, although reports suggest that many such students fail to claim the money due to them. These non-repayable awards are linked to the student's family income and vary between universities.

Living costs
Most students spend their first year in university accommodation. This is usually the highest single cost in a typical weekly budget and the costs will vary considerably between universities. Rooms may be single or shared and include catering or self-catering arrangements. Outside university in the private sector additional costs are likely to include heating, electricity, hot water and water rates.

In addition, other living expenses will need to be considered. These include insurance, healthcare, food, books and stationery, photocopying, computing and telephone calls, clothes and toiletries, local travel, travel to and from university, entertainment, socialising and sport or leisure activities.

Help towards living costs
Maintenance loans All full-time students from the UK are eligible for a means-tested maintenance loan for their first undergraduate degree. The maximum amount available is £8,200 a year, which is based on what a student from England might receive if they are studying outside London. Figures for students from Wales, Scotland and Northern Ireland will vary slightly. All students are entitled to a maintenance loan, however part of this amount will be dependent on your household income – in other words, it is means-tested. 'Household income' refers to your family's gross annual income (their income before tax) of the household you live in. Certain pensions contributions and allowances for dependent children are also deducted from the figure to achieve the total sum. This loan will be paid back in the same way as a tuition fee loan, ie once you've graduated or finished your studies, and are earning over £21,000 a year.

Other financial support
Many major organisations also provide financial help to those in various categories. These include the Lawrence Atwell's Charity for British citizens, refugees or asylum seekers aged 16–26 who are from low-income backgrounds, the Prince's Trust for disadvantaged young people aged between 13 and 30, and grants of up to £3,00 for the disabled from the Snowdon Trust.

Similarly, many scholarships are also offered by professional, commercial and other organisations. These include the armed services and the engineering professional organisations, particularly those specialising in civil or mechanical engineering, and also the Institute of Materials, Minerals and Mining. There are also sponsorships in which the student joins a firm on leaving school, combining university study with work experience and with an almost guaranteed offer of full-time employment on graduation. And there is the alternative route of taking a sandwich course and being placed with a firm for a year on full pay, often between £13,000 and £15,000 (see **Chapter 1**).

Some universities also offer additional bursaries to encourage applications from the locality. These may be available to students applying from partner schools or colleges and living in certain postcode areas, in some cases to the brothers and sisters of current students at the university, or to students who have been in care or are homeless. These awards are not repayable.

In addition, students on some health-related courses, for example Dental Hygiene, Nursing, Occupational Therapy, Physiotherapy, Radiography will be eligible for NHS student bursaries. Other bursaries are also payable for programmes funded through the General Social Care Council and also for shortage subjects for those on teacher training courses.

After starting the course, Access to Learning funds are available to help students in financial hardship or through emergency payments for unexpected financial crises. Hardship funds are also offered in very special cases, particularly to students with children or to single parents, mature students and, in particular, to students with disabilities who may also claim the Personal Independence Payment. These payments are made in instalments or as a lump sum or as a short-term loan.

Useful websites   Students from England https://www.gov.uk/student-finance
Students from Scotland www.saas.gov.uk
Students from Wales www.studentfinancewales.co.uk
Students from Northern Ireland www.studentfinanceni.co.uk

For comprehensive finance information see the useful websites above, *University Scholarships, Awards & Bursaries* and other sources listed in **Appendix 4**.

INFORMATION SOURCES

Prospectuses, websites and Open Days are key sources of the information you need to decide where to study and at the back of this book a directory of institutions is provided, with full contact details, for you to use in your research. Other sources of information include the books and websites listed in **Appendix 4**, the professional associations listed in **Appendix 3**, and the websites given in the subject tables in **Chapter 7**. It is important to take time to find out as much as you can about your preferred universities, colleges and courses, and to explore their similarities and differences. The following chapter **University and College Course and Admissions Profiles** gives you information about the types of courses offered by each university and how they are organised. This is important information that you need to know when choosing your university or college because those factors affect, for example, the amount of choice you have in what you study, and the opportunities you have for sandwich placements (see **Chapter 1**). You therefore need to read **Chapter 3** to give you an insight into universities so that you can find the one that is right for you.

UNIVERSITY AND COLLEGE COURSE AND ADMISSIONS PROFILES

UNIVERSITIES, COLLEGES AND THEIR COURSES

Choosing a degree subject is one step of the way to higher education (see **Chapter 1**), choosing a university or college is the next stage (see **Chapters 2** and **9**). However, in addition to such features as location, entry requirements, accommodation, students' facilities and the subjects offered, many universities differ in the way they organise and teach their courses. The course profiles which follow aim to identify the main course features of each of the institutions and to provide some brief notes about the types of courses they offer and how they differ.

Although universities and colleges have their own distinct identities and course characteristics, they have many similarities. Apart from full-time and sandwich courses, one-year Foundation courses are also offered in many subjects which can help the student to either convert or build on existing qualifications to enable them to start an Honours degree programme. All universities and colleges also offer one-year international Foundation courses for overseas students to provide a preliminary introduction to courses and often to provide English language tuition.

ADMISSIONS POLICIES

Although the UCAS application process is standard for all undergraduate Honours degree courses (see **Chapter 4**) the admissions policies adopted by individual departments in universities and colleges often differ, and will depend on the popularity of the course and the quality of applicants.

Mature students (defined as those aged over 21 on entry) are often interviewed. Normal published offers may not apply to mature students. In all institutions certain courses require Disclosure and Barring Service (DBS) checks or medical examinations; students should check these requirements before applying for courses.

The acceptance of deferred entry varies, depending on the chosen course, and many admissions tutors ask that the intention to take a Gap Year be included on the application if firm arrangements have been made.

Several universities and colleges advise that if a student fails to achieve the grades required for an offer, they may still be awarded a place; however, they may receive a changed offer for an alternative course. Applicants are strongly advised to be wary of such offers, unless the course is similar to the original course choice.

Applicants for places at popular universities or for popular courses cannot assume that they will receive an offer even if their predicted grades are the same or higher than a stated standard offer. Even though the government removed the cap on the number of places that universities in England are able to offer from 2015 entry onwards, meaning that they can admit an unlimited number of home and EU undergraduates, not every institution has adopted these reforms.

All institutions have a number of schemes in place to enable admissions tutors to identify and make offers to applicants who, for example, may have had their education affected by circumstances outside their control. A major initiative is Widening Participation in which various schemes can assist school and college students in getting into university. These programmes focus on specific groups of students and communities including:

- students from low participation areas
- low-performing schools and colleges or those without a strong history of progression to higher education
- students with disabilities

- people living in deprived geographical areas, including deprived rural areas
- students from black or ethnic minority backgrounds
- students from the lower socio-economic groups 4–8 including mature learners
- students requiring financial assistance or who are disadvantaged in various ways
- families with little or no experience of higher education
- students from homes with low household incomes
- students returning to study after a period of time spent away.

Applicants are strongly advised to check prospectuses and websites for up-to-date information on admissions and, in particular, on alternative qualifications to A-levels as well as any entrance test to be taken (see also **Chapter 5**). Applicants whose first language is not English should refer to **Chapter 8** for details of the English Language entry requirements.

The following information provides a selection of relevant aspects of admissions policies and practice for the institutions listed.

COURSE AND ADMISSIONS PROFILES

Aberdeen One of the oldest universities in the UK, based on two campuses. Students applying for the MA degree in Arts and Social Sciences are admitted to a degree rather than a subject, selecting from a range of courses in the first year, leading up to the final choice of subject and Honours course in the fourth year. The BSc degree is also flexible but within the Science framework. Engineering students follow a common core course in Years 1 and 2, specialising in Year 3. There is less flexibility, however, in some vocational courses such as Accountancy, Law, Medicine and Dentistry. For some degree programmes, highly qualified applicants may be admitted to the second year of the course. Courses include Divinity and Theology, Education, Music, Life Sciences, Medical Sciences and Business.

In personal statements and the referees' reports, selectors look for evidence of subject knowledge and understanding, commitment, motivation and responsibility, and the ability to cope with a university education.

Abertay A city centre university in Dundee. Courses have a strong vocational bias and are offered in the Schools of Science, Engineering and Technology, Business, Social and Health Sciences, Arts, Media, and Computer Games which is a centre of excellence.

Only applicants for courses in Computer Arts, Computing and Mental Health Nursing are interviewed. Make sure to check the website for the most up-to-date information before applying.

Aberystwyth The University offers Single, Joint and major/minor Honours courses on a modular basis. In Year 1 core topics related to the chosen subject are studied alongside optional subjects. This arrangement allows some flexibility for change when choosing final degree subjects in Years 2 and 3 provided appropriate pathways and module prerequisites are followed. Some students take a year in industry or commerce between Years 2 and 3.

All offers are made on the basis of academic criteria, and personal statements and references are important. Offers will be made predominantly on the basis of the application form but interviews are required for some subjects. Candidates will not normally be interviewed unless there are special reasons for doing so, eg the candidate has been away from study for a long time. Decisions are normally made within four weeks of receiving the application and all those receiving an offer will be invited to visit the University and their chosen academic department. *Most popular subjects 2015* Biology, Drama, English and Creative Writing, Law, Psychology.

Anglia Ruskin The University has campuses in Cambridge, Chelmsford, London and Peterborough. Courses are modular which enables students to choose from a range of topics in addition to the compulsory subject core modules. Courses are delivered by five faculties: the Lord Ashcroft International Business School, Faculty of Arts, Law & Social Sciences, Faculty of Science & Technology, Faculty of Health, Social Care & Education and Faculty of Medical Science. Many programmes have a strong vocational focus, with a focus on employability, and opportunities for placements and/or study abroad.

The University interviews all shortlisted applicants for Art and Design, Paramedic Science, Nursing, Social Work and Midwifery. Some applicants are interviewed for Business courses. Maths and English testing is also used for Nursing, Midwifery, Paramedic Science and Social Work courses.

Arts London University of the Arts London (UAL) is Europe's largest specialist art and design university, comprising six colleges: Camberwell College of Arts, Central Saint Martins, Chelsea College of Arts, London College of Communication, London College of Fashion and Wimbledon College of Arts. Together, the colleges offer a wealth of courses at pre-degree, undergraduate and postgraduate level in Art, Design, Fashion, Media, Communication and Performing Arts.

In addition to formally qualified applicants, UAL welcomes applications from candidates who can demonstrate equivalent skills and knowledge gained from work or life experience. The application process varies depending on the chosen course and whether the applicant is from the UK, EU or from a country outside the EU. Many courses require candidates to submit a portfolio of work and attend an interview as part of the selection process.

Aston A campus university in Birmingham city centre. The University offers modular courses in Single Honours degrees and Joint Honours (usually in related areas). Most degrees allow students to spend the third year on a one-year sandwich placement; over a third of students are offered graduate jobs by their placement employer. Courses are taught in the Schools of Engineering and Applied Science, Languages and Social Sciences, Life and Health Sciences and in the Aston Business School.

Offers are not normally made simply on the basis of UCAS points. Interviews are only used in special cases, for example, mature students, or those with non-standard entry qualifications. BTEC awards are acceptable and a mix of BTEC and A-levels welcomed. High-achieving Level 3 Diploma students in relevant subjects will be considered. Key Skills will be taken into account but will not be included in offers; Access programmes are accepted.

Bangor Bangor University is situated in North Wales between the mountains and the sea. There's a wide range of subjects to choose from including Ocean Sciences, Psychology, Medical Sciences, Linguistics, Chemistry, Engineering and Law. Students can study a Single Honours course or choose to combine the study of two subjects from a range of Joint Honours courses. Some courses offer a four-year undergraduate degree eg MFor, MSci, MArts. There is a placement year/year abroad for some courses. There are other study abroad schemes and taking an International Experience year is another option.

The University considers each application on its merit – assessing your potential to succeed on and benefit from the course. For 2017 entry, the new UCAS Tariff will be used in addition to the usual programme specific requirements. For a degree course, the points total should include at least two GCE A-Level or equivalent Level 3 qualifications (eg BTEC, Access, Irish Highers, International Baccalaureate, Welsh Baccalaureate, Scottish Advanced Highers and others). The University also welcomes applications from mature applicants, individuals with European qualifications and international applicants (subject to minimum English language requirements). *Most popular subjects 2015* Nursing, Psychology.

Bath The University is situated on a large campus outside the city centre. The academic year is divided into two semesters with Single and Combined Honours degrees composed of core units and optional units, allowing students some flexibility in shaping their courses with 10–12 units taken each year. A central feature of all programmes is the opportunity to take a professional placement as part of the degree: this is usually taken as either one 12-month placement or two periods of six months.

Some departments interview promising applicants; those not receiving an offer can obtain feedback on the reasons for their rejection. Students are encouraged to take the Extended Project and to provide details on their personal statement.

Bath Spa Bath Spa offers a full complement of creative, cultural and humanities-based courses, alongside social sciences and sciences. Most courses – Single Honours awards, specialised awards and Combined Honours awards – are part of a flexible modular scheme with students taking up to six modules per year. Some modules are compulsory but there is a good range of optional modules.

All eligible candidates for Art & Design and Music & Performing Arts courses are invited to attend an interview or audition. Applicants with offers for subjects which do not require an audition or interview, and are not taught at a partner college, will be invited to an Applicant Visit Day. Gap years are acceptable, except for the BA Acting course.

Bedfordshire The campuses of Bedfordshire University are situated in Luton, Bedford, Milton Keynes and Aylesbury. Its courses place a strong focus on entrepreneurship, not just employability. Many courses receive professional accreditation. A current Student Internship Scheme (SIS) operates, providing students with the opportunity to gain paid-for work experience, with flexible hours to fit around their studies. A Go Global programme gives students the opportunity to participate in two- or three-week language and cultural programmes and gain real international business experience. There is also a Get Into Sport programme offering students free membership throughout the year.

The University offers advice and guidance to enquirers and applicants throughout the admissions process via its website, http://www.beds.ac.uk/howtoapply/admissions or via its live chat function. The University considers applicants with a wide range of Level 3 qualifications and will hold interviews and auditions for a number of courses.

Birmingham The University is situated on a large campus on the edge of the city centre. Single subject and Joint Honours courses are offered. In Joint Honours courses the two chosen subjects may have common ground or can be disparate, for example Mathematics and a modern language. Some major/minor combinations are also possible. The modular system provides opportunities for students to study a subject outside their main degree. An International Foundation Year (Birmingham Foundation Academy) is available for overseas students from 12-year secondary education systems.

An Unconditional Offers Scheme applies (see website). Courses are academic and 75% of the personal statement should relate to why the applicant wants to study the subject for which they have applied. The Extended Project Qualification (EPQ) is accepted in addition to three A-levels with applicants being made an alternative offer of one grade lower plus the EPQ in addition to the standard offer. The IB offer policy has been reviewed for 2016 so the University now has a standard overall points requirement for every course and makes offers relating to the higher level subject scores. Gap years are acceptable and should be mentioned on the UCAS application or as soon as arrangements have been made. *Most popular subjects 2015* Biosciences, Chemistry, Dentistry, Economics, English, Geography, History, Law, Management, Mathematics, Medicine, Modern Languages, Nursing, Physics, Political Science, Psychology.

Birmingham (UC) The University College offers degrees within the hospitality and tourism sectors, which are awarded by the University of Birmingham. Not only is it Europe's leading specialist in management courses for the culinary arts, hospitality and tourism management, but it is also situated in the heart of Birmingham. Teaching benefits from its central location too: it's based in the conference and hotel quarter, which means opportunities for practical experience are on its doorstep. Its vocational degree courses, experienced tutors and strong links with business give students the skills they need to tackle a career in a range of rapidly expanding industries. There are international study-exchange opportunities including industrial placement opportunities throughout Europe, USA and the UK.

Applications must be made through UCAS. Students can apply online at www.ucas.com. Students wishing to apply for part-time courses should apply direct to the University College. Please contact the Admissions Office for further information.

Birmingham City Courses are offered on eight campuses throughout the city. Many courses have a vocational focus and include sandwich placements. Music is offered through the Birmingham Conservatoire, a music college of international standing. There is also an extensive International Exchange Programme, with many courses abroad being taught in English.

Admissions are administered centrally through the Admissions Unit in the Academic Registry. Some applicants will be called to interview and others invited to the department before an offer is made. If the required grades of an offer are not achieved it may still be possible to be accepted on to a course. Deferred entry is acceptable.

Bishop Grosseteste A single-site university campus close to Lincoln city centre. It has a strong reputation in Primary Education courses but also offers a varied selection of subjects at Foundation and Single

Honours degree level as well as a very large number of joint degrees in subject areas such as psychology, sport and the creative arts. Employability is central to all courses with most incorporating work placements and live projects.

Candidates are advised to attend an Open Day prior to applying. Interview days are a feature of the application process.

Bolton A small, tight-knit university family in Bolton, with an excellent reputation for student support. A range of courses are offered, designed with the workplace in mind, with many offering vocational or professional content and work experience elements.

Applications are welcomed both from those coming straight from college and from those returning to study, with a range of undergraduate, postgraduate, research, pre-degree courses and Foundation years available. They consider applications with A-level/AS General Studies, Extended Project and GCSE equivalency qualifications. Whenever possible, if admissions and academic staff consider that the course applied for is not suitable then an offer for an alternative course may be made. *Most popular subjects 2015* Art and Design, Computing, Media and Creative Technologies, Psychology.

Bournemouth The University has a strong focus on employability and offers a range of undergraduate degrees leading to BA, BSc and LLB. Courses are designed with direct input from employers, there's a work placement opportunity for every student (including opportunities to work and study abroad), and courses are accredited by the biggest names in industry. The University offers subjects in all aspects of Management, Media & Communication, Science & Technology and Health & Social Sciences.

Academic qualifications are not the only factor taken into account when assessing applications. The University looks at each application on an individual basis and offers places based on the potential to succeed on the course. The other factors it considers when assessing applications are: any work or other experience that is relevant to the course, personal achievements, references, and a passion and enthusiasm for the subject. So the personal statement is regarded as an important part of the application process. In some cases, the University will invite applicants to attend an interview and/or selection test.

Bournemouth Arts The University specialises in arts, performance, design and media courses.

Due to the high number of applications on its most popular courses, the University is unable to interview every applicant. There is a selection process which is based on each applicant's UCAS application, qualifications and an electronic portfolio.

BPP A private university with study centres throughout the UK. Courses focus on business and the professions covering business, law, accountancy, marketing and health subjects.

A range of qualifications will be considered.

Bradford A city centre university. Honours degree courses are offered, many of which are vocational, leading to professional accreditation, and include sandwich placements in industry and commerce. Subjects are taught in the Faculty of Engineering and Informatics, the Faculty of Health Studies, the Faculty of Life Sciences, the Faculty of Management and Law and the Faculty of Social Sciences.

Candidates will not be accepted on to any degree course purely on the basis of AS results (including the double award) although Tariff points from AS grades may in most cases be used towards the total Tariff points requirement. For some competitive courses, and in addition to the predicted grades and the academic references, the application will be initially assessed based on the content of your personal statement. Offers are normally based on the UCAS Tariff although subject-specific requirements may also apply. Rejected applicants may be considered for an alternative course.

Brighton BA, BSc and BEng courses are offered, 90% with industrial placements including some in Europe, the USA and Canada. Over 500 courses are on offer at this popular university on the south coast.

The University welcomes applications from students with qualifications and experience other than traditional A-levels. Access courses and BTEC are acceptable alternative qualifications. Courses usually requiring interview include Art and Design, Nursing, Medicine, Pharmacy, Paramedic Practice, Physiotherapy, Podiatry, Product Design, Social Work and Teaching.

Brighton and Sussex (MS) Students have the opportunity to use facilities on the University of Brighton and the University of Sussex campuses, and in Year 1 can choose on which campus they would like to live. However, currently as the BSMS term dates fall outside of the term dates advertised by the University of Sussex and the University of Brighton, applicants have the choice of living at Lewes Court Halls of Residence at Sussex, and Paddock Fields Halls of Residence at University of Brighton. All Year 1 Medical School students are guaranteed accommodation as long as they apply by the deadline (some students who live in the immediate local area may not be able to apply for accommodation due to more applicants requiring housing than rooms available). Students spend their first two years on the Falmer campus and then move on to associated teaching hospitals and community settings. Teaching is 'systems integrated' so students are exposed to the clinical environment from Year 1. Cadaver dissection is also part of the course from Year 1, so students get a real understanding of human anatomy, enhancing their learning experience. As the medical school is small, so are class sizes, meaning that students have a strong relationship with academic and support staff.

Standard offers usually include three A grades at A-level with a minimum of an A grade in Biology and Chemistry. All applicants are required to have a fourth AS at grade B. BSMS will also accept the Extended Project in lieu of a fourth AS at grade B, or a fourth A-level at grade B. All applicants, to include graduates and access applicants, are required to have a grade B in GCSE Maths and English.

Bristol A leading research university offering Single or Joint Honours degrees. A number of courses include a year of industrial experience or the opportunity to study or work abroad. Most courses take three or four years to complete and are modular in structure. Dentistry, Medicine and Veterinary Science are longer in duration and take five or six years to complete. Most science and engineering courses offer a choice of four-year integrated master's (MEng, MSci) as well as the three-year bachelor's (BEng, BSc) courses.

Bristol is a popular university with a high level of competition for places on all courses. A* grades may be included in the offers for some applicants depending on the application and the course applied for; where it may be included, this is shown in the typical offers published in the online course finder. Students choosing to take the Extended Project may receive two offers, one of which includes the Extended Project, for example, AAA, or AAB plus the Extended Project. Up to two applied A-levels may be considered with an A-level. Some courses may consider unit grade information when making a decision. However, as usual, decisions will be made within the context of the whole application, and will not disadvantage applicants who are unable to provide unit grade information. If unit grades are to be taken into account, this will be clearly specified in the relevant admissions statement. Most subjects will consider an application to defer entry, but you should indicate your intention to defer in your personal statement, giving information about your plans. In fairness to applicants applying in the next admissions cycle, the number of deferred places may be limited. Applicants for law will be required to sit the LNAT. The acceptability of resitting qualifications varies depending on the course, and is outlined in each course's admissions statement. The following courses always hold interviews before making an offer: Dentistry, Engineering Design, Medicine, Veterinary Nursing, Veterinary Science and courses including Innovation. Further information is available on the applicants' web pages: bristol.ac.uk/applicants. Information on how to apply can be found in the online course finder: bristol.ac.uk/study/undergraduate/apply. *Most popular subjects 2015* English, Geography, History, Law, Mathematics, Medicine, Psychology, Veterinary Science.

Brunel A campus-based university in West London (Uxbridge). All courses are made up of self-contained modules enabling students, within their scheme of studies, to choose a broad range of topics or greater specialisation as they prefer. Some modern language modules may be taken, depending on the timetable of the chosen subjects. Almost all degree courses are available in a three-year full-time mode or in four-year thick or thin sandwich courses which combine academic work with industrial experience organised through a very successful on-campus placement centre. Some exchange schemes also operate in Europe, USA and other worldwide locations. Degree programmes are offered across three Colleges: College of Engineering, Design and Physical Science (including Computing and Maths), College of Business, Arts and Social Sciences (including Theatre, Education, Journalism, English and Law) and the College of Health and Life Science (including Biomedical Science, Psychology, Physiotherapy, Occupational Therapy and Sport Science). Many courses are accredited by professional institutions recognised by employers. Please follow this link to view available courses: http://www.brunel.ac.uk/courses/course-finder.

All applicants are interviewed for Design, Electrical Engineering, Physiotherapy, Occupational Therapy, Journalism, Theatre and Education courses. The required grades for your course must normally come from at least three full A-level passes, although candidates offering a combination of AS and A-levels or BTEC and A-level courses may be considered. All applicants would need to have five GCSEs at grade C or above to include English language and maths (some courses may also require two science GCSE subjects at grade C).

Buckingham The University is an educational charity with its main income provided by the students who pay full tuition fees. A unique feature is the two-year degree programme which starts in January each year, although some courses may be extended by starting in September; some courses last three years. Courses are offered in Business, Humanities, Law, International Studies, Sciences and Medicine.

Candidates apply through UCAS in the normal way or directly online via the University's website. Applicants may be invited for interview.

Bucks New Students choose from a wide range of subjects in two faculties – Design, Media and Management (Art, Design, Music, Policing, Media, Business, Travel & Tourism, Computing, Law and Sport) and Society and Health (Nursing, Social Work, Operating Department Practitioner, Health and Social Care, Psychology, Social Sciences). The Uxbridge campus is just a short walk from a London Underground tube station and the High Wycombe campus is 40 minutes to Central London.

The University is happy to consider applicants on a case by case basis and mature students (aged 21+) with relevant experience/interest are encouraged to apply. It accepts a range of equivalent qualifications at Level 3 and requires Level 2 maths and English for the majority of its courses. Admissions tests will be used for entry to Nursing and Social Work courses. Taking an International Experience year is another option.

Cambridge The University has 29 undergraduate colleges located throughout the city: Christ's, Churchill, Clare, Corpus Christi, Downing, Emmanuel, Fitzwilliam, Girton, Gonville and Caius, Homerton, Hughes Hall (mature students only), Jesus, King's, Lucy Cavendish (mature, female students only), Magdalene, Murray Edwards (female students only), Newnham (female students only), Pembroke, Peterhouse, Queens', Robinson, St Catharine's, St Edmund's (mature students only), St John's, Selwyn, Sidney Sussex, Trinity, Trinity Hall, and Wolfson (mature students only). Undergraduate courses are offered in Arts and Sciences. Three-year degree courses (Triposes) provide a broad introduction to the subject followed by options at a later stage, and are divided into Part 1 (one or two years) and Part 2. In some Science and Engineering courses there is a fourth year (Part 3). Students studying courses in Modern and Medieval Languages and Asian and Middle Eastern Studies participate in a year abroad. In college-based teaching sessions (supervisions), essays are set for discussion to support university lectures, seminars and practicals.

The typical A-level offer for arts subjects and for Psychological and Behavioural Sciences is A*AA. For science subjects (excluding Psychological and Behavioural Sciences) it is A*A*A. Colleges modify offers to take account of individual circumstances. Self-discipline, motivation and commitment are required together with the ability to think critically and independently, plus passion or, at the very least, real enthusiasm for the chosen course. If examination predictions are good then the chance of admission may be better than one in five. Applicants are encouraged to take the Extended Project although it will not be a requirement of any offer. Although AS and A-level Critical Thinking is acceptable as a fourth AS or A-level subject, it is not considered acceptable as a third A-level. Please note that for 2017 entry onwards, the colleges at the University of Cambridge will be implementing common-format written assessments, to be taken by applicants for all subjects except Mathematics and Music. Applicants will take the written assessments either pre-interview or at interview, depending on the course for which they apply. Please see www.undergraduate.study.cam.ac.uk/applying/admissions-assessments and www.admissionstestingservice.org for further information on these assessments, and **Chapter 5** for information you need to know before completing and submitting your application. Natural Sciences receives the most applications, Classics (four years) receives the fewest. Cambridge is strongly in favour of and will continue to use UMS scores at the end of Year 12 as long as they are available. Students are strongly encouraged to take at least three and possibly four subjects, reformed or not, at the end of Year 12. Information should appear in the UCAS reference in cases where school policy limits the student's opportunity to take AS subjects. *Clearing 2015* The University of Cambridge does not accept applications through Clearing. *Most popular subjects 2015* Natural Sciences.

Canterbury Christ Church The University offers a wide range of BA, BSc, LLB and BMus programmes as well as an extensive Combined Honours scheme. The University has a main campus at Canterbury as well as undergraduate campuses at Broadstairs and Medway. The University offers undergraduate initial teacher training (primary and secondary), a wide range of degrees that lead to professions within the National Health Service as well as subjects in Arts and Humanities, Social and Applied Sciences, Childhood and Education Sciences, and Health Studies.

The UCAS form, including the reference, is highly important. Applicants for subjects where an interview is required (initial teacher training, programmes leading to professions in the NHS) must show evidence on their application of relevant experience. Other subjects that interview/audition include Multimedia Journalism, Counselling, Coaching and Mentoring, Dance and the Popular Music suite of courses.

Cardiff A city centre university. All students taking the very flexible BA degree study three subjects in the first year and then follow a Single or Joint Honours course in their chosen subject(s). Similarly, BSc Economics courses offer the option to transfer to an alternative degree course at the end of Year 1, depending on the subjects originally chosen. Many degree schemes have a vocational and professional content with a period of attachment in industry, and there are well-established links with universities abroad.

Applicants are required to take only three A-levels for degree courses. Deferred entry is acceptable. The 14–19 Diploma is an acceptable qualification for entry. Key Skills should be mentioned in an application but will not form part of an offer.

Cardiff Met Campuses are located at Llandaff, Cyncoed and in the city centre Howard Gardens. Cardiff Metropolitan University specialises in courses that are career-orientated and have been designed in conjunction with business and industry. All of the courses are created with the working world in mind and include work placements, visiting lecturers, and options for sandwich courses.

Students from Foundation degree courses or with HNC/HND qualifications should contact the course director before applying. *Most popular subjects 2015* Business and Management, Educational Studies, Fine Art, Nutrition and Dietetics, Psychology, Social Work, Sport.

Central Lancashire The University is based on a single site campus in Preston city centre, with a smaller campus at Burnley and another campus in Cyprus. It has 20 academic schools covering a wide range of subjects. Many subjects offer optional modules which gives extra choice within programmes. Foundation entry route is available for most Honours degree programmes. A number of undergraduate masters courses are offered, in addition to sandwich courses.

For entry onto Honours degree programmes, the University looks for a minimum of 104–112 points at A2 or equivalent, or 32 points at A2 or equivalent for Foundation entry. Some courses also require an interview, audition or portfolio.

Chester The University of Chester offers an extensive range of single and combined courses across its six sites: from Arts and Media, Science and Engineering, Social Sciences, Humanities, Business and Management, and specialist vocational pathways to nursing and education. Over at its Warrington Campus it runs well-established courses in Media, Business, Public Services, and Sport. The range of subject areas is set to grow as new courses are developed within the areas of Medicine, Dentistry, and Clinical Sciences. The University also accredits innovative and entrepreneurial degree courses at the University Centre Shrewsbury.

For entry requirements and to see what qualifications the University accepts, refer to the specific course page on the University of Chester's website (http://you.chester.ac.uk/undergraduate/courses). Interviews, workshops, and portfolios are required for some courses to support applications. Any questions should be directed to the admissions team using the details above.

Chichester Degree courses are offered in a range of subjects covering Acting, Dance, English, Film & Media, Fine Art, History, Music, Musical Theatre, PE, Philosophy, Politics, Psychology, Sport & Exercise Sciences and Theology at Chichester, and Accounting, Business, Data Science, Education, Maths and Product Design at the Bognor Regis campus.

Early application is advised for programmes which interview or audition applicants. Applicants will be interviewed for professional programmes (eg Early Childhood or Teacher Training). Applicants for programmes in the creative arts (eg Dance) will be auditioned. Most other decisions are made on the basis of the application form. Chichester uses more grade-based offers rather than UCAS Tariff points offers for entry. *Most popular subjects 2015* Adventure Education, Charity Development, Digital Film Production, Media and Cultural Studies, Musical Theatre, Primary Education, Psychology, Sports Therapy, Sports Coaching, Theatre.

City The University in London offers a wide range of three-year and four-year programmes leading to degrees in Business and Management, Communication, Computing, Engineering and Mathematical Sciences, Health Sciences, Law, Nursing and Social Sciences. Some schools and departments provide a common first year, allowing students to make a final decision on their degree course at the end of the first year. Some sandwich courses are optional, others compulsory. Students in some subject areas may apply to study abroad.

It is hoped that applicants will have taken four AS subjects in Year 12, going on to do three at A-level in Year 13.

Coventry Many courses are industry linked and offer sandwich placements in industry and commerce, with some opportunities to study abroad. Individual programmes of study are usually made up of compulsory modules, core options from a prescribed list and free choice modules.

The University is committed to excellence in admissions and aims to provide a professional, fair, equal and transparent service to all applicants. The University operates a centralised admissions service for full-time undergraduate applications. Applications from UK students are managed by the Recruitment and Admissions Office. Applications from the EU and overseas are managed by the International Office. Applications for courses that are commissioned by the Strategic Health Authorities are managed by the admissions unit in the Faculty of Health and Life Sciences. Each service area is responsible for handling enquiries relating to admissions, making decisions on applications and providing advice on admissions to the Faculties and Schools. The University also welcomes applications from those who have significant work or life experience and who may not necessarily meet the published academic requirements for their chosen course.

Creative Arts Foundation and Honours degree courses are offered covering Art and Design, Architecture, Media and Communications at this specialist university with campuses at Canterbury, Epsom, Farnham, Maidstone and Rochester.

Interviews and portfolios are not required for all courses. There is no minimum age requirement for entry to undergraduate courses.

Cumbria The University of Cumbria offers a wide range of courses, both taught and research-based, spanning arts, business, education, health, humanities, law, policing, social science, sport, STEM and the outdoors. The University has an extensive portfolio at both undergraduate level and postgraduate level and many courses have the option to undertake placements which gives students the much needed practical experience.

The University accepts a wide range of qualifications for course entry. Required Tariff points vary across all disciplines and some courses have specific GCSE requirements. All entry requirements and course codes can be found on its website, in its prospectus or on the UCAS website. Its institutional code is C99. The University also offers undergraduate courses with Foundation entry. A new addition to the wide range of opportunities it already offers, Foundation entry is an alternative route to accessing higher education and all the experiences you'd expect as a full-time student.

De Montfort De Montfort University Leicester (DMU) offers a wide range of undergraduate and postgraduate courses, both full-time and part-time, tailored to meet the needs of today's employers.

DMU welcomes applications from UK, European and international students with a wide range of qualifications and experience. Current entry and admissions requirements are published on its website. These may differ from criteria in printed undergraduate prospectus or course brochures – the online information is always the most up-to-date.

Derby Courses at the Derby campus are offered across three subject areas: Arts, Design and Technology, Business and Education, Health and Sciences, whilst at the Buxton campus Foundation degrees are offered as well as some BA and BSc degrees. There is also a comprehensive Joint Honours programme offering two subjects and Combined Honours courses with a choice of up to three subjects. Major/minor courses are also available.

The Level 2 Diploma is regarded as equivalent to GCSEs and the Level 3 Diploma to A-levels. Students without formal qualifications can take an Access course or the Modular Foundation course to gain entry to degree programmes.

Dundee The University of Dundee offers a wide range of undergraduate degrees. Many of its courses are vocational and offer professional accreditation. Its academic schools cover Art and Design; Science and Engineering; Education and Social Work; Humanities; Social Sciences; Life Sciences; Dentistry; Nursing and Health Sciences; and Medicine.

All applicants will be invited to visit the University after receiving an offer. Some courses interview as part of the admissions process. Advanced entry is available for most courses. For most subjects the entry requirements are shown as 'minimum' and 'typical'. Please note that the University offers a wide range of degree programmes and some have a higher level of competition for places than others. For programmes with a higher level of demand, it will make offers around the 'typical' rather than the 'minimum' level.

Durham A competitive collegiate university with two colleges in Stockton and 14 in Durham. Degree options include Single and Joint Honours courses to which subsidiary subjects can be added. There are named routes in Natural Sciences and courses in Liberal Arts and Social Sciences in which students may design their own degree course by choosing several subjects from a wide range.

The Durham admissions policy reviews the following factors: A-level or equivalent grades; GCSE performance; the personal statement (students applying for more than one type of course or institution may submit a substitute personal statement, please see www.durham.ac.uk/undergraduate/apply/ ucas/personalstatement/substitute for further details); the school/college reference; motivation for the chosen degree programme; independence of thought and working; skills derived from non-academic activities, eg sport, the arts, and voluntary and community work; and contextual evidence of merit and potential. Admission decisions are made by academic selectors. Successful applicants will be informed of the decision on their application before a college is allocated. Durham does not use interviews as a means of selection except in specific circumstances. These include applications to courses where external bodies determine that interviewing is compulsory (for example, applicants to Initial Teacher Training and Medicine), applications to the Foundation Centre, applications where the candidate is without recent and/or relevant qualifications and applications where applicants have had a break in their study prior to application. The need for an interview will be determined by academic departments on an individual basis having considered all the information provided in the application.

East Anglia The University near Norwich has four faculties (Arts and Humanities, Medicine and Health Sciences, Science and Social Sciences). The University maintains an extensive network of international exchanges in which students studying certain degree programmes are able to spend up to a year. During these placements, students are fully integrated into the culture of the host university.

Offers are normally made in terms of three A-levels although applicants with two A-levels and AS are welcome. Critical Thinking and General Studies A-levels are not accepted for most courses. Interviews are necessary for some courses. Deferred entry is acceptable.

East London The University, based on the Stratford and Docklands campuses in East London, offers Single Honours and Combined Honours programmes. Courses provide a flexibility of choice and are based on a modular structure with compulsory and optional course units. A very large number of extended degrees are also available for applicants who do not have the normal university entrance requirements.

Candidates are advised to apply as soon as possible and results are normally announced within seven days. Some students may be called for interview and in some cases an essay or a portfolio may be required. The interviewers will be looking for evidence of a real interest in the chosen subject. Rejected applicants may receive an offer of a place on an extended degree or on another course.

Edge Hill The University in Ormskirk, Lancashire has three-year programmes including Business, English, Film, Geographical Sciences, History, Law, Media, Midwifery, Nursing, Performance Studies, Social and Psychological Sciences, Sport, and Teacher Training.

With the exception of courses in Journalism, Animation, Media (Film and TV), TV Production, Performing Arts, Social and Psychological Sciences, Teacher Training, Nursing and Midwifery, most decisions are made without an interview. Those applicants who receive offers are invited to visit the University.

Edinburgh Depending on the choice of degree, three or more subjects are taken in the first year followed by second level courses in at least two of these subjects in Year 2, thus allowing a range of subjects to be studied at degree level. There is a considerable choice of subjects although there may be restrictions in the case of high-demand subjects such as English, Economics and Psychology. General or Ordinary degrees take three years and Honours degrees take four years. Joint Honours degrees are also offered.

Admission decisions are made by the admissions offices of the University's three colleges: the College of Humanities and Social Science, the College of Science and Engineering and the College of Medicine and Veterinary Medicine. Decisions on the majority of applications will be made after the UCAS deadline, once all applications have been received. All offers will be expressed in grades, not Tariff points. Make sure to check the website for the latest up-to-date information before applying.

Edinburgh Napier Students choose between Single and Joint Honours degrees from a wide range of subjects.

Entry requirements for all courses can be found at www.napier.ac.uk/courses. Applications are screened and decisions are made centrally by the Admissions Team, using entry criteria which have been agreed by the academic department. Where the admissions selection process involves an interview, audition or portfolio review, the application will be sent to the academic department for consideration. This applies to the following programmes: Nursing, Vet Nursing, Journalism, Design programmes, Music, Acting, Film, Photography and Television. *Most popular subjects 2015* The Health, Life and Social Science Faculty receives the highest number of applicants.

Essex The University is located on a large campus near Colchester. Undergraduate departments are grouped in schools of study covering Humanities and Comparative Studies, Social Sciences, Law and Sciences and Engineering. In Year 1 students take four or five courses including modules for their chosen degree. In Year 2 they may follow their chosen degree or choose another degree, including Combined and Joint courses. The four-year BA and some Law degrees include a year abroad and/or industrial placements. Degree schemes in Health, Business and the Performing Arts are also offered at the Southend campus.

Candidates are required to have three full A-levels or equivalent – students re-sitting some subjects may get a higher offer. All departments accept General Studies and Critical Thinking. Key Skills at Level 3 can be used as part of the points total providing they do not overlap with other qualifications (eg numeracy or A-level mathematics). Unit grades are not used as standard procedure. Additional aptitude tests are not used. Interviews may be required for some subjects. Admission decisions are made departmentally. *Most popular subjects 2015* Accounting, Acting, Biomedical Science, Business, Economics, Finance, Management, Nursing.

Exeter This campus university has six colleges: the Business School, the College of Engineering, Maths and Physical Sciences, the College of Humanities, the College of Life and Environmental Sciences, the College of Social Sciences and International Studies, and the University of Exeter Medical School. Most courses include an optional European or international study opportunity. Some subjects, including Biosciences, Geology and Mining Engineering, can be taken at the Cornwall campus at Penryn.

The University welcomes applications from students from all backgrounds. Key indicators include predicted and achieved academic performance in Level 2 and 3 qualifications; candidates would normally be expected to take three A-levels (or the equivalent). Deferred applications are welcome. The subjects interviewing all candidates are Applied Psychology (Clinical), Drama, Medical Imaging, Medicine and Physics, and a small number of Engineering programmes. *Most popular subjects 2015* Economics, English, History.

Falmouth A south coast university. The courses focus on Art and Design, Music and Theatre Arts, Film and TV, Photography and Journalism.

For most courses samples of works and/or interviews will be required.

Glasgow Applicants choose a degree from the Colleges of Arts; Medical, Veterinary & Life Sciences; Science & Engineering; Social Sciences. The flexible degree structure in Arts, Sciences and Social Sciences allows students to build their own degree programme from the courses on offer. Honours degrees normally take four years, with the decision for Honours taken at the end of Year 2. Primary Education, Health & Social Policy, and Environmental Science & Sustainability can be studied at the Dumfries Campus.

The University does not accept applications after the 15 January deadline. Offers are made until late March. The University does not interview applicants except for entry to Dentistry, Education, Medicine, Music and Veterinary Medicine. Deferred entry is not guaranteed for all subjects so check with the University. See the University website for up-to-date information. *Most popular subjects 2015* Business and Management, Computer Science, Dentistry, Economics, English Literature, History, Mechanical Engineering, Medicine, Primary Education, Psychology, Veterinary Medicine.

Glasgow Caledonian The University offers a wide range of career-focussed programmes offered by their Academic Schools: Glasgow School for Business and Society, School of Engineering and Built Environment, and School of Health and Life Sciences.

The University accepts a wide range of qualifications for entry, depending upon the chosen programme. Please check the website for programme-specific entry requirements.

Gloucestershire The University is located in Cheltenham with courses made up of individual study units (modules). Some are compulsory for the chosen course but other modules can be chosen from other subjects. All courses have strong employability focus with many opportunities to undertake placements and internships.

Students failing to meet the UCAS Tariff requirements may be eligible for entry based on life or work experience following an interview. Entry with BTEC, NVQ Level 3 and Access to Higher Education qualifications is acceptable.

Glyndŵr Glyndŵr University is based in Wrexham, North East Wales. The University offers a wide range of courses covering areas such as Art & Design, Business, Computing, Creative Media Technology, Education, Engineering, Health, Social Science and Sport. It also has a dedicated rural campus in nearby Northop for Animal and Environment based courses. The University places a big emphasis on developing employability and linking courses with industry requirements. As well as traditional degree pathways, it has a number of two-year fast track degree routes for those looking for faster progression. It has also added a range of four-year degree options that allow students to incorporate either a Foundation year or integrated Master's year into their degree.

Offers for all courses are made through the Admissions and Enquiries team, and are usually based on UCAS Tariff point requirements. General entry requirements for three-year bachelor's degrees are 112 UCAS Tariff points, with 120 Tariff points for four-year integrated master's courses and 48 Tariff points for courses including a Foundation year. UCAS points may be counted from a wide variety of qualifications but offers are usually made based on points from GCE A-levels or equivalent. An interview is always required for Occupational Therapy and Social Work, and usually required for all Art & Design courses, Theatre, Television and Performance, Complementary Therapies, Health and Social Care, and Youth and Community. Other subject areas do not interview as standard, but may decide to interview applicants if deemed appropriate. Deferred applications for Occupational Therapy and Social Work are not accepted. Applications are welcomed from candidates who do not possess the standard qualifications but who can demonstrate their capacity to pursue the course successfully. Entrance can be based on past experience, skills, organisational capabilities and the potential to succeed, particularly for entry onto a programme including a Foundation year.

Greenwich Many courses are on offer and there is also a flexible and comprehensive Combined Honours degree programme offering two Joint subjects of equal weight or, alternatively, major/minor combinations.

For information on admissions procedures see the University website: www.gre.ac.uk/study/apply. *Most popular subjects 2015* Architecture, Business, Computing, Education, Nursing, Science.

Harper Adams Based in Newport, Shropshire, the University focuses on agricultural, food chain and rural subjects.

All courses interview all candidates based in the UK.

Heriot-Watt This campus university near Edinburgh has six schools offering courses on the Built Environment, Engineering and Physical Sciences, Management and Languages, Mathematical and Computer Sciences, Textiles and Design and Life Sciences. There is a second campus at Galashiels.

In order to give candidates as much flexibility as possible, many will receive offers for both first and second year entry. Although one of these will be the main offer, candidates accepting this can easily change their main offer to the alternative year if they subsequently want to do so. Applicants are interviewed for some programmes.

Hertfordshire Full-time and sandwich courses are offered as well as Joint courses. All Hertfordshire students have a work exposure strand in their degrees and the close links with employers contribute to a consistently good work placement and graduate employment record. All students have the opportunity to develop self-employment skills through tailor-made packages in addition to their subject expertise and proficiency.

Applicants wanting to take a gap year should finalise their arrangements before asking for deferment and accepting a place. Once a place has been accepted for the following year it will not be possible to change their application for entry to the current year. They would need to withdraw their application and apply again through Clearing.

Huddersfield The modular approach to study provides a flexible structure to all courses, which are offered as full-time or sandwich options. All students also have the opportunity to study a modern language either as a minor option or by studying part-time through the Modern Languages Centre. Most courses are vocational.

For information on admissions procedures see the University website: www.hud.ac.uk.

Hull All full-time courses are made up of core and optional modules and are taught on the Hull campus. A 'Languages for All' programme is available for all students irrespective of their degree course subject.

All criteria for selection are set by the academic faculty. A mandatory interview process operates for shortlisted applicants for Nursing, Operating Department Practice, Midwifery, Teaching (QTS), and Social Work. Music applicants are invited to a practical session as part of an open day. A wide range of qualifications are accepted for entry to degree courses. Applications are also welcomed from those who can demonstrate Level 3 work-based learning such as Advanced Apprenticeships and NVQ 3. Bridging study may be recommended by way of a Foundation year. Most courses welcome applications for deferred entry although this should be stated on the application. Deferred entry is not available for Nursing courses.

Hull York (MS) The Medical School is a partnership between Hull and York Universities with teaching and learning facilities on both campuses.

See Medicine in Chapter 7.

IFS (UC) An independent university college. Courses focus on financial services and related professions.

Applications are submitted through UCAS and the deadline is 15 January 2017. All applications made before the closing date will be considered equally against the stated selection criteria and in the context of the number of available places. The University College will consider late applications only for courses where places are still available.

Imperial London The central site is in South Kensington. Medicine is mainly based at St Mary's Hospital, Paddington, Charing Cross Hospital and Hammersmith Hospital. The College offers world-class programmes in Science, Medicine, Engineering and Management. Joint Honours courses and degree courses with a year abroad are also available. Science courses are offered primarily in one principal subject, but flexibility is provided by the possibility to transfer at the end of the first year and by the choice of optional subjects in the later years of the course. A Humanities programme is also open to all students with a wide range of options, whilst the Tanaka Business School offers Management courses which form an integral part of undergraduate degrees. Work experience and placements are a feature of all courses.

Applicants are normally required to have three A-levels, but applicants with other qualifications of equivalent standard and students with other competencies are also welcome. The College considers candidates with the Advanced Engineering Diploma if they also have A-levels in specified subjects which meet the College's entry requirements. Applicants for entry to Year 2 of some courses can also be considered if they have completed the first year of a comparable degree at another institution with a high level of achievement, but they need to contact the relevant department before applying. A College Admissions and Appeals and Complaints procedure is available to applicants dissatisfied with the way their application has been considered. Applicants should note the College's policy on dress, health and safety published on its website. An offer for an alternative course may be made to rejected applicants.

Keele Keele University's campus in Staffordshire, in the heart of the UK, is near to cities north and south, accessible to Manchester, Birmingham and London. It also has the unique benefits of being close to a city, a vibrant university town and set within over 600 acres of beautiful campus. Flexibility is provided through either interdisciplinary Single Honours degrees, bringing together a number of topics in an integrated form, or Dual Honours degrees in which two principal subjects are studied to degree level to the same depth as a Single Honours course.

Keele's conditional offers to candidates are usually made in terms of specified grades from the qualifications they are studying. Some of its degree courses require a specific subject background and for applicants applying for a Dual Honours or Major: Minor degree, the subject specific requirements should be met for both subjects. It welcomes applications from candidates with non-traditional qualifications and will take into consideration prior learning and experience and alternative qualifications. Applicants are normally required to have completed a period of study in the last three years. Keele has taken into consideration the changes that were made to A-level and GCSE qualifications in September 2015 and reviewed its entry requirements to ensure the new post-16 curriculum does not disadvantage students in their Higher Education journey. Further information about its approach and entry requirements for September 2017 can be found on the following webpage: www.keele.ac.uk/outreach/teachersadvisers/qualificationsreform.

Kent The University's main campuses are in Canterbury and Medway in the South East of England, with specialist centres in Europe where study and research are underpinned by the exceptional facilities and resources of locations in Brussels, Paris, Athens and Rome. Many courses have a year in industry, giving valuable practical experience ahead of your final year of study. The majority of programmes offer the opportunity to study or work abroad. Single Honours courses can include the option of taking up to 25% of the degree in another subject, or to change the focus of a degree at the end of the first year. Many social sciences and humanities subjects are available as Joint Honours programmes on a 50/50 basis or as major/minor Honours degrees.

The University accepts a wide range of qualifications. Applicants returning to study after a long break are advised to contact the admissions staff before making a UCAS application. The University offers integrated Foundation year study in a number of degree subjects and an international Foundation year programme is available to non-UK students. Deferred entry is acceptable but should be mentioned on the UCAS application. The University regards the personal statement as important and recommends that applicants research their chosen courses thoroughly, and show an understanding of the curriculum. *Most popular subjects 2015* Actuarial Science, Business, Law, Mathematics.

Kingston Kingston University is based in Kingston upon Thames, a busy riverside town in Surrey which is only 25 minutes away from central London. It has four campuses, each with its own character, but all of which combine state-of-the-art facilities with a friendly study environment. Its courses have a modular structure, and several of them are available to study as Joint Honours which allows students to combine two different subjects. The two subjects can be studied equally (half-field), or one subject can be focused on more than the other (major-minor fields). All students have the opportunity to study abroad during their degree and can choose from 36 countries spanning five continents. They can also learn one of 10 languages through the Kingston Language Scheme for free during their time at the University.

Once the University has received an application from UCAS, it looks carefully at each applicant's academic record, references and personal statement. Some courses at Kingston University have an interview as part of the selection process where one or two people will interview you to find out if you have the intellectual capability, knowledge and passion to benefit from your chosen course. If you don't have an interview, you'll be invited to an applicant day instead where you will get to experience taster sessions of the course you have applied for.

Lancaster The University is situated on a large campus some distance from the city and consists of several colleges. Each college has its own social activities and events. The degree programme is split into Part 1 (Year 1) and Part 2 (Years 2 and 3). Students study up to three subjects in Year 1 and then choose to major in one or a combination of subjects in Years 2 and 3. Single and Joint courses are offered in a wide range of subjects. There are study opportunities abroad in the USA and Canada, the Far East and Australasia.

Candidates are not expected to take four or more A-levels; offers are based on the best three A-level results (except for Medicine for which one AS is also required). The University welcomes applications from students wishing to defer entry. General Studies is acceptable for the majority of courses. Admissions tutors accept a range of qualifications for entry. Some candidates are interviewed before an offer is made, but most are invited to an informal post-offer Open Day which can involve an interview or discussion with an admissions tutor.

Leeds With one of the largest city-based single-site campuses in the UK, the University of Leeds provides a vibrant experience. A member of the Russell Group, it offers excellence in learning and teaching in a wide range of courses in most subject areas, including an extensive offering of Joint Honours degrees. The size and breadth of the University allows Leeds to offer a complete student experience; studying abroad and/or industrial placements are offered as part of most courses. The research-based curriculum, combined with an unparalleled range of opportunities to complement their degree, allows students to develop skills needed for the future.

The University welcomes students with a variety of qualifications. Some courses do not accept A-level General Studies or Critical Thinking. Check the University's course finder for details of accepted qualifications: www.leeds.ac.uk/coursefinder.

Leeds Beckett (Formerly Leeds Metropolitan.) Many of the degrees are vocational with links to industry and commerce. Courses are modular with core studies and optional modules. Degree programmes are offered in the Faculties of Arts and Society, Information and Technology, Health, Sport and Recreation, the Leslie Silver International Faculty and the Leeds Business School.

Most offers are made in UCAS Tariff points, and interviews are held before an offer is made for some courses. Deferred entry is acceptable although applicants should be aware that some courses may change slightly each year.

Leeds Trinity An employer-focused, campus university located a few miles from Leeds city centre. The University offers Foundation and undergraduate degrees in a wide range of subject areas, including Business, Management and Marketing; Childhood and Education; Criminology; English; History; Journalism; Media, Film and Culture; Psychology; Secondary Education; Sociology; Sport, Health and Nutrition; and Theology and Religious Studies. Professional work placements are embedded into every undergraduate degree, and most courses include the opportunity to study abroad. With just over 3,000 students studying on a single-site campus, Leeds Trinity prides itself on offering a personalised and inclusive university experience that gives every student the support they need to realise their potential.

All applicants receiving an offer for non-interviewing courses will be invited to an Applicant Day. This gives them (and their families and friends) the opportunity to visit the campus, get a taste of student life and receive specific details about their chosen course. Some courses do require an interview and successful applicants will be invited to an Interview Day – these courses are specified in the UCAS entry requirements. The University makes Tariff-based offers for most courses, with only a few offers based on grades. All entry requirements, whether Tariff or grade-based, are listed in the course-specific entry requirements on the University's website and through UCAS. Personal statements and references are always taken into account, alongside students' academic profiles. All information is correct at the time of going to print, but please check the University website for the most up-to-date information.

Leicester Single Honours courses are offered in all the main disciplines and are taken by 75% of students. The main subject of study may be supported by one or two optional modules. Joint Honours courses are also offered which are split equally between the subjects. New for 2016 are major/minor degrees: a core area is studied in depth (75%) while an additional area (25%) is also explored. Apart from Medicine, all programmes have a common modular structure with compulsory modules and a wide choice of optional modules.

Most courses do not interview applicants although invitations to visit the University will follow any offers made. Most offers are made on the basis of three A-levels, although in some cases two A-levels and two AS may be accepted. The University welcomes the Extended Project which should be mentioned in the personal statement. The Cambridge Pre-U Diploma is also an acceptable qualification. Applications from suitably qualified students are also considered for second year entry. Contact the subject department for further information.

Lincoln A city centre university with Faculties of Art, Architecture and Design, Business and Law, Health, Life and Social Sciences, Media, Humanities and Technology. Single and Joint subject degrees are offered on a modular basis, with some subjects offering the chance to study abroad.

On some courses, notably Art and Design and Architecture, an interview with a portfolio is sometimes required before an offer can be made. The University accepts a wide range of qualifications but students without the standard entry requirements may still be offered a place on the basis of prior experience and qualifications.

Liverpool The University offers degrees in the Faculties of Humanities and Social Sciences, Science and Engineering and Health and Life Sciences. Apart from courses with a clinical component, programmes are modular. In some cases they include placements in industry or in another country and there is the opportunity for students studying many subjects to spend a year of their degree in China. The Faculty of Humanities and Social Sciences offers the 'Honours Select' programme allowing students to combine subjects from across the Faculty as Joint (50:50) or major/minor (75:25) degrees. In addition, it is possible to take a Combined Honours degree combining subjects between faculties.

Decisions on offers for most schools/departments are made centrally. The exceptions are in the Schools of Medicine, Dentistry, Health Sciences and Veterinary Science. Most departments will invite applicants to visit the University before or after an offer is made. Some departments require interviews. Offers are normally based on three A-levels or equivalent (a wide range of qualifications are accepted). Some programmes will accept two A-levels and two AS. *Most popular subjects 2015* Dentistry, Health Sciences, Management, Medicine, Veterinary Science.

Liverpool Hope Liverpool Hope offers a wide range of Single and Combined Honours undergraduate degrees. The University's excellent academic record and supportive pastoral care are complemented by the beautiful settings of the campuses. Liverpool Hope offers small group teaching, which means students are taught by research-active lecturers and benefit from insights into their research.

Each application is assessed on its own merits. The policy is to select those candidates who demonstrate they have an academic ability and personal motivation to succeed in their chosen programme of study. The admissions decision will rest primarily on the qualifications and also on the aspirations of the applicant in relation to their chosen programme of study. Selectors will take into account the evidence provided on the application form against the criteria for that particular course.

Liverpool John Moores Courses are offered in the Faculties of Business, Law and Languages, Education, Community and Leisure, Health and Applied Social Sciences, Media, Arts and Social Science, Science and Technology and the Environment. The majority of courses provide the opportunity for work-based learning or for a year-long industrial placement.

Admissions decisions are made through the Faculty 'Hubs' (Science; Health and Applied Social Sciences; Technology and Environment; Arts, Professional and Social Studies). The personal statement is regarded as highly important and students are advised to include all relevant interests and work experience. The University welcomes a wide range of entry qualifications. If an applicant fails to receive an offer for their chosen course then an offer for an alternative course may be made. All candidates are interviewed for Drama, Primary Education, Pharmacy (including an admissions test), Nursing and Social Work.

London (Birk) Part-time and full-time evening courses are offered for mature students wishing to read for first and higher degrees. Courses are offered in the Faculties of Arts, Science, Social Science and Continuing Education.

All applications are made online. Part-time undergraduate, all certificate and short course and all postgraduate applications are made directly through its website. Full-time undergraduate applications are made through UCAS.

London (Court) As a specialist institution, The Courtauld Institute of Art offers one degree programme at undergraduate level – a BA in History of Art. Teaching ranges from antiquity to the contemporary and extends across diverse cultures, from early Christian Byzantium to early modern Islamic world, from Renaissance Europe to contemporary China.

History, History of Art, English and modern European languages are the most relevant A-level subjects for the one BA course in History of Art, but applications will be considered from those studying other subjects. Art offered at A-level should normally include a history of art paper. The ability to read foreign languages is a particular asset. Candidates will be interviewed.

London (Gold) Goldsmiths is situated in New Cross, South-East London. The University takes an innovative and interdisciplinary approach to their degree courses, which include Art, Design, Drama, Computing, Media, the Arts, Education and Social Sciences. An undergraduate degree is made up of 360 credits from core and optional modules – 120 at each level. A standard module is worth 60 credits, although some degrees also contain 15-credit modules or can be made up of higher-value parts, such as a dissertation or a Major Project.

They welcome applications from students with A-levels or equivalent qualifications. While entry requirements are stipulated, candidates are assessed individually and may receive an offer that differs from the published grades. Some applicants are interviewed, in particular those for Art and Design degrees for which examples of current art and design work are required before interview. Applicants requiring deferred entry (which may or may not be acceptable depending on the course) should contact the admissions tutor before applying.

London (Hey) Heythrop College is the oldest of the London University colleges.

The College in its current form, as a constituent college of the University of London, will come to an end in 2018, although its mission and work will not. The College is currently unable to offer full undergraduate programmes for full- or part-time study. Programmes taught via distance learning through the University of London International Programmes will continue to be offered along with individual modules for visiting and auditing students.

London (Inst Paris) The Institute was established as part of London University in 1969 and offers three year courses in French Studies leading to a London University BA. Courses are taught in French.

For information on admissions procedures see Institute website: www.ulip.london.ac.uk.

London (King's) The College on the Strand offers more than 200 degree programmes in the Faculties of Arts and Humanities, Biomedical and Health Sciences, Law, Nursing and Midwifery, Physical Sciences,

Social Science and Public Policy, and Medicine and Dentistry at the Guy's or King's (Denmark Hill) or St Thomas's campuses. The degree course structure varies with the subject chosen and consists of Single Honours, Joint Honours, Combined Honours (a choice of over 60 programmes) and major/minor courses.

Applicants will normally have taken four AS subjects and pursued three of these at A-level. Most conditional offers are based on three A-level subjects, but some will ask for a fourth subject at AS, including Medicine and Dentistry. If your school or college does not permit you to take a fourth AS, they should ideally mention this in the opening paragraph of their academic reference. The majority of courses require three A-levels to be taken together in one sitting. High achievement in the fourth AS subject may compensate for an applicant who narrowly fails to achieve the A-level offer. AS and A-level General Studies and Critical Thinking are not accepted although the grade achieved may be considered when the required grades of an offer have not been met. Deferred entry is acceptable.

London (QM) Queen Mary University of London (QMUL), based in the heart of east London, is a member of the Russell Group of leading UK universities and in the top 100 universities in the world. Its flexible approach enables students to choose from a wide range of compulsory and optional modules to develop a degree programme to suit their interests. In addition, many of its degrees are accredited by professional bodies, which can give graduates a head-start in their chosen career. Many of its students also take advantage of study abroad and industrial experience opportunities, ranging from internships to a year in industry.

For all full-time programmes, students should apply online at ucas.com. The institution code for QMUL is Q50. It may be possible for students to join undergraduate degree programmes at the beginning of the second and sometimes the third year. Those wishing to transfer their degree studies from another UK higher education institution may be considered but should contact the subject department before applying.

London (RH) The College on a campus near Windsor, offers Single, Joint and major/minor Honours degrees in three faculties: Arts, History and Social Sciences, and Science. Many courses offer the opportunity to study abroad and all students can compete for international exchanges.

Applicants likely to meet the entry requirements may be called for interview or invited to an Open Day. International students may be asked to submit an example of academic work or other exercise although it would be preferable if they could visit the campus. Interviews are not intended to be nerve-wracking or daunting but rather a chance to assess the candidate's potential. In Music there may be an audition, in Drama a workshop session, and in Modern Languages some conversation in the appropriate language. Candidates who fail to meet the requirements of their offer may still be offered a place, particularly if they shone at interview.

London (RVC) Campuses in London and in Hertfordshire. Courses are offered in Veterinary Medicine, Biological Sciences and Bioveterinary Sciences (the latter two do not qualify graduates to practise as veterinary surgeons). There is also a Veterinary Gateway course and Veterinary Nursing programme.

Applications for deferred entry are considered but the offer conditions must be met in the same academic year as the application. Applicants holding offers from RVC who fall slightly below the grades required are always reconsidered and may be offered entry if places are available.

London (St George's) Courses are offered in Biomedical Science, Medicine, Paramedic Science, Healthcare Science, Physiotherapy and Diagnostic and Therapeutic Radiography.

Interviews are required for most courses and admissions tests are required for some courses. Candidates will be interviewed for all courses in Medicine, Physiotherapy, Paramedic Science, Healthcare Science and Therapeutic and Diagnostic Radiography. Once admitted students are not allowed to change courses. *Most popular subjects 2015* Biomedical Science, Medicine 4yr, Medicine 5yr.

London (SOAS) Single-subject degrees focusing on Asia, Africa and the Near East include compulsory and optional units, with two-thirds of the total units studied in the chosen subject and the remaining units or 'floaters' from a complementary course offered at SOAS or another college of the University of London. In addition, two-subject degrees give great flexibility in the choice of units, enabling students to personalise their degrees to match their interests.

Particular attention is paid to past and predicted academic performance and offers may be made without an interview. SOAS is happy to consider deferred entry, which should be stated on the UCAS application.

London (UCL) Subjects are organised in Faculties: Arts and Humanities, Brain Sciences, Built Environment (the Bartlett), Engineering Sciences, Laws, Life Sciences, Mathematical and Physical Sciences, Medical Sciences (including the UCL Medical School), Population Health Sciences, Social and Historical Sciences. In addition, there is the School of Slavonic and East European Studies and the UCL Institute of Education. UCL also offers a cross-disciplinary degree in Arts and Sciences, based on the US Liberal Arts model.

UCL welcomes applications from students proposing to spend a pre-university year engaged in constructive activity in the UK or abroad. About 9% of UCL's undergraduates take a gap year. Those wanting to enter the second year of a degree programme should make early contact with the relevant subject department to obtain approval. Applications are assessed on the basis of the personal statement, reference and the predicted academic performance, as well as additional assessment methods such as essays, questionnaires, aptitude tests and interviews. Decisions on admission are final and there is normally no right of appeal.

London (UCL Sch Pharm) The School offers the Master of Pharmacy degree. Except for hospital and extra-mural projects, all the teaching takes place on the Bloomsbury campus.

The School looks for students who are intellectually curious, willing to study hard, and who will thrive in a small, friendly environment where the emphasis is on team work and academic achievement. All students who are based in the UK and have educational qualifications which meet or are expected to meet the entry requirements are required to attend an interview before a final decision is taken on their application. Applicants whose UCAS personal statement is aimed at a subject other than Pharmacy are recommended to write a supplementary personal statement which can be sent to the Registry once the UCAS application has been submitted.

London LSE The School offers 38 degrees across a wide range of social science subjects, taught in 19 departments. Degrees are three years long, except Philosophy, Politics and Economics (PPE), which is a four-year programme. All undergraduates study a compulsory course called 'LSE 100: Understanding the causes of things' which actively challenges them to analyse questions of current public concern and develops their critical skills.

A wide range of international qualifications are accepted for direct entry to the School. Applicants offering A-levels should have taken four AS subjects, followed by three at A-level. Students will not be penalised if they have not been able to take the normal number of AS and A-level subjects, but the School asks that referees advise on such circumstances. Applicants normally offer A-levels in LSE's preferred subjects, which do not include AS/A-level Accounting, Art and Design, Business Studies, Citizenship Studies, Communication and Culture, Creative Writing, Design and Technology, Drama and Theatre Studies, Film Studies, Health and Social Care, Home Economics, ICT, Law, Leisure Studies, Media Studies, Music Technology, Sports Studies, Travel and Tourism. Standard offers range from AAB to A*AA – applicants should check individual degree requirements. Intense competition for places means that high predicted grades on the application will not guarantee an offer. Great weight is placed on the personal statement and advice on writing this can be found on the School's website. Applications are considered on a rolling basis, but they are often held in a 'gathered field' and decisions made only when all on-time applications have been received. It is unlikely there will be any vacancies when A-level results are published. *Most popular subjects 2015* Accounting and Finance, Economics, Government, Law, Management, Statistics.

London Met Single and Joint Honours courses are made up of compulsory and optional modules allowing students some flexibility to follow their particular interests.

Applicants may be required to sit a test or to submit a portfolio of work.

London Regent's A private university with a campus in Regent's Park offering a range of courses.

Contact the institution regarding their requirements and procedures.

London South Bank All courses have flexible modes of study and many vocational courses offer sandwich placements.

Applicants not achieving the grades required for their chosen course should contact the University which may still be able to make an offer of a place. All applicants are interviewed for Journalism, Midwifery, Nursing, Allied Health Professions and Architecture courses.

Loughborough Loughborough is an attractive, single-site campus university that offers a range of courses, across 19 different academic schools and departments. Degrees are structured using a combination of compulsory and optional modules so that study can be tailored to individual interest. Sandwich degree courses are an excellent way to incorporate a year of paid industry experience into study, where students can practise skills learned in a professional environment. As a result, Loughborough students have high graduate employment prospects and are often sought after by top national and international recruiters.

Loughborough University does not usually differentiate between applicants taking A-levels for the first time and applicants who are resitting subjects. Loughborough accepts the Advanced Diploma for entry to most of its undergraduate degree programmes, where this consists of the relevant Progression Diploma. Applicants may be required to take Additional or Specialist Learning (ASL) components, usually in the form of a specific A-level subject to satisfy specific course entry requirements. More information on the University's admissions and associated policies are available to view on the website: www.lboro.ac.uk/admissions. Some schools and departments will interview applicants before a decision is made, whereas others will base their decision on the information in UCAS applications alone.

Manchester A large popular university offering Single and Joint Honours courses which are divided into course units, some of which are compulsory, some optional, and some are taken from a choice of subjects offered by other schools and faculties. A comprehensive Combined Studies degree enables students to choose course units from Arts, Humanities, Social Sciences and Sciences, and this provides the flexibility for students to alter the emphasis of their studies from year to year.

Strong examination results are the main factor in the admission of students to courses and the University accepts a wide range of qualifications. All decisions are made by the academic departments according to their individual requirements. For example, some programmes may require the applicant to have GCSE maths at grade C or above for entry, others may require a compulsory subject at A-level. Other factors that are considered are prior and predicted grades, evidence of knowledge and commitment in the personal statement, and teacher references. Some courses may also take into account performance at interview, aptitude tests and portfolios. Where places are limited, they are offered to those eligible applicants who best meet the selection criteria and who, according to the admissions team, are most likely to benefit from their chosen course and to contribute both to their academic school and the wider university. *Most popular subjects 2015* Business Studies, Dentistry, English Literature, Law, Medicine.

Manchester Met A large number of courses involve industrial and commercial placements. It is also possible to take Combined Honours degrees selecting a combination of two or three subjects. Many programmes have a modular structure with compulsory and optional core modules.

Admissions staff look for personal statements showing evidence of the applicants' motivation and commitment to their chosen courses, work or voluntary experience relevant to any chosen career, and extra-curricular activities, achievements and interests which are relevant to the chosen courses.

Medway Sch Pharm The School is part of a collaboration between the Universities of Greenwich and Kent. Offers undergraduate and Master's degrees in pharmaceutical courses, accredited by The General Pharmaceutical Council.

See Medicine in Chapter 7.

Middlesex Single and Joint Honours courses are offered on a modular basis, most programmes having an optional work placement.

Some courses start in January (see www.mdx.ac.uk/courses/help-with-your-application/january-start).

NCH London The New College of the Humanities is located in Bloomsbury and is an independent university-level college, offers a liberal arts-inspired undergraduate programme featuring majors and minors in Economics, English, History, Philosophy, and Politics & International Relations, and a Single

Honours Law LLB. In addition to studying towards their degree, all students study eight core courses in subjects including Applied Ethics, Logic and Critical Thinking, Science Literacy, and a unique professional development programme. Students can also choose enrichment courses in Art History, Creative Writing, Law and Psychology. To reflect this further study, students are awarded the NCH Diploma. Students typically experience lectures of fewer than 50 students, seminars, small group tutorials and weekly one-to-one tutorials from eminent academics. Scholarships and bursaries are offered.

Students may apply direct to the College at any time or through UCAS. The application form is similar to the traditional UCAS form. NCH will consider applications individually and on their merits. Decisions are quick – usually within four to six weeks. As well as personal details and academic records, applicants are required to supply a reference and a piece of written work. An application to NCH can be made in addition to any application made to other universities through UCAS. All shortlisted students are interviewed. NCH accepts deferred entries for those wishing to take a Gap Year.

Newcastle Single, Joint and Combined Honours programmes are offered. Some programmes provide students with the opportunity to defer their choice of final degree to the end of the first or second year.

The University accepts a wide range of qualifications and combinations of qualifications for entry to its degree programmes. All qualifications that are of suitable academic level will be considered. Offers are made in terms of grades to be achieved (UCAS Tariff points are not used). *Most popular subjects 2015* Medicine, Law, Business Management, Biomedical Sciences.

Newman A full range of full-time and part-time degree courses can be chosen with a focus on Initial Teacher Training qualifications.

Applicants are advised to submit an accurate and well-presented application. Personal statements are applicants' chance to shine, show their qualities and convince admission tutors why they should offer them a place.

Northampton The University of Northampton offers Single Honours, Joint Honours, Foundation degrees, HNDs and top-up courses. The University also offers a Year 0 in some courses for those who do not meet its entry requirements. There are also placement opportunities in the third year for certain courses, particularly within the business school. A range of courses and learning options are available including full- and part-time, distance learning and two-year fast track degrees.

Entry requirements usually range from 112 to 128 UCAS points for BA/BSc degrees depending on the course.

Northumbria The University is located in Newcastle and offers a wide range of courses with an emphasis on vocational studies. Single and Joint Honours courses are offered, and a Combined Honours course allows a choice of up to three subjects.

Interviews are compulsory for courses in Architecture, most courses in Art and Design and courses in Health and Teaching. There are no admissions tests.

Norwich Arts Courses focus on Art, Design and Media Studies.

For information on admissions procedures see the University website: www.nua.ac.uk.

Nottingham Single and Joint Honours courses are available, with some industrial placements. Programmes are modular with compulsory and optional modules, the latter giving some flexibility in the selection of topics from outside the chosen subject field. Degree programmes are offered in the Faculties of Arts, Engineering, Medicine and Health Sciences, Science and Social Sciences. In addition, study-abroad opportunities are offered at over 320 institutions worldwide, through schemes such as Universitas 21 and Erasmus+; almost all students can apply to spend a period of time abroad.

Although grade predictions may match the offers published for the course there is no guarantee that an offer can be made. *Most popular subjects 2015* Economics, Medicine, Veterinary Medicine.

Nottingham Trent Degree programmes are offered in a range of subjects. Many courses are vocational with industrial and commercial placements and some students are also able to spend periods of time studying at a partner university around the world.

The UCAS personal statement is seen as a key part of the application process; the University website provides a guide on its possible content and preparation.

Open University Distance learning and part-time higher education courses. Degree and diploma courses are offered in the following subject areas: Arts and Humanities, Business and Management, Childhood and Youth, Computing and ICT, Education, Engineering and Technology, Environmental Development and International Studies, Health and Social Care, Languages, Law, Mathematics and Statistics, Psychology, Science and Social Sciences. Students study at home and are sent learning materials by the OU, maintaining contact with their tutors by email, post and telephone. See also **Chapter 1**.

There are no formal entry qualifications for admission to courses.

Oxford The University has 30 colleges and five private halls admitting undergraduates. Colleges: Balliol, Brasenose, Christ Church, Corpus Christi, Exeter, Harris Manchester (mature students only), Hertford, Jesus, Keble, Lady Margaret Hall, Lincoln, Magdalen, Mansfield, Merton, New, Oriel, Pembroke, St Anne's, St Catherine's, St Edmund Hall, St Hilda's, St Hugh's, St John's, St Peter's, Somerville, Queen's, Trinity, University, Wadham, Worcester. Permanent Private Halls: Blackfriars, Regent's Park College, St Benet's Hall, St Stephen's House, Wycliffe. Candidates apply to a college and for a Single or Joint Honours programme. Courses are offered with a core element plus a variety of options. Weekly contact with a college tutor assists students to tailor their courses to suit personal interests. Arts students are examined twice, once in the first year (Preliminary examinations) and at the end of the course (Final Honours School). Science students are similarly examined although in some subjects examinations also take place in the second year.

Entrance requirements range from A*A*A to AAA depending on the course. There are specific subject requirements for some courses, particularly in the sciences. Once any subject requirements are met, any other subjects at A-level are acceptable for admission purposes with the exception of general studies (and both general studies and critical thinking for Medicine). It is generally recommended that students take those subjects which they enjoy the most and those in which they are most likely to achieve top grades. However, as the selection criteria for Oxford University are entirely academic, it is also a good idea for students to consider how best they can demonstrate their academic abilities in their choice of subjects. Admissions tests and written work are often part of the application process. Other equivalent qualifications such as Scottish Advanced Highers, American APs and the International Baccalaureate are also very welcome. Please see www.ox.ac.uk/enreqs for further details. There are full details on admissions tests at www.ox.ac.uk/tests.

Oxford Brookes Single Honours courses are offered with modules chosen from a field of study or, alternatively, Combined Honours courses in which two subjects are chosen. These subjects may be in related or unrelated subjects. There is also a Combined Studies degree in which students 'build' their own degree by taking approved modules from a range of the subjects offered by the university.

For all applications, considerable emphasis is placed on the personal statement. Fine Art applicants wishing to take a gap year should contact the admissions tutor before applying.

Plymouth A broad portfolio of degree courses is available. Single Honours courses are offered, with many vocational programmes offering work placements.

The University looks for evidence in the UCAS personal statement of your understanding of the course, good numeracy and literacy skills, motivation and commitment, work experience or placement or voluntary work, especially if it is relevant to your course, any sponsorships or placements you have applied for, and your possible plans for a gap year.

Portsmouth Around half of the students at Portsmouth are on courses that lead to professional accreditation, and many more study on courses that offer real-life learning. Simulated learning environments include a mock courtroom, a newsroom, a health simulation suite, a £1m model pharmacy and a forensic house, where criminologists work on staged crime scenes. Placement opportunities are available in many subjects and there is also the opportunity for all students to learn a foreign language.

Applications are considered using a variety of methods and the following are taken into account: actual and predicted grades, references, personal statements, interviews and tests. Different courses use different methods to reflect, in particular, the nature and demands of the course. For all courses, academic achievement through prior learning or experience is important as is the potential to succeed, as demonstrated through commitment to the subject.

Queen Margaret QMU offers a wide range of professionally relevant courses in the areas of Healthcare; Social Sciences; Performing Arts; Film, Media and PR; and Business, Tourism and Hospitality Management.

Applicants are interviewed for some courses including Occupational Therapy, Nursing, Therapeutic and Diagnostic Radiography, and Costume Design and Construction. *Most popular subjects 2015* Diagnostic Radiography, Nursing, Physiotherapy, Psychology.

Queen's Belfast The academic year is divided into two semesters of 15 weeks each (12 teaching weeks and three examination weeks), with degree courses (pathways) normally taken over three years of full-time study. Six modules are taken each year (three in each semester) and, in theory, a degree can involve any combination of six Level 1 modules. Single, Joint and Combined Honours courses are offered and, in addition, major/minor combinations; some courses include sandwich placements.

Applications for admission to full-time undergraduate courses are made through UCAS, except for courses in Midwifery and Nursing. These should be made direct to the University's School of Nursing and Midwifery (see www.qub.ac.uk). Interviews are essential for Medicine and Dentistry.

Reading The University of Reading offers more than 200 undergraduate courses in arts, humanities, business, social science and science. The modular structure of their courses means you can specialise in the areas that interest you most, while still developing core subject knowledge. If you are interested in studying two related subjects, it also has a wide range of combined degrees to choose from. Because it recognises that 21st-century career paths typically take many turns, all their courses are designed to give you the thinking, problem-solving and creative skills that will help you thrive in any sector. You can gain professional experience that counts towards your degree by carrying out a work placement or an internship, or by spending a year working in your chosen industry. Its wide range of study abroad opportunities also offer an exciting way to enhance your future career options.

Approximately 80% of decisions on applications to undergraduate study are made by the central Admissions Office and 20% of decisions are recommended to the Admissions Office by academic departments/schools. This is agreed on an annual basis according to the requirements of the school or department. In all cases, the criteria on which successful applicants are admitted are agreed with the University's admissions steering group and the academic admissions tutor of the relevant school or department, who also maintains oversight of decisions during the year and will be involved in decisions on specific cases. Candidates are interviewed for Accounting and Business, Archaeology, Architecture, Art, Chemistry, Film and Theatre, Food and Nutritional Sciences, Graphic Communication, Meteorology, Pharmacy, Primary Education, Psychology (MSci course) and Speech and Language Therapy. Typical offers are presented in terms of A-level grades (with the exception of Single Honours Art degrees which use UCAS Tariff points), but applications are welcomed from those presenting a wide range of qualifications. For some courses, selection criteria will include interview, portfolio submission or attendance at a selection centre. *Most popular subjects 2015* Biological Sciences, Law, Maths.

Richmond (Am Int Univ) The University runs British and American courses. American courses are accredited by the Middle States Commission on Higher Education, an agency recognised by the US Department of Education. Courses are also approved by the Open University and can lead to Open University Validated Awards.

Candidates can apply through UCAS, directly to the institution, or through The Common Application. Students are encouraged to visit before applying.

Robert Gordon The University offers a wide range of vocational courses. Many courses offer work placements and there are some opportunities to study abroad in Europe, Canada and the USA.

Interviews are held for some courses, for example Nursing and Midwifery, Health Sciences, Art and Social Work.

Roehampton Roehampton has a 54-acre parkland campus in south-west London with historic buildings alongside modern, cutting edge facilities. The campus provides a close-knit community feel for students and is made up of four historic colleges and 10 academic departments. There are over 50 programmes offered at undergraduate level and Roehampton is also one of the largest providers of initial teacher training in the UK.

Tariffs for entry to undergraduate programmes vary depending on the programme; please check the website for full details. There may be additional requirements so please check before applying.

Royal Agricultural Univ The University is based in Cirencester, Gloucestershire. It currently offers 19 different undergraduate degree courses, in subjects as varied as Real Estate, Rural Land Management, International Business Management, British Wildlife Conservation, Bloodstock and Performance Horse Management, and of course Agriculture, amongst others. The RAU is ranked 3rd in the UK for graduate employability.

For information on admissions procedures see the University website: www.rau.ac.uk/study/undergraduate.

St Andrews A very wide range of subjects is offered across the Faculties of Arts, Divinity, Medicine and Science. A flexible programme is offered in the first two years when students take several subjects. The decision of Honours degree subject is made at the end of Year 2 when students choose between Single or Joint Honours degrees for the next two years. A broadly based General degree programme is also offered lasting three years. After two years of a General degree programme students may transfer onto a named Honours degree programme if they meet the requirements of the department(s).

The University highlights the importance of the personal statement and the quality of this is likely to decide which applicants receive offers. It looks for well-organised, well-written statements which include information about the applicant, their interests, relevant work experience, any voluntary work, ideas about career choice and, importantly, their reasons for their choice of course. Admissions tutors prefer candidates to achieve their grades at the first sitting. Apart from Medicine, Gateway to Physics and Gateway to Computer Science, no candidates are interviewed.

St Mark and St John The University is based in Plymouth on the edge of the city and runs 100-plus programmes which place a high emphasis on being relevant to the labour market. Students will be provided with the relevant transferable skills in demand from employers and businesses – key skills that can help put students a step ahead of the competition. The University specialises in sport, education, languages and linguistics, journalism and creative arts.

The University welcomes applications from students with disabilities, who are well catered for on campus.

St Mary's Flexible, modular degree options allow a great deal of choice to both Joint and Single Honours students. Practical and theoretical studies are followed in the Drama course.

Offers are made through the University Registry. Students for over-subscribed courses or programmes of a practical or professional nature may be called for interview and may be required to take tests. There are special studies in Applied Theatre, Physical Theatre or Theatre Arts in which applicants must take part in a short practical workshop or perform an audition piece.

Salford The University offers BA, BSc and BEng degrees with teaching methods depending on the degree. The University is equally likely to accept students with BTECs and Access qualifications as well as those with A-levels. There is a wide range of professionally accredited programmes many involving work placements. All undergraduates may study a foreign language.

The University is committed to widening participation but it does not make lower offers on the basis of educational or social disadvantage.

Sheffield The teaching year consists of two semesters (two periods of 15 weeks). Courses are fully modular, with the exceptions of Dentistry and Medicine. Students register for a named degree course which has a number of core modules, some optional modules chosen from a prescribed range of topics, and some unrestricted modules chosen from across the University.

The University considers qualifications already achieved (including GCSEs), predicted grades and personal statements as the most important parts of an application. Interviews are not a prerequisite of admission, however some departments do interview to further assess the motivation and personal qualities of applicants. Departments that interview include Medicine, Dentistry, Orthoptics and Human Communication Science (for Speech Science). The Applicant Information Desk can help with any questions applicants have about the process of applying to Sheffield and the current status of their application.

Sheffield Hallam A large number of vocational courses are offered in addition to those in Arts, Humanities and Social Sciences. The University is the largest provider of sandwich courses in the UK with most courses offering work placements, usually between the second and third years. Most students are able to study an additional language from French, German, Italian, Spanish and Japanese.

For information on admissions procedures see the University website: www.shu.ac.uk.

South Wales The University has five campuses in Cardiff, Glyntaff, Treforest, Caerleon and in Newport City. Many of the courses are vocational and can be studied as Single or Joint Honours courses or major/minor degrees.

Applicants for courses in Art and Design, Teacher Training and Social Work are interviewed.

Southampton A wide range of courses is offered in the Faculties of Law, Arts and Social Sciences, Engineering, Science and Mathematics and Medicine, Health and Life Sciences. Programmes are generally for three years. All students have the chance to study a language as part of their degree and there are many opportunities for students to study abroad or on Erasmus+-Socrates exchange programmes whether or not they are studying modern languages.

The University looks for a well-considered personal statement, focusing on your reasons for choosing a particular course, the skills you would bring to it, information about any relevant work experience, your career ideas, your personal interests related to the course, and your thoughts about 'what makes you stand out in a crowd'.

Southampton Solent Courses are offered in many vocational subjects. There are opportunities for students to gain work experience in the form of industrial placements alongside academic study.

Admissions staff look for applicants' reasons for their course choice, and for evidence of their abilities and ambitions.

Staffordshire The main campus at Stoke-on-Trent offers a diverse range of courses in Art and Design, Business, Computing, Engineering, Film, Sound & Vision, Humanities, Law, Psychology, Social Sciences, Science and Sports Science. The Centres of Excellence in Stafford and Shrewsbury offer courses in Health Professions including Nursing, Midwifery, Paramedic Science and Operating Department Practice. Courses can be taught full-time or part-time, whilst a selection of courses can be taught on a 'Fast Track' two-year basis.

The University provides various ways to support prospective students with their applications and personal statements. This includes advice over the phone, workshops on campus or at schools and colleges, online information and tailored advice at Open Days.

Stirling A flexible system operates in which students can delay their final degree choice until midway through the course. The University year is divided into two 15-week semesters, from September to December and January to May with a reading/study block and exams at the end of each semester. Innovative January entry is possible to some degree programmes. There are 200 degree combinations with the opportunity to study a range of disciplines in the first two years. In addition to Single and Combined Honours degrees, there is a General degree which allows for greater breadth of choice. Subjects range across the Arts, Social Sciences and Sciences.

Admissions are administered through a central office. It is essential to include in the personal statement your reasons for choosing your specified course. The University also looks for evidence of your transferable skills, for example communication skills and teamwork, and how you acquired these, for example through work experience, voluntary work, academic studies, hobbies and general life experience. *Most popular subjects 2015* Nursing and Primary Education.

Stranmillis (UC) This is a college of Queen's University, Belfast focusing on teacher training courses with European and international exchanges as part of the degrees.

Candidates for teacher training courses will be called for interview.

Strathclyde A credit-based modular system operates with a good degree of flexibility in course choices. The University offers many vocational courses in the Faculties of Engineering and Science and in the Strathclyde Business School. There are also degree programmes in arts subjects, Education, Law and the Social Sciences.

Formal interviews are required for some vocational courses; informal interviews are held by some science and engineering courses.

Sunderland The University of Sunderland provides a range of courses across four faculties; Arts, Design and Media; Business and Law; Education and Society; and Applied Sciences. All courses are geared towards employability, with excellent work placements and visiting lecturers from some of the biggest companies in the UK. Several courses can include an option to study abroad in various locations including Australia, USA, Germany, France and more.

The University holds informal interviews for certain courses, when applicants will be asked to present their portfolio, to give an audition, or to talk about themselves and why they want to study for that particular course. The University's admissions team are able to guide applicants through the process, via telephone 0191 515 3154, or email: admissions@sunderland.ac.uk.

Surrey The University campus at Guildford offers degree programmes in the Arts, Biomedical Sciences, Electronics and Physical Sciences, Engineering, Health and Medical Sciences and Management. Some 80% of students spend a professional training year as part of their course and in some cases there are placements abroad.

The University is willing to consider deferring an application for one year, providing it considers that this will benefit the applicant's studies. Contact the admissions staff if you are considering deferred entry.

Sussex Teaching is structured around 12 schools of study, the Brighton and Sussex Medical School and the Science and Technology Policy Research Unit. Courses cover a wide range of subjects in Humanities, Life Sciences, Science and Technology, Social Sciences and Cultural Studies. Students are registered in a school depending on the degree taken. The flexible structure allows students to interrupt their degree programme to take a year out. In addition, students can customise their degree through a range of pathways, placements and study abroad programmes.

If you are applying to do an undergraduate course in Social Work, Journalism or Medicine, you will need to attend an interview. If you do not have formal academic qualifications, you will also have to attend an interview. It also has workshops within the admissions process for Drama Studies and portfolio reviews for Product Design. If you are asked to come for an interview or workshop, this forms part of the selection process for deciding if the University can offer you a place. Interviews and workshops normally take place between January and April and it tries to give you at least two weeks' notice. It aims to keep interviewing to a minimum but depending on your chosen subject, it may need to interview you to reach a decision on your application. However, they aim to make the interview or workshop part of a structured visit to the University. You should remember that it is a two-way process – allowing you to ask questions and helping it to reach a decision about your application.

Swansea Courses are offered in Arts and Social Sciences, Business, Economics and Law, Engineering, Languages, Medicine and Health Sciences and Science. Degree courses are modular with the opportunity to take some subjects outside the chosen degree course. Part-time degrees are available and study abroad arrangements are possible in several subject areas.

Selectors take into account the candidate's ability to contribute to the cultural, sporting and social life of the University.

Teesside The Middlesbrough campus offers courses at undergraduate and postgraduate level, emphasising professionalism through work placements, volunteering, live projects, accredited courses and graduate internships. Areas of study include Animation, Games, Petroleum Technology, Chemical Engineering, Network Systems, Applied Science, Business, Computing, Design, Media, Engineering, Forensic and Crime Scene Investigation, History, Law and Criminal Justice, Psychology, Sociology and Sport.

Interviews are held for a wide range of courses, and successful applicants are given an individualised offer. Conditional offers are made in UCAS Tariff points. For some courses you may need to include points from certain subjects in your Tariff points score.

Trinity Saint David The University's main campuses are situated in various locations in and around Swansea's city centre as well as in the rural towns of Lampeter and Carmarthen in South West Wales. Study at the Lampeter campus comprises Single and Joint Honours degrees in a wide range of Humanities and Carmarthen has a strong Art and Design focus.

The University guarantees to give equal consideration to all applicants irrespective of when their applications are received. Applicants who successfully complete the residential Wales Summer School at Lampeter, Aberystwyth or Carmarthen are offered a place on an appropriate course of study on completion of their current school or college course. All other candidates will be invited to an interview to discuss their course choice. Entry is based on individual merit.

UHI The University of the Highlands and Islands offers a range of courses at centres throughout Scotland including Argyll, Inverness, Perth, Orkney and Shetland.

Contact the institution regarding its requirements and procedures.

Ulster The Faculties of Art, Design and the Built Environment, Computing and Engineering, Life and Health Sciences, Social Sciences and Ulster University Business School offer a wide range of courses. There are various styles of learning supported by formal lectures and many courses include periods of work placement.

Information is available via www.ulster.ac.uk/apply/admissions-information.

Univ Law The University of Law offers specialised Law courses and a Law with Business degree, across the country with centres in Birmingham, Bristol, Chester, Guildford, Leeds, London and Manchester. Its courses combine academic rigour and practical skills, taught by qualified lawyers, often in small group workshops. It places strong emphasis on individual tutor contact and feedback. It is possible to continue your legal education after gaining your law degree with its Legal Practice Course (LPC) to practise as a solicitor or its Bar Professional Training Course (BPTC) to prepare you for life as a barrister. De Broc School of Business (part of The University of Law) offers undergraduate business degrees with employability in mind. You have a choice of learning in the heart of London's West End at its Bloomsbury centre or in thriving city centre locations in Birmingham or Leeds. With a rich heritage and reputation for innovative teaching practices, its courses build on a strong tradition of close student support, exceptional teaching quality and career focus.

Applications are submitted through UCAS.

UWE Bristol The University consists of several campuses in Bristol including Frenchay (the largest), Bower Ashton (Creative Industries), Glenside (Health and Applied Sciences), Gloucester (Nursing), and Hartpury near Gloucester. The University offers Single and Combined Honours courses organised on a modular basis which gives much flexibility in the choice of options. Many courses include optional sandwich placements and, in addition, students have the opportunity to undertake a period of study in another EU country.

Offers may vary between applicants since selection is based on individual merit. Students applying for courses 'subject to approval' or 'subject to validation' will be kept informed of the latest developments. Most offers will be made in terms of UCAS Tariff points with specific subjects required for some programmes.

Warwick Courses are offered by departments in the Faculties of Arts, Science and Social Studies and the Warwick Medical School. Its undergraduate students can either choose single-subject degrees or combine two or more subjects in a Joint Honours degree. Options offered in each course provide some flexibility for you to tailor your course to your own areas of academic interest. Whatever course you choose, you can apply to study abroad, and many of its courses have inbuilt overseas experiences. Some of its degrees offer work placements and/or professional accreditation.

Before you decide to apply, you should check the entry requirements for your course. You will find the typical offer levels at www.warwick.ac.uk/ugoffers. Advice on the completion of your application is available at www.warwick.ac.uk/go/study. Feedback can be provided if requested for candidates whose application has been unsuccessful. The University welcomes applications for deferred entry.

West London UWL provides a high quality experience connected to the world of work. Subjects offered cover Business, Management and Law, Tourism, Hospitality and Leisure, Music, Media and Creative Technologies and Health and Human Sciences. Credit-rated Honours courses are offered, many with year-long work placements between Years 2 and 3. There are some study-abroad arrangements in Europe, Canada and the USA and there is a large mature student intake.

The University accepts a wide range of qualifications for entry to all of its undergraduate courses, providing the UCAS Tariff points achieved by applicants match or exceed the UCAS Tariff points listed in the course entry requirements. It is also possible to transfer credits achieved at another university to a course at this university.

West Scotland UWS has campuses in Ayr, Dumfries, Lanarkshire, London and Paisley and provides a range of vocationally related courses, with a unique combination of links with employers, practical opportunities and professional recognition.

Applications are considered by the Admissions Office against previously agreed academic entry qualifications provided by the following Schools: Business and Enterprise; Engineering and Computing; Media, Culture and Society; Health, Nursing and Midwifery; Education; and Science and Sport. Within the Schools of Education; Media, Culture and Society; Health, Nursing and Midwifery; Engineering and Computing; and Science and Sport, applicants may be invited to attend an audition or interview prior to an offer being made.

Westminster The University of Westminster offers practice-based courses, many with international recognition. The University's distinguished 175-year history has meant it leads the way in many areas of research, particularly politics, media, art and design, architecture and biomedical sciences. Its position in the city of London allows it to continue to build on its close connections with leading figures and organisations in these areas as well as in the worlds of business, information technology and law. The University has one of the largest study abroad programmes in the UK attracting over 1,200 students per year from the USA, Japan and across the EU. It has one of the country's largest university scholarship schemes available awarding over £2.9 million per year in scholarships.

Interviews are usually required for Media, Art and Design courses and Complementary Therapy courses. Applicants for creative courses should bring a portfolio of practical work to interviews. The University accepts transfers into Years 1, 2 and 3 of a full-time degree programme if students have studied similar units to the chosen Westminster course, and have passed Year 1 and Year 2, each with 120 credits, excluding all Westminster Business School degrees, Fashion Design and Film.

Winchester A city centre university offering Single and Joint Honours degrees (the latter with two subjects studied equally).

Interviews are required for a number of courses, including American Studies, Choreography & Dance, Comedy: Performance and Production, Drama, Musical Theatre, Performing Arts, Popular Music, Primary Education, Social Work, Theatre Production (Arts and Stage Management), and Theology, Religion & Ethics. Please make sure to check the website for the most up-to-date information before applying.

Wolverhampton A large number of specialist and Joint Honours degrees are offered and many have work placements at home or abroad. Except for courses linked to specific professional requirements, programmes are modular providing flexibility of choice.

Admissions staff make decisions on the basis of the application, and may invite applicants for interview or audition. If an applicant cannot meet the entry requirements for the chosen course, the University may offer an alternative course, or give the applicant feedback about why it was unable to offer a place.

Worcester A wide range of undergraduate courses in Education, Health, Sport, Arts, Humanities, Sciences and Business are on offer with Single and Joint Honours degrees available. The University is close to Worcester city centre, and most of its halls of residence, many of which are en-suite, are right on campus.

The University accepts a wide range of qualifications including Access to HE Diplomas. The majority of offers are based on UCAS Tariff points but some courses have specific subject or GCSE requirements. Many courses require interviews before an offer is made including Primary Education, Nursing and Health courses. The personal statement is highly important and applicants are advised to reflect on interests, work experience, voluntary experience, extra-curricular activities and achievements relevant to their chosen course. If the applicant fails to receive an offer for their chosen course then an offer for an alternative course may be made.

York Thirty departments and centres cover a range of subjects in the arts and humanities, sciences, social sciences and medicine. The 'Languages for All' programme enables any student to take a course in any one of a number of languages, in addition to which there are several opportunities to build a period abroad into a degree course.

Decisions on offers are made in the following ways. Centralised decision making: Archaeology, Economics, Education, History, History of Art, Language and Linguistic Science, Management, PEP, Philosophy, Politics, Psychology, Social Policy, Social and Political Sciences, Sociology. Semi-centralised decision making: Law, Mathematics, Physics. Devolved decision making in academic departments: Biology, Biochemistry, Biomedical Science, Chemistry, Computer Science, Electronics, English, Environment, Hull York Medical School, Music, Nursing and Midwifery, Natural Sciences, Social Work, Theatre Film and Television. All candidates are interviewed for Biology, Chemistry, Health Sciences, Law, Medicine, Music, Natural Sciences, Physics, Social Work and Theatre Film and Television. There are optional interviews for Maths.

York St John A city centre university with Faculties of Education and Theology, Business and Communication, Health and Life Sciences and Art. These offer a range of specialist degrees with Joint Honours courses offered in Business, Counselling, Design, Education, Health Studies, Information Technology, Languages and Linguistics, Management, Occupational Therapy, Physiotherapy, Psychology, Sport and Theology.

Interviews are compulsory for the following courses: Fine Art, Occupational Therapy, Physiotherapy, Primary Education, Design, and Youth and Community Work.

4 | APPLICATIONS

ENTRY REQUIREMENTS

Before applying to universities and colleges, be sure that you have the required subjects and qualifications for entry to your chosen course. Details of entry requirements are available direct from the universities and colleges. You will need to check:

 (i) the general entry requirements for courses
 (ii) any specific subject requirements to enter a particular course, for example, study of specified GCE A-levels and (where required) AS, Scottish Highers/Advanced Highers, GCSEs, Scottish Nationals, or BTEC qualifications (for example, Diploma, Certificate). The course requirements are set out in prospectuses and on websites
(iii) any age, health, Disclosure and Barring Service (DBS; formerly CRB) clearance or other requirements for entry to particular courses and universities and colleges. For entry to some specific courses such as Medicine and Nursing, offers are made subject to health screening for hepatitis B, for example, and immunisation requirements. Owing to government regulations, some universities will insist on a minimum age at entry of 18 years. Check university and college websites and prospectuses for these particular course requirements
(iv) admissions tests required by a number of universities for a range of subjects, including Dentistry, Law, Medicine and Veterinary Science/Medicine. Offers of places made by these universities are dependent on an applicant's performance in the relevant test. It is important to find out full details about universities' course requirements for possible admissions tests well before submitting the UCAS application and to make all the necessary arrangements for registering and taking any required admissions tests. See **Chapter 5** and check university/college and admissions tests websites for the latest information.

Potential applicants should ask the advice of teachers, careers advisers and university and college advisers before submitting their application.

APPLICATIONS FOR UNIVERSITY AND COLLEGE COURSES THROUGH UCAS

UCAS, the organisation responsible for managing applications to higher education courses in the UK, deals with applications for admission to full-time and sandwich first degrees, Foundation degrees, Diploma of Higher Education and Higher National Diploma courses and some full-time Higher National Certificate courses in nearly all universities (but not the Open University), university colleges, colleges and institutes of higher education, specialist colleges and some further education colleges.

The UCAS application process

Full details of application procedures and all course information can be found on the UCAS website (www.ucas.com).

Applications are made online at www.ucas.com using **Apply**. This is a secure web-based application system, which has been designed for all applicants whether they are applying through a UCAS-registered centre, such as a school or college, or applying independently from anywhere in the world.

Applications can be sent to UCAS from 1 September. The first deadline is 15 October by 18.00 (UK time) for applications to the universities of Oxford or Cambridge and applications for most courses in Medicine, Dentistry and Veterinary Science/Medicine. The deadline for UK and EU applicants to apply for all other courses is 15 January by 18.00 (UK time), except for some Art and Design courses that have a 24 March by 18.00 (UK time) deadline. You can still apply after these deadlines up to 30 June, but institutions may not be able to consider you.

On the UCAS application, you have up to five course choices unless you are applying for Dentistry, Medicine or Veterinary Science/Medicine. For these courses only four choices are permitted.

Each university or college makes any offer through the UCAS system. UCAS does not make offers, or recruit on behalf of universities and colleges. It does not advise applicants on their choice of subject although it does publish material which applicants may find useful.

Applicants may receive an 'unconditional' offer in the case of those who already hold the required qualifications, or, for those awaiting examination results, a 'conditional' offer or a rejection. When all decisions have been received from universities or colleges, applicants may finally hold up to two offers: a firm choice (first) offer and an insurance offer. Applicants who have made five choices and have no offers or have declined any offers received can use **Extra**. Applicants are told if they become eligible for **Extra** and can apply online for one further course at a time using **Track** at www.ucas.com. **Extra** runs from 25 February until 4 July. Courses available in **Extra** will be highlighted on the course search tool at www.ucas.com. Applicants not placed through this system will be eligible to contact institutions with vacancies in **Clearing** from 5 July.

If you already have your qualifications and are not waiting for any exam results, your place can be confirmed at any time after you send in your application. However, for thousands of applicants confirmation starts on the day when the A-level examination results are released. Full **Clearing** vacancy lists are also published from A-level results day (Scottish vacancy lists are published from Scottish Qualification results day). Applicants meeting the conditions of their offers for their firm choice will receive confirmation from their university or college and may still be accepted even if their results are slightly lower than those stipulated in the original offer. If rejected by their firm choice university/college, applicants will have their places confirmed by their insurance choice institution providing they have obtained the right grades. Applicants who are unsuccessful with both their institutions will be eligible to go into **Clearing** in which they can select an appropriate course in the same or a different institution where places are available. In 2015, over 60,000 applicants obtained places through **Clearing**, and over 7500 applicants found a place though **Extra**.

Each year some applicants pass their exams with better results than expected. This may mean that some will not only have met the conditions of their firm choice, but will have exceeded them. UCAS introduced **Adjustment** for these applicants – it provides an opportunity to reconsider where and what to study whilst holding a confirmed place. The **Adjustment** process is available from A-level results day (17 August 2017) until 31 August.

UCAS timetable

1 September 2016	UCAS begins accepting applications.
15 October	Deadline for UCAS to receive applications to Oxford University or the University of Cambridge, and applications to most courses in Medicine, Dentistry or Veterinary Medicine Science.
15 January 2017	Deadline for UCAS to receive applications from UK and EU applicants for all other courses, except for some Art and Design courses that have a 24 March deadline. Use the course search tool at www.ucas.com to find out whether Art and Design courses have a 15 January or 24 March deadline.
16 January–30 June	Applications received by UCAS are forwarded to the institutions for consideration at their discretion. Applications received after 30 June are processed through **Clearing**.
25 February–4 July	Applicants who have made five choices and have no offers or who have declined any offers received can use **Extra** to apply for one further course at a time on **Track** at www.ucas.com. Institutions will show which courses have vacancies in **Extra** on the UCAS website. Details of the **Extra** service can be found at www.ucas.com/extra.
24 March	Deadline for UCAS to receive applications for some Art and Design courses. Use the course search tool at www.ucas.com to find out whether Art and Design courses have a 15 January or 24 March deadline.
4 May	Applicants who have received all their decisions from universities and colleges by the end of March are asked to reply to their offers by this date.
8 June	Applicants receiving decisions from all their choices by 5 May must reply to their offers by this date.
30 June	Last date for receiving applications. Applications received after this date are entered directly into **Clearing**. On 5 July **Clearing** starts.

TBC	Scottish SQA results published. Scottish Clearing vacancy lists available.
17 August	GCE A-level and AS results published. English, Welsh and Northern Ireland Clearing vacancy lists available. (See **What To Do on Results Day ... and After** below.)

PLEASE NOTE

- You are not required to reply to any university/college offers until you have received your last decision.
- Do not send a firm acceptance to more than one offer.
- Do not try to alter a firm acceptance.
- If you decide not to go to university or college this year you can go to **Track** to completely cancel your application. But don't forget, you will not be able to reapply until next year.
- Remember to tell the institutions and UCAS if you change your address, or change your examination board, subjects or arrangements.

Information on the special arrangements for applications for Law, Medicine and Dentistry can be found under separate headings in Chapter 5.

APPLICATIONS FOR ART AND DESIGN COURSES

All art and design courses use one of two application deadlines: 15 January or 24 March. The later closing date is to allow students taking a Diploma in Foundation Studies (Art and Design) time to identify their specialisation and put together a portfolio of work which they will need to present at interview. The deadline for each course is given in the UCAS search tool.

APPLICATIONS FOR MUSIC COURSES AT CONSERVATOIRES

UCAS Conservatoires handles applications for practice-based music, dance, screen and drama courses. Applications can be made simultaneously to a maximum of six of the conservatoires listed below and simultaneous applications can also be made through both UCAS Undergraduate and UCAS Conservatoires systems. Full details of UCAS Conservatoires are given on www.ucas.com/conservatoires. The conservatoires taking part in this online admissions system are:

- Birmingham Conservatoire www.bcu.ac.uk/conservatoire
- Leeds College of Music www.lcm.ac.uk
- Royal Academy of Music www.ram.ac.uk
- Royal College of Music www.rcm.ac.uk
- Royal Conservatoire of Scotland www.rcs.ac.uk
- Royal Northern College of Music www.rncm.ac.uk
- Royal Welsh College of Music & Drama www.rwcmd.ac.uk
- Trinity Laban Conservatoire of Music & Dance www.trinitylaban.ac.uk

The Guildhall School of Music & Drama is not part of the UCAS Conservatoires scheme, so students wishing to apply will have to make their applications directly to the school. There is an application fee, which varies depending on the course for which you apply; the fee includes the audition fee, which is charged by all conservatoires. For more details, see the Guildhall website.

APPLICATIONS FOR TEACHER TRAINING COURSES

Applicants intending to start a course of initial teacher training in England, Northern Ireland and Wales leading to Qualified Teacher Status can find information on the Get Into Teaching website https://getintoteaching.education.gov.uk. See also www.ucas.com/teacher-training for full details of applying for undergraduate (and postgraduate) training courses. Scottish students should check www. gtcs.org.uk.

THE UCAS APPLICATION

Two important aspects of the UCAS application concern Sections 3 and 10. In the choices section of **Apply**, all your university/college choices (a maximum of five) are to be listed, but remember that you should not mix your subjects. For example, in popular subject areas such as English, History or Physiotherapy, it is safer to show total commitment by applying for all courses in the same subject and not to include second and/or third subject alternatives on the form. (See advice in separate tables in **Chapter 7** for **Medicine**, **Dentistry** and **Veterinary Science/Medicine**.)

A brief glance at the subject tables in **Chapter 7** will give you some idea of the popularity of various courses. In principle, institutions want the best applicants available so if there are large numbers of applicants the offers made will be higher. For Medicine and a number of other courses, offers in terms of A-level grades are now reaching AAA or A* grades, and sometimes with additional grades at AS. Conversely, for the less popular subjects, the offers can be much lower – down to CCC.

Similarly, some institutions are more popular (not necessarily better) than others. Again, this popularity can be judged easily in the tables in **Chapter 7**: the higher the offer, the more popular the institution. Popular universities often are located in attractive towns or cities such as Bristol, Exeter, Warwick, Bath or York. Because of the intense competition for places at the popular universities, applications to five of them could result in rejections from all of them! (If you are not good enough for one of them you won't be good enough for the other four!) Spread your choice of institutions.

When you have chosen your courses and your institutions, look again at the offers made and compare these with the grades projected by your teachers. It is most important to maximise your chances of a place by choosing institutions which might make you a range of offers. When all universities have considered your application you can hold only two offers (one firm and one insurance offer) and naturally it is preferable for one to be lower than the other in case you do not achieve the offer grades or equivalent points for your first choice of university or college.

The other section of the UCAS application that deserves careful thought is Section 10 (the personal statement). This seems simple enough but it is the only part of the application where you can put in a personal bid for a place! In short, you are asked to give relevant background information about yourself, your interests and your choice of course and career. Give yourself plenty of time to prepare your personal statement as this part of your application could make all the difference to getting an offer or not.

Motivation to undertake your chosen course is very important. You can show this by giving details of any work experience and work shadowing you have done (and for History courses, for example, details of visits to places of historical interest). It is a good idea to begin your statement with such evidence and explain how your interest in your chosen subject has developed. In the subject tables in **Chapter 7** under **Advice to applicants and planning the UCAS personal statement**, advice is given on what you might include in your personal statement. You should also include various activities in which you have been involved in the last three or four years. Get your parents and other members of the family to refresh your memory – it is easy to forget something quite important. You might consider planning out this section in a series of sub-sections – and if you have a lot to say, be brief. The sub-sections can include the following.

- **School activities** Are you a prefect, chairperson or treasurer of a society? Are you involved in supervisory duties of any kind? Are you in a school team? Which team? For how long? (Remember, team means any team: sports, chess, debating, even business.)
- **Intellectual activities** Have you attended any field or lecture courses in your main subjects? Where? When? Have you taken part in any school visits? Do you play in the school orchestra or have you taken part in a school drama production – on or off stage? Do you go to the theatre, art galleries or concerts?
- **Out-of-school activities** This category might cover many of the topics above, but it could also include any community or voluntary work you do, or Duke of Edinburgh Awards, the Combined Cadet Force (CCF), sport, music and drama activities etc. The countries you have visited might also be mentioned, for example, any exchange visits with friends living abroad.
- **Work experience** Details of part-time, holiday or Saturday jobs could be included here, particularly if they have some connection with your chosen course. Some applicants plan ahead and arrange to visit firms and discuss career interests with various people who already work in their chosen field.

For some courses such as Veterinary Science, work experience is essential, and it certainly helps for others, for example Medicine and Business courses.

- **Functional/Essential Skills** These cover numeracy, communication and information technology (the basics) and also advanced skills involving teamwork, problem solving and improving your own learning. If you are not offering the qualifications then evidence of your strengths in these areas may be mentioned in the school or college reference or you may include examples in your personal statement relating to your out-of-school activities.

Finally, plan your personal statement carefully. You may write short statements if you wish. It is not essential to write in prose except perhaps if you are applying for English or language courses in which case your statement will be judged grammatically! Keep a copy of your complete application for reference if you are called for interview. Almost certainly you will be questioned on what you have written.

Admissions tutors always stress the importance of the confidential reference from your head teacher or form tutors. Most schools and colleges will make some effort to find out why you want to apply for a particular course, but if they do not ask, do not take it for granted that they will know! Consequently, although you have the opportunity to write about your interests on the form, it is still a good idea to tell your teachers about them. Also, if you have to work at home under difficult conditions or if you have any medical problems, your teachers must be told since these points should be mentioned on the reference.

Deferred entry
Although application is usually made in the autumn of the year preceding the proposed year of entry, admissions tutors may be prepared to consider an application made two years before entry, so that the applicant can, perhaps, gain work experience or spend a period abroad. Policies on deferred entry may differ from department to department, so you should check with admissions tutors before applying. Simply remember that there is no guarantee that you will get the grades you need or a place at the university of your first choice at the first attempt! If not, you may need to repeat A-levels and try again. It may be better not to apply for deferred entry until you are certain in August of your grades and your place.

APPLICATIONS TO THE UNIVERSITY OF CAMBRIDGE
The universities of Oxford and Cambridge offer a wealth of resources and opportunities to students, including highly personalised teaching in tutorials (at Oxford) or supervisions (at Cambridge), where groups of two or three students meet to discuss their work with a tutor (Oxford) or supervisor (Cambridge). The college system is also a key advantage of an Oxbridge education, as students gain all the benefits of studying at a large and internationally acclaimed university, as well as the benefits of life in the smaller college community.

If you are a UK or EU applicant, you need only complete the UCAS application. You will then receive an email from the University, confirming the arrival of your application and giving you the website address of their online Supplementary Application Questionnaire (SAQ) which you will then need to complete and return by the specified date. Check with the Admissions Office or on www.study.cam.ac.uk/undergraduate/apply for the latest information.

Your UCAS application listing Cambridge as one of your university choices must be sent to UCAS by 15 October, 18.00 (UK time). If you are applying for Medicine or Veterinary Medicine you must include your BMAT registration with your application. You can indicate your choice of college or make an Open application if you have no preference. Open applicants are allocated by a computer program to colleges that have had fewer applicants per place for your chosen subject.

The Extenuating Circumstances Form (ECF) has been designed to ensure that the Cambridge colleges have the information they require in order to accurately assess any applicant who has experienced particular personal or educational disadvantage through health, personal problems, disability or difficulties with schooling. The ECF should normally be submitted by the applicant's school/college by 15 October. Further details can be obtained at www.study.cam.ac.uk/undergraduate/apply/ecf.html.

Interviews take place in Cambridge in the first three weeks of December, although some may be earlier. Please note that from 2017 entry onwards, the colleges at the University of Cambridge will be implementing common-format written assessments to be taken by all applicants for all subjects, except Mathematics and Music. Applicants will take the written assessments either pre-interview or at interview, depending on the course for which they apply. Pre-interview assessments will take place on 2 November, on the same day as those set by the University of Oxford, whilst at-interview assessments will form part of the December interview period. Please see www.undergraduate.study.cam.ac.uk/applying/admissions-assessments for further information on these assessments and **Chapter 5** for information you need to know before completing and submitting your application.

In January applicants receive either an offer conditional upon certain grades in examinations to be taken the following summer, or a rejection. Alternatively, you may be placed in a pool for further consideration. Decisions are made on the basis of academic record, reference, personal statement, submitted work/ test results and interviews. The conditions set are grades to be obtained in examinations such as A-levels, Scottish Highers/Advanced Highers or the International Baccalaureate. Offers made by some Cambridge colleges may also include Sixth Term Examination Papers (STEP) in mathematics (see **Chapter 5** under *Mathematics*). The STEPs are taken in June and copies of past papers and full details are available from www.admissionstestingservice.org.

College policies
All colleges which admit undergraduates use the selection procedures described in **Chapter 5**. However, there will be some minor variations between the various colleges, within each college and also between subjects. Further information about the policies of any particular college can be found in the Cambridge Undergraduate Prospectus and may also be obtained from the admissions tutor of the college concerned. No college operates a quota system for any subject except Medicine and Veterinary Medicine, for which there are strict quotas for the University from which places are allocated to each college.

Full details of the admissions procedures are contained in the current Cambridge Undergraduate Prospectus. Copies of the prospectus are available from Cambridge Admissions Office, Fitzwilliam House, 32 Trumpington Street, Cambridge CB2 1QY, or via the website www.undergraduate.study.cam.ac.uk.

APPLICATIONS TO THE UNIVERSITY OF OXFORD
Applications for undergraduate courses at Oxford are made through UCAS in the same way as applications to other UK universities but candidates must submit their application by 15 October, 18.00 (UK time) for entry in the following year.

You can only apply to one undergraduate course at Oxford. You can also express a preference for a particular college if you wish, or you can make an Open application. This is just like saying that you don't mind which college you go to and your application will then be allocated to a college which has relatively fewer applications for your subject in that year. The colleges have far more in common than they have differences, and all offer the same high standard of academic teaching and support, so please do not worry too much about college choice.

Applicants for most courses are required to sit a written test as part of their application, or to submit examples of their written work. See **Chapter 5** for more information and www.ox.ac.uk/apply for full details. Separate registration is required for any tests, so it's really important to check the details for your subject in good time.

When considering your application, tutors will take into account all the information that has been provided, in order to assess your suitability and potential for your chosen course. This includes your academic record, personal statement, academic reference and predicted grades, along with any written tests or written work required. If you haven't done particularly well in one area, you may still be successful if you have performed strongly in other aspects of your application. Each application is considered carefully on its individual merits, including contextual information about candidates' educational background.

A shortlist of the very best candidates will be invited to Oxford for interview, which is an important part of the selection procedure. Candidates will usually be interviewed at their college of preference and also may be interviewed by other colleges. Those from outside Europe who are not able to travel may be interviewed by telephone or Skype or some other remote means. The University works hard to ensure that the best candidates are successful, whichever college you have applied to. Any college may make you an offer of a place.

Successful candidates who have not completed their school-leaving examinations will be made conditional offers based on final grades. This will be probably be between A*A*A and AAA at A-level, 38–40 points in the International Baccalaureate, including core points, or other equivalent qualifications. Decisions are notified to candidates via UCAS by the end of January.

To find out more
The University holds three Open Days a year: two in late June or early July, and one in mid-September. These are highly recommended as a great way to visit the city and the University, meet tutors and current students and find out more. Visit the website at www.ox.ac.uk/study for further information, and details of other events around the UK and beyond.

APPLICATIONS TO THE RUSSELL GROUP
The Russell Group universities are:
University of Birmingham; University of Bristol; University of Cambridge; Cardiff University; Durham University; University of Edinburgh; University of Exeter; University of Glasgow; Imperial College London; King's College London; University of Leeds; University of Liverpool; London School of Economics and Political Science; University of Manchester; Newcastle University; University of Nottingham; University of Oxford; Queen Mary University of London; Queen's University Belfast; University of Sheffield; University of Southampton; University College London; University of Warwick; University of York. (See also under London (LSE) **Chapter 3.**)

The Russell Group published information on what it terms 'facilitating subjects', ie subjects they would prefer to be studied by A-level students. The subjects they view as 'facilitating subjects' are maths and further maths, physics, biology, chemistry, history, geography, modern and classical languages, and English literature.

APPLICATIONS TO IRISH UNIVERSITIES
All applications to universities in the Republic of Ireland are made through the Central Application Office, Tower House, Eglinton Street, Galway, Ireland; see www.cao.ie or telephone 091 509 800. The Central Application Office website gives full details of all 41 institutions and details of the application procedure. Applications are made by 1 February. Individual institutions publish details of their entry requirements for courses, but unlike applications through UCAS in the UK, no conditional offers are made. Applicants are judged purely on their academic ability except for the Royal College of Surgeons which also requires a school reference and a personal statement. The results are published in August when institutions make their offers and when successful students are required to accept or decline the offer.

APPLICATIONS TO COMMONWEALTH UNIVERSITIES
Details of universities in 37 commonwealth countries (all charge fees) are published on www.acu.ac.uk or for those in Australia, on www.australia.idp.com, and for those in Canada, www.studyincanada.com.

APPLICATIONS TO AMERICAN UNIVERSITIES
There are a very large number of universities and colleges offering degree course programmes in the USA; some institutions are independent and others state-controlled. Students applying to study in the USA can now apply to over 600 colleges through the Common Application, the new central admissions system. However, unlike the UK, where UCAS controls nearly all university and college applications, it is still necessary to apply to certain American institutions directly; a full list of participating Common Application colleges can be downloaded from the website at www.commonapp.org. Most American universities will expect applicants to have A-levels or IB qualifications and in addition, usually require students to complete a School Assessment Test (SAT) covering mathematical and verbal reasoning abilities. In some cases applicants may be required to take SAT II tests which are based on specific subjects. Tests can be taken at centres in the UK: see www.collegeboard.org.

Unlike the usual specialised subject degrees at UK universities, 'Liberal Arts' programmes in the USA have considerable breadth and flexibility, although subjects requiring greater specialised knowledge such as Medicine and Law require further study at Medical or Law School.

Because of the complexities of an application to American universities, such as financial implications, visas etc, students should initially refer to www.fulbright.co.uk. It is also important to be able to identify the differences between and the quality of institutions and valuable guides can be sourced through www.petersons.com.

THE ERASMUS+ PROGRAMME

Many universities in the UK have formal agreements with partner institutions in Europe through the Erasmus+ programme which enables UK university students to apply for courses in Europe for periods up to one year. Some of these courses are taught in English and students can receive help with accommodation and other expenses through the Erasmus+ Student Grant scheme.

The Erasmus+ programme is for undergraduates in all subject areas who would like to study or do a work placement for three to twelve months as part of their degree course in one of 32 other European countries. Most universities offer it although it is not available with every course so students are advised to check with their chosen universities before making an application. Students do not pay any fees to the European university they visit and those who go for the full academic year (24 weeks) have their UK tuition fees reduced.

AND FINALLY ... BEFORE YOU SEND IN YOUR APPLICATION

CHECK that you have passes at grade C or higher in the GCSE (or equivalent) subjects required for the course at the institutions to which you are applying. FAILURE TO HAVE THE RIGHT GCSE SUBJECTS OR THE RIGHT NUMBER OF GRADE C PASSES OR HIGHER IN GCSE WILL RESULT IN A REJECTION.

CHECK that you are taking (or have taken) the GCE A-level and, if required, AS (or equivalent) subjects required for the course at the institution to which you are applying. FAILURE TO BE TAKING OR HAVE TAKEN THE RIGHT A-LEVELS WILL ALSO RESULT IN A REJECTION.

CHECK that the GCE A-levels and other qualifications you are taking will be accepted for the course for which you are applying. Some subjects and institutions do not stipulate any specific A-levels, only that you are required to offer two or three subjects at GCE A-level. In the view of some admissions tutors NOT ALL GCE A-LEVELS CARRY THE SAME WEIGHT (see **Chapter 1**).

CHECK that you can meet the requirements for all relevant admissions/interview tests.

CHECK that you have made all the necessary arrangements for sitting any required admissions tests.

CHECK that you can meet any age, health and DBS requirements for entry to your listed courses.

WHAT TO DO ON RESULTS DAY ... AND AFTER

BE AT HOME! Do not arrange to be away when your results are published. If you do not achieve the grades you require, you will need to follow an alternative course of action and make decisions that could affect your life during the next few years. Do not expect others to make these decisions for you. If you achieve the grades or points which have been offered you will receive confirmation of a place, but this may take a few days to reach you. Once your place is confirmed contact the accommodation office at the university or college and inform them that you will need a place in a hall of residence or other accommodation.

If you achieve grades or points higher than your conditional firm (CF) choice you can reconsider where and what to study by registering with UCAS to use the **Adjustment** process in **Track**. This is available from A-level results day until 31 August and you have five days to register and secure an alternative course. You must check very carefully all the **Adjustment** information on the UCAS website (www.ucas.com) before changing your CF choice to make sure you are eligible and that a vacancy is available. There is no guarantee of a vacancy on a course you are aiming for, and it is very unlikely that competitive courses will have places. If you decide definitely to change courses advise the university or college immediately, but check with www.ucas.com and your school/college adviser for the latest information.

If your grades or points are higher than you expected and you are not holding any offers you can telephone or email the admissions tutor at the universities and colleges which rejected you and request that they might reconsider you.

If you just miss your offers then telephone or email the universities and colleges to see if they can still offer you a place. ALWAYS HAVE YOUR UCAS REFERENCE NUMBER AVAILABLE WHEN YOU CALL. Their decisions may take a few days. You should check the universities and colleges in your order of preference. Your first choice must reject you before you contact your second choice.

If you have not applied to any university or college earlier in the year then you can apply through the **Clearing** scheme which runs from the middle of July. Check the tables in **Chapter 7** to identify which institutions normally make offers matching your results, then telephone or email the institution to see if they have any vacancies before completing your **Clearing** form.

If you learn finally that you do not have a place because you have missed the grades in your offer you will receive automatically a **Clearing** form to enable you to re-apply. Before you complete this form follow the instructions above.

If an institution has vacancies they will ask you for your grades. If they can consider you they will ask you for your **Clearing** form. You can only be considered by one institution at a time.

If you have to re-apply for a place, check the vacancies on the UCAS website (www.ucas.com), in the national press and through your local careers office. If there are vacancies in your subject, check with the university or college that these vacancies have not been taken.

REMEMBER – There are many thousands of students just like you. Admissions tutors have a mammoth task checking how many students will be taking up their places since not all students whose grades match their offers finally decide to do so!

IF YOU HAVE AN OFFER AND THE RIGHT GRADES BUT ARE NOT ACCEPTING THAT OR AN ALTERNATIVE PLACE – TELL THE UNIVERSITY OR COLLEGE. Someone else is waiting for your place! If you are applying for a place through **Clearing** it may even be late September before you know you have a place so BE PATIENT AND STAY CALM!

Good luck!

ADMISSIONS TESTS, SELECTION OF APPLICANTS AND INTERVIEWS

The selection of applicants by universities and colleges takes many forms. However, with rising numbers of applicants for places (especially in the popular subjects) and increasing numbers of students with high grades, greater importance is now attached not only to applicants' predicted A-level grades and GCSE attainments, but also to other aspects of their applications, especially the school reference and the personal statement and, for some courses and some institutions, performance at interview, and performance in admissions tests.

ADMISSIONS TESTS

Admissions tests are now increasingly used for undergraduate entry to specific courses and specific institutions. These include national subject-based tests such as LNAT, BMAT and UKCAT (see below) which are used for selecting applicants for entry to specified courses at particular institutions in subjects such as Law, Medicine, Dentistry and Veterinary Sciences. Admissions tests are also set by individual universities and colleges (or commercial organisations on their behalf) for entry, again, to particular courses in the individual institutions. Examples of these include the Thinking Skills Assessment (TSA) used by, for example, the University of Oxford, and the Health Professions Aptitude Test (HPAT) used by Ulster University for entry to some health-related courses. Other examples include the subject-based admissions tests used by many universities and colleges for entry to particular courses in subjects such as Art, Dance, Construction, Design, Drama and other Performance-based courses, Education and Teacher Training, Economics, Engineering, Journalism, Languages, Music, Nursing and Social Work.

Admissions tests are usually taken before or at interview and, except for courses requiring auditions or portfolio inspections, they are generally timed, unseen, written, or online tests. They can be used on their own, or alongside other selection methods used by university and college admissions staff, including:

- questionnaires or tests to be completed by applicants prior to interview and/or offer
- examples of school work to be submitted prior to interview and/or offer
- written tests at interview
- mathematical tests at interview
- practical tests at interview
- a response to a passage at interview
- performance-based tests (for example, for Music, Dance, Drama).

Applicants should find out early from university prospectuses and websites whether admissions tests are required for entry to their preferred courses, and if so, what these will be, and the arrangements for taking them. This is important, especially for Oxford and Cambridge applicants as many of their courses and colleges also require submission of marked written work done in Years 12 or 13 at school or college.

Here is a list of commonly used admissions tests, and this is followed by degree subject lists showing subject-based and individual institutions' admissions tests.

English
English Literature Admissions Test (ELAT)
The ELAT is a pre-interview admissions test for applicants to English courses at the University of Oxford (see the ELAT pages on the Admissions Testing Service website www.admissionstestingservice.org).

Health Professions
Health Professions Admissions Test (HPAT)
The HPAT is used by Ulster University for entry to courses including Dietetics, Occupational Therapy, Physiotherapy, Podiatry, Radiography and Speech and Language Therapies.

History
History Aptitude Test (HAT)
The HAT is a two-hour test sat by all candidates applying for History courses at Oxford University (see *History* below). See www.history.ox.ac.uk.

Law
Cambridge Law Test
This is a one-hour, two-part question test designed and used by most of the Cambridge University colleges with Law applicants who are called for interview. No prior knowledge of law is required for the test. See http://ba.law.cam.ac.uk/applying/cambridge_law_test for full details.

Law National Aptitude Test (LNAT)
The LNAT is an on-screen test for applicants to specified undergraduate Law programmes at the Birmingham, Bristol, Durham, Glasgow, London (King's), London (UCL), Nottingham, Oxford and SOAS universities. (See *Law* below, and **Law** in the subject tables in **Chapter 7**.) Applicants need to check universities' websites and the LNAT website (www.lnat.ac.uk) for the UCAS codes for courses requiring applicants to sit the LNAT. (**NB** Cambridge does not require Law applicants to take the LNAT but see above and the Cambridge entry under *Law* below.) Details of LNAT (which includes multiple-choice and essay questions), practice papers, registration dates, test dates, test centres and fees are all available on the LNAT website.

Mathematics
Sixth Term Examination Paper (STEP)
Applicants with offers for Mathematics courses at Cambridge and Warwick universities are usually required to take STEP. Bath, Bristol and Oxford Universities, and Imperial London also encourage applicants for their Mathematics courses to take STEP. For details, see the STEP pages on the Admissions Testing Service website (www.admissionstestingservice.org).

Medicine, Dentistry, Veterinary Science/Medicine, and related subjects
Most medical schools require applicants to sit the UK Clinical Aptitude Test (UKCAT) or the BioMedical Admissions Test (BMAT) or, for graduate entry, the Graduate Australian Medical Schools Admissions Test (GAMSAT) for specified Medicine courses. Applicants are advised to check the websites of all universities and medical schools offering Medicine for their latest admissions requirements, including admissions and aptitude tests, to check the UKCAT website www.ukcat.ac.uk or the BMAT pages on www.admissionstestingservice.org (and for graduate entry www.gamsat.co.uk) for the latest information.

The BioMedical Admissions Test (BMAT)
This is a pen-and-paper admissions test taken by undergraduate applicants to specified Medicine, Veterinary Science/Medicine courses at Cambridge and Oxford universities, and at Imperial London, London (UCL), Leeds, Brighton and Sussex (MS) and Lancaster. Imperial London also requires BMAT for entry to Biomedical Science, and Pharmacology with Translational Medical Science; BMAT is also a requirement for entry to Biomedical Sciences at Oxford University. A list of the courses requiring BMAT is available on the BMAT pages of the Admissions Testing Service website (www.admissionstestingservice.org) and also on university websites and in their prospectuses. It is important to note BMAT's early closing date for entries and also the test dates. The two-hour test consists of three sections:

- aptitude and skills
- scientific knowledge and application
- writing task.

Applicants sit the test only once and pay one entry fee no matter how many courses they apply for. However, if they re-apply to universities the following year they will need to re-take the BMAT and pay another fee. Past question papers are available (see website) and an official study guide *Preparing for the BMAT* is also available at www.pearsonschoolsandfecolleges.co.uk. Results of the BMAT are first sent to the universities, and then to the BMAT test centres. Candidates need to contact their test centres direct for their results. See *Dentistry*, *Medicine* and *Veterinary Science/Medicine* below and relevant subject tables in **Chapter 7**.

The UK Clinical Aptitude Test (UKCAT)
The UKCAT is a clinical aptitude test used by the majority of medical and dental schools in the selection of applicants for Medicine and Dentistry, alongside their existing selection processes, for undergraduate entry. The tests are not curriculum-based and do not have a science component. No revision is necessary; there is no textbook and no course of instruction. In the first instance, the UKCAT is a test of cognitive skills involving problem-solving and critical reasoning. With over 150 test centres, it is an on-screen test (not paper-based), and is marked electronically. Some bursaries are available to help towards the cost of the test. Further details (including the most recent list of universities requiring applicants to sit the UKCAT) are found on the website www.ukcat.ac.uk. See also the **Dentistry** and **Medicine** subject tables in **Chapter 7**, the entries for *Dentistry* and *Medicine* below, and **Chapter 4** for application details. See www.ukcat.ac.uk.

Modern and Medieval Languages
The Modern and Medieval Languages Test (MML)
This written test is used by the University of Cambridge for selecting applicants for entry to courses involving modern and medieval languages. See www.mml.cam.ac.uk/applying/involve.

General Admissions Test
Thinking Skills Assessment (TSA)
The TSA is a 90-minute multiple choice test consisting of 50 questions which test applicants' critical thinking and problem-solving skills. It is used at or before interview by University College London for applicants to European Social and Political Studies, and by Oxford University for entry to several courses (see below and see the TSA web pages on www.admissionstestingservice.org).

LSE/UG Admissions Assessment
The LSE/UG Admissions Assessment is used for some applicants with non-traditional educational backgrounds. The test is not subject or course specific and consists of English comprehension exercises, essay questions and mathematical problems.

DEGREE SUBJECT LISTS OF UNIVERSITIES AND COLLEGES USING TESTS AND ASSESSMENTS
Many universities and colleges set their own tests for specific subjects so it is important to check the websites for your preferred institutions and courses for the latest information about their applications and selection processes. The following list provides a guide to the subjects and institutions requiring admissions tests and other forms of assessment.

Accountancy
Lancaster (Acc, Adt Fin) Ernst & Young assessment.
Reading (Acc Bus) Successful candidates at the interview stage will be sent a supplementary application form and an invitation to an assessment day. This is jointly run by the Henley Business School and PwC at the Whiteknights campus in Reading. The assessment centre will involve psychometric testing, a group assessment exercise and a formal interview.

Anglo Saxon, Norse and Celtic
Cambridge Check www.study.cam.ac.uk/undergraduate/apply/tests for college requirements.

Animal Management
Kirklees (Coll) Mature applicants screening test.

Anthropology
Oxford See Archaeology.

Archaeology
Bournemouth Test for mature applicants.
Cambridge Check www.study.cam.ac.uk/undergraduate/apply/tests for college requirements.
Oxford (Arch Anth) Two recent marked essays are required, preferably in different subjects, plus a statement of no more than 500 words in response to a set question – required before interview. No written test at interview. (Class Arch) Written work required. No written test at interview. Check www.ox.ac.uk/tests.

Architecture
Cambridge All colleges offering course require a portfolio of recent work at interview. Check www.study.cam.ac.uk/undergraduate/apply/tests.
Cardiff (Archit, Archit Eng) Samples of work to be sent before interview.
Dundee Samples of work required before interview.
Huddersfield Portfolio of work required.
Liverpool The interview will be based on the portfolio of work.
London Met Portfolio of work required.
London South Bank Samples of work to be sent before interview.
Nottingham Trent Examples of work are required.
Sheffield Art portfolio required for applicants without A-level Art.
Westminster Samples of work required before interview.

Art and Design
Bournemouth (Comp Animat Art) Maths, logic and life-drawing tests at interview, and portfolio of work required.
Bournemouth Arts Practical test.
Creative Arts Tests.
Glyndŵr Portfolios are required for Art and Design courses.
Oxford (Fn Art) No written work required. Portfolio to be submitted in November. Practical examination. Two pieces in different medias from a number of possible subjects. Check www.ox.ac.uk/tests.
Ravensbourne Verbal examination. (Animat) Written test.
Westminster (Fash Mrchnds Mgt) Interview and numeracy test.

Asian and Middle Eastern Studies
Cambridge Check www.study.cam.ac.uk/undergraduate/apply/tests for college requirements.

Biochemistry
London South Bank Degree subject-based test at interview.
Oxford No written test required.

Biological Sciences
London South Bank Degree subject-based test at interview.
Nottingham Trent Essay.
Oxford No written test required.

Biomedical Sciences
Hull (Coll) Essay.
Imperial London BMAT.
Nottingham Trent Essay.
Oxford BMAT is required for entry into all colleges. Check www.ox.ac.uk/tests.
Portsmouth Test of motivation and knowledge of the subject, the degree and careers to which it leads.

Bioveterinary Science
London (RVC) BMAT is not required for entry but applicants wanting to be considered for Merit Scholarships will have to take BMAT.

Broadcast Technology
Ravensbourne Written test.

Building/Construction
London South Bank (Bld Serv) Degree subject-based test and numeracy test at interview.

Business Courses
Arts London (CFash) School work to be submitted before interview. Degree subject-based test and numeracy test at interview.
Bolton Literacy and numeracy tests.
Bradford (Coll) Written test.
Newcastle Some short-listed applicants will be given a variety of assessment tests at interview.
Nottingham Trent Short-listed applicants are invited to a day-long business style assessment.
Westminster (Fash Mrchnds Mgt) Interview and numeracy test.

Chemical Engineering
Cambridge Check www.study.cam.ac.uk/undergraduate/apply/tests for college requirements.

Chemistry
Oxford No written work required. All candidates must take the Thinking Skills Assessment test. Check www.ox.ac.uk/tests.
Reading During the interview, applicants will be asked a series of chemistry-related questions from a select list. Applicants are required to discuss these in detail and may be asked to draw molecular formulas.

Classics (see also Archaeology)
Cambridge Check www.study.cam.ac.uk/undergraduate/apply/tests for college requirements.
Oxford For all Classics courses, two essays or commentaries required, normally in areas related to Classics. CAT also required. Check www.ox.ac.uk/tests.

Classics and English
Oxford Two pieces of written work required, one relevant to Classics and one to English. CAT and ELAT also required. Check www.ox.ac.uk/tests.

Classics and Modern Languages
Oxford Two Classics essays and two modern language essays required, one in the chosen language and one in English. CAT and MLAT also required. Check www.ox.ac.uk/tests.

Classics and Oriental Studies
Oxford Classics test; also language aptitude test for applicants planning to study Arabic, Hebrew, Persian or Turkish as main language; two pieces written work also required, at least one should be on a classical topic. Check www.ox.ac.uk/tests.

Computer Science
Abertay (Comp Arts) Portfolio of work required. Practical tests at interview.
Cambridge Check www.study.cam.ac.uk/undergraduate/apply/tests for college requirements.
Liverpool John Moores Questionnaire before interview. Literacy test at interview.
London (Gold) Degree subject-based test.
London (QM) Mathematical test at interview.
Oxford No written work required. MAT required. See also Mathematics. Check www.ox.ac.uk/tests.

Dance
Chichester (Perf Arts) Group practical test.

Dental Nursing
Portsmouth (Dntl Hyg Dntl Thera) Interview.

Dentistry
Cardiff UKCAT.

Dundee UKCAT.
Glasgow UKCAT.
London (King's) UKCAT.
London (QM) UKCAT.
Manchester UKCAT and interview.

Dietetics
Hertfordshire Admissions test.
London Met Interview and essay.
Ulster Health Professions Admissions Test: see www.hpat.org.uk and www.ulster.ac.uk before completing the UCAS application.

Drama
De Montfort Written papers and/or tests.
Liverpool (LIPA) (Actg) Applicants will be expected to perform one devised piece, one Shakespearean piece and a song and give a short review of a performance they have seen recently.
London (RH) Written work required at interview. The University looks for students who are mentally agile and versatile who enjoy reading as well as taking part in productions.
London (Royal Central Sch SpDr) Written papers and/or tests.
Reading (Thea) Applicants undertake a practical assessment and an interview.

Earth Sciences
Oxford No written test required.

Economics
Cambridge Check www.study.cam.ac.uk/undergraduate/apply/tests for college requirements.
Lancaster Workshop.
Oxford (Econ Mgt) No written test required. Thinking Skills Assessment. Check www.ox.ac.uk/tests.

Education Studies (see also Teacher Training)
Cambridge Check www.study.cam.ac.uk/undergraduate/apply/tests for college requirements.
Cumbria Literacy test.
Durham Key Skills tests at interview.
Newman Basic numeracy and literacy tests.
Reading Applicants are required to take part in both a group interview and an individual interview as well as completing a short essay-based written test.

Engineering
Birmingham City Mature students without GCSE English and/or mathematics are required to take a literacy and/or numeracy test. (Snd Eng Prod) Mature students to take English and mathematics tests.
Blackburn (Coll) Questionnaire and tests before interview.
Bristol (Eng Des) A-level-based test.
Cambridge Check www.study.cam.ac.uk/undergraduate/apply/tests for college requirements.
Kingston (Aerosp Eng) Numeracy and basic physics test.
London South Bank (Civ Eng; Elec Eng; Mech Eng) Degree subject-based test and numeracy test at interview.
Oxford No written work required. All candidates take the Physics Aptitude Test. Check ox.ac.uk/tests.
Southampton Literacy and numeracy tests for Foundation course applicants.
Southampton Solent Mathematical test at interview.

English
Bangor (Crea Prof Writ) Applicants are required to submit a portfolio of writing.
Birmingham City Samples of work required.
Blackpool and Fylde (Coll) Samples of work before interview.
Bristol Samples of work required.
Cambridge Check www.study.cam.ac.uk/undergraduate/apply/tests for college requirements.

Cardiff Short essay.

London (UCL) After interview, applicants are asked to write a critical commentary on an unseen passage of prose or verse.

Oxford (Engl Lang Lit) ELAT and one recent marked essay. (Engl Modn Langs) MLAT and one recent marked essay. Check www.ox.ac.uk/tests.

Portsmouth (Crea Writ) All applicants will be required to submit a short piece of creative writing to the admissions office.

Southampton Examples of written work required from Access students.

European and Middle Eastern Languages (see also Modern and Medieval Languages)

Oxford Two pieces of written work, one in the chosen language and one in English. MLAT and OLAT required. Check www.ox.ac.uk/tests.

Film Production

Bournemouth Arts Portfolio. Practical test of short film stills.

Creative Arts Portfolio at interview.

Westminster Questionnaire to be completed and samples of work required before interview.

Film Studies

Liverpool John Moores Questionnaire and test before interview.

Reading There are three stages to the interview process: a practical, a film seminar and an interview.

Roehampton Essays taken to interview and discussed.

South Wales Portfolio of work at interview.

Food Studies

Reading During the interview, applicants will be given a lead and then asked a specific question tailored to the programme applied for.

Geography

Cambridge Check www.study.cam.ac.uk/undergraduate/apply/tests for college requirements.

Cardiff Test for some Joint Honours courses.

Oxford No written work required. All candidates must take the Thinking Skills Assessment. Check www.ox.ac.uk/tests.

German (see also Modern and Medieval Languages)

Aston Written test at interview.

Healthcare Science

Hertfordshire Admissions test.

History

Bangor Samples of work only required from mature applicants without conventional qualifications.

Cambridge Check www.study.cam.ac.uk/undergraduate/apply/tests for college requirements.

Liverpool Test for mature applicants.

Liverpool John Moores Mature students not in education must submit an essay.

London (Gold) Samples of written work from non-standard applicants and from those without academic qualifications.

Oxford An essay on a historical topic is required as well as the History Aptitude Test. (Hist Modn Langs) Written work, the History Aptitude Test and Modern Language Test required. Check www.ox.ac.uk/tests.

Roehampton Essays taken to interview and discussed.

History and Modern Languages

Cambridge Check www.study.cam.ac.uk/undergraduate/apply/tests for college requirements.

History and Politics

Cambridge Check www.study.cam.ac.uk/undergraduate/apply/tests for college requirements.

History of Art
Cambridge Check www.study.cam.ac.uk/undergraduate/apply/tests for college requirements.
Oxford Two pieces of work required: (a) a marked essay from an A-level or equivalent course and (b) no more than 750 words responding to an item of art, architecture or design to which the applicant has had first-hand access with a photograph or photocopy of the item provided if possible. No written test at interview. Check www.ox.ac.uk/tests.

Human Sciences
Oxford No written work required. All candidates must take the Thinking Skills Assessment test. Check www.ox.ac.uk/tests.

Human, Social and Political Sciences
Cambridge Check www.study.cam.ac.uk/undergraduate/apply/tests for college requirements.

Italian (see also Modern and Medieval Languages)
Cardiff Test for some Joint Honours courses.

Journalism (see also Media Studies)
Brighton (Spo Jrnl) Test for those called to interview: contact admissions tutor.
City Spelling, punctuation, grammar, general knowledge tests and an essay assignment. Tests on current affairs and use of English.
Edinburgh Napier (Jrnl) Samples of work before interview.
Kent English language and academic tests for all candidates, relating to requirements of the accrediting professional bodies.
Portsmouth Candidates are subject to interview and an admissions test.
South Wales Test and interview.

Land Economy
Cambridge Check www.study.cam.ac.uk/undergraduate/apply/tests for college requirements.

Law
Birmingham LNAT.
Birmingham City Questionnaire to be completed and an IQ test.
Bolton Own diagnostic test used (logic and reasoning).
Bradford (Coll) Academic tests at interview for mature students.
Bristol LNAT.
Cambridge Check www.study.cam.ac.uk/undergraduate/apply/tests for college requirements.
Durham LNAT.
Glasgow LNAT.
Kent Internally devised test for some applicants.
London (King's) LNAT.
London (UCL) LNAT.
Manchester Met LNAT.
Nottingham LNAT.
Oxford No written work required. All applicants take the LNAT. (Law; Law St Euro) LNAT plus, at interview, a short oral test in the modern language for students taking a joint language, except for those taking European Legal Studies. Check www.ox.ac.uk/tests.

Linguistics
Cambridge Check www.study.cam.ac.uk/undergraduate/apply/tests for college requirements.

Materials Science
Oxford All candidates must take the Physics Aptitude Test. Check www.ox.ac.uk/tests.

Mathematics
Bath STEP.
Cambridge Check www.study.cam.ac.uk/undergraduate/apply/tests for college requirements.
Imperial London MAT. The paper takes two and a half hours and sample tests are available online. Students unable to sit the MAT must complete the STEP.

Liverpool John Moores Literacy and numeracy tests.
Oxford No written work required. Mathematics Aptitude Test. Check www.ox.ac.uk/tests.

Media Studies
Bolton Samples of work at interview.
Coventry Interview and portfolio.
Hull (Coll) Essay required before interview.
Liverpool John Moores Questionnaire to be completed before interview. Degree subject-based test at interview.
London Met Mathematics and written English test.

Media Technology
South Wales Portfolio and interview.

Medicine
Birmingham UKCAT.
Brighton and Sussex (MS) BMAT.
Cambridge Check www.study.cam.ac.uk/undergraduate/apply/tests for college requirements.
Cardiff UKCAT.
Dundee UKCAT.
Durham UKCAT.
East Anglia UKCAT.
Edinburgh UKCAT.
Exeter UKCAT and GAMSAT required.
Glasgow UKCAT.
Hull UKCAT.
Imperial London BMAT.
Keele UKCAT.
Lancaster BMAT.
Leeds UKCAT.
London (King's) UKCAT.
London (QM) UKCAT.
London (St George's) GAMSAT is required for the four-year Graduate Stream course. UKCAT is required for the five-year course.
London (UCL) (Six-year course) BMAT.
Manchester UKCAT and interview.
Newcastle UKCAT.
Nottingham UKCAT.
Oxford BMAT test required. Check www.ox.ac.uk/tests.
Plymouth UKCAT.
Queen's Belfast UKCAT.
St Andrews UKCAT.
Sheffield UKCAT.
Southampton UKCAT.

Meteorology
Reading (Meteor Clim MMet) All applicants will be asked to attend an interview prior to an offer being made.

Midwifery
Anglia Ruskin Literacy and numeracy tests.
Hertfordshire Admissions test.

Modern and Medieval Languages (see also Asian and Middle Eastern Studies, Oriental Studies and separate languages)
Bangor Offer may be lowered after interview.
Cambridge Check www.study.cam.ac.uk/undergraduate/apply/tests for college requirements.

Oxford (Modn Langs; Modn Lang Ling) Modern Languages Admissions Tests. Two marked essays, one in chosen language and one in English. (Euro Mid E Langs) MLAT and OLAT required. Two essays required for the European language but none for the Middle Eastern language. Check www.ox.ac.uk/tests.

Music

Bangor Candidates offered the option of an audition. Interview requirements include performance, aural and extracts for analysis or 'guessing the composer' dates etc.

Bath Spa Interview requirements include performance, harmony and counterpoint (written), essay and sight-singing.

Birmingham Interview requirements include harmony and counterpoint (written) and essay.

Birmingham City Some subject-based and practical tests. Interview requirements include performance.

Bristol Interview requirements include performance, sight-singing, keyboard tests, harmony and counterpoint (written), essay or extracts for analysis, aural.

Cambridge Check www.study.cam.ac.uk/undergraduate/apply/tests for college requirements.

Cardiff Interview requirements include performance or extracts for analysis.

Chichester Interview requirements include performance.

City Interview requirements include performance.

Colchester (Inst) Interview requirements include performance, aural, keyboard skills and essay.

Coventry Music theory exam and audition held alongside an interview. Proforma used prior to interview – some students rejected at this stage.

Derby Interview requirements include performance and essay.

Edinburgh Interview requirements include performance, harmony and counterpoint (written), essay and sight-singing.

Edinburgh Napier Audition and theory test.

Glasgow Interview requirements include performance and sight-singing.

Guildhall (Sch Mus Dr) Interviews mostly held at the School but also at Newcastle and in the USA.

Huddersfield Interview requirements include performance.

Lancaster Interview requirements include performance, aural and harmony and counterpoint (written).

Leeds Interview requirements include performance.

Leeds (CMus) (Jazz; Mus; Pop Mus St) In-house theory test to determine level of musical theory ability.

Liverpool Candidates may be asked to undertake a variety of aural tests, the performance of a prepared piece of music and some sight-reading when called for interview.

Liverpool Hope Interview requirements include performance, keyboard tests and harmony and counterpoint (written).

London (Gold) Degree subject-based test. Interview requirements include performance and extracts for analysis.

London (King's) Only borderline applicants are interviewed. Samples of written work may be requested. Interview requirements include performance, aural, sight-singing and keyboard skills.

London (RAcMus) (Mus) Interview requirements include performance, keyboard skills, harmony and counterpoint (written), and extracts for analysis.

London Met Performance tests and essay.

Oxford Interview requirements include the performance of a piece/s on the candidate's principal instrument or voice. Candidates without keyboard skills to grade 5 may be asked to take a keyboard sight-reading test. Check www.ox.ac.uk/tests.

RCMus Interview requirements include performance and sight-singing.

RConsvS Interview requirements include performance, sight-singing and aural.

Royal Welsh (CMusDr) Interview requirements include performance and essay.

Sheffield Interview requirements include performance, essay and aural.

Ulster Interview requirements include performance.

West London Students required to produce a portfolio of work and attend an audition: see www.uwl.ac.uk.

Wolverhampton Interview requirements include performance and essay.

York Interview requirements include performance, aural, keyboard skills and sight-singing.

Natural Sciences
Cambridge Check www.study.cam.ac.uk/undergraduate/apply/tests for college requirements.

Nursing
Anglia Ruskin Literacy and numeracy tests.
Birmingham City Literacy and numeracy tests at interview.
Bucks New Tests for BSc Nursing.
City Written test.
Coventry Literacy and numeracy tests.
Cumbria (Nurs; Midwif) Numeracy test.
Derby Literacy and numeracy tests at interview.
East Anglia Tests.
Hertfordshire Admissions test.
Liverpool A group of candidates are given a task to undertake during which applicants are assessed
    for their ability to work in a team, maturity, communication skills and their level of involvement.
London South Bank (Nurs A C MH) Literacy and numeracy tests at interview.
Suffolk (Univ Campus) Interview and tests.
UWE Bristol Questionnaire/test before interview.
West London Numeracy and literacy tests.
Wolverhampton Tests.
York Literacy and numeracy tests.

Occupational Therapy
Ulster Health Professions Admissions Test: see www.hpat.org.uk and www.ulster.ac.uk before completing
    the UCAS application.
UWE Bristol Questionnaire/test before interview.

Optometry
Bradford (Coll) Literacy and numeracy tests.
Hertfordshire Admissions test.

Oriental Studies
Oxford Two essays and the OLAT required. Check www.ox.ac.uk/tests.

Osteopathy
BSO All prospective students are required to attend an Interview and Evaluation Day where they are
    normally required to undertake a range of aptitude tests, a written English test and an interview
    in order to determine their suitability for the course and the BSO.

Paramedic Science
Anglia Ruskin Literacy and numeracy tests.
Hertfordshire Admissions test.

Pharmacology/Pharmaceutical Sciences
Portsmouth Test of motivation, knowledge of the subject, degree course and the careers to which it leads.

Pharmacy
Hertfordshire Admissions test.
Liverpool John Moores Literacy and numeracy tests.
Portsmouth (A-level students) Test of motivation and knowledge of pharmacy as a profession. (Other
    applicants) Test of chemistry and biology, plus literacy and numeracy tests.
Reading A simple numeracy test related to pharmacy.

Philosophy
Cambridge Check www.study.cam.ac.uk/undergraduate/apply/tests for college requirements.
Leeds Written test at interview.
Liverpool Samples of written work may be requested in cases where there is a question of the applicant's
    ability to cope with the academic skills required of them.

London (UCL) Written test at interview.
Oxford (Phil Modn Langs) MLAT; two pieces of written work required. (Phil Theol) Philosophy test and two pieces of written work. (Phil Pol Econ (PPE)) Thinking Skills Assessment; no written work required. Check www.ox.ac.uk/tests.
Warwick Written test at interview.

Physical Education
Chichester Physical test.
Liverpool John Moores Literacy and numeracy tests and gym assessment.

Physics
Oxford Physics Aptitude Test; no written work required. Check www.ox.ac.uk/tests.

Physiotherapy
East Anglia Tests.
Hertfordshire Admissions test.
Liverpool A group of candidates are given a task to undertake, during which they are assessed for their ability to work in a team, maturity, communication skills and their level of involvement.
Robert Gordon Practical testing varies from year to year.
Ulster Health Professions Admissions Test: see www.hpat.org.uk and www.ulster.ac.uk before completing the UCAS application.

Podiatry
Ulster Health Professions Admissions Test: see www.hpat.ac.uk and www.ulster.ac.uk before completing the UCAS application.

Policing
Cumbria Constabulary test.

Politics
Kent (Pol Int Rel Bidiplome) Assessment days run jointly with the IEP Lille.
Oxford See (Phil Pol Econ (PPE)) under Philosophy.

Popular Music
South Wales Audition.

Product Design
Dundee Portfolio and interview will determine the appropriate entry point for candidate (Level 1 or 2).

Psychological and Behavioural Sciences
Cambridge Check www.study.cam.ac.uk/undergraduate/apply/tests for college requirements.

Psychology
Bangor Access course entry students may be asked to submit an essay.
London (UCL) Questionnaire to be completed.
Oxford (Expmtl Psy) Thinking Skills Assessment test; no written work required. Check www.ox.ac.uk/tests.
Roehampton Questionnaire before interview; test at interview.

Radiography
Hertfordshire Admissions test.
Liverpool (Diag Radiog) A group of candidates are given a task to undertake, during which they are assessed for their ability to work in a team, maturity, communication skills and their level of involvement.
Ulster Health Professions Admissions Test: see www.hpat.org.uk and www.ulster.ac.uk before completing the UCAS application.

Social Work
Birmingham Written test at interview.

Birmingham City Some tests are set at interview.
Brunel Written test at interview.
Bucks New Tests.
Cardiff Met Scenario and subject-knowledge tests.
Coventry (Yth Wk) Literacy screening.
De Montfort Written test at interview.
Derby Literacy and numeracy tests at interview.
Dundee Literacy test.
Durham New (Coll) Written test at interview.
East Anglia Test.
Hertfordshire Admissions test.
Kent Written test followed by an interview and observed group discussions.
London (Gold) Written test at interview. Questions on social work practice and the applicant's experience of working in the social work/social care field.
London Met Pre-interview literacy test and, if successful, an interview.
London South Bank Literacy and numeracy tests.
Manchester Met (Yth Commun Wk) Tests.
Newman (Yth Commun Wk) Written test.
Portsmouth Test.
Suffolk (Univ Campus) Interview and test.
UWE Bristol Questionnaire before interview.
Wolverhampton Tests.

Sociology
Leeds Copy of written work requested.
London Met Where appropriate, separate tests in comprehension and mathematical skills that will be used to help us reach a decision.

Speech Sciences
Manchester Met Two essays and a questionnaire.
Reading A questionnaire is sent to applicants prior to an offer being made.
Sheffield Listening test and problem solving.
Ulster Health Professions Admissions Test: see www.hpat.org.uk and www.ulster.ac.uk before completing the UCAS application.

Teacher Training
Bath Spa Written test at interview.
Bishop Grosseteste Literacy and numeracy tests are part of the selection criteria at interview.
Brighton Written test at interview.
Brunel Literacy, mathematical and practical tests depending on subject.
Canterbury Christ Church All candidates are interviewed in groups of 8–10 and assessments are made based on the results of a written English test and performance in the group interview.
Cardiff Met Literacy, numeracy and subject-knowledge tests.
Chester Literacy and numeracy tests.
Chichester Written test at interview.
De Montfort Written test at interview.
Dundee Literacy and numeracy tests.
Durham Key Skills test.
Gloucestershire Mathematical test at interview. Written test at interview.
Hertfordshire Admissions test.
Liverpool John Moores Written test at interview. Mathematical and diagnostic tests on interview day.
London South Bank Literacy and numeracy tests.
Newman Basic literacy and numeracy tests for QTS and other courses.
Nottingham Trent Practical presentation. Written test at interview.
Plymouth Mathematical test at interview. Written test at interview.
Roehampton Written test at interview.

St Mary's Literacy and mathematical tests at interview. Practical tests for PE applicants.
Sheffield Hallam Interview with numeracy and literacy tests.
UWE Bristol Literacy and mathematical tests at interview.
Winchester Literacy test at interview.
Worcester Written test at interview.

Theatre and Performance
Glyndŵr An audition is required for Theatre and Performance.

Theology and Religious Studies
Cambridge Check www.study.cam.ac.uk/undergraduate/apply/tests for college requirements.
Oxford (Theol Relgn) No test; two pieces of written work required. (Theol Orntl St) Oriental Studies
Language Aptitude Test; two pieces of written work required. Check www.ox.ac.uk/tests.

Veterinary Science/Medicine
Cambridge Check www.study.cam.ac.uk/undergraduate/apply/tests for college requirements.
Liverpool Candidates are asked to write an essay on a veterinary topic prior to interview.
London (RVC) BMAT.
Myerscough (Coll) (Vet Nurs) Subject-based test at interview.

SELECTION OF APPLICANTS

University and college departmental admissions tutors are responsible for selecting candidates, basing their decisions on the policies of acceptable qualifications established by each institution and, where required, applicants' performance in admissions tests. There is little doubt that academic achievement, aptitude and promise are the most important factors although other subsidiary factors may be taken into consideration. The outline which follows provides information on the way in which candidates are selected for degree and diploma courses. **NB** Not all universities will use AS grades as part of their selection process – make sure to check individual university websites.

- Grades obtained by the applicant in GCE A-level and AS and equivalent examinations and the range of subjects studied may be considered.

- Applicant's performance in aptitude and admissions tests, as required by universities and colleges.

- Academic record of the applicant throughout his or her school career, especially up to A-level and AS, Highers, Advanced Highers or other qualifications and the choice of subjects. If you are taking general studies at A-level or AS confirm with the admissions tutor that this is acceptable.

- Time taken by the applicant to obtain good grades at GCSE/Scottish Nationals and A-level and AS/Scottish Highers/Advanced Highers.

- Forecast or the examination results of the applicant at A-level and AS (or equivalent) and head teacher's report.

- The applicant's intellectual development; evidence of ability and motivation to follow the chosen course.

- The applicant's range of interests, both in and out of school; aspects of character and personality.

- The vocational interests, knowledge and experience of the applicant particularly if they are choosing vocational courses.

INTERVIEWS

Fewer applicants are now interviewed than in the past but even if you are not called you should make an effort to visit your chosen universities and/or colleges before you accept any offer. Interviews may be arranged simply to give you a chance to see the institution and the department and to meet the staff and students. Alternatively, interviews may be an important part of the selection procedure for specific courses such as Law, Medicine and Teaching. If they are, you need to prepare yourself well. Most interviews last approximately 20–30 minutes and you may be interviewed by more than one person. For practical subjects such as Music and Drama almost certainly you will be asked to perform, and for artistic subjects, to take examples of your work. For some courses you may also have a written or other test at interview (see above).

How best can you prepare yourself?
Firstly, as one applicant advised, 'Go to the interview – at least you'll see the place.'

Secondly, on the question of dress, try to turn up looking smart (it may not matter, but it can't be wrong).

Two previous applicants were more specific: 'Dress smartly but sensibly so you are comfortable for travelling and walking round the campus.'

More general advice is also important
- 'Prepare well – interviewers are never impressed by applicants who only sit there with no willingness to take part.'
- 'Read up the prospectus and course details. Know how their course differs from any others you have applied for and be able to say why you prefer theirs.'
- 'They always ask if you have any questions to ask them: prepare some!' For example, How many students are admitted to the course each year? What are the job prospects for graduates? How easy is it to change from your chosen course to a related course?

Questions which you could ask might focus on the ways in which work is assessed, the content of the course, field work, work experience, teaching methods, accommodation and, especially for vocational courses, contacts with industry, commerce or the professions. However, don't ask questions which are already answered in the prospectus!

These are only a few suggestions and other questions may come to mind during the interview which, above all, should be a two-way flow of information. It is also important to keep a copy of your UCAS application (especially your personal statement) for reference since your interview will probably start with a question about something you have written.

Usually interviewers will want to know why you have chosen the subject and why you have chosen their particular institution. They will want to see how motivated you are, how much care you have taken in choosing your subject, how much you know about your subject, what books you have read. If you have chosen a vocational course they will want to find out how much you know about the career it leads to, and whether you have visited any places of work or had any work experience. If your chosen subject is also an A-level subject you will be asked about your course and the aspects of the course you like the most.

Try to relax. For some people interviews can be an ordeal; most interviewers know this and will make allowances. The following extract from the University of Manchester's website will give you some idea of what admissions tutors look for.

- 'You should remember that receiving an interview invite means that the admissions tutors are impressed with your application so far and you are in the running for an offer of a place at that university. It is an opportunity for you to discuss a subject that you and the interviewer share an interest in.'
- 'Interviewers will be looking for you to demonstrate how you met the criteria advertised in the prospectus and UCAS entry profiles, but will not always ask you about them directly. Some examples of criteria used by admissions tutors include: interest, motivation and commitment to the subject; the ability to study independently; the ability to work with others; the ability to manage time effectively; an interest in the university.'

In the tables in **Chapter 7** (**Selection interviews, Interview advice and questions** and **Reasons for rejection**) you will also find examples of questions which have been asked in recent years for which you might prepare, and non-academic reasons why applicants have been rejected! **Chapter 4, Applications**, provides a guide through the process of applying to your chosen universities and courses and highlights key points for your action.

The subject tables in the next chapter represent the core of the book, listing degree courses offered by all UK universities and colleges. These tables are designed to provide you with the information you need so that you can match your abilities and interests with your chosen degree subject, prepare your application and find out how applicants are selected for courses.

At the top of each table there is a brief overview of the subject area, together with a selection of websites for organisations that can provide relevant careers or course information. This is then followed by the subject tables themselves in which information is provided in sequence under the following headings.

Course offers information
- Subject requirements/preferences (GCSE/ A-level/other requirements)
- NB Offers statement
- Your target offers and examples of degree courses
- Alternative offers

Examples of colleges offering courses in this subject field

Choosing your course
- Universities and colleges teaching quality
- Top universities and colleges (research)
- Examples of sandwich degree courses

Admissions information
- Number of applicants per place
- Advice to applicants and planning the UCAS personal statement
- Misconceptions about this course
- Selection interviews
- Interview advice and questions
- Reasons for rejection (non-academic)

After-results advice
- Offers to applicants repeating A-levels

Graduate destinations and employment (Higher Education Statistics Agency (HESA))
- HESA data on graduate destinations
- Career note

Other degree subjects for consideration

When selecting a degree course it is important to try to judge the points score or grades that you are likely to achieve and compare them with the offers listed under **Your target offers and examples of degree courses**. However, even though you might be capable of achieving the indicated grades or UCAS Tariff points, it is important to note that these are likely to be the minimum grades or points required and that there is no guarantee that you will receive an offer: other factors in your application, such as the personal statement, references, and admissions test performance will be taken into consideration (see also **Chapters 3** and **5**).

University departments frequently adjust their offers, depending on the numbers of candidates applying, so you must not assume that the offers and policies published now will necessarily apply to courses starting in 2017 or thereafter. Even though offers may change during the 2016/17 application cycle, you can assume that the offers published in this book represent the typical academic levels at which you should aim.

Below are explanations of the information given under the headings in the subject tables. It is important that you read these carefully so that you understand how they can help you to choose and apply for courses that are right for you.

COURSE OFFERS INFORMATION

Subject requirements/preferences

Brief information is given on the GCSE and A-level requirements. Specific A-level subject requirements for individual institutions are listed separately. Other requirements are sometimes specified, where these are relevant to the course subject area, for example, medical requirements for health-related courses and Disclosure and Barring Service (DBS) clearance (formerly known as CRB checks). Check prospectuses and websites of universities and colleges for course requirements.

Your target offers and examples of degree courses

Universities and colleges offering degree courses in the subject area are listed in descending order according to the number of UCAS Tariff points and/or A-level grades they are likely to require applicants to achieve. The UCAS Tariff points total is listed down the left-hand side of the page, and to the right appear all the institutions (in alphabetical order) likely to make offers in this Tariff point range. (Information on the UCAS Tariff is given in **Appendix 1** and guidance on how to calculate your offers is provided on every other page of the subject tables in this book. Please also read the information in the **Important Note** box on page 81.)

The courses included on the offers line are examples of the courses available in the subject field at that university or college. You will need to check prospectuses and websites for a complete list of the institution's Single, Joint, Combined or major/minor Honours degree courses available in the subject. For each institution listed, the following information may be given.

Name of institution

Note that the name of an institution's university college or campus may be given in brackets after the institution title, for example London (King's) or Kent (Medway Sch Pharm). Where the institution is not a university, further information about its status may also be given to indicate the type of college – for example (UC) to mean University College or (CAg) to mean College of Agriculture. This is to help readers to differentiate between the types of colleges and to help them identify any specialisation a college may have, for example art or agriculture. A full list of abbreviations used is given under the heading **INSTITUTION ABBREVIATIONS** later in this chapter.

Grades/points offer

After the institution's name, a line of offers information is given, showing a typical offer made by the institution for the courses indicated in brackets. **Offers, however, may vary between applicants and the published grades and/or points offers should be regarded as targets to aim for and not necessarily the actual grades or points required**. Offers may be reduced after the publication of A-level results, particularly if a university or college is left with spare places. However, individual course offers listed in the tables in **Chapter 7** are abridged and should be used as a first source of reference and comparison only. It is not possible to publish all the variables relevant to each offer: applicants must check prospectuses and websites for full details of all offers and courses.

Depending on the details given by institutions, the offers may provide information as follows.

- **Grades** The specific grades, or average grades, required at GCE A-level or at A-level plus AS or, if specified, EPQ for the listed courses. (**NB** Graded offers may require specific grades for specific subjects.) A-level grades are always presented in capital letters; AS and EPQ grades are shown in lower case – so the offer BBBc would indicate three grade Bs at A-level, plus an additional EPQ or AS at grade c. Where necessary, the abbreviation 'AL' is used to indicate A-level, 'AS' to indicate AS and EPQ to indicate that an Extended Project Qualification is part of the offer. Offers are usually shown in terms of three A-level grades although some institutions accept two grades with the same points total or, alternatively, two A-level grades accompanied by AS grades. Two AS may generally be regarded as equivalent to one A-level, and one double award A-level as equivalent to two standard A-levels.

NB Unit grade and module information, now introduced into the admissions system, is most likely to be required by universities where a course is competitive, or where taking a specific unit is necessary or desirable for entry. Check with institutions' websites for their latest information.

- **The new UCAS Tariff points system** A-levels, AS, International Baccalaureate (IB), Scottish Highers, the Progression Diploma and a range of other qualifications have a unit value in the UCAS Tariff system (see **The UCAS 2017 Entry Tariff Points Tables** in **Appendix 1**). Where a range of Tariff points is shown, for example 112–120 points, offers are usually made within this points range for these specified courses. Note that, in some cases, an institution may require a points score which is higher than the specified grade offer given. This can be for a number of reasons – for example, you may not be offering the standard subjects that would have been stipulated in a grades offer. In such cases additional points may be added by way of AS grades, Functional/Essential Skills, the Extended Project Qualification, etc.

From the 2017 admissions cycle, UCAS Tariff points will be readjusted numerically against A-level grades as follows:

A* = 56 pts; A = 48 pts; B = 40 pts; C = 32 pts; D = 24 pts; E = 16 pts

As in the past, some universities make offers for entry to each course by way of A-level grades, others make Tariff points offers while others will make offers in both A-level grades and in Tariff points. The changes from the old numerical Tariff system to the new system will be the same and will not affect entry requirements, or students' decisions about choices in qualifications, or the preparation of applications. However, applicants should be sure that the A-level subjects they are taking are acceptable for their chosen course and for A-level grades and points offers.

A Tariff points offer will not usually discriminate between the final year exam subjects being taken by the applicant unless otherwise stated, although certain GCSE subjects may be stipulated eg English or mathematics.

Admission tutors have the unenviable task of trying to assess the number of applicants who will apply for their courses against the number of places available and so judging the offers to be made. However, as of 2015 entry, the government removed the cap on the number of places that universities in England are able to offer. English universities can now admit an unlimited number of home and EU undergraduates, though not every institution has adopted these reforms. Nevertheless, it is still important when reading the offers tables to be aware that variations occur each year. Lower offers or equivalents may be made to disadvantaged students, mature and international applicants.

The offers published in this edition therefore are based on expected admission policies operating from September to January 2016/17. They are targets to be achieved and in the case of popular courses at popular universities they should be regarded as minimum entry qualifications.

See **Chapter 3** for information from universities about their admissions policies including, for example, information about their expected use of A*, unit grades, the Progression Diploma, the Extended Project Qualification and the Cambridge Pre-U in their offers for applicants. See **Appendix 1** for **The UCAS 2017 Entry Tariff Points** tables.

- **Admissions tests for Law, Medicine and Veterinary Science/Medicine** Where admissions tests form part of a university's offer for any of these subjects, this is indicated on the offers line in the subject tables for the relevant university. This is shown by '+LNAT' (for Law), '+BMAT' or '+UKCAT' (for Medicine), and '+BMAT' (for Veterinary Science/Medicine). For example, the offers lines could read as follows:

  East Anglia – AAAb incl biol+sci +UKCAT (Med 5 yrs) (IB 36 pts HL 666 incl biol+sci)
  Durham – A*AA +LNAT (Law) (IB 38 pts)
  London (RVC) – AAA–AAB incl chem+biol +BMAT (Vet Med)

  Entry and admissions tests will be required for 2017 by a number of institutions for a wide range of subjects: see **Chapter 5** and the subject tables in **Chapter 7** for more information and check university websites and prospectuses.

Course title(s)
After the offer, an abbreviated form of the course title(s) to which the offers information refers is provided in brackets. The abbreviations used (see **COURSE ABBREVIATIONS** at the end of this chapter)

closely relate to the course titles shown in the institutions' prospectuses. When the course gives the opportunity to study abroad this can be indicated on the offers line by including 'St Abrd' after the abbreviated course title. For example:

Lancaster – A*AA–AAA incl maths (Econ (St Abrd)) (IB 38–36 pts HL 6 maths)

When experience in industry is provided as part of the course (not necessarily a sandwich course) this can be indicated on the offers line by including 'Yr Ind' after the abbreviated course title. For example:

Liverpool – AAB (Bus Mgt (Yr Ind)) (IB 33 pts)

Sometimes the information in the offers line relates to more than one course (see **Greenwich** below). In such cases, each course title is separated with a semicolon.

Greenwich – 120 pts (Lang Int Rel; Pol Int Rel)

When a number of joint courses exist in combination with a major subject, they may be presented using a list separated by slashes – for example '(Int Bus Fr/Ger/Span)' indicates International Business with French or German or Spanish. Some titles may be followed by the word 'courses' – for example, (Hist courses):

Bishop Grosseteste – 96–112 pts (Arch Hist; Hist courses)

This means that the information on the offers line refers not only to the Single Honours course in Archaeology History, but also to the range of History courses. For some institutions with extensive Combined Honours programmes, the information given on the offers line may specify (Comb Hons) or (Comb courses).

Courses awaiting validation are usually publicised in prospectuses and on websites. However, these are not included in the tables in **Chapter 7** since there is no guarantee that they will run. You should check with the university that a non-validated course will be available.

To help you understand the information provided under the **Your target offers and examples of degree courses** heading, the box below provides a few examples with their meaning explained underneath.

OFFERS LINES EXPLAINED

136 pts [University/University College name] – AAB (Acc Fin)
For the Accounting Finance course the University requires grades of AAB (136 pts) at A-level.

152 pts [University/University College name] – A*AA incl chem+biol +BMAT (Med 6 yrs)
For the 6 year Medicine course the University requires one A and two A grades at A-level, with two of these subjects in Chemistry and Biology, plus the BMAT.*

104 pts [University/University College name] – 104–120 pts (Geog)
For Geography, the University usually requires 104 UCAS Tariff points, but offers may range up to 120 UCAS Tariff points.

Alternative offers
In each of the subject tables, offers are shown in A-level grades or equivalent UCAS Tariff points, and in some cases as points offers of the International Baccalaureate Diploma (see below). However, applicants taking Scottish Highers/Advanced Highers, the Advanced Welsh Baccalaureate – Skills Challenge Certificate, the International Baccalaureate Diploma, BTEC, the Extended Project, Music examinations and Art and Design Foundation Studies should refer to **Appendix 1 – The UCAS 2017 Entry Tariff Points**. For more information, see www.ucas.com/how-it-all-works/explore-your-options/entry-requirements/tariff-tables or contact the institution direct.

IB offers

A selection of IB points offers appears at the end of some university/subject entries. For comparison of entry requirements, applicants with IB qualifications should check the A-level offers required for their course and then refer to **Appendix 1** which gives the revised IB UCAS Tariff points for 2017 entry. The figures under this subheading indicate the number or range of International Baccalaureate (IB) Diploma points likely to be requested in an offer. A range of points indicates variations between Single and Joint Honours courses. Applicants should check with the universities for any requirements for points gained from specific Higher Level (HL) subjects. Applicants offering the IB should check with prospectuses and websites and, if in doubt, contact admissions tutors for the latest information on IB offers.

Scottish offers

Scottish Honours degrees normally take four years. However, students with very good qualifications may be admitted into the second year of courses (Advanced entry). In some cases it may even be possible to enter the third year.

This year we have not included the offers details for Advanced entry. Any student with sufficient A-levels or Advanced Highers considering this option should check with the university to which they are applying. The policies at some Scottish universities are listed below:

Aberdeen Advanced entry possible for many courses, but not for Education, Law or Medicine.
Abertay Possibility of advanced entry largely dependent on content of current course.
Dundee Advanced entry possible for many courses, but not Art, Education, Law or Medicine.
Edinburgh Advanced entry possible for Science, Engineering, and Art and Design courses.
Edinburgh Napier Advanced entry to Stages 2, 3 or 4 of a programme, particularly for those with an HNC/HND or those with (or expecting to obtain) good grades in Advanced Highers or A-levels.
Glasgow Advanced entry possible in a range of subjects, including Neuroscience, Sociology and Civil Engineering.
Glasgow Caledonian Advanced entry available in a wide range of courses, including Business, Civil Engineering, Journalism and Biological Sciences.
Queen Margaret Advanced entry for some courses.
St Andrews Advanced entry for some courses.
Stirling Advanced entry for some courses.
Strathclyde Advanced entry for some courses.
West Scotland Advanced entry for some courses.

For others not on this list, please check individual university and college websites.

IMPORTANT NOTE ON THE COURSE OFFERS INFORMATION

The information provided in **Chapter 7** is presented as a first reference source as to the target levels required. Institutions may alter their standard offers in the light of the qualifications offered by applicants.

The offers they publish do not constitute a contract and are not binding on prospective students: changes may occur between the time of publication and the time of application in line with market and student demand.

The points levels shown on the left-hand side of the offers listings are for ease of reference for the reader: not all universities will be making offers using the UCAS Tariff points system and it cannot be assumed that they will accept a points equivalent to the grades they have stipulated. Check university and college prospectuses, and also their websites, for their latest information before submitting your application.

EXAMPLES OF COLLEGES OFFERING COURSES IN THIS SUBJECT FIELD

Examples of courses offered by some local colleges – but also check your local college. To check details of courses, refer to college websites and **Chapter 9** Sections 2 and 3.

CHOOSING YOUR COURSE

The information under this heading (to be read in conjunction with **Chapter 1**) covers factors that are important to consider in order to make an informed decision on which courses to apply for. The information is organised under the following subheadings.

Universities and colleges teaching quality

The Unistats website (http://unistats.direct.gov.uk) provides official information where available for different subjects and universities and colleges in the UK to help prospective students and their advisers make comparisons between them and so make informed choices about what and where to study. Information is updated annually and is available for each subject taught at each university and college (and for some further education colleges). The Quality Assurance Agency (www.qaa.ac.uk) reviews the quality and standards of all universities and colleges and official reports of their reviews are available on their website but it is important to note their dates of publication.

Top research universities and colleges (REF 2014)

In December 2014 the latest Research Excellence Framework was undertaken covering certain subject areas. The leading universities in the relevant subject areas are listed in the order of achievement. It should be noted that not all subjects were assessed.

Examples of sandwich degree courses

This section lists examples of institutions that offer sandwich placements for some of their courses in the subject field shown. The institutions listed offer placements of one-year duration and do not include language courses or work experience or other short-term placements. Check with the institutions too, since new courses may be introduced and others withdrawn depending on industrial or commercial arrangements. Further information on sandwich courses with specific information on the placements of students appears in **Chapter 1**.

NB During a period of economic uncertainty, universities and colleges may have problems placing students on sandwich courses. Applicants applying for courses are therefore advised to check with admissions tutors that these courses will run, and that placements will be available.

ADMISSIONS INFORMATION

Under this heading, information gathered from the institutions has been provided. This will be useful when planning your application.

Number of applicants per place (approx)

These figures show the approximate number of applicants initially applying for each place before any offers are made. It should be noted that any given number of applicants represents candidates who have also applied for up to four other university and college courses. In some subject areas some universities have provided details of the actual breakdown of numbers of applicants under the following headings: UK, EU (non-UK), non-EU (overseas), mature (over 21).

Advice to applicants and planning the UCAS personal statement

This section offers guidelines on information that could be included in the personal statement section of your UCAS application. In most cases, applicants will be required to indicate why they wish to follow a particular course and, if possible, to provide positive evidence of their interest. See also **Chapters 4** and **5**.

Misconceptions about this course

Admissions tutors are given the opportunity in the research for this book to set the record straight by clarifying aspects of their course they feel are often misunderstood by students, and in some cases, advisers!

Selection interviews
Institutions that normally use the interview as part of their selection procedure are listed here. Those institutions adopting the interview procedure will usually interview only a small proportion of applicants. It is important to use this section in conjunction with **Chapters 3** and **5**.

Interview advice and questions
This section includes information from institutions on what candidates might expect in an interview to cover, and examples of the types of interview questions posed in recent years. Also refer to **Chapters 3** and **5**: these chapters provide information on tests and assessments which are used in selecting students.

Reasons for rejection (non-academic)
Academic ability and potential to suceed on the course are the major factors in the selection (or rejection) of applicants. Under this subheading, admissions tutors give other reasons for rejecting applicants.

AFTER-RESULTS ADVICE
Under this heading, information for helping you decide what to do after the examination results are published is provided (see also the section on **What to do on Results Day … and After** in **Chapter 4**). Details refer to the main subject area unless otherwise stated in brackets.

Offers to applicants repeating A-levels
This section gives details of whether second-time offers made to applicants repeating their exams may be 'higher', 'possibly higher' or the 'same' as those made to first-time applicants. The information refers to Single Honours courses. It should be noted that circumstances may differ between candidates – some will be repeating the same subjects taken in the previous year, while others may be taking different subjects. Offers will also be dictated by the grades you achieved on your first sitting of the examinations. Remember, if you were rejected by all your universities and have achieved good grades, contact them by telephone on results day – they may be prepared to revise their decision. This applies particularly to medical schools.

GRADUATE DESTINATIONS AND EMPLOYMENT
The information under this heading has been provided by the Higher Education Statistics Agency (HESA) and is taken from their report *Destinations of Leavers from Higher Education 2013/14*. The report can be obtained from www.hesa.ac.uk.

Details are given of the total number of graduates surveyed whose destinations have been recorded – not the total number who graduated in that subject. Employment figures relate to those in full-time permanent paid employment after six months in a variety of occupations not necessarily related to their degree subject (part-time employment figures are not included). Figures are also given for those in voluntary, unpaid work. 'Further study' includes research into a subject-related field, higher degrees, private study or, alternatively, career training involving work and further study. The 'Assumed unemployed' category refers to those students who were believed to be unemployed for various reasons (eg travelling, personal reasons) or those students still seeking permanent employment six months after graduating. The figures given do not equal the total number of graduates surveyed as we have chosen only to include the most relevant or interesting areas.

Career note
Short descriptions of the career destinations of graduates in the subject area are provided.

OTHER DEGREE SUBJECTS FOR CONSIDERATION
This heading includes some suggested alternative courses that have similarities to the courses listed in the subject table.

ABBREVIATIONS USED IN THE SUBJECT TABLES IN CHAPTER 7

INSTITUTION ABBREVIATIONS

The following abbreviations are used to indicate specific institutions or types of institution:

Ac	Academy
AI	Arts Institute
ALRA	Academy of Live and Recorded Arts
AMD	Academy of Music and Drama
Birk	Birkbeck (London University)
BSO	British School of Osteopathy
CA	College of Art(s)
CAD	College of Art and Design
CAFRE	College of Agriculture, Food and Rural Enterprise
CAg	College of Agriculture
CAgH	College of Agriculture and Horticulture
CAT	College of Advanced Technology or Arts and Technology
CComm	College of Communication
CDC	College of Design and Communication
CECOS	London College of IT and Management
CFash	College of Fashion
CHort	College of Horticulture
CmC	Community College
CMus	College of Music
CMusDr	College of Music and Drama
Coll	College
Consv	Conservatoire
Court	Courtauld Institute (London University)
CT	College of Technology
CTA	College of Technology and Arts
Educ	Education
Gold	Goldsmiths (London University)
GSA	Guildford School of Acting
Hey	Heythrop College (London University)
IA	Institute of Art(s)
IFHE	Institute of Further and Higher Education
Inst	Institute
King's	King's College (London University)
LIPA	Liverpool Institute of Performing Arts
LSE	London School of Economics and Political Science
Met	Metropolitan
MS	Medical School
NCH	New College of the Humanities
QM	Queen Mary (London University)
RAcMus	Royal Academy of Music
RConsvS	Royal Conservatoire of Scotland
RCMus	Royal College of Music
Reg Coll	Regional College
Reg Fed	Regional Federation (Staffordshire)
RH	Royal Holloway (London University)
RNCM	Royal Northern College of Music
RVC	Royal Veterinary College (London University)
SA	School of Art
SAD	School of Art and Design

Sch	School
Sch SpDr	School of Speech and Drama
SMO	Sabhal Mòr Ostaig
SOAS	School of Oriental and African Studies (London University)
SRUC	Scotland's Rural College
UC	University College
UCFB	University College of Football Business
UCL	University College (London University)
UHI	University of the Highlands and Islands
Univ	University

COURSE ABBREVIATIONS

The following abbreviations are used to indicate course titles:

Ab	Abrahamic	**Analyt**	Analytical
Abrd	Abroad	**Anat**	Anatomy/Anatomical
Acc	Accountancy/Accounting	**Anc**	Ancient
Accs	Accessories	**Anim**	Animal
Acoust	Acoustics/Acoustical	**Animat**	Animation
Acq	Acquisition	**Animatron**	Animatronics
Act	Actuarial	**Anth**	Anthropology
Actg	Acting	**Antq**	Antique(s)
Actn	Action	**App(s)**	Applied/Applicable/Applications
Actr	Actor	**Appar**	Apparel
Actv	Active	**Appr**	Appropriate
Actvt(s)	Activity/Activities	**Apprsl**	Appraisal
Acu	Acupuncture	**Aqua**	Aquaculture/Aquatic
Add	Additional	**Ar**	Area(s)
Adlscn	Adolescence	**Arbc**	Arabic
Adlt	Adult	**Arbor**	Arboriculture
Admin	Administration/Administrative	**Arch**	Archaeology
Adt	Audit	**Archit**	Architecture
Adv	Advertising	**Archvl**	Archival
Advc	Advice	**Aroma**	Aromatherapy
Advnc	Advanced	**Arst**	Artist
Advntr	Adventure	**Artfcts**	Artefacts
Aero	Aeronautical/Aeronautics	**Artif**	Artificial
Aerodyn	Aerodynamics	**As**	Asian
Aero-Mech	Aero-mechanical	**Ass**	Assessment
Aerosp	Aerospace	**Assoc**	Associated
Aeroth	Aerothermal	**Asst**	Assistant
Af	Africa(n)	**Assyr**	Assyriology
Affrs	Affairs	**Ast**	Asset
Age	Ageing	**Astnaut**	Astronautics/Astronautical
Agncy	Agency	**Astro**	Astrophysics
Agric	Agriculture/Agricultural	**Astron**	Astronomy
Agrofor	Agroforestry	**A-Sxn**	Anglo-Saxon
Agron	Agronomy	**Ated**	Accelerated
Aircft	Aircraft	**Atel**	Atelier
Airln	Airline	**Atlan**	Atlantic
Airpt	Airport	**Atmos**	Atmospheric
Airvhcl	Airvehicle	**Attrctns**	Attractions
Akkdn	Akkadian	**Auc**	Auctioneering
Am	American	**Aud**	Audio
Amen	Amenity	**Audiol**	Audiology
Analys	Analysis	**Audtech**	Audiotechnology

Aus	Australia(n)	Buy	Buying
Austr	Australasia	Byz	Byzantine
Auth	Author/Authoring/Authorship	CAD	Computer Aided Design
Auto	Automotive	Callig	Calligraphy
Autom	Automated/Automation	Can	Canada/Canadian
Automat	Automatic	Cap	Capital
Autombl	Automobile	Cardio	Cardiology
Autsm	Autism	Cardiov	Cardiovascular
AV	Audio Video	Carib	Caribbean
Avion	Avionics	Cart	Cartography
Avn	Aviation	Cat	Catering
Ay St	Ayurvedic Studies	CATS	Credit Accumulation and Transfer Scheme
Bank	Banking	Cell	Cellular
Bch	Beach	Celt	Celtic
Bd	Based	Cent	Century
Bdwk	Bodywork	Ceram	Ceramics
Bhv	Behavioural	Cert	Certificate
Bib	Biblical	Ch Mgt	Chain Management
Bio Ins	Bio Instrumentation	Chc	Choice
Bioarch	Bioarchaeology	Chch	Church
Bioch	Biochemistry/Biochemical	Chem	Chemistry
Biocomp	Biocomputing	Cheml	Chemical
Biodiv	Biodiversity	Chin	Chinese
Bioelectron	Bioelectronics	Chiro	Chiropractic
Biogeog	Biogeography	Chld	Child/Children/Childhood
Biogeosci	Biogeoscience	Chn	Chain
Bioinform	Bioinformatics	Chng	Change
Biokin	Biokinetics	Choreo	Choreography
Biol	Biological/Biology	Chr	Christian(ity)
Biom	Biometry	Chrctr	Character
Biomed	Biomedical/Biomedicine	Chtls	Chattels
Biomol	Biomolecular	Cits	Cities
Biophys	Biophysics	Civ	Civilisation/Civil
Bioproc	Bioprocess	Class	Classical/Classics
Biorg	Bio-organic	Clim	Climate/Climatic
Biosci	Bioscience(s)	Clin	Clinical
Biotech	Biotechnology	Cllct	Collect/Collecting
Biovet	Bioveterinary	Clnl	Colonial
Bkbnd	Bookbinding	Cloth	Clothing
Bld	Build/Building	Clsrm	Classroom
Bldstck	Bloodstock	Cmbt	Combat
Blksmthg	Blacksmithing	Cmc	Comic
Blt	Built	Cmdy	Comedy
Bngli	Bengali	Cmn	Common
Braz	Brazilian	Cmnd	Command
Brew	Brewing	Cmplrs	Compilers
Brit	British	Cmpn	Companion
Brnd	Brand/Branding	Cmpsn	Composition
Broad	Broadcast(ing)	Cmpste	Composite(s)
Bspk	Bespoke	Cmwlth	Commonwealth
Bty	Beauty	Cncr	Cancer
Bulg	Bulgarian	Cnflct	Conflict
Burm	Burmese	Cnma	Cinema/Cinematics/Cinematography
Bus	Business		

Cnslg	Counselling	Crypt	Cryptography
Cnsltncy	Consultancy	Cstl	Coastal
Cnt	Central	Cstm	Costume
Cntnt	Content	Cstmd	Customised
Cntrms	Countermeasures	Ctln	Catalan
Cntry	Country/Countryside	Ctlys	Catalysis
Cntxt	Context	Ctzn	Citizenship
Cnty	Century	Culn	Culinary
Coach	Coaching	Cult	Culture/Cultural
Cog	Cognitive	Cur	Curation
Col	Colour	Cy	Cyber
Coll	Collaborative	Cyber	Cybernetics/Cyberspace
Comb	Combined	Cybertron	Cybertronics
Combus	Combustion	Cym	Cymraeg
Comm(s)	Communication(s)	Cz	Czech
Commer	Commerce/Commercial		
Commun	Community	Dan	Danish
Comp	Computer/Computerised/	Decn	Decision
	Computing	Decr	Decoration/Decorative
Compar	Comparative	Def	Defence
Complem	Complementary	Defer	Deferred Choice
Comput	Computation/al	Deg	Degree
Con	Context	Demcr	Democratic
Conc	Concept	Dept	Department
Concur	Concurrent	Des	Design(er)
Cond	Conductive	Desr	Desirable
Condit	Conditioning	Dest	Destination(s)
Cons	Conservation	Dev	Development/
Constr	Construction		Developmental
Consum	Consumer	Devsg	Devising
Cont	Contour	Df	Deaf
Contemp	Contemporary	Diag	Diagnostic
Contnl	Continental	Diet	Diet/Dietetics/Dietitian
Contr	Control	Dif	Difficulties
Conv	Conveyancing	Dig	Digital
Cord	Cordwainers	Dip	Diploma
Corn	Cornish	Dip Ing	Diplom Ingeneur
Corp	Corporate/Corporation	Dipl	Diplomacy
Cos	Cosmetic	Dir	Direct/Direction/Director/
Cosmo	Cosmology		Directing
Cr	Care	Dis	Diseases
Crcs	Circus	Disab	Disability
Crdc	Cardiac	Disas	Disaster
Crea	Creative/Creation	Discip	Disciplinary
Crfts	Crafts/Craftsmanship	Diso	Disorders
Crim	Criminal	Disp	Dispensing
Crimin	Criminological/Criminology	Dist	Distributed/Distribution
Crit	Criticism/Critical	Distil	Distillation/Distilling
Crm	Crime	Div	Divinity
Cro	Croatian	d/l	distance learning
Crr	Career	Dlvry	Delivery
Crs	Course	Dnstry	Dentistry
Crsn	Corrosion	Dntl	Dental
Crtn	Cartoon	Doc	Document/Documentary
Cru	Cruise	Dom	Domestic/Domesticated

Dr	Drama	Ergon	Ergonomics
Drg	Drawing	Est	Estate
Drs	Dress	Eth	Ethics
Dscrt	Discrete	Ethl	Ethical
Dscvry	Discovery	Eth-Leg	Ethico-Legal
Dsply	Display	Ethn	Ethnic
Dtbs	Databases	Ethnol	Ethnology
Dth	Death	Ethnomus	Ethnomusicology
Dvc	Device	EU	European Union
Dvnc	Deviance	Euro	European
Dvsd	Devised	Eval	Evaluation
Dynmcs	Dynamics	Evnglstc	Evangelistic
		Evnt(s)	Event(s)
Ecol	Ecology/Ecological	Evol	Evolution/Evolutionary
Ecomet	Econometrics	Ex	Executing
e-Commer	E-Commerce	Excl	Excellence
Econ	Economics	Exer	Exercise
Econy	Economy/ies	Exhib	Exhibition
Ecosys	Ecosystem(s)	Exmp	Exempt(ing)
Ecotech	Ecotechnology	Exp	Export
Ecotour	Ecotourism	Explor	Exploration
Ecotox	Ecotoxicology	Explsn	Explosion
Edit	Editorial/Editing	Expltn	Exploitation
Educ	Education	Expmtl	Experimental
Educr	Educare	Expnc	Experience
Efcts	Effects	Expr	Expressive
EFL	English as a Foreign	Ext	Extended
	Language	Extr	Exterior
Egypt	Egyptian/Egyptology	Extrm	Extreme
Elec	Electrical		
Elecacoust	Electroacoustics	Fabs	Fabric(s)
Electromech	Electromechanical	Fac	Faculty
Electron	Electronic(s)	Fact	Factor(s)
ELT	English Language Teaching	Facil	Facilities
Ely	Early	Fash	Fashion
Emb	Embryo	Fbr	Fibre
Embd	Embedded	Fctn	Fiction
Embr	Embroidery	Fd	Food
Emer	Emergency	Fdn	Foundation
Emp	Employment	Filmm	Filmmaking
Ener	Energy	Fin	Finance/Financial
Eng	Engineering	Finn	Finnish
Engl	English	Fish	Fisheries
Engmnt	Engagement	Fit	Fitness
Engn	Engine	Fl	Fluid
Ent	Enterprise	Fld	Field
Enter	Entertainment	Flex	Flexible
Entre	Entrepreneur/Entrepreneurship	Flor	Floristry
Env	Environment/Environmental	FMaths	Further Mathematics
EPQ	Extended Project	Fmly	Family
	Qualification	Fn	Fine
Eql	Equal	Foot	Footwear
Eqn	Equine/Equestrian	For	Foreign
Equip	Equipment	Foren	Forensic
Equit	Equitation	Foss	Fossil(s)

Fr	French	Grn	Green
Frchd	Franchised	gs	General Studies
Frcst	Forecasting	Guji	Gujerati
Frm	Farm		
Frmwk	Framework	Hab	Habitat
Frshwtr	Freshwater	Hack	Hacking
Frst	Forest	Hard	Hardware
Frsty	Forestry	Haz	Hazard
Frtlty	Fertility	Heal	Healing
Fst Trk	Fast Track	Heb	Hebrew
Fstvl	Festival	Herb	Herbal
Ftbl	Football	Herit	Heritage
Ftre	Feature(s)	Hi	High
Ftwr	Footwear	Hisp	Hispanic
Furn	Furniture	Hist	History/Historical
Fut	Futures	HL	IB Higher level
		Hlcst	Holocaust
Gael	Gaelic	Hlnds	Highlands
Gam	Gambling	Hlth	Health
Gdn	Garden	Hlthcr	Healthcare
Gdnc	Guidance	Hm	Home
Gem	Gemmology	Hnd	Hindi
Gen	General	Hol	Holistic
Genet	Genetics	Hom	Homeopathic
Geochem	Geochemistry	Homin	Hominid
Geog	Geography	Horol	Horology
Geoinform	Geoinformatics	Hort	Horticulture
Geol	Geology	Hosp	Hospital
Geophys	Geophysics	Hous	Housing
Geophysl	Geophysical	HR	Human Resources
Geopol	Geopolitics	Hrdrs	Hairdressing
Geosci	Geoscience	Hrs	Horse
Geosptl	Geospatial	Hse	House
Geotech	Geotechnics	Hspty	Hospitality
Ger	German/Germany	Htl	Hotel
Gerc	Germanic	Hum	Human(ities)
GIS	Geographical Information Systems	Hung	Hungarian
		Hydrog	Hydrography
Gk	Greek	Hydrol	Hydrology
Glf	Golf	Hyg	Hygiene
Glf Crs	Golf Course		
Gllry	Gallery/Galleries	Iber	Iberian
Glob	Global/Globalisation	Ice	Icelandic
Gls	Glass	ICT	Information and Communications Technology
Gmg	Gaming		
Gmnt	Garment	Id	Ideas
Gms	Games	Idnty	Identity
Gmtc	Geomatic	Illus	Illustration
Gndr	Gender	Imag	Image/Imaging/Imaginative
Gnm	Genome/Genomics	Immun	Immunology/Immunity
Gold	Goldsmithing	Impair	Impairment
Gov	Government	Incl	Including
Govn	Governance	Incln	Inclusion
Graph	Graphic	Inclsv	Inclusive
Grgn	Georgian	Ind	Industrial/Industry

Indep St	Independent Study	Lab	Laboratory
Indiv	Individual(s)	Lang(s)	Language(s)
Indsn	Indonesian	Las	Laser
Inf	Information	Lat	Latin
Infec	Infectious/Infection	Lcl	Local
Infml	Informal	LD	Learning Disabilities
Inform	Informatics	Ldrshp	Leadership
Infra	Infrastructure	Lea	Leather
Inftq	Informatique	Leg	Legal
Injry	Injury	Legis	Legislative
Innov	Innovation	Leis	Leisure
Ins	Insurance	Lf	Life
Inst	Institution(al)	Lfstl	Lifestyle
Instln	Installation	Lgc	Logic
Instr	Instrument/Instrumentation	Lib	Library
Int	International	Librl	Liberal
Integ	Integrated/Integration	Libshp	Librarianship
Intel	Intelligent/Intelligence	Lic	Licensed
Inter	Interior	Lic de Geog	Licence de Geographie
Interact	Interaction/Interactive	Lic de Let	Licence de Lettres
Intercult	Intercultural	Ling	Linguistics
Interd	Interdisciplinary	Lit	Literature/Literary
Intermed	Intermedia	Litcy	Literacy
Interp	Interpretation	Lnd	Land(scape)
Intlctl	Intellectual	Lndbd	Land-based
Intnet	Internet	Lns	Lens
Intr	Interest(s)	Log	Logistics
Intrmdl	Intermodal	Lrn	Learn
Inv	Investment	Lrng	Learning
Invstg	Investigating/Investigation	Ls	Loss
IPML	Integrated Professional Master	Lsr	Laser
	in Language	Ltg	Lighting
Ir	Irish	Ltr	Later
Is	Issues	Lv	Live
Isl	Islands	Lvstk	Livestock
Islam	Islamic		
Isrl	Israel/Israeli	Mach	Machine(ry)
IT	Information Technology	Mag	Magazine
Ital	Italian	Mait	Maitrise Internationale
ITE	Initial Teacher Education	Mak	Making/Maker
ITT	Initial Teacher Training	Mand	Mandarin
		Manuf	Manufacturing
Jap	Japanese	Map	Map/Mapping
Jew	Jewish	Mar	Marine
Jewel	Jewellery	Marit	Maritime
Jrnl	Journalism	Mark	Market(ing)
Jud	Judaism	Masch	Maschinenbau
Juris	Jurisprudence	Mat	Materials
Just	Justice	Mathem	Mathematical
		Maths	Mathematics
Knit	Knit/Knitted	Mbl	Mobile
Kntwr	Knitwear	Measur	Measurement
Knwl	Knowledge	Mech	Mechanical
Kor	Korean	Mecha	Mechatronics
KS	Key Stage	Mechn	Mechanisation

Mechnsms	Mechanisms	Multim	Multimedia
Med	Medicine/cal	Mus	Music(ian)
Medcnl	Medicinal	Muscskel	Musculoskeletal
Mediev	Medieval	Musl	Musical
Medit	Mediterranean	Musm	Museum
Metal	Metallurgy/Metallurgical	Mushp	Musicianship
Meteor	Meteorology/Meteorological		
Meth	Method(s)	N	New
Mgr	Manager	N Am	North America
Mgrl	Managerial	Nano	Nanoscience
Mgt	Management	Nanoelectron	Nanoelectronics
Microbiol	Microbiology/Microbiological	Nanotech	Nanotechnology
Microbl	Microbial	Nat	Nature/Natural
Microcomp	Microcomputer/	Natpth	Naturopathy
	Microcomputing	Navig	Navigation
Microelec	Microelectronics	Nbrhd	Neighbourhood
Mid E	Middle Eastern	Nds	Needs
Midwif	Midwifery	Neg	Negotiated
Min	Mining	Net	Network
Miner	Minerals	Neuro	Neuroscience
Mkup	Make-up	Neuropsy	Neuropsychology
Mling	Multilingual	News	Newspaper
Mltry	Military	NGO	Non-Governmental
MML	Master of Modern		Organisation(s)
	Languages	NI	Northern Ireland/Northern
Mnd	Mind		Irish
Mndrn	Mandarin	Nnl	National
Mnrts	Minorities	Norw	Norwegian
Mnstry	Ministry	Npli	Nepali
Mnswr	Menswear	Nrs	Norse
Mntl Hlth	Mental Health	Ntv	Native
Mntn	Mountain	Nucl	Nuclear
Mntnce	Maintenance	Nurs	Nursing
Mny	Money	Nursy	Nursery
Mod	Modular	Nutr	Nutrition(al)
Modl	Modelling/Modelmaking	Nvl	Naval
Modn	Modern	NZ	New Zealand
Modnty	Modernity		
Mol	Molecular	Obj(s)	Object(s)
Monit	Monitoring	Obs	Observational
Mov	Movement/Moving	Occ	Occupational
Mrchnds	Merchandise/Merchandising	Ocean	Oceanography
Mrchnt	Merchant	Ocn	Ocean
Mrl	Moral	Ocnc	Oceanic
Msg	Massage	Oeno	Oenology
Mslm	Muslim	Ofce	Office
Mtl	Metal(s)	Off	Offshore
Mtlsmth	Metalsmithing	Offrd	Off-road
Mtlwk	Metalworking	Okl	Oklahoma
Mtn	Motion	Onc	Oncology
Mtr	Motor	Onln	Online
Mtrcycl	Motorcycle	Op(s)	Operation(s)
Mtrg	Motoring	Oph	Ophthalmic
Mtrspo	Motorsports	Oprtg	Operating
Multid	Multi-disciplinary	Opt	Optical

Optim	Optimisation	Phon	Phonetics
Optn/s	Optional/Options	Photo	Photography/Photographic
Optoel	Optoelectronics	Photojrnl	Photojournalism
Optom	Optometry	Photon	Photonic(s)
OR	Operational Research	Phys	Physics
Ord	Ordinary	Physio	Physiotherapy
Org	Organisation	Physiol	Physiology/Physiological
Orgnc	Organic	Physl	Physical
Orgnsms	Organisms	Pks	Parks
Orn	Ornithology	Plan	Planning
Orntl	Oriental	Planet	Planetary
Orth	Orthoptics	Plas	Plastics
Orthot	Orthotics	Play	Playwork
Oseas	Overseas	Plcg	Police/Policing
Ost	Osteopathy	Plcy	Policy
Out	Outdoor	Plmt	Placement
Out Act	Outdoor Activity	Plnt	Plant
Outsd	Outside	Plntsmn	Plantsmanship
Ovrs	Overseas	Plt	Pilot
		Pltry	Poultry
P	Primary	PMaths	Pure Mathematics
P Cr	Primary Care	Pntg	Painting
Pacif	Pacific	Pod	Podiatry/Podiatric
Pack	Packaging	Pol	Politics/Political
PActv	Physical Activity	Polh	Polish
Pal	Palaeobiology	Pollut	Pollution
Palae	Palaeoecology/Palaeontology	Poly	Polymer/Polymeric
Palaeoenv	Palaeoenvironments	Pop	Popular
Paramed	Paramedic(al)	Popn	Population
Parasit	Parasitology	Port	Portuguese
Parl	Parliamentary	Postcol	Postcolonial
Part	Participation	PPE	Philosophy, Politics and
Pat	Patent		Economics or Politics,
Path	Pathology		Philosophy and Economics
Pathobiol	Pathobiological	PPI	Private Pilot Instruction
Pathogen	Pathogenesis	Ppl	People
Patt	Pattern	Ppr	Paper
Pblc	Public	Pptry	Puppetry
Pce	Peace	PR	Public Relations
PE	Physical Education	Prac	Practice/Practical
Ped	Pedagogy	Practnr	Practitioner
Per	Person/Personal	Prchsng	Purchasing
Perf	Performance	Prcrmt	Procurement
Perfum	Perfumery	Prdcl	Periodical
Pers	Personnel	Precsn	Precision
Persn	Persian	Pref	Preferable/Preferred
Petrol	Petroleum	Prehist	Prehistory
PGCE	Postgraduate Certificate in	Prem	Premises
	Education	Proc	Process/Processing
Pharm	Pharmacy	Prod	Product/Production/Produce
Pharmacol	Pharmacology	Prodg	Producing
Pharml	Pharmaceutical	Prof	Professional/Professions
Phil	Philosophy/Philosophical	Prog	Programme/Programming
Philgy	Philology	Proj	Project
Phn	Phone	Prom	Promotion

Prop	Property/ies	Rep	Representation
Pros	Prosthetics	Repro	Reproductive
Prot	Protection/Protected	Reqd	Required
Proto	Prototyping	Res	Resources
Prplsn	Propulsion	Resid	Residential
Prsts	Pursuits	Resoln	Resolution
Prt	Print	Resp	Response
Prtcl	Particle	Respir	Respiratory
Prtd	Printed	Restor	Restoration
Prtg	Printing/Printmaking	Rev	Revenue
Prvntn	Prevention	Rflxgy	Reflexology
Pst	Post	Rgby	Rugby
Pstrl	Pastoral	Rgstrn	Registration
Psy	Psychology	Rl	Real
Psychobiol	Psychobiology	Rlblty	Reliability
Psyling	Psycholinguistics	Rlwy	Railway
Psysoc	Psychosocial	Rmnc	Romance
Psytrpy	Psychotherapy	RN	Registered Nurse
Pt	Port	Rnwl	Renewal
p/t	part-time	Robot	Robotics
Ptcl	Particle	Rom	Roman
Pub	Publishing	Romn	Romanian
Pvt	Private	Rsch	Research
Pwr	Power	Rspnsb	Responsibility
Pwrcft	Powercraft	Rsrt	Resort
		Rstrnt	Restaurant
Qntm	Quantum	Rtl	Retail
Qry	Quarry	Rts	Rights
Qtrnry	Quaternary	Rur	Rural
QTS	Qualified Teacher Status	Russ	Russian
Qual	Quality	Rvr	River
Qualif	Qualification		
Quant	Quantity/Quantitative	S	Secondary
		S As	South Asian
Rad	Radio	Sansk	Sanskrit
Radiog	Radiography	Sat	Satellite
Radiothera	Radiotherapy	Sbstnce	Substance
Rbr	Rubber	Scand	Scandinavian
Rce	Race	Schlstc	Scholastic
Rcycl	Recycling	Schm	Scheme
Rdtn	Radiation	Sci	Science/Scientific
Realsn	Realisation	Scnc	Scenic
Rec	Recording	Scngrph	Scenographic/Scenography
Reclam	Reclamation	Scot	Scottish
Recr	Recreation	Scr	Secure
Reg	Regional	Script	Scriptwriting
Regn	Regeneration	Scrn	Screen
Rehab	Rehabilitation	Scrnwrit	Sreenwriting
Rel	Relations	Scrts	Securities
Relgn	Religion	Scrty	Security
Relig	Religious	Sctr	Sector
Reltd	Related	Sculp	Sculpture/Sculpting
Rem Sens	Remote Sensing	Sdlry	Saddlery
Ren	Renaissance	SE	South East
Renew	Renewable	Sec	Secretarial

Semicond	Semiconductor	SS	Solid-state
SEN	Special Educational Needs	St	Studies/Study
		St Reg	State Registration
Serb Cro	Serbo-Croat	Stats	Statistics/Statistical
Serv	Services	Std	Studio
Set	Settings	Stg	Stage
Sfc	Surface	Stgs	Settings
Sfty	Safety	Stnds	Standards
Sgnl	Signal	STQ	Scottish Teaching Qualification
Ship	Shipping	Str	Stringed
Silver	Silversmithing	Strat	Strategic/Strategy
Simul	Simulation	Strf	Stratified
Sit Lrng	Situated Learning	Strg	Strength
Sk	Skills	Strt	Street
Slav	Slavonic	Struct	Structural/Structures
Slf	Self	Stry	Story
Sln	Salon	Stt	State
Slovak	Slovakian	Stwdshp	Stewardship
Slp	Sleep	Styl	Styling
Sls	Sales	Surf	Surface
Sml	Small	Surv	Surveying
Smt	Smart	Sust	Sustainability/Sustainable
Smtc	Semitic	Swed	Swedish
Snc	Sonic	Swli	Swahili
Snd	Sound	Sxlty	Sexuality
Sndtrk	Soundtrack	Sys	System(s)
Sndwch	Sandwich	Systmtc	Systematic
Sng	Song		
Soc	Social	Tam	Tamil
Sociol	Sociology	Tap	Tapestry
SocioLeg	Socio-Legal	Tax Rev	Taxation and Revenue
Socling	Sociolinguistics	Tbtn	Tibetan
Soft	Software	Tcnqs	Techniques
Sol	Solution(s)	Teach	Teaching
Solic	Solicitors	Tech	Technology/Technician/Technical
Soty	Society		
Sov	Soviet	Technol	Technological
Sp	Speech	TEFL	Teaching English as a Foreign Language
Span	Spanish		
Spat	Spatial	Telecomm	Telecommunications
Spc	Space	Ter	Terrestrial
SPD	Surface Pattern Design	TESOL	Teaching English to Speakers of Other Languages
Spec	Special/Specialisms/Specialist		
		Testmt	Testament
Spec Efcts	Special Effects	Tex	Textiles
Sply	Supply	Thbred	Thoroughbred
Spn	Spain	Thea	Theatre
Spo	Sports	Theol	Theology
Spotrf	Sportsturf	Theor	Theory/Theoretical
Spowr	Sportswear	Ther	Therapeutic
Spptd	Supported	Thera	Therapy
Sprtng	Supporting	Tht	Thought
Sqntl	Sequential	Tiss	Tissue
Srf	Surf/Surfing	Tlrg	Tailoring
Srgy	Surgery	Tm	Time

Tmbr	Timber	**Vid**	Video
Tnnl	Tunnel/Tunnelling	**Viet**	Vietnamese
Tns	Tennis	**Virol**	Virology
Topog	Topographical	**Vis**	Visual/Visualisation
Tour	Tourism	**Vit**	Viticulture
Tox	Toxicology	**Vkg**	Viking
TQ	Teaching Qualification	**Vntr**	Venture
Tr	Trade	**Vnu**	Venue
Tr Stands	Trading Standards	**Voc**	Vocational
Trad	Traditional	**Vol**	Voluntary
Trans	Transport(ation)	**Vrtl Rlty**	Virtual Reality
Transat	Transatlantic	**Vsn**	Vision
Transl	Translation	**Vstr**	Visitor
Transnl Med Sci	Translational Medical Science		
Trav	Travel	**Wdlnd**	Woodland
Trfgrs	Turfgrass	**Welf**	Welfare
Trg	Training	**Wk**	Work
Trnrs	Trainers	**Wkg**	Working
Trpcl	Tropical	**Wlbng**	Well-being
Trpl	Triple	**Wldlf**	Wildlife
Trstrl	Terrestrial	**Wls**	Wales
Tstmnt	Testament	**Wmnswr**	Womenswear
Ttl	Total	**Wn**	Wine
Turk	Turkish	**Wrbl**	Wearable
Twn	Town	**Writ**	Writing/Writer
Typo	Typographical/Typography	**Wrld**	World
		Wrlss	Wireless
Ukr	Ukrainian	**Wst**	Waste(s)
Un	Union	**Wstn**	Western
Undwtr	Underwater	**Wtr**	Water
Unif	Unified	**Wtrspo**	Watersports
Up	Upland	**Wvn**	Woven
Urb	Urban	**www**	World Wide Web
USA	United States of America		
Util	Utilities/Utilisation	**Ycht**	Yacht
		Ychtg	Yachting
Val	Valuation	**Yng**	Young
Vcl	Vocal	**Yrs**	Years
Veh	Vehicle	**Yth**	Youth
Vert	Vertebrate		
Vet	Veterinary	**Zool**	Zoology
Vib	Vibration		
Vict	Victorian	**3D**	Three-dimensional

ACCOUNTANCY/ACCOUNTING

(see also **Finance**)

Accountancy and Accounting degree courses include accounting, finance, economics, law, management, qualitative methods and information technology. Depending on your chosen course, other topics will include business law, business computing, a study of financial institutions and markets, management accountancy, statistics, taxation and auditing, whilst at some institutions an optional language might be offered. Many, but not all, Accountancy and Accounting degrees give exemptions from the examinations of some or all of the accountancy professional bodies. Single Honours courses are more likely to give full exemptions, while Joint Honours courses are more likely to lead to partial exemptions. Students should check with universities and colleges about which professional bodies offer exemptions for their courses before applying. Most courses are strongly vocational and many offer sandwich placements or opportunities to study Accountancy/Accounting with a second subject.

Useful websites www.accaglobal.com/uk; www.cimaglobal.com; www.cipfa.org; www.tax.org.uk; www.icaew.com; www.ifa.org.uk

NB The points totals shown to the left of the institutions are for ease of reference only. It must not be assumed that Tariff points are always used by institutions or that they can be substituted for an offer in grades. The level of an offer is not necessarily indicative of the quality of a course.

COURSE OFFERS INFORMATION

Subject requirements/preferences GCSE English and mathematics required: popular universities may require A or A*. **AL** Mathematics (A or B) or accounting (A or B) required or preferred for some courses.

Your target offers and examples of degree courses
144 pts **Bath** – AAA incl maths (Acc Fin) (IB 36 pts HL 6 maths)
    Bristol – AAA/A*AB–AAB incl maths (Acc Fin; Acc Mgt; Acc Fin (Yr Abrd)) (IB 36–34 pts HL 6 maths)
    City – AAA 144 pts (Acc Fin) (IB 35 pts)
    Edinburgh – AAA–ABB (Acc Fin; Bus Acc) (IB 37–34 pts)
    Exeter – AAA–AAB (Acc Fin Euro St; Acc Fin (Yr Ind); Bus Acc) (IB 36–34 pts)
    Glasgow – AAA/A*AB–ABB incl maths (Acc Maths; Acc Fin) (IB 38–36 pts)
    Leeds – AAA (Acc Fin) (IB 35 pts)
    London LSE – AAA (Acc Fin) (IB 38 pts)
    Manchester – AAA (Acc) (IB 37 pts)
    Reading – AAA–AAB (Acc Bus; Acc Fin; Acc Mgt) (IB 35 pts)
    Strathclyde – AAA–ABB incl maths (Acc; Acc Hspty Tour Mgt; Acc Mark) (IB 36 pts HL 6 maths)
    Surrey – AAA–AAB (Acc Fin) (IB 35 pts)
    Warwick – AAA incl maths (Acc Fin) (IB 38 pts)
136 pts **Aston** – AAB–ABB (Acc Mgt) (IB 35–34 pts)
    Birmingham – AAB (Acc Fin) (IB 32 pts HL 665)
    Brunel – AAB–BBB (Bus Mgt (Acc)) (IB 33 pts)
    Cardiff – AAB (Acc; Acc Mgt; Acc Euro Lang (Fr/Ger/Span)) (IB 35 pts); (Acc (Yr Ind); Accounting St Abrd) (IB 36 pts)

Coventry – AAB (Acc Fin) (IB 31 pts)
Durham – AAB (Acc Fin; Acc Mgt) (IB 36 pts)
Lancaster – AAB (Acc Mgt St; Acc Fin) (IB 35 pts)
Liverpool – AAB (Acc Fin (Yr Ind); Acc Fin) (IB 35 pts)
London (RH) – AAB (Acc Fin) (IB 32 pts)
Loughborough – AAB–ABB (Acc Fin Mgt) (IB 34 pts)
Nottingham – AAB (Fin Acc Mgt; Acc) (IB 34 pts)
Queen's Belfast – AAB (Acc Lang (Fr/Span); Acc)
Sheffield – AAB (Acc Fin Mgt) (IB 35 pts)
Southampton – AAB–ABB (Acc Fin Plmt) (IB 34 pts)
Sussex – AAB–ABB (Acc Fin (Yr Ind); Acc Fin) (IB 34 pts)
York – AAB (Acc Bus Fin Mgt) (IB 35 pts)

128 pts **Bournemouth** – 128 pts (Int Acc Fin) (IB 32 pts)
Bradford – ABB 128 pts (Acc Fin)
East Anglia – ABB (Acc Fin) (IB 32 pts)
Essex – ABB–BBB (Acc courses; Acc Fin) (IB 32–30 pts)
Kent – ABB (Acc Fin; Acc Fin (Yr Ind)) (IB 34 pts)
Kingston – 128 pts (Acc Fin) (IB 27 pts)
Leicester – ABB (Acc Fin) (IB 30 pts)
London (QM) – ABB (Acc Mgt) (IB 34 pts)
Northumbria – ABB 128 pts (Acc) (IB 31 pts)
Roehampton – 128 pts (Acc)
Swansea – ABB–BBB (Acc; Acc Fin (Yr Ind)) (IB 33–32 pts)

120 pts **Aberdeen** – BBB (Acc Leg St; Acc Bus Mgt; Acc) (IB 32 pts)
Aberystwyth – 120 pts (Acc Fin Comp Sci; Acc Fin)
Bangor – 120 pts (Acc Fin; Acc Bank)
Bournemouth – 120 pts (Acc Fin; Acc Tax; Acc Law; Acc Bus) (IB 31 pts)
Buckingham – BBB–BCC (Acc Fin Mgt)
De Montfort – 120 pts (Acc Fin) (IB 30 pts)
Derby – 120 pts (Acc Fin)
Dundee – BBB–BCC (Acc Bus Fin; Acc) (IB 30 pts)
East London – 120 pts (Acc Fin) (IB 26 pts)
Edge Hill – BBB 120 pts (Acc)
Glasgow Caledonian – BBB incl maths+Engl (Acc) (IB 26 pts HL 4 Engl+maths)
Greenwich – 120 pts (Acc Fin)
Heriot-Watt – BBB (Acc Bus Law) (IB 29 pts)
Huddersfield – BBB 120 pts (Acc Fin)
IFS (UC) – BBB–BBC (Bank Prac Mgt) (IB 30 pts)
Keele – BBB/ABC (Acc) (IB 32 pts)
Leeds Beckett – 120 pts (Acc Fin) (IB 26 pts)
Lincoln – 120 pts (Acc Fin)
Middlesex – 120 pts (Acc Fin)
Newman – 120 pts (Acc Fin)
Oxford Brookes – BBB (Acc Fin) (IB 31 pts)
Plymouth – 120 pts (Acc Fin)
Portsmouth – 120 pts (Acc Bus) (IB 30 HL 17 pts); (Acc Fin) (IB 30 pts HL 17 pts)
Sheffield Hallam – 120 pts (Acc Fin; Foren Acc)
Staffordshire – BBB 120 pts (Acc Fin)
Stirling – BBB (Acc) (IB 32 pts)
Ulster – BBB–AAB incl maths (Acc Law; Acc) (IB 26–28 pts)
UWE Bristol – 120 pts (Acc Fin) (IB 26 pts)
Westminster – BBB (Acc) (IB 28 pts)

112 pts **Birmingham City** – BBC 112 pts (Acc) (IB 28 pts)
Brighton – BBC (Acc Fin) (IB 28 pts HL 16 pts)
Canterbury Christ Church – 112 pts (Acc Mgt; Acc)

Become an ICAEW Chartered Accountant for a career journey with limitless possibilities.
Visit icaew.com/careers today.

Accountancy/Accounting | 99

Cardiff Met – 112 pts (Acc)
Central Lancashire – 112 pts (Acc Fin Mgt) (IB 28 pts)
Chester – BBC–BCC 112 pts (Acc Fin) (IB 26 pts)
Chichester – 112–128 pts (Acc Fin) (IB 30 pts)
Coventry – BBC (Int Fin Acc) (IB 29 pts)
Gloucestershire – 112 pts (Acc Fin Mgt St)
Hull – 112 pts (Acc (Prof Expnc)) (IB 30 pts)
Liverpool John Moores – 112 pts (Acc Fin) (IB 29 pts)
London Met – 112 pts (Acc Fin)
London South Bank – BBC/A*A* 112 pts (Acc Fin)
Northampton – 112 pts (Acc Joint Hons)
Nottingham Trent – 112 pts (Acc Fin)
Robert Gordon – BBC (Acc Fin) (IB 29 pts)
West London – 112 pts (Acc Fin) (IB 29 pts)
Worcester – 112 pts (Bus Acc courses; Acc)
York St John – 112 pts (Acc Fin; Acc Bus Mgt)

104 pts
Bangor – 104–120 pts (Acc Econ)
Bath Spa – 104–120 pts (Bus Mgt (Acc))
Bolton – 104 pts (Acc courses)
BPP – BCC 104 pts (Acc Fin)
Liverpool Hope – BCC–BBB 104–120 pts (Acc Fin)
London (Birk) – 104 pts (Acc)
Manchester Met – BCC–BBC 104–112 pts (Bank Fin; Acc Fin) (IB 26 pts)
Middlesex – 104 pts (Bus Acc)
Salford – 104–120 pts (Acc Fin) (IB 24 pts)
South Wales – BCC (Acc Fin) (IB 29 pts)
Winchester – 104–120 pts (Acc Fin) (IB 26 pts)

96 pts
Abertay – CCC (Acc Fin) (IB 28 pts)
Anglia Ruskin – 96–112 pts (Acc Fin) (IB 24 pts)
Edinburgh Napier – CCC (Acc; Acc Econ; Acc Law; Acc Mark Mgt) (IB 27 pts)
Glyndŵr – 96 pts (Acc Fin)
Hertfordshire – 96–112 pts (Acc; Acc Lang (Fr/Ger/Ital/Span/Mand/Jap))
(IB 28 pts)
Teesside – 96 pts (Acc Fin)
Wolverhampton – 96–112 pts (Acc Fin; Acc Law)

88 pts
Derby – 88–120 pts (Acc Joint Hons)

80 pts
Bedfordshire – 80 pts (Acc) (IB 24 pts)
Bucks New – 80–96 pts (Acc Fin)

64 pts
Trinity Saint David – 64 pts (Acc)

24 pts
UHI – D (Acc Fin)

Alternative offers
See **Chapter 6** and **Appendix 1** for grades/new UCAS Tariff points information for other examinations.

EXAMPLES OF COLLEGES OFFERING COURSES IN THIS SUBJECT FIELD

Accrington and Rossendale (Coll); Barking and Dagenham (Coll); Bath (Coll); BITE; Blackburn (Coll); Blackpool and Fylde (Coll); Bournemouth and Poole (Coll); Bradford (Coll); Bridgwater (Coll); Bury (Coll); Central Nottingham (Coll); Chesterfield (Coll); Cornwall (Coll); Craven (Coll); Derby (Coll); East Riding (Coll); Exeter (Coll); Farnborough (CT); Grimsby (Univ Centre); Hartlepool (CFE); HOW (Coll); Leeds City (Coll); LeSoCo; London City (Coll); London UCK (Coll); LSST; Macclesfield (Coll); Manchester (Coll); Menai (Coll); Mont Rose (Coll); Neath Port Talbot (Coll); Nescot; North Nottinghamshire (Coll); North West London (Coll); Norwich City (Coll); Nottingham New (Coll); Oldham (Univ Campus); Pearson (Coll); Peterborough (Coll); Plymouth City (Coll); Redbridge (Coll); Redcar and Cleveland (Coll); Richmond-upon-Thames (Coll); St Helens (Coll); South City Birmingham (Coll); South

Your ambition...

Taking a career journey with limitless possibilities.

Thousands of employers around the world train graduates to become ICAEW Chartered Accountants. In fact, 97% of the best global brands employ our members.

Discover how you can achieve more as a chartered accountant.

icaew.com/careers

ICAEW

A WORLD LEADER OF THE ACCOUNTANCY AND FINANCE PROFESSION

New UCAS points Tariff: A* = 56 pts; A = 48 pts; B = 40 pts; C = 32 pts; D = 24 pts; E = 16 pts

Become an ICAEW Chartered Accountant for a career journey with limitless possibilities

Have you ever wanted to manage the finances of your favourite charity, or work closely with cutting edge businesses on a global scale? As an ICAEW Chartered Accountant you will find yourself at the heart of business. You will be the one making decisions that affect the strategy, direction and success of organisations around the world.

ICAEW Chartered Accountants are in demand around the world, and can be recognised by the letters ACA after their name. It's a diverse and challenging career that will give you the opportunity to experience all aspects of accountancy, finance and business, whatever your ambitions. If you are looking to gain a highly-regarded skill-set and a career filled with global opportunities to work within a range of reputable companies, then chartered accountancy could be a career to consider.

Find out why 97* of the world's 100 global leading brands employ ICAEW Chartered Accountants

The good news is there's more than one route to becoming an ICAEW Chartered Accountant. If you're bright, ambitious and want to get your career off the ground early, school leaver, apprenticeship, the ICAEW Certificate in Finance, Accounting and Business (ICAEW CFAB) and AAT-ACA Fast Track programmes offer an exciting alternative to university. If university is your chosen route, you may be interested to learn that you don't need to study an accountancy, finance or business related degree.

Discover how you can start your successful career as an ICAEW Chartered Accountant through the ACA qualification. Visit **icaew.com/careers** today!

Find out more

☐ facebook.com/icaewcareers
☐ @ICAEW_Careers
☐ youtube.com/icaewcareers

ICAEW

* ICAEW member data at January 2015, Interbrand Best Global Brands 2014.
* Includes parent companies

BUSINESS WITH CONFIDENCE   icaew.com/careers

GET AHEAD IN YOUR CAREER

with the BA Accounting & Business Flying Start degree programme

- Built in partnership with PwC, a globally renowned professional firm
- One of the fastest UK degree paths to becoming a Chartered Accountant
- A great course, a respected qualification, AND a graduate job
- Paid work placements and exemptions from 12 of the 15 ICAEW professional examinations

Find out more:
www.henley.ac.uk/flyingstart

E: ugaccounting@henley.ac.uk
T: +44 (0)118 378 4262

Business School

The spark to ignite your business education

CHALLENGE TODAY, CHANGE TOMORROW

An undergraduate degree from Newcastle University Business School will enhance your skills and understanding, enabling you to develop your influential career in global business.

Our thinking, combined with a first-class reputation for academic excellence, high graduate employability and student experience makes use a first-choice destination for students from across the world.

Explore your options at ncl.ac.uk/nubs

EFMD
EQUIS
ACCREDITED

ASSOCIATION OF MBAs
AMBA
ACCREDITED

AACSB
ACCREDITED

Business School

GRADUATE DIPLOMA IN

Finance, Accounting and Business

This innovative programme, developed in close collaboration with the ICAEW, is aimed at graduates from the UK and overseas who are interested in a career in accountancy and are looking to improve their employment prospects.

The programme has been designed to:

- enhance the personal and professional skills of students

- develop the technical and academic skills of students

- provide students with credit for seven of the 15 professional papers required to qualify as a chartered accountant

Successful completion of the programme will lead to the award of two related qualifications:

- Graduate Diploma from Newcastle University

- Certificate in Finance, Accounting and Business from the ICAEW (ICAEW CFAB)

The third cohort graduated in July with an impressive set of results and a number of them have secured training contracts.

To find out more about this career-enhancing programme, e-mail **ellen.arkless@ncl.ac.uk**.

ICAEW

PARTNER IN LEARNING

Gloucestershire and Stroud (Coll); Suffolk (Univ Campus); Sussex Coast Hastings (Coll); Tameside (Coll);
Telford New (Coll); Westminster Kingsway (Coll); Weymouth (Coll); Yeovil (Coll).

CHOOSING YOUR COURSE (SEE ALSO CH.1)

Universities and colleges teaching quality See www.qaa.ac.uk; https://unistats.direct.gov.uk.

Examples of sandwich degree courses Aston; Bath; Bedfordshire; Birmingham City; Bournemouth;
Bradford; Brighton; Brunel; Canterbury Christ Church; Cardiff Met; Central Lancashire; Chichester;
Coventry; De Montfort; Derby; Durham; Gloucestershire; Greenwich; Hertfordshire; Huddersfield; Hull;
Kent; Lancaster; Leeds Beckett; Liverpool John Moores; London (RH); Loughborough; Manchester Met;
Middlesex; Northumbria; Nottingham Trent; Oxford Brookes; Plymouth; Portsmouth; Reading; Salford;
Sheffield Hallam; South Wales; Surrey; Sussex; Teesside; Ulster; UWE Bristol; West London;
Westminster; Wolverhampton; Worcester; York.

ADMISSIONS INFORMATION

Number of applicants per place (approx) Bath 13; Birmingham 8; Bristol 10; Dundee 5; Durham 6;
East Anglia 17; Essex 7; Exeter 18; Glasgow 10; Heriot-Watt 7; Hull 8; Kent 10; Lancaster 20; Leeds
25; London LSE 17; Loughborough 12; Manchester 11; Oxford Brookes 9; Salford 8; Sheffield 40;
Staffordshire 3; Stirling 20; Strathclyde 10; Ulster 10; Warwick 14.

Advice to applicants and planning the UCAS personal statement Universities look for good
numerical and communication skills, interest in the business and financial world, teamwork, problem-
solving and computing experience. On the UCAS application you should be able to demonstrate your
interest in and understanding of accountancy and to give details of any work experience or work
shadowing undertaken. Try to arrange meetings with accountants, or work shadowing or work
experience in accountants' offices, commercial or industrial firms, town halls, banks or insurance
companies and describe the work you have done. Obtain information from the main accountancy

professional bodies (see **Appendix 3**). Refer to current affairs which have stimulated your interest from articles in the *Financial Times*, *The Economist* or the business and financial sections of the weekend press. **Bath** Gap Year welcomed. Extra-curricular activities are important and should be described on the personal statement. There should be no gaps in your chronological history. **Bristol** Deferred entry accepted. **Brunel** (Bus Mgt (Acc)) Extended Project qualification accepted in place of AS; AL Critical Thinking and General Studies acceptable. **Lancaster** (Acc Adt Fin) Selected UCAS applicants complete supplementary application form and online test. They may then be invited to a selection workshop.

Misconceptions about this course Many students believe incorrectly that you need to be a brilliant mathematician. However, you do have to be numerate and enjoy numbers (see **Subject requirements/preferences**). Many underestimate the need for a high level of attention to detail. **Buckingham** Some students think it's a maths course. **Salford** Some applicants believe the course is limited to financial knowledge when it also provides an all-round training in management skills.

Selection interviews Yes Reading, West London; **Some** Aberystwyth, Anglia Ruskin, Buckingham, Cardiff, Cardiff Met, De Montfort, Dundee, Kent, Liverpool John Moores, London LSE, Staffordshire, Stirling, Warwick, Wolverhampton; **No** Birmingham, Bristol, East Anglia, Essex, Surrey.

Interview advice and questions Be prepared to answer questions about why you have chosen the course, the qualities needed to be an accountant, and why you think you have these qualities! You should also be able to discuss any work experience you have had and to describe the differences in the work of chartered, certified, public finance and management accountants. See also **Chapter 5**. **Buckingham** Students from a non-English-speaking background are asked to write an essay. If their maths results are weak they may be asked to do a simple arithmetic test. Mature students with no formal qualifications are usually interviewed and questioned about their work experience.

Reasons for rejection (non-academic) Poor English. Lack of interest in the subject because they realise they have chosen the wrong course! No clear motivation. Course details not researched. **London South Bank** Punctuality, neatness, enthusiasm and desire to come to London South Bank not evident.

AFTER-RESULTS ADVICE

Offers to applicants repeating A-levels Higher Brunel, Glasgow Caledonian, Hull, Manchester Met; **Possibly higher** Brighton, Central Lancashire, East Anglia, Leeds, Newcastle, Oxford Brookes, Sheffield Hallam; **Same** Abertay, Aberystwyth, Anglia Ruskin, Bangor, Birmingham City, Bolton, Bradford, Buckingham, Cardiff, Cardiff Met, Chichester, De Montfort, Derby, Dundee, Durham, East London, Edinburgh Napier, Glasgow, Heriot-Watt, Huddersfield, Liverpool John Moores, Loughborough, Northumbria, Portsmouth, Salford, Staffordshire, Stirling, Trinity Saint David, West London, Wolverhampton.

GRADUATE DESTINATIONS AND EMPLOYMENT (2013/14 HESA)
Graduates surveyed 4,560 **Employed** 2,530 **In voluntary employment** 115 **In further study** 950 **Assumed unemployed** 370

Career note Most Accountancy/Accounting graduates enter careers in finance.

OTHER DEGREE SUBJECTS FOR CONSIDERATION
Actuarial Studies; Banking; Business Studies; Economics; Financial Services; Insurance; International Securities and Investment Banking; Mathematics; Quantity Surveying; Statistics.

ACTUARIAL SCIENCE/STUDIES

Actuaries deal with the evaluation and management of financial risks, particularly those associated with insurance companies and pension funds. Studies focus on business economics, financial mathematics, probability and statistics, computer mathematics, statistics for insurance, and mathematics in finance and investment. Most courses include compulsory and optional subjects.

Although Actuarial Science/Studies degrees are vocational and give full or partial exemptions from some of the examinations of the Institute and Faculty of Actuaries, students are not necessarily committed to a career as an actuary on graduation. However, many graduates go on to be actuary trainees, leading to one of the highest-paid careers.

Useful websites www.actuaries.org.uk; www.soa.org; www.beanactuary.org

NB The points totals shown to the left of the institutions are for ease of reference only. It must not be assumed that Tariff points are always used by institutions or that they can be substituted for an offer in grades. The level of an offer is not necessarily indicative of the quality of a course.

COURSE OFFERS INFORMATION

Subject requirements/preferences GCSE Most institutions require grades A or B in English and mathematics. **AL** Mathematics at a specified grade required.

Your target offers and examples of degree courses

152 pts **City** – A*AA (Act Sci) (IB 35 pts)

Manchester – A*AA–AAA incl maths (Act Sci Maths) (IB 37 pts HL 6 maths)

Queen's Belfast – A*AA–AAA incl maths (Act Sci Risk Mgt)

144 pts **Kent** – AAA incl maths (Act Sci) (IB 34 pts HL 17 pts incl 6 maths); (Act Sci (Yr Ind)) (IB 34 pts)

Leeds – A*AB–AAB incl maths (Act Maths) (IB 35 pts HL 6 maths)

London LSE – AAA incl maths (Act Sci) (IB 38 pts)

Southampton – AAA–AAB incl maths (Maths Act Sci) (IB 36 pts HL 6 maths)

136 pts **East Anglia** – AAB incl maths (Act Sci) (IB 33 pts HL 6 maths); AAB incl A maths (Act Sci (Yr Ind)) (IB 33 pts HL 6 maths)

Essex – AAB incl maths (Act Sci (Yr Ind)) (IB 33 pts HL 6 maths); AAB–ABB incl maths (Act Sci) (IB 33 pts HL 6 maths)

Leicester – AAB incl maths (Maths Act Sci) (IB 32 pts)

Liverpool – AAB incl maths (Act Maths) (IB 35 pts)

128 pts **Heriot-Watt** – ABB incl maths (Act Sci Dip Ind Trg; Act Sci) (IB 28 pts HL 6 maths)

120 pts **Kingston** – 120 pts (Act Sci)

Alternative offers

See **Chapter 6** and **Appendix 1** for grades/new UCAS Tariff points information for other examinations.

CHOOSING YOUR COURSE (SEE ALSO CH.1)

Universities and colleges teaching quality See www.qaa.ac.uk; https://unistats.direct.gov.uk.

Top research universities and colleges (REF 2014) See **Mathematics**.

Examples of sandwich degree courses East Anglia; Essex; Heriot-Watt; Kent; Kingston; Queen's Belfast.

ADMISSIONS INFORMATION

Number of applicants per place (approx) City 6; Heriot-Watt 5; Kent 6; London LSE 9; Southampton (Maths Act Sci) 9, (Econ Act Sci) 8.

Advice to applicants and planning the UCAS personal statement Demonstrate your knowledge of this career and its training, and mention any contacts you have made with an actuary. (See **Appendix 3** for contact details of professional associations for further information.) Any work experience or shadowing in insurance companies should be mentioned, together with what you have learned about the problems facing actuaries. It is important to show motivation and sheer determination for training as an actuary as it is long and tough (up to three or four years after graduation). Mathematical flair, an ability to communicate and an interest in business are paramount.

Misconceptions about this course There is a general lack of understanding of actuaries' career training and of the career itself.

Institute
and Faculty
of Actuaries

Go to
work in
the future

you love maths and relish a challenge, joining
e actuarial profession is an exciting prospect.

u'll use your numerical, statistical and analytical skills to work
t the risk of future events taking place and calculate their impact
the business you're working for. You'll be employed in banking,
urance and consultancy and apply your expertise across a range
fascinating sectors.

ere's an excellent salary from the start and great opportunities
progression. If you're a high flyer, we predict you'll make a
illiant success of it.

ww.actuaries.org.uk/become-actuary

Do you love maths? Love solving problems? Then consider a career as an actuary.

What do actuaries do?

Actuaries are experts in risk management. They use their mathematical skills to help measure the probability and risk of future events. This information is useful to many industries, including healthcare, pensions, insurance, banking and investments, where a single decision can have a major financial impact. An actuarial career can be one of the most diverse, exciting and rewarding in the world.

Where do actuaries work?

Actuaries provide financial advice on the management of assets and liabilities - especially where long term management and planning are key. Actuaries work in many areas such as finance and investment, risk management, general and life insurance, pensions and healthcare. Every area of business is subject to risks so there are no limitations to where an actuary can go; they can even be employed in the marketing and development of sophisticated financial products.

What is the salary like?

Salaries and benefit packages are excellent, even for those starting out in their career. In fact it's one of the highest paid professions wherever you go in the world. Trainees earn from £33,000 a year and newly qualified actuaries earn £55,000. In later years senior actuaries salaries range from £70,000 to £200,000. So despite the hard work, it is a very well rewarded job.

Who should become an actuary?

- A graduate with a 2:1 in a numerate subject
- Someone who loves logic and problem solving
- A good communicator
- Someone with excellent business acumen.

How do you become an actuary?

In your final year at university you need to consider applying for graduate schemes within actuarial employers. Once you secure a trainee position your employer will help you become a member of the IFoA so you can get started with actuarial exams. You can study at your own pace while working – many employers give you time off to study. In addition to passing the exams, you'll work with your employer to meet the practical work-based skills requirement.

Where can you find out more information?

If you want to find out more about becoming an actuary, visit the IFoA website at **www.actuaries.org.uk/become-actuary**.

Want to find out more?   careers@actuaries.org.uk   www.actuaries.org.uk

Selection interviews **Yes** East Anglia; **Some** Heriot-Watt, Kent, Southampton.

Interview advice and questions In view of the demanding nature of the training, it is important to have spent some time discussing this career with an actuary in practice. Questions, therefore, may focus on the roles of the actuary and the qualities you need to succeed. You should also be ready to field questions about your AL mathematics course and the aspects of it you most enjoy. See also **Chapter 5**.

Reasons for rejection (non-academic) **Kent** Poor language skills.

AFTER-RESULTS ADVICE
Offers to applicants repeating A-levels **Higher** City; **Same** Heriot-Watt, Southampton.

GRADUATE DESTINATIONS AND EMPLOYMENT (2013/14 HESA)
See **Finance**.

Career note Graduates commonly enter careers in finance, many taking further examinations to qualify as actuaries.

OTHER DEGREE SUBJECTS FOR CONSIDERATION
Accountancy; Banking; Business Studies; Economics; Financial Risk Management; Financial Services; Insurance; Mathematics; Money, Banking and Finance; Statistics.

AFRICAN STUDIES
(see also **Languages**)

African Studies courses tend to be multi-disciplinary, covering several subject areas and can include anthropology, history, geography, sociology, social psychology and languages. Most courses focus on Africa and African languages (Amharic (Ethiopia), Hausa (Nigeria), Somali (Horn of Africa), Swahili (Somalia and Mozambique), Yoruba (Nigeria, Sierra Leone, Ghana and Senegal), and Zulu (South Africa)). Courses will also include a wide range of optional topics covering African art, music, and literature, and the religions of Africa.

Useful websites www.britishmuseum.org; www.africanstudies.org; www.blackhistorymonth.org.uk; www.sasaonline.org.za

NB The points totals shown to the left of the institutions are for ease of reference only. It must not be assumed that Tariff points are always used by institutions or that they can be substituted for an offer in grades. The level of an offer is not necessarily indicative of the quality of a course.

COURSE OFFERS INFORMATION
Subject requirements/preferences **GCSE** Grade A–C in mathematics and English may be required. **AL** For language courses a language subject or demonstrated proficiency in a language is required.

Your target offers and examples of degree courses
144 pts London (UCL) – AAA incl Fr (Fr As Af Lang) (IB 38 pts HL 6 Fr)
136 pts London (SOAS) – AAB–ABB (Swli Joint Hons; Af Lang Cult; Af St) (IB 35 pts)
120 pts Birmingham – BBB (Af St; Af St Anth; Af St Dev) (IB 32 pts HL 555)

Alternative offers
See **Chapter 6** and **Appendix 1** for grades/new UCAS Tariff points information for other examinations.

CHOOSING YOUR COURSE (SEE ALSO CH.1)
Universities and colleges teaching quality See www.qaa.ac.uk; http://unistats.direct.gov.uk.

ADMISSIONS INFORMATION

Number of applicants per place (approx) Birmingham 5.

Advice to applicants and planning the UCAS personal statement Describe any visits you have made to African countries and why you wish to study this subject. Embassies in London may be able to provide information about the history, geography, politics, economics and the culture of the countries in which you are interested. Keep up-to-date with political developments in African countries. Discuss any aspects which interest you.

Selection interviews No Birmingham.

Interview advice and questions Questions are likely to be on your choice of country or geographical region, your knowledge of it and your awareness of some of the political, economic and social problems that exist. See also **Chapter 5**.

AFTER-RESULTS ADVICE

Offers to applicants repeating A-levels Higher Information not available from institutions;

GRADUATE DESTINATIONS AND EMPLOYMENT (2013/14 HESA)

Graduates surveyed 15 **Employed** 5 **In voluntary employment** 0 **In further study** 5 **Assumed unemployed** 0

Career note The language skills and knowledge acquired in African Studies courses, particularly when combined with periods of study in Africa, are relevant to a wide range of careers.

OTHER DEGREE SUBJECTS FOR CONSIDERATION

Anthropology; Geography; History; Languages; Sociology.

AGRICULTURAL SCIENCES/AGRICULTURE

(see also **Animal Sciences, Food Science/Studies and Technology, Forestry, Horticulture, Landscape Architecture, Property Management and Surveying, Zoology**)

Courses in Agriculture recognise that modern farming practice requires sound technical and scientific knowledge, together with appropriate management skills, and most courses focus to a greater or lesser extent on all these requirements. Your choice of course depends on your particular interest and aims: some courses will give greater priority than others to practical application. Most graduates enter the agriculture industry whilst others move into manufacturing, wholesale and retail work. Agricultural courses specialise in crop and animal production and will also include agri-business and environmental issues. Rural Estate and Land Management courses relate to the purchase and sale of country property, residential agency in towns, the management of commercial property, portfolios, investment funds and the provision of valuation and technical services. Countryside management courses cover the uses of the countryside including tourism, land use, and ecosystems and environmental aspects.

Useful websites www.defra.gov.uk; www.naturalengland.org.uk; www.lantra.co.uk; www.nfuonline. com; www.nfyfc.org.uk; www.iagre.org; www.bbsrc.ac.uk; www.wwoof.org.uk

NB The points totals shown to the left of the institutions are for ease of reference only. It must not be assumed that Tariff points are always used by institutions or that they can be substituted for an offer in grades. The level of an offer is not necessarily indicative of the quality of a course.

COURSE OFFERS INFORMATION

Subject requirements/preferences GCSE English and mathematics usually required; chemistry sometimes required. Practical experience may be required. **AL** One or two maths/biological science subjects may be required or preferred. Geography may be accepted as a science subject. Similar

requirements apply for Agricultural Business Management courses. (Crop Sci) Two science subjects may be required. (Cntry Mgt) Geography or Biology preferred.

Your target offers and examples of degree courses

128 pts   **Newcastle** – ABB–BBB (Agric) (IB 32–30 pts)
            Nottingham – ABB–BBB incl sci (Agric Lvstk Sci; Agric Crop Sci; Agric) (IB 32–30 pts)
            Queen's Belfast – ABB–BBB (Agric Tech)
            Reading – ABB–BBB (Agric Bus Mgt; Agric) (IB 32–30 pts)
120 pts   **CAFRE** – BBB (Agric Tech)
            Queen's Belfast – BBB–ABB incl biol/econ/geog (Lnd Use Env Mgt)
104 pts   **Harper Adams** – 104–120 pts (Agric Mark; Agric courses)
            Royal Agricultural Univ – 104 pts (Agric; Rur Lnd Mgt)
100 pts   **Aberystwyth** – 100–112 pts (Cntry Mgt; Cntry Cons; Agric; Agric Anim Sci)
 96 pts   **Hertfordshire** – 96 pts (Env Mgt Agric) (IB 24 pts)
            Royal Agricultural Univ – CCC (Bldstck Perf)

Alternative offers
See **Chapter 6** and **Appendix 1** for grades/new UCAS Tariff points information for other examinations.

EXAMPLES OF COLLEGES OFFERING COURSES IN THIS SUBJECT FIELD
Askham Bryan (Coll); Bicton (Coll); Bishop Burton (Coll); Bridgend (Coll); Bridgwater (Coll); Craven (Coll); Duchy (Coll); Easton Otley (Coll); Hadlow (Coll); Hartpury (Coll); Moulton (Coll); Myerscough (Coll); Northumberland (Coll); Plumpton (Coll); Reaseheath (Coll); Sir Gâr (Coll); Sparsholt (Coll); Suffolk (Univ Campus); UHI; Writtle (Coll).

Check **Chapter 3** for new university admission details and **Chapter 6** on how to read the subject tables.

CHOOSING YOUR COURSE (SEE ALSO CH.1)

Universities and colleges teaching quality See www.qaa.ac.uk; https://unistats.direct.gov.uk.

Top research universities and colleges (REF 2014) (Agriculture, Veterinary and Food Science) Warwick; Aberdeen; Glasgow; East Anglia; Bristol; Stirling; Queen's Belfast; Liverpool; Reading; Cambridge; Nottingham.

Examples of sandwich degree courses Aberystwyth; CAFRE; Harper Adams; Newcastle; Nottingham; Queen's Belfast; Reading.

ADMISSIONS INFORMATION

Number of applicants per place (approx) Aberystwyth (Agric courses) 2–3; Newcastle 6; Nottingham 4; Royal Agricultural Univ (Agric) 2.

Advice to applicants and planning the UCAS personal statement First-hand farming experience is essential for most courses and obviously important for all. Check prospectuses and websites. Describe the work done. Details of experience of work with agricultural or food farms (production and laboratory work), garden centres, even with landscape architects, could be appropriate. Keep up-to-date with European agricultural and fishing policies and mention any interests you have in these areas. Read farming magazines and discuss any articles which have interested you. You may even have had first-hand experience of the serious problems facing farmers. Discuss your interest or experience in practical conservation work. Ability to work both independently or as a member of a team is important. (See also **Appendix 3**.)

Selection interviews Yes Harper Adams; **Some** Bishop Burton (Coll), Derby, Edinburgh, Royal Agricultural Univ; **No** Reading.

Interview advice and questions You should be up-to-date with political and scientific issues concerning the farming community in general and how these problems might be resolved. You are likely to be questioned on your own farming background (if relevant) and your farming experience. Questions asked in the past have included: What special agricultural interests do you have? What types of farms have you worked on? What farming publications do you read and which agricultural shows have you visited? What is meant by the term 'sustainable development'? Are farmers custodians of the countryside? What are the potential sources of non-fossil-fuel electricity generation? See also **Chapter 5**.

Reasons for rejection (non-academic) Insufficient motivation. Too immature. Unlikely to integrate well. Lack of practical experience with crops or animals.

AFTER-RESULTS ADVICE

Offers to applicants repeating A-levels Possibly higher Newcastle; **Same** Harper Adams, Nottingham, Royal Agricultural Univ.

GRADUATE DESTINATIONS AND EMPLOYMENT (2013/14 HESA)

Agriculture graduates surveyed 1,370 **Employed** 695 **In voluntary employment** 25 **In further study** 330 **Assumed unemployed** 60

Career note The majority of graduates entered the agricultural industry whilst others moved into manufacturing, the wholesale and retail trades and property development.

OTHER DEGREE SUBJECTS FOR CONSIDERATION

Agroforestry; Animal Sciences; Biochemistry; Biological Sciences; Biology; Biotechnology; Chemistry; Conservation Management; Ecology (Biological Sciences); Environmental Sciences; Estate Management (Surveying); Food Science and Technology; Forestry; Horticulture; Land Surveying; Landscape Architecture; Plant Sciences; Veterinary Science; Zoology.

AMERICAN STUDIES

(see also **Latin American Studies**)

Courses normally cover American history, politics and literature, although there are opportunities to study specialist fields such as drama, film studies, history of art, linguistics, politics or sociology. In some universities, a year, term or semester spent in the USA (or Canada) is compulsory or optional whilst at other institutions the course lasts three years without a placement abroad.

Useful websites www.historynet.com; www.americansc.org.uk; www.theasa.net

NB The points totals shown to the left of the institutions are for ease of reference only. It must not be assumed that Tariff points are always used by institutions or that they can be substituted for an offer in grades. The level of an offer is not necessarily indicative of the quality of a course.

COURSE OFFERS INFORMATION

Subject requirements/preferences GCSE Specific grades in some subjects may be specified by some popular universities. **AL** English, a modern language, humanities or social science subjects preferred.

Your target offers and examples of degree courses
136 pts Birmingham – AAB-ABB (Am Can St) (IB 32 pts HL 665–655)
East Anglia – AAB (Am Lit Crea Writ) (IB 33 pts)
Loughborough – AAB incl Engl (Engl Am St) (IB 34 pts HL 5 Engl)
Sussex – AAB-ABB (Am St courses) (IB 34 pts)
128 pts East Anglia – ABB (Am St) (IB 32 pts HL 5 Engl/hist)
Essex – ABB-BBB (Am St Film) (IB 32–30 pts)
Kent – ABB (Am St) (IB 34 pts)
Manchester – ABB incl Engl lit/hist (Am St) (IB 34 pts HL 6 Engl/hist)
Northumbria – 128 pts (Am St) (IB 31 pts)
Nottingham – ABB (Am Can Lit Hist Cult) (IB 32 pts); ABB-ACC (Film TV St Am St) (IB 32 pts); ABB incl hist (Am St Hist) (IB 32 pts); ABB incl Engl (Am St Engl) (IB 32 pts)
120 pts Keele – BBB/ABC (Am St) (IB 32 pts)
Leicester – BBB (Am St) (IB 28–30 pts)
Swansea – BBB-BBC (Am St) (IB 32–30 pts)
112 pts Canterbury Christ Church – 112 pts (Am St courses)
Hertfordshire – 112 pts (Am St Joint Hons) (IB 28 pts)
Hull – 112 pts (Am St) (IB 28 pts)
York St John – 112 pts (Am St courses)
104 pts Winchester – 104-120 pts (Am St) (IB 26 pts)
 96 pts Portsmouth – 96-120 pts (Am St) (IB 30 pts HL 17 pts)
 88 pts Derby – 88-120 pts (Am St Joint Hons)

Alternative offers
See **Chapter 6** and **Appendix 1** for grades/new UCAS Tariff points information for other examinations.

EXAMPLES OF COLLEGES OFFERING COURSES IN THIS SUBJECT FIELD
Askham Bryan (Coll).

CHOOSING YOUR COURSE (SEE ALSO CH.1)
Universities and colleges teaching quality See www.qaa.ac.uk; http://unistats.direct.gov.uk.

ADMISSIONS INFORMATION
Number of applicants per place (approx) Birmingham 6; East Anglia 7; Essex 6; Hull 15; Keele 7; Leicester 7; Manchester 6; Nottingham 12; Swansea 2.

Check **Chapter 3** for new university admission details and **Chapter 6** on how to read the subject tables.

Advice to applicants and planning the UCAS personal statement Visits to America should be described, and any knowledge or interests you have of the history, politics, economics and the culture of the USA should be included on the UCAS application. The US Embassy in London may be a useful source of information. American magazines and newspapers are good reference sources and also give a good insight to life in the USA. Applicants should demonstrate an intelligent interest in both North American literature and history in their personal statement. State why you are interested in the subject and dedicate at least half of your personal statement to how and why your interest has developed – for example through extra-curricular reading, projects, films and academic study. **Manchester** Due to the detailed nature of entry requirements for American Studies courses, the prospectus is unable to include full details. For complete and up-to-date information on entry requirements for these courses, please visit the website at www.manchester.ac.uk/ugcourses.

Misconceptions about this course Swansea Some candidates feel that American Studies is a soft option. While we study many topics which students find interesting, we are very much a humanities-based degree course incorporating more traditional subjects such as history, literature and English. Our graduates also find that they are employable in the same jobs as those students taking other degrees.

Selection interviews Yes Hull, Winchester; **Some** Derby, Kent; **No** Birmingham, East Anglia, Essex.

Interview advice and questions Courses often focus on history and literature so expect some questions on any American literature you have read and also on aspects of American history, arts and culture. You may also be questioned on visits you have made to America (or Canada) and your impressions. Current political issues might also be raised, so keep up-to-date with the political scene. See also **Chapter 5**. **Birmingham** Access course and mature students are interviewed and also those students with strong applications but whose achieved grades do not meet entrance requirements. **Derby** The purpose of the interview is to help applicants understand the interdisciplinary nature of the course. **East Anglia** Admissions tutors want to see how up-to-date is the applicant's knowledge of American culture. **Swansea** Interviews are very informal, giving students the chance to ask questions about the course.

Reasons for rejection (non-academic) If personal reasons prevent year of study in America. **Birmingham** Lack of commitment to the course. **Swansea** Lack of knowledge covering literature, history and politics.

AFTER-RESULTS ADVICE
Offers to applicants repeating A-levels Higher Essex, Winchester; **Possibly higher** Nottingham; **Same** Birmingham, Derby, East Anglia, Hull, Swansea.

GRADUATE DESTINATIONS AND EMPLOYMENT (2013/14 HESA)
Graduates surveyed 555 **Employed** 275 **In voluntary employment** 30 **In further study** 120 **Assumed unemployed** 35

Career note All non-scientific careers are open to graduates. Start your career planning during your degree course and obtain work experience.

OTHER DEGREE SUBJECTS FOR CONSIDERATION
Business Studies; Cultural Studies; English Literature; Film Studies; Government; History; International History; International Relations; Latin-American Literature/Studies; Politics.

ANIMAL SCIENCES

(including **Equine Science/Studies**; see also **Agricultural Sciences/Agriculture, Biological Sciences, Biology, Physiology, Psychology, Veterinary Science/Medicine, Zoology**)

Animal science is a broad-based subject including the study of farm and companion animals and wildlife conservation and management. The more specialised courses include a range of specialisms including animal biology, nutrition and health, behavioural studies and welfare. Equine Science involves specialised studies in areas such as breeding, equine business, horsemanship, performance, stud management, event management, veterinary techniques and injuries. Some scholarships are available (eg Aberystwyth, Glyndŵr).

Useful websites www.rspca.org.uk; www.bhs.org.uk; www.wwf.org.uk; www.bsas.org.uk

NB The points totals shown to the left of the institutions are for ease of reference only. It must not be assumed that Tariff points are always used by institutions or that they can be substituted for an offer in grades. The level of an offer is not necessarily indicative of the quality of a course.

COURSE OFFERS INFORMATION

Subject requirements/preferences GCSE Mathematics/science subjects required. Also check any weight limits on equitation modules. **AL** One or two science subjects required for scientific courses, Biology and Chemistry preferred.

Your target offers and examples of degree courses

136 pts **Exeter** – AAB–ABB incl sci/maths (Anim Bhv (Cornwall)) (IB 34–32 pts HL 5 sci/maths)

128 pts **Bristol** – ABB–BBB incl biol+maths/sci (Anim Bhv Welf Sci) (IB 32–31 pts HL 5 biol+maths/sci)

Kent – ABB incl sci (Wldlf Cons; Wldlf Cons (Yr Prof Pr)) (IB 34 pts)

Newcastle – ABB–BBB incl biol+sci (Anim Sci) (IB 35–32 pts HL 6 biol)

Nottingham – ABB–BBB incl sci/maths (Anim Sci) (IB 32–30 pts)

Reading – ABB–BBB (Anim Sci) (IB 32–30 pts)

120 pts **Aberdeen** – BBB incl maths/sci (Anim Bhv) (IB 32 pts HL 5 maths/sci)

Gloucestershire – 120 pts (Anim Biol)

Lincoln – 120 pts (Anim Bhv Welf)

Stirling – BBB (Anim Biol) (IB 32 pts)

116 pts **Aberystwyth** – 116–132 pts (Anim Bhv; Anim Sci)

112 pts **Chester** – BBC–BCC incl biol/chem/sci 112 pts (Wldlf Cons Ecol) (IB 26 pts HL 5 biol/chem); BBC–BCC 112 pts (Anim Bhv Welf; Anim Bhv)

Nottingham Trent – 112 pts incl sci (Wldlf Cons); 112 pts incl biol (Anim Biol)

Oxford Brookes – BBC incl sci 112 pts (Anim Biol Cons) (IB 30 pts); BBC 112 pts (Eqn Sci; Eqn Sci Thbred Mgt) (IB 30 pts)

Plymouth – 112 pts incl biol+sci (Anim Bhv Welf) (IB 28 pts HL 5 biol+sci)

108 pts **Aberystwyth** – 108–128 pts incl biol (Eqn Sci)

104 pts **Bangor** – 104–128 pts incl biol+sci (Zool Anim Bhv)

Bournemouth – 104–128 pts (Ecol Wldlf Cons) (IB 28–32 pts)

Edinburgh Napier – BCC incl sci (Anim Biol) (IB 28 pts HL 5 sci)

Liverpool John Moores – 104–120 pts (Wldlf Cons) (IB 25 pts); 104 pts incl biol+sci (Anim Bhv) (IB 25 pts)

Manchester Met – BCC–BBC incl biol 104–112 pts (Anim Bhv) (IB 28 pts HL 5 biol)

Northampton – 104–120 pts (Wldlf Cons)

Nottingham Trent – 104 pts incl sci (Eqn Spo Sci)

South Wales – BCC incl geog/maths (Nat Hist) (IB 29 pts HL 5 geog/maths); BCC incl biol+sci (Int Wldlf Biol) (IB 29 pts HL 5 biol+sci)

SRUC – BCC incl biol+chem (App Anim Sci)

Worcester – 104–120 pts incl biol+sci/maths (Anim Biol)

Writtle (Coll) – 104 pts (Eqn courses) (IB 24 pts)
96 pts **Anglia Ruskin** – 96 pts (Anim Bhv) (IB 24 pts)
CAFRE – 96 pts incl sci (Eqn Mgt)
Canterbury Christ Church – 96 pts (Anim Sci)
Cumbria – 96 pts (Wldlf Media); (Anim Cons Sci) (IB 24 pts)
Glyndŵr – 96 pts (Eqn Sci Welf Mgt)
Royal Agricultural Univ – 96 pts (Eqn Mgt); CCC (Bldstck Perf)
88 pts **Harper Adams** – 88–104 pts (Anim Bhv Welf; Anim Hlth Welf)
80 pts **Wolverhampton** – 80 pts incl sci (Anim Bhv Wldlf Cons)
48 pts **Glyndŵr** – 48 pts (Anim St)

Alternative offers
See **Chapter 6** and **Appendix 1** for grades/new UCAS Tariff points information for other examinations.

EXAMPLES OF COLLEGES OFFERING COURSES IN THIS SUBJECT FIELD
Barnsley (Coll); Bedford (Coll); Bicton (Coll); Bishop Burton (Coll); Brooksby Melton (Coll); Bury (Coll); Calderdale (Coll); Canterbury (Coll); Central Bedfordshire (Coll); Cornwall (Coll); Craven (Coll); Derby (Coll); Duchy (Coll); Easton Otley (Coll); Grimsby (Univ Centre); Guildford (Coll); Hadlow (Coll); Hartpury (Coll); Kingston Maurward (Coll); Kirklees (Coll); Lancaster and Morecambe (Coll); Moulton (Coll); Myerscough (Coll); Northumberland (Coll); Pembrokeshire (Coll); Petroc; Plumpton (Coll); Reaseheath (Coll); Sir Gâr (Coll); South Devon (Coll); South Gloucestershire and Stroud (Coll); South Staffordshire (Coll); Sparsholt (Coll); Stamford New (Coll); Suffolk (Univ Campus); Warwickshire (Coll); West Anglia (Coll); Weston (Coll); Wiltshire (Coll); Wirral Met (Coll); Writtle (Coll).

CHOOSING YOUR COURSE (SEE ALSO CH.1)
Universities and colleges teaching quality See www.qaa.ac.uk; http://unistats.direct.gov.uk.

Top research universities and colleges (REF 2014) See **Agricultural Sciences/Agriculture** and **Biological Sciences**.

Examples of sandwich degree courses Aberystwyth; Anglia Ruskin; Cumbria; Harper Adams; Liverpool John Moores; Manchester Met; Nottingham Trent; Royal Agricultural Univ.

ADMISSIONS INFORMATION
Number of applicants per place (approx) Aberystwyth 6; Bristol 8; Harper Adams 5; Newcastle 9; Nottingham 6; Nottingham Trent (Eqn Spo Sci) 4; Reading 10; Royal Agricultural Univ 4.

Advice to applicants and planning the UCAS personal statement Describe any work you have done with animals which generated your interest in this subject. Work experience in veterinary practices, on farms or with agricultural firms would be useful. Read agricultural/scientific journals for updates on animal nutrition or breeding. For equine courses, details of practical experience with horses (eg BHS examinations, Pony Club tests) should be included.

Misconceptions about this course Students are not always aware that equine studies courses cover science, business management, nutrition, health and breeding. **Bishop Burton (Coll)** (Eqn Sci) Some students wrongly believe that riding skills and a science background are not required for this course which, in fact, is heavily focused on the scientific principles and practice of horse management.

Selection interviews Yes Bristol, Cumbria (usually), Harper Adams, Newcastle, Royal Agricultural Univ, SRUC, Writtle (Coll); **Some** Anglia Ruskin, Bishop Burton (Coll), Nottingham, Stirling, UWE Bristol; **No** Plymouth.

Interview advice and questions Questions are likely about your experience with animals and your reasons for wishing to follow this science-based subject. Other questions asked in recent years have included: What do your parents think about your choice of course? What are your views on battery hens and the rearing of veal calves? The causes of blue-tongue disease, foot and mouth disease and BSE may also feature. (Eqn courses) Students should check the level of riding ability expected (eg

BHS Level 2 or PC B-test level). Check the amount of riding, jumping and competition work on the course. (See also **Chapter 5**.) **Lincoln** (Eqn Spo Sci) Applicants required to show that they can ride to BHS Level 2. Experience with animals in general.

Reasons for rejection (non-academic) Uncertainty as to why applicants chose the course. Too immature. Unlikely to integrate well.

AFTER-RESULTS ADVICE
Offers to applicants repeating A-levels Possibly higher Nottingham; **Same** Anglia Ruskin, Bishop Burton (Coll), Chester, Harper Adams, Liverpool John Moores, Royal Agricultural Univ, Stirling, UWE Bristol.

GRADUATE DESTINATIONS AND EMPLOYMENT (2013/14 HESA)
Graduates surveyed 1,245 **Employed** 570 **In voluntary employment** 40 **In further study** 375 **Assumed unemployed** 75

Career note The majority of graduates obtained work with animals whilst others moved towards business and administration careers. This is a specialised subject area and undergraduates should start early to make contacts with organisations and gain work experience.

OTHER DEGREE SUBJECTS FOR CONSIDERATION
Agriculture; Biological Sciences; Biology; Food Science; Natural Sciences; Veterinary Science; Zoology.

Check **Chapter 3** for new university admission details and **Chapter 6** on how to read the subject tables.

ANTHROPOLOGY

(including **Social Anthropology**; see also **Archaeology, Sociology**)

Anthropology is the study of people's behaviour, beliefs and institutions and the diverse societies in which they live, and is concerned with the biological evolution of human beings. It also involves our relationships with other primates, the structure of communities and the effects of diet and disease on human groups. Alternatively, social or cultural anthropology covers aspects of social behaviour in respect of family, kinship, marriage, gender, religion, political structures, law, psychology and language. Anthropology is also offered jointly with several other subjects such as Archaeology (London (UCL), Southampton and Bristol) and Forensic Science (Dundee, Bradford).

Useful websites www.britishmuseum.org; www.therai.org.uk; www.theasa.org

NB The points totals shown to the left of the institutions are for ease of reference only. It must not be assumed that Tariff points are always used by institutions or that they can be substituted for an offer in grades. The level of an offer is not necessarily indicative of the quality of a course.

COURSE OFFERS INFORMATION

Subject requirements/preferences GCSE English and mathematics usually required. A foreign language may be required. **AL** Biology and Geography preferred for some biological anthropological courses. (Soc Anth) No specific subjects required.

Your target offers and examples of degree courses

152 pts **Cambridge** – A*AA (Hum Soc Pol Sci (Biol Anth); Hum Soc Pol Sci (Assyr Egypt); Hum Soc Pol Sci; Hum Soc Pol Sci (Soc Anth)) (IB 40–41 pts HL 776)

144 pts **Durham** – AAA (Anth) (IB 37 pts)
Edinburgh – AAA–ABB (Soc Anth courses) (IB 37–34 pts)
London (SOAS) – AAA–AAB (Soc Anth) (IB 37 pts)
Oxford – AAA (Arch Anth) (IB 38 pts)
St Andrews – AAA–AAB (Soc Anth courses) (IB 38–35 pts)

136 pts **Durham** – AAB (Anth Sociol; Anth Arch) (IB 36 pts)
Exeter – AAB–ABB (Arch Anth; Sociol Anth; Anth) (IB 34–32 pts)
London (UCL) – AAB (Arch Anth) (IB 36 pts)
London LSE – AAB (Anth Law; Soc Anth) (IB 37 pts)
Southampton – AAB–BBB 136–120 pts (Arch Anth) (IB 34–30 pts HL 17–16 pts)
Sussex – AAB–ABB (Anth courses) (IB 34 pts)

128 pts **Birmingham** – ABB–BBB (Anth courses) (IB 32 pts HL 655–555)
Bristol – ABB–BBB (Anth) (IB 32–31 pts)
Brunel – ABB (Anth Sociol; Anth) (IB 31 pts)
East Anglia – ABB (Arch Anth Art Hist) (IB 32 pts)
Edinburgh – ABB (Arch Soc Anth) (IB 34 pts)
Essex – ABB–BBB (Sociol Soc Anth) (IB 32–30 pts)
Kent – ABB (Soc Anth; Anth) (IB 34 pts); ABB incl sci/maths (Biol Anth) (IB 34 pts)
Liverpool – ABB (Evol Anth) (IB 33 pts)
London (Gold) – ABB (Anth courses) (IB 33 pts)
Manchester – ABB–BBB (Compar Relgn Soc Anth) (IB 34–31 pts)
Southampton – ABB–BBB (Sociol Anth) (IB 32 pts)

120 pts **Aberdeen** – BBB (Anth) (IB 32 pts)
Dundee – BBB–BCC incl biol (Foren Anth) (IB 30 pts)
Queen's Belfast – BBB (Soc Anth courses)

112 pts **Bradford** – BBC 112 pts (Foren Arch Anth)
Central Lancashire – 112 pts (Arch Anth) (IB 28 pts)
East London – 112 pts (Anth) (IB 24 pts)
Hull – 112 pts (Sociol Anth Gndr St; Soc Anth Sociol) (IB 28 pts)

Oxford Brookes – BBC (Anth) (IB 30 pts)
Roehampton – BBC 112 pts (Anth)
104 pts **Bournemouth** – 104–120 pts (Anth; Arch Anth) (IB 28–31 pts); 104 pts (Sociol Anth)
(IB 28 pts)
Liverpool John Moores – 104–120 pts (Foren Anth)
Portsmouth – 104–128 pts incl biol (Palae) (IB 27 pts)
96 pts **Trinity Saint David** – 96–104 pts (Anth) (IB 26 pts)

Alternative offers
See **Chapter 6** and **Appendix 1** for grades/new UCAS Tariff points information for other examinations.

CHOOSING YOUR COURSE (SEE ALSO CH.1)

Universities and colleges teaching quality See www.qaa.ac.uk; http://unistats.direct.gov.uk.

Top research universities and colleges (REF 2014) (Anthropology and Development Studies) London LSE (Int Dev); Manchester (Anth); Oxford (Int Dev); Manchester (Dev St); London (Gold); Durham; East Anglia; Cambridge; Edinburgh.

Examples of sandwich degree courses Bournemouth; Bradford; Brunel; Liverpool John Moores.

ADMISSIONS INFORMATION

Number of applicants per place (approx) Bristol 9; Cambridge 2; Durham 5; Hull 11; Kent 6; Liverpool John Moores 4; London (Gold) 7; London (SOAS) 10; London (UCL) 5; London LSE 9; Manchester 5; Oxford Brookes 8; Queen's Belfast 10; Southampton 6; Sussex 10.

Advice to applicants and planning the UCAS personal statement Visits to museums should be discussed; for example, museums of anthropology (London, Oxford, Cambridge). Describe any aspect of the subject which interests you (including books you have read) and how you have pursued this interest. Give details of any overseas travel. Give reasons for choosing course: since this is not a school subject, you will need to convince the selectors of your knowledge and interest. **Bristol** Deferred entry acceptable. **Oxford** See **Archaeology**.

Selection interviews Yes Cambridge, Dundee (Foren Anth), Hull, London (Gold) (mature students), London (UCL) (mature students), Oxford (Arch Anth) 33%, Oxford Brookes; **Some** Bristol, East Anglia, Roehampton; **No** London LSE.

Interview advice and questions This is a broad subject and questions will tend to emerge as a result of your interests in aspects of anthropology or social anthropology and your comments on your personal statement. Past questions have included: What stresses are there among the nomads of the North African desert? What is a society? What is speech? If you dug up a stone axe what could you learn from it? What are the values created by a capitalist society? Discuss the role of women since the beginning of this century. **Cambridge** See **Chapter 5** and **Archaeology**. **Oxford** See **Chapter 5** and **Archaeology**.

Reasons for rejection (non-academic) Lack of commitment. Inability to deal with a more philosophical (less positivist) approach to knowledge.

AFTER-RESULTS ADVICE

Offers to applicants repeating A-levels Possibly higher Oxford Brookes; **Same** Cambridge, Durham, East Anglia, Liverpool John Moores, London (UCL), Roehampton.

GRADUATE DESTINATIONS AND EMPLOYMENT (2013/14 HESA)

Graduates surveyed 965 **Employed** 470 **In voluntary employment** 65 **In further study** 185 **Assumed unemployed** 70

Career note All non-scientific careers are open to graduates. However, career planning should start early and efforts made to contact employers and gain work experience.

Check **Chapter 3** for new university admission details and **Chapter 6** on how to read the subject tables.

OTHER DEGREE SUBJECTS FOR CONSIDERATION
Archaeology; Egyptology; Heritage Studies; History; Human Sciences; Political Science; Psychology; Religious Studies; Social Science; Sociology.

ARABIC and ANCIENT NEAR and MIDDLE EASTERN STUDIES

(see also **History (Ancient), Religious Studies**)

Arabic is one of the world's most widely used languages, spoken by more than 300 million people in 21 countries in the Middle East and countries right across north Africa. Study of the language also includes Islamic and modern Middle Eastern history, whilst a course in Middle Eastern Studies will include an optional language such as Arabic, Persian or Turkish (Edinburgh, Exeter). Links between Britain and Arabic-speaking countries have increased considerably in recent years and most of the larger UK organisations with offices in the Middle East have only a relatively small pool of Arabic-speaking graduates from which to recruit future employees each year.

Useful websites www.ciol.org.uk; www.bbc.co.uk/languages; www.languageadvantage.com; www.languagematters.co.uk; www.upi.com; www.merip.org; www.memri.org; www.mei.edu

NB The points totals shown to the left of the institutions are for ease of reference only. It must not be assumed that Tariff points are always used by institutions or that they can be substituted for an offer in grades. The level of an offer is not necessarily indicative of the quality of a course.

COURSE OFFERS INFORMATION
Subject requirements/preferences GCSE English, mathematics and a foreign language usually required. A high grade in Arabic may be required. **AL** A modern language is usually required or preferred.

Your target offers and examples of degree courses
152 pts **Cambridge** – A*AA (As Mid E St) (IB 40–41 pts HL 776)
          Durham – A*AA (Comb Hons Soc Sci) (IB 38 pts)
144 pts **Edinburgh** – AAA–ABB (Islam St; Mid East St; Persn St; Persn Soc Anth; Arbc courses; Persn
          Pol) (IB 37–34 pts)
          Exeter – AAA–AAB incl lang (Arbc Islam St Comb Hons) (IB 34–32 pts HL 5 lang)
          Oxford – AAA (Class Orntl St; Orntl St) (IB 39 pts); AAA (Arbc courses) (IB 38 pts)
          St Andrews – AAA (Art Hist Mid E St; Arbc Mid E St) (IB 36 pts); (Arbc Econ) (IB 38 pts);
          AAA incl maths (Arbc Maths) (IB 36 pts)
136 pts **Exeter** – AAB–BBB (Mid E St) (IB 34–30 pts)
          London (SOAS) – AAB–ABB (Arbc Joint Hons; Anc Near E St; Persn Joint Hons; Mid E St; Arbc
          Islam St; Heb Joint Hons; Heb Isrl St) (IB 35 pts); (Islam St) (IB 36 pts)
128 pts **Leeds** – ABB (Arbc Islam St; Arbc Mid E St; Mid E St) (IB 34 pts)
          Manchester – ABB–BBB (Mid E St; Arbc St) (IB 34–31 pts)
          Warwick – ABB incl Fr/Ger (Fr/Ger St Arbc) (IB 34 pts HL 5 Ger)
112 pts **Central Lancashire** – 112–128 pts (Arbc Lang)
104 pts **Islamic (Coll)** – BCC 104 pts (Islam St) (IB 32 pts)
          Westminster – BCC (Arbc Ling) (IB 30 pts HL 4 Engl)

Alternative offers
See **Chapter 6** and **Appendix 1** for grades/new UCAS Tariff points information for other examinations.

CHOOSING YOUR COURSE (SEE ALSO CH.1)
Universities and colleges teaching quality See www.qaa.ac.uk; http://unistats.direct.gov.uk.

New UCAS points Tariff: A* = 56 pts; A = 48 pts; B = 40 pts; C = 32 pts; D = 24 pts; E = 16 pts

ADMISSIONS INFORMATION
Number of applicants per place (approx) Cambridge 2; Durham 5; Leeds 6; London (SOAS) 5.

Advice to applicants and planning the UCAS personal statement Describe any visits to, or your experience of living in, Arabic-speaking countries. Develop a knowledge of Middle Eastern cultures, history and politics and mention these topics on the UCAS application. Provide evidence of language-learning skills and experience.

Selection interviews Yes Cambridge, Leeds, Oxford (Orntl St) 31%.

Interview advice and questions You will need to be able to justify your reasons for wanting to study Arabic or other languages and to discuss your interest in, and awareness of, cultural, social and political aspects of the Middle East. **Cambridge** See **Chapter 5** under **Modern and Medieval Languages**. **Oxford** See **Chapter 5** under **Modern and Medieval Languages**.

AFTER-RESULTS ADVICE
Offers to applicants repeating A-levels Higher Leeds, St Andrews; **Same** Exeter, Salford.

GRADUATE DESTINATIONS AND EMPLOYMENT (2013/14 HESA)
Graduates surveyed 135 **Employed** 60 **In voluntary employment** 5 **In further study** 30 **Assumed unemployed** 10

Career note Most graduates entered business and administrative work, in some cases closely linked to their language studies.

OTHER DEGREE SUBJECTS FOR CONSIDERATION
Anthropology; Archaeology; Classical Studies; Hebrew; History; Persian; Politics; Turkish.

ARCHAEOLOGY

(see also **Anthropology, Classical Studies/Classical Civilisation, History (Ancient)**)

Courses in Archaeology differ between institutions but the majority focus on the archaeology of Europe, the Mediterranean and Middle Eastern countries and on the close examination of discoveries of prehistoric communities and ancient, medieval and post-medieval societies. Hands-on experience is involved in all courses as well as a close study of the history of the artefacts themselves. All courses will involve excavations in the UK or abroad whilst a number of universities combine archaeology with history and anthropology whilst Bournemouth, Dundee and Leicester combine it with forensic science. Southampton also has a Centre for Marine Archaeology.

Useful websites http://new.archaeologyuk.org; www.english-heritage.org.uk; www.britishmuseum.org; www.archaeologists.net

NB The points totals shown to the left of the institutions are for ease of reference only. It must not be assumed that Tariff points are always used by institutions or that they can be substituted for an offer in grades. The level of an offer is not necessarily indicative of the quality of a course.

COURSE OFFERS INFORMATION
Subject requirements/preferences GCSE English and mathematics or science usually required for BSc courses. **AL** History, Geography, English or a science subject may be preferred for some courses and two science subjects for Archaeological Science courses.

Your target offers and examples of degree courses
152 pts   **Cambridge** – A*AA (Hum Soc Pol Sci (Assyr Egypt); Hum Soc Pol Sci (Arch); Hum Soc Pol Sci) (IB 40–41 pts HL 776)
          London (UCL) – A*AA–AAA incl hist/class civ (Anc Hist Egypt) (IB 39–38 pts)
144 pts   **Durham** – AAA (Anc Hist Arch) (IB 37 pts)

Edinburgh – AAA–ABB (Anc Hist Class Arch; Class Arch Gk) (IB 40–34 pts)
Oxford – AAA (Arch Anth) (IB 38 pts); (Class Arch Anc Hist) (IB 39 pts)
St Andrews – AAA (Mediev Hist Arch) (IB 36 pts)

136 pts **Durham** – AAB (Arch; Anth Arch) (IB 36 pts)
East Anglia – AAB (Arch Anth Art Hist (St Abrd)) (IB 33 pts)
Edinburgh – AAB–ABB (Celt Arch) (IB 36–34 pts)
Exeter – AAB–BBB (Arch) (IB 34–30 pts); AAB–ABB (Arch Anth) (IB 34–32 pts)
Glasgow – AAB–BBB incl sci (Arch) (IB 36–34 pts)
London (King's) – AAB (Class Arch) (IB 35 pts)
London (UCL) – AAB–ABB (Class Arch Class Civ; Eygpt Arch; Arch) (IB 36–34 pts); AAB (Arch Anth) (IB 36 pts)
Southampton – AAB–ABB incl hist (Arch Hist) (IB 34–30 pts HL 6 hist)

128 pts **Birmingham** – ABB (Arch courses) (IB 32 pts HL 655)
Bristol – ABB–BBB (Arch Anth) (IB 32–31 pts)
Cardiff – ABB–BBC (Arch courses) (IB 36–28 pts)
East Anglia – ABB (Arch Anth Art Hist) (IB 32 pts)
Edinburgh – ABB (Arch; Arch Soc Anth) (IB 34 pts); (Archit Hist Arch) (IB 36–34 pts)
Leicester – ABB (Anc Hist Arch) (IB 28–30 pts)
Liverpool – ABB (Arch Anc Civ; Egypt; Arch) (IB 33 pts)
London (SOAS) – ABB–BBB (Hist Art Arch courses) (IB 33 pts)
Manchester – ABB–BBB (Arch Art Hist) (IB 33–32 pts); (Arch Anth; Arch) (IB 34–31 pts)
Newcastle – ABB–BBB (Arch) (IB 32 pts)
Nottingham – ABB–BBB (Arch) (IB 32–30 pts); ABB incl hist (Arch Hist) (IB 32 pts); ABB–BBB incl geog (Arch Geog) (IB 32–30 pts); ABB–AAC (Arch Class Civ; Anc Hist Arch) (IB 32 pts)
Reading – ABB–BBB (Arch courses) (IB 32–30 pts)
Sheffield – ABB–BBB (Arch Joint Hons) (IB 34 pts)
Southampton – ABB–BBB (Arch) (IB 32–30 pts); ABB–BBB incl geog (Arch Geog) (IB 32–30 pts HL 6 geog)
Warwick – ABB (Anc Hist Class Arch) (IB 34 pts)
York – ABB–BBB (Arch; Bioarch; Hist Arch) (IB 34–31 pts)

120 pts **Aberdeen** – BBB (Arch) (IB 32 pts)
Brighton – BBB (Arch Geog) (IB 30 pts)
Queen's Belfast – BBB (Arch; Arch Palae)
Sheffield – BBB–BBC (Arch; Class Hist Arch) (IB 32 pts)
Swansea – BBB–BBC (Egypt Anc Hist) (IB 32–30 pts)

112 pts **Bangor** – 112–120 pts (Herit Arch Hist; Welsh Hist Arch; Arch)
Bradford – BBC 112 pts (Arch courses)
Canterbury Christ Church – 112 pts (Arch courses)
Cardiff – BBC (Cons Objs Musm Arch) (IB 36–28 pts)
Central Lancashire – 112 pts (Arch) (IB 28 pts)
Chester – BBC–BCC 112 pts (Arch courses) (IB 26 pts)
Hull – 112 pts (Hist Arch) (IB 28 pts)

104 pts **Bournemouth** – 104–120 pts (Arch; Arch Foren Sci; Arch Anth) (IB 28–31 pts)
London (Birk) – 104 pts (Arch)
Portsmouth – 104–128 pts incl biol (Palae) (IB 27 pts)
Winchester – 104–120 pts (Arch) (IB 26 pts)

96 pts **Bishop Grosseteste** – 96–112 pts (Arch Hist)
Trinity Saint David – 96–104 pts (Arch; Arch Prof Prac) (IB 26 pts)
Winchester – 96–112 pts (Arch Prac) (IB 25 pts)
Worcester – 96–112 pts (Arch Herit St courses)

64 pts **UHI** – CC (Scot Hist Arch; Arch Env St; Arch)

Alternative offers
See **Chapter 6** and **Appendix 1** for grades/new UCAS Tariff points information for other examinations.

EXAMPLES OF COLLEGES OFFERING COURSES IN THIS SUBJECT FIELD
Peterborough (Coll); Stockton Riverside (Coll); Truro and Penwith (Coll).

CHOOSING YOUR COURSE (SEE ALSO CH.1)
Universities and colleges teaching quality See www.qaa.ac.uk; http://unistats.direct.gov.uk.

Top research universities and colleges (REF 2014) (Geography, Environmental Studies and Archaeology) Glasgow (Geog); London (RH); London LSE; Bristol (Geog); Cambridge (Geog); Oxford (Geog Env St); London (QM); St Andrews; Newcastle (Geog); Southampton (Geog); London (UCL) (Geog); Reading (Arch); Sheffield (Geog); Oxford (Arch).

Examples of sandwich degree courses Bradford.

ADMISSIONS INFORMATION
Number of applicants per place (approx) Birmingham 7; Bradford 4; Bristol 7; Cambridge 2; Cardiff 6; Durham 3; Leicester 6; Liverpool 7; London (UCL) 4; Manchester (Anc Hist Arch) 15, (Arch) 4; Newcastle 14; Nottingham 11; Sheffield 5; Southampton 6; Trinity Saint David 2; York 4.

Advice to applicants and planning the UCAS personal statement First-hand experience of digs and other fieldwork should be described. The Council for British Archaeology (see **Appendix 3**) can provide information on where digs are taking place. Describe any interests in fossils and any museum visits as well as details of visits to current archaeological sites. Your local university archaeological department or central library can also provide information on contacts in your local area (each county council employs an archaeological officer). Since this is not a school subject, the selectors will be looking for good reasons for your choice of subject. Gain practical field experience and discuss this in the personal statement. Show your serious commitment to archaeology through your out-of-school activities (fieldwork, museum experience) (see **Chapter 5**). (See also **Anthropology**.) **Bristol** Deferred entry accepted. **Cambridge** Most colleges require a school/college essay.

Misconceptions about this course Bristol We are not an elitist course: 75% of applicants and students come from state schools and non-traditional backgrounds. **Liverpool** (Egypt) Some students would have been better advised looking at courses in Archaeology or Ancient History and Archaeology which offer major pathways in the study of Ancient Egypt.

Selection interviews Yes Bangor, Bournemouth, Bradford, Cambridge, Liverpool, London (UCL), Newcastle, Oxford (Arch Anth) 33%, (Class Arch Anc Hist) 29%, Reading, Southampton, Trinity Saint David; **Some** Bristol, Cardiff, East Anglia; **No** Birmingham, Leicester, Nottingham.

Interview advice and questions Questions will be asked about any experience you have had in visiting archaeological sites or taking part in digs. Past questions have included: How would you interpret archaeological evidence, for example a pile of flints, coins? What is stratification? How would you date archaeological remains? What recent archaeological discoveries have been made? How did you become interested in archaeology? With which archaeological sites in the UK are you familiar? See also **Chapter 5**. **Birmingham** Questions may cover recent archaeological events. **Cambridge** See **Chapter 5**. **Oxford** Interviews involve artefacts, maps and other material to be interpreted. Successful entrants average 30.7% (see **Chapter 5**). **York** What are your views on the archaeology programmes on TV? What would you do with a spare weekend?

Reasons for rejection (non-academic) (Mature students) Inability to cope with essay-writing and exams. **Bournemouth** Health and fitness important for excavations. **Liverpool** (Egypt) Applicant misguided on choice of course – Egyptology used to fill a gap on the UCAS application.

AFTER-RESULTS ADVICE
Offers to applicants repeating A-levels Same Birmingham, Bradford, Cambridge, Chester, Durham, East Anglia, Leicester, Liverpool, London (UCL), Sheffield, Trinity Saint David, Winchester.

GRADUATE DESTINATIONS AND EMPLOYMENT (2013/14 HESA)
Graduates surveyed 715 **Employed** 270 **In voluntary employment** 35 **In further study** 215 **Assumed unemployed** 70

Career note Vocational opportunities closely linked to this subject are limited. However, some graduates aim for positions in local authorities, libraries and museums. A number of organisations covering water boards, forestry, civil engineering and surveying also employ field archaeologists.

OTHER DEGREE SUBJECTS FOR CONSIDERATION
Ancient History; Anthropology; Classical Studies; Classics; Geology; Heritage Studies; History; History of Art and Architecture; Medieval History.

ARCHITECTURE

(including **Architectural Technology** and **Architectural Engineering**; see also **Art and Design (Interior, Product and Industrial Design), Building and Construction, Landscape Architecture**)

Courses in Architecture provide a broad education consisting of technological subjects covering structures, construction, materials and environmental studies. Project-based design work is an integral part of all courses and in addition, history and social studies will also be incorporated into degree programmes. After completing the first three years leading to a BA (Hons), students aiming for full professional status take a further two-year course leading to, for example, a BArch, MArch or Diploma, and after a year in an architect's practice, the final professional examinations are taken. There is also a close link between architecture and civil engineering in the construction of large projects eg The Shard, Sydney Opera House and the construction of bridges and other major projects. Several architectural engineering courses are offered, for example Bath, Loughborough and Glasgow offer courses which, whilst focussing on civil engineering, also introduce creative design elements working on inventive and imaginative design solutions.

Useful websites www.ciat.org.uk; www.architecture.com; www.rias.org.uk; http://archrecord. construction.com; www.ciob.org.uk; www.citb.co.uk

NB The points totals shown to the left of the institutions are for ease of reference only. It must not be assumed that Tariff points are always used by institutions or that they can be substituted for an offer in grades. The level of an offer is not necessarily indicative of the quality of a course.

COURSE OFFERS INFORMATION
Subject requirements/preferences GCSE English and mathematics, in some cases at certain grades, are required in all cases. A science subject may also be required. **AL** Mathematics and/or Physics required or preferred for some courses. Art and Design may be preferable to Design and Technology. Art is sometimes a requirement and many schools of architecture prefer it; a portfolio of art work is often requested and, in some cases, a drawing test will be set. MEng courses not listed below unless otherwise stated.

Your target offers and examples of degree courses
152 pts Bath – A*AA incl maths (Civ Archit Eng MEng) (IB 36 pts HL 6 maths); A*AA (Archit) (IB 36 pts HL 6 maths/phys)
   Cambridge – A*AA (Archit) (IB 40–41 pts HL 776)
   Southampton – A*AA incl mats+sci/geog (Civ Eng Archit MEng) (IB 36 pts HL 6 maths+sci)
144 pts Cardiff – AAA (Archit) (IB 36 pts); AAA incl maths (Archit Eng) (IB 36–32 pts HL 5 maths+sci)
   City – 144 pts (Civ Eng Archit) (IB 30 pts HL maths)

ARCHITECTURE IN ACTION

Specialist facilities, outstanding industry connections and exciting opportunities... explore everything we have to offer!

School of Architecture Oxford Brookes University one of the largest architecture schools in the , with courses accredited the Royal Institute of tish Architects (RIBA) and Architects Registration ard (ARB). We are based Abercrombie, alongside nning, Real Estate and nstruction.

e provide plenty of portunities to get involved th community and dustry live-projects, to ild an excellent portfolio, preparation for your ofessional career.

A Architecture graduate drew Chard recently n the prestigious RIBA 015 Serjeant Award for xcellence in Drawing art 1). Andrew's designs r 'The Lost Dockyard', oposed the reconstruction ancient ships to take ace within Piraeus, Port Greece. Once the largest assenger port in Europe, e aim of this project was to tract and restore tourism ithin the area.

'The Lost Dockyard' by Andrew Chard

As a Brookes Architecture student, you will have 24 hour access, seven days a week to our open plan studios. These are equipped with flexible working areas as well as drawing and modelling spaces.

Our computers use industry-standard software, including ArchiCAD, Revit, 3D Studio MAX and Rhino3D. From laser cutters, a CNC mill, 3D printers to acid-etching, grow in your field with our latest workshop equipment.

Abercrombie

tde.bz/heap-arch

Ulster University

Building your future with Ulster University

in the School of the Built Environment

- Professional Accreditation

- Fees only **£6000** for GB students*

- Delivering career-focused education

- Campus situated only **15 MINUTES** from Belfast city centre

- One of the largest Universities in the Island of Ireland

- Top **SIX** UK Built Environment research University

- New Belfast city centre campus opening 2018

- Northern Ireland's capital **BELFAST** is the most affordable city for study in the UK

For more information visit:
study.ulster.ac.uk

*correct at time of print (2016/17)

BEng (Hons) Architectural Engineering

The programme is designed to meet the demand for graduates who are creative and innovative, and who can work in building services, architectural integration, energy use in buildings, and the application of renewable technologies. According to CITB, 182,000 jobs will be created in the UK's construction sector over the next four years, specifically for professionals who can deliver innovative and practical building engineering designs that embrace low-carbon with economic operational performance. To meet this demand for professionals with the required knowledge and skill set, this exciting new course has been launched. The programme aims to produce architecturally informed building services engineers and energy professionals, able to deliver energy efficient and environmentally conscious solutions for buildings.

The research informed curriculum offers a route to professional status in an exciting and diverse profession with excellent employment opportunities in renewable energy and sustainable built environment sectors. The graduates of this programme will be involved in the design of various building systems associated with industrial, commercial and residential buildings such as heating, ventilation and air conditioning, refrigeration, lighting, water service, drainage, plumbing, security and alarms, lifts, escalators, gas, electricity, and communication. They will also have a growing role in the deployment of renewable energy systems, sustainability and energy efficiency in buildings.

BSc (Hons) Energy

Energy is essential to our way of life. If you are interested in the major energy technologies of today and want to advance the use of renewables then study Energy at Ulster University. This course offers an exciting learning experience combining both practical and theoretical elements. It is designed to provide an in-depth knowledge of conventional and renewable energy systems, their sizing, evaluation, economics, policy agendas (environmental, planning etc.) and social acceptance. The course is delivered by the staff at the Centre of Sustainable Technologies and has a research informed curriculum on renewable energy and strong industrial links.

Embarking upon a career in Energy can open a wide variety of choices in the public or the private sector.

The Energy sector including Renewables offers significant job creation potential across the UK and EU with an estimated 3 million new jobs expected to be created by 2020. The UK's £12.5 billion renewables industry is currently supporting 110,000 jobs across the supply chain, and could support 400,000 jobs by 2020. As an Energy graduate you will be responsible for providing innovative and forward-thinking energy solutions that reduce energy consumption and associated carbon emissions, develop secure energy supplies and reduce reliance on imported fossil fuels. Career progression will take you into strategic decision making, budgetary control and wider consultancy responses.

Ulster University

Building your future with Ulster University

in the School of the Built Environment

- Professional Accreditation

- Fees only **£6000** for GB students*

- Delivering career-focused education

- Campus situated only **15 MINUTES** from Belfast city centre

- One of the largest Universities in the Island of Ireland

- Top **SIX** UK Built Environment research University

- New Belfast city centre campus opening 2018

- Northern Ireland's capital **BELFAST** is the most affordable city for study in the UK

For more information visit:
study.ulster.ac.uk

*correct at time of print (2016/17)

Ulster
University

Faculty of Art,
Design & the Built
Environment

For more
information visit:
study.ulster.ac.uk

Edinburgh – AAA–ABB (Archit) (IB 40–34 pts); AAA–ABB incl maths (Struct Eng Archit) (IB 37–32 pts)

Leeds – AAA incl maths (Archit Eng) (IB 35 pts HL 5 maths)

Liverpool – AAA (Archit) (IB 36 pts)

Manchester – AAA (Archit) (IB 37 pts)

Manchester Met – AAA 144 pts (Archit) (IB 37 pts)

Newcastle – AAA +portfolio (Archit) (IB 36 pts)

Northumbria – 144 pts (Archit) (IB 33 pts)

Nottingham – AAA (Archit) (IB 36 pts); AAA incl maths/phys (Archit Env Des MEng) (IB 36 pts)

Sheffield – AAA (Archit) (IB 37 pts); AAA–AAB incl maths (Struct Eng Archit MEng; Archit Eng Des MEng) (IB 37 pts HL 6 maths)

UWE Bristol – 144 pts (Archit) (IB 29 pts)

136 pts **Birmingham City** – AAB 136 pts (Archit) (IB 30 pts)

Coventry – AAB (Archit) (IB 31 pts)

De Montfort – 136 pts +portfolio +interview (Archit) (IB 30 pts)

Glasgow – AAB–BBB incl maths+phys (Civ Eng Archit) (IB 36–34 pts)

Huddersfield – AAB 136 pts (Archit (Int); Archit)

Kent – AAB (Archit) (IB 34 pts)

London (UCL) – AAB +portfolio (Archit; Archit Interd St) (IB 36 pts)

Nottingham – AAB–ABB (Archit Env Eng) (IB 34–32 pts)

Oxford Brookes – AAB (Archit) (IB 34–32 pts)

Queen's Belfast – AAB incl maths+sci/tech (Struct Eng Archit MEng); AAB (Archit)

UWE Bristol – 136 pts (Archit Plan) (IB 28 pts)

Westminster – AAB (Archit) (IB 35 pts)

128 pts **Arts London** – ABB 128 pts +portfolio (Archit)

Bournemouth Arts – ABB (Archit) (IB 34 pts)

Brighton – ABB (Archit) (IB 32 pts)

Creative Arts – 128 pts (Archit)

Edinburgh – ABB (Archit Hist Arch; Archit Hist) (IB 36–34 pts)

Glasgow (SA) – ABB incl maths/phys (Archit) (IB 30 pts)

Greenwich – 128 pts (Archit)

Kingston – 128 pts (Archit)

Lincoln – 128 pts (Archit)

Newcastle – ABB (Archit Urb Plan) (IB 32 pts)

Nottingham Trent – 128 pts (Archit)

Plymouth – 128 pts (Archit) (IB 32 pts)

Reading – ABB–BBB (Archit) (IB 32–30 pts)

Strathclyde – ABB 128 pts (Archit St) (IB 34 pts)

Wolverhampton – 128 pts (Archit)

120 pts **Central Lancashire** – 120 pts (Archit) (IB 30 pts)

Coventry – BBB (Archit Tech) (IB 30 pts)

Dundee – BBB–BCC incl maths/phys (Archit) (IB 30 pts)

East London – 120 pts (Archit Des Tech) (IB 26 pts); 120 pts incl art des (Archit) (IB 28 pts)

Heriot-Watt – ABC–BBB incl maths (Archit Eng) (IB 31 pts HL 5 maths)

Leeds Beckett – 120 pts (Archit; Archit Tech) (IB 26 pts)

Liverpool John Moores – 120–128 pts (Archit) (IB 31 pts)

London Met – 120 pts +portfolio (Archit)

Loughborough – 120 pts (Archit Eng Des Mgt) (IB 32 pts)

Northumbria – 120 pts (Archit Tech; Archit Eng) (IB 30 pts)

Norwich Arts – BBB incl art/des (Archit) (IB 32 pts)

Portsmouth – 120–136 pts (Archit) (IB 26 pts)

Ulster – 120 pts (Archit) (IB 26 pts)

UWE Bristol – 120 pts (Archit Env Eng; Archit Tech Des) (IB 26 pts)

112 pts **Birmingham City** – BBC 112 pts (Archit Tech) (IB 30 pts)

Central Lancashire – 112 pts (Archit Tech) (IB 28 pts)
Derby – 112 pts (Archit Tech Prac)
Northampton – 112 pts (Archit Tech)
Plymouth – 112 pts (Archit Tech Env) (IB 28 pts)
Robert Gordon – BBC incl maths/sci (Archit MArch) (IB 29 pts)
Sheffield Hallam – 112 pts (Archit Tech)
Southampton Solent – 112 pts (Archit Tech)
West London – 112 pts (Archit Des Tech)
Westminster – BBC (Archit Tech) (IB 28 pts)

108 pts **Salford** – 108–128 pts (Archit)

104 pts **Cardiff Met** – 104 pts (Archit Des Tech)
Edinburgh Napier – BCC (Archit Tech) (IB 28 pts)
Falmouth – 104–120 pts (Archit)
Liverpool John Moores – 104 pts (Archit Tech)
London South Bank – BCC 104 pts (Archit)
Nottingham Trent – 104 pts (Archit Tech)
Portsmouth – 104–120 pts (Inter Archit Des) (IB 25 pts)
UHI – BCC incl maths/phys/tech (Archit Tech)
Ulster – 104 pts incl sci/maths/tech (Archit Tech Mgt) (IB 24 pts)

96 pts **Anglia Ruskin** – 96 pts +portfolio (Archit) (IB 26 pts)
Bolton – 96 pts (Archit Tech)
Glyndŵr – 96 pts (Archit Des Tech)
Robert Gordon – CCC (Archit Tech) (IB 26 pts)
Trinity Saint David – 96 pts (Archit Tech)

88 pts **Anglia Ruskin** – 88 pts (Archit Tech) (IB 24 pts)
Derby – 88–120 pts (Archit Des Joint Hons)
London South Bank – CCD/AB 88 pts (Archit Tech)

80 pts **Wolverhampton** – 80 pts (Archit Des Tech)

64 pts **Archit Assoc Sch London** – CC +portfolio (Archit)
Ravensbourne – CC (Archit) (IB 28 pts)

Alternative offers
See **Chapter 6** and **Appendix 1** for grades/new UCAS Tariff points information for other examinations.

EXAMPLES OF COLLEGES OFFERING COURSES IN THIS SUBJECT FIELD
Basingstoke (CT); Bexley (Coll); BITE; Bournemouth and Poole (Coll); Calderdale (Coll); Hull (Coll); Suffolk (Univ Campus); Weymouth (Coll); Writtle (Coll).

CHOOSING YOUR COURSE (SEE ALSO CH.1)
Universities and colleges teaching quality See www.qaa.ac.uk; http://unistats.direct.gov.uk.

Top research universities and colleges (REF 2014) (Architecture, Built Environment and Planning) Bath; Glasgow; Cambridge; Loughborough; Aberdeen; Newcastle; Sheffield; Cardiff (Plan Geog); Liverpool; Reading; London (UCL); Sheffield Hallam.

Examples of sandwich degree courses Bath; City; Coventry; Derby; Glasgow (SA); Leeds Beckett; London South Bank; Loughborough; Northumbria; Nottingham Trent; Sheffield Hallam; Ulster; UWE Bristol; Wolverhampton.

ADMISSIONS INFORMATION
Number of applicants per place (approx) Archit Assoc Sch London 2; Bath 9; Cambridge 9; Cardiff 12; Cardiff Met 2; Creative Arts 4; Dundee 6; Edinburgh 18; Glasgow 16; London (UCL) 14; London Met 13; Manchester 7; Manchester Met 25; Newcastle 11; Nottingham 30; Oxford Brookes 15; Queen's Belfast 9; Robert Gordon 8; Sheffield 20; Southampton 10; Strathclyde 10.

Admissions tutors' advice
Bath Preference for applicants with high proportion of A and A* at GCSE.

Check **Chapter 3** for new university admission details and **Chapter 6** on how to read the subject tables.

Huddersfield 2D and 3D drawings, models, sketches and finished work in portfolio.

Kent Portfolio can be in digital form with images in JPEG format and documents in PDF.

Liverpool A lower grade offer if portfolio impressive.

Manchester Art and Art and Design as two A-levels not advised.

UWE Bristol NB Architecture and Environmental Engineering degree gives RIBA status.

Advice to applicants and planning the UCAS personal statement You should describe any visits to historical or modern architectural sites and give your opinions. Contact architects in your area and try to obtain work shadowing or work experience in their practices. Describe any such work you have done. Develop a portfolio of drawings and sketches of buildings and parts of buildings (you will probably need this for your interview). Show evidence of your reading on the history of architecture in Britain and modern architecture throughout the world. Discuss your preferences among the work of leading 20th and 21st century world architects (see **Chapter 4** and also **Appendix 3**). **Cambridge** Check College requirement for preparatory work.

Misconceptions about this course Some applicants believe that Architectural Technology is the same as Architecture. Some students confuse Architecture with Architectural Engineering.

Selection interviews The majority of universities and colleges interview or inspect portfolios for Architecture. **Yes** Archit Assoc Sch London, Bath, Birmingham City, Brighton, Cambridge, Coventry, De Montfort, Derby, Dundee, East London, Edinburgh, Falmouth, Falmouth, Glasgow (SA), Huddersfield, Kent, Kingston, Leeds Beckett, Liverpool, London (UCL), London Met, London South Bank, Manchester Met, Newcastle, Northumbria, Oxford Brookes, Queen's Belfast, Sheffield, Ulster, West London; **Some** Anglia Ruskin, Cardiff, Cardiff Met; **No** Nottingham, Portsmouth.

Interview advice and questions Most Architecture departments will expect to see evidence of your ability to draw; portfolios are often requested at interview and, in some cases, drawing tests are set prior to the interview. You should have a real awareness of architecture with some knowledge of historical styles as well as examples of modern architecture. If you have gained some work experience then you will be asked to describe the work done in the architect's office and any site visits you have made. Questions in the past have included the following: What is the role of the architect in society? Is the London Eye an eyesore? Discuss one historic and one 21st century building you admire. Who is your favourite architect? What sort of buildings do you want to design? How would you make a place peaceful? How would you reduce crime through architecture? Do you like the University buildings? Do you read any architectural journals? Which? What is the role of an architectural technologist? See also **Chapter 5**. **Archit Assoc Sch London** The interview assesses the student's potential and ability to benefit from the course. Every portfolio we see at interview will be different; sketches, models, photographs and paintings all help to build up a picture of the student's interests. Detailed portfolio guidelines are available on the website. **Cambridge** Candidates who have taken, or are going to take, A-level Art should bring with them their portfolio of work (GCSE work is not required). All candidates, including those who are not taking A-level Art, should bring photographs of any three-dimensional material. Those not taught art should bring a sketch book (for us to assess drawing abilities) and analytical drawings of a new and an old (pre-1900) building and a natural and human-made artefact. We are interested to see any graphic work in any medium that you would like to show us – please do not feel you should restrict your samples to only those with architectural reference. All evidence of sketching ability is helpful to us. (NB All colleges at Cambridge and other university departments of architecture will seek similar evidence.) **Sheffield** Art portfolio required for those without AL/GCSE Art.

Reasons for rejection (non-academic) Weak evidence of creative skills. Folio of artwork does not give sufficient evidence of design creativity. Insufficient evidence of interest in architecture. Unwillingness to try freehand sketching. **Archit Assoc Sch London** Poor standard of work in the portfolio.

AFTER-RESULTS ADVICE
Offers to applicants repeating A-levels Higher Huddersfield; **Possibly higher** Brighton, De Montfort, Glasgow, Newcastle; **Same** Archit Assoc Sch London, Bath, Birmingham City, Cambridge, Cardiff,

Cardiff Met, Creative Arts, Derby, Dundee, Greenwich, Kingston, Liverpool John Moores, London Met, London South Bank, Manchester Met, Nottingham, Nottingham Trent, Oxford Brookes, Queen's Belfast, Robert Gordon, Sheffield.

GRADUATE DESTINATIONS AND EMPLOYMENT (2013/14 HESA)
Graduates surveyed 2,810 **Employed** 1,875 **In voluntary employment** 165 **In further study** 410 **Assumed unemployed** 180

Career note Further study is needed to enter architecture as a profession. Opportunities exist in local government or private practice – areas include planning, housing, environmental and conservation fields. Architectural technicians support the work of architects and may be involved in project management, design presentations and submissions to planning authorities.

OTHER DEGREE SUBJECTS FOR CONSIDERATION
Building; Building Surveying; Civil Engineering; Construction; Heritage Management; History of Art and Architecture; Housing; Interior Architecture; Interior Design; Landscape Architecture; Property Development; Quantity Surveying; Surveying; Town and Country Planning; Urban Studies.

ART and DESIGN (GENERAL)

(including **Conservation** and **Restoration**; see also **Art and Design (3d Design)**, **Art and Design (Graphic Design)**, **Combined Courses, Communication Studies/Communication, Drama, Media Studies, Photography**)

Art and Design and all specialisms remain one of the most popular subjects. Many of the courses listed here cover aspects of fine art, graphic or three-dimensional design, but to a less specialised extent than those listed in the other Art and Design tables. Travel and visits to art galleries and museums are strongly recommended by many universities and colleges. Note that for entry to many Art and Design courses it is often necessary to follow an Art and Design Foundation course first: check with your chosen institution.

Art and Design degree courses cover a wide range of subjects. These are grouped together in six tables:

Art and Design (General),
Art and Design (Fashion and Textiles),
Art and Design (Fine Art),
Art and Design (Graphic Design),
Art and Design (Product and Industrial Design),
Art and Design (3D Design).
(History of Art and Photography are listed in separate tables.)

Useful websites www.artscouncil.org.uk; www.designcouncil.org.uk; www.theatredesign.org.uk; www.arts.ac.uk; www.dandad.org; www.csd.org.uk; www.creativefuture.org.uk

The points total shown to the left of the institutions are for ease of reference only. It must not be assumed that Tariff points are always used by institutions or that they can be substituted for an offer in grades. The level of an offer is not necessarily indicative of the quality of a course.

COURSE OFFERS INFORMATION
Subject requirements/preferences Entry requirements for Art and Design courses vary between institutions and courses (check prospectuses and websites). Most courses require an Art and Design Foundation course and a portfolio of work demonstrating potential and visual awareness. **GCSE** Five subjects at grades A–C, or a recognised equivalent. **AL** Grades or points may be required. (Des Tech) Design Technology or a physical science may be required of preferred. (Crea Arts courses) Music/Art/ Drama may be required.

Your target offers and examples of degree courses

128 pts Dundee – ABB incl art des (Art Phil Contemp Prac) (IB 34 pts)
Kent – ABB (Evnt Expnc Des) (IB 34 pts)
Leeds – ABB incl art/des (Art Des) (IB 34 pts HL 5/6 art/des)
Ulster – BBB 128 pts (Interact Multim Des) (IB 27 pts)

120 pts Cardiff Met – 120 pts (Arst Des (Maker))
De Montfort – 120 pts incl art des (Gms Art Des) (IB 30 pts HL 6 art des)
Edinburgh (CA) – BBB +portfolio (Pntg) (IB 34 pts)
Huddersfield – BBB 120 pts +portfolio +interview (Contemp Art)
Kent – BBB (Vis Perf Arts) (IB 34 pts HL 15 pts)

112 pts Birmingham City – BBC 112 pts (Art Des) (IB 28 pts)
Bournemouth Arts – BBC–BBB 112–120 pts (Crea Evnt Mgt) (IB 32 pts)
Lincoln – 112 pts (Des Exhib Musms)
Manchester Met – 112 pts +portfolio (Interact Arts) (IB 26 pts)
Nottingham Trent – 112 pts +portfolio (Decr Arts)
Staffordshire – 112 pts (Gms Art)
UWE Bristol – 112 pts (Drg Prt) (IB 25 pts)

104 pts Bath Spa – 104 pts (Contemp Arts Prac)
Falmouth – 104–120 pts +portfolio +interview (Drg)
South Wales – BCC (Crea Ther Arts) (IB 29 pts)
Worcester – 104 pts (Art Des)

96 pts Bolton – 96 pts (Art Des)
Hertfordshire – 96 pts incl art +interview +portfolio (Contemp Des Crfts courses) (IB 24 pts)
Rose Bruford (Coll) – 96 pts (Scnc Arts (Constr Props Pntg))
Salford – 96–112 pts incl art des (Vis Arts) (IB 26 pts)
Westminster – CCC–BB (Illus Vis Comm) (IB 26 pts)

88 pts Glasgow Caledonian – CCD incl art des (Comp Gms (Art Animat)) (IB 24 pts)

80 pts Hereford (CA) – 80 pts +portfolio +interview (Contemp Des Crfts; Illus)
Plymouth (CA) – 80 pts +portfolio (Des)

72 pts Robert Gordon – BC incl art/des +portfolio +interview (Pntg) (IB 24 pts); BC +interview/ portfolio (Contemp Art Prac) (IB 24 pts)

32 pts Reading – 32–136 pts (Art courses) (IB 24–35 pts)

Alternative offers
See **Chapter 6** and **Appendix 1** for grades/new UCAS Tariff points information for other examinations.

EXAMPLES OF COLLEGES OFFERING COURSES IN THIS SUBJECT FIELD
All art colleges. Banbury and Bicester (Coll); Barnet and Southgate (Coll); Barnsley (Coll); Blackburn (Coll); Blackpool and Fylde (Coll); Bradford (Coll); Brighton and Hove City (Coll); Central Nottingham (Coll); Chelmsford (Coll); Chesterfield (Coll); Chichester (Coll); Cornwall (Coll); Doncaster (Coll); Ealing, Hammersmith and West London (Coll); East Berkshire (Coll); East Surrey (Coll); Exeter (Coll); Furness (Coll); Great Yarmouth (Coll); Grimsby (Univ Centre); Highbury Portsmouth (Coll); Hugh Baird (Coll); Hull (Coll); Kingston (Coll); Llandrillo (Coll); London UCK (Coll); Loughborough (Coll); Manchester (Coll); Menai (Coll); North Nottinghamshire (Coll); North Warwickshire and Hinckley (Coll); Northumberland (Coll); Norwich City (Coll); Nottingham New (Coll); Pembrokeshire (Coll); Peter Symonds (Coll); Portsmouth (Coll); Redbridge (Coll); Richmond-upon-Thames (Coll); Somerset (Coll); South Devon (Coll); South Essex (Coll); South Tyneside (Coll); Southampton City (Coll); Southport (Coll); Stockport (Coll); Suffolk (Univ Campus); Sunderland (Coll); Sussex Coast Hastings (Coll); Totton (Coll); Truro and Penwith (Coll); Tyne Met (Coll); Wakefield (Coll); West Cheshire (Coll); West Herts (Coll); West Kent (Coll); Westminster City (Coll); Wirral Met (Coll); Writtle (Coll); Yeovil (Coll).

CHOOSING YOUR COURSE (SEE ALSO CH.1)
Top research universities and colleges (REF 2014) (Art and Design: History, Practice and Theory) London (Court); Reading (Typo/Graph Comm); St Andrews; Westminster; Essex; Open University;

Art and Design
Consult the Specialist

MPW is one of the UK's best known groups of independent sixth-form colleges. We offer a range of specialist services to those who have chosen a career in art-or design-related fields.

Two-year and one-year A level courses

Fine Art, Ceramics, Photography, Textiles and History of Art

Specialist Portfolio and Foundation preparation courses

M|P|W
Mander Portman Woodward

London	020 7835 1355
Birmingham	0121 454 9637
Cambridge	01223 350158

Getting into Art and Design Courses by MPW is published by Trotman Publishing

Check **Chapter 3** for new university admission details and **Chapter 6** on how to read the subject tables.

SCHOOL OF ARTS

Our staff are active researchers, practising artists, writers and curators - and are dedicated to sharing their expertise with you

The School of Arts offers courses in Art and Design Foundation, Music, Digital Media Production, Film and Fine Art. Students are encouraged to take part in a lively calendar of competitions, exhibitions, concerts, industry and community projects.

As part of the International Festival of Drawing – The Big Draw, October 2015, our Art and Design Foundation and Fine Art students presented their interpretation of 'Every Drawing tells a Story'. The Big Draw brought together work from all ages and abilities within the School and community and pushed the boundaries of technique and theme to include performance and storytelling.

Launched by children's illustrator Korky Paul, best-selling illustrator of *Winnie the Witch*, the programme of diverse work was exhibited in the Glass Tank Gallery.

Watch The Big Draw at Brookes online - tde.bz/heap-draw

tde.bz/heap-arts

London (UCL) (Hist Art); Manchester; Arts London; Newcastle; York; Birmingham; Lancaster; Leeds (Art); London (SOAS); Sheffield Hallam.

ADMISSIONS INFORMATION

Number of applicants per place (approx) Dundee 5; Manchester Met 10.

Advice to applicants and planning the UCAS personal statement Admissions tutors look for a wide interest in aspects of art and design. Discuss the type of work and the range of media you have explored through your studies to date. Refer to visits to art galleries and museums and give your opinions of the styles of paintings and sculpture, both historical and present day. Mention art-related hobbies. Good drawing skills and sketchbook work, creative and analytical thinking will be needed.

Selection interviews Most institutions interview and require a portfolio of work. **Yes** Bath Spa, Bedfordshire, Central Lancashire, Dundee, Edinburgh Napier, Gloucestershire, Hertfordshire, Huddersfield, Lincoln, London (Gold), London Met, Loughborough, Middlesex, Reading, Robert Gordon, South Wales, Southampton Solent, Sunderland, West London, Wolverhampton; **Some** Sheffield Hallam, Staffordshire.

Interview advice and questions All courses require a portfolio inspection. Admissions tutors will want to see both breadth and depth in the applicant's work and evidence of strong self-motivation. They will also be interested to see any sketchbooks or notebooks. However, they do not wish to see similar work over and over again! A logical, ordered presentation helps considerably. Large work, especially three-dimensional work, can be presented by way of photographs. Video or film work should be edited to a running time of no more than 15 minutes. Examples of written work may also be provided. Past questions have included: How often do you visit art galleries and exhibitions? Discuss the last exhibition you visited. What are the reactions of your parents to your choice of course and career? Do you think that modern art has anything to contribute to society compared with earlier art? Is a brick a work of art? Show signs of life – no apathy! Be eager and enthusiastic.

Reasons for rejection (non-academic) Lack of enthusiasm for design issues or to acquire design skills. Poorly presented practical work. Lack of interest or enthusiasm in contemporary visual arts. Lack of knowledge and experience of the art and design industry.

GRADUATE DESTINATIONS AND EMPLOYMENT (2013/14 HESA)

Graduates surveyed 32,140 **Employed** 16,140 **In voluntary employment** 1,500 **In further study** 4,275 **Assumed unemployed** 2,400

Career note Many Art and Design courses are linked to specific career paths which are achieved through freelance consultancy work or studio work. Some graduates enter teaching and many find other areas such as retail and management fields. Opportunities for fashion and graphic design specialists exceed those of other areas of art and design. Opportunities in industrial and product design and three-dimensional design are likely to be limited and dependent on the contacts that students establish during their degree courses. Only a very limited number of students committed to painting and sculpture can expect to succeed without seeking alternative employment.

OTHER DEGREE SUBJECTS FOR CONSIDERATION

Animation; Architecture; Art Gallery Management; Communication Studies; Computer Studies; Education; Film Studies; History of Art; Media Studies; Photography; see other **Art and Design** tables.

ART and DESIGN (FASHION and TEXTILES)

(including **Surface Design**)

Fashion Design courses involve drawing and design, research, pattern cutting and garment construction for clothing for menswear and womenswear, with specialisation often offered later in the course. First year textiles courses will involve the study of constructed textile technology techniques such as knit and stitch, leading to specialisation later. Within digital textiles, the focus is on fashion for interiors and students will experiment with techniques such as laser knitting and digital fabric printing. Courses may also cover design for textiles, commercial production and marketing. Some institutions have particularly good contacts with industry and are able to arrange sponsorships for students.

Useful websites www.fashion.net; www.londonfashionweek.co.uk; www.texi.org; www.creativefuture.org.uk; www.britishfashioncouncil.co.uk; www.designcouncil.org.uk

NB The points totals shown to the left of the institutions are for ease of reference only. It must not be assumed that Tariff points are always used by institutions or that they can be substituted for an offer in grades. The level of an offer is not necessarily indicative of the quality of a course.

COURSE OFFERS INFORMATION

Subject requirements/preferences AL Textiles or Textile Science and Technology may be required.

Your target offers and examples of degree courses

136 pts **Manchester** – AAB 136 pts (Fash Rtl) (IB 35 pts)

128 pts **Brighton** – ABB 128 pts +portfolio +interview (Fash Bus St) (IB 34 pts); ABB +portfolio (Tex Bus St) (IB 34 pts)

Glasgow (SA) – ABB (Fash Des) (IB 30 pts)

Leeds – ABB (Fash Des; Tex Des) (IB 34 pts)

Loughborough – ABB (Tex (Innov Des))

Manchester – ABB incl sci+maths (Tex Sci Tech) (IB 33 pts)

Northumbria – 128 pts (Fash; Fash Des Mark) (IB 31 pts)

120 pts **Cardiff Met** – 120 pts (Tex)

Edinburgh (CA) – BBB +portfolio (Fash; Jewel Silver; Perf Cstm; Tex) (IB 34 pts)

Heriot-Watt – BBB (Fash Comm; Fash Wmnswr; Fash Mnswr; Fash Tech; Fash)) (IB 28 pts)

Huddersfield – BBB 120 pts (Fash Tex Buy Mgt); BBB 120 pts +portfolio +interview (Fash Comm Prom; Fash Des Tex; Fash Des Mark Prod)

Norwich Arts – BBB incl art/des (Tex Des; Fash) (IB 32 pts)

Nottingham Trent – 120 pts (Fash Mark Brnd; Fash Comm Prom)

Southampton (Winchester SA) – BBB incl art/des (Fash Tex Des) (IB 30 pts); BBB (Fash Mark) (IB 30 pts)

Sunderland – 120 pts (Fash Jrnl)

Trinity Saint David – 120 pts (Sfc Pattn Des (Fash Obj); Sfc Pattn Des (Tex Fash); Sfc Pattn Des (Tex Inter)) (IB 32 pts)

112 pts **Arts London (CFash)** – BBC 112 pts +portfolio (Fash Mgt); CC 112 pts +portfolio (Fash Jrnl)

Birmingham City – BBC 112 pts (Fash Bus Prom; Fash Des courses) (IB 32 pts)

Bournemouth Arts – BBC–BBB 112–120 pts +portfolio +interview (Tex) (IB 32 pts)

Brighton – BBC (Fash Drs Hist) (IB 28 pts)

Central Lancashire – 112 pts (Fash Prom) (IB 28 pts)

De Montfort – 112 pts +portfolio +interview (Fash Des; Fash Tex Accs; Cont Fash) (IB 28 pts); 112 pts (Fash Buy) (IB 28 pts); 112 pts incl art des +portfolio +interview (Tex Des) (IB 28 pts)

Derby – 112 pts +portfolio +interview (Fash); 112 pts +portfolio (Tex Des)

East London – 112 pts +interview +portfolio (Fash Des) (IB 24 pts)

Kingston – 112 pts +portfolio (Fash)

Lincoln – 112 pts (Fash)

Liverpool John Moores – 112 pts (Fash) (IB 29 pts)

London (Royal Central Sch SpDr) – BBC +interview (Thea Prac Cstm Constr)

London Met – 112 pts (Fash Mark Bus Mgt)

Manchester Met – 112 pts +portfolio (Fash; Tex Prac) (IB 26 pts)

Middlesex – 112 pts +portfolio +interview (Fash Tex; Fash Des)

Northampton – 112 pts +portfolio +interview (Tex Fash); 112 pts +portfolio (Fash; Ftwr Accs)

Nottingham Trent – 112 pts +portfolio (Fash Des; Fash Kntwr Des Knit Tex; Tex Des; Cstm Des Mak; Fash Accs Des)

Sheffield Hallam – 112 pts (Fash Des)

Southampton Solent – 112 pts (Fash Styl)

Sunderland – 112 pts (Fash Prod Prom)

UWE Bristol – 112 pts +portfolio (Fash) (IB 25 pts)

Westminster – BBC (Fash Mrchnds Mgt) (IB 29 pts)

104 pts **Bath Spa** – 104 pts incl art des +portfolio +interview (Fash Des); 104 pts incl art des +portfolio (Tex Des Fash Inter)

Bradford (Coll) – 104 pts (Fash; Surf Des Tex Innov)

Coventry – BCC incl art/des (Fash) (IB 28 pts)

Falmouth – 104–120 pts +portfolio +interview (Fash Des; Fash Photo; Perf Spowr Des; Tex Des)

Leeds (CA) – 104 pts +portfolio (Prtd Tex Surf Patt Des; Fash (Des); Fash (Comm))

Manchester Met – BCC–BBC 104–112 pts (Int Fash Prom) (IB 25 pts); (Fash Des Tech) (IB 26 pts); 104–112 pts (Fash Buy Mrchnds) (IB 26 pts)

Northampton – 104–112 pts (Fash Mark)

Robert Gordon – BCC (Fash Mgt) (IB 28 pts)

South Wales – BCC (Fash Mark Rtl Des) (IB 29 pts); BCC incl art des +portfolio (Fash Prom) (IB 29 pts); BCC incl art des (Fash Des) (IB 29 pts)

Staffordshire – 104 pts +portfolio +interview (Tex Sfc)

West London – 104 pts incl art des (Fash Tex)

96 pts **Arts London (CFash)** – CCC 96 pts +portfolio (Fash PR Comm; Mkup Pros Perf)

Bolton – 96 pts (Tex Sfc Des)

Cleveland (CAD) – 96 pts (Fash; Tex Sfc Des)

Hertfordshire – 96 pts incl art des (Fash Fash Bus) (IB 24 pts); 96 pts incl art +portfolio +interview (Fash) (IB 24 pts)

Portsmouth – 96–112 pts (Fash Tex Des Ent) (IB 26 pts)

Salford – 96–112 pts incl art des (Fash Des) (IB 26 pts)

Southampton Solent – 96 pts (Fash Graph; Fash Prom Comm; Fash Mgt Mark; Fash courses)

Ulster – 96 pts (Tex Art Des Fash) (IB 24 pts)

Wolverhampton – 96 pts +portfolio (Fash Tex)

88 pts **Creative Arts** – 88 pts (Fash Prom Imag); 88 pts +portfolio (Fash Atel; Fash Jrnl; Tex Fash Inter)

80 pts **Anglia Ruskin** – 80–96 pts incl art/des/media (Fash Des) (IB 24 pts)

Bedfordshire – 80 pts +portfolio (Fash Des) (IB 24 pts)

Bucks New – 80–96 pts (Fash Des)

Hereford (CA) – 80 pts +portfolio +interview (Tex Des; Jewel Des)

Plymouth (CA) – 80 pts +portfolio (Fash; Print Tex Des Surf Patt)

72 pts **Robert Gordon** – BC incl art/des (Fash Tex Des) (IB 24 pts)

64 pts **Arts London (CFash)** – CC 64 pts +portfolio (Bspk Tlrg; Cord Fash Bags Accs (Prod Des Innov); Cord Ftwr (Prod Des Innov); Cstm Perf; Crea Dir Fash; Fash Cont; Fash Des Dev; Fash Des Tech (Mnswr); Fash Des Tech (Wmnswr); Fash Illus; Fash Jewel; Fash Photo; Fash Spowr; Fash Tex courses)

Colchester (Inst) – 64 pts +portfolio (Fash Tex)

Ravensbourne – CC (Fash; Fash Accs Des Proto; Fash Prom) (IB 28 pts)

UHI – CC incl Engl +portfolio (Contemp Tex; Fn Art Tex)

40 pts and below or other selection criteria (Foundation course, interview and portfolio inspection) Arts London; Arts London (CFash); Arts London (Chelsea CA); Arts London (Wimb CA); Bath Spa; Birmingham City; Brighton; Cardiff Met; Coventry; East London; Edinburgh (CA); Hertfordshire; Kingston; Leeds Beckett; Lincoln; Liverpool John Moores; London Met; Loughborough; Manchester (Coll); Middlesex; Plymouth; Robert Gordon; Southampton (Winchester SA); Staffordshire Reg Fed (SURF); UWE Bristol; Westminster.

Alternative offers

See **Chapter 6** and **Appendix 1** for grades/new UCAS Tariff points information for other examinations.

EXAMPLES OF COLLEGES OFFERING COURSES IN THIS SUBJECT FIELD

Check all art colleges. Barnet and Southgate (Coll); Barnfield (Coll); Basingstoke (CT); Bath (Coll); BITE; Blackburn (Coll); Blackpool and Fylde (Coll); Bournemouth and Poole (Coll); Bradford (Coll); Bury (Coll); Central Bedfordshire (Coll); Central Campus, Sandwell (Coll); Chelmsford (Coll); City and Islington (Coll); Doncaster (Coll); Dudley (Coll); Gloucestershire (Coll); Great Yarmouth (Coll); Hackney (CmC); Harrogate (Coll); Havering (Coll); HOW (Coll); Hull (Coll); Leicester (Coll); LeSoCo; Liverpool City (Coll); Mid-Cheshire (Coll); Newcastle (Coll); North Warwickshire and Hinckley (Coll); Northbrook (Coll); Rotherham (CAT); Sir Gâr (Coll); Somerset (Coll); South City Birmingham (Coll); South Devon (Coll); South Essex (Coll); South Gloucestershire and Stroud (Coll); South Thames (Coll); Tresham (CFHE); Walsall (Coll); West Herts (Coll); West Kent (Coll); Wigan and Leigh (Coll); York (Coll).

CHOOSING YOUR COURSE (SEE ALSO CH.1)

Universities and colleges teaching quality See www.qaa.ac.uk; http://unistats.direct.gov.uk.

Top research universities and colleges (REF 2014) See **Art and Design (General)**.

Examples of sandwich degree courses Arts London; Birmingham City; Brighton; Central Lancashire; Coventry; De Montfort; East London; Falmouth; Hertfordshire; Huddersfield; Manchester Met; Northumbria; Nottingham Trent; Portsmouth; South Wales; Ulster; Westminster; Wolverhampton.

ADMISSIONS INFORMATION

Number of applicants per place (approx) Arts London 5; Arts London (CFash) (Fash Mgt) 20; Birmingham City (Tex Des) 4; Bournemouth Arts 6; Brighton 6; Central Lancashire 4; Creative Arts 8; De Montfort 5; Derby (Tex Des) 2; Heriot-Watt 6; Huddersfield 4; Kingston 5; Leeds (CA) 4; Liverpool John Moores 6; Loughborough 5; Manchester Met 3; Middlesex 5; Northampton 4; Northumbria 8; Nottingham Trent 8, (Tex Des) 3; Southampton (Winchester SA) 6; Staffordshire 3; UWE Bristol 4; Wolverhampton 2.

Advice to applicants and planning the UCAS personal statement A well-written statement is sought, clearly stating an interest in fashion and how prior education and work experience relate to your application. You should describe any visits to exhibitions and, importantly, your views and opinions. Describe any work you have done ('making' and 'doing' skills, if any, for example, pattern cutting, sewing) or work observation in textile firms, fashion houses, even visits to costume departments in theatres can be useful. These contacts and visits should be described in detail, showing your knowledge of the types of fabrics and production processes. Give opinions on trends in haute couture, and show awareness of the work of others. Provide evidence of materials handling (see also **Appendix 3**). Show good knowledge of the contemporary fashion scene. See also **Art and Design (Graphic Design)**.

Misconceptions about this course Some students expect the Fashion degree to include textiles. (Tex) Some applicants feel that it's necessary to have experience in textiles – this is not the case. The qualities sought in the portfolio are analytical drawing, good colour sense and a sensitivity to materials.

Selection interviews Most institutions interview and require a portfolio of work. You should be familiar with current fashion trends and the work of leading designers. **Yes** Chester, Falmouth, Huddersfield, Leeds Beckett, Manchester, Northumbria, Queen Margaret, Salford, Southampton, UWE Bristol, UWE Bristol, West London; **Some** Liverpool John Moores.

Interview advice and questions Questions mostly originate from student's portfolio. See also **Art and Design (General)** and **Chapter 5**. **Birmingham City** (Tex Des) What do you expect to achieve from a degree in Fashion? **Creative Arts** Describe in detail a specific item in your portfolio and why it was selected.

Reasons for rejection (non-academic) Portfolio work not up to standard. Not enough research. Not articulate at interview. Lack of sense of humour, and inflexibility. Narrow perspective. Lack of resourcefulness, self-motivation and organisation. Complacency, lack of verbal, written and self-presentation skills. Not enough experience in designing or making clothes. See also **Art and Design (General)**.

AFTER-RESULTS ADVICE
Offers to applicants repeating A-levels Same Birmingham City, Bournemouth Arts, Creative Arts, Huddersfield, Manchester Met, Nottingham Trent, South Essex (Coll), Staffordshire.

GRADUATE DESTINATIONS AND EMPLOYMENT (2013/14 HESA)
See **Art and Design (General)**.

Career note See **Art and Design (General)**.

OTHER DEGREE SUBJECTS FOR CONSIDERATION
History of Art; Retail Management; Theatre Design.

ART and DESIGN (FINE ART)

(including **Printing, Printmaking** and **Sculpture**; see also **Art and Design (Graphic Design), Photography**)

Fine art courses are essentially practice-based courses encouraging students to find their own direction through additional intellectual and theoretical studies. The work will involve a range of activities which cover painting, illustration and sculpture. Additional studies can also involve electronic media, film, video, photography and print, although course options will vary between institutions. A more specialised study in the field of Environmental Art and Sculpture is offered at Glasgow School of Art taking sculpture outside art galleries and museums and into the public domain where students focus on drawing, wood and metal fabrication, photography, video, computers and sound. As in the case of most Art degrees, admission to courses usually requires a one-year Foundation Art course before applying.

Useful websites www.artcyclopedia.com; www.fine-art.com; www.nationalgallery.org.uk; www.britisharts.co.uk; www.tate.org.uk; www.creativefuture.org.uk; www.a-n.co.uk; www.artscouncil.org.uk

NB The points totals shown to the left of the institutions are for ease of reference only. It must not be assumed that Tariff points are always used by institutions or that they can be substituted for an offer in grades. The level of an offer is not necessarily indicative of the quality of a course.

COURSE OFFERS INFORMATION
Subject requirements/preferences See **Art and Design (General)**.

Your target offers and examples of degree courses
144 pts Oxford – AAA (Fn Art) (IB 38 pts)
136 pts Lancaster – AAB–ABB +portfolio (Fn Art) (IB 35–32 pts)
         Leeds – AAB–ABB (Fn Art) (IB 35–34 pts)
         Newcastle – AAB–BBB +portfolio (Fn Art) (IB 35–32 pts)
128 pts Dundee – ABB incl art des (Fn Art) (IB 34 pts)
         Glasgow (SA) – ABB (Sculp Env Art; Pntg Prtg; Fn Art Photo) (IB 30 pts)
         Kent – ABB–BBB incl art/hist art (Fn Art) (IB 34 pts)
         London (UCL) – ABB +portfolio (Fn Art) (IB 34 pts)
         London (UCL/Slade SA) – ABB +portfolio +interview (Fn Art)
         Loughborough – ABB (Fn Art)
120 pts Brighton – BBB +portfolio (Fn Art Pntg; Fn Art Sculp) (IB 30 pts); (Fn Art Crit Prac)
         (IB 32 pts)
         Cardiff Met – 120 pts (Fn Art)

Edinburgh – BBB (Fn Art) (IB 34 pts)
Edinburgh (CA) – BBB +portfolio (Fn Art MA; Illus) (IB 34 pts)
Huddersfield – BBB 120 pts +portfolio +interview (Contemp Art)
Leeds Beckett – 120 pts +interview (Fn Art) (IB 26 pts)
Northumbria – 120 pts incl art/photo (Fn Art) (IB 30 pts)
Norwich Arts – BBB incl art/des (Fn Art) (IB 32 pts)
Southampton (Winchester SA) – BBB incl art/des (Fn Art) (IB 30 pts)
Trinity Saint David – 120 pts +interview/portfolio (Fn Art Std Site Con)
(IB 32 pts)
York St John – 120 pts (Fn Art)
112 pts Aberystwyth – 112 pts incl art (Fn Art; Fn Art Art Hist)
Birmingham City – BBC 112 pts (Fn Art) (IB 28 pts)
Bournemouth Arts – BBC–BBB 112–120 pts +portfolio +interview (Fn Art)
(IB 32 pts)
Central Lancashire – 112 pts (Fn Art) (IB 28 pts)
Chester – BBC–BCC incl art des/fn art 112 pts (Fn Art) (IB 26 pts HL 5 vis arts)
De Montfort – 112 pts incl art des (Fn Art) (IB 28 pts)
Derby – 112 pts (Fn Art)
Gloucestershire – 112 pts +interview +portfolio (Fn Art)
Kingston – 112 pts (Fn Art)
Lincoln – 112 pts +interview (Fn Art)
Liverpool John Moores – 112–128 pts (Fn Art)
London (Gold) – BBC +portfolio (Fn Art)
London Met – 112 pts (Fn Art courses)
Manchester Met – 112 pts (Fn Art) (IB 26 pts)
Middlesex – 112 pts (Fn Art)
Northampton – 112 pts +portfolio +interview (Fn Art; Fn Art Pntg Drg)
Nottingham Trent – 112 pts +portfolio (Fn Art)
Oxford Brookes – BBC incl art (Fn Art) (IB 31 pts)
Plymouth – 112 pts (Fn Art Art Hist) (IB 24 pts)
Reading – 112 pts incl Fdn Art (IB 24–35 pts) (Fn Art)
Sheffield Hallam – 112 pts incl art des (Fn Art)
Southampton Solent – 112 pts +portfolio (Fn Art)
Sunderland – 112 pts (Fn Art)
Teesside – 112 pts +portfolio (Fn Art)
UWE Bristol – 112 pts (Fn Art) (IB 25 pts)
104 pts Bath Spa – 104 pts (Fn Art)
Coventry – BCC incl art/des (Fn Art Illus; Fn Art) (IB 28 pts)
Falmouth – 104–120 pts (Fn Art)
Leeds (CA) – 104 pts +portfolio (Fn Art)
Liverpool Hope – BCC–BBB 104–120 pts (Fn Art)
Plymouth – 104 pts +interview +portfolio (Fn Art) (IB 24 pts)
South Wales – BCC incl art des (Art Prac) (IB 29 pts)
Staffordshire – 104 pts (Fn Art)
Worcester – 104 pts (Fn Art)
96 pts Bolton – 96 pts +interview/portfolio (Fn Art)
Chichester – BCD (Fn Art courses) (IB 30 pts)
Cumbria – 96 pts (Fn Art)
East London – 96 pts +interview +portfolio (Fn Art) (IB 24 pts)
Glyndŵr – 96 pts (Fn Art)
Hertfordshire – 96 pts incl art (Fn Art) (IB 24 pts)
Ulster – 96 pts (Fn Art) (IB 24 pts)
Westminster – CCC–BB (Fn Art Mix Media) (IB 26 pts)
Wolverhampton – 96 pts +portfolio (Fn Art)
88 pts Creative Arts – 88 pts +portfolio (Fn Art courses)

New UCAS points Tariff: A* = 56 pts; A = 48 pts; B = 40 pts; C = 32 pts; D = 24 pts; E = 16 pts

80 pts   **Anglia Ruskin** – 80–96 pts (Fn Art) (IB 24 pts)
         Bedfordshire – 80 pts +portfolio (Fn Art) (IB 24 pts)
         Croydon (Univ Centre) – 80 pts (Fn Art)
         Hereford (CA) – 80 pts +portfolio +interview (Fn Art)
         Plymouth (CA) – 80 pts +portfolio (Fn Art)
64 pts   **Colchester (Inst)** – 64 pts +portfolio (Fn Art)
         UHI – CC incl Engl +portfolio (Fn Art Tex); CC +portfolio (Fn Art)
40 pts and below or other selection criteria (Foundation course, interview and portfolio inspection) Arts London; Arts London (Camberwell CA); Arts London (Chelsea CA); Arts London (Wimb CA); Bath Spa; Bedfordshire; Brighton; Bucks New; Cardiff Met; Central Lancashire; Coventry; Creative Arts; De Montfort; East London; Edinburgh (CA); Glyndŵr; HOW (Coll); Kingston; Leeds Beckett; Liverpool John Moores; London (Gold); Middlesex; Nottingham; Reading; Staffordshire Reg Fed (SURF); Trinity Saint David; UWE Bristol; West London; Westminster; West Thames (Coll).

Alternative offers
See **Chapter 6** and **Appendix 1** for grades/new UCAS Tariff points information for other examinations.

EXAMPLES OF COLLEGES OFFERING COURSES IN THIS SUBJECT FIELD
Most colleges. All are practical workshop courses. Bath (Coll); Blackpool and Fylde (Coll); Bradford (Coll); Bury (Coll); Central Bedfordshire (Coll); City and Islington (Coll); City of Oxford (Coll); Cornwall (Coll); Craven (Coll); Doncaster (Coll); Exeter (Coll); Grimsby (Univ Centre); Harrogate (Coll); Havering (Coll); Leicester (Coll); Liverpool City (Coll); Llandrillo (Coll); Menai (Coll); Newcastle (Coll); Northbrook (Coll); St Helens (Coll); Sheffield (Coll); Somerset (Coll); South Gloucestershire and Stroud (Coll); Stamford New (Coll); Sunderland (Coll); Tyne Met (Coll); Weymouth (Coll); Yorkshire Coast (Coll).

CHOOSING YOUR COURSE (SEE ALSO CH.1)
Universities and colleges teaching quality See www.qaa.ac.uk; http://unistats.direct.gov.uk.

Top research universities and colleges (REF 2014) See **Art and Design (General)**.

Examples of sandwich degree courses Coventry; Huddersfield; Ulster; Wolverhampton.

ADMISSIONS INFORMATION
Number of applicants per place (approx) Arts London (Chelsea CA) 5; Arts London (Wimb CA) (Sculp) 3; Bath Spa 8; Birmingham City 6; Bournemouth Arts 6; Cardiff Met 3; Central Lancashire 4; Creative Arts 2; Cumbria 4; De Montfort 5; Derby 3; Dundee 5; Gloucestershire 5; Kingston 9; Lincoln 4; Liverpool John Moores 3; London (Gold) 10; London (UCL) 26; London Met 11; Loughborough 4; Manchester Met 4; Middlesex 3; Newcastle 30; Northampton 3; Northumbria 4; Norwich Arts 3; Nottingham Trent 5; Portsmouth 6; Sheffield Hallam 4; Solihull (Coll) 4; Southampton (Winchester SA) 6; Staffordshire 3; Sunderland 3; UHI 2; UWE Bristol 3; Wirral Met (Coll) 3.

Advice to applicants and planning the UCAS personal statement Since this is a subject area that can be researched easily in art galleries, you should discuss not only your own style of work and your preferred subjects but also your opinions on various art forms, styles and periods. Keep up-to-date with public opinion on controversial issues. Give your reasons for wishing to pursue a course in Fine Art. Visits to galleries and related hobbies, for example reading, cinema, music, literature should be mentioned. Show the nature of your external involvement in art. (See also **Appendix 3**.) **Oxford** No deferred applications are accepted for this course; successful applicants average 11.5%.

Misconceptions about this course That Fine Art is simply art and design. Sixth-form applicants are often unaware of the importance of a Foundation Art course before starting a degree programme. **Bournemouth Arts** Applicants need to make the distinction between fine art and illustration.

Selection interviews Most institutions interview and require a portfolio of work. **Yes** Arts London (Chelsea CA), Brighton, Cardiff Met, Chester, Chichester, Cumbria, Falmouth, Kent, Leeds Beckett, Newcastle, Northumbria, Oxford (14%), Portsmouth, Southampton, York St John; **Some** Liverpool John Moores.

Interview advice and questions Questions asked on portfolio of work. Be prepared to answer questions on your stated opinions on your UCAS application and on current art trends and controversial topics reported in the press. Discussion covering the applicant's engagement with contemporary fine art practice. Visits to exhibitions, galleries etc. Ambitions for their own work. How do you perceive the world in a visual sense? Who is your favourite living artist and why? See also **Art and Design (General)** and **Chapter 5**. **UHI** Applicants are asked to produce a drawing in response to a set topic.

Reasons for rejection (non-academic) Lack of a fine art specialist portfolio. No intellectual grasp of the subject – only interested in techniques.

AFTER-RESULTS ADVICE

Offers to applicants repeating A-levels Same Anglia Ruskin, Arts London, Birmingham City, Cumbria, Manchester Met, Nottingham Trent, Staffordshire, Sunderland, UHI; **No** Oxford.

GRADUATE DESTINATIONS AND EMPLOYMENT (2013/14 HESA)

Graduates surveyed 3,175 **Employed** 1,305 **In voluntary employment** 155 **In further study** 490 **Assumed unemployed** 245

Career note See **Art and Design (General)**.

OTHER DEGREE SUBJECTS FOR CONSIDERATION

Art Gallery Management; History of Art; see other **Art and Design** tables.

ART and DESIGN (GRAPHIC DESIGN)

(including **Advertising, Animation, Design, Graphic Communication, Illustration** and **Visual Communication**; see also **Art and Design (Fine Art)**, **Art and Design (General)**, **Film, Radio, Video and TV Studies**)

Graphic Design ranges from the design of websites, books, magazines and newspapers to packaging and advertisements. Visual communication uses symbols as teaching aids and also includes TV graphics. An Art Foundation course is usually taken before entry to degree courses. Graphic Design students are probably the most fortunate in terms of the range of career opportunities open to them on graduation. These include advertising, animation, book and magazine illustration, film, interactive media design, typography, packaging, photography and work in publishing and television. Courses cover the essential element of creative thinking alongside the normal industrial practices of script-writing, character design, storyboarding, animation, and sound design.

Useful websites www.graphicdesign.about.com; www.graphic-design.com; www.allgraphicdesign.com; www.creativefuture.org.uk; www.designcouncil.org.uk

NB The points totals shown to the left of the institutions are for ease of reference only. It must not be assumed that Tariff points are always used by institutions or that they can be substituted for an offer in grades. The level of an offer is not necessarily indicative of the quality of a course.

COURSE OFFERS INFORMATION

Subject requirements/preferences See **Art and Design (General)**.

Your target offers and examples of degree courses
136 pts **Reading** – AAB–ABB (Graph Comms) (IB 35–32 pts)
128 pts **Brighton** – ABB +portfolio (Graph Des) (IB 32 pts)
        Dundee – ABB incl art des (Graph Des; Animat) (IB 34 pts)
        East Anglia – ABB (Comp Graph, Imag Multim) (IB 32 pts)
        Leeds – ABB (Graph Comm Des) (IB 34 pts)
        Loughborough – ABB (Graph Comm Illus)

Northumbria – 128 pts (Graph Des; Comp Sci Animat Graph Vision) (IB 31 pts)

120 pts **Birmingham City** – BBB 120 pts (Film Tech Vis Efcts) (IB 32 pts)

Bournemouth – 120–128 pts (Comp Vis Animat; Comp Animat Arts) (IB 31–32 pts)

Cardiff Met – 120 pts (Graph Comm)

Edinburgh – BBB (Graph Des) (IB 34 pts)

Edinburgh (CA) – BBB +portfolio (Graph Des; Intermed Art) (IB 34 pts)

Hertfordshire – 120 pts incl art (3D Comp Animat Modl; 2D Animat Chrctr Dig Media) (IB 28–30 pts)

Huddersfield – BBB 120 pts (Graph Des; Animat); BBB 120 pts +portfolio +interview (Contemp Art Illus; Illus)

Kent – BBB (Dig Art) (IB 34 pts)

Leeds Beckett – 120 pts (Gms Des; Comp Animat Vis Efcts; Graph Arts Des) (IB 26 pts)

Norwich Arts – BBB incl art/des (Graph Des; Illus; Film Mov Imag Prod; Animat; Graph Comm) (IB 32 pts)

Sheffield Hallam – 120 pts (Graph Des)

Southampton (Winchester SA) – BBB incl art/des (Graph Art) (IB 30 pts)

Trinity Saint David – 120 pts (3D Comp Animat; Illus; Graph Des) (IB 32 pts)

112 pts **Aberystwyth** – 112 pts (Comp Graph Vsn Gms)

Birmingham City – BBC 112 pts (Vis Comm (Film Animat); Vis Comm (Photo)) (IB 28 pts)

Bournemouth – 112–120 pts (Dig Media Des) (IB 30–31 pts)

Bournemouth Arts – BBC–BBB 112–120 pts +portfolio +interview (Graph Des; Illus; Animat Prod; Vis Comm) (IB 32 pts)

Bradford – BBC 112 pts (Comp Animat Vis Efcts)

Brighton – BBC +portfolio (Graph Des Dig Media) (IB 30 pts)

Central Lancashire – 112 pts (Graph Des; Adv) (IB 28 pts)

Chester – BBC–BCC 112 pts (Graph Des) (IB 26 pts HL 5 vis arts)

Derby – 112 pts +interview +portfolio (Graph Des); 112 pts (Animat)

East London – 112 pts (Animat Illus) (IB 24 pts)

Edge Hill – BBC 112 pts (Animat)

Glasgow Caledonian – BBC incl art des (3D Comp Animat) (IB 24 pts)

Gloucestershire – 112 pts +interview (Graph Des); 112 pts (Adv)

Greenwich – 112 pts (3D Dig Des Animat; Graph Dig Des)

Hull – 112 pts (Dig Des) (IB 28 pts)

Kingston – 112 pts +portfolio (Graph Des)

Lincoln – 112 pts incl art/des/media (Graph Des; Illus); 112 pts (Animat)

Liverpool John Moores – 112 pts (Graph Des Illus)

London Met – 112 pts incl art des (Graph Des)

Manchester Met – 112 pts +portfolio (Graph Des; Illus Animat) (IB 26 pts)

Middlesex – 112 pts +portfolio (Animat); 112 pts (Graph Des; Illus)

Northampton – 112 pts +portfolio +interview (Graph Comm; Illus)

Nottingham Trent – 112 pts (Graph Des)

Plymouth – 112 pts (Graph Comm Typo) (IB 24 pts); (Dig Art Tech) (IB 28 pts)

Portsmouth – 112 pts (Animat) (IB 26 pts)

Southampton Solent – 112 pts (Graph Des)

Sunderland – 112 pts (Illus Des; Adv Des; Animat Gms Art; Graph Des)

Teesside – 112 pts +interview/portfolio (Comp Gms Animat; Comp Gms Des; Comp Gms Art); 112 pts +portfolio (Graph Des)

UWE Bristol – 112 pts +portfolio (Animat; Graph Des) (IB 25 pts)

York St John – 112 pts (Graph Des)

104 pts **Bath Spa** – 104 pts (Graph Comm)

Central Lancashire – 104 pts (Animat) (IB 28 pts)

Coventry – BCC incl art/des (Illus Animat; Graph Des; Illus Graph) (IB 28 pts)

De Montfort – 104 pts incl art des (Graph Des; Graph Des Illus; Animat) (IB 28 pts HL 5 art des)

Derby – 104 pts (Illus)

Check **Chapter 3** for new university admission details and **Chapter 6** on how to read the subject tables.

Edinburgh Napier – BCC incl Engl+art/des (Graph Des) (IB 28 pts HL 5 Engl+art/des)

Falmouth – 104–120 pts +portfolio +interview (Animat Vis Efcts; Graph Des; Illus)

Leeds (CA) – 104 pts +portfolio (Graph Des; Animat; Vis Comm)

Robert Gordon – BCC (Comp Graph Animat) (IB 27 pts)

Sheffield Hallam – 104 pts (Animat)

South Wales – BCC incl art des (Graph Comm; Adv Des) (IB 29 pts)

Staffordshire – 104 pts (Graph Des; Crtn Cmc Arts; Illus)

Worcester – 104 pts (Graph Des Multim); 104 pts +interview +portfolio (Animat)

96 pts **Bolton** – 96 pts (Animat Illus)

Canterbury Christ Church – 96–112 pts (Graph Des)

Cumbria – 96 pts (Illus; Graph Des)

East London – 96 pts (Graph Des) (IB 24 pts); 96 pts +interview +portfolio (Illus) (IB 24 pts)

Glyndŵr – 96 pts (Des (Animat Vis Efcts Game Art); Des (Graph Des Multim); Graph Des Multim)

Hertfordshire – 96 pts incl art (Graph Des) (IB 24 pts)

Portsmouth – 96–112 pts (Illus) (IB 25 pts); (Graph Des) (IB 26 pts)

Staffordshire – 96 pts (Dig Film 3D Animat Tech)

Ulster – 96 pts (Animat) (IB 24 pts); 96 pts +portfolio (Graph Des Illust) (IB 24 pts)

Westminster – CCC–BB (Illus Vis Comm) (IB 26 pts); CCC (Animat) (IB 26 pts)

West Scotland – CCC (Comp Animat) (IB 24 pts); CCC incl art (Comp Animat Dig Art) (IB 24 pts)

Wolverhampton – 96 pts +portfolio (Vis Comm (Graph Des); Vis Comm (Illus))

88 pts **Creative Arts** – 88 pts (Animat; Graph Des; Graph Comm)

Glasgow Caledonian – CCD incl art des (Comp Gms (Art Animat)) (IB 24 pts)

80 pts **Anglia Ruskin** – 80–96 pts incl art/des/media (Illus Animat; Illus) (IB 24 pts); 80–96 pts (Graph Des) (IB 24 pts)

Bedfordshire – 80 pts (Animat; Adv Brnd Des) (IB 24 pts); 80 pts +portfolio (Graph Des) (IB 24 pts)

Blackburn (Coll) – 80 pts +portfolio (Illus Animat)

Bucks New – 80–96 pts (Crea Adv; Graph Arts; Animat Vis Efcts)

Hereford (CA) – 80 pts +portfolio +interview (Graph Media Des; Illus)

Plymouth (CA) – 80 pts +portfolio (Graph Des; Animat; Illus; Game Arts)

Southampton Solent – 80 pts (Animat)

Westminster – BB (Graph Comm Des) (IB 26 pts)

64 pts **Colchester (Inst)** – 64 pts +portfolio (Graph Des)

Ravensbourne – CC (Dig Adv Des; Graph Des; Mtn Graph; Animat) (IB 28 pts)

Stockport (Coll) – 64 pts (Graph Art Des)

40 pts and below or other selection criteria (Foundation course, interview and portfolio inspection) Arts London; Arts London (Camberwell CA); Arts London (Chelsea CA); Bath Spa; Bradford; Brighton; Bucks New; Coventry; Edinburgh (CA); Greenwich; Hertfordshire; HOW (Coll); Kent; Kingston; Leeds Beckett; Liverpool John Moores; Loughborough; Manchester (Coll); Oxford Brookes; Southampton (Winchester SA); UWE Bristol; West London; Westminster; Worcester.

32 pts **Arts London** – 32 pts +portfolio (Graph Des)

Alternative offers

See **Chapter 6** and **Appendix 1** for grades/new UCAS Tariff points information for other examinations.

EXAMPLES OF COLLEGES OFFERING COURSES IN THIS SUBJECT FIELD

Most colleges. Banbury and Bicester (Coll); Barking and Dagenham (Coll); Barnet and Southgate (Coll); Birmingham Met (Coll); Blackburn (Coll); Bristol City (Coll); Bury (Coll); Canterbury (Coll); Cleveland (CAD); Cornwall (Coll); Craven (Coll); Doncaster (Coll); Durham New (Coll); Exeter (Coll); Farnborough (CT); Harlow (Coll); Havering (Coll); Hugh Baird (Coll); Kirklees (Coll); Leeds (CA); Leicester (Coll); London UCK (Coll); Mid-Cheshire (Coll); Milton Keynes (Coll); Newcastle (Coll); Northbrook (Coll); Nottingham New (Coll); Oldham (Coll); Redbridge (Coll); Rotherham (CAT);

St Helens (Coll); Sheffield (Coll); Somerset (Coll); South Cheshire (Coll); South Gloucestershire and Stroud (Coll); Southport (Coll); Staffordshire Reg Fed (SURF); Stamford New (Coll); Stockport (Coll); Truro and Penwith (Coll); Tyne Met (Coll); West Kent (Coll); West Suffolk (Coll); Weston (Coll); Wigan and Leigh (Coll); York (Coll).

CHOOSING YOUR COURSE (SEE ALSO CH.1)

Universities and colleges teaching quality See www.qaa.ac.uk; http://unistats.direct.gov.uk.

Top research universities and colleges (REF 2014) See **Art and Design (General)**.

Examples of sandwich degree courses Aberystwyth; Arts London; Central Lancashire; Coventry; Hertfordshire; Huddersfield; Loughborough; Middlesex; Northumbria; Portsmouth; South Wales; Ulster; Wolverhampton.

ADMISSIONS INFORMATION

Number of applicants per place (approx) Anglia Ruskin (Illus) 3; Arts London 4; Bath Spa 9; Bournemouth Arts 6; Cardiff Met 5; Central Lancashire 5; Colchester (Inst) 3; Coventry 6; Creative Arts 5; Derby 5; Edinburgh Napier 7; Hertfordshire 6; Kingston 8; Lincoln 5; Liverpool John Moores 7; Loughborough 5; Manchester Met 8; Middlesex 3; Northampton 3; Northumbria 8; Norwich Arts 4; Nottingham Trent 6; Ravensbourne 9; Solihull (Coll) 3; Staffordshire 3; Teesside 5; Trinity Saint David 10; UWE Bristol 4; Wolverhampton 5.

Advice to applicants and planning the UCAS personal statement Discuss your special interest in this field and any commercial applications that have impressed you. Discuss the work you are enjoying at present and the range of media that you have explored. Show your interests in travel, architecture, the arts, literature, film, current affairs (see also **Appendix 3** for contact details of relevant professional associations). Have an awareness of the place of design in society.

Misconceptions about this course Bath Spa Some students think that they can start the course from A-levels; that a course in Illustration is simply 'doing small drawings'; and that Graphic Design is a soft option with little academic work.

Selection interviews All institutions interview and require a portfolio of work. **Yes** Brighton, Chester, Cumbria, Falmouth, Huddersfield, Leeds Beckett, London South Bank, Northumbria, Salford, Southampton, UWE Bristol, West London, Worcester, York St John; **Some** Liverpool John Moores.

Interview advice and questions Questions may be asked on recent trends in graphic design from the points of view of methods and designers and, particularly, art and the computer. Questions are usually asked on applicant's portfolio of work. See also **Art and Design (General)** and **Chapter 5**. **Nottingham Trent** Why graphic design? Why this course? Describe a piece of graphic design which has succeeded.

Reasons for rejection (non-academic) Not enough work in portfolio. Inability to think imaginatively. Lack of interest in the arts in general. Lack of drive. Tutor's statement indicating problems. Poorly constructed personal statement. Inability to talk about your work. Lack of knowledge about the chosen course. See also **Art and Design (General)**.

AFTER-RESULTS ADVICE

Offers to applicants repeating A-levels Same Bath Spa, Bournemouth Arts, Cardiff Met, Creative Arts, Lincoln, Manchester Met, Nottingham Trent, Staffordshire.

GRADUATE DESTINATIONS AND EMPLOYMENT (2013/14 HESA)

See **Art and Design (General)**.

Career note See **Art and Design (General)**.

OTHER DEGREE SUBJECTS FOR CONSIDERATION

Art Gallery Management; Film and Video Production; History of Art; Multimedia Design, Photography and Digital Imaging. See also other **Art and Design** tables.

Check **Chapter 3** for new university admission details and **Chapter 6** on how to read the subject tables.

ART and DESIGN (INTERIOR, PRODUCT and INDUSTRIAL DESIGN)

(including **Design Technology, Footwear Design, Furniture Design, Interior Design, Product Design, Theatre Design** and **Transport Design**; see also **Architecture, Art and Design (3d Design)**)

The field of industrial design is extensive and degree studies are usually preceded by an Art Foundation course. Product Design is one of the most common courses in which technological studies (involving materials and methods of production) are integrated with creative design in the production of a range of household and industrial products. Other courses on offer include Furniture Design, Interior, Theatre, Museum and Exhibition, Automotive and Transport Design. It should be noted that some Product Design courses have an engineering bias. Interior Design courses involve architectural considerations and courses will include aspects of building practices, materials, products and finishes. Historical studies of period designs and styles will also be included: see **Subject requirements/ preferences** below. These are stimulating courses but graduate opportunities in this field are very limited. Good courses will have good industrial contacts for sandwich courses or shorter work placements – check with course leaders (or students) before applying.

Useful websites www.ergonomics.org.uk; www.creativefuture.org.uk; www.productdesignforums.com; www.carbodydesign.com; www.shoe-design.com; www.bild.org.uk; www.csd.org.uk; www. designcouncil.org.uk; www.theatredesign.org.uk

NB The points totals shown to the left of the institutions are for ease of reference only. It must not be assumed that Tariff points are always used by institutions or that they can be substituted for an offer in grades. The level of an offer is not necessarily indicative of the quality of a course.

COURSE OFFERS INFORMATION

Subject requirements/preferences Interior Architecture Design courses require an art portfolio. **AL** Check Product Design, Industrial Design and Engineering Design course requirements since these will often require Mathematics and/or Physics.

Your target offers and examples of degree courses

144 pts **Glasgow** – AAA incl maths+phys (Prod Des Eng MEng) (IB 38–36 pts)
        Leeds – AAA (Prod Des) (IB 35 pts)
136 pts **Glasgow** – AAB–BBB incl maths+phys (Prod Des Eng) (IB 36–34 pts)
        Liverpool – AAB incl maths+sci/des tech (Ind Des MEng) (IB 35 pts HL 5 maths+phys)
        Nottingham – AAB incl maths (Prod Des Manuf) (IB 34 pts)
        Queen's Belfast – AAB incl maths+sci/tech (Prod Des Eng MEng)
        Strathclyde – AAB–BBB (Prod Des Eng MEng; Prod Eng Mgt MEng) (IB 36 pts HL 5 maths+phys)
128 pts **Brighton** – ABB incl tech (Prod Des Tech (Yr Ind); Spo Prod Des (Yr Ind); Prod Des (Yr Ind)) (IB 32 pts)
        Brunel – ABB (Ind Des Tech; Prod Des Eng; Prod Des) (IB 31 pts)
        Dundee – ABB incl art des (Inter Des) (IB 34 pts)
        Glasgow (SA) – ABB (Inter Des) (IB 30 pts); ABB incl lang (Prod Des) (IB 30 pts)
        Liverpool – ABB incl maths+sci/des tech (Ind Des) (IB 33 pts HL 5 maths+phys)
        Loughborough – ABB incl maths/phys+des/art (Prod Des Tech) (IB 34–32 pts); ABB (Ind Des Tech) (IB 34–32 pts)
        Northumbria – 128 pts (Inter Archit) (IB 31 pts)
        Oxford Brookes – ABB (Inter Archit) (IB 34–32 pts)
        Strathclyde – ABB–BBB (Prod Des Innov) (IB 34 pts HL 5 maths/phys); (Prod Eng Mgt) (IB 34 pts HL 5 maths+phys)
        Sussex – ABB–BBB incl art/des (Prod Des) (IB 34–32 pts)
120 pts **Aston** – BBB–ABB (Ind Prod Des; Trans Prod Des) (IB 32 pts)

Cardiff Met – 120 pts (Prod Des)

Edinburgh – BBB (Prod Des; Inter Des) (IB 34 pts)

Edinburgh (CA) – BBB +portfolio (Inter Des; Prod Des) (IB 34 pts)

Huddersfield – BBB 120 pts +portfolio +interview (Inter Des); BBB 120 pts +portfolio (Prod Des)

Leeds Beckett – 120 pts (Des Prod) (IB 26 pts); 120 pts incl art/des (Inter Archit Des) (IB 26 pts)

London Met – 120 pts incl art (Inter Archit Des)

Nottingham Trent – 120 pts (Inter Archit Des)

Plymouth – 120 pts (3D Des courses) (IB 24 pts)

Queen's Belfast – BBB incl maths+sci/tech (Prod Des Eng)

Sheffield Hallam – 120 pts (Prod Des)

Trinity Saint David – 120 pts (Auto Des; Prod Des) (IB 32 pts)

UWE Bristol – 120 pts (Inter Archit) (IB 26 pts)

Westminster – BBB +portfolio (Inter Archit) (IB 28 pts)

112 pts **Birmingham City** – BBC 112 pts (Prod Des; Inter Des) (IB 28 pts)

Bournemouth Arts – BBC–BBB 112–120 pts (Inter Archit Des) (IB 32 pts)

Central Lancashire – 112 pts (Inter Des; Prod Des) (IB 28 pts)

Coventry – BBC incl art/des (Prod Des) (IB 29 pts)

De Montfort – 112 pts incl art des (Inter Des; Prod Des; Ftwr Des; Prod Furn Des; Furn Des) (IB 28 pts)

Derby – 112 pts (Prod Des)

Kingston – 112 pts +portfolio (Inter Des; Prod Furn Des)

Lincoln – 112 pts incl art/des/media (Prod Des); 112 pts incl art/des (Inter Archit Des)

London (Royal Central Sch SpDr) – BBC +interview (Thea Prac Prod Ltg; Thea Prac Thea Ltg Des); BBC +interview +portfolio (Thea Prac Prop Mak; Thea Prac Scnc Art; Thea Prac Scnc Constr)

London South Bank – BBC 112 pts (Prod Des)

Manchester Met – 112 pts +portfolio (Inter Des) (IB 26 pts)

Middlesex – 112 pts (Inter Des)

Northampton – 112 pts +portfolio +interview (Inter Des)

Nottingham Trent – 112 pts +portfolio (Thea Des); 112 pts (Furn Prod Des; Prod Des)

Sheffield Hallam – 112 pts (Inter Des; Prod Des (Furn))

Southampton Solent – 112 pts (Prod Des)

Suffolk (Univ Campus) – 112 pts (App Inter Des)

Teesside – 112 pts +portfolio (Inter Des; Prod Des)

UWE Bristol – 112 pts (Crea Prod Des; Inter Des; Prod Des Tech) (IB 25 pts)

York St John – 112 pts (Prod Des; Inter Des)

104 pts **Bournemouth** – 104–120 pts (Prod Des; Ind Des) (IB 28–31 pts)

Coventry – BCC incl art/des (Inter Des) (IB 28 pts)

Dundee – BCC–CCC incl art des (Prod Des) (IB 30 pts)

Falmouth – 104 pts (Inter Des)

Manchester Met – BCC-BBC 104–112 pts (Prod Des Tech) (IB 28 pts)

Northampton – 104–112 pts (Prod Des)

Portsmouth – 104–120 pts (Inter Archit Des) (IB 25 pts)

South Wales – BCC incl art des (Inter Des) (IB 29 pts)

Staffordshire – 104 pts +portfolio +interview (Prod Des); 104 pts (Trans Des)

96 pts **East London** – 96 pts incl art des (Inter Des; Prod Des) (IB 24 pts)

Edinburgh Napier – CCC incl Engl (Inter Spat Des) (IB 26 pts HL 5 Engl); CCC (Prod Des)

Hertfordshire – 96 pts incl art +portfolio +interview (Inter Archit Des) (IB 24 pts); 96 pts incl art (Prod Des; Ind Des) (IB 24 pts)

Portsmouth – 96–120 pts incl sci/tech/des (Prod Des Innov) (IB 26 pts HL 10 pts)

Rose Bruford (Coll) – 96 pts (Ltg Des)

Salford – 96–112 pts incl art des/tech (Inter Des) (IB 26 pts)

Southampton Solent – 96 pts (Inter Des Decr)

        Ulster – 96 pts +portfolio (Prod Furn Des) (IB 24 pts)

        Wolverhampton – 96 pts +portfolio (Inter Des; Prod Des)

88 pts **Creative Arts** – 88 pts +portfolio (Prod Des)

        Glasgow Caledonian – CCD incl art des (Comp Gms (Art Animat)) (IB 24 pts)

80 pts **Anglia Ruskin** – 80–96 pts incl art/des/media (Inter Des) (IB 24 pts)

        Bangor – 80–88 pts (Prod Des)

        Bedfordshire – 80 pts (Inter Des Rtl Brnd) (IB 24 pts)

        London Met – 80 pts incl art des/tech (Furn)

64 pts **Liverpool (LIPA)** – CC 64 pts (Thea Perf Des; Thea Perf Tech)

        London Regent's – CC +portfolio (Inter Des)

        Ravensbourne – CC (Des Prod; Inter Des Env Archit) (IB 28 pts)

40 pts and below or other selection criteria (Foundation course, interview and portfolio inspection) Arts London; Arts London (Chelsea CA); Arts London (Wimb CA); Bath Spa; Bolton; Bournemouth Arts; Brighton; Bucks New; Cardiff Met; De Montfort; Dundee; Edinburgh (CA); Glasgow Caledonian; Heriot-Watt; Hertfordshire; HOW (Coll); Kingston; Lincoln; London South Bank; Royal Welsh (CMusDr); Southampton Solent.

Alternative offers

See **Chapter 6** and **Appendix 1** for grades/new UCAS Tariff points information for other examinations.

EXAMPLES OF COLLEGES OFFERING COURSES IN THIS SUBJECT FIELD

Accrington and Rossendale (Coll); Banbury and Bicester (Coll); Barking and Dagenham (Coll); Bradford (Coll); Bury (Coll); Calderdale (Coll); Chichester (Coll); Doncaster (Coll); East Riding (Coll); Gloucestershire (Coll); Grimsby (Univ Centre); Harrogate (Coll); Hartlepool (CFE); Havering (Coll); Hull (Coll); Manchester (Coll); Moulton (Coll); Newcastle (Coll); North Warwickshire and Hinckley (Coll); Sir Gâr (Coll); Somerset (Coll); South Devon (Coll); South Essex (Coll); Stockport (Coll); Truro and Penwith (Coll); West Suffolk (Coll).

CHOOSING YOUR COURSE (SEE ALSO CH.1)

Universities and colleges teaching quality See www.qaa.ac.uk; http://unistats.direct.gov.uk.

Top research universities and colleges (REF 2014) See **Art and Design (General)**.

Examples of sandwich degree courses Aston; Bournemouth; Bradford; Brighton; Brunel; Coventry; De Montfort; Huddersfield; Lincoln; Liverpool John Moores; London South Bank; Loughborough; Manchester Met; Middlesex; Nottingham Trent; Portsmouth; Queen's Belfast; Sheffield Hallam; Staffordshire; Sussex; UWE Bristol; Wolverhampton.

ADMISSIONS INFORMATION

Number of applicants per place (approx) Arts London 2; Arts London (Chelsea CA) 2; Arts London (Wimb CA) 2; Aston 6; Bath Spa 4; Birmingham City (Inter Des) 9; Bolton 1; Brunel 4; Cardiff Met 6; Central Lancashire 7; Coventry 5; Creative Arts 4; De Montfort 5; Derby 2; Edinburgh Napier 6; Loughborough 9; Manchester Met 2; Middlesex (Inter Archit Des) 4; Northampton (Prod Des) 2; Northumbria 4; Nottingham Trent (Inter Archit Des) 7, (Prod Des) 5; Portsmouth 3; Ravensbourne (Inter Des) 4, (Prod Des) 7; Salford 6; Shrewsbury (CAT) 6; Staffordshire 3; Teesside 3; Trinity Saint David 3.

Advice to applicants and planning the UCAS personal statement Your knowledge of design in all fields should be described, including any special interests you may have, for example in domestic, rail and road aspects of design, and visits to exhibitions, motor shows. **School/college reference:** tutors should make it clear that the applicant's knowledge, experience and attitude match the chosen course – not simply higher education in general. Admissions tutors look for knowledge of interior design and interior architecture, experience in three-dimensional design projects (which include problem-solving and sculptural demands), model-making experience in diverse materials, experience with two-dimensional illustration and colour work, and knowledge of computer-aided design.

Photography is also helpful, and also CAD/computer skills. See also **Art and Design (Graphic Design)**.

Misconceptions about this course Theatre Design is sometimes confused with Theatre Architecture or an academic course in Theatre Studies. **Birmingham City** (Inter Des) Some applicants believe that it is an interior decorating course (carpets and curtains). **Lincoln** (Musm Exhib Des) This is a design course, not a museum course. **Portsmouth** (Inter Des) Some students think that this is about interior decorating after Laurence Llewelyn-Bowen!

Selection interviews Most institutions will interview and require a portfolio of work. **Yes** Brunel, Cardiff Met, Chester, Dundee, Falmouth, Huddersfield, Northumbria, Salford, UWE Bristol, York St John; **Some** Staffordshire.

Interview advice and questions Applicants' portfolios of artwork form an important talking-point throughout the interview. Applicants should be able to discuss examples of current design and new developments in the field and answer questions on the aspects of industrial design which interest them. See also **Art and Design (General)** and **Chapter 5**. **Creative Arts** No tests. Discuss any visits to modern buildings and new developments, eg British Museum Great Court or the Louvre Pyramid.

Reasons for rejection (non-academic) Not hungry enough! Mature students without formal qualifications may not be able to demonstrate the necessary mathematical or engineering skills. Poor quality and organisation of portfolio. Lack of interest. Inappropriate dress. Lack of enthusiasm. Insufficient portfolio work (eg exercises instead of projects). Lack of historical knowledge of interior design. Weak oral communication. See also **Art and Design (General)**. **Creative Arts** Not enough three-dimensional model-making. Poor sketching and drawing.

AFTER-RESULTS ADVICE
Offers to applicants repeating A-levels Same Birmingham City, Bournemouth, Creative Arts, Nottingham Trent, Salford, Staffordshire.

GRADUATE DESTINATIONS AND EMPLOYMENT (2013/14 HESA)
See **Art and Design (General)**.

Career note See **Art and Design (General)**.

OTHER DEGREE SUBJECTS FOR CONSIDERATION
Architectural Studies; Architecture; Art Gallery Management; Design (Manufacturing Systems); History of Art; Manufacturing Engineering; Multimedia and Communication Design and subjects in other **Art and Design** tables.

ART and DESIGN (3D DESIGN)

(including **Ceramics, Design Crafts, Glassmaking, Jewellery, Metalwork, Silversmithing, Plastics and Woodwork**; see also **Art and Design (General), Art and Design (Interior, Product and Industrial Design)**)

This field covers a range of specialisations, which are involved in the manufacture of products in metal, ceramics, glass and wood. Some courses approach the study in a broad, comprehensive manner whilst other universities offer specialised courses in subjects such Silversmithing and Jewellery (Glasgow School of Art, London Metropolitan, and Sheffield Hallam), or Contemporary Jewellery Fashion Accessories (Staffordshire University). The Birmingham City University course in Horology is the only course in the UK offering the study of time measurement and watches and clocks, both mechanical and electronic.

Useful websites www.ergonomics.org.uk; www.creativefuture.org.uk; www.top3D.net; www.glassassociation.co.uk; www.bja.org.uk; www.cpaceramics.com; www.ccskills.org.uk; www.dandad.org; www.designcouncil.org.uk

NB The points totals shown to the left of the institutions are for ease of reference only. It must not be assumed that Tariff points are always used by institutions or that they can be substituted for an offer in grades. The level of an offer is not necessarily indicative of the quality of a course.

COURSE OFFERS INFORMATION

Subject requirements/preferences See **Art and Design (General)**.

Your target offers and examples of degree courses

128 pts **Dundee** – ABB incl art des (Jewel Metal Des) (IB 34 pts)
Glasgow (SA) – ABB (Silver Jewel) (IB 30 pts)

120 pts **Cardiff Met** – 120 pts (Ceram)
Edinburgh (CA) – BBB +portfolio (Sculp) (IB 34 pts)
Hertfordshire – 120 pts incl art (3D Comp Animat Modl) (IB 28–30 pts)
Northumbria – 120 pts (3D Des) (IB 30 pts)
Plymouth – 120 pts (3D Des courses) (IB 24 pts)

112 pts **Birmingham City** – BBC 112 pts (Horol) (IB 28 pts)
Bournemouth Arts – BBC–BBB 112–120 pts +interview (Modl) (IB 32 pts)
De Montfort – 112 pts (Des Crafts) (IB 28 pts)
Greenwich – 112 pts (3D Dig Des Animat)
Manchester Met – 112 pts (3D Des) (IB 26 pts)
Nottingham Trent – 112 pts +portfolio (Decr Arts)
Sheffield Hallam – 112 pts (Jewel Mtlwk)
Sunderland – 112 pts (Glass Ceram)

104 pts **Bath Spa** – 104 pts (3D Des (Id Mat Obj))
Liverpool Hope – BCC–BBB 104–120 pts (Des)
Staffordshire – 104 pts (3D Des (Contemp Jewel Fash Accs))
Stranmillis (UC) – BCC (Tech Des Educ QTS)

96 pts **Glyndŵr** – 96 pts (App Arts)
Wolverhampton – 96 pts (App Arts)

88 pts **Creative Arts** – 88 pts (Contemp Jewel); 88 pts +portfolio (Silver Gold Jewel)

80 pts **Hereford (CA)** – 80 pts +portfolio +interview (Jewel Des; Arst Blksmthg)
Plymouth (CA) – 80 pts +portfolio (Ceram Gls; Jewel)

72 pts **Robert Gordon** – BC incl art/des (3D Des) (IB 24 pts)

64 pts **Colchester (Inst)** – 64 pts +portfolio (3D Des Crft)

48 pts **Birmingham City** – DD 48 pts (Jewel Silver) (IB 24 pts)

40 pts and below or other selection criteria (Foundation course, interview and portfolio inspection) Arts London; Arts London (Camberwell CA); Bath Spa; Bedfordshire; Brighton; Bucks New; Central Lancashire; Dundee; East London; Edinburgh (CA); Greenwich; Hertfordshire; Lincoln; Loughborough; Menai (Coll); Middlesex; Northampton; Northbrook (Coll); Northumbria; Plymouth; Staffordshire Reg Fed (SURF); York St John.

32 pts **Arts London** – 32 pts +portfolio (3D Des) (IB 28 pts)

Alternative offers
See **Chapter 6** and **Appendix 1** for grades/new UCAS Tariff points information for other examinations.

EXAMPLES OF COLLEGES OFFERING COURSES IN THIS SUBJECT FIELD
Barking and Dagenham (Coll); Bedford (Coll); Bury (Coll); Gloucestershire (Coll); Havering (Coll); HOW (Coll); London UCK (Coll); Oldham (Coll); Sir Gâr (Coll); South Devon (Coll); York (Coll).

CHOOSING YOUR COURSE (SEE ALSO CH.1)
Universities and colleges teaching quality See www.qaa.ac.uk; http://unistats.direct.gov.uk.

Top research universities and colleges (REF 2014) See **Art and Design (General)**.

ADMISSIONS INFORMATION

Number of applicants per place (approx) Arts London (Ceram) 2; Arts London (Camberwell CA) 2, (Ceram) 3, (Jewel) 2; Bath Spa 3; Birmingham City 4, (Jewel) 5; Brighton 3; Creative Arts 4; De Montfort 3; Dundee 5; Manchester Met 5; Middlesex (3D Des) 4, (Jewel) 4; Portsmouth 3.

Advice to applicants and planning the UCAS personal statement Describe your art studies and your experience of different types of materials used. Discuss your special interest in your chosen field. Compare your work with that of professional artists and designers and describe your visits to museums, art galleries, exhibitions etc. Submit a portfolio of recent work to demonstrate drawing skills, visual awareness, creativity and innovation, showing examples of three-dimensional work in photographic or model form. See also **Art and Design (Graphic Design)**.

Selection interviews All institutions will interview and require a portfolio of work.

Interview advice and questions Questions focus on the artwork presented in the student's portfolio. See also **Art and Design (General)** and **Chapter 5**.

Reasons for rejection (non-academic) Lack of pride in their work. No ideas. See also **Art and Design (General)**.

AFTER-RESULTS ADVICE

Offers to applicants repeating A-levels Same Brighton, Creative Arts, Dundee, Manchester Met.

GRADUATE DESTINATIONS AND EMPLOYMENT (2013/14 HESA)

See **Art and Design (General)**.

Career note See **Art and Design (General)**.

OTHER DEGREE SUBJECTS FOR CONSIDERATION

Design Technology; see other **Art and Design** tables.

ASIA-PACIFIC STUDIES

(including **East** and **South Asian Studies**; see also **Chinese, Japanese, Languages**)

These courses focus on the study of the cultures, the politics, economic issues and the languages of this region of the world, such as Korean, Sanskrit, Thai and Vietnamese. The Leeds course provides Joint Honours combinations with eight options. Work experience during undergraduate years will help students to focus their interests. Many courses have a language bias or are taught jointly with other subjects.

Useful websites www.dur.ac.uk/oriental.museum; www.asia-alliance.org; www.bacsuk.org.uk

NB The points totals shown to the left of the institutions are for ease of reference only. It must not be assumed that Tariff points are always used by institutions or that they can be substituted for an offer in grades. The level of an offer is not necessarily indicative of the quality of a course.

COURSE OFFERS INFORMATION

Subject requirements/preferences GCSE A language at grade A–C. **AL** A language may be required.

Your target offers and examples of degree courses
152 pts Cambridge – A*AA (As Mid E St) (IB 40–41 pts HL 776)
144 pts Oxford – AAA (Orntl St) (IB 39 pts)
136 pts London (SOAS) – AAB–ABB (S As St 3/4 yrs; SE As St courses; Viet Joint Hons) (IB 35 pts)
          Nottingham – AAB (Mgt Chin St) (IB 34 pts)
          Sheffield – AAB–ABB (Kor St Joint Hons) (IB 35–34 pts)
128 pts Leeds – ABB (As Pacif St (Int); As Pacif St; Int Rel Thai St) (IB 34 pts)
          Sheffield – ABB (Jap St Joint Hons; E As St; Jap St; Kor St) (IB 34 pts)
112 pts Central Lancashire – 112–128 pts (As Pacif St)

Alternative offers
See **Chapter 6** and **Appendix 1** for grades/new UCAS Tariff points information for other examinations.

CHOOSING YOUR COURSE (SEE ALSO CH.1)

Universities and colleges teaching quality See www.qaa.ac.uk; http://unistats.direct.gov.uk.

Top research universities and colleges (REF 2014) See **Languages**.

Examples of sandwich degree courses Central Lancashire.

ADMISSIONS INFORMATION

Number of applicants per place (approx) London (SOAS) 4, (Thai) 2, (Burm) 1.

Advice to applicants and planning the UCAS personal statement Connections with, and visits to, South and South East Asia should be mentioned. You should give some indication of what impressed you and your reasons for wishing to study these subjects. An awareness of the geography, culture and politics of the area also should be shown on the UCAS application. Show your skills in learning a foreign language (if choosing a language course), interest in current affairs of the region, experience of travel and self-discipline.

Selection interviews Yes Cambridge, Oxford (Orntl St) 31%.

Interview advice and questions General questions are usually asked that relate to applicants' reasons for choosing degree courses in this subject area and to their background knowledge of the various cultures. See also **Chapter 5**.

GRADUATE DESTINATIONS AND EMPLOYMENT (2013/14 HESA)

South Asian Studies graduates surveyed 40 **Employed** 30 **In voluntary employment** 0 **In further study** 0 **Assumed unemployed** 0

Other Asian Studies graduates surveyed 30 **Employed** 10 **In voluntary employment** 0 **In further study** 5 **Assumed unemployed** 5

Career note Graduates enter a wide range of careers covering business and administration, retail work, education, transport, finance, community and social services. Work experience during undergraduate years will help students to focus their interests. Graduates may have opportunities of using their languages in a range of occupations.

OTHER DEGREE SUBJECTS FOR CONSIDERATION

Anthropology; Development Studies; Far Eastern Languages; Geography; History; International Relations; Politics; Social Studies.

ASTRONOMY and ASTROPHYSICS

(including **Planetary Science** and **Space Science**; see also **Geology/Geological Sciences, Physics**)

All Astronomy-related degrees are built on a core of mathematics and physics which, in the first two years, is augmented by an introduction to the theory and practice of astronomy or astrophysics. Astronomy emphasises observational aspects of the science and includes a study of the planetary system whilst Astrophysics tends to pursue the subject from a more theoretical standpoint. Some universities have onsite observatories (Central Lancashire and Lancaster). Courses often combine Mathematics or Physics with Astronomy.

Useful websites www.ras.org.uk; www.scicentral.com; www.iop.org; www.britastro.org

NB The points totals shown to the left of the institutions are for ease of reference only. It must not be assumed that Tariff points are always used by institutions or that they can be substituted for an offer in grades. The level of an offer is not necessarily indicative of the quality of a course.

COURSE OFFERS INFORMATION

Subject requirements/preferences GCSE English and a foreign language may be required by some universities; specified grades may be stipulated for some subjects. **AL** Mathematics and Physics usually required.

Your target offers and examples of degree courses

160 pts **Cambridge** – A*A*A incl sci/maths (Nat Sci (Astro)) (IB 40–41 pts HL 776)

Durham – A*A*A incl phys+maths (Phys Astron (MPhys)) (IB 38 pts)

Manchester – A*A*A–A*AA incl phys+maths (Phys Astro) (IB 39–38 pts)

152 pts **Birmingham** – A*AA–AAAA incl maths+phys (Phys Astro) (IB 32 pts HL 766)

Exeter – A*AA–AAB incl maths+phys (Phys Astro) (IB 38–34 pts HL 6 maths/phys+5 maths/ phys); A*AA–AAB incl maths+sci (Nat Sci) (IB 36–32 pts HL 5 maths+sci)

Lancaster – A*AA incl phys+maths (Phys Astro Cosmo MPhys) (IB 38 pts); A*AA incl phys and maths (Phys Ptcl Phys Cosmo MPhys) (IB 38 pts)

Nottingham – A*AA–AAA incl maths+phys (Phys Theor Astro; Phys Astron) (IB 34 pts)

144 pts **Bristol** – AAA–AAB incl maths+phys (Phys Astro) (IB 36–34 pts HL 6 maths 6/5 phys)

Cardiff – AAA–ABB incl phys+maths (Phys Astron; Phys Astron MPhys) (IB 34–32 pts HL 6 phys+maths); AAA–AAB incl maths+phys (Astro MPhys) (IB 34–32 pts HL 6 phys+maths); AAA–ABB (Astro) (IB 34–32 pts)

Edinburgh – AAA–ABB incl maths phys (Astro) (IB 37–32 pts)

Lancaster – AAA incl phys+maths (Phys Astro Cosmo; Phys Ptcl Phys Cosmo) (IB 36 pts)

London (RH) – AAA–AAB incl maths+phys (Astro) (IB 32 pts HL 6 maths+phys)

London (UCL) – AAA incl maths+phys (Astro) (IB 38 pts HL 6 maths+phys)

St Andrews – AAA incl maths+phys (Astro) (IB 38 pts)

Southampton – AAA incl maths+phys (Phys Astron MPhys) (IB 36 pts HL 6 maths+phys)

Sussex – AAA incl maths+phys (Astro) (IB 35 pts HL 6 maths+phys)

York – AAA–AAB incl maths+phys (Phys Astro) (IB 36–35 pts HL 6 maths+phys)

136 pts **Glasgow** – AAB–BBB incl maths+phys (Astron; Phys Astro) (IB 36–34 pts)

Leeds – AAB incl phys+maths (Phys Astro) (IB 35 pts HL 5 phys+maths)

Leicester – AAB incl phys+maths (Phys Astro; Phys Spc Sci Tech; Phys Planet Sci) (IB 32 pts)

London (QM) – AAB–ABB incl maths+phys 136–128 pts (Astro) (IB 34–30 pts HL 6 maths+phys); AAB–ABB incl phys+maths 136–128 pts (Astro MSci) (IB 34–30 pts HL 6 maths+phys)

Sheffield – AAB–ABB incl maths+phys (Phys Astro) (IB 35 pts HL 6 maths+phys)

Surrey – AAB incl maths+phys (Phys Astron; Phys Nucl Astro) (IB 35 pts)

Sussex – AAB–ABB incl maths+phys (Phys Astro) (IB 34 pts HL 5 maths+phys)

128 pts **Hertfordshire** – 128 pts incl maths+phys (Astro; Phys) (IB 32 pts)

Kent – ABB incl maths+phys (Astron Spc Sci Astro) (IB 34 pts); ABB incl maths+phys (Phys Astro) (IB 34 pts)

Kingston – 128 pts incl maths+sci (Aerosp Eng Astnaut Spc Tech MEng)

Liverpool – ABB incl phys+maths (Phys Astron) (IB 33 pts HL 6 phys+maths)

Loughborough – ABB incl maths+phys (Phys Astro Cosmo) (IB 34 pts)

Manchester – ABB incl maths/phys (Geol Planet Sci) (IB 33 pts HL 5 maths/phys)

Swansea – ABB–BBB incl maths+phys (Phys Ptcl Phys Cosmo) (IB 34–32 pts)

120 pts **Central Lancashire** – 120 pts (Astro) (IB 30 pts)

Keele – BBB/ABC incl phys+maths (Astro) (IB 32 pts HL 5 phys+maths)

Liverpool John Moores – 120–136 pts (Phys Astron) (IB 24–28 pts)

London (Birk) – 120 pts (Planet Sci Astron)

Nottingham Trent – 120 pts incl maths+phys (Phys Astro)

Queen's Belfast – BBB incl maths+phys (Phys Astro)

112 pts **Aberystwyth** – 112 pts incl maths+phys/comp (Spc Sci Robot)

Hull – 112 pts incl maths+phys (Phys Astro) (IB 28 pts HL 5 maths+phys)

Kingston – 112 pts incl maths+sci (Aerosp Eng Astnaut Spc Tech)

Check **Chapter 3** for new university admission details and **Chapter 6** on how to read the subject tables.

Alternative offers
See **Chapter 6** and **Appendix 1** for grades/new UCAS Tariff points information for other examinations.

CHOOSING YOUR COURSE (SEE ALSO CH.1)
Universities and colleges teaching quality See www.qaa.ac.uk; http://unistats.direct.gov.uk.

Top research universities and colleges (REF 2014) See **Physics**.

Examples of sandwich degree courses Cardiff; Hertfordshire; Kingston; Surrey.

ADMISSIONS INFORMATION
Number of applicants per place (approx) Bristol 8; Cardiff 6; Durham 3; Hertfordshire 5; Leicester 7; London (QM) 6; London (RH) 6; London (UCL) 11; Newcastle 7; Southampton 6.

Advice to applicants and planning the UCAS personal statement Books and magazines you have read on astronomy and astrophysics are an obvious source of information. Describe your interests and why you have chosen this subject. Visits to observatories would also be important. (See also **Appendix 3**.) **Bristol** Deferred entry accepted. **York** Advanced Diploma not generally accepted.

Misconceptions about this course Career opportunities are not as limited as some students think. These courses involve an extensive study of maths and physics, opening many opportunities for graduates such as geodesy, rocket and satellite studies and engineering specialisms.

Selection interviews Yes Bristol, Cambridge, London (QM), London (UCL); **Some** Cardiff.

Interview advice and questions You will probably be questioned on your study of physics and the aspects of the subject you most enjoy. Questions in the past have included: Can you name a recent development in physics which will be important in the future? Describe a physics experiment, indicating any errors and exactly what it was intended to prove. Explain weightlessness. What is a black hole? What are the latest discoveries in space? See also **Chapter 5**. **Southampton** Entrance examination for year-abroad courses.

AFTER-RESULTS ADVICE
Offers to applicants repeating A-levels Higher St Andrews; **Same** Cardiff, Durham, London (UCL); **No** Cambridge.

GRADUATE DESTINATIONS AND EMPLOYMENT (2013/14 HESA)
Graduates surveyed 295 **Employed** 115 **In voluntary employment** 5 **In further study** 145 **Assumed unemployed** 30

Career note The number of posts for professional astronomers is limited although some technological posts are occasionally offered in observatories. However, degree courses include extensive mathematics and physics so many graduates can look towards related fields including telecommunications and electronics.

OTHER DEGREE SUBJECTS FOR CONSIDERATION
Aeronautical/Aerospace Engineering; Computer Science; Earth Sciences; Geology; Geophysics; Mathematics; Meteorology; Mineral Sciences; Oceanography; Physics.

BIOCHEMISTRY

(see also **Biological Sciences, Chemistry, Food Science/Studies and Technology, Pharmacy and Pharmaceutical Sciences**)

Biochemistry is the study of life at molecular level – how genes and proteins regulate cells, tissues and ultimately whole organisms – you! It's a subject which provides the key to understanding how diseases arise and how they can be treated, it is the core of many areas of biology and is responsible for a large number of breakthroughs in medicine and biotechnology. At Newcastle, Year 1 of the course consists of modules in cell biology, biochemistry, microbiology, immunology, genetics, pharmacology and physiology with transfers between degrees possible at the end of the year. This is a pattern reflected in many other university courses. Many courses also allow for a placement in industry in the UK or in Europe or North America.

Useful websites www.biochemistry.org; www.bioworld.com; www.annualreviews.org; www.ibms.org; www.acb.org.uk; see also **Biological Sciences** and **Biology**.

NB The points totals shown to the left of the institutions are for ease of reference only. It must not be assumed that Tariff points are always used by institutions or that they can be substituted for an offer in grades. The level of an offer is not necessarily indicative of the quality of a course.

COURSE OFFERS INFORMATION

Subject requirements/preferences GCSE English, mathematics and science usually required; leading universities often stipulate A–B grades. **AL** Chemistry required and Biology usually preferred; one or two mathematics/science subjects required.

Your target offers and examples of degree courses

160 pts **Cambridge** – A*A*A incl sci/maths (Nat Sci (Bioch)) (IB 40–41 pts HL 776)

152 pts **Oxford** – A*AA incl maths/sci (Bioch (Mol Cell)) (IB 39 pts)
York – A*AA–AAB incl chem+sci/maths (Chem Biol Medcnl Chem) (IB 36–35 pts HL 6 chem)

144 pts **Bath** – AAA incl chem+sci/maths (Bioch) (IB 36 pts HL 6 chem); AAA incl chem+biol (Mol Cell Biol) (IB 36 pts HL 6 chem+biol)
Birmingham – AAA–AAB incl chem+sci (Bioch; Bioch Biotech; Bioch (Genet); Bioch Mol Cell Biol) (IB 32 pts HL 666–665)
Bristol – AAA–AAB incl chem+sci/maths (Bioch) (IB 36–34 pts HL 6 chem+sci/maths); AAA–AAB 144–136 pts (Bioch Med Bioch; Bioch Mol Biol Biotech) (IB 37–35 pts)
Edinburgh – AAA–ABB (Bioch) (IB 37–32 pts)
Imperial London – AAA incl chem+sci/maths (Bioch; Bioch (Yr Ind/Rsch); Bioch courses) (IB 38 pts HL 6 biol+chem)
Lancaster – AAA–AAB incl chem+sci (Bioch Biomed/Genet; Bioch) (IB 36–35 pts HL 6 chem+sci)
Leeds – AAA–AAB incl chem+sci (Bioch; Med Bioch) (IB 35–34 pts HL 6 chem+sci)
London (UCL) – AAA incl chem+sci/maths (Bioch) (IB 38 pts HL 6 chem 5 sci/maths)
Manchester – AAA–ABB incl chem+sci/maths (Bioch (Yr Ind); Bioch; Med Bioch) (IB 37–33 pts HL 5/6 chem+sci)
Newcastle – AAA–AAB incl biol (Bioch) (IB 35–34 pts HL 5 biol+chem)
Sheffield – AAA–AAB incl chem+sci (Bioch; Bioch Joint Hons; Med Bioch) (IB 37–35 pts HL 6 chem+sci)
York – AAA–AAB incl chem+sci/maths (Bioch) (IB 36–35 pts HL 6 chem+biol/phys)

136 pts **Birmingham** – AAB incl chem+sci (Med Bioch) (IB 32 pts HL 665)
Cardiff – AAB–ABB incl chem (Bioch) (IB 34 pts)
Dundee – AAB incl biol+chem (Bioch) (IB 30 pts)
East Anglia – AAB incl chem+maths/sci (Bioch (Yr Ind)) (IB 33 pts HL 6 chem+sci/maths)
Exeter – AAB–BBB incl biol+chem (Bioch) (IB 34–32 pts HL 5 biol+chem)
Glasgow – AAB–BBB incl biol/chem (Bioch) (IB 36–34 pts)
London (King's) – AAB incl chem+biol (Bioch) (IB 35 pts)
Nottingham – AAB incl chem+sci (Bioch Mol Med; Bioch Genet; Bioch Biol Chem; Bioch) (IB 34 pts)
St Andrews – AAB incl biol+sci/maths (Bioch) (IB 36 pts)
Southampton – AAB incl chem+sci (Bioch) (IB 34 pts HL 6 chem+sci)
Surrey – AAB–ABB incl chem+sci (Bioch) (IB 35–34 pts)
Sussex – AAB–ABB incl biol+chem (Bioch) (IB 34 pts HL 5 biol+chem)

132 pts **Aberystwyth** – 116–132 pts incl chem (Bioch)

128 pts **Aston** – ABB–BBB incl biol (Cell Mol Biol) (IB 33 pts)
East Anglia – ABB incl chem (Bioch) (IB 32 pts HL 5 chem+maths/sci)

Essex – ABB–BBB incl chem+sci/maths (Bioch) (IB 32–30 pts HL 5 chem+sci/maths)
Leicester – ABB incl chem+sci/maths (Med Bioch) (IB 30 pts); ABB incl sci/maths
(Biol Sci (Bioch)) (IB 30 pts)
Liverpool – ABB incl biol+chem (Bioch) (IB 33 pts)
London (QM) – ABB–BBB incl chem (Bioch) (IB 34 pts HL 5 chem)
London (RH) – ABB incl biol+chem (Mol Biol; Med Bioch; Bioch) (IB 32 pts)
Queen's Belfast – ABB–BBB incl chem+sci/maths (Biochem)
Reading – ABB–BBB (Bioch) (IB 32–30 pts)
Strathclyde – ABB–BBB incl biol/chem+sci (Bioch courses) (IB 30 pts HL 5 biol/chem+sci)
Warwick – ABB incl biol+chem (Bioch) (IB 34 pts HL 6 biol+chem)
120 pts   **Aberdeen** – BBB incl maths/sci (Bioch courses) (IB 32 pts HL 5 maths/sci)
Brunel – BBB (Biomed Sci (Bioch)) (IB 30 pts)
Heriot-Watt – BBB incl chem (Chem Bioch) (IB 30 pts HL 5 chem+maths)
Huddersfield – BBB incl chem+sci 120 pts (Bioch; Med Bioch)
Keele – BBB/ABC incl chem (Bioch courses) (IB 32 pts HL 6 chem)
Kent – BBB incl chem+biol (Bioch) (IB 34 pts)
Lincoln – 120 pts incl biol/chem (Bioch)
Nottingham Trent – 120 pts incl biol (Bioch)
Portsmouth – 120 pts incl biol (Bioch) (IB 30 pts HL 17 pts incl 6 biol)
Swansea – BBB–ABB incl biol+chem 120–128 pts (Bioch Genet; Bioch) (IB 32–33 pts)
116 pts   **Aberystwyth** – 116–132 pts incl chem (Genet Bioch)
112 pts   **Chester** – BBC–BCC incl chem 112 pts (Biochem) (IB 26 pts HL 5 chem)
East London – 112 pts incl biol/chem (Biotech Bioch) (IB 25 pts)
Hertfordshire – 112 pts incl chem+sci/maths (Bioch; Bioch (St Abrd)) (IB 28 pts)
Sheffield Hallam – 112 pts incl biol+chem (Bioch)
Westminster – BBC incl sci (Bioch) (IB 26 pts HL 5 sci)
104 pts   **Kingston** – 104 pts incl chem/biol (Bioch); 104–112 pts (Med Bioch)
Liverpool John Moores – 104 pts incl chem/biol (Bioch) (IB 25 pts)
Salford – 104–120 pts incl biol+chem (Bioch) (IB 28 pts)
Worcester – 104–120 pts incl biol+chem+sci/maths (Bioch)
88 pts   **London Met** – 88 pts (Bioch)
80 pts   **Wolverhampton** – 80 pts incl biol/chem (Bioch)

Alternative offers
See **Chapter 6** and **Appendix 1** for grades/new UCAS Tariff points information for other examinations.

CHOOSING YOUR COURSE (SEE ALSO CH.1)

Universities and colleges teaching quality See www.qaa.ac.uk; http://unistats.direct.gov.uk.

Top research universities and colleges (REF 2014) See **Biological Sciences**.

Examples of sandwich degree courses Aston; Bath; Bristol; Brunel; Cardiff; East London; Essex; Hertfordshire; Huddersfield; Imperial London; Kent; Kingston; Leeds; Lincoln; Liverpool John Moores; Manchester; Nottingham Trent; Queen's Belfast; Sheffield Hallam; Surrey; Sussex; York.

ADMISSIONS INFORMATION

Number of applicants per place (approx) Aberystwyth 5; Bath 8; Birmingham 5; Bradford 7; Bristol 7; Cardiff 6; Dundee 6; East Anglia 10; East London 5; Edinburgh 8; Essex 5; Imperial London 6; Keele 7; Leeds 10; Leicester (Med Bioch) 5; London (RH) 8; London (UCL) 7; Newcastle 7; Nottingham 14; Salford 4; Southampton 8; Strathclyde 7; Surrey 3; Warwick 6; York 6.

Advice to applicants and planning the UCAS personal statement It is important to show by reading scientific journals that you have interests in chemistry and biology beyond the exam syllabus. Focus on one or two aspects of biochemistry that interest you. Attend scientific lectures (often arranged by universities on Open Days), find some work experience if possible, and use these to show your understanding of what biochemistry is. Give evidence of your communication skills and time management. (See **Appendix 3**.) **Bristol** Deferred entry accepted. **Oxford** No written or work tests; successful entrants 42.7%. Further information may be obtained from the Institute of Biology and the Royal Society of Chemistry.

Misconceptions about this course York Students feel that being taught by two departments could be a problem but actually it increases their options.

Selection interviews Yes Bradford, Cambridge, East London, Essex, Kingston, Leeds, London (RH), London (UCL), Manchester, Oxford (80% (success rate 24%)), Warwick; **Some** Aberystwyth (mature students only), Bath, Birmingham (Clearing only), Cardiff, East Anglia, Keele (mature students only), Portsmouth (mature students only), Salford, Sheffield, Surrey, Wolverhampton; **No** Dundee, Liverpool John Moores.

Interview advice and questions Questions will be asked on your study of chemistry and biology and any special interests. They will also probe your understanding of what a course in Biochemistry involves and the special features offered by the university. In the past questions have been asked covering Mendel, genetics, RNA and DNA. See also **Chapter 5**. **Liverpool John Moores** Informal interviews. It would be useful to bring samples of coursework to the interview.

Reasons for rejection (non-academic) Borderline grades plus poor motivation. Failure to turn up for interviews or answer correspondence. Inability to discuss subject. Not compatible with A-level predictions or references. **Birmingham** Lack of total commitment to Biochemistry, for example intention to transfer to Medicine without completing the course.

AFTER-RESULTS ADVICE
Offers to applicants repeating A-levels Higher East Anglia, Leeds, Leicester, Nottingham, St Andrews, Strathclyde, Surrey, Warwick; **Possibly higher** Bath, Bristol, Brunel, Keele, Kent, Lancaster, Newcastle; **Same** Aberystwyth, Birmingham, Bradford, Cardiff, Dundee, Heriot-Watt, Liverpool, Liverpool John Moores, London (RH), London (UCL), Salford, Sheffield, Wolverhampton, York; **No** Cambridge.

GRADUATE DESTINATIONS AND EMPLOYMENT (2013/14 HESA)
Biochemistry, Biophysics and Molecular Biology graduates surveyed 2,200 **Employed** 855 **In voluntary employment** 60 **In further study** 785 **Assumed unemployed** 185

Career note Biochemistry courses involve several specialities which offer a range of job opportunities. These include the application of biochemistry in industrial, medical and clinical areas with additional openings in pharmaceuticals and agricultural work, environmental science and in toxicology.

OTHER DEGREE SUBJECTS FOR CONSIDERATION
Agricultural Sciences; Agriculture; Biological Sciences; Biology; Biotechnology; Botany; Brewing; Chemistry; Food Science; Genetics; Medical Sciences; Medicine; Microbiology; Neuroscience; Nursing; Nutrition; Pharmaceutical Sciences; Pharmacology; Pharmacy; Plant Science.

BIOLOGICAL SCIENCES

(including **Biomedical Materials Science**, **Biomedical Science**, **Brewing** and **Distilling**, **Cosmetic Science**, **Forensic Science**, **Immunology**, **Medical Science** and **Virology**; see also **Animal Sciences**, **Biochemistry**, **Biology**, **Biotechnology**, **Environmental Sciences**, **Genetics**, **Medicine**, **Microbiology**, **Natural Sciences**, **Neuroscience**, **Nursing and Midwifery**, **Pharmacology**, **Plant Sciences**, **Psychology**, **Zoology**)

Biological Science (in some universities referred to as Biosciences) is a fast-moving, rapidly expanding and wide subject area, ranging from, for example, conservation biology to molecular genetics. Boundaries between separate subjects are blurring and this is reflected in the content and variety of the courses offered. Many universities offer a common first year allowing final decisions to be made later in the course. Since most subjects are research-based, students undertake their own projects in

"

Leeds is really different. The lecturers
I met on the open day were genuine
and enthusiastic – I knew straight
away that it was right for me.

Karen Turner,
BSc Genetics

"

BIOLOGY

AT THE UNIVERSITY OF LEEDS

We want to inspire you to be part of the next generation of highly skilled, critical thinkers – shaping the world around you in years to come. Work alongside experienced researchers and become part of a thriving research team and environment.

The School of Biology achieved high student satisfaction rating in the latest National Student Survey with a 91% overall satisfaction score. Zoology is ranked in the top 20 among UK universities (NSS, 2015).

Study with us
You can benefit from our extensive research expertise and study at the forefront of knowledge.

All our undergraduate courses offer you the opportunity to study at postgraduate level in your fourth year with an Integrated Masters option.

- BSc/MBiol Biology
- BSc/MBiol Biology with Enterprise
- BSc/MBiol Ecology and Conservation Biology
- BSc/MBiol Genetics
- BSc/MBiol Zoology

Accredited courses
Our MBiol courses give you the benefit of recognised excellence by being awarded Advanced Accreditation by the Royal Society of Biology.

Experience more
Take the opportunity to study abroad or do an industrial placement year as part of any of our degree courses. You will participate in research activities by conducting your own research, or do our summer studentship scheme.

In the lab
With a high level of practical teaching each week you will benefit from industry-standard research facilities, specialist equipment and the latest technology.

Find out more at an open day
www.leeds.ac.uk/opendays

TOP THREE IN UK FOR STUDENT EMPLOYABILITY - QS GRADUATE EMPLOYABILITY RANKINGS 2016

WINNER OF THE ENTREPRENEURIAL UNIVERSITY OF THE YEAR 2015 - TIMES HIGHER EDUCATION

COME AND
FIND
YOUR
PLACE

> **My course is really varied so there are lots of opportunities to hone your interests.**
>
> **James Croft,**
> BSc Human Physiology

BIOMEDICAL AND SPORT SCIENCE

AT THE UNIVERSITY OF LEEDS

We want to inspire you to be part of the next generation of highly skilled, critical thinkers – shaping the world around you in years to come. Work alongside experienced researchers and become part of a thriving research team and environment.

We are number 1 in the UK for 'world-leading' research in the area of sport and exercise sciences (REF, 2014).

Study with us
You can benefit from our extensive research expertise and study at the forefront of knowledge. All our undergraduate courses offer you the opportunity to study at postgraduate level in your fourth year with an Integrated Masters option.

- BSc/MBiol Human Physiology
- BSc/MBiol Medical Science
- BSc/MBiol Neuroscience
- BSc/MBiol Pharmacology
- BSc/MSci Sport and Exercise Science
- BSc/MSci Sport Science and Physiology

Accredited courses
Our MBiol courses give you the benefit of recognised excellence by being awarded Interim Accreditation by the Royal Society of Biology.

Experience more
Take the opportunity to study abroad or do an industrial placement year as part of any of our degree courses. You will participate in research activities by conducting your own research, or do our summer studentship scheme.

In the lab
With a high level of practical teaching each week you will benefit from industry-standard research facilities, specialist equipment and the latest technology.

Find out more at an open day
www.leeds.ac.uk/opendays

TOP THREE IN UK FOR STUDENT EMPLOYABILITY - QS GRADUATE EMPLOYABILITY RANKINGS 2016

WINNER OF THE ENTREPRENEURIAL UNIVERSITY OF THE YEAR 2015 - TIMES HIGHER EDUCATION

COME AND
F I N D
YOUR
PLACE

> I never would have imagined just how many opportunities I would have to try my hand at different techniques or see them in action.

Annabel Taylor,
BSc Medical Biochemistry
with Industry

UNIVERSITY OF LEEDS

MOLECULAR & CELLULAR BIOLOGY

AT THE UNIVERSITY OF LEEDS

We want to inspire you to be part of the next generation of highly skilled, critical thinkers – shaping the world around you in years to come. Work alongside experienced researchers and become part of a thriving research team and environment.

The School of Molecular and Cellular Biology reached number 1 in the UK for student satisfaction in the latest National Student Survey (NSS, 2015).

Study with us
You can benefit from our extensive research expertise and study at the forefront of knowledge.

All our undergraduate courses offer you the opportunity to study at postgraduate level in your fourth year with an Integrated Masters option.

- BSc/MBiol Biochemistry
- BSc/MBiol Biological Sciences (Biology with Enterprise)
- BSc/MBiol Medical Biochemistry
- BSc/MBiol Medical Microbiology
- BSc/MBiol Microbiology

Accredited courses
Our MBiol courses give you the benefit of recognised excellence by being awarded Interim Accreditation by the Royal Society of Biology.

Experience more
Take the opportunity to study abroad or do an industrial placement year as part of any of our degree courses. You will participate in research activities by conducting your own research, or do our summer studentship scheme.

In the lab
With a high level of practical teaching each week you will benefit from industry-standard research facilities, specialist equipment and the latest technology.

Find out more at an open day
www.leeds.ac.uk/opendays

TOP THREE IN UK FOR STUDENT EMPLOYABILITY - QS GRADUATE EMPLOYABILITY RANKINGS 2016

WINNER OF THE ENTREPRENEURIAL UNIVERSITY OF THE YEAR 2015 - TIMES HIGHER EDUCATION

COME AND
FIND
YOUR
PLACE

the final year. It should be noted that some Medical Science courses provide a foundation for graduate entry to medical schools. Check with universities.

Useful websites bsi.immunology.org; www.ibms.org; www.scicentral.com; www.bbsrc.ac.uk; www.forensic-science-society.org.uk; www.immunology.org; see also **Biochemistry** and **Biology**.

NB The points totals shown to the left of the institutions are for ease of reference only. It must not be assumed that Tariff points are always used by institutions or that they can be substituted for an offer in grades. The level of an offer is not necessarily indicative of the quality of a course.

COURSE OFFERS INFORMATION

Subject requirements/preferences GCSE English, mathematics and science usually required. Grades AB often stipulated by popular universities. **AL** Chemistry required plus one or two other mathematics/science subjects, Biology preferred. (Ecol) Biology and one other science subject may be required or preferred. (Neuro) Mathematics/science subjects with Chemistry and/or Biology required or preferred.

Your target offers and examples of degree courses

160 pts Cambridge – A*A*A incl sci/maths (Nat Sci (Biol Biomed Sci)) (IB 40–41 pts HL 776)

152 pts Bath – A*AA incl maths (Nat Sci) (IB 36 pts HL 6 maths)
 Cambridge – A*AA (Educ Biol Sci) (IB 40–41 pts HL 776)
 London (UCL) – A*AA-AAA incl sci (Bioproc N Med (Bus Mgt)) (IB 39–38 pts HL 5 sci); A*AA-AAA incl biol (Bioproc N Med (Sci Eng)) (IB 39–38 pts HL 5 biol)
 Nottingham – A*AA incl sci/maths (Nat Sci) (IB 38 pts)
 Oxford – A*AA incl sci/maths (Biomed Sci; Biol Sci) (IB 39 pts)

144 pts Bath – AAA incl biol+chem (Biomed Sci) (IB 36 pts HL 6 chem+biol)
 Birmingham – AAA-AAB incl biol+sci (Biol Sci (Genet); Biol Sci) (IB 32 pts HL 666–665)
 Bristol – AAA-ABB incl biol+phys/chem (Palae Evol MSci) (IB 36–34 pts)
 Durham – AAA (Biomed Sci) (IB 37 pts); AAA incl biol/chem+sci (Biol Sci) (IB 37 pts)
 Edinburgh – AAA-ABB (Infec Dis; Biol Sci; Immun) (IB 37–32 pts)
 Imperial London – AAA incl biol+sci/maths (Biol Sci) (IB 38 pts HL 6 biol+chem/maths); (Med Biosci) (IB 38 pts HL 6 biol+sci/maths)
 Lancaster – AAA-AAB incl sci (Biomed Sci; Biol Sci courses) (IB 36–35 pts HL 6 sci)
 Leeds – AAA-AAB incl biol+sci (Biol Sci) (IB 35–34 pts HL 6 biol+sci); AAA-AAB incl biol/chem+sci (Med Sci) (IB 35–34 pts HL 6 biol/chem+sci)
 London (UCL) – AAA incl biol+chem (Biomed Sci) (IB 38 pts HL 5 biol+chem); (App Med Sci) (IB 38 pts HL 6 biol+chem); AAA incl biol+sci/maths (Biol Sci) (IB 38 pts HL 6 biol 5 sci/maths)
 Manchester – AAA-ABB incl sci/maths (Biomed Sci (Yr Ind); Biomed Sci) (IB 37–33 pts HL 5/6 biol+chem)
 Newcastle – AAA-ABB incl biol (Biomed Sci) (IB 35–34 pts HL 5 biol+chem); AAA-AAB incl biol (Med Sci (Defer); Biomed Genet; Exer Biomed) (IB 35–34 pts HL 5 biol+chem)
 Sheffield – AAA-AAB incl chem+sci (Med Bioch) (IB 37–35 pts HL 6 chem+sci)
 York – AAA-AAB incl biol+chem (Biomed Sci) (IB 36–35 pts HL biol+chem)

136 pts Bristol – AAB-ABB incl chem+sci/maths (Virol Immun) (IB 34–32 pts HL 6/5 chem+sci/maths); (Cell Mol Med) (IB 34–32 pts HL 6–5 chem+sci/maths)
 Cardiff – AAB-ABB incl biol (Biomed Sci (Physiol); Biomed Sci (Anat); Biomed Sci; Biomed Sci (Neuro)) (IB 34 pts HL 6 biol+chem)
 Dundee – AAB incl biol+chem (Biol Sci) (IB 30 pts)
 East Anglia – AAB (Biol Sci (Yr Ind); Biomed; Biol Sci (St Abrd)) (IB 33 pts HL 6 biol); (Foren Invstg Chem MChem) (IB 33 pts HL 6 chem+sci/maths)
 Edinburgh – AAB-ABB (Med Sci) (IB 36–32 pts)
 Exeter – AAB-ABB incl biol+sci (Hum Biosci) (IB 34–32 pts HL 5 biol+sci); (Med Sci) (IB 34–32 pts HL 65 biol+sci); AAB-ABB incl biol (Biol Sci) (IB 34–32 pts HL 5 biol)
 Glasgow – AAB-BBB incl biol/chem (Immun) (IB 36–34 pts)
 London (King's) – AAB incl chem+biol (Biomed Sci) (IB 35 pts)

London (QM) – AAB incl biol+sci (Biomed Sci) (IB 35 pts HL 6 biol+sci)

Newcastle – AAB–ABB incl biol (Biol Psy) (IB 35 pts HL 6 biol); AAB–BBB incl biol (Biol (Cell Mol Biol)) (IB 35 pts HL 6 biol)

Reading – AAB–ABB (Biol Sci (Yr Ind)) (IB 32–30 pts); (Biomed Sci) (IB 35–32 pts)

Sheffield – AAB–ABB incl biol+sci (Ecol Cons Biol) (IB 35–34 pts HL 6 biol+sci); AAB–ABB incl sci (Biomed Sci) (IB 35 pts HL 6 sci)

Southampton – AAB incl biol/chem+sci (Biomed Sci) (IB 34 pts)

Surrey – AAB–ABB incl chem+sci (Chem Foren Invstg) (IB 35–34 pts); AAB incl chem/biol+sci/maths (Biomed Sci) (IB 35 pts)

Sussex – AAB–ABB incl biol+sci/maths (Biomed Sci) (IB 34 pts HL 5 biol+sci/maths)

Warwick – AAB–ABB incl biol (Biol Sci; Biomed Sci) (IB 36–34 pts HL 6 biol)

128 pts Aberdeen – ABB incl biol+chem (Biol Sci MSci) (IB 34 pts HL 6 biol+chem); ABB incl chem/biol+maths/sci (Biomed Sci) (IB 34 pts HL 6 chem/biol+maths/sci)

Aston – ABB–BBB incl biol (Biol Sci) (IB 33 pts HL 6 biol); (Biomed Sci) (IB 33 pts); ABB–BBB incl biol (Microbiol Immun) (IB 33 pts HL 6 biol)

Birmingham – ABB incl sci/maths (Biomed Mat Sci) (IB 32 pts HL 655)

East Anglia – ABB (Biol Sci) (IB 32 pts HL 5 biol)

Essex – ABB–BBB incl biol (Biol Sci) (IB 32–30 pts HL 5 biol); ABB–BBB incl chem/biol+sci/maths (Biomed Sci) (IB 32–30 pts HL 5 chem/biol+sci/maths)

Leicester – ABB incl chem (Chem Foren Sci) (IB 30 pts); ABB incl sci/maths (Biol Sci; Biol Sci (Genet)) (IB 30 pts)

Liverpool – ABB incl biol+chem (Biol Med Sci) (IB 33 pts); ABB incl biol+sci (Biol Sci) (IB 33 pts)

London (RH) – ABB incl biol+chem (Biomed Sci; Mol Biol) (IB 32 pts)

London (St George's) – ABB incl biol+chem (Biomed Sci)

Plymouth – 128 pts incl biol+chem (Biomed Sci) (IB 30 pts HL 5 biol+sci)

Queen's Belfast – ABB–AAB incl biol/chem (Biomed Sci)

Reading – ABB–BBB (Biol Sci; Chem Foren Analys) (IB 32–30 pts)

Strathclyde – ABB–BBB incl biol/chem+sci (Biomed Sci) (IB 30 pts HL 5 biol/chem+sci); ABB–BBB incl chem+biol (Immun) (IB 32 pts HL 6 chem+biol)

Swansea – ABB–BBB incl biol (Biol Sci) (IB 33–32 pts)

UWE Bristol – 128 pts incl biol/chem+sci (Biomed Sci) (IB 27 pts HL 6 biol/chem 5 sci)

120 pts Aberdeen – BBB incl maths/sci (Immun) (IB 32 pts HL 5 maths/sci)

Bradford – BBB 120 pts (Clin Sci)

Brighton – BBB incl biol/chem (Biomed Sci) (IB 30 pts)

Brunel – BBB (Biomed Sci; Biomed Sci (Genet)) (IB 30 pts)

Central Lancashire – BBB (Med Sci)

De Montfort – 120 pts incl biol/chem (Biomed Sci) (IB 30 pts HL 6 biol/chem)

Dundee – BBB–BCC incl biol (Foren Anth) (IB 30 pts)

Greenwich – 120 pts (Biol Sci; Foren Sci; Foren Sci Crimin; Biomed Sci); (App Biomed Sci) (IB 24 pts)

Heriot-Watt – BBB (Biol Sci) (IB 27 pts HL 5 biol); BBB incl sci (Brew Distil) (IB 27 pts HL 5 biol)

Huddersfield – BBB incl chem+sci 120 pts (Med Bioch)

Keele – BBB/ABC incl chem (Foren Sci) (IB 32 pts HL 6 chem)

Kent – BBB incl biol/chem (Foren Sci) (IB 34 pts); BBB incl biol (Biomed Sci) (IB 34 pts)

Leeds Beckett – 120 pts incl biol+sci (Biomed Sci courses) (IB 26 pts HL 6 biol)

Lincoln – 120 pts incl biol/chem (Biomed Sci)

London Met – 120 pts incl biol+chem (Biomed Sci)

Northumbria – 120 pts incl chem/biol (Foren Sci) (IB 30 pts); 120 pts incl biol (Biomed Sci) (IB 30 pts)

Nottingham Trent – 120 pts incl biol+chem (Foren Sci); 120 pts incl biol (Biomed Sci)

Plymouth – 120 pts incl biol+sci (Hum Biosci) (IB 28 pts HL 5 biol+sci)

Portsmouth – BBB incl biol+sci/maths (Biomed Sci) (IB 31 pts HL 666 incl biol+chem/maths)

Queen's Belfast – BBB–ABB incl biol (Biol Sci)

Roehampton – 120 pts incl biol/chem (Biomed Sci)

Sheffield Hallam – 120 pts incl biol (Biomed Sci)

South Wales – BBB incl biol (Med Sci) (IB 32 pts HL 6 biol+sci)

Staffordshire – 120 pts incl biol/chem (Foren Sci)

Ulster – 120 pts incl sci/maths (Strtf Med) (IB 26 pts); 120 pts incl sci/maths/tech (Biomed Sci) (IB 25 pts)

UWE Bristol – 120 pts incl biol/chem (Foren Sci) (IB 26 pts HL 5 biol/chem)

112 pts **Anglia Ruskin** – 112 pts (Foren Sci) (IB 26 pts)

Bangor – 112–128 pts incl sci/maths (Med Sci); 112–128 pts incl biol (Biomed Sci) (IB 24 pts)

Bedfordshire – 112 pts incl sci (Biomed Sci) (IB 24 pts)

Brighton – BBC incl biol (Biol Sci) (IB 28 pts)

Canterbury Christ Church – 112 pts (Foren Invstg)

Cardiff Met – 112 pts incl biol+chem (Biomed Sci)

Central Lancashire – 112 pts incl biol/chem (Foren Sci) (IB 28 pts HL 5 biol/chem)

Chester – BBC–BCC incl biol/chem/env sci 112 pts (Foren Biol) (IB 26 pts HL 5 biol/chem); BBC–BCC incl biol/chem/app sci 112 pts (Biomed Sci) (IB 26 pts HL 5 biol)

De Montfort – 112 pts incl sci (Foren Sci) (IB 28 pts HL 6 sci)

East London – 112 pts incl biol/chem (Biomed Sci) (IB 25 pts)

Hertfordshire – 112 pts incl chem+sci/maths (Biol Sci; Biol (Yr Abrd)) (IB 28 pts); 112 pts incl biol/chem+sci/maths (Biomed Sci) (IB 28 pts)

Huddersfield – BBC incl chem 112 pts (Foren Analyt Sci)

Hull – 112 pts incl chem (Chem (Foren Analyt Sci)) (IB 28 pts HL chem); 112 pts incl biol (Biomed Sci) (IB 28 pts HL 5 biol)

Kingston – 112–128 pts (Biomed Sci)

Lincoln – 112 pts incl biol/chem (Foren Sci)

London (Birk) – 112 pts (Biomed)

Middlesex – 112 pts (Biomed Sci)

Northampton – 112–128 pts incl sci (Hum Biosci)

Nottingham Trent – 112 pts incl biol (Biol Sci)

Oxford Brookes – BBC (Med Sci; Biomed Sci) (IB 30 pts); BBC 112 pts (Biol Sci)

Plymouth – 112 pts incl env sci/biol+sci (Biol Sci) (IB 28 pts HL 5 biol+sci)

Roehampton – 112 pts incl biol (Biol Sci)

Staffordshire – 112 pts (Biomed Sci; Foren Biol)

Sunderland – 112 pts incl biol/chem (Biomed Sci)

Teesside – BBC incl biol/chem (Foren Sci); BBC incl biol (Foren Biol; Biol Sci)

UWE Bristol – 112 pts (Biol Sci) (IB 25 pts)

Westminster – BBC incl sci/maths (Biol Sci) (IB 26 pts HL 5 sci); BBC incl sci (Hum Med Sci; Biomed Sci) (IB 26 pts HL 5 sci)

West Scotland – BBC incl sci (App Biosci; Biomed Sci) (IB 24 pts)

Wolverhampton – 112 pts incl sci (Med Sci)

104 pts **Abertay** – BCC incl sci/maths (Psy Foren Biol) (IB 29 pts)

Bournemouth – 104–120 pts (Arch Foren Sci; Biol Sci) (IB 28–31 pts); 104–128 pts (Foren Sci) (IB 28–31 pts)

Bradford – BCC 104 pts (Foren Sci; Foren Med Sci; Biomed Sci)

Coventry – BCC incl biol (Biol Foren Sci; Med Pharmacol Sci) (IB 27 pts); BCC incl biol+sci (Biomed Sci) (IB 27 pts)

Cumbria – 104 pts incl sci (Foren Invstg Sci)

De Montfort – 104 pts incl chem+sci (Pharml Cos Sci) (IB 28 pts HL 6 chem+sci); 104 pts incl biol/chem (Med Sci) (IB 28 pts HL 6 chem+sci)

Derby – 104 pts incl biol/chem (Foren Sci; Foren Sci Crimin)

Edinburgh Napier – BCC incl sci (Biomed Sci; Biol Sci) (IB 28 pts HL 5 sci)

Glasgow Caledonian – BCC incl chem (Foren Invstg; Biomed Sci) (IB 24 pts)

Kingston – 104–112 pts (Biol Sci; Foren Sci)

Liverpool Hope – BCC–BBB 104–120 pts (Biol Sci)

Liverpool John Moores – 104 pts incl chem/biol (Biomed Sci) (IB 25 pts); 104–120 pts (Foren Anth); (Foren Sci) (IB 25 pts)

Manchester Met – BCC–BBC incl sci 104–112 pts (Foren Sci App Crimin) (IB 28 pts HL 5 sci); BCC–BBC incl biol 104–112 pts (Biomed Sci) (IB 28 pts HL 5 biol)

Robert Gordon – BCC incl chem+sci/maths (Foren Analyt Sci) (IB 28 pts HL 5 chem+sci/ maths); BCC incl biol+sci (App Biomed Sci) (IB 28 pts HL 5 biol+sci)

South Wales – BCC incl chem+biol (Foren Biol) (IB 29 pts HL 5 chem+biol)

West Scotland – BCC incl chem (Foren Sci) (IB 24 pts); BCC incl sci (App Biosci Zool) (IB 24 pts)

Worcester – 104–120 pts incl biol+sci/maths (Foren App Biol)

96 pts **Abertay** – CCC incl chem+biol/phys (Foren Sci) (IB 28 pts); CCC incl biol (Biomed Sci) (IB 28 pts)

Canterbury Christ Church – 96 pts (Biosci)

Glyndŵr – 96 pts incl sci (Foren Sci)

London Met – 96 pts incl biol+chem (Biol Sci; Med Biosci)

Salford – 96–112 pts incl biol (Hum Biol Infec Dis) (IB 28 pts)

West London – 96–112 pts incl sci (Foren Sci)

Wolverhampton – 96 pts incl sci (Biomed Sci)

88 pts **London Met** – 88 pts incl biol/chem (Foren Sci)

80 pts **Bedfordshire** – 80 pts (Biol Sci; Foren Sci) (IB 24 pts)

London South Bank – CDD–BC 80–72 pts (Biosci); CDD/BC 80–72 pts (Foren Sci)

Stirling – BB (App Biol Sci) (IB 28 pts)

Wolverhampton – 80 pts incl biol/chem (Foren Sci)

Alternative offers
See **Chapter 6** and **Appendix 1** for grades/new UCAS Tariff points information for other examinations.

EXAMPLES OF COLLEGES OFFERING COURSES IN THIS SUBJECT FIELD
Birmingham Met (Coll); Brighton and Hove City (Coll); Bromley (CFHE); Central Nottingham (Coll); Furness (Coll); Haringey, Enfield and North East London (Coll); Liverpool City (Coll); Nescot; Peterborough (Coll); Petroc; South Devon (Coll); Sunderland (Coll); Weymouth (Coll).

CHOOSING YOUR COURSE (SEE ALSO CH.1)
Universities and colleges teaching quality See www.qaa.ac.uk; http://unistats.direct.gov.uk.

Top research universities and colleges (REF 2014) Oxford; Dundee; Newcastle; Sheffield; Birmingham; Imperial London; Edinburgh; York; Exeter; Kent; Leicester; Cambridge; East Anglia; Sussex.

Examples of sandwich degree courses See **Biology**.

ADMISSIONS INFORMATION
Number of applicants per place (approx) Aston (Biomed Sci) 8; Bath 7; Bristol 8, (Neuro) 10; Cardiff 5; Durham 7; East Anglia (Biol Sci) 15; Edinburgh 8; Essex 8; Lancaster (Biol Sci) 12; Leeds (Med Sci) 25; Leicester 8; London (King's) 7; London (QM) 8; London (St George's) 15; London (UCL) 7; Newcastle 14; Nottingham 11; Southampton 8; Stirling 7; York 9.

Advice to applicants and planning the UCAS personal statement Read scientific journals and try to extend your knowledge beyond the A-level syllabus. Discuss your special interests, for example, ecology, microbiology, genetics or zoology (read up thoroughly on your interests since questions could be asked at interview). Mention any voluntary attendance on courses, work experience, voluntary work, or holiday jobs. Demonstrate good oral and written communication skills and be competent at handling numerical data. Interest in the law for Forensic Science courses. See **Appendix 3**.

Misconceptions about this course Anglia Ruskin (Foren Sci) Some students are not aware that modules in management and quality assurance are taken as part of the course. **Birmingham** We offer a range of degree labels each with different UCAS codes, for example Biological Sciences

Genetics, Biological Sciences Microbiology: all have the same first year and students can freely transfer between them. (Med Sci) Applicants often use this course as an insurance for a vocational course (usually Medicine). If they are unsuccessful for their first choice, they occasionally find it difficult to commit themselves to Medical Sciences and do not perform as well as their academic performance would predict. **Cardiff** Some students mistakenly believe that they can transfer to Medicine. **De Montfort** (Foren Sci) Students are often unaware of how much of the work is analytical biology and chemistry: they think they spend their time visiting crime scenes. **London (St George's)** It is not possible to transfer to Medicine after the first year of the Biomedical Science course. Students may be able to transfer to Year 3 of the Medical course on completion of the BSc degree. **Swansea** (Med Sci) Some applicants think the course is a form of medical training – it isn't, but it is relevant to anyone planning graduate entry for courses in Medicine or paramedical careers. (Biol Sci deferred entry) Some applicants think that this is a degree in its own right. In fact, after the first year, students have to choose one of the other degrees offered by the School of Biological Sciences. This course allows students an extra year in which to consider their final specialisation.

Selection interviews Yes Bangor, Essex, Greenwich, Hull, London (RH), London (St George's), London (UCL), Manchester, Newcastle, Nottingham Trent, Oxford (Bio Sci) 24%, (Biomed Sci) 16%, Oxford Brookes, Reading, Salford, Stirling, Strathclyde, Sunderland, Swansea (Med Sci), UWE Bristol, Warwick; **Some** Anglia Ruskin, Aston, Bristol, Cardiff, Cardiff Met, De Montfort, Derby, East Anglia, Kent, Liverpool John Moores, Roehampton, Sheffield, Sheffield Hallam, Staffordshire, Surrey (Biomed Sci), Wolverhampton; **No** Birmingham, Dundee, Nottingham.

Interview advice and questions You are likely to be asked about your main interests in biology and your choice of specialisation in the field of biological sciences or, for example, about the role of the botanist, specialist microbiologist in industry, your understanding of biotechnology or genetic engineering. Questions likely to be asked on any field courses attended. If you have a field course workbook, take it to interview. See also **Chapter 5**. **London (St George's)** (Biomed Sci) What career path do you envisage for yourself with this degree? **Oxford** No written or work tests. Interviews are rigorous but sympathetic; successful entrants average 38.8%. Applicants are expected to demonstrate their ability to understand whatever facts they have encountered and to discuss a particular aspect of biology in which they are interested. What problems does a fish face under water? Are humans still evolving?

Reasons for rejection (non-academic) Oxford Applicant appeared to have so much in his head that he tended to express his ideas in too much of a rush. He needs to slow down a bit and take more time to select points that are really pertinent to the questions.

AFTER-RESULTS ADVICE

Offers to applicants repeating A-levels Higher Bristol, Glasgow Caledonian, Hull, London (St George's), Newcastle, Sheffield, UWE Bristol; **Possibly higher** Aston, Essex, Lancaster, Manchester Met; **Same** Abertay, Anglia Ruskin, Birmingham, Cardiff, Cardiff Met, Chichester, De Montfort, Derby, Durham, East Anglia, East London, Edinburgh Napier, Exeter, Glasgow, Heriot-Watt, Huddersfield, Kingston, Leeds, Lincoln, Liverpool Hope, Liverpool John Moores, London (RH), Oxford Brookes, Plymouth, Portsmouth, Robert Gordon, Roehampton, Salford, Sheffield Hallam, Stirling, West London, West Scotland, Wolverhampton, Worcester, York; **No** Cambridge.

GRADUATE DESTINATIONS AND EMPLOYMENT (2013/14 HESA)
See also **Biology**.

Career note Degrees in biological science subjects often lead graduates into medical, pharmaceutical, veterinary, food and environmental work, research and education, in both the public and private sectors (see also **Biology**). Sandwich courses are offered at a number of institutions enabling students to gain paid experience in industry and commerce, often resulting in permanent employment on graduation. In recent years there has been a considerable increase in the number of Biomedical Science courses designed for students interested in taking a hands-on approach to studying the biology of disease. However, students should be warned that the ever-popular Forensic Science courses may not always pave the way to jobs in this highly specialised field.

OTHER DEGREE SUBJECTS FOR CONSIDERATION

Biochemistry; Biology; Biotechnology; Botany; Chemistry; Consumer Sciences; Ecology; Environmental Health; Environmental Science; Genetics; Genomics; Immunology; Microbiology; Pharmaceutical Sciences; Pharmacology; Pharmacy; Physiology; Plant Sciences; Psychology; Sport and Exercise Science; Toxicology; Virology; Zoology.

BIOLOGY

(including **Marine Biology**; see also **Animal Sciences, Biological Sciences, Biotechnology, Environmental Sciences, Microbiology, Plant Sciences, Zoology**)

The science of biology is a broad and rapidly developing subject that increasingly affects our lives. Biologists address the challenges faced by human populations such as disease, conservation and food production, and the continuing advances in such areas as genetics and molecular biology that have applications in medicine and agriculture. (See also under **Biological Sciences**.)

Useful websites www.societyofbiology.org; www.mba.ac.uk; www.bbsrc.ac.uk; see also **Biochemistry**.

NB The points totals shown to the left of the institutions are for ease of reference only. It must not be assumed that Tariff points are always used by institutions or that they can be substituted for an offer in grades. The level of an offer is not necessarily indicative of the quality of a course.

COURSE OFFERS INFORMATION

Subject requirements/preferences GCSE Mathematics and English stipulated in some cases. **AL** Biology and Chemistry important, other science subjects may be accepted. Two and sometimes three mathematics/science subjects required including Biology.

Your target offers and examples of degree courses

152 pts **Durham** – A*AA incl biol/chem (Nat Sci) (IB 38 pts); A*AA incl sci/maths (Biol Joint Hons) (IB 38 pts)

144 pts **Bath** – AAA incl chem+biol (Mol Cell Biol) (IB 36 pts HL 6 chem+biol); AAA incl biol+sci/maths (Biol) (IB 36 pts HL 6 biol)

Birmingham – AAA–AAB incl biol+sci (Hum Biol; Biol Sci (Env Biol)) (IB 32 pts HL 666–665)

Edinburgh – AAA–ABB (Evol Biol) (IB 37–32 pts)

Imperial London – AAA incl biol+sci/maths (Biol Sci Ger Sci; Ecol Env Biol) (IB 38 pts HL 6 biol+chem/maths)

Leeds – AAA–AAB incl biol (Biol) (IB 35–34 pts HL 6 biol+sci)

Manchester – AAA–ABB incl chem+sci/maths (Mol Biol) (IB 37–33 pts); AAA–ABB incl sci/maths (Biol; Cell Biol; Biol (Yr Ind); Biol Modn Lang; Cell Biol (Yr Ind); Cell Biol Modn Lang; Biol Sci Soty) (IB 37–33 pts HL 5/6 biol+chem); (Dev Biol) (IB 37–33 pts)

Sheffield – AAA incl biol+sci (Biol (Yr Abrd); Biol MBiolSci) (IB 37 pts HL 6 biol+sci)

York – AAA–AAB incl biol+chem/maths (Biol; Biol (Yr Abrd); Mol Cell Biol) (IB 36–35 pts HL 6 biol+chem/maths)

136 pts **Bristol** – AAB–ABB incl sci/maths (Biol) (IB 34–32 pts HL 5 sci/maths)

Cardiff – AAB–ABB incl biol (Biol) (IB 34 pts HL 6 biol+chem)

Dundee – AAB incl biol+chem (Mol Biol) (IB 30 pts)

Exeter – AAB–ABB incl sci/maths (Evol Biol; Cons Biol Ecol) (IB 34–32 pts HL 5 sci/maths)

Glasgow – AAB–BBB incl biol/chem (Mar Frshwtr Biol) (IB 36–34 pts)

Lancaster – AAB–AAB incl sci (Biol courses) (IB 36–35 pts HL 6 sci)

London (King's) – AAB incl chem+biol (Anat Dev Hum Biol) (IB 35 pts)

Newcastle – AAB–ABB incl biol+sci (Mar Biol Ocean; Mar Biol) (IB 35–34 pts HL 6 biol); AAB–ABB incl biol (Biol (Ecol Env Biol); Biol) (IB 35 pts HL 6 biol)

Nottingham – AAB–ABB incl biol+sci/maths (Biol) (IB 34–32 pts)

St Andrews – AAB incl biol+sci/maths (Biol courses) (IB 36 pts)

Sheffield – AAB–ABB incl biol+sci (Biol) (IB 35–34 pts HL biol+sci)

Southampton – AAB incl biol+sci (Biol) (IB 34 pts HL 6 biol+sci); AAB incl sci/maths/geog (Mar Biol) (IB 34 pts)

Sussex – AAB–ABB incl sci (Biol) (IB 34 pts HL 5 sci)

128 pts **Aston** – ABB–BBB incl biol (Hum Biol) (IB 33 pts HL 6 biol); (Cell Mol Biol) (IB 33 pts)

Edinburgh – ABB (Repro Biol) (IB 36–32 pts)

Essex – ABB–BBB (Mar Biol) (IB 32–30 pts)

Kent – BBB incl biol (Biol courses) (IB 34 pts)

Liverpool – ABB incl biol+sci (Trpcl Dis Biol) (IB 33 pts HL 6 biol); ABB incl biol+sci/maths/ geog (Mar Biol) (IB 33 pts HL 6 biol)

London (QM) – ABB–BBB incl biol (Biol) (IB 34 pts HL 5 biol)

London (RH) – ABB incl biol (Biol) (IB 32 pts); ABB incl biol+chem (Mol Biol) (IB 32 pts)

Loughborough – ABB incl sci (Hum Biol) (IB 34 pts HL 5 biol/sci)

Nottingham – ABB–BBB incl sci/maths (Env Biol) (IB 32–30 pts)

Southampton – ABB incl biol+sci/maths/geog (Mar Biol Ocean) (IB 32 pts)

Strathclyde – ABB–BBB incl chem+biol (Microbiol MSci) (IB 32 pts HL 6 chem+biol)

Swansea – ABB–BBB incl biol (Biol) (IB 33–32 pts)

120 pts **Aberdeen** – BBB incl maths/sci (Cons Biol; Mar Biol; Biol) (IB 32 pts HL 5 maths/sci)

Bangor – 120 pts (App Ter Mar Ecol)

Dundee – BBB–BCC incl maths+biol/phys (Mathem Biol) (IB 30 pts)

Edge Hill – BBB incl biol 120 pts (Biol)

Gloucestershire – 120 pts (Anim Biol; Biol)

Heriot-Watt – BBB incl sci (Mar Biol) (IB 27 pts HL 5 biol)

Huddersfield – BBB incl sci 120 pts (Med Biol; Biol (Mol Cell))

Keele – BBB/ABC incl sci/maths (Biol) (IB 32 pts HL 6 sci/maths)

Lincoln – 120 pts incl biol/chem (Biol)

Northumbria – 120 pts incl biol (App Biol; Biol Foren Biol) (IB 30 pts)

Plymouth – 120 pts incl biol+sci (Hum Biosci) (IB 28 pts HL 5 biol+sci)

Portsmouth – 120 pts incl biol (Biol; Mar Biol) (IB 30 pts HL 17 pts incl 6 biol)

Queen's Belfast – BBB–ABB incl biol+sci/maths/geog (Mar Biol)

Stirling – BBB (Biol) (IB 32 pts)

116 pts **Aberystwyth** – 116–132 pts incl biol/env sci (Env Biosci); 116–132 pts incl biol (Biol; Mar Frshwtr Biol; Plnt Biol)

112 pts **Bangor** – 112–136 pts incl biol (Mar Biol Zool; Mar Biol Ocean; Mar Biol); 112–128 pts incl biol+sci (App Mar Biol)

Central Lancashire – 112 pts incl biol/chem (Foren Sci Mol Biol) (IB 28 pts HL 5 biol/ chem)

Chester – BBC–BCC incl biol/chem/env sci 112 pts (Foren Biol) (IB 26 pts HL 5 biol/chem); BBC–BCC incl biol/chem/app sci 112 pts (Biol courses) (IB 26 pts HL 5 biol)

Derby – 112 pts (Biol)

East London – 112 pts incl biol/chem (Hum Biol) (IB 25 pts)

Hull – 112 pts incl biol (Hum Biol) (28 pts HL 5 biol); (Biol) (IB 28 pts HL 6 biol)

London (Birk) – 112 pts (Struct Mol Biol)

Middlesex – 112 pts (Biol)

Nottingham Trent – 112 pts incl biol (Zoo Biol)

Oxford Brookes – BBC (Hum Biol) (IB 30 pts); BBC 112 pts (Biol) (IB 30 pts)

Sheffield Hallam – 112 pts incl biol (Hum Biol; Biol)

Staffordshire – 112 pts (Hum Biol)

Teesside – BBC incl biol (Foren Biol)

104 pts **Bangor** – 104–128 pts incl biol (Biol)

Bath Spa – 104–120 pts incl biol/chem (Biol)

Coventry – BCC incl biol (Hum Biosci) (IB 27 pts)

Edinburgh Napier – BCC incl sci (Anim Biol; Mar Frshwtr Biol) (IB 28 pts HL 5 sci)

Glasgow Caledonian – BCC incl chem (Cell Mol Biol) (IB 24 pts)

      Liverpool Hope - BCC–BBB 104–120 pts (Biol)
      Liverpool John Moores - 104 pts incl sci (Biol) (IB 25 pts)
      Manchester Met - BCC–BBC incl biol 104–112 pts (Biol) (IB 28 pts HL 5 biol)
      Northampton - 104–120 pts (Biol)
      South Wales - BCC incl biol (Biol) (IB 29 pts HL 5 biol); BCC incl biol+sci (Int Wldlf Biol; Hum Biol) (IB 29 pts HL 5 biol+sci); BCC incl chem+biol (Foren Biol) (IB 29 pts HL 5 chem+biol)
      Staffordshire - BCC incl biol 104 pts (Biol)
      Ulster - 104 pts incl sci/maths (Biol) (IB 28 pts)
      Worcester - 104–120 pts incl biol+sci/maths (Biol)
96 pts **Anglia Ruskin** - 96 pts incl biol (Mar Biol Cons Biodiv) (IB 24 pts HL biol)
      Bolton - 96 pts incl biol (Biol)
      Canterbury Christ Church - 96 pts (Biosci)
      Cumbria - 96 pts (Cons Biol)
      Glyndŵr - 96 pts (Wldlf Plnt Biol)
      Salford - 96–112 pts incl biol (Biol) (IB 28 pts)
      Wolverhampton - 96 pts incl sci (Hum Biol)
80 pts **Queen Margaret** - BB incl chem/biol 80 pts (Hum Biol) (IB 26 pts)
      Wolverhampton - 80 pts incl biol/chem (Genet Mol Biol); 80 pts incl sci (Microbiol)

Alternative offers
See **Chapter 6** and **Appendix 1** for grades/new UCAS Tariff points information for other examinations.

EXAMPLES OF COLLEGES OFFERING COURSES IN THIS SUBJECT FIELD
Bishop Burton (Coll); Blackpool and Fylde (Coll); Bournemouth and Poole (Coll); Brighton and Hove City (Coll); HOW (Coll); Leeds City (Coll); Liverpool City (Coll); Manchester (Coll); North Hertfordshire (Coll); Solihull (Coll); South Devon (Coll); Sparsholt (Coll); SRUC; Sunderland (Coll); Truro and Penwith (Coll); Walsall (Coll); Warrington (Coll).

CHOOSING YOUR COURSE (SEE ALSO CH.1)
Universities and colleges teaching quality See www.qaa.ac.uk; http://unistats.direct.gov.uk.

Top research universities and colleges (REF 2014) See **Biological Sciences**.

Examples of sandwich degree courses Aston; Bath; Birmingham; Cardiff; Coventry; Dundee; Edinburgh Napier; Hertfordshire; Huddersfield; Kent; Kingston; Leeds; Lincoln; Liverpool John Moores; Loughborough; Manchester; Manchester Met; Middlesex; Newcastle; Northumbria; Nottingham Trent; Plymouth; Queen's Belfast; Reading; Sheffield Hallam; South Wales; Sussex; Teesside; Ulster; UWE Bristol; York.

ADMISSIONS INFORMATION
Number of applicants per place (approx) Aberdeen 8; Aberystwyth 5; Aston 6; Bath 8; Bath Spa 8; Birmingham 9; Bradford 7; Bristol 5; Cardiff 8; Dundee 6; Durham 11; Exeter 6; Hull 4; Imperial London 4; Kent 10; Leeds 6; London (RH) 5; Newcastle (Mar Biol) 15; Nottingham 9; Oxford Brookes 13; Salford 3; Southampton 7; Stirling 15; Sussex 4; Swansea (Mar Biol) 8, (Biol) 4; York 8.

Advice to applicants and planning the UCAS personal statement See **Biochemistry**, **Biological Sciences** and **Appendix 3**. **York** Advanced Diploma not generally accepted.

Misconceptions about this course Sussex Many students think that a Biology degree limits you to being a professional scientist which is not the case. **York** Some fail to realise that chemistry beyond GCSE is essential. Mature students often lack the confidence to consider the course.

Selection interviews Yes Bangor, Bath, Birmingham, Bradford (informal, after offer), Essex, Hertfordshire, Imperial London, Kent, Kingston, London (RH), Manchester, Sheffield Hallam, Southampton, SRUC, Staffordshire, Swansea, York; **Some** Anglia Ruskin, Aston, Derby, Liverpool John Moores, Sheffield, Stirling, Wolverhampton; **No** Dundee, Nottingham.

Interview advice and questions Questions are likely to focus on your studies in biology, on any work experience or any special interests you may have in biology outside school. In the past, questions have included: Is the computer like a brain and, if so, could it ever be taught to think? What do you think the role of the environmental biologist will be in the next 40–50 years? Have you any strong views on vivisection? You have a micro-organism in the blood: you want to make a culture. What conditions should be borne in mind? What is a pacemaker? What problems will a giraffe experience? How does water enter a flowering plant? Compare an egg and a potato. Discuss a family tree of human genotypes. Discuss fish farming in Britain today. What problems do fish face underwater? See also **Chapter 5**. **Liverpool John Moores** Informal interview. It is useful to bring samples of coursework to the interview. **York** Why Biology? How do you see your future?

Reasons for rejection (non-academic) Bath Spa Poor mathematical and scientific knowledge.

AFTER-RESULTS ADVICE
Offers to applicants repeating A-levels Higher Cardiff, East London, St Andrews, Strathclyde; **Possibly higher** Aston, Bath, Bradford, Durham, Leeds, London (RH), Nottingham, Portsmouth; **Same** Aberystwyth, Anglia Ruskin, Bangor, Chester, Derby, Dundee, Edinburgh Napier, Heriot-Watt, Hull, Liverpool John Moores, Loughborough, Manchester Met, Newcastle, Oxford Brookes, Plymouth, Sheffield, Southampton, Staffordshire, Stirling, Teesside, Ulster, Wolverhampton, York.

GRADUATE DESTINATIONS AND EMPLOYMENT (2013/14 HESA)
Graduates surveyed 4,730 **Employed** 1,930 **In voluntary employment** 160 **In further study** 1,415 **Assumed unemployed** 385

Career note Some graduates go into research, but many will go into laboratory work in hospitals, food laboratories, agriculture, the environment and pharmaceuticals. Others go into teaching, management and other professional and technical areas.

OTHER DEGREE SUBJECTS FOR CONSIDERATION

Anatomy; Biochemistry; Biological Sciences; Biotechnology; Chemistry; Dentistry; Ecology; Environmental Health; Environmental Science/Studies; Food Science; Genomics; Health Studies; Medicine; Midwifery; Nursing; Nutrition; Optometry; Orthoptics; Pharmaceutical Sciences; Pharmacology; Pharmacy; Physiology; Physiotherapy; Plant Sciences; Radiography; Speech and Language Therapy; Zoology.

BIOTECHNOLOGY

(including **Prosthetics**; see also **Biological Sciences, Biology, Engineering (Medical), Microbiology**)

Biotechnology is basically the application of biology to improve the quality of life. It is a multi-disciplinary subject which can involve a range of scientific disciplines covering chemistry, the biological sciences, microbiology and genetics. At Bangor for example, the course involves medical and industrial applications to the environment, the food industry, and because of its very favourable coastal location it can add marine biotechnology and fisheries genetics to its programme. Medical engineering involves the design, installation, maintenance and provision of technical support for diagnostic, therapeutic and other clinical equipment used by doctors, nurses and other clinical healthcare workers.

Useful websites www.bbsrc.ac.uk; www.bioindustry.org; www.abcinformation.org

NB The points totals shown to the left of the institutions are for ease of reference only. It must not be assumed that Tariff points are always used by institutions or that they can be substituted for an offer in grades. The level of an offer is not necessarily indicative of the quality of a course.

COURSE OFFERS INFORMATION

Subject requirements/preferences GCSE Mathematics and science subjects required. **AL** Courses vary but one, two or three subjects from Chemistry, Biology, Physics and Mathematics may be required.

Your target offers and examples of degree courses

152 pts	**Leeds** – A*AA incl maths+sci (Med Eng BEng/MEng) (IB 36 pts HL 6 maths+sci)
144 pts	**Birmingham** – AAA–AAB incl biol+sci (Biol Sci (Biotech)) (IB 32 pts HL 666–665)
	Bristol – AAA–AAB 144–136 pts (Bioch Mol Biol Biotech) (IB 37–35 pts)
	Edinburgh – AAA–ABB 144–128 pts (Biotech) (IB 37–32 pts)
	Imperial London – AAA incl chem+sci/maths (Biotech) (IB 38 pts HL 6 chem+biol/maths); (Biotech (Yr Ind/Rsch)) (IB 38 pts HL 6 chem+biol); AAA incl maths+phys (Biomat Tiss Eng) (IB 38 pts HL 6 maths+phys)
	London (UCL) – AAA incl chem+sci/maths (Biotech) (IB 38 pts HL 6 chem 5 sci/maths)
	Manchester – AAA–ABB incl sci/maths (Biotech) (IB 37–33 pts HL 5/6 biol+chem)
	Sheffield – AAA incl maths+chem (Cheml Eng Biotech MEng) (IB 37 pts HL 6 maths+chem)
	York – AAA–AAB incl biol+chem/maths (Biotech Microbiol) (IB 36–35 pts HL 6 biol+chem/maths)
136 pts	**Cardiff** – AAB–ABB incl chem (Biotech (Yr Ind)) (IB 34 pts HL 6 biol+chem)
	Glasgow – AAB–BBB incl biol/chem (Mol Cell Biol (Biotech)) (IB 36–34 pts)
	Surrey – AAB–ABB incl biol+sci/maths 136 pts (Biotech) (IB 35–34 pts)
128 pts	**Kent** – ABB incl maths+bio/chem+phys/comp (Bioeng) (IB 34 pts)
	Northumbria – 128 pts incl biol (Biotech) (IB 31 pts)
	Nottingham – ABB–BBB incl biol+sci/maths (Biotech) (IB 32–30 pts)
	Strathclyde – ABB–BBB incl maths+sci (Pros Orthot) (IB 34 pts HL 6 maths+sci)
120 pts	**Aberdeen** – BBB incl maths/sci (Biotech (App Mol Biol)) (IB 32 pts HL 5 maths/sci)
112 pts	**Chester** – BBC–BCC incl sci 112 pts (Biotech) (IB 26 pts HL 5 biol/chem)
	Middlesex – 112 pts (Biol (Biotech))
104 pts	**Bangor** – 104–128 pts incl biol (Biol Biotech)
	Edinburgh Napier – BCC incl sci (Microbiol Biotech) (IB 28 pts HL 5 sci)
96 pts	**London Met** – 96 pts incl biol+chem (Biotech)
80 pts	**Wolverhampton** – 80 pts incl sci (Biotech)

Alternative offers
See **Chapter 6** and **Appendix 1** for grades/new UCAS Tariff points information for other examinations.

CHOOSING YOUR COURSE (SEE ALSO CH.1)

Universities and colleges teaching quality See www.qaa.ac.uk; http://unistats.direct.gov.uk.

Examples of sandwich degree courses Bristol; Imperial London; Manchester; Northumbria; Surrey; York.

ADMISSIONS INFORMATION

Number of applicants per place (approx) Birmingham 6; Bristol 9; Imperial London 4; Leeds 7; London (UCL) 7; Strathclyde 4.

Advice to applicants and planning the UCAS personal statement See **Biological Sciences**, **Biochemistry** and **Appendix 3**.

Selection interviews Yes Leeds, Manchester, Strathclyde, Surrey; **Some** Wolverhampton; **No** Imperial London.

Interview advice and questions See **Biology**, **Biological Sciences** and **Chapter 5**.

AFTER-RESULTS ADVICE

Offers to applicants repeating A-levels Possibly higher Nottingham; **Same** Leeds, Wolverhampton.

GRADUATE DESTINATIONS AND EMPLOYMENT (2013/14 HESA)
Graduates surveyed 25 **Employed** 10 **In voluntary employment** 0 **In further study** 5 **Assumed unemployed** 0

Medical Technology graduates surveyed 1340 **Employed** 1065 **In voluntary employment** 10 **In further study** 100 **Assumed unemployed** 90

Career note Biotechnology, biomedical and biochemical engineering opportunities exist in medical, agricultural, food science and pharmaceutical laboratories. Some Bioengineering graduates apply for graduate medical courses and obtain both engineering and medical qualifications.

OTHER DEGREE SUBJECTS FOR CONSIDERATION
Agriculture; Biochemistry; Biological Sciences; Biomedicine; Chemistry; Food Technology; Genetics; Materials Science and Technology; Microbiology; Molecular Biology; Pharmacology.

BUILDING and CONSTRUCTION

(including **Building Design, Building Services Engineering, Building Surveying, Construction, Fire Risk Engineering, Fire Safety Management** and **Quantity Surveying.**; see also **Architecture, Engineering (Civil), Housing, Property Management** and **Surveying**)

The building and construction industry covers a wide range of specialisms and is closely allied to civil, municipal and structural engineering (see under **Engineering (Civil)**). The specialisms include Construction Management involving accountancy, economics, law and estimating in addition to main studies in building materials and methods, construction techniques, and health and safety. Then there's Building Surveying which not only involves modules on building technology but also the study of the history of building techniques and styles and enables the surveyor to diagnose and test all aspects of a building's performance and construction. Quantity Surveying is another specialism which relates to the financial planning of a building project covering costs (which can constantly change during the period of the project) as well as modifications which might be required to the original architect's plans. Finally, there is Building Services Engineering; a career which involves specialised areas such as heating, lighting, acoustics, refrigeration and air conditioning. All university courses in these subjects will offer work placements.

Useful websites www.ciob.org.uk; www.cibse.org; www.citb.co.uk; www.rics.org; www.cstt.org.uk; www.cbuilde.com

NB The points totals shown to the left of the institutions are for ease of reference only. It must not be assumed that Tariff points are always used by institutions or that they can be substituted for an offer in grades. The level of an offer is not necessarily indicative of the quality of a course.

COURSE OFFERS INFORMATION
Subject requirements/preferences GCSE English, mathematics and science usually required. **AL** Physics, Mathematics or a technical subject may be required for some courses.

Your target offers and examples of degree courses
136 pts Brunel – AAB–ABB (Mech Eng Bld Serv) (IB 33 pts)
128 pts London (UCL) – ABB (Proj Mgt Constr) (IB 34 pts)
      Newcastle – ABB (Surv Map Sci) (IB 34 pts HL 5 maths)
      Reading – ABB–BBB (Constr Mgt; Bld Surv; Quant Surv) (IB 32–30 pts)
120 pts Brighton – BBB (Bld Surv; Constr Mgt) (IB 30 pts)
      Coventry – BBB (Bld Surv; Constr Mgt) (IB 29 pts); (Quant Surv Commer Mgt) (IB 30 pts)
      Heriot-Watt – ABC–BBB (Constr Proj Mgt) (IB 29 pts)
      Huddersfield – BBB 120 pts (Surv (Bld Surv); Constr Proj Mgt)
      Leeds Beckett – 120 pts (Constr Mgt) (IB 26 pts)
      Loughborough – 120 pts (Commer Mgt Quant Surv) (IB 32 pts)

Northumbria – 120 pts (Bld Surv; Constr Proj Mgt; Quant Surv) (IB 30 pts)
Nottingham Trent – 120 pts (Bld Surv; Quant Surv Constr Commer Mgt)
Plymouth – 120 pts (Bld Surv Env) (IB 32 pts)
Ulster – 120 pts incl maths/sci (Constr Eng Mgt) (IB 26 pts); 120 pts (Quant Surv Commer; Bld Surv) (IB 26 pts)

112 pts Aston – BBC–BBB (Constr Proj Mgt) (IB 32 pts)
Birmingham City – 112 pts (Bld Surv); BBC 112 pts (Quant Surv; Constr Mgt) (IB 30 pts)
Central Lancashire – 112 pts incl maths (Bld Serv Sust Eng; Quant Surv) (IB 28 pts HL 5 maths); 112 pts (Fire Ldrshp St) (IB 25 pts); (Constr Proj Mgt; Bld Surv) (IB 28 pts)
Glasgow Caledonian – BBC (Bld Surv) (IB 24 pts)
Greenwich – 112 pts (Des Constr Mgt; Quant Surv)
Kingston – 112–120 pts (Bld Surv)
Leeds Beckett – 112 pts (Bld Surv; Quant Surv) (IB 25 pts)
London South Bank – BBC 112 pts (Quant Surv; Bld Surv)
Loughborough – 112 pts (Constr Eng Mgt) (IB 30 pts)
Oxford Brookes – BBC–BCC (Quant Surv Commer Mgt; Constr Proj Mgt) (IB 31–30 pts)
Plymouth – 112 pts (Constr Mgt Env) (IB 28 pts)
Sheffield Hallam – 112 pts (Bld Surv; Constr Proj Mgt; Quant Surv)
UWE Bristol – 112 pts (Bld Surv; Quant Surv Commer Mgt; Constr Proj Mgt) (IB 25 pts)
West London – 112 pts (Constr Proj Mgt)
Westminster – BBC (Bld Surv; Constr Mgt) (IB 28 pts); (Quant Surv Commer Mgt) (IB 29 pts)

108 pts Anglia Ruskin – 108 pts (Bld Surv; Quant Surv) (IB 25 pts)
Liverpool John Moores – 108 pts incl maths/sci (Bld Serv Eng) (IB 25 pts HL 5 maths); 108 pts (Bld Surv; Quant Surv)
Portsmouth – 108–120 pts (Quant Surv) (IB 26 pts)

104 pts Derby – 104 pts (Constr Mgt Prop Dev)
Glasgow Caledonian – BCC (Constr Mgt; Quant Surv) (IB 24 pts)
South Wales – BCC (Quant Surv Commer Mgt) (IB 29 pts)

100 pts Portsmouth – 100–120 pts (Constr Eng Mgt) (IB 26 pts)

96 pts Anglia Ruskin – 96 pts (Constr Mgt) (IB 24 pts)
Bolton – 96 pts (Quant Surv Commer Mgt; Bld Surv Prop Mgt)
Edinburgh Napier – CCC (Bld Surv; Constr Proj Mgt; Quant Surv) (IB 27 pts)
Glyndŵr – 96 pts (Constr Mgt)
Kingston – 96 pts (Constr Mgt) (IB 24 pts)
Nottingham Trent – 96 pts (Quant Surv; Constr Mgt)
Robert Gordon – CCC (Surv); (Surv) (IB 28 pts)
Southampton Solent – 96 pts (Constr Mgt)
Wolverhampton – 96 pts (Constr Mgt; Quant Surv)

88 pts Glasgow Caledonian – CCD incl maths+phys (Bld Serv Eng) (IB 24 pts)
London South Bank – CCD/AB 88 pts (Constr Mgt; Prop Mgt (Bld Surv); Commer Mgt (Quant Surv))

80 pts Colchester (Inst) – 80 pts (Constr Mgt (Site Mgt); Constr Mgt (Commer Mgt))
Wolverhampton – 80 pts (Bld Surv)

72 pts Trinity Saint David – 72 pts (Proj Constr Mgt; Quant Surv Commer Mgt)

Alternative offers
See **Chapter 6** and **Appendix 1** for grades/new UCAS Tariff points information for other examinations.

EXAMPLES OF COLLEGES OFFERING COURSES IN THIS SUBJECT FIELD

Accrington and Rossendale (Coll); Banbury and Bicester (Coll); Barnfield (Coll); Barnsley (Coll); Basingstoke (CT); Bath (Coll); Bedford (Coll); Bexley (Coll); Birmingham Met (Coll); Blackpool and Fylde (Coll); Bournemouth and Poole (Coll); Bradford (Coll); Bury (Coll); Canterbury (Coll); Carshalton (Coll); Central Nottingham (Coll); Chelmsford (Coll); Chesterfield (Coll); Croydon (Univ Centre);

Darlington (Coll); Doncaster (Coll); Dudley (Coll); Durham; Ealing, Hammersmith and West London (Coll); East Berkshire (Coll); East Kent (Coll); East Riding (Coll); East Surrey (Coll); Eastleigh (Coll); Exeter (Coll); Furness (Coll); Gateshead (Coll); Gloucestershire (Coll); Gower Swansea (Coll); Grimsby (Univ Centre); Hartlepool (CFE); Hull (Coll); Leicester (Coll); LeSoCo; Lincoln (Coll); London UCK (Coll); Menai (Coll); Mid-Kent (Coll); Nescot; North West London (Coll); Norwich City (Coll); Plymouth City (Coll); Portsmouth (Coll); Redcar and Cleveland (Coll); Richmond-upon-Thames (Coll); St Helens (Coll); South Cheshire (Coll); South City Birmingham (Coll); South Essex (Coll); South Leicestershire (Coll); Southampton City (Coll); Stamford New (Coll); Stephenson (Coll); Stockport (Coll); Suffolk (Univ Campus); Sussex Coast Hastings (Coll); Tameside (Coll); Trafford (Coll); Wakefield (Coll); Warrington (Coll); West Cheshire (Coll); West Kent (Coll); West Suffolk (Coll); Westminster City (Coll); Wigan and Leigh (Coll); Wirral Met (Coll); York (Coll); Yorkshire Coast (Coll).

CHOOSING YOUR COURSE (SEE ALSO CH.1)

Universities and colleges teaching quality See www.qaa.ac.uk; http://unistats.direct.gov.uk.

Top research universities and colleges (REF 2014) See **Architecture**.

Examples of sandwich degree courses Aston; Brighton; Brunel; Coventry; Glasgow Caledonian; Greenwich; Kingston; Leeds Beckett; Liverpool John Moores; London South Bank; Loughborough; Northumbria; Nottingham Trent; Sheffield Hallam; Ulster; UWE Bristol; Wolverhampton.

ADMISSIONS INFORMATION

Number of applicants per place (approx) Edinburgh Napier 8; Glasgow Caledonian 6; Heriot-Watt 6; Kingston 4; London (UCL) 6; Loughborough 4; Northumbria 6; UWE Bristol (Constr Mgt) 5.

Advice to applicants and planning the UCAS personal statement Details of work experience with any levels of responsibility should be included. Make contact with any building organisation to arrange a meeting with staff to discuss careers in building. Give evidence of your ability to work in a team and give details of any personal achievements in technological areas and work experience. Building also covers civil engineering, surveying, quantity surveying etc and these areas should also be explored. See also **Appendix 3**.

Misconceptions about this course Loughborough Some students fail to realise that the degree includes law, finance, economics and management plus constructional technology.

Selection interviews Yes Derby, Glasgow Caledonian, Greenwich, Kingston, Liverpool John Moores, Loughborough, Oxford Brookes, Plymouth, Sheffield Hallam, Westminster; **Some** Anglia Ruskin, Birmingham City, Brighton; **No** Reading.

Interview advice and questions Work experience in the building and civil engineering industries is important and you could be expected to describe any building project you have visited and any problems experienced in its construction. A knowledge of the range of activities to be found on a building site will be expected, for example the work of quantity and land surveyors and of the various building trades. See also **Chapter 5**. **Loughborough** The applicant should show an understanding of the role of the quantity surveyor.

Reasons for rejection (non-academic) Inability to communicate. Lack of motivation. Indecisiveness about reasons for choosing the course. **Loughborough** Applicant more suited to a hands-on course rather than an academic one.

AFTER-RESULTS ADVICE

Offers to applicants repeating A-levels Higher Liverpool John Moores; **Possibly higher** UWE Bristol; **Same** Birmingham City, Bolton, Brighton, Coventry, Heriot-Watt, Huddersfield, Kingston, London (UCL), Loughborough, Northumbria, Trinity Saint David.

GRADUATE DESTINATIONS AND EMPLOYMENT (2013/14 HESA)

Graduates surveyed 3225 **Employed** 2425 **In voluntary employment** 25 **In further study** 460 **Assumed unemployed** 120

Career note There is a wide range of opportunities within the building and construction industry for building technologists and managers. This subject area also overlaps into surveying, quantity surveying, civil engineering, architecture and planning and graduates from all these subjects commonly work together as members of construction teams.

OTHER DEGREE SUBJECTS FOR CONSIDERATION

Architectural Technology; Architecture; Civil Engineering; Property Planning and Development; Quantity Surveying; Surveying.

BUSINESS and MANAGEMENT COURSES

(see also **Business and Management Courses (International and European), Business and Management Courses (Specialised), Economics, Hospitality and Event Management, Human Resource Management, Leisure and Recreation Management/Studies, Marketing, Retail Management, Tourism and Travel**)

Business degrees attract more applicants than any other degree subject, and students should try to assess the balance between theoretical studies and hands-on approaches offered by courses. Most universities offer a range of courses such as at Durham University where in the first year of the Management course, accounting, marketing and business management are covered and students may switch to any of these degrees at the end of the year. Transfers between business courses is indeed a common feature at most institutions. As for the course content, financial studies form part of all courses with additional modules, which would include for example, marketing, business law, human resources and many others. In the following table, there is also a section focusing on European and International business courses for those with a language ability, and a further section on more specialised courses which cover advertising, airports, engineering, music, transport, travel, and sport. Since this is a vocational subject, some work experience in the field is generally required prior to application.

Useful websites www.faststream.civilservice.gov.uk; www.icsa.org.uk; www.adassoc.org.uk; www.cipr. co.uk; www.ismm.co.uk; www.export.org.uk; www.ipsos-mori.com; www.capitaresourcing.co.uk; www. tax.org.uk; www.hmrc.gov.uk; www.camfoundation.com; www.shell-livewire.org; www.iconsulting.org. uk; www.managers.org.uk; www.cipd.co.uk; www.instam.org

NB The points totals shown to the left of the institutions are for ease of reference only. It must not be assumed that Tariff points are always used by institutions or that they can be substituted for an offer in grades. The level of an offer is not necessarily indicative of the quality of a course.

COURSE OFFERS INFORMATION

Subject requirements/preferences GCSE Mathematics and English often at grade A or B required. **AL** Mathematics required for some courses. In some cases grades A, B or C may be required.

Your target offers and examples of degree courses
152 pts **Durham** – A*AA incl maths (Econ Mgt) (IB 38 pts)
　　　　 Exeter – A*AA–AAB incl maths (Maths Mgt) (IB 38–34 pts HL 6 maths)
　　　　 London (King's) – A*AA incl hum/soc sci (Bus Mgt) (IB 35 pts)
　　　　 Warwick – A*AA incl maths+phys (Phys Bus St) (IB 38 pts HL 6 maths+phys)
144 pts **Bath** – AAA/A*AB (Mgt courses) (IB 36 pts)
　　　　 Bristol – AAA/A*AB–AAB incl maths (Acc Mgt) (IB 36–34 pts HL 6 maths)
　　　　 City – AAA (Bus St) (IB 35 pts); AAA 144 pts (Mgt) (IB 35 pts)
　　　　 Edinburgh – AAA–ABB (Bus courses; Bus Acc) (IB 37–34 pts); (Econ Hist Bus)
　　　　　　 (IB 40–34 pts)
　　　　 Exeter – AAA–AAB (Bus Mgt; Bus Acc) (IB 36–34 pts)
　　　　 Lancaster – AAA (Mgt courses) (IB 36 pts)
　　　　 Leeds – AAA (Mgt Mark; Bus Econ; Econ Mgt) (IB 35 pts)

Check **Chapter 3** for new university admission details and **Chapter 6** on how to read the subject tables.

182 | Business and Management Courses

London (UCL) – AAA incl maths (Mgt Sci) (IB 38 pts HL 6 maths)

London LSE – AAA incl maths (Mgt; Bus Maths Stats) (IB 38 pts)

Loughborough – AAA–AAB incl maths (Maths Mgt) (IB 36 pts HL 6 maths)

Reading – AAA (Bus Mgt) (IB 35 pts); (Int Bus Mgt) (IB 37 pts); AAA–AAB (Entre Mgt) (IB 35 pts)

St Andrews – AAA (Mgt Span; Mgt courses; Mgt Sci) (IB 38 pts)

Surrey – AAA (Bus Econ) (IB 36 pts); AAA–AAB (Bus Mgt) (IB 36–35 pts)

Sussex – AAA–AAB (Law Bus Mgt) (IB 35 pts)

Warwick – AAA (Mgt) (IB 38 pts)

136 pts **Aston** – AAB–ABB (Acc Mgt; Bus Mgt) (IB 35–34 pts)

Birmingham – AAB (Bus Mgt courses) (IB 32 pts HL 665)

Brunel – AAB–BBB (Bus Mgt; Bus Mgt (Mark); Bus Mgt (Acc)) (IB 33 pts)

Cardiff – AAB (Bus St Jap; Bus Mgt) (IB 35 pts)

Durham – AAB (Bus Mgt) (IB 36 pts)

Glasgow – AAB–ABB (Bus Mgt Joint Hons) (IB 36–38 pts)

Lancaster – AAB (Fin Mgt St; Bus St courses; Mgt Org Bhv; Acc Mgt St) (IB 35 pts)

Leeds – AAB (Mgt) (IB 35 pts)

Liverpool – AAB (Bus Mgt (Yr Ind)) (IB 33 pts)

Loughborough – AAB–ABB (Mgt Sci) (IB 34 pts)

Manchester – AAB (Bus St; Mgt courses; Bus St Econ; Bus St Pol; Bus St Sociol; Comp Sci Bus Mgt) (IB 35 pts)

Newcastle – AAB/A*BB/A*AC incl maths (Maths Mgt) (IB 37–35 pts HL 6 maths); AAB (Bus Mgt) (IB 35 pts)

Nottingham – AAB (Mgt) (IB 34 pts)

Sheffield – AAB (Bus Mgt; Bus Mgt Joint Hons) (IB 35 pts)

Southampton – AAB–ABB incl maths/phys (Econ Mgt Sci) (IB 34 pts); AAB–ABB (Bus Mgt) (IB 34 pts); AAB–ABB incl mus +gr 8 (Mus Mgt Sci) (IB 34–30 pts HL 6 mus)

Sussex – AAB–ABB (Comp Bus Mgt; Mark Mgt; Bus Mgt St; Econ Mgt St; Fin Bus) (IB 34 pts)

Warwick – AAB incl maths+phys (Eng Bus St) (IB 36 pts HL 5 maths+phys); AAB (Law Bus St) (IB 36 pts HL 5 maths)

128 pts **Aston** – ABB (Psy Bus) (IB 33 pts)

Bournemouth – 128–136 pts (Bus St) (IB 32–33 pts)

Brighton – ABB 128 pts +portfolio +interview (Fash Bus St) (IB 34 pts)

Coventry – ABB (Bus Mgt) (IB 30 pts)

East Anglia – ABB (Bus Econ; Mark Mgt) (IB 32 pts)

Essex – ABB–BBB (Bus Mgt) (IB 32–30 pts)

Kent – ABB (Bus Admin courses) (IB 34 pts)

Kingston – 128 pts (Bus St) (IB 27 pts)

Leicester – ABB (Mgt St; Mgt St courses) (IB 30 pts)

Liverpool – ABB (Bus Mgt) (IB 33 pts); ABB incl maths (Maths Bus St) (IB 33 pts HL 6 maths)

London (QM) – ABB 128 pts (Bus Mgt) (IB 34 pts)

London (RH) – ABB (Mgt courses; Econ Mgt; Mgt Acc) (IB 32 pts)

Northumbria – ABB 128 pts (Bus Mgt) (IB 31 pts)

Nottingham – ABB incl lang (Modn Langs Bus) (IB 32 pts)

Queen's Belfast – ABB (Bus Mgt)

Strathclyde – ABB–BBB (Bus; Bus Ent courses) (IB 33 pts)

Swansea – ABB–BBB (Bus Mgt; Bus Mgt (Fin)) (IB 33–32 pts)

120 pts **Aberdeen** – BBB (Mgt St) (IB 30 pts)

Bournemouth – 120 pts (Acc Bus) (IB 31 pts)

Bradford – BBB 120 pts (Bus Mgt St)

Brighton – BBB (Bus Mgt courses; Bus Mgt Fin) (IB 30 pts HL 16 pts)

Buckingham – BBB–BCC (Bus Mgt courses); BBB (Bus Ent; Law Mgt St)

Dundee – BBB–BCC (Bus Mgt) (IB 30 pts)

Check **Chapter 3** for new university admission details and **Chapter 6** on how to read the subject tables.

KICK START YOUR CAREER

with a business and management degree from a world-leading business school

- Keep pace with business trends
- Tailor your interests with flexible modules
- Gain first-hand experience with industry placements
- Prepare for success in the business world

Find out more:
www.henley.ac.uk/ug/management

E: ugmanagement@henley.ac.uk
T: +44 (0)118 378 5058

TOP 10 IN THE UK

for graduate career prospects in Business & Management*

LONDON

READING

BA BUSINESS & MANAGEMENT

A student's perspective

" Reading about Henley's reputation, I was really impressed with its pedigree and links with local and global companies. **The standard of teaching at Henley is first class**, and the choice of modules means that you **can tailor this programme to your own ambitions** - marketing in my case. Ideally, I'd like a placement in FMCG retail, perhaps within a consumer technology company as that's where my interests lie.

Socially, I've been meeting lots of students and lecturers outside my course through working at open days, joining the Business Society and becoming a Junior Common Room Rep.

My advice? Work hard but also meet as many people as you can, from all different courses. Networking is invaluable at every stage in your life, and you never know who you're going to meet who can help you, either now or in the future. **And at Reading, the people I've met have been awesome!** "

Ben Cummings
Year 2 student,
BA Business & Management

Find out more:
www.henley.ac.uk/ug/management

E: ugmanagement@henley.ac.uk
T: +44 (0)118 378 5058

*Source: Guardian University Guide 2016

Gloucestershire – 120 pts (Bus Mgt)

Heriot-Watt – BBB (Bus Mgt HR Mgt; Bus Mgt Mark) (IB 29 pts)

Huddersfield – BBB 120 pts (Bus St; Bus St Env Mgt; Law Bus; Bus Mgt Fin; Bus Mgt)

Keele – BBB/ABC (Bus Mgt) (IB 32 pts)

Kent – BBB (Acc Mgt (Yr Ind)) (IB 34 pts)

Leeds Beckett – 120 pts (Bus St; Bus Mgt) (IB 26 pts)

Leicester – BBB (Comp Mgt) (IB 28–30 pts)

Lincoln – 120 pts (Bus Mgt)

Loughborough – BBB (Trans Bus Mgt) (IB 32 pts)

Northumbria – BBB 120 pts (Bus Mark Mgt; Bus Econ; Bus Tour Mgt; Bus Log Sply Chn Mgt) (IB 30 pts)

Oxford Brookes – BBB (Bus Mgt) (IB 31 pts)

Plymouth – 120 pts (Law Bus) (IB 30 pts)

Sheffield Hallam – 120 pts (Bus courses; Bus Econ; Bus St; Bus HR Mgt)

Staffordshire – BBB 120 pts (Bus Mgt)

Stirling – BBB (Bus St) (IB 32 pts)

Ulster – BBB–AAB (Bus St) (IB 26–28 pts)

UWE Bristol – 120 pts (Bus Mgt Ldrshp; Bus Mgt courses; Bus courses) (IB 26 pts)

112 pts **Aberystwyth** – 112 pts (Bus Mgt)

Bedfordshire – 112 pts (Bus St courses; Bus Mgt) (IB 24 pts)

Birmingham City – BBC 112 pts (Bus courses) (IB 28 pts); (Fash Bus Prom) (IB 32 pts)

Brighton – BBC incl maths (Maths Bus) (IB 28 pts); BBC (Law Bus) (IB 28 pts)

Canterbury Christ Church – 112 pts (Bus St)

Cardiff Met – 112 pts (Bus Mgt St HR Mgt; Bus Mgt St Fin; Bus Mgt St courses; Bus Mgt St Law)

Central Lancashire – 112 pts (Bus St courses) (IB 28 pts)

Chester – BBC–BCC 112 pts (Bus Mgt) (IB 26 pts)
Chichester – 112–128 pts (Bus St) (IB 30 pts)
Coventry – BBC (Span Bus) (IB 29 pts); (Glob Bus Mgt) (IB 30 pts)
De Montfort – 112 pts (Bus courses; Bus Mgt courses) (IB 28 pts)
Derby – 112 pts (Bus Mgt; Bus St)
East London – 112 pts (Bus Mgt) (IB 24 pts)
Edge Hill – BBC 112 pts (Bus Mgt)
Greenwich – 112 pts (Bus Admin; Bus Entre Innov; PR; Bus Prchsg Sply Chn Mgt; Bus Mgt; Bus Law); (Bus St) (IB 24 pts)
Hull – 112 pts (Bus courses; Bus Fin Mgt) (IB 30 pts)
Kingston – 112 pts (Bus Mgt) (IB 25 pts)
Leeds Beckett – 112 pts (Int Tour Mgt) (IB 25 pts)
Lincoln – 112 pts (Bus Mark)
Liverpool John Moores – 112 pts (Bus St; Bus Mgt) (IB 29 pts)
London Met – 112 pts (Bus Econ)
Newman – 112 pts (Bus Mgt)
Northampton – 112 pts (Bus St; Bus Entre)
Nottingham Trent – 112 pts (Law Bus; Bus Mgt courses; Bus)
Oxford Brookes – BBC (Bus Mgt) (IB 30 pts)
Portsmouth – 112 pts (Law Bus; Bus Mgt) (IB 30 pts HL 17 pts)
Southampton Solent – 112 pts (Bus Mgt)
Sunderland – 112 pts (Bus HR Mgt; Bus Mark Mgt; Bus Fin Mgt; Bus Mgt)
West London – 112 pts (Bus St; Bus St Mark; Bus St HR Mgt; Bus St Fin)
Westminster – BBC (Bus Mgt courses) (IB 28 pts)
Worcester – 112 pts (Bus courses)
York St John – 112 pts incl Ger (Bus Mgt Ger); 112 pts (Bus Mgt; Bus IT; Bus Mgt HR Mgt)

104 pts **Anglia Ruskin** – 104–120 pts (Bus Econ) (IB 24 pts)
Bangor – 104–120 pts (Bus St courses; Mgt Acc; Bus St Ital)
Bath Spa – 104–120 pts (Bus Mgt courses)
Bolton – 104 pts (Bus Mgt)
BPP – BCC 104 pts (Bus Mgt; Bus Mgt Fin)
Edinburgh Napier – BCC (Bus Mgt) (IB 28 pts)
Glasgow Caledonian – BCC (Bus Mgt) (IB 25 pts)
Kingston – 104–112 pts (Pharmacol Bus)
Leeds Trinity – 104 pts (Bus Mark; Bus Mgt; Acc Bus)
Lincoln – 104 pts (Bus St)
Liverpool Hope – BCC–BBB 104–120 pts (Bus Mgt)
Manchester Met – BCC–BBC 104–112 pts (Bus Ent HR Mgt; Bus Mgt; PR Mark) (IB 26 pts)
Middlesex – 104 pts (Bus Mgt; Bus Mgt (Mark))
Northampton – 104–120 pts (Bus Comp (Sys))
Queen Margaret – BCC 104 pts (Bus Mgt) (IB 28 pts)
Robert Gordon – BCC (Mgt) (IB 28 pts)
Salford – 104–120 pts (Bus Mgt) (IB 24 pts)
South Wales – BCC (Bus Mgt) (IB 29 pts)
SRUC – BCC (Rur Bus Mgt)
Teesside – 104 pts (Law Bus Mgt)
Westminster – BCC (Bus Mgt (Mark)) (IB 28 pts)
Winchester – 104–120 pts (Bus Mgt courses) (IB 26 pts)

96 pts **Abertay** – CCC (Mark Bus; Bus Mgt) (IB 28 pts)
Anglia Ruskin – 96–112 pts (Bus Mgt) (IB 24 pts)
Canterbury Christ Church – 96–112 pts (Bus Mgt)
Cumbria – 96 pts (Bus Mgt)
Edinburgh Napier – CCC (Bus St) (IB 27 pts)
Glyndŵr – 96 pts (Bus)

188 | Business and Management Courses

Hertfordshire – 96–112 pts (Bus St; Mgt) (IB 28 pts)
Kingston – 96 pts (Bus IT) (IB 24 pts)
London (Birk) – 96 pts (Mgt)
London Regent's – CCC (Glob Mgt courses) (IB 32 pts)
London South Bank – CCC/AA 96 pts (Bus St; Bus Admin; Bus Mgt Joint Hons)
Manchester Met – 96–112 pts (Bus Joint Hons) (IB 28 pts)
Plymouth – 96 pts (Bus St)
Roehampton – 96 pts (Bus Mgt)
Royal Agricultural Univ – 96 pts (Int Bus Mgt)
St Mary's – 96 pts (Bus Law (Joint Hons); Bus Mgt) (IB 28 pts)
Teesside – 96 pts (Bus Mgt)
West Scotland – CCC (Bus) (IB 24 pts)
Wolverhampton – 96–112 pts (Bus Mgt)
88 pts **Harper Adams** – 88–104 pts (Bus Mgt Mark)
80 pts **Bucks New** – 80–96 pts (Bus Mgt)
Central Lancashire – 80 pts (Bus Mgt Chin) (IB 24 pts)
64 pts **Trinity Saint David** – 64 pts (Bus Fin; Mgt Ldrshp; Bus Mgt)
UHI – CC (Bus Mgt)
48 pts **Colchester (Inst)** – 48 pts (Mgt)
32 pts **Greenwich (Sch Mgt)** – 32 pts (Bus Mgt)

Open University – contact +44 (0)845 300 6090 **or** www.openuniversity.co.uk/you (Bus St)

Alternative offers
See **Chapter 6** and **Appendix 1** for grades/new UCAS Tariff points information for other examinations.

EXAMPLES OF COLLEGES OFFERING COURSES IN THIS SUBJECT FIELD
Most colleges. See **Chapter 9**, Section 3.

CHOOSING YOUR COURSE (SEE ALSO CH.1)
Universities and colleges teaching quality See www.qaa.ac.uk; http://unistats.direct.gov.uk.

Top research universities and colleges (REF 2014) (Business and Management Studies) Imperial London; London LSE; Cambridge; Oxford; Cardiff; Bath; City; London (King's); Leeds; London Business School; Reading; Sheffield; Warwick; East Anglia; Lancaster.

Examples of sandwich degree courses Aston; Bath; Bedfordshire; Birmingham (UC); Birmingham City; Bournemouth; Bradford; Brighton; Brunel; Central Lancashire; Chester; Coventry; De Montfort; Derby; Glasgow Caledonian; Gloucestershire; Greenwich; Harper Adams; Hertfordshire; Huddersfield; Hull; Kingston; Liverpool John Moores; Loughborough; Manchester Met; Newcastle; Nottingham Trent; Oxford Brookes; Plymouth; Portsmouth; Royal Agricultural Univ; Sheffield Hallam; Staffordshire; Surrey; Teesside; Trinity Saint David; Ulster; UWE Bristol; West Scotland; Westminster; Wolverhampton.

ADMISSIONS INFORMATION
Number of applicants per place (approx) Abertay (Bus St) 4; Aberystwyth 3; Anglia Ruskin 5; Aston (Bus Mgt) 12, (Mgt) 5; Bangor 4; Bath 13; Birmingham 8; Birmingham (UC) 5; Blackpool and Fylde (Coll) 2; Bolton 3; Bournemouth 30; Bradford 12; Bristol 10; Brunel 12; Canterbury Christ Church 20; Cardiff 8; Central Lancashire 15; City (Bus St) 17, (Mgt Sys) 6; Colchester (Inst) 2; De Montfort (Bus Mgt) 5; Durham 6; Edge Hill 4; Glasgow Caledonian 18; Heriot-Watt 5; Hertfordshire 10; Huddersfield 5; Hull (Bus St) 19, (Mgt) 10; Kent 30; Kingston 50; Leeds 27, (Mgt St) 16; Leeds Trinity 3; Liverpool 9; London (King's) 25, (Mgt Sci) 12; London (RH) 9; London (UCL) 8; London LSE 18; London Met 10; London Regent's 25; London South Bank 4; Loughborough 5; Manchester 7; Manchester Met (Bus St) 26; Middlesex 12; Newcastle 27, (Bus Mgt) 40; Northumbria 10; Oxford Brookes 40; Plymouth 4; Portsmouth 10, (Bus Admin) 7, (Bus St) 6; Robert Gordon 5; Salford (Bus St) 9, (Mgt Sci) 2; Southampton Solent 13; Strathclyde 12; Sunderland 20; Surrey (Bus Mgt) 6; Teesside (Bus St) 4;

Trinity Saint David 7; Warwick 22; West London 4; West Scotland 5; Westminster 12; Winchester 4; Wolverhampton 7; York 6; York St John 3.

Advice to applicants and planning the UCAS personal statement There are many different kinds of businesses and any work experience is almost essential for these courses. This should be described in detail: for example, size of firm, turnover, managerial problems, sales and marketing aspects, customers' attitudes. Any special interests in business management should also be included, for example, personnel work, purchasing, marketing. Give details of travel or work experience abroad and, for international courses, language expertise and examples of leadership and organising skills. Reference can be made to any particular business topics you have studied in the *Financial Times*, *The Economist* and the business sections in the weekend press. Applicants need to be sociable, ambitious, team players. Say why you are interested in the course, identify your academic strengths, your personal strengths and interests. Check information on the websites of the Chartered Institute of Public Relations, the Chartered Institute of Marketing and the Chartered Institute of Personnel and Development. See **Appendix 3**; see also **Accountancy/Accounting**.

Misconceptions about this course Aberystwyth Students are unaware that the course addresses practical aspects of business. **Salford** (Mgt Sci) Students should appreciate that the courses are fairly mathematical. **York** A previous study of management, IT or languages at A-level is necessary.

Selection interviews Yes Birmingham City, Bradford, Coventry, Edge Hill, Essex, Glasgow Caledonian, Harper Adams, Hull, London Met, Middlesex, Northumbria, Nottingham Trent, Plymouth, Portsmouth, Robert Gordon, Roehampton, Sheffield Hallam, Strathclyde, Swansea, Teesside, Trinity Saint David, West London; **Some** Aberystwyth, Anglia Ruskin, Bath, Blackpool and Fylde (Coll), Brighton, Buckingham, Cardiff Met, City, De Montfort, Derby (Int Bus), East Anglia, Greenwich, Kent (mature and Access students), Leeds, Liverpool John Moores, Manchester Met, Salford, Southampton, Staffordshire, Stirling, Sunderland, Warwick, Winchester, Wolverhampton; **No** Birmingham, Dundee, Nottingham, West Scotland.

Interview advice and questions Any work experience you describe on the UCAS application probably will be the focus of questions which could include topics covering marketing, selling, store organisation and management and customer problems. Personal qualities are naturally important in a career in business, so be ready for such questions as: What qualities do you have which are suitable and important for this course? Describe your strengths and weaknesses. Why should we give you a place on this course? Is advertising fair? What qualities does a person in business require to be successful? What makes a good manager? What is a cash-flow system? What problems can it cause? How could supermarkets improve customer relations? See also **Chapter 5**. **Buckingham** Why Business? How do you see yourself in five years' time? Have you had any work experience? If so, discuss. **Wolverhampton** Mature students with no qualifications will be asked about their work experience.

Reasons for rejection (non-academic) Hadn't read the prospectus. Lack of communication skills. Limited commercial interest. Weak on numeracy and problem-solving. Lack of interview preparation (no questions). Lack of outside interests. Inability to cope with a year abroad. The candidate brought his parent who answered all the questions. See also **Marketing**. **Aberystwyth** Would have trouble fitting into the unique environment of Aberystwyth. Casual approach to learning. **Bournemouth** The Business Studies course is very popular. **Surrey** Hesitation about the period abroad.

AFTER-RESULTS ADVICE
Offers to applicants repeating A-levels Higher Bradford, Brunel, Greenwich, Hertfordshire, Kingston, Lancaster, Liverpool, Manchester Met, St Andrews, Sheffield, Strathclyde, Teesside, UWE Bristol; **Same** Abertay, Aberystwyth, Anglia Ruskin, Aston, Bath, Bath Spa, Birmingham City, Bolton, Bournemouth, Brighton, Brunel, Buckingham, Cardiff, Cardiff Met, Chester, De Montfort, Derby, Durham, East Anglia, East London, Glasgow, Gloucestershire, Harper Adams, Huddersfield, Hull, Kent, Leeds, Lincoln, Liverpool Hope, Liverpool John Moores, Loughborough, Newman, Northumbria, Oxford Brookes, Portsmouth, Robert Gordon, Roehampton, Royal Agricultural Univ, Salford, Sheffield Hallam, Staffordshire, Stirling, Suffolk (Univ Campus), Sunderland, Surrey, Trinity Saint David, Ulster, West London, West Scotland, Winchester, Wolverhampton, Worcester, York, York St John.

GRADUATE DESTINATIONS AND EMPLOYMENT (2013/14 HESA)

Business Studies graduates surveyed 12,715 **Employed** 7,735 **In voluntary employment** 300 **In further study** 2,010 **Assumed unemployed** 930

Management Sciences graduates surveyed 6,290 **Employed** 4,140 **In voluntary employment** 120 **In further study** 885 **Assumed unemployed** 385

Career note The majority of graduates enter trainee management roles in business-related and administrative careers, many specialising in some of the areas listed in **Other degree subjects for consideration** below. The main graduate destinations are in finance, property development, wholesale, retail and manufacturing.

OTHER DEGREE SUBJECTS FOR CONSIDERATION

Accountancy; Banking; Business Information Technology; E-Business; Economics; Estate Management; Finance; Hospitality Management; Housing Management; Human Resource Management; Insurance; Leisure Management; Logistics; Marketing; Public Administration; Retail Management; Sports Management; Surveying.

BUSINESS and MANAGEMENT COURSES (INTERNATIONAL and EUROPEAN)

(including **Business** and **Management Courses with Languages**; see also **Business and Management Courses, Business and Management Courses (Specialised), Hospitality and Event Management, Human Resource Management, Leisure and Recreation Management/Studies, Marketing, Retail Management, Tourism and Travel**)

Useful websites See **Business and Management Courses**.

NB The points totals shown to the left of the institutions are for ease of reference only. It must not be assumed that Tariff points are always used by institutions or that they can be substituted for an offer in grades. The level of an offer is not necessarily indicative of the quality of a course.

COURSE OFFERS INFORMATION

Subject requirements/preferences GCSE Mathematics and English often at grade A or B required. **AL** A language will be stipulated for most courses in this subject area. In some cases grades A, B or C may be required.

Your target offers and examples of degree courses

144 pts **Bath** – AAA/A*AB (Int Mgt) (IB 36 pts); AAA incl Span (Int Mgt Span) (IB 36 pts HL 6 Span)

Edinburgh – AAA–ABB (Int Bus Fr/Ger/Span; Int Bus) (IB 37–34 pts)

Exeter – AAA–AAB (Bus Mgt (Int St))

Leeds – AAA (Int Bus) (IB 36 pts)

London (UCL) – AAA–AAB incl maths (Econ Bus E Euro St) (IB 38–36 pts HL 5 maths)

Reading – AAA (Int Bus Mgt) (IB 37 pts); AAA–AAB (Int Mgt Bus Admin Fr/Ger/Ital) (IB 35 pts)

Warwick – AAA (Int Mgt; Int Bus) (IB 38 pts)

136 pts **Aston** – AAB–ABB (Int Bus Fr/Ger/Span) (IB 34 pts)

Bath – AAB incl Fr (Int Mgt Fr) (IB 35 pts HL 6 Fr); AAB incl Ger (Int Mgt Ger) (IB 35 pts HL 6 Ger)

Birmingham – AAB (Int Bus Lang; Int Bus) (IB 32 pts HL 665)

Brunel – AAB–BBB (Int Bus) (IB 33 pts)

Cardiff – AAB (Bus Mgt (Int Mgt); Bus Mgt Euro Lang) (IB 35 pts)

London (King's) – AAB incl Fr (Fr Mgt (Yr Abrd)) (IB 35 pts HL 6 Fr)

London (SOAS) – AAB–ABB (Int Mgt) (IB 36 pts)

Loughborough – AAB–ABB (Int Bus) (IB 34 pts)

Manchester – AAB (Int Mgt; Int Mgt Am Bus St) (IB 35 pts)

Newcastle – AAB (Int Bus Mgt) (IB 35 pts)
Nottingham – AAB incl Fr/Ger/Span (Mgt Fr/Ger/Span) (IB 34 pts); AAB (Mgt Chin St) (IB 34 pts)
Sheffield – AAB–ABB (Kor St Joint Hons) (IB 35–34 pts); AAB (Int Bus Mgt (St Abrd)) (IB 35 pts)
Southampton – AAB–ABB incl Fr/Ger/Span (Mgt Sci Fr/Ger/Span) (IB 34 pts HL 6 Fr/Ger/Span)
Surrey – AAB incl Fr/Ger/Span (Bus Mgt Fr/Ger/Span) (IB 35 pts)
Sussex – AAB–ABB (Int Bus) (IB 34 pts)

128 pts **Bournemouth** – 128–136 pts (Int Bus St) (IB 32–33 pts)
Essex – ABB–BBB (Int Bus Entre) (IB 32–30 pts)
Kent – ABB (Int Bus) (IB 34 pts)
Liverpool – ABB (Int Bus) (IB 33 pts); ABB incl langs (Modn Lang St Bus) (IB 33 pts HL 66 langs)
London (RH) – ABB (Mgt Fr/Ger/Ital/Span; Mgt Int Bus) (IB 32 pts)
Northumbria – ABB 128 pts (Int Bus Mgt) (IB 31 pts)
Queen's Belfast – ABB incl Fr/Ger (Int Bus Fr/Ger/Mand)

120 pts **Bradford** – BBB 120 pts (Int Bus Mgt)
Coventry – BBB (Int Bus Mgt) (IB 30 pts)
De Montfort – 120 pts (Int Bus) (IB 28 pts)
Dundee – BBB–BCC (Int Bus Mark; Int Bus) (IB 30 pts)
Gloucestershire – 120 pts (Int Bus Mgt)
Heriot-Watt – BBB incl lang (Int Bus Mgt Fr/Ger/Span/Chinese) (IB 30 pts)
Huddersfield – BBB 120 pts (Int Bus)
Keele – BBB/ABC (Int Bus courses) (IB 32 pts)
Leeds Beckett – 120 pts (Int Bus) (IB 26 pts)
London (QM) – BBB–ABB incl lang 120–128 pts (Russ Bus Mgt) (IB 32–34 pts HL 5 lang)
Nottingham Trent – 120 pts (Int Bus Joint Hons)
Oxford Brookes – BBB (Int Bus Mgt) (IB 33 pts)
Sheffield Hallam – 120 pts (Int Bus)
Staffordshire – BBB 120 pts (Int Bus Mgt)
Stirling – BBB (Int Mgt St Intercult St; Int Mgt St Euro Langs Soty) (IB 32 pts)
UWE Bristol – 120 pts (Int Bus) (IB 26 pts)
Westminster – BBB (Int Bus (Arbc/Chin/Fr/Russ/Span); Int Bus) (IB 28 pts)

112 pts **Bedfordshire** – 112 pts (Bus St (Int)) (IB 24 pts)
Brighton – BBC (Int Bus) (IB 28 pts HL 16 pts)
Cardiff Met – 112 pts (Int Bus Mgt)
Central Lancashire – 112 pts (Int Bus) (IB 28 pts)
Chester – BBC–BCC 112 pts (Int Bus Mgt) (IB 26 pts)
Glasgow Caledonian – BBC (Int Bus) (IB 25 pts)
Greenwich – 112 pts (Int Bus) (IB 24 pts)
Hull – 112 pts (Int Bus) (IB 30 pts)
Kingston – 112–128 pts (Int Bus) (IB 25 pts)
Lincoln – 112 pts (Int Bus Mgt)
London Met – 112 pts (Int Bus Mgt)
Middlesex – 112 pts (Int Tour Mgt Span; Int Bus)
Portsmouth – 112 pts (Int Bus St) (IB 30 pts HL 17 pts)
Robert Gordon – BBC (Int Bus Mgt) (IB 29 pts)
Roehampton – 112 pts (Int Bus)
Sheffield Hallam – 112 pts incl Fr/Ger/Span (Int Bus Fr/Ger/Span)
Southampton Solent – 112 pts (Int Bus Mgt)
York St John – 112 pts (Int Bus Mgt)

104 pts **Derby** – 104 pts (Int Spa Mgt)
Manchester Met – BCC–BBC 104–112 pts (Int Bus Mgt) (IB 26 pts); 104–112 pts incl lang (Int Bus Langs (Fr/Ger/Ital/Span)) (IB 26 pts)

          Middlesex – 104 pts (Bus Mgt Mand/Span)

          Salford – BCC 104–120 pts (Int Bus) (IB 24 pts)

96 pts   **Anglia Ruskin** – 96–112 pts (Int Bus Mgt) (IB 24 pts)

          Edinburgh Napier – CCC incl lang (Int Bus Mgt Lang) (IB 27 pts HL 5 lang)

          Euro Bus Sch London – CCC (Int Bus Chin; Int Bus)

          Hertfordshire – 96–112 pts (Int Mgt) (IB 28 pts)

          London Regent's – CCC (Int Bus); (Glob Mgt courses) (IB 32 pts)

          Plymouth – 96 pts (Int Bus); 96 pts incl Span (Int Bus Span) (IB 24 pts); 96 pts incl Fr
            (Int Bus Fr) (IB 24 pts)

          Wolverhampton – 96–112 pts (Int Bus Mgt)

          Open Univrsity – contact +44 (0)845 300 6090 **or** www.openuniversity.co.uk/you
            (Bus St Fr/Span)

Alternative offers
See **Chapter 6** and **Appendix 1** for grades/new UCAS Tariff points information for other examinations.

EXAMPLES OF COLLEGES OFFERING COURSES IN THIS SUBJECT FIELD

Most colleges. Askham Bryan (Coll); Bexley (Coll); Birmingham (UC); Blackburn (Coll); Blackpool and Fylde (Coll); Bristol City (Coll); Colchester (Inst); Cornwall (Coll); Doncaster (Coll); Duchy (Coll); Durham New (Coll); Ealing, Hammersmith and West London (Coll); Farnborough (CT); HOW (Coll); Kirklees (Coll); Knowsley (CmC); Lakes (Coll); Manchester (Coll); Mid-Cheshire (Coll); Newcastle (Coll); North Lindsey (Coll); Northbrook (Coll); Nottingham New (Coll); Riverside (Coll); St Helens (Coll); Sheffield (Coll); Somerset (Coll); South Devon (Coll); South Essex (Coll); Wakefield (Coll); Warwickshire (Coll); Westminster Kingsway (Coll); Writtle (Coll); York (Coll).

CHOOSING YOUR COURSE (SEE ALSO CH.1)

Universities and colleges teaching quality See www.qaa.ac.uk; http://unistats.direct.gov.uk.

Top research universities and colleges (REF 2014) See **Business and Management Courses**.

Examples of sandwich degree courses Anglia Ruskin; Aston; Bath; Bournemouth; Bradford; Brighton; Brunel; Cardiff Met; De Montfort; Greenwich; Hertfordshire; Leeds Beckett; Loughborough; Manchester Met; Middlesex; Northumbria; Nottingham Trent; Oxford Brookes; Plymouth; Portsmouth; Sheffield Hallam; Staffordshire; Sussex; Worcester.

ADMISSIONS INFORMATION

Number of applicants per place (approx) Anglia Ruskin 5; Aston (Int Bus) 6, (Int Bus Econ) 8; Bath 26; Birmingham 28; Birmingham (UC) 5; Blackpool and Fylde (Coll) 2; Bradford 12; Brunel 12; Cardiff 8; Central Lancashire 15; Colchester (Inst) 2; Derby 4; Glasgow Caledonian 18; Heriot-Watt 5; Hertfordshire 10; Huddersfield 5; Kent 30; Kingston 50; Leeds 27; London (King's) 25; London (RH) 9; London Met 10; London Regent's 25; Loughborough 5; Manchester Met (Int Bus) 8; Middlesex 12; Newcastle 27, (Int Bus Mgt) 25; Northumbria 10; Oxford Brookes 40; Plymouth 4; Portsmouth 10, (Int Bus) 5; Robert Gordon 5; Sheffield Hallam (Int Bus) 6; Southampton Solent 13; Warwick 22; Westminster 12; Wolverhampton 7; York St John 3.

Advice to applicants and planning the UCAS personal statement See **Business and Management Courses**.

Misconceptions about this course Aston (Int Bus Fr) Not two separate disciplines – the two subjects are integrated involving the study of language in a business and management context.

Selection interviews Yes Bradford, Coventry, Doncaster (Coll), Euro Bus Sch London, Glasgow Caledonian, Hull, Kent (mature and Access students), London Met, Middlesex, Northumbria, Nottingham Trent, Plymouth, Robert Gordon, Roehampton, Salford, Sheffield Hallam, Swansea, Teesside; **Some** Anglia Ruskin, Bath, Blackpool and Fylde (Coll), Brighton, Cardiff Met, De Montfort, Derby, Greenwich, Leeds, Manchester Met, Staffordshire, Stirling, Warwick, Wolverhampton; **No** Birmingham.

Interview advice and questions See **Business and Management Courses**. **Wolverhampton** Mature students with no qualifications will be asked about their work experience.

Reasons for rejection (non-academic) See **Business and Management Courses**. **Bournemouth** The Business Studies course is very popular. **Surrey** Hesitation about the period abroad.

AFTER-RESULTS ADVICE
Offers to applicants repeating A-levels Higher Bradford, Brunel, Greenwich, Hertfordshire, Kingston, Liverpool, Manchester Met, Sheffield, Teesside, UWE Bristol; **Same** Anglia Ruskin, Aston, Bath, Bournemouth, Brighton, Cardiff, Cardiff Met, Chester, De Montfort, Derby, Gloucestershire, Huddersfield, Hull, Kent, Leeds, Lincoln, Loughborough, Northumbria, Oxford Brookes, Robert Gordon, Roehampton, Salford, Sheffield Hallam, Staffordshire, Stirling, Surrey, Ulster, Wolverhampton, York St John.

GRADUATE DESTINATIONS AND EMPLOYMENT (2013/14 HESA)
See **Business and Management Courses**.

Career note See **Business and Management Courses**.

OTHER DEGREE SUBJECTS FOR CONSIDERATION
Accountancy; Banking; Business Information Technology; E-Business; Economics; Estate Management; Finance; Hospitality Management; Housing Management; Human Resource Management; Insurance; Leisure Management; Logistics; Marketing; Public Administration; Retail Management; Sports Management; Surveying.

BUSINESS and MANAGEMENT COURSES (SPECIALISED)

(including **Advertising, E-Commerce, Entrepreneurship, Operations Management, Public Relations** and **Publishing**; see also **Business and Management Courses, Business and Management Courses (International and European), Hospitality and Event Management, Human Resource Management, Leisure and Recreation Management/Studies, Marketing, Retail Management, Tourism and Travel**)

Useful websites See **Business and Management Courses**.

NB The points totals shown to the left of the institutions are for ease of reference only. It must not be assumed that Tariff points are always used by institutions or that they can be substituted for an offer in grades. The level of an offer is not necessarily indicative of the quality of a course.

COURSE OFFERS INFORMATION
Subject requirements/preferences GCSE Mathematics and English often at grade A or B required. **AL** Mathematics required for some courses. In some cases grades A, B or C may be required. (Publ) English required for some courses.

Your target offers and examples of degree courses
152 pts **Southampton** – A*AA incl maths+phys (Aero Astnaut (Eng Mgt) MEng) (IB 38 pts HL 6 maths+phys)
144 pts **Edinburgh** – AAA–ABB (Ecol Env Sci Mgt) (IB 37–32 pts)
        London (UCL) – AAA–AAB incl chem+sci/maths (Chem Mgt St) (IB 39–38 pts HL 5 chem+sci/maths)
136 pts **Cardiff** – AAB (Bus Mgt (Log Ops)) (IB 35 pts)
        Lancaster – AAB (Adv Mark; Euro-Am Mgt) (IB 35 pts)
        Leeds – AAB (Env Bus) (IB 35 pts)
        London (SOAS) – AAB–ABB (S E As St Int Mgt) (IB 36 pts)

Loughborough – AAB–ABB (Inf Mgt Bus) (IB 34 pts); AAB–ABB incl geog (Geog Spo Mgt) (IB 36–34 pts HL 5 geog); AAB incl Engl (Pub Engl) (IB 34 pts HL 5 Engl)

Newcastle – AAB–ABB (Agri Bus Mgt) (IB 35 pts)

Reading – AAB–ABB (Fd Sci Bus) (IB 35–32 pts)

Warwick – AAB incl maths+phys (Eng Bus Mgt) (IB 36 pts HL 5 maths+phys)

128 pts **Bournemouth** – 128–136 pts (Bus St Fin) (IB 32–33 pts)

Coventry – ABB (Bus Mark) (IB 30 pts); ABB–BBB (Disas Mgt Emer Plan; Disas Mgt) (IB 31–30 pts)

Essex – ABB–BBB (Lat Am St Bus Mgt) (IB 32–30 pts)

Ulster – ABB–AAB (Comm Adv Mark) (IB 27–28 pts)

120 pts **Aberdeen** – BBB incl maths/sci IB 32 pts (Bus Mgt Inf Sys)

Buckingham – BBB–BBC (Bus Mgt App Comp)

East Anglia – BBB (Intercult Comm Bus Mgt) (IB 31 pts)

Heriot-Watt – BBB (Bus Fin) (IB 29 pts)

Huddersfield – BBB 120 pts (Air Trans Log Mgt)

Leeds Beckett – 120 pts (PR) (IB 26 pts)

Loughborough – BBB (Air Trans Mgt) (IB 32 pts)

Middlesex – 120 pts (Mus Bus Arts Mgt)

Nottingham Trent – 120 pts (Fash Mgt; Quant Surv Constr Commer Mgt)

Sheffield Hallam – 120 pts (Bus Fin Mgt)

Ulster – 120 pts incl sci/maths/tech (Eng Mgt) (IB 26 pts)

112 pts **Arts London (CFash)** – BBC 112 pts +portfolio (Fash Mgt)

Bournemouth – 112–120 pts (PR) (IB 30–31 pts)

Cardiff Met – 112 pts (Fd Ind Mgt)

Central Lancashire – 112 pts (Fire Ldrshp St) (IB 25 pts); (Adv) (IB 28 pts)

De Montfort – 112 pts (Adv Mark Comms) (IB 28 pts)

East London – 112 pts (Adv; Bus Mgt (HR Mgt)) (IB 24 pts)

Edge Hill – BBC 112 pts (PR)

Hertfordshire – 112 pts (Mus Ind Mgt) (IB 28 pts)

Leeds Beckett – 112 pts (Spo Bus Mgt) (IB 25 pts)

Liverpool John Moores – 112 pts (Marit Bus Mgt)

London (Birk) – 112 pts (Env Mgt)

London (Royal Central Sch SpDr) – BBC +interview +portfolio (Thea Prac Stg Mgt; Thea Prac Tech Prod Mgt)

Middlesex – 112 pts (Adv PR Media)

Northampton – 112 pts (Bus Entre)

Oxford Brookes – BBC–BCC (Quant Surv Commer Mgt) (IB 31–30 pts)

Plymouth – 112 pts (Marit Bus Log; Marit Bus Marit Law)

Portsmouth – 112 pts (Bus Sys Mgt) (IB 30 pts HL 17 pts)

Sheffield Hallam – 112 pts (PR)

Sunderland – 112 pts (Tour Mgt)

Worcester – 112 pts (Bus Mark PR)

104 pts **Derby** – 104 pts (Int Spa Mgt; Int Tour Mgt)

Glasgow Caledonian – BCC (Risk Mgt) (IB 24 pts)

Harper Adams – 104–120 pts (Agric Frm Bus Mgt)

Liverpool John Moores – 104 pts (Mgt Trans Log)

Manchester Met – BCC–BBC 104–112 pts (Spo Mgt; Adv Brnd Mgt) (IB 26 pts)

Queen Margaret – BCC 104 pts (PR Mark Evnts; PR Media) (IB 28 pts)

Robert Gordon – BCC (Fash Mgt) (IB 28 pts)

Royal Agricultural Univ – 104 pts (Rur Lnd Mgt)

Staffordshire – 104 pts (Adv Brnd Mgt)

West London – 104 pts (Airln Airpt Mgt; Adv PR)

96 pts **Arts London (CFash)** – CCC 96 pts +portfolio (Fash PR Comm)

Birmingham (UC) – 96 pts (Culn Arts Mgt; Bus Ent; Bty Thera Mgt; Spa Mgt)

Edinburgh Napier – CCC (Econ Mgt) (IB 27 pts)

Liverpool (LIPA) – CCC 96 pts (Mus Thea Enter Mgt)
London South Bank – CCC 96 pts (Arts Fstvl Mgt)
Nottingham Trent – 96 pts (Constr Mgt)
Plymouth – 96 pts (Cru Mgt)
Royal Agricultural Univ – 96 pts (Int Bus Mgt (Fd Agri Bus))
Sheffield Hallam – 96 pts (IT Bus St)
Southampton Solent – 96 pts (Fash Mgt Mark; Advntr Out Mgt)
Sparsholt (Coll) – 96–112 pts (Aquacult Fish Mgt)
West London – 96 pts (Culn Arts Mgt)
West Scotland – CCC incl maths+sci (Eng Mgt) (IB 24 pts)

92 pts CEM – 92 pts (Rl Est Mgt)

88 pts Derby – 88–120 pts (Bus Mgt Joint Hons)
Southampton Solent – 88 pts (Bus IT)

80 pts Arts London – 80 pts (PR)
Bedfordshire – 80 pts (PR; Adv Mark Comms) (IB 24 pts)
Bucks New – 80–96 pts (Airln Airpt Mgt)
Colchester (Inst) – 80 pts (Constr Mgt (Site Mgt))

64 pts Trinity Saint David – 64 pts (Int Trav Tour Mgt; Mtrspo Mgt; Tour Mgt); (Spo Mgt)
(IB 24 pts)
UHI – CC (Glf Mgt)

24 pts UHI – D (Mus Bus)

Alternative offers
See **Chapter 6** and **Appendix 1** for grades/new UCAS Tariff points information for other examinations.

EXAMPLES OF COLLEGES OFFERING COURSES IN THIS SUBJECT FIELD
Most colleges. See **Chapter 9**, Section 3.

CHOOSING YOUR COURSE (SEE ALSO CH.1)
Universities and colleges teaching quality See www.qaa.ac.uk; http://unistats.direct.gov.uk.

Top research universities and colleges (REF 2014) See **Business and Management Courses**.

Examples of sandwich degree courses Birmingham (UC); Birmingham City; Bournemouth; Brighton; Central Lancashire; Coventry; De Montfort; Edinburgh Napier; Greenwich; Harper Adams; Hertfordshire; Huddersfield; Lancaster; Leeds Beckett; Liverpool John Moores; Loughborough; Manchester; Manchester Met; Newcastle; Nottingham Trent; Oxford Brookes; Plymouth; Portsmouth; Reading; Sheffield Hallam; Southampton Solent; Trinity Saint David; Ulster.

ADMISSIONS INFORMATION
Number of applicants per place (approx) Birmingham (UC) 5; Blackpool and Fylde (Coll) 2; Bournemouth (PR) 10; Canterbury Christ Church 20; Cardiff 8; Central Lancashire 15; Colchester (Inst) 2; Edge Hill 4; Edinburgh Napier (Pub) 7; Glasgow Caledonian 18; Heriot-Watt 5; Hertfordshire 10; Huddersfield 5; Kingston 50; Leeds 27; London (UCL) 8; London Met 10; London South Bank 4; Loughborough 5; Manchester 7; Middlesex 12; Newcastle 27; Oxford Brookes 40; Plymouth 4; Portsmouth 10; Robert Gordon 5; Southampton Solent 13; Sunderland 20; Trinity Saint David 7; Warwick 22; West London 4; West Scotland 5; Winchester 4.

Advice to applicants and planning the UCAS personal statement See **Business and Management Courses**.

Misconceptions about this course **Loughborough** (Pub Engl) That this is a course in Journalism: it is not!

Selection interviews **Yes** Coventry, Doncaster (Coll), Edge Hill, Glasgow Caledonian, Harper Adams, London Met, Middlesex, Nottingham Trent, Plymouth, Robert Gordon, Sheffield Hallam, Trinity Saint David, West London, Worcester; **Some** Blackpool and Fylde (Coll), Cardiff Met, De Montfort, Derby,

196 | Celtic, Irish, Scottish and Welsh Studies

East Anglia, Greenwich, Leeds, Liverpool John Moores, Manchester Met, Staffordshire, Sunderland, Warwick, Winchester.

Interview advice and questions See **Business and Management Courses**. **Loughborough** (Pub Engl) No tests at interview. We seek students with an interest in information issues within society.

Reasons for rejection (non-academic) See **Business and Management Courses**. **Bournemouth** The Business Studies course is very popular.

AFTER-RESULTS ADVICE
Offers to applicants repeating A-levels Higher Greenwich, Hertfordshire, Kingston, Lancaster, Manchester Met; **Same** Bournemouth, Cardiff, Cardiff Met, De Montfort, Derby, East Anglia, Huddersfield, Leeds, Liverpool John Moores, Loughborough, Oxford Brookes, Robert Gordon, Royal Agricultural Univ, Sheffield Hallam, Staffordshire, Sunderland, Ulster, West London, Winchester, Worcester.

GRADUATE DESTINATIONS AND EMPLOYMENT (2013/14 HESA)
See **Business and Management Courses**.

Career note See **Business and Management Courses**.

OTHER DEGREE SUBJECTS FOR CONSIDERATION
Accountancy; Banking; Business Information Technology; E-Business; Economics; Estate Management; Finance; Hospitality Management; Housing Management; Human Resource Management; Insurance; Leisure Management; Logistics; Marketing; Public Administration; Retail Management; Sports Management; Surveying.

CELTIC, IRISH, SCOTTISH and WELSH STUDIES
(including Cornish Studies and Gaelic Studies)

Evidence of Celtic civilisation and language exists in Ireland, Scotland, Wales, Cornwall, the Isle of Man and across the English Channel in Brittany. Welsh however is the only Celtic language classified as endangered and is spoken by 19% of the population, mainly in the border counties although there is a substantial number in North Wales, particularly in Gwynedd where it is reported that 70% of the population are Welsh speakers. Gaelic (Scottish Gaelic) is a Celtic language native to Scotland, although in addition to English, 'Scots' is a dialect which is spoken in the Lowlands and the Northern Isles. The content of courses in each of these languages, such as the Celtic option at Aberystwyth (the largest department of Welsh in the UK), will cover the history, literature and the language and its place in the modern world. The unique language course in the UK is Anglo Saxon, Norse and Celtic at Cambridge and covers the history and culture of the language of Britain in the Middle Ages as well as further studies on Ireland and the Scandinavian countries.

Useful websites www.webarchive.org.uk; new.wales.gov.uk; www.bbc.co.uk/wales; www.daltai.com; www.eisteddfod.org.uk; www.digitalmedievalist.com

NB The points totals shown to the left of the institutions are for ease of reference only. It must not be assumed that Tariff points are always used by institutions or that they can be substituted for an offer in grades. The level of an offer is not necessarily indicative of the quality of a course.

COURSE OFFERS INFORMATION
Subject requirements/preferences GCSE A foreign language or Welsh may be required. **AL** Welsh may be required for some courses.

Your target offers and examples of degree courses
152 pts Cambridge – A*AA (A-Sxn Nrs Celt) (IB 40–41 pts HL 776)
144 pts Edinburgh – AAA–ABB (Engl Scot Lit; Scot Hist; Scot Lit) (IB 40–34 pts)
  St Andrews – AAA (Phil Scot Hist; Scot Hist courses) (IB 36 pts)

136 pts	**Edinburgh** – AAB–ABB (Celt Ling; Scot St; Celt Engl Lit; Celt Arch; Celt; Celt Scot Hist; Scot Ethnol; Celt Scot Lit) (IB 36–34 pts)
	Glasgow – AAB–BBB (Celt Civ; Celt St courses) (IB 36–34 pts); AAB–BBB incl arts/lang (Scot Lit; Gael) (IB 36–34 pts)
128 pts	**Queen's Belfast** – ABB (Ir)
120 pts	**Aberdeen** – BBB (Engl Scot Lit) (IB 30 pts); (Celt A-Sxn St Joint Hons; Gael St; Celt A-Sxn St) (IB 32 pts)
	Aberystwyth – 120–128 pts (Hist Welsh Hist)
	Cardiff – BBB incl Welsh (Welsh) (IB 30 pts HL 5 Welsh)
	Liverpool – BBB (Ir St Joint Hons) (IB 30 pts)
	Stirling – BBB (Scot Hist) (IB 32 pts)
	Swansea – BBB–BBC (Welsh courses) (IB 32–30 pts)
112 pts	**Aberystwyth** – 112 pts (Ir Joint Hons)
	Bangor – 112–120 pts (Welsh Hist Joint Hons)
104 pts	**Aberystwyth** – 104 pts (Celt St; Welsh courses)
	Cardiff Met – 104 pts (Educ St Welsh)
	South Wales – BCC (Welsh Educ; Welsh)
64 pts	**UHI** – CC (Scot Hist Arch; Scot Cult St); CC incl hist/Engl (Scot Hist); CC +interview (Gael Dev; Gael Trad Mus; Gael Media St)

Alternative offers

See **Chapter 6** and **Appendix 1** for grades/new UCAS Tariff points information for other examinations.

CHOOSING YOUR COURSE (SEE ALSO CH.1)

Universities and colleges teaching quality See www.qaa.ac.uk; http://unistats.direct.gov.uk.

ADMISSIONS INFORMATION

Number of applicants per place (approx) Aberystwyth 6; Bangor 8; Cambridge 2; Cardiff 2; Swansea 7.

Advice to applicants and planning the UCAS personal statement Interests in this field largely develop through literature, museum visits or archaeology which should be fully described in the UCAS application.

Selection interviews Yes Aberystwyth, Cambridge, Cardiff Met.

Interview advice and questions Past questions have included: Why do you want to study this subject? What specific areas of Celtic culture interest you? What do you expect to gain by studying unusual subjects? See **Chapter 5**.

AFTER-RESULTS ADVICE

Offers to applicants repeating A-levels Higher Glasgow (AAA); **Same** Aberystwyth, Bangor, Cardiff, Swansea.

GRADUATE DESTINATIONS AND EMPLOYMENT (2013/14 HESA)

Celtic Studies graduates surveyed 250 **Employed** 90 **In voluntary employment** 0 **In further study** 90 **Assumed unemployed** 10

Career note See **Combined Courses** and **Languages**.

OTHER DEGREE SUBJECTS FOR CONSIDERATION

Anthropology; Archaeology; History.

CHEMISTRY

(see also **Biochemistry, Engineering (Chemical), Pharmacy and Pharmaceutical Sciences**)

There is a shortage of applicants for this subject despite the fact that it's the basis of many careers in the manufacturing industries, such areas as pharmaceuticals, medicine, veterinary science and health, agriculture, petroleum, cosmetics, plastics, the food industry, colour chemistry and aspects of the environment such as pollution and recycling. Most courses will offer a range of compulsory modules (possibly up to 75% of a course) and a series of optional modules. At the University of York for example, compulsory modules will include organic and inorganic chemistry and physical, theoretical, analytical and biological chemistry. Optional modules on offer cover air quality and human health, analytical and forensic science, atmospheric chemistry and climate, biological chemistry, environmental chemistry, green chemistry, industrial management, materials chemistry and medical chemistry. These options at all universities enable students to begin to focus on special studies and lay a foundation for possible future careers.

Useful websites www.rsc.org; www.chem.ox.ac.uk/vrchemistry

NB The points totals shown to the left of the institutions are for ease of reference only. It must not be assumed that Tariff points are always used by institutions or that they can be substituted for an offer in grades. The level of an offer is not necessarily indicative of the quality of a course.

COURSE OFFERS INFORMATION

Subject requirements/preferences GCSE English, mathematics/science subjects usually required. A/B grades often stipulated by popular universities. **AL** Two science subjects including Chemistry required.

Your target offers and examples of degree courses

160 pts **Cambridge** – A*A*A incl sci/maths (Nat Sci (Chem)) (IB 40–41 pts HL 776)
   Oxford – A*A*A incl chem+maths (Chem) (IB 39 pts)

152 pts **Bristol** – A*AA–AAB incl chem+maths (Chem) (IB 38–34 pts HL 6 chem+maths)
   Durham – A*AA incl chem+maths (Chem) (IB 38 pts)
   York – A*AA–AAB incl chem+sci/maths (Chem; Chem Biol Medcnl Chem; Chem Mgt Ind; Chem Res Env) (IB 36–35 pts HL 6 chem)

144 pts **Bath** – AAA–AAB incl chem+sci/maths (Chem courses) (IB 36 pts HL 6 chem+sci/maths)
   Edinburgh – AAA–ABB (Medcnl Biol Chem; Cheml Phys; Chem Env Sust Chem; Chem) (IB 37–32 pts); AAA–ABB incl chem maths (Chem Mat Chem) (IB 37–32 pts)
   Imperial London – AAA incl chem+maths (Chem (Yr Ind/Rsch)) (IB 38 pts HL 7 chem 6 maths); (Chem courses; Chem Fr/Ger/Span Sci; Chem Medcnl Chem; Chem Mol Phys) (IB 38 pts HL 7 chem 6 maths)
   Lancaster – AAA–ABB incl chem+sci (Chem) (IB 36–32 pts HL 6 chem+sci)
   London (UCL) – AAA–AAB incl chem+sci/maths (Chem; Chem Euro Lang; Medcnl Chem) (IB 38–36 pts HL 5 chem+sci/maths); (Chem Mgt St) (IB 39–38 pts HL 5 chem+sci/maths); AAA–AAB incl maths+chem (Chem Maths) (IB 38–36 pts HL 6 maths+chem); AAA incl chem+maths+phys (Cheml Phys) (IB 38 pts HL 5 chem+maths+phys)
   Nottingham – AAA incl maths+chem/phys (Chem Eng Env Eng (Yr Ind)) (IB 36 pts)
   Southampton – AAA–AAB incl chem+maths (Chem Maths MChem) (IB 34 pts); AAA–AAB incl chem+sci/maths (Chem Medcnl Sci MChem) (IB 34 pts); AAA–ABB incl chem+sci/maths (Chem) (IB 34 pts)
   Strathclyde – AAA–ABB incl sci/maths (Chem MChem) (IB 30 pts); (Chem Teach MChem; Foren Analyt Chem MChem) (IB 34 pts)

136 pts **Cardiff** – AAB incl chem (Chem) (IB 34 pts)
   Dundee – AAB incl biol+chem (Biol Chem Drug Dscvry) (IB 30 pts)
   Glasgow – AAB–BBB incl chem (Chem) (IB 36–34 pts)
   Liverpool – AAB incl chem+phys (Chem Nanotech) (IB 35 pts HL 6 chem 5 phys)

London (King's) – AAB incl chem+sci/maths (Chem Biomed) (IB 35 pts HL 6 chem+maths); (Chem) (IB 35 pts HL 6 chem+sci/maths)

Manchester – AAB incl chem+sci/maths (Chem; Chem Medcnl Chem) (IB 35 pts)

Newcastle – AAB incl chem (Chem MChem) (IB 35 pts HL 6 chem)

Nottingham – AAB incl chem+sci (Bioch Biol Chem) (IB 34 pts); AAB incl maths+phys+chem (Chem Mol Phys) (IB 34 pts); AAB–ABB incl chem (Medcnl Biol Chem; Chem) (IB 34–32 pts)

Queen's Belfast – AAB incl chem+sci+Fr/Span (Chem Fr/Span/Yr Abrd MSci)

Reading – AAB–ABB (MChem courses) (IB 35–32 pts)

St Andrews – AAB incl chem (Chem) (IB 35 pts)

Surrey – AAB–ABB incl chem+sci (Chem Foren Invstg; Medcnl Chem; Chem) (IB 35–34 pts)

Warwick – AAB incl chem+maths (Chem; Chem Medcnl Chem) (IB 36 pts HL 6 chem 5 maths)

128 pts **Birmingham** – ABB incl chem (Chem; Chem Modn Lang) (IB 32 pts HL 655); ABB incl chem+biol (Chem Pharmacol) (IB 32 pts HL 655)

East Anglia – ABB incl chem+sci/maths (Chem) (IB 32 pts HL 5 chem+sci/maths)

Kent – ABB incl chem (Chem) (IB 34 pts)

Leeds – ABB incl chem (Chem courses) (IB 35 pts HL 6 chem); ABB (Medcnl Chem) (IB 34 pts HL 6 chem)

Leicester – ABB incl chem (Pharml Chem; Chem; Chem Foren Sci) (IB 30 pts)

Liverpool – ABB incl chem+sci (Chem; Medcnl Chem; Chem (Yr Ind)) (IB 33 pts HL 6 chem 5 sci)

London (QM) – ABB–BBB incl chem (Chem) (IB 34 pts HL 5 chem)

Loughborough – ABB–BBB incl chem+sci/maths (Chem; Chem Analyt Chem; Chem MChem) (IB 34–32 pts HL 6 chem 5 sci); ABB–BBB incl chem (Medcnl Pharml Chem) (IB 34–32 pts HL 6 chem 5 sci)

Newcastle – ABB incl chem (Chem Medcnl Chem; Chem (Yr Ind); Chem) (IB 34 pts HL 6 chem)

Nottingham Trent – 128 pts incl chem (Chem MChem)

Reading – ABB–BBB (Chem) (IB 32–30 pts)

Sheffield – ABB incl chem+sci/maths (Chem) (IB 34 pts HL 6 chem+sci/maths)

Sussex – ABB incl chem (Chem) (IB 34 pts HL 5 chem)

120 pts **Aberdeen** – BBB incl chem+sci/maths (Chem) (IB 32 pts HL 5 chem+sci/maths)

Aston – BBB–ABB incl chem (Chem) (IB 32 pts HL chem); (App Chem) (IB 32 pts)

Chester – BBB–BBC incl chem 120 pts (App Chem Biotech) (IB 28 pts HL 5 chem)

Greenwich – 120 pts incl chem (Chem) (IB 28 pts)

Heriot-Watt – BBB incl chem (Chem Mat; Chem Bioch; Chem courses) (IB 30 pts HL 5 chem+maths)

Keele – BBB/ABC incl chem (Chem) (IB 32 pts HL 6 chem)

Northumbria – 120 pts incl chem (App Chem) (IB 30 pts)

Nottingham Trent – 120 pts incl chem (Chem; Pharml Medcnl Chem)

Queen's Belfast – BBB incl chem+sci (Medcnl Chem; Chem)

112 pts **Brighton** – BBC incl chem (Pharml Cheml Sci; Chem) (IB 28 pts)

Central Lancashire – 112 pts incl chem (Chem) (IB 28 pts HL 5 chem)

Huddersfield – BBC incl chem 112 pts (Chem)

Hull – 112 pts incl chem (Chem) (IB 28 pts HL chem+biol)

Lincoln – 112 pts incl chem (Chem)

Liverpool John Moores – 112 pts incl chem (App Chem MChem)

Plymouth – 112 pts incl chem (Chem) (IB 28 pts HL 5 chem+sci)

Sheffield Hallam – 112 pts incl chem (Chem)

Teesside – BBC incl chem (Chem)

104 pts **Bangor** – 104–128 pts incl chem (Chem)

Bradford – BCC incl chem 104 pts (Chem)

Coventry – BCC incl chem/biol (Analyt Chem Foren Sci) (IB 27 pts)

Kingston – 104 pts incl chem (Chem)

Check **Chapter 3** for new university admission details and **Chapter 6** on how to read the subject tables.

London Met – 104 pts incl chem+sci/maths (Chem)
Manchester Met – 104–112 pts incl chem+biol (Medcnl Biol Chem) (IB 28 pts HL 5 chem+biol); BCC–BBC incl chem 104–112 pts (Chem; Foren Chem; Pharml Chem) (IB 28 pts HL 5 chem)
South Wales – BCC incl chem+sci (Chem) (IB 29 pts HL 6 chem+sci); BCC incl chem+biol (Foren Sci) (IB 29 pts HL 5 chem+biol)
West Scotland – BCC incl chem+sci (Chem) (IB 24 pts)

96 pts **Glyndŵr** – 96 pts incl sci (Chem Grn Nanotech)
Wolverhampton – 96 pts incl chem (Chem)

Open University – contact +44 (0)845 300 6090 **or** www.openuniversity.co.uk/you (Nat Sci)

Alternative offers
See **Chapter 6** and **Appendix 1** for grades/new UCAS Tariff points information for other examinations.

EXAMPLES OF COLLEGES OFFERING COURSES IN THIS SUBJECT FIELD
Barnsley (Coll); Birmingham Met (Coll); Bromley (CFHE); Cornwall (Coll); Harrow (Coll); Leeds City (Coll); Liverpool City (Coll); Warrington (Coll); Wirral Met (Coll); Yeovil (Coll).

CHOOSING YOUR COURSE (SEE ALSO CH.1)
Universities and colleges teaching quality See www.qaa.ac.uk; http://unistats.direct.gov.uk.

Top research universities and colleges (REF 2014) Liverpool; Bath; East Anglia; Sheffield; Warwick; Cambridge; Cardiff; Bristol; Durham; Imperial London; Oxford; Leeds; Nottingham; Edinburgh; St Andrews.

Examples of sandwich degree courses Aston; Bangor; Bath; Cardiff; Dundee; East Anglia; Huddersfield; Kent; Kingston; Liverpool John Moores; Loughborough; Manchester; Manchester Met; Northumbria; Nottingham Trent; Queen's Belfast; St Andrews; Sheffield Hallam; Surrey; Teesside; West Scotland; York.

ADMISSIONS INFORMATION
Number of applicants per place (approx) Bangor (Mar Chem) 3, (Chem) 6; Bath 6; Birmingham 8; Bradford 10; Bristol 6; Cardiff 4; Durham 6; Edinburgh 5; Heriot-Watt 6; Hull 7; Imperial London 3; Kingston 4; Leeds 3; Leicester 9; Liverpool 6; London (QM) 3; London (UCL) 10; Newcastle 5; Nottingham (Chem Mol Phys) 4, (Chem) 8; Oxford (success rate 63%); Southampton 7; Surrey 3; York 5.

Advice to applicants and planning the UCAS personal statement Extend your knowledge beyond your exam studies by reading scientific journals and keeping abreast of scientific developments in the news. Discuss any visits to chemical firms and laboratories, for example, pharmaceutical, food science, rubber and plastic, paper, photographic, environmental health. See also **Appendix 3**. **Bristol** Deferred entry accepted.

Misconceptions about this course Many students do not fully appreciate the strengths of a Chemistry degree for any career despite the fact that graduates regularly go into a diverse range of careers. **Durham** Students fail to realise that they require mathematics and that physics is useful.

Selection interviews Yes Bangor, Bath, Birmingham, Bristol, Cambridge, Coventry, Greenwich, Huddersfield, Hull, Imperial London, Keele (mature students only), Kingston, Leicester, London (QM), London (UCL), London Met, Loughborough, Manchester, Newcastle, Northumbria, Nottingham, Nottingham Trent, Oxford (93% (success rate 27%)), Reading, Sheffield, Surrey, Warwick, York; **Some** Aston, Cardiff, Dundee, East Anglia, Liverpool John Moores, Plymouth; **No** Southampton.

Interview advice and questions Be prepared for questions on your chemistry syllabus and aspects that you enjoy the most. In the past a variety of questions have been asked, for example: Why is carbon a special element? Discuss the nature of forces between atoms with varying intermolecular distances. Describe recent practicals. What is acid rain? What other types of pollution are caused by the human race? What is an enzyme? What are the general properties of benzene? Why might sciences be less popular among girls at school? What can a mass spectrometer be used for? What would you do if a river turned bright blue and you were asked how to test a sample? What would be the difference between metal and non-metal pollution? What is 'turning you on' in chemistry at the moment? See also **Chapter 5**. **Bath** Why Chemistry? Discuss the practical work you are doing. **Oxford** No written or work tests. Evidence required of motivation and further potential and a capacity to analyse and use information to form opinions and a willingness to discuss them. **York** Discuss your favourite areas of chemistry, some of your extra-curricular activities, your preferred learning styles – for example, small tutorials of four or fewer, or lectures.

Reasons for rejection (non-academic) Didn't attend interview. Rude and uncooperative. Arrived under influence of drink. Poor attitude and poor commitment to chemistry. Incomplete, inappropriate, illiterate personal statements. **Southampton** Applicants called for interview are not normally rejected.

AFTER-RESULTS ADVICE
Offers to applicants repeating A-levels Higher Bangor, Dundee, Hull, Leeds, Northumbria, Nottingham, St Andrews, Warwick; **Possibly higher** Coventry, Edinburgh, Newcastle; **Same** Aston, Bath, Bristol, Cardiff, Durham, East Anglia, Greenwich, Heriot-Watt, Huddersfield, Keele, Kingston, Liverpool John Moores, London (UCL), London Met, Loughborough, Plymouth, Sheffield, Surrey; **No** Cambridge.

GRADUATE DESTINATIONS AND EMPLOYMENT (2013/14 HESA)
Graduates surveyed 3,180 **Employed** 1,440 **In voluntary employment** 60 **In further study** 1,125 **Assumed unemployed** 235

Career note A large number of Chemistry graduates choose to go on to further study as well as into scientific careers in research, analysis or development. Significant numbers also follow careers in a wide range of areas in management, teaching and retail work.

OTHER DEGREE SUBJECTS FOR CONSIDERATION
Agriculture; Biochemistry; Biological Sciences; Biomedical Science; Chemical Engineering; Environmental Science; Forensic Science; Genetics; Materials Science; Medicine; Microbiology; Oceanography; Pharmacology; Pharmacy.

CHINESE
(including **Korean**; see also **Asia-Pacific Studies, Languages**)

Oriental languages are not necessarily difficult languages but they differ considerably in their writing systems which present their own problems for the new student. Even so, Chinese is not a language to be chosen for its novelty and students should have a strong interest in China and its people. In all courses, students should prepare for intensive language learning, the focus being on the written and spoken word supported by studies covering the history, politics and culture of China and at the University of Leeds additional studies of the Asia Pacific region. At Oxford (Oriental Studies) it is also possible to take an additional language from Japanese, Korean or Tibetan whilst at Durham the course in Chinese/Japanese Studies allows for the choice of one of the languages. It is customary in all universities to spend either the second or third year at a university in China. Several universities offer joint courses with Chinese universities; at the University of Hull there is a choice of 14 such courses.

Useful websites www.ciltuk.org.uk; www.ciol.org.uk; www.bbc.co.uk/languages; www.china.org.cn/english; www.languageadvantage.com; www.languagematters.co.uk; www.chineseculture.about.com

NB The points totals shown to the left of the institutions are for ease of reference only. It must not be assumed that Tariff points are always used by institutions or that they can be substituted for an offer in grades. The level of an offer is not necessarily indicative of the quality of a course.

Check **Chapter 3** for new university admission details and **Chapter 6** on how to read the subject tables.

COURSE OFFERS INFORMATION

Subject requirements/preferences GCSE A language is required. **AL** A modern language is usually required.

Your target offers and examples of degree courses

152 pts **Cambridge** – A*AA (As Mid E St) (IB 40–41 pts HL 776)

Nottingham – A*AA–AAA (Econ Chin St) (IB 38–36 pts)

144 pts **Oxford** – AAA (Orntl St) (IB 39 pts)

136 pts **Birmingham** – AAB (Mand Chin) (IB 36 pts)

Durham – AAB (Chin St (Yr Abrd)) (IB 36 pts)

Edinburgh – AAB–ABB (Chin) (IB 36–34 pts)

Leeds – AAB–ABB (Chin courses) (IB 35–34 pts)

London (SOAS) – AAB–ABB (Chin (Modn Class); Kor; Chin St) (IB 35 pts)

Newcastle – AAB–ABB (Ling Chin/Jap) (IB 35–34 pts)

Nottingham – AAB incl geog (Geog Chin St) (IB 34 pts); AAB–ABB incl soc sci (Contemp Chin St MSci; Contemp Chin St) (IB 34–32 pts); AAB (Mgt Chin St) (IB 34 pts)

Sheffield – AAB–ABB (Chin St courses) (IB 35–34 pts)

Warwick – AAB–ABB (Chin Joint Hons) (IB 36–34 pts)

128 pts **Essex** – ABB–BBB (Mgt Mand) (IB 32–30 pts)

Leeds – ABB (Chin Pol; Chin (Modn)) (IB 34 pts)

Manchester – ABB (Chin St) (IB 34 pts); ABB–BBB incl lang (Chin courses; Russ Chin) (IB 34–32 pts); ABB incl Chin/Jap (Chin Jap) (IB 34 pts)

Newcastle – ABB–BBB (Chin St) (IB 32 pts)

Nottingham – ABB incl hist (Hist Contemp Chin St) (IB 32 pts); ABB incl Span (Span Contemp Chin St) (IB 32 pts)

120 pts **De Montfort** – 120 pts (Educ St Mand) (IB 30 pts)

London (Gold) – BBB (Int St Chin) (IB 33 pts)

112 pts **Bangor** – 112–128 pts (Law Contemp Chin St)

Chester – BBC–BCC 112 pts (Chin St) (26 pts)

Hertfordshire – 112 pts (Mand Joint Hons) (IB 28 pts)

Hull – 112 pts (Chin St) (IB 28 pts)

Nottingham Trent – 112 pts (Chin (Mand) Joint Hons)

Westminster – BBC incl lang (Chin Engl Lang) (IB 30 pts HL 4 lang)

104 pts **Manchester Met** – 104–112 pts incl lang (Ling Lang (Chin/Fr/Ger/Ital/Span)) (IB 26 pts)

Middlesex – 104 pts (Bus Mgt Mand/Span)

80 pts **Central Lancashire** – 80 pts (Bus Mgt Chin) (IB 24 pts)

Trinity Saint David – 80–104 pts (Chin St courses)

Alternative offers

See **Chapter 6** and **Appendix 1** for grades/new UCAS Tariff points information for other examinations.

CHOOSING YOUR COURSE (SEE ALSO CH.1)

Universities and colleges teaching quality See www.qaa.ac.uk; http://unistats.direct.gov.uk.

Examples of sandwich degree courses Westminster.

ADMISSIONS INFORMATION

Number of applicants per place (approx) Durham 5; Leeds 5; London (SOAS) 8; Westminster 18.

Advice to applicants and planning the UCAS personal statement It will be necessary to demonstrate a knowledge of China, its culture, political and economic background. Visits to the Far East should be mentioned, with reference to any features which have influenced your choice of degree course. See also **Appendix 3** under Languages.

Selection interviews Yes Cambridge, Oxford; **Some** Leeds, London (SOAS).

New UCAS points Tariff: A* = 56 pts; A = 48 pts; B = 40 pts; C = 32 pts; D = 24 pts; E = 16 pts

Interview advice and questions You will be expected to convince the admissions tutor why you want to study the language. Your knowledge of Chinese culture, politics and society in general, and of Far Eastern problems, could also be tested. See also **Chapter 5**.

Reasons for rejection (non-academic) Oxford Applicant's language background seemed a little weak and his written work not as strong as that of other applicants. At interview he showed himself to be a dedicated hard-working young man but lacking in the imagination, flexibility and the intellectual liveliness needed to succeed on the course.

AFTER-RESULTS ADVICE
Offers to applicants repeating A-levels Higher Leeds; **No** Cambridge.

GRADUATE DESTINATIONS AND EMPLOYMENT (2013/14 HESA)
Graduates surveyed 165 **Employed** 80 **In voluntary employment** 15 **In further study** 50 **Assumed unemployed** 10

Career note China is a country with a high economic growth rate and there are good opportunities for graduates, an increasing number being recruited by firms based in East Asia. Other opportunities exist in diplomacy, aid work and tourism throughout China, Taiwan and Mongolia as well as most non-scientific career areas in the UK. See also **Languages**.

OTHER DEGREE SUBJECTS FOR CONSIDERATION
Traditional Chinese Medicine; other Oriental languages.

CLASSICAL STUDIES/CLASSICAL CIVILISATION
(see also **Archaeology, Classics, Greek, History (Ancient), Latin**)

Two different titles but two very similar degree courses covering all aspects of the life of Ancient Greece and Rome. At the University of Leeds, Classical Civilisation is described as a study of the Greek and Roman world ranging from the earliest Greek literature to the fall of the Roman Empire, incorporating a study of history, literature, language, art, philosophy and archaeology, whilst at Newcastle, the Classical Studies course includes the same options adding architecture and medicine. As in most university courses, students will select their subject optional topics on a modular basis alongside compulsory options. At many universities, a knowledge of Greek and Latin is not necessary since degree courses may offer these languages at beginner or advanced level, but check subject requirements before applying.

Useful websites www.britishmuseum.org; see also **History** and **History (Ancient)**.

NB The points totals shown to the left of the institutions are for ease of reference only. It must not be assumed that Tariff points are always used by institutions or that they can be substituted for an offer in grades. The level of an offer is not necessarily indicative of the quality of a course.

COURSE OFFERS INFORMATION
Subject requirements/preferences GCSE English and a foreign language often required. **AL** A modern language is required for joint language courses. Relevant subjects include Classical Civilisation, English Literature, Archaeology, Latin, Greek.

Your target offers and examples of degree courses
144 pts Bristol – AAA–AAB incl Engl (Engl Class St) (IB 36–34 pts HL 6 Engl)
Durham – AAA (Class Civ) (IB 37 pts)
Edinburgh – AAA–ABB (Class Mid E St; Class Arch Gk; Class St) (IB 40–34 pts)
Exeter – AAA–ABB incl lang (Class St Modn Langs) (IB 36–32 pts HL 5 lang); AAA–ABB (Class St) (IB 36–32 pts)
St Andrews – AAA–AAB (Class St courses) (IB 36 pts)

136 pts **Bristol** – AAB–ABB (Class St) (IB 34–32 pts)

Leeds – AAB–ABB (Class Civ) (IB 35–34 pts); AAB incl Engl (Class Lit courses) (IB 35 pts HL 6 Engl)

London (King's) – AAB incl Engl (Class St Engl) (IB 35 pts HL 6 Engl); AAB (Class St; Class St Modn Gk St) (IB 35 pts)

London (UCL) – AAB–ABB (Class Arch Class Civ) (IB 36–34 pts)

Newcastle – AAB–ABB (Class St) (IB 35–32 pts)

Nottingham – AAB–ABB (Class Civ) (IB 34–32 pts)

St Andrews – AAB (Art Hist Class St) (IB 36 pts)

128 pts **Birmingham** – ABB (Class Lit Civ) (IB 32 pts HL 655)

Edinburgh – ABB (Anc Medit Civ) (IB 34 pts)

Liverpool – ABB (Egypt; Class St) (IB 33 pts)

London (RH) – ABB (Class St; Class St Ital) (IB 32 pts)

Manchester – ABB–BBB (Class St) (IB 34–31 pts)

Reading – ABB–BBB (Class St; Class Mediev St) (IB 32–30 pts)

Warwick – ABB (Class Civ) (IB 34 pts)

120 pts **Kent** – BBB (Class Arch St) (IB 34 pts)

Roehampton – 120 pts (Class Civ)

Sheffield – BBB–BBC (Class Hist Arch) (IB 32 pts)

Swansea – BBB–BBC (Class Civ) (IB 32–30 pts)

96 pts **Trinity Saint David** – 96–104 pts (Anc Civ); (Class St) (IB 26 pts)

Alternative offers
See **Chapter 6** and **Appendix 1** for grades/new UCAS Tariff points information for other examinations.

CHOOSING YOUR COURSE (SEE ALSO CH.1)

Universities and colleges teaching quality See www.qaa.ac.uk; http://unistats.direct.gov.uk.

Top research universities and colleges (REF 2014) See **Classics**.

ADMISSIONS INFORMATION

Number of applicants per place (approx) Birmingham 3; Bristol 6; Durham (Class Past) 10; Exeter 3; Leeds 7; London (RH) 4; London (UCL) 4; Manchester 6; Newcastle 8; Nottingham 6; Reading 10; Swansea 5; Trinity Saint David 2; Warwick 23.

Advice to applicants and planning the UCAS personal statement Discuss any A-level work and what has attracted you to this subject. Describe visits to classical sites or museums and what impressed you.

Misconceptions about this course Birmingham (Class Lit Civ) A study of classics at school is not necessary although while many people catch the classics bug by doing Classical Civilisation at A-level, others come to classics through reading the myths or seeing the plays and being fascinated by them. For others the interdisciplinary nature of the subject attracts them – literature, drama, history, politics and philosophy. **Exeter** (Class St) This is not a language degree. There is no requirement for either A-level Latin or Greek.

Selection interviews Yes Kent, Newcastle, Nottingham; **Some** Bristol, London (RH), Trinity Saint David, Warwick; **No** Birmingham.

Interview advice and questions In the past, questions have included: What special interests do you have in Classical Studies/Classics? Have you visited Greece, Rome or any other classical sites or museums and what were your impressions? These are the types of questions to expect, along with those to explore your knowledge of the culture, theatre and architecture of the period. See also **Chapter 5**. **Birmingham** (Class Lit Civ) The programme includes some language study and, if applicants do not have a GCSE in a foreign language, we ask them to do a short language aptitude test. Interview questions are likely to focus on your reading interests (not necessarily classical texts!) and your own reflections on them. We are interested in your ability to think for yourself and we want to be sure that you are someone who will enjoy three years of reading and talking about books. **Swansea** Reasons for choosing the subject and how the student hopes to benefit from the course.

Reasons for rejection (non-academic) Birmingham Lukewarm interest in the subject. Lack of clear idea why they wanted to do this degree.

AFTER-RESULTS ADVICE
Offers to applicants repeating A-levels Higher Nottingham, St Andrews, Warwick; **Same** Birmingham, Bristol, Durham, Exeter, Leeds, London (RH), Newcastle.

GRADUATE DESTINATIONS AND EMPLOYMENT (2013/14 HESA)
Classical Studies graduates surveyed 935 **Employed** 390 **In voluntary employment** 45 **In further study** 300 **Assumed unemployed** 65

Career note As with other non-vocational subjects, graduates enter a wide range of careers. In a small number of cases this may be subject-related with work in museums and art galleries. However, much will depend on how the student's interests develop during the undergraduate years and career planning should start early.

OTHER DEGREE SUBJECTS FOR CONSIDERATION
Archaeology; Ancient History; Classics; Greek; History; History of Art; Latin; Philosophy.

CLASSICS
(see also Classical Studies/Classical Civilisation, Greek, Latin)

These courses tend to focus on the study of Greek and Latin literature and language alongside topics such as the history, art, archaeology, drama and philosophy of Ancient Greece and Rome. Course entry requirements vary. At Oxford, with the largest Classics department in the UK, one course is offered which does not require a previous knowledge of Latin or Greek.

Useful websites www.classicspage.com; www.classics.ac.uk; www.cambridgescp.com; www.bbc.co.uk/history/ancient/greeks; www.bbc.co.uk/history/ancient/romans

NB The points totals shown to the left of the institutions are for ease of reference only. It must not be assumed that Tariff points are always used by institutions or that they can be substituted for an offer in grades. The level of an offer is not necessarily indicative of the quality of a course.

COURSE OFFERS INFORMATION
Subject requirements/preferences GCSE English and a foreign language usually required. Grades A*/A/B may be stipulated. **AL** Check courses for Latin/Greek requirements.

Your target offers and examples of degree courses
152 pts Cambridge – A*AA (Class) (IB 40–41 pts HL 776)
144 pts Bristol – AAA–AAB 144–136 pts (Class) (IB 36–34 pts)
　　　　Durham – AAA (Class) (IB 37 pts)
　　　　Edinburgh – AAA–ABB (Class; Class Engl Lang; Class Ling) (IB 40–34 pts)
　　　　Exeter – AAA–ABB incl Lat/Gk (Class) (IB 36–32 pts HL 5 Lat/Gk)
　　　　Oxford – AAA (Class Engl; Class; Class Orntl St; Class Modn Langs) (IB 39 pts)
136 pts Leeds – AAB incl Engl (Class Lit courses) (IB 35 pts HL 6 Engl)
　　　　London (King's) – AAB incl Lat/Anc Gk (Class (Gk Lat)) (IB 35 pts HL 6 Lat/Class Gk)
　　　　London (UCL) – AAB incl Gk/Lat (Class) (IB 36 pts)
　　　　Newcastle – AAB–ABB (Class) (IB 35–32 pts)
　　　　Nottingham – AAB–ABB (Class) (IB 34–32 pts)
　　　　St Andrews – AAB (Class) (IB 36 pts)
　　　　Warwick – AAB incl Lat/Anc Gk (Class) (IB 36 pts HL 6 Lat/Anc Gk)

128 pts **Birmingham** – ABB (Class Lit Civ) (IB 32 pts HL 655)
Liverpool – ABB (Class) (IB 33 pts)
London (RH) – ABB (Class) (IB 32 pts)
Manchester – ABB–BBB (Class) (IB 34–31 pts)
120 pts **Swansea** – BBB–BBC (Class) (IB 32–30 pts)
96 pts **Trinity Saint David** – 96 pts (Class) (IB 26 pts)

Alternative offers
See **Chapter 6** and **Appendix 1** for grades/new UCAS Tariff points information for other examinations.

CHOOSING YOUR COURSE (SEE ALSO CH.1)

Universities and colleges teaching quality See www.qaa.ac.uk; http://unistats.direct.gov.uk.

Top research universities and colleges (REF 2014) St Andrews; Cambridge; Durham; Reading; Birmingham; Oxford; Nottingham; Warwick.

ADMISSIONS INFORMATION

Number of applicants per place (approx) Bristol 9; Cambridge 2; Durham 8; Leeds 4; London (King's) 6; London (RH) 6; London (UCL) 5; Manchester 6; Newcastle 14; Nottingham 6; Oxford 2; Swansea 6; Trinity Saint David 5.

Advice to applicants and planning the UCAS personal statement Describe any visits made to classical sites or museums, or literature which you have read and enjoyed. Discuss any significant aspects which impressed you. Classics is an interdisciplinary subject and universities are looking for people who are versatile, imaginative and independently minded, so all types of extra-curricular activities (drama, music, philosophy, creative arts, politics, other languages and cultures) will be relevant. See also **Classical Studies/Classical Civilisation**.

Misconceptions about this course While Classics can appear irrelevant and elitist, universities aim to assist students to leave with a range of transferable skills that are of importance to employers.

Selection interviews Yes Cambridge, London (RH), London (UCL), Newcastle, Oxford (Class) 37%, (Class Eng) 32%, (Class Modn Langs) 30%, (Class Orntl St) 56%, Swansea; **Some** Bristol, Warwick; **No** Leeds, Nottingham.

Interview advice and questions What do you think it means to study Classics? Do you think Classics is still a vital and central cultural discipline? What made you apply to study Classics at this university? There are often detailed questions on the texts which the students have read, to find out how reflective they are in their reading. See also **Classical Studies/Classical Civilisation** and **Chapter 5**. **Cambridge** What would happen if the Classics department burned down? Do you think feminism is dead? Emma has become a different person since she took up yoga. Therefore she is not responsible for anything she did before she took up yoga. Discuss. **Oxford** Written tests to demonstrate ability in linguistics, competence in translation. Use of dictionaries not permitted. Classics and English applicants take the English Admissions Test.

Reasons for rejection (non-academic) Did not demonstrate a clear sense of why they wanted to study Classics rather than anything else.

AFTER-RESULTS ADVICE

Offers to applicants repeating A-levels Higher Leeds, Nottingham, St Andrews; **Same** Cambridge, Durham, Newcastle, Swansea.

GRADUATE DESTINATIONS AND EMPLOYMENT (2013/14 HESA)

See **Classical Studies/Classical Civilisation**.

Career note See **Classical Studies/Classical Civilisation**.

OTHER DEGREE SUBJECTS FOR CONSIDERATION
See **Classical Studies/Classical Civilisation**.

COMBINED COURSES

(see also **Art and Design (General)**, **Social Sciences/Studies**)

Many different subjects are offered in combined or modular arrangements. These courses are particularly useful for those applicants who have difficulty in deciding on one specialist subject to follow, allowing students to mix and match according to their interests and often enabling them to embark on new subjects.

Useful websites www.artscouncil.org.uk; www.scottisharts.org.uk; www.artsprofessional.co.uk

NB The points totals shown to the left of the institutions are for ease of reference only. It must not be assumed that Tariff points are always used by institutions or that they can be substituted for an offer in grades. The level of an offer is not necessarily indicative of the quality of a course.

COURSE OFFERS INFORMATION

Subject requirements/preferences The offers listed below are average offers. Specific offers will vary depending on the relative popularity of each subject. Check with the admissions tutor of your selected institution. **GCSE** English, mathematics or science and foreign language may be required by some universities. **AL** Some joint courses may require a specified subject.

Your target offers and examples of degree courses

160 pts **Cambridge** – A*A*A incl sci/maths (Nat Sci) (IB 40–41 pts HL 776)

152 pts **Bath** – A*AA incl maths (Nat Sci) (IB 36 pts HL 6 maths)

Birmingham – A*AA (Librl Arts Sci) (IB 32 pts HL 766)

Durham – A*AA (Comb Hons Soc Sci) (IB 38 pts)

Exeter – A*AA–AAB (Librl Arts; Flex Comb Hons) (IB 38–34 pts)

London (UCL) – A*AA–AAA (Arts Sci) (IB 39–38 pts)

144 pts **Imperial London** – AAA incl chem+sci/maths (Bioch courses) (IB 38 pts HL 6 biol+chem)

London (King's) – AAA (Librl Arts) (IB 35 pts)

London (QM) – AAA incl maths (Econ Joint Hons) (IB 36 pts HL 5 maths)

Newcastle – AAA–AAB incl Engl (Engl Lit Joint Hons) (IB 36–35 pts HL 6 Engl)

St Andrews – AAA (Gen Arts Sci) (IB 38 pts)

Sheffield – AAA–AAB incl chem+sci (Bioch Joint Hons) (IB 37–35 pts HL 6 chem+sci)

136 pts **Durham** – AAB incl mus (Mus) (IB 36 pts)

Kent – AAB (Librl Arts) (IB 34 pts)

Newcastle – AAB (Hist Art Joint Hons; Phil Joint Hons; Comb Hons) (IB 35 pts)

Sheffield – AAB–ABB (Econ Joint Hons) (IB 35 pts); AAB–BBB (Ger St Joint Hons) (IB 35–34 pts HL 6 Ger); AAB–ABB incl hist (Hist Joint Hons) (IB 35–34 pts HL 6 hist); AAB–BBB incl Fr (Fr St Joint Hons) (IB 35–34 pts HL 6 Fr); AAB–BBB incl lang (Russ St Joint Hons) (IB 35–34 pts HL 6 lang); AAB–BBB incl Span (Hisp St Joint Hons) (IB 35–34 pts HL 6 Span); AAB (Bus Mgt Joint Hons) (IB 35 pts); AAB–ABB incl maths (Maths Joint Hons) (IB 35 pts HL 6 maths); AAB–ABB incl maths+phys (Phys Joint Hons) (IB 35 pts HL 6 maths+phys)

128 pts **Cardiff** – ABB–BBB (Welsh Joint Hons) (IB 34–26 pts); (Anc Hist Joint Hons) (IB 34–30 pts)

East Anglia – ABB (Int Rel Joint Hons) (IB 32 pts)

Heriot-Watt – ABB incl maths+sci (Comb St) (IB 29 pts)

Kent – ABB (Cult St courses) (IB 34 pts)

Leeds – ABB (Film St Comb) (IB 34 pts)

Liverpool – ABB (Film St Comb Hons) (IB 33 pts); (Comb Hons) (IB 33–36 pts)

London (RH) – ABB (Librl Arts) (IB 32 pts)

Newcastle – ABB (Film Prac) (IB 32 pts)
Sheffield – ABB–BBB (Phil Joint Hons) (IB 34 pts); ABB–BBB incl mus (Mus Joint Hons)
    (IB 34 pts HL 6 mus); ABB incl Engl (Ling Joint Hons) (IB 34 pts Hl 6 Engl)
120 pts **Aberdeen** – BBB (Arts Soc Sci) (IB 32 pts)
Sunderland – 112 pts (Comb Hons)
112 pts **Bath Spa** – 112–128 pts (Psy Comb Hons)
Canterbury Christ Church – 112 pts (Joint Hons)
Hull – 112 pts (Am St; Relgn Joint Hons; Comb Lang) (IB 28 pts)
Kingston – 112 pts (Cy Scrty Comp Foren Bus Joint Hons)
Nottingham Trent – 112 pts (Euro St Joint Hons)
104 pts **Bath Spa** – 104–120 pts (Sociol Comb Hons)
Kingston – 104–144 pts (Mus Joint Hons)
South Wales – BCC (Comb St) (IB 29 pts)
Winchester – 104–120 pts (Modn Librl Arts (Phil)) (IB 26 pts)
96 pts **Leeds (CMus)** – 96 pts +gr 8 (Mus (Comb))
Manchester Met – 96–112 pts (Comb Hons)

Open University – contact +44 (0)845 300 6090 **or** www.openuniversity.co.uk/you
    (Hum Engl/Fr/Ger/Span)

Alternative offers
See **Chapter 6** and **Appendix 1** for grades/new UCAS Tariff points information for other examinations.

CHOOSING YOUR COURSE (SEE ALSO CH.1)

Universities and colleges teaching quality See www.qaa.ac.uk; http://unistats.direct.gov.uk.

Top research universities and colleges (REF 2014) See individual subject tables.

ADMISSIONS INFORMATION

Number of applicants per place (approx) Birmingham 9; Durham (Comb Arts) 7; Heriot-Watt 3; Liverpool 6; Newcastle 7.

Advice to applicants and planning the UCAS personal statement Refer to tables for those subjects you've chosen. **Bath Spa** (Crea Arts) Looks for personal statements which clarify relevant work done outside the school syllabus (eg creative writing). **Liverpool** (Comb Hons) We look for evidence of a broad interest across a range of subjects.

Misconceptions about this course Bath Spa (Crea Arts) Some applicants wish to specialise in one subject not realising it is a Joint Honours course. **Liverpool** (Comb Hons) Some students deterred because they believe that the course is too general. This is not so. The degree certificate shows the names of the two subjects taken to Honours degree level.

Selection interviews Yes Aberdeen, Manchester Met; **Some** Bristol, Liverpool.

Interview advice and questions Questions will focus on your chosen subjects. See under individual subject tables. See also **Chapter 5**.

Reasons for rejection (non-academic) Lack of clarity of personal goals.

AFTER-RESULTS ADVICE

Offers to applicants repeating A-levels Higher St Andrews; **Possibly higher** Newcastle; **Same** Bath Spa, Birmingham, Durham, Liverpool, Manchester Met.

GRADUATE DESTINATIONS AND EMPLOYMENT (2013/14 HESA)

Career note Graduates enter a wide range of careers covering business and administration, retail work, education, transport, finance, community and social services. Work experience during undergraduate years will help students to focus their interests.

OTHER DEGREE SUBJECTS FOR CONSIDERATION
See **Social Sciences/Studies**.

COMMUNICATION STUDIES/COMMUNICATION

(including **Advertising, Communications, Information Studies, Public Relations** and **Telecommunications**; see also **Art and Design (General), Computer Courses, Engineering (Communications), Film, Radio, Video and TV Studies, Journalism, Media Studies, Speech Pathology/Sciences/Therapy**)

Communication Studies courses are often linked with Media Studies and as such attract large numbers of applicants; however the course content of your chosen course should be checked since there are several variations. Some courses are purely academic, such as the City University London degree.

Useful websites www.camfoundation.com; www.aejmc.org

NB The points totals shown to the left of the institutions are for ease of reference only. It must not be assumed that Tariff points are always used by institutions or that they can be substituted for an offer in grades. The level of an offer is not necessarily indicative of the quality of a course.

COURSE OFFERS INFORMATION

Subject requirements/preferences GCSE English and mathematics grade A–C may be required. **AL** No specific subjects required.

Kingston GCSE Five subjects including mathematics and English (grade A*–C) required. **AL** English Language/Literature/related subject (80 points required), General Studies accepted when one of three A-levels or equivalent.

Your target offers and examples of degree courses
144 pts London (King's) – AAA (Librl Arts) (IB 35 pts)
136 pts Leeds – AAB (Comms Media) (IB 35 pts)
London (Gold) – AAB–ABB (Media Comms) (IB 33 pts)
Newcastle – AAB (Media Comm Cult St) (IB 34 pts)
128 pts Leeds – ABB (Graph Comm Des) (IB 34 pts)
Liverpool – ABB (Comm Media) (IB 33 pts)
Loughborough – ABB (Comm Media St) (IB 34 pts)
Northumbria – 128 pts (Fash Comm) (IB 31 pts)
Nottingham – ABB–AAC (Span Int Media Comms St) (IB 32 pts)
Sussex – ABB (Media Comms) (IB 34 pts)
Ulster – ABB–AAB (Comm Adv Mark) (IB 27–28 pts)
120 pts Buckingham – BBB–BBC (Mark Media Comms)
East Anglia – BBB (Intercult Comm Bus Mgt) (IB 31 pts)
Keele – BBB/ABC (Media Comms Cult) (IB 32 pts)
Leeds Beckett – 120 pts (Media Comm Cult) (IB 26 pts)
Sheffield Hallam – 120 pts (Mark Comms Adv)
Sunderland – 120 pts (Mass Comms)
Swansea – BBB–BBC (Pol Comm) (IB 32–30 pts); (Lang Comm) (IB 32–30 pts)
UWE Bristol – 120 pts (Mark Comms) (IB 26 pts)
112 pts Aberystwyth – 112–120 pts (Media Comm St)
Bath Spa – 112–128 pts (Media Comms)
Birmingham City – BBC 112 pts (Media Comm) (IB 28 pts)
Bournemouth – 112–120 pts (Comm Media) (IB 30–31 pts)
Brunel – BBC (Comm Media St) (IB 29 pts)
Canterbury Christ Church – 112 pts (Media Comms)
Coventry – BBC (Media Comms) (IB 28 pts)
Glasgow Caledonian – BBC (Media Comm) (IB 25 pts)

Greenwich - 112 pts (Media Comms) (IB 28 pts)
Nottingham Trent - 112 pts (Comm Soty (Joint Hons))
Oxford Brookes - BBC (Engl Lang Comm; Comm Media Cult) (IB 30 pts)
Sheffield Hallam - 112 pts (PR Media)
Westminster - BBC-AA (Comp Net Comms) (IB 28 pts)
104 pts **De Montfort** - 104 pts (Media Comm) (IB 28 pts)
Liverpool Hope - BCC-BBB 104-120 pts (Media Comm)
Manchester Met - 104-112 pts (Inf Comms; Dig Media Comms) (IB 26 pts)
Robert Gordon - BCC (PR) (IB 27 pts)
Ulster - 104-112 pts (Comm Mgt PR) (IB 24-25 pts)
96 pts **Buckingham** - CCC 96 pts (Comm Media Jrnl); CCC (Comm Media St)
Wolverhampton - 96 pts (Media Comm St)
88 pts **Creative Arts** - 88 pts (Media Comms)
80 pts **Bedfordshire** - 80 pts (Media Comms) (IB 24 pts)
Bucks New - 80-96 pts (Adv Mgt Dig Comms)

Alternative offers
See **Chapter 6** and **Appendix 1** for grades/new UCAS Tariff points information for other examinations.

CHOOSING YOUR COURSE (SEE ALSO CH.1)

Universities and colleges teaching quality See www.qaa.ac.uk; http://unistats.direct.gov.uk.

Top research universities and colleges (REF 2014) (Communication, Cultural and Media Studies, Library and Information Management) London LSE; Leicester (Musm St); Wolverhampton; Cardiff; London (Gold); Loughborough (Comm Media St); Westminster; De Montfort; Nottingham; London (RH); East Anglia; Leeds; Leicester (Media Comm); Newcastle.

Examples of sandwich degree courses Birmingham City; Bournemouth; Brunel; Central Lancashire; Coventry; Leeds Beckett; Liverpool John Moores; Loughborough; Nottingham Trent; Southampton Solent; Ulster; Westminster.

ADMISSIONS INFORMATION

Number of applicants per place (approx) Brunel 9; Leicester 15; Liverpool 6.

Advice to applicants and planning the UCAS personal statement Applicants should be able to give details of any work experience/work shadowing/discussions they have had in the media including, for example, in newspaper offices, advertising agencies, local radio stations or film companies (see also **Media Studies**). **London (Gold)** Interest in a study in depth of media theory plus some experience in media practice. **Manchester Met** Motivation more important than grades.

Selection interviews Yes Buckingham, Coventry, Glasgow Caledonian, Leicester, Southampton Solent, Ulster; **Some** London (Gold) (mature students), Sheffield Hallam (mature students).

Interview advice and questions Courses differ in this subject and, depending on your choice, the questions will focus on the type of course, either biased towards the media, or towards human communication by way of language, psychology, sociology or linguistics. See also separate subject tables and **Chapter 5**.

Reasons for rejection (non-academic) Unlikely to work well in groups. Poor writing. Misguided application, for example more practical work wanted. Poor motivation. Inability to give reasons for choosing the course. More practice needed in academic writing skills. Wrong course choice, wanted more practical work.

AFTER-RESULTS ADVICE

Offers to applicants repeating A-levels Possibly higher Coventry; **Same** Brunel, Loughborough, Nottingham Trent, Robert Gordon, Sheffield Hallam.

New UCAS points Tariff: A* = 56 pts; A = 48 pts; B = 40 pts; C = 32 pts; D = 24 pts; E = 16 pts

GRADUATE DESTINATIONS AND EMPLOYMENT (2013/14 HESA)
See **Business and Management Courses (Specialised)**, **Marketing** and **Media Studies**.

Career note Graduates have developed a range of transferable skills in their courses which open up opportunities in several areas. There are obvious links with openings in the media, public relations and advertising.

OTHER DEGREE SUBJECTS FOR CONSIDERATION
Advertising; Art and Design; Cultural Studies; Digital Communications; English; Film, Radio, Video and TV Studies; Information Studies; Journalism; Languages; Linguistics; Marketing; Media Studies; Psychology; Public Relations; Speech Sciences.

COMMUNITY STUDIES/DEVELOPMENT

(see also **Health Sciences/Studies, Nursing and Midwifery, Social and Public Policy and Administration, Social Work**)

These courses cover aspects of community social issues, for example housing, food, health, the elderly, welfare rights and counselling and features of community development such as education, arts, sport and leisure. Many courses are vocational in nature and often linked with youth work. Courses are in Education, Housing, Social Sciences and Social and Public Policy. Work experience always forms part of these courses and should also take place before you apply. Most courses will lead to professional qualifications.

Useful websites http://volunteeringmatters.org.uk; infed.org/mobi/developing-community.

NB The points totals shown to the left of the institutions are for ease of reference only. It must not be assumed that Tariff points are always used by institutions or that they can be substituted for an offer in grades. The level of an offer is not necessarily indicative of the quality of a course.

COURSE OFFERS INFORMATION
Subject requirements/preferences GCSE English and mathematics grade A–C may be required at some institutions. **AL** No specific subjects required. **Other** Minimum age 19 plus youth work experience for some courses. Health and Disclosure and Barring Service (DBS) checks required for some courses.

Your target offers and examples of degree courses
128 pts **Edinburgh** – ABB (Commun Educ) (IB 34 pts)
         Sussex – ABB–BBB (Chld Yth (Theor Prac)) (IB 32 pts)
120 pts **Glasgow** – BBB–CCC (Commun Dev) (IB 30–28 pts)
         Sunderland – 120 pts (Commun Yth Wk St)
112 pts **Huddersfield** – BBC 112 pts (Yth Commun Wk)
         Hull – 112 pts (Yth Wk Commun Dev) (IB 28 pts)
         London (Birk) – 112 pts (Commun Dev Pblc Plcy)
         London Met – 112 pts (Commun Dev Ldrshp)
         Newman – 112 pts (Yth Commun Wk)
         Sunderland – 112 pts (Commun Mus; Pblc Hlth)
         Worcester – 112 pts (Yth Commun Wrk)
104 pts **De Montfort** – 104 pts (Yth Commun Dev) (IB 28 pts)
         West Scotland – BCC incl Engl (Commun Edu) (IB 24 pts)
         Winchester – 104–120 pts (Chld Yth Commun St) (IB 26 pts)
 96 pts **Bolton** – 96 pts (Commun Nbrhd St)
         Dundee – CCC–AB (Commun Lrng Dev) (IB 29 pts)
         Glyndŵr – 96 pts (Yth Commun Wk)
         Leeds Beckett – 96 pts (Yth Wk Commun Dev) (IB 24 pts)
         Manchester Met – 96–112 pts (Yth Commun Wk) (IB 25 pts)

88 pts   **St Mark and St John** – CCD (Yth Commun Wk)
80 pts   **Bedfordshire** – 80 pts (Yth Commun Wk) (IB 24 pts)
        Cardiff Met – 80 pts (Yth Commun Educ)
        Gloucestershire – 80 pts (Yth Wk)
        Trinity Saint David – 80 pts (Yth Commun Wk)
        Ulster – 80 pts (Commun Yth Wk) (IB 24 pts)
72 pts   **St Mark and St John** – 72 pts (Commun Soc; Commun Dev)
        Sheffield Hallam – 72 pts (Yth Commun Wk)
64 pts   **London (Gold)** – CC (App Soc Sci Commun Dev Yth Wk)
48 pts   **Cumbria** – 48 pts (Yth Commun Wk)

Alternative offers
See **Chapter 6** and **Appendix 1** for grades/new UCAS Tariff points information for other examinations.

EXAMPLES OF COLLEGES OFFERING COURSES IN THIS SUBJECT FIELD
Blackburn (Coll); Bradford (Coll); Cornwall (Coll); East Kent (Coll); Grimsby (Univ Centre); North Nottinghamshire (Coll); Oldham (Univ Campus); Truro and Penwith (Coll); Weston (Coll); York (Coll).

CHOOSING YOUR COURSE (SEE ALSO CH.1)
Universities and colleges teaching quality See www.qaa.ac.uk; http://unistats.direct.gov.uk.

ADMISSIONS INFORMATION
Number of applicants per place (approx) Durham 4; Manchester Met 8; St Mark and St John 7.

Advice to applicants and planning the UCAS personal statement You should describe work you have done with people (elderly or young), particularly in a caring capacity, such as social work, or with the elderly or young children in schools, nursing, hospital work, youth work, community or charity work. You should also describe any problems arising and how staff dealt with them. See **Appendix 3**. **St Mark and St John** Strong multicultural policy. English as a Foreign Language teaching offered.

Selection interviews Yes Huddersfield (in groups), Manchester Met, Worcester, York St John; **Some** Cardiff Met, Liverpool John Moores.

Interview advice and questions This subject has a vocational emphasis and work experience, or even full-time work in the field, will be expected. Community work varies considerably, so, depending on your experiences, you could be asked about the extent of your work and how you would solve the problems which occur. See also **Chapter 5**.

Reasons for rejection (non-academic) Insufficient experience. Lack of understanding of community and youth work. Uncertain career aspirations. Incompatibility with values, methods and aims of the course. No work experience.

AFTER-RESULTS ADVICE
Offers to applicants repeating A-levels Same St Mark and St John.

GRADUATE DESTINATIONS AND EMPLOYMENT (2013/14 HESA)
See **Social Work**.

Career note Social and welfare areas of employment provide openings for those wanting to specialise in their chosen field of social work. Other opportunities will also exist in educational administration, leisure and outdoor activities.

OTHER DEGREE SUBJECTS FOR CONSIDERATION
Communication Studies; Education; Health and Social Care; Nursing; Politics; Psychology; Social Policy and Administration; Social Work; Sociology; Youth Studies.

New UCAS points Tariff: A* = 56 pts; A = 48 pts; B = 40 pts; C = 32 pts; D = 24 pts; E = 16 pts

COMPUTER COURSES

(including **Artificial Intelligence, Business Information Technology** and **Systems, Computing, Computer Networks, Computer Science, Games Technology, Information Systems** and **Web Management**; see also **Communication Studies/Communication, Information Management and Librarianship, Media Studies**)

Most universities and also colleges of further education offer Computer courses. The specialisms however are many and varied which can cause a problem when deciding which course to follow. For example, at Brunel University London, the Computer Science course has four specialisms with a choice from Artificial Intelligence, Digital Media Games, Network Computing or Software Engineering, all with sandwich placements. At Plymouth University, there are 17 Computer Science courses including Applied Computing, Digital Art Technology, Internet Design and PGCE (Secondary) Computer Science, whilst at Liverpool John Moores, Northumbria and other institutions, Computer Network Security and Forensic Computing are on offer. In all universities however there are considerable opportunities for financial support and future employment by choosing sandwich courses. Courses vary in content and in the specialisations offered, which may include software engineering, programming languages, artificial intelligence, data processing and graphics. Many universities offer sandwich placements in industry and commerce.

Useful websites www.bcs.org; www.techuk.org; www.e-skills.com; www.iap.org.uk; www.thetechpartnership.com; www.iap.org.uk

NB The points totals shown to the left of the institutions are for ease of reference only. It must not be assumed that Tariff points are always used by institutions or that they can be substituted for an offer in grades. The level of an offer is not necessarily indicative of the quality of a course.

COURSE OFFERS INFORMATION

Subject requirements/preferences GCSE Mathematics usually required. A*/A/B grades may be stipulated for some subjects. **AL** Mathematics, a science subject or Computer Science required for some courses.

Cambridge (Churchill, Magdalene) STEP used as part of the offer; (Gonville and Caius) AEA mathematics required (see **Chapter 5**).

Your target offers and examples of degree courses
160 pts **Cambridge** – A*A*A incl maths (Comp Sci) (IB 40–41 pts HL 776)
　　　　　Imperial London – A*A*A incl maths+fmaths (Maths Mathem Comput) (IB 39 pts HL 7 maths)
152 pts **Birmingham** – A*AA incl maths/comp (Comp Sci/Soft Eng MEng) (IB 32 pts HL 766)
　　　　　Bristol – A*AA–AAB incl maths/fmaths (Comp Sci; Maths Comp Sci) (IB 38–36 pts HL 6 maths)
　　　　　Imperial London – A*AA incl maths (Comp (Soft Eng) MEng; Comp (Gms Vis Interact); Comp (Comp Biol Med); Comp; Comp (Artif Intel)) (IB 41–39 pts HL 7 maths)
　　　　　London (UCL) – A*AA incl maths (Comp Sci) (IB 39 pts HL 5 maths); (Mathem Comput MEng) (IB 39 pts HL 7 maths)
　　　　　Oxford – A*AA incl maths/fmaths/comp (Comp Sci) (IB 39 pts)
　　　　　Southampton – A*AA incl maths (Comp Sci Artif Intel MEng; Comp Sci Imag Multim Sys MEng; Comp Sci Dist Sys Net MEng; Comp Sci Mbl Scr Sys MEng); A*AA incl maths+phys (Electron Eng Comp Sys MEng) (IB 38 pts)
144 pts **Bath** – AAA–A*AB incl maths (Comp Sci) (IB 36 pts HL 6 maths)
　　　　　Birmingham – AAA incl maths/comp (Comp Sci) (IB 32 pts HL 666)
　　　　　City – 144 pts (Comp Sci) (IB 29 pts)
　　　　　Durham – AAA incl maths (Comp Sci) (IB 37 pts)
　　　　　Edinburgh – AAA–ABB incl maths (Comp Sci courses; Artif Intel; Inform) (IB 37–32 pts)
　　　　　Exeter – AAA–ABB incl maths (Comp Sci) (IB 36–32 pts HL 5 maths)

Leeds – AAA incl maths/comp (Comp Sci Artif Intel; Comp Sci) (IB 35 pts HL 5 maths)

Nottingham – AAA–AAB incl comp (Comp Sci) (IB 34–32 pts)

Queen's Belfast – AAA–A*AB incl maths (Maths Comp Sci MSci)

Reading – AAA–AAB (Mgt IT) (IB 35 pts)

St Andrews – AAA–AAB incl maths (Comp Sci courses) (IB 38–36 pts); AAA incl maths (Comp Sci Psy) (IB 36 pts); AAA incl maths+phys (Comp Sci Phys) (IB 38 pts)

Southampton – AAA incl maths (Comp Sci)

Warwick – AAA incl maths (Comp Sci; Comp Mgt Sci) (IB 38 pts HL 6 maths)

136 pts **Aston** – AAB–ABB (Bus Comp IT) (IB 35–34 pts)

Cardiff – AAB–ABB (Comp Sci; Comp Sci Scrty Foren; Comp Sci Vis Comp; Comp Sci Hi Perf Comp) (IB 33 pts)

Glasgow – AAB–BBB incl maths (Comp Sci courses) (IB 36–34 pts)

Lancaster – AAB (Comp Sci courses) (IB 35 pts)

Liverpool – AAB incl maths (Comp Inf Sys; Comp Sci (Yr Ind); Comp Sci; Electron Commer Comp) (IB 35 pts HL 5 maths)

London (King's) – AAB incl sci/maths (Comp Sci Robot; Comp Sci Mgt; Comp Sci Intel Sys) (IB 35 pts HL 5 sci/maths)

London (QM) – AAB–ABB (Comp Sci courses) (IB 34–32 pts)

Loughborough – AAB (IT Mgt Bus) (IB 34 pts)

Manchester – AAB (IT Mgt Bus; IT Mgt Bus (Yr Ind)) (IB 35 pts)

Newcastle – AAB–ABB/AAC (Comp Sci courses) (IB 35–34 pts)

Queen's Belfast – AAB–AAA incl maths/tech (Comp Sci MEng)

Reading – AAB–ABB (Comp Sci courses) (IB 35–32 pts)

Sheffield – AAB–ABB incl maths (Comp Sci) (IB 35 pts HL 6 maths); AAB–ABB (IT Mgt Bus) (IB 35 pts)

Surrey – ABB (Comp IT) (IB 34 pts); ABB incl maths (Comp Sci) (IB 34 pts)

Sussex – AAB–ABB (Comp Sci; Comp Sci Artif Intel; Gms Multim Env; Comp Dig Media) (IB 34 pts)

York – AAB–ABB incl maths (Comp Sci) (IB 35–34 pts HL 6 maths)

128 pts **City** – 128–112 pts (Inf Sys) (IB 28 pts)

Coventry – ABB incl maths/sci/tech/comp (Comp Sci) (IB 29 pts)

East Anglia – ABB (Comp Sci; Bus Inf Sys) (IB 32 pts)

Greenwich – 128 pts (Comp Sys Net; Comp Scrty Foren)

Huddersfield – ABB 128 pts (Comp Gms Prog)

Kent – ABB (Comp Sci courses) (IB 34 pts)

Leicester – ABB (Comp Sci) (IB 30 pts)

London (Gold) – ABB (Crea Comp; Comp Sci) (IB 33 pts)

London (RH) – ABB (Dig Media Comms; Mgt Inf Sys) (IB 32 pts); ABB incl maths/phys/comp (Comp Sci) (IB 32 pts)

Loughborough – ABB incl maths (Comp Sci; Comp Sci Artif Intel) (IB 32 pts HL 5 maths)

Northumbria – 128 pts (Comp Sci; Comp Sci Gms Dev) (IB 31 pts)

Queen's Belfast – ABB (Bus IT (Yr Ind))

Strathclyde – ABB–BBB incl maths (Comp Sci) (IB 34 pts HL 6 maths)

Swansea – ABB–BBB (Comp Sci)

UWE Bristol – 128 pts (Comp Sci; Comp courses) (IB 27 pts)

120 pts **Aberdeen** – BBB incl maths (Comp Sci) (IB 32 pts HL 5 maths)

Aston – BBB–ABB (Comp Sci) (IB 32 pts)

Bournemouth – 120–128 pts (Comp Vis Animat; Comp Animat Arts) (IB 31–32 pts)

Bradford – BBB 120 pts (Comp Sci; Comp Sci Gms)

Brunel – BBB (Comp Sci (Artif Intel); Comp Sci; Comp Sci (Dig Media Gms); Comp Sci (Net Comp); Bus Comp) (IB 30 pts)

Buckingham – BBB 120 pts (Comp courses)

Central Lancashire – 120 pts (Web Des Dev)

City – BBB 120 pts (Comp Sci Gms Tech) (IB 32 pts)

Dundee – BBB–CCC incl maths+sci (Comp Sci) (IB 30 pts)

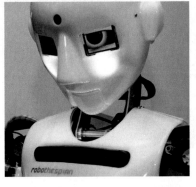

Come along to a University Open Day to find out more:
www.leeds.ac.uk/openday

Globally renowned for our teaching, research and engagement with industry, we are one of the longest established computing schools in the country.

Computing
at the University of Leeds

FLEXIBLE DEGREE OPTIONS
You can choose to study a four-year MEng or a three-year BSc degree. You also have the option of undertaking a placement year or studying abroad.

We offer the following degrees:

- Applied Computer Science
- Computer Science
- Computer Science with Artificial Intelligence
- Computer Science with Distributed Systems
- Computer Science with High-Performance Graphics and Games Engineering
- Computer Science with Mathematics
- Electronics and Computer Engineering

Many of these degree courses share a common first year, which means you can easily switch between courses.

STUDENT EXPERIENCE
We achieved 93% overall student satisfaction in the National Student Survey (NSS). You will have access to a 53 megapixel powerwall, a 3D virtual reality suite, a new cloud computing testbed and dedicated laboratories.

TAUGHT BY EXPERTS
A cutting-edge, vibrant research environment enables us to offer a range of exciting degree courses taught by experts who are national and global leaders in their fields.

HIGHLY EMPLOYABLE GRADUATES
Our recent graduates are in professional or managerial roles with organisations such as Microsoft, BAE Systems, IBM and Barclays, Amazon and BT (DLHE).

Our dedicated employability team will provide you with support and advice to help you find relevant work experience, internships and year in industry placements, as well as graduate positions.

ACCREDITED DEGREES
Our Computer Science degree is accredited by the British Computer Society (BCS).

www.engineering.leeds.ac.uk/computing

www.facebook.com/computingleeds

www.twitter.com/LeedsUniComp

UNIVERSITY OF LEEDS

Applied Computing

We offer you:

- The only two-year honours computing degree in the UK accredited by the BCS
- One of the best staff:student ratios in the UK with 1 member of staff for every 10.5 students
- Small-group teaching led by research active staff
- The best graduate employability rate in England and Wales (HESA 2015)
- Opportunities to gain industry experience
- January and September start dates
- A unique opportunity to obtain a BSc and MSc in just three years

If you didn't get the required A-Levels you can start on our 1-term Access to Computing programme, which leads on to the undergraduate degree.

THE TIMES THE SUNDAY TIMES
GOOD UNIVERSITY GUIDE 2016
UNIVERSITY OF THE YEAR FOR TEACHING

science-admissions@buckingham.ac.uk
+44 (0)1280 828204
www.buckingham.ac.uk/appliedcomputing

THE UNIVERSITY OF
BUCKINGHAM

Greenwich – 120 pts (Maths Comp; Bus Inf Sys)

Heriot-Watt – BBB incl maths (Comp Sci) (IB 28 pts HL 5 maths); BBB (Inf Sys courses) (IB 28 pts)

Huddersfield – BBB 120 pts (ICT; Comp Sci; Comp)

Keele – BBB/ABC (Comp Sci) (IB 32 pts)

Leicester – BBB (Comp) (IB 28–30 pts)

Lincoln – 120 pts (Comp Sci; Gms Comp)

Northumbria – 120 pts (IT Bus Sys) (IB 30 pts)

Norwich Arts – BBB incl art/des (Gms Art Des) (IB 32 pts)

Nottingham Trent – 120 pts incl IT/maths/sci (Comp Sci courses)

Plymouth – 120 pts (Comp Sci; Comp Inf Scrty; Comp Gms Dev) (IB 30 pts)

Queen's Belfast – BBB–ABB incl maths/tech (Comp Sci)

Sheffield Hallam – 120 pts (Comp Sci)

Stirling – BBB (Comp Sci; Bus Comp) (IB 32 pts)

Teesside – 120 pts incl tech/sci/maths (Comp Gms Prog)

Ulster – BBC 120 pts (Comp Sci (Soft Sys Dev)) (IB 26 pts); (Comp Sci) (IB 27 pts); 120 pts incl sci/maths/tech (Comp Gms Dev) (IB 26 pts)

UWE Bristol – 120 pts incl maths/sci/des/tech/eng (Gms Tech) (IB 26 pts)

112 pts **Abertay** – BBC incl maths (Comp Gms Tech) (IB 30 pts); BBC incl art des (Comp Arts) (IB 30 pts)

Aberystwyth – 112 pts (Intnt Comp Sys Admin; Bus Inf Tech; Comp Sci Artif Intel; Comp Sci)

Bath Spa – 112–128 pts (Crea Comp)

Birmingham City – BBC incl sci/tech/maths/comp 112 pts (Comp Net Scrty; Comp Sci; Foren Comp) (IB 30 pts); BBC 112 pts (Comp Gms Tech; Bus IT) (IB 30 pts)

Bradford – BBC 112 pts (Web Des Tech; Bus Comp)

Brighton – BBC (Bus Inf Sys; Comp Sci (Gms); Bus Comp Sys; Comp Sci) (IB 28 pts)

Canterbury Christ Church – 112 pts (Comp; Bus Inf Sys)
Central Lancashire – 112–120 pts (Comp Gms Dev; Comp) (IB 28 pts)
Chichester – 112–128 pts (IT Mgt Bus) (IB 30 pts)
De Montfort – 112 pts (Comp Sci courses) (IB 28 pts)
Derby – 112 pts (Comp Gms Modl Animat; Comp Gms Prog; IT)
East London – 112 pts incl Engl (Comp Gms Des (Stry Dev)) (IB 24 pts); 112 pts
    (Comp Gms Dev) (IB 24 pts)
Edge Hill – BBC 112 pts (Comp courses)
Glasgow Caledonian – BBC incl maths (Comp Gms courses) (IB 24 pts)
Gloucestershire – 112 pts (Dig Media Web Tech; Bus Comp; Comp)
Hull – 112 pts (Comp Sci; Comp Sci Gms Dev) (IB 28 pts)
Kingston – 112 pts (Comp Sci; Inf Sys)
Leeds Beckett – 112 pts (Comp; Comp Foren; Comp Foren Scrty; Bus IT) (IB 25 pts)
Liverpool John Moores – 112 pts (Comp St; Comp Gms Dev; Comp Foren)
Middlesex – 112 pts (Gms Des)
Nottingham Trent – 112 pts incl IT/sci (Inf Sys); 112 pts incl IT/maths/sci (Comp Sys
    (Foren Scrty/Net))
Oxford Brookes – BBC (Comp Sci; IT Mgt Bus) (IB 30 pts)
Salford – 112–120 pts incl maths/sci/comp (Comp Sci) (IB 30 pts)
Staffordshire – 112 pts (Bus IT; Comp Sci)
Sunderland – 112 pts (Comp Sci; Net Comp; Comp Foren; Comp; ICT)
Teesside – 112 pts +interview (Comp Sci; Crea Dig Media; IT; Web Multim Des); BBC incl
    maths/comp/IT (Comp Dig Foren); 112 pts +interview/portfolio (Comp Chrctr Animat;
    Comp Gms Animat; Comp Gms Des; Comp Gms Art); 112 pts (Comp)
West London – 112 pts (Mbl Comp; Comp Sci; IT Mgt Bus)
Westminster – BBC–AA (Comp Sci; Bus Inf Sys) (IB 26 pts); (Comp Net Comms) (IB 28 pts)
Worcester – 112 pts (Comp Gms Des Dev; Bus IT; Comp)
York St John – 112 pts (Bus IT)
104 pts **Bournemouth** – 104–120 pts (Bus IT; Comp) (IB 28–30 pts)
Brighton – BCC (Dig Media) (IB 27 pts)
De Montfort – 104 pts (ICT; Comp; Bus Inf Sys) (IB 28 pts)
Derby – 104 pts (Comp Foren Invstg; Maths Comp Sci; Comp Net Scrty; Comp Sci)
Falmouth – 104–120 pts (Comp Games)
Glasgow Caledonian – BCC incl comp/maths (IT Mgt Bus) (24 pts)
Liverpool Hope – BCC–BBB 104–120 pts (Comp Sci; IT)
Manchester Met – BCC–BBC 104–112 pts (Comp Net Tech; Comp Sci; Gms Des Dev; Comp
    Foren Scrty; Comp Gms Tech; Comp) (IB 28 pts); 104–112 pts (Web Dev) (IB 26 pts)
Northampton – 104–120 pts (Comp Gms Dev; Bus Comp (Sys))
Portsmouth – 104–120 pts (Bus Inf Sys; Comp Sci; Comp) (IB 26 pts HL 10 pts)
Robert Gordon – BCC (Comp Sci; Bus IT) (IB 27 pts)
Salford – 104–120 pts (Bus IT)
South Wales – BCC (ICT; Comp Sci) (IB 29 pts); BCC incl art des (Comp Gms Des) (IB 29 pts)
Ulster – 104–120 pts (Bus Inf Sys) (IB 24 pts)
West Scotland – BCC incl maths (Comp Gms Tech) (IB 24 pts)
96 pts **Bangor** – 96–120 pts (Comp Sci Bus; Comp Sci)
Bolton – 96 pts (Comp Net Scrty)
Canterbury Christ Church – 96–112 pts (Web Des)
Cardiff Met – 96 pts (Bus Inf Sys; Comp Sci)
Chester – 96–112 pts (Comp Sci) (IB 26 pts)
East London – 96 pts incl maths (Comp Sci) (IB 25 pts); 96 pts (Comp Bus) (IB 24 pts)
Edinburgh Napier – CCC (Comp) (IB 26 pts); (Web Des Dev; Inf Tech Mgt) (IB 27 pts)
Glyndŵr – 96 pts (Comp Net Scrty)
Hertfordshire – 96–112 pts (Bus Inf Sys) (IB 28 pts)
London Met – 96 pts (Comp Gms Prog; Comp courses)
London South Bank – CCC/AA 96 pts (Comp courses; Bus IT)

Check **Chapter 3** for new university admission details and **Chapter 6** on how to read the subject tables.

Middlesex – 96 pts (Comp Comm Net; Bus Inf Sys)
West Scotland – AA incl maths (IT) (IB 38 pts); CCC (Comp Gms Dev) (IB 24 pts)
88 pts **Anglia Ruskin** – 88 pts (Comp Gmg Tech; Comp Sci; Bus Inf Sys) (IB 24 pts)
Southampton Solent – 88 pts (Bus IT)
Trinity Saint David – 88 pts (Comp Gms Des)
Wolverhampton – 88–104 pts (Comp Sci (Gms Dev))
80 pts **Bangor** – 80 pts (Comp Inf Sys)
Bedfordshire – 80 pts (Inf Sys) (IB 24 pts)
Bucks New – 80–96 pts (Comp courses)
Colchester (Inst) – 80 pts (IT Sys Apps)
Southampton Solent – 80 pts (Net Scrty Mgt; Web Des Dev)
Trinity Saint David – 80 pts (Comp Net; Comp Inf Sys; Web Dev; Bus IT)
Wolverhampton – 80 pts (Bus Inf Sys courses)
72 pts **West Scotland** – BC incl comp sci/maths (Comp Net) (IB 24 pts); BC (Web Mbl Dev; Comp Sci) (IB 24 pts)
Wolverhampton – 72 pts (Comp Sci; Comp; IT Scrty)
64 pts **Ravensbourne** – CC (Web Media) (IB 28 pts)
24 pts **UHI** – D (Comp)

Open University – contact +44 (0)845 300 6090 **or** www.openuniversity.co.uk/you (Comp IT; Comp Joint Hons)

Alternative offers
See **Chapter 6** and **Appendix 1** for grades/new UCAS Tariff points information for other examinations.

EXAMPLES OF COLLEGES OFFERING COURSES IN THIS SUBJECT FIELD
Most colleges, check with your local college. Central Nottingham (Coll); Chesterfield (Coll); Cornwall (Coll); Doncaster (Coll); Durham New (Coll); Ealing, Hammersmith and West London (Coll); East Berkshire (Coll); Kirklees (Coll); Lakes (Coll); Leeds (CA); Llandrillo (Coll); Manchester (Coll); Mid-Cheshire (Coll); NEW (Coll); Newcastle (Coll); Northbrook (Coll); Nottingham New (Coll); Riverside (Coll); St Helens (Coll); Sheffield (Coll);Shrewsbury (CAT); Somerset (Coll); South Devon (Coll); South Essex (Coll); Staffordshire Reg Fed (SURF); Stockport (Coll); Stockton Riverside (Coll); Stoke-on-Trent (Coll); Truro and Penwith (Coll); Tyne Met (Coll); Warrington (Coll); West Cheshire (Coll); Westminster Kingsway (Coll); Wigan and Leigh (Coll); Wiltshire (Coll); York (Coll).

CHOOSING YOUR COURSE (SEE ALSO CH.1)
Universities and colleges teaching quality See www.qaa.ac.uk; http://unistats.direct.gov.uk.

Top research universities and colleges (REF 2014) (Computer Science and Informatics) Liverpool; Warwick; London (UCL); Imperial London; Manchester; Sheffield; Lancaster; London (QM); York; Cambridge; London (King's); Nottingham; Bristol; Newcastle; Oxford.

Examples of sandwich degree courses Aston; Bath; Birmingham City; Bournemouth; Bradford; Brighton; Brunel; Cardiff; City; Coventry; De Montfort; Derby; East Anglia; Edinburgh Napier; Gloucestershire; Greenwich; Huddersfield; Kent; Kingston; Leeds Beckett; Lincoln; Liverpool John Moores; London (QM); London (RH); London South Bank; Loughborough; Manchester Met; Middlesex; Newcastle; Northumbria; Nottingham Trent; Oxford Brookes; Plymouth; Portsmouth; Queen's Belfast; Reading; Salford; Sheffield Hallam; South Wales; Southampton Solent; Sunderland; Surrey; Teesside; Ulster; UWE Bristol; Westminster; Wolverhampton; York.

ADMISSIONS INFORMATION
Number of applicants per place (approx) Abertay 2; Aston (Bus Comp IT) 12; Bath 8; Birmingham 9; Bournemouth 8; Bradford 13; Bristol 8; Brunel 10; Buckingham 6; Cambridge 6; Cardiff 5; City 10; Coventry 10; Derby 3; Dundee 6; Durham 9; East Anglia (Maths Comp) 7; Edinburgh 4; Essex 2; Exeter 10; Glasgow Caledonian 8; Glyndŵr 3; Heriot-Watt 6; Hull (Comp Sci) 6; Imperial London 6; Kent 8; Kingston 10; Lancaster 5; Leeds 10; Leicester 13; Lincoln 5; Liverpool 7; Liverpool John Moores 3; London (King's) 20; London (QM) 6; London (RH) 5; London (UCL) 9; Loughborough 2; Manchester Met

10, (Bus IT) 8; Newcastle 7; Northumbria 4; Nottingham 8; Nottingham Trent 4; Oxford Brookes 18; Plymouth 12; Portsmouth 6; Robert Gordon 3; Sheffield Hallam 5; Southampton 9; Stirling 6; Strathclyde 16; Surrey 9; Swansea 5; Teesside 4; UWE Bristol 4; Warwick 11; York 6.

Advice to applicants and planning the UCAS personal statement Your computer and programming interests in and outside school or college should be described. It is also useful to give details of any visits, work experience and work shadowing relating to industrial or commercial organisations and their computer systems. (See **Appendix 3**.) Give details of your interests in, and knowledge of computer hardware, software and multimedia packages. Contact the Chartered Institute for IT for information. **Bristol** Deferred entry accepted.

Misconceptions about this course That anyone who plays computer games or uses a word processor can do a degree in Computer Studies. Some think Computing degrees are just about programming; in reality, programming is only one, albeit essential, part of computing. **City** (Bus Comp Sys) Some applicants think that it is a Business degree: it is a Computing degree focused on computing in business. **London (QM)** There are many misconceptions – among students, teachers and careers advisers – about what computer science entails. The main one is to confuse it with what schools call information and communication technology which is about the use of computer applications. Computer science is all about software – ie programming – and will generally only cover a limited study of hardware.

Selection interviews Yes Abertay, Bath, Bournemouth, Bradford, Buckingham, Cambridge, Cardiff, City, Coventry, Cumbria, Edinburgh, Edinburgh Napier, Falmouth, Hull, Imperial London, Kent, Kingston, Liverpool Hope, London (Gold), London (QM), London (UCL), London South Bank, Loughborough, Manchester, Newcastle, Northampton, Northbrook (Coll), Nottingham Trent, Oxford (Comp Sci) 9%, (Comp Sci Phil) 16%, Plymouth, Portsmouth, St Andrews, Salford, Sheffield Hallam, Southampton, Surrey, UWE Bristol, West London, Wigan and Leigh (Coll); **Some** Anglia Ruskin, Birmingham City, Brighton, East Anglia, Liverpool John Moores, London Met, Manchester Met, Sunderland, Warwick (5%–10%); **No** Dundee, Nottingham, West Scotland.

Interview advice and questions While A-level Computer Studies is not usually required, you will be questioned on your use of computers and aspects of the subject which interest you. How do you organise your homework/social life? What are your strengths and weaknesses? Do you have any idea of the type of career you would like? See also **Chapter 5**. **City** The aim of the interview is to obtain a full picture of the applicant's background, life experiences etc, before making an offer. **York** No tests. Questions for discussion at the whiteboard are usually mathematical or are about fundamental computer science such as sorting.

Reasons for rejection (non-academic) Little practical interest in computers/electronics. Inability to work as part of a small team. Mismatch between referee's description and performance at interview. Unsatisfactory English. Can't communicate. Inability to convince interviewer of the candidate's worth. Incoherent, unmotivated, arrogant and without any evidence of good reason. **London (QM)** Misunderstanding of what computer science involves as an academic subject – especially in personal statements where some suggest that they are interested in a course with business and administrative skills. Lack of sufficient mathematics. Computer science is a mathematical subject and we cannot accept applicants who are unable to demonstrate good mathematical skills. **Southampton** Lack of motivation; incoherence; carelessness.

AFTER-RESULTS ADVICE
Offers to applicants repeating A-levels Higher Brighton, De Montfort, Greenwich, Kingston, St Andrews, Surrey, Sussex, Warwick; **Possibly higher** Bath, Edinburgh, Lancaster, Leeds, Newcastle, Oxford Brookes, Portsmouth, Sheffield, Teesside, UWE Bristol; **Same** Abertay, Anglia Ruskin, Aston, Brunel, Buckingham, Cambridge, Cardiff, Cardiff Met, City, Derby, Dundee, Durham, East Anglia, East London, Exeter, Huddersfield, Hull, Kent, Lincoln, Liverpool, Liverpool Hope, Liverpool John Moores, London (RH), London (UCL), London South Bank, Loughborough, Manchester Met, Northumbria, Nottingham Trent, Robert Gordon, Salford, Sheffield Hallam, Sunderland, Ulster, West London, Wolverhampton, Worcester, York.

GRADUATE DESTINATIONS AND EMPLOYMENT (2013/14 HESA)

Computer Science graduates surveyed 7,780 **Employed** 4,860 **In voluntary employment** 180 **In further study** 1,000 **Assumed unemployed** 865

Information Systems graduates surveyed 2,315 **Employed** 1,370 **In voluntary employment** 55 **In further study** 330 **Assumed unemployed** 225

Artificial Intelligence graduates surveyed 70 **Employed** 40 **In voluntary employment** 0 **In further study** 10 **Assumed unemployed** 5

Career note A high proportion of graduates go to work in the IT sector with some degrees leading towards particular fields (usually indicated by the course title). Significant areas include software design and engineering, web and internet-based fields, programming, systems analysis and administration.

OTHER DEGREE SUBJECTS FOR CONSIDERATION

Business Studies; Communications Engineering; Computer Engineering; Electrical and Electronic Engineering; Geographical Information Systems; Information Studies; Mathematics; Physics; Software Engineering.

CONSUMER STUDIES/SCIENCES

(including **Consumer Product Design** and **Trading Standards**; see also **Food Science/Studies and Technology, Hospitality and Event Management**)

There are relatively few Consumer Studies degree courses by name, but this does not mean it is not an important subject: it offers such a varied range of career opportunities. The University College Birmingham course is a good example covering marketing, retail management, public relations, food product development, food and recipe development, and even food journalism. There are of course more specialised courses listed in this chapter, but consumer courses provide an excellent taster for applicants unsure of their final career choice.

Useful websites www.which.co.uk; www.tradingstandards.uk

NB The points totals shown to the left of the institutions are for ease of reference only. It must not be assumed that Tariff points are always used by institutions or that they can be substituted for an offer in grades. The level of an offer is not necessarily indicative of the quality of a course.

COURSE OFFERS INFORMATION

Subject requirements/preferences GCSE Mathematics and English usually required. **AL** No specific subjects required.

Your target offers and examples of degree courses
136 pts **Reading** – AAB–ABB (Nutr Fd Consum Sci) (IB 35–32 pts)
 96 pts **Abertay** – CCC (Fd Consum Sci) (IB 28 pts)
        Birmingham (UC) – 96 pts (Food Consum Mgt)
        Edinburgh Napier – CCC (Mark Mgt Consum St) (IB 27 pts)

Alternative offers
See **Chapter 6** and **Appendix 1** for grades/new UCAS Tariff points information for other examinations.

CHOOSING YOUR COURSE (SEE ALSO CH.1)

Universities and colleges teaching quality See www.qaa.ac.uk; http://unistats.direct.gov.uk.

Examples of sandwich degree courses Birmingham (UC); Harper Adams.

ADMISSIONS INFORMATION

Number of applicants per place (approx) Birmingham (UC) 2.

New UCAS points Tariff: A* = 56 pts; A = 48 pts; B = 40 pts; C = 32 pts; D = 24 pts; E = 16 pts

Advice to applicants and planning the UCAS personal statement Relevant work experience or work shadowing in, for example, business organisations, restaurants, cafes, or the school meals service, would be appropriate. See also **Hospitality and Event Management** and **Dietetics** and **Appendix 3**.

Interview advice and questions Questions will stem from your special interests in this subject and in the past have included: What interests you in consumer behaviour? What are the advantages and disadvantages of measuring consumer behaviour? What is ergonomics? What do you understand by the term sustainable consumption? What world or national news has annoyed, pleased or upset you? What relevance do textiles and dress have to home economics? How would you react in a room full of fools? See also **Chapter 5**.

AFTER-RESULTS ADVICE
Offers to applicants repeating A-levels Same Ulster.

GRADUATE DESTINATIONS AND EMPLOYMENT (2013/14 HESA)
Career note The various specialisms involved in these courses allow graduates to look for openings in several other career areas, for example, food quality assurance, consumer education and advice. Many graduates enter business administration and careers in retailing, evaluating new products and liaising with the public.

OTHER DEGREE SUBJECTS FOR CONSIDERATION
Biological Sciences; Business Studies; Dietetics; Environmental Health; Food Science; Health Studies; Hospitality Management; Marketing; Nutrition; Psychology; Retail Management.

DANCE/DANCE STUDIES
(see also **Drama**)

Dance courses abound, most offering a balance of theoretical and practical studies across a range of dance styles. The Royal Academy of Dance for example offers ballet, adult ballet, boys' ballet, creative and contemporary dance, West End jazz, street dance, and song and dance. Other institutions offer Dance combined with other subjects equally, or at the University of Surrey, Dance can be taken as a major subject or as a minor subject with Film Studies or Theatre and Performance. Some universities offer Performance Arts with many courses covering the study of choreography, acting and directing, and acting and dance. Whilst entry to Dance courses usually requires A-level grades, competitive entry to the most popular courses, such as the Contemporary Dance course at Trinity Laban, is by a demanding audition.

Useful websites www.cdet.org.uk; www.ndta.org.uk; www.rad.org.uk; www.royalballetschool.org.uk

NB The points totals shown to the left of the institutions are for ease of reference only. It must not be assumed that Tariff points are always used by institutions or that they can be substituted for an offer in grades. The level of an offer is not necessarily indicative of the quality of a course.

COURSE OFFERS INFORMATION
Subject requirements/preferences GCSE English usually required. **AL** No specific subjects required. **Other** Disclosure and Barring Service (DBS) checks required for some courses: check websites. Practical dance experience essential.

Your target offers and examples of degree courses
136 pts   **Kingston** – 136 pts (Dance)
           Roehampton – 136 pts +audition +interview (Dance St)
           Surrey – AAB–ABB incl dance (Dance) (IB 35–34 pts)
128 pts   **East London** – 128 pts +audition +interview (Dance (Urb Prac)) (IB 27 pts)
           Edge Hill – ABB 128 pts offer may be altered based on audition (Dance; Dance Dr)
120 pts   **Leeds Beckett** – 120 pts (Dance) (IB 26 pts)
           West London – 120 pts (Musl Thea)
112 pts   **Bedfordshire** – 112 pts +audition +interview (Dance Prof Prac) (IB 24 pts)

Canterbury Christ Church – 112 pts (Dance)
Cardiff Met – 112 pts (Dance)
Chester – BBC–BCC 112 pts +audition (Dance) (IB 26 pts)
Chichester – 112–128 pts (Dance)
Coventry – BBC incl dance/perf arts (Dance) (IB 28 pts HL 5 dance)
Cumbria – 112 pts (Dance Musl Thea)
De Montfort – 112 pts (Dance) (IB 28 pts)
Lincoln – 112 pts (Dance)
Liverpool John Moores – 112 pts (Dance Prac)
Middlesex – 112 pts +audition +interview (Dance St; Dance Perf)
RAc Dance – BBC +RAD Intermediate (Ballet Educ)
Sunderland – 112 pts (Dance)

104 pts **Bath Spa** – 104–120 pts (Dance)
Central Lancashire – 104 pts (Dance Perf Teach) (IB 28 pts)
Falmouth – 104–120 pts (Dance Choreo)
Liverpool Hope – BCC–BBB 104–120 pts (Dance)
Plymouth – 104 pts (Dance Thea) (IB 28 pts)
Salford – BCC–BBB 104 pts (Dance) (IB 24 pts)

96 pts **Birmingham City** – 96 pts incl dr (App Perf (Commun Educ))
Canterbury Christ Church – 96 pts (Dance Educ)
Cumbria – 96 pts (Dance)
Manchester Met – 96–112 pts (Dance) (IB 28 pts)
Winchester – 96–112 pts (Choreo Dance) (IB 25 pts)
Wolverhampton – 96 pts (Dance Dr; Dance)

88 pts **Derby** – 88–120 pts (Dance Mov St Joint Hons)
London Met – 88 pts incl dance/PE/biol/spo sci (Spo Dance Thera)

80 pts **Bucks New** – 80–96 pts (Dance Perf) (IB 24 pts)

64 pts **Greenwich** – 64 pts (Prof Dance Musl Thea) (IB 28 pts)
Liverpool (LIPA) – 64 pts (Dance)

32 pts **Northern (Sch Contemp Dance)** – 32 pts +audition +interview (Contemp Dance)
RAc Dance – 32 pts +RAD Intermediate Dist learn (Dance Educ)
RConsvS – +audition check with School (Modn Ballet)
Teesside – +audition (Dance)
Trinity Laban Consv – +audition check with Conservatoire (Contemp Dance)

Alternative offers
See **Chapter 6** and **Appendix 1** for grades/new UCAS Tariff points information for other examinations.

EXAMPLES OF COLLEGES OFFERING COURSES IN THIS SUBJECT FIELD
Barking and Dagenham (Coll); Bournemouth and Poole (Coll); Brooksby Melton (Coll); City and Islington (Coll); Coventry City (Coll); Doncaster (Coll); Ealing, Hammersmith and West London (Coll); East Durham (Coll); Gateshead (Coll); Grimsby (Univ Centre); Havering (Coll); Hull (Coll); Kingston (Coll); Leeds City (Coll); Leicester (Coll); LeSoCo; Liverpool City (Coll); Manchester (Coll); Northbrook (Coll); Nottingham New (Coll); Petroc; South Essex (Coll); South Gloucestershire and Stroud (Coll); Southampton City (Coll); Stratford-upon-Avon (Coll); Suffolk (Univ Campus); Sunderland (Coll); Sussex Downs (Coll); Wakefield (Coll); West Thames (Coll).

CHOOSING YOUR COURSE (SEE ALSO CH.1)
Universities and colleges teaching quality See www.qaa.ac.uk; http://unistats.direct.gov.uk.

Top research universities and colleges (REF 2014) (Music, Drama, Dance and Performing Arts) Open University; Roehampton (Dance); London (QM); Warwick; London (SOAS); Durham; London (RH) (Mus); Southampton; Oxford; Birmingham (Mus); City; London (King's) (Film); Manchester (Dr); London (RH) (Dr Thea); Huddersfield; Manchester (Mus); Cardiff.

Examples of sandwich degree courses Coventry; Surrey.

New UCAS points Tariff: A* = 56 pts; A = 48 pts; B = 40 pts; C = 32 pts; D = 24 pts; E = 16 pts

ADMISSIONS INFORMATION

Number of applicants per place (approx) Chichester 6; De Montfort (Dance) 13; Derby 12; Liverpool (LIPA) 24; Liverpool John Moores 3; Middlesex 12; Northern (Sch Contemp Dance) 6; Roehampton 17; Surrey 5; Trinity Laban Consv 5.

Advice to applicants and planning the UCAS personal statement Full details should be given of examinations taken and practical experience in contemporary dance or ballet. Refer to your visits to the theatre and your impressions. You should list the dance projects in which you have worked, productions in which you have performed and the roles. State any formal dance training you have had and the grades achieved. Applicants need to have dedication, versatility, inventiveness and individuality, practical experience of dance, theoretical ability and language competency. **Bath Spa** Dance experience outside education should be mentioned.

Misconceptions about this course That Performing Arts is only an acting course: it also includes music.

Selection interviews Yes Bedfordshire, Birmingham City, Cardiff Met, Chester, Chichester, Falmouth, Leeds Beckett, Plymouth, Roehampton, Worcester; **Some** RAc Dance.

Interview advice and questions Nearly all institutions will require auditions or interviews or attendance at a workshop. The following scheme required by **Liverpool (LIPA)** may act as a guide:

1 Write a short essay (500 words) on your own views and experience of dance. You should take into account the following.
   - (i) Your history and how you have developed physically and intellectually in your run-up to applying to LIPA.
   - (ii) Your main influences and what inspires you.
   - (iii) What you want to gain from training as a dancer.
   - (iv) Your ideas on health and nutrition as a dancer, taking into account gender and physicality.
2 All candidates must prepare **two** practical audition pieces.
   - (i) Whatever you like, in whatever style you wish, as long as the piece does not exceed two minutes (please note: panel will stop anyone exceeding this time limit). There will be no pianist at this part of the session, so if you're using music please bring it with you. This devised piece should be created by you and this means that you should feel comfortable with it and that it expresses something personal about you. You should wear your regular practice clothes for your presentation.
   - (ii) You are asked to sing a musical theatre solo as part of the audition and will be accompanied by a pianist. An accompanist is provided, but you must provide the sheet music for your song, fully written out for piano accompaniment and in the key you wish to sing (the accompanist will **not** transpose at sight). **Important** Do NOT choreograph your song. You should expect to sit on a high stool or stand when singing for the audition.
3 Additionally, all candidates will participate in a class given on the day of audition.
   - (i) Please ensure that you are dressed appropriately for class with clothing you are comfortable in but allows your movement to be seen. In preparing the practical elements of the audition, please remember that audition panels are not looking for a polished performance. The panel will be looking for candidates' ability to make a genuine emotional and physical connection with the material that they are presenting which shows clear intent and focus.

Remember that it is in your best interest to prepare thoroughly. Nerves inevitably play a part in any audition and can undermine even the best-prepared candidate. Your best defence is to feel confident in your preparation. See also **Chapter 5**. **Chichester** Applicants will be asked to prepare a set-piece in advance and to perform the piece in front of a group. **De Montfort** (Perf Arts) Practical workshops in dance and theatre plus a written paper. **Salford** Audition and Interview **Surrey** Applicants invited to spend a day at the University for interview and a practical class to assess dance skills. An audition fee may be charged. **Wolverhampton** Audition in the form of a dance class

Reasons for rejection (non-academic) Applicants more suitable for an acting or dance school course than a degree course. No experience of dance on the UCAS application. Limited dance skills. **Surrey** Inadequate dance background. Had not seen/read about/done any dance.

Check **Chapter 3** for new university admission details and **Chapter 6** on how to read the subject tables.

AFTER-RESULTS ADVICE

Offers to applicants repeating A-levels Same Chester, Chichester, De Montfort, Liverpool John Moores, Salford, Surrey, Trinity Laban Consv, Winchester, Wolverhampton.

GRADUATE DESTINATIONS AND EMPLOYMENT (2013/14 HESA)

Graduates surveyed 1,105 **Employed** 485 **In voluntary employment** 30 **In further study** 270 **Assumed unemployed** 25

Career note Teaching is the most popular career destination for the majority of graduates. Other opportunities exist as dance animators working in education or in the community to encourage activity and participation in dance. There is a limited number of openings for dance or movement therapists who work with the emotionally disturbed, the elderly or physically disadvantaged.

OTHER DEGREE SUBJECTS FOR CONSIDERATION

Arts Management; Drama; Education (Primary); Music; Performance Studies; Physical Education; Sport and Exercise Science.

DENTISTRY

(including **Dental Technology, Dental Hygiene** and **Oral Health Science**)

Dentistry involves the treatment and prevention of a wide range of mouth diseases from tooth decay and gum disease to mouth cancer. Courses in Dentistry/Dental Surgery cover the basic medical sciences, human disease, clinical studies and clinical dentistry. The amount of patient contact will vary between institutions but will be considerable in all dental schools. Intercalated courses in other science subjects are offered on most courses. Courses in Oral Health Science and Dental Therapy and Hygiene lead to professional qualifications as therapists and hygienists providing advice and non-surgical treatment for children and adults to prevent tooth decay. Dental Technology courses similarly lead to a professional qualification to prepare crowns, bridges, partial and complete sets of dentures, and other orthodontic devices to replace and correct teeth.

Useful websites www.bda.org; www.bsdht.org.uk; www.dla.org.uk

NB The points totals shown to the left of the institutions are for ease of reference only. It must not be assumed that Tariff points are always used by institutions or that they can be substituted for an offer in grades. The level of an offer is not necessarily indicative of the quality of a course.

COURSE OFFERS INFORMATION

Subject requirements/preferences GCSE English, mathematics and science subjects required in most cases for Dentistry courses. A*/A/B grades stipulated in certain subjects by many dental schools. **AL** Chemistry plus Biology or another science subject usually required for Dentistry: see offers lines below. (Dntl Tech, Oral Hlth Sci) Science subject required or preferred. Many dental schools use admissions tests (eg UKCAT: see **Chapter 5**). Evidence of non-infectivity or hepatitis B immunisation required and all new dental students screened for hepatitis C. Disclosure and Barring Service (DBS) check at enhanced level is also required.

London (King's) GCSE English and maths grade B.

Manchester GCSE 6 subjects at grade A.

Your target offers and examples of degree courses

164 pts **Birmingham** – AAAa–AAAb incl chem+biol +UKCAT (Dnstry) (IB 32 pts HL 666)

        Queen's Belfast – AAAa incl chem+sci/maths +UKCAT (Dntl Srgy)

152 pts **London (King's)** – A*AA incl biol+chem +UKCAT (Dnstry) (IB 35 pts HL 6 biol+chem)

144 pts **Bristol** – AAA–AAB incl chem+biol/phys (Dnstry) (IB 36–34 pts HL 6 chem+biol/phys)

        Cardiff – AAA incl chem+biol +UKCAT (Dnstry) (IB 36 pts HL 6 chem+biol)

        Dundee – AAA incl chem+sci +UKCAT (Dnstry) (IB 37 pts)

Glasgow – AAA incl biol+chem +UKCAT (Dnstry) (IB 36 pts)
Leeds – AAA incl biol+chem (Dntl Srgy) (IB 35 pts HL 6 biol+chem)
Liverpool – AAA incl chem/biol (Dntl Srgy) (IB 36 pts HL 6 chem+biol)
London (QM) – AAA incl chem/biol+sci/maths +UKCAT (Dnstry) (IB 38 pts HL 6 sci)
Manchester – AAA incl chem+biol +UKCAT (Dnstry) (IB 37 pts)
Newcastle – AAA incl chem+biol +UKCAT (Dntl Srgy) (IB 37 pts HL 6 chem+biol)
Sheffield – AAA incl chem+biol +UKCAT (Dntl Srgy) (IB 37 pts HL 6 chem+biol)

128 pts **Birmingham** – ABB incl biol (Dntl Hyg Thera) (IB 32 pts HL 655)
London (QM) – ABB incl maths/phys/chem (Dntl Mat) (IB 34 pts HL 6 maths/phys/chem)
Newcastle – ABB incl biol (Oral Dntl Hlth Sci) (IB 34 pts HL 5 biol)

120 pts **Cardiff** – BBB incl biol (Dntl Thera Hyg)
Dundee – BBB incl biol (Oral Hlth Sci) (IB 30 pts)
Edinburgh – BBB incl biol (Oral Hlth Sci) (IB 32 pts)
Portsmouth – 120 pts incl sci (Dntl Hyg Dntl Thera) (IB 30 pts HL 17 pts incl 6 sci)

112 pts **Cardiff Met** – 112 pts (Dntl Tech)

104 pts **Glasgow Caledonian** – BCC incl biol (Oral Hlth Sci) (IB 24 pts HL 6 biol)
Teesside – 104–112 pts incl biol +interview (Dntl Hyg Dntl Thera)
UHI – BCC incl sci (Oral Hlth Sci)

Alternative offers
See **Chapter 6** and **Appendix 1** for grades/new UCAS Tariff points information for other examinations.

EXAMPLES OF COLLEGES OFFERING COURSES IN THIS SUBJECT FIELD
Birmingham Met (Coll); Bury (Coll); Neath Port Talbot (Coll); Plumpton (Coll).

CHOOSING YOUR COURSE (SEE ALSO CH.1)
Universities and colleges teaching quality See www.qaa.ac.uk; http://unistats.direct.gov.uk.

Top research universities and colleges (REF 2014) (Allied Health Professions, Dentistry, Nursing and Pharmacy) Birmingham; Sheffield (Biomed Sci); Bangor; Swansea (Allied Hlth); Aston; Coventry; Southampton; Cardiff; Surrey; Glasgow; Nottingham (Pharm); Bradford; East Anglia (Allied Hlth); London (QM); Sheffield (Dnstry); Queen's Belfast (Pharm); Bath; London (King's) (Pharm); Leeds.

ADMISSIONS INFORMATION
Number of applicants per place (approx) Birmingham 7, (Dntl Hyg Thera) 8; Bristol 13; Cardiff 4; Cardiff Met (Dntl Tech) 1; Dundee 8, (Pre-Dntl) 5; Edinburgh (Oral Hlth Sci) 10 places every 2nd yr; Glasgow 7; Leeds 11; Liverpool 15; London (King's) 128 (offers to 1 in 9); London (QM) 18; Manchester 12, (Pre-Dntl) 21, (Oral Hlth Sci) 26; Manchester Met 16; Newcastle 12; Portsmouth 2; Queen's Belfast 5; Sheffield 12.

Admissions tutors' advice
Bristol Places in Clearing for international students.

Buckingham The course is specially designed for the international student market and takes place at the Leicester Dental Academy and Clinic. Applications go through UCAS and should be submitted in June (check with University) for a September entry. Results of medical or dental examinations taken in the applicant's country should also be submitted, eg the All India Pre-Medical Test (AIPMT) for Indian applicants.

Advice to applicants and planning the UCAS personal statement UCAS applications listing four choices only should be submitted by 15 October. Applicants may add one alternative (non-Dentistry) course. However, if they receive an offer for this course and are rejected for Dentistry, they will not be considered for Dentistry courses in Clearing if they perform better than expected in the examinations. On your UCAS application show evidence of your manual dexterity, work experience and awareness of problems experienced by dentists. Details should be provided of discussions with dentists and work shadowing in dental surgeries. Employment (paid or voluntary) in any field, preferably dealing with people in an environment widely removed from your home or school, could be described. Discuss any specialised fields of dentistry in which you might be interested. See also **Appendix 3**. **Bristol** Applications are not segregated by type of educational institution. Candidates are assessed on general presentation. At least 20 days of work experience is expected, if possible in different fields of dentistry. Re-sit candidates only considered if they failed to get the grades by a small margin and they had originally placed Bristol as their first firm choice. **Cardiff** Applicants must be able to demonstrate: (a) evidence of, and potential for, high academic achievement, (b) an understanding of the demands of dental training and practice, (c) a caring and committed attitude towards people, (d) a willingness to accept resonsibility, (e) an ability to communicate effectively, (f) evidence of broad social, cultural or sporting interests. **Glasgow** Applicants invited to submit a portfolio as evidence of their suitability. This will be assessed against the BDS Person Specification available from the Dental School. Candidates who do not submit a portfolio are not invited to selection interview. **London (King's)** School activities desirable, for example, general reading, debating, theological interests. Community activities very desirable. General activities desirable, for example, sport, first-aid, handiwork (which can be shown at interview to demonstrate manual dexterity). Work shadowing and paid or voluntary work very desirable (check website). **Manchester** Re-sit offers normally only made to students who firmly accepted an offer the previous year. Re-sit offers AAA. Applicants are required to have observed a general dental practitioner at work before applying; a minimum of two weeks is expected. **Newcastle** Applications from students with disabilities welcomed.

Misconceptions about this course Cardiff Met (Dntl Tech) Some think that the course allows them to practise as a dentist. Some think the degree is entirely practical.

Selection interviews Most dental schools will interview candidates. **Yes** Aberdeen, Birmingham (400–450 applicants; 50% get through initial sort), Bristol, Cardiff, Dundee, Glasgow, Leeds, Liverpool, London (King's), London (QM), Manchester, Newcastle, Plymouth, Portsmouth, Queen's Belfast, Sheffield; **Some** Cardiff Met.

Interview advice and questions Dental work experience or work shadowing is essential (check with university websites) and, as a result, questions will be asked on your reactions to the work and your understanding of the different types of treatment that a dentist can offer. In the past, questions at interview have included: What is conservative dentistry? What does integrity mean? Do you think the first-year syllabus is a good one? What qualities are required by a dentist? What are prosthetics, periodontics, orthodontics? What causes tooth decay? Questions asked on the disadvantages of being a dentist, the future of dentistry and how you could show that you are manually dexterous. Other questions on personal attributes and spare time activities. What are the careers within the profession open to dentists? Questions on the future of dentistry (preventative and cosmetic dentistry), the problems facing dentists, the skills needed and the advantages and disadvantages of fluoride in water. How do you relax? How do you cope with stress? See also **Chapter 5**. **Bristol** All candidates called for interview must attend in order to be considered for a place; 200 are selected for interview for the five-year course and 15 for the six-year course. Offers are made to 180 and six respectively. An essay is set on a dental subject and will be assessed for spontaneity, written content and clear thought processes. Candidates at interview are assessed on general presentation, response to questions, knowledge of dentistry, evidence of teamwork, leadership, general interests, manual dexterity and good eyesight (a practical test is taken). Examples of practical work, for example, art work, needlework etc may be taken to interview as evidence of manual dexterity. **Leeds** The interview assesses personality, verbal and communication skills and knowledge of dentistry. **London (King's)** 220 applicants are interviewed of whom 180 will receive offers. All applicants receiving offers will have been interviewed. Applicants complete a questionnaire prior to interview and the interviews last about 20 minutes. Applicants may take to interview any examples of practical work, for example, art, woodwork, needlework etc as evidence of manual dexterity.

Reasons for rejection (non-academic) Lack of evidence of a firm commitment to dentistry. Lack of breadth of interests. Lack of motivation for a health care profession. Unprofessional attitude. Poor manual dexterity. Poor communication skills. Poor English. Lack of evidence of ability to work in groups. Not for the faint-hearted! More interested in running a business and making money than in caring for people. **Cardiff Met** (Dntl Tech) Target numbers need to be precise so the course fills at a late stage.

New UCAS points Tariff: A* = 56 pts; A = 48 pts; B = 40 pts; C = 32 pts; D = 24 pts; E = 16 pts

Mature students The following universities/dental schools offer shortened (usually four years) courses in Dentistry/Dental Surgery for graduates with at least 2.1 degrees in specified subjects. GCE A-level subjects and grades are also specified. Check with universities: Liverpool, London (King's), (QM).

AFTER-RESULTS ADVICE

Offers to applicants repeating A-levels Higher Cardiff (preference given to students who previously applied), Dundee, Leeds (very few), Manchester (AAA for applicants who firmly accepted offer of a place); **Same** Cardiff Met (Dntl Tech), Queen's Belfast.

GRADUATE DESTINATIONS AND EMPLOYMENT (2013/14 HESA)

Clinical Dentistry graduates surveyed 945 **Employed** 855 **In voluntary employment** 10 **In further study** 50 **Assumed unemployed** 0

Career note The great majority of Dental Technology graduates gain employment in this career with job opportunities excellent in both the UK and Europe. There are openings in the NHS, commercial dental laboratories and the armed services.

OTHER DEGREE SUBJECTS FOR CONSIDERATION

Anatomy; Biochemistry; Biological Sciences; Biomedical Materials Science; Chemistry; Medical Sciences; Medicine; Nursing; Optometry; Pharmacy; Physiology; Physiotherapy; Radiography; Speech Therapy/Sciences; Veterinary Medicine/Science.

DEVELOPMENT STUDIES

(see also **International Relations, Politics, Town and Country Planning**)

Development Studies courses are multi-disciplinary and cover a range of subjects including economics, geography, sociology, social anthropology, politics, natural resources, with special reference to countries overseas. Courses obviously overlap with International Relations degrees which should also be checked. The main focus of Development Studies is to identify and recognise problems arising overseas and how countries may be assisted in terms of poverty and health, as well as exploring wider issues concerning social and political perspectives. The unique degree course in this category is Charity Development at the University of Chichester with either Single Honours or Joint Honours. The course covers fund-raising practices, through events and campaigns, marketing and planning.

Useful websites www.devstud.org.uk; www.gov.uk/government/organisations/department-for-international-development; www.ids.ac.uk; see also **Politics**.

NB The points totals shown to the left of the institutions are for ease of reference only. It must not be assumed that Tariff points are always used by institutions or that they can be substituted for an offer in grades. The level of an offer is not necessarily indicative of the quality of a course.

COURSE OFFERS INFORMATION

Subject requirements/preferences GCSE Mathematics, English and a foreign language may be required. **AL** Science or social science subjects may be required or preferred for some courses.

Your target offers and examples of degree courses
144 pts   **London (SOAS)** – AAA–AAB (Dev St) (IB 37 pts)
          Warwick – AAA (Glob Sust Dev Bus St) (IB 38 pts)
136 pts   **Bath** – AAB (Int Dev Econ) (IB 35 pts)
          London (King's) – AAB (Int Dev) (IB 35 pts)
          Manchester – AAB (Dev St) (IB 35 pts)
          Sussex – AAB–ABB (Econ Int Dev) (IB 34 pts); AAB (Int Rel Dev; Int Dev) (IB 35 pts)
128 pts   **Birmingham** – ABB (Plan Econ) (IB 32 pts HL 655)
          East Anglia – ABB (Int Dev Anth; Int Dev Pol; Int Dev) (IB 32 pts)

      Leeds – ABB (Int Dev courses) (IB 34 pts)
      Sussex – ABB–BBB (Sociol Int Dev) (IB 34–32 pts)
120 pts **Birmingham** – BBB (Af St Dev) (IB 32 pts HL 555)
112 pts **Aberystwyth** – 112 pts (Educ Int Dev)
      Chichester – 112 pts +interview (Charity Dev)
      East London – 112 pts (Int Dev NGO Mgt) (IB 24 pts)
      Leeds Beckett – 112 pts (Int Rel Glob Dev) (IB 25 pts)
      London (Birk) – 112 pts (Dev Glob)
      Northampton – 112 pts (Int Dev courses)
      Westminster – BBC (Int Rel Dev) (IB 30 pts)
104 pts **Bath Spa** – 104–120 pts (Glob Dev Sust)
      Derby – 104–120 pts geog/sci/soc sci (Thrd Wrld Dev Joint Hons)
 96 pts **Bradford** – CCC 96 pts (Dev Pce St)
      Portsmouth – 96–120 pts (Int Dev St) (IB 30 pts HL 17 pts)
 64 pts **UHI** – CC (Sust Dev); CC +interview (Gael Dev)

Alternative offers
See **Chapter 6** and **Appendix 1** for grades/new UCAS Tariff points information for other examinations.

EXAMPLES OF COLLEGES OFFERING COURSES IN THIS SUBJECT FIELD
Blackpool and Fylde (Coll); Harrogate (Coll); Hull (Coll); Myerscough (Coll); Newcastle (Coll); South Devon (Coll); SRUC; Truro and Penwith (Coll); Wakefield (Coll); Yeovil (Coll).

CHOOSING YOUR COURSE (SEE ALSO CH.1)
Universities and colleges teaching quality See www.qaa.ac.uk; http://unistats.direct.gov.uk.

Top research universities and colleges (REF 2014) (Anthropology and Development Studies) London LSE (Int Dev); Manchester (Anth); Oxford (Int Dev); Manchester (Dev St); London (Gold); Durham; East Anglia; Cambridge; Edinburgh.

ADMISSIONS INFORMATION
Number of applicants per place (approx) Bradford 6; East Anglia 8; Leeds 8.

Admissions tutors' advice Discuss aspects of development studies which interest you, for example in relation to geography, economics, politics. Interests in Third World countries should be mentioned. Knowledge of current events.

Advice to applicants and planning the UCAS personal statement Some students think that Development Studies has something to do with property, with plants or with childhood. It is none of these and is about international processes of change, development, progress and crisis.

Interview advice and questions Since this is a multi-disciplinary subject, questions will vary considerably. Initially they will stem from your interests and the information given on your UCAS application and your reasons for choosing the course. In the past, questions at interview have included: Define a Third World country. What help does the United Nations provide in the Third World? Could it do too much? What problems does the United Nations face in its work throughout the world? Why Development Studies? What will you do in your gap year, and what do you want to achieve? See also **Chapter 5**.

AFTER-RESULTS ADVICE
Offers to applicants repeating A-levels Same East Anglia.

GRADUATE DESTINATIONS AND EMPLOYMENT (2013/14 HESA)
Career note The range of specialisms offered on these courses will encourage graduates to make contact with and seek opportunities in a wide range of organisations, not necessarily limited to the Third World and government agencies.

OTHER DEGREE SUBJECTS FOR CONSIDERATION

Economics; Environmental Science/Studies; Geography; Government; International Relations; Politics; Sociology; Sustainable Development.

DIETETICS

(see also **Food Science/Studies and Technology, Health Sciences/Studies, Nutrition**)

Courses are often linked with nutrition and train students for a career as a dietitian. In addition to the scientific aspects of dietetics covering biochemistry, human physiology, food and clinical medicine, students are also introduced to health promotion, psychology, counselling and management skills. (See **Appendix 3**.)

Useful websites www.nutrition.org; www.bda.uk.com; www.dietetics.co.uk; www.skillsforhealth.org.uk

NB The points totals shown to the left of the institutions are for ease of reference only. It must not be assumed that Tariff points are always used by institutions or that they can be substituted for an offer in grades. The level of an offer is not necessarily indicative of the quality of a course.

COURSE OFFERS INFORMATION

Subject requirements/preferences GCSE English, mathematics and science usually required. **AL** Biology and/or Chemistry may be required. **Other** Health and Disclosure and Barring Service (DBS) checks required and possible immunisation against hepatitis B for practice placements.

Your target offers and examples of degree courses

136 pts London (King's) – AAB incl chem+biol (Nutr Diet) (IB 35 pts)
Nottingham – AAB–ABB incl sci (Nutr Diet MNutr) (IB 34–32 pts)
Surrey – AAB–ABB incl biol+sci (Nutr Diet) (IB 35–34 pts HL 6 biol 5 sci)

128 pts Coventry – ABB incl biol (Diet)
Leeds – ABB incl sci (Fd Sci) (IB 35–34 pts HL 5 sci); (Fd Sci Nutr) (IB 35–34 pts HL 5 sci)
Plymouth – 128 pts incl biol+chem (Diet) (IB 31 pts)

120 pts Cardiff Met – 120 pts (Hum Nutr Diet) (IB 26 pts)
Chester – BBB–BBC incl biol+sci 120 pts (Nutr Diet) (IB 28 pts HL 5 biol/chem)
Hertfordshire – 120 pts incl chem+biol (Diet) (IB 30 pts)
Leeds Beckett – 120 pts incl chem+sci (Diet) (IB 26 pts HL 6 chem)
London Met – 120 pts incl biol+chem (Diet Nutr)
Ulster – BBB incl sci/maths +HPAT (Diet)

104 pts Bath Spa – 104–120 pts incl sci/maths (Hum Nutr)
Glasgow Caledonian – BCC incl chem (Hum Nutr Diet) (IB 24 pts)
Robert Gordon – BCC incl chem+biol (Nutr Diet) (IB 27 pts)

88 pts Queen Margaret – AB incl chem+biol 88 pts (Diet) (IB 28 pts)

Alternative offers
See **Chapter 6** and **Appendix 1** for grades/new UCAS Tariff points information for other examinations.

CHOOSING YOUR COURSE (SEE ALSO CH.1)

Universities and colleges teaching quality See www.qaa.ac.uk; http://unistats.direct.gov.uk.

Top research universities and colleges (REF 2014) See **Health Sciences/Studies**.

Examples of sandwich degree courses Cardiff Met; Glasgow Caledonian; Leeds Beckett; Surrey; Ulster.

ADMISSIONS INFORMATION

Number of applicants per place (approx) Glasgow Caledonian 11; Nottingham 7; Queen Margaret 5; Surrey 1.

Advice to applicants and planning the UCAS personal statement Discuss the work with a hospital dietitian and describe fully work experience gained in hospital dietetics departments or with the schools meals services, and the problems of working in these fields. Admissions tutors expect applicants to have at least visited a dietetics department, and to be outgoing with good oral and written communication skills. Contact the British Dietetic Association (see **Appendix 3**).

Selection interviews Yes Cardiff Met, Chester, Coventry, Leeds Beckett, Ulster.

Interview advice and questions Your knowledge of a career in dietetics will be fully explored and questions will be asked on your work experience and how you reacted to it. See also **Chapter 5**.

AFTER-RESULTS ADVICE
Offers to applicants repeating A-levels Possibly higher Glasgow Caledonian.

GRADUATE DESTINATIONS AND EMPLOYMENT (2013/14 HESA)
See **Nutrition**.

Career note Dietitians are professionally trained to advise on diets and aspects of nutrition and many degree courses combine both subjects. They may work in the NHS as hospital dietitians collaborating with medical staff on the balance of foods for patients, or in local health authorities working with GPs, or in health centres or clinics dealing with infant welfare and ante-natal problems. In addition, dietitians advise consumer groups in the food industry and government and may be involved in research. Courses can lead to professional registration: check with admissions tutors.

OTHER DEGREE SUBJECTS FOR CONSIDERATION
Biological Sciences; Biochemistry; Biology; Consumer Studies; Food Science; Health Studies; Hospitality Management; Human Nutrition; Nursing; Nutrition.

DRAMA

(including **Performing Arts/Studies, Theatre Arts, Theatre Studies** and **Theatre Design**; see also **Art and Design (General), Dance/Dance Studies**)

Drama courses are popular, with twice as many women as men applying each year. Lack of confidence in securing appropriate work at the end of the course, however, tends to encourage many applicants to bid for joint courses although these are usually far more competitive since there are fewer places available. Most schools of acting and drama provide a strong vocational bias whilst university drama departments offer a broader field of studies combining theory and practice. For example, at London (Goldsmiths) the Drama and Theatre Arts degree offers a balance between acting and production whilst their Arts Management degree focuses on planning and organisation across the whole spectrum of arts activities, museums, galleries, theatres, dance, live venues and film companies.

Useful websites www.equity.org.uk; www.abtt.org.uk; www.thestage.co.uk; www.uktw.co.uk; www.ukperformingarts.co.uk; www.stagecoach.co.uk; www.dramauk.co.uk; www.rada.ac.uk; www.artscouncil.org.uk

NB The points totals shown to the left of the institutions are for ease of reference only. It must not be assumed that Tariff points are always used by institutions or that they can be substituted for an offer in grades. The level of an offer is not necessarily indicative of the quality of a course.

COURSE OFFERS INFORMATION
Subject requirements/preferences GCSE English usually required. **AL** English, Drama, Theatre Studies may be required or preferred. (Thea Arts) English, Theatre Studies or Drama may be required for some courses. **Other** Disclosure and Barring Service (DBS) clearance required for some courses: check websites.

Your target offers and examples of degree courses
152 pts Cambridge – A*AA (Educ Engl Dr) (IB 40–41 pts HL 776)

GS/A Guildford
School
of Acting

GSA HAS BUILT AN INTERNATIONAL REPUTATION FOR EXCELLENCE IN TRAINING FOR ACTORS AND TECHNICIANS IN ALL AREAS OF THEATRE AND THE RECORDED MEDIA.

Situated in a brand new building where it is part of the School of Arts at the University of Surrey, GSA offers quality vocational training in Acting, Musical Theatre, Actor Musician and Professional Production Skills with courses ranging from National Diplomas and Foundation Degrees through to postgraduate qualifications in Acting, Musical Theatre and Creative Practices and Direction.

We currently offer both funded places as well as private ones. The state-of-the-art Ivy Arts Centre ensures outstanding facilities for Professional Production Skills training and a versatile theatre space for productions. An excellent film and TV department and access to a number of other local theatres and a very special creative community make GSA a top choice amongst candidates wishing to train for the performing arts industry.

GSA offers full-time Foundation courses with Acting or Musical Theatre pathways at an accredited drama school. In addition GSA offers a part-time evening course for students who intend to complete their A Levels prior to applying for full-time training. These courses complement GSA's existing Saturday School and well subscribed Easter and Summer Schools.

High profile graduates include Tom Chambers, Brenda Blethyn OBE, Celia Imrie, Michael Ball, Bill Nighy, Luke Kempner, Chris Geere, Ellie Paskell, Emma Barton, Claire Cooper, Rob Kazinsky, Ian Kelsey, Jordan Lee Davies, Ayden Callaghan and Justin Fletcher MBE. Virtually every West End show features performers who trained at GSA. Students have performed at the Olivier Awards ceremony, the opening of G-Live, Guildford, The Festival of Remembrance at The Royal Albert Hall and numerous other prestigious events, most recently Sam Bailey Live in the West End.

Guildford School of Acting
Stag Hill Campus,
Guildford, Surrey
GU2 7XH, UK

t: +44 (0)1483 684040
f: +44 (0)1483 684070
e: gsaenquiries@gsa.surrey.ac.uk
w: www.gsauk.org

TRINITY
COLLEGE LONDON
Validated Course Provider 27006

drama uk
Accredited

COURSES FOR
2017 ENTRY

GSA /est. 1935
UNIVERSITY OF SURREY

UNDERGRADUATE COURSES
- BA (HONS) ACTING
- BA (HONS) ACTOR MUSICIAN
- BA (HONS) MUSICAL THEATRE
- BA (HONS) PROFESSIONAL PRODUCTION SKILLS
- BA (HONS) THEATRE (CONVERSION BY DISTANCE LEARNING)

POSTGRADUATE COURSES
- MA ACTING
- MA MUSICAL THEATRE
- MA CREATIVE PRACTICES & DIRECTION

WE ALSO OFFER
- FOUNDATION COURSE
- PART-TIME COURSE
- EASTER/SUMMER SCHOOLS
- SATURDAY SCHOOL

For an application form/further
details contact:

t: +44 (0)1483 684040
f: +44 (0)1483 684070
e: gsaenquiries@gsa.surrey.ac.uk
w: www.gsauk.org

Guildford School of Acting
Stag Hill Campus,
Guildford, Surrey
GU2 7XH, UK

TRINITY
COLLEGE LONDON
Validated Course Provider 27006

drama uk
Accredited

144 pts	**Bristol** – AAA–AAB incl Engl (Thea Engl) (IB 36–34 pts HL 6 Engl)
	Exeter – AAA–ABB (Dr) (IB 36–32 pts)
	Lancaster – AAA–AAB incl Engl (Thea Engl Lit) (IB 36–35 pts HL 6 Engl)
	Leeds – AAA–ABB (Thea Perf) (IB 34 pts)
136 pts	**Birmingham** – AAB–ABB (Dr Thea Arts) (IB 32 pts HL 665–655)
	Bristol – AAB–ABB (Thea Perf St) (IB 34–32 pts); AAB–ABB incl lang (Thea Modn Lang) (IB 34–32 pts HL 5 lang)
	East Anglia – AAB (Dr) (IB 33 pts HL 5 Engl/thea st); AAB incl dr/thea st/Engl (Script Perf) (IB 33 pts HL 5 Engl/thea st)
	Glasgow – AAB–BBB incl arts/lang (Thea St) (IB 36–34 pts)
	Kingston – 136–144 pts (Dr)
	Lancaster – AAB–ABB (Thea) (IB 35–32 pts)
	Loughborough – AAB–ABB (Dr) (IB 34 pts HL 5 Engl/thea arts); AAB incl Engl (Engl Dr) (IB 34 pts HL 5 Engl)
	Manchester – AAB incl Engl (Dr) (IB 35 pts); AAB (Dr Engl/Scrn St/Mus) (IB 35 pts)
	Sheffield – AAB–ABB incl Engl (Engl Thea) (IB 35 pts HL 6 Engl)
	Surrey – AAB–ABB incl art/hum/soc sci (Thea Perf) (IB 35–34 pts)
	Surrey (GSA Consv) – AAB–ABB +audition +interview (Actg; Musl Thea) (IB 35–34 pts)
	Sussex – AAB–ABB (Dr (Thea Perf); Dr St Span; Dr St Film St) (IB 34 pts)
	Warwick – AAB incl Engl (Engl Thea St) (IB 36 pts HL 6 Engl); AAB (Thea Perf St) (IB 36 pts)
	York – AAB (Thea (Writ Dir Perf)) (IB 35 pts)
128 pts	**Essex** – ABB–BBB (Dr; Dr Lit) (IB 32–30 pts)
	Kent – ABB (Dr Thea) (IB 34 pts)
	London (Gold) – ABB (Dr Thea Arts) (IB 33 pts)
	London (QM) – ABB incl art/hum+lang 128 pts (Fr/Ger/Russ Dr) (IB 34 pts HL 6 art/hum 5 lang); 128–136 pts (Dr) (IB 34 pts)

New UCAS points Tariff: A* = 56 pts; A = 48 pts; B = 40 pts; C = 32 pts; D = 24 pts; E = 16 pts

London (RH) – ABB incl mus (Dr Mus) (IB 32 pts); ABB (Dr Thea St; Dr Ger/Ital; Dr Phil; Fr Dr) (IB 32 pts); ABB incl Engl lit/dr (Dr Crea Writ) (IB 32 pts); ABB incl Engl (Engl Dr) (IB 32 pts)

Reading – ABB–BBB (Engl Lit Film Thea; Thea) (IB 32–30 pts)

Surrey (GSA Consv) – ABB +interview (Prof Prod Sk) (IB 34 pts)

120 pts **Brunel** – BBB (Thea; Thea Engl; Thea Crea Writ; Thea Film TV St) (IB 30 pts)

Derby – 120 pts +audition (Perf Arts)

Edge Hill – BBB 120 pts (Dr)

Huddersfield – BBB 120 pts (Dr; Dr Engl Lang/Lit)

Kent – BBB (Vis Perf Arts) (IB 34 pts HL 15 pts)

Leeds Beckett – 120 pts (Perf) (IB 26 pts)

London (Birk) – 120 pts (Thea Dr St)

London (Royal Central Sch SpDr) – BBB +interview (Dr App Thea Educ)

Northumbria – 120 pts incl perf arts (Perf) (IB 30 pts); 120 pts incl dr/perf arts (Dr App Thea) (IB 30 pts)

Queen's Belfast – BBB (Dr courses)

Queen Margaret – BBB 120 pts (Dr Perf) (IB 30 pts)

Sunderland – 120 pts (Dr Engl)

West London – 120 pts (Actg; Musl Thea)

112 pts **Aberystwyth** – 112–120 pts (Dr Thea St; Scngrph Thea Des)

Bangor – 112–120 pts incl Engl (Engl Lit Thea Perf) (IB 26 pts)

Bath Spa – 112–128 pts incl dr/thea st (Dr)

Birmingham City – BBC incl Engl 112 pts (Engl Dr) (IB 26 pts); BBC 112 pts (Des Thea Perf Evnts) (IB 28 pts)

Bournemouth Arts – BBC–BBB 112–120 pts (Actg) (IB 32 pts)

Canterbury Christ Church – 112 pts (Perf Arts)

Chester – BBC–BCC incl dr/thea arts 112 pts (Dr Thea St courses) (IB 26 pts HL 5 thea arts)

Chichester – BBC–BCC +interview/audition (Thea) (IB 30 pts)

Cumbria – 112 pts (Perf Arts; Dr Musl Thea; Dr Perf Musl Thea Perf)

De Montfort – 112 pts (Dr St; Perf Arts) (IB 28 pts)

East London – 112 pts (Dr App Thea Perf) (IB 24 pts)

Greenwich – 112 pts (Dr)

Hull – 112 pts (Dr Engl; Dr Thea Prac) (IB 28 pts)

Lincoln – 112 pts (Dr) (IB 25 pts)

London (Royal Central Sch SpDr) – BBC +interview (Thea Prac Perf Arts); BBC +interview +portfolio (Thea Prac Pptry Des Perf; Thea Prac Stg Mgt; Thea Prac Tech Prod Mgt; Thea Prac Thea Snd)

London Met – 112 pts (Thea Perf Prac)

London South Bank – BBC 112 pts (Dr Perf)

Manchester Met – 112 pts (Actg) (IB 26 pts)

Middlesex – 112 pts (Thea Arts)

Newman – 112 pts (Dr courses)

Northampton – 112 pts +audition (Actg); 112 pts (Dr courses)

Oxford Brookes – BBC (Dr) (IB 29 pts)

Plymouth – 112 pts (Thea Perf) (IB 28 pts)

Roehampton – 112 pts (Dr Thea Perf St)

Rose Bruford (Coll) – 112 pts (Am Thea Arts; Euro Thea Arts)

St Mary's – 112 pts (Dr Physl Thea; Dr Thea Arts; Dr App Thea) (IB 28 pts)

Sunderland – 112 pts (Dr; Perf Arts)

UWE Bristol – 112 pts (Dr; Dr courses) (IB 25 pts)

York St John – 112 pts (Dr Thea)

104 pts **Cardiff Met** – 104 pts (Engl Dr)

Central Lancashire – 104 pts (Mus Thea; Thea; Actg) (IB 28 pts)

Coventry – BCC incl dr/thea/perf arts (Thea Prof Prac) (IB 28 pts)

Falmouth – 104–120 pts (Actg)

Liverpool Hope – BCC–BBB 104–120 pts (Dr Thea St)
Liverpool John Moores – 104 pts (Dr) (IB 28 pts)
Portsmouth – 104–120 pts (Dr Perf) (IB 25 pts)
St Mark and St John – BCC (Actg)
Salford – 104–120 pts incl Engl/dr (Engl Dr) (IB 26 pts)
Sheffield Hallam – 104 pts (Perf Stg Scrn)
South Wales – BCC +audition (Thea Dr; Perf Media) (IB 29 pts)
Worcester – 104 pts (Dr Perf)

96 pts **Birmingham City** – 96 pts (Stg Mgt)
Bishop Grosseteste – 96–112 pts (App Dr courses)
Colchester (Inst) – 96 pts +audition (Crea Perf (Actg))
Glyndŵr – 96 pts (Thea TV Perf)
Liverpool (LIPA) – CCC 96 pts (Mus Thea Enter Mgt)
Manchester Met – 96–112 pts (Dr; Contemp Thea Perf) (IB 28 pts)
Rose Bruford (Coll) – 96 pts (Stg Mgt; Cstm Prod; Actr Mushp; Actg)
Royal Welsh (CMusDr) – 96 pts +interview (Stg Mgt Tech Thea)
Southampton Solent – 96 pts (Perf)
Winchester – 96–112 pts (Perf Arts; Dr; Cmdy (Perf Prod); Thea Chld Yng Ppl) (IB 25 pts)
Wolverhampton – 96 pts (Dr; Dance Dr)

88 pts **Anglia Ruskin** – 88–104 pts (Dr; Dr Engl Lit) (IB 24 pts)
Derby – 88–120 pts +audition (Thea St Joint Hons)

80 pts **Bedfordshire** – 80 pts (Thea Prof Prac) (IB 24 pts)
Bucks New – 80–96 pts (Perf Arts (Film TV Stg))
Trinity Saint David – 80 pts (Perf Arts)

72 pts **Liverpool (LIPA)** – BC–BB 72–80 pts (App Thea Commun Dr)

64 pts **Birmingham City** – 64 pts audition (Actg)
Colchester (Inst) – 64 pts +audition (Musl Thea); 64 pts +interview (Tech Thea)
Essex – 64 pts +audition (Actg; Actg Contemp Thea)
Liverpool (LIPA) – CC 64 pts (Thea Perf Des; Thea Perf Tech; Actg)
London (Royal Central Sch SpDr) – CC +audition (Actg; Actg (Coll Dvsd Thea); Act (Musl Thea))
London Regent's – CC +audition (Actg Glob Thea)
Trinity Saint David – 64 pts +audition (Actg) (IB 26 pts)

40 pts **Guildhall (Sch Mus Dr)** – 40 pts (Actg; Stg Mgt Tech Thea)

32 pts **Arts London** – 32 pts +interview +portfolio (Thea Scrn (Set Des Scrn); Thea Scrn (Thea Des); Dir; Perf Des Prac); 32 pts +audition +interview (Actg)
RConsvS – EE +audition (Contemp Perf Prac; Actg) (IB 24 pts); EE (Prod Arts Des) (IB 24 pts)
Arts Educ Sch – entry by audition; contact admissions tutor (Actg; Musl Thea)
Bristol Old Vic (Thea Sch) – +audition +interview (Prof Actg); +interview (Prof Stg Mgt)
LAMDA – +audition (Prof Actg); +interview (Stg Mgt Tech Thea)
London (RADA) – +audition (Actg)
London Mountview (Ac Thea Arts) – +audition (Perf (Musl Thea); Perf (Actg))
Royal Welsh (CMusDr) – +audition (Actg)
Teesside – +audition (Perf Lv Rec Media)

Alternative offers
See **Chapter 6** and **Appendix 1** for grades/new UCAS Tariff points information for other examinations.

EXAMPLES OF COLLEGES OFFERING COURSES IN THIS SUBJECT FIELD
Amersham and Wycombe (Coll); Blackpool and Fylde (Coll); Bradford (Coll); Brooksby Melton (Coll); Bury (Coll); Calderdale (Coll); Chichester (Coll); Coventry City (Coll); Craven (Coll); Croydon (Univ Centre); Doncaster (Coll); Ealing, Hammersmith and West London (Coll); East Durham (Coll); Exeter (Coll); Gateshead (Coll); Gloucestershire (Coll); Grimsby (Univ Centre); Guildford (Coll); Havering (Coll); Hopwood Hall (Coll); Hugh Baird (Coll); Hull (Coll); Kingston (Coll); Leicester (Coll); Liverpool City

(Coll); Manchester (Coll); Mid-Cheshire (Coll); Middlesbrough (Coll); Nescot; Newcastle (Coll); North Nottinghamshire (Coll); North Shropshire (Coll); Northbrook (Coll); Nottingham New (Coll); Oldham (Univ Campus); Peterborough (Coll); Plymouth City (Coll); Redbridge (Coll); Richmond-upon-Thames (Coll); Rotherham (CAT); St Helens (Coll); Sheffield (Coll); South Devon (Coll); South Gloucestershire and Stroud (Coll); Southampton City (Coll); Stamford New (Coll); Stratford-upon-Avon (Coll); Sunderland (Coll); Tresham (CFHE); Wakefield (Coll); Warrington (Coll); West Herts (Coll); West Thames (Coll); Westminster City (Coll); Weymouth (Coll); Wigan and Leigh (Coll); Yeovil (Coll); Yorkshire Coast (Coll).

CHOOSING YOUR COURSE (SEE ALSO CH.1)

Universities and colleges teaching quality See www.qaa.ac.uk; http://unistats.direct.gov.uk.

Top research universities and colleges (REF 2014) (Music, Drama, Dance and Performing Arts) Open University; Roehampton (Dance); London (QM); Warwick; London (SOAS); Durham; London (RH) (Mus); Southampton; Oxford; Birmingham (Mus); City; London (King's) (Film); Manchester (Dr); London (RH) (Dr Thea); Huddersfield; Manchester (Mus); Cardiff.

ADMISSIONS INFORMATION

Number of applicants per place (approx) Aberystwyth 10; Arts London (Actg) 32, (Dir) 10; Bath Spa 10; Birmingham 15; Bristol 19; Brunel 9; Chester 14; Cumbria 4; De Montfort (Perf Arts) 5; East Anglia 13; Edge Hill 8; Essex 15; Exeter 20; Huddersfield 5; Hull 16, (Scarborough) 2; Hull (Coll) 2; Kent 24; Lancaster 18; Leeds 10; Liverpool (LIPA) (Actg) 48; Liverpool John Moores 10; London (Gold) 28; London (RH) 10; London (Royal Central Sch SpDr) (Thea Prac) 5; London Met 20; London Mountview (Ac Thea Arts) (Musl Thea) 8; Loughborough 6; Manchester (Dr) 6, (Dr Engl Lit) 7; Manchester (Coll) 10; Manchester Met 48; Middlesex 26; Northampton 3; Northumbria 25; Queen Margaret 4; Reading 17; Roehampton 6; Royal Welsh (CMusDr) (Actg) 50, (Stg Mgt) 10; Warwick 18; Winchester (Dr) 6; Worcester 4; York 4; York St John 9.

Advice to applicants and planning the UCAS personal statement List the plays in which you have performed and specify the characters played. Indicate any experience in other areas of theatre, especially directing or writing. Add any information on projects you have initiated or developed or worked on in theatre craft, such as set design, costume design, lighting design, prop-making, scene painting. List any community arts projects such as work with youth clubs, hospital radio, amateur dramatics, music/drama workshops and voluntary work within the arts. Show your strengths in dance and theatre, and your commitment to drama in all its aspects. See **Chapter 5** and also **Appendix 3**. **Bristol** Deferred entry accepted. **London (Royal Central Sch SpDr)** (Dr App Thea Educ) We look for an interest in theatre and performance in different social and cultural settings, for example, community, schools, prisons. We also look for an enquiring mind, practical drama skills, flexibility and focus. **Manchester** Due to the detailed nature of entry requirements for Drama courses, the University is unable to include full details in the prospectus. For complete and up-to-date information on the entry requirements for these courses, please visit the website at www.manchester.ac.uk/ ugcourses. **Warwick** Gap year only acceptable in exceptional circumstances. **York** (Writ Dir Perf) Strong analytical ability plus experience in a related field, eg stage management/design, drama, writing are important factors.

Misconceptions about this course That a Theatre Studies course is a training for the stage: it is not. **Arts London** Provides a long-established classical conservatoire-type training for actors, and not Theatre Studies or Performance Arts courses, contrary to the views of some students. It is no longer a private school and home and EU students pay the standard degree fee. **De Montfort** (Perf Arts) Students are unaware that the course involves music. **Kent** This is not like an acting school. **Staffordshire** We stress to applicants that this is not a drama school course. **Winchester** This is not an acting course although practical work is involved. **York St John** This is not a course for intending actors.

Selection interviews Most institutions, usually with auditions which are likely to involve solo and group tests. **Yes** Bath Spa, Bedfordshire, Bishop Grosseteste, Brunel, Cardiff Met, Chester, Chichester, Cumbria, East Anglia, Edge Hill, Essex, Exeter, Falmouth, Huddersfield, Leeds Beckett, Liverpool John

Moores, London (Gold), Manchester, Middlesex, Northumbria, Plymouth, Portsmouth, Reading, St Mary's, Warwick, West London, Winchester, Wolverhampton, York; **Some** Anglia Ruskin, Bristol, Bucks New, Liverpool John Moores, Liverpool John Moores, London (QM).

Interview advice and questions See also **Chapter 5**. **Arts London** (Actg) Two three-minute speeches or scenes, one of which must be from the classical repertoire. (Dir) Interview and practical workshop which may involve directing actors. **Bristol** Assesses each case on its merits, paying attention to candidate's educational and cultural opportunities. Particularly interested in applicants who have already shown some evidence of commitment in their approach to drama in practical work, theatre-going, film viewing or reading. One fifth of applicants are called for interview and take part in practical sessions. They may present any art work, photography or similar material. (London Board Practical Music not acceptable for Drama/Music unless offered with theoretical music plus one other A-level.) **Brunel** All applicants to whom an offer may be made will be auditioned, involving a practical workshop, voice, movement improvisation and a short prepared speech. Offers unlikely to be made to those with less than a grade B in drama or theatre studies. **Chichester** Applicants will be asked to prepare a set-piece in advance and to perform it before a group. **De Montfort** (Perf Arts) What do you hope to gain on a three-year course in Performing Arts? Interviews involve practical workshops in drama and theatre and a written paper. **East Anglia** Looks for candidates with a sound balance of academic and practical skills. Applicants will be expected to analyse performance and to understand what is entailed in the production of a drama. **Hull** Interviews two groups of 18 for whole day which presents a mini-version of the course, with entire staff and a number of current students present. Offers then made to about half. Selection process is all-important. More applicants for the Joint Honours courses with English, Theology, American Studies or a modern language, who have a conventional half-hour interview. Drama/English is the most popular combination and the offer includes a B in English. **Kent** No Single Honours candidate accepted without interview. Emphasis equally on academic and practical abilities. Questions asked to probe the applicant's creative and analytical grasp of theatre. **Lancaster** (Thea St) Candidates invited for interview and should be prepared to take part in a workshop with other candidates. We are just as interested in backstage people as actors and now have an arts administration option. **Loughborough** Candidates judged as individuals. Applicants with unconventional subject combinations and mature students considered. Final selection based on interview and audition. Applicants ought to show experience of practical drama, preferably beyond school plays. **Royal Welsh (CMusDr)** (Actg) Audition; (Stg Mgt) interview; (Thea Des) interview and portfolio presentation. All applicants are charged an audition/interview fee. **Warwick** Interview is important to assess academic potential and particularly commitment to, and suitability for, teaching; offers therefore variable.

Reasons for rejection (non-academic) Poor ambition. Wrong expectations of the course. Several students clearly want drama school acting training rather than a degree course. Not enough background reading. **Arts London** Insufficient clarity about career aims. **De Montfort** (Perf Arts) Candidate more suitable for a drama or dance school than for a degree course. No genuine engagement with the subject. Evidence of poor attendance at school.

AFTER-RESULTS ADVICE
Offers to applicants repeating A-levels Higher Bristol, Glasgow (AAA), Hull, Warwick; **Possibly higher** London (RH); **Same** Brunel, Chichester, De Montfort (Perf Arts), East Anglia, Huddersfield, Kent, Leeds (further audition required), Liverpool Hope, Liverpool John Moores, Loughborough, Manchester (Coll), Newman, Nottingham Trent, Roehampton, Royal Welsh (CMusDr), St Mary's, Staffordshire, Sunderland, Surrey (GSA Consv), Winchester, York St John.

GRADUATE DESTINATIONS AND EMPLOYMENT (2013/14 HESA)
Graduates surveyed 5,075 **Employed** 2,545 **In voluntary employment** 150 **In further study** 700 **Assumed unemployed** 335

Career note Some graduates develop careers in performance, writing, directing and producing as well as wider roles within the theatre. Others go on to careers such as teaching, media management and retail where their creativity and communication skills are valued.

OTHER DEGREE SUBJECTS FOR CONSIDERATION
Art and Design (Costume Design, Stage Design); Arts Management; Dance; Education (Primary);
English; Performance Studies.

ECONOMICS

(see also **Business and Management Courses, Mathematics, Statistics**)

Economics is about how society makes good use of the limited resources available. Degree
courses cover all aspects of finance, taxation and monetary union between countries, aiming to
equip the student to analyse economic problems in a systematic way and thus acquire an
understanding of how economic systems work. Economics involves mathematics and statistics,
and applicants without economics at AS or A-level should be prepared for this although for BA
courses, such as at the University of Leicester, mathematics is not required at A-level. All courses
are quite flexible with specialisms coming later in the course, leading to a range of career choices.
Many joint courses are often offered with combinations such as Politics, Management and Finance.
The course at Cambridge in Land Economy focuses on the legal and economic aspects relative to
the natural environment, covering business regulations and the financial aspects of real estate
and development. The course is accredited by the Royal Institution of Chartered Surveyors and
has a very high success rate of graduate employment. (See also the Property Development and
Surveying table.)

Useful websites www.iea.org.uk; www.res.org.uk; www.economist.com; www.neweconomics.org; see
also **Finance**.

*NB The points totals shown to the left of the institutions are for ease of reference only. It must not
be assumed that Tariff points are always used by institutions or that they can be substituted for an
offer in grades. The level of an offer is not necessarily indicative of the quality of a course.*

COURSE OFFERS INFORMATION

Subject requirements/preferences GCSE English, mathematics and occasionally a foreign language
required. A*/A/B may be stipulated by some universities. **AL** Mathematics, Economics or Business
Studies may be required or preferred. Business Studies may be preferred if Economics is not offered.
Applicants should note that many courses will accept students without Economics (check prospectuses
and websites).

Your target offers and examples of degree courses
152 pts **Bath** – A*AA incl maths (Econ Pol; Econ) (IB 36 pts HL 6 maths)
Bristol – A*AA–AAB incl maths (Econ courses) (IB 38–34 pts HL 6 maths)
Cambridge – A*AA incl maths (Econ) (IB 40–41 pts HL 776); A*AA (Lnd Econ) (IB 40–41 pts
HL 776)
Durham – A*AA incl maths (Econ Mgt; Econ Pol; PPE; Econ) (IB 38 pts)
Exeter – A*AA–AAB incl maths (Maths Econ) (IB 38–34 pts HL 6 maths); A*AA–AAB
(Bus Econ (Euro St); Econ; Econ Pol (Euro St); Bus Econ; Econ Ecomet) (IB 38–34 pts)
Lancaster – A*AA–AAA incl maths (Econ (St Abrd)) (IB 38–36 pts HL 6 maths)
London (King's) – A*AA (PPE) (IB 35 pts HL 766)
London (UCL) – A*AA incl geog+maths (Econ Geog) (IB 39 pts HL 7 maths 6 geog); A*AA
incl maths (Econ) (IB 39 pts HL 7 maths); A*AA–AAA incl maths (PPE; Stats Econ Fin;
Econ Stats) (IB 39–38 pts HL 7 maths)
London LSE – A*AA incl A* maths (PPE) (IB 38 pts); A*AA incl maths (Ecomet Mathem Econ;
Maths Econ; Econ Econ Hist; Econ) (IB 38 pts)
Nottingham – A*AA–AAA (PPE) (IB 38–36); (Econ Chin St; Econ Ger; Econ Phil) (IB 38–36
pts); (Econ Fr) (IB 38–36 pts); A*AA–AAA incl maths (Econ courses) (IB 38–36 pts);
A*AA–AAA (Econ Hisp St) (IB 38–36 pts)
Oxford – A*AA (Econ Mgt) (IB 39 pts)

Warwick – A*AA incl maths (Econ; Econ Ind Org) (IB 38 pts HL 6 maths); A*AA (PPE) (IB 38 pts); A*AA (Econ Pol Int St) (IB 38 pts HL 4 maths)

York – A*AA–AAA incl maths (Econ Fin) (IB 36 pts); (PPE) (IB 37 pts)

144 pts **Birmingham** – AAA (Econ) (IB 32 pts HL 666); AAA incl lang (Econ Lang) (IB 32 pts HL 666); AAA incl maths (Mathem Econ Stats) (IB 32 pts HL 666)

Bristol – AAA/A*AB–AAB/A*BB incl maths (Econ Acc) (IB 36–34 pts HL 6 maths); AAA–AAB 144–136 pts (Phil Econ) (IB 37–35 pts)

Edinburgh – AAA–ABB (Econ Fin; Econ courses; Econ Stats) (IB 37–34 pts)

Exeter – AAA–AAB (PPE) (IB 36–34 pts)

Leeds – AAA (Bus Econ; Econ Fin; Econ Mgt; PPE; Econ) (IB 35 pts)

Liverpool – AAA incl maths (Econ) (IB 36 pts HL 6 maths)

London (QM) – AAA incl maths (Econ; Econ Fin Mgt; Econ Joint Hons) (IB 36 pts HL 5 maths)

London (SOAS) – AAA–AAB (Econ Joint Hons) (IB 37 pts)

London (UCL) – AAA–AAB incl maths (Econ Bus E Euro St) (IB 38–36 pts HL 5 maths)

London LSE – AAA (Gov Econ) (IB 38 pts)

NCH London – AAA–ABB (PPE); AAA–ABB incl maths (Econ)

Newcastle – AAA–ABB (Pol Econ) (IB 37–34 pts)

Oxford – AAA (Hist Econ) (IB 38 pts); (PPE) (IB 39 pts)

St Andrews – AAA (Econ courses) (IB 38 pts)

Southampton – AAA–AAB incl maths (Maths OR Stats Econ) (IB 36 pts HL 6 maths)

Surrey – AAA (Bus Econ; Econ Fin; Econ) (IB 36 pts)

Sussex – AAA–AAB (PPE) (IB 35 pts)

York – AAA incl maths (Econ Maths) (IB 36 pts HL 6 maths); (Econ Ecomet Fin; Econ) (IB 36 pts); AAA incl hist+maths (Hist Econ) (IB 36 pts HL 6 hist)

136 pts **Aston** – AAB–ABB (Econ Mgt) (IB 35–34 pts)

Cardiff – AAB incl Fr/Ger/Span (Bus Econ Euro Lang (Fr/Ger/Span)) (IB 35 pts); AAB (Bus Econ; Econ) (IB 35 pts)

City – AAB–ABB 136–128 pts (Econ; Fin Econ; Econ Acc) (IB 33 pts)

East Anglia – AAB (Econ) (IB 33 pts)

Glasgow – AAB–BBB incl Engl (Econ Joint Hons) (IB 38–36 pts)

Lancaster – AAB (Fin Econ; PPE; Acc Econ; Econ; Econ Joint Hons) (IB 35 pts)

London LSE – AAB incl maths (Env Plcy Econ) (IB 37 pts); AAB (Soc Plcy Econ) (IB 37 pts)

Loughborough – AAB incl geog (Geog Econ) (IB 36–34 pts HL 5 geog); AAB–ABB (Econ Acc; Econ Pol; Bus Econ Fin; Econ) (IB 34 pts)

Manchester – AAB (Econ Pol; Econ Sociol; Econ courses; Econ; PPE; Bus St Econ) (IB 35 pts)

Newcastle – AAB (Econ; Econ Bus Mgt; Econ Fin) (IB 35 pts)

Nottingham – AAB (Ind Econ; Ind Econ Ins) (IB 34 pts)

Queen's Belfast – AAB (PPE)

Reading – AAB–ABB (Econ; Bus Econ) (IB 35–32 pts)

Sheffield – AAB–ABB (Econ Joint Hons) (IB 35 pts)

Southampton – AAB–ABB incl maths/phys (Econ Mgt Sci; Acc Econ) (IB 34 pts); AAB–ABB incl maths (Econ; Econ Fin) (IB 34 pts HL 5 maths); (Econ Act Sci) (IB 34 pts HL 6 maths); AAB–ABB (Econ Phil) (IB 34–32 pts)

Sussex – AAB–ABB (Econ; Econ Int Dev; Econ Int Rel; Econ Mgt St; Econ Pol) (IB 34 pts)

128 pts **Birmingham** – ABB (Pol Econ) (IB 32 pts HL 655)

East Anglia – ABB (Bus Fin Econ; PPE; Econ Acc; Bus Econ) (IB 32 pts)

Essex – ABB–BBB (Econ Pol; PPE; Econ Fr; Econ; Fin Econ; Int Econ; Mgt Econ; Econ Langs) (IB 32–30 pts)

Kent – ABB–BBB incl maths (Econ; Euro Econ) (IB 34 pts)

Leicester – ABB (Econ Courses) (IB 30 pts)

Liverpool – ABB (Bus Econ) (IB 33 pts)

London (RH) – ABB (Fin Bus Econ; Econ Mgt; Econ Pol Int Rel) (IB 32 pts); (PPE) (IB 34 pts); ABB incl maths (Econ) (IB 32 pts); (Econ Maths) (IB 35 pts)

Economics

THE UNIVERSITY OF BUCKINGHAM

- Top for employment among non-specialist institutions *(HESA 2015)*
- Unique two-year honours degrees
- Three entry points: January, July and September

"Studying Economics at Buckingham has been a pleasure. The programme is so diverse and covers almost everything that can possibly interest an economics student. The small tutorials, especially, really engage you with the subject. The lecturers and tutors are some of the best economists from around the world and there are few better places."
Donald Dauti, Economics 2014

international-studies-admissions@buckingham.ac.uk
+44 (0)1280 820369
www.buckingham.ac.uk/economics-international

THE TIMES
THE SUNDAY TIMES
GOOD UNIVERSITY GUIDE 2016
UNIVERSITY OF THE YEAR FOR TEACHING

Queen's Belfast – ABB (Econ courses)
Reading – ABB–BBB (Fd Mark Bus Econ) (IB 32–30 pts)
Southampton – ABB–BBB incl maths/phys (Pol Econ) (IB 32 pts HL 4 maths)
Stirling – ABB (PPE) (IB 35 pts)
Strathclyde – ABB–BBB (Econ Psy; Econ) (IB 33 pts); ABB–BBB incl maths (Maths Stats Econ) (IB 32 pts HL 6 maths)
Swansea – ABB–BBB (Econ courses) (IB 33–32 pts)
120 pts **Aberdeen** – BBB (Econ) (IB 32 pts)
Aberystwyth – 120 pts (Econ; Bus Econ)
Bournemouth – 120 pts (Fin Econ; Econ) (IB 31 pts)
Brunel – BBB (Econ; Pol Econ; Econ Bus Fin) (IB 30 pts)
Buckingham – BBB (Law Econ)
Coventry – BBB (Econ courses; Bus Econ; Int Econ Tr) (IB 30 pts)
De Montfort – 120 pts (Econ Fin) (IB 28 pts)
Dundee – BBB–BCC incl sci/maths (Bus Econ Mark; Econ St; Bus Econ Mark Hist) (IB 30 pts)
Greenwich – 120 pts (Econ; Econ Bank)
Heriot-Watt – BBB (Econ) (IB 29 pts)
Huddersfield – BBB 120 pts (Econ courses; Econ)
Keele – BBB/ABC (Bus Econ; Econ courses) (IB 32 pts)
Leeds Beckett – 120 pts (Econ Fin) (IB 26 pts)
London (Birk) – 120 pts p/t, for under 21s (over 21s varies) (Econ Soc Pol)
Northampton – 120 pts (Econ courses)
Sheffield Hallam – 120 pts (Bus Econ)
Stirling – BBB (Econ) (IB 32 pts)
UWE Bristol – 120 pts (Econ) (IB 26 pts)
Westminster – BBB (Bus Econ) (IB 28 pts)

Check **Chapter 3** for new university admission details and **Chapter 6** on how to read the subject tables.

112 pts **Birmingham City** – BBC 112 pts (Econ Fin) (IB 28 pts)
        Bradford – BBC (Fin Econ); BBC 112 pts (Econ; Econ Int Rel)
        Cardiff Met – 112 pts (Int Econ Fin; Econ)
        Central Lancashire – 112 pts (Econ) (IB 28 pts)
        Chester – BBC–BCC 112 pts (Econ (Joint Hons)) (IB 26 pts)
        East London – 112 pts (Econ) (IB 24 pts)
        Hull – 112 pts (Econ; Bus Econ; Econ (Int)) (IB 30 pts)
        Kingston – 112 pts (Bus Econ); (Fin Econ) (IB 25 pts)
        London Met – 112 pts (Bus Econ; Econ)
        Nottingham Trent – 112 pts (Econ; Econ Bus; Econ Int Fin Bank)
        Plymouth – 112 pts (Econ courses) (IB 25 pts)
        Portsmouth – 112 pts (Econ) (IB 30 pts HL 17 pts)
        Sheffield Hallam – 112 pts (Int Fin Econ)
        Worcester – 112 pts (Bus Econ Fin)
104 pts **Anglia Ruskin** – 104–120 pts (Bus Econ) (IB 24 pts)
        Bangor – 104–120 pts (Econ Joint Hons; Bus Econ)
        Dundee – BCC (Spat Econ) (IB 30 pts)
        Kingston – 104 pts (Econ) (IB 24 pts)
        Manchester Met – BCC–BBC 104–112 pts (Econ) (IB 26 pts); 104–112 pts (Econ Joint Hons)
          (IB 28 pts)
        Salford – 104–120 pts (Bus Econ) (IB 24 pts)
 96 pts **Edinburgh Napier** – CCC (Econ Mgt) (IB 27 pts)
        Hertfordshire – 96–112 pts (Bus Econ; Econ) (IB 28 pts)
        Leeds Beckett – 96 pts (Econ Bus) (IB 24 pts)

        Open University – contact +44 (0)845 300 6090 **or** www.openuniversity.co.uk/you (Econ
        Mathem Sci; PPE; Soc Sci Econ)

Alternative offers
See **Chapter 6** and **Appendix 1** for grades/new UCAS Tariff points information for other examinations.

EXAMPLES OF COLLEGES OFFERING COURSES IN THIS SUBJECT FIELD
Greenwich (Sch Mgt); Plymouth City (Coll).

CHOOSING YOUR COURSE (SEE ALSO CH.1)
Universities and colleges teaching quality See www.qaa.ac.uk; http://unistats.direct.gov.uk.

Top research universities and colleges (REF 2014) (Economics and Econometrics) London (UCL); Cambridge; Warwick; Essex; London LSE; Nottingham; Oxford; Bristol; East Anglia; Edinburgh.

Examples of sandwich degree courses Aston; Bath; Birmingham City; Bournemouth; Brunel; Coventry; De Montfort; Essex; Greenwich; Hertfordshire; Leeds Beckett; Liverpool; Loughborough; Manchester Met; Newcastle; Nottingham Trent; Plymouth; Portsmouth; Salford; Sheffield Hallam; Surrey; UWE Bristol; Westminster.

ADMISSIONS INFORMATION
Number of applicants per place (approx) Aberystwyth 3; Anglia Ruskin 10; Aston 8; Bangor 4; Bath 6; Birmingham 3; Birmingham City 16; Bradford 5; Bristol 8; Brunel 12; Buckingham 4; Cambridge 7; Cardiff 8; Central Lancashire 5; City 18, (Econ Acc) 12; Coventry 10; Dundee 5; Durham 8; East Anglia 15; Essex 6; Exeter 12; Greenwich 8; Heriot-Watt 4; Hull 15; Kent 11; Kingston 9; Lancaster 14; Leeds 16; Leicester 10; Liverpool 4; London (UCL) 12; London LSE (Econ) 15, (Ecomet Mathem Econ) 20; Loughborough 15; Manchester 8; Manchester Met 5; Middlesex 8; Newcastle 11, (Econ Bus Mgt) 27; Northampton 8; Nottingham (Econ Chin) 8; Nottingham Trent 2; Plymouth 4; Portsmouth 6; Queen's Belfast 10; St Andrews 5; Salford 6; Sheffield 10; Southampton 8; Stirling 6; Surrey 5; Swansea 7; Warwick 16; York 4.

Advice to applicants and planning the UCAS personal statement Visits, work experience and work shadowing in banks, insurance companies, accountants' offices etc should be described. Keep up-to-date with economic issues by reading *The Economist* and the *Financial Times* and find other sources of information. Describe any particular aspects of economics which interest you – and why. Make it clear on the statement that you know what economics is and why you want to study it. Give evidence of your interest in economics and your reasons for choosing the course and provide information about your sport/extra-curricular activities and positions of responsibility.

Misconceptions about this course Bradford That the Economics course is very mathematical and that students will not get a good job, eg management. **Kent** That the Economics course is mathematical, has a high failure rate and has poorer job prospects than Business Studies courses. **London (UCL)** Some think the Economics course is a Business course.

Selection interviews Yes Birmingham, Cambridge, Coventry, East Anglia, East London, Edinburgh, Essex, Keele, London (RH), London (UCL), Manchester Met, Middlesex, Nottingham, Nottingham Trent, Oxford (27% (success rate 7%)), Reading, Southampton (Acc Econ), Surrey, UWE Bristol; **Some** Aberystwyth, Anglia Ruskin, Bangor, Buckingham, Dundee, Kent, Leeds, London Met (mature students), Loughborough, Swansea; **No** Bristol, London LSE.

Interview advice and questions If you have studied economics at A-level or in other examinations, expect to be questioned on aspects of the subject. This is a subject which is constantly in the news, so keep abreast of developments and be prepared to be asked questions such as: What is happening to sterling at present? What is happening to the dollar? How relevant is economics today? What are your views on the government's economic policy? Do you think that the family is declining as an institution? Discuss Keynesian economics. Is the power of the Prime Minister increasing? What is a recession? How would you get the world out of recession? What causes a recession? See also **Chapter 5**. **Cambridge** What is the point of using NHS money to keep old people alive? **Oxford** (Econ Mgt) 'I was asked questions on a newspaper article I had been given to read 45 minutes beforehand, followed by a few maths problems and an economics question.' Explain why teachers might be changing jobs to become plumbers. (Econ Mgt) What is the difference between the buying and selling of slaves and the buying and selling of football players? Should a Wal-Mart store be opened in the middle of Oxford?

Reasons for rejection (non-academic) Lack of knowledge about the course offered and the subject matter; lack of care in preparing personal statement; poor written English; the revelation on the statement that they want a course different from that for which they have applied! **Aberystwyth** Would have trouble fitting into the unique environment at Aberystwyth.

AFTER-RESULTS ADVICE
Offers to applicants repeating A-levels Higher Birmingham City, City, East Anglia, Essex, Leeds, Newcastle, Nottingham, Queen's Belfast, St Andrews, Warwick, York; **Possibly higher** Bradford, Brunel, Durham, Lancaster; **Same** Aberystwyth, Anglia Ruskin, Bangor, Bath, Buckingham, Cambridge, Cardiff, Coventry, Dundee, East London, Edinburgh Napier, Heriot-Watt, Hull, Kingston, Liverpool, London (RH), London Met, Loughborough, Nottingham Trent, Salford, Sheffield, Surrey, Swansea.

GRADUATE DESTINATIONS AND EMPLOYMENT (2013/14 HESA)
Graduates surveyed 4,930 **Employed** 2,880 **In voluntary employment** 150 **In further study** 1,040 **Assumed unemployed** 380

Career note Most graduates work within areas of business and finance, and in a range of jobs including management and administration posts across both public and private sectors.

OTHER DEGREE SUBJECTS FOR CONSIDERATION
Accountancy; Actuarial Studies; Administration; Banking; Business Studies; Development Studies; Estate Management; Financial Services; Government; Politics; Management Sciences/Studies; Property Development; Quantity Surveying; Social Sciences; Sociology; Statistics.

Check **Chapter 3** for new university admission details and **Chapter 6** on how to read the subject tables.

EDUCATION STUDIES

(see also **Physical Education, Social Sciences/Studies, Teacher Training**)

There are four types of degree courses in Education. Firstly, there are those universities providing an academic study of the subject at Single Honours level covering the study of childhood and aspects of education such as psychology, sociology, philosophy and history (check with your chosen institution). Secondly, there are institutions offering degrees in Education with a professional practice qualification to teach, as in the degree course in Contemporary Education at Brunel University London. Thirdly, as in all degree subjects, there are many Joint Honours degrees in which Education is taken with another academic subject, in which the two subjects may be taken equally or on a major/minor basis. Finally, there are specific degree courses in teacher training and professional practice leading directly to the classroom (see the **Teacher Training** table).

Useful websites www.gtcs.org.uk; www.gttr.ac.uk; www.education.gov.uk; https://set.et-foundation. co.uk; www.et-foundation.co.uk

NB The points totals shown to the left of the institutions are for ease of reference only. It must not be assumed that Tariff points are always used by institutions or that they can be substituted for an offer in grades. The level of an offer is not necessarily indicative of the quality of a course.

COURSE OFFERS INFORMATION
Your target offers and examples of degree courses

152 pts Cambridge – A*AA (Educ Geog/Hist/Lang/Mus/Phys/Relig St; Educ Engl Dr; Educ Engl; Educ Class; Educ Biol Sci) (IB 40–41 pts HL 776)

144 pts Durham – AAA (Educ St (Biol Sci/Engl St/Geog/Hist/Phil/Psy/Sociol/Theol)) (IB 37 pts)
Loughborough – AAA–AAB incl maths (Maths Maths Educ) (IB 36 pts HL 6 maths)

136 pts Glasgow – AAB–BBB incl tech/sci (Technol Educ) (IB 34–32 pts)

128 pts Bath – ABB (Educ Psy) (IB 35 pts)
Birmingham – ABB (Educ) (IB 32 pts HL 655)
Cardiff – ABB–BBB (Educ) (IB 34–32 pts)
Edinburgh – ABB (Commun Educ) (IB 34 pts)
Gloucestershire – 128 pts (Physl Educ)
Keele – ABB incl Engl (Educ) (IB 34 pts HL 6 Engl)
Newcastle – ABB–BBB (Educ) (IB 32–30 pts)
Sheffield – ABB–BBB (Educ Cult Chld) (IB 34 pts)
Southampton – ABB (Educ) (IB 32 pts)
York – ABB (Sociol Educ) (IB 34 pts)

120 pts Cardiff – BBB (Educ Sociol; Educ Welsh) (IB 32 pts)
De Montfort – 120 pts (Educ St Psy; Educ St; Educ St Mand) (IB 30 pts)
East Anglia – BBB (Educ) (IB 31 pts)
Liverpool John Moores – 120 pts (P Educ)
Northumbria – 120 pts (Ely P Educ) (IB 30 pts)
Sunderland – 120 pts (Educ St)
York – BBB (Engl Educ; Educ) (IB 31 pts)

112 pts Aberystwyth – 112–120 pts (Educ Joint Hons)
Brighton – BBC (Educ) (IB 28 pts)
Brunel – BBC (Contemp Educ) (IB 29 pts)
Canterbury Christ Church – 112 pts (Ely Chld St; Educ St)
Central Lancashire – 112 pts (Df St Educ; Educ courses)
Chester – BBC–BCC 112 pts (Educ St courses) (IB 26 pts)
Dundee – BBC (Educ) (IB 30 pts)
East London – 112 pts incl soc sci (Ely Chld St) (IB 24 pts); 112 pts (Educ St; Spec Educ) (IB 24 pts)

New UCAS points Tariff: A* = 56 pts; A = 48 pts; B = 40 pts; C = 32 pts; D = 24 pts; E = 16 pts

Edge Hill – BBC 112 pts (Ely Yrs Educ)
Huddersfield – BBC 112 pts (Relgn Educ)
Leeds Beckett – 112 pts (Chld St) (IB 25 pts)
London (Gold) – BBC (Educ Cult Soty) (IB 33 pts)
London Met – 112 pts (Educ St)
Manchester Met – BBC (P Educ) (IB 27 pts)
Newman – 112 pts (Educ St courses; Ely Chld Educ Care; St P Educ; Phil Relgn Educ)
Oxford Brookes – BBC (Educ St) (IB 30 pts)
Plymouth – 112 pts (Ely Chld St) (IB 26 pts)
Roehampton – 112 pts (Educ)
Suffolk (Univ Campus) – 112 pts (Ely Chld St)
Worcester – 112 pts (Educ courses)

104 pts **Bath Spa** – 104–120 pts (Yth Commun St; Educ St)
Brighton – BCC incl biol (Hum Biol Educ) (IB 27 pts)
Cardiff Met – 104 pts (Educ St Ely Chld St)
Chichester – 104–120 pts (Educ Ely Chld)
Derby – 104 pts (Ely Chld St; Maths Educ; Educ St)
Hertfordshire – 104 pts (Educ St; Ely Chld Educ) (IB 26 pts)
Hull – 104 pts (Educ St courses) (IB 28 pts)
Liverpool Hope – BCC–BBB 104–120 pts (Educ; SEN)
Liverpool John Moores – 104 pts (Educ St Spec Inclsv Nds; Educ St Ely Yrs; Out Educ)
Manchester Met – BCC–BBC 104–112 pts (Educ St) (IB 25 pts)
Nottingham Trent – 104 pts (Psy Spec Inclsv Educ; Educ St)
St Mark and St John – BCC (Educ St; Ely Chld Educ; SEN Disab St)
Sheffield Hallam – 104 pts (Educ St; Educ Psy Cnslg)
South Wales – BCC (Welsh Educ); (Sociol Educ; Ely Yrs Educ Prac) (IB 29 pts)
York St John – 104 pts (Educ St)

96 pts **Aberystwyth** – 96 pts (Chld St)
Bangor – 96 pts (Chld St)
Bedfordshire – 96 pts (Ely Yrs Educ; Educ St) (IB 24 pts)
Birmingham (UC) – 96 pts (Chld St)
Bishop Grosseteste – 96–112 pts (Educ St courses)
Chichester – 96–104 pts (Out Advntr Educ) (IB 29 pts)
Glyndŵr – 96 pts (Educ)
Leeds Trinity – 96 pts (Educ St)
Nottingham Trent – 96 pts (Chld St)
Oldham (Univ Campus) – CCC 96 pts (Ely Yrs)
Plymouth – 96 pts (Educ St) (IB 25 pts)
Portsmouth – 96–120 pts (Ely Chld St) (IB 28 pts HL 15 pts)
St Mark and St John – CCC (Out Advntr Educ)
St Mary's – 96 pts (Educ Soc Sci) (IB 28 pts)
Staffordshire – 96 pts (Ely Chld St)

88 pts **Bradford (Coll)** – 88 pts (Educ St)
Teesside – 88 pts (Ely Chld St; Chld Yth St)
Trinity Saint David – 88 pts (P Educ St; Educ St; Educ St Psy)

80 pts **Anglia Ruskin** – 80 pts (Educ St) (IB 24 pts)
Cardiff Met – 80 pts (Yth Commun Educ)
Kent – CDD (Autsm St) (IB 34 pts)

72 pts **Trinity Saint David** – 72–96 pts (Ely Chld)

64 pts **Colchester (Inst)** – 64 pts (Ely Yrs)
South Essex (Coll) – 64 pts (Ely Yrs Educ)

EXAMPLES OF COLLEGES OFFERING COURSES IN THIS SUBJECT FIELD

Most colleges, check with your local college. Amersham and Wycombe (Coll); Barnet and Southgate (Coll); Barnfield (Coll); Barnsley (Coll); Blackburn (Coll); Blackpool and Fylde (Coll); Bournville (Coll);

Check **Chapter 3** for new university admission details and **Chapter 6** on how to read the subject tables.

Bridgwater (Coll); Bristol City (Coll); Bromley (CFHE); Calderdale (Coll); Chesterfield (Coll); Cliff (Coll); Cornwall (Coll); Craven (Coll); Derby (Coll); Duchy (Coll); East Riding (Coll); Exeter (Coll); Farnborough (CT); Grimsby (Univ Centre); Guildford (Coll); Harrogate (Coll); Havering (Coll); Hillcroft (Coll); Hopwood Hall (Coll); Hull (Coll); Kensington and Chelsea (Coll); Kirklees (Coll); Lakes (Coll); Lincoln (Coll); Liverpool City (Coll); Llandrillo (Coll); London City (Coll); Macclesfield (Coll); Mid-Cheshire (Coll); Nescot; Newcastle (Coll); Newham (CFE); Norland (Coll); North Lindsey (Coll); Norwich City (Coll); Nottingham New (Coll); Peter Symonds (Coll); Peterborough (Coll); Petroc; RAc Dance; Sheffield (Coll); Somerset (Coll); South Cheshire (Coll); South City Birmingham (Coll); South Devon (Coll); Stockport (Coll); Sunderland (Coll); Truro and Penwith (Coll); Wakefield (Coll); Warrington (Coll); Warwickshire (Coll); West Anglia (Coll); Westminster City (Coll); Wirral Met (Coll); Yeovil (Coll).

CHOOSING YOUR COURSE (SEE ALSO CH.1)

Universities and colleges teaching quality See www.qaa.ac.uk; http://unistats.direct.gov.uk.

Top research universities and colleges (REF 2014) (Education) Sheffield; Oxford; London (King's); Queen's Belfast; Loughborough; Exeter; Nottingham; Cardiff; Durham; York; Stirling; Bristol.

ADMISSIONS INFORMATION

Number of applicants per place (approx) Aberystwyth 6; Anglia Ruskin 1; Bangor 5; Bath 5; Bath Spa 5; Birmingham 8; Bishop Grosseteste 12; Bristol (Chld St) 6; Brunel (PE) 5; Cambridge 3; Canterbury Christ Church 15; Cardiff (Educ) 8; Cardiff Met 3; Central Lancashire 5; Chester 25; Chichester 12; Derby 13; Dundee 5; Durham 2; Edge Hill 17; Gloucestershire 20; Glyndŵr 15; Greenwich 3; Hull 7; Hull (Coll) 4; Leeds 4; Liverpool Hope 5; Liverpool John Moores 3; London (Gold) 5; London (UCL) 10; Manchester (Lrn Disab St) 2; Manchester Met 23; Middlesex 7; Northampton 7; Northumbria 8; Nottingham Trent 11; Oxford Brookes 6; Plymouth 14; Roehampton 6; St Mark and St John 5; St Mary's 19; Sheffield Hallam 7; Southampton 8; Trinity Saint David 10; UWE Bristol 20; Winchester 4; Wolverhampton 4; Worcester 21; York 3.

Advice to applicants and planning the UCAS personal statement Chichester Applicants should have spent a minimum of two weeks observing/helping out in a state school.

Misconceptions about this course That Childhood Studies is a childcare, child health or teaching course: it is not. That Educational Studies leads to a teaching qualification – it does not. **Bath Spa** (Educ St) Applicants should note that this is not a teacher training course – it leads on to PGCE teacher training (this applies to other Education Studies courses).

Selection interviews Yes Aberdeen, Bishop Grosseteste, Brunel, Cambridge, Chester, Chichester, Cumbria, Derby, Glasgow, Glyndŵr, Manchester Met (group interviews), Newman, Nottingham, Nottingham Trent, Oxford Brookes, Plymouth, Reading, Sheffield Hallam, Stirling, Stockport (Coll), UWE Bristol, Worcester, York St John; **Some** Anglia Ruskin, Bangor, Cardiff, Roehampton, St Mark and St John, Winchester; **No** East Anglia.

Interview advice and questions Cambridge The stage is a platform for opinions or just entertainment? **Derby** Applicants are asked about an aspect of education. **Liverpool John Moores** Discussion regarding any experience the applicant has had with children. **Worcester** Interviewees are asked to write a statement concerning their impressions of the interview.

Reasons for rejection (non-academic) Unable to meet the requirements of written standard English. Ungrammatical personal statements.

AFTER-RESULTS ADVICE

Offers to applicants repeating A-levels Higher Oxford Brookes, Warwick; **Same** Anglia Ruskin, Bangor, Bishop Grosseteste, Brighton, Brunel, Cambridge, Canterbury Christ Church, Cardiff, Chester, Chichester, De Montfort, Derby, Dundee, Durham, East Anglia, Liverpool Hope, Liverpool John Moores, London (Gold), Manchester Met, Newman, Northumbria, Nottingham Trent, Roehampton, St Mark and St John, St Mary's, Sunderland, Winchester, Wolverhampton, Worcester, York, York St John.

GRADUATE DESTINATIONS AND EMPLOYMENT (2013/14 HESA)
Academic Studies in Education graduates surveyed 10,300 **Employed** 4,545 **In voluntary employment** 140 **In further study** 3,285 **Assumed unemployed** 330

Career note Education Studies degrees prepare graduates for careers in educational administration although many will move into more general areas of business or into aspects of work with Social Services. Prospects are generally good. Courses in Childhood Studies could lead to work in health or childcare-related posts, in social work or administration.

OTHER DEGREE SUBJECTS FOR CONSIDERATION
Psychology; Social Policy; Social Sciences; Social Work.

ENGINEERING/ENGINEERING SCIENCES

(including **General Engineering, Integrated Engineering, Engineering Design** and **Product Design**; see also **Engineering (Manufacturing and Production), Transport Management and Planning**)

Mathematics and physics provide the basis of all Engineering courses although several universities and colleges now provide one-year Foundation courses for applicants without science A-levels. Many of the Engineering courses listed below enable students to delay the decision of their final engineering specialism. Engineering courses at most universities offer a range of specialisms in which, after a common first or second year, the choice of specialism is made. The flexibility of these courses is considerable, for example, it is sometimes possible to transfer from the BEng degree to the MEng degree at the end of the first or second year. At some universities, eg Durham, the first two years of the course cover a broad engineering education for all students enabling them to decide on their specialism in Year 3 from Civil, Electronic or Mechanical Engineering. A similar scheme operates at Lancaster University, whilst at Bath, the Mechanical Engineering department offers a choice of five courses at the end of Year 2. Many institutions offer sandwich courses and firms also offer valuable sponsorships.

Engineering Council UK (ECUK) Statement
Recent developments in the engineering profession and the regulations that govern registration as a professional engineer (UK-SPEC) mean that MEng and bachelor's degrees are the typical academic routes to becoming registered.

Chartered Engineers (CEng) develop solutions to engineering problems, using new or existing technologies, through innovation, creativity and change. They might develop and apply new technologies, promote advanced designs and design methods, introduce new and more efficient production techniques, marketing and construction concepts, and pioneer new engineering services and management methods.

Incorporated Engineers (IEng) act as exponents of today's technology through creativity and innovation. They maintain and manage applications of current and developing technology, and may be involved in engineering design, development, manufacture, construction and operation. Both Chartered and Incorporated Engineers are variously engaged in technical and commercial leadership and possess effective interpersonal skills.

You should confirm with universities whether their courses are accredited for CEng or IEng by relevant professional engineering institutions. To become a Chartered or Incorporated Engineer, you will have to demonstrate competence and commitment appropriate to the registration category. On top of your academic knowledge, you will also need to demonstrate your professional development and experience. Most of this will come after you graduate but placements in industry during your degree course are also available. Both Chartered and Incorporated Engineers usually progress to become team leaders or to take other key management roles. For full information check www.engc.org.uk/ukspec.

Useful websites www.scicentral.com; www.engc.org.uk; www.epsrc.ac.uk; www.etrust.org.uk

NB The points totals shown to the left of the institutions are for ease of reference only. It must not be assumed that Tariff points are always used by institutions or that they can be substituted for an offer in grades. The level of an offer is not necessarily indicative of the quality of a course.

COURSE OFFERS INFORMATION

Subject requirements/preferences GCSE English, mathematics and a science subject required. **AL** Mathematics and/or Physics, Engineering or another science usually required. Design Technology may be acceptable or in some cases required. Offers shown below refer to BEng or BSc courses unless otherwise stated.

Cambridge (Churchill, Peterhouse) STEP may be used as part of conditional offer; (Trinity) if student does not have A-level Further Mathematics, AEA Mathematics is required.

Oxford AL Mathematics and mechanics modules are recommended, Further Mathematics is helpful.

Your target offers and examples of degree courses

160 pts **Cambridge** – A*A*A incl maths+phys (Eng) (IB 40–41 pts HL 776)
Oxford – A*A*A incl maths+phys (Eng Sci) (IB 40 pts)

152 pts **Bristol** – A*AA/AABB–AAB incl maths+phys/fmaths (Eng Des (Yr Ind) MEng) (IB 38–34 pts HL 6 maths+phys)

144 pts **Bristol** – AAA–AAB incl maths (Eng Maths) (IB 36–34 pts HL 6 maths)
Durham – AAA incl maths+phys (Gen Eng) (IB 37 pts)
Edinburgh – AAA–ABB incl maths (Eng; Eng Sust Ener) (IB 37–32 pts)
Exeter – AAA–ABB incl maths+sci (Eng Mgt MEng; Eng MEng; Eng; Eng Mgt) (IB 36–32 pts HL 5 maths+sci)
Lancaster – AAA incl maths+sci (Eng (St Abrd) MEng) (IB 36 pts HL 6 maths+sci)
London (QM) – AAA incl sci/maths/des (Des Innov Crea Eng MEng) (IB 36 pts HL 6 sci/maths/des)
Nottingham – AAA incl maths+chem/phys (Chem Eng Env Eng (Yr Ind)) (IB 36 pts); AAA incl maths+sch/phys (Env Eng) (IB 36 pts)

136 pts **Cardiff** – AAB (Integ Eng courses) (IB 36–32 pts)
Lancaster – AAB–ABB incl maths+sci (Eng) (IB 35–32 pts HL 6 maths+sci)
Liverpool – AAB incl maths+sci (Eng MEng) (IB 35 pts HL 5 maths+phys)
Newcastle – AAB–ABB incl maths (Mar Tech Off Eng) (IB 35–34 pts HL 5 maths+phys)
Warwick – AAB incl maths+phys (Eng; Eng Bus Mgt; Eng Bus St) (IB 36 pts HL 5 maths+phys)

128 pts **Brunel** – ABB (Prod Des Eng) (IB 31 pts)
City – 128 pts (Eng Mgt Entre) (IB 32 pts)
Liverpool – ABB incl maths+sci (Eng) (IB 33 pts HL 5 maths+phys)
Loughborough – ABB incl maths/phys+des/art (Prod Des Tech) (IB 34–32 pts); ABB incl maths+phys/des/eng (Prod Des Eng) (IB 32 pts); ABB incl maths/phys (Eng Mgt) (IB 33 pts)
Strathclyde – ABB–BBB (Prod Des Eng) (IB 34 HL 5 maths+phys); (Prod Eng Mgt) (IB 34 pts HL 5 maths+phys)

120 pts **Aberdeen** – BBB incl maths+phys/des tech/eng (Eng) (IB 32 pts HL 5 maths+phys)
Aston – BBB–ABB incl maths+phys (Des Eng) (IB 32 pts)
Cardiff Met – 120 pts (Prod Des)
Greenwich – 120 pts (Eng Bus Mgt)
Heriot-Watt – BBB incl maths+phys/tech (Eng) (IB 31 pts)
Leicester – BBB incl maths+sci (Gen Eng) (IB 28 pts)
Queen's Belfast – BBB incl maths+sci/tech (Prod Des Eng)
Ulster – 120 pts incl sci/maths/tech (Eng Mgt) (IB 26 pts)
UWE Bristol – 120 pts (Archit Env Eng) (IB 26 pts)

112 pts **Central Lancashire** – 112 pts incl maths+sci/tech/eng (Robot Eng)
Derby – 112 pts (Prod Des)
London South Bank – BBC 112 pts (Eng Prod Des)

New UCAS points Tariff: A* = 56 pts; A = 48 pts; B = 40 pts; C = 32 pts; D = 24 pts; E = 16 pts

UWE Bristol – 112 pts (Prod Des Tech) (IB 25 pts)
104 pts **Bournemouth** – 104–120 pts (Des Eng) (IB 28–31 pts)
Manchester Met – BCC–BBC incl maths+sci 104–112 pts (Auto Eng) (IB 28 pts)
Northampton – 104–120 pts (Eng)
Staffordshire – 104 pts +portfolio +interview (Prod Des)
96 pts **East London** – 96 pts incl art des (Prod Des) (IB 24 pts)
Hertfordshire – 96 pts incl art (Ind Des) (IB 24 pts)
Portsmouth – 96–120 pts incl sci/tech/des (Prod Des Innov) (IB 26 pts HL 10 pts)
64 pts **UHI** – CC incl maths (Ener Eng)

Open University – contact +44 (0)845 300 6090 **or** www.openuniversity.co.uk/you (Eng)

Alternative offers
See **Chapter 6** and **Appendix 1** for grades/new UCAS Tariff points information for other
examinations.

EXAMPLES OF COLLEGES OFFERING COURSES IN THIS SUBJECT FIELD
See under separate Engineering tables. Blackburn (Coll); Blackpool and Fylde (Coll); Bristol City (Coll);
Bury (Coll); City and Islington (Coll); Cornwall (Coll); Coventry City (Coll); East Berkshire (Coll); East
Kent (Coll); East Surrey (Coll); Harlow (Coll); Highbury Portsmouth (Coll); Lancaster and Morecambe
(Coll); Llandrillo (Coll); Loughborough (Coll); Manchester (Coll); Mid-Cheshire (Coll); Middlesbrough
(Coll); Newcastle (Coll); North Kent (Coll); Northumberland (Coll); Portsmouth (Coll); Redcar and
Cleveland (Coll); Richmond-upon-Thames (Coll); St Helens (Coll); Selby (Coll); Somerset (Coll); South
Devon (Coll); South Essex (Coll); Stockport (Coll); Trafford (Coll); Tyne Met (Coll); Warwickshire (Coll);
West Nottinghamshire (Coll); West Suffolk (Coll); Westminster City (Coll).

CHOOSING YOUR COURSE (SEE ALSO CH.1)
Universities and colleges teaching quality See www.qaa.ac.uk; http://unistats.direct.gov.uk.

Top research universities and colleges (REF 2014) (General Engineering) London (King's); Cardiff;
Oxford; Sheffield; Cambridge; Imperial London; Liverpool; London (UCL); Glasgow.

Examples of sandwich degree courses Aston; Brunel; Cardiff; Central Lancashire; De Montfort; East
London; Huddersfield; Leicester; London South Bank; Loughborough; Manchester Met; Nottingham;
Nottingham Trent; Portsmouth; Staffordshire; Ulster; UWE Bristol; Wolverhampton.

ADMISSIONS INFORMATION
Number of applicants per place (approx) Aberdeen 6; Aston 8; Birmingham 6; Bournemouth 5;
Bristol (Eng Des) 3, (Eng Maths) 5; Brunel 10; Cambridge 7; Cardiff 5; City 3; Durham 9; Edinburgh 5;
Exeter 6; Lancaster 15; Leicester 10; Loughborough 9; Manchester Met 2; Northampton 3; Strathclyde
5; Warwick 10.

Advice to applicants and planning the UCAS personal statement Details of careers in the various
engineering specialisms should be obtained from the relevant engineering institutions (see **Appendix
3**). This will enable you to describe your interests in various aspects of engineering. Contact
engineers to discuss their work with them. Try to visit an engineering firm relevant to your choice of
specialism.

Selection interviews Yes Bournemouth, Bristol, Cambridge, Exeter, Lancaster, London (QM),
Loughborough, Manchester Met, Oxford (53% (success rate 17%)), Strathclyde; **Some** Cardiff, Leicester
(mature students only).

Interview advice and questions Since mathematics and physics are important subjects, it is
probable that you will be questioned on the applications of these subjects too, for example, the
transmission of electricity, nuclear power, aeronautics, mechanics etc. Past questions have included:
Explain the theory of an arch; what is its function? What is the connection between distance and
velocity and acceleration and velocity? How does a car ignition work? See also separate **Engineering**
tables and **Chapter 5**. **Nottingham Trent** What is Integrated Engineering?

Reasons for rejection (non-academic) Made no contribution whatsoever to the project discussions during the UCAS interview. Forged reference! Poor work ethic. Lack of motivation towards the subject area. Better suited to an alternative Engineering course. Failure to attend interview. Poor interview preparation.

AFTER-RESULTS ADVICE

Offers to applicants repeating A-levels Higher Loughborough, Warwick; **Possibly higher** Edinburgh, Lancaster, Manchester Met; **Same** Brunel (good reasons needed for repeating), Cambridge, Cardiff, Derby, Durham, Exeter, Heriot-Watt, Liverpool, Nottingham Trent.

GRADUATE DESTINATIONS AND EMPLOYMENT (2013/14 HESA)

Graduates surveyed 1690 **Employed** 1130 **In voluntary employment** 25 **In further study** 335 **Assumed unemployed** 75

Career note A high proportion of Engineering graduates go into industry as engineers, technicians, IT specialists or managers, irrespective of their engineering speciality. However, the transferable skills gained during their courses are also valued by employers in other sectors.

OTHER DEGREE SUBJECTS FOR CONSIDERATION

Computer Science; Materials Science; Mathematics; Physics; Technology; all branches of Engineering (see also following **Engineering** tables).

ENGINEERING (ACOUSTICS and SOUND)

(including **Audio Engineering** and **Sound Technology**; see also **Engineering (Electrical and Electronic), Film, Radio, Video and TV Studies, Media Studies, Music**)

These courses, such as the one at the University of Southampton, focus on sound and vibration engineering which covers many aspects of society, such as the motor industry, airlines, the environment, underwater communication, ultrasound, as used in medicine, and all communication systems. Courses also involve sound measurement, hearing, environmental health, and legal aspects of sound and vibration. Acoustics and sound are also extensively involved in the music industry, perhaps the most prestigious course being the Tonmeister degree at the University of Surrey comprising music theory and practice, sound, acoustics, electronics and computer systems. The department has good links with and a high reputation in the music industry.

Engineering Council statement See **Engineering/Engineering Sciences**.

Useful websites www.ioa.org.uk; www.engc.org.uk

NB The points totals shown to the left of the institutions are for ease of reference only. It must not be assumed that Tariff points are always used by institutions or that they can be substituted for an offer in grades. The level of an offer is not necessarily indicative of the quality of a course.

COURSE OFFERS INFORMATION

Subject requirements/preferences AL Mathematics and Physics usually required; Music is also required for some courses. See also **Engineering/Engineering Sciences**. Offers shown below refer to BEng or BSc courses unless otherwise stated.

Your target offers and examples of degree courses

152 pts Surrey – A*AA–AAA incl maths+mus+phys (Mus Snd Rec (Tonmeister)) (IB 38–36 pts HL 6 maths+mus+phys)

144 pts Glasgow – AAA 144 pts (Electron Mus MEng) (IB 36–38 pts)

   Southampton – AAA incl maths+phys (Acoust Eng) (IB 36 pts HL 6 maths+phys)

   York – AAA incl maths+sci (Mus Tech Sys MEng; Electron Eng Mus Tech Sys MEng) (IB 36–32 pts HL 5/6 maths+phys)

136 pts **Glasgow** – AAB–BBB incl maths+phys (Electron Mus) (IB 36–34 pts)
London (QM) – AAB 136 pts (Electron Mus Aud Sys MEng) (IB 34 pts)
Southampton – AAB incl maths+phys+mus (Acoust Mus) (IB 34 pts HL 6 maths+phys)

128 pts **York** – ABB incl maths+sci (Mus Tech Sys; Electron Eng Mus Tech Sys) (IB 36–32 pts HL 5/6 maths+phys)

120 pts **Birmingham City** – BBB incl sci/tech/maths/comp 120 pts (Snd Eng Prod) (IB 32 pts)
Brunel – BBB incl mus (Snc Arts) (IB 30 pts)
Huddersfield – BBB incl mus 120 pts (Mus Tech courses)

112 pts **Bournemouth** – 112–120 pts (Mus Aud Tech; Mus Snd Prod Tech) (IB 30–31 pts)
Lincoln – 112 pts (Aud Prod)
Liverpool (LIPA) – BBC 112 pts (Snd Tech)
Liverpool John Moores – 112 pts (Aud Mus Prod)
London (Royal Central Sch SpDr) – BBC +interview +portfolio (Thea Prac Thea Snd)
London Met – 112 pts (Mus Bus Lv Enter)
Portsmouth – 112 pts (Mus Snd Tech) (IB 26 pts)
Salford – 112–120 pts incl maths/sci (Aud Acoust) (IB 35 pts)
Southampton Solent – 112 pts (Aud Acoust Eng MEng; Pop Mus Prod)
West London – 112 pts (App Snd Eng)

104 pts **Bolton** – 104 pts incl maths/sci/tech/mus (Snd Eng Des)
De Montfort – 104 pts (Aud Rec Tech) (IB 28 pts)
South Wales – BCC (Snd Eng) (IB 29 pts)

96 pts **Glyndŵr** – 96 pts (Snd Tech)
Hertfordshire – 96 pts incl mus/sci/tech (Snd Des Tech; Aud Rec Prod) (IB 24 pts)
Rose Bruford (Coll) – 96 pts (Perf Snd (Lv Des Eng))

64 pts **Ravensbourne** – CC (Snd Des; Broad Aud Tech; Broad Comp; Broad Sys Tech; Outsd Broad Tech) (IB 28 pts)

32 pts **Arts London** – 32 pts +interview +portfolio (Snd Arts Des)

24 pts **UHI** – D (Aud Eng)

Alternative offers
See **Chapter 6** and **Appendix 1** for grades/new UCAS Tariff points information for other examinations.

EXAMPLES OF COLLEGES OFFERING COURSES IN THIS SUBJECT FIELD
Amersham and Wycombe (Coll); Barnsley (Coll); Bristol City (Coll); Calderdale (Coll); Hugh Baird (Coll); Leicester (Coll); Newcastle (Coll); Northbrook (Coll); Plymouth City (Coll); Redcar and Cleveland (Coll); St Helens (Coll); Salford; South City Birmingham (Coll); Sussex Downs (Coll); Truro and Penwith (Coll).

CHOOSING YOUR COURSE (SEE ALSO CH.1)
Universities and colleges teaching quality See www.qaa.ac.uk; http://unistats.direct.gov.uk.

Examples of sandwich degree courses Birmingham City; De Montfort; Huddersfield; Portsmouth; Surrey; York.

ADMISSIONS INFORMATION
Number of applicants per place (approx) Anglia Ruskin 5; Salford 4; Southampton 4.

Advice to applicants and planning the UCAS personal statement See **Engineering/Engineering Sciences**. See also **Appendix 3**.

Misconceptions about this course Anglia Ruskin Failure to appreciate the emphasis that the course gives to science and technology.

Selection interviews Yes Salford, Southampton; **Some** Anglia Ruskin.

Interview advice and questions What interests you about acoustics engineering? What career do you have in mind on graduating? See also **Chapter 5**.

Reasons for rejection (non-academic) See **Engineering/Engineering Sciences**.

AFTER-RESULTS ADVICE
Offers to applicants repeating A-levels Same Anglia Ruskin, Salford.

GRADUATE DESTINATIONS AND EMPLOYMENT (2013/14 HESA)
See **Engineering/Engineering Sciences**.

Career note Specialist topics on these courses will enable graduates to make decisions as to their future career destinations.

OTHER DEGREE SUBJECTS FOR CONSIDERATION
Audiology; Broadcast Engineering; Communications Engineering; Computer Engineering; Computer Science; Media Technology; Music; Radio and TV; Technology; Telecommunications Engineering and Electronic Engineering.

ENGINEERING (AERONAUTICAL and AEROSPACE)

(see also **Engineering (Electrical and Electronic)**)

Courses cover the manufacture of military and civil aircraft, theories of mechanics, thermodynamics, electronics, computing and engine design. Avionics courses include flight and energy control systems, airborne computing, navigation, optical and TV displays, airborne communications, and radar systems for navigation and power. Aeronautical Engineering involves the design, construction and powering of aircraft, and similarly Aerospace Engineering covers aerodynamics, flight design and control propulsion and communications. Pilot training, with an additional fee, is also included in some courses as at the universities of Brunel, Bucks New, Leeds, Kingston, Hertfordshire, Liverpool, Salford and Southampton. Some courses also include spaceflight studies and the Electronics course at Bath can be combined with Space Science Technology. (See also under **Business Management Courses (Specialised)** for details of Aviation Management degrees.)

Engineering Council statement See **Engineering/Engineering Sciences**.

Useful websites aerosociety.com; www.engc.org.uk; www.theiet.org

NB The points totals shown to the left of the institutions are for ease of reference only. It must not be assumed that Tariff points are always used by institutions or that they can be substituted for an offer in grades. The level of an offer is not necessarily indicative of the quality of a course.

COURSE OFFERS INFORMATION
Subject requirements/preferences See **Engineering/Engineering Sciences**. Offers shown below refer to BEng or BSc courses unless otherwise stated.

Your target offers and examples of degree courses

160 pts **Cambridge** – A*A*A incl maths+phys (Aerosp Aeroth Eng) (IB 40–41 pts HL 776)

Imperial London – A*A*A incl phys+maths (Aero Eng MEng; Aero Eng (Yr Abrd)) (IB 40 pts HL 7 maths 6 phys)

152 pts **Bath** – A*AA incl maths+phys (Aerosp Eng) (IB 36 pts HL 6 maths+phys)

Bristol – A*AA–AAA incl maths+phys (Aerosp Eng; Aerosp Eng (St Abrd) MEng) (IB 38–36 pts HL 6 maths+phys)

Leeds – A*AA incl maths+phys (Aero Aerosp Eng) (IB 36 pts HL 6 maths+phys)

Southampton – A*AA incl maths+phys (Aero Astnaut (Aerodyn) MEng; Aero Astnaut (Airvhcl Sys Des) MEng; Aero Astnaut (Spcrft Eng) MEng; Aero Astnaut (Mat Struct) MEng; Aero Astnaut (Eng Mgt) MEng) (IB 38 pts HL 6 maths+phys); (Aero Astnaut; Aero Astnaut MEng) (IB 38 pts); A*AA incl maths/phys (Mech Eng (Aerosp) MEng) (IB 38 pts HL 6 maths+phys)

144 pts **Brunel** – AAA (Avn Eng Plt St MEng; Avn Eng MEng; Aerosp Eng MEng; Mech Eng Aero MEng) (IB 34 pts)

City – 144 pts (Aero Eng MEng) (IB 35 pts)

Glasgow – AAA incl maths+phys (Aerosp Sys MEng; Aero Eng MEng) (IB 38–36 pts)

Imperial London – AAA incl maths+phys (Aerosp Mat) (IB 38 pts HL 6 maths+phys)

Leeds – AAA incl maths/phys (Avn Tech Mgt; Avn Tech Plt St) (IB 35 pts HL 5 maths/phys)

Liverpool – AAA incl maths+sci (Aerosp Eng MEng; Aerosp Eng Plt St MEng) (IB 35 pts HL 5 maths+phys)

London (QM) – AAA incl maths+phys (Aerosp Eng MEng) (IB 36 pts HL 6 maths+phys)

Loughborough – AAA–AAB incl maths+phys (Aero Eng) (IB 34 pts HL 6 maths+phys)

Manchester – AAA incl maths+phys (Aerosp Eng MEng; Aerosp Eng Mgt) (IB 37 pts HL 6 maths+phys)

Nottingham – AAA–AAB incl maths+sci/tech (Aerosp Eng) (IB 36–34 pts)

Sheffield – AAA incl maths+phys (Aerosp Eng MEng; Aerosp Eng (PPI) MEng) (IB 37 pts HL 6 maths+phys)

Surrey – AAA–AAB incl maths+phys (Aerosp Eng) (IB 36–35 pts)

136 pts **Bath** – AAB incl maths+sci/tech (Electron Eng Spc Sci Tech) (IB 35 pts HL 6 maths/phys)

Brunel – AAB–ABB (Mech Eng Aero; Aerosp Eng; Avn Eng; Avn Eng Plt St) (IB 33 pts)

Glasgow – AAB–BBB incl maths+phys (Aero Eng; Aerosp Sys) (IB 36–34 pts)

London (QM) – AAB incl maths+phys (Aerosp Eng) (IB 34 pts HL 6 maths+phys)

Manchester – AAB incl maths+phys (Aerosp Eng) (IB 35 pts HL 6 maths+phys)

Queen's Belfast – AAB incl maths+sci/tech (Prod Des Eng MEng); AAB incl maths+sci/fmaths (Aerosp Eng MEng)

Sheffield – AAB–ABB incl maths+phys (Aero Eng (Yr Ind)) (IB 35 pts HL 6 maths+phys); AAB incl maths+phys (Aerosp Eng (PPI); Aerosp Eng) (IB 35 pts HL 6 maths+phys)

Strathclyde – AAB–BBB (Mech Eng Aero MEng) (IB 36 pts HL 6 maths+phys); AAB–BBB incl maths+phys (Aero Mech Eng MEng) (IB 36 pts HL 6 maths+phys)

Swansea – AAB incl maths (Aerosp Eng MEng) (IB 34 pts)

128 pts **City** – 128 pts (Aero Eng) (IB 33 pts)

Coventry – ABB (Avn Mgt) (IB 31 pts); ABB incl maths+phys/tech (Aerosp Sys Eng) (IB 31 pts)

Hertfordshire – 128 pts incl maths+phys/tech/eng (Aerosp Eng MEng; Aerosp Sys Eng Plt St MEng; Aerosp Sys Eng MEng) (IB 32 pts)

Kingston – 128 pts incl maths+sci (Aerosp Eng Astnaut Spc Tech MEng; Aerosp Eng MEng)

Liverpool – ABB incl maths+sci (Aerosp Eng) (IB 33 pts HL 5 maths+phys)

Strathclyde – ABB–BBB (Aero-Mech Eng) (IB 32 pts HL 5 maths+phys)

Swansea – ABB–BBB incl maths (Aerosp Eng) (IB 32 pts)

UWE Bristol – 128 pts incl maths+sci/tech/des/eng (Aerosp Eng MEng) (IB 27 pts HL 6 maths)

120 pts **Brighton** – BBB incl maths+sci (Aero Eng MEng) (IB 30 pts)

Leicester – BBB incl maths+sci (Aerosp Eng) (IB 28 pts)

Loughborough – BBB (Air Trans Mgt) (IB 32 pts)

Queen's Belfast – BBB incl maths+sci/fmaths/tech/des (Aerosp Eng)

UWE Bristol – 120 pts incl maths+sci/des/tech/eng (Aerosp Eng) (IB 26 pts HL 5 maths)

112 pts **Brighton** – BBC incl maths+sci (Aero Eng) (IB 28 pts)

Glyndŵr – 112 pts incl maths/phys (Aero Mech Eng MEng)

Kingston – 112 pts incl maths+sci (Aerosp Eng Astnaut Spc Tech; Aerosp Eng)

Sheffield Hallam – 112 pts incl maths+sci/eng/tech (Aerosp Eng)

Teesside – BBC incl maths+phys (Aerosp Eng)

104 pts **Hertfordshire** – 104 pts incl maths+phys/tech/eng (Aerosp Eng; Aerosp Sys Eng Plt St; Aerosp Sys Eng) (IB 26 pts)

South Wales – BCC incl maths+sci (Aero Eng) (IB 29 pts HL 5 maths+sci); BCC incl maths/sci (Aircft Mntnce Eng) (IB 29 pts HL 5 maths/sci)

96 pts **Glyndŵr** – 96 pts incl maths/sci (Aero Mech Eng)

Hertfordshire – 96 pts (Aerosp Tech Mgt; Aerosp Tech Plt St) (IB 24 pts)

64 pts **UHI** – CC incl maths (Aircft Eng)

MANCHESTER
1824

The University of Manchester

Undergraduate studies in

Engineering

The facts

» One of Europe's leading Schools of Engineering

» Eighty teaching staff, with up to 350 undergraduate places each year

» Seventy percent of graduates are awarded First or Upper Second Class Honours degrees

Your experience

From the flexible, 24/7 learning environment of the Alan Gilbert Learning Commons to the personal development opportunities and specialist support services we offer, we will empower you to be your best. We're well underway with the biggest investment programme ever seen in UK higher education, having invested £750 million in our facilities since 2004, with another £1 billion to follow. Away from your studies you'll have access to the UK's largest student union, almost 300 student societies, and excellent sports and fitness facilities. The only thing you won't experience is boredom.

Nine reasons we should be your number one choice

1. Professionally accredited courses
2. Top-rated for graduate employment
3. Student clubs and groups
4. Strong industrial partnerships
5. Peer Assisted Study Scheme (PASS)
6. Excellent research rankings
7. Extensive laboratory facilities
8. Cross-disciplinary
9. Teamwork

Courses

Aerospace Engineering

~~SWL 6.2~~

Civil Engineering

Mechanical Engineering

BEng MEng

Profile

Katherine Woolley
MEng(Hons) Civil Engineering
Senior Tunnel Engineer, AECOM

"A good degree in engineering from Manchester impresses the employers. My MEng degree has given me a great benchmark. It also meant that I've been able to get chartered without a Masters

degree. After University I worked for Mott MacDonald in Croydon, UK as a tunnel engineer. I moved to Auckland in New Zealand in July 2011 to work for AECOM as a senior tunnel engineer. My main responsibilities are management, design and construction supervision of tunnels. "

MEng or BEng?

We offer a range of degree courses at both MEng (Master of Engineering) or BEng (Bachelor of Engineering) level. The most obvious difference between these is duration: four or five years for MEng, and three years for BEng. Transfer between BEng and MEng is possible. The first three years cover most of the engineering science whereas the fourth year looks in more depth at particular applications. But what else could influence your choice?

Many students studying for a degree in engineering aim to become Chartered Engineers, and accredited MEng courses give you the required educational base to achieve this. Accredited BEng courses require you to complete further study in order to achieve the same status.

Student Recruitment and Admissions

School of Mechanical, Aerospace and Civil Engineering

Pariser Building, Sackville Street, Manchester, M13 9PL

Tel +44 (0) 161 306 9210
email ug-mace@manchester.ac.uk

School of Mechanical, Aerospace and Civil Engineering

www.manchester.ac.uk/mace/undergraduate

Alternative offers
See **Chapter 6** and **Appendix 1** for grades/new UCAS Tariff points information for other examinations.

EXAMPLES OF COLLEGES OFFERING COURSES IN THIS SUBJECT FIELD
Blackpool and Fylde (Coll); Bristol City (Coll); Exeter (Coll); Farnborough (CT); Macclesfield (Coll); Newcastle (Coll); Solihull (Coll); Yeovil (Coll).

CHOOSING YOUR COURSE (SEE ALSO CH.1)
Universities and colleges teaching quality See www.qaa.ac.uk; http://unistats.direct.gov.uk.

Top research universities and colleges (REF 2014) (Aeronautical, Mechanical, Chemical and Manufacturing Engineering) Cambridge; London (UCL); Manchester (Chem Eng); Bath; Imperial London; Sheffield (Mech Eng Advnc Manuf); Sheffield (Chem Biol Eng); Queen's Belfast; Birmingham (Chem Eng).

Examples of sandwich degree courses Bath; Brighton; Brunel; City; Coventry; Hertfordshire; Kingston; Leeds; Loughborough; Queen's Belfast; Sheffield Hallam; South Wales; Surrey; Teesside; UWE Bristol.

ADMISSIONS INFORMATION
Number of applicants per place (approx) Bath 10; Bristol 7; City 17; Coventry 7; Farnborough (CT) 7; Glyndŵr 5; Hertfordshire 17; Kingston 9; London (QM) 8; Loughborough 10; Queen's Belfast 6; Salford 6; Southampton 10; UWE Bristol 4; York 3 av.

Advice to applicants and planning the UCAS personal statement Interest in engineering and aerospace. Work experience in engineering. Flying experience. Personal attainments. Relevant hobbies. Membership of Air Training Corps. See also **Engineering/Engineering Sciences**. **Bristol** Deferred entry accepted. **Imperial London** Deferred entry acceptable.

Misconceptions about this course That Aeronautical Engineering is not a highly analytical subject: it is.

Selection interviews Yes Bristol, Cambridge, Farnborough (CT), Hertfordshire, Imperial London, Kingston, London (QM), Loughborough, Southampton.

Interview advice and questions Why Aeronautical Engineering? Questions about different types of aircraft and flight principles of helicopters. Range of interests in engineering. See also **Chapter 5**.

Reasons for rejection (non-academic) See **Engineering/Engineering Sciences**.

AFTER-RESULTS ADVICE
Offers to applicants repeating A-levels Higher Bristol, Queen's Belfast; **Possibly higher** Hertfordshire; **Same** Bath, City, Farnborough (CT), Kingston, Liverpool, Loughborough, Southampton, York; **No** Cambridge.

GRADUATE DESTINATIONS AND EMPLOYMENT (2013/14 HESA)
Aerospace Engineering graduates surveyed 1030 **Employed** 545 **In voluntary employment** 10 **In further study** 300 **Assumed unemployed** 100

Career note Specialist areas of study on these courses will open up possible career directions. See also **Engineering/Engineering Sciences**.

OTHER DEGREE SUBJECTS FOR CONSIDERATION
Astronomy; Astrophysics; Computer Science; Electronics and Systems Engineering; Materials Science; Mathematics; Naval Architecture; Physics.

ENGINEERING (CHEMICAL)

(including **Fire Engineering, Fire Safety** and **Nuclear Engineering**; see also **Chemistry**)

Chemical engineers explore solutions to problems across the whole spectrum of industries involving oil and gas, petroleum, pharmaceuticals, including cosmetics, food and drink, biotechnology, bioengineering and biomedical engineering, their role being concerned with the chemical properties of materials and also the safety aspects of projects. Petroleum engineers work in oil and gas projects which can include exploration, excavation, and refining and courses include the study of geology. Another branch is Fire Risk Engineering which invariably overlaps to some extent with Civil Engineering as in the course at the University of Edinburgh, and also Safety Engineering and Disaster Management courses as at Ulster University. Finally, Nuclear Engineering focuses on the uses of nuclear energy, such as the provision of non-fossil fuels and also covers power generation and the decommissioning of nuclear waste.

Engineering Council statement See **Engineering/Engineering Sciences**.

Useful websites www.icheme.org; www.engc.org.uk; www.whynotchemeng.com; www.bceca.org.uk; www.semta.org.uk

NB The points totals shown to the left of the institutions are for ease of reference only. It must not be assumed that Tariff points are always used by institutions or that they can be substituted for an offer in grades. The level of an offer is not necessarily indicative of the quality of a course.

COURSE OFFERS INFORMATION

Subject requirements/preferences AL Mathematics and Chemistry required. See also **Engineering/ Engineering Sciences**. Offers shown below refer to BEng or BSc courses unless otherwise stated.

Your target offers and examples of degree courses

160 pts **Cambridge** – A*A*A incl maths+phys (Cheml Eng) (IB 40–41 pts HL 776)

    Imperial London – A*A*A incl maths+chem+sci (Cheml Nucl Eng MEng; Cheml Eng MEng) (IB 39 pts HL 7 maths 6 chem+sci)

    Oxford – A*A*A incl maths+phys (Cheml Eng MEng) (IB 40 pts)

152 pts **Bath** – A*AA incl maths+chem (Cheml Eng BEng/MEng; Bioch Eng MEng) (IB 36 pts HL 6 maths+chem)

    Birmingham – A*AA–AAAA incl chem+maths (Cheml Eng MEng (Yr Abrd); Cheml Eng MEng; Cheml Eng) (IB 32 pts HL 766)

    Leeds – A*AA incl maths+phys/chem (Chem Nucl Eng; Cheml Eng courses) (IB 36 pts HL 6 maths+phys/chem)

    London (UCL) – A*AA–AAA incl maths+sci (Eng (Bioch) MEng; Eng (Bioch)) (IB 39–38 pts HL 5 maths+sci); A*AA–AAB incl maths+chem/phys (Eng (Cheml)) (IB 39–36 pts HL 5 maths+chem/phys)

144 pts **Birmingham** – AAA incl maths+phys (Nucl Eng MEng) (IB 32 pts HL 666)

    Edinburgh – AAA–ABB (Cheml Eng; Cheml Eng Mgt) (IB 37–32 pts); AAA–ABB incl maths (Struct Fire Sfty Eng) (IB 37–32 pts)

    Lancaster – AAA incl maths+chem (Cheml Eng MEng) (IB 36 pts HL 6 maths+chem)

    Leeds – AAA incl maths+phys/chem (Petrol Eng) (IB 35 pts HL 5 maths+phys/chem)

    Loughborough – AAA incl maths+chem/phys (Cheml Eng MEng; Cheml Eng Mgt) (IB 36 pts)

    Manchester – AAA incl maths+sci (Petrol Eng) (IB 37 pts HL 5 maths+sci); (Cheml Eng) (IB 37 pts)

    Nottingham – AAA incl maths+chem/phys (Cheml Eng; Cheml Eng Env Eng; Cheml Eng MEng) (IB 36 pts)

    Sheffield – AAA incl maths+chem (Cheml Eng; Cheml Eng MEng Joint Hons; Cheml Eng Biotech MEng) (IB 37 pts HL 6 maths+chem)

    Surrey – AAA incl maths+chem (Cheml Eng MEng) (IB 36 pts)

136 pts **Aston** – AAB–AAA incl chem+maths (Cheml Eng MEng) (IB 34 pts HL 6 maths+chem)
 Lancaster – AAB–ABB incl maths+chem (Cheml Eng) (IB 35–32 pts HL 6 maths+chem); AAB–
  ABB incl maths+phys (Nucl Eng) (IB 35–32 pts HL 6 maths+phys)
 Newcastle – AAB incl maths+chem (Cheml Eng) (IB 36 pts HL 6 maths+chem)
 Surrey – AAB incl maths+chem (Cheml Eng) (IB 35 pts)
128 pts **Liverpool** – ABB incl phys+maths (Phys Nucl Sci) (IB 33 pts HL 6 phys+maths)
 Strathclyde – ABB–BBB (Cheml Eng) (IB 32 pts HL 6 maths 5 chem+phys)
 Swansea – ABB–BBB incl maths+chem (Cheml Eng) (IB 32 pts)
120 pts **Aberdeen** – BBB incl maths+phys/des tech/eng (Cheml Eng; Petrol Eng) (IB 32 pts HL 5
  maths+phys)
 Aston – BBB–ABB incl chem+maths (Cheml Eng) (IB 32 pts HL chem)
 Heriot-Watt – BBB incl maths+chem (Cheml Eng; Cheml Eng Ener Eng MEng) (IB 29 pts HL
  maths+chem); (Cheml Eng Oil Gas Tech MEng; Cheml Eng Pharml Chem MEng) (IB 29 pts)
 Queen's Belfast – BBB incl maths+sci/tech (Cheml Eng)
 Teesside – BBB incl maths+chem (Cheml Eng MEng)
112 pts **Bradford** – BBC 112 pts (Cheml Eng)
 Central Lancashire – 112 pts incl maths/sci (Fire Eng BEng/MEng) (IB 24 pts HL 5
  maths/sci)
 Glasgow Caledonian – BBC incl maths/phys (Fire Risk Eng) (IB 25 pts)
 Huddersfield – BBC incl chem+maths 112 pts (Chem Cheml Eng)
 Hull – 112 pts incl maths+chem (Cheml Eng) (IB 28 pts HL 5 maths+chem)
 Nottingham Trent – 112 pts incl maths+phys (Phys Nucl Tech)
 Portsmouth – 112–128 pts incl maths+sci/tech (Petrol Eng) (IB 27 pts HL 14 pts incl 6
  maths+sci/tech)
 Teesside – BBC incl maths+chem (Cheml Eng)
 West Scotland – BBC incl maths+sci (Cheml Eng) (IB 24 pts)

Alternative offers
See **Chapter 6** and **Appendix 1** for grades/new UCAS Tariff points information for other examinations.

EXAMPLES OF COLLEGES OFFERING COURSES IN THIS SUBJECT FIELD
Bridgwater (Coll); (Nucl Tech) Lakes (Coll).

CHOOSING YOUR COURSE (SEE ALSO CH.1)
Universities and colleges teaching quality See www.qaa.ac.uk; http://unistats.direct.gov.uk.

Top research universities and colleges (REF 2014) See **Engineering (Aeronautical and
Aerospace)**.

Examples of sandwich degree courses Aston; Bath; Bradford; Huddersfield; Hull; London South
Bank; Loughborough; Manchester; Queen's Belfast; Surrey; Teesside.

ADMISSIONS INFORMATION
Number of applicants per place (approx) Aston 4; Bath 9; Birmingham 6; Heriot-Watt 8;
Huddersfield 7; Imperial London 4, (MEng) 4; Leeds 9; London (UCL) 7; Loughborough 7; Newcastle 6;
Nottingham 6; Sheffield 14; Strathclyde 6; Surrey 5; Swansea 3.

Misconceptions about this course Surrey That chemical engineering is chemistry on a large scale:
physics is as applicable as chemistry.

Selection interviews Yes Bath, Birmingham, Cambridge, Imperial London, Leeds, London (UCL),
Loughborough, Manchester, Newcastle, Oxford, Surrey, Teesside; **No** Nottingham.

Interview advice and questions Past questions have included the following: How would you justify
the processing of radioactive waste to people living in the neighbourhood? What is public health
engineering? What is biochemical engineering? What could be the sources of fuel and energy in the
year 2020? Discuss some industrial applications of chemistry. Regular incidents occur in which
chemical spillage and other problems affect the environment – be prepared to discuss these social

Join the fastest growing engineering discipline:

- UK graduate salaries in the region of £30,000
- Opportunities to travel
- Wide variety of career options
- Excellent graduate job prospects

Discover chemical engineering at

whynotchemeng.com

Why chemical engineering matters

whynotchemeng.com

Chemical engineers are the problem-solvers of the STEM community. Whether it's working out how to make industrial processes more environmentally-friendly or investigating an alternative energy source, a chemical engineer's work is never dull.

Power to the people

Society needs fuel to power heating, cooking and transport. Electricity is used to power industry and commerce, operate equipment and light our lives.

This energy demand is rapidly increasing - not only is the world's population rising, but global development and new technologies are making that population more energy-hungry.

Meeting this demand presents a crucial challenge for chemical engineers in the decades ahead. Our main energy sources are running out, and the climate change challenge increases the need for environmentally-friendly solutions: carbon-capture, nuclear, solar, biomass, wind, hydrogen – where does the future of power generation lie?

Food glorious food

The pressures of a growing population and improved living standards in the developing world means a demand for more food – particularly protein-rich foods that put pressure on water and land availability.

The demand for more food has led to a greater awareness of these challenges and the need for scientific and engineering solutions to food production.

Chemical and biochemical engineers are working with agricultural industry to solve problems throughout the global food chain, to meet demand for sufficient, safe food without increasing energy, water or land use, as well as minimising waste production and environmental impact.

Water, water everywhere…

More than a billion people lack access to a clean, safe, treated water supply. Population growth and industrialisation are putting increasing pressure on already stretched supplies.

Water shortages are being caused by a wide range of factors. Environmental problems such as pollution, climate change and waste management all need to be looked at in order to improve the safety of drinking water for global communities.

Different countries have different needs, demands and challenges, however chemical and biochemical engineers will play a vital role in improving water quality by developing more efficient process technologies and practices.

Live long and prosper

People are living longer thanks to recent developments in healthcare. Infectious diseases common in previous generations have largely been erased as medicines become more widely available in developing countries.

Our wellbeing is not just about health, but also about quality of life. Improvements in lifestyle bring their own issues with a rising global population presenting new challenges for the healthcare industry.

Chemical and biochemical engineers are involved with producing new and better solutions for our health and wellbeing while addressing the pressures on limited resources such as energy, water and raw materials.

why not CHEMENG
shape the future…

The
University
Of
Sheffield.

• Fully accredited by the IChemE
• World-class facilities
• 95% student satisfaction

A professional engineer from day one.

BEng/MEng Chemical Engineering • MEng Chemical Engineering with a Year in Industry
MEng Chemical Engineering with Chemistry • MEng Chemical Engineering with Energy
MEng Chemical Engineering with Biotechnology • MEng Chemical Engineering with
Nuclear Technology • MEng Chemical Engineering with a Modern Language

Department of Chemical and Biological Engineering
www.sheffield.ac.uk/cbe • chemeng@sheffield.ac.uk • +44 (0)114 222 7601

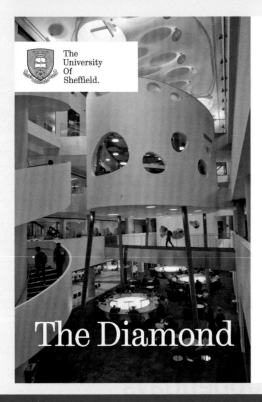

The
University
Of
Sheffield.

The Diamond

The Diamond is home to all engineering undergraduates and highlights the University's commitment to developing innovative learning and teaching.

The seventeen laboratories provide specialised engineering facilities, offering you an excellent practical experience and giving you an advantage in the graduate job market. As a chemical engineering student, you will take part in lectures and tutorials in an extensive lab programme focussing on the principles and application of chemical engineering. Our pilot plant is a unique facility, providing you with a safe environment in which to apply your learning to larger-scale process equipment, through hands-on experimentation. The control room will simulate a true industrial plant, with industry-standard software. You'll have the opportunity to carry out virtual experiments using the simulation software, giving you experience of the breadth of practical industrial chemical processing.

Check **Chapter 3** for new university admission details and **Chapter 6** on how to read the subject tables.

Come along to a University Open Day to find out more:
www.leeds.ac.uk/opendays

Globally renowned for our teaching and research, the School of Chemical and Process Engineering has an established reputation across the entire spectrum of chemical, energy and petroleum engineering.

Chemical Engineering
at the University of Leeds

FLEXIBLE DEGREE OPTIONS

You can choose to study a four-year MEng or a three-year BEng degree. You also have the option of undertaking a placement year or studying abroad.

We offer the following degrees:

- Chemical Engineering
- Chemical and Energy Engineering
- Chemical and Materials Engineering
- Chemical and Nuclear Engineering
- Petroleum Engineering

The first two years of our chemical engineering degrees are common, focusing on the fundamental science and engineering concepts associated with the subject, which means you can easily switch between courses.

HIGHLY EMPLOYABLE GRADUATES

95% of our students go on to work or further study within six months of graduating, with graduates employed in professional and managerial positions at Arup, GlaxoSmithKline, Unilever, P&G, Atkins and many more (DLHE).

Our dedicated employability team will provide you with support and advice to help you find relevant work experience, internships and year in industry placements, as well as graduate positions.

ACCREDITED DEGREES

Our chemical engineering courses are accredited by the Institution of Chemical Engineers (IChemE), the only organisation to award Chartered Chemical Engineer status.

HIGH RANKINGS IN UNIVERSITY LEAGUE TABLES

We are ranked 6th in the UK for Chemical Engineering by the Guardian League table 2016 and are a top 100 university for Chemical Engineering in the QS World Rankings by subject.

www.engineering.leeds.ac.uk/chemical

 www.facebook.com/facultyofengineeringleeds

 www.twitter.com/LeedsUniEng

UNIVERSITY OF LEEDS

The University of Nottingha

UNITED KINGDOM · CHINA · MALAY

"

Our students can experience the global opportunities, challenges and careers available in Chemical and Environmental Engineering

Ed Lester
Professor of Chemical Technologies

Why study Chemical and Environmental Engineering **at Nottingham**?

Courses

All our courses are available as three-year BEng and four-year MEng degree programmes.

Across your first year you'll learn applied process engineering such as reaction engineering, separations, material selection, plant design and process operations, before preparing for the commercial environment with laboratory-based learning and industry-led teaching in your second and third years.

Year in industry

All our courses come with an optional year in industry, which allows you to develop your skills; professional experience is a key step towards Chartered Engineer status.

This significantly boosts employment prospects and has a positive impact on degree results.

- World top 1% university*
- Top 10 UK chemical engineering department**
- 94.3% of first-degree graduates available for employment secured work or further study within six months
- Support from engineers and scientists with extensive teaching and industrial experience

*QS World University Rankings 2014/15
**7th in *The Guardian University Guide 2016*

Find out more at **www.nottingham.ac.uk/chemev**

issues. See also **Chapter 5**. **Imperial London** Interviews can be conducted in South East Asia if necessary.

Reasons for rejection (non-academic) See **Engineering/Engineering Sciences**.

AFTER-RESULTS ADVICE

Offers to applicants repeating A-levels Higher Swansea; **Possibly higher** Bath, Leeds, London South Bank, Queen's Belfast; **Same** Aston, Birmingham, Cambridge, Loughborough, Newcastle, Nottingham, Sheffield, Surrey, Teesside.

GRADUATE DESTINATIONS AND EMPLOYMENT (2013/14 HESA)

Chemical, Process and Energy Engineering graduates surveyed 1,040 **Employed** 615 **In voluntary employment** 20 **In further study** 215 **Assumed unemployed** 95

Career note Chemical engineering is involved in many aspects of industry and scientific development. In addition to the oil and chemical-based industries, graduates enter a wide range of careers including the design and construction of chemical process plants, food production, pollution control, environmental protection, energy conservation, waste recovery and recycling, medical science, health and safety, and alternative energy sources.

OTHER DEGREE SUBJECTS FOR CONSIDERATION

Biochemistry; Biotechnology; Chemistry; Cosmetic Science; Environmental Science; Food Science and Technology; Materials Science; Mathematics; Nuclear Engineering; Physics.

ENGINEERING (CIVIL)

(including **Architectural, Coastal, Disaster Management, Environmental, Offshore, Structural** and **Transportation Engineering**; see also **Building and Construction, Environmental Sciences**)

Civil engineers translate the work of architectural designs into reality, dealing with large scale projects such as high rise buildings, bridges, dock and harbour projects, roads, railways, dams, water supplies and reservoirs. In all major projects, civil engineers and architects work in close liaison as demonstrated at the University of Bath which has the only interdisciplinary Architecture and Civil Engineering department in the UK in which students following either degree work together. The University of Leeds also offers a common first Engineering year for all students, who can switch courses with a choice from Architectural Engineering or Civil Engineering with specialisms in either Environmental Engineering, Project Management, or Structural Engineering which focuses on the materials used in construction.

Engineering Council statement See **Engineering/Engineering Sciences**.

Useful websites www.ice.org.uk; www.engc.org.uk; www.wisecampaign.org.uk; www.istructe.org.uk

NB The points totals shown to the left of the institutions are for ease of reference only. It must not be assumed that Tariff points are always used by institutions or that they can be substituted for an offer in grades. The level of an offer is not necessarily indicative of the quality of a course.

COURSE OFFERS INFORMATION

Subject requirements/preferences See **Engineering/Engineering Sciences**. Offers shown below refer to BEng or BSc courses unless otherwise stated.

Your target offers and examples of degree courses

160 pts **Cambridge** – A*A*A incl maths+phys (Civ Struct Env Eng) (IB 40–41 pts HL 776)
           Imperial London – A*A*A incl maths+phys (Civ Eng MEng) (IB 39 pts HL 7 maths 6 phys)
152 pts **Bath** – A*AA incl maths (Civ Archit Eng MEng; Civ Eng) (IB 36 pts HL 6 maths)
           Bristol – A*AA–AAA incl maths+sci (Civ Eng MEng; Civ Eng) (IB 38–36 pts HL 6 maths+sci)
           London (UCL) – A*AA–AAA (Eng (Civ)) (IB 39–38 pts)

Oxford – A*AA 152 pts (Civ Eng MEng) (IB 40 pts)

Southampton – A*AA incl mats+sci/geog (Civ Eng Archit MEng) (IB 36 pts HL 6 maths+sci); A*AA incl maths+sci (Civ Eng) (IB 36 pts HL 6 maths+sci); A*AA incl maths+sci/geog (Civ Eng MEng) (IB 36 pts HL 6 maths+sci)

144 pts **Birmingham** – AAA incl maths (Civ Eng MEng; Civ Ener Eng MEng) (IB 32 pts HL 666)

Brunel – AAA (Mech Eng Bld Serv MEng; Civ Eng MEng; Civ Eng Sust MEng) (IB 34 pts)

Cardiff – AAA incl maths (Archit Eng) (IB 36–32 pts HL 5 maths+sci); (Civ Eng; Civ Env Eng) (IB 36–32 pts)

City – 144 pts (Civ Eng Archit) (IB 30 pts HL maths); (Civ Eng MEng) (IB 32 pts)

Edinburgh – AAA–ABB incl maths (Civ Eng; Struct Eng Archit) (IB 37–32 pts)

Exeter – AAA–ABB incl maths+sci (Civ Eng MEng) (IB 36–32 pts HL 5 maths+sci)

Glasgow – AAA incl maths+phys (Civ Eng MEng) (IB 38–36 pts)

Leeds – AAA incl maths (Civ Env Eng) (IB 35 pts HL 5 maths)

Newcastle – AAA incl maths (Civ Eng MEng; Civ Struct Eng MEng) (IB 37 pts HL 6 maths)

Nottingham – AAA–AAB incl maths+sci/tech (Civ Eng) (IB 36–34 pts); AAA incl maths+sci/tech (Civ Eng MEng) (IB 36 pts)

Sheffield – AAA–AAB incl maths (Civ Struct Eng MEng; Civ Eng; Civ Eng Modn Lang) (IB 37 pts HL 6 maths)

136 pts **Birmingham** – AAB incl maths (Civ Eng) (IB 32 pts HL 665)

Coventry – AAB incl maths (Civ Eng MEng) (IB 31 pts)

Exeter – AAB–ABB incl maths+sci (Civ Eng) (IB 36–32 pts HL 5 maths+sci)

Glasgow – AAB–BBB incl maths+phys (Civ Eng Archit; Civ Eng) (IB 36–34 pts)

Liverpool – AAB incl maths (Civ Struct Eng MEng; Civ Eng MEng) (IB 35 pts HL 5 maths)

Manchester – AAB (Civ Eng) (IB 35 pts)

Newcastle – AAB incl maths (Mar Tech Off Eng MEng) (IB 36 pts HL 5 maths+phys); (Civ Surv Eng; Civ Struct Eng; Civ Eng) (IB 35 pts HL 6 maths)

Queen's Belfast – AAB incl maths+sci/tech (Civ Eng MEng; Env Civ Eng MEng; Struct Eng Archit MEng)

Surrey – AAB incl maths+sci/tech (Civ Eng) (IB 35 pts)

Warwick – AAB incl maths+phys (Civ Eng) (IB 36 pts HL 5 maths+phys)

128 pts **Aberdeen** – ABB incl maths+phys/des tech/eng (Civ Env Eng MEng; Civ Struct Eng MEng) (IB 34 pts HL 6 maths+phys)

Brunel – ABB (Civ Eng; Civ Eng Sust) (IB 31 pts)

City – 128 pts (Civ Eng) (IB 30 pts)

Liverpool – ABB incl maths (Civ Eng) (IB 33 pts HL 5 maths)

Liverpool John Moores – 128 pts (Civ Eng MEng) (IB 27 pts)

Loughborough – ABB incl maths (Civ Eng) (IB 34 pts HL 5 maths)

Strathclyde – ABB–BBB incl maths+phys/eng (Civ Eng) (IB 32 pts HL 5 maths+phys/eng)

Swansea – ABB–BBB incl maths (Civ Eng) (IB 32 pts)

120 pts **Aberdeen** – BBB incl maths+phys/des tech/eng (Civ Eng) (IB 32 pts HL 5 maths+phys)

Brighton – BBB incl maths (Civ Eng) (IB 30 pts HL 5 maths)

Coventry – BBB incl maths (Civ Eng) (IB 30 pts)

Dundee – BBB–BCC incl maths+sci/eng (Civ Eng) (IB 30 pts)

Greenwich – 120 pts (Civ Eng)

Heriot-Watt – ABC–BBB incl maths (Civ Eng) (IB 31 pts HL 5 maths); BBB incl maths (Civ Eng Int St) (IB 31 pts HL 5 maths)

Leeds Beckett – 120 pts (Civ Eng) (IB 26 pts)

Northumbria – 120 pts (Archit Eng) (IB 30 pts)

Queen's Belfast – BBB incl maths+sci/tech (Civ Eng)

112 pts **Bradford** – BBC 112 pts (Civ Struct Eng)

Central Lancashire – 112 pts (Fire Ldrshp St) (IB 25 pts)

Edinburgh Napier – BBC incl maths+sci (Civ Eng MEng) (IB 30 pts HL 5 maths+sci)

Glasgow Caledonian – BBC incl maths+phys (Env Civ Eng) (IB 24 pts)

Kingston – 112 pts (Civ Eng)

Plymouth – 112 pts incl maths (Civ Eng; Civ Cstl Eng) (IB 28 pts HL 5 maths)

Come along to a University Open Day to find out more:

www.leeds.ac.uk/openday

Ulster University

Building your future with Ulster University

in the School of the Built Environment

- Professional Accreditation

- Fees only **£6000** for GB students*

- Delivering career-focused education

- Campus situated only **15 MINUTES** from Belfast city centre

- One of the largest Universities in the Island of Ireland

- Top **SIX** UK Built Environment research University

- New Belfast city centre campus opening 2018

- Northern Ireland's capital **BELFAST** is the most affordable city for study in the UK

For more information visit:
study.ulster.ac.uk

*correct at time of print (2016/17)

BEng (Hons) / MEng (Hons) Civil Engineering and BSc (Hons) Civil Engineering (Geo)

Would you like a career that leaves a legacy for years to come, in addition to meeting the needs of the current generation? Civil Engineering links old with new. The second oldest engineering discipline influences the environment for future generations, encompassing all elements of infrastructure, from building structures, through roads, drainage, tunnels and sea defences. Innovation and practical solutions are combined to produce sustainable outcomes. Civil Engineering allows you to work on numerous projects throughout your career each requiring a different solution so you will never be bored.

The well-established Civil Engineering degrees at Ulster University are ranked 9 in the UK in the Guardian League tables for Civil Engineering 2016. High levels of student satisfaction saw the courses joint top of the national student league tables in the UK for Civil Engineering in 2014-2015. The Guardian League tables for Civil Engineering show the highest levels of Student Satisfaction with the teaching element – 96% satisfied.

The courses are well established and have high employment. The MEng (Hons) Civil Engineering has had 100% employment since it commenced and produces graduates that have all the academic background needed for the highest level within the industry – Chartered Status.

The BEng (Hons) and BSc (Hons) Civil Engineering courses are also close to 100% employment or further learning. These courses can be topped up to the academic learning required for Chartered Status within the industry via the MSc Infrastructure Engineering.

In addition to enabling students to benefit from well tested theories and technologies, the courses include an introduction to Building Information Modelling and other current developments. The courses have just received admission to the CDIO (Conceive - Design - Implement - Operate) educational framework. The course has invited lecturers from industry and includes industrial placement (for 1 year). It integrates the core themes required for accreditation by the Joint Board of Moderators: Design, Sustainability, Management, Health and Safety and Analysis. This accreditation allows the degree to be recognised in 17 different countries through the Washington Accord.

Research informed teaching applies throughout the course. The Highways laboratory is one of the best in the UK with clients such as Red Bull Racing, DRD and the Highways Agency. The Fire Laboratory is the second biggest in the UK. Experimental data for creation of the Euro codes for Castellated Beams in Fire was produced on site. Depending on the selection of optional modules students can benefit from these facilities.

Students can also apply for Incorporated Engineer status within the industry. There is currently a shortfall in the number of engineers graduating and those required, ranking Civil Engineering second in the skills deficit for Northern Ireland, so high employment levels are set to continue.

Ulster
University

Building your future with Ulster University

in the School of the Built Environment

- Professional Accreditation

- Fees only **£6000** for GB students*

- Delivering career-focused education

- Campus situated only **15 MINUTES** from Belfast city centre

- One of the largest Universities in the Island of Ireland

- Top **SIX** UK Built Environment research University

- New Belfast city centre campus opening 2018

- Northern Ireland's capital **BELFAST** is the most affordable city for study in the UK

For more information visit:
study.ulster.ac.uk

*correct at time of print (2016/17)

BEng (Hons) / MEng Safety Engineering and Disaster Management

Would you like a career as a professional engineer providing a leadership role in the design of highly creative technological solutions for the delivery of complex engineering projects and humanitarian relief responses? Are you keen to apply science and technology to solve real world problems?

If you want to save lives and make a meaningful difference in the world, then this is the course for you. Come and study Safety Engineering and Disaster Management at Ulster.

Through this course you will develop a full understanding of your ethical role in terms of designing critical solutions to highly sophisticated problems with the primary aim of preserving or improving human life. The two key focal points of the course, safety engineering and disaster management, intertwine perfectly to educate and prepare you for roles within industry. This new and innovative BEng (Hons) / MEng degree combines the professional engineering discipline of Safety Engineering with Disaster Management. Increasing concerns over climate change and energy security, the resultant new technologies, and the growing threat of natural and manmade disasters mean that today's engineers face a new set of challenges. This degree will equip you with specialist skills to design structures and systems to withstand potential disasters

in the natural and the built environment. The nature of disasters may include those caused by extreme weather such as flooding, forest fires or earthquakes, or industrial incidents including chemical, biological, radiological and nuclear.

This course transcends industrial sectors and as such you will be employable across a wide range of industries as varied as nuclear and renewable energies, oil and gas, pharmaceutical, manufacturing, international aid agencies, engineering consultancies, governmental emergency response roles, and disaster and crisis management arenas. Job opportunities are vast on the global stage as the nature of the role applies to most business sectors. A one year industrial placement is an integral component of this degree course.

Engineers have the skills to help people and communities most in need and in the face of adversity. As a student on this course you will learn to recognise the hazards and modes of failure of a system or structure, and you will learn how to plan for emergencies and provide solutions in the event of a disaster. As a graduate from this course you will have engineering skills that can be used where human benefit is the primary concern.

If you have an eye for innovation, a creative mind and a passion for compassion; if you have an educational background mix of science, technology, mathematics and geography and ultimately a desire to make a meaningful difference in the world then this course will appeal to you.

Teesside – BBC incl maths (Civ Eng; Civ Eng Disas Mgt)

UWE Bristol – 112 pts incl maths (Civ Env Eng) (IB 25 pts HL 5 maths)

West London – 112 pts incl maths/phys (Civ Env Eng)

108 pts **Liverpool John Moores** – 108 pts incl maths/sci (Bld Serv Eng) (IB 25 pts HL 5 maths); 108 pts (Civ Eng)

Portsmouth – 108–120 pts incl maths (Civ Eng) (IB 26 pts HL 10 pts incl maths)

Ulster – 108 pts incl maths+sci/tech (Civ Eng) (IB 25 pts)

104 pts **Bolton** – 104 pts incl maths (Civ Eng)

Coventry – BCC incl maths/sci/tech/eng (Civ Eng BSc) (IB 29 pts)

London South Bank – BCC/BB 104–80 pts (Civ Eng)

Nottingham Trent – 104–120 pts (Civ Eng BSc/BEng)

Salford – 104–112 pts incl maths+phys/des tech (Civ Eng) (IB 30 pts)

South Wales – BCC incl maths+sci (Civ Eng) (IB 29 pts HL 5 maths+sci)

West Scotland – BCC incl maths+sci (Civ Eng) (IB 24 pts)

96 pts **Abertay** – CCC incl sci (Civ Env Eng) (IB 28 pts)

Derby – 96 pts (Civ Eng)

East London – 96 pts incl maths (Civ Eng) (IB 27 pts); 96 pts (Surv Map Sci) (IB 24 pts)

Edinburgh Napier – CCC incl maths+sci (Civ Eng; Civ Trans Eng) (IB 27 pts HL 5 maths+sci)

Ulster – 96 pts incl sci/tech (Civ Eng (Geoinform)) (IB 24 pts)

92 pts **Wolverhampton** – 92 pts incl maths (Civ Eng)

80 pts **Anglia Ruskin** – 80 pts (Civ Eng) (IB 24 pts)

72 pts **Trinity Saint David** – 72 pts (Civ Eng Env Mgt)

Alternative offers

See **Chapter 6** and **Appendix 1** for grades/new UCAS Tariff points information for other examinations.

EXAMPLES OF COLLEGES OFFERING COURSES IN THIS SUBJECT FIELD

Birmingham Met (Coll); Blackburn (Coll); Bolton (Coll); Bradford (Coll); Chelmsford (Coll); Chesterfield (Coll); Exeter (Coll); Guildford (Coll); Lakes (Coll); Leeds Building (Coll); Lincoln (Coll); London UCK (Coll); Mid-Kent (Coll); Moulton (Coll); Norwich City (Coll); Plymouth City (Coll); Sheffield (Coll); Somerset (Coll); South Cheshire (Coll); South Devon (Coll); South Leicestershire (Coll); Wakefield (Coll); Wigan and Leigh (Coll).

CHOOSING YOUR COURSE (SEE ALSO CH.1)

Universities and colleges teaching quality See www.qaa.ac.uk; http://unistats.direct.gov.uk.

Top research universities and colleges (REF 2014) (Civil and Construction Engineering) Cardiff; Imperial London; Sheffield; Manchester; Dundee.

Examples of sandwich degree courses Bath; Bradford; Brighton; Cardiff; City; Coventry; East London; Kingston; Liverpool John Moores; London South Bank; Loughborough; Nottingham Trent; Plymouth; Portsmouth; Queen's Belfast; Salford; Surrey; Teesside; Ulster; UWE Bristol; West Scotland; Wolverhampton.

ADMISSIONS INFORMATION

Number of applicants per place (approx) Abertay 8; Bath 7; Birmingham 11; Bradford 5; Bristol 8; Brunel 4; Cardiff 5; City 11; Coventry 10, (Civ Eng) 11; Dundee 5; Durham 6; Edinburgh Napier 4; Glasgow Caledonian 4; Greenwich 11; Heriot-Watt 7; Imperial London 4; Kingston 8; Leeds 10; Liverpool John Moores 16; London (UCL) 7; London South Bank 5; Loughborough 6; Newcastle 11, (Off Eng) 9; Nottingham 6; Nottingham Trent 11; Plymouth 3; Portsmouth 3; Queen's Belfast 6; Salford 5; Sheffield 7; South Wales 6; Southampton 10; Strathclyde 4; Surrey 5; Swansea 3; Teesside 6; West Scotland 4; Wolverhampton 3.

Advice to applicants and planning the UCAS personal statement See **Engineering/Engineering Sciences**. Also read the magazine *The New Civil Engineer* and discuss articles which interest you on your application. See also **Appendix 3**. **Bristol** Deferred entry accepted.

New UCAS points Tariff: A* = 56 pts; A = 48 pts; B = 40 pts; C = 32 pts; D = 24 pts; E = 16 pts

Selection interviews Yes Bath, Birmingham, Brighton, Bristol, Cambridge, Coventry, Edinburgh Napier, Greenwich, Heriot-Watt, Imperial London, Kingston, Leeds, London (UCL), Loughborough, Newcastle, Oxford, Salford, Surrey, Warwick; **Some** Anglia Ruskin, Cardiff, Dundee, Nottingham Trent, Southampton; **No** Nottingham.

Interview advice and questions Past questions have included: Why have you chosen Civil Engineering? Have you contacted the Institution of Civil Engineers/Institution of Structural Engineers? How would you define the difference between the work of a civil engineer and the work of an architect? What would happen to a concrete beam if a load were applied? Where would it break and how could it be strengthened? The favourite question: Why do you want to be a civil engineer? What would you do if you were asked to build a concrete boat? Do you know any civil engineers? What problems were faced in building the Channel Tunnel? See also **Chapter 5**. **Cambridge** Why did they make mill chimneys so tall?

Reasons for rejection (non-academic) Lack of vitality. Lack of interest in buildings, the built environment or in civil engineering. Poor communication skills. See also **Engineering/Engineering Sciences**.

AFTER-RESULTS ADVICE
Offers to applicants repeating A-levels Higher East London, Kingston, Liverpool John Moores, Nottingham, Queen's Belfast, Teesside, Warwick; **Possibly higher** Portsmouth, Southampton; **Same** Abertay, Bath, Birmingham, Bradford, Brighton, Bristol, Cardiff, City, Coventry, Dundee, Durham, Greenwich, Heriot-Watt, Leeds, London (UCL), London South Bank, Loughborough, Newcastle, Nottingham Trent, Salford, Sheffield, Wolverhampton; **No** Cambridge.

GRADUATE DESTINATIONS AND EMPLOYMENT (2013/14 HESA)
Graduates surveyed 2,845 **Employed** 1,965 **In voluntary employment** 35 **In further study** 465 **Assumed unemployed** 145

Career note The many aspects of this subject will provide career directions for graduates with many openings with local authorities and commercial organisations.

OTHER DEGREE SUBJECTS FOR CONSIDERATION
Architecture; Building; Surveying; Town and Country Planning.

ENGINEERING (COMMUNICATIONS)

(including **Mobile Communications**; see also **Communication Studies/Communication, Engineering (Electrical and Electronic)**)

Communications engineering impacts on many aspects of the engineering and business world. Courses overlap considerably with Electronic, Computer, Digital, Media and Internet Engineering and provide graduates with expertise in such fields as telecommunications, mobile communications and microwave engineering, optoelectronics, radio engineering and internet technology. Sandwich courses and sponsorships are offered by several universities.

Engineering Council statement See **Engineering/Engineering Sciences**.

Useful websites See **Computer Courses** and **Engineering (Electrical and Electronic)**.

NB The points totals shown to the left of the institutions are for ease of reference only. It must not be assumed that Tariff points are always used by institutions or that they can be substituted for an offer in grades. The level of an offer is not necessarily indicative of the quality of a course.

COURSE OFFERS INFORMATION
Subject requirements/preferences See **Engineering/Engineering Sciences**. Offers shown below refer to BEng or BSc courses unless otherwise stated.

Your target offers and examples of degree courses

152 pts **Southampton** – A*AA incl maths+phys (Electron Eng Wrlss Comms MEng) (IB 38 pts)

144 pts **Bath** – AAA incl maths+sci/tech (Comp Sys Eng MEng; Electron Comm Eng MEng) (IB 36 pts HL 6 maths+sci/tech)

Bristol – AAA–AAB incl maths (Electron Comms Eng; Electron Comms Eng MEng) (IB 36–34 pts HL 6 maths)

Brunel – AAA–AAB (Electron Comms Eng MEng) (IB 34 pts)

Edinburgh – AAA–ABB incl maths (Electron Elec Eng Mgt) (IB 37–32 pts)

Newcastle – AAA incl maths+phys/chem (Electron Comms MEng (Yr Abrd)) (IB 37 pts HL 5 maths+phys/chem)

Nottingham – AAA–ABB incl maths+sci/electron (Electron Comms Eng) (IB 36–32 pts)

York – AAA incl maths+sci (Electron Comm Eng MEng) (IB 36–32 pts HL 5/6 maths+phys)

136 pts **Aston** – AAB–ABB (Bus Comp IT) (IB 35–34 pts)

Bath – AAB incl maths+sci/tech (Electron Comm Eng) (IB 35 pts HL 6 maths/phys); (Comp Sys Eng) (IB 35 pts HL 6 maths+sci/tech)

Newcastle – AAB incl maths+phys/chem (Electron Comms) (IB 35 pts HL 5 maths+phys/chem)

Sheffield – AAB–ABB incl maths+sci/electron (Electron Comms Eng MEng) (IB 35 pts HL 6 maths+sci/electron)

128 pts **Essex** – ABB–BBB incl maths (Telecomm Eng) (IB 32–30 pts HL 5 maths)

Kent – ABB incl maths+sci/tech (Electron Comms Eng MEng) (IB 34 pts)

Leicester – ABB–AAB incl maths+sci (Comms Electron Eng MEng) (IB 30–32 pts)

London (QM) – ABB incl maths (Electron Eng Telecomm) (IB 32 pts HL 5 maths)

Sheffield – ABB incl maths+sci/electron (Electron Comms Eng) (IB 34 pts HL 6 maths+sci/electron)

York – ABB incl maths+sci (Electron Comm Eng) (IB 36–32 pts HL 5/6 maths+phys)

120 pts **Aberdeen** – BBB incl maths/sci IB 32 pts (Bus Mgt Inf Sys)

Aston – BBB–ABB incl maths+phys (Comms Eng) (IB 32 pts HL maths+phys)

Brunel – BBB (Bus Comp) (IB 30 pts)

Buckingham – BBB–BBC (Bus Mgt App Comp)

City – 120 pts (Telecomm) (IB 32 pts)

Heriot-Watt – BBB (Inf Sys courses) (IB 28 pts)

Huddersfield – BBB incl maths+sci/tech 120 pts (Electron Comm Eng)

Kent – BBB maths+sci/tech (Electron Comms Eng) (IB 34 pts)

Leicester – BBB incl maths+sci (Comms Electron Eng) (IB 28 pts)

112 pts **Birmingham City** – BBC incl maths+sci/tech/comp 112 pts (Electron Eng (Telecomm)) (IB 30 pts HL 5 maths); BBC 112 pts (Bus IT) (IB 30 pts)

Bradford – BBC 112 pts (Bus Comp)

Brighton – BBC incl sci/maths (Comp Sys Comms) (IB 28 pts); BBC (Bus Inf Sys) (IB 28 pts)

Kingston – 112 pts (Comp Sci (Net Comms))

London South Bank – BBC 112 pts (Telecomm Eng)

Nottingham Trent – 112 pts incl IT/sci (Inf Sys; ICT)

Westminster – BBC–AA (Bus Inf Sys) (IB 26 pts)

104 pts **Bournemouth** – 104–120 pts (Bus IT) (IB 28–30 pts)

De Montfort – 104 pts (ICT) (IB 28 pts)

Hertfordshire – 104 pts incl maths+phys/tech/eng (Dig Comms Electron) (IB 26 pts)

Liverpool Hope – BCC–BBB 104–120 pts (IT)

Manchester Met – 104–112 pts (Inf Comms) (IB 26 pts)

Northampton – 104–120 pts (Comp (Comp Net Eng))

South Wales – BCC (ICT) (IB 29 pts)

Wolverhampton – 104 pts incl maths+sci/tech (Electron Telecomm Eng (MEng))

96 pts **Cardiff Met** – 96 pts (Bus Inf Sys)

Edinburgh Napier – CCC (Inf Tech Mgt) (IB 27 pts)

Middlesex – 96 pts (Bus Inf Sys; Mob Sys Comm Eng)

New UCAS points Tariff: A* = 56 pts; A = 48 pts; B = 40 pts; C = 32 pts; D = 24 pts; E = 16 pts

88 pts   **Anglia Ruskin** – 88 pts (Bus Inf Sys) (IB 24 pts)
       London Met – 88 pts incl maths (Electron Comms Eng)
       Southampton Solent – 88 pts (Bus IT)
80 pts   **Bangor** – 80 pts (Comp Inf Sys)
       Bedfordshire – 80 pts (Inf Sys; Telecomm Net Eng; Bus Inf Sys) (IB 24 pts)

Alternative offers
See **Chapter 6** and **Appendix 1** for grades/new UCAS Tariff points information for other examinations.

EXAMPLES OF COLLEGES OFFERING COURSES IN THIS SUBJECT FIELD
Barking and Dagenham (Coll); Birmingham Met (Coll); Blackpool and Fylde (Coll); Bromley (CFHE); Cornwall (Coll); Plymouth.

CHOOSING YOUR COURSE (SEE ALSO CH.1)
Universities and colleges teaching quality See www.qaa.ac.uk; http://unistats.direct.gov.uk.

Examples of sandwich degree courses Aston; Bath; Bradford; Brunel; Kent; Kingston; Manchester Met; Portsmouth; Wolverhampton; York.

ADMISSIONS INFORMATION
Number of applicants per place (approx) Bath 10; Birmingham 10; Bradford 9; Bristol 2; Coventry 7; Hull 8; London Met 5; London South Bank 3; York 8 av.

Advice to applicants and planning the UCAS personal statement See **Engineering (Electrical and Electronic)** and **Appendix 3**.

Selection interviews Yes Bradford, Bristol, Hertfordshire, Kent, London Met.

Interview advice and questions See **Engineering (Electrical and Electronic)**.

Reasons for rejection (non-academic) See **Engineering (Electrical and Electronic)**.

GRADUATE DESTINATIONS AND EMPLOYMENT (2013/14 HESA)
See **Engineering (Electrical and Electronic)** and **Engineering/Engineering Sciences**.

Career note Many commercial organisations offer opportunities in the specialist areas described at the top of this table. Work placements and sandwich courses have, in the past, resulted in over 60% of graduates gaining employment with their firms.

OTHER DEGREE SUBJECTS FOR CONSIDERATION
Computer Science; Engineering (Computer, Control, Electrical, Electronic, Systems); Physics.

ENGINEERING (COMPUTER, CONTROL, SOFTWARE and SYSTEMS)

The design and application of modern computer systems is fundamental to a wide range of disciplines which also include electronic, software and computer-aided engineering. Most courses give priority to reinforcing the essential transferable skills consisting of management techniques, leadership skills, literacy, presentation skills, business skills and time management. At many universities Computer Engineering is offered as part of a range of Electronics degree programmes where the first and even the second year courses are common to all students, who then choose to specialise later. A year in industry is a common feature of many of these courses.

Engineering Council statement See **Engineering/Engineering Sciences**.

Useful websites See **Computer Courses** and **Engineering/Engineering Sciences**.

NB The points totals shown to the left of the institutions are for ease of reference only. It must not be assumed that Tariff points are always used by institutions or that they can be substituted for an offer in grades. The level of an offer is not necessarily indicative of the quality of a course.

COURSE OFFERS INFORMATION

Subject requirements/preferences See **Engineering/Engineering Sciences**. Offers shown below refer to BEng or BSc courses unless otherwise stated.

Your target offers and examples of degree courses

160 pts Cambridge – A*A*A incl maths+sci (Eng (Inf Comp Eng)) (IB 40–41 pts HL 776)
Oxford – A*A*A incl maths+phys (Inf Eng) (IB 40 pts)

152 pts Birmingham – A*AA incl maths/comp (Comp Sci/Soft Eng MEng) (IB 32 pts HL 766)
Imperial London – A*AA incl maths+phys (Electron Inf Eng) (IB 38 pts HL 6 maths+phys); A*AA incl maths (Comp (Soft Eng) MEng); A*AA incl maths 152 pts (Electron Inf Eng (St Abrd)) (IB 38 pts HL 6 maths+phys)

144 pts Bath – AAA incl maths+sci/tech (Comp Sys Eng MEng) (IB 36 pts HL 6 maths+sci/tech)
Brunel – AAA–AAB (Electron Comp Eng MEng; Comp Sys Eng MEng) (IB 34 pts)
Edinburgh – AAA–ABB incl maths (Electron Comp Sci MEng; Electron Soft Eng MEng) (IB 37–32 pts)
Loughborough – AAA incl maths+sci (Electron Comp Sys Eng) (IB 37 pts HL 5 maths+sci)
Manchester – AAA (Comp Sys Eng) (IB 37 pts)
Southampton – AAA incl maths 144 pts (Soft Eng) (IB 37 pts HL 18 pts)
Warwick – AAA incl maths (Comp Sys Eng) (IB 38 pts HL 6 maths)

136 pts Aberystwyth – 136 pts (Soft Eng MEng)
Bath – AAB incl maths+sci/tech (Comp Sys Eng) (IB 35 pts HL 6 maths+sci/tech)
Cardiff – AAB–ABB (App Soft Eng) (33 pts)
Glasgow – AAB–BBB incl maths (Electron Soft Eng) (IB 36–34 pts)
Greenwich – 136 pts (Soft Eng)
Liverpool – AAB incl maths (Soft Dev) (IB 35 pts HL 5 maths)
Loughborough – AAB (Electron Comp Sys Eng MEng; Sys Eng MEng) (IB 36–34 pts)
Newcastle – AAB incl maths+phys/chem (Electron Comp Eng) (IB 35 pts HL 5 maths+phys/chem)
Sheffield – AAB 136 pts (Comp Sys Eng) (IB 35 pts); AAB–ABB incl maths+sci (Sys Contr Eng; Sys Contr Eng (Eng Mgt); Mecha Robot Eng) (IB 35 pts HL 6 maths+sci)
Strathclyde – AAB–BBB incl maths+phys (Comp Electron Sys MEng) (IB 36 pts HL 6 maths+phys)
York – AAB–ABB incl maths (Comp Sci Embd Sys Eng) (IB 35–34 pts HL 6 maths)

128 pts Brunel – ABB–BBB (Comp Sys Eng courses) (IB 31 pts)
Central Lancashire – 128 pts incl maths+phys (Comp Aid Eng MEng) (IB 31 pts)
East Anglia – ABB (Comp Sys Eng; Comp Sys Eng (Yr Ind)) (IB 32 pts)
Essex – ABB–BBB (Comp Electron; Comp Sys Eng; Comp Net) (IB 32–30 pts)
Leicester – ABB–AAB incl maths+sci (Soft Electron Eng MEng) (IB 30–32 pts)
Liverpool – ABB incl maths+sci/tech (Comp Sci Electron Eng; Avion Sys) (IB 33 pts HL 5 maths+phys/electron); (Comp Sci Electron Eng MEng; Avion Sys MEng) (IB 33 pts HL 5 maths+sci)
London (RH) – ABB incl maths/phys/comp (Comp Sci Soft Eng) (IB 32 pts)
Loughborough – ABB incl maths+sci (Sys Eng) (IB 34 pts HL 5 maths+sci)
Northumbria – 128 pts (Comp Net Cy Scrty) (IB 31 pts)
Queen's Belfast – AAB–AAA incl sci/maths/tech (Soft Eng MEng)
Strathclyde – ABB–BBB (Comp Electron Sys) (IB 32 pts HL 6 maths+phys/eng); ABB–BBB incl maths (Soft Eng) (IB 34 pts HL 6 maths)
Sussex – ABB–BBB incl maths (Comp Eng) (IB 34–32 pts HL 5 maths)
UWE Bristol – 128 pts (Comp Sys Integ) (IB 27 pts)

120 pts Aberdeen – BBB (Electron Comp Eng) (IB 30 pts)
Bangor – 120–128 pts incl phys+maths (Comp Sys Eng MEng)

Bradford – BBB 120 pts (Soft Eng)

Brunel – BBB incl mus (Snc Arts) (IB 30 pts); BBB (Gms Des; Comp Sci (Soft Eng); Gms Des Film TV St) (IB 30 pts)

City – 120 pts (Comp Sys Eng) (IB 32 pts)

Heriot-Watt – BBB incl maths+phys/tech (Comp Electron) (IB 29 pts HL maths+phys)

Huddersfield – BBB incl maths+sci/tech 120 pts (Comp Sys Eng)

Kent – BBB incl maths+sci/tech (Comp Sys Eng) (IB 34 pts)

Leicester – BBB incl maths+sci (Soft Electron Eng) (IB 28 pts)

Nottingham Trent – 120 pts incl IT/maths/sci (Soft Eng)

Plymouth – 120 pts (Comp Sys Net) (IB 30 pts)

Stirling – BBB (Soft Eng) (IB 32 pts)

Teesside – BBB incl maths+phys (Instr Contr Eng MEng)

Ulster – BBC incl sci/maths/tech 120 pts (Comp Eng) (IB 26 pts)

112 pts **Aberystwyth** – 112 pts incl maths+phys/comp (Spc Sci Robot); 112 pts (Soft Eng)

Central Lancashire – 112 pts incl maths/phys (Comp Aid Eng) (IB 28 pts)

Coventry – BBC incl maths+sci/tech/eng (Comp Hard Soft Eng) (IB 29 pts)

De Montfort – 112 pts (Soft Eng) (IB 28 pts)

Greenwich – 112 pts (Comp Eng)

Hertfordshire – 112 pts (Soft Dev Bus) (IB 28 pts)

Hull – 112 pts (Comp Sci (Soft Eng)) (IB 28 pts)

Kingston – 112 pts (Gms Tech; Soft Eng)

London South Bank – BBC 112 pts (Comp Sys Net)

Nottingham Trent – 112 pts incl IT/maths/sci (Comp Sys Eng)

Sheffield Hallam – 112 pts (Comp Sys Eng; Gms Soft Dev)

Staffordshire – BBC/CCCc 112 pts (Soft Eng); 112 pts (Comp Gms Prog)

Sunderland – 112 pts (Gms Soft Dev)

Teesside – BBC incl maths+phys (Instr Contr Eng)

Westminster – BBC-AA (Comp Sys Eng) (IB 28 pts)

104 pts **Bournemouth** – 104–120 pts (Soft Eng) (IB 28–30 pts)

Hertfordshire – 104 pts incl maths+phys/tech/eng (Dig Sys Comp Eng) (IB 26 pts)

Liverpool John Moores – 104 pts (Soft Eng) (IB 24 pts)

Manchester Met – BCC–BBC 104–112 pts (Soft Eng) (IB 28 pts)

Northampton – 104–120 pts (Comp (Comp Sys Eng))

96 pts **Bangor** – 96–104 pts incl maths+phys (Comp Sys Eng)

Cardiff Met – 96 pts (Soft Eng)

Edinburgh Napier – CCC (Comp Sys Net) (IB 26 pts)

Glasgow Caledonian – CCC incl maths+phys (Comp Aided Mech Eng) (IB 24 pts)

Middlesex – 96 pts (Comp Comm Net)

Portsmouth – 96–112 pts incl maths+sci/tech (Comp Eng) (IB 26 pts HL 10 pts incl maths+sci/tech)

Sheffield Hallam – 96 pts (Soft Eng)

88 pts **London Met** – 88 pts (Comp Sys Eng)

Trinity Saint David – 88 pts (Soft Eng)

Wolverhampton – 88 pts (Comp Sys Eng); 88–104 pts (Comp Sci (Soft Eng))

80 pts **Bedfordshire** – 80 pts (Comp Sys Eng; Comp Sci Soft Eng) (IB 24 pts)

Bucks New – 80–96 pts (Soft Eng)

Southampton Solent – 80 pts (Comp Sys Net; Net Scrty Mgt)

Trinity Saint David – 80 pts (Comp Sys Electron)

Alternative offers

See **Chapter 6** and **Appendix 1** for grades/new UCAS Tariff points information for other examinations.

EXAMPLES OF COLLEGES OFFERING COURSES IN THIS SUBJECT FIELD

Accrington and Rossendale (Coll); Barking and Dagenham (Coll); Barnfield (Coll); Birmingham Met (Coll); Blackburn (Coll); Blackpool and Fylde (Coll); Bristol City (Coll); Bromley (CFHE); Cornwall (Coll); Doncaster (Coll); Farnborough (CT); Gateshead (Coll); Highbury Portsmouth (Coll); Manchester (Coll); Newcastle (Coll); North Lindsey (Coll); Nottingham New (Coll); SAE Inst; Somerset (Coll); Tyne Met (Coll).

CHOOSING YOUR COURSE (SEE ALSO CH.1)

Universities and colleges teaching quality See www.qaa.ac.uk; http://unistats.direct.gov.uk.

Top research universities and colleges (REF 2014) See **Computer Courses**.

Examples of sandwich degree courses Aberystwyth; Bath; Bradford; Brunel; Cardiff; City; Greenwich; Huddersfield; Kent; London South Bank; Loughborough; Manchester; Manchester Met; Northumbria; Nottingham Trent; Plymouth; Portsmouth; Reading; Sheffield Hallam; South Wales; UWE Bristol; Westminster; York.

ADMISSIONS INFORMATION

Number of applicants per place (approx) Bath 10; Birmingham 9; Bournemouth 3; Cardiff 6; Central Lancashire 12; Coventry 2; East Anglia 4; Edinburgh 3; Huddersfield 2; Imperial London 5; Kent 5; Lancaster 12; Liverpool John Moores 2; London South Bank 3; Loughborough 17; Sheffield 10; Sheffield Hallam 8; Southampton 4; Staffordshire 5; Stirling 7; Strathclyde 7; Teesside 3; Trinity Saint David 4; UWE Bristol 12; Westminster 5; York 3 av.

Advice to applicants and planning the UCAS personal statement See **Computer Courses**, **Engineering (Electrical and Electronic)** and **Appendix 3**.

Selection interviews Yes Bradford, Cambridge, East Anglia, Hertfordshire, Huddersfield, Kent, Manchester, Nottingham Trent, Sheffield Hallam, Trinity Saint David, Westminster; **Some** Loughborough; **No** Bath, Cardiff, Liverpool John Moores, Reading.

Interview advice and questions See **Computer Courses**, **Engineering (Electrical and Electronic)** and **Chapter 5**.

Reasons for rejection (non-academic) Lack of understanding that the course involves engineering. See also **Computer Courses** and **Engineering (Electrical and Electronic)**.

AFTER-RESULTS ADVICE

Offers to applicants repeating A-levels Higher Strathclyde, Warwick, York; **Possibly higher** City, Huddersfield, Sheffield; **Same** Bath, Birmingham, Coventry, East Anglia, Lancaster, Liverpool John Moores, London South Bank, Loughborough, Teesside; **No** Cambridge.

GRADUATE DESTINATIONS AND EMPLOYMENT (2013/14 HESA)

Software Engineering graduates surveyed 750 **Employed** 445 **In voluntary employment** 10 **In further study** 100 **Assumed unemployed** 85

Career note Career opportunities extend right across the whole field of electronics, telecommunications, control and systems engineering.

OTHER DEGREE SUBJECTS FOR CONSIDERATION

Computer Science; Computing; Engineering (Aeronautical, Aerospace, Communications, Electrical and Electronic); Mathematics; Media (Systems/Engineering/Technology); Physics.

ENGINEERING (ELECTRICAL and ELECTRONIC)

(see also **Engineering (Acoustics and Sound), Engineering (Aeronautical and Aerospace), Engineering (Communications))**

Electrical and Electronic Engineering courses provide a sound foundation for those looking for a career in electricity generation and transmission, communications or control systems, including robotics. All courses cater for students wanting a general or more specialist engineering education and options should be considered when choosing degree courses. These could include optoelectronics and optical communication systems, microwave systems, radio frequency engineering and circuit technology. Many courses have common first years, allowing transfer in Year 2. Courses in electronic engineering also overlap closely with information technology and information systems engineering which involves electronic and digital information covering the internet and mobile phones. Most institutions have good industrial contacts and applicants should look closely at sandwich courses.

Engineering Council statement See **Engineering/Engineering Sciences**.

Useful websites www.theiet.org; www.engc.org.uk

NB The points totals shown to the left of the institutions are for ease of reference only. It must not be assumed that Tariff points are always used by institutions or that they can be substituted for an offer in grades. The level of an offer is not necessarily indicative of the quality of a course.

COURSE OFFERS INFORMATION

Subject requirements/preferences See **Engineering/Engineering Sciences**. Offers shown below refer to BEng or BSc courses unless otherwise stated.

Your target offers and examples of degree courses

160 pts **Cambridge** – A*A*A incl maths+phys (Eng (Elec Inf Sci/Elec Electron Eng)) (IB 40–41 pts HL 776)

Oxford – A*A*A incl maths+phys (Elec Eng Sci) (IB 40 pts)

152 pts **Imperial London** – A*AA incl maths+phys (Elec Electron Eng MEng; Elec Electron Eng Mgt MEng; Electron Inf Eng) (IB 38 pts HL 6 maths+phys); A*AA incl maths 152 pts (Electron Inf Eng (St Abrd)) (IB 38 pts HL 6 maths+phys)

Southampton – A*AA incl maths+phys (Electron Eng Comp Sys MEng; Electron Eng Artif Intel MEng; Electron Eng Nanotech MEng; Electron Eng Mbl Scr Sys MEng; Electron Eng Wrlss Comms MEng) (IB 38 pts)

Surrey – A*AA–AAA incl maths+phys/electron (Electron Eng Comp Sys MEng; Electron Eng MEng) (IB 38–36 pts)

144 pts **Bath** – AAA incl maths+sci/tech (Elec Electron Eng MEng; Electron Comm Eng MEng; Elec Pwr Eng MEng) (IB 36 pts HL 6 maths+sci/tech)

Bristol – AAA–AAB incl maths (Elec Electron Eng; Electron Comms Eng; Electron Comms Eng MEng) (IB 36–34 pts HL 6 maths)

Brunel – AAA–AAB (Electron Comp Eng MEng; Electron Elec Eng MEng) (IB 34 pts)

City – 144 pts (Elec Electron Eng MEng) (IB 35 pts)

Edinburgh – AAA–ABB (Elec Eng Renew Ener; Elec Mech Eng) (IB 37–32 pts); AAA–ABB incl maths (Electron; Electron Elec Eng; Electron Elec Eng Mgt; Electron Soft Eng MEng) (IB 37–32 pts)

Exeter – AAA–ABB incl maths+sci (Electron Eng Comp Sci) (IB 36–32 pts HL 5 maths+sci)

Glasgow – AAA 144 pts (Electron Mus MEng) (IB 36–38 pts); AAA incl maths+phys (Electron Elec Eng MEng) (IB 38–36 pts)

Lancaster – AAA incl maths+sci (Electron Elec Eng MEng) (IB 36 pts HL 6 maths+sci)

Leeds – AAA incl maths (Electron Eng) (IB 35 pts HL 5 maths); (Electron Elec Eng) (IB 35 pts HL 5 maths)

London (UCL) – AAA incl maths+phys/fmaths (Eng (Electron Elec)) (IB 38 pts HL 5 maths)

Loughborough – AAA incl maths+sci (Electron Comp Sys Eng) (IB 37 pts HL 5 maths+sci); (Electron Elec Eng MEng) (IB 37 pts HL 6 maths+sci)

Manchester – AAA (Comp Sys Eng) (IB 37 pts)

Newcastle – AAA incl maths+phys/chem (Electron Comms MEng (Yr Abrd)) (IB 37 pts HL 5 maths+phys/chem)

Nottingham – AAA-ABB incl maths+sci/electron (Electron Comms Eng; Electron Eng; Elec Electron Eng; Electron Comp Eng; Elec Eng) (IB 36-32 pts); AAA-ABB 144-128 pts (Elec Eng Renew Ener Sys) (IB 32-36 pts)

Sheffield – AAA-AAB incl maths/phys/chem (Electron Elec Eng Modn Lang MEng) (IB 37 pts HL 6 maths/phys/chem)

Southampton – AAA incl maths+phys (Electron Eng) (IB 36 pts)

Surrey – AAA-AAB incl maths+phys/electron (Electron Eng; Electron Eng Comp Sys) (IB 36-35 pts)

York – AAA incl maths+sci (Electron Eng MEng; Electron Eng Nanotech MEng; Electron Comm Eng MEng) (IB 36-32 pts HL 5/6 maths+phys)

136 pts **Aston** – AAB-AAA incl maths+phys (Elec Electron Eng MEng) (IB 34 pts HL 6 maths+phys)

Bath – AAB incl maths/phys+sci/tech (Elec Electron Eng) (IB 35 pts HL 6 maths+sci/tech); AAB incl maths+sci/tech (Electron Comm Eng; Electron Eng Spc Sci Tech) (IB 35 pts HL 6 maths/phys); (Elec Pwr Eng) (IB 36 pts HL 6 maths+sci/tech)

Birmingham – AAB incl maths (Electron Eng Bus Mgt; Elec Ener Eng; Electron Elec Eng) (IB 32 pts HL 665)

Cardiff – AAB incl maths (Elec Electron Eng) (IB 36-32 pts)

Glasgow – AAB-BBB incl maths+phys (Electron Elec Eng; Electron Mus) (IB 36-34 pts)

Lancaster – AAB-ABB incl maths+sci (Electron Elec Eng) (IB 35-32 pts HL 6 maths+sci)

Loughborough – AAB (Electron Comp Sys Eng MEng) (IB 36-34 pts)

Manchester – AAB incl maths+phys/electron (Elec Electron Eng) (IB 35 pts HL 6 maths+phys)

Newcastle – AAB incl maths+phys/chem (Electron Comms; Electron Comp Eng; Elec Electron Eng) (IB 35 pts HL 5 maths+phys/chem)

Queen's Belfast – AAB incl maths+sci/tech (Elec Electron Eng MEng)

Sheffield – AAB incl maths+sci/electron (Dig Electron; Microelec; Elec Eng MEng) (IB 35 pts HL 6 maths+sci/electron); AAB-ABB incl maths+sci/electron (Electron Comms Eng MEng; Electron Eng MEng) (IB 35 pts HL 6 maths+sci/electron)

Southampton – AAB incl maths+phys (Elec Eng; Electromech Eng) (IB 34 pts)

Strathclyde – AAB-BBB incl maths+phys (Electron Dig Sys MEng) (IB 36 pts HL 6 maths+phys)

Warwick – AAB incl maths+phys (Electron Eng) (IB 36 pts HL 5 maths+phys)

128 pts **Coventry** – ABB incl maths+sci/des/eng (Elec Electron Eng) (IB 31 pts)

Essex – ABB-BBB (Electron Eng; Comp Electron) (IB 32-30 pts)

Kent – ABB incl maths+sci/tech (Electron Comms Eng MEng) (IB 34 pts)

Liverpool – ABB incl maths+sci/tech (Elec Electron Eng; Elec Eng Electron (Yr Ind)) (IB 33 pts HL 5 maths+phys/electron); (Elec Eng Electron MEng) (IB 33 pts HL 5 maths+sci)

London (QM) – ABB incl maths (Electron Eng Telecomm) (IB 32 pts HL 5 maths); ABB incl maths+sci (Electron Eng courses; Elec Electron Eng) (IB 32 pts HL 5 maths+phys)

Plymouth – 128 pts incl maths+sci/tech (Elec Electron Eng MEng) (IB 32 pts)

Sheffield – ABB incl maths+sci/electron (Electron Eng) (IB 34 pts HL 6 maths+electron); (Elec Eng; Electron Comms Eng) (IB 34 pts HL 6 maths+sci/electron)

Strathclyde – ABB-BBB incl maths+phys (Electron Elec Eng) (IB 32 pts HL 6 maths+phys)

Sussex – ABB-BBB incl maths (Elec Electron Eng) (IB 34-32 pts HL 5 maths)

York – ABB incl maths+sci (Electron Eng; Electron Comm Eng; Electron Eng Nanotech) (IB 36-32 pts HL 5/6 maths+phys)

120 pts **Aberdeen** – BBB incl maths+phys/des tech/eng (Elec Electron Eng) (IB 32 pts HL 5 maths+phys)

Aston – BBB-ABB incl maths+phys (Electron Eng Comp Sci; Electromech Eng) (IB 32 pts)

Bangor – 120-128 pts incl maths+phys (Electron Eng MEng)

The University Of Sheffield.

WORLD-CLASS FACILITIES
STRONG INDUSTRIAL LINKS

Choose from a range of BEng and MEng degrees

- Electronic Engineering
- Electrical Engineering
- Electrical & Electronic Engineering
- Electronic & Communications Engineering
- Digital Electronics
- Microelectronics
- Electronic & Electrical Engineering with a Modern Language
- Foundation Year

Include a Year in Industry option or you might want to take a Study Abroad year - the choice is yours

DEPARTMENT OF ELECTRONIC & ELECTRICAL ENGINEERING
Website: www.sheffield.ac.uk/eee   **Email:** eee-rec@sheffield.ac.uk
Telephone: 0114 2225382

ELECTRONIC ENGINEER OR ELECTRICAL ENGINEER?

We are often asked what the difference is between the two professions. Electronic Engineers are concerned with the design, manufacture and management of the circuits and systems that contribute to almost all areas of our technological lives. Think of laptops, mobile phones, communication satellites. Perhaps less well known to you are semiconductors, nanotechnology and bio-electronics.

Electrical Engineers design systems that generate and move power between distances of just a few millimetres up to miles. They need to know how to use the laws governing electromagnetics to convert energy into motion and back. Their products include machines such as rotary electric motors, power transformers, heaters and lighting. But they also develop fault tolerant actuators for use in aerospace, electrically powered transport and natural energy converters.

Although there are differences as well as overlaps, our electronics graduates are competent electrical engineers and vice-versa. We will teach you all the theories and tools necessary to prepare you for an exciting career in a profession that touches all areas of human civilisation.

Flexibility and Choice

You can tailor your degree to suit your interests. Our flexible course structure means you can transfer from one EEE specialisation to another. For most of our degrees, the first two years offer a common core, giving you a broad educational base in the subject. You can then make an informed decision on your future specialisations.

Taught by Experts

You'll learn from internationally acclaimed academics in a creative and supportive environment. We work with industry to develop our courses so you acquire the knowledge and skills employers are looking for. The world-leading research we're doing feeds directly into your learning, so you understand the very latest innovations in the field of electrical science.

Our courses are very practical and you'll get to grips with the sort of challenges that professionals face, exploring your ideas using the latest test facilities.

We are home to a number of research centres, including the Rolls-Royce University Technology Centre for Advanced Electrical Machines and Drives, the Sheffield-Siemens Wind Power Research Centre and the EPSRC National Centre for III-V Technologies.

Year in Industry Options

Put theory into practice and gain industrial experience as part of your degree course. It will enhance your employment prospects and, of course, you will benefit financially from earning!

What Next?

Find out more about us by booking online for a University Open Day (June to October), or visit us on one of our own Departmental Visit Days (November to March).

For more about courses and modules, see the online prospectus:
www.sheffield.ac.uk/undergraduate

All courses accredited by the Institution of Engineering and Technology

Scholarships and Bursaries available

Come to EEE at Sheffield for the best student experience

UNIVERSITY *of York*
DEPARTMENT OF ELECTRONICS

📞 **01904 322365**   ✉ ***elec-ug-admissions@york.ac.uk***   💻 ***www.york.ac.uk/electronics/undergraduate***

The Department of Electronics at the University of York has been consistently ranked amongst the best electronics departments in the country for its teaching quality and world-leading research in electromagnetic compatibility, biologically-inspired computing, music technology, wireless communications and nanotechnology. Programmes include:

- **Electronic Engineering:** provides a very wide range of knowledge and techniques in modern electronics.
- **Electronic and Communication Engineering:** gives students a strong electronics background with an emphasis on application to communication technologies.
- **Electronic and Computer Engineering:** a Computer Systems Engineering programme combining the use of electronics and computer hardware/software.
- **Music Technology Systems:** focuses on the internal design and function of contemporary music technology systems within an electronic engineering programme.
- **Music Technology Systems with a Foundation Year:** an entry route for students wishing to pursue our Music Technology Systems courses but don't have appropriate qualifications. The foundation year includes music technology work alongside maths, physics, and electronics.
- **Electronic Engineering with Nanotechnology:** gives students a strong electronics background with an emphasis on its application to nanotechnologies.
- **Electronic Engineering with Business Management:** comprises 35 percent business management, 65 percent electronics. It meets the needs of those with ambitions to progress to a management position.
- **Foundation Year:** an entry route for those who do not have relevant qualifications, particularly mature students.

The Department has a wide range of facilities used to support the teaching and research activities. Most of these facilities are also available in collaboration with industry, allowing direct input to project work.

Facilities include: interactive BioWall; Nanotechnology Clean Room; Computing Labs; Electromagnetic Test Facilities; FPGA and ARM-based Development Systems; Audio Recording Studios; Teaching Laboratories for practical work, project work and iPad/iPhone workstations. Also, the Department's Technical Support provide design and construction facilities, including PCB design and manufacture, digital manufacturing technology 3D printing and a surface-mount assembly line.

New UCAS points Tariff: A* = 56 pts; A = 48 pts; B = 40 pts; C = 32 pts; D = 24 pts; E = 16 pts

Studying Nanotechnology and Electronic Engineering

Stories about nanotechnology are commonplace, from current uses in CPU design to very speculative ideas. But what does it mean to study the engineering of nanotechnology?

At the University of York, students study nanotechnology in all 3 or 4 years of an electronic engineering degree. The applications vary widely, but to carry out such engineering it is necessary to acquire the complex fundamental knowledge. This ranges from core electronic engineering through to aspects of physics and chemistry.

The practical skills also required are considerable – at York students are taken into the clean room fabrication facilities from their First Year on. They carry out full fabrication exercises to become familiar with the many stages required to build electronic devices starting with pristine silicon wafers and finishing with devices that can be measured in a normal electronics laboratory or imaged in one of the electron microscopes.

But on top of the fundamentals, there is often surprise due to the range of applications the students may study in their course. Some applications are to core aspects of electronics – improving the performance of processors and memory. The fabrication and use of nano-wires can be studied to improve the speed of such devices. Imaging of nano-devices is challenging, so novel electron sources within electron microscopes can be investigated – perhaps using beams of electrons from carbon nano-tubes to probe the magnetic structure of devices.

Using small (10 nanometre) nano-particles within nano-fluids can give interesting effects. The physical properties of such materials can be controlled by magnetic or electric fields. Students have investigated these fluids in shock absorbers for cars – behaving fluidly or stiffly by applying voltage, giving shock absorbers with smoothly varying properties depending on the driver or the road.

Many potential medical applications exist to extend the major impact electronics has on diagnostics and treatment. Integrated electronic sensors can detect proteins, enzymes and small molecule biomarkers. With nanoelectronic devices, such as single-electron transistors, not only large samples but the properties of individual molecules can be investigated.

The diversity of nanotechnology applications is growing rapidly – what is required to sustain this are good engineering graduates with the knowledge and practical skills to push these forward!

📞 **01904 322365**   ✉️ *elec-ug-admissions@york.ac.uk*   💻 *www.elec.york.ac.uk/ugrad/*

Check **Chapter 3** for new university admission details and **Chapter 6** on how to read the subject tables.

Bradford – BBB 120 pts (Elec Electron Eng)

City – 120 pts (Elec Electron Eng) (IB 32 pts)

Derby – 120 pts incl sci/maths (Elec Electron Eng)

Dundee – BBB–BBC incl maths+sci/eng (Electron Eng Phys) (IB 30 pts); BBB–BCC incl maths+sci/eng (Electron Eng) (IB 30 pts)

Greenwich – 120 pts (Elec Electron Eng)

Heriot-Watt – BBB incl maths+phys/tech (Comp Electron) (IB 29 pts HL maths+phys); (Elec Electron Eng courses) (IB 29 pts)

Huddersfield – BBB incl maths+sci/tech 120 pts (Electron Comm Eng; Electron Eng)

Kent – BBB maths+sci/tech (Electron Comms Eng) (IB 34 pts)

Leicester – BBB incl maths+sci (Elec Electron Eng) (IB 28 pts)

Northumbria – 120 pts incl maths+sci (Elec Electron Eng) (IB 30 pts)

Plymouth – 120 pts incl maths+sci/tech (Elec Electron Eng) (IB 30 pts)

Queen's Belfast – BBB incl maths+sci/tech (Elec Electron Eng)

Swansea – BBB incl maths (Electron Elect Eng) (IB 32 pts)

Ulster – 120 pts incl sci/maths/tech (Electron Eng) (IB 26 pts)

UWE Bristol – 120 pts incl maths+sci/des/tech/eng (Electron Eng) (IB 26 pts HL 5 maths+sci/tech)

112 pts **Bedfordshire** – 112 pts incl maths/phys/comp (Electron Eng) (IB 24 pts)

Birmingham City – BBC incl maths+sci/tech/comp 112 pts (Electron Eng (Microelec)) (IB 30 pts HL 5 maths)

Brighton – BBC incl maths+sci (Elec Electron Eng) (IB 28 pts)

Central Lancashire – 112 pts incl maths+phys (Electron Eng)

Chester – BBC incl maths+phys/chem 112 pts (Electron Elec Eng) (IB 28 pts HL 5 maths+physl sci)

Hull – 112 pts incl maths (Electron Eng MEng; Electron Eng) (IB 28 pts HL 5 maths)

London South Bank – BBC 112 pts (Elec Electron Eng) (IB 24 pts)

Sheffield Hallam – 112 pts incl maths+sci (Elec Electron Eng)

Staffordshire – BBC/CCCc incl maths/phys/eng 112 pts (Elec Eng; Electron Eng)

Sunderland – 112 pts incl maths/phys (Electron Elec Eng)

Teesside – BBC incl maths+phys (Elec Electron Eng)

Westminster – BBC (Electron Eng) (IB 28 pts)

104 pts **De Montfort** – 104 pts incl maths/phys (Electron Eng) (IB 28 pts)

Hertfordshire – 104 pts incl maths+phys/tech/eng (Elec Electron Eng; Dig Comms Electron) (IB 26 pts)

Liverpool John Moores – 104–120 pts (Elec Electron Eng)

Manchester Met – BCC–BBC incl maths+sci/eng/tech 104–112 pts (Elec Electron Eng) (IB 28 pts)

Robert Gordon – BCC incl maths+phys/eng/des tech (Electron Elec Eng) (IB 28 pts); (Electron Elec Eng MEng) (IB 29 pts)

South Wales – BCC incl maths+sci (Elec Electron Eng) (IB 29 HL 5 maths+sci); BCC incl maths/sci/tech (Ltg Des Tech) (IB 29 pts HL 5 maths/sci)

Wolverhampton – 104 pts incl maths+sci/tech (Electron Telecomm Eng (MEng))

96 pts **Bangor** – 96–104 pts incl maths+phys (Comp Sys Eng; Electron Eng)

Edinburgh Napier – CCC incl maths+sci (Elec Eng; Electron Elec Eng) (IB 27 pts HL 5 maths+sci)

Glasgow Caledonian – CCC incl maths+phys (Elec Pwr Eng) (IB 24 pts)

Glyndŵr – 96 pts incl maths/sci (Elec Electron Eng)

Portsmouth – 96–112 pts incl maths+sci/tech (Electron Eng) (IB 26 pts HL 10 pts incl maths+sci/tech)

Southampton Solent – 96 pts (Electron Eng)

88 pts **London Met** – 88 pts incl maths (Electron Comms Eng)

Alternative offers
See **Chapter 6** and **Appendix 1** for grades/new UCAS Tariff points information for other examinations.

EXAMPLES OF COLLEGES OFFERING COURSES IN THIS SUBJECT FIELD
Banbury and Bicester (Coll); Barking and Dagenham (Coll); Basingstoke (CT); Bedford (Coll); Birmingham Met (Coll); Blackburn (Coll); Blackpool and Fylde (Coll); Bournemouth and Poole (Coll); Bradford (Coll); Canterbury (Coll); Carshalton (Coll); Central Nottingham (Coll); Chesterfield (Coll); Darlington (Coll); Doncaster (Coll); Dudley (Coll); Ealing, Hammersmith and West London (Coll); East Surrey (Coll); Exeter (Coll); Farnborough (CT); Furness (Coll); Gateshead (Coll); Gloucestershire (Coll); Gower Swansea (Coll); Grimsby (Univ Centre); Hartlepool (CFE); Havering (Coll); Highbury Portsmouth (Coll); Hopwood Hall (Coll); Hull (Coll); Leeds City (Coll); Lincoln (Coll); Liverpool City (Coll); London City (Coll); London UCK (Coll); Loughborough (Coll); Mid-Kent (Coll); Milton Keynes (Coll); Newcastle (Coll); North Lindsey (Coll); North Nottinghamshire (Coll); North Warwickshire and Hinckley (Coll); Northbrook (Coll); Norwich City (Coll); Pembrokeshire (Coll); Plymouth City (Coll); St Helens (Coll); Solihull (Coll); Southport (Coll); Stephenson (Coll); Stockport (Coll); Stoke-on-Trent (Coll); Sunderland (Coll); Sussex Coast Hastings (Coll); Tameside (Coll); Tyne Met (Coll); Uxbridge (Coll); Wakefield (Coll); Warrington (Coll); Warwickshire (Coll); Wigan and Leigh (Coll); York (Coll).

CHOOSING YOUR COURSE (SEE ALSO CH.1)
Universities and colleges teaching quality See www.qaa.ac.uk; http://unistats.direct.gov.uk.

Top research universities and colleges (REF 2014) (Electrical and Electronic Engineering, Metallurgy and Materials) Leeds; London (QM) (Electron Elec Comp Eng); Oxford; Cambridge; Imperial London (Metal Mat); London (UCL); Sheffield (Electron Elec Comp Eng); Southampton.

Examples of sandwich degree courses Aston; Bath; Birmingham City; Bradford; Brighton; Brunel; Cardiff; Central Lancashire; City; Coventry; De Montfort; Glasgow Caledonian; Greenwich; Hertfordshire; Huddersfield; Kent; Leicester; Liverpool John Moores; London South Bank; Loughborough; Manchester Met; Northumbria; Plymouth; Portsmouth; Queen's Belfast; Reading; Sheffield Hallam; South Wales; Staffordshire; Sunderland; Surrey; Teesside; Ulster; UWE Bristol; Westminster; Wolverhampton; York.

ADMISSIONS INFORMATION
Number of applicants per place (approx) Aston 6; Bath 10; Birmingham 10; Birmingham City 11; Bradford (Elec Electron Eng) 8; Bristol 10; Cardiff 7; Central Lancashire 4; City 10; Coventry 8; De Montfort 1; Derby 8; Dundee 5; Edinburgh Napier 8; Glasgow Caledonian 5; Greenwich 10; Heriot-Watt 6; Hertfordshire 7; Huddersfield 5; Hull 8; Kent 5; Lancaster 7; Leeds 15; Leicester 15; Liverpool John Moores 2; London (UCL) 7; London South Bank 5; Manchester Met 5; Newcastle 9; Northumbria 7; Nottingham 8; Plymouth 22; Portsmouth 4; Robert Gordon 3; Sheffield 15; Sheffield Hallam 2; South Wales 2; Southampton 8; Staffordshire 7; Strathclyde 7; Sunderland 6; Surrey 6, (MEng) 3; Swansea 3; Teesside 4; UWE Bristol 8; Warwick 8; Westminster 5; York 5.

Advice to applicants and planning the UCAS personal statement Applicants should show enthusiasm for the subject, for example career ambitions, hobbies, work experience, attendance at appropriate events, competitions etc, and evidence of good ability in mathematics and a scientific mind. Applicants should also show that they can think creatively and have the motivation to succeed on a demanding course. See also **Engineering/Engineering Sciences** and **Appendix 3**. **Bristol** Deferred entry accepted.

Selection interviews Yes Aston, Bangor (Electron Eng), Bath, Birmingham, Bradford, Bristol, Brunel, Cambridge, Central Lancashire, De Montfort, Derby, Essex, Heriot-Watt, Hertfordshire, Huddersfield, Hull, Imperial London, Lancaster, Liverpool, London (UCL), Manchester, Newcastle, Nottingham, Oxford, Plymouth, Portsmouth, Southampton, Strathclyde, Sunderland, Surrey, UWE Bristol, West London, Westminster; **Some** Brighton, Cardiff, Dundee, Kent, Leicester, Loughborough, Staffordshire; **No** Liverpool John Moores.

Interview advice and questions Past questions have included: How does a combustion engine work? How does a trumpet work? What type of position do you hope to reach in five to 10 years' time? Could you sack an employee? What was your last physics practical? What did you learn from it? What are the methods of transmitting information from a moving object to a stationary observer? Wire bending exercise – you are provided with an accurate diagram of a shape that could be produced by bending a length of wire in a particular way. You are supplied with a pair of pliers and the exact length of wire required and you are given 10 minutes to reproduce as accurately as possible the shape drawn. A three-minute talk had to be given on one of six subjects (topics given several weeks before the interview); for example, 'The best is the enemy of the good'. Is there a lesson here for British industry? 'I was asked to take my physics file and discuss some of my conclusions in certain experiments.' Explain power transmission through the National Grid. How would you explain power transmission to a friend who hasn't done physics? See also **Chapter 5**. **York** Questions based on a mathematical problem.

Reasons for rejection (non-academic) Poor English. Inability to communicate. Frightened of technology or mathematics. Poor motivation and work ethic. Better suited to a less specialised engineering/science course. Some foreign applicants do not have adequate English. See also **Engineering/Engineering Sciences**. **Surrey** Can't speak English (it has happened!).

AFTER-RESULTS ADVICE
Offers to applicants repeating A-levels Higher Brighton, Central Lancashire, Greenwich, Huddersfield, Newcastle, Queen's Belfast, Strathclyde, Warwick; **Possibly higher** Aston, City, De Montfort, Derby, Glasgow, Hertfordshire, London Met, Portsmouth, Sheffield; **Same** Bangor, Bath, Birmingham, Bradford, Cardiff, Coventry, Dundee, Durham, Hull, Kent, Leeds, Liverpool, Liverpool John Moores, London South Bank, Loughborough, Northumbria, Nottingham (usually), Nottingham Trent, Robert Gordon, Southampton, Staffordshire, Surrey, Wolverhampton, York; **No** Cambridge.

GRADUATE DESTINATIONS AND EMPLOYMENT (2013/14 HESA)
Graduates surveyed 3,230 **Employed** 1,990 **In voluntary employment** 65 **In further study** 625 **Assumed unemployed** 250

Career note Electrical and Electronic Engineering is divided into two main fields – heavy current (electrical machinery, distribution systems, generating stations) and light current (computers, control engineering, telecommunications). Opportunities exist with many commercial organisations.

OTHER DEGREE SUBJECTS FOR CONSIDERATION
Computer Science; Engineering (Aeronautical, Communications, Computer, Control); Mathematics; Physics.

ENGINEERING (MANUFACTURING AND PRODUCTION)
(see also **Engineering/Engineering Sciences**)

Manufacturing engineering is sometimes referred to as production engineering. It is a branch of the subject concerned with management aspects of engineering such as industrial organisation, purchasing, and the planning and control of operations. Manufacturing Engineering courses are therefore geared to providing the student with a broad-based portfolio of knowledge in both the technical and business areas. Mechanical, product and design engineers develop systems and production processes relating to the overall progress and management of a product from its design to its final completion, including the materials used, the efficiency of the production line and development costs. For those students from an artistic background however, who wish to combine their design skills with the technical aspects of engineering, the BA Industrial Design Technology course at Brunel University London is ideal, in which mechanical, and electrical engineers, practical designers and psychologists combine to provide solutions to design problems. As in all engineering courses, those offering industrial placements through sandwich courses provide many financial benefits (see **Chapter 1**).

Engineering Council statement See **Engineering/Engineering Sciences**.

Useful websites www.engc.org.uk; www.imeche.org; www.theiet.org; www.semta.org.uk

NB The points totals shown to the left of the institutions are for ease of reference only. It must not be assumed that Tariff points are always used by institutions or that they can be substituted for an offer in grades. The level of an offer is not necessarily indicative of the quality of a course.

COURSE OFFERS INFORMATION

Subject requirements/preferences See **Engineering/Engineering Sciences**. Offers shown below refer to BEng or BSc courses unless otherwise stated.

Your target offers and examples of degree courses
160 pts   **Cambridge** – A*A*A (Eng (Manuf Eng)) (IB 40–41 pts HL 776)
152 pts   **Bath** – A*AA incl maths+phys (Mech Eng Manuf Mgt MEng) (IB 36 pts HL 6 maths+phys)
144 pts   **Glasgow** – AAA incl maths+phys (Prod Des Eng MEng) (IB 38–36 pts)
              Newcastle – AAA incl maths+chem/phys/fmaths (Mech Des Manuf Eng MEng) (IB 37 pts
                 HL 5 maths)
              Nottingham – AAA incl maths (Manuf Eng MEng) (IB 36 pts)
136 pts   **Liverpool** – AAB incl maths+sci/des tech (Ind Des MEng) (IB 35 pts HL 5 maths+phys)
              Newcastle – AAB–ABB incl maths+phys/chem/fmaths (Mech Des Manuf Eng) (IB 35 pts
                 HL 5 maths+phys)
              Strathclyde – AAB–BBB (Prod Des Eng MEng) (IB 36 pts HL 5 maths+phys)
              Warwick – AAB incl maths+phys (Manuf Mech Eng) (IB 36 pts HL 5 maths+phys)
128 pts   **Brunel** – ABB (Ind Des Tech) (IB 31 pts)
              Liverpool – ABB incl maths+sci/des tech (Ind Des) (IB 33 pts HL 5 maths+phys)
              Strathclyde – ABB–BBB (Prod Des Eng) (IB 34 HL 5 maths+phys)
120 pts   **Aston** – BBB–ABB (Prod Des Mgt) (IB 32 pts)
              Derby – 120 pts (Manuf Prod Eng)
              Loughborough – ABB incl maths+phys/des/eng (Manuf Eng) (IB 33 pts)
112 pts   **Liverpool John Moores** – 112 pts incl sci/maths/eng/tech (Prod Des Eng)
              Trinity Saint David – 112 pts incl maths/phys (Mech Manuf Eng)
104 pts   **South Wales** – BCC incl maths+sci (Mech Eng) (IB 29 pts HL 5 maths+sci)
  96 pts   **Plymouth** – 96 pts incl sci (Mech Des Manuf)
              Southampton Solent – 96 pts (Eng Des Manuf)
  80 pts   **Portsmouth** – 80–96 pts incl maths+sci/tech (Mech Manuf Eng) (IB 26 pts HL 10 pts
                 incl maths+sci/tech)

Alternative offers
See **Chapter 6** and **Appendix 1** for grades/new UCAS Tariff points information for other examinations.

EXAMPLES OF COLLEGES OFFERING COURSES IN THIS SUBJECT FIELD

Basingstoke (CT); Birmingham Met (Coll); Blackpool and Fylde (Coll); Bristol City (Coll); Central Bedfordshire (Coll); Central Nottingham (Coll); City and Islington (Coll); Darlington (Coll); Doncaster (Coll); Dudley (Coll); Exeter (Coll); Farnborough (CT); Hartlepool (CFE); Leeds City (Coll); Lincoln (Coll); Newcastle (Coll); North Warwickshire and Hinckley (Coll); Petroc; Solihull (Coll); Somerset (Coll); Sunderland (Coll); Tyne Met (Coll); Warrington (Coll); Warwickshire (Coll); Weymouth (Coll); Wigan and Leigh (Coll).

CHOOSING YOUR COURSE (SEE ALSO CH.1)

Universities and colleges teaching quality See www.qaa.ac.uk; http://unistats.direct.gov.uk.

Top research universities and colleges (REF 2014) See **Engineering (Aeronautical and Aerospace)**.

Examples of sandwich degree courses Aston; Bath; Bradford; Brunel; Loughborough.

ADMISSIONS INFORMATION

Number of applicants per place (approx) Aston 6; Bath 10; Loughborough 6; Nottingham 5; Strathclyde 8; Warwick 8.

Advice to applicants and planning the UCAS personal statement Work experience or work shadowing in industry should be mentioned. See **Engineering/Engineering Sciences** and **Appendix 3**.

Selection interviews Yes Cambridge, Loughborough, Nottingham, Strathclyde.

Interview advice and questions Past questions include: What is the function of an engineer? Describe something interesting you have recently done in your A-levels. What do you know about careers in manufacturing engineering? Discuss the role of women engineers in industry. Why is a disc brake better than a drum brake? Would you be prepared to make people redundant to improve the efficiency of a production line? See also **Chapter 5**.

Reasons for rejection (non-academic) Mature students failing to attend interview are rejected. One applicant produced a forged reference and was immediately rejected. See also **Engineering/ Engineering Sciences**.

AFTER-RESULTS ADVICE

Offers to applicants repeating A-levels Higher Strathclyde; **Same** Cambridge, Loughborough, Nottingham.

GRADUATE DESTINATIONS AND EMPLOYMENT (2013/14 HESA)

Production and Manufacturing Engineering graduates surveyed 655 **Employed** 460 **In voluntary employment** 5 **In further study** 80 **Assumed unemployed** 45

Career note Graduates with experience in both technical and business skills have the flexibility to enter careers in technology or business management.

OTHER DEGREE SUBJECTS FOR CONSIDERATION

Business Studies; Computer Science; Engineering (Electrical, Mechanical); Physics; Technology.

ENGINEERING (MECHANICAL)

(including Agricultural Engineering, Automotive Engineering and Motorsport Engineering)

Mechanical Engineering is one of the most wide-ranging engineering disciplines. All courses involve the design, installation and maintenance of equipment used in industry. Whilst Automotive Engineering deals with all forms of transport, specialisms are also offered in Motorsport Engineering at several universities, in Transport Product Design at Aston University and in Agricultural Machinery and Off-road Vehicle Design at Harper Adams University. Several universities include a range of Engineering courses with a common first year allowing students to specialise from Year 2. Agricultural Engineering involves all aspects of off-road vehicle design and maintenance of other machinery used in agriculture.

Engineering Council statement See **Engineering/Engineering Sciences**.

Useful websites www.imeche.org; www.engc.org.uk; www.iagre.org

NB The points totals shown to the left of the institutions are for ease of reference only. It must not be assumed that Tariff points are always used by institutions or that they can be substituted for an offer in grades. The level of an offer is not necessarily indicative of the quality of a course.

COURSE OFFERS INFORMATION

Subject requirements/preferences (Prod Des courses) Design Technology or Art may be required or preferred. See also **Engineering/Engineering Sciences**. Offers shown below refer to BEng or BSc courses unless otherwise stated.

Your target offers and examples of degree courses

160 pts **Cambridge** – A*A*A incl maths+sci (Eng (Mech Eng) MEng) (IB 40–41 pts HL 776)

Imperial London – A*A*A incl maths+phys (Mech Eng MEng) (IB 40 pts HL 6 maths+phys)

Oxford – A*A*A incl maths+phys (Mech Eng) (IB 40 pts)

152 pts **Bath** – A*AA incl maths+phys (Mech Auto Eng; Mech Eng MEng) (IB 36 pts HL 6 maths+phys)

Bristol – A*AA–AAA incl maths+phys (Mech Eng) (IB 38–36 pts HL 6 maths+phys)

Leeds – A*AA incl maths+phys (Mech Eng; Auto Eng) (IB 36 pts HL 18 pts incl 6 maths+phys)

London (UCL) – A*AA–AAA incl maths+phys/fmaths (Eng (Mech Bus Fin) MEng) (IB 39–38 pts HL 6 maths+phys); A*AA–AAA incl maths+phys (Eng (Mech) MEng) (IB 39–38 pts HL 6 maths+phys)

Loughborough – A*AA incl maths+phys (Mech Eng MEng) (IB 36 pts HL 6 maths+phys); (Auto Eng MEng) (IB 38 pts HL 6 maths+phys)

Southampton – A*AA incl maths+phys (Mech Eng (Nvl Eng) MEng) (IB 38 pts HL 6 maths+phys); A*AA incl maths/phys (Mech Eng (Advnc Mat) MEng; Mech Eng; Mech Eng (Biomed Eng) MEng; Mech Eng (Auto) MEng; Mech Eng (Aerosp) MEng; Mech Eng (Eng Mgt) MEng; Mech Eng (Mecha) MEng; Mech Eng (Sust Ener Sys) MEng) (IB 38 pts HL 6 maths+phys)

144 pts **Bath** – AAA incl maths+phys (Integ Mech Elec Eng) (IB 36 pts HL 6 maths+phys)

Birmingham – AAA incl maths (Mech Eng MEng) (IB 32 pts HL 666)

Brunel – AAA (Mtrspo Eng MEng; Mech Eng Auto Des MEng; Mech Eng MEng; Mech Eng Aero MEng; Mech Eng Bld Serv MEng) (IB 34 pts)

Cardiff – AAA incl maths (Mech Eng) (IB 36–32 pts HL 5 maths+sci)

City – 144 pts (Auto Mtrspo Eng MEng) (IB 32 pts HL 6 maths); (Mech Eng MEng) (IB 35 pts)

Edinburgh – AAA–ABB (Mech Eng; Elec Mech Eng; Mech Eng Mgt; Mech Eng Renew Ener) (IB 37–32 pts)

Exeter – AAA–ABB incl maths+sci (Mech Eng; Mech Eng MEng) (IB 36–32 pts HL 5 maths+sci)

Lancaster – AAA incl maths+sci (Mech Eng MEng) (IB 36 pts HL 6 maths+sci)

Leeds – AAA incl maths (Mecha Robot) (IB 35 pts HL 5 maths)

Liverpool – AAA incl maths+sci (Mech Mat Eng MEng; Mech Eng MEng) (IB 35 pts HL 5 maths+phys)

London (QM) – AAA incl maths+phys/chem (Mech Eng MEng) (IB 36 pts HL 6 maths+phys/chem)

London (UCL) – AAA–AAB incl maths+phys/fmaths (Eng (Mech Bus Fin)) (IB 38–36 pts HL 5 maths+phys)

Manchester – AAA incl maths+phys (Mech Eng MEng) (IB 37 pts HL 6 maths+phys)

Newcastle – AAA incl maths+chem/phys/fmaths (Mech Low Carbon Trans Eng MEng) (IB 37 pts HL 5 maths)

Nottingham – AAA incl maths (Mech Eng MEng) (IB 36 pts)

Sheffield – AAA incl maths+phys/chem (Mech Eng; Mech Eng MEng; Mech Eng (Ind Mgt) MEng; Mech Eng Fr/Ger/Ital MEng) (IB 37 pts HL 6 maths+phys/chem)

Surrey – AAA–AAB incl maths+phys (Auto Eng; Mech Eng) (IB 36–35 pts)

136 pts **Aston** – AAB–AAA incl maths+phys (Mech Eng MEng) (IB 34 pts HL 6 maths+phys)

Birmingham – AAB incl maths (Mech Eng; Mech Eng (Auto)) (IB 32 pts HL 665)

Brunel – AAB–ABB (Mtrspo Eng; Mech Eng Aero; Mech Eng; Mech Eng Auto Des) (IB 33 pts)

Exeter – AAB–BBB incl phys/chem+sci (Min Eng) (IB 34–30 pts)

Glasgow – AAB–BBB incl maths+phys (Mech Eng; Mech Des Eng) (IB 36–34 pts)

Glasgow (SA) – AAB incl maths+phys (Prod Des Eng) (IB 36 pts)

Huddersfield – AAB incl maths+sci/tech 136 pts (Auto Mtrspo Eng MEng; Mech Eng MEng)

Lancaster – AAB–ABB incl maths+sci (Mech Eng) (IB 35–32 pts HL 6 maths+sci)

London (QM) – AAB incl math+phys/chem (Mech Eng) (IB 34 pts HL 6 maths+phys/chem)

Loughborough – AAB–ABB incl maths+phys (Auto Eng) (IB 34 pts HL 6 maths+phys); AAB incl maths+phys (Mech Eng) (IB 33 pts)

Manchester – AAB incl maths+phys/eletron (Mecha Eng) (IB 35 pts HL 6 maths+phys); AAB incl maths+phys (Mech Eng Mgt; Mech Eng) (IB 35 pts HL 6 maths+phys)

Newcastle – AAB–ABB incl maths+phys/chem/fmaths (Mech Des Manuf Eng) (IB 35 pts HL 5 maths+phys); AAB–AAA incl maths+phys/chem/fmaths (Mech Eng) (IB 37–35 pts HL 5 maths)

Nottingham – AAB incl maths (Mech Eng) (IB 34 pts)

Queen's Belfast – AAB incl maths+sci/fmaths (Mech Eng MEng)

Ulster – 136 pts incl maths+sci/tech (Mech Eng MEng) (IB 28 pts)

Warwick – AAB incl maths+phys (Mech Eng; Manuf Mech Eng; Auto Eng) (IB 36 pts HL 5 maths+phys)

128 pts **Aberdeen** – ABB incl maths+phys/des tech/eng (Mech Eng Bus Mgt MEng) (IB 34 pts HL 6 maths+phys)

City – 128 pts (Auto Mtrspo Eng) (IB 28 pts); (Mech Eng) (IB 33 pts)

Coventry – ABB incl maths+sci/tech/eng (Mech Eng; Mtrspo Eng) (IB 31 pts)

Leicester – ABB–AAB incl maths+sci (Mech Eng MEng) (IB 30–32 pts)

Liverpool – ABB incl maths+sci/tech (Mecha Robot Sys MEng) (IB 33 pts HL 5 maths+sci); ABB incl maths+sci (Mech Mat Eng; Mech Eng) (IB 33 pts HL 5 maths+phys)

Liverpool John Moores – 128 pts (Mech Eng MEng; Mech Mar Eng MEng)

Northumbria – 128 pts incl maths+sci/tech (Mech Eng; Mech Auto Eng BEng/MEng) (IB 31 pts)

Oxford Brookes – ABB (Mech Eng MEng) (IB 33 pts HL 5 maths+phys)

Sheffield Hallam – 128 pts incl maths+sci (Mech Eng MEng)

Strathclyde – ABB–BBB (Mech Eng) (IB 32 pts HL 5 maths+phys)

Sussex – ABB–BBB incl maths (Auto Eng; Mech Eng) (IB 34–32 pts HL 5 maths)

Swansea – ABB–BBB incl maths (Mech Eng) (IB 32 pts)

120 pts **Aberdeen** – BBB incl maths+phys/des tech/eng (Eng (Mech Oil Gas St); Mech Eng) (IB 32 pts HL 5 maths+phys)

Aston – BBB–ABB incl maths+phys (Mech Eng) (IB 32 pts); BBB–ABB (Trans Prod Des) (IB 32 pts)

Brighton – BBB incl maths+sci (Auto Eng MEng) (IB 30 pts)

Derby – 120 pts (Mech Eng; Mtrcycl Eng; Mtrspo Eng)

Dundee – BBB–BCC incl maths+sci/eng (Mech Eng) (IB 30 pts)

Glasgow – BBB–AAB (Mech Eng Aero) (IB 34–36 pts)

Greenwich – 120 pts (Mech Eng)

Heriot-Watt – BBB incl maths+phys/tech/eng (Mech Eng Ener Eng; Mech Eng) (IB 30 pts)

Huddersfield – BBB incl maths+sci/tech 120 pts (Auto Mtrspo Eng; Mech Eng)

Leicester – BBB incl maths+sci (Mech Eng) (IB 28 pts)

Loughborough – ABC–BBB (Des Ergon) (IB 32 pts)

Oxford Brookes – BBB incl maths+phys (Auto Eng) (IB 30 pts HL 5 maths+phys); (Mtrspo Eng) (IB 30 pts HL 5 maths); BBB (Mech Eng BEng) (IB 30 pts HL 5 maths+phys)

Plymouth – 120 pts incl maths+sci/tech (Mech Eng); (Mech Eng Cmpstes) (IB 28 pts)

Portsmouth – 120–144 pts incl maths+sci/tech (Mech Eng MEng) (IB 28 pts HL 15 pts incl 6 maths+sci/tech)

Queen's Belfast – BBB incl maths+sci/fmaths (Mech Eng)

Salford – 120–128 pts incl maths+phys/des tech (Mech Eng MEng) (IB 35 pts)

Ulster – 120 pts incl sci/maths/tech (Mech Eng) (IB 26 pts)

UWE Bristol – 120 pts incl maths+sci/des/tech/eng (Auto Eng; Mech Eng) (IB 26 pts HL 5 maths+sci/tech)

112 pts **Birmingham City** – BBC incl maths 112 pts (Auto Eng) (IB 30 pts HL 5 maths); (Mech Eng; Mtrspo Tech) (IB 30 pts)

Bradford – BBC 112 pts (Mech Eng; Mech Auto Eng)

Brighton – BBC incl maths+sci (Mech Eng) (IB 28 pts); BBC (Auto Eng) (IB 28 pts)

Central Lancashire – 112 pts incl maths+phys/sci (Mtrspo Eng)

De Montfort – 112 pts (Mech Eng) (IB 28 pts)

Edinburgh Napier – BBC incl maths+sci (Mech Eng MEng) (IB 29 pts HL 5 maths+sci)

Glyndŵr – 112 pts incl maths/phys (Aero Mech Eng MEng)

Hull – 112 pts incl maths (Mech Med Eng MEng; Mech Med Eng) (IB 28 pts HL 5 maths); 112 pts (Mech Eng; Mech Eng MEng) (IB 28 pts HL 5 maths)

Kingston – 112 pts (Mech Eng)

Lincoln – 112 pts incl maths (Mech Eng)

Liverpool John Moores – 112 pts (Mech Mar Eng)

London South Bank – BBC 112 pts (Mech Eng)

Oxford Brookes – BBC (Eng Mech BSc) (IB 30 pts)

Robert Gordon – BBC incl maths+phys/eng/des tech (Mech Elec Eng MEng; Mech Eng; Mech Eng MEng) (IB 29 pts)

Sheffield Hallam – 112 pts incl maths+sci (Mech Eng); 112 pts incl maths+sci/eng/tech (Auto Eng)

Staffordshire – BBC/CCCc 112 pts (Mtrspo Tech; Auto Eng; Mech Eng); BBC/CCCc incl maths/phys/eng 112 pts (Mecha)

Sunderland – 112 pts incl maths/phys (Auto Eng; Mech Eng)

Teesside – BBC incl maths+phys (Mech Eng)

Trinity Saint David – 112 pts incl maths/phys (Mech Eng)

104 pts **De Montfort** – 104 pts incl maths/phys (Mecha) (IB 28 pts)

Hertfordshire – 104 pts incl maths+phys/tech/eng (Auto Eng; Mech Eng; Auto Eng Mtrspo) (IB 26 pts)

Liverpool John Moores – 104 pts (Mech Eng)

Manchester Met – BCC–BBC incl maths+sci/eng/tech 104–112 pts (Mech Eng) (IB 28 pts); BCC–BBC incl maths+sci 104–112 pts (Auto Eng) (IB 28 pts)

Portsmouth – 104–120 pts incl maths+sci/tech (Mech Eng) (IB 27 pts HL 12 pts incl 5 maths+sci/tech)

Robert Gordon – BCC incl maths+phys/eng/des tech (Mech Off Eng; Mech Elec Eng) (IB 28 pts)

South Wales – BCC incl maths+sci (Mech Eng) (IB 29 pts HL 5 maths+sci)

West Scotland – BCC incl maths+sci (Mech Eng) (IB 24 pts)

96 pts **Bolton** – 96 pts (Auto Perf Eng (Mtrspo)); 96 pts incl maths/sci/tech/eng (Mtrspo Tech); 96 pts incl maths+sci/tech/eng (Mech Eng)

Edinburgh Napier – CCC incl maths+sci (Mech Eng) (IB 27 pts HL 5 maths+sci)

Glasgow Caledonian – CCC incl maths+phys (Comp Aided Mech Eng; Mech Electron Sys Eng) (IB 24 pts)

Glyndŵr – 96 pts incl maths/sci (Aero Mech Eng)

Harper Adams – 96–112 pts incl maths (Agric Eng; Auto Eng)

Kingston – 96 pts (Mtrspo Eng (Mtrcycl); Mtrspo Eng)

Plymouth – 96 pts incl sci (Mech Des Manuf)

Southampton Solent – 96 pts (Eng Des Manuf)

Trinity Saint David – 96 pts incl maths/phys (Auto Eng; Mtrcycl Eng; Mtrspo Eng)

80 pts **Portsmouth** – 80–96 pts incl maths+sci/tech (Mech Manuf Eng) (IB 26 pts HL 10 pts incl maths+sci/tech)

Wolverhampton – 80 pts incl maths+sci/tech (Mech Eng; Auto Sys Eng)

72 pts **Harper Adams** – 72–88 pts (Auto Eng Mark Mgt; Agric Eng Mark Mgt)

60 pts **Anglia Ruskin** – 60–72 pts incl maths (Mech Eng) (IB 24 pts)

Alternative offers

See **Chapter 6** and **Appendix 1** for grades/new UCAS Tariff points information for other examinations.

EXAMPLES OF COLLEGES OFFERING COURSES IN THIS SUBJECT FIELD

Banbury and Bicester (Coll); Barking and Dagenham (Coll); Barnet and Southgate (Coll); Basingstoke (CT); Bath (Coll); Bedford (Coll); Blackburn (Coll); Blackpool and Fylde (Coll); Bradford (Coll); Bridgwater (Coll); Canterbury (Coll); Chesterfield (Coll); Cornwall (Coll); Darlington (Coll); Doncaster (Coll); Dudley (Coll); Ealing, Hammersmith and West London (Coll); East Surrey (Coll); Exeter (Coll); Farnborough (CT); Furness (Coll); Gateshead (Coll); Gloucestershire (Coll); Gower Swansea (Coll); Grimsby (Univ Centre); Hartlepool (CFE); Highbury Portsmouth (Coll); Lincoln (Coll); Loughborough (Coll); Mid-Kent (Coll); Milton Keynes (Coll); Newcastle (Coll); North Lindsey (Coll); North Warwickshire and Hinckley (Coll); Northbrook (Coll); Norwich City (Coll); Pembrokeshire (Coll); Petroc; Plymouth City (Coll); Portsmouth (Coll); South Devon (Coll); South Gloucestershire and Stroud (Coll); South Tyneside (Coll); Southampton City (Coll); Southport (Coll); Stephenson (Coll); Sussex Coast Hastings (Coll); Tameside (Coll); Tyne Met (Coll); Uxbridge (Coll); Wakefield (Coll); Warrington (Coll); Warwickshire (Coll); Wigan and Leigh (Coll); Wiltshire (Coll); Wirral Met (Coll); Yeovil (Coll); Yorkshire Coast (Coll).

CHOOSING YOUR COURSE (SEE ALSO CH.1)

Universities and colleges teaching quality See www.qaa.ac.uk; http://unistats.direct.gov.uk.

Top research universities and colleges (REF 2014) See **Engineering (Aeronautical and Aerospace)**.

Examples of sandwich degree courses Aston; Bath; Birmingham City; Bradford; Brighton; Cardiff; Central Lancashire; City; Coventry; De Montfort; Glasgow Caledonian; Harper Adams; Hertfordshire; Huddersfield; Kingston; Leicester; Liverpool John Moores; London South Bank; Loughborough; Manchester Met; Northumbria; Oxford Brookes; Plymouth; Portsmouth; Queen's Belfast; Salford; Sheffield Hallam; South Wales; Staffordshire; Sunderland; Surrey; Teesside; Ulster; UWE Bristol; West Scotland; Wolverhampton.

ADMISSIONS INFORMATION

Number of applicants per place (approx) Aston 8; Bath 10; Birmingham 9; Bradford 4; Brighton 10; Bristol 9; Cardiff 8; City 13; Coventry 8; Dundee 5; Durham 6; Glyndŵr 4; Heriot-Watt 9; Hertfordshire 10; Huddersfield 1; Hull 11; Kingston 8; Lancaster 8; Leeds 15; Leicester 11; Liverpool 6; Liverpool John Moores 2; London (QM) 6; London (UCL) 11; London South Bank 4; Loughborough 8, (Mech Eng) 12, (Auto Eng) 7; Manchester Met 6, (Mech Eng) 6; Newcastle 10; Northumbria 4; Nottingham 8; Plymouth 6; Portsmouth 6; Sheffield 10; South Wales 6; Southampton 9; Staffordshire 6; Strathclyde 6; Surrey 9; Teesside 7; UWE Bristol 17; Warwick 8.

Admissions tutors' advice Bristol Places in Clearing for international students.

Advice to applicants and planning the UCAS personal statement Work experience; hands-on skills. An interest in solving mathematical problems related to physical concepts. Enjoyment in designing mechanical devices or components. Interest in engines, structures, dynamics or fluid flow and efficient use of materials or energy. Apply to the Year in Industry Scheme (www.etrust.org.uk) for placement. Scholarships are available to supplement the scheme. See **Engineering/Engineering Sciences** and **Appendix 3**.

Misconceptions about this course Loughborough Although organised by the Wolfson School of Manufacturing and Mechanical Engineering, the degree does not include manufacturing.

Selection interviews Yes Aston, Birmingham, Bolton, Bradford, Brighton, Bristol, Cambridge, Cardiff, Harper Adams, Hertfordshire, Huddersfield, Imperial London, Kingston, Lancaster, Leeds, Leicester, Liverpool John Moores, London (QM), Loughborough (Auto Eng), Manchester Met, Newcastle, Nottingham, Oxford, Sheffield, Sheffield Hallam, Strathclyde, Sunderland, Surrey; **Some** Blackpool and Fylde (Coll), Dundee, Liverpool, Staffordshire.

Interview advice and questions Past questions include: What mechanical objects have you examined and/or tried to repair? How do you see yourself in five years' time? What do you imagine you would be doing (production, management or design engineering)? What engineering interests do you have? What qualities are required to become a successful mechanical engineer? Do you like sixth-form work? Describe the working of parts on an engineering drawing. How does a fridge work? What is design in the context of mechanical engineering? What has been your greatest achievement to date? What are your career plans? See also **Engineering/Engineering Sciences** and **Chapter 5**. **Hertfordshire** All interviewees receive a conditional offer. Provide an example of working as part of a team, meeting a deadline, working on your own.

Reasons for rejection (non-academic) See **Engineering/Engineering Sciences**.

AFTER-RESULTS ADVICE
Offers to applicants repeating A-levels Higher Brighton, Dundee, Kingston, Newcastle, Queen's Belfast, Swansea, Warwick; **Possibly higher** City, Huddersfield; **Same** Aston, Bath, Bradford, Bristol, Coventry, Derby, Durham, Edinburgh Napier, Harper Adams, Heriot-Watt, Leeds (usually), Lincoln, Liverpool, Liverpool John Moores, London South Bank, Loughborough, Manchester Met, Northumbria, Nottingham, Oxford Brookes, Sheffield, Sheffield Hallam, Southampton, Staffordshire, Sunderland, Surrey, Teesside, Wolverhampton; **No** Cambridge.

GRADUATE DESTINATIONS AND EMPLOYMENT (2013/14 HESA)
Graduates surveyed 3,965 **Employed** 2,630 **In voluntary employment** 45 **In further study** 665 **Assumed unemployed** 265

Career note Mechanical Engineering graduates have a wide choice of career options. Apart from design and development of plant and machinery, they are also likely to be involved in production processes and working at various levels of management. Mechanical engineers share interests such as structures and stress analysis with civil and aeronautical engineers, and electronics and computing with electrical and software engineers.

OTHER DEGREE SUBJECTS FOR CONSIDERATION
Engineering (Aeronautical/Aerospace, Building, Computer (Control, Software and Systems), Electrical/ Electronic, Manufacturing, Marine); Materials Science; Mathematics; Physics; Product Design; Technologies.

ENGINEERING (MEDICAL)

(including **Clinical Engineering, Medical Electronics** and **Instrumentation, Mechanical** and **Medical Engineering, Medical Physics, Medical Product Design, Product Design for Medical Devices** and **Rehabilitation Engineering**; see also **Biotechnology**)

Biomedical Engineering lies at the interface between engineering, mathematics, physics, chemistry, biology and clinical practice. This makes it a branch of engineering that has the most direct effect on human health. It is a rapidly expanding interdisciplinary field that applies engineering principles and technology to medical and biological problems. Biomedical engineers work in fields as diverse as neuro-technology, fluid mechanics of the blood and respiratory systems, bone and joint biomechanics, biosensors, medical imaging, synthetic biology and biomaterials. These can lead to novel devices such as joint replacements and heart valves, new surgical instruments, rehabilitation protocols and even prosthetic limbs.

Useful websites www.assclinsci.org; www.nhsclinicalscientists.info; www.ipem.ac.uk

NB The points totals shown to the left of the institutions are for ease of reference only. It must not be assumed that Tariff points are always used by institutions or that they can be substituted for an offer in grades. The level of an offer is not necessarily indicative of the quality of a course.

COURSE OFFERS INFORMATION
Subject requirements/preferences GCSE/AL Subjects taken from mathematics, physics, chemistry and biology. Offers shown below refer to BEng or BSc courses unless otherwise stated.

Your target offers and examples of degree courses

152 pts **Imperial London** – A*AA incl maths+phys+sci (Biomed Eng MEng) (IB 38 pts HL 6 maths+phys)
Leeds – A*AA incl maths+sci (Med Eng BEng/MEng) (IB 36 pts HL 6 maths+sci)
Surrey – A*AA-AAA incl maths (Med Eng MEng) (IB 38 pts)

144 pts **Cardiff** – AAA incl maths (Med Eng) (IB 36-32 pts HL 5 maths+sci)
Glasgow – AAA incl maths+phys (Biomed Eng MEng) (IB 38-36 pts)
London (King's) – AAA incl maths+phys (Phys Med Apps) (IB 35 pts HL 6 maths+phys)
London (QM) – AAA incl maths+phys/chem (Med Eng MEng) (IB 36 pts HL 6 maths+phys/chem)
London (UCL) – AAA-ABB incl maths+phys (Med Phys) (IB 38-34 pts HL 6 maths 5 phys)
Manchester – AAA-ABB incl sci/maths (Biomed Sci) (IB 37-33 pts HL 5/6 biol+chem)
Sheffield – AAA incl maths+sci (Bioeng MEng) (IB 37 pts HL 6 maths+sci)
Surrey – AAA-AAB incl maths (Med Eng) (IB 36-35 pts)

136 pts **Glasgow** – AAB-BBB incl maths+phys (Biomed Eng) (IB 36-34 pts)
London (King's) – AAB incl maths+phys (Biomed Eng) (IB 35 pts)
London (QM) – AAB incl maths+phys/chem (Med Eng) (IB 34 pts HL 6 maths+phys/chem)
Queen's Belfast – AAB incl maths+phys (Phys Med Apps MSci)
Sheffield – AAB incl maths+sci (Bioeng) (IB 35 pts HL 6 maths+sci)
Swansea – AAB-ABB incl maths (Med Eng MEng) (IB 34-33 pts)

128 pts **City** – 128 pts incl sci/maths (Biomed Eng) (IB 32 pts HL 5 sci/maths)
Hertfordshire – 128 pts incl maths+sci/tech/eng (Biomed Eng MEng) (IB 32 pts)

120 pts **Queen's Belfast** – BBB incl maths+phys (Phys Med Apps)
Swansea – BBB incl maths (Med Eng) (IB 32 pts)

112 pts **Bradford** – BBC 112 pts (Med Eng)
Hertfordshire – 112 pts incl maths+sci/eng/tech (Biomed Eng) (IB 28 pts)
Hull – 112 pts incl maths (Mech Med Eng; Mech Med Eng MEng) (IB 28 pts HL 5 maths)

Alternative offers
See **Chapter 6** and **Appendix 1** for grades/new UCAS Tariff points information for other examinations.

CHOOSING YOUR COURSE (SEE ALSO CH.1)

Universities and colleges teaching quality See www.qaa.ac.uk; http://unistats.direct.gov.uk.

Examples of sandwich degree courses Bradford; Cardiff; City; Hull; Leeds; Surrey.

ADMISSIONS INFORMATION

Number of applicants per place (approx) Cardiff 4; London (UCL) 5; Swansea 5.

Advice to applicants and planning the UCAS personal statement **Cardiff** An appreciation of the typical careers available within medical engineering and an interest in engineering and anatomy would be preferable. **London (UCL)** Evidence of interest in medical physics/physics, eg visits to hospitals or internships.

Selection interviews Yes Cardiff (all applicants), London (UCL); **Some** Swansea.
Interview advice and questions London (UCL) Searching questions at interview. Test may be included.

AFTER-RESULTS ADVICE

Offers to applicants repeating A-levels Same Cardiff, London (UCL), Swansea.

GRADUATE DESTINATIONS AND EMPLOYMENT (2013/14 HESA)
See **Biotechnology**.

Career note High rate of graduate employment. *Money* magazine ranks Biomedical Engineering number 1 for job growth prospects for the next 10 years.

OTHER DEGREE SUBJECTS FOR CONSIDERATION
Biological Sciences; Prosthetic; Orthotics.

New UCAS points Tariff: A* = 56 pts; A = 48 pts; B = 40 pts; C = 32 pts; D = 24 pts; E = 16 pts

ENGLISH

(including **Creative Writing**; see also **Journalism, Languages, Linguistics, Literature**)

English courses continue to be extremely popular and competitive and cover English Literature, English, and English Language, bearing in mind that the content of courses can vary considerably. English Literature courses are popular because they are often an extension of A-level or equivalent studies and will offer a wide range of modules. At the University of Sheffield, the course covers the study of literature, poetry, fiction and drama from Old English to the 21st century along with modules such as American Literature, Gothic Literature, the Australian cinema and Renaissance lyrics. However, English Language courses break the mould and offer a broader interpretation of English with studies in the use of language, grammar, the meaning of words, language in the workplace, in broadcasting and other aspects of society, Pidgin and Creole English, methods of communication and linguistics. Admissions tutors will expect students to have read widely outside their A-level syllabus.

Useful websites www.bl.uk; www.lrb.co.uk; www.literature.org; www.bibliomania.com

NB The points totals shown to the left of the institutions are for ease of reference only. It must not be assumed that Tariff points are always used by institutions or that they can be substituted for an offer in grades. The level of an offer is not necessarily indicative of the quality of a course.

COURSE OFFERS INFORMATION

Subject requirements/preferences GCSE English language and English literature required and a foreign language may be preferred. Grades may be stipulated. **AL** English with specific grades usually stipulated. Modern languages required for joint courses with languages.

Your target offers and examples of degree courses

152 pts **Bristol** – A*AA–AAB incl Engl (Engl) (IB 38–34 pts HL 6 Engl)
  Cambridge – A*AA (Educ Engl Dr; A-Sxn Nrs Celt) (IB 40–41 pts HL 776); A*AA incl Engl (Engl) (IB 40–41 pts HL 776)
  Durham – A*AA incl Engl lit (Engl Lit) (IB 38 pts)
  Exeter – A*AA–AAB incl Engl lit (Engl; Engl (St Abrd)) (IB 38–34 pts HL 6 Engl)
144 pts **Birmingham** – AAA incl Engl (Engl Crea Writ) (IB 32 pts HL 666)
  Bristol – AAA–AAB incl Engl (Thea Engl; Engl Class St) (IB 36–34 pts HL 6 Engl)
  East Anglia – AAA incl Engl (Engl Lit Crea Writ) (IB 34 pts HL 6 Engl)
  Edinburgh – AAA–ABB (Engl Lang) (IB 37–34 pts); (Class Engl Lang; Engl Lit; Engl Scot Lit) (IB 40–34 pts)
  Lancaster – AAA–AAB incl Engl (Engl Lit) (IB 36–35 pts HL 6 lit); AAA–AAB (Engl Lang; Engl Lang Lit; Engl Lang Crea Writ; Mediev Ren St) (IB 36–35 pts)
  Leeds – AAA incl Engl (Engl Lang Lit) (IB 35 pts HL 6 Engl)
  London (King's) – AAA incl Engl+lang (Compar Lit) (IB 35 pts HL 6 Engl lit)
  London (UCL) – AAA incl Engl lit (Engl) (IB 38 pts HL 6 Engl)
  Manchester – AAA–AAB incl Engl (Engl Lit courses) (IB 37–35 pts HL 7 Engl)
  NCH London – AAA–ABB (Engl)
  Newcastle – AAA–AAB incl Engl (Engl Lang Lit) (IB 36–35 pts HL 6 Engl)
  Nottingham – AAA–BBB (Engl St) (IB 34–36 pts); AAA–AAB incl Engl (Engl Crea Writ; Engl Lang Lit; Engl) (IB 36–34 pts)
  Oxford – AAA (Engl Modn Langs) (IB 38 pts); AAA (Engl Lang Lit) (IB 38 pts)
  St Andrews – AAA incl Engl (Engl courses) (IB 38 pts)
  Sussex – AAA–ABB incl Engl (Engl Joint Hons) (IB 35–34 pts HL 6 Engl); AAA–AAB incl Engl (Engl) (IB 35 pts HL 6 Engl)
  Warwick – AAA/A*AB incl Engl lit (Engl Lit) (IB 38 pts HL 6 Engl); AAA incl Engl (Engl Lit Crea Writ) (IB 38 pts HL 6 Engl)
  York – AAA incl Engl (Engl) (IB 36 pts HL 6 Engl); AAA incl Engl+hist (Engl Hist) (IB 36 pts HL 6 Engl+hist)

136 pts **Birmingham** – AAB incl Engl (Engl) (IB 32 pts HL 665); AAB (Engl Lang) (IB 32 pts HL 665)

Cardiff – AAB incl Engl lit (Engl Lit) (IB 36 pts)

East Anglia – AAB (Am Engl Lit) (IB 33 pts HL 5 Engl); AAB incl Engl (Engl Lit Joint Hons; Engl Lit) (IB 33 pts HL 5 Engl); AAB incl dr/thea st/Engl (Script Perf) (IB 33 pts HL 5 Engl/thea st)

Glasgow – AAB–BBB incl arts/lang (Engl Lit; Engl Lang) (IB 36–34 pts)

Liverpool – AAB–ABB incl Engl (Engl) (IB 35–33 pts HL 6 Engl)

London (Gold) – AAB (Engl Crea Writ) (IB 33 pts)

London (King's) – AAB incl Engl/lang/psy (Engl Lang Ling) (IB 35 pts HL 6 Engl/lang/psy); AAB incl anc Gk+Engl (Gk Engl) (IB 35 pts HL 6 anc Gk+Engl); AAB incl Engl (Class St Engl) (IB 35 pts HL 6 Engl)

Loughborough – AAB incl Engl (Pub Engl; Engl Am St; Engl; Engl Spo Sci) (IB 34 pts HL 5 Engl)

Sheffield – AAB–ABB (Engl Lang Ling) (IB 35 pts); AAB–ABB incl Engl (Engl Lang Lit; Engl Lit; Engl Joint Hons) (IB 35 pts HL 6 Engl)

Southampton – AAB–ABB incl Engl+Fr/Ger/Span (Engl Fr/Ger/Span) (IB 34 pts HL 6 Engl+Fr/Ger/Span); AAB–ABB incl Engl+hist (Engl Hist) (IB 34 pts HL 6 Engl+hist); AAB–ABB incl Engl (Film Engl) (IB 32 pts HL 6 Engl); (Engl) (IB 34 pts HL 6 Engl); (Phil Engl) (IB 34–32 pts HL 6 Engl); AAB–ABB incl Engl+mus +gr 8 (Engl Mus) (IB 34 pts HL 6 Engl+mus)

Surrey – AAB incl Engl+Fr/Ger/Span (Engl Lit Fr/Ger/Span) (IB 35–34 pts); AAB–ABB incl Engl (Engl Lit; Engl Lit Crea Writ) (IB 35–34 pts)

Sussex – AAB–ABB incl Engl (Engl Lang Lit) (IB 34 pts HL 6 Engl)

Warwick – AAB incl Engl lit+Fr (Engl Fr) (IB 36 pts HL 6 Engl lit 5 Fr)

York – AAB incl Engl (Engl Ling; Engl Hist Art; Engl Pol; Engl Phil) (IB 35 pts HL 6 Engl)

128 pts **Aston** – ABB–BBB incl Engl (Engl Lang) (IB 33–32 pts); ABB (Pol Engl Lang; Int Rel Engl Lang) (IB 33 pts)

Cardiff – ABB (Engl Lang) (IB 34 pts)

East Anglia – ABB (Film Engl St) (IB 32 pts HL 5 Engl)

Essex – ABB–BBB (Engl Lit; Crea Writ; Engl Lang; Engl Lang Lit) (IB 32–30 pts)

Huddersfield – ABB incl Engl 128 pts (Engl Lang courses; Engl Lit; Engl Lang Lit)

Keele – ABB (Engl) (IB 34 pts HL 6 Engl)

Kent – ABB (Engl Lang Ling) (IB 34 pts); ABB incl Engl (Engl Am Postcol Lit; Engl Lang Ling Engl Am Lit) (IB 34 pts)

Leicester – ABB incl Engl (Engl courses) (IB 30 pts)

London (Gold) – ABB (Engl; Engl Compar Lit) (IB 33 pts)

London (QM) – ABB–AAB incl Engl 128–136 pts (Engl Lit Ling; Engl) (IB 34 pts HL 6 Engl); 128–136 pts (Engl Lang Ling) (IB 34 pts)

London (RH) – ABB incl Engl lit/dr (Dr Crea Writ) (IB 32 pts); ABB incl Engl (Engl; Engl Dr) (IB 32 pts)

Newcastle – ABB (Engl Lang) (IB 34 pts)

Northumbria – 128 pts incl Engl (Engl Lit; Engl Lang Lit; Engl Lit Crea Writ) (IB 31 pts HL 5 Engl)

Nottingham – ABB (Engl Hisp St) (IB 32 pts)

Queen's Belfast – ABB inc Engl (Engl courses)

Reading – ABB–BBB (Engl Lang courses) (IB 32–30 pts); (Engl Lang Engl Lit) (IB 33–30 pts)

Roehampton – ABB incl Engl 128 pts (Engl Lit)

Sheffield – ABB incl Engl (Engl Lang Sociol) (IB 34 pts HL 6 Engl)

Strathclyde – ABB–BBB (Engl courses) (IB 34 pts)

Winchester – 128–144 pts (Engl Am Lit) (IB 27 pts)

120 pts **Aberdeen** – BBB (Engl Scot Lit) (IB 30 pts); (Engl) (IB 32 pts)

Aberystwyth – 120 pts incl Engl (Engl Lit)

Brunel – BBB incl Engl (Engl) (IB 30 pts); BBB (Engl Crea Writ; Thea Engl; Thea Crea Writ; Engl Film TV St) (IB 30 pts)

Buckingham – BBB (Engl Lit courses)

English

Of the 105 English departments in the UK, Buckingham is ranked:

- 2nd for overall satisfaction *(NSS 2015)*
- 5th for academic support *(NSS 2015)*
- 7th for organisation and management *(NSS 2015)*
- 8th=(with Oxford) for course satisfaction *(The Guardian University Guide 2016)*

Our personal approach means you get lots of individual attention. An excellent staff-student ratio is used for small-group teaching and weekly tutorials on each module. If you are fascinated by English literature, or want to study English language to a high level or learn to teach it, look at the different degrees we offer.

THE TIMES
THE SUNDAY TIMES
GOOD
UNIVERSITY
GUIDE
2016
UNIVERSITY
OF THE YEAR
FOR TEACHING

english-admissions@buckingham.ac.uk
+44 (0)1280 820156
ww.buckingham.ac.uk/humanities

THE UNIVERSITY OF
BUCKINGHAM

Chester – 120 pts (Engl Lang) (IB 28 pts HL 5 Engl); BBB–BBC 120 pts (Engl Lit) (IB 28 pts HL 5 Engl)

Coventry – BBB (Engl) (IB 29 pts); (Engl Jrnl) (IB 30 pts)

De Montfort – 120 pts incl Engl (Engl) (IB 30 pts); 120 pts (Engl Lang; Crea Writ Joint Hons) (IB 30 pts)

Dundee – BBB–BCC incl Engl (Engl Film St; Engl) (IB 30 pts)

East London – 120 pts (Engl Lit) (IB 26 pts)

Edge Hill – BBB 120 pts (Engl; Crea Writ; Engl Lang; Engl Lit; Engl Film St; Engl Lit Hist)

Gloucestershire – 120 pts (Engl Lit; Engl Lang)

Huddersfield – BBB 120 pts (Dr Engl Lang/Lit)

Keele – BBB/ABC incl Engl (Engl Joint Hons) (IB 32 pts HL 6 Engl)

Kingston – 120 pts (Engl Lit) (IB 30 pts)

Leeds Beckett – 120 pts (Engl Lit) (IB 26 pts)

London (Birk) – 120 pts (Engl)

Plymouth – 120 pts incl Engl+Span (Engl Span) (IB 30 pts); 120 pts incl Engl+Fr (Engl Fr) (IB 30 pts)

Sheffield Hallam – 120 pts incl Engl lit (Engl Lit); 120 pts incl Engl (Engl; Crea Writ); 120 pts incl Engl lit/lang (Engl Lang); 120 pts incl Engl lit/hist (Engl Hist)

Stirling – BBB (Engl St) (IB 32 pts)

Sunderland – 120 pts (Engl; Engl Crea Writ; Dr Engl; Engl Lang Ling; Engl Film; Engl Lang Lit)

Swansea – BBB–BBC incl Engl (Engl Lit Lang St) (IB 32–30 pts); BBB–BBC (Engl courses) (IB 32–30 pts)

UWE Bristol – 120 pts (Engl Writ; Engl) (IB 26 pts)

Winchester – 120–136 pts (Crea Writ) (IB 27 pts)

York – BBB (Engl Educ) (IB 31 pts)

Check **Chapter 3** for new university admission details and **Chapter 6** on how to read the subject tables.

112 pts **Bangor** – 112–128 pts incl Engl (Engl Lit courses) (IB 26 pts); 112–120 pts incl Engl (Engl Lit Thea Perf; Engl Lit Engl Lang) (IB 26 pts)

Bath Spa – 112–128 pts incl Engl lit (Engl Lit); 112–128 pts (Crea Writ)

Bedfordshire – 112 pts (Engl courses) (IB 24 pts)

Birmingham City – 112 pts incl Engl (Engl) (IB 26 pts); BBC incl Engl 112 pts (Engl Crea Writ; Engl Lang Engl Lit) (IB 26 pts)

Bournemouth – 112–120 pts (Engl) (IB 30–31 pts)

Brighton – BBC incl Engl lit (Engl Lit) (IB 28 pts)

Canterbury Christ Church – 112 pts incl Engl (Engl Lit); 112 pts (Engl Lang Comm)

Chester – BBC–BCC 112 pts (Engl (Comb); Crea Writ) (IB 26 pts)

Derby – 112 pts incl Engl (Engl; Crea Prof Writ)

East London – 112 pts incl Engl (Crea Prof Writ) (IB 24 pts)

Edinburgh Napier – BBC incl Engl (Engl) (IB 29 pts Hl 5 Engl); (Engl Film) (IB 29 pts HL 5 Engl)

Gloucestershire – 112 pts (Crea Writ)

Greenwich – 112 pts (Crea Writ; Engl Lang Lit)

Hertfordshire – 112 pts (Engl Lang Comm; Engl Lit) (IB 28 pts)

Hull – 112 pts (Engl; Dr Engl) (IB 28 pts)

Liverpool John Moores – 112 pts (Crea Writ Flm St) (IB 29 pts)

London Met – 112 pts (Crea Prof Writ; Engl Lit)

Middlesex – 112 pts (Engl)

Newman – 112 pts (Engl)

Northampton – 112 pts (Engl courses; Crea Writ courses)

Nottingham Trent – 112 pts (Engl)

Oxford Brookes – BBC (Engl Lang Comm) (IB 30 pts)

Reading – 112 pts (P Educ Engl) (IB 28 pts)

Roehampton – 112 pts (Crea Writ; Engl Lang Ling)

Southampton Solent – 112 pts (Engl; Engl Mag Jrnl; Engl Film)

Teesside – 112 pts incl Engl (Engl St; Engl St Crea Writ)

Westminster – BBC incl lang (Chin Engl Lang) (IB 30 pts HL 4 lang)

York St John – 112 pts (Engl Lang Ling; Engl Lit; Crea Writ)

104 pts **Bangor** – 104–120 pts (Engl Lang courses; Mus Crea Writ)

Cardiff Met – 104 pts (Engl Media; Educ St Engl; Engl Crea Writ; Engl Dr)

Central Lancashire – 104 pts (Engl Lang Lit; Engl Lang Crea Writ); (Engl Lit) (IB 28 pts)

Chichester – 104–128 pts incl Engl (Engl Lit); 104–120 pts incl Engl (Crea Writ Engl)

Falmouth – 104–120 pts (Engl; Engl Crea Writ)

Leeds Trinity – 104 pts (Engl; Engl Writ; Engl Film St; Engl Media)

Liverpool Hope – BCC–BBB 104–120 pts (Engl Lit; Engl Lang)

Liverpool John Moores – 104 pts (Hist Engl; Crea Writ; Engl) (IB 28 pts)

Manchester Met – 104–112 pts (Engl Am Lit; Engl) (IB 26 pts)

Portsmouth – 104–120 pts (Crea Media Writ) (IB 25 pts)

St Mark and St John – BCC (Engl Crea Writ; Engl Lang Ling)

St Mary's – 104 pts (Engl; Crea Prof Writ) (IB 28 pts)

South Wales – BCC incl Engl (Engl; Engl Crea Writ) (IB 29 pts HL 5 Engl)

Staffordshire – 104 pts (Engl)

Westminster – BCC (Engl Lang courses) (IB 30 pts HL 4 lang)

Winchester – 104–120 pts incl Engl (Engl courses) (IB 26 pts)

Worcester – 104–112 pts (Engl Lang courses; Engl Lit courses)

96 pts **Bishop Grosseteste** – 96–112 pts (Engl courses)

Bolton – 96 pts (Crea Writ; Engl)

Cumbria – 96 pts (Engl Crea Writ; Engl)

Glyndŵr – 96 pts (Engl; Engl Crea Writ)

London South Bank – CCC 96 pts (Engl Crea Writ)

Manchester Met – 96–112 pts (Crea Writ) (IB 28 pts)

      Portsmouth – 96–120 pts incl Engl (Engl Lang courses) (IB 30 pts HL 17 pts incl 6 Engl); 96–120 pts incl Engl+hist (Engl Hist) (IB 30 pts HL 17 pts incl 6 Engl+hist)

      Trinity Saint David – 96 pts (Engl) (IB 26 pts)

      Wolverhampton – 96 pts (Engl courses; Crea Prof Writ courses)

88 pts **Anglia Ruskin** – 88–104 pts incl Engl (Writ Engl Lit) (IB 28 pts HL 4 Engl); 88–104 pts (Engl Lang Engl Lang Teach) (IB 26 pts)

      Derby – 88–120 pts incl Engl (Crea Prof Writ Joint Hons)

      Kingston – 88–144 pts (Crea Writ)

80 pts **Anglia Ruskin** – 80–104 pts incl Engl (Engl Lit) (IB 28 pts)

      Arts London – 80 pts (Mag Jrnl Pub)

      Bedfordshire – 80 pts (Crea Writ) (IB 24 pts)

      Bucks New – 80–96 pts (Crea Writ Pub)

64 pts **Norwich City (Coll)** – 64 pts (Engl Soc Sci)

      UHI – CC incl Engl (Lit)

48 pts **Anglia Ruskin** – DD (Hist Engl)

Alternative offers
See **Chapter 6** and **Appendix 1** for grades/new UCAS Tariff points information for other examinations.

EXAMPLES OF COLLEGES OFFERING COURSES IN THIS SUBJECT FIELD

Accrington and Rossendale (Coll); Birmingham Met (Coll); Blackburn (Coll); Blackpool and Fylde (Coll); Bournemouth and Poole (Coll); Bradford (Coll); Bury (Coll); Craven (Coll); Doncaster (Coll); Farnborough (CT); Grimsby (Univ Centre); Llandrillo (Coll); Neath Port Talbot (Coll); Newham (CFE); North Lindsey (Coll); Norwich City (Coll); Peterborough (Coll); Petroc; South Devon (Coll); Suffolk (Univ Campus); Truro and Penwith (Coll); West Anglia (Coll); West Suffolk (Coll); Yeovil (Coll).

CHOOSING YOUR COURSE (SEE ALSO CH.1)

Universities and colleges teaching quality See www.qaa.ac.uk; http://unistats.direct.gov.uk.

Top research universities and colleges (REF 2014) (English Language and Literature) Warwick; Aberdeen; Durham; Newcastle; London (QM); York; Birmingham; Cardiff; St Andrews; Liverpool; London (UCL); Oxford Brookes.

Examples of sandwich degree courses Aston; Brighton; Coventry; Hertfordshire; Huddersfield; Loughborough; Southampton Solent; Surrey.

ADMISSIONS INFORMATION

Number of applicants per place (approx) Bangor 5; Bath Spa 8; Birmingham 7, (Engl Educ) 4; Birmingham City 9; Blackpool and Fylde (Coll) 2; Bristol 7; Brunel 10; Buckingham 2; Cambridge 4; Cardiff (Engl Lit) 6; Central Lancashire 10; Chester 20; Chichester 4; Cumbria 24; De Montfort 7; Derby 6; Dundee 6; Durham 12; East Anglia (Engl Lit Crea Writ) 17; Edge Hill 4; Exeter 13; Gloucestershire 35; Glyndŵr 2; Hertfordshire 6; Huddersfield 5; Hull 14; Kingston 6; Lancaster 12; Leeds 10; Leeds Trinity 7; Leicester 6; Liverpool (Engl Comm St) 7; London (Gold) 9; London (QM) 9; London (RH) 9; London (UCL) 17; London South Bank 5; Loughborough 40; Manchester 10; Manchester Met 7; Middlesex 8; Newman 3; Northampton 3; Nottingham 22; Nottingham Trent 21; Oxford (success rate 25%), (Magdalen) 15; Oxford Brookes 15; Portsmouth 8; Reading 11; Roehampton 5; Sheffield 12; Sheffield Hallam 4; South Wales 8; Southampton 8; Stirling 9; Sunderland 10; Teesside 5; Trinity Saint David 4; UWE Bristol 4; Warwick 15; Winchester 3; York 8; York St John 3.

Advice to applicants and planning the UCAS personal statement Applicants should read outside their subject. Details of any writing you have done (for example poetry, short stories) should be provided. Theatre visits and play readings are also important. Keep up-to-date by reading literary and theatre reviews in the national newspapers (keep a scrapbook of reviews for reference). Evidence is needed of a good writing style. Favourite authors, spare-time reading. Ability to write lucidly, accurately and succinctly. Evidence of literary enthusiasm. General interest in communications –

verbal, visual, media. **Bristol** Deferred entry accepted in some cases. Late applications may not be accepted. **Manchester** Due to the detailed nature of entry requirements for English Literature and American Studies courses, we are unable to include full details in the prospectus. For complete and up-to-date information on our entry requirements for these courses, please visit our website at www. manchester.ac.uk/ugcourses.

Misconceptions about this course Birmingham City The study of English language means descriptive linguistics – the course won't necessarily enable students to speak or write better English. **Buckingham** Native speakers of English often do not realise that the EFL degree courses are restricted to non-native speakers of English. **East Anglia** (Engl Lit Crea Writ) This is not simply a creative writing course: English literature is the predominant element.

Selection interviews Yes Bangor (mature students), Birmingham, Bishop Grosseteste, Cambridge, Canterbury Christ Church, Chichester, Cumbria, East Anglia, Essex, Falmouth, Gloucestershire, Huddersfield, Hull, Kingston, Lancaster, Leeds Trinity, London (Gold), London (RH), London (UCL), Middlesex, Newcastle, Nottingham, Oxford (Engl Lang Lit) 21%, (Engl Modn Langs) 16%, Portsmouth, Reading, Roehampton, Warwick; **Some** Bangor, Birmingham City, Blackburn (Coll), Blackpool and Fylde (Coll), Bristol, Cardiff Met, Chester, De Montfort, Derby, Dundee, Leeds, London (King's), London (QM), London Met, Loughborough, Southampton, Trinity Saint David, Truro and Penwith (Coll), Wolverhampton.

Interview advice and questions Questions will almost certainly be asked on set A-level texts and any essays which have been submitted prior to the interview. You will also be expected to have read outside your A-level subjects and to answer questions about your favourite authors, poets, dramatists etc. Questions in the past have included: Do you think that class discussion plays an important part in your English course? What is the value of studying a text in depth rather than just reading it for pleasure? What is the difference between satire and comedy? Are books written by women different from those written by men? Why would you go to see a production of *Hamlet*? What are your views on the choice of novels for this year's Booker Prize? What books are bad for you? If you could make up a word, what would it be? Short verbal tests and a précis may be set. See also **Chapter 5**. **Buckingham** It is useful to know if there is any particular reason why students want a particular programme; for example, for the TEFL degree is a member of the family a teacher? **Cambridge** We look for interviewees who respond positively to ideas, can think on their feet, engage intelligently with critical issues and sustain an argument. If they don't evince any of these we reject them. What books are bad for you? **Leeds** Interview questions based on information supplied in the personal statement. One third of the applicants are interviewed. Academic ability; current reading interests. **London (King's)** Interview questions are based on the information in the personal statement. Applicants are asked to prepare a short literary text which will be discussed at interview. **London (UCL)** The interview will focus on an ability to discuss literature in terms of language, plot, characters and genre. Following the interview applicants will be asked to write a critical commentary on an example of unseen prose or verse. **Oxford** Is there a difference between innocence and naivety? If you could make up a word, what would it be? Why? Do you think *Hamlet* is a bit long? No? Well I do. Is the Bible a fictional work? Was Shakespeare a rebel? **Roehampton** Samples of work taken to interview and discussed. **Warwick** We may ask students to sight-read or to analyse a text. **York** Written essays are required to be submitted at interview.

Reasons for rejection (non-academic) Some are well-informed about English literature – others are not. Inability to respond to questions about their current studies. Lack of enthusiasm for the challenge of studying familiar subjects from a different perspective. Must be able to benefit from the course. Little interest in how people communicate with each other. They don't know a single thing about our course. **Bangor** We reject those who decline interviews. **Bristol** Not enough places to make offers to all those whose qualifications deserve one. **Cambridge** See **Interview advice and questions**. **East Anglia** (Engl Am Lit) Personal statement unconvincing in its commitment to American literature. (Other courses) Poor examples of work submitted. **Leeds** Unsuitable predictions. **Oxford** (1) The essay she submitted was poorly written, careless and reductive and, in general, lacking in attention to the subject. She should be encouraged to write less and think more about what she is saying. She seems to put down the first thing that comes into her head. (2) We had the feeling that he rather tended to dismiss texts which did not satisfy the requirements of his personal canon and that he therefore might not be happy pursuing a course requiring the study of texts from all periods. (3) In her essay on Bronte she took a phrase from Arnold which was metaphorical (to do with hunger) and applied it literally, writing at length about the diet of the characters. **Reading** None. If they have reached the interview we have already eliminated all other factors. **Sheffield Hallam** Apparent lack of eagerness to tackle all three strands of the course (literature, language and creative writing). **Southampton** Insufficient or patchy academic achievement. Applicants coming from non-standard academic backgrounds are assessed in terms of their individual situations.

AFTER-RESULTS ADVICE
Offers to applicants repeating A-levels Higher Sheffield Hallam, Southampton (varies), Warwick; **Possibly higher** Lancaster, Newcastle, Oxford Brookes; **Same** Bangor, Birmingham City, Blackpool and Fylde (Coll), Bristol, Cambridge, Cardiff, Cardiff Met, Chester, Chichester, Cumbria, De Montfort, Derby, Dundee, Durham, East Anglia, Edge Hill, Hull, Leeds, Leeds Trinity, Liverpool, Liverpool Hope, London (Gold), London (RH), Loughborough, Manchester Met, Newman, Nottingham, Nottingham Trent, Portsmouth, Reading, Roehampton, St Mary's, Sheffield, Stirling, Suffolk (Univ Campus), Trinity Saint David, Ulster, Winchester, Wolverhampton, York, York St John.

GRADUATE DESTINATIONS AND EMPLOYMENT (2013/14 HESA)
English Studies graduates surveyed 10,025 **Employed** 4,705 **In voluntary employment** 525 **In further study** 2,480 **Assumed unemployed** 675

Career note English graduates work in the media, management, public and social services, business, administration and IT, retail sales, the cultural industries and the teaching profession. Those who have undertaken courses in creative writing could aim for careers in advertising, public relations, journalism or publishing.

OTHER DEGREE SUBJECTS FOR CONSIDERATION
Communication Studies; Drama; Language courses; Linguistics; Literature; Media Studies.

ENVIRONMENTAL SCIENCES

(including **Climate Science, Conservation, Ecology, Environmental Health, Environmental Hazards, Environmental Management** and **Meteorology;** see also **Biological Sciences, Biology, Engineering (Civil), Geography, Geology/Geological Sciences, Health Sciences/Studies, Marine/Maritime Studies, Town and Country Planning**)

Environmental Sciences courses need to be researched carefully since the content offered by different institutions can vary considerably. The emphasis may be biological or geographical and courses can cover marine, legal, social and political issues. Some courses focus on ecological issues, either environmental or industrial, others on environmental hazards and health, so expect some overlap in many courses. The vocational courses in this category with professional status are those of an environmental health officer whose role is concerned with all aspects of public health, covering food safety, housing, health and safety, and environmental protection.

Useful websites www.cieh.org; www.ends.co.uk; www.enn.com; www.iagre.org.uk; www.defra.gov. uk; www.socenv.org.uk; www.ies-uk.org.uk; www.noc.soton.ac.uk; www.britishecologicalsociety.org; www.rmets.org

NB The points totals shown to the left of the institutions are for ease of reference only. It must not be assumed that Tariff points are always used by institutions or that they can be substituted for an offer in grades. The level of an offer is not necessarily indicative of the quality of a course.

Check **Chapter 3** for new university admission details and **Chapter 6** on how to read the subject tables.

COURSE OFFERS INFORMATION

Subject requirements/preferences GCSE English, mathematics and a science (often chemistry or biology) usually required. **AL** One or two science subjects are usually stipulated; Mathematics may be required. (Meteor) Mathematics, Physics and another science may be required sometimes with specified grades, eg Mathematics and Physics grade B.

Your target offers and examples of degree courses

152 pts **Leeds** – A*AA (Sust Env Mgt (Int)) (IB 35 pts); A*AA incl maths+phys/chem (Meteor Clim Sci (Int)) (IB 35 pts)

York – A*AA–AAB incl chem+sci/maths (Chem Res Env) (IB 36–35 pts HL 6 chem)

144 pts **Birmingham** – AAA–AAB incl biol+sci (Biol Sci (Env Biol)) (IB 32 pts HL 666–665)

Edinburgh – AAA–ABB (Ecol; Ecol Env Sci Mgt; Ecol Env Sci; Chem Env Sust Chem; Geophys Meteor; Phys Meteor) (IB 37–32 pts)

Imperial London – AAA incl biol+sci/maths (Ecol Env Biol) (IB 38 pts HL 6 biol+chem/maths)

Lancaster – AAA–ABB incl chem (Env Chem) (IB 36–32 pts HL 6 chem)

Leeds – AAA–AAB incl biol (Ecol Env Bio) (IB 35–34 pts HL 6 biol+sci)

London (UCL) – AAA–AAB incl geog (Env Geog) (IB 38–36 pts HL 6 geog)

Sheffield – AAA–AAB incl biol+sci (Ecol Cons Biol MBiolSci) (IB 37 pts HL 6 biol+sci)

York – AAA–AAB (Ecol) (IB 36–35 pts)

136 pts **Cardiff** – AAB–ABB (Ecol) (IB 34 pts)

East Anglia – AAB 136 pts (Env Sci MSci) (IB 33 pts HL 6 sci); AAB/ABBB incl sci (Env Earth Sci MSci) (IB 33 pts HL 6 sci)

Exeter – AAB–ABB incl sci (Env Sci) (IB 34–32 pts HL 5 sci); AAB–ABB incl sci/maths (Cons Biol Ecol) (IB 34–32 pts HL 5 sci/maths); AAB–BBB incl sci (Renew Ener) (IB 34–30 pts HL 5 sci)

London (QM) – AAB–BBB (Env Sci) (IB 32–30 pts)

London LSE – AAB incl maths (Env Plcy Econ) (IB 37 pts)

Newcastle – ABB (Env Sci) (IB 34 pts)

Reading – AAB–ABB (Ecol Wldlf Cons; Maths Meteor) (IB 35–32 pts)

St Andrews – AAB incl biol+sci/maths (Ecol Cons) (IB 36 pts)

Sheffield – AAB–ABB incl biol+sci (Ecol Cons Biol) (IB 35–34 pts HL 6 biol+sci)

Sussex – AAB–ABB incl sci/env st (Ecol Cons Env) (IB 34 pts HL 5 sci)

128 pts **Birmingham** – ABB incl sci (Env Sci) (IB 32 pts HL 655); ABB (Pal Palaeoenv) (IB 32–34 pts)

Coventry – ABB–BBB (Geog Nat Haz) (IB 29 pts)

East Anglia – ABB incl geog (Env Geog Clim Chng) (IB 32 pts HL 5 geog); ABB (Env Sci) (IB 32 pts HL 5 sci); ABB incl maths (Meteor Ocean) (IB 32 pts HL 5 maths)

Kent – ABB (Env Soc Sci (Yr Prof Pr); Env Soc Sci) (IB 34 pts)

Lancaster – ABB incl sci (Ecol Cons; Env Biol; Env Sci) (IB 32 pts HL 6 sci)

Leeds – ABB (Sust Env Mgt; Env Sci) (IB 34 pts); ABB incl maths+phys/chem (Meteor Clim Sci) (IB 34 pts)

Leicester – ABB incl sci/maths/geog (App Env Geol) (IB 30 pts)

Liverpool – ABB incl sci/maths/geog (Env Sci) (IB 33 pts HL 4 sci); ABB incl biol+sci (Ecol Env) (IB 33 pts HL 6 biol)

London (RH) – ABB incl biol (Ecol Env) (IB 32 pts)

Manchester – ABB incl sci (Env Sci; Env Res Geol) (IB 33 pts HL 5 sci); ABB (Env Mgt) (IB 34 pts)

Nottingham – ABB–BBB incl sci/maths (Env Biol; Env Sci) (IB 32–30 pts)

Plymouth – 128 pts (Mar Biol Cstl Ecol) (IB 30 pts)

Reading – ABB–BBB (Meteor Clim; Env Sci; Env Mgt) (IB 32–30 pts)

Sheffield – ABB–BBB (Lnd Archit) (IB 34 pts); ABB incl sci/maths/geog (Env Sci) (IB 34 pts HL 6 sci/maths/geog)

Southampton – ABB incl sci (Env Mgt Bus; Env Sci) (IB 32 pts HL 5 sci)

York – ABB incl sci/maths/geog (Env Sci) (IB 34 pts)

120 pts **Aberdeen** – BBB incl maths/sci (Env Sci; Ecol) (IB 32 pts HL 5 maths/sci)

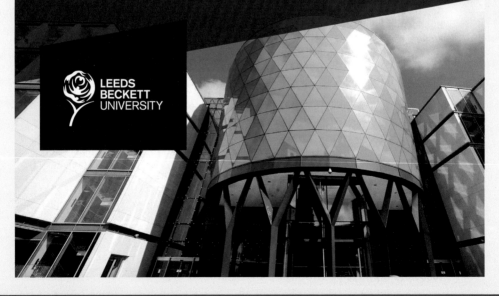

LEEDS BECKETT UNIVERSITY

BSc (Hons) Environmental Health

This course, accredited by the Chartered Institute of Environmental Health, will teach you how to examine complex environmental health problems and understand how to formulate effective solutions. You will be taught by environmental health practitioners with experience in key areas of food safety, health and safety, environmental protection and housing.

BSc (Hons) Safety, Health & Environmental Management

Accredited by the Institution of Occupational Safety and Health and taught by leading experts in the industry, this course will expand your knowledge of safety, health and environmental management and control. With our fresh approach to teaching you will learn and develop innovative approaches to managing health and safety issues in a positive and effective way.

To find out more, visit courses.leedsbeckett.ac.uk and search for 'environmental health'

Bangor – 120 pts (App Ter Mar Ecol)

Brighton – BBB (Env Sci) (IB 30 pts)

Dundee – BBB–BCC (Env Sust) (IB 30 pts); BBB–BCC incl sci (Env Sci) (IB 30 pts); BBB–BCC incl maths+sci/eng (Renew) (IB 30 pts)

Edge Hill – BBB 120 pts (Env Sci)

Glasgow – BBB–CCC incl sci/maths/geog (Env Sci Sust) (IB 30–28 pts)

Gloucestershire – 120 pts (Ecol Env Sci)

Greenwich – 120 pts (Env Sci)

Huddersfield – BBB 120 pts (Bus St Env Mgt)

Keele – BBB/ABC (Env Sust) (IB 32 pts); BBB/ABC incl sci/geog (App Env Sci courses) (IB 32 pts HL 6 sci/geog)

Liverpool – BBB (Env Plan) (IB 31 pts)

Northumbria – 120 pts incl geog/sci (Env Sci) (IB 30 pts); 120 pts incl geog (Geog Env Mgt) (IB 30 pts)

Queen's Belfast – BBB–ABB incl biol/econ/geog (Lnd Use Env Mgt)

Stirling – BBB (Ecol; Env Sci; Cons Biol Mgt; Env Sci Out Educ) (IB 32 pts)

Ulster – 120 pts incl sci/maths (Env Hlth) (IB 26 pts)

116 pts **Aberystwyth** – 116–132 pts incl biol/env sci (Env Biosci); 116–132 pts incl biol (Ecol)

112 pts **Bangor** – 112 pts incl sci (Env Sci; Env Cons; Env Mgt); 112–128 pts incl sci (Mar Env St)

Brighton – BBC incl biol+geog (Ecol) (IB 28 pts)

Central Lancashire – 112 pts (Env Mgt) (IB 28 pts)

Chester – BBC–BCC incl biol/chem/sci 112 pts (Wldlf Cons Ecol) (IB 26 pts HL 5 biol/chem); BBC–BCC 112 pts (Nat Haz Mgt) (IB 26 pts HL 5 geog)

Glasgow Caledonian – BBC (Env Mgt) (IB 24 pts)

Hull – 112 pts incl biol (Ecol Env) (IB 28 pts HL 5 biol)

Leeds Beckett – 112 pts (Env Hlth) (IB 25 pts)

London (Birk) – 112 pts (Env Mgt)

     Northampton – 112–120 pts (Env Sci courses)
     Nottingham Trent – 112 pts incl sci (Env Sci)
     Oxford Brookes – BBC 112 pts (Env Sci) (IB 30 pts)
     Plymouth – 112 pts incl sci (Env Sci) (IB 28 pts); 112 pts (Archit Tech Env) (IB 28 pts)
     Sheffield Hallam – 112 pts (Env Sci)
     Teesside – BBC incl sci/geog (Env Sci)
     UWE Bristol – 112 pts incl sci (Wldlf Ecol Cons Sci; Env Sci) (IB 25 pts HL 5 sci)
104 pts **Bath Spa** – 104–120 pts (Env Sci)
     Bournemouth – 104–128 pts (Env Sci) (IB 31 pts)
     Cardiff Met – 104 pts (Env Hlth)
     Derby – 104–112 pts incl geog/sci (Env Haz Joint Hons)
     Liverpool Hope – BCC–BBB 104–120 pts (Env Sci)
     Manchester Met – BCC–BBC incl geog/sci 104–112 pts (Env Mgt Sust (St Abrd); Env Sci (St
        Abrd); Ecol Cons (St Abrd)) (IB 28 pts HL 5 geog/sci); BCC–BBC incl geog 104–112 pts
        (Physl Geog) (IB 28 pts HL 5 geog/sci)
     Nottingham Trent – 104 pts (Env Cons)
     Portsmouth – 104–128 pts incl sci/maths (Mar Env Sci) (IB 26 pts HL 5 sci)
     West Scotland – BCC incl biol/chem (Env Hlth) (IB 28 pts)
96 pts **Canterbury Christ Church** – 96 pts (Env Sci; Ecol Cons)
     Glyndŵr – 96 pts (Geog Ecol Env)
     Hertfordshire – 96 pts (Env Mgt; Hum Geog Env St) (IB 24 pts)
     Kingston – 96–112 pts (Env Mgt; Env Sci); (Env Haz Dis Mgt) (IB 26 pts)
     Manchester Met – 96–112 pts (Ent Out St) (IB 28 pts)
     Southampton Solent – 96 pts (Geog Env St)
     Sparsholt (Coll) – 96–112 pts (Aquacult Fish Mgt)
     Worcester – 96–112 pts incl biol+sci (Ecol); 96–112 pts incl geog+sci (Env Sci)
88 pts **Ulster** – 88–104 pts incl sci/maths/tech (Env Sci) (IB 24 pts)
80 pts **Wolverhampton** – 80 pts (Env Hlth)
72 pts **Trinity Saint David** – 72 pts incl geog (Env Cons)
64 pts **UHI** – CC (Arch Env St); CC incl sci (Env Sci)

     Open University – contact +44 (0)845 300 6090 **or** www.openuniversity.co.uk/you (Env St)

Alternative offers
See **Chapter 6** and **Appendix 1** for grades/new UCAS Tariff points information for other
examinations.

EXAMPLES OF COLLEGES OFFERING COURSES IN THIS SUBJECT FIELD
Askham Bryan (Coll); Bedford (Coll); Birmingham Met (Coll); Bishop Burton (Coll); Cornwall (Coll);
Duchy (Coll); Durham New (Coll); Easton Otley (Coll); Hadlow (Coll); Hartpury (Coll); Kingston
Maurward (Coll); Leeds City (Coll); Manchester (Coll); Moulton (Coll); Myerscough (Coll); Petroc;
Plymouth City (Coll); Sparsholt (Coll); Truro and Penwith (Coll); Weston (Coll); Writtle (Coll); York
(Coll).

CHOOSING YOUR COURSE (SEE ALSO CH.1)
Universities and colleges teaching quality See www.qaa.ac.uk; http://unistats.direct.gov.uk.

Top research universities and colleges (REF 2014) (Earth Systems and Environmental Sciences)
Bristol; Cambridge; Oxford; London (RH); Birmingham; Southampton; London (Birk); London (UCL);
Leicester; Manchester; Leeds.

Examples of sandwich degree courses Brighton; Coventry; Glasgow Caledonian; Greenwich;
Hertfordshire; Keele; Kingston; Leeds; Manchester Met; Middlesex; Nottingham Trent; Reading;
Teesside; Ulster; UWE Bristol.

ADMISSIONS INFORMATION

Number of applicants per place (approx) Aberystwyth 3; Bangor 3; Bath Spa 2; Birmingham 5; Bournemouth 4; Bristol 6; Cardiff Met 4; Coventry 9; Dundee 6; Durham 5; East Anglia 7; Edinburgh 1; Essex 3; Glasgow Caledonian 1; Gloucestershire 11; Glyndŵr 3; Greenwich 2; Hertfordshire 5; Hull 8; Kingston 3; Lancaster 11; Liverpool John Moores 5; London (RH) 8; London (UCL) 7; London LSE 7; Manchester Met (Env Sci) 5; Northampton 4; Northumbria 8; Nottingham 6; Nottingham Trent 3; Oxford Brookes 13; Plymouth 8; Portsmouth 5; Sheffield Hallam 8; Southampton 4; Stirling 10; Trinity Saint David 3; Ulster 16; UWE Bristol 1; Wolverhampton 2; Worcester 7; York 4.

Advice to applicants and planning the UCAS personal statement 'We want doers, not just thinkers' is one comment from an admissions tutor. Describe any field courses which you have attended; make an effort to visit one of the National Parks. Discuss these visits and identify any particular aspects which impressed you. Outline travel interests. Give details of work as a conservation volunteer and other outside-school activities. Strong communication skills, people-oriented work experience. Watch your spelling and grammar! What sparked your interest in Environmental Science? Discuss your field trips. (Env Hlth courses) A basic knowledge of environmental health as opposed to environmental sciences. Work experience in an environmental health department is looked upon very favourably. See also **Appendix 3**. **Lancaster** Two A-level subjects required from Biology, Chemistry, Computing, Environmental Science, Geography or Geology.

Misconceptions about this course Bangor Students should note that only simple mathematical skills are required for this course. **Southampton** This is not just a course for environmentalists, for example links with BP, IBM etc. **Wolverhampton** This is a course in environmental science, not environmental studies: there is a difference.

Selection interviews Yes Coventry, Gloucestershire, Greenwich, Hertfordshire, Kingston, Manchester Met, Newcastle, Nottingham, Nottingham Trent, Oxford Brookes, Reading, Sheffield Hallam, Trinity Saint David, UWE Bristol; **Some** Bangor, Birmingham, Cardiff Met, Derby, East Anglia, Plymouth, Southampton, Staffordshire; **No** Dundee.

Interview advice and questions Environmental issues are constantly in the news, so keep abreast of developments. You could be asked to discuss any particular environmental problems in the area in which you live and to justify your stance on any environmental issues on which you have strong opinions. See also **Chapter 5**. **Bath Spa** Questions on school work, current affairs and field courses. **East Anglia** Can you display an informed interest in any aspect of environmental science?

Reasons for rejection (non-academic) Inability to be aware of the needs of others.

AFTER-RESULTS ADVICE

Offers to applicants repeating A-levels Higher Greenwich, Lancaster, Nottingham, Nottingham Trent; **Possibly higher** Aberystwyth, Bradford, Northumbria; **Same** Bangor, Birmingham, Brighton, Cardiff Met, Derby, Dundee, East Anglia, Leeds, Liverpool John Moores, Manchester Met, Plymouth, Southampton, Ulster, Wolverhampton.

GRADUATE DESTINATIONS AND EMPLOYMENT (2013/14 HESA)

See **Biological Sciences**.

Career note Some graduates find work with government departments, local authorities, statutory and voluntary bodies in areas like land management and pollution control. Others go into a range of non-scientific careers.

OTHER DEGREE SUBJECTS FOR CONSIDERATION

Biological Sciences; Biology; Chemistry; Earth Sciences; Environmental Engineering; Geography; Geology; Meteorology; Ocean Sciences/Oceanography; Town and Country Planning.

EUROPEAN STUDIES

(see also **French, German, International Relations, Languages, Russian and East European Studies**)

European Studies courses provide the opportunity to study one or two main languages along with a broad study of economic, political, legal, social and cultural issues within the broad context of the European community. Other similar specific courses such as European History or European Politics allow the student to focus on an individual subject area.

Useful websites www.europa.eu; www.britishcouncil.org/erasmus; see also **Languages**.

NB The points totals shown to the left of the institutions are for ease of reference only. It must not be assumed that Tariff points are always used by institutions or that they can be substituted for an offer in grades. The level of an offer is not necessarily indicative of the quality of a course.

COURSE OFFERS INFORMATION

Subject requirements/preferences GCSE English and a foreign language for all courses and possibly mathematics. Grades may be stipulated. **AL** A modern language usually required.

Your target offers and examples of degree courses

152 pts **Durham** – A*AA incl maths+fmaths (Maths (Euro St)) (IB 38 pts)
London (UCL) – A*AA (Euro Soc Pol St) (IB 39 pts)

144 pts **London (King's)** – AAA–AAB incl Fr/Ger/Span (Euro St (Fr/Ger/Span) (Yr Abrd)) (IB 35 pts HL 6 Fr/Ger/Span)
London (UCL) – AAA–AAB (Pol E Euro St) (IB 38–36 pts)
Newcastle – AAA–ABB (Gov EU St) (IB 32 pts)

136 pts **Glasgow** – AAB–BBB (Cnt E Euro St) (IB 38–36 pts)
London (UCL) – AAB incl lang (Lang Cult) (IB 36 pts HL 6 lang)
Southampton – AAB–ABB incl lang (Langs Contemp Euro St) (IB 34 pts HL 6 lang)

128 pts **Bath** – ABB–AAB incl langs (Modn Langs Euro St) (IB 34 pts HL 6 5 langs)
Essex – ABB–BBB (Euro St; Euro St Fr/Ger/Ital/Span) (IB 32–30 pts)
Kent – ABB–BBB incl maths (Euro Econ) (IB 34 pts)
Leeds – ABB (Euro St Langs) (IB 34 pts)
Leicester – ABB incl Fr/Ital/Span (Euro St) (IB 30 pts)
London (RH) – ABB (Euro St Fr/Ger/Ital/Span) (IB 34 pts)
Manchester – ABB incl Engl lang (Euro St Modn Lang) (IB 34 pts)
Nottingham – ABB incl lang (Modn Euro St) (IB 32 pts)
Swansea – ABB–BBB incl geog (Geog Euro St) (IB 33–32 pts)

120 pts **Aberdeen** – BBB 120 pts (Euro St) (IB 32 pts)
Dundee – BBB–BBC (Euro St) (IB 30 pts)
Kent – BBB incl lang (Euro St (Comb Langs)) (IB 34 pts); BBB incl Fr/Ger/Span (Euro St (Fr/Ger/Span)) (IB 34 pts)
Stirling – BBB (Euro Film Media) (IB 32 pts)

112 pts **Nottingham Trent** – 112 pts (Euro St Joint Hons)

96 pts **Portsmouth** – 96–120 pts (Euro St Int Rel) (IB 30 pts HL 17 pts)

Open University – contact +44 (0)845 300 6090 **or** www.openuniversity.co.uk/you (Euro St)

Alternative offers
See **Chapter 6** and **Appendix 1** for grades/new UCAS Tariff points information for other examinations.

CHOOSING YOUR COURSE (SEE ALSO CH.1)

Universities and colleges teaching quality See www.qaa.ac.uk; http://unistats.direct.gov.uk.

Top research universities and colleges (REF 2014) See **Languages**.

ADMISSIONS INFORMATION
Number of applicants per place (approx) Bath 5; Dundee 6; Durham 2; Kent 11; Leicester 15; London (King's) 7; London (UCL) 8; Nottingham 6; Nottingham Trent 12; Portsmouth 5.

Advice to applicants and planning the UCAS personal statement Try to identify an interest you have in the country relevant to your studies. Visits to that country should be described. Read the national newspapers and magazines and keep up-to-date with political and economic developments. Show your interest in the culture and civilisation of Europe as a whole, through, for example, European travel. Show your motivation for choosing the course and give details of your personal achievements and any future career plans, showing your international awareness and perspective.

Selection interviews Some Dundee, Kent (not usually); **No** Essex, Portsmouth, Reading.

Interview advice and questions Whilst your interest in studying a language may be the main reason for applying for this subject, the politics, economics and culture of European countries are constantly in the news. You should keep up-to-date with any such topics concerning your chosen country and be prepared for questions. A language test may occupy part of the interview. See also **Chapter 5**.

Reasons for rejection (non-academic) Poor powers of expression. Lack of ideas on any issues. Lack of enthusiasm.

AFTER-RESULTS ADVICE
Offers to applicants repeating A-levels **Same** Dundee.

GRADUATE DESTINATIONS AND EMPLOYMENT (2013/14 HESA)
Graduates surveyed 180 **Employed** 90 **In voluntary employment** 10 **In further study** 50 **Assumed unemployed** 10

Career note See **Languages**.

OTHER DEGREE SUBJECTS FOR CONSIDERATION
Business and Management; History; International Relations; Politics; Language courses.

FILM, RADIO, VIDEO and TV STUDIES

(see also **Art and Design (Graphic Design), Communication Studies/Communication, Engineering (Acoustics and Sound), Media Studies, Photography**)

Many courses are offered in this subject field, some combined with TV studies, photography and media studies as in the course at the University of Leeds which combines theory with practice offering a knowledge in digital film and photography with options in TV production, film editing, and documentary production. By contrast, the Exeter course presents a broad chronological and geographical coverage from the silent film to the Hollywood classics. It's therefore important to choose courses with care, particularly the theoretical and practical content of courses. At Brunel University London, practical studies occupy 40% of the course whilst at Chichester the Digital Film Production course offers a 50/50 balance between production work and screenwriting.

Useful websites www.bfi.org.uk; www.film.com; www.allmovie.com; www.bksts.com; www.imdb.com; www.fwfr.com; www.bafta.org; www.movingimage.us; http://film.britishcouncil.org; www.filmsite.org; www.festival-cannes.com/en; www.bbc.co.uk/careers/home; www.rogerebert.com; www.bectu.org.uk

NB The points totals shown to the left of the institutions are for ease of reference only. It must not be assumed that Tariff points are always used by institutions or that they can be substituted for an offer in grades. The level of an offer is not necessarily indicative of the quality of a course.

COURSE OFFERS INFORMATION

Subject requirements/preferences GCSE English usually required. Courses vary, check prospectuses. **AL** English may be stipulated for some courses.

Your target offers and examples of degree courses

144 pts Lancaster – AAA–AAB incl Engl (Film Engl Lit) (IB 36–35 pts HL 6 lit)
            London (King's) – AAA incl Engl+lang (Compar Lit Film St) (IB 35 pts HL 6 Engl lit)
            St Andrews – AAA–AAB (Film St courses) (IB 38–36 pts)

136 pts Bristol – AAB–ABB (Film TV) (IB 34–32 pts)
            East Anglia – AAB (Film TV St) (IB 33 pts)
            Exeter – AAB–ABB (Film St) (IB 34–32 pts)
            Glasgow – AAB–BBB incl arts/lang (Film TV St Joint Hons) (IB 36–34 pts)
            Kent – AAB (Film courses) (IB 34 pts)
            Lancaster – AAB–ABB (Film St; Film Sociol) (IB 35–32 pts)
            Leeds – AAB (Film Photo Media) (IB 35 pts)
            Manchester – AAB–BBB incl Engl (Scrn St courses) (IB 36–31 pts)
            Southampton – AAB–ABB (Film Phil; Film St) (IB 32 pts); AAB–ABB incl hist (Film Hist) (IB 32 pts HL 6 hist); AAB–ABB incl Engl (Film Engl) (IB 32 pts HL 6 Engl)
            Surrey – AAB–ABB (Film St Joint Hons) (IB 36–34 pts)
            Sussex – AAB–ABB (Dr St Film St; Film St) (IB 34 pts)
            Warwick – AAB incl Engl/film st/hist (Film St) (IB 36 pts HL 6 Engl/film st/hist); AAB incl Engl (Film Lit) (IB 36 pts HL 6 Engl)
            York – AAB (Film TV Prod) (IB 35 pts)

128 pts East Anglia – ABB (Film Engl St) (IB 32 pts HL 5 Engl); ABB incl hist (Film Hist) (IB 32 pts HL 5 hist)
            Essex – ABB–BBB (Film St Lit; Film St) (IB 32–30 pts)
            Keele – ABB (Film St) (IB 34 pts)
            Kent – ABB (Film) (IB 34 pts)
            Leeds – ABB (Film St Comb) (IB 34 pts)
            Liverpool – ABB (Film St Comb Hons) (IB 33 pts)
            London (QM) – 128–136 pts incl film/media (Film St) (IB 34 pts HL 5 film/media)
            London (RH) – ABB (Film St) (IB 32 pts)
            Newcastle – ABB (Film Prac; Film Media) (IB 32 pts)
            Northumbria – 128 pts (Film TV St) (IB 31 pts)
            Nottingham – ABB/AAC (Film TV St) (IB 32 pts); ABB–ACC (Film TV St Am St) (IB 32 pts)
            Reading – ABB–BBB (Engl Lit Film Thea; Film Thea; Art Film Thea; Film) (IB 32–30 pts)
            Westminster – ABB (Film) (IB 32 pts)

120 pts Aberdeen – BBB (Film Vis Cult) (IB 32 pts)
            Birmingham City – BBB 120 pts (Film Prod Tech; Film Tech Vis Efcts) (IB 32 pts)
            Bournemouth – 120–128 pts (TV Prod) (IB 31–32 pts)
            Brunel – BBB (Gms Des Film TV St; Thea Film TV St; Engl Film TV St) (IB 30 pts)
            Derby – 120 pts +interview +portfolio (Film Prod); 120 pts (Media Prod)
            Dundee – BBB–BCC incl Engl (Engl Film St) (IB 30 pts)
            Edge Hill – BBB 120 pts (Film TV Prod; Engl Film St; Film St)
            Edinburgh (CA) – BBB +portfolio (Film TV) (IB 34 pts)
            Gloucestershire – 120 pts (Film Prod)
            Greenwich – 120 pts (Dig Film Prod)
            Hertfordshire – 120 pts (Film TV (Prod)) (IB 30 pts)
            Kent – BBB (Art Hist Film) (IB 34 pts)
            Leeds Beckett – 120 pts (Filmm) (IB 26 pts)
            Leicester – BBB (Film Media St) (IB 28 pts)
            Lincoln – 120 pts (Film TV)
            Norwich Arts – BBB incl art/des (Film Mov Imag Prod) (IB 32 pts)
            Queen's Belfast – BBB (Film St courses)
            Sheffield Hallam – 120 pts (Film Media Prod)

Check **Chapter 3** for new university admission details and **Chapter 6** on how to read the subject tables.

Stirling – BBB (Glob Cnma; Film Media) (IB 32 pts)

Sunderland – 120 pts (Film Media; Dig Film Prod; Engl Film)

112 pts **Aberystwyth** – 112–120 pts (Film TV St)

Bath Spa – 112–128 pts (Film Scrn St courses)

Bedfordshire – 112 pts (TV Prod) (IB 24 pts)

Birmingham City – BBC 112 pts (Media Comm (Rad)) (IB 28 pts)

Bournemouth – 112–120 pts (Rad; Film Prod Cnma) (IB 30–31 pts)

Bournemouth Arts – BBC–BBB 112–120 pts +portfolio +interview (Film Prod; Animat Prod) (IB 32 pts)

Bradford – BBC 112 pts (Film TV Prod; Film Media St)

Brunel – BBC (Film TV St) (IB 29 pts)

Canterbury Christ Church – 112 pts (Film Rad TV St)

Chester – 112 pts (Rad Prod) (IB 28 pts); BBC–BCC 112 pts (Film St; Rad Prod courses; TV Prod) (IB 26 pts)

Chichester – 112–128 pts (Film TV St) (IB 30 pts)

Creative Arts – 112 pts (Film Prod)

East London – 112 pts (Film) (IB 24 pts)

Edge Hill – BBC 112 pts (Media Film TV)

Edinburgh Napier – BBC incl Engl (Engl Film) (IB 29 pts HL 5 Engl)

Gloucestershire – 112 pts (Film St)

Greenwich – 112 pts (Film St; Film TV Prod)

Hertfordshire – 112 pts (Engl Lang Comm Film) (IB 28 pts)

Huddersfield – BBC incl dr/thea/perf arts 112 pts (Film St courses)

Hull – 112 pts (Film St) (IB 28 pts)

Liverpool John Moores – 112 pts (Film St; Crea Writ Flm St) (IB 29 pts)

London Met – 112 pts (Film Broad Prod; Film TV St; Jrnl Film TV St)

Manchester Met – 112 pts (Filmm) (IB 26 pts)

Middlesex – 112 pts (Film)

Northampton – 112 pts (Film Scrn St Joint Hons)

Nottingham Trent – 112 pts incl IT/sci (Dig Media Tech); 112 pts (Des Film TV; Film TV Joint Hons)

Oxford Brookes – BBC (Film St) (IB 30 pts)

Roehampton – 112 pts (Film)

Southampton Solent – 112 pts (Film TV; Film; Engl Film; TV Vid Prod; TV Std Prod)

Suffolk (Univ Campus) – 112 pts (Dig Film Prod)

Sunderland – 112 pts (Photo Vid Dig Imag)

Teesside – 112 pts (TV Film Prod)

UWE Bristol – 112 pts (Filmm) (IB 25 pts)

West London – 112 pts (Film Prod)

York St John – 112 pts (Film St)

104 pts **Arts London** – BCC 104 pts (Film TV)

Bangor – 104–120 pts (Mus Film St; Film St courses)

Central Lancashire – 104 pts (TV Prod; Scrnwrit Film TV Rad; Film Prod); (Film Media St) (IB 28 pts)

De Montfort – 104 pts (Film St Joint Hons; Aud Rec Tech) (IB 28 pts)

Falmouth – 104–120 pts (Film)

Leeds Trinity – 104 pts (Engl Film St; TV Prod; Film TV St)

Manchester Met – 104–112 pts (Film Media St) (IB 26 pts)

Portsmouth – 104–120 pts (Film St courses) (IB 25 pts)

Queen Margaret – BCC 104 pts (Film Media; Thea Film) (IB 28 pts)

St Mary's – 104 pts (Film Scrn Media) (IB 28 pts)

Sheffield Hallam – 104 pts incl film/media st (Film St); 104 pts incl film/Engl/hist/jrnl (Film St Scrnwrit)

South Wales – BCC incl art/film/media (Film; Film St) (IB 29 pts)

Staffordshire – 104 pts (Media (Film) Prod; Film TV Rad St)

      Worcester – 104 pts (Film St Scrn Writ); 104 pts +interview +portfolio (Film Prod)
96 pts **Cumbria** – 96 pts (Film TV)
      Derby – 96 pts (Film TV St)
      Kingston – 96 pts (Film St)
      London South Bank – CCC 96 pts (Film Prac; Film St)
      Manchester Met – 96–112 pts (Film TV Cult St) (IB 28 pts)
      Staffordshire – 96 pts (Dig Film 3D Animat Tech)
      West Scotland – CCC incl Engl (Filmm Scrnwrit; Broad Prod) (IB 24 pts)
      Winchester – 96–112 pts (Film St) (IB 25 pts)
      Wolverhampton – 96 pts (Film St courses; Film Media Cult St)
88 pts **Anglia Ruskin** – 88–104 pts (Film St) (IB 24 pts)
      Derby – 88–120 pts (Film TV St Joint Hons)
80 pts **Anglia Ruskin** – 80–96 pts (Film TV Prod) (IB 24 pts)
      Bucks New – 80–96 pts (Film TV Prod)
      Plymouth (CA) – 80 pts +portfolio (Film)
64 pts **Ravensbourne** – CC (Dig Film Prod) (IB 28 pts)
32 pts **RConsvS** – EE (Dig Film TV) (IB 24 pts)

Alternative offers
See **Chapter 6** and **Appendix 1** for grades/new UCAS Tariff points information for other examinations.

EXAMPLES OF COLLEGES OFFERING COURSES IN THIS SUBJECT FIELD
Accrington and Rossendale (Coll); Amersham and Wycombe (Coll); Barking and Dagenham (Coll); Barnsley (Coll); Birmingham Met (Coll); Bournemouth and Poole (Coll); Bournville (Coll); Bradford (Coll); Brooksby Melton (Coll); Bury (Coll); Central Film Sch; Chesterfield (Coll); Chichester (Coll); Cleveland (CAD); Cornwall (Coll); Croydon (Univ Centre); Doncaster (Coll); East Surrey (Coll); Exeter (Coll); Farnborough (CT); Gloucestershire (Coll); Grimsby (Univ Centre); Harrow (Coll); Hereford (CA); Hull (Coll); Kensington and Chelsea (Coll); Manchester (Coll); Northbrook (Coll); Nottingham New (Coll); Rotherham (CAT); South Devon (Coll); South Staffordshire (Coll); Truro and Penwith (Coll); Warwickshire (Coll); West Thames (Coll); Weston (Coll); Wiltshire (Coll).

CHOOSING YOUR COURSE (SEE ALSO CH.1)
Universities and colleges teaching quality See www.qaa.ac.uk; http://unistats.direct.gov.uk.

Top research universities and colleges (REF 2014) See **Drama**.

Examples of sandwich degree courses Birmingham City; Bradford; Canterbury Christ Church; Greenwich; Hertfordshire; Huddersfield; Portsmouth; Southampton Solent; Surrey; UWE Bristol; Wolverhampton.

ADMISSIONS INFORMATION
Number of applicants per place (approx) Bournemouth 30; Bournemouth Arts 9; Bristol 15; Brunel 10; Canterbury Christ Church 50; Central Lancashire 5; East Anglia (Film Engl St) 7, (Film Am St) 5; Kent 30; Leicester 9; Liverpool John Moores 17; London Met 7; Portsmouth 20; Sheffield Hallam 60; Southampton 6; Southampton Solent 7; Staffordshire 31; Stirling 12; Warwick 18; Westminster 41; York 4; York St John 6.

Advice to applicants and planning the UCAS personal statement Bournemouth Arts Any experience in film making (beyond home videos) should be described in detail. Knowledge and preferences of types of films and the work of some producers should be included on the UCAS application. Read film magazines and other appropriate literature to keep informed of developments. Show genuine interest in a range of film genres and be knowledgeable about favourite films, directors and give details of work experience or film projects undertaken. You should also be able to discuss the ways in which films relate to broader cultural phenomena, social, literary, historical.

Misconceptions about this course That an A-level in Film or Media Studies is required; it is not. That it's Film so it's easy! That the course is all practical work. Some applicants believe that these are Media courses. Some applicants believe that Film and TV Studies is a training for production work. **Bournemouth Arts** (Animat Prod) This is not a Film Studies course but a course based on traditional animation with supported computer image processing. **De Montfort** Some believe that this is a course in practical film making: it is not, it is for analysts and historians. **Winchester** That graduation automatically leads to a job in broadcasting!

Selection interviews Most institutions will interview applicants in this subject. **Yes** Birmingham City, Bournemouth, Bournemouth Arts, Canterbury Christ Church, Chichester, Cumbria, Falmouth, Hertfordshire, Leeds Beckett, London South Bank, Middlesex, Reading, Warwick, Worcester, York; **Some** Bristol, East Anglia, Liverpool John Moores, Southampton, Staffordshire, Wolverhampton; **No** Essex, Nottingham.

Interview advice and questions Questions will focus on your chosen field. In the case of films be prepared to answer questions not only on your favourite films but on the work of one or two directors you admire and early Hollywood examples. See also **Chapter 5**. **Bournemouth Arts** Written piece prior to interview. Questions at interview relevant to the portfolio/reel. **Staffordshire** We assess essay-writing skills.

Reasons for rejection (non-academic) Not enough drive or ambition. No creative or original ideas. Preference for production work rather than practical work. Inability to articulate the thought process behind the work in the applicant's portfolio. Insufficient knowledge of media affairs. Lack of knowledge of film history. Wrong course choice, wanted more practical work.

AFTER-RESULTS ADVICE
Offers to applicants repeating A-levels Higher Bournemouth Arts, Glasgow, Manchester Met; **Same** De Montfort, East Anglia, Liverpool Hope, St Mary's, Staffordshire, Stirling, Winchester, Wolverhampton, York St John.

GRADUATE DESTINATIONS AND EMPLOYMENT (2013/14 HESA)
See **Media Studies**.

Career note Although this is a popular subject field, job opportunities in film, TV and radio are limited. Successful graduates frequently have gained work experience with companies during their undergraduate years. The transferable skills (verbal communication etc) will open up other career opportunities.

OTHER DEGREE SUBJECTS FOR CONSIDERATION
Animation; Communication Studies; Creative Writing; Media Studies; Photography.

FINANCE

(including **Banking**, **Financial Services** and **Insurance**; see also **Accountancy/Accounting**)

Courses involving finance are wide ranging and can involve accountancy, actuarial work, banking, economics, financial services, insurance, international finance, marketing, quantity surveying, real estate management, and risk management. Some courses are theoretical, others, such as accountancy and real estate management, are vocational, providing accreditation to professional bodies. A large number of courses are offered with commercial and industrial placements over six months or a year (which includes paid employment) and many students have found that their connection with a firm has led to offers of full-time employment upon graduation.

Useful websites www.cii.co.uk; www.financialadvice.co.uk; www.efinancialnews.com; www.worldbank.org; www.ifslearning.ac.uk; www.ft.com

NB The points totals shown to the left of the institutions are for ease of reference only. It must not be assumed that Tariff points are always used by institutions or that they can be substituted for an offer in grades. The level of an offer is not necessarily indicative of the quality of a course.

COURSE OFFERS INFORMATION

Subject requirements/preferences GCSE Most institutions will require English and mathematics grade C minimum. **AL** Mathematics may be required or preferred.

Your target offers and examples of degree courses

160 pts Imperial London – A*A*A incl maths+fmaths (Maths Stats Fin) (IB 39 pts HL 7 maths)

152 pts Exeter – A*AA–AAB (Econ Fin; Econ Fin (Int St)) (IB 38–34 pts)

London (UCL) – A*AA–AAA incl maths+phys/fmaths (Eng (Mech Bus Fin) MEng) (IB 39–38 pts HL 6 maths+phys); A*AA–AAA incl maths (Stats Econ Fin) (IB 39–38 pts HL 7 maths)

Manchester – A*AA–AAA incl maths (Maths Fin; Maths Fin Maths) (IB 37 pts HL 6 maths)

Nottingham – A*AA–AAA/A*AB incl maths (Fin Maths) (IB 36 pts)

York – A*AA–AAA incl maths (Econ Fin) (IB 36 pts)

144 pts Bath – AAA incl maths (Acc Fin) (IB 36 pts HL 6 maths)

Birmingham – AAA (Mny Bank Fin) (IB 32 pts HL 666); AAA incl lang (Mny Bank Fin Lang) (IB 32 pts HL 666)

Bristol – AAA/A*AB–AAB incl maths (Acc Fin) (IB 36–34 pts HL 6 maths)

City – AAA (Bank Int Fin) (IB 35 pts); AAA 144 pts (Inv Fin Risk Mgt) (IB 35 pts)

Edinburgh – AAA–ABB (Acc Fin; Econ Fin) (IB 37–34 pts)

Exeter – AAA–AAB (Acc Fin) (IB 36–34 pts)

Glasgow – AAA/A*AB–ABB incl maths (Acc Fin; Fin Stats) (IB 38–36 pts)

Lancaster – AAA–AAB incl maths/fmaths (Fin Maths) (IB 36 pts HL 6 maths)

Leeds – AAA (Acc Fin; Int Bus Fin; Econ Fin) (IB 35 pts); AAA/A*AB–AAB/A*BB/A*AC incl maths (Maths Fin) (IB 35 pts HL 6 maths)

London (UCL) – AAA–AAB incl maths+phys/fmaths (Eng (Mech Bus Fin)) (IB 38–36 pts HL 5 maths+phys)

London LSE – AAA (Acc Fin) (IB 38 pts); AAA incl maths (Stats Fin) (IB 38 pts)

Reading – AAA–AAB (Fin Inv Bank; Acc Fin) (IB 35 pts)

St Andrews – AAA (Fin Econ) (IB 38 pts)

Southampton – AAA–AAB incl maths (Maths Fin) (IB 36 pts HL 6 maths)

Strathclyde – AAA–ABB incl maths (Acc Fin) (IB 36 pts HL 6 maths)

Surrey – AAA (Econ Fin) (IB 36 pts); AAA–AAB incl maths (Fin Maths) (IB 36 pts HL 6 maths); AAA–AAB (Acc Fin) (IB 35 pts)

Warwick – AAA incl maths (Acc Fin) (IB 38 pts)

York – AAA incl maths (Econ Ecomet Fin) (IB 36 pts)

136 pts Aston – AAB–ABB (Fin) (IB 35–34 pts)

Birmingham – AAB (Acc Fin) (IB 32 pts HL 665)

Cardiff – AAB 136 pts (Bank Fin Euro Lang) (IB 35 pts); AAB (Acc Fin; Bank Fin; Fin Mgt) (IB 35 pts)

City – AAB–ABB 136–128 pts (Fin Econ) (IB 33 pts)

Durham – AAB (Acc Fin) (IB 36 pts)

IFS (UC) – AAB–ABB (Fin Inv Risk) (IB 32 pts)

Lancaster – AAB (Fin; Fin Econ; Acc Fin Comp Sci; Acc Fin; Acc Fin Maths) (IB 35 pts)

Leicester – AAB incl maths (Fin Maths) (IB 32 pts)

Liverpool – AAB incl maths (Maths Fin) (IB 35 pts HL 6 maths); AAB (Acc Fin) (IB 35 pts)

London (QM) – AAB incl maths (Maths Fin Acc) (IB 34 pts HL 6 maths)

Loughborough – AAB–ABB (Bus Econ Fin; Acc Fin Mgt; Bank Fin Mgt) (IB 34 pts)

Manchester – AAB (Fin; Acc Fin) (IB 35 pts)

Newcastle – AAB/A*BB/A*AC incl maths (Maths Fin) (IB 37–35 pts HL 6 maths); AAB (Bus Acc Fin; Acc Fin; Econ Fin) (IB 35 pts)

Nottingham – AAB–ABB (Acc Fin Contemp Chin MSci) (IB 34–32 pts); AAB (Ind Econ Ins; Fin Acc Mgt) (IB 34 pts)

Professional degrees for a career in finance

ifs *University College*
Incorporated by Royal Charter

We focus only in banking and finance degrees and are located in the heart of London's financial district.

With over 135 years experience in the finance industry, a degree from *ifs University College* gives you an edge in a competitive world.

- BSc (Hons) in Banking Practice and Management
- BSc (Hons) in Finance, Investment and Risk

I really couldn't ask for a more relevant course while pursuing a career in banking. I am based right in the heart of the City, surrounded by multi-billion pound financial services organisations. What more could I ask for?

Cole Mills, Third year student
BSc (Hons) in Banking Practice and Management

Why not come and visit us?

Visit our City of London campus to see the facilities on offer, meet with the programme team and learn more about the experience of studying at *ifs University College*.

There are many degrees you can choose from, such as the standard Business Management, whereas **ifs** University College provide you with a degree dedicated to providing you with an understanding of the financial environment, specifically targeting banking and management.

The networking opportunities were key for me, most events I went to I made a new contact who was very supportive, I often attended other events with my contacts to widen my knowledge and experience – plus more networking!

I was fortunate enough to be able to participate in a Work Place Learning module in my third year – this started my career as I continued to work part-time at Barclays throughout my 3rd year and was privileged to be offered a full-time contract with my employer – not many universities offer the chance for this module.

Elliot Seal
Analyst within Barclays Internal Audit Investment Bank Team
BSc graduate 2014

www.ifslearning.ac.uk/BSc

Sheffield – AAB–ABB incl maths (Fin Maths) (IB 35 pts HL 6 maths); AAB (Acc Fin Mgt) (IB 35 pts)

Southampton – AAB–ABB incl maths (Econ Fin) (IB 34 pts HL 5 maths); AAB–ABB (Acc Fin Plmt; Acc Fin) (IB 34 pts)

Strathclyde – AAB–BBB (Mech Eng Fin Mgt MEng) (IB 36 pts HL 6 maths+phys)

Sussex – AAB–ABB (Fin Bus; Acc Fin) (IB 34 pts)

York – AAB (Acc Bus Fin Mgt) (IB 35 pts)

128 pts **Bournemouth** – 128–136 pts (Bus St Fin) (IB 32–33 pts)

Bradford – ABB 128 pts (Acc Fin)

Brunel – ABB (Fin Acc) (IB 31 pts)

East Anglia – ABB (Bus Fin Econ) (IB 32 pts)

Essex – ABB–BBB (Fin; Fin Econ; Acc Fin; Bank Fin) (IB 32–30 pts)

Kent – ABB (Acc Fin) (IB 34 pts); ABB–BBB incl maths (Fin Econ) (IB 34 pts)

Kingston – 128 pts (Acc Fin) (IB 27 pts)

Leicester – ABB (Acc Fin; Bank Fin) (IB 30 pts)

Liverpool – ABB (Law Acc Fin) (IB 33 pts)

London (RH) – ABB (Fin Bus Econ) (IB 32 pts)

Northumbria – ABB 128 pts (Fin Inv Mgt) (IB 31 pts)

Plymouth – 128 pts incl maths (Maths Fin) (IB 30 pts HL 5 maths)

Queen's Belfast – ABB–AAB incl maths (Fin (Yr Ind))

Strathclyde – ABB–BBB (Fin courses) (IB 33 pts)

Swansea – ABB–BBB (Acc Fin; Bus Mgt (Fin)) (IB 33–32 pts)

120 pts **Aberdeen** – BBB (Fin) (IB 32 pts)

Aberystwyth – 120 pts (Acc Fin; Bus Fin)

Bangor – 120 pts (Acc Fin)

Bournemouth – 120 pts (Acc Fin; Fin Econ) (IB 31 pts)

Brunel – BBB (Econ Bus Fin) (IB 30 pts)

Buckingham – BBB–BCC (Acc Fin Mgt); BBB (Law Bus Fin)
De Montfort – 120 pts (Econ Fin) (IB 28 pts)
Dundee – BBB–BCC (Fin; Int Fin) (IB 30 pts)
East London – 120 pts (Acc Fin) (IB 26 pts)
Greenwich – 120 pts (Acc Fin; Fin Maths; Fin Inv Bank)
Heriot-Watt – BBB (Bus Fin; Acc Fin) (IB 29 pts)
Huddersfield – BBB 120 pts (Bus St Fin Serv; Acc Fin)
IFS (UC) – BBB–BBC (Bank Prac Mgt) (IB 30 pts)
Keele – BBB/ABC (Fin courses; Acc Fin) (IB 32 pts)
Leeds Beckett – 120 pts (Acc Fin) (IB 26 pts)
Lincoln – 120 pts (Acc Fin)
Middlesex – 120 pts (Acc Fin)
Nottingham Trent – 120 pts (Prop Fin Inv)
Oxford Brookes – BBB (Acc Fin) (IB 31 pts)
Plymouth – 120 pts (Acc Fin)
Portsmouth – 120 pts (Acc Fin) (IB 30 pts HL 17 pts)
Sheffield Hallam – 120 pts (Acc Fin; Bus Fin Mgt)
Staffordshire – BBB 120 pts (Acc Fin)
Stirling – BBB (Fin) (IB 32 pts)
Ulster – 120 pts (Econ Fin)
UWE Bristol – 120 pts (Acc Fin; Bank Fin) (IB 26 pts)

112 pts **Birmingham City** – BBC 112 pts (Acc Fin; Bus Fin; Econ Fin) (IB 28 pts)
Brighton – BBC incl maths (Maths Fin) (IB 28 pts); BBC (Acc Fin; Fin Inv) (IB 28 pts HL 16 pts)
Bucks New – 112–128 pts (Ftbl Bus Fin)
Cardiff Met – 112 pts (Bus Mgt St Fin; Int Econ Fin)
Central Lancashire – 112 pts (Acc Fin St) (IB 28 pts)
Chester – BBC–BCC 112 pts (Bank Bus Fin) (IB 26 pts)
Chichester – 112–128 pts (Acc Fin; Fin Econ) (IB 30 pts)
East London – 112 pts (Fin) (IB 24 pts)
Gloucestershire – 112 pts (Acc Fin Mgt St)
Greenwich – 112 pts (Bus Fin)
Hertfordshire – 112 pts incl maths (Fin Maths) (IB 28 pts)
Hull – 112 pts (Fin Mgt; Bus Fin Mgt) (IB 30 pts)
Lincoln – 112 pts (Bus Fin)
Liverpool John Moores – 112 pts (Acc Fin) (IB 29 pts)
London Met – 112 pts (Bank Fin)
London South Bank – BBC/A*A* 112 pts (Acc Fin)
Middlesex – 112 pts (Bank Fin)
Northampton – 112 pts (Bank Fin Plan)
Nottingham Trent – 112 pts (Econ Int Fin Bank; Acc Fin)
Oxford Brookes – BBC (Econ Fin Int Bus) (IB 30 pts)
Portsmouth – 112 pts (Econ Fin Bank; Fin Mgt Bus) (IB 30 pts HL 17 pts)
Robert Gordon – BBC (Acc Fin) (IB 29 pts)
Sheffield Hallam – 112 pts (Int Fin Econ; Int Fin Inv; Int Fin Bank)
Southampton Solent – 112 pts (Acc Fin)
Sunderland – 112 pts (Bus Fin Mgt; Acc Fin)
West London – 112 pts (Bus St Fin); (Acc Fin) (IB 29 pts)
Westminster – BBC (Fin) (IB 28 pts)
York St John – 112 pts (Bus Mgt Fin; Acc Fin)

104 pts **Bangor** – 104–120 pts (Bank Fin)
Coventry – 104 pts (Fin Serv)
Glasgow Caledonian – BCC (Fin Inv Risk) (IB 24 pts)
Manchester Met – BCC–BBC 104–112 pts (Acc Fin; Bank Fin) (IB 26 pts)
Plymouth – 104 pts (Fin Econ) (IB 24 pts)

Check **Chapter 3** for new university admission details and **Chapter 6** on how to read the subject tables.

Portsmouth – 104–120 pts incl maths (Maths Fin Mgt) (IB 26 pts HL 10 pts incl maths)
South Wales – BCC (Acc Fin; Fin Plan Inv Risk) (IB 29 pts)
Winchester – 104–120 pts (Acc Fin) (IB 26 pts)

96 pts **Abertay** – CCC (Acc Fin) (IB 28 pts)
Anglia Ruskin – 96–112 pts (Bus Mgt Fin; Bank Fin) (IB 24 pts)
Edinburgh Napier – CCC (Fin Serv) (IB 27 pts)
Hertfordshire – 96–112 pts (Acc Econ; Fin) (IB 28 pts)
London Regent's – CCC (Glob Mgt courses) (IB 32 pts)
Manchester Met – 96–112 pts (Fin Mgt (Joint Hons)) (IB 28 pts)
Teesside – 96 pts (Acc Fin)
Wolverhampton – 96–112 pts (Acc Fin)

80 pts **Bedfordshire** – 80 pts (Int Fin Bank) (IB 24 pts)
Bucks New – 80–96 pts (Bus Fin; Acc Fin)

64 pts **Trinity Saint David** – 64 pts (Bus Fin)

Alternative offers
See **Chapter 6** and **Appendix 1** for grades/new UCAS Tariff points information for other examinations.

EXAMPLES OF COLLEGES OFFERING COURSES IN THIS SUBJECT FIELD
Barnet and Southgate (Coll); Blackburn (Coll); Bradford (Coll); Croydon (Univ Centre); Manchester (Coll); Menai (Coll); Newcastle (Coll); Norwich City (Coll); Pearson (Coll); Peterborough (Coll); Plymouth City (Coll); Suffolk (Univ Campus).

CHOOSING YOUR COURSE (SEE ALSO CH.1)
Universities and colleges teaching quality See www.qaa.ac.uk; http://unistats.direct.gov.uk.

Examples of sandwich degree courses Aston; Bath; Birmingham City; Bournemouth; Bradford; Brighton; Brunel; Chichester; City; Coventry; De Montfort; Durham; Gloucestershire; Greenwich; Hertfordshire; Huddersfield; Kent; Kingston; Lancaster; Leeds Beckett; Liverpool John Moores; London Met; Loughborough; Manchester Met; Middlesex; Nottingham Trent; Oxford Brookes; Plymouth; Portsmouth; Queen's Belfast; Sheffield Hallam; Surrey; Sussex; Teesside; Trinity Saint David; UWE Bristol; West London; Westminster; Wolverhampton; York.

ADMISSIONS INFORMATION
Number of applicants per place (approx) Aberystwyth 4; Bangor 10; Birmingham 3; Birmingham City 13; Buckingham 4; Cardiff 10; Central Lancashire 6; City 10; Dundee 5; Durham 6; Loughborough 35; Manchester 11; Middlesex 3; Northampton 3; Portsmouth 4; Sheffield Hallam 4; UWE Bristol 4.

Advice to applicants and planning the UCAS personal statement Visits to banks or insurance companies should be described, giving details of any work experience or work shadowing done in various departments. Discuss any particular aspects of finance etc which interest you. See also **Appendix 3**.

Misconceptions about this course Many applicants believe that they can only enter careers in banking and finance when they graduate. In fact, business and industry provide wide-ranging opportunities.

Selection interviews **Yes** Buckingham (pref), Huddersfield; **Some** Dundee, Staffordshire, Stirling; **No** City.

Interview advice and questions Banking involves both high street and merchant banks, so a knowledge of banking activities in general will be expected. In the past mergers have been discussed and also the role of the Bank of England in the economy. The work of the accountant may be discussed. See also **Chapter 5**.

Reasons for rejection (non-academic) Lack of interest. Poor English. Lacking in motivation and determination to complete the course.

AFTER-RESULTS ADVICE

Offers to applicants repeating A-levels Higher Glasgow; **Possibly higher** Bangor; **Same** Birmingham, Birmingham City, Bradford, Cardiff, City, Dundee, Edinburgh Napier, London Met, Loughborough, Northumbria, Stirling.

GRADUATE DESTINATIONS AND EMPLOYMENT (2013/14 HESA)

Graduates surveyed 1,820 **Employed** 1,045 **In voluntary employment** 40 **In further study** 365 **Assumed unemployed** 160

Career note Most graduates enter financial careers. Further study is required to qualify as an accountant and to obtain other professional qualifications, eg Institute of Banking.

OTHER DEGREE SUBJECTS FOR CONSIDERATION

Accountancy; Actuarial Studies; Business Studies; Economics.

FOOD SCIENCE/STUDIES and TECHNOLOGY

(see also **Agricultural Sciences/Agriculture, Biochemistry, Consumer Studies/Sciences, Dietetics, Hospitality and Event Management, Nutrition**)

Food Science courses are purely scientific and technical in their approach with the study of food composition and storage in order to monitor food quality, safety and preparation. Scientific elements cover biochemistry, chemistry and microbiology, focussing on human nutrition and, in some courses, dietetics, food processing and management. These courses however are not to be confused with Culinary Arts subjects which lead to careers in food preparation. There are also several business courses specialising in food, such as Food Product Management and Marketing options. The unique course in this category however is the Viticulture and Oenology course at the University of Brighton offered through Plumpton College, which involves the study of grape growing and wine-making.

Useful websites www.sofht.co.uk; www.ifst.org; www.defra.gov.uk; www.iagre.org

NB The points totals shown to the left of the institutions are for ease of reference only. It must not be assumed that Tariff points are always used by institutions or that they can be substituted for an offer in grades. The level of an offer is not necessarily indicative of the quality of a course.

COURSE OFFERS INFORMATION

Subject requirements/preferences GCSE English, mathematics and a science. **AL** One or two mathematics/science subjects; Chemistry may be required.

Your target offers and examples of degree courses

136 pts **Reading** – AAB–ABB (Fd Sci Bus) (IB 35–32 pts); AAB–ABB (Fd Sci; Nutr Fd Sci; Fd Tech Bioproc) (IB 35–32 pts)
        Surrey – AAB–ABB incl sci/maths (Fd Sci Microbiol) (IB 35–34 pts HL 6 biol 5 sci/maths); (Nutr Fd Sci) (IB 35–34 pts)

128 pts **Leeds** – ABB incl sci (Fd Sci) (IB 35–34 pts HL 5 sci)
        Newcastle – ABB–BBB incl sci (Fd Mark Nutr) (IB 34–32 pts HL 6 biol); ABB–BBB incl biol+sci (Fd Hum Nutr) (IB 34–32 pts HL 6 biol)
        Nottingham – ABB–BBB incl sci/maths (Fd Sci; Nutr Fd Sci) (IB 32–30 pts)
        Reading – ABB–BBB (Fd Mark Bus Econ) (IB 32–30 pts)

120 pts **Heriot-Watt** – BBB incl sci (Biol Sci (Fd Bev Sci)) (IB 27 pts HL 5 biol)
        Northumbria – 120 pts incl sci/fd tech/hm econ (Fd Sci Nutr) (IB 30 pts)
        Queen's Belfast – BBB–ABB incl biol/chem (Fd Qual Sfty Nutr)

112 pts **Cardiff Met** – 112 pts (Fd Ind Mgt; Fd Sci Tech)
        Huddersfield – BBC 112 pts (Fd Nutr Hlth)
        Sheffield Hallam – 112 pts (Fd Nutr; Fd Mark Mgt)
        Teesside – BBC incl sci/fd tech/nutr (Fd Nutr)

104 pts **Bath Spa** – 104–120 pts (Fd Nutr)
Coventry – BCC incl biol/chem/fd tech (Fd Nutr) (IB 27 pts)
Glasgow Caledonian – BCC incl chem (Fd Biosci) (IB 24 pts)
Liverpool John Moores – 104 pts (Fd Dev Nutr)
Royal Agricultural Univ – 104 pts (Fd Prod Sply Mgt)
96 pts **Abertay** – CCC (Fd Consum Sci; Fd Nutr Hlth) (IB 28 pts)
Birmingham (UC) – 96 pts (Culn Arts Mgt; Fd Mark Mgt)
CAFRE – 96 pts incl sci/hm econ (Food Tech; Fd Des Nutr)
Royal Agricultural Univ – 96 pts (Int Bus Mgt (Fd Agri Bus))
Ulster – 96 pts incl sci/maths/tech (Fd Nutr) (IB 24 pts)
88 pts **Harper Adams** – 88–104 pts (Fd Prod Mark; Agri-Fd Mark Bus St)
80 pts **London South Bank** – CDD 80 pts (Fd Nutr)

Alternative offers
See **Chapter 6** and **Appendix 1** for grades/new UCAS Tariff points information for other examinations.

EXAMPLES OF COLLEGES OFFERING COURSES IN THIS SUBJECT FIELD
Bridgwater (Coll); CAFRE; Cornwall (Coll); Duchy (Coll); Grimsby (Univ Centre); Plumpton (Coll); Warwickshire (Coll); Westminster Kingsway (Coll).

CHOOSING YOUR COURSE (SEE ALSO CH.1)
Universities and colleges teaching quality See www.qaa.ac.uk; http://unistats.direct.gov.uk.

Top research universities and colleges (REF 2014) See **Agricultural Sciences/Agriculture**.

Examples of sandwich degree courses Birmingham (UC); Cardiff Met; Coventry; Huddersfield; London South Bank; Northumbria; Queen's Belfast; Reading; Sheffield Hallam.

ADMISSIONS INFORMATION
Number of applicants per place (approx) Bath Spa 4; Cardiff Met 1; Huddersfield 4; Leeds 5; Liverpool John Moores 2; London South Bank 3; Newcastle 13; Nottingham 7; Queen's Belfast 10; Sheffield Hallam 4; Surrey 17.

Advice to applicants and planning the UCAS personal statement Visits, work experience or work shadowing in any food manufacturing firm, or visits to laboratories, should be described on your UCAS application. Keep up-to-date with developments by reading journals relating to the industry.

Misconceptions about this course Some applicants confuse food technology with catering or hospitality management. Applicants under-estimate the job prospects. **Leeds** Food Science is not food technology, catering or cooking. It aims to understand why food materials behave in the way they do, in order to improve the nutritive value, safety and quality of the food we eat.

Selection interviews Yes Harper Adams, Reading; **Some** Leeds, Nottingham, Surrey; **No** Liverpool John Moores.

Interview advice and questions Food science and technology is a specialised field and admissions tutors will want to know your reasons for choosing the subject. You will be questioned on any experience you have had in the food industry. More general questions may cover the reasons for the trends in the popularity of certain types of food, the value of junk food and whether scientific interference with food is justifiable. See also **Chapter 5**. **Leeds** Questions asked to ensure that the student understands, and can cope with, the science content of the course.

Reasons for rejection (non-academic) Too immature. Unlikely to integrate well. Lack of vocational commitment.

AFTER-RESULTS ADVICE
Offers to applicants repeating A-levels Higher Heriot-Watt, Leeds; **Possibly higher** Nottingham; **Same** Abertay, Liverpool John Moores, Queen's Belfast, Sheffield Hallam, Surrey.

New UCAS points Tariff: A* = 56 pts; A = 48 pts; B = 40 pts; C = 32 pts; D = 24 pts; E = 16 pts

GRADUATE DESTINATIONS AND EMPLOYMENT (2013/14 HESA)

Food and Beverage Studies graduates surveyed 450 **Employed** 285 **In voluntary employment** 5 **In further study** 80 **Assumed unemployed** 15

Career note Employment levels for food science/studies and technology graduates are high mainly in manufacturing and retailing and increasingly with large companies.

OTHER DEGREE SUBJECTS FOR CONSIDERATION

Biochemistry; Biological Sciences; Biology; Biotechnology; Chemistry; Consumer Studies; Crop Science; Dietetics; Health Studies; Hospitality Management; Nutrition; Plant Science.

FORESTRY

(see also **Agricultural Sciences/Agriculture**)

Courses cover all aspects of the importance of forests from the biological, ecological, environmental, economic and sociological aspects with practical involvement in the establishment of forests and their control, growth, health and quality. Courses in woodland conservation including the topic of wildlife conservation are also offered.

Useful websites www.iagre.org.uk; www.forestry.gov.uk; www.rfs.org.uk; www.charteredforesters.org; www.iom3.org/content/wood-technology; www.woodlandtrust.org.uk/learn/british-trees

NB The points totals shown to the left of the institutions are for ease of reference only. It must not be assumed that Tariff points are always used by institutions or that they can be substituted for an offer in grades. The level of an offer is not necessarily indicative of the quality of a course.

COURSE OFFERS INFORMATION

Subject requirements/preferences GCSE English, mathematics or science usually required. Check prospectuses. **AL** Two science subjects are usually stipulated which can include Mathematics, Geography or Geology.

Your target offers and examples of degree courses
120 pts **Aberdeen** – BBB incl maths/sci (Frsty; Frst Sci) (IB 32 pts HL 5 maths/sci)
104 pts **Bangor** – 104 pts incl sci (Frsty; Cons Frsty)
96 pts **Cumbria** – 96 pts (Frst Mgt; Wdlnd Ecol Cons)
         Myerscough (Coll) – CCC 96 pts (Arbor Urb Frsty) (IB 24 pts)
         Sparsholt (Coll) – 96–112 pts (Wdlnd Cons Mgt)
24 pts **UHI** – D (Sust Frst Mgt)

Alternative offers
See **Chapter 6** and **Appendix 1** for grades/new UCAS Tariff points information for other examinations.

EXAMPLES OF COLLEGES OFFERING COURSES IN THIS SUBJECT FIELD

Duchy (Coll); Hadlow (Coll); Myerscough (Coll); Plumpton (Coll); Sparsholt (Coll).

CHOOSING YOUR COURSE (SEE ALSO CH.1)

Universities and colleges teaching quality See www.qaa.ac.uk; http://unistats.direct.gov.uk.

Examples of sandwich degree courses Bangor; Cumbria.

ADMISSIONS INFORMATION

Number of applicants per place (approx) Bangor 2.

Advice to applicants and planning the UCAS personal statement Contact the Forestry Commission and the Woodland Trust and try to arrange visits to forestry centres, local community woodlands and forests and to the Woodland Trust's sites. Discuss the work with forest officers and learn about future plans for specific forest areas and describe any visits made. Mention any experience of forestry or wood processing industries (for example, visits to forests and mills, work experience in relevant organisations). See also **Appendix 3**.

Misconceptions about this course Bangor That the course provides practical training in forestry (for example, in the use of chainsaws and pesticides) or wood processing. It does not: it is intended to educate future managers, for example; not to train forestry or mill workers.

Selection interviews Most institutions.

Interview advice and questions Work experience or field courses attended are likely to be discussed and questions asked such as: What is arboriculture? On a desert island how would you get food from wood? How do you see forestry developing in the next hundred years? What aspects of forestry are the most important? See also **Chapter 5**. **Bangor** Why are you interested in forestry?

AFTER-RESULTS ADVICE
Offers to applicants repeating A-levels Same Bangor.

GRADUATE DESTINATIONS AND EMPLOYMENT (2013/14 HESA)
Graduates surveyed 90 **Employed** 60 **In voluntary employment** 0 **In further study** 5 **Assumed unemployed** 10

Career note Opportunities exist with the Forestry Commission as supervisors, managers and in some cases, scientists. Other employers include private landowners (especially in Scotland), co-operative forest societies, local authorities and commercial firms.

OTHER DEGREE SUBJECTS FOR CONSIDERATION
Agriculture; Biological Sciences; Countryside Management; Crop Science; Ecology; Environmental Sciences; Woodland and Wildlife Management.

FRENCH
(see also **European Studies, Languages**)

Applicants should select courses according to the emphasis which they prefer. Courses could focus on literature or language (or both), or on the written and spoken word, as in the case of interpreting and translating courses, or on the broader study of French culture, political and social aspects found on European Studies courses.

Useful websites http://europa.eu; www.visavis.org; www.bbc.co.uk/languages; www.languageadvantage.com; www.languagematters.co.uk; www.ciol.org.uk; www.reed.co.uk/multilingual; www.ciltuk.org.uk; www.lemonde.fr; www.institut-francais.org.uk; www.academie-francaise.fr; www.institut-de-france.fr; www.sfs.ac.uk; http://fs.oxfordjournals.org

NB The points totals shown to the left of the institutions are for ease of reference only. It must not be assumed that Tariff points are always used by institutions or that they can be substituted for an offer in grades. The level of an offer is not necessarily indicative of the quality of a course.

COURSE OFFERS INFORMATION
Subject requirements/preferences GCSE French, mathematics (for business courses), grade levels may be stipulated. **AL** French is usually required at a specific grade and in some cases a second language may be stipulated.

Your target offers and examples of degree courses
152 pts **Nottingham** – A*AA–AAA (Econ Fr) (IB 38–36 pts)
144 pts **Durham** – AAA incl lang (Modn Langs Cult (Yr Abrd)) (IB 37 pts)

Edinburgh – AAA–ABB (Fr; Int Bus Fr/Ger/Span) (IB 37–34 pts)
Imperial London – AAA incl chem+maths (Chem Fr/Ger/Span Sci) (IB 38 pts HL 7 chem
   6 maths)
London (King's) – AAA–AAB incl Fr/Ger/Span (Euro St (Fr/Ger/Span) (Yr Abrd)) (IB 35 pts
   HL 6 Fr/Ger/Span); AAA incl Fr+hist (Fr Hist (Yr Abrd)) (IB 35 pts HL 6 Fr+hist); AAA incl
   Fr (Fr Phil (Yr Abrd)) (IB 35 pts HL 6 Fr)
London (UCL) – AAA incl Fr (Fr; Fr As Af Lang) (IB 38 pts HL 6 Fr)
Oxford – AAA incl Fr (Fr) (IB 38 pts)
St Andrews – AAA–AAB (Fr courses) (IB 36 pts)
Southampton – AAA–AAB incl maths+Fr/Ger/Span (Maths Fr/Ger/Span) (IB 36 pts HL
   6 maths)
Surrey – AAA–AAB incl Fr (Fr courses) (IB 36–35 pts)

136 pts **Aston** – AAB–ABB (Int Bus Fr/Ger/Span) (IB 34 pts)
Bath – AAB incl Fr (Int Mgt Fr) (IB 35 pts HL 6 Fr)
Birmingham – AAB incl Fr (Fr St Joint Hons) (IB 32 pts HL 665)
Exeter – AAB–ABB incl Fr (Fr Arbc) (IB 34–32 pts HL 5 Fr); AAB–ABB incl Fr+Lat (Fr Lat)
   (IB 34–32 pts HL 5 Fr+Lat)
Glasgow – AAB–BBB incl arts/lang (Fr Joint Hons) (IB 36–34 pts)
Lancaster – AAB–ABB (Fr St) (IB 35–32 pts)
Leeds – AAB incl Fr+maths (Fr Maths) (IB 35 pts HL 6 Fr+maths)
London (King's) – AAB incl Fr+Ger (Fr Ger (Yr Abrd)) (IB 35 pts HL 6 Fr+Ger); AAB incl
   Fr+Span (Fr Span (Yr Abrd)) (IB 35 pts HL 5 Fr+Span); AAB incl Fr (Fr; Fr Mgt (Yr Abrd))
   (IB 35 pts HL 6 Fr)
Nottingham – AAB incl Fr/Ger/Span (Mgt Fr/Ger/Span) (IB 34 pts)
Sheffield – AAB–BBB incl Fr (Fr St Joint Hons) (IB 35–34 pts HL 6 Fr)
Southampton – AAB–ABB incl Engl+Fr/Ger/Span (Engl Fr/Ger/Span) (IB 34 pts HL 6
   Engl+Fr/Ger/Span); AAB–ABB incl Fr (Fr) (IB 34 pts HL 6 Fr); AAB incl sci/maths/geog
   (Ocean Fr) (IB 34 pts); AAB–ABB incl Fr/Ger/Span (Film Fr/Ger/Span) (IB 32 pts HL 6
   Fr/Ger/Span)
Warwick – AAB incl Fr (Fr Joint Hons; Fr Ger/Ital St) (IB 36 pts HL 5 Fr)
York – AAB–ABB (Fr Ger Lang (Yr Abrd); Fr Ling (Yr Abrd); Fr Ital Lang (Yr Abrd); Fr Sp Lang
   (Yr Abrd)) (IB 34 pts)

128 pts **Aston** – ABB–BBB incl Fr (Fr courses) (IB 33–32 pts HL 6 Fr)
Bath – ABB–AAB incl langs (Modn Langs Euro St) (IB 34 pts HL 6 5 langs)
Bristol – ABB–BBB incl Fr (Fr courses) (IB 32–31 pts HL 5 Fr)
Cardiff – ABB incl Fr (Fr courses)
Dundee – ABB incl Engl+lang (Law Langs) (IB 32 pts)
Essex – ABB–BBB (Econ Fr; Fr St Modn Langs) (IB 32–30 pts)
Leeds – ABB (Fr) (IB 34 pts HL 6 Fr)
Leicester – ABB incl lang (Fr Joint Hons) (IB 30 pts)
Liverpool – ABB incl Fr (Fr) (IB 33 pts HL 6 Fr); (Fr Joint Hons) (IB 33 pts HL 6 Fr)
London (Inst Paris) – ABB incl Fr (Fr St) (IB 36 pts HL 6 Fr)
London (QM) – ABB incl art/hum+lang 128 pts (Fr/Ger/Russ Dr) (IB 34 pts HL 6 art/hum 5
   lang)
London (RH) – ABB incl mus (Mus Fr/Ger/Ital/Span) (IB 32 pts); ABB (Fr Dr; Mgt Fr/Ger/
   Ital/Span; Fr Lat) (IB 32 pts); (Euro St Fr/Ger/Ital/Span) (IB 34 pts); ABB incl Fr (Fr) (IB
   34 pts); ABB incl Span (Span Fr/Ger/Ital) (IB 32 pts)
Manchester – ABB incl lang (Fr courses) (IB 34 pts)
Newcastle – ABB–BBB incl Fr (Fr Joint Hons) (IB 32 pts HL 6 Fr)
Northumbria – ABB 128 pts (Int Bus Mgt Fr) (IB 31 pts)
Nottingham – ABB (Fr Joint Hons) (IB 32 pts); ABB incl Fr (Fr St) (IB 32 pts)
Queen's Belfast – ABB incl Fr (Fr)
Reading – ABB–BBB (Fr courses) (IB 32–30 pts)
Sheffield – ABB (Fr St) (IB 34 pts)
Strathclyde – ABB–BBB (Fr courses) (IB 34 pts)

Check **Chapter 3** for new university admission details and **Chapter 6** on how to read the subject tables.

Sussex – ABB–BBB incl Fr (Fr Ital/Span) (IB 32 pts HL 5 Fr)

Warwick – ABB incl Fr (Fr St) (IB 34 pts HL 5 Fr)

120 pts **Aberdeen** – BBB (Fr) (IB 32 pts)

Buckingham – BBB (Law Fr)

Heriot-Watt – BBB incl lang (App Langs Transl (Fr/Span) (Ger/Span)) (IB 30 pts)

Kent – BBB incl Fr (Fr) (IB 34 pts)

London (QM) – 120–128 pts incl Fr (Fr courses) (IB 32–34 pts HL 5 Fr)

Plymouth – 120 pts incl Engl+Fr (Engl Fr) (IB 30 pts)

Queen's Belfast – BBB–ABB incl Fr (Fr Joint Hons)

Stirling – BBB (Fr) (IB 32 pts)

Sunderland – 120 pts (Fr courses)

Swansea – BBB–BBC incl lang (Fr) (IB 32–30 pts)

112 pts **Aberystwyth** – 112–128 pts incl lang (Fr Joint Hons)

Canterbury Christ Church – 112 pts incl Fr (Fr)

Central Lancashire – 112–128 pts (Fr/Ger/Span/Jap)

Chester – BBC–BCC incl Fr 112 pts (Fr) (IB 26 pts HL 5 Fr)

Coventry – BBC (Fr courses) (IB 29 pts)

Hertfordshire – 112 pts (Fr Joint Hons) (IB 28 pts)

Hull – 112 pts incl lang (Fr; Fr Joint Hons; Fr/Ger/Ital/Span Hist) (IB 28 pts)

Nottingham Trent – 112 pts incl Fr (Fr Joint Hons)

Oxford Brookes – BBC incl Fr (Fr St) (IB 31 pts)

104 pts **Central Lancashire** – 104 pts (Fr (Comb))

London (Birk) – 104 pts (Modn Langs (Fr, Ger, Jap, Port, Span); Fr Mgt; Fr St)

Manchester Met – 104–112 pts incl lang (Ling Lang (Chin/Fr/Ger/Ital/Span)) (IB 26 pts); 104–112 pts incl Fr (Fr St) (IB 26 pts)

Plymouth – 104 pts incl Fr (Int Rel Fr)

Westminster – BCC (Fr courses) (IB 30 pts HL 4 lang)

96 pts **Bangor** – 96–104 pts incl Fr (Fr courses)

Kingston – 96 pts (Fr)

Plymouth – 96 pts (Pol Fr) (IB 26 pts)

Portsmouth – 96–120 pts (Fr St) (IB 30 pts HL 17 pts)

Alternative offers

See **Chapter 6** and **Appendix 1** for grades/new UCAS Tariff points information for other examinations.

EXAMPLES OF COLLEGES OFFERING COURSES IN THIS SUBJECT FIELD

Birmingham Met (Coll); Greenwich (Sch Mgt); Manchester (Coll); Newcastle (Coll); Richmond-upon-Thames (Coll).

CHOOSING YOUR COURSE (SEE ALSO CH.1)

Universities and colleges teaching quality See www.qaa.ac.uk; http://unistats.direct.gov.uk.

Top research universities and colleges (REF 2014) See **Languages**.

ADMISSIONS INFORMATION

Number of applicants per place (approx) Aston 6; Bangor 4; Bath (Modn Langs Euro St) 6; Birmingham 5; Bristol 4; Cardiff 6; Central Lancashire 5; Durham 5; Exeter 8; Hull 12; Kent 10; Kingston 4; Lancaster 7; Leicester (Fr Ital) 5; Liverpool 5; London (Inst Paris) 9; London (King's) 9; London (RH) 5; London (UCL) 5; Manchester Met 13; Newcastle 17; Northampton 3; Nottingham 16; Oxford Brookes 8; Portsmouth 20; Warwick 7; York 8.

Advice to applicants and planning the UCAS personal statement Visits to France (including exchange visits) should be described, with reference to any particular cultural or geographical features of the region visited. Providing information about your contacts with French friends and experience in speaking the language are also important. Express your willingness to work/live/travel abroad and show your interests in French life and culture. Read French newspapers and magazines and keep up-to-date with news stories etc. See also **Appendix 3**. **Bristol** Deferred entry accepted in some cases. Late applications may not be accepted.

Misconceptions about this course Leeds See **Languages**. **Swansea** Some applicants are not aware of the range of subjects which can be combined with French in our flexible modular system. They sometimes do not know that linguistics and area studies options are also available as well as literature options in French.

Selection interviews Yes Bangor, Birmingham, East Anglia (after offer), Essex, Heriot-Watt, Hull, Kingston, Lancaster, Liverpool, London (Inst Paris), London (RH), London (UCL), Oxford, Surrey, Warwick; **Some** Canterbury Christ Church (mature students), Leeds; **No** Nottingham, Portsmouth, Reading.

Interview advice and questions Questions will almost certainly be asked on your A-level texts, in addition to your reading outside the syllabus – books, magazines, newspapers etc. Part of the interview may be conducted in French and written tests may be involved. See also **Chapter 5**. **Leeds** See **Languages**.

Reasons for rejection (non-academic) Unstable personality. Known alcoholism. Poor motivation. Candidate unenthusiastic, unmotivated, ill-informed about the nature of the course (had not read the prospectus). Not keen to spend a year abroad.

AFTER-RESULTS ADVICE
Offers to applicants repeating A-levels Higher Aberystwyth, Glasgow, Leeds, Oxford Brookes, Warwick; **Possibly higher** Aston (Fr; Fr Ger); **Same** Aston, Chester, Durham, East Anglia, Lancaster, Liverpool, London (RH), Newcastle, Nottingham (Fr Ger; Fr Lat), Sheffield, Surrey, Sussex, Ulster.

GRADUATE DESTINATIONS AND EMPLOYMENT (2013/14 HESA)
Graduates surveyed 1530 **Employed** 785 **In voluntary employment** 80 **In further study** 360 **Assumed unemployed** 80

Career note See **Languages**.

OTHER DEGREE SUBJECTS FOR CONSIDERATION
European Studies; International Business Studies; Literature; other language.

GENETICS
(see also **Biological Sciences, Microbiology**)

Genetics is at the cutting edge of modern biology, as demonstrated by the recent developments in genomics and biotechnology leading to considerable advances in the treatment of disease and genetic engineering. Studies

can cover such fields as genetic counselling, population genetics, pharmaceuticals, pre-natal diagnoses, cancer biology, evolution, forensic genetics, plant biology and food quality. Possibly an ideal option for keen science students looking for a degree allied to medicine.

Useful websites www.genetics.org; www.nature.com/genetics; www.genetics.org.uk; see also **Biological Sciences**.

NB The points totals shown to the left of the institutions are for ease of reference only. It must not be assumed that Tariff points are always used by institutions or that they can be substituted for an offer in grades. The level of an offer is not necessarily indicative of the quality of a course.

COURSE OFFERS INFORMATION

Subject requirements/preferences GCSE English, mathematics and science subjects. **AL** Chemistry and/or Biology are usually required or preferred.

Your target offers and examples of degree courses

160 pts **Cambridge** – A*A*A incl sci/maths (Nat Sci (Genet)) (IB 40–41 pts HL 776)

144 pts **Bath** – AAA incl chem+biol (Mol Cell Biol) (IB 36 pts HL 6 chem+biol)

Birmingham – AAA–AAB incl chem+sci (Bioch (Genet)) (IB 32 pts HL 666–665); AAA–AAB incl biol+sci (Biol Sci (Genet)) (IB 32 pts HL 666–665)

Lancaster – AAA–AAB incl chem+sci (Bioch Biomed/Genet) (IB 36–35 pts HL 6 chem+sci)

Leeds – AAA–AAB incl biol (Genet) (IB 35–34 pts HL 6 biol+sci)

Manchester – AAA–ABB incl sci/maths (Genet; Genet (Yr Ind); Genet Modn Lang) (IB 37–33 pts)

Newcastle – AAA–AAB incl biol (Biomed Genet) (IB 35–34 pts HL 5 biol+chem)

Sheffield – AAA–AAB incl chem+sci (Genet Microbiol; Genet; Genet Mol Cell Biol; Med Genet) (IB 37–35 pts HL 6 chem+sci)

York – AAA–AAB incl biol+chem/maths (Genet (Yr Abrd); Genet) (IB 36–35 pts HL 6 biol+chem/maths)

136 pts **Cardiff** – AAB–ABB incl biol (Genet) (IB 34 pts HL 6 biol+chem)

Dundee – AAB incl biol+chem (Mol Genet) (IB 30 pts)

Glasgow – AAB–BBB incl biol/chem (Genet) (IB 36–34 pts)

London (King's) – AAB incl chem+biol (Mol Genet) (IB 35 pts HL 6 chem+biol); (Pharmacol Mol Genet) (IB 35 pts)

Nottingham – AAB–ABB incl biol+sci (Genet) (IB 34–32 pts); AAB incl chem+sci (Bioch Genet) (IB 34 pts)

128 pts **East Anglia** – ABB incl biol (Mol Biol Genet) (IB 32 pts HL 5 biol)

Essex – ABB–BBB (Genet) (IB 32–30 pts)

Leicester – ABB incl sci/maths (Med Genet) (IB 30 pts)

Liverpool – ABB incl biol+sci (Genet) (IB 33 pts HL 6 biol)

London (QM) – ABB incl biol (Genet) (IB 34 pts HL 5 biol)

120 pts **Aberdeen** – BBB incl maths/sci (Genet; Genet (Immun)) (IB 32 pts HL 5 maths/sci)

Brunel – BBB (Biomed Sci (Genet)) (IB 30 pts)

Huddersfield – BBB incl sci 120 pts (Med Genet)

Swansea – BBB–ABB incl biol 120–128 pts (Genet) (IB 32–33 pts); BBB–ABB incl biol+chem 120–128 pts (Bioch Genet) (IB 32–33 pts); BBB–ABB 120–128 pts (Med Genet) (IB 32–33 pts)

116 pts **Aberystwyth** – 116–132 pts incl biol (Genet)

112 pts **Hertfordshire** – 112 pts incl biol/chem+sci/maths (Mol Biol) (IB 28 pts)

80 pts **Wolverhampton** – 80 pts incl biol/chem (Genet Mol Biol)

Alternative offers

See **Chapter 6** and **Appendix 1** for grades/new UCAS Tariff points information for other examinations.

CHOOSING YOUR COURSE (SEE ALSO CH.1)

Universities and colleges teaching quality See www.qaa.ac.uk; http://unistats.direct.gov.uk.

Top research universities and colleges (REF 2014) See **Biological Sciences**.

Examples of sandwich degree courses See also **Biological Sciences**. Brunel; Cardiff; Essex; Huddersfield; Leeds; Manchester; York.

ADMISSIONS INFORMATION

Number of applicants per place (approx) Bath 8; Cardiff 8; Dundee 5; Leeds 7; Leicester (Biol Sci) 10; Newcastle 8; Nottingham 6; Swansea 7; Wolverhampton 4; York 9.

Advice to applicants and planning the UCAS personal statement See **Biological Sciences**.

New UCAS points Tariff: A* = 56 pts; A = 48 pts; B = 40 pts; C = 32 pts; D = 24 pts; E = 16 pts

Misconceptions about this course York Some fail to realise that chemistry (beyond GCSE) is essential to an understanding of genetics.

Selection interviews Yes Cambridge, Liverpool, Manchester, Swansea, Wolverhampton; **No** Cardiff, Dundee.

Interview advice and questions Likely questions will focus on your A-level science subjects, particularly biology, why you wish to study genetics, and on careers in genetics. See also **Chapter 5**.

AFTER-RESULTS ADVICE

Offers to applicants repeating A-levels Higher Aberystwyth, Leeds, Newcastle, Nottingham, Swansea; **Same** Cardiff, Dundee, London (UCL), Wolverhampton, York; **No** Cambridge.

GRADUATE DESTINATIONS AND EMPLOYMENT (2013/14 HESA)

Graduates surveyed 305 **Employed** 100 **In voluntary employment** 10 **In further study** 135 **Assumed unemployed** 25

Career note See **Biological Sciences**.

OTHER DEGREE SUBJECTS FOR CONSIDERATION

Biochemistry; Biological Sciences; Biology; Biotechnology; Human Sciences; Immunology; Life Sciences; Medical Biochemistry; Medical Biology; Medicine; Microbiology; Molecular Biology; Natural Sciences; Physiology; Plant Sciences.

GEOGRAPHY

(see also **Environmental Sciences**)

The content and focus of geography courses will vary between universities although many similarities exist between BA and BSc courses apart from entry requirements. For example, at the University of Birmingham, the course is flexible offering topics from migration and urban and social changes, to natural hazards and global environmental changes, with decisions on the paths to take between human and physical geography being delayed. At Leeds, the BA course focuses on human geography and the BSc course on physical aspects. This is a subject deserving real research between the offerings of a wide range of institutions in view of the variety of topics on offer, for example, rural, historical, political or cultural geography at Exeter, environmental geography and climate change at East Anglia, and physical oceanography as part of the BSc course at Plymouth.

Useful websites www.metoffice.gov.uk; www.rgs.org; www.ordnancesurvey.co.uk; www.geographical. co.uk; www.nationalgeographic.com; www.cartography.org.uk; www.naturalengland.org.uk; www. geography.org.uk; www.thepowerofgeography.co.uk; www.publicprofiler.org; www.esri.com/what-is-gis

NB The points totals shown to the left of the institutions are for ease of reference only. It must not be assumed that Tariff points are always used by institutions or that they can be substituted for an offer in grades. The level of an offer is not necessarily indicative of the quality of a course.

COURSE OFFERS INFORMATION

Subject requirements/preferences GCSE Geography usually required. Mathematics/sciences often required for BSc courses. **AL** Geography is usually required for most courses. Mathematics/science subjects required for BSc courses.

Your target offers and examples of degree courses
152 pts **Bristol** – A*AA–AAB (Geog) (IB 38–34pts)
Cambridge – A*AA (Geog) (IB 40–41 pts HL 776)
Durham – A*AA (Comb Hons Soc Sci) (IB 38 pts)
London (UCL) – A*AA incl geog+maths (Econ Geog) (IB 39 pts HL 7 maths 6 geog)
Oxford – A*AA (Geog) (IB 39 pts)

144 pts **Cardiff** – AAA–AAB incl geog (Geog (Hum) Plan) (IB 38–36 pts HL 6 geog); (Geog (Hum)) (IB 38–36 pts)

        Durham – AAA (Geog) (IB 37 pts)

        Edinburgh – AAA–ABB (Geol Physl Geog) (IB 37–32 pts)

        Exeter – AAA–AAB incl hum/soc sci (Geog) (IB 36–34 pts HL 5 hum/soc sci)

        London (UCL) – AAA–AAB incl geog (Env Geog; Geog) (IB 38–36 pts HL 6 geog)

        London LSE – AAA (Geog; Geog Econ) (IB 38 pts)

        St Andrews – AAA (Geog; Geog Lang; Geog Int Rel; Geog Psy) (IB 38 pts)

136 pts **Birmingham** – AAB (Geog) (IB 32 pts HL 665)

        Glasgow – AAB–BBB incl sci (Geog) (IB 36–34 pts)

        Lancaster – AAB incl geog (Geog; Physl Geog) (IB 35 pts HL 6 geog)

        Leeds – AAB (Geog) (IB 35 pts)

        London (King's) – AAB (Geog) (IB 35 pts HL 665)

        London (QM) – AAB–BBB (Hum Geog) (IB 32–30 pts)

        London (SOAS) – AAB incl geog (Geog Joint Hons) (IB 35 pts)

        Loughborough – AAB incl geog (Geog Spo Sci; Geog Econ) (IB 36–34 pts HL 5 geog); AAB–ABB incl geog (Geog Spo Mgt) (IB 36–34 pts HL 5 geog)

        Manchester – AAB (Geog) (IB 35 pts)

        Newcastle – AAB–ABB incl geog (Geog) (IB 35–32 pts HL 6 geog); AAB (Earth Sci) (IB 35 pts)

        Nottingham – AAB incl geog (Geog Chin St; Geog Bus) (IB 34 pts)

        Sheffield – AAB–ABB incl geog (Geog) (IB 35 pts HL 6 geog)

        Southampton – AAB–ABB incl geog (Geog; Physl Geog Ocean) (IB 34–32 pts)

        Sussex – AAB–ABB (Geog; Geog Anth) (IB 34 pts)

128 pts **Birmingham** – ABB (Geog Urb Reg Plan (Joint Hons)) (IB 32 pts HL 655)

        Coventry – ABB–BBB (Geog Nat Haz) (IB 29 pts); (Disas Mgt Emer Plan; Disas Mgt; Geog) (IB 31–30 pts)

        East Anglia – ABB incl geog (Env Geog Clim Chng) (IB 32 pts HL 5 geog); ABB (Geog) (IB 32 pts HL 5 geog)

        Leicester – ABB (Geog; Hum Geog; Physl Geog) (IB 30 pts)

        Liverpool – ABB (Geog) (IB 33 pts)

        London (QM) – AAB–BBB (Geog) (IB 32–30 pts)

        London (RH) – ABB (Geog; Hum Geog; Physl Geog; Geog Pol Int Rel) (IB 32 pts)

        Loughborough – ABB (Hist Geog) (IB 34 pts)

        Newcastle – ABB incl geog+sci (Physl Geog) (IB 32 pts HL 6 geog); ABB–BBB incl geog (Geog Plan) (IB 32–30 pts)

        Northumbria – 128 pts incl geog (Geog) (IB 31 pts)

        Nottingham – ABB–BBB incl geog (Arch Geog) (IB 32–30 pts)

        Reading – ABB–BBB (Hum Geog; Physl Geog; Geog Econ (Reg Sci); Hum Physl Geog) (IB 32–30 pts)

        Southampton – ABB incl geog+sci/maths (Geol Physl Geog; Ocean Physl Geog) (IB 32 pts); ABB–BBB incl geog (Popn Geog) (IB 32 pts)

        Swansea – ABB–BBB incl geog (Geog; Geog Geoinform; Geog Euro St) (IB 33–32 pts)

        York – ABB incl geog+sci/maths (Env Geog) (IB 34 pts)

120 pts **Aberdeen** – BBB (Geog (Arts/Sci)) (IB 32 pts)

        Aberystwyth – 120–128 pts incl geog (Hum Geog; Physl Geog; Geog)

        Bangor – 120 pts incl geog (Geog)

        Brighton – BBB (Geog) (IB 30 pts)

        Chester – BBB–BBC incl geog/sci 120 pts (Geog) (IB 28 pts HL 5 geog)

        Dundee – BBB–BCC incl sci (Geog) (IB 30 pts)

        Edge Hill – BBB 120 pts (Physl Geog; Physl Geog Geol)

        Gloucestershire – 120 pts (Geog courses)

        Greenwich – 120 pts (Geog)

        Keele – BBB/ABC (Geog) (IB 32 pts HL 6 geog); BBB/ABC incl geog (Physl Geog; Hum Geog) (IB 32 pts HL 6 geog)

Leeds Beckett – 120 pts (Hum Geog; Hum Geog Plan) (IB 26 pts)
Northumbria – 120 pts incl geog (Geog Env Mgt) (IB 30 pts)
Plymouth – 120–128 pts (Physl Geog Geol) (IB 28–30 pts)
Queen's Belfast – BBB incl geog (Geog); BBB incl geog+Fr/Span (Geog Ext St Euro)
Sheffield Hallam – 120 pts incl geog (Geog)
Stirling – BBB (Geog) (IB 32 pts)
UWE Bristol – 120 pts (Geog) (IB 26 pts)

112 pts **Bangor** – 112–128 pts incl sci (Mar Geog)
Canterbury Christ Church – 112 pts incl geog (Geog)
Central Lancashire – 112 pts (Geog) (IB 28 pts)
Derby – 112 pts incl sci/soc sci/geog (Geog)
Edge Hill – BBC 112 pts (Geog; Hum Geog)
Hull – 112 pts incl sci (Geol Physl Geog) (IB 28 pts); 112 pts (Physl Geog; Hum Geog; Geog) (IB 28 pts)
London (Birk) – 112 pts (Geog)
Nottingham Trent – 112 pts incl geog (Geog; Geog (Physl))
Oxford Brookes – BBC incl geog (Geog) (IB 30 pts)
Plymouth – 112 pts incl geog (Geog) (IB 28 pts HL 5 geog)
Portsmouth – 112 pts (Hum Geog; Physl Geog) (IB 26 pts HL 13 pts); 112 pts incl geog (Geog) (IB 26 pts HL 13 pts incl 5 geog)
Sheffield Hallam – 112 pts incl geog/soc sci (Hum Geog)

104 pts **Bath Spa** – 104–120 pts (Geog)
Bournemouth – 104–128 pts (Geog) (IB 30–32 pts)
Liverpool Hope – BCC–BBB 104–120 pts (Geog)
Liverpool John Moores – 104–120 pts (Geog) (IB 25 pts)
Manchester Met – BCC–BBC incl geog 104–112 pts (Physl Geog) (IB 28 pts HL 5 geog/sci); (Geog (St Abrd)) (IB 28 pts HL 5 geog); (Hum Geog (St Abrd)) (IB 28 pts HL 5 geog)
Northampton – 104–120 pts (Geog (Physl Geog); Geog)
South Wales – BCC incl geog/maths (Geog; Geol Physl Geog) (IB 29 pts HL 5 geog/maths)
Winchester – 104–120 pts (Geog) (IB 26 pts)
Worcester – 104–120 pts (Geog; Hum Geog); 104–112 pts (Geog courses)

96 pts **Glyndŵr** – 96 pts (Geog Ecol Env)
Hertfordshire – 96 pts (Hum Geog; Geog) (IB 24 pts)
Kingston – 96–112 pts (Geog Joint Hons; Hum Geog)
St Mary's – 96 pts (Geog) (IB 28 pts)
Southampton Solent – 96 pts (Geog Mar St; Geog Env St)
Staffordshire – CCC 96 pts (Geog; Geog Mntn Ldrshp)

88 pts **Ulster** – 88–104 pts incl geog (Geog) (IB 24 pts)

Open University – contact +44 (0)845 300 6090 **or** www.openuniversity.co.uk/you (Soc Sci Geog)

Alternative offers
See **Chapter 6** and **Appendix 1** for grades/new UCAS Tariff points information for other examinations.

EXAMPLES OF COLLEGES OFFERING COURSES IN THIS SUBJECT FIELD
Hopwood Hall (Coll); Truro and Penwith (Coll).

CHOOSING YOUR COURSE (SEE ALSO CH.1)
Universities and colleges teaching quality See www.qaa.ac.uk; http://unistats.direct.gov.uk.

Top research universities and colleges (REF 2014) (Geography, Environmental Studies and Archaeology) Glasgow (Geog); London (RH); London LSE; Bristol (Geog); Cambridge (Geog); Oxford (Geog Env St); London (QM); St Andrews; Newcastle (Geog); Southampton (Geog); London (UCL) (Geog); Reading (Arch); Sheffield (Geog); Oxford (Arch).

Examples of sandwich degree courses Brighton; Cardiff; Coventry; Hertfordshire; Kingston; Loughborough; Manchester Met; Northumbria; Nottingham Trent; Plymouth; Sheffield Hallam; Ulster; UWE Bristol.

ADMISSIONS INFORMATION

Number of applicants per place (approx) Aberystwyth 3; Birmingham 5; Bristol 6; Cambridge 3; Cardiff 5; Central Lancashire 3; Chester 10; Coventry 12; Derby 4; Dundee 5; Durham 4; Edge Hill 8; Edinburgh 8; Exeter 10; Gloucestershire 40; Greenwich 2; Hull 10; Kingston 7; Lancaster 13; Leeds 12; Leicester 5; Liverpool 3; Liverpool John Moores 6; London (King's) 5; London (QM) 5; London (RH) 7; London (SOAS) 5; London (UCL) 7; London LSE 8; Loughborough 6, (Geog Spo Sci) 20; Manchester 6; Newcastle 14; Northampton 4; Northumbria 16; Nottingham 7; Portsmouth 5; St Mary's 4; Sheffield (BA) 13, (BSc) 10; South Wales 5; Southampton 7; Staffordshire 10; Strathclyde 8; Swansea 5; UWE Bristol 10; Worcester 5.

Advice to applicants and planning the UCAS personal statement Visits to, and field courses in, any specific geographical region should be fully described. Study your own locality in detail and get in touch with the area planning office to learn about any future developments. Read geographical magazines and describe any special interests you have – and why. Be aware of world issues and have travel experience. **Bristol** Deferred entry accepted.

Misconceptions about this course Birmingham Some students think that the BA and BSc Geography courses are very different; in fact they do not differ from one another. All course options are available for both degrees. **Liverpool** Some applicants assume that a BSc course restricts them to physical geography modules. This is not so since human geography modules can be taken. Some students later specialise in human geography.

Selection interviews Yes Cambridge, Canterbury Christ Church, Central Lancashire, Coventry, Edge Hill, Greenwich, Kingston, London (King's), London (QM), London (RH), London (UCL), Manchester, Manchester Met, Northumbria, Oxford (24%), UWE Bristol, Worcester; **Some** Bristol, Cardiff, Dundee, East Anglia, Liverpool, London (SOAS), Loughborough, Newcastle, Southampton, Staffordshire; **No** Birmingham, Nottingham, Reading.

Interview advice and questions Geography is a very broad subject and applicants can expect to be questioned on their syllabus and those aspects which they find of special interest. Some questions in the past have included: What fieldwork have you done? What are your views on ecology? What changes in the landscape have you noticed on the way to the interview? Explain in simple meteorological terms today's weather. Why are earthquakes almost unknown in Britain? What is the value of practical work in geography to primary school children? (BEd course) What do you enjoy about geography and why? Are there any articles of geographical importance in the news at present? Discuss the current economic situation in Britain and give your views. Questions on the Third World, on world ocean currents and drainage and economic factors world-wide. What do you think about those people who consider global warming nonsense? Expect to comment on local geography and on geographical photographs and diagrams. See also **Chapter 5**. **Cambridge** Are Fairtrade bananas really fair? Imagine you are hosting the BBC radio show on New Year's day, what message would you send to listeners? **Liverpool** Looks for why students have chosen Geography and the aspects of the subject they enjoy. **Oxford** Is nature natural? **Southampton** Applicants selected on academic ability only.

Reasons for rejection (non-academic) Lack of awareness of the content of the course. Failure to attend interview. Poor general knowledge. Lack of geographical awareness. **Hull** (BSc) Usually insufficient science background. **Liverpool** Personal statement gave no reason for choosing Geography.

AFTER-RESULTS ADVICE

Offers to applicants repeating A-levels Higher Bournemouth, Glasgow, Hull, Kingston, Nottingham, St Andrews, Sussex (Geog Lang); **Possibly higher** Edinburgh; **Same** Aberystwyth, Birmingham, Bradford, Brighton, Bristol, Cardiff, Chester, Coventry, Derby, Dundee, Durham, East Anglia, Edge Hill, Lancaster, Leeds, Liverpool, Liverpool Hope, Liverpool John Moores, London (RH), London (SOAS),

Loughborough, Manchester Met, Newcastle, Northumbria, Oxford Brookes, St Mary's, Southampton, Staffordshire, Ulster; **No** Cambridge.

GRADUATE DESTINATIONS AND EMPLOYMENT (2013/14 HESA)
Human and Social Geography graduates surveyed 2380 **Employed** 1290 **In voluntary employment** 115 **In further study** 550 **Assumed unemployed** 135

Physical Geography graduates surveyed 3120 **Employed** 1510 **In voluntary employment** 110 **In further study** 770 **Assumed unemployed** 195

Career note Geography graduates enter a wide range of occupations, many in business and administrative careers. Depending on specialisations, areas could include agriculture, forestry, hydrology, transport, market research and retail. Teaching is also a popular option.

OTHER DEGREE SUBJECTS FOR CONSIDERATION
Agriculture; Anthropology; Civil Engineering; Countryside Management; Development Studies; Environmental Engineering/Science/Studies; Forestry; Geology; Geomatic Engineering; Surveying; Town Planning; Urban Land Economics; Urban Studies.

GEOLOGY/GEOLOGICAL SCIENCES

(including **Earth Sciences, Geophysics** and **Geoscience**; see also **Astronomy and Astrophysics, Environmental Sciences**)

Topics in Geology courses include the physical and chemical constitution of the earth, exploration geophysics, oil and marine geology (oceanography) and seismic interpretation. Earth Sciences cover geology, environmental science, physical geography and can also include business studies and language modules. No previous knowledge of geology is required for most courses.

Useful websites www.geolsoc.org.uk; www.bgs.ac.uk; www.noc.soton.ac.uk; www.scicentral.com; www.geophysics.org.uk

NB The points totals shown to the left of the institutions are for ease of reference only. It must not be assumed that Tariff points are always used by institutions or that they can be substituted for an offer in grades. The level of an offer is not necessarily indicative of the quality of a course.

COURSE OFFERS INFORMATION
Subject requirements/preferences GCSE English, mathematics and a science required. **AL** One or two mathematics/science subjects usually required. Geography may be accepted as a science subject.

Your target offers and examples of degree courses
160 pts **Cambridge** – A*A*A incl sci/maths (Nat Sci (Earth Sci)) (IB 40–41 pts HL 776)
152 pts **Leeds** – A*AA (Geophysl Sci (Int); Geol Sci (Int)) (IB 35 pts)
Oxford – A*AA/AAAA (Earth Sci (Geol)) (IB 39 pts)
144 pts **Birmingham** – AAA incl sci (Geol MSci (Yr Abrd)) (IB 32 pts HL 666)
Bristol – AAA–ABB incl sci (Env Geosci) (IB 36–34 pts); AAA–AAB (Geol) (IB 36–34 pts)
Cardiff – AAA (Explor Res Geol (Int)) (IB 32–30 pts); (Env Geosci (Int); Geol (Int) MESci) (IB 34 pts)
Durham – AAA incl sci (Earth Sci) (IB 37 pts)
Edinburgh – AAA–ABB (Geol Physl Geog; Geophys; Geophys Meteor; Geophys Geol; Geol) (IB 37–32 pts)
Imperial London – AAA (Geol) (IB 38 pts); AAA 144 pts (Petrol Geosci MSci) (IB 38 pts); AAA incl maths+phys (Geophys; Geol Geophys) (IB 38 pts HL 6 maths+phys)
Leicester – AAA incl sci/maths/geog (Geol MGeol; Geol Pal MGeol) (IB 34 pts)

The
University
Of
Sheffield.

Department
Of
Landscape.

SHAPE YOUR WORLD

Landscape Architecture, **Undergraduate Courses**

BA Hons or BSc Hons in Landscape Architecture

www.sheffield.ac.uk/**landscape**

SHEFFIE
LANDSCA
ARCHITECTU

TUDYING
ANDSCAPE
RCHITECTURE
T SHEFFIELD

Department of Landscape at the University of ffield is one of the leading places to study Landscape hitecture in the UK. As one of the largest academic itutions in our field, we offer internationally renowned earch and taught courses that span arts, design, ial sciences, geography, planning, ecology and nagement.

ne to the Department of Landscape and you will joining one of the world's leading departments for dscape education and research. Our staff are involved ome of the most exciting contemporary landscape ign projects. They are committed to developing next generation of Landscape Architects to create ing, functional and inspirational places.

94%
of students secured graduate jobs in Landscape Architecture in 2014

Hons Landscape Architecture
AS code: K3K4

s course aims to educate Landscape chitects who, as well as being skilled signers, have a sound understanding landscape issues at the large scale. If u enjoy subjects such as geography, litics, economics or history you will oreciate the scope and challenge of s course. By learning about urban sign theory, planning and practice, you l acquire a better understanding of context in which design takes place d the wider implications of your design oposals. On completing this course, u will be uniquely placed to understand wider societal picture, into which fits piring design.

BSc Hons Landscape Architecture
UCAS code: KC39

This course aims to educate Landscape Architects to have an in-depth understanding of ecology and habitat creation. If you are interested in the natural world or enjoy biology or environmental sciences, you will enjoy the focus of this course. You will learn about ecological processes and how they work within designed landscape to give you an understanding of the impact that design proposals have on habitat. In a world of increasing environmental pressure, this course will give you the specialist training to protect and restore existing habitats as well as create new places where nature thrives.

London (UCL) – AAA–ABB (Earth Sci) (IB 38–34 pts); AAA–ABB incl maths+phys (Geophys) (IB 38–34 pts HL 5 maths+phys); AAA–ABB incl sci (Earth Sci (Int)) (IB 38–34 pts HL 5 sci/maths); (Geol; Env Geosci) (IB 38–34 pts HL 5 sci)

136 pts **Cardiff** – AAB (Explor Res Geol MESci) (IB 32–30 pts); (Geol MESci) (IB 33–32 pts)

Durham – AAB incl sci+maths (Geophys Geol) (IB 36 pts); AAB incl sci (Geosci; Geol) (IB 36 pts)

East Anglia – AAB/ABBB incl sci (Env Earth Sci MSci) (IB 33 pts HL 6 sci)

Exeter – AAB–ABB incl sci/geol (Geol (Cornwall)) (IB 34–32 pts HL 5 sci); AAB–ABB (App Geol) (IB 34–32 pts)

Glasgow – AAB–BBB incl sci (Earth Sci) (IB 36–34 pts)

Leeds – AAB (Geol Sci) (IB 35 pts)

Liverpool – AAB incl maths+phys (Geol Geophys MESci) (IB 35 pts HL 4 maths+phys); AAB incl sci (Geol MESci) (IB 35 pts HL 4 sci); (Geol Physl Geog MESci) (IB 35 pts)

Manchester – AAB incl sci (Earth Sci MEarthSci) (IB 35 pts)

St Andrews – AAB incl sci/maths/geog (Env Earth Sci; Geol) (IB 36 pts)

Southampton – AAB incl maths+phys (Geophys MSci) (IB 34 pts); AAB–ABB incl geog (Physl Geog Geol) (IB 34–32 pts)

128 pts **Birmingham** – ABB incl sci (Geol) (IB 32 pts HL 655); ABB (Geol Arch) (IB 32–34 pts)

Cardiff – ABB (Explor Res Geol; Env Geosci; Geol) (IB 32–30 pts); (Earth Sci incl Fdn Yr) (IB 34 pts)

East Anglia – ABB (Env Geophys) (IB 32 pts HL 5 maths); (Env Earth Sci) (IB 32 pts HL 5 sci)

Lancaster – ABB incl sci (Earth Env Sci) (IB 32 pts HL 6 sci)

Leicester – ABB incl sci/maths/geog (App Env Geol; Geol) (IB 30 pts); ABB incl maths/phys (Geol Geophys) (IB 30 pts)

Liverpool – ABB incl sci (Geol; Geol Physl Geog) (IB 33 pts)

London (RH) – ABB incl sci (Geosci; Geol; Geol (Yr Ind)) (IB 32 pts)

Manchester – ABB incl chem (Geochem) (IB 33 pts HL 5 chem); ABB incl sci (Geol; Env Res Geol) (IB 33 pts HL 5 sci); ABB incl sci+geog (Geog Geol) (IB 33 pts HL 5 sci); ABB incl maths/phys (Geol Planet Sci) (IB 33 pts HL 5 maths/phys)

Southampton – ABB incl geog+sci/maths (Geol Physl Geog) (IB 32 pts); ABB sci/maths/geog (Geol) (IB 32 pts); ABB incl maths+phys (Geophys Sci) (32 pts)

Swansea – ABB–BBB incl geog (Physl Earth Sci) (IB 33–32 pts)

120 pts **Aberdeen** – BBB incl maths/sci (Geol Petrol Geol) (IB 32 pts HL 5 maths/sci)

Brighton – BBB incl geog/sci (Physl Geog Geol) (IB 30 pts); BBB incl sci (Geol) (IB 30 pts)

Edge Hill – BBB 120 pts (Physl Geog Geol)

Keele – BBB/ABC incl sci/geog (Geol courses) (IB 32 pts HL 6 sci/geog)

London (Birk) – 120 pts (Geol)

Plymouth – 120–128 pts (Geol Ocn Sci; App Geol; Physl Geog Geol) (IB 28–30 pts)

112 pts **Aberystwyth** – 112 pts incl sci (Env Earth Sci)

Bangor – 112–128 pts incl sci (Geol Ocean)

Derby – 112 pts incl sci/maths/geog (Geol)

Hull – 112 pts incl sci (Geol Physl Geog) (IB 28 pts)

Portsmouth – 112–136 pts incl maths/phys/chem+sci/tech (Eng Geol Geotech) (IB 29 pts HL 12 pts incl maths/phys/chem+sci/tech)

104 pts **Portsmouth** – 104–128 pts incl biol (Geol) (IB 27 pts); 104–128 pts incl sci/tech (Geol Haz) (IB 28 pts HL 11 pts incl sci/tech)

South Wales – BCC incl geog/maths (Geol) (IB 29 pts)

96 pts **Kingston** – 96–112 pts (Geol)

Open University – contact +44 (0)845 300 6090 **or** www.openuniversity.co.uk/you (Geol St)

Alternative offers

See **Chapter 6** and **Appendix 1** for grades/new UCAS Tariff points information for other examinations.

CHOOSING YOUR COURSE (SEE ALSO CH.1)

Universities and colleges teaching quality See www.qaa.ac.uk; http://unistats.direct.gov.uk.

Top research universities and colleges (REF 2014) See **Environmental Sciences**.

Examples of sandwich degree courses Brighton; Cardiff; Leeds; London (RH); Plymouth; Portsmouth.

ADMISSIONS INFORMATION

Number of applicants per place (approx) Aberystwyth 5; Bangor 4; Birmingham 4; Bristol 6; Cardiff 5; Derby 4; Durham 4; East Anglia 7; Edinburgh 5; Exeter 5; Imperial London 5; Kingston 19; Leeds 8; Leicester 5; Liverpool 5; London (RH) 5; London (UCL) 7; Oxford 1.2; Plymouth 7; Portsmouth (Eng Geol Geotech) 2, (Geol) 2; Southampton 5.

Advice to applicants and planning the UCAS personal statement Visits to any outstanding geological sites and field courses you have attended should be described in detail. Apart from geological formations, you should also be aware of how geology has affected humankind in specific areas in the architecture of the region and artefacts used. Evidence of social skills could be given. See also **Appendix 3**. **Bristol** Only accepting a limited number of deferred applicants in fairness to next year's applicants. Apply early.

Misconceptions about this course East Anglia Many applicants fail to realise that environmental earth science extends beyond geology to the links between the solid earth and its behaviour and society in general. **London (UCL)** Environmental geoscience is sometimes mistaken for environmental science; they are two different subjects.

Selection interviews Yes Cambridge, Imperial London, Kingston, Liverpool, London (RH), Oxford (89% (success rate 23%)), Southampton; **Some** Aberystwyth (mature students only), Bristol, Derby; **No** Birmingham, East Anglia, Edinburgh.

Interview advice and questions Some knowledge of the subject will be expected and applicants could be questioned on specimens of rocks and their origins. Past interviews have included questions on the field courses attended, and the geophysical methods of exploration in the detection of metals. How would you determine the age of this rock (sample shown)? Can you integrate a decay curve function and would it help you to determine the age of rocks? How many planes of crystallisation could this rock have? What causes a volcano? What is your local geology? See also **Chapter 5**. **Oxford** (Earth Sci) Candidates may be asked to comment on specimens of a geological nature, based on previous knowledge of the subject.

Reasons for rejection (non-academic) Exeter Outright rejection uncommon but some applicants advised to apply for other programmes.

AFTER-RESULTS ADVICE

Offers to applicants repeating A-levels Higher Bristol, St Andrews; **Possibly higher** Cardiff, Portsmouth; **Same** Aberystwyth, Derby, Durham, East Anglia, Leeds, London (RH), Plymouth, Southampton; **No** Cambridge.

GRADUATE DESTINATIONS AND EMPLOYMENT (2013/14 HESA)

Graduates surveyed 1410 **Employed** 620 **In voluntary employment** 35 **In further study** 395 **Assumed unemployed** 105

Career note Areas of employment include mining and quarrying, the oil and gas industry, prospecting and processing.

OTHER DEGREE SUBJECTS FOR CONSIDERATION

Archaeology; Civil and Mining Engineering; Environmental Science; Geography; Meteorology; Oceanography; Physics.

Check **Chapter 3** for new university admission details and **Chapter 6** on how to read the subject tables.

GERMAN

(see also **European Studies, Languages**)

There are fewer Single Honours German courses than formerly, although the subject is offered jointly with other subjects, particularly other languages and business and management studies, at many universities. German courses range between those which focus on language and literature (eg Edinburgh), those which emphasise fluency of language and communication (eg Hull), those offering translation studies (eg Heriot-Watt), and German Studies courses which cover economic and political aspects of modern Germany, such as at the University of Portsmouth.

Useful websites www.ciltuk.org.uk; www.goethe.de; www.bbc.co.uk/languages; www.ciol.org.uk; www.languageadvantage.com; www.languagematters.co.uk; www.faz.net; www.sueddeutsche.de; www.europa.eu; www.gslg.org.uk; www.amgs.org.uk; www.wigs.ac.uk

NB The points totals shown to the left of the institutions are for ease of reference only. It must not be assumed that Tariff points are always used by institutions or that they can be substituted for an offer in grades. The level of an offer is not necessarily indicative of the quality of a course.

COURSE OFFERS INFORMATION

Subject requirements/preferences GCSE English and German are required. **AL** German required usually at a specified grade.

Your target offers and examples of degree courses

152 pts **Cambridge** – A*AA incl lang (Modn Mediev Langs) (IB 40–41 pts HL 776)
Nottingham – A*AA-AAA (Econ Ger) (IB 38–36 pts)

144 pts **Birmingham** – AAA +LNAT (Law Ger Law) (IB 32 pts HL 666)
Bristol – AAA-AAB incl Ger +LNAT (Law Ger) (IB 36–34 pts HL 6 Ger)
Edinburgh – AAA-ABB (Int Bus Fr/Ger/Span) (IB 37–34 pts)
Imperial London – AAA incl chem+maths (Chem Fr/Ger/Span Sci) (IB 38 pts HL 7 chem 6 maths); AAA incl biol+sci/maths (Biol Sci Ger Sci) (IB 38 pts HL 6 biol+chem/maths)
London (King's) – AAA incl mus+Ger (Ger Mus (Yr Abrd)) (IB 35 pts HL 6 mus+Ger); AAA-AAB incl Fr/Ger/Span (Euro St (Fr/Ger/Span) (Yr Abrd)) (IB 35 pts HL 6 Fr/Ger/Span)
London (UCL) – AAA-ABB incl lang (Modn Langs) (IB 38–34 pts HL 6 lang)
Oxford – AAA (Ger courses) (IB 38 pts)
St Andrews – AAA-AAB (Ger courses) (IB 36 pts)
Southampton – AAA-AAB incl maths+Fr/Ger/Span (Maths Fr/Ger/Span) (IB 36 pts HL 6 maths)
Surrey – AAA-AAB incl Ger (Ger courses) (IB 36–35 pts)

136 pts **Aston** – AAB-ABB (Int Bus Fr/Ger/Span) (IB 34 pts)
Bath – 136 pts AAB incl Ger (Int Mgt Ger) (IB 35 pts HL 6 Ger)
Birmingham – AAB (Ger St courses) (IB 32 pts HL 665)
Edinburgh – AAB-ABB (Ger) (IB 36–34 pts)
Exeter – AAB-ABB incl Ger/Arbc (Ger Arbc) (IB 34–32 pts HL 5 Ger/Arbc)
Glasgow – AAB-BBB incl arts/lang (Ger Joint Hons) (IB 36–34 pts)
Lancaster – AAB-ABB (Ger St courses) (IB 35–32 pts)
London (King's) – AAB incl Fr+Ger (Fr Ger (Yr Abrd)) (IB 35 pts HL 6 Fr+Ger)
Nottingham – AAB incl Fr/Ger/Span (Mgt Fr/Ger/Span) (IB 34 pts)
Sheffield – AAB-BBB (Ger St Joint Hons) (IB 35–34 pts HL 6 Ger)
Southampton – AAB-ABB incl Engl+Fr/Ger/Span (Engl Fr/Ger/Span) (IB 34 pts HL 6 Engl+Fr/Ger/Span); AAB-ABB incl Fr/Ger/Span (Film Fr/Ger/Span) (IB 32 pts HL 6 Fr/Ger/Span)
Warwick – AAB incl Engl lit+lang (Engl Ger Lit) (IB 36 pts HL 5 Engl lit+lang); AAB incl Fr (Fr Ger/Ital St) (IB 36 pts HL 5 Fr); AAB incl lang/Lat/Anc Gk (Ger Joint Hons) (IB 36 pts HL 5 lang/Lat/Anc Gk)

York – AAB–ABB incl Ger (Ger courses) (IB 35–34 pts); AAB–ABB (Fr Ger Lang (Yr Abrd)) (IB 34 pts)

128 pts **Aston** – ABB–BBB incl Ger (Ger courses) (IB 33–32 pts HL 6 Ger)

Bath – ABB incl Ger+lang (Ger courses) (IB 34 pts HL 65 Ger+lang); ABB–AAB incl langs (Modn Langs Euro St) (IB 34 pts HL 6 5 langs)

Bristol – ABB–BBB incl lang (Ger courses) (IB 32–31 pts HL 5 lang); ABB–BBB incl Ger (Ger) (IB 32–31 pts HL 5 Ger)

Cardiff – ABB incl lang (Ger)

Dundee – ABB incl Engl+lang (Law Langs) (IB 32 pts)

Leeds – ABB incl Ger (Ger courses) (IB 34 pts HL 6 Ger)

Liverpool – ABB incl Ger (Ger courses) (IB 33 pts HL 6 Ger)

London (QM) – ABB incl art/hum+lang 128 pts (Fr/Ger/Russ Dr) (IB 34 pts HL 6 art/hum 5 lang)

London (RH) – ABB incl mus (Mus Fr/Ger/Ital/Span) (IB 32 pts); ABB (Ger courses; Dr Ger/Ital; Mgt Fr/Ger/Ital/Span) (IB 32 pts); (Euro St Fr/Ger/Ital/Span) (IB 34 pts); ABB incl Span (Span Fr/Ger/Ital) (IB 32 pts)

Manchester – ABB–BBB incl lang (Ger courses) (IB 34–32 pts)

Nottingham – ABB incl Ger (Ger) (IB 32 pts); ABB (Ger Joint Hons) (IB 32 pts)

Warwick – ABB incl Ger (Ger St courses; Ger Ital) (IB 34 pts HL 5 Ger)

120 pts **Aberdeen** – BBB (Ger) (IB 32 pts)

Dundee – BBB–BCC (Ger Joint Hons; Int Bus Ger; Phil Ger) (IB 30 pts)

Heriot-Watt – BBB incl lang (App Langs Transl (Fr/Span) (Ger/Span)) (IB 30 pts)

Kent – BBB incl lang (Ger) (IB 34 pts); BBB (Ger courses) (IB 34 pts)

London (QM) – 120–128 pts incl lang (Ger Ling; Ger Compar Lit; Ger courses) (IB 32–34 pts HL 5 lang)

Manchester – BBB incl Ger (Ger St) (IB 31 pts)

Reading – BBB/ABC (Ger courses) (IB 30 pts)

Sheffield – BBB–BBC incl Ger (Ger St) (IB 32 pts HL 6 Ger)

Swansea – BBB–BBC incl lang (Ger courses) (IB 32–30 pts)

112 pts **Aberystwyth** – 112–128 pts (Ger Joint Hons)

Central Lancashire – 112–128 pts (Ger (Comb); Fr/Ger/Span/Jap)

Chester – 112 pts incl Ger (Ger courses) (IB 26 pts HL 5 Ger)

Hertfordshire – 112 pts (Ger Joint Hons) (IB 28 pts)

Hull – 112 pts incl lang (Ger; Fr/Ger/Ital/Span Hist; Ger Joint Hons; Ger Transl St) (IB 28 pts)

Nottingham Trent – 112 pts incl Ger (Ger Joint Hons)

York St John – 112 pts incl Ger (Bus Mgt Ger)

104 pts **London (Birk)** – 104 pts (Modn Langs (Fr, Ger, Jap, Port, Span); Ger)

Manchester Met – 104–112 pts incl lang (Ling Lang (Chin/Fr/Ger/Ital/Span)) (IB 26 pts)

96 pts **Bangor** – 96–104 pts incl Ger (Ger courses)

Portsmouth – 96–120 pts (Ger St) (IB 30 pts HL 17 pts)

Alternative offers

See **Chapter 6** and **Appendix 1** for grades/new UCAS Tariff points information for other examinations.

CHOOSING YOUR COURSE (SEE ALSO CH.1)

Universities and colleges teaching quality See www.qaa.ac.uk; http://unistats.direct.gov.uk.

Top research universities and colleges (REF 2014) See **Languages**.

ADMISSIONS INFORMATION

Number of applicants per place (approx) Aston 4; Bangor 6; Bath 5; Birmingham 6; Bristol 4; Cardiff 6; Central Lancashire 2; Durham 5; Exeter 4; Heriot-Watt 10; Hull 12; Kent 10; Lancaster 7;

Leeds (Joint Hons) 8; London (King's) 5; London (QM) 6; London (RH) 5; London (UCL) 5; Nottingham 5; Portsmouth 5; Staffordshire 5; Surrey 2; Swansea 4; Warwick 8; York 6.

Advice to applicants and planning the UCAS personal statement Describe visits to Germany or a German-speaking country and the particular cultural and geographical features of the region. Contacts with friends in Germany and language experience should also be mentioned, and if you are bilingual, say so. Read German newspapers and magazines and keep up-to-date with national news.

Misconceptions about this course Leeds See **Languages**. **Swansea** Some students are afraid of the year abroad, which is actually one of the most enjoyable parts of the course.

Selection interviews Yes Bangor, Birmingham, Cambridge, Heriot-Watt, Hull, Liverpool, London (RH), London (UCL), Oxford, Sheffield, Southampton, Surrey (always); **Some** Cardiff, Leeds, Portsmouth, Swansea; **No** Nottingham.

Interview advice and questions Questions asked on A-level syllabus. Part of the interview may be in German. What foreign newspapers and/or magazines do you read? Questions on German current affairs, particularly politics and reunification problems, books read outside the course, etc. See also **Chapter 5**. **Leeds** See **Languages**.

Reasons for rejection (non-academic) Unstable personality. Poor motivation. Insufficient commitment. Unrealistic expectations. Not interested in spending a year abroad.

AFTER-RESULTS ADVICE

Offers to applicants repeating A-levels Higher Birmingham, Glasgow, Leeds, Warwick; **Same** Aston, Cardiff, Chester, Durham, London (RH), Nottingham, Surrey, Swansea, Ulster, York; **No** Cambridge.

GRADUATE DESTINATIONS AND EMPLOYMENT (2013/14 HESA)

Graduates surveyed 570 **Employed** 305 **In voluntary employment** 25 **In further study** 80 **Assumed unemployed** 25

Career note See **Languages**.

OTHER DEGREE SUBJECTS FOR CONSIDERATION

East European Studies; European Studies; International Business Studies.

GREEK

(see also Classical Studies/Classical Civilisation, Classics, Languages, Latin)

Courses are offered in Ancient and Modern Greek, covering the language and literature from ancient times to the present day. Some Classics and Classical Studies courses (see separate tables) also provide the opportunity to study Greek from scratch.

Useful websites www.greek-language.com; www.arwhead.com/Greeks; www.greekmyth.org; www.fhw.gr; www.culture.gr; www.greeklanguage.gr

NB The points totals shown to the left of the institutions are for ease of reference only. It must not be assumed that Tariff points are always used by institutions or that they can be substituted for an offer in grades. The level of an offer is not necessarily indicative of the quality of a course.

COURSE OFFERS INFORMATION

Subject requirements/preferences GCSE English and a foreign language required. Greek required by some universities. **AL** Latin, Greek or a foreign language may be specified by some universities.

Your target offers and examples of degree courses
152 pts Cambridge – A*AA (Class) (IB 40–41 pts HL 776); A*AA 152 pts (Modn Mediev Langs (Class Gk)) (IB 40–41 pts HL 776)

144 pts **Edinburgh** – AAA–ABB (Gk St courses; Anc Hist Gk) (IB 40–34 pts)
   Oxford – AAA (Modn Langs (Modn Gk)) (IB 38 pts)
136 pts **Glasgow** – AAB–BBB incl arts/lang (Gk) (IB 36–34 pts)
   London (King's) – AAB incl anc Gk+Engl (Gk Engl) (IB 35 pts HL 6 anc Gk+Engl); AAB
      (Class St Modn Gk St) (IB 35 pts)
   London (UCL) – AAB incl Gk (Gk Lat) (IB 36 pts HL 6 Gk); AAB incl Lat (Lat Gk)
      (IB 36 pts HL 6 Lat)
   St Andrews – AAB (Gk courses) (IB 36 pts)
128 pts **London (RH)** – ABB (Gk) (IB 32 pts)
 96 pts **Trinity Saint David** – 96 pts (Lat Joint Hons)

Alternative offers
See **Chapter 6** and **Appendix 1** for grades/new UCAS Tariff points information for other examinations.

CHOOSING YOUR COURSE (SEE ALSO CH.1)

Universities and colleges teaching quality See www.qaa.ac.uk; http://unistats.direct.gov.uk.

Top research universities and colleges (REF 2014) See **Classics**.

ADMISSIONS INFORMATION

Number of applicants per place (approx) Leeds 2; London (King's) 3; London (UCL) 5.

Advice to applicants and planning the UCAS personal statement See **Classical Studies/Classical Civilisation**.

Selection interviews Yes Cambridge, London (RH).

Interview advice and questions Questions asked on A-level syllabus: Why do you want to study Greek? What aspects of this course interest you? (Questions will develop from answers.) See also **Chapter 5**.

Reasons for rejection (non-academic) Poor language ability.

AFTER-RESULTS ADVICE

Offers to applicants repeating A-levels Higher St Andrews; **Same** Leeds; **No** Cambridge.

GRADUATE DESTINATIONS AND EMPLOYMENT (2013/14 HESA)

Classical Greek Studies graduates surveyed 5 **Employed** 0 **In voluntary employment** 0 **In further study** 0 **Assumed unemployed** 0

Career note See **Languages**.

OTHER DEGREE SUBJECTS FOR CONSIDERATION

Ancient History; Classical Studies; Classics; European Studies; Philosophy.

HEALTH SCIENCES/STUDIES

(including **Audiology, Chiropractic, Deaf Studies, Orthoptics, Orthotics, Osteopathy, Paramedic Science** and **Prosthetics**; see also **Community Studies/Development, Dietetics, Environmental Sciences, Nursing and Midwifery, Nutrition, Pharmacology, Pharmacy and Pharmaceutical Sciences, Physiotherapy, Radiography, Social Sciences/Studies, Speech Pathology/Sciences/ therapy**)

Health Sciences/Studies is a broad subject field which offers courses covering both practical applications concerning health and well-being (some of which border on nursing) and also the administrative activities involved in the promotion of health in the community. Also included are some specialised careers which include chiropractic, involving the healing process by way of

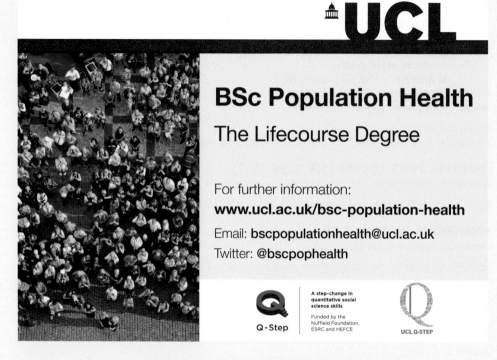

UCL FACULTY OF POPULATION HEALTH SCIENCES

UCL

BSc Population Health
The Lifecourse Degree

For further information:
www.ucl.ac.uk/bsc-population-health
Email: **bscpopulationhealth@ucl.ac.uk**
Twitter: **@bscpophealth**

Q-Step
A step-change in quantitative social science skills
Funded by the Nuffield Foundation, ESRC and HEFCE

UCL Q-STEP

manipulation, mainly in the spinal region, and osteopathy in which joints and tissues are manipulated to correct abnormalities. Audiology is concerned with the treatment and diagnosis of hearing and balance disorders while prosthetics involves the provision and fitting of artificial limbs and orthotics is concerned with making and fitting braces, splints and special footwear to ease pain and to assist movement.

Useful websites www.rsph.org.uk; www.bmj.com; www.aor.org.uk; www.baap.org.uk; www.chiropractic-uk.co.uk; www.osteopathy.org.uk; www.who.int; www.csp.org.uk; www.baaudiology.org; www.thebsa.org.uk; www.nhscareers.nhs.uk; www.gcc-uk.org; www.bso.ac.uk; www.osteopathy.org; www.collegeofparamedics.co.uk

NB The points totals shown to the left of the institutions are for ease of reference only. It must not be assumed that Tariff points are always used by institutions or that they can be substituted for an offer in grades. The level of an offer is not necessarily indicative of the quality of a course.

COURSE OFFERS INFORMATION
Subject requirements/preferences GCSE English, mathematics and a science important or essential for some courses. **AL** Mathematics, Chemistry or Biology may be required for some courses. **Other** Health checks and Disclosure and Barring Service (DBS) clearance required for many courses.

Your target offers and examples of degree courses
136 pts **Exeter** – AAB–ABB incl biol+sci (Med Sci) (IB 34–32 pts HL 65 biol+sci)
London (UCL) – AAB–ABB (Popn Hlth) (IB 36–34 pts)
Southampton – AAB–BBB (Hlthcr (Mgt Plcy Rsch)) (IB 34 pts)
Surrey – AAB–ABB incl sci (Paramed Prac) (IB 35 pts)
128 pts **Aston** – ABB incl sci (Hlthcr Sci (Audiol)) (IB 33 pts)
Durham – ABB (Hlth Hum Sci) (IB 34 pts)

New UCAS points Tariff: A* = 56 pts; A = 48 pts; B = 40 pts; C = 32 pts; D = 24 pts; E = 16 pts

Leeds – ABB incl sci (Hlthcr Sci (Audiol)) (IB 34 pts HL 5 sci)
Manchester – ABB incl sci/maths (Hlthcr Sci (Audiol)) (IB 34–33 pts)
Plymouth – 128 pts (Paramed Practnr) (IB 27 pts)
Salford – ABB incl maths/phys/eng 128 pts (Pros Orthot) (IB 28 pts)
Sheffield – ABB–BBB (Hlth Hum Sci) (IB 34–32 pts)
Southampton – ABB incl sci (Hlthcr Sci (Cardiov Respir Slp Sci)) (IB 32 pts)
South Wales – ABB incl biol+sci (MChiro) (IB 32 pts)
Strathclyde – ABB–BBB incl maths+sci (Pros Orthot) (IB 34 pts HL 6 maths+sci)
Surrey – ABB +interview (Midwif) (IB 34 pts)
UWE Bristol – 128 pts incl sci/soc sci (Paramed Sci) (IB 27 pts HL 6 sci/soc sci);
  128 pts incl biol/chem+sci (Hlthcr Sci (Physiol Sci); Hlthcr Sci (Lf Sci)) (IB 27 pts
  HL 6 biol/chem 5 sci)

120 pts **Bradford** – BBB 120 pts (Clin Sci)
Brighton – BBB (Paramed Prac) (IB 30 pts)
Brunel – BBB (Biomed Sci (Hum Hlth)) (IB 30 pts)
Cardiff Met – 120 pts (Hlthcr Sci) (IB 26 pts)
De Montfort – 120 pts incl sci (Hlthcr Sci Audiol) (IB 30 pts HL 6 sci)
Dundee – BBB incl biol (Oral Hlth Sci) (IB 30 pts)
East Anglia – BBB incl biol/chem/PE (Paramed Sci) (IB 31 pts HL sci)
Glasgow – BBB–CCC (Hlth Soc Plcy) (IB 30–28 pts)
Glasgow Caledonian – BBB incl sci (Orth) (IB 28 pts HL 6 sci)
Hertfordshire – 120 pts incl sci (Paramed Sci) (IB 30 pts)
Kent – BBB (Hlth Soc Cr) (IB 34 pts)
Liverpool – BBB incl biol (Orth) (IB 30 pts HL 6 biol)
London (St George's) – BBB incl biol (Hlthcr Sci (Physiol Sci))
Manchester Met – 120 pts incl biol (Hlthcr Sci) (IB 28 pts HL 5 biol)
Sheffield – BBB incl sci/maths (Orth) (IB 32 pts HL 6 sci/maths)
Sunderland – 120 pts (Hlth Soc Cr)
Swansea – BBB incl sci/maths (Hlthcr Sci (Audiol)); BBB (Ost)

112 pts **Brit Coll Ost Med** – BBC incl biol 112 pts (MOst)
Canterbury Christ Church – 112 pts (Hlth St)
Central Lancashire – 112 pts (Df St Educ; Sex Hlth St)
Chester – 112 pts (Hlth Soc Cr) (IB 26 pts)
East London – 112 pts (Hlth Prom) (IB 24 pts)
Edge Hill – BBC 112 pts (Hlth Soc Wlbng)
Greenwich – 112 pts (Hlth Wlbng; Pblc Hlth)
Hertfordshire – 112 pts incl biol/chem+sci/maths (Hlthcr Sci (Lf Sci)) (IB 28 pts)
Lincoln – 112 pts (Hlth Soc Cr)
London Met – 112 pts (Hlth Soc Cr; Hlth Soc Plcy)
Middlesex – 112 pts incl sci (Hlthcr Sci (Audiol))
Nottingham Trent – 112 pts incl sci/PE (Exer Nutr Hlth)
Portsmouth – 112 pts incl sci (Paramed Sci) (IB 26 pts HL 5 sci)
Salford – 112 pts incl sci (Exer Physl Actvt Hlth) (IB 29 pts)
Sheffield Hallam – 112 pts (Nutr Pblc Hlth)
Southampton Solent – 112 pts (Hlth Exer Physl Actvt; Psy (Hlth Psy))
Sunderland – 112 pts (Pblc Hlth; Hlthcr Sci (Physiol/Lf Sci))
Swansea – BBC (Hlth Soc Cr)
Ulster – 112 pts (Hlth Soc Cr Plcy) (IB 25 pts)
Westminster – BBC (Herb Med) (IB 26 pts HL 5 sci)

104 pts **Anglo-Euro (Coll Chiro)** – BCC (Chiro) (IB 26 pts)
Derby – 104 pts (Hlth Soc Cr)
European Sch Ost – BCC incl sci/maths (Ost) (IB 26 pts HL 5 sci)
Kingston – 104–144 pts (Exer Nutr Hlth)
Liverpool Hope – BCC–BBB 104–120 pts (Hlth Wlbng)
Liverpool John Moores – 104 pts (Hlth Soc Cr Indiv Fmly Commun)

Northampton – 104–120 pts (Hlth St Joint Hons)
UHI – BCC incl sci (Oral Hlth Sci)
West Scotland – BCC incl biol/chem (Env Hlth) (IB 28 pts)
96 pts **Bangor** – 96–112 pts (Hlth Soc Cr)
BPP – CCC incl sci 96 pts (Chiro MChiro)
Cardiff Met – 96 pts (Hlth Soc Cr)
Nescot – CCC incl sci 96 pts (Ost Med)
Nottingham Trent – 96 pts (Hlth Soc Cr)
Oldham (Univ Campus) – 96 pts (Hlth Commun St)
St Mary's – 96 pts incl sci (Hlth Exer Sci) (IB 28 pts)
Trinity Saint David – 96 pts (Hlth Nutr Lfstl)
West London – 96 pts (Hlth Prom Pblc Hlth)
Wolverhampton – 96–112 pts (Df St courses)
88 pts **Winchester** – 88–104 pts (Hlth Commun Soc Cr St) (IB 24 pts)
80 pts **Anglia Ruskin** – 80 pts (Pblc Hlth) (IB 24 pts)
Wolverhampton – 80 pts (Soc Cr Hlth St; Hlth St)
64 pts **UHI** – CC (Hlth St)
Worcester – 64 pts (Paramed Sci)

Open University – contact +44 (0)845 300 6090 **or** www.openuniversity.co.uk/you (Hlth Soc Cr)

Alternative offers
See **Chapter 6** and **Appendix 1** for grades/new UCAS Tariff points information for other examinations.

EXAMPLES OF COLLEGES OFFERING COURSES IN THIS SUBJECT FIELD

See also **Social and Public Policy and Administration**. Most colleges, check with your local college. Accrington and Rossendale (Coll); Amersham and Wycombe (Coll); Bedford (Coll); Blackburn (Coll); Blackpool and Fylde (Coll); Bradford (Coll); Bridgwater (Coll); Bristol City (Coll); Chesterfield (Coll); City of Oxford (Coll); Cornwall (Coll); Doncaster (Coll); Duchy (Coll); Durham New (Coll); Exeter (Coll); Grimsby (Univ Centre); Hugh Baird (Coll); Hull (Coll); Leeds City (Coll); Lincoln (Coll); Llandrillo (Coll); Manchester (Coll); Myerscough (Coll); Newcastle (Coll); Norwich City (Coll); Petroc; St Helens (Coll); Sir Gâr (Coll); Somerset (Coll); Sparsholt (Coll); Stockport (Coll); Tresham (CFHE); Truro and Penwith (Coll); Wakefield (Coll); Warwickshire (Coll); West Cheshire (Coll); Westminster City (Coll); Weston (Coll); Wigan and Leigh (Coll); York (Coll).

CHOOSING YOUR COURSE (SEE ALSO CH.1)

Universities and colleges teaching quality See www.qaa.ac.uk; http://unistats.direct.gov.uk.

Top research universities and colleges (REF 2014) (Public Health, Health Services and Primary Care) Cambridge; Liverpool; Oxford; Imperial London; Keele; London (UCL); Southampton; Bristol; London (King's); London (QM).

(Allied Health Professions, Dentistry, Nursing and Pharmacy) Birmingham; Sheffield (Biomed Sci); Bangor; Swansea (Allied Hlth); Aston; Coventry; Southampton; Cardiff; Surrey; Glasgow; Nottingham (Pharm); Bradford; East Anglia (Allied Hlth); London (QM); Sheffield (Dnstry); Queen's Belfast (Pharm); Bath; London (King's) (Pharm); Leeds.

ADMISSIONS INFORMATION

Number of applicants per place (approx) Anglo-Euro (Coll Chiro) 1; Bangor 2; Brit Coll Ost Med 5; Brunel 2; Central Lancashire 6; Chester 6; Cumbria 4; European Sch Ost 3; Liverpool John Moores 10; London Met 7; Manchester 18; Manchester Met 10; Northampton 3; Portsmouth 12; Salford 8; Southampton 4; Swansea 1.

Admissions tutors' advice You should describe any work with people you have done, particularly in a caring capacity, for example, working with the elderly, nursing, hospital work. Show why you wish to study this subject. You should give evidence of your ability to communicate and to work in a group. Evidence needed of applicants' understanding of the NHS and health care systems. Osteopathy applicants should provide clear evidence of why they want to work as an osteopath: work shadowing in an osteopath's practice is important and should be described. Give details of any work using your hands.

Misconceptions about this course There is a mistaken belief that Health Science courses include nursing. **Bangor** (Hlth Soc Cr) This is an administration course, not a nursing course. **Brit Coll Ost Med** Some students think that we offer an orthodox course in medicine. **European Sch Ost** Some applicants think we teach in French: we do not although we do have a franchise with a French school based in St Etienne and a high percentage of international students. All lectures are in English. Applicants should note that cranial osteopathy – one of our specialisms – is only one aspect of the programme.

Selection interviews Yes Anglia Ruskin, Bournemouth, Brighton, Cardiff Met, Central Lancashire, Coventry, Edinburgh, European Sch Ost, Lincoln, London (St George's), London South Bank, Nottingham Trent, Plymouth, Portsmouth, Robert Gordon, Salford, Southampton, Swansea, West Scotland, Worcester, York; **Some** Canterbury Christ Church, Derby, Liverpool John Moores; **No** Dundee.

Interview advice and questions Courses vary considerably and you are likely to be questioned on your reasons for choosing the course at that university or college. If you have studied biology then questions are possible on the A-level syllabus and you could also be asked to discuss any work experience you have had. (Ost) What personal qualities would you need to be a good osteopath? What have you done that you would feel demonstrates a sense of responsibility? What would you do if you were not able to secure a place on an Osteopathy course this year? See also **Chapter 5**. **Liverpool John Moores** Interviews are informal. It would be useful for you to bring samples of coursework to the interview.

Reasons for rejection (non-academic) Some students are mistakenly looking for a professional qualification in, for example, occupational therapy, nursing. **Coventry** Inadequate mathematics knowledge.

AFTER-RESULTS ADVICE
Offers to applicants repeating A-levels Same Bangor, Brighton, Chester, Derby, European Sch Ost, Lincoln, Liverpool John Moores, Salford, Surrey, Swansea.

GRADUATE DESTINATIONS AND EMPLOYMENT (2013/14 HESA)
See also **Biotechnology**, **Dentistry**, **Medicine**, **Nursing and Midwifery**, **Nutrition** and **Optometry**.

Complementary Medicine graduates surveyed 595 **Employed** 260 **In voluntary employment** 0 **In further study** 130 **Assumed unemployed** 15

Aural and Oral Sciences graduates surveyed 700 **Employed** 495 **In voluntary employment** 5 **In further study** 55 **Assumed unemployed** 20

Career note Graduates enter a very broad variety of careers depending on their specialism. Opportunities exist in the public sector, for example, management and administrative positions with health and local authorities and in health promotion.

OTHER DEGREE SUBJECTS FOR CONSIDERATION
Audiology; Biological Sciences; Biology; Community Studies; Consumer Studies; Dentistry; Dietetics; Medicine; Environmental Health; Nursing; Nutrition; Occupational Therapy; Optometry; Physiotherapy; Psychology; Podiatry; Radiography; Speech Therapy; Sport Science.

HISTORY

(including **Heritage Management** and **Medieval Studies**; see also **History (Ancient), History (Economic and Social), History of Art)**

Degrees in History cover a very broad field with many courses focusing on British and European history. However, specialised History degrees are available which cover other regions of the world and, in addition, all courses will offer a wide range of modules.

Useful websites www.english-heritage.org.uk; www.historytoday.com; www.archives.com; www. historynet.com; www.archives.org.uk; www.royalhistoricalsociety.org; www.nationalarchives.gov.uk; www.historesearch.com; www.history.ac.uk

NB The points totals shown to the left of the institutions are for ease of reference only. It must not be assumed that Tariff points are always used by institutions or that they can be substituted for an offer in grades. The level of an offer is not necessarily indicative of the quality of a course.

COURSE OFFERS INFORMATION

Subject requirements/preferences GCSE English and a foreign language may be required or preferred. **AL** History usually required at a specified grade. (Mediev St) History or English Literature required for some courses. (Vkg St) English or History.

Your target offers and examples of degree courses

152 pts **Bristol** – A*AA–AAB incl hist (Hist) (IB 38–34 pts HL 6 hist)
Cambridge – A*AA (Hist) (IB 40–41 pts HL 776)
Durham – A*AA incl hist (Hist) (IB 38 pts HL 6 hist)
Exeter – A*AA–AAB (Hist) (IB 38–34 pts)
London (UCL) – A*AA–AAA incl hist+Euro lang (Hist Euro Langs) (IB 39–38 pts HL 6 hist+Euro lang); A*AA–AAA incl hist (Hist; Hist (Yr Abrd)) (IB 39–38 pts HL 6 hist)

144 pts **Birmingham** – AAA–AAB incl hist (Hist) (IB 32 pts HL 666–665)
Cardiff – AAA–ABB incl hist (Hist) (IB 33 pts HL 6 hist)
Edinburgh – AAA–ABB (Hist Pol; Scot Hist) (IB 40–34 pts); AAA–AAB (Hist) (IB 40–34 pts)
Lancaster – AAA–AAB (Hist Phil; Hist; Hist Pol; Hist Int Rel; Mediev Ren St) (IB 36–35 pts)
Leeds – AAA incl hist (Hist) (IB 35 pts HL 6 hist)
Liverpool – AAA–AAB (Hist) (IB 36–35 pts)
London (King's) – AAA incl hist (War St Hist; Hist) (IB 35 pts HL 6 hist); AAA incl Fr+hist (Fr Hist (Yr Abrd)) (IB 35 pts HL 6 Fr+hist)
London LSE – AAA (Hist; Gov Hist; Int Rel Hist) (IB 38 pts)
Manchester – AAA–AAB incl hist (Hist) (IB 37 pts)
NCH London – AAA–ABB (Hist)
Newcastle – AAA–AAB incl hist (Hist) (IB 37–35 pts HL 6 hist)
Nottingham – AAA incl hist (Hist; Hist Pol) (IB 36 pts); AAA–AAB incl Engl+hist (Engl Hist) (IB 36–34 pts)
Oxford – AAA (Hist Pol; Hist Econ; Hist Modn Langs; Hist; History (Anc Modn)) (IB 38 pts); (Class Arch Anc Hist) (IB 39 pts)
St Andrews – AAA (Mediev Hist Arch; Mediev Hist courses; Scot Hist courses) (IB 36 pts); (Modn Hist courses) (IB 38–36 pts)
Warwick – AAA incl hist (Hist (Ren/Modn Modn)) (IB 38 pts HL 6 hist)
York – AAA incl hist+Fr (Hist Fr) (IB 36 pts HL 6 hist+Fr); AAA incl Engl+hist (Engl Hist) (IB 36 pts HL 6 Engl+hist); AAA incl hist/class civ (Hist) (IB 36 pts HL 6 hist)

136 pts **Birmingham** – AAB incl hist (Hist Joint Hons) (IB 32 pts HL 665)
Cardiff – AAB incl hist (Modn Hist Pol) (IB 34 pts)
East Anglia – AAB incl hist (Hist; Modn Hist; Hist Pol) (IB 33 pts HL 5 hist)
Edinburgh – AAB–ABB (Celt Scot Hist) (IB 36–34 pts)
Glasgow – AAB–BBB incl arts/lang (Scot Hist; Hist) (IB 36–34 pts)

A PLACE TO
INSPIRE YOU/AN
APPROACH TO
CHALLENGE YOU

The School of History at the University of Kent combines
research excellence with inspirational teaching to offer a superb
student experience.

- Ranked 8th for Research Intensity (REF 2014)
- Offering flexible, research-led teaching
- Modules include: medieval, early modern, modern British and European,
  American, imperial and colonial, military, scientific and medical history
- Scored 93% for student satisfaction in the most recent National Student Survey
  (*NSS* 2013)
- Based in the historic cathedral city of Canterbury, across 300 acres of parkland
- Outstanding employability support – 96% of History graduates go on to
  employment or further study after six months

To find out more go to
www.kent.ac.uk/history,
or come along to an Open Day
www.kent.ac.uk/opendays
01227 827272

University of
Kent

50
1965-2015
THE UK'S
EUROPEAN
UNIVERSITY

COMBINING RESEARCH EXCELLENCE WITH INSPIRATIONAL TEACHING

The School of History at the University of Kent is recognised as one of the leading history departments in the country. Ranked eighth for Research Intensity in the most recent Research Excellence Framework, students are taught by world-class academics, actively working at the forefront of their fields.

The School prides itself on its flexible programmes, offering students the opportunity to tailor their degree to their own interests. Undergraduate students have access to over 80 modules covering British, Irish, European, American, Pacific and African history, as well as a wide range of courses on military history. An unparalleled range of joint honours degrees are also on offer, for those wishing to pursue a cross-disciplinary programme.

For the past five years, the School of History has consistently scored over 90% for student satisfaction in the National Student Survey – reflecting its inspiring teaching, lively and engaging student body and fantastic student support. A student-led History Society maintains a vibrant undergraduate community, organising extra-curricular lectures, field trips to places such as Rome and Vienna, and a host of social events.

The School is situated on Canterbury's leafy campus, where students have access to the University library, which holds over one million items, as well as the British Cartoon Archive. The medieval city provides a dramatic backdrop to the study of history, and students have privileged access to the Canterbury Cathedral Library and archives. High-speed trains link Canterbury to London and the continent, placing many of the most influential and historic sites in Europe a stone's throw away.

The School of History also has strong and established links with institutions across Europe as well as in Canada, the United States and South Africa allowing for a truly global outlook and opportunities to study abroad.

The strength of the School's degrees means that graduates are highly sought after; in 2014 96% of students were in employment or further study shortly after graduation.

A superb student experience

"Every part of the School of History made my time at Kent exciting and enjoyable. The School offers a wide range of modules to choose from, and staff are always there to help you with any questions you might have.

Kent is a brilliant place to go for a History degree. It is one of the most exciting and innovative Universities in the UK and is at the forefront of research. The amount of extracurricular activities available to you is brilliant. Having a degree from the University of Kent is brilliant for my future career prospects, and in many job interviews employers have commented on Kent being a great University to have been to.

Since graduating I have completed a work placement with Channel 5 in their PR department, and have recently begun an internship with Sony Music."

Jessie Martin
History graduate

Fantastic prospects

"I was attracted to Kent by the modules available, the fact that it was a campus university, and the impressive student satisfaction rating. Kent is second in the country for History too, so I felt I'd be in safe hands.

My course was great; the teaching was one of its finest features. I always felt my seminars were valuable to my learning, and really built my confidence in each topic.

My studies have definitely helped my career prospects. The day after results day I was offered a full time job as a Trainee Oral Historian, working for an organisation which provides cultural, educational and historical activities. The work involves setting up exhibitions, interviewing people, conducting research, and archiving material. I am proud to be able to directly put my degree to use."

Emily Richards
History graduate

Further details

For more information please contact:
history@kent.ac.uk
01227 823710
www.kent.ac.uk/history

London (RH) – AAB–ABB (Hist) (IB 32 pts)

London (SOAS) – AAB–ABB (Hist) (IB 35 pts)

London (UCL) – AAB–ABB (Hist Phil Sci) (IB 36–34 pts); ABB incl hist (Hist (Cnt E Euro) Jew St) (IB 34 pts HL 5 hist); AAB–ABB incl hist (Russ Hist) (IB 36–34 pts HL 5 hist)

Manchester – AAB–ABB incl hist/pol (Pol Modn Hist) (IB 35–34 pts)

Nottingham – AAB incl hist (Anc Hist Hist; Hist Art Hist) (IB 34 pts)

Reading – AAB–ABB (Hist) (IB 32 pts)

Sheffield – AAB incl hist (Hist Pol) (IB 35 pts HL 6 hist); AAB–ABB incl hist (Hist) (IB 35 pts HL 6 hist); (Hist Joint Hons) (IB 35–34 pts HL 6 hist)

Southampton – AAB–ABB incl Engl+hist (Engl Hist) (IB 34 pts HL 6 Engl+hist); AAB–ABB incl hist (Film Hist) (IB 32 pts HL 6 hist); (Hist; Modn Hist Pol) (IB 34 pts HL 6 hist); (Arch Hist) (IB 34–30 pts HL 6 hist); (Phil Hist) (IB 34–32 pts HL 6 hist)

Sussex – AAB–ABB (Hist Joint Hons; Hist) (IB 34 pts)

128 pts **Chichester** – ABB–CCC (Hist) (IB 31 pts)

East Anglia – ABB (Lit Hist) (IB 32 pts HL 5 Engl); (Phil Hist; Am Hist) (IB 32 pts HL 5 hist); ABB incl hist (Film Hist; Hist Hist Art) (IB 32 pts HL 5 hist)

Edinburgh – ABB (Archit Hist) (IB 36–34 pts)

Essex – ABB–BBB (Hist; Modn Hist; Am Hist; Soc Cult Hist) (IB 32–30 pts)

Huddersfield – ABB 128 pts (Comb Hons); ABB incl hist 128 pts (Hist)

Keele – ABB (Hist) (IB 34 pts)

Kent – ABB incl hist (Am St (Hist); Hist courses) (IB 34 pts); ABB incl B hist (War St) (IB 34 pts HL 16 pts incl 5 hist)

Leeds – ABB incl biol (Biol Hist Phil Sci) (IB 34 pts HL 6 biol); ABB incl hist (Hist Phil Sci courses) (IB 34 pts HL 6 hist)

Leicester – ABB (Anc Hist Hist) (IB 28–30 pts); (Hist; Hist Am St; Contemp Hist; Hist courses) (IB 30 pts)

Liverpool – ABB (Hist Comb Hons) (IB 33 pts)

London (Gold) – ABB (Hist; Hist Hist Ideas) (IB 33 pts); ABB–BBB (Hist Pol) (IB 33 pts)

London (QM) – 128 pts incl hist (Hist) (IB 34 pts HL 5 hist); ABB incl hist 128 pts (Mediev Hist; Hist Compar Lit; Hist Pol) (IB 34 pts HL 5 hist)

London (UCL) – ABB (Scand St Hist) (IB 34 pts)

Loughborough – ABB (Hist Pol; Hist Int Rel; Hist Geog; Hist; Hist Engl) (IB 34 pts)

Manchester – ABB incl hist (Hist courses) (IB 35 pts)

Northumbria – 128 pts incl hist/pol (Hist Pol) (IB 31 pts HL 5 hist/pol); 128 pts incl hist (Hist) (IB 31 pts HL 5 hist)

Nottingham – ABB (Am Can Lit Hist Cult) (IB 32 pts); ABB incl hist (Am St Hist; Hist East Euro Cult St; Hist Contemp Chin St) (IB 32 pts); ABB incl Span (Hisp St Hist) (IB 32 pts)

Queen's Belfast – ABB–BBB (Hist courses)

Roehampton – 128 pts (Hist)

Sheffield – ABB (Jap St Joint Hons) (IB 34 pts)

Strathclyde – ABB–BBB (Hist) (IB 34 pts)

120 pts **Aberdeen** – BBB (Hist) (IB 32 pts)

Aberystwyth – 120–128 pts (Hist; Hist Welsh Hist; Mediev Ely Modn Hist; Modn Contemp Hist)

Brunel – BBB (Hist) (IB 30 pts)

Buckingham – BBB (Engl Lit Hist)

Chester – BBB–BBC incl hist/class civ/pol/sociol 120 pts (Hist) (IB 28 pts HL 5 hist)

Chichester – BBB–CCC (Modn Hist) (IB 30 pts)

Coventry – BBB (Hist courses) (IB 29 pts)

De Montfort – 120 pts incl hist (Hist) (IB 30 pts)

Dundee – BBB–BCC (Hist; Scot Hist St) (IB 30 pts); BBB–BCC incl sci/maths (Bus Econ Mark Hist) (IB 30 pts)

Edge Hill – BBB 120 pts (Hist; Engl Lit Hist; Hist Pol)

Gloucestershire – 120 pts (Hist)

Greenwich – 120 pts (Hist) (IB 28 pts)

Leeds Beckett – 120 pts (Hist) (IB 26 pts)

Leicester – BBB (Int Rel Hist) (IB 28 pts)
Oxford Brookes – BBB (Hist) (IB 32 pts)
Queen's Belfast – BBB–ABB incl Fr (Fr Joint Hons)
Sheffield Hallam – 120 pts incl Engl lit/hist (Engl Hist)
Stirling – BBB (Scot Hist; Hist) (IB 32 pts)
Sunderland – 120 pts (Hist courses)
Swansea – BBB–BBC incl hist (Hist) (IB 32–30 pts); BBB–BBC (Mediev St Anc Hist)
  (IB 32–30 pts)
UWE Bristol – 120 pts (Hist) (IB 26 pts)

112 pts Bangor – 112–120 pts (Hist; Mediev Ely Modn Hist; Modn Contemp Hist; Welsh Hist Joint
  Hons; Herit Arch Hist)
Brighton – BBC (Hist Lit Cult) (IB 28 pts)
Canterbury Christ Church – 112 pts (Hist; Hist Arch)
Derby – 112 pts incl class/hist/pol (Hist)
East London – 112 pts (Hist) (IB 24 pts)
Hertfordshire – 112 pts (Hist; Hist Ital) (IB 28 pts)
Hull – 112 pts incl lang (Fr/Ger/Ital/Span Hist) (IB 28 pts); 112 pts (Hist; Hist Arch)
  (IB 28 pts)
Lincoln – 112 pts (Hist)
Liverpool John Moores – 112 pts (Hist) (IB 28 pts)
Manchester Met – BBC 112 pts (Mediev Ely Modn Hist; Hist) (IB 26 pts); 112 pts
  (Modn Hist) (IB 26 pts)
Newman – 112 pts (Hist)
Northampton – 112–120 pts (Hist courses) (IB 24 pts)
Nottingham Trent – 112 pts (Pol Hist; Hist)
Plymouth – 112 pts (Hist courses) (IB 28 pts)
Sheffield Hallam – 112 pts incl hist (Hist)
Teesside – 112 pts incl hist (Hist)
Westminster – BBC incl Engl (Engl Lit Hist) (IB 30 pts HL 5 Engl)
York St John – 112 pts (Hist)

104 pts Bath Spa – 104–120 pts (Hist)
Brighton – BCC (Sociol Soc Hist) (IB 27 pts)
Central Lancashire – 104 pts (Hist) (IB 28 pts)
Coventry – BCC (Pol Hist) (IB 28 pts)
Leeds Trinity – 104 pts (Hist)
Liverpool Hope – BCC–BBB 104–120 pts (Hist)
London (Birk) – 104 pts (Pol Phil Hist; Hist)
Manchester Met – 104–112 pts (Hist Joint Hons) (IB 26 pts)
St Mary's – 104 pts (Hist) (IB 28 pts)
South Wales – BCC (Hist) (IB 29 pts)
Staffordshire – 104 pts (Modn Hist)
Winchester – 104–120 pts (Hist; Hist Mediev Wrld) (IB 26 pts)
Worcester – 104–112 pts (Hist courses)

96 pts Bishop Grosseteste – 96–112 pts (Arch Hist; Hist courses)
Bradford – CCC 96 pts (Hist Pol)
Glyndŵr – 96 pts (Hist)
Kingston – 96 pts (Hist)
Portsmouth – 96–120 pts incl hist (Hist; Am St Hist) (IB 30 pts HL 17 pts incl 6 hist);
  96–120 pts incl Engl+hist (Engl Hist) (IB 30 pts HL 17 pts incl 6 Engl+hist)
Trinity Saint David – 96–104 pts (Herit St); (Hist courses) (IB 26 pts)
Wolverhampton – 96–112 pts (Pol Hist; Hist)

88 pts Anglia Ruskin – 88–104 pts (Hist) (IB 24 pts)
80 pts Trinity Saint David – 80–104 pts (Mediev St Joint Hons)
64 pts UHI – CC (Scot Hist Arch); CC incl hist/Engl (Scot Hist); CC incl hist/Engl/pol (Hist Pol)
48 pts Anglia Ruskin – DD (Hist Engl)

Alternative offers
See **Chapter 6** and **Appendix 1** for grades/new UCAS Tariff points information for other examinations.

EXAMPLES OF COLLEGES OFFERING COURSES IN THIS SUBJECT FIELD
Blackpool and Fylde (Coll); Bury (Coll); Farnborough (CT); North Lindsey (Coll); Peterborough (Coll); Petroc; South Devon (Coll); Stockton Riverside (Coll); Suffolk (Univ Campus); Truro and Penwith (Coll); West Anglia (Coll); West Suffolk (Coll); Yeovil (Coll).

CHOOSING YOUR COURSE (SEE ALSO CH.1)
Universities and colleges teaching quality See www.qaa.ac.uk; http://unistats.direct.gov.uk.

Top research universities and colleges (REF 2014) York; Birmingham; Southampton; London (King's); Sheffield; London (Birk); Hertfordshire; Leeds; Leicester; Queen's Belfast; Sussex; Warwick; Edinburgh; Cardiff.

ADMISSIONS INFORMATION
Number of applicants per place (approx) Aberystwyth 6; Anglia Ruskin 4; Bangor 6; Bath Spa 6; Birmingham 8; Bristol 7; Brunel 6; Buckingham 10; Cambridge 3; Cardiff 7; Central Lancashire 5; Chichester 4; De Montfort 10; Dundee 6; Durham 11; East Anglia 8; Edge Hill 8; Exeter 9; Gloucestershire 26; Glyndŵr 2; Huddersfield 4; Hull 5; Kent 12; Kingston 6; Lancaster 11; Leeds 12; Leeds Trinity 14; Leicester 7; Liverpool 6; London (Gold) 6; London (King's) 10; London (QM) 5; London (RH) 9; London (UCL) 5; London LSE 19; Manchester 6; Manchester Met 8; Newcastle 13; Newman 2; Northampton 4; Nottingham 20; Oxford Brookes 25; Portsmouth 5; Roehampton 3; St Mary's 5; Sheffield Hallam 21; Southampton 8; Staffordshire 8; Stirling 2; Teesside 4; Trinity Saint David 6; UWE Bristol 6; Warwick 17; York 5; York St John 3.

Advice to applicants and planning the UCAS personal statement Show your passion for the past! Visits to places of interest should be mentioned, together with any particular features which impressed you. Read historical books and magazines outside your A-level syllabus. Mention these and describe any special areas of study which interest you. (Check that these areas are covered in the courses for which you are applying!) **Bristol** Only accepting a limited number of deferred applicants in fairness to next year's applicants. Apply early. **Manchester** Due to the detailed nature of entry requirements for History courses, we are unable to include full details in the prospectus. For complete and up-to-date information on our entry requirements for these courses, please visit our website at www.manchester.ac.uk/ugcourses.

Misconceptions about this course Students sometimes underestimate the amount of reading required. **Lincoln** Some students expect the subject to be assessed only by exams and essays. It is not – we use a wide range of assessment methods. **Liverpool John Moores** Some applicants think that they have to study ancient and medieval history as well as modern; we actually only cover post-1750 history. **Stirling** Some applicants think that we only teach British history. We also cover European, American, African and environmental history.

Selection interviews Yes Bangor, Birmingham, Bishop Grosseteste, Brighton, Cambridge, Canterbury Christ Church, Chichester, Edge Hill, Hertfordshire, Hull, Lancaster, Leeds Trinity, London (King's), London (RH), London (UCL), Oxford (Hist) 23%, (Hist Econ) 19%, (Hist Engl) 11%, (Hist Modn Lang) 22%, (Hist Pol) 11%, Oxford Brookes, Portsmouth, Roehampton, Warwick; **Some** Anglia Ruskin, Bristol, Buckingham, Cardiff, De Montfort, East Anglia, Huddersfield, Kent, Liverpool, London (QM), London LSE (rarely), Sheffield Hallam, Staffordshire, Trinity Saint David, Winchester, Wolverhampton; **No** Dundee, Essex, Nottingham, Reading, Southampton.

Interview advice and questions Questions are almost certain to be asked on those aspects of the History A-level syllabus which interest you. Examples of questions in previous years have included: Why did imperialism happen? If a Martian arrived on Earth what aspect of life would you show him/her to sum up today's society? Has the role of class been exaggerated by Marxist historians? What is the difference between power and authority and between patriotism and nationalism? Did Elizabeth I have a foreign policy? What is the relevance of history in modern society? Who are your favourite monarchs? How could you justify your study of history to the taxpayer? What are the origins of your Christian name? See also **Chapter 5**. **Cambridge** How would you compare Henry VIII to Stalin? In the 1920s did the invention of the Henry Ford car lead to a national sub-culture or was it just an aspect of one? Is there such a thing as 'race'? Should historians be allowed to read sci-fi novels? **De Montfort** Why History? Why is history important? **Oxford** Questions on submitted work and the capacity to think independently. What are the origins of your name? Why are you sitting in this chair? **Sheffield** Written work may be required. **Swansea** We ask applicants to explain something – a hobby, an historical problem or a novel. The subject is less important than a coherent and enthusiastic explanation.

Reasons for rejection (non-academic) Personal statements which read like job applications, focusing extensively on personal skills and saying nothing about the applicant's passion for history. Poor use of personal statement combined with predicted grades. Little commitment and enthusiasm. No clear reason for choice of course. Little understanding of history. Absence or narrowness of intellectual pursuits. Deception or concealment on the UCAS application. Knowledge of 19th century history (chosen subject) did not have any depth. Unwillingness to learn. Narrow approach to subject. Failure to submit requested information. **Birmingham** Commitment insufficient to sustain interest over three years. **London (King's)** Inability to think analytically and comparatively. **London (UCL)** The vast majority of applications are of a very high standard, many applicants being predicted AAA grades. We view each application as a complete picture, taking into account personal statement, reference and performance at any interview as well as actual and predicted academic performance. There is no single rule by which applicants are selected and therefore no single reason why they are rejected. **Nottingham** No discrimination against Oxbridge applicants.

AFTER-RESULTS ADVICE
Offers to applicants repeating A-levels Higher Exeter, Glasgow, Huddersfield, Leeds, Liverpool, St Andrews, Trinity Saint David, Warwick; **Possibly higher** Aberystwyth, Birmingham, Cambridge, Portsmouth; **Same** Anglia Ruskin, Bangor, Bristol, Buckingham, Cardiff, Chester, Chichester, De Montfort, Dundee, Durham, East Anglia, Edge Hill, Hull, Kent, Lancaster, Lincoln, Liverpool Hope, Liverpool John Moores, London (QM), London (RH), London (SOAS), Newcastle, Newman, Nottingham Trent, Oxford Brookes, Roehampton, St Mary's, Staffordshire, Stirling, Suffolk (Univ Campus), Winchester, Wolverhampton, York, York St John.

GRADUATE DESTINATIONS AND EMPLOYMENT (2013/14 HESA)
Graduates surveyed 9,445 **Employed** 4,320 **In voluntary employment** 470 **In further study** 2,405 **Assumed unemployed** 610

Career note Graduates enter a broad spectrum of careers. Whilst a small number seek positions with museums and galleries, most will enter careers in management, public and social services and retail as well as the teaching profession.

OTHER DEGREE SUBJECTS FOR CONSIDERATION
Ancient History; Anthropology; Archaeology; Economic and Social History; Government; History of Art; International Relations; Medieval History; Politics.

HISTORY (ANCIENT)
(see also **Arabic and Ancient Near and Middle Eastern Studies, Archaeology, Classical Studies/ Classical Civilisation, History**)

Ancient History covers the Greek and Roman world, the social, religious, political and economic changes taking place in the Byzantine period and the medieval era which followed.

Useful websites www.royalhistoricalsociety.org; www.guardians.net; www.arwhead.com/Greeks; www.ancientworlds.net; www.bbc.co.uk/history/ancient; www.historesearch.com/ancient.html

NB The points totals shown to the left of the institutions are for ease of reference only. It must not be assumed that Tariff points are always used by institutions or that they can be substituted for an offer in grades. The level of an offer is not necessarily indicative of the quality of a course.

COURSE OFFERS INFORMATION

Subject requirements/preferences GCSE A foreign language or classical language may be required. **AL** History or Classical Civilisation may be preferred subjects.

Your target offers and examples of degree courses

152 pts **Cambridge** – A*AA (Hum Soc Pol Sci (Assyr Egypt)) (IB 40–41 pts HL 776)
London (UCL) – A*AA–AAA incl hist/class civ (Anc Hist; Anc Hist Egypt) (IB 39–38 pts)

144 pts **Durham** – AAA (Anc Hist Arch; Anc Hist) (IB 37 pts)
Edinburgh – AAA–ABB (Anc Hist Lat; Anc Hist; Anc Hist Gk; Anc Hist Class Arch) (IB 40–34 pts)
Exeter – AAA–ABB (Anc Hist) (IB 36–32 pts)
Oxford – AAA (History (Anc Modn)) (IB 38 pts)
St Andrews – AAA (Anc Hist Econ) (IB 38 pts)

136 pts **Bristol** – AAB–ABB (Anc Hist) (IB 34–32 pts)
London (King's) – AAB (Anc Hist) (IB 35 pts)
London (UCL) – AAB (Anc Wrld) (IB 36 pts)
Nottingham – AAB incl hist (Anc Hist Hist) (IB 34 pts)
St Andrews – AAB (Anc Hist Art Hist; Anc Hist Film St) (IB 36 pts)

128 pts **Birmingham** – ABB (Arch Anc Hist; Anc Mediev Hist; Anc Hist) (IB 32 pts HL 655)
Cardiff – ABB–BBB (Anc Hist Joint Hons) (IB 34–30 pts)
Edinburgh – ABB (Anc Medit Civ) (IB 34 pts)
Leicester – ABB (Anc Hist Hist; Anc Hist Arch) (IB 28–30 pts)
Liverpool – ABB (Anc Hist; Arch Anc Civ) (IB 33 pts)
London (RH) – ABB (Anc Hist Phil) (IB 32 pts); ABB (Anc Hist) (IB 32 pts)
Manchester – ABB–BBB (Anc Hist) (IB 34–31 pts)
Nottingham – ABB–AAC (Anc Hist Arch) (IB 32 pts)
Warwick – ABB (Anc Hist Class Arch) (IB 34 pts)

120 pts **Kent** – BBB (Anc Hist) (IB 34 pts)
Swansea – BBB–BBC (Egypt Anc Hist; Anc Hist Hist; Anc Mediev Hist) (IB 32–30 pts)

96 pts **Trinity Saint David** – 96 pts (Anc Mediev Hist; Anc Hist) (IB 26 pts)

Alternative offers
See **Chapter 6** and **Appendix 1** for grades/new UCAS Tariff points information for other examinations.

CHOOSING YOUR COURSE (SEE ALSO CH.1)

Universities and colleges teaching quality See www.qaa.ac.uk; http://unistats.direct.gov.uk.

Top research universities and colleges (REF 2014) See **Classics**.

ADMISSIONS INFORMATION

Number of applicants per place (approx) Birmingham 7; Bristol 6; Cardiff 4; Durham 11; Leicester 32; London (RH) 3; London (UCL) 5; Manchester 7; Nottingham 10; Oxford 4.

Advice to applicants and planning the UCAS personal statement Any information about experience of excavation or museum work should be given. Visits to Greece and Italy to study archaeological sites should be described. Show how your interest in, for example, Ancient Egypt developed through, for example, reading, television and the internet. Be aware of the work of the career archaeologist, for example, sites and measurement officers, field officers and field researchers (often specialists in pottery, glass, metalwork). See also **History**.

Misconceptions about this course Liverpool (Egypt) Some students would have been better advised looking at V400 Archaeology or VV16 Ancient History and Archaeology, both of which offer major pathways in the study of Ancient Egypt.

Selection interviews Yes London (RH), Oxford (25%); **Some** Bristol, Cardiff; **No** Birmingham.

Interview advice and questions See **History**.

Reasons for rejection (non-academic) **Liverpool** (Egypt) Egyptology used to fill a gap on the UCAS application. Applicant misguided in choice of subject.

AFTER-RESULTS ADVICE
Offers to applicants repeating A-levels **Same** Birmingham, Cardiff, Durham, Newcastle.

GRADUATE DESTINATIONS AND EMPLOYMENT (2013/14 HESA)
See **History**.

Career note See **History**.

OTHER DEGREE SUBJECTS FOR CONSIDERATION
Anthropology; Archaeology; Classical Studies; Classics; Greek; History of Art; Latin.

HISTORY (ECONOMIC and SOCIAL)
(see also **History**)

Economic and Social History is a study of societies and economies and explores the changes that have taken place in the past and the causes and consequences of those changes. The study can cover Britain, Europe and other major powers.

Useful websites www.royalhistoricalsociety.org; www.ehs.org.uk; see also **Economics** and **History**.

NB The points totals shown to the left of the institutions are for ease of reference only. It must not be assumed that Tariff points are always used by institutions or that they can be substituted for an offer in grades. The level of an offer is not necessarily indicative of the quality of a course.

COURSE OFFERS INFORMATION
Subject requirements/preferences **GCSE** Mathematics usually required and a language may be preferred. **AL** History preferred.

Your target offers and examples of degree courses
152 pts **London LSE** – A*AA incl maths (Econ Econ Hist) (IB 38 pts)
144 pts **Edinburgh** – AAA–ABB (Sociol Soc Econ Hist) (IB 37–34 pts)
  York – AAA incl hist+maths (Hist Econ) (IB 36 pts HL 6 hist)
136 pts **Glasgow** – AAB–BBB incl Engl (Econ Soc Hist) (IB 38–36 pts)
128 pts **Essex** – ABB–BBB (Soc Cult Hist) (IB 32–30 pts)
  Manchester – ABB incl hist/sociol (Hist Sociol) (IB 34 pts)
120 pts **Aberdeen** – BBB 120 pts (Econ Hist)
  Aberystwyth – 120–128 pts (Hist Econ Soc Hist)
  Edinburgh – AAA–ABB (Soc Hist) (IB 40–34 pts)
112 pts **Manchester Met** – BBC 112 pts (Soc Hist) (IB 26 pts)

Alternative offers
See **Chapter 6** and **Appendix 1** for grades/new UCAS Tariff points information for other examinations.

CHOOSING YOUR COURSE (SEE ALSO CH.1)
Universities and colleges teaching quality See www.qaa.ac.uk; http://unistats.direct.gov.uk.

ADMISSIONS INFORMATION
Number of applicants per place (approx) London LSE (Econ Hist) 3, (Econ Hist Econ) 5; York 8.

Advice to applicants and planning the UCAS personal statement See **History**.

Selection interviews **Yes** Aberystwyth.

Interview advice and questions See **History**.

AFTER-RESULTS ADVICE
Offers to applicants repeating A-levels **Higher** York.

GRADUATE DESTINATIONS AND EMPLOYMENT (2013/14 HESA)
See **History**.

Career note See **History**.

OTHER DEGREE SUBJECTS FOR CONSIDERATION
Economics; Government; History; Politics; Social Policy and Administration; Sociology.

HISTORY OF ART
(see also **History**)

History of Art (and Design) courses differ slightly between universities although most will focus on the history and appreciation of European art and architecture from the 14th to 20th centuries. Some courses also cover the Egyptian, Greek and Roman periods and at London (SOAS), Asian, African and European Art. The history of all aspects of design and film can also be studied in some courses. There has been an increase in the popularity of these courses in recent years.

Useful websites www.artchive.com; www.artcyclopedia.com; theartguide.com; www.galleries.co.uk; www.fine-art.com; www.nationalgallery.org.uk; www.britisharts.co.uk; www.tate.org.uk

NB The points totals shown to the left of the institutions are for ease of reference only. It must not be assumed that Tariff points are always used by institutions or that they can be substituted for an offer in grades. The level of an offer is not necessarily indicative of the quality of a course.

COURSE OFFERS INFORMATION
Subject requirements/preferences **GCSE** English required and a foreign language usually preferred. **AL** History is preferred for some courses.

Your target offers and examples of degree courses
152 pts **Cambridge** – A*AA (Hist Art) (IB 40–41 pts HL 776)
144 pts **Edinburgh** – AAA–ABB (Hist Art; Hist Art Hist Mus) (IB 37–34 pts)
 Exeter – AAA–AAB (Art Hist Vis Cult) (IB 36–34 pts)
 London (UCL) – AAA–ABB (Hist Art) (IB 36–34 pts)
 Oxford – AAA (Hist Art) (IB 38 pts)
 St Andrews – AAA (Art Hist Mid E St; Art Hist Psy) (IB 36 pts)
136 pts **Bristol** – AAB–ABB (Hist Art) (IB 34–32 pts); AAB–ABB incl lang (Hist Art Modn Lang)
 (IB 34–32 pts HL 5 lang)
 East Anglia – AAB (Hist Art; Arch Anth Art Hist (St Abrd)) (IB 33 pts)
 Glasgow – AAB–BBB incl arts/lang (Hist Art) (IB 36–34 pts)
 Leeds – AAB (Hist Art) (IB 34–35 pts)
 London (Court) – AAB (Hist Art) (IB 35 pts)
 Newcastle – AAB (Hist Art Joint Hons) (IB 35 pts)
 Nottingham – AAB incl hist (Hist Art Hist) (IB 34 pts); AAB incl Engl (Hist Art Engl)
 (IB 34 pts); AAB (Hist Art) (IB 34 pts)
 St Andrews – AAB (Art Hist) (IB 35 pts); (Art Hist Class St; Art Hist Lang) (IB 36 pts)
 Sussex – AAB–ABB (Art Hist) (IB 34 pts)
 York – AAB incl hist/class civ (Hist Hist Art) (IB 35 pts HL 6 hist); AAB–ABB (Hist Art)
 (IB 35–34 pts); AAB incl Engl (Engl Hist Art) (IB 35 pts HL 6 Engl)

128 pts **Birmingham** – ABB (Hist Art) (IB 32 pts HL 655); ABB incl lang (Modn Langs Hist Art) (IB 32 pts HL 655)

East Anglia – ABB incl hist (Hist Hist Art) (IB 32 pts HL 5 hist)

Essex – ABB–BBB (Lit Art Hist; Art Hist) (IB 32–30 pts)

London (SOAS) – ABB (Hist Art (As Af Euro)) (IB 33 pts); ABB–BBB (Hist Art Arch courses; Hist Art) (IB 33 pts)

Manchester – ABB–BBB (Arch Art Hist) (IB 33–32 pts); (Hist Art) (IB 34–31 pts)

Nottingham – ABB–BBB (Arch Hist Art) (IB 32–30 pts)

Warwick – ABB (Hist Art) (IB 34 pts)

120 pts **Aberdeen** – BBB (Hist Art) (IB 32 pts)

Buckingham – BBB (Art Hist Herit Mgt)

Kent – BBB (Art Hist Film; Art Hist) (IB 34 pts)

Leicester – BBB (Hist Art) (IB 28 pts)

112 pts **Aberystwyth** – 112 pts incl art (Fn Art Art Hist); 112 pts (Art Hist)

Brighton – BBC (Fash Drs Hist; Hist Art Des) (IB 28 pts)

Liverpool John Moores – 112 pts (Hist Art) (IB 29 pts)

London (Birk) – 112 pts (Hist Art)

Manchester Met – 112–120 pts (Art Hist) (IB 26 pts)

Plymouth – 112 pts (Fn Art Art Hist) (IB 24 pts)

104 pts **Plymouth** – 104 pts (Art Hist) (IB 28 pts)

Alternative offers
See **Chapter 6** and **Appendix 1** for grades/new UCAS Tariff points information for other examinations.

EXAMPLES OF COLLEGES OFFERING COURSES IN THIS SUBJECT FIELD
South Gloucestershire and Stroud (Coll).

CHOOSING YOUR COURSE (SEE ALSO CH.1)
Universities and colleges teaching quality See www.qaa.ac.uk; http://unistats.direct.gov.uk.

Top research universities and colleges (REF 2014) See **Art and Design (General)**.

ADMISSIONS INFORMATION
Number of applicants per place (approx) Aberystwyth 9; Birmingham 14; Brighton 8; Bristol 4; Cambridge 3; East Anglia 7; Essex 5; Kent 3; Leeds 29; Leicester 6; London (Gold) 10; London (SOAS) 4; London (UCL) 8; Manchester 3; Manchester Met 10; Nottingham 10; York 4.

Advice to applicants and planning the UCAS personal statement Applicants for History of Art courses should have made extensive visits to art galleries, particularly in London, and should be familiar with the main European schools of painting. Evidence of lively interest required. Discuss your preferences and say why you prefer certain types of work or particular artists. You should also describe any visits to museums and any special interests in furniture, pottery or other artefacts.
Bristol Deferred entry may be considered. **London (Court)** A-levels in History, History of Art, English, and modern European languages are the most relevant; however, other subjects are considered. Art offered as an A-level should include a history of art paper.

Misconceptions about this course Kent The History of Art is not a practical course in fine arts. **York** Students do not need a background in art or art history. It is not a course with a studio element in it.

Selection interviews Yes Brighton, Cambridge, Essex, London (Court), London (UCL), Manchester Met, Oxford (11%); **Some** Bristol, Buckingham, Kent, Manchester, Warwick; **No** Birmingham, East Anglia, Nottingham.

Interview advice and questions Some universities set slide tests on painting and sculpture. Those applicants who have not taken History of Art at A-level will be questioned on their reasons for choosing the subject, their visits to art galleries and museums and their reactions to the art work which has impressed them. See **Chapter 5**. **Kent** Do they visit art galleries? Have they studied art history previously? What do they expect to get out of the degree? Sometimes they are given images to compare and discuss.

Reasons for rejection (non-academic) Poorly presented practical work. Students who do not express any interest or enthusiasm in contemporary visual arts are rejected.

AFTER-RESULTS ADVICE
Offers to applicants repeating A-levels Possibly higher St Andrews; **Same** Aberystwyth, East Anglia, Kent, Leeds, Warwick, York; **No** Cambridge.

GRADUATE DESTINATIONS AND EMPLOYMENT (2013/14 HESA)
Career note Work in galleries, museums and collections will be the objective of many graduates, who should try to establish contacts by way of work placements and experience during their undergraduate years. The personal skills acquired during their studies, however, open up many opportunities in other careers.

OTHER DEGREE SUBJECTS FOR CONSIDERATION
Art; Archaeology; Architecture; Classical Studies; Photography.

HORTICULTURE

(including **Garden Design**; see also **Agricultural Sciences/Agriculture, Landscape Architecture, Plant Sciences**)

Horticulture is a broad subject area covering amenity or landscape horticulture, production horticulture and retail horticulture.

Useful websites www.iagre.org; www.rhs.org.uk; www.horticulture.org.uk; www.growcareers.info; www.sgd.org.uk

NB The points totals shown to the left of the institutions are for ease of reference only. It must not be assumed that Tariff points are always used by institutions or that they can be substituted for an offer in grades. The level of an offer is not necessarily indicative of the quality of a course.

COURSE OFFERS INFORMATION
Subject requirements/preferences GCSE Mathematics sometimes required. **AL** A science subject may be required or preferred for some courses.

Your target offers and examples of degree courses
104 pts **Hadlow (Coll)** – 104 pts (Gdn Des; Hort (Commer))
       SRUC – BCC (Hort); BCC incl sci (Hort Plntsmn)
 96 pts **Duchy (Coll)** – 96 pts (Hort (Gdn Lnd Des))
       Writtle (Coll) – 96–112 pts (Hort) (IB 24 pts)
 64 pts **Worcester** – 64 pts (Hort)

Alternative offers
See **Chapter 6** and **Appendix 1** for grades/new UCAS Tariff points information for other examinations.

EXAMPLES OF COLLEGES OFFERING COURSES IN THIS SUBJECT FIELD
Askham Bryan (Coll); Bicton (Coll); Bishop Burton (Coll); Bridgend (Coll); Bridgwater (Coll); Brooksby Melton (Coll); CAFRE; Capel Manor (Coll); Craven (Coll); Myerscough (Coll); Warwickshire (Coll).

CHOOSING YOUR COURSE (SEE ALSO CH.1)
Universities and colleges teaching quality See www.qaa.ac.uk; http://unistats.direct.gov.uk.

Examples of sandwich degree courses Nottingham Trent.

New UCAS points Tariff: A* = 56 pts; A = 48 pts; B = 40 pts; C = 32 pts; D = 24 pts; E = 16 pts

ADMISSIONS INFORMATION
Number of applicants per place (approx) Greenwich 4; SRUC 1; Writtle (Coll) 3.

Advice to applicants and planning the UCAS personal statement Practical experience is important and visits to botanical gardens (the Royal Botanic Gardens, Kew or Edinburgh and the Royal Horticultural Society gardens at Wisley) could be described. Contact your local authority offices for details of work in parks and gardens departments. See also **Appendix 3**.

Misconceptions about this course Greenwich (Hort) Students are unaware of the scope of this degree. The course covers commercial horticulture, nursery retail and production, commercial and medicinal crop production, horticultural chemistry, plant physiology, hydroponics and fruit practice and production.

Selection interviews Yes Worcester; **Some** Greenwich, SRUC.

Interview advice and questions Past questions have included: How did you become interested in horticulture? How do you think this course will benefit you? Could you work in all weathers? What career are you aiming for? Are you interested in gardening? Describe your garden. What plants do you grow? How do you prune rose trees and fruit trees? Are there any EU policies at present affecting the horticulture industry? Topics relating to the importance of science and horticulture. See also **Chapter 5**.

AFTER-RESULTS ADVICE
Offers to applicants repeating A-levels Same Greenwich, SRUC.

GRADUATE DESTINATIONS AND EMPLOYMENT (2013/14 HESA)
See **Agricultural Sciences/Agriculture**.

Career note Graduates seeking employment in horticulture will look towards commercial organisations for the majority of openings. These will include positions as growers and managers with fewer vacancies for scientists involved in research and development and advisory services.

OTHER DEGREE SUBJECTS FOR CONSIDERATION
Agriculture; Biology; Crop Science; Ecology; Forestry; Landscape Architecture; Plant Sciences.

HOSPITALITY and EVENT MANAGEMENT

(see also **Business and Management Courses, Business and Management Courses (International and European), Business and Management Courses (Specialised), Consumer Studies/Sciences, Food Science/Studies and Technology, Leisure and Recreation Management/Studies, Tourism and Travel**)

Courses cover the full range of skills required for those working in the industry. Specific studies include hotel management, food and beverage supplies, equipment design, public relations and marketing. Depending on the course, other topics may include events management, tourism and the international trade.

Useful websites www.thebapa.org.uk; www.cordonbleu.net; www.instituteofhospitality.org; www.people1st.co.uk; www.abpco.org

NB The points totals shown to the left of the institutions are for ease of reference only. It must not be assumed that Tariff points are always used by institutions or that they can be substituted for an offer in grades. The level of an offer is not necessarily indicative of the quality of a course.

COURSE OFFERS INFORMATION
Subject requirements/preferences GCSE English and mathematics usually required together with a foreign language for International Management courses. **AL** No specified subjects.

Your target offers and examples of degree courses

136 pts **Surrey** – AAB (Int Hspty Mgt) (IB 35 pts)

128 pts **Coventry** – ABB (Evnt Mgt) (IB 29 pts)

Kent – ABB (Evnt Expnc Des) (IB 34 pts)

Strathclyde – ABB–BBB (Mgt Hspty Tour Mgt) (IB 33 pts)

120 pts **Coventry** – BBB (Int Hspty Tour Mgt) (IB 30 pts)

Leeds Beckett – 120 pts (Spo Evnt Mgt; Evnts Mgt) (IB 26 pts)

Staffordshire – BBB 120 pts (Evnts Mgt)

112 pts **Birmingham City** – BBC 112 pts (Media Comm (Evnt Exhib Ind)) (IB 28 pts)

Bournemouth – 112–120 pts (Evnts Mgt) (IB 30–31 pts)

Bournemouth Arts – BBC–BBB 112–120 pts (Crea Evnt Mgt) (IB 32 pts)

Brighton – BBC (Int Hspty Mgt; Int Evnt Mgt) (IB 28 pts)

Canterbury Christ Church – 112 pts (Evnts Mgt)

Cardiff Met – 112 pts (Int Tour Hspty Mgt; Evnts Mgt)

Central Lancashire – 112 pts (Evnt Mgt) (IB 25 pts); (Int Hspty Mgt) (IB 28 pts)

Chester – BBC–BCC 112 pts (Evnts Mgt) (IB 26 pts)

Chichester – 112–128 pts (Evnt Mgt) (IB 30 pts)

De Montfort – 112 pts (Arts Fstvl Mgt) (IB 28 pts)

East London – 112 pts (Hspty Mgt) (IB 24 pts)

Glasgow Caledonian – BBC (Int Evnts Mgt) (IB 25 pts)

Gloucestershire – 112 pts (Evnts Mgt)

Greenwich – 112 pts (Evnt Mgt)

Huddersfield – BBC 112 pts (Evnts Mgt; Hspty Bus Mgt)

Lincoln – 112 pts (Evnts Mgt)

Liverpool John Moores – 112 pts (Evnts Mgt) (IB 28 pts)

London Met – 112 pts (Evnts Mgt)

Northampton – 112 pts (Evnts Mgt; Evnts Mgt Joint Hons)

Oxford Brookes – BBC (Int Hspty Mgt) (IB 30 pts)

Plymouth – 112 pts (Evnt Mgt)

Southampton Solent – 112 pts (Evnts Mgt)

Sunderland – 112 pts (Int Tour Hspty Mgt)

Ulster – BBC–BBB (Int Hspty Mgt) (IB 25 pts)

104 pts **Birmingham (UC)** – 104 pts (Evnts Mgt)

Derby – 104 pts (Int Hspty Mgt; Evnt Mgt)

Edinburgh Napier – BCC (Fstvl Evnt Mgt) (IB 28 pts)

Queen Margaret – BCC 104 pts (Evnts Mgt) (IB 28 pts)

Robert Gordon – BCC (Evnts Mgt) (IB 28 pts)

Salford – BCC 104–120 pts (Int Evnts Mgt) (IB 24 pts)

South Wales – BCC (Evnt Mgt) (IB 29 pts)

West London – 104 pts (Hspty Mgt; Evnt Mgt)

96 pts **Birmingham (UC)** – 96 pts (Spa Mgt; Hspty courses; Culn Arts Mgt; Spec Hair Media Mkup)

CAFRE – 96 pts incl bus/sci/hm econ (Fd Bus Mgt)

Edinburgh Napier – CCC (Hspty Mark Mgt) (IB 27 pts)

Essex – 96 pts (Htl Mgt)

Euro Bus Sch London – CCC (Int Evnts Mgt)

Hertfordshire – 96–112 pts (Evnt Mgt) (IB 28 pts)

London Regent's – CCC (Int Evnts Mgt)

Manchester Met – 96–112 pts (Evnts Mgt) (IB 26 pts); CCC–BBC 96–112 pts (Hspty Bus Mgt) (IB 26 pts)

Plymouth – 96 pts (Cru Mgt); (Int Hspty Mgt; Hspty Mgt) (IB 24 pts)

Robert Gordon – CCC (Hspty Mgt) (IB 26 pts)

Sheffield Hallam – 96–112 pts (Int Htl Rsrt Mgt)

West Scotland – CCC (Evnts Mgt) (IB 24 pts)

Winchester – 96–112 pts (Evnt Mgt) (IB 25 pts)

New UCAS points Tariff: A* = 56 pts; A = 48 pts; B = 40 pts; C = 32 pts; D = 24 pts; E = 16 pts

Wolverhampton – 96–112 pts (Int Hspty Mgt; Evnt Vnu Mgt)
Writtle (Coll) – 96 pts (Evnt Mgt)
88 pts **Portsmouth** – 88 pts (Hspty Mgt; Hspty Mgt Tour) (IB 28 pts HL 15 pts)
80 pts **Bedfordshire** – 80 pts (Evnt Mgt) (IB 24 pts)
Bucks New – 80–96 pts (Evnts Fstvl Mgt; Mus Live Evnts Mgt)
64 pts **Trinity Saint David** – 64 pts (Evnts Mgt)
UHI – CC (Hosp Mgt)
48 pts **Colchester (Inst)** – 48 pts +interview (Hspty Mgt)

Alternative offers
See **Chapter 6** and **Appendix 1** for grades/new UCAS Tariff points information for other examinations.

EXAMPLES OF COLLEGES OFFERING COURSES IN THIS SUBJECT FIELD
Accrington and Rossendale (Coll); Askham Bryan (Coll); Barnsley (Coll); Bedford (Coll); Birmingham Met (Coll); Bishop Burton (Coll); Blackburn (Coll); Blackpool and Fylde (Coll); Bournemouth and Poole (Coll); Bournville (Coll); Bradford (Coll); Brighton and Hove City (Coll); Bury (Coll); Cornwall (Coll); Craven (Coll); Darlington (Coll); Derby (Coll); Doncaster (Coll); Durham New (Coll); Ealing, Hammersmith and West London (Coll); East Riding (Coll); Furness (Coll); Grimsby (Univ Centre); Guildford (Coll); Hartlepool (CFE); Highbury Portsmouth (Coll); Hull (Coll); Leicester (Coll); Liverpool City (Coll); Llandrillo (Coll); London City (Coll); London UCK (Coll); Loughborough (Coll); LSST; Macclesfield (Coll); Manchester (Coll); Mid-Kent (Coll); Neath Port Talbot (Coll); Nescot; Newcastle (Coll); North Nottinghamshire (Coll); Northumberland (Coll); Norwich City (Coll); Petroc; Plumpton (Coll); Plymouth City (Coll); Portsmouth (Coll); Reaseheath (Coll); Redbridge (Coll); Richmond-upon-Thames (Coll); Sheffield (Coll); South Cheshire (Coll); South Devon (Coll); South Essex (Coll); Southampton City (Coll); Stratford-upon-Avon (Coll); Suffolk (Univ Campus); Walsall (Coll); Warwickshire (Coll); West Cheshire (Coll); West Herts (Coll); West Suffolk (Coll); Westminster Kingsway (Coll); Weymouth (Coll); Wirral Met (Coll).

CHOOSING YOUR COURSE (SEE ALSO CH.1)
Universities and colleges teaching quality See www.qaa.ac.uk; http://unistats.direct.gov.uk.

Examples of sandwich degree courses Birmingham (UC); Bournemouth; Brighton; Cardiff Met; Central Lancashire; Derby; Gloucestershire; Huddersfield; Leeds Beckett; London Met; Manchester Met; Oxford Brookes; Plymouth; Portsmouth; Salford; Sheffield Hallam; Staffordshire; Sunderland; Surrey; Ulster; West London; Wolverhampton.

ADMISSIONS INFORMATION
Number of applicants per place (approx) Bournemouth 9; Cardiff Met 12; Central Lancashire 8; Edinburgh Napier 17; London Met 10; Manchester Met (Hspty Mgt) 12; Oxford Brookes 9; Portsmouth 10; Robert Gordon 3; Strathclyde 8; Surrey 12.

Advice to applicants and planning the UCAS personal statement Experience in dealing with members of the public is an important element in this work which, coupled with work experience in cafés, restaurants or hotels, should be described fully. All applicants are strongly recommended to obtain practical experience in catering or hotel work. Admissions tutors are likely to look for experience in industry and for people who are ambitious, sociable and team players. See also **Appendix 3**.

Misconceptions about this course Cardiff Met The course is not about cooking! We are looking to create managers, not chefs.

Selection interviews Yes Salford; **Some** Cardiff Met, Manchester Met, Robert Gordon; **No** Bucks New, Portsmouth, Surrey.

Interview advice and questions Past questions have included: What books do you read? What do you know about hotel work and management? What work experience have you had? What kind of job do you have in mind when you have qualified? How did you become interested in this course?

Do you eat in restaurants? What types of restaurants? Discuss examples of good and bad restaurant organisation. What qualities do you have which make you suitable for management? See also **Chapter 5**.

Reasons for rejection (non-academic) Lack of suitable work experience or practical training. Inability to communicate. Lack of awareness of workload, for example shift working, weekend work. **Cardiff Met** Students looking specifically for licensed trade courses or a cookery course. **Oxford Brookes** Lack of commitment to the hotel and restaurant industry.

AFTER-RESULTS ADVICE
Offers to applicants repeating A-levels Higher Bournemouth, Huddersfield, Oxford Brookes, Surrey; **Same** Brighton, Cardiff Met, Manchester Met, Salford, Strathclyde, Suffolk (Univ Campus), Ulster, West London, Wolverhampton.

GRADUATE DESTINATIONS AND EMPLOYMENT (2013/14 HESA)
Including Leisure, Tourism and Transport graduates surveyed 5,190 **Employed** 3,160 **In voluntary employment** 115 **In further study** 720 **Assumed unemployed** 310

Career note These business-focused hospitality programmes open up a wide range of employment and career opportunities in both hospitality and other business sectors. The demand for employees has been high in recent years. Events Management is currently a growth area with graduates working in sports and the arts, tourist attractions, hospitality, business and industry.

OTHER DEGREE SUBJECTS FOR CONSIDERATION
Business; Consumer Studies; Dietetics; Food Science; Health Studies; Leisure and Recreation Management; Management; Tourism and Travel.

HOUSING
(see also **Building and Construction, Property Management and Surveying, Town and Country Planning**)

These courses prepare students for careers in housing management although topics covered will also be relevant to other careers in business and administration. Modules will be taken in housing, law, finance, planning policy, public administration and construction.

Useful websites www.gov.uk/government/topics/housing; www.rtpi.org.uk; www.freeindex.co.uk/categories/property/construction/Property_Development

NB The points totals shown to the left of the institutions are for ease of reference only. It must not be assumed that Tariff points are always used by institutions or that they can be substituted for an offer in grades. The level of an offer is not necessarily indicative of the quality of a course.

COURSE OFFERS INFORMATION
Subject requirements/preferences GCSE English and mathematics required. **AL** No specified subjects.

Your target offers and examples of degree courses
120 pts **Birmingham** – BBB (Soc Pol (Hous Commun)) (IB 32 pts HL 555)
112 pts **Central Lancashire** – 112 pts (Commun Soc Care Plcy Prac) (IB 28 pts)
 96 pts **London South Bank** – CCC 96 pts (Hous St)
 72 pts **Cardiff Met** – 72 pts (Hous (Supptd Hous/Plcy Prac))

Alternative offers
See **Chapter 6** and **Appendix 1** for grades/new UCAS Tariff points information for other examinations.

New UCAS points Tariff: A* = 56 pts; A = 48 pts; B = 40 pts; C = 32 pts; D = 24 pts; E = 16 pts

EXAMPLES OF COLLEGES OFFERING COURSES IN THIS SUBJECT FIELD
Birmingham Met (Coll); Blackburn (Coll); Nescot; St Helens (Coll); Truro and Penwith (Coll).

CHOOSING YOUR COURSE (SEE ALSO CH.1)
Universities and colleges teaching quality See www.qaa.ac.uk; http://unistats.direct.gov.uk.

ADMISSIONS INFORMATION
Number of applicants per place (approx) Cardiff Met 1.

Advice to applicants and planning the UCAS personal statement An interest in people, housing problems, social affairs and the built environment is important for this course. Contacts with local housing managers (through local authority offices or housing associations) are important. Describe any such contacts and your knowledge of the housing types and needs in your area. The planning department in your local council office will be able to provide information on the various types of developments taking place in your locality and how housing needs have changed during the past 50 years. See also **Appendix 3**.

Misconceptions about this course Applicants do not appreciate that the course is very close to social work/community work and is most suitable for those wishing to work with people.

Selection interviews Yes Cardiff Met.

Interview advice and questions Since the subject is not studied at school, questions are likely to be asked on reasons for choosing this degree. Other past questions include: What is a housing association? Why were housing associations formed? In which parts of the country would you expect private housing to be expensive and, by comparison, cheap? What is the cause of this? Have estates of multi-storey flats fulfilled their original purpose? If not, why not? What causes a slum? What is an almshouse? See also **Chapter 5**.

Reasons for rejection (non-academic) Lack of awareness of current social policy issues.

AFTER-RESULTS ADVICE
Offers to applicants repeating A-levels Same Cardiff Met, London South Bank.

GRADUATE DESTINATIONS AND EMPLOYMENT (2013/14 HESA)
See **Building and Construction**.

Career note Graduates aiming for openings in housing will be employed mainly as managers with local authorities; others will be employed by non-profit-making housing associations and trusts and also by property companies owning blocks of flats.

OTHER DEGREE SUBJECTS FOR CONSIDERATION
Architecture; Building; Business Studies; Community Studies; Environmental Planning; Estate Management; Property Development; Social Policy and Administration; Social Studies; Surveying; Town Planning; Urban Regeneration.

HUMAN RESOURCE MANAGEMENT

(see also Business and Management Courses, Business and Management Courses (International and European), Business and Management Courses (Specialised))

This is one of the many branches of the world of business and has developed from the role of the personnel manager. HR managers may be involved with the induction and training of staff, disciplinary and grievance procedures, redundancies and equal opportunities issues. In large organisations some HR staff may specialise in one or more of these areas. Work experience dealing with the public should be stressed in the UCAS personal statement.

Useful websites www.hrmguide.co.uk; www.cipd.co.uk

NB The points totals shown to the left of the institutions are for ease of reference only. It must not be assumed that Tariff points are always used by institutions or that they can be substituted for an offer in grades. The level of an offer is not necessarily indicative of the quality of a course.

COURSE OFFERS INFORMATION

Subject requirements/preferences **GCSE** English and mathematics at C or above. **AL** No subjects specified.

Your target offers and examples of degree courses

136 pts **Aston** – AAB–ABB (HR Mgt) (IB 35–34 pts)
Cardiff – AAB (Bus Mgt (HR)) (IB 35 pts)
Lancaster – AAB (Mgt HR) (IB 35 pts)
Leeds – AAB (HR Mgt) (IB 35 pts)
Manchester – AAB (Mgt HR) (IB 35 pts)

128 pts **Bournemouth** – 128–136 pts (Bus St HR Mgt) (IB 32–33 pts)
Coventry – ABB (Bus HR Mgt) (IB 30 pts)
London (RH) – ABB (Mgt HR) (IB 32 pts)
Swansea – ABB–BBB (Bus Mgt (HR Mgt)) (IB 33–32 pts)

120 pts **Bradford** – BBB 120 pts (HR Mgt)
De Montfort – 120 pts (HR Mgt) (IB 28 pts)
Heriot-Watt – BBB (Bus Mgt HR Mgt) (IB 29 pts)
Huddersfield – BBB 120 pts (Bus HR Mgt)
Keele – BBB/ABC (HR Mgt Joint Hons) (IB 32 pts)
Leeds Beckett – 120 pts (Bus HR Mgt) (IB 26 pts)
Northumbria – BBB 120 pts (HR Mgt) (IB 30 pts)
Sheffield Hallam – 120 pts (Bus HR Mgt)
Stirling – BBB (HR Mgt) (IB 32 pts)
Ulster – BBB (Law HR Mgt) (IB 26 pts)

112 pts **Birmingham City** – BBC 112 pts (Bus HR Mgt) (IB 28 pts)
Brighton – BBC (Bus HR Mgt) (IB 28 pts HL 16 pts)
Canterbury Christ Church – 112 pts (HR Mgt)
Cardiff Met – 112 pts (Bus Mgt St HR Mgt)
Chichester – 112–128 pts (Evnt Mgt HR Mgt) (IB 30 pts)
East London – 112 pts (Bus Mgt (HR Mgt)) (IB 24 pts)
Greenwich – 112 pts (HR Mgt)
Middlesex – 112 pts (Psy HR Mgt)
Northampton – 112 pts (HR Mgt courses)
Nottingham Trent – 112 pts (Bus Mgt HR)
Portsmouth – 112 pts (HR Mgt Psy) (IB 30 pts HL 17 pts)
Sunderland – 112 pts (Bus HR Mgt)
West London – 112 pts (Bus St HR Mgt)
Westminster – BBC (Bus Mgt HR Mgt) (IB 28 pts)
Worcester – 112 pts (Bus Mark HR Mgt; HR Mgt courses)
York St John – 112 pts (Bus Mgt HR Mgt)

104 pts **Bath Spa** – 104–120 pts (Bus Mgt (HR Mgt))
Liverpool John Moores – 104 pts (HR Mgt) (IB 27 pts)
Manchester Met – BCC–BBC 104–112 pts (HR Mgt) (IB 26 pts)
Middlesex – 104 pts (Bus Mgt (HR))
Robert Gordon – BCC (Mgt HR Mgt) (IB 28 pts)
South Wales – BCC (HR Mgt) (IB 29 pts)
Ulster – 104–120 pts (Adv HR Mgt; HR Mgt Mark) (IB 24 pts)

96 pts **Anglia Ruskin** – 96–112 pts (Bus HR Mgt) (IB 24 pts)
Edinburgh Napier – CCC (Bus St HR Mgt) (IB 27 pts)

New UCAS points Tariff: A* = 56 pts; A = 48 pts; B = 40 pts; C = 32 pts; D = 24 pts; E = 16 pts

Hertfordshire – 96–112 pts (Bus HR; HR Mgt) (IB 28 pts)
West Scotland – CCC (HR Mgt) (IB 24 pts)
Wolverhampton – 96–112 pts (HR Mgt)
88 pts **Derby** – 88–120 pts (HR Mgt)
80 pts **Bedfordshire** – 80 pts (HR Mgt) (IB 24 pts)
Bucks New – 80–96 pts (Bus HR Mgt)
64 pts **Trinity Saint David** – 64 pts (HR Mgt)
32 pts **Greenwich (Sch Mgt)** – 32 pts (HR Mgt)

Alternative offers
See **Chapter 6** and **Appendix 1** for grades/new UCAS Tariff points information for other examinations.

EXAMPLES OF COLLEGES OFFERING COURSES IN THIS SUBJECT FIELD
Barking and Dagenham (Coll); Basingstoke (CT); Bath (Coll); Birmingham Met (Coll); Bournemouth and Poole (Coll); Croydon (Univ Centre); Greenwich (Sch Mgt); London City (Coll); London UCK (Coll); Manchester (Coll); Newcastle (Coll); North Lindsey (Coll); Plymouth City (Coll); St Helens (Coll); South Gloucestershire and Stroud (Coll); Suffolk (Univ Campus); Wigan and Leigh (Coll).

CHOOSING YOUR COURSE (SEE ALSO CH.1)
Universities and colleges teaching quality See www.qaa.ac.uk; http://unistats.direct.gov.uk.

Examples of sandwich degree courses Aston; Bath Spa; Bedfordshire; Birmingham City; Bournemouth; Bradford; Brighton; Central Lancashire; Chichester; Coventry; De Montfort; Hertfordshire; Huddersfield; Leeds; Leeds Beckett; Liverpool John Moores; Manchester Met; Northampton; Northumbria; Portsmouth; Sheffield Hallam; Trinity Saint David; Ulster; West Scotland; Westminster; Wolverhampton; Worcester.

ADMISSIONS INFORMATION
Number of applicants per place (approx) Anglia Ruskin 10; Aston 10.

Advice to applicants and planning the UCAS personal statement See **Business and Management Courses**.

Selection interviews Yes De Montfort; **Some** Anglia Ruskin. (See **Business and Management Courses**.)

Interview advice and questions See **Business and Management Courses**.

Reasons for rejection (non-academic) See **Business and Management Courses**.

AFTER-RESULTS ADVICE
Offers to applicants repeating A-levels Higher Anglia Ruskin.

GRADUATE DESTINATIONS AND EMPLOYMENT (2013/14 HESA)
Graduates surveyed 715 **Employed** 455 **In voluntary employment** 10 **In further study** 85 **Assumed unemployed** 60

Career note See under **Business and Management Courses**.

OTHER DEGREE SUBJECTS FOR CONSIDERATION
Business Studies; Information Systems; Management Studies/Sciences; Marketing; Psychology; Retail Management; Sociology; Sports Management.

HUMAN SCIENCES/HUMAN BIOSCIENCES

(see also **Medicine, Neuroscience**)

Human Sciences is a multi-disciplinary study relating to biological and social sciences and focuses on social and cultural behaviour. Topics range from genetics and evolution to health, disease, social behaviour and industrial societies. A typical course may include anatomy, physiology, bio-mechanics, anthropology and psychology.

Useful websites www.bbsrc.ac.uk; www.becominghuman.org; see also **Biology** and **Geography**.

NB The points totals shown to the left of the institutions are for ease of reference only. It must not be assumed that Tariff points are always used by institutions or that they can be substituted for an offer in grades. The level of an offer is not necessarily indicative of the quality of a course.

COURSE OFFERS INFORMATION

Subject requirements/preferences GCSE Science essential and mathematics usually required. **AL** Chemistry/Biology usually required or preferred for some courses.

Your target offers and examples of degree courses

144 pts **Exeter** – AAA–ABB (Hum Sci (Cornwall)) (IB 36–32 pts)
London (UCL) – AAA incl sci (Hum Sci) (IB 38 pts HL 6 sci)
Oxford – AAA (Hum Sci) (IB 38 pts)
Sussex – AAA–AAB (Psy Cog Sci; Psy Neuro) (IB 35 pts)

128 pts **Durham** – ABB (Hlth Hum Sci) (IB 34 pts)
Sheffield – ABB–BBB (Hlth Hum Sci) (IB 34–32 pts)
Swansea – ABB (Med Sci Hum)

120 pts **Loughborough** – ABC/BBB (Ergon (Hum Fact Des)) (IB 32 pts)
Northumbria – 120 pts incl biol (Hum Biosci) (IB 30 pts)
Plymouth – 120 pts incl biol+sci (Hum Biosci) (IB 28 pts HL 5 biol+sci)

112 pts **Westminster** – BBC incl sci (Hum Med Sci) (IB 26 pts HL 5 sci)
West Scotland – BBC incl sci (Biomed Sci; App Biomed Sci) (IB 24 pts)

104 pts **Coventry** – BCC incl biol (Hum Biosci) (IB 27 pts)
Manchester Met – BCC–BBC incl geog 104–112 pts (Hum Geog (St Abrd)) (IB 28 pts HL 5 geog); BCC–BBC incl biol 104–112 pts (Hum Biol) (IB 28 pts HL 5 biol)
West Scotland – BCC incl chem (Foren Sci) (IB 24 pts)

Alternative offers
See **Chapter 6** and **Appendix 1** for grades/new UCAS Tariff points information for other examinations.

EXAMPLES OF COLLEGES OFFERING COURSES IN THIS SUBJECT FIELD

Blackpool and Fylde (Coll); Farnborough (CT); Suffolk (Univ Campus).

CHOOSING YOUR COURSE (SEE ALSO CH.1)

Universities and colleges teaching quality See www.qaa.ac.uk; http://unistats.direct.gov.uk.

ADMISSIONS INFORMATION

Number of applicants per place (approx) London (UCL) 3; Oxford 4–5.

Advice to applicants and planning the UCAS personal statement See **Biology** and **Anthropology**.

Selection interviews Yes London (UCL), Oxford (14%).

Interview advice and questions Past questions have included: What do you expect to get out of a degree in Human Sciences? Why are you interested in this subject? What problems do you think you will be able to tackle after completing the course? Why did you drop PE as an A-level given that it's relevant to Human Sciences? How do you explain altruism, given that we are surely programmed by our genes to be selfish? How far is human behaviour determined by genes? What do you think are the key differences between animals and human beings? See also **Chapter 5**. **Oxford** Are there too many people in the world?

GRADUATE DESTINATIONS AND EMPLOYMENT (2013/14 HESA)
See **Biology**.

Career note As a result of the multi-disciplinary nature of these courses, graduates could focus on openings linked to their special interests or look in general at the scientific and health sectors. Health administration and social services work and laboratory-based careers are some of the more common career destinations of graduates.

OTHER DEGREE SUBJECTS FOR CONSIDERATION
Anthropology; Biology; Community Studies; Environmental Sciences; Life Sciences; Psychology; Sociology.

INFORMATION MANAGEMENT and LIBRARIANSHIP

(including **Library Studies**; see also **Computer Courses, Media Studies**)

Information Management and Library Studies covers the very wide field of information. Topics covered include retrieval, indexing, computer and media technology, classification and cataloguing are all included in these courses.

Useful websites www.aslib.co.uk; www.ukoln.ac.uk; www.cilip.org.uk; www.bl.uk

NB The points totals shown to the left of the institutions are for ease of reference only. It must not be assumed that Tariff points are always used by institutions or that they can be substituted for an offer in grades. The level of an offer is not necessarily indicative of the quality of a course.

COURSE OFFERS INFORMATION
Subject requirements/preferences GCSE English, mathematics and occasionally a foreign language. **AL** No specified subjects.

Your target offers and examples of degree courses
144 pts **Edinburgh** – AAA–ABB incl maths (Inform) (IB 37–32 pts)
           Reading – AAA–AAB (Mgt IT) (IB 35 pts)
136 pts **Lancaster** – AAB (Mgt IT) (IB 35 pts)
           London (UCL) – AAB (Inf Mgt Bus) (IB 36 pts)
           Loughborough – AAB–ABB (Inf Mgt Bus) (IB 34 pts); AAB (IT Mgt Bus) (IB 34 pts)
           Manchester – AAB (IT Mgt Bus (Yr Ind); IT Mgt Bus) (IB 35 pts)
           Sheffield – AAB–ABB (IT Mgt Bus) (IB 35 pts)
           Southampton – AAB (IT Org) (IB 34 pts)
128 pts **Kent** – ABB (Comp) (IB 34 pts)
           UWE Bristol – 128 pts (IT Mgt Bus) (IB 27 pts)
120 pts **Huddersfield** – BBB 120 pts (ICT)
           Northumbria – 120 pts (IT Mgt) (IB 30 pts)
112 pts **Chichester** – 112–128 pts (IT Mgt Bus) (IB 30 pts)
           Edge Hill – BBC 112 pts (IT Mgt Bus)
           Oxford Brookes – BBC (IT Mgt Bus) (IB 30 pts)
104 pts **Bournemouth** – 104–120 pts (IT Mgt) (IB 28–30 pts)
 88 pts **Southampton Solent** – 88 pts (Bus IT)

Alternative offers
See **Chapter 6** and **Appendix 1** for grades/new UCAS Tariff points information for other examinations.

EXAMPLES OF COLLEGES OFFERING COURSES IN THIS SUBJECT FIELD
Most colleges offer ICT courses. Birmingham Met (Coll); Blackburn (Coll); Llandrillo (Coll); North Shropshire (Coll); Northumberland (Coll); Nottingham New (Coll); St Helens (Coll); Selby (Coll); Somerset (Coll); South Essex (Coll); Stockport (Coll); Totton (Coll); Trafford (Coll); Truro and Penwith (Coll); West Cheshire (Coll); West Herts (Coll); West Thames (Coll).

CHOOSING YOUR COURSE (SEE ALSO CH.1)
Universities and colleges teaching quality See www.qaa.ac.uk; http://unistats.direct.gov.uk.

Top research universities and colleges (REF 2014) (Communication, Cultural and Media Studies, Library and Information Management) London LSE; Leicester (Musm St); Wolverhampton; Cardiff; London (Gold); Loughborough (Comm Media St); Westminster; De Montfort; Nottingham; London (RH); East Anglia; Leeds; Leicester (Media Comm); Newcastle.

Examples of sandwich degree courses Birmingham City; Bournemouth; De Montfort; Gloucestershire; Huddersfield; Kent; Kingston; Lancaster; Loughborough; Manchester; Nottingham Trent; Reading; UWE Bristol.

ADMISSIONS INFORMATION
Number of applicants per place (approx) London (UCL) 8; Loughborough 5; Manchester Met 4; Sheffield 30; Southampton 5.

Advice to applicants and planning the UCAS personal statement Work experience or work shadowing in local libraries is important but remember that reference libraries provide a different field of work. Visit university libraries and major reference libraries and discuss the work with librarians. Describe your experiences in the personal statement. See also **Appendix 3**.

Misconceptions about this course Read the prospectus carefully. The course details can be confusing. Some courses have a bias towards the organisation and retrieval of information, others towards information systems technology.

Selection interviews Yes London (UCL), Southampton; **Some** Loughborough.

Interview advice and questions Past questions include: What is it about librarianship that interests you? Why do you think you are suited to be a librarian? What does the job entail? What is the role of the library in school? What is the role of the public library? What new developments are taking place in libraries? Which books do you read? How often do you use a library? What is the Dewey number for the history section in the library? (Applicant studying A-level History.) See also **Chapter 5**.

AFTER-RESULTS ADVICE
Offers to applicants repeating A-levels Higher Loughborough; **Same** Sheffield.

GRADUATE DESTINATIONS AND EMPLOYMENT (2013/14 HESA)
Career note Graduates in this subject area and in communications enter a wide range of public and private sector jobs where the need to process information as well as to make it easily accessible and user-friendly, is very high. Areas of work could include web content, design and internet management and library management.

OTHER DEGREE SUBJECTS FOR CONSIDERATION
Business Information Systems; Communication Studies; Computer Science; Geographic Information Systems; Media Studies.

New UCAS points Tariff: A* = 56 pts; A = 48 pts; B = 40 pts; C = 32 pts; D = 24 pts; E = 16 pts

INTERNATIONAL RELATIONS

(including **International Development, Peace Studies** and **War Studies**; see also **Development Studies, European Studies, Politics**)

A strong interest in international affairs is a prerequisite for these courses which often allow students to focus on a specific area such as African, Asian or West European politics.

Useful websites www.sipri.org; www.un.org; www.un.int; rightweb.irc-online.org; see also **Politics**.

NB The points totals shown to the left of the institutions are for ease of reference only. It must not be assumed that Tariff points are always used by institutions or that they can be substituted for an offer in grades. The level of an offer is not necessarily indicative of the quality of a course.

COURSE OFFERS INFORMATION

Subject requirements/preferences GCSE English; a foreign language usually required. **AL** No specified subjects. (War St) History may be required.

Your target offers and examples of degree courses

152 pts Cambridge – A*AA (Hum Soc Pol Sci (Pol Int Rel)) (IB 40–41 pts HL 776)
  Warwick – A*AA (Econ Pol Int St) (IB 38 pts HL 4 maths)

144 pts Bath – AAA (Pol Int Rel) (IB 36 pts)
  Bristol – AAA–AAB (Pol Int Rel) (IB 36–34 pts)
  Durham – AAA incl soc sci/hum (Int Rel) (37 pts)
  Edinburgh – AAA–ABB (Int Rel; Int Rel Law) (IB 40–34 pts)
  Exeter – AAA–ABB incl lang (Int Rel Modn Lang) (IB 36–32 pts HL 5 lang); AAA–BBB
    (Pol Int Rel (Cornwall)) (IB 36–30 pts); AAA–AAB (Hist Int Rel (St Abrd); Hist Int Rel)
    (IB 36–34 pts)
  Lancaster – AAA–AAB (Hist Int Rel) (IB 36–35 pts)
  London (King's) – AAA (War St Phil; War St) (IB 35 pts); AAA incl hist (War St Hist) (IB 35
    pts HL 6 hist)
  London LSE – AAA (Int Rel Hist; Int Rel) (IB 38 pts)
  Nottingham – AAA (Int Rel Glob Is MSci) (IB 36 pts)
  St Andrews – AAA (Int Rel courses; Geog Int Rel) (IB 38 pts)
  Surrey – AAA–AAB (Law Int St) (IB 36–35 pts)
  Sussex – AAA–AAB (Law Int Rel) (IB 35 pts)

136 pts Cardiff – AAB incl lang (Pol Int Rel (incl lang)) (IB 34 pts)
  Lancaster – AAB–ABB (Pce St Int Rel; Pol Int Rel) (IB 35–32 pts)
  Leeds – AAB (Int Rel) (IB 34 pts)
  Manchester – AAB (Pol Int Rel) (IB 35 pts)
  Reading – AAB–ABB (Int Dev) (IB 35–32 pts)
  Sheffield – AAB incl hist (Hist Pol) (IB 35 pts HL 6 hist); AAB (Int Rel Pol; Int Pol Scrty St)
    (IB 35 pts)
  Sussex – AAB–ABB (Econ Int Rel) (IB 34 pts); AAB (Int Rel; Int Rel Dev) (IB 35 pts)
  York – AAB (Pol Int Rel) (IB 35 pts)

128 pts Aston – ABB (Int Rel Engl Lang; Pol Int Rel) (IB 33 pts); ABB–BBB (Bus Int Rel) (IB 33 pts)
  Birmingham – ABB (Int Rel; Int Rel Joint Hons; Pol Sci Int Rel) (IB 32 pts HL 655)
  East Anglia – ABB (Int Rel; Int Rel Joint Hons) (IB 32 pts)
  Essex – ABB–BBB (Int Rel; Pol Hum Rts; Sociol Hum Rts) (IB 32–30 pts)
  Leeds – ABB (Int Rel Thai St) (IB 34 pts)
  Leicester – BBB (Int Rel) (IB 28 pts)
  London (QM) – ABB 128 pts (Int Rel) (IB 34 pts)
  London (RH) – ABB (Geog Pol Int Rel; Econ Pol Int Rel; Pol Int Rel) (IB 32 pts)
  Loughborough – ABB (Hist Int Rel; Int Rel) (IB 34 pts)
  Queen's Belfast – ABB (Int Pol Cnflct St)

Check **Chapter 3** for new university admission details and **Chapter 6** on how to read the subject tables.

Reading – ABB–BBB (War Pce Int Rel) (IB 32 pts); (Int Rel courses; Pol Int Rel) (IB 32–30 pts)
Southampton – ABB–BBB (Pol Int Rel; Int Rel) (IB 32 pts)

120 pts **Aberdeen** – BBB (Int Rel courses) (IB 32 pts)
Aberystwyth – 120 pts (Int Pol; Int Pol Strat St)
Brunel – BBB (Int Pol) (IB 30 pts)
Coventry – BBB (Int Rel) (IB 29 pts)
Dundee – BBB–BCC (Int Rel Pol) (IB 30 pts)
Greenwich – 120 pts (Lang Int Rel; Pol Int Rel)
Heriot-Watt – BBB incl maths (Civ Eng Int St) (IB 31 pts HL 5 maths)
Keele – BBB/ABC (Int Rel) (IB 32 pts)
Kent – BBB (War Cnflct) (IB 34 pts)
Leicester – BBB (Int Rel Hist) (IB 28 pts)
London (Gold) – BBB (Int St) (IB 33 pts)
Nottingham Trent – 120 pts (Int Law)
Stirling – BBB (Pol (Int Pol)) (IB 32 pts)
Swansea – BBB–BBC (Int Rel; Int Rel Am St; War Soty) (IB 32–30 pts)

112 pts **Bradford** – BBC 112 pts (Econ Int Rel)
Brighton – BBC (Hum War Cnflct Modnty) (IB 28 pts)
Canterbury Christ Church – 112 pts (Int Rel)
Chester – BBC–BCC 112 pts (Int Dev St) (IB 26 pts)
De Montfort – 112 pts (Int Rel; Int Rel Pol) (IB 28 pts)
Hull – 112 pts (Pol Int Rel) (IB 28 pts)
Leeds Beckett – 112 pts (Int Rel Glob Dev; Int Rel Pce St) (IB 25 pts)
Lincoln – 112 pts (Int Rel)
London Met – 112 pts (Law (Int Rel))
Nottingham Trent – 112 pts (Glob St Joint Hons; Int Rel Joint Hons)
Oxford Brookes – BBC (Int Rel) (IB 31 pts)
Portsmouth – 112 pts (Law Int Rel)
Sheffield Hallam – 112 pts (Int Fin Bank)
Westminster – BBC (Int Rel) (IB 30 pts)

104 pts **Buckingham** – BCC (Int St)
Derby – 104–120 pts incl soc sci (Int Rel Dip Joint Hons); 104–120 pts geog/sci/soc sci (Thrd Wrld Dev Joint Hons)
Liverpool Hope – BCC–BBB 104–120 pts (Int Rel)
London (Birk) – 104 pts (Glob Pol Int Rel)
Manchester Met – 104–112 pts (Int Pol Phil) (IB 26 pts); 104–112 pts incl lang (Int Pol Langs (Fr/Ger/Ital/Span)) (IB 26 pts)
Middlesex – 104 pts (Int Pol)
Plymouth – 104 pts incl Fr (Int Rel Fr); 104 pts (Int Rel); (Int Rel Law; Int Bus Econ) (IB 24 pts); (Int Rel Pol) (IB 26 pts)
Westminster – BCC (Int Rel Lang) (IB 30 pts HL 4 lang)

96 pts **Bradford** – CCC 96 pts (Pce St; Dev Pce St; Int Rel Scrty St)
London Met – 96 pts (Int Rel; Int Rel Pce Cnflct St)
Nottingham Trent – 96 pts (Pol Int Rel)
Portsmouth – 96–120 pts (Euro St Int Rel; Int Rel) (IB 30 pts HL 17 pts)
Wolverhampton – 96–112 pts (War St; War St Phil)

Open University – contact +44 (0)845 300 6090 **or** www.openuniversity.co.uk/you (Int St)

Alternative offers
See **Chapter 6** and **Appendix 1** for grades/new UCAS Tariff points information for other examinations.

CHOOSING YOUR COURSE (SEE ALSO CH.1)

Universities and colleges teaching quality See www.qaa.ac.uk; http://unistats.direct.gov.uk.

Top research universities and colleges (REF 2014) See **Politics.**

New UCAS points Tariff: A* = 56 pts; A = 48 pts; B = 40 pts; C = 32 pts; D = 24 pts; E = 16 pts

Examples of sandwich degree courses Aston; Bath; Brunel; Coventry; Nottingham Trent; Oxford Brookes; Plymouth; Portsmouth; Westminster.

ADMISSIONS INFORMATION
Number of applicants per place (approx) Aberystwyth 6; Bath 6; Birmingham 10; De Montfort 6; Derby 3; Exeter 8; Leeds 13; London (King's) 6; London LSE (Int Rel) 21; Nottingham 5; Portsmouth 2; Reading 5; Southampton (Int Rel) 6.

Advice to applicants and planning the UCAS personal statement Describe any special interests you have in the affairs of any particular country. Contact embassies for information on cultural, economic and political developments. Follow international events through newspapers and magazines. Give details of any voluntary work you have done. **London (King's)** Substantial experience required in some area of direct relevance to War Studies. **St Andrews** Give reasons for choice of course and evidence of your interest.

Misconceptions about this course Some students think that this degree will give direct entry into the Diplomatic Service.

Selection interviews Yes London (King's), London Met; **Some** De Montfort, East Anglia, Nottingham Trent, Wolverhampton; **No** Birmingham, Nottingham.

Interview advice and questions Applicants are likely to be questioned on current international events and crises between countries. See also **Chapter 5**. **Nottingham Trent** Be prepared to be challenged on your existing views!

AFTER-RESULTS ADVICE
Offers to applicants repeating A-levels Same Chester, De Montfort, Exeter, Lincoln, Wolverhampton.

GRADUATE DESTINATIONS AND EMPLOYMENT (2013/14 HESA)
See **Politics**.

Career note See **Politics**.

OTHER DEGREE SUBJECTS FOR CONSIDERATION
Development Studies; Economics; European Studies; Government; Politics.

ITALIAN
(see also **Languages**)

The language and literature of Italy will feature strongly on most Italian courses. The majority of applicants have no knowledge of Italian. They will need to give convincing reasons for their interest and to show that they have the ability to assimilate language quickly. See also **Appendix 3** under **Languages**.

Useful websites www.europa.eu; www.italia.gov.it; www.bbc.co.uk/languages; www.languageadvantage.com; www.italianstudies.org.uk; www.languagematters.co.uk; see also **Languages**.

NB The points totals shown to the left of the institutions are for ease of reference only. It must not be assumed that Tariff points are always used by institutions or that they can be substituted for an offer in grades. The level of an offer is not necessarily indicative of the quality of a course.

COURSE OFFERS INFORMATION
Subject requirements/preferences GCSE English and a foreign language required. **AL** Italian may be required for some courses.

Your target offers and examples of degree courses
152 pts Cambridge – A*AA incl lang (Modn Mediev Langs) (IB 40–41 pts HL 776)

144 pts **Birmingham** – AAA (Ital Joint Hons) (IB 32 pts HL 666)

Durham – AAA incl lang (Modn Langs Cult (Yr Abrd)) (IB 37 pts)

Oxford – AAA (Ital courses) (IB 38 pts)

St Andrews – AAA–AAB (Ital courses) (IB 38–36 pts)

136 pts **Edinburgh** – AAB–ABB (Ital Ling; Ital) (IB 36–34 pts)

Exeter – AAB–ABB incl Ital/Arbc (Ital Arbc) (IB 34–32 pts HL 5 Ital/Arbc)

Glasgow – AAB–BBB incl arts/lang (Ital Joint Hons) (IB 36–34 pts)

London (UCL) – AAB (Ital) (IB 36 pts)

Warwick – AAB incl Engl lit+lang (Engl Ital Lit) (IB 36 pts HL 5 Engl lit+lang); AAB incl Fr (Fr Ger/Ital St) (IB 36 pts HL 5 Fr); AAB incl lang (Ital Joint Hons) (IB 36 pts HL 5 lang)

York – AAB–ABB (Fr Ital Lang (Yr Abrd)) (IB 34 pts)

128 pts **Bath** – ABB–AAB incl langs (Modn Langs Euro St) (IB 34 pts HL 6 5 langs)

Bristol – ABB–BBB incl lang (Ital) (IB 32–31 pts HL 5 lang)

Cardiff – ABB incl Ital (Ital)

Leeds – ABB incl Ital (Ital; Ital Joint Hons) (IB 34 pts HL 6 Ital)

Leicester – ABB incl lang (Ital Joint Hons) (IB 30 pts)

London (RH) – ABB incl mus (Mus Fr/Ger/Ital/Span) (IB 32 pts); ABB (Mgt Fr/Ger/Ital/Span; Class St Ital; Dr Ger/Ital) (IB 32 pts); (Ital Joint Hons; Euro St Fr/Ger/Ital/Span) (IB 34 pts); ABB incl Span (Span Fr/Ger/Ital) (IB 32 pts)

Manchester – ABB–BBB (Ital courses) (IB 34–32 pts)

Strathclyde – ABB–BBB (Ital courses) (IB 34 pts)

Sussex – ABB–BBB incl Ital/Span (Ital Span) (IB 32 pts HL 5 Ital/Span)

Warwick – ABB incl Ger (Ger Ital) (IB 34 pts HL 5 Ger); ABB incl lang (Ital courses) (IB 34 pts HL 5 lang)

120 pts **Kent** – BBB (Ital courses) (IB 34 pts)

Manchester – BBB (Ital St) (IB 31 pts)

Reading – BBB/ABC (Ital) (IB 30 pts)

Swansea – BBB–BBC incl lang (Ital courses) (IB 32–30 pts)

112 pts **Bangor** – 112–128 pts (Euro Law Ital)

Hertfordshire – 112 pts (Phil Ital; Hist Ital; Engl Lit Ital) (IB 28 pts)

Hull – 112 pts incl lang (Ital Joint courses; Fr/Ger/Ital/Span Hist) (IB 28 pts)

Nottingham Trent – 112 pts (Ital Joint Hons)

104 pts **Bangor** – 104–120 pts (Bus St Ital)

Manchester Met – 104–112 pts incl lang (Ling Lang (Chin/Fr/Ger/Ital/Span)) (IB 26 pts)

96 pts **Bangor** – 96–104 pts (Hist Ital)

Portsmouth – 96–120 pts incl lang (Comb Modn Lang) (IB 29 pts HL 16 pts incl 5 lang)

Alternative offers

See **Chapter 6** and **Appendix 1** for grades/new UCAS Tariff points information for other examinations.

CHOOSING YOUR COURSE (SEE ALSO CH.1)

Universities and colleges teaching quality See www.qaa.ac.uk; http://unistats.direct.gov.uk.

Top research universities and colleges (REF 2014) See **Languages**.

ADMISSIONS INFORMATION

Number of applicants per place (approx) Birmingham 5; Bristol 4; Cardiff 3; Durham 5; Hull 8; Leeds 3; London (RH) 4; London (UCL) 5.

Admissions tutors' advice **Bristol** Places in Clearing for international students.

Advice to applicants and planning the UCAS personal statement Describe any visits to Italy and experience of speaking the language. Interests in Italian art, literature, culture, society and architecture could also be mentioned. Read Italian newspapers and magazines and give details if you have a bilingual background. Give evidence of your interest and your reasons for choosing the course. See also **Appendix 3** under **Languages**.

New UCAS points Tariff: A* = 56 pts; A = 48 pts; B = 40 pts; C = 32 pts; D = 24 pts; E = 16 pts

Misconceptions about this course **Leeds** See **Languages**.

Selection interviews Yes Birmingham (majority receive offers), Cambridge, London (RH), Oxford; **No** Reading.

Interview advice and questions Past questions include: Why do you want to learn Italian? What foreign newspapers or magazines do you read (particularly if the applicant has taken A-level Italian)? Have you visited Italy? What do you know of the Italian people, culture, art? See also **Chapter 5**. **Leeds** See **Languages**.

AFTER-RESULTS ADVICE
Offers to applicants repeating A-levels Higher Birmingham, Glasgow, Warwick; **Same** Cardiff, Hull, Leeds.

GRADUATE DESTINATIONS AND EMPLOYMENT (2013/14 HESA)
Graduates surveyed 315 **Employed** 130 **In voluntary employment** 10 **In further study** 60 **Assumed unemployed** 15

Career note See **Languages**.

OTHER DEGREE SUBJECTS FOR CONSIDERATION
European Studies; International Business Studies; other languages.

JAPANESE
(see also **Asia-Pacific Studies, Languages**)

A strong interest in Japan and its culture is expected of applicants. A number of four-year joint courses are now offered, all of which include a period of study in Japan. Potential employers are showing an interest in Japanese. Students report that 'it is not a soft option'. They are expected to be firmly committed to a Japanese degree (for example, by listing only Japanese on the UCAS application), to have an interest in using their degree in employment and to be prepared for a lot of hard work. See **Appendix 3** under **Languages**.

Useful websites www.ciltuk.org.uk; www.ciol.org.uk; www.bbc.co.uk/languages; www.languageadvantage.com; www.languagematters.co.uk; www.japanese-online.com; www.gojapango.com; www.thejapanesepage.com; www.japanesestudies.org.uk

NB The points totals shown to the left of the institutions are for ease of reference only. It must not be assumed that Tariff points are always used by institutions or that they can be substituted for an offer in grades. The level of an offer is not necessarily indicative of the quality of a course.

COURSE OFFERS INFORMATION
Subject requirements/preferences GCSE A foreign language usually required. **AL** Modern language required for some courses.

Your target offers and examples of degree courses
152 pts Cambridge – A*AA (As Mid E St) (IB 40–41 pts HL 776)
144 pts Edinburgh – AAA–ABB (Jap Ling; Jap) (IB 40–34 pts)
       Oxford – AAA (Orntl St; Class Orntl St) (IB 39 pts)
136 pts Birmingham – AAB incl lang (Modn Langs) (IB 32 pts HL 665)
       Cardiff – AAB (Bus St Jap) (IB 35 pts)
       Leeds – AAB–ABB (Jap courses) (IB 35–34 pts)
       Sheffield – AAB–ABB (Kor St Joint Hons) (IB 35–34 pts)
128 pts Manchester – ABB (Jap St) (IB 34 pts); ABB incl Chin/Jap (Chin Jap) (IB 34 pts); ABB incl Russ/Jap (Russ Jap) (IB 34 pts)

Newcastle – ABB–BBB (Jap St) (IB 32 pts)

Sheffield – ABB (Jap St Joint Hons; Jap St) (IB 34 pts)

112 pts **Central Lancashire** – 112–128 pts (Fr/Ger/Span/Jap)

104 pts **London (Birk)** – 104 pts (Modn Langs (Fr, Ger, Jap, Port, Span))

Alternative offers
See **Chapter 6** and **Appendix 1** for grades/new UCAS Tariff points information for other examinations.

CHOOSING YOUR COURSE (SEE ALSO CH.1)
Universities and colleges teaching quality See www.qaa.ac.uk; http://unistats.direct.gov.uk.

ADMISSIONS INFORMATION
Number of applicants per place (approx) Cardiff 8; Durham 5; Sheffield 10.

Advice to applicants and planning the UCAS personal statement Discuss your interest in Japan and your reasons for wishing to study the language. Know Japan, its culture and background history. Discuss any visits you have made or contacts with Japanese nationals. See also **Appendix 3** under **Languages**. **Leeds** See **Languages**.

Selection interviews **Yes** Cambridge, Oxford; **Some** Leeds.

Interview advice and questions Japanese is an extremely demanding subject and applicants are most likely to be questioned on their reasons for choosing this degree. They will be expected also to have some knowledge of Japanese culture, history and current affairs. See also **Chapter 5**.

Reasons for rejection (non-academic) Insufficient evidence of genuine motivation.

AFTER-RESULTS ADVICE
Offers to applicants repeating A-levels **No** Cambridge.

GRADUATE DESTINATIONS AND EMPLOYMENT (2013/14 HESA)
Graduates surveyed 130 **Employed** 55 **In voluntary employment** 5 **In further study** 15 **Assumed unemployed** 15

Career note See **Languages**.

OTHER DEGREE SUBJECTS FOR CONSIDERATION
Asia-Pacific Studies; International Business Studies; Oriental Languages; South East Asia Studies.

JOURNALISM

(see also Communication Studies/Communication, English, Media Studies)

A passion for writing, good spelling, grammar and punctuation and the ability to work under pressure are some of the qualities which all journalists require. The opportunities within journalism range from covering day-to-day news stories in the local and national press to periodicals and magazines covering specialist subjects. Journalism is also the foundation for work in local radio.

Useful websites www.journalism.co.uk; www.wannabehacks.co.uk; www.bjtc.org.uk; www.nctj.com; www.nuj.org.uk

The points totals shown to the left of the institutions are for ease of reference only. It must not be assumed that Tariff points are always used by institutions or that they can be substituted for an offer in grades. The level of an offer is not necessarily indicative of the quality of a course.

COURSE OFFERS INFORMATION
Subject requirements/preferences **GCSE** English and maths often required. **AL** No specific subjects required.

Your target offers and examples of degree courses

144 pts **City** – AAA 144 pts (Jrnl) (IB 35 pts)

136 pts **Cardiff** – AAB (Jrnl Media Engl Lit) (IB 36 pts)
Leeds – AAB (Broad Jrnl) (IB 35 pts)
London (Gold) – AAB–ABB (Jrnl) (IB 33 pts)

128 pts **Cardiff** – ABB (Jrnl Media Sociol) (IB 36 pts)
Central Lancashire – 128–112 pts (Spo Jrnl; Jrnl)
Kent – ABB (Jrnl News Ind) (IB 34 pts)
Kingston – 128 pts (Pol Jrnl) (IB 28 pts); ABB 128 pts (Jrnl)
Newcastle – ABB (Jrnl Media Cult) (IB 34 pts)
Northumbria – 128 pts incl Engl (Jrnl; Jrnl Engl Lit) (IB 31 pts HL 5 Engl)
Nottingham Trent – 128 pts (Jrnl; Broad Jrnl)
Sheffield – ABB–BBB (Jrnl St) (IB 34 pts)
Strathclyde – ABB–BBB (Jrnl Crea Writ courses) (IB 34 pts)
Sussex – ABB (Jrnl) (IB 34 pts)

120 pts **Bournemouth** – 120–128 pts (Multim Jrnl) (IB 31–32 pts)
Brighton – BBB (Spo Jrnl) (IB 30 pts)
Brunel – BBB (Jrnl) (IB 30 pts)
Coventry – BBB (Engl Jrnl) (IB 30 pts); BBB incl Engl/media (Jrnl) (IB 30 pts)
Gloucestershire – 120 pts (Jrnl)
Leeds Beckett – 120 pts (PR Jrnl; Jrnl; Photo Jrnl) (IB 26 pts)
Lincoln – 120 pts (Jrnl)
Staffordshire – 120 pts (Jrnl)
Stirling – BBB (Jrnl St) (IB 32 pts)
Sunderland – 120 pts (Mag Jrnl; Jrnl; Broad Jrnl; Fash Jrnl; Spo Jrnl)

Check **Chapter 3** for new university admission details and **Chapter 6** on how to read the subject tables.

Trinity Saint David – 120 pts (Photojrnl Doc Photo)
UWE Bristol – 120 pts (Jrnl PR; Engl Writ; Jrnl) (IB 26 pts)
Westminster – BBB (Jrnl) (IB 28 pts)

112 pts **Birmingham City** – BBC 112 pts (Media Comm (Jrnl)) (IB 28 pts)
Brighton – BBC (Multim Broad Jrnl) (IB 28 pts)
Buckingham – BBC–BCC (Jrnl Comm St)
Canterbury Christ Church – 112 pts (Multim Jrnl)
Chester – 112 pts (Spo Jrnl) (IB 26 pts); BBC–BCC 112 pts (Jrnl) (IB 26 pts)
Derby – 112 pts (Jrnl)
East London – 112 pts (Jrnl; Spo Jrnl) (IB 24 pts)
Glasgow Caledonian – BBC (Multim Jrnl)
Gloucestershire – 112 pts +interview +portfolio (Photojrnl Doc Photo)
Hertfordshire – 112 pts (Jrnl Joint Hons) (IB 28 pts)
Huddersfield – BBC 112 pts (Spo Jrnl; Jrnl)
Leeds Trinity – 112 pts (Spo Jrnl; Jrnl; Broad Jrnl)
Liverpool John Moores – 112 pts (Jrnl) (IB 29 pts)
London Met – 112 pts (Jrnl Film TV St; Fash Mark Jrnl)
Middlesex – 112 pts (Crea Writ Jrnl; Jrnl Media)
Northampton – 112 pts incl Engl (Multim Jrnl)
Robert Gordon – BBC incl Engl (Jrnl) (IB 28 pts)
Roehampton – 112 pts (Jrnl)
Sheffield Hallam – 112 pts (Jrnl)
Southampton Solent – 112 pts (Jrnl; Spo Jrnl; Engl Mag Jrnl)
Teesside – 112 pts +interview (Multim Jrnl); 112 pts +interview/portfolio (Broad Media Prod)
West London – 112 pts (Broad Jrnl)
Worcester – 112 pts (Jrnl)

104 pts **De Montfort** – 104 pts (Jrnl) (IB 28 pts)
Edinburgh Napier – BCC incl Engl (Jrnl) (IB 28 pts HL 5 Engl)
Falmouth – 104–120 pts (Jrnl; Spo Jrnl)
London Met – 104 pts (Jrnl)
St Mark and St John – BCC (Jrnl; Spo Jrnl)
South Wales – BCC (Jrnl) (IB 29 pts)
Staffordshire – 104 pts (Photojrnl) (IB 24 pts)
Winchester – 104–120 pts (Jrnl Media St); (Jrnl) (IB 26 pts)

96 pts **Bangor** – 96–104 pts (Jrnl Media St)
Glyndŵr – 96 pts (Broad Jrnl Media Comms)
London South Bank – CCC 96 pts (Jrnl)
Portsmouth – 96–120 pts (Jrnl) (IB 30 pts HL 17 pts)
West Scotland – CCC incl Engl (Jrnl) (IB 24 pts)
Wolverhampton – 96 pts (Broad Jrnl)

88 pts **Creative Arts** – 88 pts (Jrnl; Mus Jrnl); 88 pts +portfolio (Fash Jrnl)
80 pts **Arts London** – 80 pts (Jrnl)
Bedfordshire – 80 pts (Jrnl) (IB 24 pts)
72 pts **Anglia Ruskin** – 72–80 pts (Jrnl (Multim))

Alternative offers
See **Chapter 6** and **Appendix 1** for grades/new UCAS Tariff points information for other examinations.

EXAMPLES OF COLLEGES OFFERING COURSES IN THIS SUBJECT FIELD
Blackburn (Coll); Blackpool and Fylde (Coll); Chesterfield (Coll); Cornwall (Coll); Darlington (Coll); Ealing, Hammersmith and West London (Coll); Exeter (Coll); Grimsby (Univ Centre); Harlow (Coll); London UCK (Coll); Milton Keynes (Coll); Oaklands (Coll); Peterborough (Coll); Portsmouth (Coll); Somerset (Coll); South Essex (Coll); West Thames (Coll).

New UCAS points Tariff: A* = 56 pts; A = 48 pts; B = 40 pts; C = 32 pts; D = 24 pts; E = 16 pts

CHOOSING YOUR COURSE (SEE ALSO CH.1)

Universities and colleges teaching quality See www.qaa.ac.uk; http://unistats.direct.gov.uk.

Examples of sandwich degree courses Coventry; Hertfordshire; Huddersfield; Leeds; Portsmouth; Southampton Solent.

ADMISSIONS INFORMATION

Number of applicants per place (approx) Southampton Solent 20; Strathclyde (Jrnl) 20.

Selection interviews Yes Bedfordshire, Brunel, Edinburgh Napier, Falmouth, Kent, Leeds Trinity, London South Bank, Northumbria, Sussex, Winchester; Most institutions will interview candidates, some requiring auditions and/or a portfolio.

GRADUATE DESTINATIONS AND EMPLOYMENT (2013/14 HESA)

Graduates surveyed 2,395 **Employed** 1,405 **In voluntary employment** 125 **In further study** 215 **Assumed unemployed** 205

LANDSCAPE ARCHITECTURE

(including **Garden Design** and **Landscape Design** and **Management**; see also **Agricultural Sciences/Agriculture, Architecture, Horticulture**)

Landscape architects shape the world you live in, they are responsible for urban design and the integration of ecology and the quality of the built environment. Courses in Landscape Architecture include project-based design, landscape theory, management, planning and design, ecology, construction, plant design and design practice. After completing the first three years leading to a BSc (Hons) or BA (Hons), students aiming for full professional status take a further one year in practice and one year to achieve their Master of Landscape Architecture (MLA).

Useful websites www.landscapeinstitute.org; www.bealandscapearchitect.com; www.landscape.co.uk; www.bali.org.uk

NB The points totals shown to the left of the institutions are for ease of reference only. It must not be assumed that Tariff points are always used by institutions or that they can be substituted for an offer in grades. The level of an offer is not necessarily indicative of the quality of a course.

COURSE OFFERS INFORMATION

Subject requirements/preferences GCSE English, geography, art and design, mathematics and at least one science usually required. **AL** Preferred subjects for some courses include Biology, Geography and Environmental Science. A portfolio may also be required.

Sheffield AL Art and Design or Design Technology required.

Your target offers and examples of degree courses
144 pts **Sheffield** – AAA (Archit Lnd) (IB 37 pts)
136 pts **Edinburgh** – AAB–ABB (Lnd Archit) (IB 36–34 pts)
128 pts **Edinburgh (CA)** – ABB (Lnd Archit MA) (IB 34 pts)
           Greenwich – 128 pts (Lnd Archit)
           Sheffield – ABB–BBB (Lnd Archit) (IB 34 pts)
120 pts **Leeds Beckett** – 120 pts (Lnd Archit Des) (IB 26 pts)
112 pts **Birmingham City** – BBC 112 pts (Land Archit) (IB 28 pts)
           Gloucestershire – 112 pts (Lnd Archit)
104 pts **Hadlow (Coll)** – 104 pts (Lnd Mgt; Gdn Des)
 96 pts **Writtle (Coll)** – 96–112 pts (Lnd Gdn Des; Gdn Des Restor Mgt; Lnd Archit) (IB 24 pts)

Alternative offers
See **Chapter 6** and **Appendix 1** for grades/new UCAS Tariff points information for other examinations.

The University Of Sheffield.

Department Of Landscape.

SHAPE YOUR WORLD.

The Department of Landscape at the University of Sheffield is the top rated Landscape Architecture department in the UK[1].

Landscape Architecture involves the design, planning and management of places that benefit people and nature. Landscape Architects create spaces between buildings that are inspirational and functional. If you have a flair for creativity and a passion for improving the environment and people's lives, Landscape Architecture could be for you.

Come to the Department of Landscape and you will be joining one of the world's leading departments for landscape education and research. Our staff are involved in some of the most exciting contemporary landscape design projects. They are committed to developing the next generation of Landscape Architects to create lasting, functional and inspirational places.

Why study Landscape Architecture?

"I was initially looking into Architecture, but discovered Landscape Architecture at a careers meeting during year 12 at school and then as soon as I visited the department and the city I knew this is where I wanted to go. I was so impressed with the facilities and the staff were all really friendly.

The course is so varied and dynamic beyond anything I really expected, you learn about everything across the whole Landscape Architecture discipline.

The best thing about the course at Sheffield is how it has really encouraged my graphic skills. I had no idea how to use Photoshop or InDesign before I started the course and now I would consider my graphic skills as one of my main strengths."

Daniel Bilsborough, Final Year, Landscape Architecture

Sheffield is the ideal place to study Landscape Architecture, whether large-scale urban renewal, complex planning issues natural habitat. More than a third of our city is within the boundary of the breathtaking Peak District National Park.

Our students are highly sought after within the landscape profession. We aim to develop graduates with outstanding skills, who are able to take the lead in multidisciplinary projects. Study with us and you will develop design skills as well as the ability to understand the cultural, social and ecological drivers that underpin successful landscapes.

Our courses also equip students with excellent transferable skills. Through working in teams, solving complex problems, undertaking live projects for community groups and developing your own personal portfolio, you will acquire professional standards in communication, graphic design, report writing and presentation.

Our graduates are in demand: graduates from the Department of Landscape work in the private sector, where many have set up their own companies. Others work in the public or Third sectors, helping to improve local communities.

Whatever path you choose, a degree in Landscape Architecture from Sheffield will set you up to make a real, positive difference to the world around you.

94%
of students secured graduate jobs in Landscape Architecture in 2014

Contact Us

Email: emma.shaw@sheffield.ac.uk

Telephone: +44 (0)114 222 0602

Website: www.sheffield.ac.uk/landscape **Twitter:** @LandscapeSheff

For more information about our profession visit:

www.landscapeinstitute.org www.iwanttobealandscapearchitect.com

SHEFFIELD
LANDSCAPE
ARCHITECTURE

EXAMPLES OF COLLEGES OFFERING COURSES IN THIS SUBJECT FIELD
Craven (Coll); Duchy (Coll).

CHOOSING YOUR COURSE (SEE ALSO CH.1)
Universities and colleges teaching quality See www.qaa.ac.uk; http://unistats.direct.gov.uk.

ADMISSIONS INFORMATION
Number of applicants per place (approx) Edinburgh (CA) 7; Gloucestershire 9; Greenwich 3; Manchester Met 9; Writtle (Coll) 5.

Advice to applicants and planning the UCAS personal statement Knowledge of the work of landscape architects is important. Arrange a visit to a landscape architect's office and try to organise some work experience. Read up on historical landscape design and visit country house estates with examples of outstanding designs. Describe these visits in detail and your preferences. Membership of the National Trust could be useful. See also **Appendix 3**.

Selection interviews Yes Gloucestershire, Greenwich, Manchester Met, Sheffield, Writtle (Coll); **Some** Birmingham City.

Interview advice and questions Applicants will be expected to have had some work experience and are likely to be questioned on their knowledge of landscape architectural work and the subject. Historical examples of good landscaping could also be asked for. See also **Chapter 5**.

Reasons for rejection (non-academic) Lack of historical knowledge and awareness of current developments. Poor portfolio.

AFTER-RESULTS ADVICE
Offers to applicants repeating A-levels Same Birmingham City, Edinburgh (CA), Greenwich, Manchester Met.

GRADUATE DESTINATIONS AND EMPLOYMENT (2013/14 HESA)
Landscape Design graduates surveyed 175 **Employed** 100 **In voluntary employment** 0 **In further study** 45 **Assumed unemployed** 5

Career note Opportunities at present in landscape architecture are good. Openings exist in local government or private practice and may cover planning, housing, and conservation.

OTHER DEGREE SUBJECTS FOR CONSIDERATION
Architecture; Art and Design; Environmental Planning; Forestry; Horticulture.

LANGUAGES

(including **British Sign Language, European Language Studies, Modern Languages** and **Translation Studies; see separate language tables;** see also **African Studies, Asia-Pacific Studies, Chinese, English, European Studies, French, German, Greek, Italian, Japanese, Latin, Linguistics, Russian and East European Studies, Scandinavian Studies, Spanish**)

Modern language courses usually offer three main options: a single subject degree commonly based on literature and language, a European Studies course, or two-language subjects which can often include languages different from those available at school (such as Scandinavian Studies, Russian and the languages of Eastern Europe, the Middle and Far East).

Useful websites www.ciol.org.uk; www.iti.org.uk; www.europa.eu; www.ciltuk.org.uk; www.bbc.co.uk/languages; www.languageadvantage.com; www.omniglot.com; www.languagematters.co.uk

NB The points totals shown to the left of the institutions are for ease of reference only. It must not be assumed that Tariff points are always used by institutions or that they can be substituted for an offer in grades. The level of an offer is not necessarily indicative of the quality of a course.

COURSE OFFERS INFORMATION

Subject requirements/preferences GCSE English and a modern language required. In some cases grades A and/or B may be stipulated. **AL** A modern foreign language required usually with a specified grade.

Your target offers and examples of degree courses

152 pts **Cambridge** – A*AA incl lang (Modn Mediev Langs) (IB 40–41 pts HL 776); A*AA (As Mid E St) (IB 40–41 pts HL 776)

London (UCL) – A*AA–AAA incl hist+Euro lang (Hist Euro Langs) (IB 39–38 pts HL 6 hist+Euro lang)

Nottingham – A*AA–AAA incl maths+phys (Phys Euro Lang) (IB 34 pts)

144 pts **Birmingham** – AAA (Port Joint Hons) (IB 32 pts HL 666); AAA incl lang (Econ Lang) (IB 32 pts HL 666)

Durham – AAA incl lang (Modn Langs Cult (Yr Abrd); Modn Langs Hist (Yr Abrd)) (IB 37 pts)

Edinburgh – AAA–BBB (Span Port) (IB 34 pts)

Exeter – AAA–ABB incl lang (Int Rel Modn Lang) (IB 36–32 pts HL 5 lang)

Imperial London – AAA incl chem+maths (Chem Fr/Ger/Span Sci) (IB 38 pts HL 7 chem 6 maths)

London (UCL) – AAA–ABB incl lang (Modn Langs) (IB 38–34 pts HL 6 lang)

Manchester – AAA–ABB incl sci/maths (Anat Sci Modn Lang; Biol Modn Lang) (IB 37–33 pts HL 5/6 biol+chem); (Zool Modn Lang; Microbiol Modn Langs; Plnt Sci Modn Lang; Genet Modn Lang) (IB 37–33 pts)

Oxford – AAA (Hist Modn Langs; Engl Modn Langs; Modn Langs Ling) (IB 38 pts); (Class Modn Langs; Orntl St; Phil Modn Langs) (IB 39 pts)

St Andrews – AAA (Heb courses) (IB 36–38 pts); AAA incl maths (Maths Langs) (IB 36 pts)

Sheffield – AAA–AAB incl maths (Civ Eng Modn Lang) (IB 37 pts HL 6 maths); AAA–AAB incl maths/phys/chem (Electron Elec Eng Modn Lang MEng) (IB 37 pts HL 6 maths/phys/chem)

136 pts **Bath** – AAB incl lang (Lang Pol) (IB 36 pts)

Birmingham – AAB incl lang (Modn Langs) (IB 32 pts HL 665)

Bristol – AAB–ABB incl langs (Modn Langs courses) (IB 34–32 pts HL 6/5 langs); AAB–ABB incl lang (Phil Modn Lang; Hist Art Modn Lang; Pol Modn Lang) (IB 34–32 pts HL 5 lang)

Exeter – AAB–ABB incl Fr+Lat (Fr Lat) (IB 34–32 pts HL 5 Fr+Lat)

Lancaster – AAB–ABB (Modn Langs) (IB 35–32 pts); AAB (Mgt St Euro Langs) (IB 35 pts)

London (SOAS) – AAB–ABB (Burm (Myan) courses; Indsn Joint Hons; Kor; Swli Joint Hons; Thai Joint Hons; Turk) (IB 35 pts)

London (UCL) – AAB incl lang (Lang Cult) (IB 36 pts HL 6 lang)

St Andrews – AAB (Modn Lang courses; Art Hist Lang) (IB 36 pts)

Southampton – AAB–ABB incl Fr/Ger/Span (Mgt Sci Fr/Ger/Span) (IB 34 pts HL 6 Fr/Ger/Span); AAB–ABB incl lang (Langs Contemp Euro St) (IB 34 pts HL 6 lang)

128 pts **Aston** – ABB–BBB incl Fr/Ger/Span (Transl St (Fr/Ger/Span)) (IB 33–32 pts HL 6 Fr/Ger/Span)

Bath – ABB–AAB incl langs (Modn Langs Euro St) (IB 34 pts HL 6 5 langs)

Bristol – ABB–BBB incl mus+lang (Mus Modn Lang) (IB 34–32 pts HL 6 mus 5 lang); ABB–BBB incl lang (Span Modn Lang) (IB 32–31 pts HL 5 lang); (Russ Port) (IB 32–31 pts)

East Anglia – ABB (Transl Media Modn Lang) (IB 32 pts); ABB incl A Fr/Span/Jap (Transl Interp Lang (Yr Abrd)) (IB 32 pts HL 6 Fr/Span/Jap); ABB incl Fr/Jap/Span (Modn Langs 4 yrs (Double Hons)) (IB 32 pts)

Essex – ABB–BBB (Modn Langs; Lang St; Euro St Fr/Ger/Ital/Span; Span St Modn Langs; Port St Modn Langs) (IB 32–30 pts)

Leeds – ABB (Port Russ) (IB 34 pts)

Liverpool – ABB (Lat Am Hisp St Comb Hons) (IB 33 pts); ABB incl langs (Modn Euro Langs; Modn Lang St Bus) (IB 33 pts HL 66 langs); ABB incl maths+Euro lang (Mathem Sci Euro Lang) (IB 33 pts HL 6 maths+Euro lang)

London (RH) – ABB incl Fr/Ger/Ital/Span (Mling St Int Rel) (IB 34 pts)

Manchester – ABB–BBB (Span Port) (IB 34–32 pts); ABB incl Engl lang (Euro St Modn Lang) (IB 34 pts)

Newcastle – ABB–BBB incl lang (Modn Langs) (IB 32 pts HL 6 lang); ABB–BBB incl Fr/Ger/Span (Modn Langs Ling) (IB 32 pts HL 6 Fr/Ger/Span); ABB incl Fr/Span/Ger (Mod Langs Transl Interp) (IB 32 pts HL 6 Fr/Span/Ger); ABB–BBB incl Fr (Fr Joint Hons) (IB 32 pts HL 6 Fr)

Nottingham – ABB incl lang (Modn Euro St; Modn Lang St; Modn Langs Bus) (IB 32 pts)

Sheffield – ABB incl lang (Modn Langs) (IB 34 pts HL 6 lang)

120 pts **Aberdeen** – BBB 120 pts (Euro St) (IB 32 pts); BBB (Lang Ling; Langs Lit Scot) (IB 32 pts)

Dundee – BBB–BBC (Euro St) (IB 30 pts)

Greenwich – 120 pts (Lang Int Rel)

Heriot-Watt – BBB incl lang (App Langs Transl (Fr/Span) (Ger/Span); Langs (Interp Transl) (Fr/Ger) (Ger/Span)) (IB 30 pts); BBB (Brit Sign Lang) (IB 30 pts)

Middlesex – 120 pts (Interp Transl)

Roehampton – 120 pts (Transl)

Stirling – BBB (Int Mgt St Euro Langs Soty; Modn Langs) (IB 32 pts)

Swansea – BBB–BBC incl lang (Modn Lang Transl Inter) (IB 32–30 pts)

112 pts **Aberystwyth** – 112 pts incl lang (Euro Langs; Rmnc Langs)

Central Lancashire – 112–128 pts (Modn Langs)

Chester – BBC–BCC incl Fr/Ger/Span 112 pts (Modn Langs) (IB 26 pts HL 5 Span/Fr/Ger)

Greenwich – 112 pts (Adv Mark Comm Lang)

Hull – 112 pts incl lang (Modn Lang St) (IB 28 pts); 112 pts (Comb Lang) (IB 28 pts)

London Met – 112 pts (Transl)

Nottingham Trent – 112 pts incl Fr (Fr Joint Hons)

York St John – 112 pts incl lang (Langs)

104 pts **London (Birk)** – 104 pts (Ling Lang)

Westminster – BCC (Transl St (Fr); Transl St (Span); Int Rel Lang) (IB 30 pts HL 4 lang)

96 pts **Edinburgh Napier** – CCC incl lang (Int Bus Mgt Lang) (IB 27 pts HL 5 lang)

Plymouth – 96 pts incl Fr (Int Bus Fr) (IB 24 pts)

Wolverhampton – 96–112 pts (Interp (Brit Sign Lang/Engl))

Open University – contact +44 (0)845 300 6090 **or** www.openuniversity.co.uk/you (Modn Lang St)

Alternative offers
See **Chapter 6** and **Appendix 1** for grades/new UCAS Tariff points information for other examinations.

CHOOSING YOUR COURSE (SEE ALSO CH.1)

Universities and colleges teaching quality See www.qaa.ac.uk; http://unistats.direct.gov.uk.

Top research universities and colleges (REF 2014) (Modern Languages and Linguistics) London (QM) (Ling); Queen Margaret; Edinburgh (Ling); Kent; York; Queen's Belfast; Southampton; Cardiff; Essex; Warwick; Glasgow (Celt St); Cambridge; Manchester; London (RH).

ADMISSIONS INFORMATION

Number of applicants per place (approx) Aston 4; Bath 6; Birmingham 5; Bristol 15; Cambridge 2; Cardiff 6; Durham 6; East Anglia 15; Heriot-Watt 5; Lancaster 10; Leeds 8; Liverpool 5; London (UCL) 5; Newcastle 22; Roehampton 3; Swansea 4; Wolverhampton 10.

Advice to applicants and planning the UCAS personal statement Discuss any literature studied outside your course work. Students applying for courses in which they have no previous knowledge (for example, Italian, Portuguese, Modern Greek, Czech, Russian) would be expected to have done a considerable amount of language work on their own in their chosen language before starting the course. See also **Appendix 3**.

New UCAS points Tariff: A* = 56 pts; A = 48 pts; B = 40 pts; C = 32 pts; D = 24 pts; E = 16 pts

Misconceptions about this course Leeds Some applicants think that studying languages means studying masses of literature – wrong. At Leeds, generally speaking, it's up to you; you study as much or as little literature as you choose. Residence abroad does not inevitably mean a university course (except where you are taking a language from scratch). Paid employment is usually another option.

Selection interviews Yes Aston, Cambridge, Heriot-Watt, Liverpool, London (RH), Oxford (Modn Lang) 33%, (Modn Lang Ling) 44%, Roehampton, Salford, Southampton; **Some** Leeds, Swansea; **No** Dundee, East Anglia.

Interview advice and questions See also **Chapter 5**. **Cambridge** Think of a painting of a tree. Is the tree real? **Leeds** Give an example of something outside your studies that you have achieved over the past year. **London (RH)** Conversation in the appropriate language.

Reasons for rejection (non-academic) Lack of commitment to spend a year abroad. Poor references. Poor standard of English. No reasons for why the course has been selected. Poor communication skills. Incomplete applications, for example missing qualifications and reference.

AFTER-RESULTS ADVICE
Offers to applicants repeating A-levels Possibly higher Aston; **Same** Birmingham, Bristol, Durham, East Anglia, Leeds, Liverpool, Newcastle, Nottingham Trent, Stirling, Wolverhampton; **No** Cambridge.

GRADUATE DESTINATIONS AND EMPLOYMENT (2013/14 HESA)
See separate language tables.

Career note The only career-related fields for language students are teaching, which attracts some graduates, and the demanding work of interpreting and translating, to which only a small number aspire. The majority will be attracted to work in management and administration, financial services and a host of other occupations which may include the social services, law and property development.

OTHER DEGREE SUBJECTS FOR CONSIDERATION
Communication Studies; Linguistics; Modern Languages Education/Teaching.

LATIN
(see also Classical Studies/Classical Civilisation, Classics, Greek, Languages)

Latin courses provide a study of the language, art, religion and history of the Roman world. This table should be read in conjunction with the **Classical Studies/Classical Civilisation** and **Classics** tables.

Useful websites www.thelatinlibrary.com; https://en.wikipedia.org/wiki/Latin; www.arlt.co.uk

NB The points totals shown to the left of the institutions are for ease of reference only. It must not be assumed that Tariff points are always used by institutions or that they can be substituted for an offer in grades. The level of an offer is not necessarily indicative of the quality of a course.

COURSE OFFERS INFORMATION
Subject requirements/preferences GCSE English, a foreign language and Latin may be stipulated. **AL** Check courses for Latin requirement.

Your target offers and examples of degree courses
152 pts Cambridge – A*AA (Class) (IB 40–41 pts HL 776); (Modn Mediev Langs (Class Lat)) (IB 40–41 pts)
144 pts Edinburgh – AAA–ABB (Anc Hist Lat; Lat St) (IB 40–34 pts)
 St Andrews – AAA (Lat Mediev Hist) (IB 36 pts); AAA–AAB (Lat courses) (IB 38–36 pts)

136 pts **Exeter** – AAB–ABB incl Fr+Lat (Fr Lat) (IB 34–32 pts HL 5 Fr+Lat)
         Glasgow – AAB–BBB incl arts/lang (Latin Joint Hons) (IB 36–34 pts)
         London (UCL) – AAB incl Gk (Gk Lat) (IB 36 pts HL 6 Gk); AAB incl Lat (Lat Gk)
            (IB 36 pts HL 6 Lat)
         Nottingham – AAB–ABB (Lat courses) (IB 34–32 pts)
         Warwick – AAB inc Engl lit+Lat (Engl Lat Lit) (IB 36 pts HL 6 Engl lit+Lat)
128 pts **London (RH)** – ABB (Fr Lat; Lat) (IB 32 pts)
112 pts **Swansea** – BBC (Lat Joint Hons) (IB 30 pts)
 96 pts **Trinity Saint David** – 96 pts (Lat Joint Hons)

Alternative offers
See **Chapter 6** and **Appendix 1** for grades/new UCAS Tariff points information for other examinations.

CHOOSING YOUR COURSE (SEE ALSO CH.1)

Universities and colleges teaching quality See www.qaa.ac.uk; http://unistats.direct.gov.uk.

Top research universities and colleges (REF 2014) See **Classics**.

ADMISSIONS INFORMATION

Number of applicants per place (approx) Leeds 2; London (UCL) 5; Nottingham 6; Trinity Saint David 6.

Advice to applicants and planning the UCAS personal statement See **Classical Studies/Classical Civilisation** and **Classics**.

Selection interviews Yes Cambridge, London (RH), London (UCL), Nottingham, Trinity Saint David.

Interview advice and questions See **Classical Studies/Classical Civilisation** and **Classics**.

AFTER-RESULTS ADVICE

Offers to applicants repeating A-levels Higher Leeds, St Andrews, Warwick.

GRADUATE DESTINATIONS AND EMPLOYMENT (2013/14 HESA)

Graduates surveyed 20 **Employed** 10 **In voluntary employment** 0 **In further study** 0 **Assumed unemployed** 0

Career note Graduates enter a broad range of careers within management, the media, commerce and tourism as well as social and public services. Some graduates choose to work abroad and teaching is a popular option.

OTHER DEGREE SUBJECTS FOR CONSIDERATION

Ancient History; Archaeology; Classical Studies; Classics.

LATIN AMERICAN STUDIES

(including **Hispanic Studies**; see also **American Studies, Spanish**)

Latin American courses provide a study of Spanish and of Latin American republics, covering both historical and present-day conditions and problems. Normally a year is spent in Latin America.

Useful websites www.ciol.org.uk; www.bbc.co.uk/languages; www.languageadvantage.com; www.languagematters.co.uk; www.ciltuk.org.uk; www.wola.org; www.latinamericalinks.com; www.thelaa.org; see also **Languages** and **Spanish**.

NB The points totals shown to the left of the institutions are for ease of reference only. It must not be assumed that Tariff points are always used by institutions or that they can be substituted for an offer in grades. The level of an offer is not necessarily indicative of the quality of a course.

COURSE OFFERS INFORMATION

Subject requirements/preferences GCSE English and a foreign language required by most universities. **AL** Spanish may be required for some courses.

Aberdeen English, mathematics or science and a foreign language.

Your target offers and examples of degree courses

152 pts **Nottingham** – A*AA–AAA (Econ Hisp St) (IB 38–36 pts)

136 pts **Birmingham** – AAB incl hist (Hisp St Hist) (IB 32 pts HL 665)

Glasgow – AAB–BBB incl arts/lang (Hisp St) (IB 36–34 pts)

London (UCL) – AAB incl Span (Span Lat Am St) (IB 36 pts HL 6 Span)

Sheffield – AAB–BBB incl Span (Hisp St Joint Hons) (IB 35–34 pts HL 6 Span)

Southampton – AAB–ABB incl Span (Span (Lat Am St)) (IB 34 pts HL 6 Span); AAB–ABB incl Span/Port (Pol Span/Port Lat Am St) (IB 34 pts HL 6 Span/Port)

128 pts **Bristol** – ABB–BBB incl Span (Hisp St) (IB 32–31 pts HL 5 Span)

Essex – ABB–BBB (Lat Am St courses) (IB 32–30 pts)

Liverpool – ABB (Lat Am Hisp St Comb Hons) (IB 33 pts)

London (RH) – ABB (Comp Lit Cult Span) (IB 32 pts)

Manchester – ABB–BBB incl Span (Span Port Lat Am St) (IB 34–32 pts)

Newcastle – ABB–BBB incl Span (Span Port Lat Am St) (IB 32 pts HL 6 Span)

Nottingham – ABB incl Span/Russ (Hisp St Russ) (IB 32 pts); ABB (Am St Lat Am St) (IB 32 pts); ABB incl Span (Hisp St Hist) (IB 32 pts)

Sheffield – ABB–BBB incl Span (Hisp St) (IB 34 pts HL 6 Span)

Warwick – ABB incl lang (Hisp St courses) (IB 34 pts HL 5 lang)

120 pts **Aberdeen** – BBB (Hisp St (Lat Am/Spn)) (IB 32 pts)

Kent – BBB (Hisp St courses) (IB 34 pts)

London (QM) – 120–128 pts incl lang (Hisp St) (IB 32–34 pts HL 5 lang); 120–128 pts (Hisp St courses) (IB 32–34 pts HL 5 lang)

Stirling – BBB (Span Lat Am St) (IB 32 pts)

112 pts **Hull** – 112 pts incl lang (Hisp St Relgn Joint Hons) (IB 28 pts)

96 pts **Portsmouth** – 96–120 pts (Span Lat Am St) (IB 30 pts HL 17 pts)

Alternative offers
See **Chapter 6** and **Appendix 1** for grades/new UCAS Tariff points information for other examinations.

CHOOSING YOUR COURSE (SEE ALSO CH.1)

Universities and colleges teaching quality See www.qaa.ac.uk; http://unistats.direct.gov.uk.

ADMISSIONS INFORMATION

Number of applicants per place (approx) Essex 3; Liverpool 3; Nottingham 7; Portsmouth 5; Southampton 8.

Advice to applicants and planning the UCAS personal statement Visits and contacts with Spain and Latin American countries should be described. An awareness of the economic, historical and political scene of these countries is also important. Information may be obtained from respective embassies.

Selection interviews Yes Southampton; **No** Portsmouth.

Interview advice and questions Past questions include: Why are you interested in studying Latin American Studies? What countries related to the degree course have you visited? What career are you planning when you finish your degree? Applicants taking Spanish are likely to be asked questions on their syllabus and should also be familiar with some Spanish newspapers and magazines. See also **Chapter 5**.

AFTER-RESULTS ADVICE

Offers to applicants repeating A-levels Higher Essex; **Same** Portsmouth.

GRADUATE DESTINATIONS AND EMPLOYMENT (2013/14 HESA)
See **American Studies**.

Career note See **Languages**.

OTHER DEGREE SUBJECTS FOR CONSIDERATION
American Studies; Portuguese; Spanish.

LAW
(including **Law** and **Criminology**; see also **Social Sciences/Studies**)

Law courses are usually divided into two parts. Part I occupies the first year and introduces the student to criminal and constitutional law and the legal process. Thereafter, many different specialised topics can be studied in the second and third years. Consult the subsection '**Interview advice and questions**' in order to gain a flavour of the types of questions raised in studying this subject. The course content is very similar for most courses. Applicants are advised to check with universities for their current policies concerning their use of the National Admissions Test for Law (LNAT). See **Subject requirements/preferences** below and also **Chapter 5**.

Useful websites www.barcouncil.org.uk; www.cilex.org.uk; www.lawcareers.net; www.lawsociety.org. uk; www.cps.gov.uk; www.justice.gov.uk/about/hmcts; www.lawscot.org.uk; www.lawsoc-ni.org; www.rollonfriday.com; www.lnat.ac.uk

NB The points totals shown to the left of the institutions are for ease of reference only. It must not be assumed that Tariff points are always used by institutions or that they can be substituted for an offer in grades. The level of an offer is not necessarily indicative of the quality of a course.

COURSE OFFERS INFORMATION
Subject requirements/preferences GCSE Many universities will expect high grades. **AL** Arts, humanities, social sciences and sciences plus languages for courses combined with a foreign language. **All universities** Applicants offering Art and Music A-levels should check whether these subjects are acceptable.

Manchester GCSE Requirements are often higher than normal – minimum of five A grades.

Your target offers and examples of degree courses
152 pts **Cambridge** – A*AA (Lnd Econ; Law) (IB 40–41 pts HL 776)
    Durham – A*AA +LNAT (Law) (IB 38 pts)
    London (King's) – A*AA incl Fr/Ger +LNAT (Engl Law Fr Law/Ger Law) (IB 35 pts
        HL 6 Fr/Ger); A*AA +LNAT (Pol Phil Law; Law) (IB 35 pts)
    London (QM) – A*AA (Law) (IB 37 pts)
    London (SOAS) – A*AA–AAB (Law) (IB 37 pts)
    London (UCL) – A*AA +LNAT (Law) (IB 39 pts); A*AA incl Fr/Ger/Span +LNAT
        (Law Fr Law/Ger Lat/Hisp Law) (IB 39 pts HL 6 Fr/Ger/Span)
    London LSE – A*AA (Law) (IB 38 pts)
    Nottingham – A*AA +LNAT (Law) (IB 38 pts)
144 pts **Birmingham** – AAA +LNAT (Law; Law Bus St; Law Ger Law) (IB 32 pts HL 666)
    Bristol – AAA–AAB incl Fr +LNAT (Law Fr) (IB 36–34 pts HL 6 incl Fr); AAA–AAB +LNAT (Law)
        (IB 36–34 pts); AAA–AAB incl Ger +LNAT (Law Ger) (IB 36–34 pts HL 6 Ger)
    Cardiff – AAA–AAB (Law Crimin; Law) (IB 34 pts)
    East Anglia – AAA (Law Am Law) (IB 34 pts)
    Edinburgh – AAA–ABB (Law courses; Law Acc) (IB 40–34 pts)
    Exeter – AAA–AAB (Law; Law (Euro St)) (IB 36–34 pts)
    Glasgow – AAA–BBB incl Engl +LNAT (Law Joint Hons) (IB 39–34 pts)

The University of Law

WE SHARE
YOUR AMBITION

EXPERIENCE AND EXPERTISE

The University of Law (ULaw) is the UK's largest law school and has trained more lawyers than anyone else. No other institution can match our reputation, passion and commitment to preparing students for today's workplace. We combine years of experience with a fresh, modern approach to ensure our students achieve their career ambitions.

ULaw's success is built on continual innovation, and ensuring we always reflect the needs of today's employers. Our tutors are qualified solicitors, barristers or judges with extensive professional experience. Many continue to practise law, so know exactly the skills and qualities future employers need, passing unique knowledge directly to students.

EXCELLENT EMPLOYABILITY

We develop leading legal minds and business leaders.

Lawyers today are among the best-paid professionals. Law firms offer high starting salaries to graduates, and successful solicitors and barristers enjoy excellent earning potential. At ULaw we enjoy close relationships with employers, working with more than 90 of the top 100 UK law firms and over 30 leading law firms send their trainees exclusively to us.

Career benefits also extend beyond financial remuneration, with a high percentage of law students wanting to make a difference and to make positive changes in society.

Law degrees are a great foundation to a huge range of careers. Our students gain a formidable range of skills that are essential and welcomed throughout the business world. From working in multinational companies, banking and finance, to technology, media and charities, a legal qualification is highly valued by employers.

97% of our students **are employed** within 9 months*

88% STUDENT SATISFACTION WITH THE QUALITY OF THE COURSE 2015**

1ST LEARNING RESOURCES & ACADEMIC SUPPORT†

*Statistics taken from full-time LPC students graduating in summer 2014
**National Student Survey †Excludes further education colleges that offer higher education courses

SEE YOURSELF
AT A LEADING
LAW SCHOOL

Law

- Obtain a qualifying law degree (LLB) in only two years
- Excellent staff:student ratio with classes of six students
- Buckingham students are amongst the most satisfied in the UK *(NSS 2015)*
- Flexible entry points in January, July and September

"The small tutorial groups give everyone the opportunity to have lots of individual contact with the tutors, who are incredibly supportive, approachable and friendly. They take time to pay close attention to the needs of everyone, and they knew all our names within the first week!"
Willin Belliard, LLB (Hons) 2013

THE TIMES
THE SUNDAY TIMES
GOOD
UNIVERSITY
GUIDE
2016
UNIVERSITY
OF THE YEAR
FOR TEACHING

law-admissions@buckingham.ac.uk
+44 (0)1280 828321 / 828344
ww.buckingham.ac.uk/law

THE UNIVERSITY OF
BUCKINGHAM

Kent – AAA (Int Legal St (Yr Abrd)) (IB 34 pts); AAA–AAB incl Fr/Ger/Ital/Span (Engl Fr Law/ Ger Law/Ital Law/Span Law) (IB 34 pts); AAA–AAB (Law Joint Hons; Law) (IB 34 pts)

Lancaster – AAA (Law (Int); Law) (IB 36 pts); AAA–AAB (Law Crimin) (IB 36 pts)

Leeds – AAA (Law) (IB 38 pts)

London (QM) – AAA (Law Pol) (IB 37 pts)

Manchester – AAA (Law) (IB 37 pts)

NCH London – AAA–ABB (Law)

Newcastle – AAA (Law) (IB 34 pts)

Nottingham – AAA incl Fr/Ger/Span +LNAT (Law Fr Fr Law/Ger Ger Law/Span Span Law) (IB 38 pts)

Oxford – AAA +LNAT (Law; Law Law St Euro) (IB 38 pts)

Reading – AAA–AAB (Law; Law Leg St Euro) (IB 35 pts)

Sheffield – AAA–AAB (Law; Law (Euro Int)) (IB 37 pts)

Southampton – AAA–AAB (Law; Law (Euro Leg St); Law (Int Leg St)) (IB 36 pts)

Surrey – AAA–AAB (Law Int St; Law) (IB 36–35 pts)

Sussex – AAA–AAB incl Fr/Ital/Span (Law Lang (Yr Abrd)) (IB 35 pts HL 5 Fr/Ital/Span); AAA–AAB (Law Bus Mgt; Law Int Rel; Law Pol; Law) (IB 35 pts); (Law Am St) (IB 35 pts)

Warwick – AAA (Law; Law (St Abrd)) (IB 38 pts); AAA incl Fr/Ger (Euro Law) (IB 38 pts HL 6 Fr/Ger)

York – AAA/A*AB/A*A*C (Law) (IB 36 pts)

136 pts **Aston** – AAB–ABB (Law Mgt) (IB 35–34 pts)

Durham – AAB (Crimin) (IB 36 pts)

East Anglia – AAB (Law; Law Euro Leg St) (IB 33 pts)

Huddersfield – AAB 136 pts (Law (Exmp))

Leicester – AAB incl Fr (Maîtrise Engl Fr Law) (IB 33 pts); AAB incl modn lang (Law Modn Lang (Fr/Span/Ital)) (IB 33 pts); AAB (Law) (IB 33 pts)

Check **Chapter 3** for new university admission details and **Chapter 6** on how to read the subject tables.

394 | Law

          London (RH) – AAB (Law) (IB 32 pts)
          London LSE – AAB (Anth Law) (IB 37 pts)
          Manchester – AAB (Law Crimin; Law Pol) (IB 35 pts)
          Queen's Belfast – AAB (Law)
          Sheffield – AAB–ABB (Law Crimin) (IB 35 pts)
          Surrey – AAA–AAB (Law Crimin) (IB 36–35 pts)
          Swansea – AAB–BBB (Bus Law)
          Warwick – AAB (Law Bus St) (IB 36 pts HL 5 maths); (Law Sociol) (IB 36 pts)

128 pts   **Aberdeen** – ABB (Law) (IB 34 pts)
          Brunel – ABB (Law) (IB 31 pts)
          City – ABB–BBB 128 pts (Law) (IB 29 pts)
          Coventry – ABB (Law) (IB 31 pts)
          Dundee – ABB incl Engl+lang (Law Langs) (IB 32 pts); ABB incl Engl (Engl Law; Law (Scot Engl); Scot Law) (IB 32 pts)
          Essex – ABB–BBB (Law Hum Rts (LLB); Phil Law; Law; Engl Fr Law (Mait)) (IB 32–30 pts)
          Keele – ABB (Law courses) (IB 34 pts)
          Kingston – 128 pts (Law)
          Leicester – ABB (Crimin) (IB 30 pts)
          Liverpool – ABB (Law Acc Fin; Law) (IB 33 pts)
          Middlesex – 128 pts (Law)
          Northumbria – 128 pts (Law (Exmp)) (IB 31 pts)
          Portsmouth – 128 pts (Law) (IB 31 pts HL 18 pts)
          Stirling – ABB (Law) (IB 36 pts)
          Westminster – ABB (Law) (IB 32 pts)

120 pts   **Aberystwyth** – 120 pts (Law; Crim Law; Euro Law)
          Bangor – 120–128 pts (Law courses)
          Bournemouth – 120 pts (Acc Law; Law; Law Tax; Bus Law; Enter Law) (IB 31 pts)
          Bradford – BBB 120 pts (Law; Bus St Law)
          Buckingham – BBB (Law Bus Fin; Law Econ; Law Mgt St; Law; Law Fr; Law Pol)
          Bucks New – 120–136 pts (Law; Bus Law)
          Canterbury Christ Church – BBB (Law)
          Central Lancashire – 120 pts (Law Crimin; Law)
          Chester – BBC–BCC 120 pts (Law Crimin) (IB 28 pts); BBB–BBC 120 pts (Law) (IB 28 pts)
          De Montfort – 120 pts (Law) (IB 30 pts)
          Derby – 120 pts (Law; Law Crimin)
          Edge Hill – BBB 120 pts (Crimin; Law; Law Crimin)
          Gloucestershire – 120 pts (Law)
          Greenwich – 120 pts (Crimin); (Law) (IB 28 pts)
          Huddersfield – BBB 120 pts (Law Bus; Law)
          Leeds Beckett – 120 pts (Law) (IB 26 pts)
          Lincoln – 120 pts (Law; Crimin)
          Liverpool John Moores – 120 pts (Law Crim Just; Law) (IB 30 pts)
          London (Birk) – 120 pts (Law; Crimin Crim Just)
          Northampton – 120 pts (Law courses)
          Nottingham Trent – 120 pts (Law)
          Oxford Brookes – BBB–BBC (Law) (IB 32 pts)
          Plymouth – 120 pts (Law; Law Bus) (IB 30 pts)
          Portsmouth – 120 pts (Law Crimin) (IB 30 pts HL 17 pts)
          Sheffield Hallam – 120 pts (Law; Law Crimin)
          Staffordshire – 120 pts (Law (Crimin))
          Sunderland – 120 pts (Law Comb Hons)
          Swansea – BBB (Law Span)
          Ulster – BBB (Law; Law HR Mgt; Law Ir; Law Mark) (IB 26 pts)
          Univ Law – BBB (Law Int; Law) (IB 31 pts)

        UWE Bristol – 120 pts (Law; Crimin Law) (IB 26 pts)

        Westminster – ABC incl Fr (Law Fr Law) (IB 30 pts); ABC (Euro Leg St) (IB 30 pts)

112 pts **Bangor** – 112–128 pts (Law Crimin)

        Birmingham City – 112 pts (Law; Law Am Leg St; Law Crimin; Sociol Crimin) (IB 28 pts)

        Brighton – BBC (Law Bus) (IB 28 pts)

        Cardiff Met – 112 pts (Bus Mgt St Law)

        Chester – BBC–BCC 112 pts (Law (Comb)) (IB 26 pts)

        Cumbria – 112 pts (Law)

        De Montfort – 112 pts (Law Hum Rts Soc Just) (IB 28 pts)

        East London – 112 pts (Law) (IB 26 pts)

        Edinburgh Napier – BBC incl Engl (Law; Crimin) (IB 29 pts HL 5 Engl)

        Greenwich – 112 pts (Bus Law)

        Hertfordshire – 112 pts (Law; Law (Gov Pol)) (IB 28 pts)

        Hull – 112 pts (Law Phil; Law; Law Pol) (IB 28 pts)

        Kingston – 112–128 pts (Crimin courses)

        London Met – 112 pts (Law; Bus Law; Law (Int Rel))

        Manchester Met – BBC–BBB 112–120 pts (Law) (IB 26 pts)

        Middlesex – 112 pts (Crimin courses)

        Nottingham Trent – 112 pts (Law Bus; Law Psy; Law Crimin)

        Plymouth – 112 pts (Marit Bus Marit Law)

        Portsmouth – 112 pts (Law Int Rel); (Law Bus) (IB 30 pts HL 17 pts)

        Robert Gordon – BBC incl Engl (Law) (IB 29 pts HL 5 Engl)

        Roehampton – 112 pts (Crimin)

        Southampton Solent – 112 pts (Law; Crimin)

        Strathclyde – BBC (Scots Engl Law (Clin)) (IB 32 pts HL 5 Engl)

        Sunderland – 112 pts (Law)

        West London – 112 pts (Law)

        Wolverhampton – 112 pts (Law)

104 pts **Abertay** – BCC (Law) (IB 29 pts)

        BPP – BCC 104 pts (Law)

        De Montfort – 104 pts (Crimin Crim Just) (IB 28 pts)

        Liverpool Hope – BCC–BBB 104–120 pts (Law Comb Hons)

        London South Bank – BCC 104 pts (Law)

        Plymouth – 104 pts (Int Rel Law) (IB 24 pts)

        St Mary's – 104 pts (Law) (IB 28 pts)

        South Wales – BCC (Law Crimin Crim Just; Law) (IB 29 pts)

        Teesside – 104 pts (Law Bus Mgt; Law)

        West London – 104 pts (Crimin)

        Winchester – 104–120 pts (Law) (IB 26 pts)

96 pts **Anglia Ruskin** – 96–112 pts (Law) (IB 30 pts)

        Bradford – CCC 96 pts (App Crim Just St)

        Cumbria – 96 pts (Crimin Law)

        Glyndŵr – 96 pts (Crimin Crim Just)

        St Mary's – 96 pts (Bus Law (Joint Hons)) (IB 28 pts)

        Teesside – 96 pts (Crimin courses)

        West Scotland – CCC (Law Bus) (IB 24 pts)

        Winchester – 96–112 pts (Law (Comb Hons))

        Wolverhampton – 96 pts (Law Phil)

88 pts **Bolton** – 88 pts (Law)

        Derby – 88–120 pts (Law Joint Hons)

80 pts **Bedfordshire** – 80 pts (Law; Crimin) (IB 24 pts)

        Bucks New – 80–96 pts (Crimin) (IB 24 pts)

        Open University – contact +44 (0)845 300 6090 **or** www.openuniversity.co.uk/you (Law)

Check **Chapter 3** for new university admission details and **Chapter 6** on how to read the subject tables.

Alternative offers
See **Chapter 6** and **Appendix 1** for grades/new UCAS Tariff points information for other examinations.

EXAMPLES OF COLLEGES OFFERING COURSES IN THIS SUBJECT FIELD
Barnsley (Coll); Birmingham Met (Coll); Blackburn (Coll); Blackpool and Fylde (Coll); Bury (Coll); Croydon (Univ Centre); Derby (Coll); Grimsby (Univ Centre); London UCK (Coll); Menai (Coll); Nottingham New (Coll); Pearson (Coll); Petroc; St Helens (Coll); South Devon (Coll); South Thames (Coll); South Tyneside (Coll); Truro and Penwith (Coll); West Suffolk (Coll).

CHOOSING YOUR COURSE (SEE ALSO CH.1)
Universities and colleges teaching quality See www.qaa.ac.uk; http://unistats.direct.gov.uk.

Top research universities and colleges (REF 2014) Durham; London (King's); York; Sheffield; Cambridge; Leeds; London LSE; Ulster; London (QM); Warwick; Bristol; Exeter.

Examples of sandwich degree courses Aston; Bournemouth; Bradford; Brighton; Brunel; Coventry; De Montfort; Essex; Greenwich; Hertfordshire; Huddersfield; Leeds; Nottingham Trent; Plymouth; Portsmouth; Surrey; Teesside; UWE Bristol; Westminster.

ADMISSIONS INFORMATION
Number of applicants per place (approx) Abertay 3; Aberystwyth 8; Anglia Ruskin 10; Aston 10; Bangor 3; Birmingham 6; Birmingham City 20; Bournemouth 9; Bradford 2; Bristol 5; Brunel 2; Buckingham 3; Cambridge 5; Cardiff 12; Central Lancashire 36; City 23; Coventry 15; De Montfort 6; Derby 7; Dundee 6; Durham 6; East Anglia 14; East London 13; Edinburgh 5; Edinburgh Napier 7; Essex 26; Exeter 15; Glasgow 8; Glasgow Caledonian 10; Huddersfield 10; Hull 15; Kent 11; Kingston 25; Lancaster 8; Leeds 15; Leicester 9; Liverpool 10; Liverpool John Moores 10; London (King's) 14; London (QM) 17; London (SOAS) 8; London (UCL) 14; London LSE 14; London Met 13; London South Bank 4; Manchester 7; Manchester Met 21; Middlesex 25; Newcastle 13; Northampton 4; Northumbria 12; Nottingham 9; Nottingham Trent 15; Oxford Brookes 18; Plymouth 14; Robert Gordon 4; Sheffield 16; Sheffield Hallam 6; Southampton 7; Southampton Solent 5; Staffordshire 16; Strathclyde 10; Sussex 10; Teesside 3; UWE Bristol 27; Warwick 20; West London 18; Westminster 29; Wolverhampton 12; York 8.

Admissions tutors' advice Bristol Places in Clearing for international students.

Advice to applicants and planning the UCAS personal statement Visit the law courts and take notes on cases heard. Follow leading legal arguments in the press. Read the law sections in the *Independent*, *The Times* and the *Guardian*. Discuss the career with lawyers and, if possible, obtain work shadowing in lawyers' offices. Describe these visits and experiences and indicate any special areas of law which interest you. (Read *Learning the Law* by Glanville Williams.) Commitment is essential to the study of law as an academic discipline, not necessarily with a view to taking it up as a career.

When writing to admissions tutors, especially by email, take care to present yourself well: text language is not acceptable. You should use communication as an opportunity to demonstrate your skill in the use of English. Spelling mistakes, punctuation errors and bad grammar suggest that you will struggle to develop the expected writing ability (see **Misconceptions about this course**) and may lead to your application being rejected. When writing to an admissions tutor do not demand an answer immediately or by return or urgently. If your query is reasonable the tutor will respond without such urging. Adding these demands is bad manners and suggests that you are doing everything at the last minute and increases your chances of a rejection.

The criteria for admission are: motivation and capacity for sustained and intense work; the ability to analyse and solve problems using logical and critical approaches; the ability to draw fine distinctions, to separate the relevant from the irrelevant; the capacity for accurate and critical observation, for sustained and cogent argument; creativity and flexibility of thought and lateral thinking; competence in English; the ability to express ideas clearly and effectively; a willingness to listen and to be able to give considered responses. See also **Appendix 3**. **Deferred entry** Check with your university choices since deferred entry will not necessarily be accepted. **Bristol** Deferred entry is limited. Second time applicants rarely considered. **Manchester** Deferred entry is not accepted. **Warwick** Deferred entry is usually acceptable.

Misconceptions about this course Aberystwyth Some applicants believe that all Law graduates enter the legal profession – this is incorrect. **Birmingham** Students tend to believe that success in the law centres on the ability to learn information. Whilst some information does necessarily have to be learnt, the most important skills involve (a) developing an ability to select the most relevant pieces of information and (b) developing the ability to write tightly argued, persuasively reasoned essays on the basis of such information. **Bristol** Many applicants think that most of our applicants have been privately educated: the reverse is true. **Derby** Many applicants do not realise the amount of work involved to get a good degree classification.

Selection interviews Approximately four well-qualified candidates apply for every place on undergraduate Law courses in the UK and the National Admissions Test for Law (LNAT) is used by a number of universities (see Your target offers and examples of degree courses and **Chapter 5**). **Yes** Aberystwyth, Anglia Ruskin, Buckingham, Cambridge, Canterbury Christ Church, Central Lancashire, Coventry, East London, Edinburgh Napier, Essex, Kent, Lancaster, Liverpool, London (King's), London (UCL), Oxford (Law) 15%, (Law Euro Law) 12%, Teesside, West London, York; **Some** Bangor, Cardiff, Derby, Huddersfield, Liverpool John Moores, Northumbria, Nottingham Trent (mature students), Oxford Brookes (mature students), Sheffield Hallam, Southampton (mature students), Staffordshire, Sunderland, Surrey, UWE Bristol, Warwick; **No** Birmingham, Bristol, Dundee, East Anglia, Nottingham, Reading, Southampton Solent.

Interview advice and questions Law is a highly competitive subject and applicants will be expected to have a basic awareness of aspects of law and to have gained some work experience, on which they are likely to be questioned. It is almost certain that a legal question will be asked at interview and applicants will be tested on their responses. Questions in the past have included: What interests you in the study of law? What would you do to overcome the problem of prison overcrowding if you were (a) a judge, (b) a prosecutor, (c) the Prime Minister? What legal cases have you read about recently? What is jurisprudence? What are the causes of violence in society? A friend bought a bun which, unknown to him, contained a stone. He gave it to you to eat and you broke a tooth. Could you sue anyone? Have you visited any law courts? What cases did you see? A person arrives in England unable to speak the language. He lights a cigarette in a restaurant where smoking is not allowed. Can he be charged and convicted? What should be done in the case of an elderly person who steals a bar of soap? What, in your opinion, would be the two basic laws in Utopia? Describe, without using your hands, how you would do the butterfly stroke. What would happen if there were no law? Should we legalise euthanasia? If you could change any law, what would it be? How would you implement the changes? If a person tries to kill someone using black magic, are they guilty of attempted murder? If a jury uses a ouija board to reach a decision, is it wrong? If so, why? Jane attends a university interview. As she enters the building she sees a diamond brooch on the floor. She hands it to the interviewer who hands it to the police. The brooch is never claimed. Who is entitled to it? Jane? The interviewer? The police? The University authorities? The Crown? Mr Grabbit who owns the building? Where does honesty fit into law? For joint courses: what academic skills are needed to succeed? Why have you applied for a joint degree? See also **Chapter 5**. **Cambridge** Logic questions. If I returned to the waiting room and my jacket had been taken and I then took another one, got home and actually discovered it was mine, had I committed a crime? If the interviewer pulled out a gun and aimed it at me, but missed as he had a bad arm, had he committed a crime? If the interviewer pulled out a gun and aimed it at me, thinking it was loaded but, in fact, it was full of blanks and fired it at me with the intention to kill, had he committed a crime? Which of the three preceding situations are similar and which is the odd one out? If a law is immoral, is it still a law and must people abide by it? For example, when Hitler legalised the systematic killing of Jews, was it still law? **Oxford** Should the use of mobile phones be banned on public transport? Is wearing school uniform a breach of human rights? If you could go back in time to any period of time, when would it be and why? Would you trade your scarf for my bike, even if you have no idea what state it's in or if I even have one? Is someone guilty of an offence if they did not set out to commit a crime but ended up doing so? Does a girl who joins the Scouts have a political agenda?

Reasons for rejection (non-academic) 'Dreams' about being a lawyer! Poorly informed about the subject. Badly drafted application. Underestimated workload. Poor communication skills. **Manchester Met** Some were rejected because they were obviously more suited to Psychology.

AFTER-RESULTS ADVICE
Offers to applicants repeating A-levels Higher Aberystwyth, Coventry, Dundee, Essex, Glasgow, Hull, Leeds, London Met, Manchester Met, Newcastle, Nottingham, Oxford Brookes, Queen's Belfast, Sheffield, Sheffield Hallam, Strathclyde, UWE Bristol, Warwick; **Possibly higher** Liverpool; **Same** Anglia Ruskin, Bangor, Birmingham, Bradford, Brighton, Bristol, Brunel, Cardiff, De Montfort, Derby, Durham, East Anglia, Huddersfield, Kingston, Lincoln, Liverpool Hope, Liverpool John Moores, Northumbria, Nottingham Trent, Staffordshire, Stirling, Sunderland, Surrey, Wolverhampton; **No** Cambridge.

GRADUATE DESTINATIONS AND EMPLOYMENT (2013/14 HESA)
Graduates surveyed 10,880 **Employed** 4,655 **In voluntary employment** 395 **In further study** 3,920 **Assumed unemployed** 570

Career note Recent reports (Oct 2013) suggest that at the present time there are too many students training to be lawyers at a time when jobs in the legal profession are scarce. Thus, applicants intending to aim for a career in the profession should note that at the present time training places for the bar and solicitors' examinations are in short supply. There are, however, alternative legal careers such as legal journalism, patent law, legal publishing and teaching. The course also proves a good starting point for careers in industry, commerce and the public service, whilst the study of consumer protection can lead to qualification as a Trading Standards officer.

OTHER DEGREE SUBJECTS FOR CONSIDERATION
Criminology; Economics; Government; History; International Relations; Politics; Social Policy and Administration; Sociology.

LEISURE and RECREATION MANAGEMENT/STUDIES

(see also **Business and Management Courses, Business and Management Courses (International and European), Business and Management Courses (Specialised), Hospitality and Event Management, Sports Sciences/Studies, Tourism and Travel**)

The courses cover various aspects of leisure and recreation and in particular a wide range of outdoor activities. Specialist options include recreation management, tourism and countryside management, all of which are offered as individual degree courses in their own right. Look out for other 'outdoor' activities in sport such as the two-year Foundation Studies course in Surf Science and Technology at Cornwall College through Plymouth University. There is also an obvious link with Sports Studies, Physical Education and Tourism and Travel courses. See also **Appendix 3**.

Useful websites www.cimspa.co.uk; www.leisuremanagement.co.uk; www.thebapa.org.uk; www.leisureopportunities.co.uk; www.recmanagement.com; www.uksport.gov.uk

NB The points totals shown to the left of the institutions are for ease of reference only. It must not be assumed that Tariff points are always used by institutions or that they can be substituted for an offer in grades. The level of an offer is not necessarily indicative of the quality of a course.

COURSE OFFERS INFORMATION
Subject requirements/preferences GCSE Normally English and mathematics grades A–C. **AL** No specified subjects. **Other** Disclosure and Barring Service (DBS) clearance and health checks required for some courses.

Your target offers and examples of degree courses

128 pts **Manchester** – ABB–BBB (Mgt Ldrshp Leis) (IB 34–32 pts)

120 pts **Stirling** – BBB (Env Sci Out Educ) (IB 32 pts)

112 pts **Canterbury Christ Church** – 112 pts (Spo Leis Mgt)
Central Lancashire – 112 pts (Out Ldrshp) (IB 25 pts)
Derby – 112 pts (Out Ldrshp Mgt)
Leeds Beckett – 112 pts (Enter Mgt) (IB 25 pts)

104 pts **Cumbria** – 104 pts (Out Ldrshp; Out Advntr Env)
Gloucestershire – 104 pts (Spo Mgt Dev)
Stranmillis (UC) – BCC (Hlth Physl Actvt Spo)
Ulster – 104–120 pts (Leis Evnts Mgt) (IB 24 pts)

96 pts **Birmingham (UC)** – 96 pts (Spa Mgt)
Bournemouth – 96–112 pts (Evnts Leis Mark) (IB 26–30 pts)
Manchester Met – 96–112 pts (Out St) (IB 28 pts)
Southampton Solent – 96 pts (Advntr Out Mgt)
Worcester – 96 pts (Out Advntr Ldrshp Mgt)

80 pts **Bucks New** – 80–96 pts (Spo Bus Mgt) (IB 20 pts)

64 pts **Trinity Saint David** – 64 pts (Leis Mgt)
UHI – CC (Advntr Tour Mgt)

Alternative offers
See **Chapter 6** and **Appendix 1** for grades/new UCAS Tariff points information for other examinations.

EXAMPLES OF COLLEGES OFFERING COURSES IN THIS SUBJECT FIELD
See also **Tourism and Travel**. Bedford (Coll); Blackburn (Coll); Bradford (Coll); Brighton and Hove City (Coll); Cornwall (Coll); Durham New (Coll); Exeter (Coll); Grimsby (Univ Centre); Leicester (Coll); Loughborough (Coll); Manchester (Coll); Mid-Kent (Coll); Myerscough (Coll); Newcastle (Coll); Norwich City (Coll); Pembrokeshire (Coll); South Devon (Coll); SRUC; Suffolk (Univ Campus); Totton (Coll); Wakefield (Coll); West Cheshire (Coll); West Herts (Coll); Wirral Met (Coll); Yorkshire Coast (Coll).

CHOOSING YOUR COURSE (SEE ALSO CH.1)
Universities and colleges teaching quality See www.qaa.ac.uk; http://unistats.direct.gov.uk.

Top research universities and colleges (REF 2014) See **Sports Sciences/Studies**.

Examples of sandwich degree courses Bournemouth; Trinity Saint David; Ulster.

ADMISSIONS INFORMATION
Number of applicants per place (approx) Brighton 10; Gloucestershire 7; Hull 3.

Advice to applicants and planning the UCAS personal statement Work experience, visits to leisure centres and national parks and any interests you have in particular aspects of leisure should be described, for example, art galleries, museums, countryside management, sport. An involvement in sports and leisure as a participant or employee is an advantage. See also **Appendix 3**.

Misconceptions about this course The level of business studies in leisure management courses is higher than many students expect.

Interview advice and questions In addition to sporting or other related interests, applicants will be expected to have had some work experience and can expect to be asked to discuss their interests. What do you hope to gain by going to university? See also **Chapter 5**.

Reasons for rejection (non-academic) Poor communication or presentation skills. Relatively poor sporting background or knowledge.

GRADUATE DESTINATIONS AND EMPLOYMENT (2013/14 HESA)
See **Hospitality and Event Management**.

Career note Career opportunities exist in public and private sectors within leisure facilities, health clubs, the arts, leisure promotion, marketing and events management. Some graduates work in sports development and outdoor activities.

OTHER DEGREE SUBJECTS FOR CONSIDERATION

Business Studies; Events Management; Hospitality Management; Sports Studies; Tourism.

LINGUISTICS

(see also **English, Languages**)

Hi/Hello/Good day/Good morning – Linguistics is the study of language, the way we speak to our friends, or at an interview, the expressions we use, how we express ideas or emotions. The way in which children speak, the types of language used in advertising, or in sports reporting. Courses will include morphology – the formation of words, phonetics – the study of sounds, and semantics – the study of meanings. OK?/Understand?/Cheers!

Useful websites www.ciol.org.uk; www.cal.org; www.applij.oxfordjournals.org; www.linguisticsociety. org; www.sil.org; www.baal.org.uk

NB The points totals shown to the left of the institutions are for ease of reference only. It must not be assumed that Tariff points are always used by institutions or that they can be substituted for an offer in grades. The level of an offer is not necessarily indicative of the quality of a course.

COURSE OFFERS INFORMATION

Subject requirements/preferences GCSE English required and a foreign language preferred. **AL** English may be required or preferred for some courses.

Your target offers and examples of degree courses

152 pts **Cambridge** – A*AA (Ling) (IB 40–41 pts)

144 pts **Edinburgh** – AAA–ABB (Ling Engl Lang; Ling) (IB 37–34 pts); (Class Ling; Jap Ling; Phil Ling) (IB 40–34 pts)

Lancaster – AAA–AAB (Ling; Ling Phil; Ling (St Abrd)) (IB 36–35 pts)

136 pts **Edinburgh** – AAB–ABB (Ital Ling) (IB 36–34 pts)

Lancaster – AAB (Ling Psy) (IB 35 pts)

Leeds – AAB–ABB (Ling Joint Hons) (IB 35–34 pts HL 16 pts); (Ling Phon) (IB 35–34 pts)

London (SOAS) – AAB–ABB (Ling) (IB 35 pts)

Newcastle – AAB–ABB (Ling Chin/Jap; Ling) (IB 35–34 pts)

Sheffield – AAB–ABB (Engl Lang Ling) (IB 35 pts)

Southampton – AAB–ABB incl lang (Lang Soty) (IB 34 pts HL 6 lang)

York – AAB–ABB (Fr Ling (Yr Abrd); Ling) (IB 34 pts); AAB (Phil Ling) (IB 35 pts)

128 pts **Essex** – ABB–BBB (Ling) (IB 32–30 pts)

Kent – ABB (Engl Lang Ling) (IB 34 pts); ABB incl Engl (Engl Lang Ling Engl Am Lit) (IB 34 pts)

London (QM) – ABB–AAB incl Engl 128–136 pts (Engl Lit Ling) (IB 34 pts HL 6 Engl); 128–136 pts (Engl Lang Ling) (IB 34 pts)

Manchester – ABB (Ling courses) (IB 34 pts)

Newcastle – ABB–BBB incl Fr/Ger/Span (Modn Langs Ling) (IB 32 pts HL 6 Fr/Ger/Span)

Queen's Belfast – ABB incl Engl (Engl Ling)

Sheffield – ABB incl Engl (Ling Joint Hons) (IB 34 pts Hl 6 Engl)

120 pts **Aberdeen** – BBB (Lang Ling) (IB 32 pts)

Gloucestershire – 120 pts (Engl Lang Ling)

London (QM) – 120–128 pts incl lang (Ger Ling) (IB 32–34 pts HL 5 lang)

UWE Bristol – 120 pts (Engl Lang Ling) (IB 27 pts)

112 pts **Brighton** – BBC incl Engl lang/lit (Engl Lang Ling) (IB 28 pts)
Nottingham Trent – 112 pts (Ling Joint Hons)
Roehampton – 112 pts (Engl Lang Ling)
Westminster – BBC–BB incl Engl (Engl Lang Ling) (IB 30 pts HL 5 Engl)
104 pts **Bangor** – 104–120 pts (Ling Engl Lang; Ling; Ling Engl Lit)
Central Lancashire – 104 pts (Engl Lang Ling)
London (Birk) – 104 pts (Ling Lang)
Manchester Met – 104–112 pts incl lang (Ling Lang (Chin/Fr/Ger/Ital/Span)) (IB 26 pts)
St Mark and St John – BCC (Engl Lang Ling)
Ulster – 104–112 pts (Lang Ling Cnslg St) (IB 24–25 pts)
Westminster – BCC (Arbc Ling) (IB 30 pts HL 4 Engl)
96 pts **Wolverhampton** – 96 pts (Ling courses)
88 pts **Anglia Ruskin** – 88–104 pts (Engl Lang Ling) (IB 26 pts)
80 pts **Bedfordshire** – 80 pts (Engl Lang Ling) (IB 24 pts)

Alternative offers
See **Chapter 6** and **Appendix 1** for grades/new UCAS Tariff points information for other examinations.

CHOOSING YOUR COURSE (SEE ALSO CH.1)
Universities and colleges teaching quality See www.qaa.ac.uk; http://unistats.direct.gov.uk.

Top research universities and colleges (REF 2014) (Modern Languages and Linguistics) London (QM) (Ling); Queen Margaret; Edinburgh (Ling); Kent; York; Queen's Belfast; Southampton; Cardiff; Essex; Warwick; Glasgow (Celt St); Cambridge; Manchester; London (RH).

Examples of sandwich degree courses Leeds; Nottingham Trent; Westminster.

ADMISSIONS INFORMATION
Number of applicants per place (approx) Bangor 3; Cambridge 3; Essex 1; Lancaster 12; Leeds 12; London (UCL) 4; York 11.

Advice to applicants and planning the UCAS personal statement Give details of your interests in language and how it works, and about your knowledge of languages and their similarities and differences.

Selection interviews Yes Brighton, Cambridge, Essex, Lancaster; **Some** Newcastle, Sheffield.

Interview advice and questions Past questions include: Why do you want to study linguistics? What does the subject involve? What do you intend to do at the end of your degree course? What answer do you give to your parents or friends when they ask why you want to study the subject? How and why does language vary according to sex, age, social background and regional origins? See also **Chapter 5**.

Reasons for rejection (non-academic) Lack of knowledge of linguistics. Hesitation about the period to be spent abroad.

AFTER-RESULTS ADVICE
Offers to applicants repeating A-levels Higher Essex; **Same** Brighton, Leeds, Newcastle, York.

GRADUATE DESTINATIONS AND EMPLOYMENT (2013/14 HESA)
Graduates surveyed 610 **Employed** 35 **In voluntary employment** 30 **In further study** 145 **Assumed unemployed** 35

Career note Students enter a wide range of careers, with information management and editorial work in publishing offering some interesting and useful outlets.

OTHER DEGREE SUBJECTS FOR CONSIDERATION
Cognitive Science; Communication Studies; Education Studies; English; Psychology; Speech Sciences.

Check **Chapter 3** for new university admission details and **Chapter 6** on how to read the subject tables.

LITERATURE

(see also **English**)

This is a very broad subject introducing many aspects of the study of literature and aesthetics. Courses will vary in content. Degree courses in English and foreign languages will also include a study of literature.

Useful websites www.lrb.co.uk; www.literature.org; www.bibliomania.com; www.bl.uk; www.acla.org

NB The points totals shown to the left of the institutions are for ease of reference only. It must not be assumed that Tariff points are always used by institutions or that they can be substituted for an offer in grades. The level of an offer is not necessarily indicative of the quality of a course.

COURSE OFFERS INFORMATION

Subject requirements/preferences GCSE English and a foreign language usually required. **AL** English may be required or preferred for some courses.

Ulster (Ir Lang Lit) Applicants need at least grade B (or equivalent) in A-level Irish.

Your target offers and examples of degree courses

152 pts Durham – A*AA incl hist+Engl lit (Engl Lit Hist) (IB 38 pts); A*AA incl Engl lit
(Engl Lit; Engl Lit Phil) (IB 38 pts)

144 pts Edinburgh – AAA–ABB (Engl Lit; Scot Lit) (IB 40–34 pts)
Lancaster – AAA–AAB incl Engl (Thea Engl Lit) (IB 36–35 pts HL 6 Engl); (Engl Lit; Film Engl
Lit) (IB 36–35 pts HL 6 lit); AAA–AAB (Engl Lang Lit) (IB 36–35 pts)
Leeds – AAA incl Engl (Engl Lang Lit) (IB 35 pts HL 6 Engl)
London (King's) – AAA incl Engl+lang (Compar Lit; Compar Lit Film St) (IB 35 pts HL
6 Engl lit)
Manchester – AAA–AAB incl Engl (Engl Lit courses) (IB 37–35 pts HL 7 Engl)
Newcastle – AAA–AAB incl Engl (Engl Lit Joint Hons; Engl Lit; Engl Lang Lit) (IB 36–35 pts
HL 6 Engl)
Nottingham – AAA–AAB incl Engl (Engl Lang Lit) (IB 36–34 pts)
Oxford – AAA (Engl Lang Lit) (IB 38 pts)
Warwick – AAA/A*AB incl Engl lit (Engl Lit) (IB 38 pts HL 6 Engl); AAA incl Engl
(Engl Lit Crea Writ) (IB 38 pts HL 6 Engl)

136 pts Cardiff – AAB incl Engl lit (Engl Lit) (IB 36 pts); AAB (Jrnl Media Engl Lit) (IB 36 pts)
East Anglia – AAB incl Engl (Engl Lit; Engl Lit Joint Hons) (IB 33 pts HL 5 Engl); AAB
(Am Engl Lit) (IB 33 pts HL 5 Engl); (Am Lit Crea Writ) (IB 33 pts)
Edinburgh – AAB–ABB (Celt Scot Lit) (IB 36–34 pts)
Glasgow – AAB–BBB (Compar Lit Joint Hons) (IB 36–34 pts); AAB–BBB incl arts/lang
(Engl Lit; Scot Lit) (IB 36–34 pts)
Leeds – AAB incl Engl (Class Lit courses) (IB 35 pts HL 6 Engl)
London (Gold) – AAB (Am Lit) (IB 34 pts)
Sheffield – AAB–ABB incl Engl (Engl Lang Lit; Engl Lit; Bib Lit Engl) (IB 35 pts HL 6 Engl)
Surrey – AAB–ABB incl Engl (Engl Lit; Engl Lit Crea Writ) (IB 35–34 pts)
Sussex – AAB–ABB incl Engl (Engl Lang Lit) (IB 34 pts HL 6 Engl)
Warwick – AAB incl Engl lit+lang (Engl Ital Lit; Engl Ger Lit) (IB 36 pts HL 5 Engl lit+lang);
AAB incl Engl (Film Lit) (IB 36 pts HL 6 Engl)

128 pts East Anglia – ABB (Lit Hist; Cult Lit Pol) (IB 32 pts HL 5 Engl)
Essex – ABB–BBB (Film St Lit; Lit Art Hist; Dr Lit; Engl Lit; Engl Lang Lit) (IB 32–30 pts)
Huddersfield – ABB incl Engl 128 pts (Engl Lit; Engl Lit Crea Writ)
Kent – ABB (Compar Lit; Wrld Lit) (IB 34 pts); ABB incl Engl (Engl Am Postcol Lit; Engl Lang
Ling Engl Am Lit; Contemp Lit) (IB 34 pts)

London (Gold) – ABB (Engl Compar Lit) (IB 33 pts)
London (QM) – ABB–AAB incl Engl 128–136 pts (Engl Lit Ling) (IB 34 pts HL 6 Engl);
ABB incl hist 128 pts (Hist Compar Lit) (IB 34 pts HL 5 hist)
London (RH) – ABB (Comp Lit Cult Span; Compar Lit Cult) (IB 32 pts)
Northumbria – 128 pts incl Engl/hist (Engl Lit Hist) (IB 31 pts HL 5 Engl/hist); 128 pts incl
Engl (Engl Lit; Engl Lang Lit; Engl Lit Crea Writ; Jrnl Engl Lit) (IB 31 pts HL 5 Engl)
Nottingham – ABB (Am Can Lit Hist Cult) (IB 32 pts)
Reading – ABB–BBB (Engl Lit Film Thea) (IB 32–30 pts); (Engl Lang Engl Lit)
(IB 33–30 pts)
Roehampton – ABB incl Engl 128 pts (Engl Lit)
Winchester – 128–144 pts (Engl Am Lit) (IB 27 pts)
120 pts Aberdeen – BBB (Engl Scot Lit; Lit Wrld Cntxt courses) (IB 30 pts); (Langs Lit Scot) (IB 32
pts)
Aberystwyth – 120 pts incl Engl (Engl Lit Crea Writ; Engl Lit)
Buckingham – BBB (Engl Lit Hist; Engl Lit courses)
East London – 120 pts (Engl Lit) (IB 26 pts)
Edge Hill – BBB 120 pts (Engl Lit)
Gloucestershire – 120 pts (Engl Lit)
Greenwich – 120 pts (Engl Lit)
Kingston – 120 pts (Engl Lit) (IB 30 pts)
Leeds Beckett – 120 pts (Engl Lit) (IB 26 pts)
London (QM) – 120–136 pts (Compar Lit courses) (IB 32–34 pts); 120–128 pts incl lang
(Ger Compar Lit) (IB 32–34 pts HL 5 lang)
Sheffield Hallam – 120 pts incl Engl lit (Engl Lit)
Sunderland – 120 pts (Engl Lang Lit)
Swansea – BBB–BBC incl Engl (Engl Lit Lang St) (IB 32–30 pts)
York – BBB (Engl Educ) (IB 31 pts)
112 pts Bangor – 112–120 pts incl Engl (Engl Lit Engl Lang) (IB 26 pts)
Bath Spa – 112–128 pts incl Engl lit (Engl Lit)
Birmingham City – BBC incl Engl 112 pts (Engl Lit courses) (IB 26 pts)
Brighton – BBC (Hist Lit Cult) (IB 28 pts); BBC incl Engl lit/lit+lang (Media Engl Lit)
(IB 28 pts); BBC incl Engl lit (Engl Lit) (IB 28 pts)
Hertfordshire – 112 pts (Engl Lit Ital; Engl Lit) (IB 28 pts)
Hull – 112 pts (Engl Am Lit Cult) (IB 28 pts)
London Met – 112 pts (Engl Lit)
Westminster – BBC incl Engl (Engl Lit Hist) (IB 30 pts HL 5 Engl)
York St John – 112 pts (Engl Lit; Crea Writ)
104 pts Bangor – 104–120 pts (Ling Engl Lit)
Central Lancashire – 104 pts (Engl Lit) (IB 28 pts)
Liverpool Hope – BCC–BBB 104–120 pts (Engl Lit)
Manchester Met – 104–112 pts (Engl Am Lit) (IB 26 pts)
Worcester – 104–112 pts (Engl Lit courses)
96 pts Bishop Grosseteste – 96–112 pts (Engl courses)
Portsmouth – 96–120 pts incl Engl (Engl Lit courses)
88 pts Anglia Ruskin – 88–104 pts incl Engl (Writ Engl Lit) (IB 28 pts HL 4 Engl); 88–104 pts
(Phil Engl Lit; Dr Engl Lit) (IB 24 pts)
64 pts UHI – CC incl Engl (Lit)

Alternative offers
See **Chapter 6** and **Appendix 1** for grades/new UCAS Tariff points information for other
examinations.

CHOOSING YOUR COURSE (SEE ALSO CH.1)
Universities and colleges teaching quality See www.qaa.ac.uk; http://unistats.direct.gov.uk.

Top research universities and colleges (REF 2014) See **English**.

Check **Chapter 3** for new university admission details and **Chapter 6** on how to read the subject tables.

ADMISSIONS INFORMATION

Number of applicants per place (approx) East Anglia 12; Essex 4.

Advice to applicants and planning the UCAS personal statement See **English**. **Kent** An interest in literatures other than English.

Misconceptions about this course Kent Some students think that a foreign language is required – it is not.

Interview advice and questions See **English**. See also **Chapter 5**. **Kent** Which book would you take on a desert island, and why? What is the point of doing a Literature degree in the 21st century?

Reasons for rejection (non-academic) Kent Perceived inability to think on their feet.

GRADUATE DESTINATIONS AND EMPLOYMENT (2013/14 HESA)
See **English**.

Career note Students enter a wide range of careers, with information management and editorial work in publishing offering some interesting and useful outlets. See also **English**, **Linguistics** and **Celtic, Irish, Scottish and Welsh Studies**.

MARINE/MARITIME STUDIES

(including **Marine Biology, Marine Engineering** and **Oceanography**; see also **Environmental Sciences, Naval Architecture**)

A wide range of courses come in this category. These include Marine Business; Marine Law – world shipping, transport of goods, shipbroking, salvage rights, piracy; Marine Technology – marine engineering/nautical design; Marine Technology Offshore Engineering – marine structures, oil rigs, offshore engineering; Navigation Marine Science – merchant navy, yachts, superyachts; Naval Architecture with High Performance Crafts – design, construction, operation, large and small vessels, hydrofoils, hovercrafts; Shipping Port Management – international shipping, shipbroking, ship agency work; Yacht and Powercraft Design – powerboats, yachts, superyachts. Other scientific courses eg marine applications with biology, chemistry, freshwater biology, geography.

Useful websites www.ukchamberofshipping.com; uksa.org; www.rya.org.uk; www.royalnavy.mod.uk; www.sstg.org; www.noc.soton.ac.uk; www.nautinst.org; www.mcsuk.org; www.nmm.ac.uk; www.imo. org; www.mcga.gov.uk; www.cefas.defra.gov.uk; www.mba.ac.uk

NB The points totals shown to the left of the institutions are for ease of reference only. It must not be assumed that Tariff points are always used by institutions or that they can be substituted for an offer in grades. The level of an offer is not necessarily indicative of the quality of a course.

COURSE OFFERS INFORMATION

Subject requirements/preferences GCSE Mathematics and science are required for several courses. **AL** Science or Mathematics will be required or preferred for some courses.

Your target offers and examples of degree courses

144 pts **Cardiff** – AAA (Mar Geog (Int)) (IB 34 pts)
    Strathclyde – AAA–AAB incl maths+phys (Nvl Archit Ocn Eng MEng) (IB 36 pts HL 6 maths+phys)

136 pts **Cardiff** – AAB (Mar Geog MESci) (IB 33–32 pts)
    East Anglia – AAB/ABBB incl maths (Meteor Ocean MSci; Meteor Ocean (Yr Abrd)) (IB 33 pts HL 6 maths)
    Glasgow – AAB–BBB incl biol/chem (Mar Frshwtr Biol) (IB 36–34 pts)
    Newcastle – AAB–ABB incl biol+sci (Mar Biol; Mar Biol Ocean) (IB 35–34 pts HL 6 biol); AAB incl maths (Mar Tech Off Eng MEng) (IB 36 pts HL 5 maths+phys); AAB–ABB incl maths (Mar Tech Mar Eng; Mar Tech Sml Crft Tech) (IB 35–34 pts HL 5 maths+phys)

New UCAS points Tariff: A* = 56 pts; A = 48 pts; B = 40 pts; C = 32 pts; D = 24 pts; E = 16 pts

St Andrews – AAB incl biol+sci/maths (Mar Biol) (IB 36 pts)

Southampton – AAB incl sci/maths/geog (Ocean Fr; Mar Biol) (IB 34 pts); AAB–ABB incl geog (Physl Geog Ocean) (IB 34–32 pts)

128 pts Cardiff – ABB (Mar Geog) (IB 32–30 pts)

East Anglia – ABB incl maths (Meteor Ocean) (IB 32 pts HL 5 maths)

Essex – ABB–BBB (Mar Biol) (IB 32–30 pts)

Liverpool – ABB incl biol+sci/maths/geog (Mar Biol Ocean) (IB 33 pts HL 5 biol)

Plymouth – 128 pts (Mar Biol Cstl Ecol) (IB 30 pts); ABB incl biol+sci 128 pts (Mar Biol Ocean) (IB 30 pts)

Southampton – ABB incl sci/maths/geog (Ocean) (IB 32 pts); ABB incl geog+sci/maths (Ocean Physl Geog) (IB 32 pts); ABB incl biol+sci/maths/geog (Mar Biol Ocean) (IB 32 pts)

Strathclyde – ABB–BBB incl maths+phys (Nvl Archit Mar Eng; Nvl Archit Ocn Eng) (IB 32 pts HL 5 maths+phys)

120 pts Aberdeen – BBB incl maths/sci (Mar Biol) (IB 32 pts HL 5 maths/sci)

Bangor – 120 pts (App Ter Mar Ecol); 120–136 pts incl phys/maths+sci (Ocean Comp)

Heriot-Watt – BBB incl sci (Mar Biol) (IB 27 pts HL 5 biol)

Liverpool – BBB incl sci (Ocn Sci) (IB 30 pts)

Plymouth – 120 pts incl maths+sci/tech (Mar Tech) (IB 28 pts); 120 pts (Ocn Sci)

Portsmouth – 120 pts incl biol (Mar Biol) (IB 30 pts HL 17 pts incl 6 biol)

Queen's Belfast – BBB–ABB incl biol+sci/maths/geog (Mar Biol)

Stirling – BBB (Mar Biol) (IB 32 pts)

116 pts Aberystwyth – 116–132 pts incl biol (Mar Frshwtr Biol)

112 pts Bangor – 112–136 pts incl biol (Mar Biol Ocean); 112–128 pts incl sci (Mar Env St; Ocn Sci; Geol Ocean; Mar Geog); 112–128 pts incl biol+sci (App Mar Biol)

Hull – 112 pts incl biol (Mar Biol) (IB 30 pts)

Liverpool John Moores – 112 pts (Marit St; Marit Bus Mgt)

Plymouth – 112 pts (Marit Bus Log; Marit Bus Marit Law); 112–104 pts (Ocn Explor Surv)

104 pts Edinburgh Napier – BCC incl sci (Mar Frshwtr Biol) (IB 28 pts HL 5 sci)

Falmouth – 104–120 pts +portfolio +interview (Mar Nat Hist Photo)

Portsmouth – 104–128 pts incl sci/maths (Mar Env Sci) (IB 26 pts HL 5 sci)

UHI – BCC incl sci (Mar Sci)

96 pts Aberdeen – 96 pts (Mar Cstl Res Mgt Mar Biol)

Anglia Ruskin – 96 pts incl biol (Mar Biol Cons Biodiv) (IB 24 pts HL biol)

Plymouth – 96 pts (Mar Cmpste Tech)

Southampton Solent – 96 pts (Geog Mar St; Ycht Des Prod; Ship Pt Mgt)

80 pts Plymouth – 80–112 pts (Navig Marit Sci) (IB 24 pts)

Alternative offers

See **Chapter 6** and **Appendix 1** for grades/new UCAS Tariff points information for other examinations.

EXAMPLES OF COLLEGES OFFERING COURSES IN THIS SUBJECT FIELD

Blackpool and Fylde (Coll); Cornwall (Coll); Plymouth City (Coll); South Devon (Coll); South Tyneside (Coll); Southampton City (Coll); Sparsholt (Coll).

CHOOSING YOUR COURSE (SEE ALSO CH.1)

Universities and colleges teaching quality See www.qaa.ac.uk; http://unistats.direct.gov.uk.

Examples of sandwich degree courses Anglia Ruskin; Bangor; Cardiff; Essex; Liverpool John Moores; Plymouth; Portsmouth; Southampton Solent.

ADMISSIONS INFORMATION

Number of applicants per place (approx) Glasgow 2; Liverpool John Moores (Marit St) 3; Southampton 6; Southampton Solent (Ocean) 6, (Ocn Chem) 6.

Advice to applicants and planning the UCAS personal statement This is a specialised field and, in many cases, applicants will have experience of marine activities. Describe these experiences, for example, sailing, snorkelling, fishing. See also **Appendix 3**.

Selection interviews Yes Southampton, UHI.

Interview advice and questions Most applicants will have been stimulated by their studies in science or will have strong interests or connections with marine activities. They are likely to be questioned on their reasons for choosing the course. See also **Chapter 5**.

AFTER-RESULTS ADVICE

Offers to applicants repeating A-levels Same Bangor, Liverpool John Moores, Plymouth, UHI.

GRADUATE DESTINATIONS AND EMPLOYMENT (2013/14 HESA)

Maritime Technology graduates surveyed 250 **Employed** 160 **In voluntary employment** 0 **In further study** 40 **Assumed unemployed** 10

Career note This subject area covers a wide range of vocational courses, each offering graduates an equally wide choice of career openings in either purely scientific or very practical areas.

OTHER DEGREE SUBJECTS FOR CONSIDERATION

Biology; Civil Engineering; Environmental Studies/Sciences; Geography; Marine Engineering; Marine Transport; Naval Architecture; Oceanography.

MARKETING

(including **Public Relations**; see also **Business and Management Courses, Business and Management Courses (International and European), Business and Management Courses (Specialised), Retail Management**)

Marketing courses are very popular and applications should include evidence of work experience or work shadowing. Whilst Marketing is also a subject included in all Business Studies courses, specialist marketing courses are also available focussing on Advertising (also included in Marketing and Graphic Design courses), Agriculture, Consumer Behaviour, Design, Fashion, Food, Leisure, Retail and Sport.

Useful websites www.adassoc.org.uk; www.cim.co.uk; www.camfoundation.com; www.ipa.co.uk; www.ipsos-mori.com; www.marketingtoday.com

NB The points totals shown to the left of the institutions are for ease of reference only. It must not be assumed that Tariff points are always used by institutions or that they can be substituted for an offer in grades. The level of an offer is not necessarily indicative of the quality of a course.

COURSE OFFERS INFORMATION

Subject requirements/preferences GCSE English and mathematics. **AL** No specified subjects required.

Your target offers and examples of degree courses
152 pts Lancaster – A*AA–AAA (Mark (St Abrd); Mark Mgt (St Abrd)) (IB 38–36 pts)
144 pts Exeter – AAA–AAB (Mgt Mark) (IB 36–34 pts)
       Leeds – AAA (Mgt Mark) (IB 35 pts)
136 pts Aston – AAB–ABB (Mark) (IB 35–34 pts)
       Cardiff – AAB (Bus Mgt (Mark)) (IB 35 pts)
       Durham – AAB (Mark) (IB 36 pts)
       Lancaster – AAB (Mark Mgt) (IB 34 pts); (Adv Mark; Mark Des; Mark) (IB 35 pts)
       Loughborough – AAB–ABB (Rtl Mark Mgt) (IB 34 pts)
       Manchester – AAB (Mgt (Mark); Fash Mark) (IB 35 pts)
       Newcastle – AAB (Mark; Mark Mgt) (IB 35 pts)

Southampton – AAB–ABB (Mark; Int Mark) (IB 34 pts)

Sussex – AAB–ABB (Mark Mgt) (IB 34 pts)

128 pts **Coventry** – ABB (Mark; Adv Mark) (IB 30 pts)

Essex – ABB–BBB (Mark) (IB 32–30 pts); ABB–ABB (Mgt Mark) (IB 32–30 pts)

Kent – ABB (Evnt Expnc Des; Mark) (IB 34 pts)

Liverpool – ABB (Mark) (IB 33 pts)

London (RH) – ABB (Mgt Mark) (IB 32 pts)

Northumbria – 128 pts (Fash Des Mark) (IB 31 pts); ABB 128 pts (Mark Mgt) (IB 31 pts)

Reading – ABB/AAC (Consum Bhv Mark) (IB 35–32 pts); ABB–BBB (Fd Mark Bus Econ)
(IB 32–30 pts)

Strathclyde – ABB–BBB (Mark courses) (IB 33 pts)

Swansea – ABB–BBB (Bus Mgt (Mark)) (IB 33–32 pts)

Ulster – ABB–AAB (Comm Adv Mark) (IB 27–28 pts)

120 pts **Birmingham City** – BBB 120 pts (Mark Adv PR) (IB 30 pts)

Bournemouth – 120–128 pts (Mark) (IB 31–32 pts)

Bradford – BBB 120 pts (Mark)

Buckingham – BBB–BBC (Mark Media Comms; Mark Psy; Mark Span; Mark Joint courses)

Coventry – BBB (Spo Mark) (IB 29 pts)

De Montfort – 120 pts (Mark) (IB 28 pts)

Dundee – BBB–BCC (Int Bus Mark) (IB 30 pts); BBB–BCC incl sci/maths (Bus Econ Mark Hist;
Bus Econ Mark) (IB 30 pts)

Edge Hill – BBB 120 pts (Mark)

Heriot-Watt – BBB (Bus Mgt Mark) (IB 29 pts)

Huddersfield – BBB 120 pts (Adv Mark Comm; Mark; Mark PR; Spo Sci); BBB 120 pts
+portfolio +interview (Fash Comm Prom)

Keele – BBB/ABC (Mark courses) (IB 32 pts)

Leeds Beckett – 120 pts (Mark; Mark Adv Mgt) (IB 26 pts)

Northumbria – BBB 120 pts (Bus Mark Mgt) (IB 30 pts); 120 pts (Adv) (IB 30 pts)

Nottingham Trent – 120 pts (Fash Comm Prom; Fash Mark Brnd; Mark)

Oxford Brookes – BBB (Bus Mark Mgt) (IB 31 pts)

Sheffield Hallam – 120 pts (Bus Mark; Mark; Mark Comms Adv)

Southampton (Winchester SA) – BBB (Fash Mark) (IB 30 pts)

Staffordshire – BBB 120 pts (Bus Mark Mgt)

Stirling – BBB (Mark; Rtl Mark) (IB 32 pts)

Trinity Saint David – 120 pts (Adv Brnd Des) (IB 32 pts)

Ulster – BBB (Law Mark) (IB 26 pts); BBB–ABB (Mark) (IB 26–27 pts)

UWE Bristol – 120 pts (Mark Comms) (IB 26 pts)

Westminster – BBB (PR Adv) (IB 28 pts)

112 pts **Aberystwyth** – 112 pts (Mark)

Birmingham City – BBC 112 pts (Mark) (IB 28 pts)

Bournemouth – 112–120 pts (Adv) (IB 30–31 pts)

Brighton – BBC (Mark) (IB 28 pts)

Canterbury Christ Church – 112 pts (Mark; Adv)

Cardiff Met – 112 pts (Mark Mgt)

Central Lancashire – 112 pts (Mark Mgt) (IB 28 pts)

Chester – BBC–BCC 112 pts (Adv; Mark PR; Mark Mgt) (IB 26 pts)

Chichester – 112–128 pts (Mark) (IB 30 pts)

Creative Arts – 112 pts (Fash Mgt Mark; Adv)

De Montfort – 112 pts (Int Mark Bus; Adv Mark Comms) (IB 28 pts)

Derby – 112 pts (Mark courses; Mark (PR Adv))

East London – 112 pts +interview +portfolio (Fash Mark) (IB 24 pts); 112 pts (Bus Mgt
(Mark)) (IB 24 pts)

Edge Hill – BBC 112 pts (Adv)

Glasgow Caledonian – BBC (Int Mark) (IB 25 pts)

Gloucestershire – 112 pts (Adv)

Greenwich – 112 pts (Adv Mark Comms; Mark; Adv Mark Comm Lang)

Hull – 112 pts (Mark) (IB 30 pts)

Lincoln – 112 pts (Mark; Bus Mark; Adv Mark)

Liverpool John Moores – 112 pts (Mark; Bus PR) (IB 29 pts)

London Met – 112 pts (Mark Comms; Fash Mark Bus Mgt; Fash Mark Jrnl; Adv Mark Comms PR)

Middlesex – 112 pts (Adv PR Media)

Northampton – 112 pts (Mark Joint Hons; Evnts Mgt Joint Hons; Adv Joint Hons)

Plymouth – 112 pts (Mark)

Portsmouth – 112 pts (Mark; Mark Psy) (IB 30 pts HL 17 pts)

Roehampton – 112 pts (Mark)

Southampton Solent – 112 pts (Adv; PR Comm)

Sunderland – 112 pts (Bus Mark Mgt; Adv Des; Fash Prod Prom)

West London – 112 pts (Bus St Mark)

Westminster – BBC (Mark Comms; Mark Mgt) (IB 28 pts)

Worcester – 112 pts (Bus Mark PR; Bus Mark HR Mgt; Mark courses; Bus Mark Adv; Adv courses)

York St John – 112 pts (Tour Mgt Mark; Mark Mgt)

104 pts   **Bangor** – 104–120 pts (Mark)

Bath Spa – 104–120 pts (Bus Mgt (Mark))

Falmouth – 104–120 pts (Crea Adv)

Harper Adams – 104–120 pts (Agric Mark)

Leeds (CA) – 104 pts +portfolio (Crea Adv)

Leeds Trinity – 104 pts (Media Mark)

Liverpool Hope – BCC–BBB 104–120 pts (Mark)

Manchester Met – BCC–BBC 104–112 pts (Int Fash Prom) (IB 25 pts); (Dig Media Mark; Mark Mgt; Rtl Mgt Mark; PR Mark) (IB 26 pts); 104–112 pts (Spo Mark Mgt) (IB 26 pts)

Middlesex – 104 pts (Mark)

Northampton – 104–120 pts (Psy Mark); 104–112 pts (Fash Mark)

Queen Margaret – BCC 104 pts (PR Mark Evnts) (IB 28 pts)

Robert Gordon – BCC (Mgt Mark) (IB 28 pts)

South Wales – BCC (Mark; Fash Mark Rtl Des) (IB 29 pts); BCC incl art des +portfolio (Fash Prom) (IB 29 pts); BCC incl art des (Adv Des) (IB 29 pts)

Ulster – 104–120 pts (Adv courses; Adv HR Mgt; HR Mgt Mark) (IB 24 pts)

Westminster – BCC (Bus Mgt (Mark)) (IB 28 pts)

Winchester – 104–120 pts (Media Comm Adv) (IB 26 pts)

96 pts   **Abertay** – CCC (Mark Bus) (IB 28 pts)

Anglia Ruskin – 96–112 pts (Mark) (IB 24 pts)

Bedfordshire – 96 pts (Mark) (IB 24 pts)

Birmingham (UC) – 96 pts (Mark Mgt; Mark Evnts Mgt)

Bournemouth – 96–112 pts (Evnts Leis Mark) (IB 26–30 pts)

Edinburgh Napier – CCC (Mark Mgt Consum St; Mark Mgt; Mark Dig Media) (IB 27 pts)

Hertfordshire – 96–112 pts (Mark Adv; Mark) (IB 28 pts)

London South Bank – CCC 96 pts (Bus Mgt Mark; Mark)

Manchester Met – 96–112 pts (Mark Comb Hons) (IB 28 pts)

Southampton Solent – 96 pts (Mark; Mark Adv Mgt; Fash Prom Comm)

Teesside – 96 pts (Mark)

West Scotland – CCC (Mark) (IB 24 pts)

Wolverhampton – 96–112 pts (Mark Mgt)

88 pts   **Creative Arts** – 88 pts (Fash Prom Imag)

Harper Adams – 88–104 pts (Bus Mgt Mark; Agri-Fd Mark Bus St)

80 pts   **Bedfordshire** – 80 pts (PR; Adv Mark Comms) (IB 24 pts)

Bucks New – 80–96 pts (Mark)

Plymouth (CA) – 80 pts +portfolio (Crea Adv Brnd)

New UCAS points Tariff: A* = 56 pts; A = 48 pts; B = 40 pts; C = 32 pts; D = 24 pts; E = 16 pts

64 pts **Ravensbourne** – CC (Fash Prom) (IB 28 pts)
      Trinity Saint David – 64 pts (Mark Mgt)

Alternative offers
See **Chapter 6** and **Appendix 1** for grades/new UCAS Tariff points information for other examinations.

EXAMPLES OF COLLEGES OFFERING COURSES IN THIS SUBJECT FIELD

Arts London (CFash); Bath (Coll); Birmingham Met (Coll); Blackpool and Fylde (Coll); Bradford (Coll); CAFRE; Croydon (Univ Centre); Doncaster (Coll); ESE; Grimsby (Univ Centre); Kensington Bus (Coll); Leeds City (Coll); LeSoCo; London UCK (Coll); Loughborough (Coll); LSAS; LSST; Manchester (Coll); Newcastle (Coll); North Shropshire (Coll); Northbrook (Coll); Nottingham New (Coll); Pearson (Coll); Peterborough (Coll); Petroc; Plymouth City (Coll); South City Birmingham (Coll); South Essex (Coll); Suffolk (Univ Campus); Wakefield (Coll); Warwickshire (Coll); Yeovil (Coll).

CHOOSING YOUR COURSE (SEE ALSO CH.1)

Universities and colleges teaching quality See www.qaa.ac.uk; http://unistats.direct.gov.uk.

Examples of sandwich degree courses Aston; Bath Spa; Bedfordshire; Birmingham City; Bournemouth; Bradford; Brighton; Brunel; Cardiff Met; Central Lancashire; Chichester; Coventry; De Montfort; Derby; Durham; Gloucestershire; Greenwich; Harper Adams; Hertfordshire; Huddersfield; Lancaster; Leeds Beckett; Liverpool John Moores; London (RH); London South Bank; Loughborough; Manchester Met; Newcastle; Northumbria; Nottingham Trent; Oxford Brookes; Plymouth; Portsmouth; Sheffield Hallam; Southampton Solent; Staffordshire; Sussex; Teesside; Trinity Saint David; Ulster; UWE Bristol; Westminster; Wolverhampton; Worcester.

ADMISSIONS INFORMATION

Number of applicants per place (approx) Abertay 6; Aberystwyth 3; Anglia Ruskin 5; Aston 9; Birmingham City 4; Bournemouth 10; Brunel 10; Central Lancashire 13; De Montfort 3; Derby 5; Glasgow Caledonian 15; Harper Adams 3; Huddersfield 7; Lancaster 28; Lincoln 3; London Met 10; Manchester 7; Northampton 4; Northumbria 8; Nottingham Trent 2; Plymouth 12; Portsmouth 4; Staffordshire 6; Stirling 10; Teesside 3.

Advice to applicants and planning the UCAS personal statement See **Business and Management Courses** and **Appendix 3**.

Selection interviews **Yes** Harper Adams, Middlesex; **Some** Aberystwyth, Anglia Ruskin, Aston, Buckingham, De Montfort, Manchester Met, Staffordshire; **No** Essex.

Interview advice and questions Past questions include: What is marketing? Why do you want to take a Marketing degree? Is sales pressure justified? How would you feel if you had to market a product which you considered to be inferior? See also **Chapter 5**. **Buckingham** What job do you see yourself doing in five years' time?

Reasons for rejection (non-academic) Little thought of reasons for deciding on a Marketing degree. Weak on numeracy and problem-solving. Limited commercial awareness. Poor inter-personal skills. Lack of leadership potential. No interest in widening their horizons, either geographically or intellectually. 'We look at appearance, motivation and the applicant's ability to ask questions.' Not hungry enough. Limited understanding of the career. No clear reasons for wishing to do the course.

AFTER-RESULTS ADVICE

Offers to applicants repeating A-levels **Same** Abertay, Aberystwyth, Anglia Ruskin, Aston, Buckingham, De Montfort, Lincoln, Manchester Met, Queen Margaret, Staffordshire.

GRADUATE DESTINATIONS AND EMPLOYMENT (2013/14 HESA)

Graduates surveyed 3,450 **Employed** 2405 **In voluntary employment** 145 **In further study** 235 **Assumed unemployed** 210

Career note See **Business and Management Courses**.

OTHER DEGREE SUBJECTS FOR CONSIDERATION
Advertising; Art and Design; Business courses; Communications; Graphic Design; Psychology; Public Relations.

MATERIALS SCIENCE/METALLURGY

Materials Science is a broad subject which covers physics, chemistry and engineering at one and the same time! From its origins in metallurgy, materials science has now moved into the processing, structure and properties of materials – ceramics, polymers, composites and electrical materials. Materials science and metallurgy are perhaps the most misunderstood of all careers and applications for degree courses are low with very reasonable offers. Valuable bursaries and scholarships are offered by the Institute of Materials, Minerals and Mining (check with Institute – see **Appendix 3**). Polymer Science is a branch of materials science and is often studied in conjunction with Chemistry and covers such topics as polymer properties and processing relating to industrial applications with, for example, plastics, paints, adhesives. Other courses under this heading include Fashion and Leather Technology. See also **Appendix 3**.

Useful websites www.eef.org.uk/uksteel; www.iom3.org; www.epsrc.ac.uk; www.imm.org; www.icme.org.uk

NB The points totals shown to the left of the institutions are for ease of reference only. It must not be assumed that Tariff points are always used by institutions or that they can be substituted for an offer in grades. The level of an offer is not necessarily indicative of the quality of a course.

COURSE OFFERS INFORMATION

Subject requirements/preferences GCSE (Eng/Sci courses) Science/mathematics subjects. **AL** Mathematics, Physics and/or Chemistry required for most courses. (Poly Sci) Mathematics and/or Physics usually required; Design Technology encouraged.

Your target offers and examples of degree courses

160 pts Cambridge – A*A*A incl sci/maths (Nat Sci (Mat Sci)) (IB 40–41 pts HL 776)

152 pts Imperial London – A*AA incl maths+phys (Mat Sci Eng) (IB 38 pts HL 6 maths+phys); A*AA incl maths+ phys (Mat courses) (IB 38 pts HL 6 maths+phys); A*AA incl maths+phys (Mat Mgt) (IB 38 pts HL 6 maths+phys)

Oxford – A*AA incl maths+phys (Mat Sci) (IB 40 pts)

Southampton – A*AA incl maths/phys (Mech Eng (Advnc Mat) MEng) (IB 38 pts HL 6 maths+phys)

144 pts Birmingham – AAA incl maths+phys/chem/des tech (Mat Eng; Mat Sci Eng Bus Mgt MEng) (IB 32 pts HL 666)

Exeter – AAA–ABB incl maths+sci (Mat Eng; Mat Eng MEng) (IB 36–32 pts HL 5 maths+sci)

Imperial London – AAA incl maths+phys (Biomat Tiss Eng; Aerosp Mat) (IB 38 pts HL 6 maths+phys)

Liverpool – AAA incl maths+sci (Mech Mat Eng MEng) (IB 35 pts HL 5 maths+phys)

London (QM) – AAA incl sci/maths (Mat Sci Eng MEng (Yr Ind); Mat Sci MEng) (IB 36 pts HL 6 sci/maths); AAA incl maths/phys/chem (Dntl Mat MEng) (IB 36 pts HL 6 maths/phys/chem)

Loughborough – AAA incl maths/sci/des (Des Eng Mat MEng) (IB 36 pts); AAA incl maths/phys/chem (Mat Eng MEng; Auto Mat MEng) (IB 36 pts)

Sheffield – AAA–AAB incl sci/maths (Mat Sci Eng (Biomat) MEng) (IB 37 pts HL 6 sci/maths); AAA–AAB incl maths/phys/chem (Mat Sci Eng (Ind Mgt) MEng; Mat Sci Eng MEng) (IB 37 pts HL 6 maths/phys/chem); AAA incl maths/phys/chem (Metal) (IB 37 pts IB 6 maths/phys/chem)

Southampton – AAA incl maths+phys (Ship Sci (Advncd Mat) MEng) (IB 36 pts HL 6 maths+phys)

136 pts **Birmingham** – AAB incl maths/sci/des tech (Spo Mat Sci) (IB 32 pts HL 665); AAB incl maths+phys (Nucl Sci Mat) (IB 32 pts HL 665); AAB incl maths+phys/chem/des tech (Mat Sci Ener Eng; Mat Sci Eng Bus Mgt; Metal) (IB 32 pts HL 665)

Exeter – AAB–BBB incl phys/chem+sci (Min Eng) (IB 34–30 pts)

Loughborough – AAB incl maths+sci (Biomat Eng) (IB 34 pts HL 5 maths+sci); AAB incl maths/phys/chem (Mat Eng; Auto Mat) (IB 34 pts)

Manchester – AAB (Mat Sci Eng) (IB 35 pts)

St Andrews – AAB incl chem (Mat Chem) (IB 35 pts)

Sheffield – AAB–ABB incl maths+phys (Aerosp Mat) (IB 35 pts HL 6 maths+phys); AAB–ABB incl maths/phys/chem (Mat Sci Eng (Ind Mgt); Mat Sci Eng) (IB 35 pts HL 6 maths/phys/chem); AAB–ABB incl sci/maths (Mat Sci Eng (Biomat)) (IB 35 pts HL 6 sci/maths); AAB (Mat Sci Eng (Modn Lang)) (IB 35 pts)

Strathclyde – AAB–BBB (Mech Eng Mat Eng MEng) (IB 36 pts HL 6 maths+phys)

Swansea – AAB–ABB (Mat Sci Eng MEng) (IB 34–33 pts)

128 pts **Liverpool** – ABB incl maths+sci (Mech Mat Eng) (IB 33 pts HL 5 maths+phys)

London (QM) – ABB maths/sci (Med Mat) (IB 34 pts HL 6 maths/sci); ABB incl sci/maths (Mat Sci Eng) (IB 34 pts HL 6 sci/maths); ABB incl sci/maths/des (Mat Des) (IB 34 pts HL 6 sci/maths/des); ABB incl maths/phys/chem (Dntl Mat) (IB 34 pts HL 6 maths/phys/chem)

120 pts **Heriot-Watt** – BBB incl chem (Chem Mat) (IB 30 pts HL 5 chem+maths)

Swansea – BBB (Mat Sci Eng) (IB 32 pts)

112 pts **Sheffield Hallam** – 112 pts (Mat Eng)

96 pts **Edinburgh Napier** – CCC incl maths+sci (Poly Eng) (IB 27 pts HL 5 maths+sci)

72 pts **Northampton** – 72 pts (Lea Tech (Sci/Mark/Bus))

Alternative offers
See **Chapter 6** and **Appendix 1** for grades/new UCAS Tariff points information for other examinations.

EXAMPLES OF COLLEGES OFFERING COURSES IN THIS SUBJECT FIELD
Hereford (CA).

CHOOSING YOUR COURSE (SEE ALSO CH.1)
Universities and colleges teaching quality See www.qaa.ac.uk; http://unistats.direct.gov.uk.

Top research universities and colleges (REF 2014) See **Engineering (Electrical and Electronic)**.

Examples of sandwich degree courses Exeter; London (QM); Loughborough; St Andrews; Sheffield Hallam.

ADMISSIONS INFORMATION
Number of applicants per place (approx) Birmingham 8; Imperial London 3; Liverpool 3; Nottingham 7; Southampton 8; Swansea 4.

Advice to applicants and planning the UCAS personal statement Read scientific and engineering journals and describe any special interests you have. Try to visit chemical or technological installations (rubber, plastics, glass etc) and describe your visits. See also **Appendix 3**.

Misconceptions about this course Students are generally unaware of what this subject involves or the opportunities within the industry.

Selection interviews Yes Birmingham, Imperial London, Nottingham, Oxford (28%).

Interview advice and questions Questions are likely to be based on AS/A-level science subjects. Recent examples include: Why did you choose Materials Science? How would you make each part of this table lamp (on the interviewer's desk)? Identify this piece of material. How was it manufactured? How has it been treated? (Questions related to metal and polymer samples.) What would you consider the major growth area in materials science? See also **Chapter 5**. **Birmingham** We try to gauge understanding; for example, an applicant would be unlikely to be questioned on specific facts, but might be asked what they have understood from a piece of coursework at school. **Oxford** Tutors look for an ability to apply logical reasoning to problems in physical science and an enthusiasm for thinking about new concepts in science and engineering.

AFTER-RESULTS ADVICE
Offers to applicants repeating A-levels Higher Swansea; **Same** Birmingham, Liverpool; **No** Cambridge.

GRADUATE DESTINATIONS AND EMPLOYMENT (2013/14 HESA)
Metallurgy graduates surveyed 10 **Employed** 5 **In voluntary employment** 0 **In further study** 5 **Assumed unemployed** 0

Polymers and Textiles graduates surveyed 175 **Employed** 100 **In voluntary employment** 5 **In further study** 15 **Assumed unemployed** 5

Materials Science graduates surveyed 35 **Employed** 15 **In voluntary employment** 0 **In further study** 15 **Assumed unemployed** 0

Career note Materials scientists are involved in a wide range of specialisms in which openings are likely in a range of industries. These include manufacturing processes in which the work is closely linked with that of mechanical, chemical, production and design engineers.

OTHER DEGREE SUBJECTS FOR CONSIDERATION
Aerospace Engineering; Biotechnology; Chemistry; Dentistry; Engineering Sciences; Mathematics; Mechanical Engineering; Medical Engineering; Plastics Technology; Physics; Product Design and Materials; Prosthetics and Orthotics; Sports Technology.

MATHEMATICS
(including **Mathematical Sciences/Studies**; see also **Economics, Statistics**)

Mathematics at degree level is an extension of A-level mathematics, covering pure and applied mathematics, statistics, computing, mathematical analysis and mathematical applications. Mathematics is of increasing importance and is used in the simplest of design procedures and not only in applications in the physical sciences and engineering. It also plays a key role in management, economics, medicine and the social and behavioural sciences.

Useful websites www.ima.org.uk; www.theorsociety.com; www.m-a.org.uk; www.mathscareers.org.uk; www.imo-official.org; www.bmoc.maths.org; www.maths.org; www.ukmt.org.uk

NB The points totals shown to the left of the institutions are for ease of reference only. It must not be assumed that Tariff points are always used by institutions or that they can be substituted for an offer in grades. The level of an offer is not necessarily indicative of the quality of a course.

COURSE OFFERS INFORMATION
Subject requirements/preferences GCSE English often required and mathematics is obviously essential at a high grade for leading universities. **AL** Mathematics, in several cases with a specified grade, required for all courses. AS Further Mathematics may be required. **Other** Mathematics AEA or STEP papers may be required by some universities (eg Imperial, Warwick). See also **Chapter 4**. NB The level of an offer may depend on whether an applicant is taking AS/A-level Further Maths; check websites.

Imperial London GCSE 5 A/A* grades.

Your target offers and examples of degree courses
168 pts Warwick – A*A*A*–A*AA incl maths+fmaths +STEP (Maths MMaths) (IB 39 pts HL 6 maths); (Maths Joint Hons; Maths) (IB 39 pts HL 6 maths); A*A*A*–AAA incl maths +STEP (MORSE) (IB 38 pts HL 7 maths)

160 pts **Cambridge** – A*A*A incl maths +STEP (Maths) (IB 40–41 pts HL 776); A*A*A +STEP (Maths Phys) (IB 40–42 pts HL 766–777)

Imperial London – A*A*A incl maths+fmaths (Maths; Maths Stats; PMaths; Maths Optim Stats; Maths Mathem Comput; Maths Stats Fin) (IB 39 pts HL 7 maths)

London (UCL) – A*A*A–A*AA incl maths/fmaths +STEP (Maths) (IB 40–39 pts HL 7 maths); A*A*A–A*AA incl maths+fmaths (Maths courses) (IB 40–39 pts HL 7 maths)

Manchester – A*A*A–A*AA incl phys+maths (Maths Phys) (IB 39–38 pts)

Oxford – A*A*A incl maths (Maths Stats) (IB 39 pts HL 7 maths); (Maths; Maths Phil) (IB 39 pts)

152 pts **Bath** – A*AA incl maths+phys (Maths Phys) (IB 36 pts HL 6 maths+phys); A*AA incl maths (Mathem Sci) (IB 39 pts HL 6 maths)

Bristol – A*AA–AAB incl maths+sci/fmaths (Maths) (IB 38–34 pts HL 6 maths+sci); A*AA–AAB incl maths/fmaths (Maths Comp Sci) (IB 38–36 pts HL 6 maths)

Durham – A*AA incl maths+fmaths (Maths (Euro St); Maths) (IB 38 pts)

Exeter – A*AA–AAB incl maths+phys (Maths Phys) (IB 38–34 pts HL 56 maths+phys); A*AA–AAB incl maths (Maths; Maths Acc; Maths Fin; Maths Econ) (IB 38–34 pts HL 6 maths)

London (UCL) – A*AA incl maths (Mathem Comput MEng) (IB 39 pts HL 7 maths)

London LSE – A*AA incl maths (Ecomet Mathem Econ; Maths Econ) (IB 38 pts)

Manchester – A*AA–AAA incl maths (Maths Phil; Maths; Maths Fin; Maths Fin Maths; Act Sci Maths) (IB 37 pts HL 6 maths)

Nottingham – A*AA–AAA incl maths+phys (Mathem Phys) (IB 34 pts); A*AA–AAA/A*AB incl maths (Maths; Fin Maths) (IB 36 pts)

Southampton – A*AA–AAB incl maths (Maths; Maths MMaths) (IB 37 pts HL 6 maths)

Warwick – A*AA incl maths/fmaths (Dscrt Maths) (IB 39 pts HL 6 maths)

144 pts **Birmingham** – AAA incl maths (Maths; Maths Bus Mgt) (IB 32 pts HL 666)

Bristol – AAA–AAB incl maths (Eng Maths) (IB 36–34 pts HL 6 maths); AAA–AAB incl maths (Maths Phil) (IB 36–34 pts HL 6 maths)

Cardiff – AAA–A*AB incl maths (Maths MMaths) (IB 36 pts HL 6 maths)

City – AAA 144 pts (Mathem Sci; Mathem Sci Stats) (IB 32 pts)

Edinburgh – AAA–ABB (Maths Mus; Maths Stats; App Maths; Maths; Maths Mgt; Maths MA; Mathem Phys) (IB 37–32 pts)

Glasgow – AAA/A*AB–ABB incl maths (Acc Maths) (IB 38–36 pts)

Lancaster – AAA–AAB incl maths/fmaths (Maths; Fin Maths) (IB 36 pts HL 6 maths); AAA incl phys+maths (Theor Phys Maths) (IB 36 pts); AAA–ABB incl maths/fmaths (Maths Stats) (IB 36 pts HL 6 maths)

Leeds – A*AB–AAB incl maths (Act Maths) (IB 35 pts HL 6 maths); AAA/A*AB–AAB/A*BB/A*AC incl maths (Maths; Maths Stats) (IB 35 pts HL 6 maths); (Maths Fin) (IB 35 pts HL 6 maths)

London (King's) – AAA incl maths+fmaths (Maths) (IB 35 pts HL 6 maths); (Maths Phil) (IB 35 pts HL 6 maths); AAA incl phys+maths+fmaths (Maths Phys) (IB 35 pts HL 6 maths+phys)

London (QM) – AAA incl maths (Maths Stats Fin Econ; Maths MSci) (IB 36 pts HL 6 maths)

London (UCL) – AAA–AAB incl maths+chem (Chem Maths) (IB 38–36 pts HL 6 maths+chem)

Loughborough – AAA–AAB incl maths (Maths; Maths Maths Educ; Maths Mgt) (IB 36 pts HL 6 maths)

Newcastle – AAA/A*AB incl maths (Maths MMaths) (IB 37 pts HL 6 maths)

Nottingham – AAA–AAB incl comp (Comp Sci) (IB 34–32 pts)

Queen's Belfast – AAA–A*AB incl maths (Maths Comp Sci MSci; Maths MSci; Maths Stats OR MSci); A*AB/AAA incl maths (App Maths Phys MSci)

St Andrews – AAA (Anc Hist Maths; Maths) (IB 36 pts); AAA incl maths (App Maths; Maths Langs; Arbc Maths; Maths Span) (IB 36 pts); (PMaths) (IB 38 pts)

Sheffield – AAA–AAB incl maths (Maths MMaths; Maths MMath (Yr Abrd)) (IB 37 pts HL 6 maths)

Southampton – AAA–AAB incl maths+phys (Maths Phys) (IB 36 pts HL 6 maths); AAA–AAB incl maths+mus (Maths Mus) (IB 36 pts HL 6 maths); AAA–AAB incl maths (Maths Stats;

Mathem St; Maths OR Stats Econ; Maths Fin; Maths Act Sci; Maths Comp Sci) (IB 36 pts HL 6 maths); AAA–AAB incl maths+Fr/Ger/Span (Maths Fr/Ger/Span) (IB 36 pts HL 6 maths); AAA–AAB incl maths+biol (Maths Biol) (IB 36 pts HL 6 maths); AAA incl maths+phys (Phys Maths MPhys) (IB 36 pts HL 6 maths+phys)

Surrey – AAA–AAB incl maths (Fin Maths; Maths Stats) (IB 36 pts HL 6 maths); (Maths courses) (IB 36–35 pts HL 6 maths)

Sussex – AAA incl maths+fmaths (Maths MMaths) (IB 35 pts HL 6 maths)

Swansea – AAA incl maths (Maths MMaths) (IB 36 pts)

York – AAA–AAB incl maths (Maths; Maths Stats) (IB 36 pts HL 6 maths); AAA incl maths (Maths Fin; Econ Maths) (IB 36 pts HL 6 maths); AAA–AAB incl maths+phys (Maths Phys) (IB 36–35 pts HL 6 maths+phys)

136 pts **Brunel** – AAB incl maths/fmaths (Fin Maths MMaths) (IB 33 pts HL 6 maths)

Cardiff – AAB/A*BB/A*AC incl maths (Maths; Maths Apps; Maths OR Stats) (IB 34 pts HL 6 maths)

Central Lancashire – 136 pts incl maths (Maths) (IB 32 pts)

City – 136 pts (Maths Fin) (IB 32 pts)

East Anglia – AAB–ABB incl maths (Maths MMath) (IB 33 pts HL 6 maths); AAB (Maths) (IB 33 pts HL 6 maths)

Glasgow – AAB–BBB incl maths (Maths) (IB 36–34 pts)

Kent – AAB incl maths (Fin Maths) (IB 34 pts)

Lancaster – AAB (Acc Fin Maths) (IB 35 pts); AAB–ABB incl maths/fmaths (Maths Phil) (IB 35 pts HL 6 maths)

Leicester – AAB incl maths (Maths; Fin Maths; Maths Mgt; Maths Econ) (IB 32 pts)

Liverpool – AAB incl maths (Maths Fin) (IB 35 pts HL 6 maths); AAB incl maths+phys (Mathem Phys MMath) (IB 35 pts HL 6 maths+phys)

London (QM) – AAB incl maths (Maths Fin Acc; Maths) (IB 34 pts HL 6 maths); (Maths Stats) (IB 34 pts HL 6 maths)

London (RH) – AAB–ABB incl maths/fmaths (Maths) (IB 32 pts); (Maths Stats) (IB 32 pts)

Manchester – AAB (Comp Sci Maths) (IB 35 pts)

Newcastle – AAB/A*BB/A*AC incl maths (Maths Stats; Maths; Maths Mgt; Maths Fin) (IB 37–35 pts HL 6 maths)

Reading – AAB–ABB (Maths; Maths Stats; Maths Meteor; Comput Maths) (IB 35–32 pts)

Sheffield – AAB–ABB incl maths (Maths; Maths Joint Hons; Comp Sci Maths; Fin Maths) (IB 35 pts HL 6 maths)

Southampton – AAB–ABB incl maths (Phil Maths) (IB 34–32 pts HL 6 maths)

Sussex – AAB–ABB incl maths (Maths Econ; Maths courses) (IB 34 pts HL 5 maths)

128 pts **Aston** – ABB–AAB incl maths (Maths; Maths Joint Hons) (IB 32 pts HL 6 maths)

Brunel – ABB (Maths Stats Mgt; Maths Comp Sci; Maths) (IB 31 pts)

Coventry – ABB incl maths (Maths courses) (IB 31 pts HL 5 maths)

Essex – ABB–BBB (Maths) (IB 32–30 pts)

Kent – ABB incl maths (Maths; Maths Stats) (IB 34 pts)

Liverpool – ABB incl maths (Maths; Maths Bus St; Maths Econ) (IB 33 pts HL 6 maths); (Maths Stats) (IB 33 pts HL 6 maths); ABB incl maths+Euro lang (Mathem Sci Euro Lang) (IB 33 pts HL 6 maths+Euro lang)

London (RH) – ABB incl maths (Econ Maths) (IB 35 pts)

Loughborough – ABB incl maths+phys (Phys Maths) (IB 34 pts)

Northumbria – 128 pts incl maths (Maths) (IB 31 pts)

Plymouth – 128 pts incl maths (Maths Fin) (IB 30 pts HL 5 maths)

Queen's Belfast – ABB incl maths (App Maths Phys; Maths Comp Sci; Maths; Maths Stats OR); ABB incl maths+Fr/Ger (Maths Ext St Euro)

Strathclyde – ABB–BBB incl maths (Maths Stats Econ; Maths courses) (IB 32 pts HL 6 maths)

Swansea – ABB–BBB incl maths (Maths) (IB 34–32 pts)

120 pts **Aberdeen** – BBB incl maths (Maths; App Maths) (IB 32 pts HL 5 maths)

Coventry – BBB incl maths (Maths Stats) (IB 29 pts HL 4 maths)

Dundee – BBB–BCC incl maths+biol/phys (Mathem Biol) (IB 30 pts); BBB–BCC incl maths (Maths) (IB 30 pts)

Greenwich – 120 pts (Fin Maths; Maths Comp; Maths)

Heriot-Watt – BBB incl maths (Maths Span; Maths; Maths Joint Hons) (IB 28 pts HL 5 maths)

Keele – ABC incl maths (Maths) (IB 32 pts HL 6 maths)

Nottingham Trent – 120 pts incl maths (Maths)

Oxford Brookes – ABC (Mathem Sci; Maths courses) (IB 30 pts HL 5 maths)

South Wales – BBB incl maths (Maths) (IB 29 pts HL 5 maths)

Stirling – BBB (Maths Apps) (IB 32 pts)

UWE Bristol – 120 pts incl maths (Maths) (IB 26 pts HL 6 maths)

112 pts **Aberystwyth** – 112–128 pts incl maths (Maths; App Maths Stats; App Maths PMaths)

Brighton – BBC incl maths (Maths) (IB 28 pts HL 5 maths); (Maths Fin; Maths Bus) (IB 28 pts)

Canterbury Christ Church – 112 pts (Maths S Educ QTS)

Chester – BBC–BCC 112 pts (Maths) (IB 26 pts)

De Montfort – 112 pts incl maths (Maths) (IB 28 pts HL 6 maths)

Hertfordshire – 112 pts incl maths (Maths; Fin Maths) (IB 28 pts)

Kingston – 112 pts (Act Maths Stats; Maths)

Liverpool John Moores – 112 pts (Maths) (IB 24 pts)

London (Birk) – 112 pts (Maths Stats)

Nottingham Trent – 112 pts incl maths+PE/sci (Spo Sci Maths)

Sheffield Hallam – 112 pts incl maths (Maths)

104 pts **Bolton** – 104 pts incl maths (Maths)

Chichester – BCC–CCC incl maths (Maths Mathem Lrng) (IB 28 pts HL 4 maths)

Derby – 104 pts (Maths Comp Sci; Maths Educ; Maths)

Liverpool Hope – BCC–BBB 104–120 pts (Maths)

Manchester Met – BCC–BBC incl maths 104–112 pts (Maths) (IB 28 pts HL 5 maths)

Portsmouth – 104–120 pts incl maths (Maths; Maths Stats; Maths Fin Mgt) (IB 26 pts HL 10 pts incl maths)

Staffordshire – 104 pts incl maths (Maths) (IB 24 pts HL 4 maths)

Wolverhampton – 104 pts incl maths (Maths)

96 pts **Bishop Grosseteste** – 96–112 pts (Spo Maths) (IB 24 pts)

80 pts **Bedfordshire** – 80 pts incl maths (Comp Maths) (IB 24 pts)

London Met – 80 pts (Maths)

72 pts **London Met** – 72 pts (Mathem Sci)

Open University – contact +44 (0)845 300 6090 **or** www.openuniversity.co.uk/you (Maths)

Alternative offers
See **Chapter 6** and **Appendix 1** for grades/new UCAS Tariff points information for other examinations.

EXAMPLES OF COLLEGES OFFERING COURSES IN THIS SUBJECT FIELD
Accrington and Rossendale (Coll); Bournemouth and Poole (Coll); Bradford (Coll); Bury (Coll); Greenwich (Sch Mgt); Westminster City (Coll).

CHOOSING YOUR COURSE (SEE ALSO CH.1)
Universities and colleges teaching quality See www.qaa.ac.uk; http://unistats.direct.gov.uk.

Top research universities and colleges (REF 2014) (Mathematical Sciences) Oxford; Dundee; Cambridge; Warwick; Imperial London; Lancaster; London (RH); St Andrews; Manchester; Cardiff; Sheffield; Glasgow; Bath; Newcastle; Nottingham.

Examples of sandwich degree courses Aston; Bath; Bradford; Brighton; Brunel; Cardiff; Coventry; East Anglia; Greenwich; Hertfordshire; Kent; Kingston; Lancaster; Liverpool John Moores;

Loughborough; Northumbria; Nottingham Trent; Portsmouth; Reading; Staffordshire; Surrey; UWE Bristol; Wolverhampton; York.

ADMISSIONS INFORMATION

Number of applicants per place (approx) Aberystwyth 8, (App Maths) 5; Aston 8; Bath 6; Birmingham 6; Bristol 8; Brunel 5; Cambridge 6; Cardiff 5; Central Lancashire 7; City 6; Coventry 8; Derby 4; Dundee 5; Durham 9; East Anglia 5; Edinburgh 4; Exeter 6; Greenwich 2; Heriot-Watt 5; Hertfordshire 9; Kent 8; Lancaster 12; Leeds (Maths) 5, (Maths Fin) 4; Leicester 14; Liverpool 5; London (King's) 8; London (QM) 5; London (RH) 8; London (UCL) 9; London LSE (Maths) 11; London Met 3; Manchester Met 3; Newcastle 7; Northumbria 7; Nottingham Trent 7; Oxford Brookes 21; Plymouth 8; Portsmouth 7; Sheffield 5; Sheffield Hallam 3; Southampton 10; Strathclyde 6; Surrey 7; UWE Bristol 7; Warwick 6; York 6.

Advice to applicants and planning the UCAS personal statement Any interests you have in careers requiring mathematical ability could be mentioned, for example, engineering, computers (hardware and software) and business applications. Show determination, love of mathematics and an appreciation of the rigour of the course. Give details of your skills, work experience, positions of responsibility. A variety of non-academic interests to complement the applicant's academic abilities preferred. For non-UK students fluency in oral and written English required. **Manchester** Unit grades may form part of an offer. **Warwick** Offers for courses in Statistics (MORSE, Mathematics and Statistics) include achievement requirements in STEP and other requirements. Check University websites for latest information. See also **Appendix 3**.

Misconceptions about this course London (QM) Some believe that a study of mechanics is compulsory – it is not. **Surrey** Maths is not just about calculations: it focuses on reasoning, logic and applications. **York** Further maths is not required.

Selection interviews Yes Aberystwyth, Bath, Bishop Grosseteste, Cambridge, Central Lancashire, City, Coventry, Imperial London, Kingston, Lancaster, Leeds, London (King's), London (RH), Manchester, Northampton, Nottingham, Oxford (Maths) 18%, (Maths Comp Sci) 18%, (Maths Phil) 18%, (Maths Stats) 9%, Sheffield, Southampton, UWE Bristol, Warwick; **Some** Brighton, Bristol, Cardiff, East Anglia, Greenwich, Heriot-Watt, Kent, London (UCL), London LSE (rarely), London Met, Loughborough, Manchester Met, Newcastle, York; **No** Birmingham, Dundee, Essex, Liverpool, Liverpool John Moores, Reading.

Interview advice and questions Questions are likely to be asked arising from the information you have given in your UCAS application and about your interests in the subject. Questions in recent years have included: How many ways are there of incorrectly setting up the back row of a chess board? A ladder on a rough floor leans against a smooth wall. Describe the forces acting on the ladder and give the maximum possible angle of inclination possible. There are three particles connected by a string; the middle one is made to move – describe the subsequent motion of the particles. What mathematics books have you read outside your syllabus? Why does a ball bounce? Discuss the work of any renowned mathematician. Balance a pencil on your index fingers and then try to move both towards the centre of the pencil. Explain what is happening in terms of forces and friction. See also **Chapter 5**. **Cambridge** If you could spend half an hour with any mathematician past or present, who would it be? **Oxford** What makes you think I'm having thoughts? What was the most beautiful proof in A-level mathematics? I am an oil baron in the desert and I need to deliver oil to four different towns which happen to lie in a straight line. In order to deliver the correct amount to each town I must visit each town in turn, returning to my warehouse in between each visit. Where would I position my warehouse in order to drive the shortest possible distance? Roads are no problem since I have a friend who will build me as many roads as I like for free. **Southampton** Personal statements generate discussion points. Our interviews are informal chats and so technical probing is kept low key.

Reasons for rejection (non-academic) Usually academic reasons only. Lack of motivation. Uneasiness about how much mathematics will be remembered after a gap year. **Birmingham** A poorly written and poorly organised personal statement.

New UCAS points Tariff: A* = 56 pts; A = 48 pts; B = 40 pts; C = 32 pts; D = 24 pts; E = 16 pts

AFTER-RESULTS ADVICE

Offers to applicants repeating A-levels Higher Brighton, Coventry, Essex, Glasgow, London Met, Strathclyde, Surrey, Swansea, Warwick; **Possibly higher** Cambridge (Hom), Durham, Lancaster, Leeds, Newcastle, Sheffield; **Same** Aberystwyth, Aston, Bath, Birmingham, Bristol, Brunel, Chester, East Anglia, Liverpool, Liverpool Hope, London (RH), Loughborough (usually), Manchester Met, Nottingham, Nottingham Trent, Oxford Brookes, Sheffield Hallam, Southampton, Stirling, Wolverhampton, York; **No** Cambridge.

GRADUATE DESTINATIONS AND EMPLOYMENT (2013/14 HESA)

Graduates surveyed 5,440 **Employed** 2,580 **In voluntary employment** 145 **In further study** 1,660 **Assumed unemployed** 420

Career note Graduates enter a range of careers. Whilst business, finance and retail areas are popular options, mathematicians also have important roles in the manufacturing industries. Mathematics offers the pleasure of problem-solving, the satisfaction of a rigorous argument and the most widely employable non-vocational degree subject. A student's view: 'Maths trains you to work in the abstract, to think creatively and to come up with concrete conclusions.' These transferable skills are much sought-after by employers. Employment prospects are excellent, with high salaries.

OTHER DEGREE SUBJECTS FOR CONSIDERATION

Accountancy; Actuarial Studies; Astronomy; Astrophysics; Computer Science; Economics; Engineering Sciences; Operational Research; Physics; Statistics.

MEDIA STUDIES

(including **Broadcasting** and **Journalism**; see also **Art and Design (General), Communication Studies/Communication, Computer Courses, Engineering (Acoustics and Sound), Film, Radio, Video and TV Studies, Information Management and Librarianship, Journalism, Photography**)

Intending Media applicants need to check course details carefully since this subject area can involve graphic design, illustration and other art courses as well as the media in the fields of TV, radio and journalism.

Useful websites www.bbc.co.uk/jobs; www.newspapersoc.org.uk; www.ppa.co.uk; careers. thomsonreuters.com; www.nctj.com; www.ipa.co.uk; www.camfoundation.com; www.mediastudies.com

NB The points totals shown to the left of the institutions are for ease of reference only. It must not be assumed that Tariff points are always used by institutions or that they can be substituted for an offer in grades. The level of an offer is not necessarily indicative of the quality of a course.

COURSE OFFERS INFORMATION

Subject requirements/preferences GCSE English and mathematics often required. **AL** No specified subjects required.

Your target offers and examples of degree courses

136 pts **Lancaster** – AAB–ABB (Media Cult St) (IB 35–32 pts)
Leeds – AAB (Comms Media) (IB 35 pts)
London (Gold) – AAB–ABB (Media Comms) (IB 33 pts)
Loughborough – AAB incl Engl (Pub Engl) (IB 34 pts HL 5 Engl)
Newcastle – AAB (Media Comm Cult St) (IB 34 pts)
Surrey – AAB–ABB (Media Cult Soty) (IB 35–34 pts)
York – AAB (Interact Media) (IB 35 pts)

128 pts **Cardiff** – ABB (Jrnl Media Sociol) (IB 36 pts)
East Anglia – ABB (Transl Media Modn Lang; Media St; Media Int Dev) (IB 32 pts)
Essex – ABB–BBB (Media Cult Soc) (IB 32–30 pts)
Leicester – ABB (Media Soty) (IB 30 pts)

Check **Chapter 3** for new university admission details and **Chapter 6** on how to read the subject tables.

Lincoln – 128 pts (Media Prod)
Liverpool – ABB (Comm Media) (IB 33 pts)
London (RH) – ABB (Dig Media Comms) (IB 32 pts)
Loughborough – ABB (Comm Media St) (IB 34 pts)
Newcastle – ABB (Jrnl Media Cult) (IB 34 pts)
Northumbria – 128 pts (Media Jrnl) (IB 31 pts)
Nottingham – ABB/AAC (Int Media Comm St) (IB 32 pts); ABB–AAC (Span Int Media Comms St) (IB 32 pts)
Sussex – ABB (Media Prac; Media Cult St) (IB 34 pts)

120 pts **Aberystwyth** – 120–128 pts (Hist Media)
Bournemouth – 120–128 pts (Media Prod) (IB 31–32 pts)
Brighton – BBB (Env Media St) (IB 30 pts)
Brunel – BBB (Vis Efcts Mtn Graph) (IB 30 pts)
Derby – 120 pts (Media Prod)
Keele – BBB/ABC (Media Comms Cult) (IB 32 pts)
Leeds Beckett – 120 pts (Broad Media Tech; Crea Media Tech; Media Comm Cult) (IB 26 pts)
Leicester – BBB (Film Media St) (IB 28 pts)
Oxford Brookes – BBB (Pub Media) (IB 31 pts)
Stirling – BBB (Euro Film Media) (IB 32 pts)
Sunderland – 120 pts (Media St Comb Hons; Media Cult Comm)
Swansea – BBB–BBC (Media) (IB 32–30 pts)
Trinity Saint David – 120 pts (Dig Arts) (IB 32 pts)

112 pts **Aberystwyth** – 112–120 pts (Media Comm St)
Arts London (CFash) – CC 112 pts +portfolio (Fash Jrnl)
Bath Spa – 112–128 pts (Media Comms)
Birmingham City – BBC 112 pts (Media Comm (Evnt Exhib Ind); Media Comm (Jrnl); Media Comm (Mus Ind)) (IB 28 pts)
Bournemouth – 112–120 pts (Dig Media Des; Film Prod Cnma; Comm Media) (IB 30–31 pts)
Brighton – BBC (Media St) (IB 28 pts); BBC incl Engl lit/lit+lang (Media Engl Lit) (IB 28 pts)
Brunel – BBC (Comm Media St; Sociol Media St) (IB 29 pts)
Buckingham – BBC–BCC (Jrnl Comm St)
Canterbury Christ Church – 112 pts (Media Comms)
Central Lancashire – 112 pts (Media Prod)
Chester – BBC–BCC 112 pts (Media) (IB 26 pts)
Chichester – 112–128 pts (Media) (IB 30 pts)
Coventry – BBC incl media/film st (Media Prod) (IB 27 pts); BBC (Media Comms) (IB 28 pts)
East London – 112 pts (Media Comm) (IB 24 pts)
Edge Hill – BBC 112 pts (Media Mus Snd)
Glasgow Caledonian – BBC (Media Comm) (IB 25 pts)
Greenwich – 112 pts (Media Comms) (IB 28 pts)
Huddersfield – BBC 112 pts (Media Pop Cult)
Hull – 112 pts (Media Scrn St) (IB 28 pts)
Kingston – 112 pts (Media Comm)
London Met – 112 pts (Media Comms)
Middlesex – 112 pts (Pub Dig Cult; Jrnl Media)
Northampton – 112 pts (Media Prod Mov Imag)
Nottingham Trent – 112 pts (Media; Media Joint Hons)
Oxford Brookes – BBC (Comm Media Cult) (IB 30 pts)
Plymouth – 112 pts (Media Arts) (IB 25 pts)
Portsmouth – 112 pts (Dig Media) (IB 26 pts)
Sheffield Hallam – 112 pts (PR Media; Dig Media Prod; Media)
Teesside – 112 pts +interview (Crea Dig Media); 112 pts +interview/portfolio (Broad Media Prod); 112 pts (Media St)
UWE Bristol – 112 pts (Media Jrnl; Media Cult Prac) (IB 25 pts)
West London – 112 pts (Media Comms)

New UCAS points Tariff: A* = 56 pts; A = 48 pts; B = 40 pts; C = 32 pts; D = 24 pts; E = 16 pts

York St John – 112 pts (Media courses)
104 pts   **Bangor** – 104–120 pts (Media St courses)
Brighton – BCC (Media St Sociol/Educ) (IB 27 pts)
Cardiff Met – 104 pts (Engl Media)
Central Lancashire – 104 pts (Film Media St) (IB 28 pts)
De Montfort – 104 pts (Media Comm; Jrnl) (IB 28 pts)
Falmouth – 104–120 pts (Jrnl)
Leeds Trinity – 104 pts (Media; Media Mark; Engl Media)
Liverpool Hope – BCC–BBB 104–120 pts (Media Comm)
Liverpool John Moores – 104 pts (Int Jrnl; Media Cult Comm) (IB 28 pts)
Manchester Met – BCC–BBC 104–112 pts (Dig Media Mark) (IB 26 pts); 104–112 pts
    (Film Media St; Dig Media Comms) (IB 26 pts)
Middlesex – 104 pts (Media Cult St)
Portsmouth – 104–120 pts (Media St Joint Hons) (IB 25 pts)
Queen Margaret – BCC 104 pts (Media; PR Media) (IB 28 pts)
St Mary's – 104 pts (Media Arts) (IB 28 pts)
South Wales – BCC +audition (Perf Media) (IB 29 pts); BCC incl art/film/media
    (Media Prod) (IB 29 pts)
Winchester – 104–120 pts (Jrnl Media St); (Media Comm Adv; Media Comm courses;
    Broad TV Media Prod) (IB 26 pts)
Worcester – 104 pts (Media Cult)
96 pts   **Bangor** – 96–104 pts (Jrnl Media St)
Bolton – 96 pts (Media Writ Prod)
Buckingham – CCC 96 pts (Comm Media Jrnl); CCC (Comm Media St)
Chichester – 96–120 pts (Spo Media)
Cumbria – 96 pts (Wldlf Media)
Edinburgh Napier – CCC (Dig Media Glob) (IB 27 pts)
Glyndŵr – 96 pts (Broad Jrnl Media Comms)
Portsmouth – 96–120 pts (Sociol Media St) (IB 30 pts HL 17 pts)
Robert Gordon – CCC incl Engl (Media) (IB 26 pts)
Roehampton – 96 pts (Media Cult Idnty)
Southampton Solent – 96 pts (Media Cult Prod)
Wolverhampton – 96 pts (Media Cult St; Media Comm St; Film Media Cult St)
88 pts   **Anglia Ruskin** – 88–104 pts (Media courses) (IB 26 pts)
Creative Arts – 88 pts (Media Comms; Media Crea Writ; Spo Jrnl)
Derby – 88–120 pts (Media St)
80 pts   **Arts London** – 80 pts (Mag Jrnl Pub; Contemp Media Cult)
Bedfordshire – 80 pts (Media Prod courses; Media Comms) (IB 24 pts)
Hull (Coll) – 80 pts (Jrnl Dig Media; Filmm Crea Media Prod; Broad Media)
Plymouth (CA) – 80 pts +portfolio (Fash Media Mark)
64 pts   **Ravensbourne** – CC (Edit Pst Prod) (IB 28 pts)
UHI – CC +interview (Gael Media St)
Teesside – +audition (Perf Lv Rec Media)

Alternative offers
See **Chapter 6** and **Appendix 1** for grades/new UCAS Tariff points information for other
examinations.

EXAMPLES OF COLLEGES OFFERING COURSES IN THIS SUBJECT FIELD
Most colleges, check with your local college. Accrington and Rossendale (Coll); Blackpool and Fylde
(Coll); Bridgwater (Coll); Brooksby Melton (Coll); Central Film Sch; East Riding (Coll); Farnborough (CT);
Gloucestershire (Coll); HOW (Coll); Hugh Baird (Coll); Kingston (Coll); Leeds City (Coll); London UCK
(Coll); LSST; Macclesfield (Coll); Mid-Cheshire (Coll); Newcastle (Coll); Northbrook (Coll); Peterborough
(Coll); South Essex (Coll); Stratford-upon-Avon (Coll); Truro and Penwith (Coll); Westminster Kingsway
(Coll); Weston (Coll); Yeovil (Coll).

CHOOSING YOUR COURSE (SEE ALSO CH.1)

Universities and colleges teaching quality See www.qaa.ac.uk; http://unistats.direct.gov.uk.

Top research universities and colleges (REF 2014) See **Communication Studies/Communication**.

Examples of sandwich degree courses Bedfordshire; Bournemouth; Bradford; Brighton; Brunel; Coventry; De Montfort; Essex; Hertfordshire; Huddersfield; Kingston; Leeds; Leeds Beckett; Liverpool John Moores; Manchester Met; Nottingham Trent; Portsmouth; Sheffield Hallam; Surrey; Ulster.

ADMISSIONS INFORMATION

Number of applicants per place (approx) Bath Spa 4; Bournemouth (Media Prod) 24; Bradford 13; Canterbury Christ Church 23; Cardiff 11; Cardiff Met 3; Central Lancashire 33; Chichester 6; Creative Arts 3; Cumbria 4; De Montfort 11; East London 27; Falmouth 4; Greenwich 12; Lincoln 4; London (Gold) 13; London (RH) 11; Northampton 4; Northumbria 14; Nottingham Trent 5; Portsmouth 5; Sheffield Hallam 56; South Essex (Coll) 10; Teesside 33; Trinity Saint David 5; UWE Bristol 20; Winchester 7.

Advice to applicants and planning the UCAS personal statement Work experience or work shadowing is important. Contact local newspaper offices to meet journalists and to discuss their work. Contact local radio stations and advertising agencies, read newspapers (all types) and be able to describe the different approaches of newspapers. Watch TV coverage of news stories and the way in which the interviewer deals with politicians or members of the public. Give your opinions on the various forms of media. School magazine and/or any published work should be mentioned. A balance of academic and practical skills preferred. Creativity, problem-solving, cultural awareness, communication skills and commitment required. (International students: Fluency in written and spoken English required.) See also **Communication Studies/Communication** and **Appendix 3**.

Misconceptions about this course Birmingham City That Media courses are soft options: they are not! **Cardiff Met** Some applicants believe that the course will automatically lead to a job in the media: it won't. This depends on the student developing other employment skills and experience. **Cumbria** This is not a Media Studies course: it is a highly practical media production course. **Lincoln** (Media Prod) BTEC applicants may think that this is a technology-based course.

Selection interviews Yes Birmingham City, Bournemouth, Chichester, Creative Arts, East Anglia, Gloucestershire, Hertfordshire, London (Gold), London (RH), St Mark and St John, Salford, Southampton Solent, West London, Winchester, Worcester; **Some** Anglia Ruskin, Edge Hill, Huddersfield, Liverpool John Moores, Nottingham Trent, Sheffield Hallam, Sunderland, Wolverhampton; **No** Cardiff, Cardiff Met, Nottingham, Portsmouth, South Essex (Coll).

Interview advice and questions Past questions include: Which newspapers do you read? Discuss the main differences between the national daily newspapers. Which radio programmes do you listen to each day? Which television programmes do you watch? Should the BBC broadcast advertisements? What do you think are the reasons for the popularity of *EastEnders*? Film or video work, if required, should be edited to a running time of 15 minutes unless otherwise stated. See also **Chapter 5**. **Cardiff Met** What is your favourite area in respect of popular culture? Are you considering taking up the work placement module? If so where would you plan to go? **Cumbria** Role of journalism in society. What is today's main news story? Who is Rupert Murdoch? **Lincoln** Give a written or verbal critique of a media product.

Reasons for rejection (non-academic) No clear commitment (to Broadcast Journalism) plus no evidence of experience (now proving to be essential). Mistaken expectations of the nature of the course. Can't write and doesn't work well in groups. Too specific and narrow areas of media interest, for example, video or script-writing. Lack of knowledge of current affairs. **Cardiff Met** Lack of experience in the field. Application arrived too late.

AFTER-RESULTS ADVICE

Offers to applicants repeating A-levels Same Birmingham City, Cardiff, Cardiff Met, Chester, Chichester, De Montfort, Huddersfield, Lincoln, Loughborough, Manchester Met, Nottingham Trent, St Mary's, South Essex (Coll), Sunderland, Winchester, Wolverhampton.

GRADUATE DESTINATIONS AND EMPLOYMENT (2013/14 HESA)
Graduates surveyed 5,065 **Employed** 2,715 **In voluntary employment** 240 **In further study** 520 **Assumed unemployed** 480

Career note See **Film, Radio, Video and TV Studies**.

OTHER DEGREE SUBJECTS FOR CONSIDERATION
Advertising; Communication; English; Film, Radio, Video and TV Studies; Journalism; Photography; Public Relations.

MEDICINE

(including **Medical Sciences**; see also **Biological Sciences, Human Sciences/Human Biosciences**)

Medicine is a highly popular choice of degree subject and career. All courses listed below include the same areas of study and all lead to a qualification and career in medicine. Medical schools aim to produce doctors who are clinically competent, who are able to see patients as people and have a holistic and ethical approach (including the ability to understand and manage each patient's case in a family and social context as well as in hospital), who treat patients and colleagues with respect, dignity and sensitivity, are skilled at teamwork and are prepared for continual learning. In several ways, these aims reflect the qualities selectors seek when interviewing applicants. In all cases, close attention will be paid to the confidential report on the UCAS application to judge the applicant's personality, communication skills, academic potential and commitment to a medical career. Methods of teaching may vary slightly, depending on the medical school. To achieve these aims, some medical schools adopt the system of self-directed learning (SDL) in which objectives are set to assess students' progress, and problem-based learning (PBL) which helps students to develop critical thinking and clinical problem-solving skills.

Whilst there is a core curriculum of knowledge, the first three years integrate scientific and clinical experience, and there are fewer formal lectures than before, with more group and individual work. For outstanding students without science A-levels, some pre-medical courses are available. Most medical schools also offer an extra year of study, usually in the middle of the medical degree, to enable students to research a scientific subject leading to an 'intercalated' BSc degree. Additionally, elective periods abroad in the final year can sometimes be taken.

Medical students' and doctors' advice to applicants
'I did not fully appreciate how diverse medicine is as a career. Everyone has their own particular reasons for wishing to pursue it but these will change as you progress through your career. There are many different pathways you can take which makes it all the more exciting ... and daunting! Choose your university carefully; in most medical degrees you will only be based at university for the first two years and thereafter you will be in hospitals around the area so choose a city or an area you want to work and live in.'

'Medicine is a career which can open many doors – as a family or hospital doctor, working in Africa treating children with infectious diseases, in a war zone, in a laboratory, in sport, in journalism, and in law, going on to study law, to specialise in medical law, I have friends who have done all of these things.'

'Get to know what the real working lives of doctors are. The attributes needed to see sick and needy people. The fact that the NHS is a public and not a private organisation and what this means in the changing world of medical knowledge. Some of this is very difficult to learn in the sixth form but periods of work experience will help. In addition to talking to medical students and family friends who are doctors, browse through medical journals and medical websites. Every doctor has had their own individual experiences, good and bad, but the majority would still apply to medicine again if they were 17!'

Useful websites www.scicentral.com; www.ipem.ac.uk; www.bmj.com; www.admissionstestingservice.org; www.gmc-uk.org; www.nhscareers.nhs.uk; www.bma.org.uk; www.rcgp.org.uk; www.rcpath.org

NB The points totals shown to the left of the institutions are for ease of reference only. It must not be assumed that Tariff points are always used by institutions or that they can be substituted for an offer in grades. The level of an offer is not necessarily indicative of the quality of a course.

COURSE OFFERS INFORMATION

Subject requirements/preferences GCSE In all cases a good spread of science and non-science subjects will be expected at high grades.

Aberdeen English, mathematics, biology, physics or dual award science. Combinations of AB grades expected, especially in sciences.

Birmingham Five subjects at A* or A including chemistry, English language and mathematics normally at grade A. Dual science award grade A acceptable as an alternative to physics and biology.

Brighton and Sussex (MS) Mathematics and English at grade B, biology and chemistry.

Bristol Five A/A* grades to include mathematics, English and two sciences.

Buckingham Eight subjects (minimum) including biology, mathematics, chemistry and English.

Cambridge Mathematics, physics, chemistry or dual science award.

Cardiff Four or five A* in nine subjects (minimum). English or Welsh at grade B, mathematics at grade B or above, grades AA in dual science or AAA in three sciences.

Dundee Chemistry and biology or human biology essential.

Durham See **Newcastle**.

East Anglia Six subjects at grade A or above including mathematics, English and two science subjects.

Edinburgh English, mathematics, biology, chemistry or dual science award at grade B or higher.

Glasgow English, chemistry, biology (preferred), mathematics and physics.

Hull York (MS) Six subjects at grades A*–C including English language at grade A or B, English literature at grade A, mathematics at grade B or higher plus chemistry and biology.

Imperial London Chemistry, biology, physics (or dual science award) plus mathematics and English. At least three subjects are required at grade A, and two subjects at grade B.

Keele Chemistry, physics, biology (dual science award acceptable, grades BB minimum), English language and mathematics at grade B minimum. A broad spread of subjects is expected with a minimum of four at grade A or A*.

Lancaster See **Liverpool**.

Leeds Six subjects at grade B minimum including English, mathematics, chemistry and biology or dual science award.

Leicester English language and sciences (including chemistry) or dual science award.

Liverpool Nine subjects at grades A–C, including dual science (or biology, chemistry and physics), English language and mathematics at grade B minimum.

London (King's) Grade B (minimum) in chemistry, biology and physics (or dual science award), English and mathematics.

London (QM) Six subjects at AB minimum grades including English, mathematics and science subjects.

London (St George's) Typically eight subjects at grade A are required including English language, mathematics and science subjects. Contact the admissions team for a more detailed breakdown of grade requirements.

London (UCL) English and mathematics at grade B minimum plus grade C in a foreign language.

Manchester Seven subjects with five at grades A/A*. Chemistry, biology and physics required at grade C (or AS) minimum, with English and mathematics at grade B minimum.

Newcastle At least five subjects with grades AAAAB to include English, mathematics and either biology, chemistry, physics or dual science award.

Nottingham Six subjects at grade A/A* to include biology, chemistry and physics or dual science award. (Grade A AS physics can compensate for a B at **GCSE**.)

Oxford Chemistry, mathematics, biology and physics or dual science award acceptable.

Queen's Belfast Chemistry, biology, mathematics and either physics or dual science award.

Medicine

Consult the Specialist

MPW is one of the
UK's best known
groups of independent
sixth-form colleges.
We offer a range of
specialist services to
those who have chosen
a career in Medicine.

Specialist two-year and
one-year A level courses

Detailed UCAS advice

"Insight into Medicine" work
experience courses

Seminars on applications
procedures and interview
preparation

Interview training

MPW

Mander Portman Woodward

London	020 7835 1355
Birmingham	0121 454 9637
Cambridge	01223 350158

Getting into Medical School by MPW is published by Trotman Publishing

Check **Chapter 3** for new university admission details and **Chapter 6** on how to read the subject tables.

St Andrews Chemistry, biology, mathematics and physics. If mathematics and biology are not offered at A2 then each must have been passed at grade B or higher. English is required at grade B or higher.

Sheffield At least six subjects at grade A. English, mathematics, chemistry and a science or a dual science award required.

Southampton A minimum of seven subjects at grade A including English, mathematics and dual science award or equivalent. (Widening Access course BM6) Five at grade C including English, mathematics and dual science award or equivalent. (Students join the five-year programme on completion of Year Zero.)

AL See **Your target offers and examples of degree courses** below. Candidates applying for A104 courses at **Cardiff**, **Dundee**, **East Anglia**, **London (King's)**, **Manchester** and **Sheffield** are not accepted if they are offering more than one laboratory-based subject (check with university). **London (UCL)** Mathematics and Further Mathematics will not both be counted towards three AL subjects. Applicants should note that A-levels in General Studies and Critical Thinking may not be accepted for entry.

Medicine Foundation courses These are designed for students who have demonstrated high academic potential but who have taken non-science subjects or a combination including no more than one of Biology, Chemistry and Physics.

Other requirements: See **Health Requirements** below; DBS clearance is also required.

NB Home and EU-funded students applying for entry to Medicine are required by many universities to sit either the UKCAT or BMAT tests before applying. See **Your target offers and examples of degree courses** below, **Chapter 4** and **Chapter 5** for further information.

Your target offers and examples of degree courses

164 pts **Queen's Belfast** – AAAa incl chem+sci/maths +UKCAT (Med 5 yrs)

160 pts **Cambridge** – A*A*A incl chem+sci/maths +BMAT (Med 6 yrs) (IB 40–41 pts HL 776)
East Anglia – AAAb incl biol+sci +UKCAT (Med 5 yrs) (IB 36 pts HL 666 incl biol+sci)
Edinburgh – AAAb incl chem +maths/sci +UKCAT (Med) (IB 37 pts)
Liverpool – AAAb incl chem+biol (Med Srgy 5 yrs) (IB 36 pts HL 666 incl biol+chem)
London (St George's) – AAAb incl chem+biol +UKCAT (Med 5 yrs) (IB 36 pts HL 6 chem+biol)

152 pts **Birmingham** – A*AA incl chem+biol (Med Srgy) (IB 32 pts HL 766)
Exeter – A*AA–AAA incl biol+chem +UKCAT +interview (Med) (IB 38–36 pts HL 6 biol+chem)
London (UCL) – A*AA incl chem+biol +BMAT (Med 6 yrs) (IB 39 pts HL 7 biol/chem 6 biol/chem)
Oxford – A*AA incl chem+sci/maths +BMAT (Med 6 yrs) (IB 39 pts)
Plymouth – A*AA–AAA incl chem+biol +UKCAT (Med Srgy BMBS) (IB 38–36 pts HL 6 biol+chem)

144 pts **Aberdeen** – AAA chem+sci/maths +UKCAT (Med 5 yrs) (IB 36 pts HL 6 chem+sci/maths)
Brighton and Sussex (MS) – AAA incl biol+chem +BMAT (Med 5 yrs) (IB 36 pts HL 6 biol+chem)
Bristol – AAA–AAB incl chem+biol/phys (Med 5 yrs) (IB 36–34 pts HL 6 chem+biol/phys)
Cardiff – AAA incl sci/maths +UKCAT (Med 5 yrs) (IB 38 pts); AAA +UKCAT (Med 6 yrs) (IB 38 pts)
Dundee – AAA incl chem+sci +UKCAT (Med 5 yrs) (IB 37 pts)
Durham – AAA incl chem/biol +UKCAT Applications through Newcastle (Med 5 yrs) (IB 38 pts)
Glasgow – AAA incl chem+sci/maths +UKCAT (Med 5 yrs) (IB 38 pts)
Hull York (MS) – AAA incl chem+biol +UKCAT (Med) (IB 36 pts HL 665 incl chem+biol)
Imperial London – AAA–A*AA incl biol+chem +BMAT (Med) (IB 38 pts HL 6 biol+chem)
Keele – AAA–A*AB incl chem/biol+sci/maths +UKCAT (Med) (IB 35 pts)
Lancaster – AAA incl biol+chem +BMAT (Med Srgy) (IB 36 pts HL 6 biol+chem)
Leeds – AAA incl chem +BMAT (Med Srgy 5 yrs) (IB 35 pts HL 6 chem)
Leicester – AAA incl chem+biol +UKCAT (Med 5 yrs) (IB 36 pts)
London (King's) – AAA incl chem+biol +UKCAT (Med 5 yrs) (IB 35 pts HL 6 chem+biol)
London (QM) – AAA incl chem/biol+sci/maths +UKCAT (Med 5 yrs) (IB 38 pts HL 6 sci)

Manchester – AAA incl chem+sci/maths +UKCAT (Med 5 yrs) (IB 37 pts)
Newcastle – AAA incl chem/biol +UKCAT (Med Srgy (5 yrs)) (IB 38 pts HL 6 chem/biol)
Nottingham – AAA incl chem+biol +UKCAT (Med 5 yrs) (IB 36 pts)
St Andrews – AAA incl chem+sci/maths +UKCAT (Med 5/6 yrs) (IB 38 pts)
Sheffield – AAA incl chem+sci +UKCAT (Med) (IB 37 pts HL 6 chem+sci)
Southampton – AAA incl chem+biol +UKCAT (Med 5 yrs) (IB 36 pts)
136 pts Buckingham – AAB incl chem+maths/sci (Med)
Exeter – AAB–ABB incl biol+sci (Med Sci) (IB 34–32 pts HL 65 biol+sci)
Manchester – AAB (Med 6 yrs) (IB 35 pts)
120 pts South Wales – BBB incl biol (Med Sci) (IB 32 pts HL 6 biol+sci)

Widening Access and Foundation Courses (Check websites)
LWP – Local Widening Participation
Bradford (Leeds) – BCC 260 pts (Course B991) **LWP**
Bristol – BBC incl chem+sci/maths (A108) (IB 29 pts) **LWP**
Cardiff – AAA +UKCAT (Course A104) (IB 38 pts)
Dundee – AABBB at Higher in S5 +UKCAT (Course A104) **LWP**
Dundee – AAA +UKCAT (Course A104) (IB 37 pts)
Durham – AAB–BCC incl biol+chem +UKCAT (Course A190)
East Anglia – ABB +UKCAT (Course A104) (IB 32 pts)
Keele – AAA–A*AB +UKCAT (Course A104) (IB 35 pts)
London (King's) – BBB–AAA incl chem+biol +UKCAT (Course A101)
Liverpool – Zero Yr prog (Course 789S)
Manchester – AAB +arts/hum (Course A104) (IB 35 pts)
Nottingham – BBC incl biol+chem +UKCAT (Course A108) (IB 28 pts)
Sheffield – AAA +UKCAT (Course A104) (IB 37 pts)
Southampton – BBC incl chem+biol +UKCAT (Course A102)
St Andrews – 85%/3.2 GPA incl chem +UKCAT (Int students only)

Alternative offers
See **Chapter 6** and **Appendix 1** for grades/new UCAS Tariff points information for other examinations.

EXAMPLES OF COLLEGES OFFERING COURSES IN THIS SUBJECT FIELD
Furness (Coll).

CHOOSING YOUR COURSE (SEE ALSO CH.1)
Universities and colleges teaching quality See www.qaa.ac.uk; http://unistats.direct.gov.uk.

Top research universities and colleges (REF 2014) (Clinical Medicine) London (King's); Oxford; London (QM); Cardiff; Edinburgh; Cambridge; Imperial London; Sheffield; Leeds; Manchester.

ADMISSIONS INFORMATION
Number of applicants per place (approx) Aberdeen 9; Brighton and Sussex (MS) 10; Bristol 15; Cambridge 6; Cardiff 9; Dundee 13; East Anglia 7; Edinburgh 16; Glasgow 8; Hull York (MS) 3; Imperial London 8; Leicester 12; Liverpool 8; London (King's) 12; London (QM) 5; London (UCL) 8; Manchester 5; Newcastle 10; Nottingham 10; St Andrews 8.

Numbers of applicants (a UK b EU (non-UK) c non-EU d mature) Birmingham **a**5 **b**25, (Grad entry) 12; Leeds **a**17; Oxford **a**26% success rate **c**10; Queen's Belfast **a**4 **c**(a small number of places are allocated); Sheffield **a**17 (ave 30 applicants per place for 6yr courses); Cambridge **c**22.

Admissions tutors' advice Policies adopted by all medical schools are very similar, although some medical schools use the Multiple Mini-Interview format (MMI) when candidates rotate around different question stations each one devoted to one question. Each interview lasts seven minutes. However, a brief outline of the information provided by admissions tutors is given below. Further information should be obtained direct from institutions. Applicants wishing to contact medical schools should do so either by letter or by telephone and not by email.

Aberdeen Applicants must take the UKCAT in the year of application. A cut-off score is not used. Overseas applicants may be interviewed abroad or in Aberdeen. MMI interviews take place lasting up to an hour. Total intake 152 including 12 international students. Most offers are made by end of March. Points equivalent results not accepted. Re-sits only accepted in exceptional circumstances. These must be submitted in good time to be considered. Feedback for unsuccessful applicants upon request. International students English language entry requirement (or equivalent): IELTS 7.0 and 7.0 in speaking.

Birmingham UKCAT required. Non-academic interests and extra-curricular activities noted in addition to academic factors. General studies not accepted. MMI interview format used (see Admission tutors' advice). Approximately 1,000 called for interview; 28 places for EU students and 12 for graduate entry. 10% take a year off which does not jeopardise the chances of an offer but candidates must be available for interview. Candidates must have achieved AAAA at AS to be considered for interview. Re-sit candidates who failed by a small margin are only considered in exceptional circumstances. Transfers of undergraduates from other medical schools not considered. International applicants must show a good standard of written and spoken English. Second time applicants considered if not previously rejected at interview.

Brighton and Sussex (MS) BMAT used to assess each applicant. All applicants required to have grade B in maths and English GCSE. Candidates are interviewed if they have passed the first two stages of assessment (academic and personal statement). Work experience necessary. Interviews (20 mins) for Medicine are currently held in January, February and March. Re-sit applicants are welcome to apply but only if they have dropped in one grade and one subject (eg AAB). Applicants with lower grades but re-sitting can apply to us once they have re-sat their subjects and obtained AAA. All Year 1 medical school students are guaranteed accommodation as long as they apply by the deadline (some students who live in the local area may not be able to apply for accommodation due to more applicants requiring housing than rooms available). Teaching is 'systems integrated' so students are exposed to the clinical environment from Year 1. Cadaver dissection is also part of the course from Year 1, so students get a real understanding of human anatomy, enhancing their learning experience. As the medical school is small, so are class sizes, meaning that students have a strong relationship with academic and support staff.

Bristol No places are offered without an interview. MMI interview format (see above). Second time applicants rarely considered. The top 10% of applicants are called for an interview lasting an hour; the remainder grouped into three categories: 'high reserve', 'hold' and 'unsuccessful' – some from the first two categories will be interviewed. Full details of the interview process are offered on the Bristol website. Widening participation panel considers appropriate candidates, an additional 50 of whom will be interviewed. UKCAT and BMAT not used. Criteria for selection: realistic and academic interest in medicine, commitment to helping others, wide range of interests, contribution to school/college activities, personal achievements. Interview criteria: reasons for wanting to study Medicine, awareness of current developments, communication skills, self-confidence, enthusiasm and determination to study, ability to cope with stress, awareness of the content of the course and career. General Studies and Critical Thinking not acceptable. Subject content overlap (eg Biology/PE/Sports Science) not allowed. Deferred entry welcomed (except for A101 (Graduate Entry)) but applicants must be available for interview. Points equivalent results not accepted. International students English language requirement (or equivalent): IELTS 7.5. Places in Clearing for international students. Some candidates are still applying without the right subjects or grade predictions. Their medicine curriculum is being reviewed. Visit www.bristol.ac.uk/study/undergraduate/ for up-to-date course and entry information.

Cambridge Most applicants for Medicine at Cambridge have at least three science/mathematics A-levels and some colleges require this or ask for particular A-level subject(s). BMAT used to assess each applicant. The standard course is offered at all colleges except Hughes Hall. Normally two interviews, of 20 minutes each. Films of interviews on www.cam.ac.uk/interviews/. 80% of applicants are interviewed and tests may be set or school/college essays submitted. Gap year acceptable but for positive reasons. Clinical studies from Year 4; 50% of students continue at the Cambridge Clinical School (Addenbrooke's Hospital).

Cardiff Admission is determined by a combination of academic performance, non-academic skills, knowledge and completion of the UKCAT test. Applications can be made in the Welsh language. 1,500 of the 3,500 applicants are called for interview. Applications are assessed and scored as follows: 1. Medical motivation and awareness of career. 2. Caring ethos. 3. Sense of responsibility. 4. Evidence of a balanced approach to life. 5. Evidence of self-directed learning. 6. Referee's report.

Dundee No minimum UKCAT cut-off score used, although candidates receiving offers in recent years have typically achieved around 2720 pts. A fully integrated hospital and medical school. Preference given to candidates who achieve the right grades at the first sitting. A system of 10 seven-minute mini-interviews has been introduced which gives students separate opportunities to sell themselves. Deferred entry acceptable. Clinical attachments in Year 4. World-wide experience in final year electives.

Durham (See also **Newcastle**) The medical course is offered in partnership with Newcastle University. Applicants can apply to the Durham or Newcastle campus. Study is at Queen's Campus, Stockton. It places a greater value on whether its applicants can demonstrate the personal qualities and attributes that will help make them the good doctors of the future. This could be through work experience. It has a small number of places for local students who fulfil the Universities' widening participation who engage with their Gateway Programme, and a Foundation route into medicine for mature applicants. But there is no preference for local students in its direct route into medicine. It has an eight-station MMI. This does not include a written PQA. It requires a 2:1 or a First Class Honours degree. Applicants from non-EU countries must apply to Newcastle where there is a quota of places for overseas students. Clinical contact begins in Year 1.

East Anglia Criteria include academic requirements, capacity to cope with self-directed learning, teamwork, responsibility, motivation and UKCAT. Unusual for applicants with less than 2400 pts to be interviewed. Interview regarded as the acid test; seven-stations MMI format (see above) are used for the interviews, candidates visit each station for one question with six minutes at each station. Two scenario questions (see www.med.uea.ac.uk/mbbs/mbbs application). English entry requirement IELTS 7.5. Clinical experience from Year 1. Re-sits considered if grades of ABB were obtained at the first sitting. Those re-sitting three A-levels require predictions of A*AA, two A-levels A*A, one A-level A*.

Edinburgh All examination grades must be achieved at the first sitting; only in extenuating circumstances will re-sits be considered. All UKCAT scores considered. The situation judgement section of the UKCAT test is also considered. Equal weighting given to academic and non-academic criteria. Non-academic criteria score based on personal qualities and skills, evidence of career exploration prior to application, breadth and level of non-academic achievements and interests. Work experience and work shadowing, particularly in a hospital, viewed positively but the admissions panel recognises that not all applicants have equal opportunities to gain such experience. School-leaving applicants are not normally interviewed so references are important. Shortlisted graduate and mature applicants will be interviewed; 190 UK/EU fee rate places available, around one in ten receive an offer. International applicants not normally called for interview. Some clinical experience from Year 1. The six-year programme includes an intercalated research Honours year in Year 3.

Exeter See also under **Plymouth**. Selection procedures include the assessment of UKCAT.

Glasgow UKCAT is considered with all other aspects of the application. All aspects are considered in equal measure. The range of scores considered changes each year as the performance of each admissions cohort varies. Obtaining work experience in a medical setting is not necessary to study or obtain entry to medicine but it is expected that candidates will have a realistic understanding of what a career in medicine entails and be aware of current issues facing the medical profession. A commitment to caring for others is also expected, which can be demonstrated through voluntary or paid work in a community setting. Any commitment to work experience or similar is expected to last beyond the offer-making stage of the admissions process. The interview session will last around 30 minutes. It is expected that applicants will be interviewed by two panels, with two interviewers on each panel. Applicants may be assessed against some or all of the following criteria: Why Medicine?, What makes a good Doctor?, Why Glasgow Medical School?, Suitability to study Medicine, Teamwork and getting on with people, Problem solving in a scenario setting: Candidates will be given the option to select one of two scenarios prior to their interview. Candidates will be expected to discuss the issues around the scenario with their panel. General Studies and Critical Thinking are not acceptable as third subjects. Maths and Further Maths are NOT considered as separate subjects at A-level.

Hull York (MS) Students apply to HYMS not to either the University of Hull or York. Students allocated places at Hull or York by ballot for Years 1 and 2. Transfers from other medical schools not accepted. Disabilities listed on UCAS application do not affect the assessment of the application. UKCAT required; 560 called for interview, 300 offered places. Group interviews of 20 minutes and a personal interview of 10 minutes. Formally structured interviews exploring academic ability, motivation, understanding of healthcare issues, communication skills, conscientiousness, empathy, tolerance and maturity. Questions are drawn from a bank of possible topics (sample questions available online prior to interview). UKCAT test scores of 2,450 or less will be rejected including 400 or less in the verbal reasoning sub-test and less than 500 in any other sub-test. A fourth AS is not required. A-level re-sits not usually accepted. Feedback to unsuccessful candidates after February. Clinical placements from Year 1. Non-EU applicants English language (or equivalent requirement) IELTS 7.5 with at least 7 in each component.

Imperial London 302 places. Fifteen-minute interviews with panel of four or five selectors. Not aimed at being an intimidating experience – an evaluation of motivation, capacity to deal with stress, evidence of commitment to the values of the NHS constitution, evidence of working as a leader and team member, ability to multitask, likely contribution to university life, communication skills and maturity. BMAT test cut-off scores calculated each year depending on applications. Admissions tutor's comment: 'We look for resourceful men and women with wide interests and accomplishments, a practical concern for others and for those who will make a contribution to the life of the school and hospital.' Results within two weeks. Re-sits are only considered for candidates with extenuating circumstances. Candidates may also write directly to the School. Clinical contact in Year 1.

Keele Please check our website for details of our application process http://www.keele.ac.uk/ medicine/undergraduatemedicalcourse/entryrouteshowtoapply/.

Lancaster The University delivers the curriculum at the academic base at Lancaster University and clinical placements in Years 2–5 at acute hospitals and primary care settings in Lancashire and Cumbria. To apply, use Liverpool University's UCAS code and see www.liv.ac.uk/medicine for course and application information. BMAT required. Interviews in the MMI format with 12–14 different stations. See Admission tutors' advice.

Leeds BMAT required. No cut-off point when assessing the results. 218 home students plus 19 non-EU students. Admissions tutor's comment: 'We use the MMI format for interviews [see above]. Consider your motivation carefully – we do!' Good verbal, non-verbal and presentational skills required. Candidates should: (i) be able to report on some direct experience of what a career in medicine is about; (ii) show evidence of social activities on a regular basis (eg part-time employment, organised community experiences); (iii) show evidence of positions of responsibility and interests outside medical and school activities. Disabled students should indicate their disability status on the UCAS form. Candidates must be available for interview; approximately 25% of all applicants interviewed. Points-equivalent results not accepted. International students' English language requirement (or equivalent): IELTS 7.5 including 7.5 in spoken English. Re-applications accepted from students who have achieved the right grades. Re-sits only considered in exceptional circumstances and with good supporting evidence; offer AAA. Transfers from other medical schools not encouraged. Ward based attachments begin in Year 1 and 2; clinical practice from Year 3. Applicants should hold the required A-level grades or a high class science or medically related degree.

Leicester New purpose built medical school opening 2016. UKCAT required. Interview is MMI format – 8 x 7-minute stations looking at attributes laid down by the NHS constitution, Values Based Recruitment, and GMC Tomorrow's Doctors. Deferred entry considered. Resits rarely considered and only on prior agreement from the admissions tutors; offer predicted or achieved AAA including Chemistry and Biology to at least AS. Transfers from other medical schools not considered. Patient contact in first semester, full body dissection. Integrated course.

Liverpool UKCAT is required for all non-graduate applicants applying to the A100 programme. Graduate applicants to the A100 programme must offer GAMSAT. 255 Home/EU places are available on the A100 Liverpool medical programme. Evidence of healthcare insight and awareness, caring contribution to the community, excellent communication and values that embody and underpin good healthcare practice is necessary. Interview is via Multiple Mini Interview. Applicants wishing to take a gap year may be considered but applicants must be available for interview. The Liverpool A100 medical programme usually has 23 places available for international students. Under-qualified international students may be able to apply to Liverpool International College prior to placing an application for the Liverpool A100 medical programme. The selection process at Liverpool is a three stage process which is competitive at each stage. Applications are placed via UCAS. For international students, certain minimum language requirements for the course may exist (IELTS of no less than 7.0 in each component).

London (King's) UKCAT required. Personal statement a significant factor in selection. Emphasis placed on appreciation of academic, physical and emotional demands of the course, commitment, evidence of working in a caring environment, communication skills and interaction with the general public. Approximately 30% of applicants are called for interview. 25 places for non-EU applicants and all of them are interviewed. Usually interviews are of 15–20 minutes' duration with two interviewers. Clinical contact in Year 1.

London (St George's) Applicants must be taking A-level Chemistry and Biology (or one to A-level and the other to AS). You will be required to complete your A-levels within two years of study and the standard offer is AAA and b in a distinct AS. Applicants must have an average grade of A across their top eight GCSEs including English language, maths and double award or the single sciences. Applicants are also required to take the UKCAT test in the year of application. Applicants who meet our A-level and GCSE requirements and achieve our required overall and section scores in UKCAT will be offered an interview. All offers are made post-interview. Applicants are expected to have relevant work experience which is assessed at interview. The English language requirement for international students is IELTS 7.0 with no section less than 6.5. Deferred entry welcome. Medicine (six years, including Foundation year) is for mature non-graduate students only. Medicine (four years, Graduate stream) is for graduates with a 2.2 Hons degree in any discipline. Graduates are not eligible for the five-year Medicine programme. UKCAT selection and overall scores for entry were introduced for the five-year Medicine programme for 2012 onwards.

London (UCL) All candidates are required to take the BMAT. Two or three selectors interview applicants, each interview lasting 15–20 minutes; 30% of applicants interviewed. Qualities sought include motivation, awareness of scientific and medical issues, ability to express and defend opinions, maturity and individual strengths. Deferred entry for good reason is acceptable. Minimum age of entry 18 years. Transfers from other medical schools not accepted. International students may take the University Preparation Certificate for Science and Engineering (UPCSE) which is the minimum entry requirement for entry to Medicine. 24 places for non-EU applicants. Patient contact starts in Year 1.

Manchester Minimum age of entry 17 years; 372 places for around 2,500 applicants. UKCAT scores important. Threshold not disclosed. Seven interviews based on the MMI format (see above). Mitigating circumstances regarding the health or disposition of the candidate should appear in the referee's report. Any applicant who feels unwell before the interview should inform the admissions team and the interview will be re-scheduled; pleas of infirmity cannot be accepted after the interview! Candidates should be aware of the advantages and disadvantages of enquiry-based learning and opinions may be asked. Ethical questions may be raised. Decisions will be made by the end of March. Re-sit offers only made to applicants with extenuating circumstances; having AAB at first attempt A-level. Clinical attachments from Year 3. Application details on www.mms.manchester.ac.uk/undergraduate.

Newcastle (See also **Durham**) 219 places at Newcastle; 99 places at Durham. Applicants can apply to spend Years 1 and 2 at either Newcastle or the Durham, Queen's campus, Stockton. UKCAT threshold not stipulated. From 2017 both campuses will be running Multiple Mini Interviews. Retakes not considered except in extreme circumstances. Deferred entry accepted. Clinical experience from Year 3. Make sure to check the website for the latest up-to-date information before applying.

Nottingham Up to date information on the Medicine programmes at the University of Nottingham and the application process is provided on the University's website.

Oxford Critical Thinking and General Studies are not acceptable. BMAT required. Biology is recommended at AS. 425 applicants called for interview on the basis of academic performance, test score and information on the application form. Ratio of interviewees to places approximately 2.5 to 1. No student admitted without an interview. All colleges use a common set of selection criteria: 11% success rate. Candidate's comment (Lincoln College): 'Two interviewers and two interviews. Questions covered my hobbies and social life, and scientific topics to test my logical train of thought. A great university, but it's not the be-all and end-all if you don't get in.' Clinical experience commences in Year 4.

Plymouth The Plymouth University Peninsula School of Medicine and Dentistry opened for entry in 2013. The typical offers published are not necessarily the threshold for selection for interview, which takes approx. 20 minutes. UKCAT must be taken; thresholds vary (approx 2550–2600 pts).

Queen's Belfast Majority of applicants are school-leavers; 95% from Northern Ireland. When considering applicants' GCSE performance, the best nine subjects will be scored on the basis of 4 points for an A* and 3 points for an A. Points will also be given or deducted on each UKCAT paper. Offers for re-sitting applicants will be restricted. These applicants will have been expected to have missed their offer by one grade. A proportion of candidates will be called for interview. Interviews based on the MMI format (see Admission tutors' advice). A small number of places are allocated to non-EU applicants. Number of places restricted for re-sit applicants who have narrowly missed an offer at Queen's. Clinical experience from Year 1.

St Andrews Medical Science students take a full three-year programme leading to BSc (Hons), followed by clinical medicine at one of its partner medical schools. UKCAT required. MMI interview format (see above) with six mini interviews or stations. Special attention given to international students and those who achieve qualifications at more than one sitting. As far as possible the interview panel will reflect the gender and ethnic distribution of candidates for interview.

Sheffield Applications processed between October and end of March. Candidates may send additional information concerning extenuating circumstances or health problems via the University's Disrupted Studies form, which can be found at: www.sheffield.ac.uk/undergraduate/apply/applying/disrupted. UKCAT required; threshold available at: www.sheffield.ac.uk/medicine/prospective_ug/applying/ entryrequire. MMI interview format with eight, eight-minute interviews. A2 re-sits are not accepted. Gap year acceptable; medicine-related work very helpful. Clinical experience from Year 1. For more information, please see: www.sheffield.ac.uk/medicine/prospective_ug.

Southampton Please refer to the website for further information: www.southampton.ac.uk/medicine.

Swansea Graduate entry only.

Warwick Graduate entry only.

Advice to applicants and planning the UCAS personal statement (See also **Admissions tutors' advice**) Nearly all universities now require either the UKCAT or BMAT entry tests to be taken before applying for Medicine. Check websites (www.ukcat.ac.uk; www.bmat.org.uk) for details of test dates and test centres and with universities for their requirements. It is essential that you check for the latest information before applying and that you give yourself plenty of time to make arrangements for sitting these tests (see also **Chapter 5**).

Admissions tutors look for certain personal qualities (see **Admissions tutors' advice**) and these will emerge in your personal statement, at the interview and on your school or college reference. There should be evidence of scientific interest, commitment, enthusiasm, determination, stability, self-motivation, ability to organise your own work, interest in the welfare of others, communication skills, modesty (arrogance and over-confidence could lead to rejection!), breadth of interest, leadership skills, stamina, good physical and mental health.

Some kind of first-hand experience in a medical setting is almost obligatory for those applying for Medicine (see also under **Admissions tutors' advice**). Depending on your personal contacts in the medical profession, this could include observing operations (for example, orthopaedic surgery), working in hospitals and discussing the career with your GP. Remember that your friends and relatives may have medical conditions that they would be willing to discuss with you – and all this will contribute to your knowledge and show that you are informed and interested. Read medical and scientific magazines and keep up-to-date with important current issues – AIDS, swine 'flu, assisted dying, abortion. Community work, clubs, societies, school and social activities should be mentioned. Show that you have an understanding of the role of health professionals in society and the social factors that influence health and disease. And finally, a comment from one admissions tutor: 'Don't rush around doing things just for your CV. If you are a boring student, be an incredibly well-read boring student! You can play netball, rugby, hockey, make beautiful music and paint with your feet, but if you fail to get the grades you'll be rejected.'

Bristol Deferred places are limited. Late applications may not be accepted.

Misconceptions about this course Liverpool Some applicants think that three science subjects at A-level are required to study Medicine – wrong! **London (St George's)** That you should be white, middle class and male: 60% of medical students are now female and 53% of our students are not white.

Selection interviews Yes Aberdeen, Birmingham, Brighton, Bristol, Cambridge, Dundee, Durham, East Anglia, Exeter, Glasgow, Hull York (MS), Keele, Lancaster, London (King's), London (St George's), Manchester, Newcastle, Nottingham, Oxford (11%), Plymouth, Queen's Belfast, St Andrews, Sussex, Swansea, Warwick, York; **No** Edinburgh.

Interview advice and questions Questions will vary between applicants, depending on their UCAS statements and their AS/A-level subjects. Questions are likely to relate to A-level specific subjects, general medicine topics and unconnected topics (see also **Admissions tutors' advice**). The following questions will provide a guide to the range of topics covered in past interviews. Outline the structure of DNA. What is meant by homeostasis? Is a virus a living organism? What has been the most important advance in biology in the last 50 years? What interests you about (i) science, (ii) biology, (iii) chemistry? Why did you choose the particular AS/A-level subjects you are doing? Why do you want to study Medicine/become a doctor? Do you expect people to be grateful? Why do you want to study here? Why should we take you? What do you do to relax? What do you do when you have three or four things to do, and they are all equally urgent? How do you balance work and all the outside activities you do? Do you agree with the concept of Foundation hospitals? What do you think about polyclinics? Do you think NHS doctors and staff should be able to take private patients? If you were in charge of finances for a large health authority, what would be your priorities for funding? If you had to decide between saving the life of a young child and that of an old person, what would you do? Would you treat lung cancer patients who refuse to give up smoking? What do you understand by 'gene therapy'? Can you give any examples? In your opinion what is the most serious cause for concern for the health of the UK? What do you want to do with your medical degree? What do you think the human genome project can offer medicine? Should we pay for donor organs? Where do you see yourself in 15 years' time? What was the last non-technical book you read? What is your favourite piece of classical music? List your top five novels. What is your favourite play? What politician do you admire the most? Who made the most valuable contribution to the 20th century? Why do you think research is important? Why is teamwork important? What do you think about the NHS's problems? Do you think that sport is important? What did you gain from doing work experience in a nursing home? What were the standards like? How does the medical profession deal with social issues? What societies will you join at university? How could you compare your hobby of rowing to medicine? Do you agree that it is difficult to balance the demands of being a doctor with those of starting a family? In doing a medical course, what would you find the most emotionally challenging aspect? How would you cope with emotional strain? Who should have priority for receiving drugs in a flu epidemic/pandemic? How would you deal with the death of a patient? What are stem cells? Why are they controversial? How is cloning done? What constitutes a human being? Describe an egg. How can you measure intelligence? How do we combat genetic diseases? How are genes actually implanted? What do you want to talk about? If you were a cardiothoracic surgeon, would you perform a heart by-pass operation on a smoker? What are the negative aspects of becoming a doctor? At some interviews essays may be set, eg (i) 'A scientific education is a good basis for a medical degree: discuss'; (ii) 'Only drugs that are safe and effective should be prescribed to patients: discuss'. Should someone sell their kidney? How would you describe a human to a person from Mars? Should obese people have treatment on the NHS? Occasionally applicants at interview may be given scenarios to discuss (see **East Anglia** under **Admissions tutors' advice**). See also **Chapter 5**. **Oxford** Tell me about drowning. What do you think of assisted suicide? Would you give a 60-year-old woman IVF treatment? When are people dead?

Reasons for rejection (non-academic) Insufficient vocation demonstrated. No steps taken to gain practical experience relevant to medicine. Doubts as to the ability to cope with the stress of a medical career. Not enough awareness about the career. Lack of knowledge about the course. Applicant appears dull and lacking in enthusiasm and motivation. Lacking a caring, committed attitude towards people. No evidence of broad social, cultural or sporting interests or of teamwork. Poor or lack of communication skills. Arrogance. Over-confident at interview. Unrealistic expectations about being a doctor.

Age at entry Applicants must be 17 years old on 30 September of the year of entry. However, some medical schools stipulate 17 years 6 months, and a small number stipulate 18 years. Those considering entry at 17 would probably be advised to take a gap year. **London (St George's)** (Med with Fdn Yr) minimum age of applicants is 21.

Health requirements Medical schools require all students to have their immunity status for hepatitis B, tuberculosis and rubella checked on entry. Offers are usually made subject to satisfactory health screening for hepatitis B. In line with advice from the General Medical Council, students will not be admitted to courses who are found to be e-antigen positive when screened within the first week of the course. Candidates accepting offers should assure themselves of their immunity status.

Mature students Medical schools usually accept a small number of mature students each year. However, several, if not the majority, reject applicants over 30 years of age. Some medical schools accept non-graduates although A-level passes at high grades are usually stipulated. The majority of applicants accepted are likely to be graduates with a first or 2.1 degree. **Birmingham** Maximum age at entry is 30 years. **Bristol** Maximum age at entry is 30 years. **Leeds** Maximum age at entry is 30 years. Applicants should hold the required A-level grades or a high class science degree; 15–20 places. **Southampton** 36 places available, maximum age 40. Applicants with nursing qualifications should hold two grade B A-levels including Chemistry. Mature students taking Access courses must achieve 70% in A2 chemistry.

Advice to graduate applicants Graduate applicants are considered by all medical schools. At some medical schools the Graduate Australian Medical Schools Admission Test (GAMSAT) and the Medical Schools Admissions Test (MSAT) are now being used to assess the aptitude of prospective applicants. Applicants at some institutions are selected on the basis of three criteria: (i) an Honours degree at 2.2 or above; (ii) the GAMSAT score; (iii) performance at interview. All applicants must be EU students. **London (St George's)** Some students think that science graduates are the only ones to do well in GAMSAT: 40% of those on the course do not have a science degree or A-levels; however, work experience is essential.

GRADUATE DESTINATIONS AND EMPLOYMENT (2013/14 HESA)
Clinical Medicine graduates surveyed 4,800 **Employed** 4,670 **In voluntary employment** 10 **In further study** 95 **Assumed unemployed** 0

Career note Applicants should also bear in mind that while most doctors do work in the NHS, either in hospital services or in general practice, many graduates choose to work in other fields such as public health, pharmacology, the environment, occupational medicine with industrial organisations, the armed services and opportunities abroad.

OTHER DEGREE SUBJECTS FOR CONSIDERATION
Biomedical/Medical Materials Science; Biology; Biotechnology; Clinical Sciences; Dentistry; Dietetics; Genetics; Health Sciences; Immunology; Medical Biochemistry; Medical Engineering; Medical Microbiology; Medical Physics; Medical Product Design; Medical Sciences; Medicinal Chemistry; Midwifery; Nursing; Nutrition; Occupational Therapy; Optometry; Osteopathy; Pharmacology; Pharmacy; Physiology; Physiotherapy; Psychology; Radiography; Speech Sciences; Sports Medicine; Veterinary Medicine; Virology – and Law! (The work of doctors and lawyers is similar: both are required to identify the relevant information – clinical symptoms or legal issues!)

MICROBIOLOGY

(see also **Biological Sciences, Biology, Biotechnology, Genetics**)

Microbiology is a branch of biological science specialising in the study of micro-organisms: bacteria, viruses and fungi. The subject covers the relationship between these organisms and disease and industrial applications such as food and drug production, waste-water treatment and future biochemical uses.

Useful websites www.sgm.ac.uk; www.nature.com/micro; www.asm.org; www.microbiologynetwork. com; see also **Biochemistry**, **Biological Sciences** and **Biology**.

NB The points totals shown to the left of the institutions are for ease of reference only. It must not be assumed that Tariff points are always used by institutions or that they can be substituted for an offer in grades. The level of an offer is not necessarily indicative of the quality of a course.

COURSE OFFERS INFORMATION

Subject requirements/preferences GCSE English and mathematics and science subjects. **AL** One or two mathematics/science subjects including Chemistry and/or Biology, required or preferred; grades sometimes specified.

Your target offers and examples of degree courses

144 pts **Birmingham** – AAA–AAB incl biol+sci (Biol Sci (Microbiol)) (IB 32 pts HL 666–665)
Edinburgh – AAA–ABB (Mol Biol; Dev Regn Stem Cells) (IB 37–32 pts)
Imperial London – AAA incl biol+sci/maths (Microbiol) (IB 38 pts HL 6 biol+chem/maths)
Leeds – AAA–ABB incl chem/biol+sci (Microbiol; Med Microbiol) (IB 35–34 pts HL 6 chem/ biol+sci)
Manchester – AAA–ABB incl sci/maths (Microbiol (Yr Ind); Microbiol Modn Langs) (IB 37–33 pts)
Sheffield – AAA–AAB incl chem+sci (Genet Microbiol; Mol Biol; Microbiol; Genet Mol Cell Biol) (IB 37–35 pts HL 6 chem+sci); (Med Microbiol) (IB 37–35 pts HL chem+sci)
York – AAA–AAB incl biol+chem/maths (Biotech Microbiol) (IB 36–35 pts HL 6 biol+chem/ maths)
136 pts **Bristol** – AAB–ABB incl chem+sci (Med Microbiol) (IB 34–32 pts HL 6/5 chem+sci); AAB–ABB incl chem+sci/maths (Cell Mol Med) (IB 34–32 pts HL 6–5 chem+sci/maths)
Cardiff – AAB–ABB incl chem (Mol Biol) (IB 34 pts HL 6 biol+chem)
Dundee – AAB incl biol+chem (Microbiol) (IB 30 pts)
Glasgow – AAB–BBB incl biol/chem (Microbiol; Mol Cell Biol (Biotech); Mol Cell Biol (Plnt Sci)) (IB 36–34 pts)
Nottingham – AAB–ABB incl sci/maths/geog (Microbiol) (IB 34–32 pts)
Surrey – AAB–ABB incl biol+sci/maths (Microbiol; Microbiol (Med)) (IB 35–34 pts HL 6 biol 5 sci); AAB–ABB incl sci/maths (Fd Sci Microbiol) (IB 35–34 pts HL 6 biol 5 sci/maths)
Warwick – AAB–ABB incl biol (Med Microbiol Virol) (IB 36–34 pts HL 6 biol)
128 pts **Aston** – ABB–BBB incl biol (Cell Mol Biol) (IB 33 pts)
Leicester – ABB incl sci/maths (Med Microbiol) (IB 30 pts)
Liverpool – ABB incl biol+sci (Microbiol) (IB 33 pts HL 6 biol)
Reading – ABB–BBB incl biol+sci (Microbiol) (IB 32–30 pts)
Strathclyde – ABB–BBB incl biol/chem+sci (Immun Microbiol) (IB 30 pts HL 5 biol/ chem+sci); ABB–BBB incl chem+biol (Microbiol MSci) (IB 32 pts HL 6 chem+biol)
120 pts **Aberdeen** – BBB incl maths+sci (Microbiol) (IB 32 pts HL 5 maths/sci)
Aston – ABB–BBB incl biol (Microbiol Immun) (IB 33 pts HL 6 biol)
Heriot-Watt – BBB incl sci (Biol Sci (Microbiol)) (IB 27 pts HL 5 biol)
Huddersfield – BBB incl sci 120 pts (Biol (Mol Cell))
Leeds Beckett – 120 pts incl biol+sci (Biomed Sci (Microbiol)) (IB 26 pts HL 6 biol)

Nottingham Trent – 120 pts incl biol (Microbiol)
Queen's Belfast – BBB–ABB incl biol+sci (Microbiol)
Stirling – BBB (Cell Biol) (IB 32 pts)
116 pts **Aberystwyth** – 116–132 pts incl biol (Microbiol; Microbiol Zool)
112 pts **Hertfordshire** – 112 pts incl biol/chem+sci/maths (Mol Biol) (IB 28 pts)
104 pts **Edinburgh Napier** – BCC incl sci (Microbiol Biotech) (IB 28 pts HL 5 sci)
Glasgow Caledonian – BCC (Microbiol) (IB 32 pts); BCC incl chem (Cell Mol Biol) (IB 24 pts)
Manchester Met – BCC–BBC incl biol 104–112 pts (Microbiol Mol Biol) (IB 28 pts HL 5 biol)
80 pts **Wolverhampton** – 80 pts incl sci (Microbiol)

Alternative offers
See **Chapter 6** and **Appendix 1** for grades/new UCAS Tariff points information for other examinations.

EXAMPLES OF COLLEGES OFFERING COURSES IN THIS SUBJECT FIELD
St Helens (Coll).

CHOOSING YOUR COURSE (SEE ALSO CH.1)
Universities and colleges teaching quality See www.qaa.ac.uk; http://unistats.direct.gov.uk.

Top research universities and colleges (REF 2014) See **Biological Sciences**.

Examples of sandwich degree courses See also **Biochemistry** and **Biological Sciences**. Aston; Bristol; Leeds; Manchester; Manchester Met; Nottingham Trent; Queen's Belfast; Surrey; York.

ADMISSIONS INFORMATION
Number of applicants per place (approx) Aberystwyth 5; Bradford 6; Bristol 8; Cardiff 4; Dundee 5; Leeds 7; Liverpool 3; Nottingham 7; Strathclyde 10; Surrey 4; Wolverhampton 4.

Advice to applicants and planning the UCAS personal statement Relevant experience, particularly for mature students. See **Biological Sciences** and also **Appendix 3**.

Selection interviews Yes Bristol, Manchester, Surrey; **Some** Aberystwyth (mature students only), Cardiff, Leeds, Nottingham, Wolverhampton; **No** Dundee.

Interview advice and questions Examples of past questions include: How much does the country spend on research and on the armed forces? Discuss reproduction in bacteria. What do you particularly like about your study of biology? What would you like to do after your degree? Do you have any strong views on vivisection? Discuss the differences between the courses you have applied for. What important advances have been made in the biological field recently? How would you describe microbiology? Do you know anything about the diseases caused by micro-organisms? What symptoms would be caused by which particular organisms? See also **Chapter 5**.

AFTER-RESULTS ADVICE
Offers to applicants repeating A-levels Higher Bristol, Strathclyde, Warwick; **Possibly higher** East Anglia, Nottingham; **Same** Aberystwyth, Bradford, Cardiff, Leeds, Liverpool, Wolverhampton.

GRADUATE DESTINATIONS AND EMPLOYMENT (2013/14 HESA)
Graduates surveyed 410 **Employed** 155 **In voluntary employment** 15 **In further study** 145 **Assumed unemployed** 40

Career note See **Biology**.

OTHER DEGREE SUBJECTS FOR CONSIDERATION
Animal Sciences; Biochemistry; Biological Sciences; Biology; Biotechnology; Genetics; Medical Sciences; Medicine; Molecular Biology; Pharmacology; Physiology.

New UCAS points Tariff: A* = 56 pts; A = 48 pts; B = 40 pts; C = 32 pts; D = 24 pts; E = 16 pts

MUSIC

(including **Music Technology**; see also **Engineering (Acoustics and Sound)**)

Theory and practice are combined to a greater or lesser extent in most university Music courses and from which about 50% or more of graduates will go on to non-music careers. However, courses are also offered by conservatoires and schools of music where the majority of applicants are aiming to become professional musicians. For these courses the ability to perform on an instrument is more important than academic ability and offers are therefore likely to be lower. When choosing music courses the applicant should also be aware of the specialisms offered such as classical, jazz, new music, popular music and film music (Leeds College of Music) in addition to courses in music production and music business. Music Journalism is also an option on some courses. See also **Appendix 2**. Some applications are made through the Conservatoires Admissions Service (CUKAS): see **Chapter 6** for details.

Useful websites www.ism.org; www.roh.org.uk; www.nyo.org.uk; www.cukas.ac.uk; www.artscouncil. org.uk; www.soundandmusic.org; http://gb.abrsm.org/en/home

NB The points totals shown to the left of the institutions are for ease of reference only. It must not be assumed that Tariff points are always used by institutions or that they can be substituted for an offer in grades. The level of an offer is not necessarily indicative of the quality of a course.

COURSE OFFERS INFORMATION

Subject requirements/preferences GCSE A foreign language and mathematics may be required. A good range of As and Bs for popular universities. **AL** Music plus an instrumental grade usually required.

Your target offers and examples of degree courses

160 pts Imperial London – A*A*A incl maths+phys (Phys Mus Perf) (IB 39 pts)

152 pts Cambridge – A*AA incl mus (Mus) (IB 40–41 pts HL 776)

Surrey – A*AA-AAA incl maths+mus+phys (Mus Snd Rec (Tonmeister)) (IB 38–36 pts HL 6 maths+mus+phys)

144 pts Birmingham – AAA-AAB (Mus) (IB 32 pts HL 666–665)

Edinburgh – AAA-ABB (Maths Mus; Phys Mus) (IB 37–32 pts); (Hist Art Hist Mus) (IB 37–34 pts)

London (King's) – AAA incl mus+Ger (Ger Mus (Yr Abrd)) (IB 35 pts HL 6 mus+Ger); AAA incl mus (Mus) (IB 35 pts HL 6 mus)

London (RH) – AAA incl maths+phys+mus (Phys Mus) (IB 32 pts)

Oxford – AAA incl mus (Mus) (IB 38 pts)

Southampton – AAA-AAB incl maths+mus (Maths Mus) (IB 36 pts HL 6 maths)

136 pts Bristol – AAB-BBB incl mus (Mus) (IB 34–32 pts HL 6 mus)

Cardiff – AAB-BBB incl music +gr 8 theor+prac (Mus courses) (IB 32 pts HL 6 music)

City – AAB 136 pts (Mus)

Durham – AAB incl mus (Mus) (IB 36 pts)

Glasgow – AAB-BBB incl mus +gr 8 +audition +interview (Mus) (IB 34–32 pts); AAB-BBB incl mus +gr 8 (Mus MA) (IB 36–34 pts)

Leeds – AAB incl mus (Mus; Mus (Perf)) (IB 35 pts HL 6 mus)

Manchester – AAB incl mus +gr 8 instr/voice (Mus) (IB 36–35 pts); AAB incl mus +gr 8 instr/voice +gr 6 piano (Mus Dr) (IB 36–35 pts)

Newcastle – AAB-BBB (Folk Trad Mus) (IB 34–33 pts HL mus)

Nottingham – AAB-ABB incl mus (Mus Phil; Mus) (IB 32 pts)

Southampton – AAB incl maths+phys+mus (Acoust Mus) (IB 34 pts HL 6 maths+phys); AAB-ABB incl mus +gr 8 (Mus Mgt Sci) (IB 34–30 pts HL 6 mus); (Phil Mus) (IB 34–32 pts HL 6 mus); AAB-BBB incl mus +gr 8 (Mus) (IB 34–30 pts HL 6 mus); AAB-ABB incl Engl+mus +gr 8 (Engl Mus) (IB 34 pts HL 6 Engl+mus)

Surrey – AAB–ABB incl mus +gr 7/8 (Mus) (IB 35–34 pts)

York – AAB–ABB incl mus (Mus) (IB 35–34 pts HL 6 mus)

128 pts **Edinburgh** – ABB (Mus Tech; Mus) (IB 34 pts)

Kent – ABB–BBB incl mus (Mus Tech; Mus; Pop Mus) (IB 34 pts)

Leeds – ABB incl mus (Mus Joint Hons) (IB 34 pts HL 6 music)

Liverpool – ABB (Mus Pop Mus) (IB 33 pts)

London (Gold) – ABB (Mus) (IB 33 pts); ABB–BBB (Pop Mus) (IB 33 pts)

London (RH) – ABB incl mus (Mus Fr/Ger/Ital/Span; Mus Pol St; Dr Mus; Mus Phil)
(IB 32 pts)

Newcastle – ABB incl mus (Mus) (IB 32 pts)

Sheffield – ABB–BBB incl mus (Mus; Mus Joint Hons; Theol Mus) (IB 34 pts HL 6 mus)

Sussex – ABB–BBB incl mus +gr 7 (Mus; Mus Tech) (IB 32 pts HL 5 mus)

120 pts **Aberdeen** – BBB (Mus St) (IB 32 pts)

Birmingham City – BBC incl sci/tech/maths/comp 120 pts (Mus Tech) (IB 29 pts)

Brunel – BBB incl mus (Mus; Perf; Cmpsn; Snc Arts) (IB 30 pts)

Derby – 120 pts incl sci/maths/comp/tech +interview (Mus Tech Prod); 120 pts incl sci/
maths/comp/tech (Pop Mus Prod Joint Hons)

Huddersfield – BBB incl mus 120 pts (Mus Tech courses; Mus)

Leeds Beckett – 120 pts (Mus Tech; Perf; Mus Prod) (IB 26 pts)

London (SOAS) – BBB incl mus (Mus Joint Hons) (IB 31 pts)

Middlesex – 120 pts (Mus Bus Arts Mgt)

Queen's Belfast – BBB incl mus (Mus); BBB (Mus Tech Snc Arts)

Trinity Saint David – 120 pts (Mus Tech) (IB 32 pts)

UWE Bristol – 120 pts incl mus+sci/mus tech (Crea Mus Tech) (IB 26 pts HL 5 music/sci)

West London – 120 pts (Musl Thea)

112 pts **Bangor** – 112–120 pts incl mus (Mus)

Birmingham City – 112 pts (Mus Bus)

Bournemouth – 112–120 pts (Mus Aud Tech) (IB 30–31 pts)

Brighton – BBC (Dig Mus Snd Arts) (IB 28 pts)

Canterbury Christ Church – 112 pts (Mus)

Chester – BBC–BCC 112 pts (Pop Mus Perf; Mus Commer Mus Prod) (IB 26 pts)

Coventry – BBC (Mus Perf; Mus Cmpsn) (IB 28 pts); BBC incl maths/phys/tech/mus
(Mus Tech) (IB 29 pts)

Cumbria – 112 pts (Dr Perf Musl Thea Perf)

Derby – 112 pts (Pop Mus Mus Tech)

East London – 112 pts incl mus (Mus Perf Prod) (IB 24 pts)

Edge Hill – BBC 112 pts (Media Mus Snd)

Gloucestershire – 112 pts +interview +portfolio (Pop Mus); 112 pts (Mus Media Mgt)

Huddersfield – BBC 112 pts (Mus Jrnl)

Hull – 112 pts incl mus (Mus) (IB 28 pts)

Liverpool (LIPA) – BBC 112 pts (Snd Tech)

Middlesex – 112 pts (Mus; Pop Mus)

Northampton – 112 pts (Pop Mus courses)

Plymouth – 112 pts (P Mus BEd (QTS))

Portsmouth – 112 pts (Mus Snd Tech) (IB 26 pts)

Reading – 112 pts (P Ed Mus) (IB 28 pts)

Southampton Solent – 112 pts (Pop Mus Prod)

Staffordshire – 112 pts (Crea Mus Tech; Mus Tech)

Sunderland – 112 pts (Commun Mus; Jazz Pop Commer Mus)

West London – 112 pts incl mus (Mus Tech Pop Mus Perf; Mus Perf Mus Tech)

York St John – 112 pts (Mus courses)

104 pts **Bangor** – 104–120 pts (Mus Crea Writ; Mus Film St)

Bath Spa – 104–128 pts (Commer Mus)

Central Lancashire – 104 pts (Mus Thea; Mus; Mus Prod) (IB 28 pts)

Chichester – BCC (Musl Thea) (IB 30 pts)

De Montfort – 104 pts incl mus (Mus Tech Innov; Mus Tech Perf) (IB 28 pts HL 5 mus); 104 pts (Mus Tech) (IB 28 pts)

Falmouth – 104–120 pts (Crea Mus Tech; Mus; Pop Mus)

Hertfordshire – 104 pts incl mus (Mus Cmpsn Tech) (IB 26 pts)

Keele – BCC (Mus Tech) (IB 28 pts); BCC +gr 7 (Mus) (IB 28 pts)

Kingston – 104–144 pts (Mus Joint Hons); 104 pts (Mus; Crea Mus Tech)

Liverpool Hope – BCC–BBB 104–120 pts (Mus)

Oxford Brookes – BCC (Mus) (IB 29 pts)

Plymouth – 104 pts incl mus (Mus) (IB 26 pts)

RConsvS – BCC incl mus +audition (Mus BEd)

South Wales – BCC (Pop Commer Mus; Crea Mus Tech) (IB 29 pts)

96 pts   **Canterbury Christ Church** – 96–112 pts (Commer Mus)

Edinburgh Napier – BCD incl mus+Engl (Pop Mus) (IB 27 pts HL 5 music+Engl); BCD incl mus+Engl +gr 8 (Mus) (IB 27 pts HL 5 mus/Engl)

Glyndŵr – 96 pts (Mus Tech)

Hertfordshire – 96 pts incl mus/sci/tech (Mus Tech) (IB 24 pts)

Leeds (CMus) – 96 pts (Mus (Prod)); 96 pts +gr 8 (Mus (Comb); Mus (Class Mus); Mus (Jazz); Mus (Pop Mus))

Liverpool (LIPA) – CCC 96 pts (Mus; Mus Thea Enter Mgt)

Manchester Met – 96–112 pts (Crea Mus Prod; Pop Mus; Mus) (IB 28 pts)

Middlesex – 96 pts (Jazz)

Rose Bruford (Coll) – 96 pts (Actr Mushp)

Southampton Solent – 96 pts (Mus Prom)

Teesside – 96–112 pts (Mus Tech)

Westminster – CCC (Commer Mus) (IB 26 pts)

West Scotland – CCC incl Engl (Commer Mus) (IB 24 pts); CCC incl mus+maths/phys/comp sci (Mus Tech) (IB 24 pts)

Wolverhampton – 96 pts (Mus; Mus Pop Mus; Mus Tech)

88 pts   **Anglia Ruskin** – 88 pts (Aud Mus Tech) (IB 24 pts); 88–104 pts incl mus/mus tech (Mus) (IB 26 pts HL 5 mus)

Chichester – CCD (Mus) (IB 28 pts); CCD +audition (Choral Dir)

Creative Arts – 88 pts (Mus Jrnl)

80 pts   **Bedfordshire** – 80 pts +interview (Mus Tech) (IB 24 pts)

Bucks New – 80–96 pts (Aud Mus Prod; Mus Mgt Arst Dev)

64 pts   **London (Royal Central Sch SpDr)** – CC +audition (Act (Musl Thea))

Ravensbourne – CC (Mus Prod Media) (IB 28 pts)

UHI – CC +interview (Gael Trad Mus)

32 pts   **Guildhall (Sch Mus Dr)** – 32 pts (Perf Crea Ent); EE (Mus) (IB 24 pts)

London (RAcMus) – EE incl mus +audition (Mus BMus)

RCMus – EE incl mus +audition (BMus)

RConsvS – EE +audition (BMus courses; Musl Thea) (IB 24 pts)

RNCM – EE (BMus)

Royal Welsh (CMusDr) – EE incl mus +audition apply through CUKAS (BMus)

Trinity Laban Consv – EE incl mus +gr 8 check with admissions tutor (Mus)

24 pts   **UHI** – D (Pop Mus)

Alternative offers
See **Chapter 6** and **Appendix 1** for grades/new UCAS Tariff points information for other examinations.

EXAMPLES OF COLLEGES OFFERING COURSES IN THIS SUBJECT FIELD
Most colleges, check with your local college. Accrington and Rossendale (Coll); Amersham and Wycombe (Coll); Barnfield (Coll); Barnsley (Coll); Bath (Coll); Bedford (Coll); Birmingham Met (Coll); Blackpool and Fylde (Coll); Bournemouth and Poole (Coll); Bradford (Coll); Brighton and Hove City (Coll); Calderdale (Coll); Canterbury (Coll); Carshalton (Coll); City and Islington (Coll); Colchester (Inst);

Cornwall (Coll); Coventry City (Coll); Doncaster (Coll); Dudley (Coll); Ealing, Hammersmith and West London (Coll); East Surrey (Coll); Exeter (Coll); Fareham (Coll); Gateshead (Coll); Gloucestershire (Coll); Grimsby (Univ Centre); Havering (Coll); Hertford (Reg Coll); HOW (Coll); Hull (Coll); Kingston (Coll); Leicester (Coll); Liverpool City (Coll); Manchester (Coll); Mid-Cheshire (Coll); Mid-Kent (Coll); Neath Port Talbot (Coll); Nescot; Newcastle (Coll); Northbrook (Coll); Oaklands (Coll); Petroc; Rotherham (CAT); Sheffield (Coll); South Downs (Coll); South Essex (Coll); South Gloucestershire and Stroud (Coll); Telford New (Coll); Tresham (CFHE); Truro and Penwith (Coll); Westminster City (Coll); Wigan and Leigh (Coll).

CHOOSING YOUR COURSE (SEE ALSO CH.1)

Universities and colleges teaching quality See www.qaa.ac.uk; http://unistats.direct.gov.uk.

Top research universities and colleges (REF 2014) (Music, Drama, Dance and Performing Arts) Open University; Roehampton (Dance); London (QM); Warwick; London (SOAS); Durham; London (RH) (Mus); Southampton; Oxford; Birmingham (Mus); City; London (King's) (Film); Manchester (Dr); London (RH) (Dr Thea); Huddersfield; Manchester (Mus); Cardiff.

Examples of sandwich degree courses Birmingham City; Bournemouth; Coventry; Gloucestershire; Hertfordshire; Huddersfield; Leeds; Leeds Beckett; Oxford Brookes; Portsmouth; Staffordshire; Surrey; Teesside; UWE Bristol.

ADMISSIONS INFORMATION

Number of applicants per place (approx) Anglia Ruskin 5; Bangor 4; Bath Spa 8; Birmingham 8; Bristol 8; Brunel 7; Cambridge 2; Cardiff 6; Chichester 4; City 7; Colchester (Inst) 4; Cumbria 7; Durham 4; Edinburgh 11; Edinburgh Napier 3; Glasgow 4; Huddersfield 2; Hull 21; Kingston 18; Lancaster 8; Leeds 18; Liverpool 9; Liverpool (LIPA) 12; London (Gold) 7; London (King's) 10; London (RAcMus) 7; London (RH) 7; London (SOAS) 4; London Met 10; Manchester 6; Middlesex 23; Newcastle 24; Northampton 3; Nottingham 7; Oxford Brookes 12; Queen's Belfast 6; RCMus 10; RConsvS 6; RNCM 8; Roehampton 4; Rose Bruford (Coll) 15; Southampton 6; Strathclyde 15; Surrey 6; (Tonmeister) 12; Trinity Laban Consv 4; Ulster 8; York 8; York St John 2.

Advice to applicants and planning the UCAS personal statement In addition to your ability and expertise with your chosen musical instrument(s), it is also important to know your composers and to take a critical interest in various kinds of music. Reference should be made to these, visits to concerts listed and any special interests indicated in types of musical activity, for example, opera, ballet. Work with orchestras, choirs and other musical groups should also be included and full details given of any competitions entered and awards obtained. See **Chapter 4** for details of applications for Music courses at conservatoires. **Guildhall (Sch Mus Dr)** International applicants sending extra documentation from overseas must make sure that for Customs purposes they indicate that they will pay any import tax charged. **London (Gold)** We encourage students to bring examples of their written and creative work. **Royal Welsh (CMusDr)** Evidence of performance-related experience, eg youth orchestras, solo work, prizes, scholarships etc. Our course is a conservatoire course as opposed to a more academic university course. We offer a very high standard of performance tuition balanced with academic theory modules. **Surrey** (Snd Rec (Tonmeister)) Demonstration of motivation towards professional sound recording.

Misconceptions about this course Cardiff Some mistakenly think that the BMus scheme is either performance-based or something inferior to the principal music-based degree. **Surrey** Some believe that the Music course is exclusively performance-based (the course includes substantial academic and compositional elements).

Selection interviews Most institutions, plus audition to include a performance of a prepared piece (or pieces) on main instrument. **Yes** Aberdeen, Anglia Ruskin, Bath Spa, Birmingham, Birmingham City, Cambridge, Canterbury Christ Church, Cardiff, Chester, Chichester, Doncaster (Coll), Edinburgh, Edinburgh Napier, Falmouth, Glasgow, Guildhall (Sch Mus Dr), Hertfordshire, Huddersfield, Kent, Leeds Beckett, Liverpool (LIPA), London (Gold), Manchester, Oxford (32%), West London, York; **Some** Bristol, Bucks New, Coventry, Staffordshire (Mus Tech), Surrey.

New UCAS points Tariff: A* = 56 pts; A = 48 pts; B = 40 pts; C = 32 pts; D = 24 pts; E = 16 pts

Interview advice and questions See also **Chapter 4** under Applications for Music Courses at Conservatoires.

Anglia Ruskin In addition to A-levels, Grade 7 is required (with a good pass, first study) plus Grade 5 minimum keyboard standard. AS points are not counted towards the Tariff required for this subject. A demo CD may be required.

Bangor Offer depends on proven ability in historical or compositional fields plus acceptable performance standard. Options include music therapy, recording techniques, jazz.

Bath Spa Some candidates interviewed. Required to perform and sight-read on main instrument, and given aural and critical listening tests. Discussion of previous performing, composing and academic experience. (Crea Mus Tech) Applicants will be required to submit an audio portfolio demonstrating technical and creative skills.

Bristol (Mus Fr/Ger/Ital) No in-depth interviews; candidates invited to Open Days.

Cambridge (St Catharine's) At interview candidates may have to undergo some simple keyboard or aural tests (such as harmonisation of an unseen melody or memorisation of a rhythm). More importantly, they will have to comment on some unseen musical extracts from a stylistic and analytical point of view. Candidates are asked to submit some examples of work before the interview, from the fields of harmony and counterpoint, history and analysis; they are also encouraged to send any other material such as compositions, programme notes or an independent essay on a subject of interest to the candidate. (Taking the STEP examination is not a requirement for admission.) Above all this, though, the main prerequisite for reading Music at St Catharine's is an academic interest in the subject itself.

Canterbury Christ Church Associated Board examinations in two instruments (or one instrument and voice); keyboard competence essential, particularly for the BEd course.

Colchester (Inst) Great stress laid on candidate's ability to communicate love of the subject.

Cumbria Admission by live performance or as a demo. QTS applicants interviewed for teaching suitability. See also **Chapter 5**.

Durham Grade 6 piano (Associated Board), a foreign language (GCSE grade A–C), and A-level Music grade B required.

Edinburgh Napier Most candidates are called for interview, although very well-qualified candidates may be offered a place without interview. All are asked to submit samples of their work. Associated Board Grade 7 on piano is usually expected.

Huddersfield Have an open and inquisitive outlook with regard to all aspects of music from performing to composing, musicology to listening. Candidates auditioned on their principal instrument or voice. They will be asked about playing technique, interpretation and interests.

Hull (Coll) Good instrumental grades can improve chances of an offer and of confirmation in August. Students are not normally required to attend an audition/interview. Decisions will be made according to the information supplied on the UCAS application. Successful applicants will be invited to attend a departmental Open Day. We welcome applications from mature students and those with unconventional qualifications: in such cases an interview may be required.

Kingston Associated Board Grade 8 on main instrument is required, with at least Grade 4 on a keyboard instrument (where this is not the main instrument). Audition and interview may be required. Candidates with non-standard qualifications are interviewed and asked to bring samples of written work.

Lancaster Grade 8 Associated Board required on an instrument or voice and some keyboard proficiency (Grade 6) usually expected. We do not accept candidates without interview. For the Music degree, instrumental or vocal skills equivalent to Grade 8 required. For Music Technology, applicants should hold music theory Grade 5 or be able to demonstrate the ability to read a score. Applicants wishing to take practical studies will need instrumental or vocal skills equivalent to Grade 8.

Leeds Intending students should follow an academic rather than practical-oriented A-level course. The University is experimenting with abandoning the formal interview in favour of small group Open Days for those holding offers made on the UCAS information, to focus on a practical exchange of information relevant to the applicant's decision to accept or reject the offer. Grade 8 Associated Board on an instrument is a normal expectation.

Leeds (CMus) There will be an audition and an essay on music theory.

Liverpool (LIPA) In addition to performing in orchestras etc, give details of any compositions you have completed (the number and styles). Instrumentalists (including vocalists) should describe any performance/gig experience together with any musical instrument grades achieved. (Mus) Candidates should prepare two pieces of contrasting music to play on their chosen instrument. Candidates who have put song-writing/composition as either first or second choice should have a CD of their work to play to the panel. (Snd Tech) Applicants must prepare a critical review of a sound recording of their choice which highlights the technical and production values that they think are the most important. Examples of recorded work they have undertaken should also be available at interview, eg on CD. (Mus Perf Arts) Applicants should have A-levels (or equivalent) and have completed Grade 5 Music Theory before the course commences.

London (Gold) The interview will include a discussion of music and the personal interests of the applicant.

London (RAcMus) All candidates are called for audition, and those who are successful are called for a further interview; places are offered later, subject to the minimum GCSE requirements being achieved. (BMus) Applicants sit a 50-minute written paper, and may also be tested on keyboard and aural performance.

London (RH) Candidates are tested with an aural test, a harmony/counterpoint test, a conceptual essay, and a viva at which they are asked questions and asked to perform. On the basis of the results in these tests we make offers. There is a tradition of caring for each individual and we strive to give each applicant a fair hearing. Musicality, a good intellect and real enthusiasm are the qualities we look for.

London (SOAS) Candidates are judged on individual merits. Applicants are expected to have substantial practical experience of musical performance, but not necessarily Western music.

Newcastle We expect a reasonable background knowledge of musical history, basic harmony and counterpoint and keyboard skills of approximately Grade 8 standard; if the main instrument is not piano or organ – Grade 5. While practical skills are important, academic ability is the primary requisite. Practical Music or Music Technology accepted in place of Music.

Nottingham A high standard of aural ability is expected. Interviewees take two short written papers, intellectual enquiry and attainment are looked for, together with a good range of knowledge and sense of enterprise. Only borderline/mature students are interviewed, successful applicants are invited to an Open Day.

RCMus All UK and Eire candidates are required to attend an audition in person but recordings are acceptable from overseas applicants. It must be stressed, however, that personal audition is preferable and those students offered places on the basis of a recorded audition may be required to take a confirmatory audition on arrival. Candidates are required to perform on the principal study instrument as well as undertaking sight-reading, aural tests and paperwork. There is also an interview. Potential scholars sometimes proceed to a second audition, usually on the same day. The academic requirement for the BMus (RCM) course is two A-levels at pass grades. Acceptance is ultimately based on the quality of performance at audition, performing experience and perceived potential as a performer. As a guide, applicants should be of at least Grade 8 distinction standard.

RNCM All applicants are called for audition. Successful applicants proceed to an academic interview which will include aural tests and questions on music theory and history. Student comment: 'A 45-minute interview with a panel of three. Focus was on portfolio of compositions sent in advance. Prior to interview was asked to harmonise a short passage and study an orchestral excerpt followed up at interview. Aural test waived.'

Royal Welsh (CMusDr) All UK and Eire applicants are called to audition in person; overseas candidates may audition by sending a recording. Candidates are required to perform on their sight-reading ability. Candidates who are successful in the audition proceed to interview in which there will be a short aural test. Candidates for the BA (Music) course are required to bring recent examples of harmony, counterpoint and essays.

Surrey (Music) Applicants may expect to be questioned in the interview about their musical experience, enthusiasm and any particular compositions they have studied. They will also be asked to perform on their first instrument. (Snd Rec (Tonmeister)) Applicants can expect to be questioned about their recording interests and motivation and show an ability to relate A-level scientific knowledge to simple recording equipment. They may be asked to perform on their first instrument.

Trinity Laban Consv Applicants for the BMus degree must attend an audition and show that they have attained a certain level of competence in their principal and second studies, musical subjects and in musical theory. Grade 8 practical and theory can count as one A-level, but not if the second A-level is in music. Overseas applicants may submit a tape recording in the first instance when a place may be offered for one year. Thereafter they will have to undergo a further test. They must also show evidence of good aural perception in musical techniques and musical analysis.

Wolverhampton The audition will involve playing/singing a piece of own-choice music (up to five minutes – no longer). Accompanists may be brought along or the department may be able to provide one if requested in advance. Candidates will be requested to produce a short piece of written work. It would be helpful to see any music certificates and a Record of Achievement if available, together with examples of recent work in music (an essay, harmony, composition etc).

Reasons for rejection (non-academic) Usually academic (auditions, practical, aural/written test). Dull, unenthusiastic students, ignorant about their subject, showing lack of motivation and imagination. **Cambridge** Her harmony was marred by elementary technical errors and her compositions lacked formal and stylistic focus. **London (King's)** Apparent lack of interest, performance not good enough, lack of music history knowledge. Foreign students: language skills inadequate. **Royal Welsh (CMusDr)** Performing/technical ability not of the required standard.

AFTER-RESULTS ADVICE
Offers to applicants repeating A-levels Higher Leeds; **Same** Anglia Ruskin, Bath Spa, Bristol, Cardiff, City, Colchester (Inst), De Montfort, Durham, Guildhall (Sch Mus Dr), Huddersfield, Hull, Kingston, Leeds (CMus), London (RAcMus), London (RH), Nottingham, Rose Bruford (Coll), Royal Welsh (CMusDr), Staffordshire, Surrey, York, York St John.

GRADUATE DESTINATIONS AND EMPLOYMENT (2013/14 HESA)
Graduates surveyed 4,435 **Employed** 1,830 **In voluntary employment** 140 **In further study** 1,130 **Assumed unemployed** 250

Career note Some graduates go into performance-based careers, many enter the teaching profession and others go into a wide range of careers requiring graduate skills.

OTHER DEGREE SUBJECTS FOR CONSIDERATION
Acoustics; Drama; Musical Theatre; Performance Arts.

NATURAL SCIENCES
(see also **Biological Sciences**)

These are flexible courses allowing the student to gain a broad view of the origins and potential of sciences in general and then to focus in Years 2 and 3 on a specialist area of scientific study.

Useful websites www.scicentral.com; www.nature.com; see also **Biology**, **Chemistry** and **Physics**.

NB The points totals shown to the left of the institutions are for ease of reference only. It must not be assumed that Tariff points are always used by institutions or that they can be substituted for an offer in grades. The level of an offer is not necessarily indicative of the quality of a course.

COURSE OFFERS INFORMATION
Subject requirements/preferences GCSE Strong results, particularly in the sciences. **AL** Science subjects required.

Cambridge (Emmanuel) One AEA science may be required when only two sciences taken; (Peterhouse) STEP may be used as part of conditional offer.

Your target offers and examples of degree courses

160 pts **Cambridge** – A*A*A incl sci/maths +TSA test (Nat Sci (Neuro)) (IB 40–41 pts HL 776); A*A*A incl sci/maths (Nat Sci (Physiol Dev Neuro); Nat Sci (Bioch); Nat Sci (Biol Biomed Sci); Nat Sci (Chem); Nat Sci (Genet); Nat Sci (Earth Sci); Nat Sci (Mat Sci); Nat Sci (Zool); Nat Sci; Nat Sci (Hist Phil Sci)) (IB 40–41 pts HL 776); (Nat Sci (Astro)) (IB 40–41 pts HL 776)

152 pts **Bath** – A*AA incl maths (Nat Sci) (IB 36 pts HL 6 maths); A*AA (Nat Sci (St Abrd)) (IB 36 pts)

Birmingham – A*AA (Nat Sci) (IB 32 pts HL 766)

Cambridge – A*AA (Educ Biol Sci) (IB 40–41 pts HL 776)

Durham – A*AA incl biol/chem (Nat Sci) (IB 38 pts)

East Anglia – A*AA/A*ABB incl sci (Nat Sci MNatSci; Nat Sci (Yr Ind/St Abrd)) (IB 35 pts HL 6 sci)

Exeter – A*AA–AAB incl maths+sci (Nat Sci) (IB 36–32 pts HL 5 maths+sci)

Lancaster – A*AA–AAA incl sci (Nat Sci; Nat Sci (St Abrd)) (IB 38–36 pts HL 6 sci)

Leeds – A*AA (Nat Sci) (IB 36 pts)

London (UCL) – A*AA–AAA incl sci/maths/geol (Nat Sci) (IB 39–38 pts HL 5 sci/maths)

Nottingham – A*AA incl sci/maths (Nat Sci) (IB 38 pts)

144 pts **East Anglia** – AAA/AABB incl sci (Nat Sci) (IB 34 pts HL 6 sci)

Leicester – AAA incl sci (Nat Sci) (IB 34 pts)

Open University – contact +44 (0)845 300 6090 **or** www.openuniversity.co.uk/you (Nat Sci)

Alternative offers

See **Chapter 6** and **Appendix 1** for grades/new UCAS Tariff points information for other examinations.

CHOOSING YOUR COURSE (SEE ALSO CH.1)

Universities and colleges teaching quality See www.qaa.ac.uk; http://unistats.direct.gov.uk.

Top research universities and colleges (REF 2014) See separate science tables.

Examples of sandwich degree courses Bath; East Anglia; Leeds.

ADMISSIONS INFORMATION

Number of applicants per place (approx) Bath 8; Birmingham 10; Cambridge 5; Durham 6; London (UCL) 5; Nottingham 7.

Advice to applicants and planning the UCAS personal statement See **Biology**, **Chemistry**, **Physics** and **Appendix 3**.

Selection interviews Yes Bath, Cambridge, East Anglia, Southampton, York; **No** Birmingham.

Interview advice and questions See also **Chapter 5**. **Cambridge** Questions depend on subject choices and studies at A-level and past questions have included the following: Discuss the setting up of a chemical engineering plant and the probabilities of failure of various components. Questions on the basic principles of physical chemistry, protein structure and functions and physiology. Questions on biological specimens. Comment on the theory of evolution and the story of the Creation in Genesis. What are your weaknesses? Questions on electro-micrographs. What do you talk about with your friends? How would you benefit from a university education? What scientific magazines do you read? Questions on atoms, types of bonding and structures. What are the problems of being tall? What are the differences between metals and non-metals? Why does graphite conduct? Questions on quantum physics and wave mechanics. How could you contribute to life here? What do you see yourself doing in five years' time? If it is common public belief that today's problems, for example industrial pollution, are caused by scientists, why do you wish to become one? Questions on the gyroscopic motion of cycle wheels, the forces on a cycle in motion and the design of mountain bikes. What do you consider will be the most startling scientific development in the future? What do you estimate is the mass of air in this room? If a carrot can grow from one carrot cell, why not a human?

AFTER-RESULTS ADVICE
Offers to applicants repeating A-levels No Cambridge.

GRADUATE DESTINATIONS AND EMPLOYMENT (2013/14 HESA)
See **Biology**, **Chemistry**, **Mathematics** and **Physics**.

Career note These courses offer a range of science and in some cases non-scientific subjects, providing students with the flexibility to develop particular interests as they progress through the course.

OTHER DEGREE SUBJECTS FOR CONSIDERATION
Anatomy; Anthropology; Archaeology; Astrophysics; Biochemistry; Biological Sciences; Biology; Chemistry; Earth Sciences; Ecology; Genetics; Geography; Geology; History and Philosophy of Science; Neuroscience; Pharmacology; Physics; Plant Sciences; Psychology; Zoology.

NAVAL ARCHITECTURE

(including **Marine Engineering** and **Ship Science**; see also **Marine/Maritime Studies**)

Professional naval architects or marine engineers are responsible for the design, construction and repair of cruise liners, yachts, submarines, container ships and oil tankers. Ship Science focuses on, for example, vehicles and structures that use the oceans for transport, recreation and energy generation. Courses cover marine structures, transport and operations, design, propulsion and mathematics. Ship design has many similarities to the design of aircraft.

Useful websites www.rina.org.uk; www.strath.ac.uk/na-me; www.naval-architecture.co.uk

NB The points totals shown to the left of the institutions are for ease of reference only. It must not be assumed that Tariff points are always used by institutions or that they can be substituted for an offer in grades. The level of an offer is not necessarily indicative of the quality of a course.

COURSE OFFERS INFORMATION
Subject requirements/preferences GCSE Grades A–C in mathematics and physics are normally required. **AL** Mathematics and Physics usually required.

Your target offers and examples of degree courses
144 pts Southampton – AAA incl maths+phys (Ship Sci (Advncd Mat) MEng; Ship Sci (Eng Mgt) MEng; Ship Sci (Nvl Archit) MEng; Ship Sci (Nvl Eng) MEng; Ship Sci (Ycht Sml Crft) MEng; Ship Sci) (IB 36 pts HL 6 maths+phys)
Strathclyde – AAA–AAB incl maths+phys (Nvl Archit Mar Eng MEng; Nvl Archit Ocn Eng MEng) (IB 36 pts HL 6 maths+phys)
136 pts Newcastle – AAB incl maths (Mar Tech Mar Eng MEng; Mar Tech Sml Crft Tech MEng; Mar Tech Off Eng MEng) (IB 36 pts HL 5 maths+phys); AAB–ABB incl maths (Mar Tech Sml Crft Tech; Mar Tech Mar Eng) (IB 35–34 pts HL 5 maths+phys)
128 pts Liverpool John Moores – 128 pts (Mech Mar Eng MEng)
Strathclyde – ABB–BBB incl maths+phys (Nvl Archit Mar Eng; Nvl Archit Ocn Eng) (IB 32 pts HL 5 maths+phys)
120 pts Plymouth – 120 pts incl maths+sci/tech (Mar Tech) (IB 28 pts); 120 pts (Ocn Sci)
112 pts Liverpool John Moores – 112 pts (Mech Mar Eng; Naut Sci)
96 pts Southampton Solent – 96 pts (Ycht Des Prod)

Alternative offers
See **Chapter 6** and **Appendix 1** for grades/new UCAS Tariff points information for other examinations.

EXAMPLES OF COLLEGES OFFERING COURSES IN THIS SUBJECT FIELD
Cornwall (Coll); Plymouth City (Coll); South Tyneside (Coll).

CHOOSING YOUR COURSE (SEE ALSO CH.1)
Universities and colleges teaching quality See www.qaa.ac.uk; http://unistats.direct.gov.uk.

Examples of sandwich degree courses Plymouth.

ADMISSIONS INFORMATION
Number of applicants per place (approx) Newcastle 9; Southampton 4.

Advice to applicants and planning the UCAS personal statement Special interests in this subject area should be described fully. Visits to shipyards and awareness of ship design from the *Mary Rose* in Portsmouth to modern speedboats should be fully explained and the problems noted. See also **Engineering/Engineering Sciences**, **Marine/Maritime Studies** and **Appendix 3**.

Selection interviews **Some** Newcastle, Southampton.

Interview advice and questions Because of the highly vocational nature of this subject, applicants will naturally be expected to discuss any work experience and to justify their reasons for choosing the course. See also **Chapter 5**.

AFTER-RESULTS ADVICE
Offers to applicants repeating A-levels **Higher** Newcastle.

GRADUATE DESTINATIONS AND EMPLOYMENT (2013/14 HESA)
Graduates surveyed 90 **Employed** 70 **In voluntary employment** 0 **In further study** 5 **Assumed unemployed** 5

Career note A small proportion of naval architects work in the shipbuilding and repair industry, others are involved in the construction of oil rigs or may work for ship-owning companies. There are also a number of firms of marine consultants employing naval architects as managers or consultants.

OTHER DEGREE SUBJECTS FOR CONSIDERATION
Aeronautical Engineering; Civil Engineering; Electrical/Electronic Engineering; Geography; Marine Biology; Marine Engineering; Marine/Maritime Studies; Marine Technology; Mechanical Engineering; Oceanography; Physics; Shipping Operations; Transport Management.

NEUROSCIENCE

(including **Anatomical Science**; see also **Biological Sciences, Human Sciences/Human Biosciences, Physiology, Psychology**)

Courses in neuroscience include the study of biochemistry, cell and molecular biology, genetics and physiology and focus on the structure and functions of the brain. It also overlaps into neurobiology, neuroanatomy, neurophysiology, pharmacology and psychology which in turn can involve the study of behavioural problems and mental processes, both conscious and unconscious. It is a field of research contributing to the treatment of such medical conditions as Parkinson's disease, Alzheimer's, schizophrenia, epilepsy and autism. Studies will cover anatomical structures such as skeletal, muscular, cardiovascular and nervous systems and components such as muscle cells.

Useful websites www.innerbody.com; www.instantanatomy.net

NB The points totals shown to the left of the institutions are for ease of reference only. It must not be assumed that Tariff points are always used by institutions or that they can be substituted for an offer in grades. The level of an offer is not necessarily indicative of the quality of a course.

COURSE OFFERS INFORMATION
Subject requirements/preferences **GCSE** Mathematics usually required. **AL** One or two mathematics/science subjects usually required;

Biology and Chemistry preferred.

Your target offers and examples of degree courses
160 pts **Cambridge** – A*A*A incl sci/maths +TSA test (Nat Sci (Neuro)) (IB 40–41 pts HL 776)
144 pts **Birmingham** – AAA incl biol (Hum Neuro) (IB 32 pts HL 666 incl biol)
         Edinburgh – AAA–ABB (Neuro) (IB 37–32 pts)
         Leeds – AAA–AAB incl biol/chem+sci (Neuro) (IB 35–34 pts HL 6 biol/chem+sci)
         Liverpool – AAA–ABB incl biol (Anat Hum Biol) (IB 36–33 pts HL 6 biol)
         London (RH) – AAA–AAB (Psy Clin Cog Neuro) (IB 32 pts)
         London (UCL) – AAA incl chem+sci/maths (Neuro) (IB 38 pts HL 5 chem+sci/maths)
         Manchester – AAA–ABB (Cog Neuro Psy) (IB 37–33 pts); AAA–ABB incl sci/maths
            (Anat Sci; Anat Sci (Yr Ind)) (IB 37–33 pts HL 5/6 biol+chem); (Neuro) (IB 37–33 pts)
         Reading – AAA–AAB (Psy Neuro) (IB 35 pts)
         Sussex – AAA–AAB (Psy Cog Sci; Psy Neuro) (IB 35 pts)
136 pts **Bangor** – 136–112 pts (Psy Neuropsy)
         Bristol – AAB–ABB incl sci/maths (Neuro) (IB 34–32 pts HL 6/5 sci/maths)
         Cardiff – AAB–ABB incl biol (Biomed Sci; Biomed Sci (Neuro); Biomed Sci (Anat))
            (IB 34 pts HL 6 biol+chem)
         Glasgow – AAB–BBB incl biol/chem (Anat; Neuro) (IB 36–34 pts)
         Leicester – AAB (Psy Cog Neuro) (IB 32 pts)
         London (Gold) – AAB–ABB (Psy Cog Neuro) (IB 33 pts)
         London (King's) – AAB incl chem+biol (Anat Dev Hum Biol; Neuro) (IB 35 pts)
         Nottingham – AAB incl biol/chem+sci/maths (Neuro) (IB 34 pts)
         St Andrews – AAB incl sci/maths (Neuro) (IB 35 pts)
         Sussex – AAB–ABB incl sci/psy (Med Neuro; Neuro Cog Sci) (IB 34 pts HL 5 sci/psy)
128 pts **Essex** – ABB–BBB (Psy Cog Neuro) (IB 32–30 pts)
120 pts **Aberdeen** – BBB incl maths+sci (Neuro Psy) (IB 32 pts HL 5 maths+sci)
         Dundee – BBB–BCC incl biol+chem (Anat Sci) (IB 30 pts)
         Keele – BBB/ABC incl sci/maths (Neuro) (IB 32 pts HL 6 chem)
112 pts **Central Lancashire** – 112–128 pts (Neuropsy) (IB 28–30 pts)
         Middlesex – 112 pts (Med Physiol (Neuro))

Alternative offers
See **Chapter 6** and **Appendix 1** for grades/new UCAS Tariff points information for other examinations.

CHOOSING YOUR COURSE (SEE ALSO CH.1)
Universities and colleges teaching quality See www.qaa.ac.uk; http://unistats.direct.gov.uk.

Top research universities and colleges (REF 2014) See **Biological Sciences**.

Examples of sandwich degree courses Bristol; Cardiff; Leeds; Manchester.

ADMISSIONS INFORMATION
Number of applicants per place (approx) Bristol 10; Cardiff 9; Liverpool 7; London (UCL) 7.

Advice to applicants and planning the UCAS personal statement Give reasons for your interest in this subject (usually stemming from school work in biology). Discuss any articles in medical and other scientific journals which have attracted your attention and any new developments in medicine related to neuroscience.

Selection interviews Yes Liverpool; **Some** Cardiff; **No** Bristol.

Interview advice and questions Questions are likely on your particular interests in biology and anatomy, why you wish to study the subject and your future career intentions. See also **Chapter 5**.

Reasons for rejection (non-academic) Liverpool Unfocused applications with no evidence of basic knowledge of the course.

AFTER-RESULTS ADVICE
Offers to applicants repeating A-levels Higher Bristol; **Possibly higher** Liverpool; **Same** Cardiff.

Check **Chapter 3** for new university admission details and **Chapter 6** on how to read the subject tables.

Aston University
Birmingham

BSc Neuroscience

The development of an undergraduate programme in Neuroscience at Aston University reflects our longstanding expertise in this area.

What is Neuroscience?

Neuroscience is a subject with broad scope, covering everything from how psychology can help us understand the mind, memory and consciousness, right down to how the machinery at the presynaptic terminal controls neurotransmitter release at individual brain synapses. It can be mathematical/theoretical, for example in the study of neuronal network architectures and graph theory, or it can be wet laboratory science using reduced preparations such as the in vitro brain slice. Often, these approaches are aimed at answering similar questions. Neuroscience is one of the most rapidly expanding areas of research in the world – check out the BlueBrain or Connectome projects (google 'bluebrain' or 'humanconnectome.org') - you could be part of this type of groundbreaking work!

Why choose this degree?

> Neuroscience research at Aston University is pioneering and is taught by active internationally renowned researchers. This ensures your course content is always up to date and relevant.
> The degree has a large practical element to give you hands-on experience of working at whole brain and in vitro levels including local field potential recording and receptor pharmacology.
> You can specialise in your final year in areas that most interest you.
> You will learn the elements of Biochemistry, Molecular Biology, Anatomy, Developmental Biology, Pharmacology,Psychology and Cellular and Network Physiology that underlie modern Neuroscience.
> You will learn about how the brain functions in disease states, for example epilepsy, schizophrenia, Parkinson's disease and Alzheimer's.
> You will gain an understanding of ethical and social issues surrounding research in Neuroscience and its application to medical conditions.
> A BSc in Neuroscience will open the path to postgraduate study in this exciting area.

Course Content

The course is designed to provide a sound academic understanding of neuroscience, alongside extensive, solid practical experience of research, both at the whole-brain (human) level and in vitro, using reduced preparations. You will develop a rigorous understanding of neuroscience from the molecular to the whole brain, including: how receptors and ion channels operate, neuronal behaviour and communication, local network function and how brain circuits produce rhythmic activity. At the other end of the spectrum you will learn about cognition, visual and auditory attention and brain development. By the final year, you will be ready to undertake your independent project, supervised by a member of academic staff and focusing on the area of neuroscience that interests you most.

 For further details visit **www.aston.ac.uk/lhs**

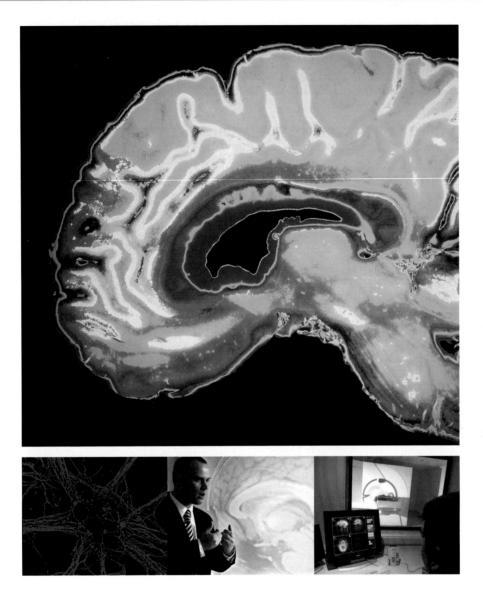

Career prospects after graduation

Many graduates of the BSc Neuroscience programme may wish to enter into academic research at PhD level, either at Aston or at other institutions worldwide. Recent PhD students from Aston have gone on to work at prestigious Neuroscience research institutions, for example, in Chicago, Philadelphia and Helsinki, gaining the experience they require to start their own laboratories. However, there exist many opportunities for neuroscience graduates to work in pharmaceutical company drug development, clinical neurophysiology, contract research, neuropsychology and psychiatry, regulatory affairs, policy and research administration, the media, publishing and teaching. Neuroscience is growing globally, and as more is discovered about the brain, there will be many more as yet unimagined career opportunities in future!

GRADUATE DESTINATIONS AND EMPLOYMENT (2013/14 HESA)
Including Pathology and Physiology graduates surveyed 3,015 **Employed** 1,820 **In voluntary employment** 25 **In further study** 615 **Assumed unemployed** 150

Career note The subject leads to a range of careers in various laboratories, in government establishments, the NHS, pharmaceutical and food industries. It can also lead to postgraduate studies in physiotherapy, nursing, osteopathy and, in exceptional cases, in medicine, dentistry and veterinary science.

OTHER DEGREE SUBJECTS FOR CONSIDERATION
Biological Sciences; Biology; Genetics; Microbiology; Osteopathy; Physiology; Physiotherapy.

NURSING and MIDWIFERY
(see also **Biological Sciences, Community Studies/Development, Health Sciences/Studies**)

Nursing and Midwifery courses are designed to equip students with the scientific and caring skills demanded by medical science in the 21st century. Courses follow a similar pattern with an introductory programme of study covering clinical skills, nursing practice and the behavioural and social sciences. Thereafter, specialisation starts in adult, child or mental health nursing, or with patients with learning disabilities. Throughout the three-year course students gain extensive clinical experience in hospital wards, clinics, accident and emergency and high-dependency settings. UCAS handles applications for Nursing degree courses. From 2013 nursing became an all-graduate profession.

Useful websites www.scicentral.com; www.nhscareers.nhs.uk; www.nursingtimes.net; www.nmc-uk.org; www.rcn.org.uk; www.rcm.org.uk; see also **Health Sciences/Studies** and **Medicine**.

NB The points totals shown to the left of the institutions are for ease of reference only. It must not be assumed that Tariff points are always used by institutions or that they can be substituted for an offer in grades. The level of an offer is not necessarily indicative of the quality of a course.

COURSE OFFERS INFORMATION
Subject requirements/preferences GCSE English and a science subject. Mathematics required at several universities. **AL** Science subjects required for some courses. **Other** All applicants holding firm offers will require an occupational health check and Disclosure and Barring Service (DBS) clearance and are required to provide documentary evidence that they have not been infected with hepatitis B. (Paramed Sci) Full clean manual UK driving licence with at least a provisional C1 category.

Your target offers and examples of degree courses
144 pts **Southampton** – AAA incl sci (Midwif) (IB 36 pts)
136 pts **Bournemouth** – 136 pts (Midwif) (IB 33 pts)
         Edinburgh – AAB–ABB (Nurs St) (IB 36–34 pts)
         UWE Bristol – 136 pts incl sci/soc sci (Midwif) (IB 28 pts HL 6 sci/soc sci)
128 pts **Birmingham City** – ABB 128 pts (Midwif) (IB 36 pts)
         Bradford – ABB 128 pts (Midwif St)
         Cardiff – ABB (Midwif) (IB 28 pts)
         Central Lancashire – ABB incl biol (Midwif St) (IB 25 pts)
         City – 128 pts (Midwif) (IB 33 pts)
         East Anglia – ABB (Midwif) (IB 32 pts)
         Edge Hill – ABB 128 pts (Midwif)
         Glasgow – ABB incl sci/maths (Nurs A/C/LD/MH) (IB 32 pts)
         Huddersfield – ABB incl biol 128 pts (Midwif St)
         Leeds – ABB incl biol (Midwif) (IB 34 pts HL 5 biol)
         London (King's) – ABB (Midwif Reg) (IB 34 pts)
         Manchester – ABB incl sci (Midwif) (IB 34 pts)
         Sheffield Hallam – 128 pts incl nat/soc sci (Midwif)
         Southampton – ABB–BBB (Nurs A/C/MH) (IB 32–30 pts)

Surrey – ABB +interview (Midwif) (IB 34 pts)
York – ABB (Midwif) (IB 32 pts)

120 pts **Anglia Ruskin** – 120 pts (Midwif) (IB 26 pts)
Bangor – 120 pts (Nurs A/C/LD/MH; Midwif)
Birmingham – BBB (Nurs A/MH/C) (IB 32 pts HL 555)
Birmingham City – BBB 120 pts (Nurs A/C/LD/MH) (IB 26 pts)
Bournemouth – 120 pts (Nurs A/C/LD/MH) (IB 31 pts)
Bradford – BBB 120 pts (Nurs A/C/MH)
Brighton – BBB incl sci/soc sci (Nurs A/C/MH) (IB 30 pts); BBB (Midwif) (IB 30 pts)
Canterbury Christ Church – BBB (Midwif)
Cardiff – BBB (Nurs A/C/MH) (IB 28 pts)
Chester – BBB–BBC incl biol/app sci 120 pts (Midwif) (IB 28 pts HL 5 biol)
City – 120 pts +interview+test (Nurs A/C/MH)
Coventry – BBB incl biol (Midwif) (IB 27)
Cumbria – 120 pts incl biol (Midwif)
De Montfort – 120 pts (Midwif) (IB 30 pts)
East Anglia – BBB (Nurs A/C/LD/MH) (IB 31 pts)
Hertfordshire – 120 pts incl biol/soc sci (Midwif RM) (IB 30 pts)
Huddersfield – BBB incl biol/maths/soc sci 120 pts (Nurs A/C/LD/MH)
Kingston – 120–128 pts (Midwif)
Leeds – BBB (Nurs A/C/LD/MH) (IB 33 pts)
Leeds Beckett – 120 pts (Nurs A/MH) (IB 26 pts)
Liverpool – BBB (Nurs) (IB 30 pts)
Liverpool John Moores – 120 pts (Midwif) (IB 26 pts)
London (King's) – BBB (Nurs A/C/MH) (IB 32 pts)
London South Bank – BBB 120 pts (Midwif)
Northumbria – 120 pts incl sci/hlth (Midwif) (IB 30 pts)
Nottingham – BBB (Nurs A/C/LD/MH) (IB 30 pts)
Oxford Brookes – BBB incl biol (Midwif) (IB 32 pts HL 4 biol)
South Wales – BBB (Midwif; Nurs A/C/LD/MH) (IB 32 pts)
Swansea – BBB (Nurs A/C/MH; Midwif)
UWE Bristol – 120 pts incl sci/soc sci (Nurs A/C/LD/MH) (IB 26 pts HL 5 sci/soc sci)
West London – 120 pts (Midwif)
Worcester – 120 pts (Nurs A/C/MH); BBB incl sci/soc sci 120 pts (Midwif)
York – BBB (Nurs A/C/LD/MH) (IB 31 pts)

112 pts **Anglia Ruskin** – 112 pts (Nurs A/C/LD/MH) (IB 24 pts)
Bedfordshire – 112 pts +interview (Midwif; Nurs A/C/MH) (IB 24 pts)
Canterbury Christ Church – BBC (Nurs A/C/MH)
Central Lancashire – 112 pts (Nurs Pre Reg)
Chester – 112 pts (Nurs A/C/LD/MH) (IB 28 pts)
De Montfort – 112 pts (Nurs A/C/MH) (IB 28 pts)
Derby – 112 pts (Nurs A/MH)
Edge Hill – BBC 112 pts (Nurs A/C/LD/MH)
Greenwich – 112 pts (Nurs A/C/LD/MH; Midwif)
Hull – 112 pts (Nurs A/C/MH/LD) (IB 24 pts)
Keele – BBC incl biol/soc sci 112 pts (Midwif) (IB 25 pts)
Kingston – 112 pts (Nurs A/C/LD/MH)
Lincoln – 112 pts (Nurs)
Liverpool John Moores – 112 pts (Nurs (MH/A/C))
Manchester – BBC incl sci/soc sci (Nurs A/C/MH) (IB 30 pts)
Manchester Met – BBC 112 pts (Nurs A) (IB 29 pts)
Middlesex – 112 pts (Midwif; Nurs A/C/MH)
Northampton – 112–120 pts incl sci (Midwif); 112 pts (Nurs A/C/MH/LD)
Northumbria – 112 pts (Nurs St A/C/LD/MH) (IB 29 pts)
Oxford Brookes – BBC (Nurs A/C/MH)

Queen's Belfast – BBC–BCC incl sci/maths (Midwif Sci)
Salford – 112–128 pts (Midwif) (IB 26 pts)
Sheffield Hallam – 112 pts (Nurs A/C/MH)
Staffordshire – BBC (Midwif Prac) (IB 25 pts)
Teesside – 112–128 pts incl sci (Midwif)
Ulster – 112 pts (Nurs A/MH) (IB 25 pts)
West London – 112 pts (Nurs A/C/LD/MH)
Wolverhampton – 112 pts incl sci (Midwif); 112 pts (Nurs A/C/MH)

104 pts **Abertay** – BCC (Nurs MH) (IB 29 pts)
Coventry – BCC (Nurs A/C/LD/MH) (IB 27 pts)
Hertfordshire – 104 pts (Nurs (A/C/LD/MH)) (IB 26 pts)
Keele – 104 pts (Nurs A/C/LD/MH) (IB 24 pts)
London South Bank – A*A/BCC 104 pts (Nurs A/C/MH)
Queen's Belfast – BCC–BBC incl sci (Nurs A/C/LD/MH)
Queen Margaret – BCC 104 pts (Nurs) (IB 30 pts)
Robert Gordon – BCC incl Engl+sci (Midwif)
Staffordshire – CCC IB 24 pts (Nurs Prac A/C/MH)

96 pts **Bucks New** – 96–112 pts (Nurs A/C/MH)
Cumbria – 96 pts incl sci/soc sci (Nurs A/C/LD/MH)
Edinburgh Napier – CCC incl biol (Midwif)
Stirling – CCC (Nurs A/MH) (IB 28 pts)
Teesside – 96–108 pts +interview (Nurs St A/C/LD/MH)
West Scotland – CCC (Midwif) (IB 28 pts)

72 pts **Glasgow Caledonian** – BC (Nurs St A/C/MH) (IB 24 pts)
64 pts **Dundee** – CC (Nurs A/C/MH) (IB 24 pts)
Edinburgh Napier – CC (Nurs A/C/LD/MH)
Robert Gordon – CC incl Engl+sci (Nurs A/C/MH)
West Scotland – CC (Nurs A/MH) (IB 24 pts)

Open University – contact +44 (0)845 300 6090 **or** www.openuniversity.co.uk/you (Nurs Prac)

Abbreviations used in this table A – Adult; C – Child; LD – Learning Disability; MH – Mental Health.

Alternative offers
See **Chapter 6** and **Appendix 1** for grades/new UCAS Tariff points information for other examinations.

EXAMPLES OF COLLEGES OFFERING COURSES IN THIS SUBJECT FIELD
Central Campus, Sandwell (Coll); East Kent (Coll); Mid-Kent (Coll); Norwich City (Coll); Oaklands (Coll); Somerset (Coll); Suffolk (Univ Campus).

CHOOSING YOUR COURSE (SEE ALSO CH.1)
Universities and colleges teaching quality See www.qaa.ac.uk; http://unistats.direct.gov.uk.

Top research universities and colleges (REF 2014) (Allied Health Professions, Dentistry, Nursing and Pharmacy) Birmingham; Sheffield (Biomed Sci); Bangor; Swansea (Allied Hlth); Aston; Coventry; Southampton; Cardiff; Surrey; Glasgow; Nottingham (Pharm); Bradford; East Anglia (Allied Hlth); London (QM); Sheffield (Dnstry); Queen's Belfast (Pharm); Bath; London (King's) (Pharm); Leeds.

ADMISSIONS INFORMATION
Number of applicants per place (approx) Abertay 10; Anglia Ruskin 10; Bangor 10; Birmingham 8; Birmingham City 15; Bournemouth 9; Brighton 3; Cardiff 7; Central Lancashire (Midwif) 14; City (Nurs MH) 4, (Nurs C) 8, (Midwif) 5; Cumbria 8; De Montfort 10; Glasgow Caledonian 12; Huddersfield (Midwif St) 10; Hull 10; Leeds (Midwif) 12; Liverpool John Moores (Nurs) 5; London (King's) 4; London South Bank 16; Middlesex 10; Northampton 17; Northumbria 16; Nottingham 3; Queen Margaret 3; Salford 10; Sheffield Hallam 8; Southampton (Nurs) 15, (Midwif) 25; Staffordshire (Midwif Prac) 10; Surrey 10; Swansea 10; UWE Bristol 27; York (Nurs Prac) 8, (Midwif) 2.

Numbers of applicants (**a** UK **b** EU (non-UK) **c** non-EU **d** mature) Cardiff **c**6.

Advice to applicants and planning the UCAS personal statement Experience of care work – for example in hospitals, old people's homes, children's homes – is important. Describe what you have done and what you have learned. Read nursing journals in order to be aware of new developments in the treatment of illnesses. Note, in particular, the various needs of patients and the problems they experience. Try to compare different nursing approaches with, for example, children, people with learning disabilities, old people and terminally ill people. If you under-performed at GCSE, give reasons. If you have had work experience or a part-time job, describe how your skills have developed, for example responsibility, communication, team-building, organisational skills. How do you spend your spare time? Explain how your interests help with stress and pressure. See also **Appendix 3**. Admission is subject to eligibility for an NHS bursary. Contact NHS Student Grants Unit, tel 01253 655655.

Misconceptions about this course That Nursing programmes are not demanding. Midwives and nurses don't do shift work and are not involved in travelling! **City** Midwives are only involved at the birth stage and not at the ante-natal and post-natal stages, or in education and support.

Selection interviews Most institutions **Yes** Abertay, Anglia Ruskin, Bangor, Bedfordshire, Birmingham, Birmingham City, Bournemouth, Brighton, Cardiff, Central Lancashire, City, Coventry, Cumbria, Dundee, Dundee, East Anglia, Edge Hill, Edinburgh, Edinburgh Napier, Greenwich, Hertfordshire, Huddersfield, Hull, Keele, Leeds Beckett, Lincoln, Liverpool John Moores, London (King's), London South Bank, Manchester, Middlesex, Nottingham, Plymouth, Queen Margaret, Queen's Belfast, Robert Gordon, Salford, Sheffield Hallam, Southampton, Stirling, Surrey, Swansea, UWE Bristol, West London, West Scotland, Wolverhampton, Worcester; **Some** Bucks New.

Interview advice and questions Past questions have included: Why do you want to be a nurse? What experience have you had in nursing? What do you think of the nurses' pay situation? Should nurses go on strike? What are your views on abortion? What branch of nursing most interests you? How would you communicate with someone who can't speak English? What is the nurse's role in the community? How should a nurse react in an emergency? How would you cope with telling a patient's relative that the patient was dying? Admissions tutors look for communication skills, team interaction and the applicant's understanding of health/society-related subjects. See also **Chapter 5**. **London South Bank** What do you understand by equal opportunities? **Swansea** What is your perception of the role of the nurse? What qualities do you have that would be good for nursing?

Reasons for rejection (non-academic) Insufficient awareness of the roles and responsibilities of a midwife or nurse. Lack of motivation. Poor communication skills. Lack of awareness of nursing developments through the media. (Detailed knowledge of the NHS or nursing practice not usually required.) Failed medical. Unsatisfactory health record. Not fulfilling the hepatitis B requirements or police check requirements. Poor preparation for the interview. Too shy. Only wants nursing as a means to something else, for example commission in the armed forces. Too many choices on the UCAS application, for example Midwifery, Physiotherapy, Occupational Therapy. No care experience. Some applicants have difficulty with maths – multiplication and division – used in calculating dosage for medicines. **De Montfort** No insight as to nursing as a career or the various branches of nursing. **Swansea** Poor communication skills.

AFTER-RESULTS ADVICE
Offers to applicants repeating A-levels Higher Cardiff, Hull, Liverpool John Moores (Midwif), UWE Bristol; **Same** De Montfort, Huddersfield, Liverpool John Moores, London South Bank, Queen Margaret, Salford, Staffordshire, Stirling, Suffolk (Univ Campus), Surrey, Swansea, Wolverhampton; **No** Birmingham City.

GRADUATE DESTINATIONS AND EMPLOYMENT (2013/14 HESA)
Nursing graduates surveyed 21,085 **Employed** 16,165 **In voluntary employment** 50 **In further study** 1,195 **Assumed unemployed** 320

Career note The majority of graduates aim to enter the nursing profession.

OTHER DEGREE SUBJECTS FOR CONSIDERATION
Audiology; Biological Sciences; Biology; Community Studies; Dietetics; Education; Health Studies; Medicine; Nutrition; Occupational Therapy; Optometry; Pharmacology; Pharmacy; Physiotherapy; Podiatry; Psychology; Radiography; Social Policy and Administration; Social Work; Sociology; Speech Therapy; Veterinary Nursing.

NUTRITION
(see also **Dietetics, Food Science/Studies and Technology, Health Sciences/Studies**)

Nutrition attracts a great deal of attention in society and whilst controversy, claim and counter-claim seem to focus daily on the merits and otherwise of food, it is, nevertheless, a scientific study in itself. Courses involve topics relating to diet, health, nutrition and food policy and are designed to prepare students to enter careers as specialists in nutrition and dietetics.

Useful websites www.nutrition.org.uk; www.nutritionsociety.org; see also under **Dietetics**.

NB The points totals shown to the left of the institutions are for ease of reference only. It must not be assumed that Tariff points are always used by institutions or that they can be substituted for an offer in grades. The level of an offer is not necessarily indicative of the quality of a course.

COURSE OFFERS INFORMATION
Subject requirements/preferences GCSE Mathematics and science usually required. **AL** Science subjects required for most courses, Biology and/or Chemistry preferred.

Your target offers and examples of degree courses
136 pts Glasgow – AAB–BBB incl biol/chem (Physiol Spo Sci Nutr) (IB 36–34 pts)
Leeds – AAB (Nutr) (IB 34 pts)
London (King's) – AAB incl chem+biol (Nutr Diet) (IB 35 pts)
Nottingham – AAB–ABB incl sci (Nutr Diet MNutr) (IB 34–32 pts)
Reading – AAB–ABB (Nutr Fd Consum Sci; Fd Sci; Nutr Fd Sci) (IB 35–32 pts)
Surrey – AAB–ABB incl biol+sci (Nutr; Nutr Diet) (IB 35–34 pts HL 6 biol 5 sci); AAB–ABB incl sci/maths (Nutr Fd Sci) (IB 35–34 pts)
128 pts Leeds – ABB incl sci (Fd Sci Nutr) (IB 35–34 pts HL 5 sci)
London (King's) – ABB incl chem+biol (Nutr) (IB 34 pts)
Newcastle – ABB–BBB incl sci (Fd Mark Nutr) (IB 34–32 pts HL 6 biol); ABB–BBB incl biol+sci (Fd Hum Nutr) (IB 34–32 pts HL 6 biol)
Nottingham – ABB–BBB incl sci (Nutr) (IB 32–30 pts); ABB–BBB incl sci/maths (Nutr Fd Sci) (IB 32–30 pts)
120 pts Cardiff Met – 120 pts (Hum Nutr Diet) (IB 26 pts)
Chester – BBB–BBC incl biol+sci 120 pts (Nutr Diet) (IB 28 pts HL 5 biol/chem)
Greenwich – 120 pts (Hum Nutr)
Leeds Beckett – 120 pts incl chem+sci (Diet) (IB 26 pts HL 6 chem); 120 pts incl biol/chem (Nutr) (IB 26 pts HL 6 biol)
London Met – 120 pts incl biol+chem (Diet Nutr)
Northumbria – 120 pts incl biol (Hum Nutr) (IB 30 pts); 120 pts incl sci/fd tech/hm econ (Fd Sci Nutr) (IB 30 pts)
Plymouth – 120 pts incl biol+sci (Nutr Exer Hlth) (IB 28 pts HL 5 biol+sci)
Queen's Belfast – BBB–ABB incl biol/chem (Fd Qual Sfty Nutr)
112 pts Bournemouth – 112 pts (Nutr) (IB 30 pts)
Cardiff Met – 112 pts (Spo Biomed Nutr)
Central Lancashire – 112–128 pts (Nutr Exer Sci) (IB 25–27 pts)
Chester – BBC–BCC incl biol/chem/env sci 112 pts (Hum Nutr) (IB 26 pts HL 5 biol/chem)
Edge Hill – BBC 112 pts (Nutr Hlth)
Huddersfield – BBC 112 pts (Nutr Pblc Hlth; Fd Nutr Hlth)
Hull – 112 pts (Spo Exer Nutr) (IB 28 pts)

BSc (Hons) Nutrition

Nutrition is an exciting, growing and contemporary career choice.

At Leeds Beckett University we are passionate about teaching the application of nutrition to promote good health and prevent diet-related illness in individual groups, communities and populations. Our BSc (Hons) Nutrition course is accredited by the Association for Nutrition and aims to produce registered nutritionists equipped to practise within the UK and overseas.

Through work placements you will experience the wide variety of roles available to registered nutritionists. You could undertake an extended placement in the UK or overseas, working in the food industry, community nutrition or research.

To find out more, visit courses.leedsbeckett.ac.uk and search for 'nutrition'

AfN ACCREDITED PROGRAMME
ACCREDITATION NO: AC206

Leeds Trinity – 112 pts (Spo Exer Sci (Spo Nutr))
Nottingham Trent – 112 pts incl sci/PE (Exer Nutr Hlth)
Oxford Brookes – BBC 112 pts (Nutr) (IB 30 pts)
Roehampton – 112 pts (Nutr Hlth)
Sheffield Hallam – 112 pts (Fd Nutr; Nutr Pblc Hlth; Nutr Diet Lfstl)
Teesside – BBC incl sci/fd tech/nutr (Fd Nutr)
Westminster – BBC incl sci (Hum Nutr) (IB 26 pts HL 5 sci)
York St John – 112 pts (Nutr Exer Hlth)

104 pts **Bath Spa** – 104–120 pts (Fd Nutr); 104–120 pts incl sci/maths (Hum Nutr)
Coventry – BCC incl biol/chem/fd tech (Fd Nutr) (IB 27 pts)
Glasgow Caledonian – BCC incl chem (Hum Nutr Diet) (IB 24 pts)
Kingston – 104–144 pts (Exer Nutr Hlth); 104–112 pts (Nutr)
Liverpool Hope – BCC–BBB 104–120 pts (Nutr)
Liverpool John Moores – 104 pts (Fd Dev Nutr)
Robert Gordon – BCC incl chem+biol (Nutr Diet) (IB 27 pts)
Ulster – 104 pts incl sci/maths/tech (Hum Nutr) (IB 24 pts)
Worcester – 104–120 pts incl biol+sci/maths (Hum Nutr)

96 pts **Abertay** – CCC (Fd Nutr Hlth) (IB 28 pts)
Bedfordshire – 96 pts (Hlth Nutr Exer) (IB 24 pts)
CAFRE – 96 pts incl sci/hm econ (Fd Des Nutr)
Hertfordshire – 96 pts incl chem+biol (Nutr) (IB 24 pts)
Manchester Met – CCC–BBC 96–112 pts (Nutr Sci) (IB 26 pts)
Robert Gordon – CCC incl chem+sci (Nutr) (IB 26 pts)
St Mary's – 96 pts (Nutr) (IB 28 pts)
Trinity Saint David – 96 pts (Hlth Nutr Lfstl)
Ulster – 96 pts incl sci/maths/tech (Fd Nutr) (IB 24 pts)

88 pts **Harper Adams** – 88–104 pts (Fd Pblc Hlth Nutr)
London Met – 88 pts incl biol (Hum Nutr)

80 pts **London South Bank** – CDD/BC 80–72 pts (Hum Nutr)
   Queen Margaret – BB incl chem/biol 80 pts (Nutr) (IB 26 pts)

Alternative offers
See **Chapter 6** and **Appendix 1** for grades/new UCAS Tariff points information for other examinations.

EXAMPLES OF COLLEGES OFFERING COURSES IN THIS SUBJECT FIELD
Bradford (Coll); Grimsby (Univ Centre); Suffolk (Univ Campus); Truro and Penwith (Coll).

CHOOSING YOUR COURSE (SEE ALSO CH.1)
Universities and colleges teaching quality See www.qaa.ac.uk; http://unistats.direct.gov.uk.

Top research universities and colleges (REF 2014) See **Agricultural Sciences/Agriculture**.

Examples of sandwich degree courses Bedfordshire; Coventry; Glasgow Caledonian; Harper Adams; Hertfordshire; Huddersfield; Kingston; Leeds; Leeds Beckett; Liverpool John Moores; Manchester Met; Newcastle; Northumbria; Queen's Belfast; Reading; Sheffield Hallam; Surrey; Teesside; Ulster.

ADMISSIONS INFORMATION
Number of applicants per place (approx) Cardiff Met 5; Glasgow Caledonian 8; Liverpool John Moores 10; London (King's) 6; London Met 9; London South Bank 5; Newcastle 5; Nottingham 7; Robert Gordon 4; Surrey 5.

Advice to applicants and planning the UCAS personal statement Information on relevant experience, reasons for wanting to do the degree and careers sought would be useful. See also **Dietetics** and **Appendix 3**. **Surrey** Overseas students not eligible for Nutrition and Dietetics course.

Misconceptions about this course Some applicants do not realise that this is a science course.

Selection interviews Yes London Met, Surrey; **Some** Nottingham, Robert Gordon, Roehampton; **No** Liverpool John Moores.

Interview advice and questions Past questions have focused on scientific A-level subjects studied and aspects of subjects enjoyed by the applicants. Questions then arise from answers. Extensive knowledge expected of nutrition as a career and candidates should have talked to people involved in this type of work, for example dietitians. They will also be expected to discuss wider problems such as food supplies in developing countries and nutritional problems resulting from famine. See also **Chapter 5**. **Liverpool John Moores** Interviews are informal. It would be useful for you to bring samples of coursework to the interview.

AFTER-RESULTS ADVICE
Offers to applicants repeating A-levels Possibly higher Nottingham; **Same** Liverpool John Moores, Manchester Met, Roehampton, St Mary's, Surrey.

GRADUATE DESTINATIONS AND EMPLOYMENT (2013/14 HESA)
Graduates surveyed 925 **Employed** 525 **In voluntary employment** 15 **In further study** 140 **Assumed unemployed** 55

Career note Nutritionists work in retail, health promotion and sport; others specialise in dietetics.

OTHER DEGREE SUBJECTS FOR CONSIDERATION
Biological Sciences; Biology; Consumer Studies; Dietetics; Food Sciences; Health Studies/Sciences.

OCCUPATIONAL THERAPY

Everyday life involves washing, dressing, eating, walking, driving, shopping and going to work, all aspects which we take for granted – until we have an injury or illness. If this happened to you then during the recovery period, you would realise the importance of the occupational therapist's role. They assist people of all ages, not only those being treated with physical injuries/illness but others with mental health issues, the work being to identify the special problems they face and the practical solutions that are required to help them recover and maintain their daily living and working skills. The focus of the OT is on meaningful and functional activity. This may be achieved by advising on physical modifications to the home environment and potentially introducing new equipment and devices to make various activities easier along with task analysis. In the case of mental health OTs, they assist clients to re-establish routines and skills to allow them to return to living fulfilling lives. To achieve these results, occupational therapists often work with physiotherapists, psychologists, speech therapists and social workers amongst others. Most courses therefore involve anatomy, physiology, psychology, sociology, mental health and ethics. OTs can work in a very wide range of settings, acute care, long term care, social services and mental health plus many more. There are opportunities to specialise in burns, hand therapy, oncology and surgery, forensic psychology and prison rehabilitation to name but a few. Selectors look for maturity, initiative, tact, sound judgement, team work and organising ability.

Useful websites www.cot.co.uk; www.ot-direct.com

NB The points totals shown to the left of the institutions are for ease of reference only. It must not be assumed that Tariff points are always used by institutions or that they can be substituted for an offer in grades. The level of an offer is not necessarily indicative of the quality of a course.

COURSE OFFERS INFORMATION
Subject requirements/preferences GCSE English, mathematics and science grade A–C. **AL** A social science or science subjects required or preferred for most courses. **Other** All applicants need to pass an occupational health check and obtain Disclosure and Barring Service (DBS) clearance.

Your target offers and examples of degree courses
136 pts Southampton – AAB–ABB incl sci/soc sci (Occ Thera) (IB 34–32 pts)
UWE Bristol – 136 pts incl sci/soc sci (Occ Thera) (IB 28 pts HL 6 sci/soc sci)
128 pts Bournemouth – 128 pts (Occ Thera) (IB 32 pts)
Bradford – ABB 128 pts (Occ Thera)
Cardiff – ABB (Occ Thera) (IB 35 pts)
Plymouth – 128 pts incl sci (Occ Thera) (IB 27 pts)
120 pts Brunel – BBB (Occ Thera) (IB 30 pts)
East Anglia – BBB (Occ Thera) (IB 31 pts HL 655)
Huddersfield – BBB incl biol/psy 120 pts (Occ Thera)
Liverpool – BBB incl soc sci/biol/PE (Occ Thera) (IB 29 pts)
London South Bank – BBB 120 pts (Occ Thera) (IB 26 pts)
Northumbria – 120 pts incl sci/hlth (Occ Thera) (IB 30 pts)
Oxford Brookes – BBB (Occ Thera) (IB 32 pts)
Ulster – BBB +HPAT (Occ Thera) (IB 26 pts)
Worcester – 120–136 pts incl biol/soc sci (Occ Thera)
York St John – 120 pts (Occ Thera)
112 pts Canterbury Christ Church – BBC (Occ Thera)
Coventry – BBC (Occ Thera)
Cumbria – 112 pts (Occ Thera)
Derby – 112 pts (Occ Thera)
Northampton – 112–120 pts (Occ Thera)
104 pts Glasgow Caledonian – BCC (Occ Thera) (IB 24 pts)
Glyndŵr – 104 pts (Occ Thera)
Robert Gordon – BCC incl Engl+biol (Occ Thera) (IB 27 pts)
Teesside – 104–112 pts incl sci (Occ Thera)

Brighton – p/t, individual offers may vary, NHS bursaries are available for all courses (Occ Thera)

Alternative offers
See **Chapter 6** and **Appendix 1** for grades/new UCAS Tariff points information for other examinations.

CHOOSING YOUR COURSE (SEE ALSO CH.1)

Universities and colleges teaching quality See www.qaa.ac.uk; http://unistats.direct.gov.uk.

Top research universities and colleges (REF 2014) See **Health Sciences/Studies**.

ADMISSIONS INFORMATION

Number of applicants per place (approx) Canterbury Christ Church 5; Cardiff 10; Coventry 15; Cumbria 20; Derby 5; East Anglia 5; Northampton 4; Northumbria 4; Oxford Brookes 12; Robert Gordon 6; Southampton 7; Ulster 13; York St John 5.

Advice to applicants and planning the UCAS personal statement Contact your local hospital and discuss this career with the occupational therapists. Try to obtain work shadowing experience and make notes of your observations. Describe any such visits in full (see also **Reasons for rejection (non-academic)**). Applicants are expected to have visited two occupational therapy departments, one in a physical or social services setting, one in the mental health field. Good interpersonal skills. Breadth and nature of health-related work experience is important. Also skills, interests (for example, sports, design). Applicants should have a high standard of communication skills and experience of working with people with disabilities. See also **Appendix 3**. **York St John** Contact with the profession essential; very competitive course.

Selection interviews Most institutions. **Yes** Bournemouth, Brighton, Brunel, Canterbury Christ Church, Coventry, Cumbria, East Anglia, Huddersfield, Queen Margaret, Robert Gordon, Sheffield Hallam, Ulster, Worcester, York St John.

Interview advice and questions Since this is a vocational course, work experience is nearly always essential and applicants are likely to be questioned on the types of work involved and the career. Some universities may use admissions tests: check websites and see **Chapter 5**.

Reasons for rejection (non-academic) Poor communication skills. Lack of knowledge of occupational therapy. Little evidence of working with people. Uncertain about their future career. Lack of maturity. Indecision regarding the profession.

AFTER-RESULTS ADVICE

Offers to applicants repeating A-levels Same Derby, York St John.

GRADUATE DESTINATIONS AND EMPLOYMENT (2013/14 HESA)

Career note Occupational therapists (who work mostly in hospital departments) are involved in the rehabilitation of those who have required medical treatment and work with the young, aged and, for example, people with learning difficulties.

OTHER DEGREE SUBJECTS FOR CONSIDERATION

Audiology; Community Studies; Dietetics; Education; Health Studies/Sciences; Nursing; Nutrition; Physiotherapy; Podiatry; Psychology; Radiography; Social Policy and Administration; Social Work; Sociology; Speech Sciences.

OPTOMETRY (OPHTHALMIC OPTICS)

(including Ophthalmic Dispensing and Orthoptics)

Optometry courses (which are increasingly popular) lead to qualification as an optometrist (previously known as an ophthalmic optician). They provide training in detecting defects and diseases in the eye and in prescribing treatment with, for example, spectacles, contact lenses and other appliances to correct or improve vision. Orthoptics includes the study of general anatomy, physiology and normal child development and leads to a career as an orthoptist. This involves the investigation, diagnosis and treatment of defects of binocular vision and other eye conditions. The main components of degree courses include the study of the eye, the use of diagnostic and measuring equipment and treatment of eye abnormalities. See also **Appendix 3**.

Useful websites www.optical.org; www.orthoptics.org.uk; www.abdo.org.uk; www.college-optometrists.org

NB The points totals shown to the left of the institutions are for ease of reference only. It must not be assumed that Tariff points are always used by institutions or that they can be substituted for an offer in grades. The level of an offer is not necessarily indicative of the quality of a course.

COURSE OFFERS INFORMATION

Subject requirements/preferences GCSE Good grades in English and science subjects usually required. **AL** Science subjects required for all Optometry courses. Mathematics usually acceptable.

Your target offers and examples of degree courses

144 pts **Aston** – AAA–AAB incl sci (Optom) (IB 34 pts HL 6 biol+chem/phys 5 maths)
Cardiff – AAA incl sci/maths (Optom) (IB 34 pts incl sci/maths)
City – AAA 144 pts (Optom) (IB 34 pts)
Plymouth – AAA incl maths/sci 144 pts (Optom) (IB 35 pts HL 5 maths/sci)

136 pts **Anglia Ruskin** – AAB incl sci/maths (Optom) (IB 33 pts HL 6 sci/maths)
Bradford – AAB 136 pts (Optom)
Glasgow Caledonian – AAB–AAA incl sci/maths (Optom) (IB 30 pts HL 4 sci+maths)
Hertfordshire – 136 pts incl sci/maths (MOptom) (IB 34 pts)
Manchester – AAB incl sci/maths (Optom) (IB 35 pts)
Ulster – AAB incl sci/maths (Optom) (IB 37 pts)

120 pts **Liverpool** – BBB incl biol (Orth) (IB 30 pts HL 6 biol)
Sheffield – BBB incl sci/maths (Orth) (IB 32 pts HL 6 sci/maths)

80 pts **Anglia Ruskin** – 80 pts incl sci (Oph Disp) (IB 24 pts)

72 pts **City** – 72 pts (Oph Disp)

64 pts **Bradford (Coll)** – 64 pts incl sci/maths (Oph Disp)
Glasgow Caledonian – CC (Oph Disp) (IB 24 pts)

Alternative offers
See **Chapter 6** and **Appendix 1** for grades/new UCAS Tariff points information for other examinations.

EXAMPLES OF COLLEGES OFFERING COURSES IN THIS SUBJECT FIELD

Anglia Ruskin; Bradford (Coll); City; City and Islington (Coll).

CHOOSING YOUR COURSE (SEE ALSO CH.1)

Universities and colleges teaching quality See www.qaa.ac.uk; http://unistats.direct.gov.uk.

ADMISSIONS INFORMATION

Number of applicants per place (approx) Anglia Ruskin 12; Aston 7; Bradford 6; Cardiff 13; City 11; Glasgow Caledonian 9.

Advice to applicants and planning the UCAS personal statement For Optometry courses contact with optometrists is essential, either work shadowing or gaining some work experience. Make notes of your experiences and the work done and report fully on the UCAS application on why the career interests you. See also **Appendix 3**.

Selection interviews Yes Bradford, City, Manchester; **Some** Anglia Ruskin, Aston, Cardiff; **No** Glasgow Caledonian.

Interview advice and questions Optometry is a competitive subject requiring applicants to have had some work experience on which they will be questioned. See also **Chapter 5**. **Anglia Ruskin** Why will you make a good optometrist? Describe the job.

AFTER-RESULTS ADVICE

Offers to applicants repeating A-levels Higher City; **Possibly higher** Aston; **Same** Anglia Ruskin, Cardiff.

GRADUATE DESTINATIONS AND EMPLOYMENT (2013/14 HESA)

Graduates surveyed 685 **Employed** 545 **In voluntary employment** 20 **In further study** 110 **Assumed unemployed** 15

Career note The great majority of graduates enter private practice either in small businesses or in larger organisations (which have been on the increase in recent years). A small number work in eye hospitals. Orthoptists tend to work in public health and education dealing with children and the elderly.

OTHER DEGREE SUBJECTS FOR CONSIDERATION

Health Studies; Nursing; Occupational Therapy; Physics; Physiotherapy; Radiography; Speech Studies.

PHARMACOLOGY

(including Toxicology; see also Biological Sciences, Health Sciences/Studies)

Pharmacology is the study of drugs and medicines and courses focus on physiology, biochemistry, toxicology, immunology, microbiology and chemotherapy. Pharmacologists are not qualified to work as pharmacists. Toxicology involves the study of the adverse effects of chemicals on living systems. See also **Appendix 3** under Pharmacology.

Useful websites www.thebts.org; www.bps.ac.uk

NB The points totals shown to the left of the institutions are for ease of reference only. It must not be assumed that Tariff points are always used by institutions or that they can be substituted for an offer in grades. The level of an offer is not necessarily indicative of the quality of a course.

COURSE OFFERS INFORMATION

Subject requirements/preferences GCSE English, science and mathematics. **AL** Chemistry and/or Biology required for most courses.

Your target offers and examples of degree courses

160 pts **Cambridge** – A*A*A incl sci/maths (Nat Sci (Pharmacol)) (IB 40–41 pts HL 776)

144 pts **Leeds** – AAA–ABB incl biol/chem+sci (Pharmacol) (IB 35–34 pts HL 6 chem/biol+sci)

London (UCL) – AAA–AAB incl chem+sci/maths (Pharmacol) (IB 38–36 pts HL 5 chem+sci/maths)

Manchester – AAA–ABB incl sci/maths (Pharmacol; Pharmacol (Yr Ind)) (IB 37–33 pts HL 5/6 sci); (Pharmacol Physiol (Yr Ind)) (IB 37–33 pts)

Newcastle – AAA–AAB incl biol (Pharmacol) (IB 35–34 pts HL 5 chem+biol)

136 pts **Bath** – AAB incl chem+sci/maths (Pharmacol) (IB 36 pts)

Bristol – AAB–ABB incl chem+sci/maths (Pharmacol (Yr Ind)) (IB 34–32 pts HL 6/5 chem+sci/maths)

Glasgow – AAB–BBB incl biol/chem (Pharmacol) (IB 36–34 pts)

London (King's) – AAB incl chem+biol (Pharmacol Mol Genet; Pharmacol) (IB 35 pts)

Southampton – AAB incl chem+sci/maths (Pharmacol) (IB 34 pts HL 6 chem+sci/maths)

128 pts **Birmingham** – ABB incl chem+biol (Chem Pharmacol) (IB 32 pts HL 655)

Dundee – ABB incl biol+chem (Pharmacol) (IB 30 pts)

Edinburgh – ABB (Pharmacol) (IB 36–32 pts)

Leicester – ABB incl sci/maths (Biol Sci (Physiol Pharmacol)) (IB 30 pts)

Liverpool – ABB incl chem+sci (Pharmacol) (IB 33 pts HL 6 chem)

Strathclyde – ABB–BBB incl chem+biol (Pharmacol MSci) (IB 32 pts HL 6 chem+biol)

New UCAS points Tariff: A* = 56 pts; A = 48 pts; B = 40 pts; C = 32 pts; D = 24 pts; E = 16 pts

120 pts **Aberdeen** – BBB incl maths/sci (Pharmacol) (IB 32 pts HL 5 maths/sci)
Kent – BBB incl biol+chem+maths (Pharmacol Physiol) (IB 26–30 pts)
Leeds Beckett – 120 pts incl biol+sci (Biomed Sci (Physiol/Pharmacol)) (IB 26 pts HL 6 biol)
Nottingham Trent – 120 pts incl biol (Pharmacol)
112 pts **Central Lancashire** – 112 pts incl chem/biol/env sci (Physiol Pharmacol) (IB 28 pts HL 5 biol/chem)
East London – 112 pts incl biol+chem (Pharmacol) (IB 25 pts)
Hertfordshire – 112 pts incl sci/maths/geog (Pharmacol) (IB 28 pts)
Portsmouth – BBC incl biol/chem+sci/maths (Pharmacol) (IB 30 pts HL 665 incl biol+chem/maths)
Westminster – BBC incl sci (Pharmacol Physiol) (IB 26 pts HL 5 sci); BBC (Herb Med) (IB 26 pts HL 5 sci)
104 pts **Coventry** – BCC incl biol (Med Pharmacol Sci) (IB 27 pts)
Glasgow Caledonian – BCC incl chem (Pharmacol) (IB 24 pts)
Kingston – 104–112 pts (Pharmacol Bus); (Pharmacol) (IB 26–28 pts)
88 pts **London Met** – 88 pts incl biol+chem (Pharmacol)
80 pts **Queen Margaret** – BB incl chem/biol 80 pts (App Pharmacol) (IB 26 pts)
Wolverhampton – 80 pts (Pharmacol) (IB 25 pts)

Alternative offers
See **Chapter 6** and **Appendix 1** for grades/new UCAS Tariff points information for other examinations.

CHOOSING YOUR COURSE (SEE ALSO CH.1)
Universities and colleges teaching quality See www.qaa.ac.uk; http://unistats.direct.gov.uk.

Examples of sandwich degree courses Bath; Bristol; East London; Kingston; Leeds; Manchester; Nottingham Trent; Southampton.

ADMISSIONS INFORMATION
Number of applicants per place (approx) Bath 7; Birmingham 6; Bristol 7; Dundee 5; East London 4; Hertfordshire 10; Leeds 7; Liverpool 5; London (King's) 6; London (UCL) 5; Portsmouth 4; Southampton 8; Strathclyde 10; Wolverhampton 4.

Advice to applicants and planning the UCAS personal statement Contact with the pharmaceutical industry is important in order to be aware of the range of work undertaken. Read pharmaceutical journals (although note that Pharmacology and Pharmacy courses lead to different careers). See also **Pharmacy and Pharmaceutical Sciences**. **Bath** Interests outside A-level studies. Important to produce evidence that there is more to the student than A-level ability. **Bristol** Be aware that a Pharmacology degree is mainly biological rather than chemical although both subjects are important.

Misconceptions about this course Mistaken belief that Pharmacology and Pharmaceutical Sciences is the same as Pharmacy and that a Pharmacology degree will lead to work as a pharmacist.

Selection interviews Yes Bath, Birmingham, Cambridge, Manchester, Newcastle; **Some** Dundee; **No** Portsmouth.

Interview advice and questions Past questions include: Why do you want to do Pharmacology? Why not Pharmacy? Why not Chemistry? How are pharmacologists employed in industry? What are the issues raised by anti-vivisectionists on animal experimentation? Questions relating to the A-level syllabus in chemistry and biology. See also **Chapter 5**.

Reasons for rejection (non-academic) Confusion between Pharmacology, Pharmacy and Pharmaceutical Sciences. One university rejected two applicants because they had no motivation or understanding of the course (one had A-levels at AAB!). Insurance against rejection for Medicine. Lack of knowledge about pharmacology as a subject.

AFTER-RESULTS ADVICE

Offers to applicants repeating A-levels Higher Bristol, Glasgow, Leeds; **Same** Bath, Dundee, Portsmouth.

GRADUATE DESTINATIONS AND EMPLOYMENT (2013/14 HESA)

Pharmacology,Toxicology and Pharmacy graduates surveyed 2,840 **Employed** 2,185 **In voluntary employment** 110 **In further study** 400 **Assumed unemployed** 90

Career note The majority of pharmacologists work with the large pharmaceutical companies involved in research and development. A small number are employed by the NHS in medical research and clinical trials. Some will eventually diversify and become involved in marketing, sales and advertising.

OTHER DEGREE SUBJECTS FOR CONSIDERATION

Biochemistry; Biological Sciences; Biology; Biotechnology; Chemistry; Life Sciences; Medical Biochemistry; Medicinal Chemistry; Microbiology; Natural Sciences; Pharmaceutical Sciences; Pharmacy; Physiology; Toxicology.

PHARMACY and PHARMACEUTICAL SCIENCES

(including **Herbal Medicine**; see also **Biochemistry, Chemistry, Health Sciences/Studies**)

Pharmacy is the science of medicines, involving research into chemical structures and natural products of possible medicinal value, the development of dosage and the safety testing of products. This table also includes information on courses in Pharmaceutical Science (which should not be confused with Pharmacy) which is a multi-disciplinary subject covering chemistry, biochemistry, pharmacology and medical issues. Pharmaceutical scientists apply their knowledge of science and the biology of disease to the design and delivery of therapeutic agents. Note: All Pharmacy courses leading to MPharm are four years. Only Pharmacy degree courses accredited by the Royal Phamaceutical Society of Great Britain lead to a qualification as a pharmacist. Check prospectuses and websites.

Useful websites www.pharmweb.net; www.rpharms.com; www.chemistanddruggist.co.uk

NB The points totals shown to the left of the institutions are for ease of reference only. It must not be assumed that Tariff points are always used by institutions or that they can be substituted for an offer in grades. The level of an offer is not necessarily indicative of the quality of a course.

COURSE OFFERS INFORMATION

Subject requirements/preferences GCSE English, mathematics and science subjects. **AL** Chemistry and one or two other sciences required for most courses.

Your target offers and examples of degree courses

144 pts London (UCL Sch Pharm) – AAA–AAB incl chem+sci/maths (MPharm) (IB 38–36 pts HL 18–17 pts incl chem+sci/maths)

136 pts Aston – AAB–ABB incl chem+sci/maths (MPharm) (IB 33 pts HL 6 chem+biol/phys 5 maths)
Bath – AAB incl chem+sci/maths (MPharm) (IB 36 pts)
Birmingham – AAB incl chem+sci/maths (MPharm) (IB 32 pts HL 665)
Cardiff – AAB–ABB incl chem+sci/maths (MPharm) (IB 34 pts HL 6 chem+sci/maths)
East Anglia – AAB (MPharm) (IB 33 pts HL 6 chem+sci/maths)
Huddersfield – AAB–ABB incl chem+biol (MPharm) (IB 32 pts)
Keele – AAB–ABB incl biol/chem (MPharm) (IB 32 pts HL 6 biol/chem)
London (King's) – AAB incl chem+sci/maths (MPharm) (IB 35 pts)
Nottingham – AAB incl chem+sci/maths (Pharm MPharm) (IB 34 pts)
Queen's Belfast – AAB incl chem+sci/maths (MPharm)
Reading – AAB–ABB (MPharm) (IB 35–32 pts)

Aston University
Birmingham

School of Life & Health Sciences

Acknowledged as UK-leading with an outstanding reputation for teaching and research. Our excellence in research is integrated into lectures, giving students the distinct advantage of access to the latest trends, thinking, issues and research in their particular field.

Prepare for your future with our range of professionally relevant courses:

- Foundation Degree in Hearing Aid Audiology 2 years full-time with integrated work-based learning
- BSc Healthcare Science (Audiology) 3 years full-time with integrated placements
- BSc Biological Sciences 3 years full-time/4 years full-time with a placement
- BSc Cell and Molecular Biology 3 years full-time/4 years full-time with a placement
- BSc Human Biology 3 years full-time/4 years full-time with a placement
- BSc Microbiology and Immunology 3 years full-time/4 years full-time with a placement
- MBiol Biological Sciences 4 years full-time/5 years full-time with a placement
- BSc Biomedical Science 3 years full-time/4 years full-time with a placement
- BSc Optometry 3 years full-time

- Masters in Optometry 4 years with an integrated pre-registration year
- Pharmacy – MPharm 4 years full time
- BSc Psychology 3 years full-time/4 years full-time with a placement
- BSc Psychology and Business (Joint Honours) 4 years full-time with a placement
- BSc Psychology and Sociology (Joint Honours) 4 years full-time with a placement
- BEng/MEng Biomedical Engineering 3 years full-time/4 years full-time
- BSc Audiological Sciences for International Students only. Years 1 & 2 on campus and year 3 in your home country.
- BSc Neuroscience 4 years full-time with a placement.

We prepare our graduates for professional roles as scientists and practitioners who make a real difference to the communities in which they work and live.

96%
Student Satisfaction
2015 NSS

www.aston.ac.uk/lhs

Strathclyde – AAB–BBB incl chem (MPharm) (IB 36 pts HL 7 chem 6 maths+biol+Engl)

Ulster – AAB incl chem+sci/maths (MPharm) (IB 28 pts)

128 pts **Bradford** – ABB incl chem+sci 128 pts (MPharm)

Brighton – ABB incl chem+sci (MPharm) (IB 32 pts HL 5 chem+biol)

Central Lancashire – ABB incl chem+sci/maths (MPharm) (IB 27 pts HL 665 incl chem+sci/maths)

De Montfort – 128 pts incl chem+sci/maths (MPharm) (IB 30 pts HL 6 chem+sci/maths)

Greenwich – ABB incl chem+sci (MPharm) (IB 32 pts HL 15 pts incl 5 chem+sci)

Hertfordshire – 128 pts incl chem+sci/maths (MPharm) (IB 32 pts)

Kent – ABB incl chem+sci/maths (MPharm) (IB 32 pts)

Leicester – ABB incl chem (Pharml Chem) (IB 30 pts)

London (QM) – ABB incl chem (Pharml Chem) (IB 34 pts HL 5 chem)

Loughborough – ABB–BBB incl chem (Medcnl Pharml Chem) (IB 34–32 pts HL 6 chem 5 sci)

Manchester – ABB–AAA incl chem+maths/biol (MPharm) (IB 35 pts HL 6 chem 6/5 maths/biol)

Portsmouth – 128 pts incl chem+sci (MPharm) (IB 31 pts HL 18 pts incl 5 chem+sci/maths)

Sunderland – 128–120 pts incl chem+sci (MPharm)

120 pts **Greenwich** – 120 pts (Pharml Sci)

Kingston – 120 pts (MPharm)

Liverpool John Moores – 120 pts incl chem (Pharm MPharm) (IB 26 pts)

Nottingham Trent – 120 pts incl chem (Pharml Medcnl Chem)

Robert Gordon – BBB incl chem+maths/sci (MPharm) (IB 32 pts)

Wolverhampton – BBB incl chem+sci/maths 120 pts (MPharm) (IB 34 pts HL 6 chem)

112 pts **Arts London** – BBC incl chem+sci 112 pts (Cos Sci)

Brighton – BBC incl chem (Pharml Cheml Sci) (IB 28 pts)

East London – 112 pts incl biol/chem (Pharml Sci) (IB 25 pts)

Hertfordshire – 112 pts incl sci/maths/geog (Pharml Sci) (IB 28 pts)

Huddersfield – BBC incl chem 112 pts (Pharml Chem)

Westminster – BBC (Herb Med) (IB 26 pts HL 5 sci)

104 pts **De Montfort** – 104 pts incl chem+sci (Pharml Cos Sci) (IB 28 pts HL 6 chem+sci)

Kingston – 104 pts (Pharml Sci)

Manchester Met – BCC–BBC incl chem 104–112 pts (Pharml Chem) (IB 28 pts HL 5 chem)

South Wales – BCC incl chem+sci (Pharml Sci) (IB 29 pts HL 5 chem+sci)

96 pts **London Met** – 96 pts incl biol+chem (Pharml Sci)

80 pts **Wolverhampton** – 80 pts incl chem (Pharml Sci)

Alternative offers

See **Chapter 6** and **Appendix 1** for grades/new UCAS Tariff points information for other examinations.

EXAMPLES OF COLLEGES OFFERING COURSES IN THIS SUBJECT FIELD

Birmingham Met (Coll); Bromley (CFHE).

CHOOSING YOUR COURSE (SEE ALSO CH.1)

Universities and colleges teaching quality See www.qaa.ac.uk; http://unistats.direct.gov.uk.

Top research universities and colleges (REF 2014) (Allied Health Professions, Dentistry, Nursing and Pharmacy) Birmingham; Sheffield (Biomed Sci); Bangor; Swansea (Allied Hlth); Aston; Coventry; Southampton; Cardiff; Surrey; Glasgow; Nottingham (Pharm); Bradford; East Anglia (Allied Hlth); London (QM); Sheffield (Dnstry); Queen's Belfast (Pharm); Bath; London (King's) (Pharm); Leeds.

Examples of sandwich degree courses Bradford; De Montfort; Greenwich; Hertfordshire.

ADMISSIONS INFORMATION

Number of applicants per place (approx) Aston 10; Bath 6; Bradford 10; Brighton 24 (apply early); Cardiff 8; De Montfort 14; Durham 4; Liverpool John Moores (Pharm) 7; London (King's) 15, (Sch

Pharm) 6; London (UCL) 6; Manchester 9; Nottingham 8; Portsmouth 20; Robert Gordon 11; Strathclyde 10; Sunderland 20.

Advice to applicants and planning the UCAS personal statement Work experience and work shadowing with a retail and/or hospital pharmacist is important, and essential for Pharmacy applicants. Read pharmaceutical journals, extend your knowledge of well-known drugs and antibiotics. Read up on the history of drugs. Attend Open Days or careers conferences. See also **Appendix 3**. **Manchester** Students giving preference for Pharmacy are likely to be more successful than those who choose Pharmacy as an alternative to Medicine or Dentistry.

Misconceptions about this course That a degree in Pharmaceutical Science is a qualification leading to a career as a pharmacist. It is not: it is a course which concerns the application of chemical and biomedical science to the design, synthesis and analysis of pharmaceuticals for medicinal purposes. See also **Pharmacology**.

Selection interviews Yes Bath, Bradford, Brighton, Cardiff, De Montfort, East Anglia, Huddersfield, Keele, Liverpool John Moores, London (UCL Sch Pharm), Manchester, Nottingham, Portsmouth, Reading, Robert Gordon, Strathclyde, Wolverhampton; **Some** Aston.

Interview advice and questions As work experience is essential for Pharmacy applicants, questions are likely to focus on this and what they have discovered. Other relevant questions could include: Why do you want to study Pharmacy? What types of work do pharmacists do? What interests you about the Pharmacy course? What branch of pharmacy do you want to enter? Name a drug – what do you know about it (formula, use etc)? Name a drug from a natural source and its use. Can you think of another way of extracting a drug? Why do fungi destroy bacteria? What is an antibiotic? Can you name one and say how it was discovered? What is insulin? What is its source and function? What is diabetes? What type of insulin is used in its treatment? What is a hormone? What drugs are available over the counter without prescription? What is the formula of aspirin? What is genetic engineering? See also **Chapter 5**. **Bath** Informal and relaxed; 400 approx selected for interview – very few rejected at this stage. **Cardiff** Interviews cover both academic and vocational aspects; candidates must reach a satisfactory level in both areas. **Liverpool John Moores** What are the products of a reaction between an alcohol and a carboxylic acid? **Manchester** Candidates failing to attend interviews will have their applications withdrawn. The majority of applicants are called for interview.

Reasons for rejection (non-academic) Poor communication skills. Poor knowledge of pharmacy and the work of a pharmacist.

AFTER-RESULTS ADVICE
Offers to applicants repeating A-levels Higher Bradford, Cardiff, De Montfort, Liverpool John Moores, London (UCL Sch Pharm), Nottingham (offers rarely made), Portsmouth, Queen's Belfast, Strathclyde; **Possibly higher** Aston, Robert Gordon; **Same** Bath, Brighton, East Anglia, Sunderland, Wolverhampton.

GRADUATE DESTINATIONS AND EMPLOYMENT (2013/14 HESA)
See **Pharmacology**.

Career note The majority of Pharmacy graduates proceed to work in the commercial and retail fields, although opportunities also exist with pharmaceutical companies and in hospital pharmacies. There are also opportunities in agricultural and veterinary pharmacy.

OTHER DEGREE SUBJECTS FOR CONSIDERATION
Biochemistry; Biological Sciences; Biology; Biotechnology; Chemistry; Drug Development; Life Sciences; Medicinal Chemistry; Microbiology; Natural Sciences; Pharmacology; Physiology.

PHILOSOPHY

(see also **Psychology**)

Philosophy is one of the oldest and most fundamental disciplines, which examines the nature of the universe and humanity's place in it. Philosophy seeks to discover the essence of the mind, language and physical reality and discusses the methods used to investigate these topics.

Useful websites www.iep.utm.edu; www.philosophypages.com; www.philosophy.eserver.org; see also **Religious Studies**.

NB The points totals shown to the left of the institutions are for ease of reference only. It must not be assumed that Tariff points are always used by institutions or that they can be substituted for an offer in grades. The level of an offer is not necessarily indicative of the quality of a course.

COURSE OFFERS INFORMATION

Subject requirements/preferences GCSE English and mathematics. A foreign language may be required. **AL** No specific subjects except for joint courses.

Your target offers and examples of degree courses

160 pts **Cambridge** – A*A*A incl sci/maths (Nat Sci (Hist Phil Sci)) (IB 40–41 pts HL 776)
Oxford – A*A*A incl maths (Maths Phil) (IB 39 pts)

152 pts **Cambridge** – A*AA (Phil) (IB 40–41 pts HL 776)
Durham – A*AA incl maths (PPE) (IB 38 pts); A*AA incl Engl lit (Engl Lit Phil) (IB 38 pts)
London (King's) – A*AA +LNAT (Pol Phil Law) (IB 35 pts); A*AA (PPE) (IB 35 pts HL 766)
London (UCL) – A*AA-AAA incl maths (PPE) (IB 39-38 pts HL 7 maths)
London LSE – A*AA incl A* maths (PPE) (IB 38 pts)
Manchester – A*AA-AAA incl maths (Maths Phil) (IB 37 pts HL 6 maths)
Nottingham – A*AA-AAA (PPE) (IB 38–36)
Oxford – A*AA (Psy Phil Ling) (IB 39 pts)
Warwick – A*AA (PPE) (IB 38 pts)
York – A*AA-AAA incl maths (PPE) (IB 37 pts)

144 pts **Bristol** – AAA-AAB incl maths+phys (Phys Phil) (IB 36–34 pts HL 6 maths 6/5 phys); AAA-AAB incl maths (Maths Phil) (IB 36–34 pts HL 6 maths); AAA-AAB 144–136 pts (Phil Econ) (IB 37–35 pts); AAA-AAB (Phil; Phil Theol) (IB 36–34 pts)
Durham – AAA (Phil Psy; Phil) (IB 37 pts); AAA incl soc sci/hum (Phil Pol) (IB 37 pts)
Edinburgh – AAA-ABB (Phil Ling; Phil) (IB 40–34 pts)
Exeter – AAA-AAB (Phil Pol; Phil; PPE) (IB 36–34 pts)
Lancaster – AAA-AAB (Ling Phil) (IB 36–35 pts)
Leeds – AAA (PPE) (IB 35 pts)
London (King's) – AAA (War St Phil) (IB 35 pts); (Phil courses) (IB 35 pts); AAA incl maths+fmaths (Maths Phil) (IB 35 pts HL 6 maths); AAA incl Fr (Fr Phil (Yr Abrd)) (IB 35 pts HL 6 Fr)
London (UCL) – AAA (Phil) (IB 38 pts)
London LSE – AAA (Phil Lgc Sci Meth; Pol Phil) (IB 38 pts); AAA incl maths (Phil Econ) (IB 38 pts)
NCH London – AAA-ABB (Phil; PPE)
Oxford – AAA (Phil Theol; Phil Modn Langs; PPE) (IB 39 pts)
St Andrews – AAA (Phil Scot Hist) (IB 36 pts); AAA-AAB (Phil courses) (IB 35–38 pts)
Sussex – AAA-AAB (PPE) (IB 35 pts)
Warwick – AAA-AAB (Phil Joint Hons) (IB 38–36 pts)
York – AAA (Phil Pol) (IB 36 pts); AAA-AAB incl maths+phys (Phys Phil) (IB 36–35 pts HL 6 maths+phys)

136 pts **Birmingham** – AAB (Phil) (IB 32 pts HL 665)

New UCAS points Tariff: A* = 56 pts; A = 48 pts; B = 40 pts; C = 32 pts; D = 24 pts; E = 16 pts

Bristol – AAB–ABB (Sociol Phil) (IB 34–32 pts); AAB–ABB incl lang (Phil Modn Lang) (IB 34–32 pts HL 5 lang)

Glasgow – AAB–BBB incl arts/lang (Phil) (IB 36–34 pts)

Lancaster – AAB (PPE) (IB 35 pts); AAB–ABB (Phil; Phil Relig St; Eth Phil Relgn) (IB 35–32 pts); AAB–ABB incl maths/fmaths (Maths Phil) (IB 35 pts HL 6 maths)

Leeds – AAB (Phil; Phil Joint Hons) (IB 35 pts)

Liverpool – AAB–ABB 136–128pts (Phil Joint Hons) (IB 35–33 pts HL 665)

London (King's) – AAB (Relgn Phil Eth) (IB 35 pts)

London (UCL) – AAB–ABB (Hist Phil Sci) (IB 36–34 pts)

Manchester – AAB (PPE) (IB 35 pts)

Nottingham – AAB/A*BB/A*A*C (Phil; Phil Theol; Class Civ Phil) (IB 34 pts); AAB incl Engl (Engl Phil) (IB 34 pts); AAB (Psy Phil) (IB 34 pts)

Queen's Belfast – AAB (PPE)

Sheffield – AAB–ABB (Phil) (IB 35 pts); AAB (Pol Phil) (IB 35 pts)

Southampton – AAB–ABB (Film Phil) (IB 32 pts); (Phil; Econ Phil; Phil Sociol; Phil Pol) (IB 34–32 pts); AAB–ABB incl maths (Phil Maths) (IB 34–32 pts HL 6 maths); AAB–ABB incl hist (Phil Hist) (IB 34–32 pts HL 6 hist); AAB–ABB incl Engl (Phil Engl) (IB 34–32 pts HL 6 Engl); AAB–ABB incl mus +gr 8 (Phil Mus) (IB 34–32 pts HL 6 mus)

Sussex – AAB–ABB (Phil) (IB 34 pts)

Warwick – AAB (Phil) (IB 36 pts)

York – AAB incl Engl (Engl Phil) (IB 35 pts HL 6 Engl); AAB (Phil; Phil Ling) (IB 35 pts)

128 pts **Cardiff** – ABB (Phil) (IB 34 pts)

Dundee – ABB incl art des (Art Phil Contemp Prac) (IB 34 pts)

East Anglia – ABB (Phil Hist) (IB 32 pts HL 5 hist); (Phil; Phil Pol; PPE) (IB 32 pts)

Essex – ABB–BBB (Phil; Phil Hist; PPE; Phil Law) (IB 32–30 pts)

Kent – ABB (Phil Joint courses) (IB 34 pts)

Leeds – ABB incl biol (Biol Hist Phil Sci) (IB 34 pts HL 6 biol); ABB incl hist (Hist Phil Sci courses) (IB 34 pts HL 6 hist)

Liverpool – ABB (Phil) (IB 33 pts)

London (RH) – ABB incl mus (Mus Phil) (IB 32 pts); ABB (Pol Phil) (IB 32 pts); (Phil) (IB 34 pts); (PPE) (IB 34 pts)

Manchester – ABB (Phil) (IB 34 pts); ABB–BBB (Theol St Phil Eth) (IB 34–31 pts)

Reading – ABB–BBB (Phil courses; Art Phil) (IB 32–30 pts)

Sheffield – ABB–BBB (Phil Joint Hons) (IB 34 pts)

Stirling – ABB (PPE; Phil) (IB 35 pts)

Warwick – ABB (Class Civ Phil) (IB 34 pts)

120 pts **Aberdeen** – BBB incl maths+phys (Nat Phil (Phys)) (IB 32 pts HL 5 maths+phys); BBB (Phil Joint Hons) (IB 32 pts)

Chichester – BBB (Phil Eth) (IB 30 pts)

Dundee – BBB–BCC (Phil; Euro Phil) (IB 30 pts)

Gloucestershire – 120 pts (Relgn Phil Eth)

Keele – BBB/ABC (Phil) (IB 32 pts)

London (Birk) – 120 pts (Phil)

Queen's Belfast – BBB (Phil courses)

Roehampton – 120 pts (Phil)

UWE Bristol – 120 pts (Phil) (IB 26 pts)

112 pts **Brighton** – BBC (Phil Pol Eth) (IB 28 pts)

Canterbury Christ Church – 112 pts (Relgn Phil Eth)

Hertfordshire – 112 pts (Phil; Phil Ital) (IB 28 pts)

Hull – 112 pts (Phil; Phil Pol) (IB 28 pts)

Newman – 112 pts (Phil Relgn Educ)

Nottingham Trent – 112 pts (Phil Joint Hons)

Oxford Brookes – BBC (Phil) (IB 30 pts)

York St John – 112 pts (Relgn Phil Eth)

104 pts **Bath Spa** – 104–120 pts (Relgn Phil Eth)

Check **Chapter 3** for new university admission details and **Chapter 6** on how to read the subject tables.

      Central Lancashire – 104 pts (Phil Pol; Phil) (IB 28 pts)
      Leeds Trinity – 104 pts (Phil Eth Relgn)
      Liverpool Hope – BCC–BBB 104–120 pts (Phil Eth Relgn; Phil Eth)
      London (Birk) – 104 pts (Pol Phil Hist)
      Manchester Met – 104–112 pts (Phil; Int Pol Phil) (IB 26 pts)
      St Mary's – 104 pts (Phil) (IB 28 pts)

96 pts **Bangor** – 96–112 pts (Phil Relgn)
      Bishop Grosseteste – 96–112 pts (Theol Eth Soty)
      Manchester Met – 96–112 pts (Phil Joint Hons) (IB 28 pts)
      Trinity Saint David – 96–104 pts (Phil; Phil Joint Hons) (IB 26 pts)
      Wolverhampton – 96 pts (Law Phil; Phil Sociol; Relig St Phil); 96–112 pts (War St Phil;
        Pol Phil)

88 pts **Anglia Ruskin** – 88–104 pts (Phil; Phil Engl Lit) (IB 24 pts)

      Open University – (Phil Psy); contact +44 (0)845 300 6090 **or** www.openuniversity.co.uk/
      you (PPE)

Alternative offers
See **Chapter 6** and **Appendix 1** for grades/new UCAS Tariff points information for other examinations.

CHOOSING YOUR COURSE (SEE ALSO CH.1)
Universities and colleges teaching quality See www.qaa.ac.uk; http://unistats.direct.gov.uk.

Top research universities and colleges (REF 2014) Warwick; Essex; Sheffield; Edinburgh; Birmingham; London LSE; St Andrews; Bristol; Oxford; Cambridge (Hist Phil Sci); London (King's).

ADMISSIONS INFORMATION
Number of applicants per place (approx) Birmingham 4; Bristol 19; Cambridge 6; Cardiff 8; Dundee 6; Durham 8; East Anglia 6; Hull 19; Kent 9; Lancaster 6; Leeds 10; Liverpool 5; London (King's) 6; London (UCL) 12; London LSE 11; Manchester 6; Northampton 3; Nottingham 7; Oxford (success rate 44%), (PPE) 29%; Sheffield 6; Southampton 6; Trinity Saint David 4; Warwick 9; York 6.

Advice to applicants and planning the UCAS personal statement Read Bertrand Russell's *Problems of Philosophy*. Refer to any particular aspects of philosophy which interest you (check that these are offered on the courses for which you are applying). Since Philosophy is not a school subject, selectors will expect applicants to have read around the subject. Explain what you know about the nature of studying philosophy. Say what you have read in philosophy and give an example of a philosophical issue that interests you. Universities do not expect applicants to have a wide knowledge of the subject, but evidence that you know what the subject is about is important. **Bristol** Deferred entry considered.

Misconceptions about this course Applicants are sometimes surprised to find what wide-ranging Philosophy courses are offered.

Selection interviews Yes Cambridge, Essex, Lancaster, Leeds, Liverpool, London (UCL), Newcastle, Oxford (Phil Mod Lang) 23%, (PPE) 15%, (Phil Theol) 21%, Southampton, Trinity Saint David, Warwick; **Some** Bristol, Cardiff, Hull, London LSE (rare); **No** Birmingham, Dundee, East Anglia, Nottingham, Reading.

Interview advice and questions Philosophy is a very wide subject and initially applicants will be asked for their reasons for their choice and their special interests in the subject. Questions in recent years have included: Is there a difference between being tactless and being insensitive? Can you be tactless and thin-skinned? Define the difference between knowledge and belief. Was the vertical distortion of El Greco's paintings a product of a vision defect? What is the point of studying philosophy? What books on philosophy have you read? Discuss the work of a renowned philosopher. What is a philosophical novel? Who has the right to decide your future – yourself or another? What do you want to do with your life? What is a philosophical question? John is your husband, and if John is your husband then necessarily you must be his wife; if you are necessarily his wife then it is not possible that you could not be his wife; so it was impossible for you not to have married him – you were destined for each other. Discuss. What is the difference between a man's entitlements, his deserts and his attributes? What are morals? A good understanding of philosophy is needed for entry to degree courses, and applicants are expected to demonstrate this if they are called to interview. As one admissions tutor stated, 'If you find Bertrand Russell's *Problems of Philosophy* unreadable – don't apply!' See also **Chapter 5**. **Cambridge** If you were to form a government of philosophers what selection process would you use? Is it moral to hook up a psychopath (whose only pleasure is killing) to a really stimulating machine so that he can believe he is in the real world and kill as much as he likes? **Oxford** If you entered a teletransporter and your body was destroyed and instantly recreated on Mars in exactly the same way with all your memories intact etc, would you be the same person? Tutors are not so much concerned with what you know as how you think about it. Evidence required concerning social and political topics and the ability to discuss them critically. (PPE) Is being hungry the same thing as wanting to eat? Why is there not a global government? What do you think of teleport machines? Should there be an intelligence test to decide who should vote? **York** Do human beings have free will? Do we perceive the world as it really is?

Reasons for rejection (non-academic) Evidence of severe psychological disturbance, criminal activity, drug problems (evidence from referees' reports). Lack of knowledge of philosophy. **Oxford** He was not able to explore his thoughts deeply enough or with sufficient centrality. **York** No evidence of having read any philosophical literature.

AFTER-RESULTS ADVICE
Offers to applicants repeating A-levels Higher Bristol (Phil Econ), Essex, Glasgow, Leeds, Warwick; **Same** Birmingham, Bristol, Cardiff, Dundee, Durham, East Anglia, Hull, Liverpool Hope, Newcastle, Nottingham (in some cases), Nottingham Trent, St Mary's, Southampton, Stirling, Wolverhampton, York; **No** Cambridge.

GRADUATE DESTINATIONS AND EMPLOYMENT (2013/14 HESA)
Graduates surveyed 1,860 **Employed** 835 **In voluntary employment** 85 **In further study** 490 **Assumed unemployed** 140

Career note Graduates have a wide range of transferable skills that can lead to employment in many areas, eg management, public administration, publishing, banking and social services.

OTHER DEGREE SUBJECTS FOR CONSIDERATION
Divinity; History and Philosophy of Science; History of Art; Human Sciences; Psychology; Religious Studies; Science; Theology.

PHOTOGRAPHY
(see also Art and Design (Fine Art), Art and Design (General), Film, Radio, Video and TV Studies, Media Studies)

Photography courses offer a range of specialised studies involving commercial, industrial and still photography, portraiture and film, digital and video work. Increasingly this subject is featuring in Media courses. See also **Appendix 3**.

Useful websites www.the-aop.org; www.rps.org; www.bjp-online.com; www.bipp.com

NB The points totals shown to the left of the institutions are for ease of reference only. It must not be assumed that Tariff points are always used by institutions or that they can be substituted for an offer in grades. The level of an offer is not necessarily indicative of the quality of a course.

COURSE OFFERS INFORMATION

Subject requirements/preferences GCSE Art and/or a portfolio usually required. **AL** One or two subjects may be required, including an art/design or creative subject. Most institutions will make offers on the basis of a portfolio of work.

Your target offers and examples of degree courses

136 pts **Leeds** – AAB (Film Photo Media) (IB 35 pts)

128 pts **Brighton** – ABB +portfolio (Photo) (IB 34 pts)

Glasgow (SA) – ABB (Fn Art Photo) (IB 30 pts)

120 pts **Derby** – 120 pts +portfolio +interview (Photo; Commer Photo)

Edinburgh (CA) – BBB +portfolio (Photo) (IB 34 pts)

Huddersfield – BBB 120 pts (Photo)

Leeds Beckett – 120 pts (Photo Jrnl) (IB 26 pts)

Norwich Arts – BBB incl art/des (Photo) (IB 32 pts)

Sheffield Hallam – 120 pts (Photo)

Sunderland – 120 pts (Photo Comb Hons)

Trinity Saint David – 120 pts (Photojrnl Doc Photo); (Photo Arts) (IB 32 pts)

112 pts **Birmingham City** – BBC 112 pts (Media Comm (Media Photo); Vis Comm (Photo)) (IB 28 pts)

Bournemouth – 112–128 pts (Photo) (IB 32 pts)

Bournemouth Arts – BBC–BBB 112–120 pts +portfolio +interview (Commer Photo; Photo) (IB 32 pts)

Central Lancashire – 112 pts (Fash Prom) (IB 28 pts)

Chester – BBC–BCC incl art/des/photo 112 pts (Photo) (IB 26 pts HL 5 vis arts); BBC–BCC 112 pts (Photo Dig Photo) (IB 26 pts)

Coventry – BBC incl art/media/photo (Photo) (IB 28 pts)

De Montfort – 112 pts incl art des (Photo Vid) (IB 28 pts)

Gloucestershire – 112 pts +interview +portfolio (Photojrnl Doc Photo; Photo)

Kingston – 112 pts (Photo)

Lincoln – 112 pts incl art/des/media (Photo)

Manchester Met – 112 pts +portfolio (Photo) (IB 26 pts)

Middlesex – 112 pts (Photo)

Northampton – 112 pts incl art/des/photo (Photo)

Nottingham Trent – 112 pts (Photo)

Plymouth – 112 pts (Photo) (IB 24 pts)

Roehampton – 112 pts (Photo)

Southampton Solent – 112 pts (Photo)

Sunderland – 112 pts (Photo Vid Dig Imag)

UWE Bristol – 112 pts (Photo) (IB 25 pts)

West London – 112 pts incl art des (Photo)

104 pts **Bath Spa** – 104 pts incl art des +portfolio +interview (Photo)

Central Lancashire – 104 pts (Photo)

Falmouth – 104–120 pts +portfolio +interview (Press Edit Photo; Mar Nat Hist Photo; Photo; Fash Photo)

Leeds (CA) – 104 pts +portfolio (Photo)

South Wales – BCC incl art des +interview +portfolio (Doc Photo) (IB 29 pts); BCC +interview +portfolio (Photo) (IB 29 pts)

Staffordshire – 104 pts (Photo; Photojrnl) (IB 24 pts)

96 pts **Bolton** – 96 pts (Photo)

Canterbury Christ Church – 96–112 pts (Photo)

Cleveland (CAD) – 96 pts (Photo)

Cumbria – 96 pts (Photo)

East London – 96 pts (Photo) (IB 24 pts)

Hertfordshire – 96 pts incl art +portfolio +interview (Photo) (IB 24 pts)

Portsmouth – 96–112 pts (Photo) (IB 25 pts)

New UCAS points Tariff: A* = 56 pts; A = 48 pts; B = 40 pts; C = 32 pts; D = 24 pts; E = 16 pts

        Ulster – 96 pts incl art des (Photo) (IB 24 pts)
        Westminster – CCC–BB incl photo (Photo) (IB 28 pts)
        Wolverhampton – 96 pts +portfolio (Photo)
88 pts **Creative Arts** – 88 pts (Photo)
80 pts **Anglia Ruskin** – 80–96 pts (Photo) (IB 24 pts)
        Bedfordshire – 80 pts +portfolio (Photo Vid Art) (IB 24 pts)
        Hereford (CA) – 80 pts +portfolio +interview (Photo)
        Plymouth (CA) – 80 pts +portfolio (Photo)
64 pts **Arts London (CFash)** – CC 64 pts +portfolio (Fash Photo)
        Colchester (Inst) – 64 pts +portfolio (Photo)
        Ravensbourne – CC (Dig Photo) (IB 28 pts)
32 pts **Arts London** – 32 pts (Photo)

Alternative offers
See **Chapter 6** and **Appendix 1** for grades/new UCAS Tariff points information for other examinations.

EXAMPLES OF COLLEGES OFFERING COURSES IN THIS SUBJECT FIELD
Amersham and Wycombe (Coll); Barking and Dagenham (Coll); Bedford (Coll); Birmingham Met (Coll); Blackburn (Coll); Blackpool and Fylde (Coll); Bournemouth and Poole (Coll); Bradford (Coll); Brighton and Hove City (Coll); Bristol City (Coll); Canterbury (Coll); Central Bedfordshire (Coll); Central Campus, Sandwell (Coll); Central Nottingham (Coll); City and Islington (Coll); Coventry City (Coll); Doncaster (Coll); East Surrey (Coll); Exeter (Coll); Farnborough (CT); Gloucestershire (Coll); Great Yarmouth (Coll); Grimsby (Univ Centre); Havering (Coll); Hugh Baird (Coll); Hull (Coll); Kensington and Chelsea (Coll); Kirklees (Coll); Leeds City (Coll); Leicester (Coll); LeSoCo; Lincoln (Coll); Llandrillo (Coll); LSST; Manchester (Coll); Mid-Cheshire (Coll); Milton Keynes (Coll); Myerscough (Coll); Nescot; Newcastle (Coll); North Shropshire (Coll); North Warwickshire and Hinckley (Coll); Northbrook (Coll); Northumberland (Coll); Nottingham New (Coll); Rotherham (CAT); St Helens (Coll); Sheffield (Coll); Sir Gâr (Coll); Solihull (Coll); South Devon (Coll); South Essex (Coll); South Gloucestershire and Stroud (Coll); South Staffordshire (Coll); Southampton City (Coll); Southport (Coll); Stamford New (Coll); Stockport (Coll); Suffolk (Univ Campus); Sussex Coast Hastings (Coll); Tresham (CFHE); Truro and Penwith (Coll); Wakefield (Coll); Walsall (Coll); West Kent (Coll); Westminster City (Coll); Weston (Coll); Weymouth (Coll); Wiltshire (Coll); Wirral Met (Coll); Yeovil (Coll).

CHOOSING YOUR COURSE (SEE ALSO CH.1)
Universities and colleges teaching quality See www.qaa.ac.uk; http://unistats.direct.gov.uk.

Examples of sandwich degree courses Coventry; Hertfordshire; Huddersfield; Leeds; Portsmouth; Wolverhampton.

ADMISSIONS INFORMATION
Number of applicants per place (approx) Arts London 10; Birmingham City 6; Blackpool and Fylde (Coll) 3; Bournemouth Arts 7; Cleveland (CAD) 2; Derby 20; Falmouth 3; Nottingham Trent 4; Plymouth 2; Plymouth (CA) 7; Portsmouth 4; Staffordshire 3; Stockport (Coll) 6; Trinity Saint David 12.

Advice to applicants and planning the UCAS personal statement Discuss your interest in photography and your knowledge of various aspects of the subject, for example, digital, video, landscape, medical, wildlife and portrait photography. Read photographic journals to keep up-to-date on developments, particularly in photographic technology. You will also need first-hand experience of photography and to be competent in basic skills. See also **Appendix 3**. **Derby** (Non-UK students) Fluency in written and spoken English important. Portfolio of work essential.

Misconceptions about this course Some believe that courses are all practical work with no theory. **Cumbria** They didn't realise the facilities were so good!

Selection interviews Most institutions will interview applicants and expect to see a portfolio of work. **Yes** Brighton, Chester, Cumbria, Falmouth, Huddersfield, Salford, Southampton Solent, West London.

Interview advice and questions Questions relate to the applicant's portfolio of work which, for these courses, is of prime importance. Who are your favourite photographers? What is the most recent exhibition you have attended? Have any leading photographers influenced your work? Questions regarding contemporary photography. Written work sometimes required. See **Chapter 5**.

Reasons for rejection (non-academic) Lack of passion for the subject. Lack of exploration and creativity in practical work. Poorly presented portfolio.

AFTER-RESULTS ADVICE

Offers to applicants repeating A-levels Same Birmingham City, Blackpool and Fylde (Coll), Chester, Cumbria, Manchester Met, Nottingham Trent, Staffordshire.

GRADUATE DESTINATIONS AND EMPLOYMENT (2013/14 HESA)

Cinematics and Photography graduates surveyed 4,415 **Employed** 2,195 **In voluntary employment** 200 **In further study** 340 **Assumed unemployed** 430

Career note Opportunities for photographers exist in a range of specialisms including advertising and editorial work, fashion, medical, industrial, scientific and technical photography. Some graduates also go into photojournalism and other aspects of the media.

OTHER DEGREE SUBJECTS FOR CONSIDERATION

Art and Design; Digital Animation; Film, Radio, Video and TV Studies; Media Studies; Moving Image; Radiography.

PHYSICAL EDUCATION

(see also **Education Studies, Sports Sciences/Studies, Teacher Training**)

Physical Education courses are very popular and unfortunately restricted in number. Ability in gymnastics or an involvement in sport are obviously important factors.

Useful websites www.afpe.org.uk; www.uksport.gov.uk; see also **Education Studies** and **Teacher Training**.

NB The points totals shown to the left of the institutions are for ease of reference only. It must not be assumed that Tariff points are always used by institutions or that they can be substituted for an offer in grades. The level of an offer is not necessarily indicative of the quality of a course.

COURSE OFFERS INFORMATION

Subject requirements/preferences GCSE English, mathematics and a science. **AL** PE, sports studies and science are preferred subjects and for some courses one of these may be required. Disclosure and Barring Service (DBS) check before starting the course. Declaration of Health usually required.

Your target offers and examples of degree courses
144 pts **Birmingham** – AAA–ABB incl maths/sci (Spo PE Coach Sci) (IB 32 pts HL 666–665)
128 pts **Bangor** – 128–104 pts (Spo Hlth PE)
         East Anglia – ABB (PE) (IB 32 pts)
         Edge Hill – ABB 128 pts (PE Sch Spo)
         Edinburgh – ABB (PE) (IB 34 pts)
         Sheffield Hallam – 128 pts (PE Sch Spo)
120 pts **Brighton** – BBB (PE) (IB 30 pts)
         Cardiff Met – 120 pts (Spo PE)

        Chichester – BBB–BBC incl PE (PE Spo Coach) (IB 30 pts)

        Greenwich – 120 pts incl sci (Spo Sci Coach) (IB 24 pts)

        Leeds Beckett – 120 pts incl sci (PE Out Educ) (IB 26 pts); 120 pts incl sci/PE (PE courses) (IB 26 pts)

        St Mark and St John – BBB incl PE/sci (PE)

112 pts **Brunel** – BBC (PE Yth Spo; Spo Hlth Exer Sci (Spo Dev)) (IB 29 pts)

        Canterbury Christ Church – 112 pts (PE Spo Exer Sci)

        East London – 112 pts incl PE/spo/sci (Spo PE Dev) (IB 24 pts)

        Leeds Trinity – 112 pts (P PE Spo Dev; S PE courses)

        Liverpool John Moores – 112 pts (Spo Dev)

        Newman – 112 pts (Spo Educ St)

        Oxford Brookes – BBC (Spo Coach PE) (IB 30 pts)

        Plymouth – 112 pts (P PE BEd (QTS))

        St Mark and St John – 112 pts (Coach PE)

        Staffordshire – 112 pts (PE Yth Spo Coach)

        Wolverhampton – 112 pts (PE)

        Worcester – 112 pts (PE Spo St)

        York St John – 112 pts (Spo Coach)

104 pts **Bedfordshire** – 104 pts +interview (PE S) (IB 24 pts)

        Cardiff Met – 104 pts (Educ St Spo Physl Actvt)

        Glyndŵr – 104 pts (Spo Coach)

        Greenwich – 104 pts (PE Spo)

        Liverpool Hope – BCC–BBB 104–120 pts (Spo PE)

        Winchester – 104–120 pts (P Educ PE QTS)

 96 pts **Anglia Ruskin** – 96 pts (Spo Coach PE) (IB 24 pts)

        Cumbria – 96 pts (PE)

        Manchester Met – 96–112 pts (Coach Spo Dev; PE Spo Ped) (IB 28 pts)

        Trinity Saint David – 96 pts (PE) (IB 26 pts)

 80 pts **Bedfordshire** – 80 pts (Spo St) (IB 24 pts)

        London Met – 80 pts incl biol/PE/spo sci (Spo Sci PE)

        Wolverhampton – 80 pts (Exer Hlth)

Alternative offers

See **Chapter 6** and **Appendix 1** for grades/new UCAS Tariff points information for other examinations.

EXAMPLES OF COLLEGES OFFERING COURSES IN THIS SUBJECT FIELD

City and Islington (Coll); Doncaster (Coll); Hartpury (Coll); Mid-Cheshire (Coll); Peterborough (Coll).

CHOOSING YOUR COURSE (SEE ALSO CH.1)

Universities and colleges teaching quality See www.qaa.ac.uk; http://unistats.direct.gov.uk.

Top research universities and colleges (REF 2014) See **Sports Sciences/Studies**.

ADMISSIONS INFORMATION

Number of applicants per place (approx) Bangor 19; Birmingham 5; Brunel 10; Chichester 5; Edge Hill 40; Leeds Trinity 33; Liverpool John Moores 4; Newman 5; St Mark and St John 18; Sheffield Hallam 60; Worcester 31.

Advice to applicants and planning the UCAS personal statement Ability in gymnastics, athletics and all sports and games is important. Full details of these activities should be given on the UCAS application – for example, teams, dates and awards achieved, assisting in extra-curricular activities. Involvement with local sports clubs, health clubs, summer camps, gap year. Relevant experience in coaching, teaching, community and youth work. **Liverpool John Moores** Commitment to working with children and a good sports background.

Selection interviews Most institutions. In most cases, applicants will take part in physical education practical tests and games/gymnastics, depending on the course. The results of these tests could affect the level of offers. See also **Chapter 5**. **Yes** Worcester.

Interview advice and questions The applicant's interests in physical education will be discussed, with specific questions on, for example, sportsmanship, refereeing, umpiring and coaching. Questions in the past have also included: What qualities should a good netball goal defence possess? How could you encourage a group of children into believing that sport is fun? Do you think that physical education should be compulsory in schools? Why do you think you would make a good teacher? What is the name of the education minister? **Liverpool John Moores** Questions on what the applicant has gained or learned through experiences with children.

Reasons for rejection (non-academic) Poor communication and presentational skills. Relatively poor sporting background or knowledge. Lack of knowledge about the teaching of physical education and the commitment required. Lack of ability in practicalities, for example, gymnastics, dance when relevant. Poor self-presentation. Poor writing skills.

AFTER-RESULTS ADVICE
Offers to applicants repeating A-levels Same Liverpool John Moores, Newman.

GRADUATE DESTINATIONS AND EMPLOYMENT (2013/14 HESA)
See **Sports Sciences/Studies**.

Career note The majority of graduates go into teaching although, depending on any special interests, they may also go on into the sport and leisure industry.

OTHER DEGREE SUBJECTS FOR CONSIDERATION
Coach Education; Exercise and Fitness; Exercise Physiology; Human Biology; Leisure and Recreation; Physiotherapy; Sport and Exercise Science; Sport Health and Exercise; Sport Studies/Sciences; Sports Coaching; Sports Development; Sports Engineering; Sports Psychology; Sports Therapy.

PHYSICS
(see also Astronomy and Astrophysics)

Physics is an increasingly popular subject and a wide variety of courses are available which enables students to follow their own interests and specialisations. Some course options are nanotechnology, medical physics, cosmology, environmental physics and biophysics.

Useful websites www.myphysicscourse.org; www.iop.org; www.physics.org; www.scicentral.com; www.ipem.ac.uk; www.epsrc.ac.uk; jobs.newscientist.com; www.nature.com/physics

NB The points totals shown to the left of the institutions are for ease of reference only. It must not be assumed that Tariff points are always used by institutions or that they can be substituted for an offer in grades. The level of an offer is not necessarily indicative of the quality of a course.

COURSE OFFERS INFORMATION
Subject requirements/preferences GCSE English, mathematics and science. **AL** Physics and mathematics are required for most courses.

Your target offers and examples of degree courses
160 pts **Cambridge** – A*A*A incl sci/maths (Nat Sci (Phys/Physl Sci/Astro)) (IB 40–41 pts HL 776)
     Durham – A*A*A incl phys+maths (Phys Astron (MPhys); Theor Phys (MPhys); Phys) (IB 38 pts)
     Imperial London – A*A*A incl maths+phys (Phys; Phys Mus Perf; Phys (Yr Abrd)) (IB 39 pts)
     Manchester – A*A*A–A*AA incl phys+maths (Phys; Phys Astro) (IB 39–38 pts)

New UCAS points Tariff: A* = 56 pts; A = 48 pts; B = 40 pts; C = 32 pts; D = 24 pts; E = 16 pts

UNIVERSITY *of York*

Department of Physics

The Department of Physics offers the highest quality physics education in a leading research environment. An enthusiasm for teaching and excellent staff–student rapport ensure an extremely supportive atmosphere.

Physics studies the fundamental forces of nature in order to understand the structure, function and workings of the world around us. Our flexible programmes allow students to experience a wide-ranging approach to physics or to specialise in a particular area of study.

Offered as an integrated Masters or Bachelors degree, our courses are accredited by the Institute of Physics and are available with a placement years abroad and in industry.

- Physics
- Physics with Astrophysics
- Theoretical Physics
- Physics with Philosophy
- Mathematics and Physics

For further information on our courses contact please visit: www.york.ac.uk/physics

UNIVERSITY *of York*

Department of Physics

Studying Physics

Physics is fundamental to our understanding of how the universe works. By choosing to take a degree in Physics, you choose to study an enormously stimulating subject that also sits right at the heart of technology development. Physics today is a very rewarding and exciting field with new discoveries occurring at the frontiers of human knowledge. Its methods and insights are widely applicable and its practitioners widely sought.

Physics at York

Our flexible programmes allow students to maintain a wide ranging approach to physics or to specialise in a particular area. Students are able to further tailor their course to their interests by studying abroad or by conducting a research placement. All our programmes are accredited by the Institute of Physics (IOP) and are structured around core teaching which ensures that students have a solid grounding in the key concepts of physics.

We offer an integrated Year Abroad programme alongside all of our Physics programs. Studying or working abroad during your degree is a life-changing etxperience that can boost your self-confidence, independence and ambition. It also broadens your cultural and social perspectives, develops language skills and significantly increases your employability in the global jobs market.

The White Rose Industrial Physics Academy (WRIPA), a new collaboration between the Universities of York and Sheffield and technical industry partners aims to improve the industry-relevant skills of physics graduates. The Academy is setting up industry-led undergraduate projects, enhancing the industry focus of the taught curriculum and organising joint workshops and recruitment events to enhance the industry skills of our graduates.

You will be taught by world leading academics at the cutting edge of their research field who posses an enthusiasm for teaching. This fosters excellent staff-student rapport and ensures an extremely friendly and supportive atmosphere. Regular supervisions meetings, small group tutorials and our 'open door' policy for approaching our academic staff are distinctive in our teaching approach and enable students to share their insights and develop a deeper understanding of their subject.

Our department is rapidly expanding with world leading research programmes in several areas of physics including Condensed Matter Physics, Nuclear Physics, Plasma Physics, Quantum Computing, Nanophysics, Nuclear Astrophysics and Fusion. There has recently been significant major investment in our laboratories and facilities including our new Quantum Technology Hub, York-JEOL Nanocentre, York Plasma Institute and our Astrocampus.

You will have excellent career prospects with over 80% of graduates in employment or further study after six months after graduating. We pride ourselves on being a friendly and supportive department, helping students to unlock their academic potential and develop skills that are highly sought after by employers

We are one of only nine Physics departments to achieve the Juno Champion Award for support of women in physics and have achieved a Silver Athena SWAN accreditation for our ongoing support of women in science.

Find out more:

For further information on studying at York:
www.york.ac.uk/physics
+44 (0)1904 322241
physics-admissions@york.ac.uk

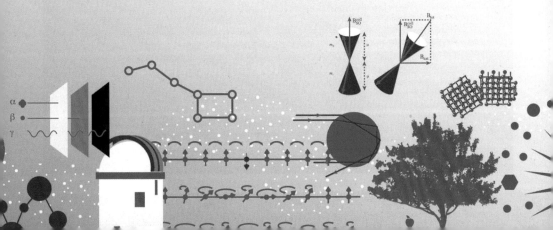

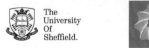

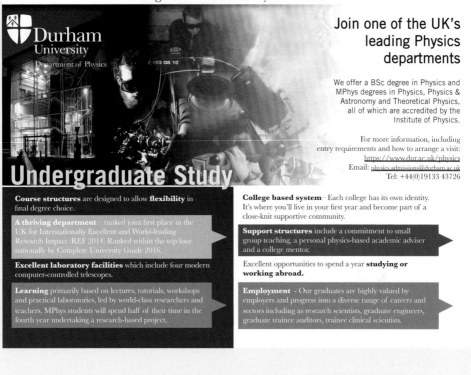

Together we'll create your future

Durham University
Department of Physics

Undergraduate Study

Join one of the UK's leading Physics departments

We offer a BSc degree in Physics and MPhys degrees in Physics, Physics & Astronomy and Theoretical Physics, all of which are accredited by the Institute of Physics.

For more information, including entry requirements and how to arrange a visit:
https://www.dur.ac.uk/physics
Email: physics.admissions@durham.ac.uk
Tel: +44(0)19133 43726

Course structures are designed to allow **flexibility** in final degree choice.

A thriving department - ranked joint first place in the UK for Internationally Excellent and World-leading Research Impact (REF 2014). Ranked within the top four nationally by Complete University Guide 2016.

Excellent laboratory facilities which include four modern computer-controlled telescopes.

Learning primarily based on lectures, tutorials, workshops and practical laboratories, led by world-class researchers and teachers. MPhys students will spend half of their time in the fourth year undertaking a research-based project.

College based system - Each college has its own identity. It's where you'll live in your first year and become part of a close-knit supportive community.

Support structures include a commitment to small group teaching, a personal physics-based academic adviser and a college mentor.

Excellent opportunities to spend a year **studying or working abroad.**

Employment - Our graduates are highly valued by employers and progress into a diverse range of careers and sectors including as research scientists, graduate engineers, graduate trainee auditors, trainee clinical scientists.

152 pts
Bath – A*AA incl maths+phys (Phys; Maths Phys) (IB 36 pts HL 6 maths+phys)
Birmingham – A*AA–AAAA incl maths+phys (Phys) (IB 32 pts HL 766)
Durham – A*AA incl biol/chem (Nat Sci) (IB 38 pts)
Exeter – A*AA–AAB incl maths+phys (Maths Phys) (IB 38–34 pts HL 56 maths+phys); (Phys Astro; Phys) (IB 38–34 pts HL 6 maths/phys+5 maths/phys)
Lancaster – A*AA incl phys+maths (Phys Astro Cosmo MPhys; MPhys) (IB 38 pts); A*AA incl phys and maths (Phys Ptcl Phys Cosmo MPhys) (IB 38 pts)
Nottingham – A*AA–AAA incl maths+phys (Phys; Phys Euro Lang; Phys Med Phys; Phys Theor Phys; Mathem Phys; Phys Theor Astro; Phys Astron) (IB 34 pts)
Oxford – A*AA incl phys+maths (Phys) (IB 39 pts)
Surrey – A*AA–AAA incl maths+mus+phys (Mus Snd Rec (Tonmeister)) (IB 38–36 pts HL 6 maths+mus+phys)
Warwick – A*AA incl maths+phys (Phys Bus St; Phys) (IB 38 pts HL 6 maths+phys)

144 pts
Bristol – AAA–AAB incl maths+phys (Phys) (IB 35–34 pts HL 6 maths 6/5 phys); (Phys Astro; Phys Phil) (IB 36–34 pts HL 6 maths 6/5 phys)
Cardiff – AAA–ABB incl phys+maths (Phys) (IB 34–32 pts HL 6 maths+phys); (Phys Astron; Phys MPhys; Phys Med Phys; Theor Comput Phys; Phys Astron MPhys) (IB 34–32 pts HL 6 phys+maths)
East Anglia – AAA/AABB incl sci (Nat Sci) (IB 34 pts HL 6 sci)
Edinburgh – AAA–ABB (Phys; Phys Mus; Geophys; Geophys Meteor; Phys Meteor; Theor Phys; Comput Phys; Mathem Phys) (IB 37–32 pts)
Lancaster – AAA incl phys+maths (Phys; Phys Astro Cosmo; Phys Ptcl Phys Cosmo; Theor Phys Maths) (IB 36 pts)
London (King's) – AAA incl phys+maths+fmaths (Maths Phys) (IB 35 pts HL 6 maths+phys); AAA incl maths+phys (Phys; Phys Theor Phys; Phys Med Apps; Phys Phil) (IB 35 pts HL 6 maths+phys)

Check **Chapter 3** for new university admission details and **Chapter 6** on how to read the subject tables.

London (RH) – AAA incl maths+phys+mus (Phys Mus) (IB 32 pts); AAA–AAB incl maths+phys (Phys; Theor Phys; Phys Ptcl Phys) (IB 32 pts)

London (UCL) – AAA–ABB (Phys Med Phys) (IB 38–34 pts HL 6 maths 5 phys); AAA–ABB incl maths+phys (Med Phys) (IB 38–34 pts HL 6 maths 5 phys); AAA incl maths+phys (Phys) (IB 38 pts HL 6 maths+phys); AAA incl chem+maths+phys (Cheml Phys) (IB 38 pts HL 5 chem+maths+phys)

Newcastle – AAA incl maths+phys (MPhys) (IB 37 pts HL 6 maths+phys)

St Andrews – AAA incl maths+phys (Comp Sci Phys; Phys) (IB 38 pts)

Sheffield – AAA–AAB incl maths+phys (Phys MPhys) (IB 37 pts HL 6 maths+phys)

Southampton – AAA–AAB incl maths+phys (Maths Phys) (IB 36 pts HL 6 maths); AAA incl maths+phys (Phys Photon MPhys; Phys Spc Sci MPhys; Phys Nanotech MPhys; Phys Maths MPhys; Phys Astron MPhys) (IB 36 pts HL 6 maths+phys)

Swansea – AAA–AAB incl maths+phys (Phys MPhys) (IB 36–34 pts)

York – AAA–AAB incl maths+phys (Phys Astro; Maths Phys; Phys; Phys MPhys; Phys Phil; Theor Phys) (IB 36–35 pts HL 6 maths+phys)

136 pts **Glasgow** – AAB–BBB incl maths+phys (Phys Astro; Phys) (IB 36–34 pts)

Leeds – AAB incl phys+maths (Theor Phys) (IB 34 pts HL 5 phys+maths); (Phys Astro; Phys) (IB 35 pts HL 5 phys+maths)

Leicester – AAB incl phys+maths (Phys Spc Sci Tech; Phys Astro; Phys; Phys Nanotech; Phys Planet Sci) (IB 32 pts)

Liverpool – AAB incl maths+phys (Mathem Phys MMath) (IB 35 pts HL 6 maths+phys); (Theor Phys MPhys) (IB 35 pts HL 6 phys+maths); AAB incl phys+maths (Phys MPhys) (IB 35 pts HL 6 phys+maths)

Liverpool John Moores – AAB incl maths+phys (Astro MPhys)

London (QM) – AAB–ABB incl maths+phys 136–128 pts (Astro) (IB 34–30 pts HL 6 maths+phys); AAB–ABB incl phys+maths 136–128 pts (Astro MSci) (IB 34–30 pts HL 6 maths+phys); (Theor Phys) (IB 30–34 pts HL 6 phys+maths); (Phys Ptcl Phys) (IB 34–30 pts HL 6 phys+maths); 136 pts incl phys+maths (Phys MSci) (IB 34 pts HL 6 maths+phys); (Theor Phys MSci) (IB 34 pts HL 6 phys+maths)

Loughborough – AAB incl maths+phys (Eng Phys) (IB 36 pts HL 6 maths+phys)

Nottingham – AAB incl maths+phys+chem (Chem Mol Phys) (IB 34 pts)

Queen's Belfast – AAB incl maths+phys (Phys Astro MSci; Phys MSci; Phys Med Apps MSci)

Sheffield – AAB incl mus+phys (Theor Phys) (IB 35 pts HL 6 maths+phys); AAB–ABB incl maths+phys (Phys Joint Hons; Phys Astro; Phys) (IB 35 pts HL 6 maths+phys)

Southampton – AAB incl maths+phys (Phys) (IB 34 pts)

Surrey – AAB incl maths+phys (Phys Astron; Phys; Phys Nucl Astro; Phys Qntm Tech) (IB 35 pts)

Sussex – AAB–ABB incl maths+phys (Phys Astro; Phys; Theor Phys) (IB 34 pts HL 5 maths+phys)

Swansea – AAB–BBB incl maths+phys (Phys Nanotech; Theor Phys) (IB 34–32 pts)

128 pts **Aberdeen** – ABB (Phys Complex Sys Modl)

East Anglia – ABB incl chem+maths (Cheml Phys) (IB 32 pts HL 5 chem+maths)

Heriot-Watt – ABB incl maths+phys (Phys courses) (IB 29 pts)

Hertfordshire – 128 pts incl maths+phys (Phys) (IB 32 pts)

Kent – ABB incl maths+phys (Phys) (IB 34 pts)

Liverpool – ABB incl phys+maths (Phys Nucl Sci; Phys Med Apps; Phys) (IB 33 pts HL 6 phys+maths); ABB incl maths+phys (Geophys (Geol/Phys)) (IB 33 pts HL 4 maths+phys)

Loughborough – ABB incl maths+phys (Phys; Phys Maths) (IB 34 pts)

Queen's Belfast – ABB incl maths (Theor Phys)

Reading – ABB–AAC incl maths phys (Env Phys) (IB 32–30 pts)

Strathclyde – ABB–BBB (Phys) (IB 32 pts HL 5 phys+maths)

Swansea – ABB–BBB incl maths+phys (Phys Ptcl Phys Cosmo; Phys) (IB 34–32 pts)

120 pts **Aberdeen** – BBB incl maths+phys (Phys; Nat Phil (Phys)) (IB 32 pts HL 5 maths+phys)

Central Lancashire – 120 pts incl phys+maths (App Phys; Phys) (IB 30 pts)

Dundee – BBB–BCC incl maths+phys/eng (Phys) (IB 30 pts)

Keele – BBB/ABC incl phys/maths (Phys courses) (IB 31 pts HL 5 maths 4 phys)
Liverpool John Moores – 120–136 pts (Phys Astron) (IB 24–28 pts)
Nottingham Trent – 120 pts incl maths+phys (Phys Astro)
Queen's Belfast – BBB incl maths+phys (Phys Astro; Phys; Phys Med Apps)

112 pts **Aberystwyth** – 112 pts incl maths+phys (Phys courses); 112 pts incl maths+phys/comp (Spc Sci Robot)
De Montfort – 112 pts incl maths/phys (Phys) (IB 28 pts HL maths/phys)
Hull – 112 pts incl maths+phys (Phys) (IB 28 HL 5 maths+phys); (Phys Astro) (IB 28 pts HL 5 maths+phys)
Nottingham Trent – 112 pts incl maths+phys (Phys; Phys Nucl Tech)

104 pts **Manchester Met** – 104–112 pts incl maths+phys (App Phys) (IB 28 pts)
Portsmouth – 104 pts incl maths/phys/electron (App Phys) (IB 26 pts HL 5 phys/maths/electron)
Salford – 104–112 pts incl maths+phys (Phys) (IB 28 pts); 104–112 pts (Phys Acoust)
West Scotland – BCC incl maths/phys (Phys) (IB 24 pts)

96 pts **Nottingham Trent** – 96 pts incl maths+phys (Phys Foren Apps)
St Mary's – 96 pts incl phys (App Phys) (IB 28 pts)

Open University – contact +44 (0)845 300 6090 **or** www.openuniversity.co.uk/you (Physl Sci)

Alternative offers
See **Chapter 6** and **Appendix 1** for grades/new UCAS Tariff points information for other examinations.

EXAMPLES OF COLLEGES OFFERING COURSES IN THIS SUBJECT FIELD
Birmingham Met (Coll); South Devon (Coll).

CHOOSING YOUR COURSE (SEE ALSO CH.1)
Universities and colleges teaching quality See www.qaa.ac.uk; http://unistats.direct.gov.uk.

Top research universities and colleges (REF 2014) Cardiff; Durham; Nottingham; Edinburgh; St Andrews; Strathclyde; Southampton; Warwick; Imperial London; Manchester; Oxford; Bath; Cambridge; Leeds.

Examples of sandwich degree courses Bath; Bristol; Cardiff; East Anglia; Hertfordshire; Kent; Loughborough; Nottingham Trent; Portsmouth; Surrey; Sussex; West Scotland.

ADMISSIONS INFORMATION
Number of applicants per place (approx) Bath 7; Birmingham 6; Bristol 7; Cardiff 4, (Phys Astron) 6; Dundee 5; Durham 7; Edinburgh 9; Exeter 5; Heriot-Watt 5; Hull 7; Imperial London 3; Kent 8; Lancaster 8; Leeds 7; Leicester 7; Liverpool 4; London (King's) 7; London (QM) 6; London (RH) 9; London (UCL) 11; Loughborough 6; Manchester 4; Nottingham 10; Salford 5; Southampton 6; Strathclyde 5; Surrey 5; Swansea 3; Warwick 8; York 5.

Advice to applicants and planning the UCAS personal statement Admissions tutors look for potential, enthusiasm and interest in the subject so interests relating to maths and physics must be mentioned. An awareness of the range of careers in which physics is involved should also be mentioned on the UCAS application together with a demonstration of any particular interests, such as details on a physics or maths book you have read recently (not science fiction!). Make sure to mention if you have attended any courses, summer schools or day conferences on physics and engineering. See also **Appendix 3**. **Bristol** Deferred entry accepted.

Selection interviews Yes Aberystwyth, Cambridge, East Anglia, Exeter, Heriot-Watt, Hull, Imperial London, Lancaster, Liverpool, London (QM), London (RH), Loughborough, Manchester, Oxford (Phys) 16%, (Phys Phil) 12%, St Andrews, Salford, Sheffield, Warwick, York; **Some** Bristol, Cardiff; **No** Bath, Birmingham, Dundee, Nottingham, Strathclyde, Surrey, Swansea.

486 | Physiology

Interview advice and questions Questions will almost certainly focus on those aspects of the physics AS/A-level course which the student enjoys. See also **Chapter 5**. **Bristol** Why Physics? Questions on mechanics, physics and pure maths. Given paper and calculator and questions asked orally; best to take your own calculator. Tutors seek enthusiastic and highly motivated students and the physicist's ability to apply basic principles to unfamiliar situations.

AFTER-RESULTS ADVICE
Offers to applicants repeating A-levels Higher Bristol, Glasgow, St Andrews, Warwick; **Possibly higher** Aberystwyth, Hull, Leeds, Loughborough, York; **Same** Birmingham, Cardiff, Dundee, Durham, East Anglia, Exeter, Lancaster, Leicester, Liverpool, Salford, Swansea; **No** Cambridge.

GRADUATE DESTINATIONS AND EMPLOYMENT (2013/14 HESA)
Graduates surveyed 2,380 **Employed** 925 **In voluntary employment** 55 **In further study** 930 **Assumed unemployed** 205

Career note Many graduates go into scientific and technical work in the manufacturing industries. However, in recent years, financial work, management and marketing have also attracted many seeking alternative careers.

OTHER DEGREE SUBJECTS FOR CONSIDERATION
Astronomy; Astrophysics; Computer Science; Earth Sciences; Engineering subjects; Geophysics; Materials Science and Metallurgy; Mathematics; Meteorology; Natural Sciences; Oceanography; Optometry; Radiography.

PHYSIOLOGY
(see also Animal Sciences, Neuroscience, Psychology)

Physiology is the study of body function. Courses in this wide-ranging subject will cover the central nervous system, special senses and neuro-muscular mechanisms, and body-regulating systems such as exercise, stress and temperature regulation. The Bristol course is available for intercalation in which it is possible to follow a one-year stand-alone degree in any of the following subjects: Anatomical Science, Global Health, Health Science, Medical Humanities, or Transfusion and Transplanting Science.

Useful websites www.physoc.org; www.physiology.org; www.bases.org.uk/Physiology; see also **Biological Sciences**.

NB The points totals shown to the left of the institutions are for ease of reference only. It must not be assumed that Tariff points are always used by institutions or that they can be substituted for an offer in grades. The level of an offer is not necessarily indicative of the quality of a course.

COURSE OFFERS INFORMATION
Subject requirements/preferences GCSE Science and mathematics at grade A. **AL** Two science subjects are usually required; Chemistry and Biology are the preferred subjects.

Your target offers and examples of degree courses
160 pts Cambridge – A*A*A incl sci/maths (Nat Sci (Physiol Dev Neuro)) (IB 40–41 pts HL 776)
144 pts Leeds – AAA–ABB (Hum Physiol) (IB 35–34 pts); AAA–ABB incl sci (Spo Sci Physiol) (IB 35–34 pts HL 6 sci)
Manchester – AAA–ABB incl maths/sci (Physiol (Yr Ind)) (IB 37–33 pts); AAA–ABB incl sci/maths (Pharmacol Physiol (Yr Ind); Physiol) (IB 37–33 pts)
Newcastle – AAA–AAB incl biol (Physiol Sci) (IB 35–34 pts HL 5 biol+chem)
136 pts Bristol – AAB–ABB incl sci/maths (Physiol Sci) (IB 34–32 pts HL 6/5 sci/maths)
Cardiff – AAB–ABB incl biol (Biomed Sci (Physiol)) (IB 34 pts HL 6 biol+chem)
Dundee – AAB incl biol+chem (Physiol Sci) (IB 30 pts)

       Edinburgh – AAB–ABB (Physiol) (IB 37–32 pts)

       Glasgow – AAB–BBB incl biol/chem (Physiol Spo Sci; Physiol; Physiol Spo Sci Nutr) (IB 36–34 pts)

       London (King's) – AAB incl chem+biol (Med Physiol) (IB 35 pts)

128 pts **Leeds** – ABB incl sci (Hlthcr Sci (Crdc Physiol)) (IB 34 pts HL 5 sci)

       Leicester – ABB incl sci/maths (Med Physiol) (IB 30 pts)

       UWE Bristol – 128 pts incl biol/chem+sci (Hlthcr Sci (Physiol Sci); Hlthcr Sci (Lf Sci)) (IB 27 pts HL 6 biol/chem 5 sci)

120 pts **Aberdeen** – BBB incl maths/sci (Physiol (Yr Ind)) (IB 32 pts HL 5 maths/sci); (Physiol) (IB 32 pts HL 5 maths+sci)

       London (St George's) – BBB incl biol (Hlthcr Sci (Physiol Sci))

       Plymouth – 120 pts incl biol+sci (Hlthcr Sci (Physiol Sci))

112 pts **BSO** – BBC incl biol+sci (MOst)

       Central Lancashire – 112 pts incl chem/biol/env sci (Physiol Pharmacol) (IB 28 pts HL 5 biol/chem)

       East London – 112 pts incl biol/chem (Med Physiol) (IB 25 pts)

       Portsmouth – 112–128 pts (Hum Physiol) (IB 26 pts)

       Sunderland – 112 pts incl biol/chem (Physiol Sci)

       Ulster – 112 pts incl sci/maths (Hlth Physiol) (IB 25 pts)

       Westminster – BBC incl sci (Pharmacol Physiol) (IB 26 pts HL 5 sci)

104 pts **Manchester Met** – BCC–BBC incl biol 104–112 pts (Physiol (Physl Actvt Hlth)) (IB 28 pts HL 5 biol)

       Wolverhampton – 104 pts incl sci (Hlthcr Sci (Physiol Sci))

Alternative offers

See **Chapter 6** and **Appendix 1** for grades/new UCAS Tariff points information for other examinations.

CHOOSING YOUR COURSE (SEE ALSO CH.1)

Universities and colleges teaching quality See www.qaa.ac.uk; http://unistats.direct.gov.uk.

Top research universities and colleges (REF 2014) See **Biological Sciences**.

Examples of sandwich degree courses Cardiff; Leeds; Manchester; Manchester Met; Wolverhampton.

ADMISSIONS INFORMATION

Number of applicants per place (approx) Bristol 6; Cardiff 8; Dundee 5; Leeds 4; Leicester 5; Liverpool 10; London (King's) 5; Newcastle 6.

Advice to applicants and planning the UCAS personal statement See **Neuroscience** and **Biological Sciences**.

Selection interviews Yes Cambridge, Leeds, Manchester, Newcastle; **Some** Bristol, Cardiff, Dundee; **No** Leicester.

Interview advice and questions Past questions include: What made you decide to do a Physiology degree? What experimental work have you done connected with physiology? What future career do you have in mind? What is physiology? Why not choose Medicine instead? What practicals do you do at school? See also **Chapter 5**. **Cardiff** Interviewer expects to see outside interests and ability to mix with people as well as an interest in biological sciences.

AFTER-RESULTS ADVICE

Offers to applicants repeating A-levels Higher Bristol, Glasgow, Leeds, Leicester, Newcastle; **Same** Cardiff, Dundee; **No** Cambridge.

GRADUATE DESTINATIONS AND EMPLOYMENT (2013/14 HESA)

See **Neuroscience**.

Career note See **Biology**.

OTHER DEGREE SUBJECTS FOR CONSIDERATION

Anatomy; Biochemistry; Biological Sciences; Biotechnology; Dentistry; Genetics; Health Studies; Medicine; Microbiology; Neuroscience; Nursing; Optometry; Pharmacology; Radiography; Sports Science.

PHYSIOTHERAPY

(including **Osteopathy**, **Sports Therapy** and **Veterinary Physiotherapy**; see also
Health Sciences/Studies)

Physiotherapists work as part of a multi-disciplinary team with other health professionals and are involved in the treatment and rehabilitation of patients of all ages and with a wide variety of medical problems. It includes periods of clinical practice. On successful completion of the three-year course, graduates are eligible for State Registration and Membership of the Chartered Society of Physiotherapy. Courses are very competitive. A-levels in Biology or Human Biology and PE are usually specified with high grades. Check websites. Tuition fees are paid by the NHS Bursary Scheme in England (and similar support is available in the rest of the UK, but arrangements differ so it is important to consult the relevant authority). Bursaries are available based on individual circumstances. All courses expect applicants to have gained some work experience which can include caring and voluntary work.

Useful websites www.csp.org.uk; www.thephysiotherapysite.co.uk; www.nhscareers.nhs.uk; www.physiotherapy.co.uk; www.hpc-uk.org

NB The points totals shown to the left of the institutions are for ease of reference only. It must not be assumed that Tariff points are always used by institutions or that they can be substituted for an offer in grades. The level of an offer is not necessarily indicative of the quality of a course.

COURSE OFFERS INFORMATION

Subject requirements/preferences GCSE English, mathematics and science subjects. Many universities stipulate A/B grades in specific subjects. **AL** One or two science subjects are required. **Other** Occupational health check and Disclosure and Barring Service (DBS) clearance.

Your target offers and examples of degree courses
144 pts **Southampton** – AAA incl sci (Physio) (IB 36 pts)
136 pts **Birmingham** – AAB incl biol/PE (Physio) (IB 32 pts HL 665)
 Bournemouth – 136 pts (Physio) (IB 33 pts)
 Bradford – AAB 136 pts (Physio)
 Brunel – AAB–ABB (Physio) (IB 33 pts)
 Cardiff – AAB incl biol (Physio) (IB 34 pts)
 Coventry – AAB inc biol (Physio)
 East Anglia – AAB incl biol/hum biol/PE (Physio) (IB 33 pts HL 666 incl biol)
 London (King's) – AAB incl sci/maths/soc sci (Physio) (IB 35 pts)
 Nottingham – AAB incl biol/physl sci (Physio) (IB 34 pts)
 Oxford Brookes – AAB incl biol (Physio) (IB 34 pts HL 5 biol)
 Plymouth – 136 pts incl biol (Physio) (IB 33 pts)
 Queen Margaret – AAB incl sci/maths 136 pts (Physio) (IB 32 pts)
 UWE Bristol – 136 pts incl biol (Physio) (IB 28 pts HL 6 biol)
128 pts **Brighton** – ABB incl biol/PE (Physio) (IB 32 pts HL biol)
 Central Lancashire – ABB incl sci (Physio)
 Harper Adams – ABB incl biol+sci (Vet Physio)
 Hertfordshire – ABB incl lf sci (Physio) (IB 32 pts)
 Huddersfield – ABB incl biol/PE 128 pts (Physio)

Keele – ABB/A*BC incl biol/PE (Physio) (IB 34 pts HL 6 biol)
Kingston – see under London (St George's) (Physio)
Leeds Beckett – 128 pts incl sci (Physio) (IB 27 pts HL 6 sci)
Liverpool – ABB incl biol/PE (Physio) (IB 30 pts HL 6 biol)
London (St George's) – ABB (Physio)
Manchester Met – ABB incl biol sci (Physio) (IB 29 pts)
Northumbria – 128 pts incl sci/hlth (Physio) (IB 31 pts HL sci/hlth)
Sheffield Hallam – 128 pts incl biol/PE (Physio)
Teesside – 128–144 pts incl sci/soc sci +interview (Physio)
York St John – ABB incl biol/PE (Physio)
120 pts **Chichester** – 120 pts incl sci (Spo Thera) (IB 32 pts HL 5 sci)
Cumbria – 120 pts (Physio)
East London – 120 pts incl sci/maths/PE (Physio) (IB 28 pts)
Glasgow Caledonian – BBB incl sci (Physio) (IB 30 pts HL 6 biol+sci)
Robert Gordon – BBB incl sci/maths (Physio) (IB 32 pts)
Ulster – BBB incl sci/maths +HPAT (Physio) (IB 26 pts)
Worcester – 120–136 pts incl biol/PE (Physio)

Alternative offers
See **Chapter 6** and **Appendix 1** for grades/new UCAS Tariff points information for other examinations.

EXAMPLES OF COLLEGES OFFERING COURSES IN THIS SUBJECT FIELD
Warwickshire (Coll); Writtle (Coll).

CHOOSING YOUR COURSE (SEE ALSO CH.1)
Universities and colleges teaching quality See www.qaa.ac.uk; http://unistats.direct.gov.uk.

Top research universities and colleges (REF 2014) See **Health Sciences/Studies**.

ADMISSIONS INFORMATION
Number of applicants per place (approx) Birmingham 9; Bradford 22; Brighton 30, (overseas) 6; Brunel 11; Cardiff 17; Coventry 15; East Anglia 14; East London 10; Glasgow Caledonian 12; Hertfordshire 13; Huddersfield 18; Kingston 9; Liverpool 20; London (King's) 16; Northumbria 37; Queen Margaret 11; Robert Gordon 13; Sheffield Hallam 12; Southampton 36; Teesside 33; Ulster 12; UWE Bristol 12.

Advice to applicants and planning the UCAS personal statement Visits to, and work experience in, hospital physiotherapy departments are important although many universities publicly state that this is not necessary. However, with the level of competition for this subject I would regard this as doubtful (see Reasons for rejection). Applicants must demonstrate a clear understanding of the nature of the profession. Give details of voluntary work activities. Take notes of the work done and the different aspects of physiotherapy. Explain your experience fully on the UCAS application. Outside interests and teamwork are considered important. Good communication skills are required. Observation placement within a physiotherapy department. See also **Appendix 3**. **Coventry** The University of Leicester part-delivers a BSc Physiotherapy degree. This course is a Coventry University degree that has 30 places based at the Leicester campus. Teaching takes place at Leicester and Coventry. Students are admitted by Coventry but live and mostly study at Leicester. **Manchester Met** We need to know why you want to be a physiotherapist. We also look for work shadowing a physiotherapist or work experience in another caring role. Evidence is also required of good communication skills, ability to care for people and of teamwork and leadership.

Misconceptions about this course Some applicants think that physiotherapy has a sports bias.

Selection interviews Most institutions. **Yes** Birmingham, Bournemouth, Bradford, Brighton, Brunel, Coventry, Cumbria, East Anglia, East London, Huddersfield, Keele, London (St George's), Northumbria,

Nottingham, Robert Gordon, Sheffield Hallam, Ulster, Worcester, York St John; **Some** Cardiff (mature students), Kingston, Southampton (mature students).

Interview advice and questions Physiotherapy is one of the most popular courses at present and work experience is very important, if not essential. A sound knowledge of the career, types of treatment used in physiotherapy and some understanding of the possible problems experienced by patients will be expected. Past interview questions include: How does physiotherapy fit into the overall health care system? If one patient was a heavy smoker and the other not, would you treat them the same? What was the most emotionally challenging thing you have ever done? Give an example of teamwork in which you have been involved. Why should we make you an offer? What is chiropractic? What is osteopathy? See also **Chapter 5**.

Reasons for rejection (non-academic) Lack of knowledge of the profession. Failure to convince the interviewers of a reasoned basis for following the profession. Failure to have visited a hospital physiotherapy unit. Lack of awareness of the demands of the course. **Birmingham** Poor communication skills. Lack of career insight. **Cardiff** Lack of knowledge of physiotherapy; experience of sports injuries only. **UWE Bristol** Applicants re-sitting A-levels are not normally considered.

AFTER-RESULTS ADVICE
Offers to applicants repeating A-levels Higher East Anglia, East London, Glasgow Caledonian, Kingston, Teesside, UWE Bristol; **Same** Coventry, Queen Margaret, Southampton.

GRADUATE DESTINATIONS AND EMPLOYMENT (2013/14 HESA)
See **Health Sciences/Studies**.

Career note The professional qualifications gained on graduation enable physiotherapists to seek posts in the NHS where the majority are employed. A small number work in the community health service, particularly in rural areas, whilst others work in residential homes. In addition to private practice, there are also some opportunities in professional sports clubs.

OTHER DEGREE SUBJECTS FOR CONSIDERATION
Anatomy; Audiology; Biological Sciences; Health Studies; Leisure and Recreation; Nursing; Occupational Therapy; Osteopathy; Physical Education; Psychology; Sport Science/Studies.

PLANT SCIENCES
(including **Botany**; see also **Biological Sciences, Biology, Horticulture**)

Plant Sciences cover such areas as plant biochemistry, plant genetics, plant conservation and plant geography. Botany encompasses all aspects of plant science and also other subject areas including agriculture, forestry and horticulture. Botany is basic to these subjects and others including pharmacology and water management. As with other biological sciences, some universities introduce Plant Sciences by way of a common first year with other subjects. Plant sciences has applications in the agricultural, biotechnological, horticultural and food industries.

Useful websites www.kew.org; www.anbg.gov.au; www.bsbi.org.uk; www.botany.net; www.botany.org

NB The points totals shown to the left of the institutions are for ease of reference only. It must not be assumed that Tariff points are always used by institutions or that they can be substituted for an offer in grades. The level of an offer is not necessarily indicative of the quality of a course.

COURSE OFFERS INFORMATION
Subject requirements/preferences GCSE Mathematics if not offered at A-level. **AL** One or two science subjects are usually required.

Your target offers and examples of degree courses

160 pts **Cambridge** – A*A*A incl sci/maths (Nat Sci (Plnt Sci)) (IB 40–41 pts HL 776)
144 pts **Birmingham** – AAA–AAB incl biol+sci (Biol Sci (Plnt Biol)) (IB 32 pts HL 666–665)
       Edinburgh – AAA–ABB (Plnt Sci) (IB 37–32 pts)
       Manchester – AAA–ABB incl sci/maths (Plnt Sci; Plnt Sci Modn Lang; Plnt Sci (Yr Ind))
          (IB 37–33 pts)
       Sheffield – AAA–AAB incl biol+sci (Plnt Sci MBiolSci) (IB 37 pts HL 6 biol+sci)
136 pts **Glasgow** – AAB–BBB incl biol/chem (Mol Cell Biol (Plnt Sci)) (IB 36–34 pts)
       Sheffield – AAB–ABB incl biol+sci (Plnt Sci) (IB 35–34 pts HL 6 biol+sci)
128 pts **Nottingham** – ABB–BBB incl sci (Plnt Sci) (IB 32–30 pts)
120 pts **Aberdeen** – BBB incl maths+sci (Plnt Soil Sci) (IB 32 pts HL 5 maths+sci)
116 pts **Aberystwyth** – 116–132 pts incl biol (Plnt Biol)
104 pts **Worcester** – 104–120 pts incl biol+sci/maths (Plnt Sci)
  96 pts **Canterbury Christ Church** – 96 pts (Plnt Sci) (IB 24 pts)
       Myerscough (Coll) – CCC 96 pts (Arbor Urb Frsty) (IB 24 pts)

Alternative offers
See **Chapter 6** and **Appendix 1** for grades/new UCAS Tariff points information for other examinations.

CHOOSING YOUR COURSE (SEE ALSO CH.1)
Universities and colleges teaching quality See www.qaa.ac.uk; http://unistats.direct.gov.uk.

Top research universities and colleges (REF 2014) See **Biological Sciences**.

Examples of sandwich degree courses Manchester.

ADMISSIONS INFORMATION
Number of applicants per place (approx) Edinburgh 6; Glasgow 4; Nottingham 7; Sheffield 5.

Advice to applicants and planning the UCAS personal statement Visit botanical gardens. See also **Biological Sciences** and **Appendix 4**.

Selection interviews Yes Cambridge; **Some** Nottingham.

Interview advice and questions You are likely to be questioned on your biology studies, your reasons for wishing to study Plant Sciences and your ideas about a possible future career. In the past, questions have been asked about Darwin's theory of evolution, photosynthesis and DNA and the value of gardening programmes on TV! See also **Chapter 5**.

AFTER-RESULTS ADVICE
Offers to applicants repeating A-levels Possibly higher Nottingham; **Same** Birmingham, Sheffield; **No** Cambridge.

GRADUATE DESTINATIONS AND EMPLOYMENT (2013/14 HESA)
Botany graduates surveyed 55 **Employed** 25 **In voluntary employment** 0 **In further study** 15 **Assumed unemployed** 0

Career note See **Biology** and **Horticulture**.

OTHER DEGREE SUBJECTS FOR CONSIDERATION
Agriculture; Biochemistry; Biological Sciences; Biology; Crop Science (Agronomy); Ecology; Food Science; Forestry; Herbal Medicine; Horticulture; Landscape Architecture; Traditional Chinese Medicine.

PODIATRY (CHIROPODY)

A podiatrist's primary aim is to improve the mobility, independence and quality of life for their patients. They are autonomous healthcare professionals who deliver preventative, palliative, biomechanical, pharmacological and surgical interventions for lower limb problems. They work alone or are part of a multidisciplinary team. Courses lead to the eligibility for registration with the Health and Care Professions Council and some work shadowing prior to application is preferred by admissions tutors.

Useful websites www.careersinpodiatry.com; www.nhscareers.nhs.uk; www.podiatrynetwork.com; www.podiatrytoday.com; www.healthcommunities.com/health-topics/foot-health.shtml; www.feetforlife.org

NB The points totals shown to the left of the institutions are for ease of reference only. It must not be assumed that Tariff points are always used by institutions or that they can be substituted for an offer in grades. The level of an offer is not necessarily indicative of the quality of a course.

COURSE OFFERS INFORMATION

Subject requirements/preferences GCSE Mathematics and science subjects. **AL** Biology usually required or preferred. **Other** Hepatitis B, tuberculosis and tetanus immunisation; Disclosure and Barring Service (DBS) clearance (a pre-existing record could prevent a student from participating in the placement component of the course and prevent the student from gaining state registration).

Your target offers and examples of degree courses
120 pts **East London** – 120 pts incl sci/maths/PE (Pod) (IB 28 pts)
          Huddersfield – BBB incl biol/spo sci/PE 120 pts (Pod)
          Plymouth – 120 pts (Pod) (IB 28 pts)
          Southampton – BBB incl sci/soc sci (Pod) (IB 30 pts)
          Ulster – BBB incl sci/maths +HPAT (Pod) (IB 26 pts)
112 pts **Birmingham Met (Coll)** – 112 pts (Pod)
          Brighton – BBC (Pod) (IB 28 pts)
          Cardiff Met – 112 pts (Pod)
          Northampton – 112–128 pts (Pod)
104 pts **Glasgow Caledonian** – BCC incl sci (Pod) (IB 24 pts)
 96 pts **Queen Margaret** – CCC 96 pts (Pod) (IB 28 pts)
 64 pts **Durham New (Coll)** – 64 pts (Pod)

Alternative offers
See **Chapter 6** and **Appendix 1** for grades/new UCAS Tariff points information for other examinations.

EXAMPLES OF COLLEGES OFFERING COURSES IN THIS SUBJECT FIELD
Birmingham Met (Coll); Durham New (Coll).

CHOOSING YOUR COURSE (SEE ALSO CH.1)
Universities and colleges teaching quality See www.qaa.ac.uk; http://unistats.direct.gov.uk.

ADMISSIONS INFORMATION
Number of applicants per place (approx) Birmingham Met (Coll) 4; Cardiff Met 8; Huddersfield 2–3; Northampton 2; Southampton 4.

Advice to applicants and planning the UCAS personal statement Visit a podiatrist's clinic to gain work experience/work shadowing experience. Applicants need the ability to communicate with all age ranges, to work independently, to be resourceful and to possess a focused approach to academic work. Admissions tutors look for evidence of an understanding of podiatry, some work experience,

Profile: College of Podiatry

The world around us is dominated by science in one way or another, be it biology in plants or the human body, physics in engineering or communications and chemistry in food or DNA research.

Podiatry is no exception . . . it's full of science!

To understand how the lower limb works and to help patients you need to know all sorts about biology, physics and chemistry

Biology

Biology is probably the main science people associate with working in the medical profession. As a podiatrist it's really important to understand the structure of the body as well as how things interact. Podiatrists measure the blood flow in the legs and feet and to do this they have to know exactly how to find the arteries and veins. They can test blood flow in a number of ways by using their hands, ultrasound devices and blood pressure tests.

Treatment of painful or ingrowing toenails is achieved using simple surgical techniques. To do this podiatrists have to give patients injections of anaesthetic, which must be placed accurately near the nerves in the toe. To do the surgery effectively they have to understand the structure of the nail and surrounding tissues. So you can see how important it is to know your anatomy!

Physics

Physics is also important. Podiatrists treat a lot of different patients with biomechanical problems and understanding levers and forces really helps to diagnose the problem and work out how to treat the patient.

Participating in sports puts increased forces through the joints in the legs, which can cause pain and injury. Runners for example can develop foot or leg problems that may need treatment from a podiatrist. Using a treadmill, video equipment and their knowledge a podiatrist can assess the patient, diagnose the problem and potentially provide custom-made insoles that can alter the mechanics of the foot and reduce unwanted forces going through the foot.

Chemistry

Chemistry is also important in podiatry. Chemical reactions are essential for normal body function. Podiatrists need to know how illnesses and medicines may affect different chemical processes in the body to provide appropriate treatment.

Wounds in the skin contain all sorts of biochemicals. Podiatrists must understand what potential interactions there might be with anything they are using to treat a wound that would slow down the healing process. They need to know about different kinds of medication and how they react with the body.

For example understanding chemistry enables a podiatrist to calculate the maximum safe dose of anaesthetic for a patient.

If you would like further information about podiatry training please visit www.careersinpodiatry.com

good people skills, and effective communication. Mature applicants must include an academic reference (not an employer reference). See also **Appendix 3**.

Misconceptions about this course Cardiff Met Prospective students are often not aware of the demanding requirements of the course: 1000 practical clinical hours augmented by a rigorous academic programme. Applicants are often unaware that whilst the elderly are a significant sub-population of patients with a variety of foot problems, increasingly the role of the podiatrist is the diagnosis and management of biomechanical/developmental disorders as well as the management of the diabetic or rheumatoid patient and those who require surgical intervention for nail problems. **Huddersfield** Many people think that podiatry is limited in its scope of practice to treating toe nails, corns and calluses: FALSE. As professionals, we do treat such pathologies but the scope of practice is much wider. It now includes surgery, biomechanics, sports injuries, treating children and high-risk patients. Because offers are low it is considered an easier course than, for example, Physiotherapy: FALSE. The course is academically demanding in addition to the compulsory clinical requirement.

Selection interviews Most institutions. **Yes** Cardiff Met, Huddersfield, Southampton, Ulster.

Interview advice and questions Past questions include: Have you visited a podiatrist's surgery? What do your friends think about your choice of career? Do you think that being a podiatrist could cause you any physical problems? With which groups of people do podiatrists come into contact? What are your perceptions of the scope of practice of podiatry? What transferable skills do you think you will need? See also **Chapter 5**. **Cardiff Met** What made you consider podiatry as a career? Have you researched your career choice and where did you find the information? What have you discovered and has this altered your original perception of podiatry? What personal characteristics do you think you possess which might be useful for this work? **Southampton** Applicants should show an interest in medical topics. Communication skills are important, as is an insight into the implications of a career in podiatry.

Reasons for rejection (non-academic) Unconvincing attitude; poor communication and inter-personal skills; lack of motivation; medical condition or physical disabilities which are incompatible with professional practice; no knowledge of chosen profession; lack of work experience.

AFTER-RESULTS ADVICE
Offers to applicants repeating A-levels Same Cardiff Met, Huddersfield.

GRADUATE DESTINATIONS AND EMPLOYMENT (2013/14 HESA)
Career note Many state-registered podiatrists are employed by the NHS whilst others work in private practice or commercially run clinics.

OTHER DEGREE SUBJECTS FOR CONSIDERATION
Audiology; Biological Sciences; Health Studies; Nursing; Occupational Therapy; Osteopathy; Physiotherapy.

POLITICS

(including **Government** and **International Politics**; see also **Development Studies, International Relations, Social Sciences/Studies**)

Politics is often described as the study of 'who gets what, where, when and how'. Courses have become increasingly popular in recent years and usually cover the politics and government of the major powers. Because of the variety of degree courses on offer, it is possible to study the politics of almost any country in the world.

Useful websites www.europa.eu; www.gov.uk/government/organisations/foreign-commonwealth-office; www.psa.ac.uk; www.parliament.uk; www.whitehouse.gov; www.amnesty.org; www.gov.uk; www.un.org; www.un.int

NB The points totals shown to the left of the institutions are for ease of reference only. It must not be assumed that Tariff points are always used by institutions or that they can be substituted for an offer in grades. The level of an offer is not necessarily indicative of the quality of a course.

COURSE OFFERS INFORMATION

Subject requirements/preferences GCSE English, mathematics and a foreign language may be required. **AL** No subjects specified; History useful but an arts or social science subject an advantage.

Your target offers and examples of degree courses

152 pts **Bath** – A*AA incl maths (Econ Pol) (IB 36 pts HL 6 maths)
   Cambridge – A*AA (Hum Soc Pol Sci; Hum Soc Pol Sci (Pol Int Rel)) (IB 40–41 pts HL 776)
   Durham – A*AA incl maths (Econ Pol; PPE) (IB 38 pts)
   Exeter – A*AA–AAB (Econ Pol (Euro St)) (IB 38–34 pts)
   London (King's) – A*AA +LNAT (Pol Phil Law) (IB 35 pts); A*AA (PPE) (IB 35 pts HL 766)
   London (UCL) – A*AA–AAA incl maths (PPE) (IB 39–38 pts HL 7 maths)
   London LSE – A*AA incl A* maths (PPE) (IB 38 pts)
   Nottingham – A*AA–AAA (PPE) (IB 38–36)
   Warwick – A*AA (PPE) (IB 38 pts); A*AA (Econ Pol Int St) (IB 38 pts HL 4 maths)
   York – A*AA–AAA incl maths (PPE) (IB 37 pts)

144 pts **Bath** – AAA (Pol Int Rel) (IB 36 pts)
   Bristol – AAA–AAB (Pol Int Rel) (IB 36–34 pts)
   Durham – AAA incl soc sci/hum (Pol; Phil Pol) (IB 37 pts)
   Edinburgh – AAA–ABB (Persn Pol) (IB 37–34 pts); (Hist Pol; Pol) (IB 40–34 pts)
   Exeter – AAA–BBB (Pol Int Rel (Cornwall)) (IB 36–30 pts); AAA–AAB (Pol; PPE) (IB 36–34 pts)
   Lancaster – AAA–AAB (Pol (St Abrd); Hist Pol) (IB 36–35 pts)
   Leeds – AAA (PPE) (IB 35 pts)
   London (King's) – AAA (War St) (IB 35 pts)
   London (QM) – AAA (Law Pol) (IB 37 pts)
   London (SOAS) – AAA (Pol) (IB 37 pts)
   London (UCL) – AAA–AAB (Pol E Euro St) (IB 38–36 pts)
   London LSE – AAA (Int Rel; Gov; Gov Econ; Gov Hist; Pol Phil) (IB 38 pts)
   NCH London – AAA–ABB (Pol Int Rel; PPE)
   Newcastle – AAA–ABB (Gov EU St; Pol) (IB 32 pts); (Pol Econ) (IB 37–34 pts)
   Nottingham – AAA incl hist (Hist Pol) (IB 36 pts)
   Oxford – AAA (Hist Pol) (IB 38 pts); (PPE) (IB 39 pts)
   Sussex – AAA–AAB (Law Pol; PPE) (IB 35 pts)
   Warwick – AAA (Pol courses) (IB 38 pts)
   York – AAA (Phil Pol) (IB 36 pts)

136 pts **Bath** – AAB incl lang (Lang Pol) (IB 36 pts)
   Bristol – AAB–ABB (Pol Sociol; Soc Plcy Pol) (IB 34–32 pts); AAB–ABB incl lang (Pol Modn Lang) (IB 34–32 pts HL 5 lang)
   Cardiff – AAB incl lang (Pol Int Rel (incl lang)) (IB 34 pts); AAB (Pol; Int Rel Pol) (IB 34 pts)
   East Anglia – AAB incl hist (Hist Pol) (IB 33 pts HL 5 hist)
   Glasgow – AAB–BBB incl Engl (Pol) (IB 38–36 pts)
   Lancaster – AAB–ABB (Pol Relig St; Pol; Pol Sociol; Pol Int Rel) (IB 35–32 pts); AAB (PPE) (IB 35 pts)
   Leeds – AAB (Pol Parl St; Pol) (IB 36 pts)
   London (Gold) – AAB–ABB (PPE) (IB 33 pts)
   London (King's) – AAB (Euro Pol) (IB 35 pts)
   London LSE – AAB (Soc Plcy Gov) (IB 37 pts)
   Loughborough – AAB–ABB (Econ Pol) (IB 34 pts)
   Manchester – AAB (PPE) (IB 35 pts)
   Queen's Belfast – AAB (PPE; Law Pol)
   Reading – AAB (PPE) (IB 35 pts)

Sheffield – AAB incl hist (Hist Pol) (IB 35 pts HL 6 hist); AAB (Int Rel Pol; Pol Phil; Pol; Int Pol Scrty St) (IB 35 pts)

Southampton – AAB–ABB (PPE) (IB 34–32 pts HL 5 maths); (Phil Pol) (IB 34–32 pts); AAB–ABB incl Span/Port (Pol Span/Port Lat Am St) (IB 34 pts HL 6 Span/Port); AAB–ABB incl Fr/Ger (Pol Fr/Ger) (IB 34 pts HL 6 Fr/Ger); AAB–ABB incl hist (Modn Hist Pol) (IB 34 pts HL 6 hist)

Surrey – AAB incl soc sci/hum (Int Pol; Pol) (IB 35 pts)

Sussex – AAB–ABB (Pol courses; Econ Pol) (IB 34 pts)

Warwick – AAB (Pol Sociol) (IB 36 pts)

York – AAB incl Engl (Engl Pol) (IB 35 pts HL 6 Engl); AAB (Pol; Pol Int Rel; Soc Pol Sci) (IB 35 pts)

128 pts **Aston** – ABB (Pol Soc Plcy; Pol Sociol; Pol Int Rel; Pol Engl Lang) (IB 33 pts)

Birmingham – ABB (Pol Sci; Pol Econ; Pol Sci Int Rel; Pol Sci Soc Plcy (Yr Abrd)) (IB 32 pts HL 655)

Chichester – ABB–BBC incl pol/hist (Pol)

City – ABB–BBB 128–120 pts (Int Pol) (IB 32 pts)

East Anglia – ABB (Pol; PPE) (IB 32 pts)

Essex – ABB–BBB (Pol Hum Rts; Econ Pol; PPE; Pol) (IB 32–30 pts)

Kent – ABB–BBB (Econ Pol) (IB 34 pts)

Kingston – 128 pts (Pol Jrnl) (IB 28 pts)

Leeds – ABB (Pol Port/Russ/Span; Chin Pol; Int Dev courses) (IB 34 pts)

Liverpool – ABB (Int Pol Plcy; Pol) (IB 33 pts)

London (QM) – ABB 128 pts (Pol) (IB 34 pts); ABB incl hist 128 pts (Hist Pol) (IB 34 pts HL 5 hist)

London (RH) – ABB incl mus (Mus Pol St) (IB 32 pts); ABB (Pol Phil; Pol; Econ Pol Int Rel; Pol Int Rel; Geog Pol Int Rel) (IB 32 pts); (PPE) (IB 34 pts)

Loughborough – ABB (Hist Pol; Pol courses) (IB 34 pts)

Manchester – ABB (Pol Soc Anth; Pol Sociol) (IB 34 pts)

Newcastle – ABB–BBB (Pol Sociol) (IB 32–30 pts)

Northumbria – 128 pts incl hist/pol (Hist Pol) (IB 31 pts HL 5 hist/pol)

Nottingham – ABB (Pol courses) (IB 32 pts)

Reading – ABB–BBB (War Pce Int Rel) (IB 32 pts); (Pol Int Rel) (IB 32–30 pts)

Sheffield – ABB (Pol Sociol) (IB 34 pts)

Southampton – ABB–BBB incl maths/phys (Pol Econ) (IB 32 pts HL 4 maths); ABB–BBB (Pol Int Rel; Pol) (IB 32 pts)

Stirling – ABB (PPE) (IB 35 pts)

Strathclyde – ABB–BBB (Pol courses) (IB 34 pts)

120 pts **Aberdeen** – BBB (Pol courses) (IB 32 pts)

Aberystwyth – 120 pts (Int Pol; Pol St); 120–128 pts (Pol courses)

Brunel – BBB (Int Pol; Pol Econ; Pol) (IB 30 pts)

Chichester – BBB–CCC (Pol Contemp Hist) (IB 31 pts)

Dundee – BBB–BCC (Pol) (IB 30 pts); BBB–BCC incl sci (Geopol) (IB 30 pts)

Edge Hill – BBB 120 pts (Hist Pol)

Greenwich – 120 pts (Pol Int Rel)

Keele – BBB/ABC (Pol) (IB 32 pts)

Kent – BBB (Pol Int Rel (Yr Abrd); Pol) (IB 34 pts)

Leicester – BBB (Pol Econ; Pol) (IB 28 pts)

Lincoln – 120 pts (Pol; Int Rel Pol)

London (Gold) – BBB (Pol; Int St) (IB 33 pts)

Queen's Belfast – BBB–ABB incl Fr (Fr Joint Hons); BBB–ABB (Pol Joint Hons)

Stirling – BBB (Pol; Pol (Int Pol)) (IB 32 pts)

Sunderland – 120 pts (Pol Comb Hons)

Swansea – BBB–BBC (Pol; Pol Soc Plcy; Pol Comm; War Soty) (IB 32–30 pts); BBB–BBC incl lang (Pol Span) (IB 32–30 pts)

112 pts **Brighton** – BBC (Pol; Phil Pol Eth) (IB 28 pts)

Canterbury Christ Church – 112 pts (Pol)
Chester – BBC–BCC 112 pts (Pol) (IB 26 pts)
De Montfort – 112 pts (Pol Sociol); (Int Rel Pol; Pol Gov) (IB 28 pts)
Huddersfield – BBC 112 pts (Pol; Int Pol)
Hull – 112 pts (PPE; Phil Pol; Law Pol; Pol Int Rel) (IB 28 pts)
Leeds Beckett – 112 pts (Pol) (IB 25 pts)
London Met – 112 pts (Pol)
Northampton – 112 pts (Int Rel Pol)
Nottingham Trent – 112 pts (Pol Hist)
Oxford Brookes – BBC (Pol; Econ Pol Int Rel; Int Rel Pol) (IB 30 pts)
Westminster – BBC (Pol Int Rel; Pol) (IB 30 pts)

104 pts **Central Lancashire** – 104 pts (Pol courses; Phil Pol) (IB 28 pts)
Coventry – BCC (Pol; Pol Hist) (IB 28 pts)
Liverpool Hope – BCC–BBB 104–120 pts (Pol Int Rel; Pol)
London (Birk) – 104 pts (Pol Phil Hist)
Manchester Met – 104–112 pts (Int Pol Phil; Pol; Int Pol) (IB 26 pts)
Middlesex – 104 pts (Int Pol)
Nottingham Trent – 104 pts (Pol)
Plymouth – 104 pts (Int Rel Pol) (IB 26 pts)
Sheffield Hallam – 104 pts (Pol)
Ulster – 104–112 pts (Sociol Pol; Pol) (IB 24–25 pts)
Worcester – 104 pts (Pol (Ppl Pwr))

96 pts **Bradford** – CCC 96 pts (Pol)
Kingston – 96 pts (Pol Int Rel)
London Met – 96 pts (Int Rel Pce Cnflct St)
London South Bank – CCC 96 pts (Pol)
Nottingham Trent – 96 pts (Pol Int Rel)
Plymouth – 96 pts (Pol Fr) (IB 26 pts)
Portsmouth – 96–120 pts (Pol) (IB 30 pts HL 17 pts)
West Scotland – CCC incl Engl (Soty Pol Plcy) (IB 24 pts)
Wolverhampton – 96–112 pts (Pol Phil; Pol Hist; Sociol Pol)

64 pts **UHI** – CC (Sociol Pol; PPE); CC incl Engl/hist/pol (Scot Hist Pol); CC incl hist/Engl/pol (Hist Pol)

Open University – contact +44 (0)845 300 6090 **or** www.openuniversity.co.uk/you (PPE)

Alternative offers
See **Chapter 6** and **Appendix 1** for grades/new UCAS Tariff points information for other examinations.

EXAMPLES OF COLLEGES OFFERING COURSES IN THIS SUBJECT FIELD
Blackburn (Coll); Newham (CFE).

CHOOSING YOUR COURSE (SEE ALSO CH.1)
Universities and colleges teaching quality See www.qaa.ac.uk; http://unistats.direct.gov.uk.

Top research universities and colleges (REF 2014) (Politics and International Studies) London LSE; London (UCL); Sheffield; Essex; Exeter; Oxford; Cardiff; Warwick; York.

Examples of sandwich degree courses Aston; Bath; Brunel; Coventry; De Montfort; Essex; Leeds; Loughborough; Middlesex; Nottingham Trent; Oxford Brookes; Plymouth; Surrey.

ADMISSIONS INFORMATION
Number of applicants per place (approx) Aberystwyth 4; Aston 4; Bath 6; Birmingham 5; Bradford 10; Bristol 14; Brunel 5; Cambridge 5; Cardiff 14; De Montfort 6; Dundee 6; Durham (Pol) 9, (PPE) 8; East Anglia 15; Exeter 8; Hull 11, (PPE) 20; Kent 14; Lancaster 14; Leeds 18; Leicester 7; Liverpool 9; London (QM) 10; London (SOAS) 5; London LSE (Gov) 17, (Gov Econ) 10, (Gov Hist) 17; London Met 5;

Loughborough 4; Newcastle 9; Northampton 4; Nottingham 5; Nottingham Trent 3; Oxford (PPE) 7; Oxford Brookes 12; Portsmouth 6; Southampton 6; Stirling 9; Swansea 3; Warwick 10; York 6, (PPE) 9.

Advice to applicants and planning the UCAS personal statement Study the workings of government in the UK, Europe and other areas of the world, such as the Middle East, the Far East, America and Russia. Describe visits to the Houses of Commons and Lords and the debates taking place. Attend council meetings – county, town, district, village halls. Describe these visits and agendas. Read current affairs avidly. Be aware of political developments in the major countries and regions of the world including the Middle East, South America, the UK, Europe, USA, China, Korea and Russia. Keep abreast of developments in theatres of war, for example, Afghanistan. Explain your interests in detail. **Aberystwyth** We look for degree candidates with a strong interest in political and social issues and who want to inquire into the way in which the world is organised politically, socially and economically. **Bristol** Deferred entry accepted. **De Montfort** Demonstration of active interest in current affairs and some understanding of how politics affects our daily lives.

Misconceptions about this course Aberystwyth Many students believe that they need to study politics at A-level for Politics courses – this is not the case. **De Montfort** Some applicants believe that a Politics course only covers the mechanics of government and parliament.

Selection interviews Yes Bath (mature students), Cambridge, Hull, Kent, Leeds (Pol Parl St), Liverpool, London (Gold), Oxford, Portsmouth; **Some** Aberystwyth, Bristol, De Montfort, Dundee, London (SOAS), London Met, Loughborough, Surrey, Ulster, Warwick; **No** Birmingham, East Anglia, Essex, Huddersfield, Leicester, London LSE, Nottingham, Reading, Sheffield, Swansea.

Interview advice and questions Questions may stem from AS/A-level studies but applicants will also be expected to be up-to-date in their knowledge and opinions of current events. Questions in recent years have included: What constitutes a 'great power'? What is happening at present in the Labour Party? Define capitalism. What is a political decision? How do opinion polls detract from democracy? Is the European Union a good idea? Why? What are the views of the present government on the European Union? What is a 'spin doctor'? Are politicians hypocrites? See also **Chapter 5**. **De Montfort** Why Politics? What political issues motivate your interests, for example environmentalism, human rights?

AFTER-RESULTS ADVICE
Offers to applicants repeating A-levels Higher Essex, Glasgow, Leeds, Newcastle, Nottingham, Warwick, York; **Possibly higher** Hull, Lancaster, Oxford Brookes, Swansea; **Same** Aberystwyth, Birmingham, Bristol, De Montfort, Dundee, Durham, East Anglia, Lincoln, Liverpool Hope, London (SOAS), London Met, London South Bank, Loughborough, Nottingham Trent, Portsmouth, Stirling, Sussex, Wolverhampton; **No** Cambridge.

GRADUATE DESTINATIONS AND EMPLOYMENT (2013/14 HESA)
Graduates surveyed 4,775 **Employed** 2,435 **In voluntary employment** 290 **In further study** 1,140 **Assumed unemployed** 345

Career note The transferable skills gained in this degree open up a wide range of career opportunities. Graduates seek positions in management, public services and administration and in some cases in political activities.

OTHER DEGREE SUBJECTS FOR CONSIDERATION
Development Studies; Economics; Government; History; International Relations; Public Policy and Administration; Social Policy and Administration; Sociology.

PROPERTY MANAGEMENT and SURVEYING

(including **Property Management/Development, Quantity Surveying** and **Real Estate Management. For Financial Investment in Property see under Finance;** see also **Agricultural Sciences/Agriculture, Building and Construction, Housing, Town and Country Planning**)

Surveying covers a very diverse range of careers and courses and following a Royal Institution of Chartered Surveyors (RICS) accredited course is the accepted way to become a Chartered Surveyor. There are three main specialisms, which involve the Built Environment (Building Surveying, Project Management and Quantity Surveying); Land Surveying (Rural, Planning, Environmental, Minerals and Waste Management); Property Surveying (Commercial and Residential Property and Valuation, Facilities Management, Arts and Antiques). Student membership of the RICS is possible. Not all the courses listed below receive RICS accreditation; check with the university or college prior to applying.

Useful websites www.rics.org/ru/join/student; www.cstt.org.uk

NB The points totals shown to the left of the institutions are for ease of reference only. It must not be assumed that Tariff points are always used by institutions or that they can be substituted for an offer in grades. The level of an offer is not necessarily indicative of the quality of a course.

COURSE OFFERS INFORMATION

Subject requirements/preferences GCSE English and mathematics grade A–C. **AL** No subjects specified; mathematics useful.

Your target offers and examples of degree courses

152 pts **Cambridge** – A*AA (Lnd Econ) (IB 40–41 pts HL 776)

144 pts **Reading** – AAA–AAB (Rl Est) (IB 35 pts)

128 pts **Newcastle** – ABB (Surv Map Sci) (IB 34 pts HL 5 maths)
Oxford Brookes – ABB–BBB (Rl Est Mgt) (IB 33–32 pts)
Reading – ABB–BBB (Quant Surv) (IB 32–30 pts)

120 pts **Aberdeen** – BBB (Rl Est Mgt)
Coventry – BBB (Quant Surv Commer Mgt) (IB 30 pts)
Kingston – 120 pts (Rl Est Mgt)
Loughborough – 120 pts (Commer Mgt Quant Surv) (IB 32 pts)
Northumbria – 120 pts (Rl Est; Quant Surv) (IB 30 pts)
Nottingham Trent – 120 pts (Quant Surv Constr Commer Mgt; Rl Est)
Ulster – 120 pts (Quant Surv Commer) (IB 26 pts)

112 pts **Birmingham City** – BBC 112 pts (Rl Est; Quant Surv) (IB 30 pts)
Central Lancashire – 112 pts incl maths (Quant Surv) (IB 28 pts HL 5 maths)
Greenwich – 112 pts (Quant Surv)
Leeds Beckett – 112 pts (Quant Surv) (IB 25 pts)
London South Bank – BBC 112 pts (Quant Surv)
Oxford Brookes – BBC–BCC (Quant Surv Commer Mgt) (IB 31–30 pts); BBC (Plan Prop Dev) (IB 31 pts)
Sheffield Hallam – 112 pts (Quant Surv)
UWE Bristol – 112 pts (Quant Surv Commer Mgt; Rl Est) (IB 25 pts)
Westminster – BBC (Rl Est) (IB 28 pts); (Quant Surv Commer Mgt) (IB 29 pts)

108 pts **Anglia Ruskin** – 108 pts (Quant Surv) (IB 25 pts)
Liverpool John Moores – 108 pts (Rl Est Mgt Bus; Quant Surv)
Portsmouth – 108–120 pts (Prop Dev) (IB 26 pts HL 10 pts); (Quant Surv) (IB 26 pts)

104 pts **Derby** – 104 pts (Constr Mgt Prop Dev)
Glasgow Caledonian – BCC (Quant Surv) (IB 24 pts)
Royal Agricultural Univ – 104 pts (Rl Est)
South Wales – BCC (Proj Mgt (Surv); Quant Surv Commer Mgt) (IB 29 pts)

96 pts **Bolton** – 96 pts (Quant Surv Commer Mgt)

Edinburgh Napier – CCC (Rl Est Surv) (IB 27 pts HL 5 maths); (Quant Surv) (IB 27 pts)
Nottingham Trent – 96 pts (Quant Surv)
Robert Gordon – CCC (Surv); (Surv) (IB 28 pts)
Wolverhampton – 96 pts (Quant Surv)
88 pts **Derby** – 88-120 pts (Prop Dev Joint Hons)
Harper Adams – 88 pts (Rur Prop Mgt)
London South Bank – CCD/AB 88 pts (Commer Mgt (Quant Surv))
72 pts **Trinity Saint David** – 72 pts (Quant Surv Commer Mgt)

Alternative offers
See **Chapter 6** and **Appendix 1** for grades/new UCAS Tariff points information for other examinations.

EXAMPLES OF COLLEGES OFFERING COURSES IN THIS SUBJECT FIELD
Bexley (Coll); Blackburn (Coll); CEM; South Cheshire (Coll).

CHOOSING YOUR COURSE (SEE ALSO CH.1)
Universities and colleges teaching quality See www.qaa.ac.uk; http://unistats.direct.gov.uk. Check on RICS accreditation.

Examples of sandwich degree courses Anglia Ruskin; Birmingham City; Central Lancashire; Coventry; Glasgow Caledonian; Kingston; Leeds Beckett; Liverpool John Moores; London South Bank; Loughborough; Northumbria; Nottingham Trent; Oxford Brookes; Sheffield Hallam; Ulster; UWE Bristol; Wolverhampton.

ADMISSIONS INFORMATION
Number of applicants per place (approx) Anglia Ruskin 2; Birmingham City 4; Cambridge 4; Edinburgh Napier 12; Glasgow Caledonian 3; Greenwich 8; Harper Adams 4; London South Bank 2; Loughborough 9; Nottingham Trent (Quant Surv) 10; Oxford Brookes (Quant Surv) 4, (Prop) 5; Portsmouth 5; Robert Gordon 5; Royal Agricultural Univ 3; Sheffield Hallam (Quant Surv) 7; Westminster 10; Wolverhampton 6.

Admissions tutors' advice Nottingham Trent Candidates should demonstrate that they have researched the employment opportunities in the property and construction sectors.

Advice to applicants and planning the UCAS personal statement Surveyors work with architects and builders as well as in their own consultancies dealing with commercial and residential property. Work experience with various firms is strongly recommended depending on the type of surveying speciality preferred. Read surveying magazines. **Cambridge** Statements should be customised to the overall interests of students, not to the Land Economy Tripos specifically. **Oxford Brookes** Apply early. Applicants should be reflective. We are looking for at least 50%-60% of the personal statement to cover issues surrounding why they want to do the course, what motivates them about the subject, how they have developed their interest, how their A-levels have helped them and what they have gained from any work experience. Extra-curricular activities are useful but should not dominate the statement.

Misconceptions about this course Students underestimate the need for numerical competence.

Selection interviews Yes Birmingham City, Cambridge, Glasgow Caledonian, Harper Adams, Heriot-Watt, Kingston, Loughborough, Oxford Brookes, Royal Agricultural Univ, Salford, Ulster; **Some** Anglia Ruskin, East London, Robert Gordon; **No** Edinburgh Napier, Liverpool John Moores, Nottingham Trent.

Interview advice and questions What types of work are undertaken by surveyors? How do you qualify? What did you learn on your work experience? See also **Chapter 5**. **Cambridge** (Land Econ) Questions on subsidies and the euro and economics. Who owns London? How important is the modern day church in town planning? How important are natural resources to a country? Is it more important to focus on poverty at home or abroad? Is the environment a bigger crisis than poverty? Do you think that getting involved with poverty abroad is interfering with others 'freedoms'?

(The questions were based on information given in the personal statement.) Students sit a thinking test and a written exam. **Oxford Brookes** Interviews for applicants who are likely to be offered a place. Telephone interviews for those who cannot attend. Group exercise at interview. No offers without an interview.

Reasons for rejection (non-academic) Inability to communicate. Lack of motivation. Indecisiveness about reasons for choosing the course. **Loughborough** Applicants more suited to a practical type of course rather than an academic one. **Nottingham Trent** Incoherent and badly written application forms.

AFTER-RESULTS ADVICE
Offers to applicants repeating A-levels Higher Bolton, Nottingham Trent; **Possibly higher** Liverpool John Moores; **Same** Coventry, Edinburgh Napier, Oxford Brookes, Portsmouth, Robert Gordon, Salford.

GRADUATE DESTINATIONS AND EMPLOYMENT (2013/14 HESA)
Career note See **Building and Construction**.

OTHER DEGREE SUBJECTS FOR CONSIDERATION
Architecture; Building and Construction; Civil Engineering; Estate Management; Town Planning; Urban Studies.

PSYCHOLOGY

(including **Behavioural Science, Cognitive Sciences, Counselling** and **Neuroscience**; see also **Animal Sciences, Biological Sciences, Neuroscience, Philosophy, Physiology, Social Sciences/Studies**)

Psychology is a very popular subject, with the number of applications rising by 40,000 in the last 10 years. The study attracts three times more women than men. It covers studies in development, behaviour, perception, memory, language, learning and personality as well as social relationships and abnormal psychology. Psychology is a science and you will be involved in experimentation and statistical analysis. The degree is usually offered as a BSc or a BA course and there are many similarities between them; the differences are in the elective subjects which can be taken in the second and third years. Contrary to popular belief, psychology is not a study to enable you to psycho-analyse your friends – psychology is not the same as psychiatry!

To qualify as a chartered psychologist (for which a postgraduate qualification is required) it is necessary to obtain a first degree (or equivalent) qualification which gives eligibility for both Graduate Membership (GM) and the Graduate Basis for Registration (GBR) of the British Psychological Society (BPS). A full list of courses accredited by the British Psychological Society is available on the Society's website www.bps.org.uk. Specialisms in the subject include Educational, Clinical, Occupational and Forensic Psychology (see **Appendix 3**).

Behavioural Science covers the study of animal and human behaviour and offers an overlap between Zoology, Sociology, Psychology and Biological Sciences. Psychology, however, also crosses over into Education, Management Sciences, Human Resource Management, Counselling, Public Relations, Advertising, Artificial Intelligence, Marketing, Retail and Social Studies.

Useful websites www.psychology.org; www.bps.org.uk; www.socialpsychology.org; www.psychcentral.com

NB The points totals shown to the left of the institutions are for ease of reference only. It must not be assumed that Tariff points are always used by institutions or that they can be substituted for an offer in grades. The level of an offer is not necessarily indicative of the quality of a course.

COURSE OFFERS INFORMATION
Subject requirements/preferences GCSE English, mathematics and a science. **AL** A science subject is usually required. Psychology may be accepted as a science subject.

Your target offers and examples of degree courses

160 pts **Cambridge** – A*A*A incl sci/maths (Nat Sci (Psy)) (IB 40–41 pts HL 776)

152 pts **Bath** – A*AA (Psy) (IB 36 pts)

Cambridge – A*AA (Psy Bhv Sci) (IB 40–41 pts HL 776)

London (UCL) – A*AA–AAA incl sci/maths/psy (Psy) (IB 39–38 pts HL 6 sci/maths/psy)

Oxford – A*AA (Psy Phil Ling) (IB 39 pts); A*AA (Psy (Expmtl)) (IB 39 pts)

144 pts **Birmingham** – AAA–AAB (Psy) (IB 32 pts HL 666–665)

Bristol – AAA–AAB incl sci/psy/geog (Psy) (IB 36–34 pts)

Cardiff – AAA/A*AB–AAB (Psy) (IB 36 pts)

Durham – AAA (Phil Psy; Psy) (IB 37 pts)

Edinburgh – AAA–ABB (Cog Sci (Hum)) (IB 37–34 pts)

Exeter – AAA–AAB incl sci (App Psy (Clin); Psy Spo Exer Sci; Psy) (IB 36–34 pts HL 5 sci)

Kent – AAA (App Psy; App Psy Clin Psy) (IB 34 pts)

Leeds – AAA (Psy) (IB 35 pts)

London (RH) – AAA–AAB (Psy Clin Cog Neuro; Psy) (IB 32 pts)

Manchester – AAA–ABB (Cog Neuro Psy) (IB 37–33 pts)

Newcastle – AAA–ABB incl sci (Psy) (IB 35 pts)

Nottingham – AAA–AAB incl sci (Psy) (IB 36–34 pts); AAA–AAB (Psy Cog Neuro) (IB 36–34 pts)

Reading – AAA–AAB (Psy; Psy Neuro; Art Psy) (IB 35 pts)

St Andrews – AAA (Art Hist Psy; Psy) (IB 36 pts); (Econ Psy; Geog Psy) (IB 38 pts); AAA incl maths (Comp Sci Psy) (IB 36 pts)

Southampton – AAA–AAB incl sci/maths (Psy) (IB 34 pts)

Surrey – AAA (Psy) (IB 36 pts)

Sussex – AAA–AAB (Psy; Psy Cog Sci; Psy Neuro) (IB 35 pts)

York – AAA–AAB incl sci/maths (Psy) (IB 36–35 pts)

136 pts **Bangor** – 136–112 pts (Psy; Psy Neuropsy; Psy Clin Hlth Psy); 136–128 pts (Spo Exer Psy)

City – AAB 136 pts (Psy) (IB 33 pts)

Durham – AAB (Psy (App)) (IB 36 pts)

Edinburgh – AAB–ABB (Psy) (IB 36–34 pts)

Glasgow – AAB–BBB incl sci (Psy) (IB 38–36 pts)

Kent – AAB incl Fr/Ger (Psy St Euro) (IB 34 pts); AAB (Psy Clin Psy; Soc Psy; Psy) (IB 34 pts)

Lancaster – AAB (Psy; Ling Psy) (IB 35 pts)

Leicester – AAB (Psy; Psy Sociol; Psy Cog Neuro) (IB 32 pts)

London (Gold) – AAB–ABB (Psy) (IB 33 pts); AAB–ABB (Psy Cog Neuro) (IB 33 pts)

London (QM) – AAB incl sci/maths (Psy) (IB 35 pts Hl 6 sci/maths)

Loughborough – AAB (Soc Psy; Psy; Spo Exer Psy) (IB 35 pts)

Manchester – AAB (Psy) (IB 35 pts)

Newcastle – AAB–ABB incl biol (Biol Psy) (IB 35 pts HL 6 biol); AAB–ABB (Nutr Psy) (IB 35 pts HL 6 biol)

Nottingham – AAB (Psy Phil) (IB 34 pts)

Sheffield – AAB (Psy) (IB 35 pts)

Southampton – AAB (Educ Psy) (IB 34 pts)

Sussex – AAB–ABB incl sci/psy (Neuro Cog Sci) (IB 34 pts HL 5 sci/psy)

Swansea – AAB–ABB (Psy) (IB 34–33 pts)

UWE Bristol – 136 pts (Psy courses) (IB 28 pts)

Warwick – AAB (Psy) (IB 36 pts)

128 pts **Aston** – ABB (Psy) (IB 32 pts)

Coventry – ABB (Psy; Spo Psy) (IB 31 pts)

De Montfort – 128 pts (Psy; Psy Crimin) (IB 30 pts)

East Anglia – ABB (Psy) (IB 32 pts)

Essex – ABB–BBB (Psy; Psy Cog Neuro) (IB 32–30 pts)

Greenwich – 128 pts (Psy; Crimin Crim Psy)

Lincoln – 128 pts incl sci (Psy; Psy Clin Psy)

Join now as a Subscriber

The British Psychological Society is the representative body for psychology and psychologists in the UK. We are responsible for the development, promotion and application of psychology for the public good.

As a Subscriber you can:

- Receive full online access to *The Psychologist*, our monthly magazine;
- Keep up-to-date with the latest developments affecting psychology;
- Contribute to our discussion groups;
- Attend our events to find out more about a career in psychology;
- Benefit from high street discounts.

Find out more and to join online

www.bps.org.uk/join

Why choose a BPS accredited degree?

Accreditation is a mark of quality; studying an accredited degree in psychology can be the first step towards becoming a psychologist, but it will also give you valuable skills that can be used in a variety of sectors such as education, business, health and the media.

Studying an accredited psychology degree gives you eligibility for Graduate Basis for Chartered Membership (GBC).

GBC is required to train to become a Chartered psychologist.

For more information about accreditation and to see which courses are accredited visit **www.bps.org.uk/accreditation**

Student membership

Once you're studying an accredited undergraduate degree, membership will broaden your appreciation and understanding of psychology, and open up a network of like-minded students, academics and professionals, not to mention future opportunities.

For more information on Student membership visit **www.bps.org.uk/student**

 The British Psychological Society

THINK PSYCHOLOGY
THINK BANGOR

PRIFYSGOL
BANGOR
UNIVERSITY

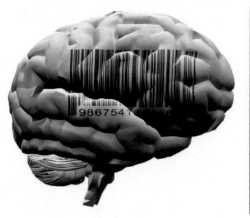

Why Psychology at Bangor?

We are one of very few UK Psychology departments able to boast a consistent track record of being highly ranked for 'Student Satisfaction', 'Research Excellence' and 'Employability'. That mean we are confident our students are happy, study with world leading academics and are well placed to get a job when they graduate. Not a bad combination!

Student satisfaction and student life

We offer our students an exceptional lifestyle, a few highlights of which are:

- Top 10 in the UK and No.1 in Wales for 'Student Satisfaction' in the National Student Survey 2015.
- Unlike most universities, Bangor offers free membership of all clubs and societies – so there are no expensive subscriptions.
- Bangor is a friendly, safe city whose nightlife is dominated by the influx of over 11,000 students. About 1 in 3 of the town's inhabitants are students!
- WhatUni? 2015 awards saw Bangor's Clubs and Societies ranked No.1 in the UK, the Halls ranked 3rd in the UK and the University ranked 7th overall.
- Bangor is "one of the cheapest places in Britain" to be a student (The Independent's A-Z of Universities).

Teaching excellence

We focus on caring for and supporting our students and have specialist International, Employability and Disability Tutors who can help you reach your maximum potential. Our independent external examiner has said we are *"producing some of the best quality psychology graduates in the UK"*.

Bangor boosts your job prospects

To help you go further with your Bangor degree, you can develop additional skills, gain qualifications and complete work experience that's relevant both to your degree and to your future career.

- UK Top 20 for Graduate Prospects according to The Times Good University Guide 2015.
- 89% of our Psychology students are either working or in further study within six month of graduating (Psychology, UniStats).

BSc/MSci

Psychology

Psychology with Clinical and Health Psychology

BSc

Psychology with Neuropsychology

Psychology with Business

Please feel free to contact us:

Tel: 01248 382629
E-mail: psychology@bangor.ac.uk

"The quality of the lecturers and staff make the School of Psychology such a great department to be a part of".

Ashleigh Johnstone -2015 Graduate

The British
Psychological Society
Accredited

THINK PSYCHOLOGY
THINK BANGOR

PRIFYSGOL
BANGOR
UNIVERSITY

There are lots of reasons why we think you should consider studying Psychology with us. Here are just a few:

- Ranked Top 10 in the UK for **'Student Satisfaction'** in the 2015 NSS
- Ranked Top 20 in the UK for **Research** in REF 2014
- Ranked Top 20 in the UK for 'Employability by **THE TIMES** 2016 Good University Guide
- Each year about **75%** of our students graduate with a 1st or 2:1
- Bangor provides students with an excellent mix of transferable skills and **employability** courses giving access to a varied range of professions
- A compact affordable **friendly city** dominated by over 11000 students and in a stunning location
- **Easy to reach:** about 90 minutes from Liverpool & Manchester and around 3 hours on the train from London

Contact us for more information:

School of Psychology, Bangor University, Gwynedd LL57 2AS

t. +44(0)1248 382629 **e.** psychology@bangor.ac.uk
www.bangor.ac.uk/psychology @PsychBangor

SEICOLEG
BANGOR
PSYCHOLOGY

Psychology

Buckingham offers Psychology students the very best experience and prospects, with a focus on skills training to prepare students for postgraduate study and employment.

- Department ranked 7th in *The Guardian University League Table 2016*
- Combination of lecture and small-group tutorial teaching, providing students with quality contact time with teaching staff
- Opportunity for students to obtain a BSc (Hons) and MSc in three years
- The course covers all seven areas of professional psychology
- Safest campus in the UK
- September and January starting points

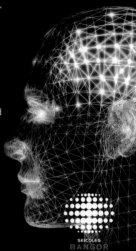

THE TIMES
THE SUNDAY TIMES
GOOD
UNIVERSITY
GUIDE
2016

UNIVERSITY
OF THE YEAR
FOR TEACHING

science-admissions@buckingham.ac.uk
+44 (0)1280 828204
ww.buckingham.ac.uk/psychology

THE UNIVERSITY OF
BUCKINGHAM

Check **Chapter 3** for new university admission details and **Chapter 6** on how to read the subject tables.

Liverpool – ABB (Psy) (IB 33 pts)
Liverpool John Moores – 128 pts (Foren Psy Crim Just) (IB 33 pts)
London (Birk) – 128 pts (Psy)
Northumbria – 128 pts (Psy) (IB 31 pts)
Queen's Belfast – ABB (Psy)
Strathclyde – ABB–BBB (Econ Psy) (IB 33 pts); (Psy) (IB 34 pts)
UWE Bristol – 128 pts (Crimin Psy) (IB 27 pts)
York – ABB (Sociol Soc Psy) (IB 34 pts)

120 pts **Aberdeen** – BBB (Psy) (IB 32 pts); BBB incl maths+sci (Neuro Psy) (IB 32 pts HL 5 maths+sci)
Aston – BBB (Psy Sociol) (IB 33 pts)
Brighton – BBB (App Psy Sociol; App Psy Crimin) (IB 30 pts)
Brunel – BBB (Psy courses) (IB 30 pts)
Buckingham – BBB–BBC (Mark Psy); BBB 120 pts (Psy Span; Psy)
Chester – BBB–BBC 120 pts (Psy courses) (IB 28 pts)
Chichester – BBB–CCC incl psy/sci/soc sci (Psy) (IB 30 pts HL 5 sci)
De Montfort – 120 pts (Educ St Psy) (IB 30 pts)
Derby – 120 pts (Psy)
Dundee – BBB–BCC (Psy) (IB 30 pts)
Edge Hill – BBB 120 pts (Psy)
Heriot-Watt – BBB (Psy courses) (IB 27 pts)
Huddersfield – BBB 120 pts (Psy; Psy Crimin; Psy Cnslg)
Keele – BBB/ABC (Psy) (IB 32 pts)
Kingston – 120 pts (Foren Psy)
Leeds Beckett – 120 pts incl sci/maths (Psy courses) (IB 26 pts HL 6 sci)
Loughborough – ABC/BBB (Ergon (Hum Fact Des)) (IB 32 pts)
Manchester Met – BBB–BBC (Psy) (IB 26 pts)
Oxford Brookes – BBB (Psy) (IB 33 pts)
Plymouth – BBB 120 pts (Psy Sociol) (IB 28 pts); 120 pts (Psy) (IB 28 pts)
Portsmouth – 120 pts incl sci (Psy; Foren Psy) (IB 30 pts HL 17 pts incl 6 sci)
Roehampton – 120 pts (Psy Cnslg; Psy)
Sheffield Hallam – 120 pts (Psy)
Staffordshire – 120 pts (Psy Crimin; Psy; Foren Psy)
Stirling – BBB (Psy) (IB 32 pts)
Sunderland – 120 pts (Psy Comb Hons)
Westminster – BBB incl sci/maths (Cog Clin Psy) (IB 32 pts); BBB (Psy) (IB 32 pts)
York St John – 120 pts (Psy)

112 pts **Abertay** – BBC (Psy; Psy Cnslg) (IB 30 pts)
Aberystwyth – 112 pts (Psy Crimin; Psy)
Bath Spa – 112–128 pts (Psy; Psy Comb Hons)
Bedfordshire – 112 pts (Psy; Psy Crim Bhv) (IB 24 pts)
Birmingham City – 112 pts (Psy) (IB 28 pts)
Bolton – 112 pts (Psy Psytrpy Cnslg; Crimin Foren Psy); (Psy) (IB 26 pts)
Bournemouth – 112 pts (Psy) (IB 30 pts)
Canterbury Christ Church – BBC (Psy)
Cardiff Met – 112 pts (Psy)
Central Lancashire – 112–128 pts (Foren Psy; Hlth Psy; Neuropsy) (IB 28–30 pts); 112–120 pts (Psy) (IB 28–30 pts)
Chester – BBC–BCC 112 pts (Cnslg Sk) (IB 26 pts)
East London – 112 pts (Psy; Foren Psy) (IB 24 pts)
Hertfordshire – 112 pts incl sci (Psy) (IB 28 pts)
Hull – 112 pts (Psy; Psy Crimin) (IB 28 pts)
Leeds Beckett – 112 pts (Crimin Psy; Psy Soty) (IB 25 pts)
Leeds Trinity – 112 pts (Psy; Foren Psy)
Liverpool John Moores – 112 pts (App Spo Psy) (IB 25 pts); (Crimin Psy) (IB 29 pts)

London South Bank – BBC 112 pts (Psy (Clin Psy); Psy; Psy (Chld Dev))
Manchester Met – BBC–BBB 112–120 pts (Psy Sociol) (IB 26 pts)
Middlesex – 112 pts (Psy HR Mgt; Psy Comb courses)
Newman – 112 pts (Psy)
Northampton – 112–120 pts (Psy courses)
Nottingham Trent – 112 pts (Law Psy; Psy)
Portsmouth – 112 pts (Mark Psy) (IB 30 pts HL 17 pts)
Queen Margaret – BBC 112 pts (Psy) (IB 30 pts)
Salford – 112 pts (Psy) (IB 27 pts)
Sheffield Hallam – 112 pts (Crimin Psy)
Southampton Solent – 112 pts (Psy; Psy (Hlth Psy))
Sunderland – 112 pts (Psy; Psy Cnslg)
Ulster – 112–120 pts (Psy courses) (IB 25–26 pts)
Worcester – 112 pts (Psy)

104 pts **Abertay** – BCC incl sci/maths (Psy Foren Biol) (IB 29 pts)
Bournemouth – 104–120 pts (Spo Psy Coach Sci) (IB 28–31 pts)
BPP – BCC 104 pts (Psy)
Bradford – BCC 104 pts (Psy; Psy Crm)
Central Lancashire – 104–120 pts (Spo Psy)
Edinburgh Napier – BCC incl Engl (Psy; Psy Sociol) (IB 28 pts HL 5 Engl)
Glyndŵr – 104 pts (Psy)
Kingston – 104 pts (Psy courses) (IB 30 pts)
Liverpool Hope – BCC–BBB 104–120 pts (Psy; Psy Comb Hons)
Liverpool John Moores – 104 pts (App Psy) (IB 25 pts)
London Met – 104 pts (Psy)
Northampton – 104–120 pts (Psy Mark)
Nottingham Trent – 104 pts (Ely Yrs Psy; Psy Spec Inclsv Educ)
St Mary's – 104 pts (Psy) (IB 28 pts)
Sheffield Hallam – 104 pts (Educ Psy Cnslg)
South Wales – BCC (Psy Cnslg St; Psy; Psy Dev Diso) (IB 29 pts)
Teesside – 104 pts (Psy Crimin; Psy; Foren Psy; Psy Cnslg)
West London – 104–120 pts (Psy; Psy Crimin/Cnslg Theor)

96 pts **Anglia Ruskin** – 96 pts (Psy; Psy Crimin) (IB 24 pts)
Bishop Grosseteste – 96–112 pts (Psy Joint Hons)
Bradford – CCC 96 pts (Sociol Psy)
Bucks New – 96–112 pts (Psy; Psy Crimin; Psy Sociol)
Derby – 96 pts (Crea Expr Thera (Dance/Dr/Mus/Art))
Manchester Met – 96–112 pts (Psy Spo Exer) (IB 28 pts)
Portsmouth – 96–120 pts (Sociol Psy) (IB 30 pts HL 17 pts)
Trinity Saint David – 96 pts (Psy)
West Scotland – CCC (Psy) (IB 24 pts)

88 pts **Queen Margaret** – CCD 88 pts (Psy Sociol) (IB 26 pts)
Trinity Saint David – 88 pts (Cnslg St Psy; Educ St Psy)
Wolverhampton – 88 pts (Psy; Psy (Cnslg Psy))

80 pts **Bedfordshire** – 80 pts (App Psy; Hlth Psy) (IB 24 pts)
Cumbria – 80 pts (App Psy)
Kent – CDD (Autsm St) (IB 34 pts)

72 pts **UHI** – BC (Psy)

Open University – contact +44 (0)845 300 6090 **or** www.openuniversity.co.uk/you
(Psy; Soc Sci Psy St)

Alternative offers
See **Chapter 6** and **Appendix 1** for grades/new UCAS Tariff points information for other examinations.

EXAMPLES OF COLLEGES OFFERING COURSES IN THIS SUBJECT FIELD

Barking and Dagenham (Coll); Bedford (Coll); Birmingham Met (Coll); Blackburn (Coll); Bradford (Coll); Bury (Coll); Canterbury (Coll); Chesterfield (Coll); Colchester (Inst); Cornwall (Coll); Croydon (Univ Centre); Doncaster (Coll); Durham New (Coll); Eastleigh (Coll); Farnborough (CT); Great Yarmouth (Coll); Grimsby (Univ Centre); Guildford (Coll); Haringey, Enfield and North East London (Coll); Harrogate (Coll); Havering (Coll); Lambeth (Coll); London UCK (Coll); Metanoia (Inst); Milton Keynes (Coll); Nescot; Newham (CFE); North Lindsey (Coll); North Nottinghamshire (Coll); Norwich City (Coll); Oldham (Coll); Oldham (Univ Campus); Peter Symonds (Coll); Peterborough (Coll); Petroc; Riverside (Coll); South City Birmingham (Coll); South Devon (Coll); South Gloucestershire and Stroud (Coll); South Tyneside (Coll); Southport (Coll); Suffolk (Univ Campus); Sussex Downs (Coll); Totton (Coll); Truro and Penwith (Coll); Tyne Met (Coll); Warwickshire (Coll); West Anglia (Coll); West Suffolk (Coll); West Thames (Coll); Weston (Coll); Wirral Met (Coll).

CHOOSING YOUR COURSE (SEE ALSO CH.1)

Universities and colleges teaching quality See www.qaa.ac.uk; https://unistats.direct.gov.uk.

Top research universities and colleges (REF 2014) (Psychology, Psychiatry and Neuroscience) Oxford; York; Cambridge; London (RH); Imperial London; Cardiff; Sussex; Warwick; Essex; London (Birk); Birmingham; Dundee; Bangor.

Examples of sandwich degree courses Aston; Bath; Bedfordshire; Bournemouth; Brunel; Cardiff; Coventry; Hertfordshire; Huddersfield; Kent; Lancaster; Leeds; Loughborough; Middlesex; Newcastle; Nottingham Trent; Plymouth; Portsmouth; Reading; Surrey; Ulster; UWE Bristol; Westminster.

ADMISSIONS INFORMATION

Number of applicants per place (approx) Abertay 5; Aston 6; Bangor 5; Bath 8; Bath Spa 10; Birmingham 6; Bolton 5; Bournemouth 4; Bradford 2; Bristol 8; Brunel 20; Buckingham 1; Cambridge 6; Cardiff 5; Cardiff Met 5; Central Lancashire 13; Chester 20; City 6; Coventry 7; De Montfort 10; Derby 6; Dundee 6; Durham 9; Edinburgh Napier 6; Exeter 14; Glasgow Caledonian 15; Gloucestershire 50; Greenwich 8; Hertfordshire 22; Huddersfield 3; Hull 14; Kent 15; Lancaster 20; Leeds 12; Leeds Trinity 13; Leicester 6; Liverpool 21; Liverpool John Moores 8; London (RH) 10; London (UCL) 11; London South Bank 7; Loughborough 8; Manchester 7; Manchester Met 14; Middlesex 10; Newcastle 20; Newman 3; Northampton 4; Northumbria 2; Nottingham 9; Nottingham Trent 3; Oxford Brookes 29; Plymouth 5; Portsmouth 10; Roehampton 7; Salford 4; Sheffield 12; Sheffield Hallam 10; Southampton 10; Staffordshire 6; Stirling 9; Surrey 10; Sussex 5; Swansea 7; Teesside 10; UWE Bristol 12; Warwick 13; Westminster 6; Worcester 9; York 9; York St John 3.

Advice to applicants and planning the UCAS personal statement Psychology is heavily over-subscribed so prepare well in advance by choosing suitable AS and A-level subjects. Contact the Education and Social Services departments in your local authority office to arrange meetings with psychologists to gain a knowledge of the work. Make notes during those meetings and of any work experience gained and describe these fully on the UCAS application. Reference to introductory reading in psychology is important (many students have a distorted image of it). Demonstrate your interest in psychology through, for example, voluntary or other work experience. See also **Appendix 3**.
Bristol General scientific interests are important. Only consider this course if you have some aptitude and liking for scientific study (either in biological or physical sciences). Deferred entry accepted.
Glasgow Maths A-level grade B required for all courses. **Leeds** One A-level subject must be taken from Psychology, Geography, Maths, Chemistry, Physics or Biology.

Misconceptions about this course Some believe a Psychology course will train them as therapists or counsellors – it will not. **Bath** They think that they are going to learn about themselves. **Birmingham** Some applicants underestimate the scientific nature of the course. **Exeter** It's scientific! **Lincoln** Applicants should be aware that this is a science-based course. Academic psychology is an empirical science requiring research methodologies and statistical analysis. **Reading** Not all applicants are aware that it is a science-based course and are surprised at the high science and statistics content. **Sussex** Applicants should note that the BSc course is not harder than the BA course. Many students mistakenly believe that psychology consists of counselling and that there is no maths. Psychology is a science. **York** Some students think psychology means Freud which it hasn't done for 50 years or more. They do not realise that psychology is a science in the same vein as biology, chemistry or physics. Only 20% of Psychology graduates become professional psychologists. This involves taking a postgraduate degree in a specialist area of psychology.

Selection interviews Yes Birmingham, Bishop Grosseteste, Cambridge, Exeter, Glyndŵr, London (QM), Manchester, Middlesex, Northampton, Oxford (Psy (Expmtl)) 19%, (Psy Phil Ling) 15%, Oxford Brookes, Plymouth, Reading (MSci courses), Southampton; **Some** Anglia Ruskin, Aston, Bangor, Bolton, Bristol, Cardiff, Derby (non-standard applications), East Anglia, Glasgow Caledonian, Leeds (mature students), London (UCL) (300 out of 1500 applicants), London Met, Nottingham Trent (non-standard applications), Roehampton, Salford, Sunderland, Swansea; **No** Buckingham, Chichester, Dundee, Essex, Huddersfield, Keele, Leeds Trinity, Leicester, Liverpool John Moores, Newcastle, Nottingham, Surrey.

Interview advice and questions Although some applicants will have studied the subject at A-level and will have a broad understanding of its coverage, it is still essential to have gained some work experience or to have discussed the career with a professional psychologist. Questions will focus on this and in previous years they have included: What have you read about psychology? What do you expect to gain by studying psychology? What are your parents' and teachers' views on your choice of subject? Are you interested in any particular branch of the subject? Is psychology an art or a science? Do you think you are well suited to this course? Why? Do you think it is possible that if we learn enough about the functioning of the brain we can create a computer that is functionally the same? What is counselling? Is it necessary? Know the differences between the various branches of psychology and discuss any specific interests, for example, in clinical, occupational, educational, criminal psychology and cognitive, neuro-, social or physiological psychology. What influences young children's food choices? What stereotypes do we have of people with mental illness? See also **Chapter 5**. **Bangor** Each application is treated individually and considered on its own merits. **Oxford** Ability to evaluate evidence and to have the capacity for logical and creative thinking.

Reasons for rejection (non-academic) Lack of background reading and lack of awareness of psychology; poor communication skills; misunderstanding of what is involved in a degree course. Poor personal statement. Poor grades, especially in GCSE maths. **Exeter** Competition for places – we can select those with exceptional grades. **Surrey** Inarticulate. **Warwick** (BSc) Lack of science background.

AFTER-RESULTS ADVICE
Offers to applicants repeating A-levels Higher Birmingham, City, Loughborough, Newcastle, Portsmouth, Southampton, Swansea, Warwick, York; **Possibly higher** Aston, Northampton; **Same** Bangor, Bolton, Brunel, Cardiff, Cardiff Met, Chester, Derby, Dundee, Durham, East Anglia, Huddersfield, Hull, Lincoln, Liverpool Hope, Liverpool John Moores, London (RH), London South Bank, Manchester Met, Newman, Nottingham, Nottingham Trent, Oxford Brookes, Roehampton, Salford, Sheffield Hallam, Staffordshire, Stirling, Suffolk (Univ Campus), Sunderland, Surrey, Ulster, West London, Wolverhampton, York St John; **No** Cambridge.

GRADUATE DESTINATIONS AND EMPLOYMENT (2013/14 HESA)
Graduates surveyed 12,225 **Employed** 5,630 **In voluntary employment** 480 **In further study** 2,910 **Assumed unemployed** 770

Career note Clinical, educational and occupational psychology are the three main specialist careers for graduate psychologists, all involving further study. Ergonomics, human–computer interaction, marketing, public relations, human resource management, advertising, the social services, the prison and rehabilitation services also provide alternative career routes.

OTHER DEGREE SUBJECTS FOR CONSIDERATION
Anthropology; Behavioural Science; Cognitive Sciences; Education; Health Studies; Neuroscience; Sociology.

Check **Chapter 3** for new university admission details and **Chapter 6** on how to read the subject tables.

RADIOGRAPHY

(including **Medical Imaging** and **Radiotherapy**; see also **Health Sciences/Studies**)

Many institutions offer both Diagnostic and Therapeutic Radiography but applicants should check this, and course entry requirements, before applying. Information on courses is also available from the Society of Radiographers (see **Appendix 3**). Diagnostic Radiography is the demonstration on film (or other imaging materials) of the position and structure of the body's organs using radiation or other imaging media. Therapeutic Radiography is the planning and administration of treatment for patients suffering from malignant and non-malignant disease using different forms of radiation. Courses lead to state registration.

Useful websites www.sor.org; www.radiographycareers.co.uk; www.nhscareers.nhs.uk

NB The points totals shown to the left of the institutions are for ease of reference only. It must not be assumed that Tariff points are always used by institutions or that they can be substituted for an offer in grades. The level of an offer is not necessarily indicative of the quality of a course.

COURSE OFFERS INFORMATION

Subject requirements/preferences GCSE Five subjects including English, mathematics and a science subject (usually at one sitting). **AL** One or two sciences required; mathematics may be acceptable. (Radiothera) One science subject required for some courses. Psychology may not be considered a science subject at some institutions. **Other** Applicants required to have an occupational health check and a Disclosure and Barring Service (DBS) clearance. Visit to, or work experience in, a hospital imaging department often required/expected.

Your target offers and examples of degree courses

136 pts **Exeter** – AAB–BBB incl sci (Med Imag (Diag Radiog)) (IB 34–30 pts HL 4 sci)
128 pts **Leeds** – ABB incl sci (Radiog) (IB 34 pts HL 5 sci)
    Sheffield Hallam – 128 pts incl sci/maths (Diag Radiog)
120 pts **Bangor** – 120 pts incl biol/phys (Diag Radiog)
    Birmingham City – BBB incl sci 120 pts (Radiothera; Diag Radiog) (IB 26 pts)
    Cardiff – BBB (Diag Radiog Imag; Radiother Onc) (IB 28 pts)
    City – 120 pts (Radiog (Radiothera Onc); Radiog (Diag Imag)) (IB 33 pts)
    Cumbria – 120 pts incl sci (Diag Radiog)
    Derby – 120 pts incl sci (Diag Radiog)
    Hertfordshire – 120 pts incl sci/maths (Radiothera Onc) (IB 30 pts); 120 pts incl sci (Diag Radiog Imag) (IB 30 pts)
    Liverpool – BBB incl sci/maths/PE (Radiothera) (IB 30 pts HL 5 maths+biol/phys); BBB incl biol sci (Diag Radiog) (IB 30 pts HL 6 maths+biol/phys)
    London (St George's) – BBB incl sci 120 pts (Diag Radiog; Ther Radiog) (IB 26 pts)
    Portsmouth – 120 pts incl sci (Radiog (Diag)); (Radiog (Ther)) (IB 30 pts HL 17 pts incl 5 sci/maths)
    Sheffield Hallam – 120 pts incl sci (Radiothera Onc)
    UWE Bristol – 120 pts incl sci (Diag Imag) (IB 26 pts HL 5 sci)
112 pts **London South Bank** – A*A*/BBC (Diag Radiog); A*A*/BBC 112 pts (Thera Radiog)
104 pts **Glasgow Caledonian** – BCC incl sci (Radiothera Onc; Diag Imag) (IB 24 pts)
    Robert Gordon – BCC incl sci/maths (Diag Radiog) (IB 27 pts)
 96 pts **Queen Margaret** – CCC incl sci 96 pts (Ther Radiog) (IB 28 pts)

Alternative offers
See **Chapter 6** and **Appendix 1** for grades/new UCAS Tariff points information for other examinations.

EXAMPLES OF COLLEGES OFFERING COURSES IN THIS SUBJECT FIELD
Birmingham Met (Coll).

CHOOSING YOUR COURSE (SEE ALSO CH.1)
Universities and colleges teaching quality See www.qaa.ac.uk; http://unistats.direct.gov.uk.

Top research universities and colleges (REF 2014) See **Health Sciences/Studies**.

ADMISSIONS INFORMATION
Number of applicants per place (approx) Birmingham City (Radiothera) 8; Cardiff 3; Derby 6; Glasgow Caledonian 7; Hertfordshire (Diag Radiog Imag) 8; Leeds 10; Liverpool 13; London (St George's) 7; London South Bank 9; Portsmouth 10; Robert Gordon 5; Sheffield Hallam 8, (Radiothera Onc) 3.

Advice to applicants and planning the UCAS personal statement Contacts with radiographers and visits to the radiography departments of hospitals should be discussed in full on the UCAS application. See also **Appendix 3**. **Birmingham City** Evidence needed of a visit to at least one imaging department or oncology (radiotherapy) department before completing the UCAS application. Evidence of good research into the career. **Liverpool** Choice between therapeutic and diagnostic pathways should be made before applying.

Misconceptions about this course There is often confusion between radiotherapy and diagnostic imaging and between diagnostic and therapeutic radiography.

Selection interviews **Yes** Bangor, Birmingham City, Cardiff, City, Cumbria, Derby, Exeter, Hertfordshire, London (St George's), London South Bank, Portsmouth, Queen Margaret, Sheffield Hallam.

Interview advice and questions All applicants should have discussed this career with a radiographer and visited a hospital radiography department. Questions follow from these contacts. Where does radiography fit into the overall health care system? See also **Chapter 5**.

Reasons for rejection (non-academic) Lack of interest in people. Poor communication skills. Occasionally students may be unsuitable for the clinical environment, for example, they express a fear of blood and needles; poor grasp of radiography as a career. Unable to meet criteria for employment in the NHS, for example, health factors, criminal convictions, severe disabilities.

AFTER-RESULTS ADVICE
Offers to applicants repeating A-levels **Higher** London (St George's); **Same** Derby.

GRADUATE DESTINATIONS AND EMPLOYMENT (2013/14 HESA)
See **Health Sciences/Studies**.

Career note Most radiographers work in the NHS in hospital radiography departments undertaking diagnostic or therapeutic treatment. Others work in private healthcare.

OTHER DEGREE SUBJECTS FOR CONSIDERATION
Audiology; Forensic Engineering; Health Studies; Medical Physics; Nursing; Occupational Therapy; Physics; Podiatry; Speech Sciences.

RELIGIOUS STUDIES

(including **Biblical Studies, Divinity, Islamic Studies, Jewish Studies** and **Theology**; see also **Arabic and Ancient Near and Middle Eastern Studies**)

The subject content of these courses varies and students should check prospectuses carefully. They are not intended as training courses for ministry; an adherence to a particular religious denomination is not a necessary qualification for entry. Courses offer the study of the major religions – Christianity,

Judaism, Islam, Buddhism and Hinduism. The comprehensive Lancaster course offers optional modules covering theological, sociological, anthropological, psychological and philosophical perspectives.

Useful websites www.theguardian.com/world/religion; www.cwmission.org; www.miraclestudies. net; www.academicinfo.net/religindex.html; www.theologywebsite.com; www.jewishstudies.org; www.jewish-studies.com; www.jewfaq.org; www.virtualreligion.net; www.jis.oxfordjournals.org

NB The points totals shown to the left of the institutions are for ease of reference only. It must not be assumed that Tariff points are always used by institutions or that they can be substituted for an offer in grades. The level of an offer is not necessarily indicative of the quality of a course.

COURSE OFFERS INFORMATION

Subject requirements/preferences GCSE English and mathematics. For teacher training, English and mathematics and science. **AL** Religious Studies or Theology may be required or preferred for some courses.

Your target offers and examples of degree courses

152 pts Cambridge – A*AA (Theol Relig St) (IB 40–41 pts HL 776)

144 pts Durham – AAA (Phil Theol) (IB 37 pts)
Edinburgh – AAA–ABB (Islam St) (IB 37–34 pts)
Oxford – AAA (Theol Relgn; Theol Orntl St) (IB 38 pts); (Phil Theol) (IB 39 pts)
St Andrews – AAA (Bib St; Theol St; Theol) (IB 36 pts); (Heb courses) (IB 36–38 pts); AAA incl Engl (Bib St Engl) (IB 38 pts)

136 pts Bristol – AAB–ABB (Relgn Theol) (IB 34–32 pts)
Cardiff – AAB–BBB (Relig Theol St) (IB 36–28 pts)
Durham – AAB (Theol courses) (IB 36 pts)
Edinburgh – AAB–ABB (Div Class) (IB 36–34 pts); (Relig St) (IB 36–34 pts)
Exeter – AAB–BBB (Theol Relgn) (IB 34–30 pts)
Glasgow – AAB–BBB incl arts/lang (Theol Relig St) (IB 36–34 pts)
Lancaster – AAB–ABB (Pol Relig St; Phil Relig St; Relig St; Relig St Sociol) (IB 35–32 pts)
London (King's) – AAB (Relgn Pol Soty; Theol; Relgn Phil Eth) (IB 35 pts)
London (SOAS) – AAB–ABB (Islam St) (IB 36 pts)
Sheffield – AAB–ABB incl Engl (Bib Lit Engl) (IB 35 pts HL 6 Engl)

128 pts Birmingham – ABB (Theol Relgn) (IB 32 pts HL 655)
Cardiff – ABB (Relig St Ger/Ital) (IB 32 pts HL 5 lang); ABB incl Span (Relig St Span) (IB 26 pts)
Leeds – ABB (Russ Civ Theol Relig St; Theol Relig St; Islam St) (IB 34 pts)
London (SOAS) – ABB–BBB (St Relgns) (IB 33 pts)
London (UCL) – ABB incl hist (Hist (Cnt E Euro) Jew St) (IB 34 pts HL 5 hist)
Manchester – ABB–BBB (Relgns Theol) (IB 34–31 pts)
Sheffield – ABB–BBB (Relgn Theol Bib) (IB 34 pts); ABB incl Engl/lang (Relgn Theol Bib Ling) (IB 34 pts HL 6 Engl/lang); ABB–BBB incl mus (Theol Mus) (IB 34 pts HL 6 mus)
Stranmillis (UC) – ABB +interview (Relig St Educ QTS)

120 pts Aberdeen – BBB (Theol; Div; Relig St) (IB 32 pts)
Chichester – BBB (Theol Relgn) (IB 30 pts)
Gloucestershire – 120 pts (Relgn Phil Eth)
Kent – BBB (Relig St) (IB 34 pts)
Queen's Belfast – BBB (Theol)

112 pts Canterbury Christ Church – 112 pts (Theol)
Chester – BBC–BCC 112 pts (Theol Relig St; Relig St; Theol) (IB 26 pts)
Huddersfield – BBC 112 pts (Relgn Educ)
Hull – 112 pts incl lang (Hisp St Relgn Joint Hons) (IB 28 pts); 112 pts (Phil Relgn; Relgn Joint Hons) (IB 28 pts)
Newman – 112 pts (Phil Relgn Educ; Theol)
Roehampton – 112 pts (Theol Relig St)

Stirling – BBC (Relgn) (IB 32 pts)
York St John – 112 pts (Relgn Phil Eth; Theol Relig St)
104 pts **Bath Spa** – 104–120 pts (Relgn Phil Eth; St Relgn Comb)
Central Lancashire – 104 pts (Relgn Cult Soty) (IB 28 pts)
Islamic (Coll) – BCC 104 pts (Islam St) (IB 32 pts)
Leeds Trinity – 104 pts (Theol Relig St; Phil Eth Relgn)
Liverpool Hope – BCC–BBB 104–120 pts (Theol Relig St; Phil Eth Relgn)
St Mary's – 104 pts (Theol Relig St) (IB 28 pts)
South Wales – BCC (Relig St) (IB 29 pts)
Winchester – 104–120 pts (Theol Relgn Eth) (IB 26 pts)
96 pts **Bangor** – 96–112 pts (Phil Relgn)
Bishop Grosseteste – 96–112 pts (Theol Eth Soty)
Trinity Saint David – 96–104 pts (Relig St Islam St)
Wolverhampton – 96 pts (Relig St Phil; Relig St Sociol; Relig St courses)
88 pts **Trinity Saint David** – 88–120 pts (Theol Relig St) (IB 26 pts)
80 pts **Trinity Saint David** – 80–112 pts (Theol Joint Hons)
64 pts **UHI** – CC (Theol St)

Alternative offers
See **Chapter 6** and **Appendix 1** for grades/new UCAS Tariff points information for other examinations.

CHOOSING YOUR COURSE (SEE ALSO CH.1)
Universities and colleges teaching quality See www.qaa.ac.uk; http://unistats.direct.gov.uk.

Top research universities and colleges (REF 2014) (Theology and Religious Studies) Durham; Exeter; Leeds; Cambridge; Birmingham; London (UCL); London (SOAS); Edinburgh.

ADMISSIONS INFORMATION
Number of applicants per place (approx) Bangor 5; Birmingham 4; Bristol 9; Cambridge 2; Chichester 6; Cumbria 12; Durham 4; Edinburgh 3; Exeter 7; Glasgow 4; Hull 10; Kent 13; Lancaster 6; Leeds 4; Leeds Trinity 4; Liverpool Hope 6; London (Hey) 4; London (King's) 6; Manchester 4; Newman 2; Nottingham 10; Sheffield 7; Trinity Saint David 7; Winchester 6; York St John 2.

Advice to applicants and planning the UCAS personal statement An awareness of the differences between the main religions is important as is any special research you have done to help you decide on your preferred courses. Interests in the religious art and architecture of various periods and styles should be noted. Applicants should have an open-minded approach to studying a diverse range of religious traditions. **Bristol** Deferred entry accepted.

Misconceptions about this course Some students think that you must be religious to study Theology – in fact, people of all faiths and none study the subject. A study of religions is not Christian theology. **Leeds** Some applicants are not aware of the breadth of the subject. We offer modules covering New Testament, Christian theology, Islamic studies, Hinduism, Buddhism, Sikhism, Christian ethics, sociology of religion. **Newman** That the Theology course only concentrates on the Christian/ Catholic religions – all major religions are covered.

Selection interviews Yes Bishop Grosseteste, Cambridge, Hull, Lancaster, London (Hey), Manchester, Oxford (Theol Relgn) 33%, Oxford Brookes, Trinity Saint David, Winchester; **Some** Bristol, Cardiff, Leeds, London (SOAS); **No** Birmingham, Chester, Chichester, Edinburgh, Leeds Trinity, Nottingham, Sheffield.

Interview advice and questions Past questions have included: Why do you want to study Theology/ Biblical Studies/Religious Studies? What do you hope to do after obtaining your degree? Questions relating to the A-level syllabus. Questions on current theological topics. Do you have any strong religious convictions? Do you think that your religious beliefs will be changed at the end of the course? Why did you choose Religious Studies rather than Biblical Studies? How would you explain the miracles to a 10-year-old? (BEd course). Do you agree with the National Lottery? How do you think you can apply theology to your career? See also **Chapter 5**. **Cambridge** There is a Christian priest who regularly visits India and converted to a Hindu priest. When he is in England he still practises as a Christian priest. What problems might this pose? Do you believe we should eradicate Christmas on the basis that it offends other religious groups? **Oxford** The ability to defend one's opinions and willingness to engage in a lively dialogue are both important.

Reasons for rejection (non-academic) Students not attending Open Days may be rejected. Too religiously conservative. Failure to interact. Lack of motivation to study a subject which goes beyond A-level. **Cardiff** Insufficiently open to an academic study of religion.

AFTER-RESULTS ADVICE
Offers to applicants repeating A-levels Higher Hull, Manchester, St Andrews; **Possibly higher** Cambridge (Hom); **Same** Bangor, Birmingham, Cardiff, Chester, Durham, Glasgow, Lancaster, Leeds, Liverpool Hope, London (SOAS), Nottingham, St Mary's, Sheffield, Stirling, Trinity Saint David, Winchester, Wolverhampton, York St John; **No** Cambridge.

GRADUATE DESTINATIONS AND EMPLOYMENT (2013/14 HESA)
Theology and Religious Studies graduates surveyed 1,830 **Employed** 740 **In voluntary employment** 160 **In further study** 545 **Assumed unemployed** 75

Career note Although a small number of graduates may regard these courses as a preparation for entry to religious orders, the great majority enter other careers, with teaching particularly popular.

OTHER DEGREE SUBJECTS FOR CONSIDERATION
Community Studies; Education; History; Philosophy; Psychology; Social Policy and Administration; Social Work.

RETAIL MANAGEMENT

(see also **Business and Management Courses, Business and Management Courses (International and European), Business and Management Courses (Specialised), Marketing**)

This subject attracts a large number of applicants each year and it is necessary to have work experience before applying. The work itself varies depending on the type of retail outlet. After completing their courses graduates in a large department store will be involved in different aspects of the business, for example supervising shop assistants, warehouse and packing staff. They could also receive special training in the sales of particular goods, for example food and drink, clothing, furniture. Subsequently there may be opportunities to become buyers. In more specialised shops, for example shoes, fashion and food, graduates are likely to work only with these products, with opportunities to reach senior management.

Useful websites www.brc.org.uk; www.retailweek.com; www.theretailbulletin.com; www.retailcareers.co.uk; www.retailchoice.com; www.nrf.com

NB The points totals shown to the left of the institutions are for ease of reference only. It must not be assumed that Tariff points are always used by institutions or that they can be substituted for an offer in grades. The level of an offer is not necessarily indicative of the quality of a course.

COURSE OFFERS INFORMATION
Subject requirements/preferences GCSE English and mathematics at grade C or above. **AL** No subjects specified.

Your target offers and examples of degree courses
136 pts **Loughborough** – AAB–ABB (Rtl Mark Mgt) (IB 34 pts)
　　　　Manchester – AAB 136 pts (Fash Rtl) (IB 35 pts)
　　　　Surrey – AAB–ABB (Bus Rtl Mgt) (IB 35–34 pts)

128 pts **Roehampton** – 128 pts (Rtl Mark Mgt)
120 pts **Heriot-Watt** – BBB (Fash Mark Rtl) (IB 28 pts)
        Huddersfield – BBB 120 pts (Fash Tex Buy Mgt)
        Leeds Beckett – 120 pts (Rtl Mgt) (IB 26 pts)
        Nottingham Trent – 120 pts (Fash Mgt)
        Stirling – BBB (Rtl Mark) (IB 32 pts)
112 pts **Arts London** – 112 pts (Fash Mgt)
        Birmingham City – BBC 112 pts (Fash Bus Prom) (IB 32 pts)
        Brighton – BBC (Rtl Mgt) (IB 28 pts)
        Cardiff Met – 112 pts (Mark Mgt)
        Central Lancashire – 112 pts (Rtl Mgt (Buy Fash Mark)) (IB 28 pts)
        De Montfort – 112 pts (Fash Buy) (IB 28 pts)
        London Met – 112 pts (Fash Rtl Mgt)
104 pts **Bournemouth** – 104–120 pts (Rtl Mgt) (IB 26–30 pts)
        Manchester Met – BCC–BBC 104–112 pts (Rtl Mgt Mark) (IB 26 pts)
        South Wales – BCC (Rtl Mgt) (IB 29 pts)
  96 pts **Canterbury Christ Church** – 96–112 pts (Bus Mgt (Rtl))
  88 pts **Creative Arts** – 88 pts (Fash Buy Rtl Mgt)

Alternative offers
See **Chapter 6** and **Appendix 1** for grades/new UCAS Tariff points information for other examinations.

EXAMPLES OF COLLEGES OFFERING COURSES IN THIS SUBJECT FIELD
Blackburn (Coll); Blackpool and Fylde (Coll); Durham New (Coll); Hugh Baird (Coll); Hull (Coll); Leeds City (Coll); Llandrillo (Coll); Newcastle (Coll).

CHOOSING YOUR COURSE (SEE ALSO CH.1)
Universities and colleges teaching quality See www.qaa.ac.uk; http://unistats.direct.gov.uk.

Examples of sandwich degree courses Arts London; Birmingham City; Bournemouth; Brighton; Central Lancashire; De Montfort; Huddersfield; Leeds Beckett; Manchester Met; Surrey.

ADMISSIONS INFORMATION
Number of applicants per place (approx) See also **Business and Management Courses**. Bournemouth 8; Manchester Met 10.

Advice to applicants and planning the UCAS personal statement See also **Business and Management Courses**. **Manchester Met** (Rtl Mark Mgt) Evidence of working with people or voluntary work experience (department unable to assist with sponsorships).

Misconceptions about this course See **Business and Management Courses**.

Selection interviews Yes Birmingham City.

Interview advice and questions See **Business and Management Courses**.

Reasons for rejection (non-academic) See **Business and Management Courses**.

GRADUATE DESTINATIONS AND EMPLOYMENT (2013/14 HESA)
See **Business and Management Courses**.

Career note Majority of graduates work in business involved in marketing and retail work. Employment options include brand design, product management, advertising, PR, sales and account management.

OTHER DEGREE SUBJECTS FOR CONSIDERATION
Business Studies; Consumer Sciences/Studies; E-Commerce; Human Resource Management; Psychology; Supply Chain Management.

RUSSIAN and EAST EUROPEAN STUDIES

(including **Bulgarian, Croatian, Czech, Finnish, Georgian, Hungarian, Polish, Romanian, Russian** and **Serbian**; see also **European Studies, Languages**)

East European Studies cover a wide range of the less popular language courses and should be considered by anyone with a love of and gift for languages. Many natural linguists often devote themselves to one of the popular European languages studied up to A-level, when their language skills could be extended to the more unusual languages, thereby increasing their future career opportunities.

Useful websites www.ciol.org.uk; www.bbc.co.uk/languages; www.languageadvantage.com; www.languagematters.co.uk; www.ciltuk.org.uk

NB The points totals shown to the left of the institutions are for ease of reference only. It must not be assumed that Tariff points are always used by institutions or that they can be substituted for an offer in grades. The level of an offer is not necessarily indicative of the quality of a course.

COURSE OFFERS INFORMATION

Subject requirements/preferences GCSE A foreign language. **AL** One or two modern languages may be stipulated.

Your target offers and examples of degree courses

152 pts **Cambridge** – A*AA incl lang (Modn Mediev Langs) (IB 40–41 pts HL 776)
144 pts **Edinburgh** – AAA–ABB (Russ St) (IB 37–34 pts)
Oxford – AAA (Modn Langs (Russ+2nd Lang); Euro Mid E Langs (Cz/Russ); Russ) (IB 38 pts)
St Andrews – AAA–AAB (Russ courses) (IB 38–36 pts)
136 pts **Bath** – AAB (Russ Pol) (IB 36 pts)
Birmingham – AAB (Russ St courses) (IB 32 pts HL 665)
Exeter – AAB–ABB incl Russ/Arbc (Russ Arbc) (IB 34–32 pts HL 5 Russ/Arbc)
Glasgow – AAB–BBB (Cnt E Euro St) (IB 38–36 pts); AAB–BBB incl arts/lang (Russ) (IB 36–34 pts)
Leeds – AAB incl Span (Russ Span) (IB 35 pts HL 6 Span)
London (UCL) – AAB–ABB (Russ St; Bulg/Czech/Finn/Hung/Polh/Romn/Slovak E Euro St) (IB 36–34 pts); AAB–ABB incl hist (Russ Hist) (IB 36–34 pts HL 5 hist)
Sheffield – AAB–BBB incl lang (Russ St Joint Hons) (IB 35–34 pts HL 6 lang)
128 pts **Bath** – ABB (Russ courses) (IB 34 pts); ABB–AAB incl langs (Modn Langs Euro St) (IB 34 pts HL 6 5 langs)
Bristol – ABB–BBB incl lang (Russ) (IB 32–31 pts HL 5 lang); (Russ Port) (IB 32–31 pts)
Leeds – ABB (Russ Sociol; Russ Civ Theol Relig St; Russ) (IB 34 pts)
London (QM) – ABB incl art/hum+lang 128 pts (Fr/Ger/Russ Dr) (IB 34 pts HL 6 art/hum 5 lang)
Manchester – ABB–BBB incl lang (Russ Chin) (IB 34–32 pts); ABB incl Russ/Jap (Russ Jap) (IB 34 pts)
Nottingham – ABB incl Span/Russ (Hisp St Russ) (IB 32 pts); ABB (Russ courses) (IB 32 pts); ABB incl hist (Hist East Euro Cult St) (IB 32 pts)
Sheffield – ABB (Jap St Joint Hons) (IB 34 pts)
120 pts **London (QM)** – BBB–ABB incl lang 120–128 pts (Russ Bus Mgt; Russ) (IB 32–34 pts HL 5 lang)
Manchester – BBB incl lang (Russ St) (IB 31 pts)
Sheffield – BBB–BBC incl lang (Russ St) (IB 32 pts HL 6 lang)

Alternative offers
See **Chapter 6** and **Appendix 1** for grades/new UCAS Tariff points information for other examinations.

New UCAS points Tariff: A* = 56 pts; A = 48 pts; B = 40 pts; C = 32 pts; D = 24 pts; E = 16 pts

CHOOSING YOUR COURSE (SEE ALSO CH.1)
Universities and colleges teaching quality See www.qaa.ac.uk; http://unistats.direct.gov.uk.

ADMISSIONS INFORMATION
Number of applicants per place (approx) Bath 5; Birmingham 3; Bristol 4; Durham 5; Leeds 3; London (UCL) 3; Nottingham 5.

Advice to applicants and planning the UCAS personal statement Visits to Eastern Europe should be mentioned, supported by your special reasons for wishing to study the language. A knowledge of the cultural, economic and political scene could be important. Fluent English important for non-UK students. Evidence of wide reading, travel and residence abroad. See also **Appendix 3** under Languages.

Selection interviews Yes Cambridge, London (UCL), Oxford (Euro Mid E Langs) 29%; **No** Nottingham.

Interview advice and questions Since many applicants will not have taken Russian at A-level, questions often focus on their reasons for choosing a Russian degree, and their knowledge of, and interest in, Russia. Those taking A-level Russian are likely to be questioned on the course and on any reading done outside A-level work. East European Studies applicants will need to show some knowledge of their chosen country/countries and any specific reasons why they wish to follow the course. See also **Chapter 5**. **Leeds** See **Languages**.

Reasons for rejection (non-academic) Lack of perceived commitment for a demanding *ab initio* subject.

AFTER-RESULTS ADVICE
Offers to applicants repeating A-levels Higher Bristol, Glasgow, Leeds, St Andrews; **Same** Durham; **No** Cambridge.

GRADUATE DESTINATIONS AND EMPLOYMENT (2013/14 HESA)
Graduates surveyed 170 **Employed** 85 **In voluntary employment** 5 **In further study** 30 **Assumed unemployed** 10

Career note See **Languages**.

OTHER DEGREE SUBJECTS FOR CONSIDERATION
Economics; European Studies; International Relations; Linguistics; Politics; other languages.

SCANDINAVIAN STUDIES
(see also **Languages**)

Scandinavian Studies provides students who enjoy languages with the opportunity to extend their language expertise to learn a modern Scandinavian language – Danish, Norwegian or Swedish – from beginner's level to Honours level in four years, including a year in Scandinavia. The three languages are very similar to each other and a knowledge of one makes it possible to access easily the literature and cultures of the other two. Viking Studies includes Old Norse, runology and archaeology.

Useful websites www.ciltuk.org.uk; www.ciol.org.uk; www.bbc.co.uk/languages; www.languageadvantage.com; www.languagematters.co.uk; www.scandinaviahouse.org; www.scandinavianstudy.org

NB The points totals shown to the left of the institutions are for ease of reference only. It must not be assumed that Tariff points are always used by institutions or that they can be substituted for an offer in grades. The level of an offer is not necessarily indicative of the quality of a course.

COURSE OFFERS INFORMATION

Subject requirements/preferences GCSE Foreign language preferred for all courses. **AL** A modern language may be required.

Your target offers and examples of degree courses
152 pts **Cambridge** – A*AA (A-Sxn Nrs Celt) (IB 40–41 pts HL 776)
144 pts **Edinburgh** – AAA–ABB (Scand St (Dan Norw Swed)) (IB 37–34 pts)
128 pts **London (UCL)** – ABB (Vkg Old Nrs St; Ice; Scand St) (IB 34 pts)

Alternative offers
See **Chapter 6** and **Appendix 1** for grades/new UCAS Tariff points information for other examinations.

CHOOSING YOUR COURSE (SEE ALSO CH.1)

Universities and colleges teaching quality See www.qaa.ac.uk; http://unistats.direct.gov.uk.

ADMISSIONS INFORMATION

Number of applicants per place (approx) London (UCL) 3.

Advice to applicants and planning the UCAS personal statement Visits to Scandinavian countries could be the source of an interest in studying these languages. You should also be aware of cultural, political, geographical and economic aspects of Scandinavian countries. Knowledge of these should be shown in your statement.

Selection interviews Yes Cambridge.

Interview advice and questions Applicants in the past have been questioned on why they have chosen this subject area, on their visits to Scandinavia and on their knowledge of the country/ countries and their people. Future career plans are likely to be discussed. See also **Chapter 5**.

Reasons for rejection (non-academic) One applicant didn't know the difference between a noun and a verb.

AFTER-RESULTS ADVICE

Offers to applicants repeating A-levels No Cambridge.

GRADUATE DESTINATIONS AND EMPLOYMENT (2013/14 HESA)

See **Languages**.

Career note See **Languages**.

OTHER DEGREE SUBJECTS FOR CONSIDERATION

Archaeology; European History/Studies; History; other modern languages, including, for example, Russian and East European languages.

SOCIAL and PUBLIC POLICY and ADMINISTRATION

(see also **Community Studies/Development, Social Work, Sociology**)

Social Policy is a multi-disciplinary degree that combines elements from sociology, political science, social and economic history, economics, cultural studies and philosophy. It is a study of the needs of society and how best to provide such services as education, housing, health and welfare services.

Useful websites www.local.gov.uk

NB The points totals shown to the left of the institutions are for ease of reference only. It must not be assumed that Tariff points are always used by institutions or that they can be substituted for an offer in grades. The level of an offer is not necessarily indicative of the quality of a course.

New UCAS points Tariff: A* = 56 pts; A = 48 pts; B = 40 pts; C = 32 pts; D = 24 pts; E = 16 pts

COURSE OFFERS INFORMATION

Subject requirements/preferences GCSE English and mathematics normally required. **AL** No subjects specified.

Your target offers and examples of degree courses

152 pts **Cambridge** – A*AA (Hum Soc Pol Sci) (IB 40–41 pts HL 776)
Durham – A*AA (Comb Hons Soc Sci) (IB 38 pts)

144 pts **Glasgow** – AAA–BBB incl Engl (Soc Pblc Plcy) (IB 39–34 pts)

136 pts **Bath** – AAB (Soc Plcy) (IB 35 pts)
Bristol – AAB–ABB (Soc Plcy Pol) (IB 34–32 pts)
Edinburgh – AAB–ABB (Soc Plcy courses) (IB 36–34 pts)
London LSE – AAB (Soc Plcy Sociol) (IB 37 pts HL 666); (Soc Plcy; Soc Plcy Econ; Soc Plcy Gov) (IB 37 pts)

128 pts **Aston** – ABB (Pol Soc Plcy) (IB 33 pts); ABB–BBB (Bus Mgt Pblc Plcy) (IB 33 pts)
Birmingham – ABB (Pol Sci Soc Plcy (Yr Abrd); Plan Soc Plcy) (IB 32 pts HL 655)
Bristol – ABB–BBB (Soc Plcy; Soc Plcy Sociol) (IB 32–31 pts)
Cardiff – ABB (Crimin Soc Plcy) (IB 32 pts)
Leeds – ABB (Interd Soc Pol Sociol; Soc Plcy courses) (IB 34 pts)
Loughborough – ABB (Crimin Soc Plcy) (IB 32 pts)
Nottingham – ABB (Sociol Soc Plcy) (IB 32 pts); ABB 128 pts (Soc Wk) (IB 32 pts)
Sheffield – ABB (Soc Plcy Crimin) (IB 34 pts)
Southampton – ABB–BBB (Sociol Soc Plcy) (IB 32 pts)

120 pts **Aston** – BBB (Sociol Soc Pol) (IB 33–32 pts)
Birmingham – BBB (Soc Plcy) (IB 32 pts HL 555)
Cardiff – BBB (Educ Soc Plcy; Soc Plcy Sociol) (IB 32 pts)
Kent – BBB (Soc Plcy) (IB 34 pts)
Lincoln – 120 pts (Crimin Soc Plcy)
Liverpool – BBB (Sociol Soc Plcy) (IB 30 pts)
London (Gold) – BBB (Econ Pol Pblc Plcy) (IB 33 pts)
Queen's Belfast – BBB (Soc Plcy courses)
Sheffield – BBB (Soc Plcy Sociol) (IB 32 pts)
Stirling – BBB (Sociol Soc Plcy) (IB 32 pts)
Swansea – BBB (Soc Plcy; Crimin Soc Plcy)
York – BBB (Soc Plcy) (IB 31 pts)

112 pts **Central Lancashire** – 112 pts (Soc Plcy Sociol) (IB 28 pts)
Lincoln – 112 pts (Soc Plcy)
London Met – 112 pts (Hlth Soc Plcy; Sociol Soc Plcy)

104 pts **Bath Spa** – 104–120 pts (Yth Commun St; Educ St)
Bournemouth – 104 pts (Sociol) (IB 30 pts)
Liverpool Hope – BCC–BBB 104–120 pts (Soc Plcy courses)
Manchester Met – 104–112 pts (Pblc Serv) (IB 26 pts)
Ulster – 104–112 pts (Soc Plcy) (IB 24–25 pts)

96 pts **Bangor** – 96–112 pts (Soc Plcy Joint Hons; Sociol Soc Pol)
Manchester Met – 96–112 pts (Chld Fmly St) (IB 25 pts)
West Scotland – CCC incl Engl (Soty Pol Plcy) (IB 24 pts)
Wolverhampton – 96–112 pts (Soc Plcy courses)

80 pts **Anglia Ruskin** – 80 pts (Soc Plcy) (IB 24 pts)

64 pts **Trinity Saint David** – 64 pts (Pblc Serv)

Open University – contact +44 (0)845 300 6090 **or** www.openuniversity.co.uk/you (Soc Plcy Sociol)

Alternative offers
See **Chapter 6** and **Appendix 1** for grades/new UCAS Tariff points information for other examinations.

Check **Chapter 3** for new university admission details and **Chapter 6** on how to read the subject tables.

EXAMPLES OF COLLEGES OFFERING COURSES IN THIS SUBJECT FIELD

Barnfield (Coll); Blackburn (Coll); Blackpool and Fylde (Coll); Bournville (Coll); Bromley (CFHE); Calderdale (Coll); Canterbury (Coll); Central Bedfordshire (Coll); Central Campus, Sandwell (Coll); Chesterfield (Coll); City of Oxford (Coll); Craven (Coll); Dearne Valley (Coll); Derby (Coll); Dudley (Coll); Durham New (Coll); East Surrey (Coll); Exeter (Coll); Hull (Coll); Lancaster and Morecambe (Coll); Llandrillo (Coll); Loughborough (Coll); Macclesfield (Coll); Manchester (Coll); Milton Keynes (Coll); Nescot; Norwich City (Coll); Plymouth City (Coll); St Helens (Coll); South Gloucestershire and Stroud (Coll); Walsall (Coll); Warrington (Coll); West Herts (Coll); Weston (Coll); Wigan and Leigh (Coll); Yeovil (Coll).

CHOOSING YOUR COURSE (SEE ALSO CH.1)

Universities and colleges teaching quality See www.qaa.ac.uk; http://unistats.direct.gov.uk.

Top research universities and colleges (REF 2014) See **Social Work**.

Examples of sandwich degree courses Aston; Bath; Leeds.

ADMISSIONS INFORMATION

Number of applicants per place (approx) Aston 8; Bangor 6; Bath 6; Birmingham 5; Bristol 3; Cardiff 4; Central Lancashire 6; Kent 5; Leeds 10; London LSE (Soc Plcy) 4, (Soc Plcy Sociol) 8, (Soc Plcy Econ) 7, (Soc Plcy Gov) 14; Loughborough 5; Manchester Met 4; Nottingham 3; Southampton 6; Stirling 11; Swansea 6; York 3.

Advice to applicants and planning the UCAS personal statement Careers in public and social administration are covered by this subject; consequently a good knowledge of these occupations and contacts with the social services should be discussed fully on your UCAS application. Gain work experience if possible. (See **Appendix 3** for contact details of some relevant organisations.) **Aston** The course is specially tailored for students aiming for careers in NHS management, the civil service and local government. **Bangor** Ability to communicate and work in a group. **Bristol** Deferred entry accepted. **York** Work experience, including voluntary work relevant to social policy.

Misconceptions about this course York Some applicants imagine that the course is vocational and leads directly to social work – it does not. Graduates in this field are well placed for a wide range of careers.

Selection interviews Yes London LSE, Nottingham, Swansea; **Some** Anglia Ruskin, Bangor, Bath (mature students), Cardiff, Kent, Leeds (mature students), Loughborough, Southampton; **No** Birmingham.

Interview advice and questions Past questions have included: What relevance has history to social administration? What do you understand by 'public policy'? What advantage do you think studying social science gives when working in policy fields? How could the image of public management of services be improved? Applicants should be fully aware of the content and the differences between all the courses on offer, why they want to study Social Policy and their career objectives. See also **Chapter 5**.

Reasons for rejection (non-academic) Some universities require attendance when they invite applicants to Open Days (check). Lack of awareness of current social issues. See also **Social Work**. **Bath** Applicant really wanted Business Studies: evidence that teacher, careers adviser or parents are pushing the applicant into the subject or higher education.

AFTER-RESULTS ADVICE

Offers to applicants repeating A-levels Higher Glasgow, Leeds; **Same** Anglia Ruskin, Bangor, Bath, Birmingham, Brighton, Cardiff, Loughborough, Southampton, York.

GRADUATE DESTINATIONS AND EMPLOYMENT (2013/14 HESA)

Social Policy graduates surveyed 1,515 **Employed** 765 **In voluntary employment** 45 **In further study** 330 **Assumed unemployed** 90

Career note See **Social Sciences/Studies**.

OTHER DEGREE SUBJECTS FOR CONSIDERATION

Behavioural Science; Community Studies; Criminology; Economic and Social History; Economics; Education; Government; Health Studies; Human Resource Management; Law; Politics; Psychology; Social Work; Sociology; Women's Studies.

SOCIAL SCIENCES/STUDIES

(including **Combined Social Sciences, Criminology, Criminal Justice, Human Rights** and **Police Studies**; see also **Combined Courses, Education Studies, Health Sciences/Studies, Law, Politics, Psychology, Teacher Training**)

Most Social Sciences/Studies courses take a broad view of aspects of society, for example, economics, politics, history, social psychology and urban studies. Applied Social Studies usually focuses on practical and theoretical preparation for a career in social work. These courses are particularly popular with mature students and some universities and colleges offer shortened degree courses for those with relevant work experience.

Useful websites http://volunteeringmatters.org.uk

NB The points totals shown to the left of the institutions are for ease of reference only. It must not be assumed that Tariff points are always used by institutions or that they can be substituted for an offer in grades. The level of an offer is not necessarily indicative of the quality of a course.

COURSE OFFERS INFORMATION

Subject requirements/preferences GCSE Usually English and mathematics; a science may be required. **AL** No subjects specified. **Other** A Disclosure and Barring Service (DBS) check and relevant work experience required for some courses.

Your target offers and examples of degree courses
152 pts Durham – A*AA (Comb Hons Soc Sci) (IB 38 pts)
144 pts Exeter – AAA–ABB (Crimin) (IB 36–32 pts)
    Lancaster – AAA–ABB (Crimin) (IB 36–32 pts); AAA–AAB (Law Crimin) (IB 36 pts)
    Manchester – AAA–ABB incl sci/maths (Biol Sci Soty) (IB 37–33 pts HL 5/6 biol+chem)
    York – AAA–AAB incl biol+chem/maths (Crimin) (IB 36–35 pts HL 6 biol+chem/maths)
136 pts Cardiff – AAB (Crimin) (IB 34 pts)
    Durham – AAB (Crimin) (IB 36 pts)
    London (UCL) – AAB–ABB (Sci Soty; Popn Hlth) (IB 36–34 pts)
    Manchester – AAB (Law Crimin) (IB 35 pts)
    Surrey – AAB (Crimin Sociol) (IB 35 pts); AAA–AAB (Law Crimin) (IB 36–35 pts)
    York – AAB (Soc Pol Sci) (IB 35 pts)
128 pts Bath – ABB (Soc Sci) (IB 34 pts)
    Bristol – ABB–BBB (Chld St) (IB 32–31 pts)
    Cardiff – ABB (Crimin Educ) (IB 32 pts); ABB–BBB (Soc Sci) (IB 34–32 pts); ABB
      (Crimin Soc Plcy) (IB 32 pts); (Crimin Sociol) (IB 34 pts)
    City – ABB 128 pts (Crimin Sociol) (IB 33 pts)
    Essex – ABB–BBB (Sociol Crimin; Law Hum Rts (LLB); Crimin) (IB 32–30 pts)
    Greenwich – 128 pts (Crimin Crim Psy)
    Leeds – ABB (Soc Pol Crim; Chld St) (IB 34 pts)
    Leicester – ABB (Crimin) (IB 30 pts)
    Liverpool John Moores – 128 pts (Foren Psy Crim Just) (IB 33 pts)
    London (RH) – ABB (Crimin Sociol) (IB 32 pts)
    Loughborough – ABB (Crimin Soc Plcy) (IB 32 pts)

Manchester – ABB (Crimin) (IB 33 pts); (Soc Anth Crimin) (IB 34 pts)
Queen's Belfast – ABB (Crimin)
Sheffield – ABB (Soc Plcy Crimin) (IB 34 pts)
UWE Bristol – 128 pts (Crimin; Crimin Psy) (IB 27 pts)
120 pts **Aberystwyth** – 120 pts (Hum Rts)
Brighton – BBB (App Psy Crimin; Crimin Sociol) (IB 30 pts)
Chester – BBC–BCC 120 pts (Law Crimin) (IB 28 pts)
Coventry – BBB (Sociol Crimin) (IB 29 pts)
Edge Hill – BBB 120 pts (Crimin)
Glasgow Caledonian – BBB (Soc Sci) (IB 26 pts)
Gloucestershire – 120 pts (Crimin)
Greenwich – 120 pts (Crimin; Foren Sci Crimin)
Huddersfield – BBB 120 pts (Psy Crimin)
Keele – BBB/ABC (Crimin; Crimin Joint Hons) (IB 32 pts)
Kent – BBB (Crimin Joint Hons; Crimin) (IB 34 pts)
Lincoln – 120 pts (Crimin Soc Plcy; Crimin)
Liverpool – BBB (Crimin) (IB 30 pts)
Liverpool John Moores – 120 pts (Law Crim Just) (IB 30 pts)
London (Birk) – 120 pts (Crimin Crim Just; Soc Sci)
Northumbria – 120 pts (Crimin) (IB 30 pts); 120 pts incl sci (Crimin Foren Sci) (IB 30 pts)
Staffordshire – 120 pts (Psy Crimin; Plcg Crim Invstg)
Stirling – BBB (Crimin Sociol; Crimin) (IB 32 pts)
Stranmillis (UC) – BBB (Ely Chld St)
Sunderland – 120 pts (Crimin)
Ulster – 120–128 pts (Crimin Crim Just) (IB 26 pts)
York – BBB (App Soc Sci (Chld Yng Ppl/Crm Crim Just); App Soc Sci) (IB 31 pts)
112 pts **Aberystwyth** – 112 pts (Crimin)
Birmingham City – 112 pts (Crimin courses; Crimin Plcg Invstg) (IB 28 pts)
Bolton – 112 pts (Crimin Foren Psy)
Brighton – BBC (Hum War Cnflct Modnty) (IB 28 pts)
Brunel – BBC (Spo Hlth Exer Sci (Spo Dev)) (IB 29 pts)
Canterbury Christ Church – 112 pts (App Crimin; Plcg)
Central Lancashire – 112 pts (Crimin Comb courses; BSL Df St); (Plcg Crim Invstg) (IB 28 pts)
Chester – BBC–BCC 112 pts (Crimin) (IB 26 pts)
Coventry – BBC (Crimin) (IB 28 pts)
De Montfort – 112 pts (Law Hum Rts Soc Just) (IB 28 pts)
Derby – 112 pts (Crimin)
East London – 112 pts (Crimin Crim Just) (IB 24 pts)
Edinburgh Napier – BBC incl Engl (Crimin) (IB 29 pts HL 5 Engl)
Huddersfield – BBC 112 pts (Crimin)
Hull – 112 pts (Psy Crimin; Crimin) (IB 28 pts)
Kingston – 112–128 pts (Crimin courses)
Leeds Beckett – 112 pts (Crimin Psy; Psy Soty; Crimin) (IB 25 pts)
Liverpool John Moores – 112 pts (Crimin; Crim Just; Crimin Psy) (IB 29 pts)
London Met – 112 pts (Crimin courses)
Manchester Met – 112 pts (Crimin; Crimin Joint Hons) (IB 26 pts)
Middlesex – 112 pts (Crimin (Plcg); Crimin courses)
Northampton – 112–128 pts (Crimin)
Nottingham Trent – 112 pts (Law Crimin; Comm Soty (Joint Hons))
Roehampton – 112 pts (Crimin)
Sheffield Hallam – 112 pts (Crimin; Crimin Sociol; Crimin Psy)
Southampton Solent – 112 pts (Crimin; Crim Invstg Psy)
Teesside – BBC (Crm Scene Sci)
Westminster – BBC (Crimin) (IB 28 pts)

UCL FACULTY OF POPULATION HEALTH SCIENCES

UCL

BSc Population Health

WHAT IS POPULATION HEALTH?

Population health studies the factors that shape our health – the social and physical environment, the way we live, health care systems and our genes.

This BSc programme will ground you in the different social science disciplines used to study population health and prepare you for research and professional practice in the health sector and beyond.

For further information:

www.ucl.ac.uk/bsc-population-health

Email: bscpopulationhealth@ucl.ac.uk

Twitter: @bscpophealth

The Lifecourse Degree

WHAT WILL I LEARN?

- World leading researchers will teach you the social, economic and demographic distribution of health and disease, and train you to analyse data to address health inequalities.

- You will develop quantitative data analysis skills, which are in high demand by employers, especially in the health sector and beyond.

- Complementing this you will also learn the theory, history and policy of population health creating a unique multidisciplinary educational experience.

 Q-Step

A step-change in quantitative social science skills

Funded by the Nuffield Foundation, ESRC and HEFCE

 UCL Q-STEP

104 pts **Abertay** – BCC (Crimin) (IB 29 pts)
Bradford – BCC 104 pts (Psy Crm)
Brighton – BCC (Soc Sci) (IB 27 pts)
De Montfort – 104 pts (Crimin Crim Just) (IB 28 pts)
Derby – 104 pts incl biol/chem (Foren Sci Crimin)
Edinburgh Napier – BCC incl Engl (Soc Sci) (IB 28 pts HL 5 Engl)
Kent – BCC (Soc Sci; Crim Just Crimin) (IB 34 pts)
Liverpool Hope – BCC–BBB 104–120 pts (Crimin)
Liverpool John Moores – 104 pts (Crimin Sociol) (IB 27 pts)
Middlesex – 104 pts (Crimin (Yth Just))
Nottingham Trent – 104 pts (Crimin)
Plymouth – 104 pts (Crimin Crim Just St)
Robert Gordon – BCC (App Soc Sci) (IB 27 pts)
Sheffield Hallam – 104 pts (App Soc Sci)
South Wales – BCC (Crimin Crim Just; Plcg Sci) (IB 29 pts)
Teesside – 104 pts (Psy Crimin)
West London – 104–120 pts (Psy Crimin/Cnslg Theor); 104 pts (Crimin)
Winchester – 104–120 pts (Crimin) (IB 26 pts)
96 pts **Bangor** – 96–112 pts (Crimin Crim Just)
Bishop Grosseteste – 96–112 pts (Ely Chld St courses)
Bradford – CCC 96 pts (App Crim Just St)
Bucks New – 96–112 pts (Plcg St courses)
Cumbria – 96 pts (Crimin Soc Sci; Crimin Law; Crimin Plcg Invstg)
Glyndŵr – 96 pts (Crimin Crim Just)
Kingston – 96–144 pts (Hum Rts)
London South Bank – CCC 96 pts (Crimin)

Check **Chapter 3** for new university admission details and **Chapter 6** on how to read the subject tables.

Manchester Met – 96–112 pts (Crm St) (IB 28 pts)
Portsmouth – 96–128 pts (Crimin Crim Just) (IB 30 pts HL 17 pts)
St Mary's – 96 pts (Educ Soc Sci) (IB 28 pts)
Teesside – 96 pts (Crimin courses; Crim Invstg)
West Scotland – CCC incl Engl (Crim Just) (IB 24 pts)
Wolverhampton – 96–112 pts (Plcg Intel; Crimin Crim Just)

88 pts **Anglia Ruskin** – 88–104 pts (Crimin courses) (IB 24 pts)
80 pts **Bedfordshire** – 80 pts (Crimin; App Soc St) (IB 24 pts)
Bucks New – 80–96 pts (Crimin) (IB 24 pts)
Wolverhampton – 80 pts incl biol/chem (Foren Sci Crimin)
72 pts **Farnborough (CT)** – 72 pts (Psy Crimin)
64 pts **London (Gold)** – CC (App Soc Sci Commun Dev Yth Wk)
UHI – CC (Soc Sci)

Open University – contact +44 (0)845 300 6090 **or** www.openuniversity.co.uk/you
(Crimin Psy St; Soc Sci Econ; Soc Sci Geog; Soc Sci Media St; Soc Sci Pol; Soc Sci Psy St)

Alternative offers
See **Chapter 6** and **Appendix 1** for grades/new UCAS Tariff points information for other examinations.

EXAMPLES OF COLLEGES OFFERING COURSES IN THIS SUBJECT FIELD

See also **Social and Public Policy and Administration**. Accrington and Rossendale (Coll); Blackburn (Coll); Blackpool and Fylde (Coll); Bolton (Coll); Central Campus, Sandwell (Coll); Cornwall (Coll); Coventry City (Coll); Derby (Coll); Doncaster (Coll); Ealing, Hammersmith and West London (Coll); Exeter (Coll); Gloucestershire (Coll); Lincoln (Coll); Llandrillo (Coll); London UCK (Coll); Middlesbrough (Coll); Mid-Kent (Coll); Newcastle (Coll); North Lindsey (Coll); Norwich City (Coll); Peter Symonds (Coll); Peterborough (Coll); Richmond-upon-Thames (Coll); Sir Gâr (Coll); Somerset (Coll); South Essex (Coll); Stamford New (Coll); Suffolk (Univ Campus); Truro and Penwith (Coll); Warwickshire (Coll); West Anglia (Coll); Wirral Met (Coll); York (Coll).

CHOOSING YOUR COURSE (SEE ALSO CH.1)

Universities and colleges teaching quality See www.qaa.ac.uk; http://unistats.direct.gov.uk.

Top research universities and colleges (REF 2014) See individual social science subjects.

Examples of sandwich degree courses Bath; Coventry; De Montfort; Middlesex; Portsmouth; Surrey; Teesside.

ADMISSIONS INFORMATION

Number of applicants per place (approx) Abertay 1; Bangor 2; Bath 6; Bradford 15; Cambridge 5; Cardiff 5; Cornwall (Coll) 2; Coventry 7; Cumbria 4; De Montfort 1; Durham 3; East London 10; Edge Hill 5; Glasgow Caledonian 9; Hull 5; Kingston 5; Leicester (Crimin) 9; Liverpool 13; London LSE 14; London South Bank 3; Manchester Met 10; Middlesex 26; Northampton 5; Nottingham Trent 2; Portsmouth 3; Roehampton 6; Sheffield Hallam 7; Southampton 6; Staffordshire 2; Sunderland 11; West Scotland 5; Westminster 14; Winchester 3; York 5.

Advice to applicants and planning the UCAS personal statement The Social Sciences/Studies subject area covers several topics. Focus on these (or some of these) and state your main areas of interest, outlining your work experience, personal goals and motivation to follow the course. Show your interest in current affairs and especially in social issues and government policies.

Misconceptions about this course **Cornwall (Coll)** That students transfer to Plymouth at the end of Year 1: this is a three-year course in Cornwall.

Selection interviews **Yes** Anglia Ruskin, Bangor, Birmingham, Birmingham City, Coventry, Cumbria, Edge Hill, Essex, Glasgow Caledonian, Hull, Kingston, Nottingham Trent, Roehampton, Sunderland, West London, West Scotland; **Some** Bath (mature students), Cornwall (Coll), East London, Robert Gordon, Staffordshire, Westminster, Winchester.

New UCAS points Tariff: A* = 56 pts; A = 48 pts; B = 40 pts; C = 32 pts; D = 24 pts; E = 16 pts

Interview advice and questions Past questions have included: Define democracy. What is the role of the Church in nationalistic aspirations? Does today's government listen to its people? Questions on current affairs. How would you change the running of your school? What are the faults of the Labour Party/Conservative Party? Do you agree with the National Lottery? Is money from the National Lottery well spent? Give examples of how the social services have failed. What is your understanding of the social origins of problems? See also **Chapter 5**.

Reasons for rejection (non-academic) Stated preference for other institutions. Incompetence in answering questions.

AFTER-RESULTS ADVICE

Offers to applicants repeating A-levels Higher Essex, Glasgow; **Same** Abertay, Anglia Ruskin, Bangor, Bradford, Chester, Cornwall (Coll), Coventry, Cumbria, Durham, East Anglia, Gloucestershire, Leeds, Liverpool, London Met, London South Bank, Manchester Met, Nottingham Trent, Roehampton, Sheffield Hallam, Staffordshire, Stirling, Winchester, Wolverhampton.

GRADUATE DESTINATIONS AND EMPLOYMENT (2013/14 HESA)

See **Law**, **Politics** and **Psychology**

Career note Graduates find careers in all aspects of social provision, for example health services, welfare agencies such as housing departments, the probation service, police forces, the prison service, personnel work and residential care and other careers not necessarily linked with their degree subjects.

OTHER DEGREE SUBJECTS FOR CONSIDERATION

Business Studies; Community Studies; Economics; Education; Geography; Government; Health Studies; Law; Politics; Psychology; Public Administration; Social Policy; Social Work; Sociology; Urban Studies.

SOCIAL WORK

(see also **Community Studies/Development, Social and Public Policy and Administration**)

Social Work courses (which lead to careers in social work) have similarities to those in Applied Social Studies, Social Policy and Administration, Community Studies and Health Studies. If you are offered a place on a Social Work course which leads to registration as a social worker, you must undergo the Disclosure and Barring Service (DBS) check. You will also have to provide health information and certification. Check for full details of training and careers in social work with the General Social Care Council (see **Appendix 3**). Students from England receive full payment of fees and student bursaries from the General Social Care Council.

Useful websites www.ageuk.org.uk; www.samaritans.org; www.ccwales.org.uk; www.sssc.uk.com; www.niscc.info; www.basw.co.uk

NB The points totals shown to the left of the institutions are for ease of reference only. It must not be assumed that Tariff points are always used by institutions or that they can be substituted for an offer in grades. The level of an offer is not necessarily indicative of the quality of a course.

COURSE OFFERS INFORMATION

Subject requirements/preferences GCSE English and mathematics usually required. **AL** No subjects specified. **Other** Disclosure and Barring Service (DBS) check and an occupational health check required. Check also with universities for applicant minimum age requirements.

Your target offers and examples of degree courses
136 pts Edinburgh – AAB–ABB (Soc Wk) (IB 36–34 pts)
128 pts Bath – ABB–BBB (Soc Wk App Soc St) (IB 34–32 pts)
        Birmingham – ABB (Soc Wk) (IB 32 pts HL 655)

Check **Chapter 3** for new university admission details and **Chapter 6** on how to read the subject tables.

Brighton – ABB (Soc Wk) (IB 32 pts)
Lancaster – ABB (Soc Wk) (IB 32 pts)
Leeds – ABB (Soc Wk) (IB 34 pts)
Nottingham – ABB 128 pts (Soc Wk) (IB 32 pts)
Queen's Belfast – ABB (Soc Wk)
Strathclyde – ABB–BBB (Soc Wk)
Sussex – ABB (Soc Wk) (IB 34 pts); ABB–BBB (Chld Yth (Theor Prac)) (IB 32 pts)

120 pts **Bournemouth** – BBB (Soc Wk) (IB 31 pts)
Bradford – BBB 120 pts (Soc Wk)
Coventry – BBB (Soc Wk) (IB 27 pts)
De Montfort – 120 pts (Soc Wk) (IB 30 pts)
East Anglia – BBB (Soc Wk) (IB 31 pts)
Edge Hill – BBB 120 pts (Soc Wk)
Greenwich – 120 pts (Soc Wk)
Huddersfield – BBB 120 pts (Soc Wk)
Kent – BBB (Soc Wk) (IB 34 pts)
Leeds Beckett – 120 pts (Soc Wk) (IB 26 pts)
London (Gold) – BBB (Soc Wk) (IB 33 pts)
Middlesex – BBB 120 pts (Soc Wk)
Northumbria – 120 pts (Soc Wk) (IB 30 pts)
Nottingham Trent – 120 pts (Soc Wk)
Plymouth – 120 pts (Soc Wk) (IB 24 pts)
Stirling – BBB (Soc Wk) (IB 32 pts)
Sunderland – 120 pts (Soc Wk)
UWE Bristol – 120 pts (Soc Wk) (IB 26 pts)
York – BBB (Soc Wk) (IB 31 pts)

112 pts **Bedfordshire** – 112 pts (Soc Wk) (IB 24 pts)
Birmingham City – 112 pts (Soc Wk) (IB 32 pts)
Canterbury Christ Church – BBC (Soc Wk)
Central Lancashire – 112 pts (Soc Wk) (IB 28 pts)
Chester – 112 pts (Soc Wk) (IB 26 pts)
East London – 112 pts (Soc Wk) (IB 24 pts)
Hull – 112 pts (Soc Wk) (IB 28 pts)
Keele – BBC (Soc Wk) (IB 30 pts)
Kingston – 112 pts (Soc Wk)
Lincoln – 112 pts (Soc Wk)
London Met – 112 pts (Soc Wk)
London South Bank – BBC 112 pts (Soc Wk)
Manchester Met – BBC 112 pts (Soc Wk) (IB 29 pts)
Newman – 112 pts (Wk Chld Yng Ppl Fmly)
Oxford Brookes – BBC (Soc Wk) (IB 32 pts)
Portsmouth – 112 pts (Soc Wk) (IB 29 pts HL 12 pts)
Sheffield Hallam – 112 pts (Soc Wk)
Southampton Solent – 112 pts (Soc Wk)
South Wales – BBC (Soc Wk) (IB 29 pts)
Staffordshire – 112 pts (Soc Wk)
West London – 112 pts (Soc Wk)

104 pts **Chichester** – BCC (Soc Wk) (IB 30 pts)
Derby – 104 pts (App Soc Wk)
Gloucestershire – 104 pts +interview (Soc Wk)
Glyndŵr – 104–120 pts (Soc Wk)
Hertfordshire – 104 pts (Soc Wk) (IB 26 pts)
Liverpool Hope – BCC–BBB 104–120 pts (Soc Wk)
Liverpool John Moores – 104 pts (Hlth Soc Cr Indiv Fmly Commun)
Northampton – 104–120 pts (Soc Cr courses; Soc Wk)

    South Wales – BCC (Yth Commun Wk) (IB 29 pts)
    Swansea – 104 pts (Soc Wk)
    Wolverhampton – 104 pts (Soc Wk)
96 pts **Anglia Ruskin** – 96 pts (Soc Wk)
    Bucks New – 96–112 pts (Soc Wk)
    Cardiff Met – 96 pts (Soc Wk; Hlth Soc Cr)
    Cumbria – 96 pts (Soc Wk)
    Derby – 96 pts (Wk Yng Ppl Commun)
    Glasgow Caledonian – CCC (Soc Wk) (IB 24 pts)
    HOW (Coll) – 96 pts (Soc Wk)
    Manchester Met – 96–112 pts (Chld Fmly St) (IB 25 pts); BCD–BBC 96–112 pts (Soc Cr)
      (IB 25 pts)
    Nottingham Trent – 96 pts (Yth St)
    Robert Gordon – CCC (Soc Wk) (IB 26 pts)
    Teesside – 96–108 pts +interview (Soc Wk)
    West Scotland – CCC (Soc Wk) (IB 24 pts)
    Winchester – 96–112 pts (Soc Wk) (IB 25 pts)
88 pts **Dundee** – AB–CCC (Soc Wk) (IB 29 pts)
    St Mark and St John – CCD (Yth Commun Wk)
    Winchester – 88–104 pts (Hlth Commun Soc Cr St) (IB 24 pts)
80 pts **Bedfordshire** – 80 pts (Hlth Soc Cr) (IB 24 pts)
    Cumbria – 80 pts (Wkg Chld Fmly)
72 pts **St Mark and St John** – 72 pts (Commun Dev)
64 pts **London (Gold)** – CC (App Soc Sci Commun Dev Yth Wk)
48 pts **Colchester (Inst)** – 48 pts +interview (Hlth Soc Cr)

    Open University – contact +44 (0)845 300 6090 **or** www.openuniversity.co.uk/you
      (Soc Wk)

Alternative offers
See **Chapter 6** and **Appendix 1** for grades/new UCAS Tariff points information for other examinations.

EXAMPLES OF COLLEGES OFFERING COURSES IN THIS SUBJECT FIELD
See also **Social and Public Policy and Administration**. Barnfield (Coll); Birmingham Met (Coll); Blackburn (Coll); Bradford (Coll); Bromley (CFHE); Central Nottingham (Coll); Cornwall (Coll); Durham New (Coll); Exeter (Coll); Furness (Coll); Gateshead (Coll); Great Yarmouth (Coll); Harrogate (Coll); Hartlepool (CFE); HOW (Coll); Hull (Coll); Leeds City (Coll); Liverpool City (Coll); Llandrillo (Coll); Mid-Kent (Coll); Newcastle (Coll); North Lindsey (Coll); Norwich City (Coll); Sir Gâr (Coll); Somerset (Coll); South Cheshire (Coll); South City Birmingham (Coll); South Gloucestershire and Stroud (Coll); South Thames (Coll); Southport (Coll); Stockport (Coll); Suffolk (Univ Campus); Truro and Penwith (Coll); Warrington (Coll); Warwickshire (Coll); Wiltshire (Coll); Wirral Met (Coll); Yorkshire Coast (Coll).

CHOOSING YOUR COURSE (SEE ALSO CH.1)
Universities and colleges teaching quality See www.qaa.ac.uk; http://unistats.direct.gov.uk.

Top research universities and colleges (REF 2014) (Social Work and Social Policy) London LSE; Oxford; East Anglia; Kent; Teesside; York; Leicester; London (UCL); Southampton; Glasgow; Edinburgh; Bath; Bristol.

ADMISSIONS INFORMATION
Number of applicants per place (approx) Bath 7; Birmingham 13; Bradford 10; Coventry 22; Dundee 6; Durham 4; London Met 27; Northampton 7; Nottingham Trent 6; Sheffield Hallam 4; Staffordshire 3.

Advice to applicants and planning the UCAS personal statement The statement should show motivation for social work, relevant work experience, awareness of the demands of social work and give relevant personal information, for example disabilities. Awareness of the origins of personal and family difficulties, commitment to anti-discriminatory practice. Most applicants for these courses will have significant experience of a statutory care agency or voluntary/private organisation providing a social work or social care service. See also **Social and Public Policy and Administration** and **Appendix 4**.

Selection interviews Yes Anglia Ruskin, Bedfordshire, Birmingham, Birmingham City, Bournemouth, Bradford, Brighton, Canterbury Christ Church, Cardiff Met, Central Lancashire, Chester, Chichester, Coventry, Cumbria, East Anglia, Edge Hill, Edinburgh, Gloucestershire, Glyndŵr, Greenwich, Hertfordshire, Huddersfield, Hull, Keele, Kent, Leeds Beckett, Liverpool Hope, London Met, Middlesex, Northumbria, Nottingham, Nottingham Trent, Portsmouth, Queen's Belfast, Robert Gordon, Sheffield Hallam, South Wales, Staffordshire, Sunderland, Sussex, Swansea, UWE Bristol, West London, West Scotland, Winchester, Wolverhampton, Worcester, York; **Some** Bath, Dundee, Liverpool John Moores.

Interview advice and questions What qualities are needed to be a social worker? What use do you think you will be to society as a social worker? Why should money be spent on prison offenders? Your younger brother is playing truant and mixing with bad company. Your parents don't know. What would you do? See also **Social and Public Policy and Administration** and **Chapter 5**.

Reasons for rejection (non-academic) Criminal convictions.

AFTER-RESULTS ADVICE
Offers to applicants repeating A-levels Same Lincoln, Liverpool Hope, Staffordshire, Suffolk (Univ Campus), Wolverhampton.

GRADUATE DESTINATIONS AND EMPLOYMENT (2013/14 HESA)
Graduates surveyed 8,610 **Employed** 4,960 **In voluntary employment** 110 **In further study** 1,515 **Assumed unemployed** 445

Career note See **Social Sciences/Studies**.

OTHER DEGREE SUBJECTS FOR CONSIDERATION
Community Studies; Conductive Education; Criminology; Economics; Education; Health Studies; Law; Psychology; Public Sector Management and Administration; Social Policy; Sociology; Youth Studies.

SOCIOLOGY
(see also **Anthropology, Social and Public Policy and Administration**)

Sociology is the study of social organisation, social structures, systems, institutions and practices. Courses are likely to include the meaning and structure of, for example, race, ethnicity and gender, industrial behaviour, crime and deviance, health and illness. **NB** Sociology is not a training course for social workers, although some graduates take additional qualifications to qualify in social work.

Useful websites www.britsoc.co.uk; www.asanet.org; www.sociology.org.uk; www.sociology.org

NB The points totals shown to the left of the institutions are for ease of reference only. It must not be assumed that Tariff points are always used by institutions or that they can be substituted for an offer in grades. The level of an offer is not necessarily indicative of the quality of a course.

COURSE OFFERS INFORMATION
Subject requirements/preferences GCSE English and mathematics usually required. **AL** No subjects specified.

Your target offers and examples of degree courses
152 pts Cambridge – A*AA (Hum Soc Pol Sci) (IB 40–41 pts HL 776); (Hum Soc Pol Sci (Sociol)) (IB 40–41 pts HL 776)

144 pts **Edinburgh** – AAA–ABB (Sociol; Sociol Soc Econ Hist) (IB 37–34 pts)
Exeter – AAA–ABB (Sociol Comb Hons) (IB 36–32 pts)
Lancaster – AAA–ABB (Crimin Sociol) (IB 36–32 pts)

136 pts **Bath** – AAB (Sociol) (IB 35 pts)
Bristol – AAB–ABB (Sociol Phil; Pol Sociol) (IB 34–32 pts)
Durham – AAB (Anth Sociol; Sociol) (IB 36 pts)
Exeter – AAB–ABB (Sociol) (IB 34–32 pts)
Glasgow – AAB–BBB incl arts/lang (Sociol) (IB 36–34 pts)
Lancaster – AAB–ABB (Sociol; Pol Sociol; Relig St Sociol; Film Sociol) (IB 35–32 pts)
Leicester – AAB (Psy Sociol) (IB 32 pts)
London LSE – AAB (Soc Plcy Sociol) (IB 37 pts HL 666); (Sociol) (IB 37 pts)
Manchester – AAB (Econ Sociol; Bus St Sociol) (IB 35 pts)
Sheffield – AAB (Sociol Bus Mgt) (IB 35 pts)
Southampton – AAB–ABB (Phil Sociol) (IB 34–32 pts)
Surrey – AAB–ABB (Sociol) (IB 35–34 pts)
Warwick – AAB (Law Sociol) (IB 36 pts)

128 pts **Aston** – ABB (Pol Sociol) (IB 33 pts)
Birmingham – ABB (Sociol) (IB 32 pts HL 655)
Bristol – ABB–BBB (Soc Plcy Sociol; Sociol) (IB 32–31 pts)
Brunel – ABB (Anth Sociol) (IB 31 pts)
Cardiff – ABB (Jrnl Media Sociol) (IB 36 pts); ABB–BBB (Sociol) (IB 34–32 pts)
City – ABB (Sociol) (IB 33 pts); ABB–BBB 128–120 pts (Sociol Psy) (IB 32 pts)
Essex – ABB–BBB (Sociol Crimin; Sociol Hum Rts; Sociol Soc Anth) (IB 32–30 pts); ABB–BBB (Sociol) (IB 32–30 pts)
Leeds – ABB (Sociol; Russ Sociol; Interd Soc Pol Sociol) (IB 34 pts)
Leicester – ABB (Sociol) (IB 30 pts)
London (Gold) – ABB–BBB (Sociol) (IB 33 pts)
Loughborough – ABB (Sociol) (IB 34 pts)
Manchester – ABB (Pol Sociol) (IB 34 pts); ABB–BBB (Sociol) (IB 34–32 pts)
Newcastle – ABB–BBB (Sociol) (IB 32–30 pts)
Nottingham – ABB (Sociol Soc Plcy; Sociol) (IB 32 pts)
Sheffield – ABB (Pol Sociol) (IB 34 pts); ABB incl Engl (Engl Lang Sociol) (IB 34 pts HL 6 Engl)
Southampton – ABB–BBB (Sociol Soc Plcy; Sociol) (IB 32 pts)
Sussex – ABB–BBB (Sociol) (IB 34–32 pts)
Warwick – ABB (Sociol) (IB 34 pts)
York – ABB (Sociol; Sociol Soc Psy; Sociol Educ) (IB 34 pts)

120 pts **Aberdeen** – BBB (Sociol) (IB 32 pts)
Aston – BBB (Psy Sociol) (IB 33 pts); (Sociol courses) (IB 33–32 pts)
Brighton – BBB (Crimin Sociol; App Psy Sociol) (IB 30 pts)
Cardiff – BBB (Sociol Welsh; Educ Sociol) (IB 32 pts)
Coventry – BBB (Sociol; Sociol Crimin) (IB 29 pts)
Greenwich – 120 pts (Sociol)
Keele – BBB/ABC (Sociol; Sociol Joint Hons) (IB 32 pts)
Kent – BBB (Sociol; Sociol (Yr Abrd)) (IB 34 pts)
Liverpool – BBB (Sociol) (IB 30 pts)
Northumbria – 120 pts (Sociol) (IB 30 pts)
Plymouth – BBB 120 pts (Psy Sociol) (IB 28 pts)
Queen's Belfast – BBB–ABB (Sociol courses)
Sheffield – BBB (Soc Plcy Sociol) (IB 32 pts)
Stirling – BBB (Sociol Soc Plcy) (IB 32 pts)
Sunderland – 120 pts (Sociol)

112 pts **Birmingham City** – 112 pts (Sociol; Sociol Crimin) (IB 28 pts)
Brighton – BBC (Sociol) (IB 28 pts)
Brunel – BBC (Sociol Media St; Sociol) (IB 29 pts)

Canterbury Christ Church – 112 pts (Sociol)
Chester – BBC–BCC 112 pts (Sociol) (IB 26 pts)
De Montfort – 112 pts (Pol Sociol)
East London – 112 pts (Sociol) (IB 24 pts)
Edge Hill – BBC 112 pts (Sociol)
Gloucestershire – 112 pts (Sociol)
Huddersfield – BBC 112 pts (Sociol)
Hull – 112 pts (Soc Anth Sociol; Sociol) (IB 28 pts)
Kingston – 112 pts (Sociol)
Leeds Beckett – 112 pts (Sociol) (IB 25 pts)
London Met – 112 pts (Sociol)
Manchester Met – BBC–BBB 112–120 pts (Psy Sociol) (IB 26 pts); 112 pts (Sociol) (IB 26 pts)
Northampton – 112–120 pts (Sociol)
Oxford Brookes – BBC (Sociol) (IB 30 pts)
Roehampton – 112 pts (Sociol)
Sheffield Hallam – 112 pts (Sociol)
UWE Bristol – 112 pts (Sociol) (IB 25 pts)
Westminster – BBC (Sociol) (IB 28 pts)

104 pts **Abertay** – BCC (Sociol) (IB 29 pts)
Bath Spa – 104–120 pts (Sociol; Sociol Comb Hons)
Brighton – BCC (Media St Sociol/Educ; Sociol Soc Hist) (IB 27 pts)
Central Lancashire – 104 pts (Sociol) (IB 28 pts)
Derby – 104 pts (Sociol)
Edinburgh Napier – BCC incl Engl (Psy Sociol) (IB 28 pts HL 5 Engl)
Liverpool John Moores – 104 pts (Crimin Sociol) (IB 27 pts); (Sociol) (IB 28 pts)
Middlesex – 104 pts (Sociol)
Nottingham Trent – 104 pts (Sociol)
Plymouth – 104 pts (Sociol) (IB 26 pts)
St Mary's – 104 pts (Sociol) (IB 28 pts)
Salford – 104–112 pts (Sociol) (IB 25 pts)
South Wales – BCC (Sociol Educ; Sociol Crimin Crim Just) (IB 29 pts)
Staffordshire – 104 pts (Sociol)
Ulster – 104–112 pts (Sociol; Sociol Pol) (IB 24–25 pts)
Winchester – 104–120 pts (Sociol) (IB 26 pts)
Worcester – 104 pts (Sociol)

96 pts **Bangor** – 96–120 pts (Sociol Joint Hons) (IB 24 pts); 96–112 pts (Sociol Soc Pol; Sociol)
Bedfordshire – 96 pts (Crimin Sociol) (IB 24 pts)
Bradford – CCC 96 pts (Sociol; Sociol Psy)
Bucks New – 96–112 pts (Psy Sociol)
London South Bank – CCC 96 pts (Sociol)
Portsmouth – 96–120 pts (Sociol; Sociol Media St; Sociol Psy) (IB 30 pts HL 17 pts)
Wolverhampton – 96 pts (Phil Sociol; Relig St Sociol); 96–112 pts (Sociol Pol; Sociol)

88 pts **Anglia Ruskin** – 88–104 pts (Sociol) (IB 24 pts)
Derby – 88–120 pts (Sociol Joint Hons)
Queen Margaret – CCD 88 pts (Psy Sociol) (IB 26 pts)
Teesside – 88 pts +interview (Sociol)

Alternative offers
See **Chapter 6** and **Appendix 1** for grades/new UCAS Tariff points information for other examinations.

EXAMPLES OF COLLEGES OFFERING COURSES IN THIS SUBJECT FIELD
Blackburn (Coll); Bury (Coll); Cornwall (Coll); Croydon (Univ Centre); Farnborough (CT); Hull (Coll); Lincoln (Coll); Milton Keynes (Coll); Newham (CFE); North Lindsey (Coll); Norwich City (Coll);

Peterborough (Coll); Petroc; Richmond-upon-Thames (Coll); South Devon (Coll); Suffolk (Univ Campus); Totton (Coll); West Anglia (Coll); West Suffolk (Coll).

CHOOSING YOUR COURSE (SEE ALSO CH.1)
Universities and colleges teaching quality See www.qaa.ac.uk; http://unistats.direct.gov.uk.

Top research universities and colleges (REF 2014) York; Cardiff; Manchester; Lancaster; Edinburgh; Oxford; London LSE; Essex; Exeter.

Examples of sandwich degree courses Aston; Bath; Brunel; Coventry; Middlesex; Plymouth; Surrey; UWE Bristol.

ADMISSIONS INFORMATION
Number of applicants per place (approx) Aston 8; Bangor 1; Bath 6; Birmingham 8; Birmingham City 12; Bristol 6; Brunel 24; Cardiff 5; City 11; Durham 3; East London 8; Exeter 5; Gloucestershire 8; Greenwich 5; Hull 11; Kent 10; Kingston 9; Lancaster 12; Leeds 14; Leicester 4; Liverpool 9; Liverpool John Moores 10; London (Gold) 5; London LSE 10; London Met 3; Loughborough 10; Manchester 8; Northampton 3; Northumbria 18; Nottingham 7; Plymouth 9; Portsmouth 12; Roehampton 4; Sheffield Hallam 7; Southampton 4; Staffordshire 10; Sunderland 5; Surrey 6; Warwick 20; Worcester 5; York 5.

Advice to applicants and planning the UCAS personal statement Show your ability to communicate and work as part of a group and your curiosity about issues such as social conflict and social change between social groups. Discuss your interests in sociology on the personal statement. Demonstrate an intellectual curiosity about sociology and social problems. See also **Social Sciences/ Studies**. **Bristol** Deferred entry accepted.

Misconceptions about this course Some applicants believe that all sociologists want to become social workers. **Birmingham** Students with an interest in crime and deviance may be disappointed that we do not offer modules in this area. **London Met** That it is the stamping ground of student activists and has no relevance to the real world.

Selection interviews Yes Birmingham City, Cambridge, City, Derby, East London, Lancaster, Liverpool, London (Gold), Newcastle, Nottingham, Salford, Southampton; **Some** Anglia Ruskin, Aston, Bath (mature applicants), Cardiff, Hull, Kent, Leeds, Leicester, London Met, Loughborough, Nottingham Trent, Sheffield Hallam, Staffordshire; **No** Birmingham, Bristol, Essex, Liverpool John Moores, Portsmouth, St Mary's, Surrey, Warwick.

Interview advice and questions Past questions have included: Why do you want to study Sociology? What books have you read on the subject? How do you see the role of women changing in the next 20 years? See also **Chapter 5**. **London Met** Questions will focus on existing level of interest in the subject and the applicant's expectations about studying.

Reasons for rejection (non-academic) Evidence of difficulty with written work. Non-attendance at Open Days (find out from your universities if your attendance will affect their offers). 'In the middle of an interview for Sociology a student asked us if we could interview him for Sports Studies instead!' See also **Social and Public Policy and Administration**. **Durham** No evidence of awareness of what the course involves. **London Met** References which indicated that the individual would not be able to work effectively within a diverse student group; concern that the applicant had not put any serious thought into the choice of subject for study.

AFTER-RESULTS ADVICE
Offers to applicants repeating A-levels Higher Brunel, East London, Essex, Glasgow, Hull, Newcastle, Nottingham Trent, Warwick, York; **Possibly higher** Leeds, Liverpool, Portsmouth; **Same** Aston, Bangor, Bath, Birmingham, Birmingham City, Bristol, Cardiff, Coventry, Derby, Durham, Gloucestershire, Kingston, Lancaster, Liverpool John Moores, London Met, Loughborough, Northumbria, Roehampton, St Mary's, Salford, Sheffield Hallam, Southampton, Staffordshire; **No** Cambridge.

GRADUATE DESTINATIONS AND EMPLOYMENT (2013/14 HESA)
Graduates surveyed 6,785 **Employed** 3,405 **In voluntary employment** 265 **In further study** 1,210 **Assumed unemployed** 505

Career note See **Social Sciences/Studies**.

OTHER DEGREE SUBJECTS FOR CONSIDERATION
Anthropology; Economic and Social History; Economics; Education; Geography; Government; Health Studies; History; Law; Politics; Psychology; Social Policy; Social Work.

SPANISH

(including **Hispanic Studies** and **Portuguese**; see also **Languages, Latin American Studies**)

Spanish can be studied by focusing on the language and literature of Spain. Broader courses in Hispanic Studies (see also **Latin American Studies**) are available which also include Portuguese and Latin American studies. See also **Appendix 3** under Languages.

Useful websites www.donquijote.co.uk; www.europa.eu; www.ciltuk.org.uk; www.ciol.org.uk; www. bbc.co.uk/languages; www.languageadvantage.com; www.languagematters.co.uk; www.studyspanish. com; www.spanishlanguageguide.com; see also **Latin American Studies**.

NB The points totals shown to the left of the institutions are for ease of reference only. It must not be assumed that Tariff points are always used by institutions or that they can be substituted for an offer in grades. The level of an offer is not necessarily indicative of the quality of a course.

COURSE OFFERS INFORMATION
Subject requirements/preferences GCSE English, mathematics or science and a foreign language. **AL** Spanish required for most courses.

Your target offers and examples of degree courses
152 pts **Cambridge** – A*AA incl lang (Modn Mediev Langs) (IB 40–41 pts HL 776)
144 pts **Bath** – AAA incl Span (Int Mgt Span) (IB 36 pts HL 6 Span)
    Edinburgh – AAA-ABB (Int Bus Fr/Ger/Span) (IB 37–34 pts)
    Imperial London – AAA incl chem+maths (Chem Fr/Ger/Span Sci) (IB 38 pts HL 7 chem 6 maths)
    London (King's) – AAA-AAB incl Fr/Ger/Span (Euro St (Fr/Ger/Span) (Yr Abrd)) (IB 35 pts HL 6 Fr/Ger/Span)
    London (UCL) – AAA-ABB incl lang (Modn Langs) (IB 38–34 pts HL 6 lang)
    Oxford – AAA incl Span (Span courses) (IB 38 pts); AAA (Port courses) (IB 38 pts)
    St Andrews – AAA (Mgt Span) (IB 38 pts); AAA incl maths (Maths Span) (IB 36 pts); AAA-AAB (Span courses) (IB 38–36 pts)
    Southampton – AAA-AAB incl maths+Fr/Ger/Span (Maths Fr/Ger/Span) (IB 36 pts HL 6 maths)
    Surrey – AAA-AAB incl Span (Span courses) (IB 36–35 pts)
136 pts **Aston** – AAB-ABB (Int Bus Fr/Ger/Span) (IB 34 pts)
    Birmingham – AAB incl hist (Hisp St Hist) (IB 32 pts HL 665)
    Exeter – AAB-ABB incl Span/Arbc (Span Arbc) (IB 34–32 pts HL 5 Span/Arbc)
    Glasgow – AAB-BBB incl arts/lang (Span; Hisp St) (IB 36–34 pts)
    Lancaster – AAB incl geog (Span St Geog) (IB 35 pts HL 6 geog); AAB-ABB (Span St) (IB 35–32 pts)
    Leeds – AAB incl Span (Russ Span) (IB 35 pts HL 6 Span)
    London (King's) – AAB incl Fr+Span (Fr Span (Yr Abrd)) (IB 35 pts HL 5 Fr+Span)
    London (UCL) – AAB incl Span (Span Lat Am St) (IB 36 pts HL 6 Span)
    Nottingham – AAB incl Fr/Ger/Span (Mgt Fr/Ger/Span) (IB 34 pts)
    Southampton – AAB-ABB incl Engl+Fr/Ger/Span (Engl Fr/Ger/Span) (IB 34 pts HL 6 Engl+Fr/Ger/Span); AAB-ABB incl Span (Span (Lat Am St); Span courses) (IB 34 pts

HL 6 Span); AAB–ABB incl Fr/Ger/Span (Film Fr/Ger/Span) (IB 32 pts HL 6 Fr/Ger/
Span); AAB–ABB incl Span/Port (Pol Span/Port Lat Am St) (IB 34 pts HL 6 Span/Port)

Sussex – AAB–ABB (Dr St Span) (IB 34 pts)

York – AAB–ABB (Fr Sp Lang (Yr Abrd)) (IB 34 pts); AAB (Span courses) (IB 34 pts)

128 pts **Aston** – ABB–BBB incl Span (Span Comb Hons) (IB 33–32 pts HL 6 Span)

Bath – ABB–AAB incl langs (Modn Langs Euro St) (IB 34 pts HL 6 5 langs)

Birmingham – ABB incl lang (Modn Langs Hist Art) (IB 32 pts HL 655)

Bristol – ABB–BBB incl Span (Span) (IB 32–31 pts HL 5 Span); (Hisp St) (IB 32–31 pts
HL 5 Span)

Cardiff – ABB incl Span (Span)

Dundee – ABB incl Engl+lang (Law Langs) (IB 32 pts)

Essex – ABB–BBB (Span St Modn Langs; Lat Am St courses) (IB 32–30 pts)

Leeds – ABB incl Span (Span; Span Port Lat Am St) (IB 34 pts HL 6 Span)

Liverpool – ABB incl Span (Hisp St) (IB 33 pts HL 6 Span)

London (RH) – ABB incl mus (Mus Fr/Ger/Ital/Span) (IB 32 pts); ABB (Mgt Fr/Ger/Ital/
Span) (IB 32 pts); (Euro St Fr/Ger/Ital/Span) (IB 34 pts); ABB incl Span (Span courses;
Span Fr/Ger/Ital) (IB 32 pts)

Manchester – ABB–BBB (Span Port) (IB 34–32 pts); ABB incl lang (Span courses)
(IB 34 pts); ABB–BBB incl Span (Span Port Lat Am St) (IB 34–32 pts)

Northumbria – ABB 128 pts (Int Bus Mgt Span) (IB 31 pts)

Nottingham – ABB (Engl Hisp St) (IB 32 pts); ABB incl Span (Hisp St) (IB 32 pts); ABB–AAC
(Span Int Media Comms St) (IB 32 pts)

Queen's Belfast – ABB incl Span (Span Port St)

Sheffield – ABB (Jap St Joint Hons) (IB 34 pts); ABB–BBB incl Span (Hisp St) (IB 34 pts
HL 6 Span)

Strathclyde – ABB–BBB (Span courses) (IB 34 pts)

Sussex – ABB–BBB incl Ital/Span (Ital Span) (IB 32 pts HL 5 Ital/Span)

Warwick – ABB incl lang (Hisp St courses) (IB 34 pts HL 5 lang)

120 pts **Dundee** – BBB–BCC (Span courses) (IB 30 pts)

Heriot-Watt – BBB incl maths (Maths Span) (IB 28 pts HL 5 maths); BBB incl lang (App
Langs Transl (Fr/Span) (Ger/Span); Span App Lang St) (IB 30 pts)

London (QM) – 120–128 pts incl lang (Hisp St) (IB 32–34 pts HL 5 lang); 120–128 pts
(Hisp St courses) (IB 32–34 pts HL 5 lang)

Plymouth – 120 pts incl Engl+Span (Engl Span) (IB 30 pts)

Queen's Belfast – BBB–ABB incl Span (Span)

Roehampton – 120 pts (Span)

Stirling – BBB (Span Lat Am St) (IB 32 pts)

Sunderland – 120 pts (Span Comb Hons)

Swansea – BBB (Law Span); BBB–BBC incl lang (Span; Pol Span) (IB 32–30 pts)

112 pts **Aberystwyth** – 112 pts incl lang (Span Joint Hons)

Central Lancashire – 112–128 pts (Span Int Bus; Fr/Ger/Span/Jap)

Chester – BBC–BCC incl Span 112 pts (Span courses) (IB 26 pts HL 5 Span)

Coventry – BBC (Span Bus) (IB 29 pts)

Greenwich – 112 pts (Span)

Hull – 112 pts incl lang (Fr/Ger/Ital/Span Hist; Span) (IB 28 pts)

Kingston – 112–128 pts incl Span (Span courses)

Nottingham Trent – 112 pts (Span Joint Hons)

104 pts **London (Birk)** – 104–120 pts (Span courses); 104 pts (Modn Langs (Fr, Ger, Jap, Port, Span))

Manchester Met – 104–112 pts incl Span (Span St) (IB 26 pts); 104–112 pts incl lang
(Ling Lang (Chin/Fr/Ger/Ital/Span)) (IB 26 pts)

Middlesex – 104 pts (Bus Mgt Mand/Span)

Westminster – BCC (Transl St (Span)) (IB 30 pts HL 4 lang)

96 pts **Bangor** – 96–104 pts incl Span (Span courses)

Plymouth – 96 pts incl Span (Int Bus Span) (IB 24 pts)

Portsmouth – 96–120 pts (Span St; Span Lat Am St) (IB 30 pts HL 17 pts)

Alternative offers
See **Chapter 6** and **Appendix 1** for grades/new UCAS Tariff points information for other examinations.

EXAMPLES OF COLLEGES OFFERING COURSES IN THIS SUBJECT FIELD
Euro Bus Sch London; Richmond-upon-Thames (Coll).

CHOOSING YOUR COURSE (SEE ALSO CH.1)
Universities and colleges teaching quality See www.qaa.ac.uk; http://unistats.direct.gov.uk.

Top research universities and colleges (REF 2014) See **Languages**.

ADMISSIONS INFORMATION
Number of applicants per place (approx) Birmingham 9; Bristol 4; Cardiff 3; Durham 5; Exeter 5; Hull 14; Leeds 10; Liverpool 3; London (King's) 6; London (QM) 5; London (UCL) 6; Middlesex 2; Nottingham 7; Portsmouth 4; Southampton 8.

Advice to applicants and planning the UCAS personal statement Visits to Spanish-speaking countries should be discussed. Study the geography, culture, literature and politics of Spain (or Portugal) and discuss your interests in full. Further information could be obtained from embassies in London. See also **Appendix 3** under **Languages**.

Selection interviews Yes Cambridge, Hull, London (UCL), Oxford, Southampton; **Some** Cardiff, Leeds, London (QM), London (RH), Nottingham, Roehampton, Swansea.

Interview advice and questions Candidates offering A-level Spanish are likely to be questioned on their A-level work, their reasons for wanting to take the subject and on their knowledge of Spain and its people. Interest in Spain is important for all applicants. Student comment: 'Mostly questions about the literature I had read and I was given a poem and asked questions on it.' Questions were asked in the target language. 'There were two interviewers for the Spanish interview; they did their best to trip me up and to make me think under pressure by asking aggressive questions.' See **Chapter 5**.

AFTER-RESULTS ADVICE
Offers to applicants repeating A-levels Higher Glasgow, Leeds; **Same** Cardiff, Chester, Hull, Liverpool, London (RH), Nottingham, Roehampton, Swansea; **No** Cambridge.

GRADUATE DESTINATIONS AND EMPLOYMENT (2013/14 HESA)
Spanish Studies graduates surveyed 1,125 **Employed** 575 **In voluntary employment** 40 **In further study** 205 **Assumed unemployed** 65

Career note See **Languages**.

OTHER DEGREE SUBJECTS FOR CONSIDERATION
International Business Studies; Latin American Studies; Linguistics; see other language tables.

SPEECH PATHOLOGY/SCIENCES/THERAPY

(including **Deaf Studies** and **Phonetics**; see also **Communication Studies/Communication, Health Sciences/Studies**)

Speech Pathology/Sciences/Therapy is the study of speech defects caused by accident, disease or psychological trauma. These can include failure to develop communication at the usual age, voice disorders, physical and learning disabilities and stammering. Courses lead to qualification as a speech therapist. This is one of many medical courses. See also **Medicine** and **Appendix 3**.

Useful websites www.rcslt.org; www.speechteach.co.uk; www.asha.org

New UCAS points Tariff: A* = 56 pts; A = 48 pts; B = 40 pts; C = 32 pts; D = 24 pts; E = 16 pts

NB The points totals shown to the left of the institutions are for ease of reference only. It must not be assumed that Tariff points are always used by institutions or that they can be substituted for an offer in grades. The level of an offer is not necessarily indicative of the quality of a course.

COURSE OFFERS INFORMATION

Subject requirements/preferences GCSE English language, modern foreign language and biology/ dual award science at grade B or above. **AL** At least one science subject; Biology may be stipulated, Psychology and English Language may be preferred. **Other** Disclosure and Barring Service (DBS) and occupational health checks essential for Speech Sciences/Speech Therapy applicants.

Your target offers and examples of degree courses
136 pts **East Anglia** – AAB (Sp Lang Thera) (IB 33 pts HL 666)
         Manchester – AAB (Sp Lang Thera) (IB 35 pts)
         Newcastle – AAB incl biol (Sp Lang Sci) (IB 35 pts)
         Queen Margaret – AAB incl sci/maths 136 pts (Sp Lang Thera) (IB 32 pts)
         Reading – AAB (Sp Lang Thera) (IB 35 pts)
         Sheffield – AAB 136 pts (Sp Sci) (IB 34 pts)
         Strathclyde – AAB–ABB incl Engl+maths+sci (Sp Lang Path) (IB 32 pts HL 6 Engl+maths+sci)
128 pts **Cardiff Met** – ABB (Sp Lang Thera)
         City – ABB–BBB 128–120 pts (Sp Lang Thera) (IB 33 pts)
         De Montfort – 128 pts (Hum Comm (Sp Lang Thera)) (IB 30 pts)
         Leeds Beckett – 128 pts incl sci/psy/sociol/lang (Sp Lang Thera) (IB 27 pts)
         Manchester Met – ABB (Sp Path Thera) (IB 30 pts)
         St Mark and St John – ABB (Sp Lang Thera)
         Sheffield – ABB–BBB (Sp Lang Sci) (IB 34 pts)
120 pts **Birmingham City** – BBB incl sci 120 pts (Sp Lang Thera) (IB 30 pts)
104 pts **St Mark and St John** – BCC (Sp Lang Sci)

Alternative offers
See **Chapter 6** and **Appendix 1** for grades/new UCAS Tariff points information for other examinations.

EXAMPLES OF COLLEGES OFFERING COURSES IN THIS SUBJECT FIELD
Portsmouth.

CHOOSING YOUR COURSE (SEE ALSO CH.1)
Universities and colleges teaching quality See www.qaa.ac.uk; http://unistats.direct.gov.uk.

ADMISSIONS INFORMATION

Number of applicants per place (approx) Birmingham City 28; Cardiff Met 10; City 16; De Montfort 5; Manchester 13; Manchester Met 21; Newcastle 23; Queen Margaret 12.

Advice to applicants and planning the UCAS personal statement Contact with speech therapists and visits to their clinics are an essential part of the preparation for this career. Discuss your contacts in full, giving details of any work experience or work shadowing you have done and your interest in helping people to communicate, showing evidence of good 'people skills'. See also **Appendix 3** and **Chapter 5**. **Manchester** Selectors look for some practical experience with individuals who have communication or swallowing difficulties. (International students) Good English required because of placement periods.

Misconceptions about this course Some students fail to differentiate between speech therapy, occupational therapy and physiotherapy. They do not realise that to study speech and language therapy there are academic demands, including the study of linguistics, psychology, medical sciences and clinical dynamics, so the course is intensive. **Cardiff Met** Some are under the impression that good grades are not necessary, that it is an easy option and one has to speak with a standard pronunciation.

Selection interviews Yes Birmingham City, Cardiff Met, East Anglia, Leeds Beckett, Manchester Met, St Mark and St John, Sheffield, Ulster, Worcester; **No** De Montfort.

Interview advice and questions Have you visited a speech and language therapy clinic? What did you see there? What made you want to become a speech therapist? What type of speech problems are there? What type of person would make a good speech therapist? Interviews often include an ear test (test of listening ability). See also **Chapter 5**. **Cardiff Met** Interviewees must demonstrate an insight into communication problems and explain how one speech sound is produced.

Reasons for rejection (non-academic) Insufficient knowledge of speech and language therapy. Lack of maturity. Poor communication skills. Written language problems.

AFTER-RESULTS ADVICE
Offers to applicants repeating A-levels Higher Birmingham City, Cardiff Met; **Possibly higher** Manchester Met; **Same** City, De Montfort, Newcastle.

GRADUATE DESTINATIONS AND EMPLOYMENT (2013/14 HESA)
Career note Speech therapists work mainly in NHS clinics, some work in hospitals and others in special schools or units for the mentally or physically handicapped. The demand for speech therapists is high.

OTHER DEGREE SUBJECTS FOR CONSIDERATION
Audiology; Communication Studies; Deaf Studies; Education; Health Studies; Linguistics; Psychology.

SPORTS SCIENCES/STUDIES
(see also Leisure and Recreation Management/Studies, Physical Education)

In addition to the theory and practice of many different sporting activities, Sports Sciences/Studies courses also cover the psychological aspects of sports and of sports business administration. The geography, economics and sociology of recreation may also be included. The England and Wales Cricket Board has introduced the Universities Centres of Cricketing Excellence scheme (UCCE).

Useful websites www.uksport.gov.uk; www.laureus.com; www.wsff.org.uk; www.sta.co.uk; www.olympic.org; www.sportscotland.org.uk; www.thebapa.org.uk; www.planet-science.com; www.olympic.org/london-2012-summer-olympics; www.bases.org.uk; www.eis2win.co.uk

NB The points totals shown to the left of the institutions are for ease of reference only. It must not be assumed that Tariff points are always used by institutions or that they can be substituted for an offer in grades. The level of an offer is not necessarily indicative of the quality of a course.

COURSE OFFERS INFORMATION
Subject requirements/preferences GCSE English, mathematics and, often, a science subject. **AL** Science required for Sport Science courses. PE required for some Sport Studies courses. **Other** Disclosure and Barring Service (DBS) disclosure required for many courses. Evidence of commitment to sport.

Your target offers and examples of degree courses

144 pts **Bath** – AAA incl sci/maths (Spo Exer Sci) (IB 36 pts HL 6 sci/maths)
  Birmingham – AAA–AAB incl sci/maths (Spo Exer Sci) (IB 32 pts HL 666–665)
  Exeter – AAA–AAB incl sci (Exer Spo Sci) (IB 36–34 pts HL 5 sci)
  Leeds – AAA–ABB incl sci (Spo Exer Sci; Spo Sci Physiol) (IB 35–34 pts HL 6 sci)
  Loughborough – AAA (Spo Exer Sci) (IB 36 pts)

136 pts **Bangor** – 136–128 pts (Spo Exer Psy)
  Bath – AAB/A*AC/A*BB (Spo Soc Sci) (IB 35 pts)
  Birmingham – AAB incl maths/sci/des tech (Spo Mat Sci) (IB 32 pts HL 665); AAB–ABB (App Glf Mgt St) (IB 32 pts HL 665–655)

EXPLORE MORE AT ONE OF THE UK'S BEST SPORT SCIENCE SCHOOLS.

Bangor University's School of Sport, Health and Exercise Sciences is regularly rated as one of the Top 10 schools in the UK for degree performance and student satisfaction.

Equally impressive are our research credentials. All our staff are research-active and 100% of our research is either world-leading or at an international level making us 7th in the UK. So if you're seeking a Sport Science School with no-limits learning

potential that will help you push boundaries and go beyond normal expectations then we're just what you're looking for.

Along with state-of-the-art laboratories and the opportunity to study abroad as part of your degree, Bangor also promises a stunning setting in the heart of Snowdonia; probably the most ideal university location in the country for pursuing sport and outdoor activities.

Bangor University

WHY CHOOSE **BANGOR** FOR SPORT SCIENCE?

At Bangor, you'd be studying at one of the best research-led Sport Science Schools in the UK. We've been teaching high-calibre undergraduate degrees for nearly ＿ years. Over this time, we've attracte＿ world-leading academic staff who have ongoing links at the highest levels of sport and performance (eg UK Sport, English Institute of Sport, the England and Wales Cricket Boar＿ Sport Wales, Ministry of Defence, a＿ England Rugby) and health (eg NHS MENCAP). All of these professional links have contributed to the development of one of the UK's bes＿ degree programmes.

What does this mean for you?

Our research activities lead to new, revised and state-of-the-art content being included in our teaching. Furthermore, many students choosing to study Sports Science at Bangor will have the opportunity to get directly involved with these exciting and world leading research processes! This leads to high student engagement and means we are in the Top Ten in the UK (Guardian University Guide 2016).

Opportunity of a Lifetime

Study Abroad as part of your degree and gain valuable 'real life' experience to enhance your CV. Our students have been to universities in West Florida, Maine and Iowa, USA and Melbourne, Australia.

With the **Bangor Employability Award**, you have the opportunity to obtain qualifications and complete work experience related to your future career aspirations. This ensures that you graduate, not only with a degree of the highest calibre, but with a CV full of transferable skills that will support your future career and help you to excel in today's competitive job market.

Sport and Outdoor Activities at Bangor

In our experience, most of our students like to do sport as well as learn about it. You will be studying in one of the best university locations in the UK. As well as providing an enjoyable learning environment, this fantastic location gives you an excellent opportunity to become actively involved in life outside the lecture hall.

Our award-winning clubs and societies offer free membership so there are no expensive subscriptions to pay.

"There is so much support and commitme＿ from the lecturers... I love the location of Bangor, with beaches and mountains close by meaning that there is always something to do.＿

Courtney Lightfoot, BSc/MSc student

PRIFYSGOL
BANGOR
UNIVERSITY

Follow SHES on 🐦 **@SportSciBangor**
www.bangor.ac.uk/sport

FOR LIFE'S EXPLORERS

Durham – AAB (Spo Exer Physl Actvt) (IB 36 pts)

Glasgow – AAB–BBB incl biol/chem (Physiol Spo Sci Nutr; Physiol Spo Sci) (IB 36–34 pts)

Loughborough – AAB incl geog (Geog Spo Sci) (IB 36–34 pts HL 5 geog); AAB incl Engl (Engl Spo Sci) (IB 34 pts HL 5 Engl); AAB (Spo Sci Mgt) (IB 34 pts)

Strathclyde – AAB–BBB (Spo Physl Actvt) (IB 34 pts)

Ulster – AAB incl sci/maths/spo (Spo Exer Sci) (IB 28 pts); AAB incl hum/soc sci/spo (Spo St) (IB 28 pts)

128 pts **Bangor** – 128–104 pts (Spo Sci; Spo Hlth PE; Spo Sci (Out Act); Spo Hlth Exer Sci)

Brighton – ABB (Spo Exer Sci; Spo Coach) (IB 32 pts)

Cardiff Met – 128 pts (Spo Exer Sci; Spo Condit Rehab Msg)

Central Lancashire – 128–112 pts (Spo Jrnl)

Coventry – ABB (Spo Mgt) (IB 29 pts); (Spo Psy) (IB 31 pts)

Derby – 128 pts incl biol/PE (Spo Exer Sci)

Edinburgh – ABB (App Spo Sci; Spo Recr Mgt) (IB 34 pts)

Essex – ABB–BBB (Spo Exer Sci) (IB 32–30 pts)

Gloucestershire – 128 pts (Physl Educ; Spo Thera; Spo Dev Coach)

Kent – ABB incl sci/maths (Spo Thera; Spo Exer Sci) (IB 34 pts)

Lincoln – 128 pts incl sci/spo (Spo Exer Sci)

Loughborough – ABB (Spo Mgt) (IB 32 pts)

Northumbria – 128 pts (Spo Mgt) (IB 31 pts)

Nottingham Trent – 128 pts incl sci/PE (Spo Exer Sci)

Sheffield Hallam – 128 pts incl PE/soc sci/sci (Spo Exer Sci); 128 pts incl PE/spo sci/sci (Spo Coach; Physl Actvt Spo Hlth)

UWE Bristol – 128 pts incl biol/PE (Spo Rehab) (IB 27 pts HL 5 biol/PE)

120 pts **Aberdeen** – BBB incl maths/sci (Spo Exer Sci) (IB 32 pts HL 5 maths/sci)

Brighton – BBB (Spo Jrnl) (IB 30 pts)

Cardiff Met – 120 pts (Spo PE)

Chester – 120 pts (Spo Exer Sci) (IB 28 pts)

Coventry – BBB (Spo Mark) (IB 29 pts)

Derby – 120 pts (Spo Thera Rehab)

Edge Hill – BBB 120 pts (Spo Thera; Spo Dev; Spo Exer Sci)

Gloucestershire – 120 pts (Spo Exer Sci)

Greenwich – 120 pts (Spo Sci); 120 pts incl sci (Spo Sci Coach) (IB 24 pts)

Kent – BBB incl sci/maths (Spo Exer Hlth) (IB 34 pts); BBB (Spo Exer Mgt) (IB 34 pts)

Leeds Beckett – 120 pts (Spo courses) (IB 26 pts); 120 pts incl sci/PE (Spo Physl Actv Hlth) (IB 26 pts)

Nottingham Trent – 120 pts incl sci/PE (Spo Sci Mgt)

St Mark and St John – BBB (Spo Thera; Spo Coach)

Stirling – BBB (Spo St; Spo Exer Sci) (IB 32 pts)

Sunderland – 120 pts (Spo Comb Hons)

Swansea – BBB–ABB (Spo Sci)

112 pts **Aberystwyth** – 112 pts (Spo Exer Sci)

Bournemouth – 112–128 pts (Spo Dev Coach Sci) (IB 30–32 pts)

Brighton – BBC (Spo St) (IB 28 pts)

Brunel – BBC (Spo Hlth Exer Sci (Coach); Spo Hlth Exer Sci; Spo Hlth Exer Sci (Hum Perf)) (IB 29 pts)

Canterbury Christ Church – 112 pts (Spo Exer Sci courses)

Central Lancashire – 112–128 pts incl biol/PE/spo sci (Spo Thera) (IB 25–27 pts); 112 pts (Advntr Spo Sci) (IB 25 pts); 112–128 pts (Spo Sci) (IB 25–27 pts)

Chester – BBC–BCC (Spo Dev Coach) (IB 26 pts); 112 pts (Spo Jrnl) (IB 26 pts)

Coventry – BBC incl biol/PE (Spo Thera) (IB 28 pts)

Derby – 112 pts (Spo Coach Dev)

East London – 112 pts incl PE/spo/sci (Spo Exer Sci) (IB 24 pts); 112 pts (Spo Jrnl) (IB 24 pts)

Hertfordshire – 112 pts incl sci (Spo Exer Sci) (IB 28 pts); 112 pts (Spo St) (IB 28 pts)

Huddersfield – BBC 112 pts (Spo Jrnl)

Hull – 112 pts (Spo Coach Perf; Spo Exer Nutr; Spo Rehab) (IB 28 pts)

Leeds Trinity – 112 pts (Spo Exer Sci (Spo Nutr); Spo Psy; Spo Jrnl)

Liverpool John Moores – 112–128 pts (Sci Ftbl; Spo Coach; Spo Exer Sci)

Manchester Met – 112–120 pts (Spo Exer Sci) (IB 28 pts)

Middlesex – 112 pts (Spo Exer Sci; Spo Exer Rehab)

Newman – 112 pts (Spo St)

Nottingham Trent – 112 pts incl maths+PE/sci (Spo Sci Maths); 112 pts incl sci/PE (Coach Spo Sci)

Oxford Brookes – BBC (Spo Exer Sci) (IB 30 pts)

Portsmouth – 112–128 pts incl sci (Spo Exer Sci) (IB 28 pts HL 11 pts incl 5 sci); 112 pts (Spo Mgt Bus Comm) (IB 26 pts)

Roehampton – 112 pts incl sci/PE (Spo Exer Sci)

St Mary's – 112 pts incl sci (Strg Condit Sci) (IB 28 pts)

Sheffield Hallam – 112 pts (Spo Bus Mgt; Spo Dev Coach)

Staffordshire – 112 pts (Spo St; Spo Exer Sci)

Sunderland – 112 pts (Spo Dev; Spo Exer Sci; Spo Coach)

West Scotland – BBC incl sci (Spo Exer Sci) (IB 28 pts)

Worcester – 112 pts (Spo St; Spo Bus Mgt); 112 pts incl PE/hum biol (Spo Thera)

York St John – 112 pts (Spo Dev Coach; Spo Sci Injry Rehab)

104 pts   **Abertay** – BCC incl sci/PE/maths (Spo Exer) (IB 29 pts)

Birmingham (UC) – 104 pts (Spo Thera)

Bournemouth – 104–120 pts (Spo Psy Coach Sci; Spo Mgt) (IB 28–31 pts)

Central Lancashire – 104–120 pts (Spo Psy)

Chichester – 104–120 pts incl sci (Spo courses) (IB 30 pts HL 5 sci)

Cumbria – 104–120 pts (Spo Exer Sci)

Edinburgh Napier – BCC incl sci/psy (Spo Exer Sci courses) (IB 28 pts HL 5 sci)

Glyndŵr – 104 pts (Spo Exer Sci; Spo Coach)

Kingston – 104–144 pts (Spo Sci; Spo Analys Coach)

Liverpool Hope – BCC–BBB 104–120 pts (Spo Psy; Spo Exer Sci)

Manchester Met – BCC–BBC 104–112 pts (Spo Mgt) (IB 26 pts); 104–112 pts (Spo Mark Mgt) (IB 26 pts)

Northampton – 104–120 pts (Spo St courses)

Robert Gordon – BCC incl Engl+sci (App Spo Exer Sci) (IB 28 pts HL 5 sci)

St Mark and St John – BCC (Spo Dev)

St Mary's – 104 pts incl sci (Spo Coach Sci; Spo Sci) (IB 28 pts); 104 pts incl biol/PE+spo/sci (Spo Rehab) (IB 28 pts)

South Wales – BCC incl sci/maths/PE (Rgby Coach Perf) (IB 29 pts); BCC incl sci/maths (Ftbl Coach Perf) (IB 29 pts HL 5 sci/maths); BCC incl sci/PE (Spo St; Spo Exer Sci) (IB 29 pts); BCC (Spo Ldrshp Dev; Spo Psy) (IB 29 pts)

Sunderland – 104 pts (Spo St)

Teesside – 104 pts incl spo/sci/PE (Spo Thera Rehab); 104 pts (Spo Exer (Spo St); Spo Exer (App Spo Sci); Spo Exer (Coach Sci); Spo Dev)

96 pts   **Anglia Ruskin** – 96 pts (Spo Sci) (IB 24 pts)

Bolton – 96 pts incl spo/PE/sci (Spo Rehab; Spo Exer Sci)

Central Lancashire – 96–112 pts (Spo Evnt Mgt)

Cumbria – 96–112 pts (Coach Spo Dev; Spo Rehab; Spo Coach Dev)

East London – (Spo Dev)

Manchester Met – 96–112 pts (Psy Spo Exer; Coach Spo Dev; Spo Dev (Joint Hons); Coach St (Joint Hons)) (IB 28 pts)

Southampton Solent – 96 pts (Spo St Bus)

Winchester – 96–112 pts (Spo Coach; Spo Bus Mark) (IB 25 pts)

Wolverhampton – 96 pts (Spo Coach Prac); 96 pts incl sci (Spo Exer Sci)

88 pts   **Derby** – 88–120 pts incl biol/PE (Spo Exer St Joint Hons)

London Met – 88 pts incl biol/PE/spo sci (Spo Sci)

London South Bank – CCD/BC 88–72 pts (Spo Exer Sci)

New UCAS points Tariff: A* = 56 pts; A = 48 pts; B = 40 pts; C = 32 pts; D = 24 pts; E = 16 pts

80 pts **Bedfordshire** – 80 pts (Ftbl St; Spo St) (IB 24 pts)
64 pts **Trinity Saint David** – 64 pts (Spo Mgt) (IB 24 pts)

Alternative offers
See **Chapter 6** and **Appendix 1** for grades/new UCAS Tariff points information for other examinations.

EXAMPLES OF COLLEGES OFFERING COURSES IN THIS SUBJECT FIELD

Most colleges, check with your local college. Accrington and Rossendale (Coll); Askham Bryan (Coll); Bishop Burton (Coll); Blackpool and Fylde (Coll); Bradford (Coll); Colchester (Inst); Easton Otley (Coll); Hackney (CmC); Hartpury (Coll); Lakes (Coll); Leeds City (Coll); Manchester (Coll); Myerscough (Coll); Newcastle (Coll); North Kent (Coll); North Lindsey (Coll); Peterborough (Coll); Plumpton (Coll); Reaseheath (Coll); Sir Gâr (Coll); South Devon (Coll); South Essex (Coll); Stamford New (Coll); Suffolk (Univ Campus); Tameside (Coll); Warwickshire (Coll); Westminster City (Coll); Weston (Coll); Writtle (Coll); York (Coll).

CHOOSING YOUR COURSE (SEE ALSO CH.1)

Universities and colleges teaching quality See www.qaa.ac.uk; http://unistats.direct.gov.uk.

Top research universities and colleges (REF 2014) (Sports and Exercise Science, Leisure and Tourism) Bristol; Liverpool John Moores; Leeds; Bath; Birmingham; Exeter; London (King's); Bangor; Cardiff Met.

Examples of sandwich degree courses Bath; Bedfordshire; Bournemouth; Brighton; Brunel; Central Lancashire; Coventry; Essex; Hertfordshire; Kingston; Leeds; Loughborough; Manchester Met; Nottingham Trent; Portsmouth; Southampton Solent; Trinity Saint David; Ulster.

ADMISSIONS INFORMATION

Number of applicants per place (approx) Aberystwyth 5; Bangor 15; Bath 8; Birmingham 7; Brunel 6; Canterbury Christ Church 30; Cardiff Met 10; Chichester 4; Cumbria 14, (Spo St) 6; Durham 7; Edinburgh 11; Exeter 23; Gloucestershire 8; Kingston 13; Leeds 25; Leeds Trinity 35; Liverpool John Moores 4; Loughborough 20; Manchester Met 16; Northampton 4; Northumbria 30; Nottingham Trent 8; Portsmouth 12; Roehampton 8; St Mary's 4; Sheffield Hallam 7; South Essex (Coll) 1; Staffordshire 12; Stirling 10; Strathclyde 28; Sunderland 2; Swansea 6; Teesside 15; Winchester 5; Wolverhampton 4; Worcester 10; York St John 4.

Advice to applicants and planning the UCAS personal statement See also **Physical Education** and **Appendix 3**. **Cardiff Met** A strong personal statement required which clearly identifies current performance profile and indicates a balanced lifestyle.

Misconceptions about this course Bath (Spo Exer Sci) This is not a sports course with a high component of practical sport: it is a science programme with minimal practical sport. (Coach Educ Spo Dev) This is not necessarily a course for elite athletes. **Birmingham** (App Glf Mgt St) Applicants do not appreciate the academic depth required across key areas (it is, in a sense, a multiple Honours course – business management, sports science, coaching theory, materials science). **Sheffield Hallam** (Spo Tech) Some applicants expect an engineering course! **Swansea** (Spo Sci) Applicants underestimate the quantity of maths on the course. Many applicants are uncertain about the differences between Sports Studies and Sports Science.

Selection interviews Yes Bishop Grosseteste, Chichester, Essex, Leeds, Nottingham, Nottingham Trent, Robert Gordon, Sheffield Hallam, Stirling, West Scotland, Wolverhampton, Worcester; **Some** Anglia Ruskin, Bath, Cardiff Met, Cumbria, Derby, Leeds Trinity, Liverpool John Moores, Roehampton, St Mary's, Sheffield Hallam, Staffordshire; **No** Birmingham, Edinburgh.

Interview advice and questions Applicants' interests in sport and their sporting activities are likely to be discussed at length. Past questions include: How do you strike a balance between sport and academic work? How many, and which, sports do you coach? For how long? Have you devised your own coaching programme? What age range do you coach? Do you coach unsupervised? See also **Chapter 5**. **Loughborough** A high level of sporting achievement is expected

Reasons for rejection (non-academic) Not genuinely interested in outdoor activities. Poor sporting background or knowledge. Personal appearance. Inability to apply their science to their specialist sport. Illiteracy. Using the course as a second option to Physiotherapy. Arrogance. Expectation that they will be playing sport all day. When the course is explained to them some applicants realise that a more arts-based course would be more appropriate.

AFTER-RESULTS ADVICE

Offers to applicants repeating A-levels Higher Swansea; **Same** Cardiff Met, Chichester, Derby, Dundee, Lincoln, Liverpool John Moores, Loughborough, Roehampton, St Mary's, Sheffield Hallam, Staffordshire, Stirling, Sunderland, Winchester, Wolverhampton, York St John.

GRADUATE DESTINATIONS AND EMPLOYMENT (2013/14 HESA)

Graduates surveyed 9,600 **Employed** 4,630 **In voluntary employment** 235 **In further study** 2,300 **Assumed unemployed** 420

Career note Career options include sport development, coaching, teaching, outdoor centres, sports equipment development, sales, recreation management and professional sport.

OTHER DEGREE SUBJECTS FOR CONSIDERATION

Anatomy; Biology; Human Movement Studies; Leisure and Recreation Management; Nutrition; Physical Education; Physiology; Physiotherapy; Sports Equipment Product Design.

STATISTICS

(see also Economics, Mathematics)

Statistics has mathematical underpinnings but is primarily concerned with the collection, interpretation and analysis of data. Statistics are used to analyse and solve problems in a wide range of areas, particularly in the scientific, business, government and public services.

Useful websites www.rss.org.uk; www.statistics.gov.uk; www.ons.gov.uk/ons/index.html

NB The points totals shown to the left of the institutions are for ease of reference only. It must not be assumed that Tariff points are always used by institutions or that they can be substituted for an offer in grades. The level of an offer is not necessarily indicative of the quality of a course.

COURSE OFFERS INFORMATION

Subject requirements/preferences GCSE English and mathematics. **AL** Mathematics required for all courses.

Your target offers and examples of degree courses
168 pts   Warwick – A*A*A*–AAA incl maths +STEP (MORSE) (IB 38 pts HL 7 maths)
160 pts   Imperial London – A*A*A incl maths+fmaths (Maths Stats; Maths Optim Stats; Maths Stats Fin) (IB 39 pts HL 7 maths)
　　　　　 Oxford – A*A*A incl maths (Maths Stats) (IB 39 pts HL 7 maths)
152 pts   Bath – A*AA incl maths (Stats) (IB 39 pts HL 6 maths)
　　　　　 London (UCL) – A*AA–AAA/A*AB incl maths (Stats Mgt Bus; Stats) (IB 39–38 pts HL 7 maths); A*AA–AAA incl maths (Stats Sci (Int); Stats Econ Fin) (IB 39–38 pts HL 7 maths)
　　　　　 Manchester – A*AA–AAA incl maths (Maths Stats) (IB 37 pts HL 6 maths)
144 pts   Birmingham – AAA incl maths (Mathem Econ Stats) (IB 32 pts HL 666)
　　　　　 City – AAA 144 pts (Mathem Sci Stats) (IB 32 pts)
　　　　　 Edinburgh – AAA–ABB (Maths Stats) (IB 37–32 pts)
　　　　　 Glasgow – AAA/A*AB–ABB incl maths (Fin Stats) (IB 38–36 pts)
　　　　　 Lancaster – AAA–AAB incl maths/fmaths (Stats; Stats (St Abrd) MSci) (IB 36 pts HL 6 maths); AAA–ABB incl maths/fmaths (Maths Stats) (IB 36 pts HL 6 maths)

Leeds – AAA/A*AB–AAB/A*BB/A*AC incl maths (Maths Stats) (IB 35 pts HL 6 maths)

London LSE – AAA incl maths (Bus Maths Stats; Stats Fin) (IB 38 pts)

Queen's Belfast – AAA–A*AB incl maths (Maths Stats OR MSci)

St Andrews – AAA incl maths (Stats) (IB 36 pts)

Southampton – AAA–AAB incl maths (Maths OR Stats Econ; Maths Stats) (IB 36 pts HL 6 maths)

Surrey – AAA–AAB incl maths (Maths Stats) (IB 36 pts HL 6 maths)

York – AAA–AAB incl maths (Maths Stats) (IB 36 pts HL 6 maths)

136 pts **Cardiff** – AAB/A*BB/A*AC incl maths (Maths OR Stats) (IB 34 pts HL 6 maths)

Glasgow – AAB–BBB incl maths (Stats) (IB 36–34 pts)

London (QM) – AAB incl maths (Maths Stats) (IB 34 pts HL 6 maths)

London (RH) – AAB–ABB incl maths/fmaths (Maths Stats) (IB 32 pts)

Newcastle – AAB/A*BB/A*AC incl maths (Maths Stats; Stats) (IB 37–35 pts HL 6 maths)

Reading – AAB–ABB (Maths Stats; Comput Maths) (IB 35–32 pts)

128 pts **Brunel** – ABB (Maths Stats Mgt) (IB 31 pts)

East Anglia – ABB incl maths (Bus Stats) (IB 32 pts HL 6 maths)

Heriot-Watt – ABB incl maths (Stats Modl) (IB 28 pts HL 6 maths)

Kent – ABB incl maths (Maths Stats) (IB 34 pts)

Liverpool – ABB incl maths (Maths Stats) (IB 33 pts HL 6 maths)

Plymouth – 128 pts incl maths (Maths Stats) (IB 30 pts HL 5 maths)

Queen's Belfast – ABB incl maths (Maths Stats OR)

Reading – ABB/AAC (Consum Bhv Mark) (IB 35–32 pts)

Strathclyde – ABB–BBB incl maths (Maths Stats Econ) (IB 32 pts HL 6 maths)

120 pts **Coventry** – BBB incl maths (Maths Stats) (IB 29 pts HL 4 maths)

Greenwich – 120 pts (Stats) (IB 25 pts)

Kent – BBB (Stat Soc Rsch) (IB 34 pts)

112 pts **Aberystwyth** – 112–128 pts incl maths (App Maths PMaths)

Kingston – 112 pts (Act Maths Stats)

London (Birk) – 112 pts (Maths Stats)

104 pts **Portsmouth** – 104–120 pts incl maths (Maths Stats) (IB 26 pts HL 10 pts incl maths)

Staffordshire – 104 pts incl maths (Maths) (IB 24 pts HL 4 maths)

Alternative offers

See **Chapter 6** and **Appendix 1** for grades/new UCAS Tariff points information for other examinations.

CHOOSING YOUR COURSE (SEE ALSO CH.1)

Universities and colleges teaching quality See www.qaa.ac.uk; http://unistats.direct.gov.uk.

Top research universities and colleges (REF 2014) See **Mathematics**.

Examples of sandwich degree courses Bath; Brunel; Cardiff; Coventry; Greenwich; Kent; Kingston; Portsmouth; Reading; Surrey; UWE Bristol.

ADMISSIONS INFORMATION

Number of applicants per place (approx) Bath 6; Coventry 3; Heriot-Watt 6; Lancaster 11; London (UCL) 9; London LSE 9; Newcastle 5; Southampton 10; York 5.

Advice to applicants and planning the UCAS personal statement Love mathematics, don't expect an easy life. See also **Mathematics** and **Appendix 3**.

Selection interviews Yes Bath, Birmingham, Liverpool, London (UCL), Newcastle; **Some** East Anglia, Greenwich; **No** Reading.

Interview advice and questions Questions could be asked on your A-level syllabus (particularly in mathematics). Applicants' knowledge of statistics and their interest in the subject are likely to be tested, together with their awareness of the application of statistics in commerce and industry. See also **Chapter 5**.

AFTER-RESULTS ADVICE
Offers to applicants repeating A-levels Higher Kent, Leeds, Liverpool, Newcastle; **Same** Birmingham.

GRADUATE DESTINATIONS AND EMPLOYMENT (2013/14 HESA)
Graduates surveyed 385 **Employed** 215 **In voluntary employment** 10 **In further study** 100 **Assumed unemployed** 25

Career note See **Mathematics**.

OTHER DEGREE SUBJECTS FOR CONSIDERATION
Accountancy; Actuarial Sciences; Business Information Technology; Business Studies; Computer Science; Economics; Financial Services; Mathematical Studies; Mathematics.

TEACHER TRAINING

(see also **Education Studies, Physical Education, Social Sciences/Studies**)

Abbreviations used in this table: ITE – Initial Teacher Education; ITT – Initial Teacher Training; P – Primary Teaching; QTS – Qualified Teacher Status; S – Secondary Teaching; STQ – Scottish Teaching Qualification.

Teacher training courses are offered in the following subject areas: Art and Design (P); Biology (P S); Business Studies (S); Chemistry (P S); Childhood (P); Computer Education (P); Creative and Performing Arts (P); Dance (P S); Design and Technology (P S); Drama (P S); English (P S); Environmental Science (P S); Environmental Studies (P); French (P S); General Primary; Geography (P S); History (P S); Maths (P S); Music (P S); Physical Education/Movement Studies (P S); Religious Studies (P); Science (P S); Sociology (S); Textile Design (S); Welsh (P). For further information on teaching as a career see websites below and **Appendix 3** for contact details. Over 50 taster courses are offered each year to those considering teaching as a career. Early Childhood Studies has been introduced in recent years by a number of universities. The courses focus on child development, from birth to eight years of age, and the provision of education for children and their families. It is a multi-disciplinary subject and can cover social problems and legal and psychological issues. Note that many institutions listed below also offer one-year Postgraduate Certificate in Education (PGCE) courses which qualify graduates to teach other subjects.

Useful websites www.gtcs.org.uk; www.gttr.ac.uk; teachertrainingcymru.org; www.gov.uk/dfe

NB The points totals shown to the left of the institutions are for ease of reference only. It must not be assumed that Tariff points are always used by institutions or that they can be substituted for an offer in grades. The level of an offer is not necessarily indicative of the quality of a course.

COURSE OFFERS INFORMATION
Subject requirements/preferences See **Education Studies**.

Your target offers and examples of degree courses
152 pts **Cambridge** – A*AA (Educ Engl Dr; Educ Engl; Educ Class; Educ Geog/Hist/Lang/Mus/Phys/
        Relig St; Educ Biol Sci) (IB 40–41 pts HL 776)
144 pts **Durham** – AAA (Educ St (Biol Sci/Engl St/Geog/Hist/Phil/Psy/Sociol/Theol))
        (IB 37 pts)
        Strathclyde – AAA–ABB incl sci/maths (Chem Teach MChem) (IB 34 pts)
136 pts **Edinburgh** – AAB–ABB (P Educ courses) (IB 36–34 pts)
        Glasgow – AAB–BBB incl Engl (Relig Phil Educ; Educ P QTS) (IB 34–32 pts)
        Stranmillis (UC) – AAB (P Educ QTS)
128 pts **Durham** – ABB (P Educ) (IB 34 pts)
        Edge Hill – ABB 128 pts (P Educ QTS)

New UCAS points Tariff: A* = 56 pts; A = 48 pts; B = 40 pts; C = 32 pts; D = 24 pts; E = 16 pts

Stranmillis (UC) – ABB +interview (Relig St Educ QTS)

Strathclyde – ABB–BBB (P Educ) (IB 34 pts)

120 pts **Brighton** – BBB (P Educ) (IB 30 pts)

Canterbury Christ Church – BBB (P Educ QTS)

Chester – BBB–BBC 120 pts (Teach Trg P Ely Yrs QTS) (IB 28 pts)

Chichester – 120 pts (P Teach Ely Yrs QTS) (IB 30 pts)

Cumbria – 120 pts (P Educ QTS)

Gloucestershire – 120 pts +interview (P Educ BEd QTS)

Leeds Beckett – 120 pts (P Educ (QTS); Ely Chld Educ QTS) (IB 26 pts)

Northampton – 120 pts (Ely Yrs Educ QTS)

Nottingham Trent – 120 (P Educ QTS)

Roehampton – 120–128 pts (P Educ QTS)

Sheffield Hallam – 120 pts (P Educ QTS)

Stirling – BBB (Educ P; Educ S) (IB 32 pts)

Sunderland – 120 pts (P Educ)

UWE Bristol – 120 pts (P Educ ITE) (IB 26 pts)

West Scotland – BBB incl Engl (Educ) (IB 32 pts)

Winchester – 120–136 pts (P Educ Geog QTS); 120–128 pts (P Educ QTS)

Worcester – 120 pts (P ITE)

York St John – 120 pts (P Educ)

112 pts **Bath Spa** – 112–128 pts (P Educ (BA + PGCE))

Bedfordshire – 112 pts (P Educ BEd QTS) (IB 24 pts)

Birmingham City – BBC 112 pts (P Educ QTS) (IB 26 pts)

Bishop Grosseteste – 112 pts (P Educ QTS)

Canterbury Christ Church – 112 pts (Maths S Educ QTS)

Chichester – BBC–CCC (Maths Teach KS 2+3) (IB 28 pts)

Edge Hill – BBC 112 pts (S Educ QTS courses)

Gloucestershire – 112 pts (Educ St courses)

Greenwich – 112 pts (Educ P BA QTS)

Hertfordshire – 112 pts (Educ P BEd QTS) (IB 28 pts)

Hull – 112 pts (P Teach) (IB 28 pts)

Leeds Beckett – 112 pts (Chld St) (IB 25 pts)

Leeds Trinity – BBC (P Educ courses (QTS))

Middlesex – 112 pts (P Educ QTS)

Oxford Brookes – BBC (P Teach Educ) (IB 30 pts)

Plymouth – 112 pts (P Mus BEd (QTS); P PE BEd (QTS))

RAc Dance – BBC +RAD Intermediate (Ballet Educ)

Reading – 112 pts (P Educ courses; P Ed Mus; P Educ Engl) (IB 28 pts)

Sheffield Hallam – 112 pts incl des tech (Des Tech Educ QTS)

Winchester – 112–128 pts (Educ St (Ely Chld)) (IB 26 pts)

Wolverhampton – 112 pts (P Educ)

104 pts **Cardiff Met** – 104 pts (S Educ (Mus/Welsh) QTS)

Gloucestershire – 104 pts (Ely Chld St)

Liverpool Hope – BCC–BBB 104–120 pts (P Educ QTS)

Northampton – 104–120 pts (Educ St courses); 104 pts (Ely Chld St; Chld Yth)

Nottingham Trent – 104 pts (Ely Yrs Spec Inclsv Educ; Spec Inclsv Educ Dig Lrng)

RConsvS – BCC incl mus +audition (Mus BEd)

St Mark and St John – BCC (PE (S Educ QTS))

St Mary's – 104 pts (P Educ QTS) (IB 28 pts)

South Wales – BCC (P St QTS) (IB 29 pts)

Stranmillis (UC) – BCC (Tech Des Educ QTS)

Winchester – 104–120 pts (P Educ PE QTS); (Educ St courses) (IB 26 pts)

96 pts **Bangor** – 96 pts (P Educ QTS)

Bedfordshire – 96 pts (Ely Yrs Educ; Educ St) (IB 24 pts)

Birmingham City – 96 pts (Cond Educ)

Check **Chapter 3** for new university admission details and **Chapter 6** on how to read the subject tables.

       Cumbria – 96–112 pts (Ely Yrs Educ Dev QTS)
       Huddersfield – CCC 96 pts (Ely Yrs)
       Kingston – 96 pts (P Teach QTS)
       Middlesex – 96 pts (Educ St; Ely Chld St)
       Portsmouth – 96–120 pts (Ely Chld St) (IB 28 pts HL 15 pts)
       St Mark and St John – 96 pts (P Educ QTS)
       Staffordshire – 96 pts (Ely Chld St)
88 pts **Nottingham Trent** – 88 pts (S Des Tech Educ)
       Teesside – 88 pts (Ely Chld St; Chld Yth St)
80 pts **Bangor** – 80–96 pts (Des Tech S Educ QTS)
72 pts **Trinity Saint David** – 72–96 pts (Ely Chld)

Alternative offers
See **Chapter 6** and **Appendix 1** for grades/new UCAS Tariff points information for other examinations.

EXAMPLES OF COLLEGES OFFERING COURSES IN THIS SUBJECT FIELD
Most colleges, check with your local college. Bedford (Coll); Bishop Burton (Coll); Bradford (Coll); Bromley (CFHE); Carshalton (Coll); Cornwall (Coll); Kensington Bus (Coll); Leeds City (Coll); Llandrillo (Coll); Loughborough (Coll); Mid-Cheshire (Coll); Myerscough (Coll); Nottingham New (Coll); Sir Gâr (Coll); South Cheshire (Coll); South Devon (Coll); South Essex (Coll); Wakefield (Coll); Warwickshire (Coll); Wigan and Leigh (Coll); Wiltshire (Coll); Yeovil (Coll).

CHOOSING YOUR COURSE (SEE ALSO CH.1)
Universities and colleges teaching quality See www.qaa.ac.uk; http://unistats.direct.gov.uk.

Top research universities and colleges (REF 2014) See **Education Studies**.

ADMISSIONS INFORMATION
Number of applicants per place (approx) Bangor 5; Bishop Grosseteste 12; Canterbury Christ Church 15; Cardiff Met 3; Chester 25; Cumbria 5; Derby 13; Dundee 5; Durham 8; Edge Hill 17; Gloucestershire 20; Greenwich 3; Hull 7; Kingston 9; Liverpool Hope 5; Middlesex 7; Northampton 7; Nottingham Trent 11; Oxford Brookes 6; Plymouth 14; Roehampton 6; St Mark and St John 5; St Mary's 19; Sheffield Hallam 7; Strathclyde 7; UWE Bristol 20; West Scotland 7; Winchester 4; Wolverhampton 4; Worcester 21.

Advice to applicants and planning the UCAS personal statement Too many candidates are applying without the required GCSE requirements in place or pending (Maths, English, Science). Any application for teacher training courses requires candidates to have experience of observation in schools and with children relevant to the choice of age range. Describe what you have learned from this. Any work with young people should be described in detail, indicating any problems which you may have seen which children create for the teacher. Applicants are strongly advised to have had some teaching practice prior to interview and should give evidence of time spent in a primary or secondary school and give an analysis of activity undertaken with children. Give details of music qualifications, if any. Admissions tutors look for precise, succinct, well-reasoned, well-written statements (no mistakes!). See also **Chapter 5**.

Selection interviews Check all institutions. It is a requirement that all candidates for teacher training are interviewed. **Yes** Bedfordshire, Birmingham City, Brighton, Cardiff Met, Cumbria, Dundee, Durham, Edge Hill, Edinburgh, Glasgow, Gloucestershire, Greenwich, Hertfordshire, Huddersfield, Leeds Beckett, Leeds Trinity, Liverpool John Moores, London (Gold), London Met, Middlesex, Northumbria, Roehampton, St Mark and St John, South Wales, Sunderland, UWE Bristol, Winchester, Wolverhampton, York St John.

Interview advice and questions Questions invariably focus on why you want to teach and your experiences in the classroom. In some cases you may be asked to write an essay on these topics. Questions in the past have included: What do you think are important issues in education at present? Discussion of course work will take place for Art applicants. **Derby** Applicants are asked about an aspect of education.

Reasons for rejection (non-academic) Unable to meet the requirements of written standard English. Ungrammatical personal statements. Lack of research about teaching at primary or secondary levels. Lack of experience in schools. Insufficient experience of working with people; tendency to be racist.

AFTER-RESULTS ADVICE

Offers to applicants repeating A-levels Higher Oxford Brookes; **Possibly higher** Cumbria; **Same** Bangor, Bishop Grosseteste, Brighton, Canterbury Christ Church, Chester, Derby, Dundee, Durham, Liverpool Hope, Nottingham Trent, Roehampton, St Mark and St John, St Mary's, Stirling, Sunderland, UHI, Winchester, Wolverhampton, Worcester, York St John; **No** Kingston.

GRADUATE DESTINATIONS AND EMPLOYMENT (2013/14 HESA)

Graduates surveyed 11,505 **Employed** 9,110 **In voluntary employment** 45 **In further study** 755 **Assumed unemployed** 230

Career note See **Education Studies**.

OTHER DEGREE SUBJECTS FOR CONSIDERATION

Education Studies; Psychology; Social Policy; Social Sciences; Social Work.

TOURISM and TRAVEL

(see also **Business and Management Courses, Business and Management Courses (International and European), Business and Management Courses (Specialised), Hospitality and Event Management, Leisure and Recreation Management/Studies**)

Tourism and Travel courses are popular; some are combined with Hospitality Management which thus provides students with two possible career paths. Courses involve business studies and a detailed study of tourism and travel. Industrial placements are frequently involved and language options are often included. See also **Appendix 3**.

Useful websites www.wttc.org; www.abta.com; www.thebapa.org.uk; www.itt.co.uk; www.tmi.org.uk

NB The points totals shown to the left of the institutions are for ease of reference only. It must not be assumed that Tariff points are always used by institutions or that they can be substituted for an offer in grades. The level of an offer is not necessarily indicative of the quality of a course.

COURSE OFFERS INFORMATION

Subject requirements/preferences GCSE English and mathematics required. **AL** No subjects specified.

Your target offers and examples of degree courses
136 pts **Surrey** – AAB (Int Hspty Tour Mgt; Int Tour Mgt) (IB 35 pts)
128 pts **Strathclyde** – ABB–BBB (Mgt Hspty Tour Mgt) (IB 33 pts)
120 pts **Northumbria** – BBB 120 pts (Bus Tour Mgt; Tour Evnts Mgt) (IB 30 pts)
        Staffordshire – BBB 120 pts (Tour Mgt)
        Sunderland – 120 pts (Tour Comb Hons)
112 pts **Aberystwyth** – 112 pts (Tour Mgt)
        Brighton – BBC (Int Tour Mgt) (IB 28 pts)
        Canterbury Christ Church – 112 pts (Tour Leis St; Tour Mgt)
        Cardiff Met – 112 pts (Int Tour Hspty Mgt)
        Central Lancashire – 112 pts (Int Tour Mgt) (IB 28 pts)
        Chichester – 112–128 pts (Sust Tour Mgt)
        East London – 112 pts (Int Tour Mgt); (Tour Mgt) (IB 24 pts)
        Gloucestershire – 112 pts (Htl Rsrt Tour Mgt)
        Greenwich – 112 pts (Tour Mgt)
        Leeds Beckett – 112 pts (Int Tour Mgt) (IB 25 pts)

Lincoln – 112 pts (Int Tour Mgt)
London Met – 112 pts (Tour Trav Mgt)
Southampton Solent – 112 pts (Tour Mgt; Int Tour Mgt)
Suffolk (Univ Campus) – 112 pts (Tour Mgt)
Sunderland – 112 pts (Tour Mgt; Int Tour Hspty Mgt)
Westminster – BBC (Tour Bus; Tour Plan Mgt) (IB 28 pts)
York St John – 112 pts (Tour Mgt; Tour Mgt Mark)

104 pts **Bath Spa** – 104–120 pts (Bus Mgt (Tour Mgt))
Birmingham (UC) – 104 pts (Int Tour Mgt)
Bournemouth – 104–120 pts (Tour Mgt) (IB 28–31 pts)
Coventry – 104 pts (Strat Tour Hspty Mgt)
Derby – 104 pts (Int Tour Mgt)
Liverpool Hope – BCC–BBB 104–120 pts (Tour)
Liverpool John Moores – 104 pts (Tour Leis Mgt)
Middlesex – 104 pts (Int Tour Mgt)
Queen Margaret – BCC 104 pts (Int Hspty Tour Mgt) (IB 28 pts)
Ulster – 104–120 pts (Int Trav Tour Mgt) (IB 24–26 pts)
West London – 104 pts (Trav Tour Mgt)

96 pts **Anglia Ruskin** – 96–112 pts (Tour Mgt) (IB 24 pts)
Birmingham (UC) – 96 pts (Int Tour Bus Mgt)
Edinburgh Napier – CCC (Tour Mgt Entre; Tour Mgt; Tour Mgt HR Mgt) (IB 27 pts)
Hertfordshire – 96–112 pts (Tour Joint Hons) (IB 24–28 pts); (Tour Mgt; Int Tour Mgt)
    (IB 28 pts)
London South Bank – CCC 96 pts (Tour Hspty Leis Mgt)
Manchester Met – CCC–BBC 96–112 pts (Tour Mgt) (IB 26 pts)
Plymouth – 96 pts (Cru Mgt); (Tour Mgt; Bus Tour; Int Tour Mgt) (IB 24 pts)
Robert Gordon – CCC (Int Tour Mgt) (IB 26 pts)
St Mary's – 96 pts (Tour; Tour Mgt) (IB 28 pts)
Wolverhampton – 96–112 pts (Tour Mgt)

88 pts **Portsmouth** – 88 pts (Hspty Mgt Tour) (IB 28 pts HL 15 pts)
80 pts **Bedfordshire** – 80 pts (Trav Tour; Int Tour Mgt) (IB 24 pts)
64 pts **Trinity Saint David** – 64 pts (Int Trav Tour Mgt; Tour Mgt)
UHI – CC (Advntr Tour Mgt)
32 pts **Greenwich (Sch Mgt)** – 32 pts (Trav Tour)

Alternative offers
See **Chapter 6** and **Appendix 1** for grades/new UCAS Tariff points information for other examinations.

EXAMPLES OF COLLEGES OFFERING COURSES IN THIS SUBJECT FIELD

Barnet and Southgate (Coll); Barnsley (Coll); Basingstoke (CT); Bedford (Coll); Birmingham Met (Coll); Bishop Burton (Coll); Blackburn (Coll); Blackpool and Fylde (Coll); Bournemouth and Poole (Coll); Bournville (Coll); Bradford (Coll); Brighton and Hove City (Coll); Bury (Coll); Central Bedfordshire (Coll); Central Nottingham (Coll); Chelmsford (Coll); Cornwall (Coll); Craven (Coll); Dearne Valley (Coll); Derby (Coll); Dudley (Coll); Durham New (Coll); East Berkshire (Coll); East Surrey (Coll); Grimsby (Univ Centre); Guildford (Coll); Highbury Portsmouth (Coll); Hugh Baird (Coll); Hull (Coll); Kingston (Coll); Lancaster and Morecambe (Coll); Leeds City (Coll); Leicester (Coll); Liverpool City (Coll); Llandrillo (Coll); London City (Coll); London UCK (Coll); Loughborough (Coll); Manchester (Coll); Mid-Cheshire (Coll); Mid-Kent (Coll); Neath Port Talbot (Coll); Nescot; Newcastle (Coll); North Kent (Coll); North Nottinghamshire (Coll); North Warwickshire and Hinckley (Coll); Northumberland (Coll); Norwich City (Coll); Nottingham New (Coll); Plumpton (Coll); Portsmouth (Coll); Redcar and Cleveland (Coll); South Cheshire (Coll); South Devon (Coll); Suffolk (Univ Campus); Sunderland (Coll); Uxbridge (Coll); West Cheshire (Coll); West Herts (Coll); West London; West Nottinghamshire (Coll); West Thames (Coll); Westminster City (Coll); Westminster Kingsway (Coll); Weston (Coll); Wirral Met (Coll); Yorkshire Coast (Coll).

CHOOSING YOUR COURSE (SEE ALSO CH.1)

Universities and colleges teaching quality See www.qaa.ac.uk; http://unistats.direct.gov.uk.

Examples of sandwich degree courses Birmingham (UC); Bournemouth; Brighton; Chester; Chichester; Gloucestershire; Greenwich; Hertfordshire; Leeds Beckett; Lincoln; Liverpool John Moores; Manchester Met; Middlesex; Northumbria; Plymouth; Portsmouth; Sheffield Hallam; Southampton Solent; Sunderland; Surrey; Trinity Saint David; Ulster; Wolverhampton.

ADMISSIONS INFORMATION

Number of applicants per place (approx) Aberystwyth 3; Birmingham (UC) 10; Bournemouth 16; Derby 4; Liverpool John Moores 10; Northumbria 6; Sheffield Hallam 12; Sunderland 2.

Advice to applicants and planning the UCAS personal statement Work experience in the travel and tourism industry is important – in agencies, in the airline industry or hotels. This work should be described in detail. Any experience with people in sales work, dealing with the public – their problems and complaints – should also be included. Travel should be outlined, detailing places visited. Genuine interest in travel, diverse cultures and people. Good communication skills required. See also **Appendix 3**.

Misconceptions about this course Wolverhampton Some applicants are uncertain whether or not to take a Business Management course instead of Tourism Management. They should be aware that the latter will equip them with a tourism-specific knowledge of business.

Selection interviews Yes Brighton, Derby; **Some** Anglia Ruskin, Sunderland; **No** Liverpool John Moores, Surrey.

Interview advice and questions Past questions have included: What problems have you experienced when travelling? Questions on places visited. Experiences of air, rail and sea travel. What is marketing? What special qualities do you have that will be of use in the travel industry? See also **Chapter 5**.

Reasons for rejection (non-academic) Wolverhampton English language competence.

AFTER-RESULTS ADVICE

Offers to applicants repeating A-levels Same Anglia Ruskin, Birmingham (UC), Chester, Derby, Lincoln, Liverpool John Moores, Manchester Met, Northumbria, St Mary's, Wolverhampton.

GRADUATE DESTINATIONS AND EMPLOYMENT (2013/14 HESA)

See **Hospitality and Event Management**.

Career note See **Business and Management Courses**.

OTHER DEGREE SUBJECTS FOR CONSIDERATION

Airline and Airport Management; Business Studies; Events Management; Heritage Management; Hospitality Management; Leisure and Recreation Management; Travel Management.

TOWN and COUNTRY PLANNING

(including **Environmental Planning** and **Urban Studies**; see also **Development Studies, Environmental Sciences, Housing, Property Management and Surveying, Transport Management and Planning**)

Town and Country Planning courses are very similar and some lead to qualification or part of a qualification as a member of the Royal Town Planning Institute (RTPI). Further information from the RTPI (see **Appendix 3**).

Useful websites www.rtpi.org.uk

NB The points totals shown to the left of the institutions are for ease of reference only. It must not be assumed that Tariff points are always used by institutions or that they can be substituted for an offer in grades. The level of an offer is not necessarily indicative of the quality of a course.

COURSE OFFERS INFORMATION

Subject requirements/preferences GCSE English and mathematics required. **AL** Geography may be specified.

Your target offers and examples of degree courses

152 pts Cambridge – A*AA (Lnd Econ) (IB 40–41 pts HL 776)

144 pts Cardiff – AAA–ABB (Urb Plan Dev) (IB 38–34 pts); AAA–AAB incl geog (Geog (Hum) Plan)
(IB 38–36 pts HL 6 geog)
Reading – AAA–AAB (Rl Est; Rur Prop Mgt) (IB 35 pts)

136 pts London (UCL) – AAB (Plan Rl Est) (IB 36 pts)
London LSE – AAB (Env Dev) (IB 37 pts)
Reading – AAB (Rl Est Plan Dev)

128 pts Birmingham – ABB (Plan Soc Plcy; Geog Urb Reg Plan (Joint Hons); Plan Econ)
(IB 32 pts HL 655)
Liverpool – ABB (Twn Reg Plan) (IB 33 pts)
London (UCL) – ABB (Urb St; Urb Plan Des Mgt) (IB 34 pts)
Manchester – ABB (Env Mgt) (IB 34 pts)
Newcastle – ABB–BBC (Urb Plan) (IB 32–28 pts)
Sheffield – ABB–BBB incl geog (Geog Plan) (IB 34 pts HL 6 geog)

120 pts Dundee – BBB–BCC (Twn Reg Plan) (IB 30 pts)
Heriot-Watt – ABC–BBB (Urb Plan Prop Dev) (IB 29 pts)
Leeds Beckett – 120 pts (Hum Geog Plan) (IB 26 pts)
Liverpool – BBB (Env Plan; Urb Regn Plan) (IB 31 pts)
Nottingham Trent – 120 pts (Plan Dev)
Queen's Belfast – BBB (Plan Env Dev)
Sheffield – BBB–BBC (Urb St; Urb St Plan) (IB 32 pts)

112 pts Oxford Brookes – BBC (Plan Prop Dev) (IB 31 pts); BBC–BBB (City Reg Plan) (IB 31 pts)
Westminster – BBC (Prop Plan) (IB 28 pts)

96 pts London South Bank – CCC 96 pts (Urb Env Plan)

Alternative offers
See **Chapter 6** and **Appendix 1** for grades/new UCAS Tariff points information for other examinations.

CHOOSING YOUR COURSE (SEE ALSO CH.1)

Universities and colleges teaching quality See www.qaa.ac.uk; http://unistats.direct.gov.uk.

Top research universities and colleges (REF 2014) See **Architecture**.

Examples of sandwich degree courses Cardiff; Northumbria; Nottingham Trent.

ADMISSIONS INFORMATION

Number of applicants per place (approx) Birmingham 2; Cardiff 6; Dundee 5; London (UCL) 6; London South Bank 3; Manchester 9; Newcastle 9; Oxford Brookes 3; UWE Bristol 6.

Advice to applicants and planning the UCAS personal statement Visit your local planning office and discuss the career with planners. Know plans and proposed developments in your area and any objections to them. Study the history of town planning worldwide and the development of new towns in the UK during the 20th century, for example Bournville, Milton Keynes, Port Sunlight, Welwyn Garden City, Cumbernauld, and the advantages and disadvantages which became apparent. See also **Appendix 3**. **Oxford Brookes** See **Property Development and Management**.

Selection interviews Yes Harper Adams, London (UCL), Newcastle, Oxford Brookes; **Some** Cardiff; **No** Dundee.

Interview advice and questions Since Town and Country Planning courses are vocational, work experience in a planning office is relevant and questions are likely to be asked on the type of work done and the problems faced by planners. Questions in recent years have included: If you were re-planning your home county for the future, what points would you consider? How are statistics used in urban planning? How do you think the problem of inner cities can be solved? Have you visited your local planning office? See also **Chapter 5**.

Reasons for rejection (non-academic) Lack of commitment to study for a professional qualification in Town Planning.

AFTER-RESULTS ADVICE
Offers to applicants repeating A-levels Higher Newcastle, UWE Bristol; **Same** Cardiff, Dundee, London South Bank, Oxford Brookes.

GRADUATE DESTINATIONS AND EMPLOYMENT (2013/14 HESA)
Planning (urban, rural and regional) graduates surveyed 820 **Employed** 545 **In voluntary employment** 15 **In further study** 140 **Assumed unemployed** 30

Career note Town Planning graduates have a choice of career options within local authority planning offices. In addition to working on individual projects on urban development, they will also be involved in advising, co-ordinating and adjudicating in disputes and appeals. Planners also work closely with economists, surveyors and sociologists and their skills open up a wide range of other careers.

OTHER DEGREE SUBJECTS FOR CONSIDERATION
Architecture; Countryside Management; Environmental Studies; Geography; Heritage Management; Housing; Land Economy; Property; Public Administration; Real Estate; Sociology; Surveying; Transport Management.

TRANSPORT MANAGEMENT and PLANNING

(including **Logistics**, **Transport Design** and **Supply Chain Management**; see also **Engineering/ Engineering Sciences, Town and Country Planning**)

Transport Management and Planning is a specialised branch of business studies with many applications on land, sea and air. It is not as popular as the less specialised Business Studies courses but is just as relevant and will provide the student with an excellent introduction to management and its problems.

Useful websites www.transportweb.com; www.nats.aero; www.ciltuk.org.uk

NB The points totals shown to the left of the institutions are for ease of reference only. It must not be assumed that Tariff points are always used by institutions or that they can be substituted for an offer in grades. The level of an offer is not necessarily indicative of the quality of a course.

COURSE OFFERS INFORMATION
Subject requirements/preferences GCSE English and mathematics required. **AL** No subjects specified.

Birmingham GCSE Mathematics grade B required.

Your target offers and examples of degree courses
136 pts **Cardiff** – AAB (Bus Mgt (Log Ops)) (IB 35 pts)
        Leeds – AAB (Geog Trans Plan) (IB 35 pts)
128 pts **Coventry** – ABB (Avn Mgt) (IB 31 pts)
120 pts **Aston** – BBB (Log Trans Mgt) (IB 32 pts)
        Huddersfield – BBB 120 pts (Air Trans Log Mgt)

Loughborough – BBB (Air Trans Mgt; Trans Bus Mgt) (IB 32 pts)
Northumbria – BBB 120 pts (Bus Log Sply Chn Mgt) (IB 30 pts)
112 pts **Coventry** – BBC incl art/des (Auto Trans Des) (IB 29 pts)
Greenwich – 112 pts (Bus Log Trans Mgt)
Huddersfield – BBC 112 pts (Trans Log Mgt)
104 pts **Liverpool John Moores** – 104 pts (Mgt Trans Log)
Staffordshire – 104 pts (Trans Des)
West London – 104 pts (Airln Airpt Mgt)
96 pts **Bucks New** – 96–112 pts (Air Trans Comm Plt Trg)
Plymouth – 96 pts (Cru Mgt)
80 pts **Bucks New** – 80–96 pts (Airln Airpt Mgt)
64 pts **Trinity Saint David** – 64 pts (Log Sply Chn Mgt)

Alternative offers
See **Chapter 6** and **Appendix 1** for grades/new UCAS Tariff points information for other examinations.

EXAMPLES OF COLLEGES OFFERING COURSES IN THIS SUBJECT FIELD
Bedford (Coll); Blackburn (Coll); Brighton and Hove City (Coll); Craven (Coll); Grimsby (Univ Centre); Mid-Kent (Coll); Myerscough (Coll); Newcastle (Coll); Norwich City (Coll); South Devon (Coll); Wirral Met (Coll).

CHOOSING YOUR COURSE (SEE ALSO CH.1)
Universities and colleges teaching quality See www.qaa.ac.uk; http://unistats.direct.gov.uk.

Examples of sandwich degree courses Aston; Coventry; Huddersfield; Liverpool John Moores; Loughborough; Plymouth.

ADMISSIONS INFORMATION
Number of applicants per place (approx) Aston 5; Coventry 5; Huddersfield 5; Loughborough 11.

Advice to applicants and planning the UCAS personal statement Air, sea, road and rail transport are the main specialist areas. Contacts with those involved and work experience or work shadowing should be described in full. See also **Appendix 3**.

Selection interviews Yes Loughborough, Plymouth; **Some** Aston, Bucks New; **No** Huddersfield, Loughborough.

Interview advice and questions Some knowledge of the transport industry (land, sea and air) is likely to be important at interview. Reading around the subject is also important, as are any contacts with management staff in the industries. Past questions have included: What developments are taking place to reduce the number of cars on the roads? What transport problems are there in your own locality? How did you travel to your interview? What problems did you encounter? How could they have been overcome? See also **Chapter 5**.

AFTER-RESULTS ADVICE
Offers to applicants repeating A-levels Same Aston.

GRADUATE DESTINATIONS AND EMPLOYMENT (2013/14 HESA)
Career note Many graduates will aim for openings linked with specialisms in their degree courses. These could cover air, rail, sea, bus or freight transport in which they will be involved in the management and control of operations as well as marketing and financial operations.

OTHER DEGREE SUBJECTS FOR CONSIDERATION
Air Transport Engineering; Civil Engineering; Environmental Studies; Logistics; Marine Transport; Town and Country Planning; Urban Studies.

New UCAS points Tariff: A* = 56 pts; A = 48 pts; B = 40 pts; C = 32 pts; D = 24 pts; E = 16 pts

VETERINARY SCIENCE/MEDICINE

(including **Bioveterinary Sciences** and **Veterinary Nursing**; see also **Animal Sciences**)

Veterinary Medicine/Science degrees enable students to acquire the professional skills and experience to qualify as veterinary surgeons. Courses follow the same pattern and combine rigorous scientific training with practical experience. The demand for these courses is considerable (see below) and work experience is essential prior to application. Graduate entry programmes provide a route to qualifying as a vet to graduates with good degrees in specified subjects. See also **Appendix 3**. Veterinary Nursing Honours degree courses combine both the academic learning and the nursing training required by the Royal College of Veterinary Surgeons, and can also include practice management. Foundation degrees in Veterinary Nursing are more widely available. Bioveterinary Sciences are usually three-year full-time BSc degree courses focusing on animal biology, management and disease but do not qualify graduates to work as vets. For places in Veterinary Science/Medicine, applicants may select only four universities. Applicants to the University of Cambridge Veterinary School and the Royal Veterinary College, University of London are required to sit the BioMedical Admissions Test (BMAT) (see **Chapter 5**).

Useful websites www.rcvs.org.uk; www.admissionstestingservice.org; www.bvna.org.uk; www.spvs. org.uk; www.bva.co.uk

NB The points totals shown to the left of the institutions are for ease of reference only. It must not be assumed that Tariff points are always used by institutions or that they can be substituted for an offer in grades. The level of an offer is not necessarily indicative of the quality of a course.

COURSE OFFERS INFORMATION

Subject requirements/preferences GCSE (Vet Sci/Med) Grade B English, mathematics, physics, dual science if not at A-level. **AL** (Vet Sci/Med) See offers below. (Vet Nurs) Biology and another science may be required. **Other** Work experience essential for Veterinary Science/Medicine and Veterinary Nursing courses and preferred for other courses: check requirements. Health checks may be required.

Bristol (Vet Sci/Med) **GCSE** Grade A in five or six subjects. Grade A or B in physics.

Glasgow (Vet Sci/Med) **GCSE** Grade A or B in physics.

Liverpool (Vet Sci/Med) **GCSE** English, mathematics, physics, dual science grade B if not at A-level. (Vet Nurs) **GCSE** Five subjects including English and two sciences.

Your target offers and examples of degree courses
160 pts **Cambridge** – A*A*A +BMAT (Vet Med) (IB 40–41 pts)
152 pts **Glasgow** – A*AA incl chem+biol (Vet Med Srgy) (IB 38 pts)
144 pts **Bristol** – AAA–AAB incl chem+biol 144–136 pts (Vet Sci) (IB 36–34 pts HL 6 chem 6/5 biol)
       Edinburgh – AAA incl chem+biol+maths/phys (Vet Med) (IB 38 pts)
       Liverpool – AAA incl biol+chem (Vet Sci) (IB 36 pts HL 6 biol+chem)
       London (RVC) – AAA–AAB incl chem+biol +BMAT (Vet Med)
       Surrey – AAA incl chem+biol (Vet Med Sci) (IB 36 pts HL 6 chem+biol)
136 pts **Glasgow** – AAB incl chem+biol (Vet Biosci) (IB 36–34 pts)
       Nottingham – AAB incl chem+biol (Vet Med Srgy) (IB 34 pts); AAB (Vet Med +Prelim Yr)
         (IB 34 pts)
       Surrey – AAB incl biol+sci (Vet Biosci) (IB 35 pts)
128 pts **Harper Adams** – ABB incl biol+sci (Vet Physio)
       Liverpool – ABB incl biol+sci (Biovet Sci) (IB 33 pts)
       London (RVC) – ABB–BBB incl chem/biol+sci/maths (Biovet Sci 3 yrs)
120 pts **Lincoln** – 120 pts incl biol/chem (Biovet Sci)
112 pts **Bristol** – BBC incl biol+chem (Vet Nurs Biovet Sci) (IB 29 pts HL 5 biol+chem)
104 pts **Edinburgh Napier** – BCC incl sci (Vet Nurs) (IB 28 pts HL 5 sci)
       Harper Adams – 104–120 pts incl biol (Biovet Sci)

96 pts **London (RVC)** – CCC incl chem+biol (Vet Gateway prog 1 yr); BCD incl biol (Vet Nurs)
Middlesex – 96 pts (Vet Nurs)

Alternative offers
See **Chapter 6** and **Appendix 1** for grades/new UCAS Tariff points information for other examinations.

EXAMPLES OF COLLEGES OFFERING COURSES IN THIS SUBJECT FIELD
Askham Bryan (Coll) (Vet Nurs); Bedford (Coll); Bishop Burton (Coll); Canterbury (Coll); Chichester (Coll); Cornwall (Coll); Derby (Coll); Duchy (Coll) (Vet Nurs); Easton Otley (Coll); Guildford (Coll); Hadlow (Coll) (Vet Nurs); Hartpury (Coll) (Vet Nurs); Kingston Maurward (Coll); Leeds City (Coll); Moulton (Coll); Myerscough (Coll) (Vet Nurs); Northumberland (Coll) (Vet Nurs); Plumpton (Coll) (Vet Nurs); Sheffield (Coll); Sir Gâr (Coll); South Devon (Coll); Sparsholt (Coll); Stamford New (Coll); Warwickshire (Coll); West Anglia (Coll); Writtle (Coll) (Vet Nurs).

CHOOSING YOUR COURSE (SEE ALSO CH.1)
Author's note Veterinary Science/Medicine is an intensely competitive subject and, as in the case of Medicine, one or two offers and three rejections are not uncommon. As a result, the Royal College of Veterinary Surgeons has raised a number of points which are relevant to applicants and advisers.

1 Every candidate for a Veterinary Medicine/Science degree course should be advised to spend a suitable period with a veterinarian in practice.

2 A period spent in veterinary work may reveal a hitherto unsuspected allergy or sensitivity following contact with various animals.

3 Potential applicants should be under no illusions about the difficulty of the task they have set themselves: at least five applicants for every available place, with no likelihood of places being increased at the present time.

4 There are so many candidates who can produce the necessary level of scholastic attainment that other considerations have to be taken into account in making the choice. In most cases, the number of GCSE grade As will be crucial. This is current practice. Headteachers' reports and details of applicants' interests, activities and background are very relevant and are taken fully into consideration; applicants are reminded to include details of periods of time spent with veterinary surgeons.

5 Any applicant who has not received an offer but who achieves the grades required for admission ought to get in touch, as soon as the results are known, with the schools and enquire about the prospects of entry at the Clearing stage. All courses cover the same subject topics.

Universities and colleges teaching quality See www.qaa.ac.uk; http://unistats.direct.gov.uk.

Top research universities and colleges (REF 2014) (Agriculture, Veterinary and Food Science) Warwick; Aberdeen; Glasgow; East Anglia; Bristol; Stirling; Queen's Belfast; Liverpool; Reading; Cambridge; Nottingham.

Examples of sandwich degree courses Harper Adams; UWE Bristol.

ADMISSIONS INFORMATION
Number of applicants per place (approx) Bristol (Vet Sci) 9, (Vet Nurs Biovet Sci) 12; Cambridge 5; Edinburgh 17; Glasgow 20; Liverpool 12; London (RVC) 5; Nottingham 11.

Admissions tutors' advice Bristol Places in Clearing for international students.

Advice to applicants and planning the UCAS personal statement Applicants for Veterinary Science must limit their choices to four universities and submit their applications by 15 October. They may add one alternative course. Work experience is almost always essential so discuss this in full, giving information about the size and type of practice and the type of work in which you were involved. See also **Appendix 3. Bristol** Six weeks of work experience including two weeks in a veterinary practice, one week lambing and one week on a dairy farm. **Cambridge** Work experience expected. **Edinburgh** Competition for places is intense: 72 places are available and only one in seven applicants will receive an offer. The strongest candidates are interviewed and are normally required to take with them an additional reference outlining recent work experience with large and small animals;

examples include dairy or lambing experience, kennels or catteries, or an abattoir visit. **Glasgow** A minimum of two weeks in a veterinary practice plus experience of work on a dairy farm, working at a stables, assisting at lambing, work at a cattery or kennels and if possible a visit to an abattoir. Additional experience at a zoo or wildlife park. **Liverpool** The selection process involves three areas: academic ability to cope with the course; knowledge of vocational aspects of veterinary science acquired through work experience in veterinary practice and six further weeks of experience working with animals; personal attributes that demonstrate responsibility and self-motivation. **London (RVC)** Hands-on experience needed: two weeks in a veterinary practice, and two weeks in another animal environment, for example riding school, zoo, kennels. **Nottingham** Six weeks (minimum) of work experience required and preferably one day at an abattoir.

Misconceptions about this course Liverpool (Biovet Sci) Some applicants think that the course allows students to transfer to Veterinary Science: it does not. **UWE Bristol** (Vet Nurs Sci) Students think that the degree qualifies them as veterinary nurses but in fact RCVS assessment/training is additional.

Selection interviews (Vet Sci and Vet Nurs) All institutions **Yes** Cambridge, Edinburgh, Edinburgh Napier, Glasgow, Harper Adams, London (RVC), Nottingham; **Some** Surrey (Vet Biosci).

Interview advice and questions Past questions have included: Why do you want to be a vet? Have you visited a veterinary practice? What did you see? Do you think there should be a Vet National Health Service? What are your views on vivisection? What are your views on intensive factory farming? How can you justify thousands of pounds of taxpayers' money being spent on training you to be a vet when it could be used to train a civil engineer? When would you feel it your responsibility to tell battery hen farmers that they were being cruel to their livestock? What are your views on vegetarians? How does aspirin stop pain? Why does it only work for a certain length of time? Do you eat beef? Outline the bovine TB problem. Questions on A-level science syllabus. See also **Chapter 5**. **Glasgow** Applicants complete a questionnaire prior to interview. Questions cover experience with animals, reasons for choice of career, animal welfare, teamwork, work experience, stressful situations.

Reasons for rejection (non-academic) Failure to demonstrate motivation. Lack of basic knowledge or understanding of ethical and animal issues.

AFTER-RESULTS ADVICE
Offers to applicants repeating A-levels Higher London (RVC); **Same** Liverpool, UWE Bristol (Vet Nurs Sci); **No** Cambridge, Edinburgh, Glasgow.

GRADUATE DESTINATIONS AND EMPLOYMENT (2013/14 HESA)
Graduates surveyed 590 **Employed** 535 **In voluntary employment** 20 **In further study** 20 **Assumed unemployed** 15

Career note Over 80% of veterinary surgeons work in private practice with the remainder involved in research in universities, government-financed research departments and in firms linked with farming, foodstuff manufacturers and pharmaceutical companies.

OTHER DEGREE SUBJECTS FOR CONSIDERATION
Agricultural Science; Agriculture; Animal Sciences; Biological Sciences; Biology; Dentistry; Equine Dental Science; Equine Management; Equine Studies; Medicine; Zoology.

ZOOLOGY

(including **Animal Biology**; see also **Agricultural Sciences/Agriculture, Animal Sciences, Biological Sciences, Biology**)

Zoology courses have a biological science foundation and could cover animal ecology, marine and fisheries biology, animal population, development and behaviour and, on some courses, wildlife management and fisheries.

Useful websites www.biaza.org.uk; www.zsl.org; www.academicinfo.net/zoo.html; www.abwak.co.uk

NB The points totals shown to the left of the institutions are for ease of reference only. It must not be assumed that Tariff points are always used by institutions or that they can be substituted for an offer in grades. The level of an offer is not necessarily indicative of the quality of a course.

COURSE OFFERS INFORMATION

Subject requirements/preferences GCSE English and science/mathematics required or preferred. **AL** One or two sciences will be required.

Your target offers and examples of degree courses

160 pts **Cambridge** – A*A*A incl sci/maths (Nat Sci (Zool)) (IB 40–41 pts HL 776)

144 pts **Birmingham** – AAA–AAB incl biol+sci (Biol Sci (Zool)) (IB 32 pts HL 666–665)

Edinburgh – AAA–ABB (Zool) (IB 37–32 pts)

Leeds – AAA–AAB incl biol+sci (Zool) (IB 35–34 pts HL 6 biol+sci)

Manchester – AAA–ABB 144–128 pts (Zool) (IB 37–33 pts); AAA–ABB incl sci/maths (Zool Modn Lang; Zool (Yr Ind)) (IB 37–33 pts)

Sheffield – AAA incl biol+sci (Zool MBiol) (IB 37 pts HL 6 biol+sci)

136 pts **Bristol** – AAB–ABB incl sci/maths (Zool) (IB 34–32 pts HL 6/5 sci/maths)

Cardiff – AAB–ABB incl biol (Zool) (IB 34 pts HL 6 biol+chem)

Exeter – AAB–ABB incl sci/maths (Zool (Cornwall)) (IB 34–32 pts HL 5 sci/maths)

Glasgow – AAB–BBB incl biol/chem (Zool) (IB 36–34 pts)

Newcastle – AAB–ABB incl biol+sci (Mar Zool) (IB 35–34 pts HL 6 biol); AAB–ABB incl biol (Zool) (IB 35 pts HL 6 biol)

Nottingham – AAB–ABB incl biol+sci (Zool) (IB 34–32 pts)

St Andrews – AAB incl biol+sci/maths (Zool) (IB 36 pts)

Sheffield – AAB–ABB incl biol+sci (Zool) (IB 35–34 pts HL 6 biol+sci)

Southampton – AAB incl biol+sci/maths (Zool) (IB 34 pts HL 6 biol+sci/maths)

128 pts **Leicester** – ABB incl sci/maths (Biol Sci (Zool)) (IB 30 pts)

Liverpool – ABB incl biol+sci (Zool) (IB 33 pts HL 6 biol)

London (QM) – ABB incl biol (Zool) (IB 34 pts HL 5 biol)

London (RH) – ABB incl biol (Zool) (IB 32 pts)

Reading – ABB–BBB (Zool) (IB 32–30 pts)

Roehampton – 128 pts incl biol+sci (Zool)

Swansea – ABB–BBB incl biol (Zool) (IB 33–32 pts)

120 pts **Aberdeen** – BBB incl maths/sci (Zool) (IB 32 pts HL 5 maths/sci)

Gloucestershire – 120 pts (Anim Biol)

Lincoln – 120 pts incl biol (Zool)

Queen's Belfast – BBB–ABB incl biol+sci/maths/geog (Zool)

Stirling – BBB (Anim Biol) (IB 32 pts)

116 pts **Aberystwyth** – 116–132 pts (Anim Bhv); 116–132 pts incl biol (Zool; Microbiol Zool)

112 pts **Bangor** – 112–136 pts incl biol (Mar Biol Zool); 112–136 pts incl biol+sci (Mar Vert Zool)

Chester – BBC–BCC 112 pts (Anim Bhv Biol/Psy)

Derby – 112 pts incl biol (Zool)

Hull – 112 pts incl biol (Zool) (IB 28 pts HL 5 biol)

Nottingham Trent – 112 pts incl biol (Zoo Biol)

Oxford Brookes – BBC incl sci 112 pts (Anim Biol Cons) (IB 30 pts)

Staffordshire – 112 pts (Anim Biol Cons)

104 pts **Bangor** – 104–128 pts incl biol+sci (Zool; Zool Cons; Zool Mar Zool)

Edinburgh Napier – BCC incl sci (Anim Biol) (IB 28 pts HL 5 sci)

Liverpool John Moores – 104–120 pts (Zool) (IB 25 pts)

Manchester Met – BCC–BBC incl biol 104–112 pts (Anim Bhv; Wldlf Biol) (IB 28 pts HL 5 biol)

Northampton – 104–120 pts (Wldlf Cons)

South Wales – BCC incl geog/maths (Nat Hist) (IB 29 pts HL 5 geog/maths); BCC incl biol+sci (Int Wldlf Biol) (IB 29 pts HL 5 biol+sci)

New UCAS points Tariff: A* = 56 pts; A = 48 pts; B = 40 pts; C = 32 pts; D = 24 pts; E = 16 pts

West Scotland – BCC incl sci (App Biosci Zool) (IB 24 pts)
Worcester – 104–120 pts incl biol+sci/maths (Anim Biol)
96 pts Anglia Ruskin – 96 pts (Zool) (IB 24 pts)
Cumbria – 96 pts (Wldlf Media)

Alternative offers
See **Chapter 6** and **Appendix 1** for grades/new UCAS Tariff points information for other examinations.

EXAMPLES OF COLLEGES OFFERING COURSES IN THIS SUBJECT FIELD
See also **Animal Sciences**. Bishop Burton (Coll); Cornwall (Coll); Craven (Coll); Dudley (Coll); Guildford (Coll); Leeds City (Coll); South Gloucestershire and Stroud (Coll); Sparsholt (Coll).

CHOOSING YOUR COURSE (SEE ALSO CH.1)
Universities and colleges teaching quality See www.qaa.ac.uk; http://unistats.direct.gov.uk.

Examples of sandwich degree courses Cardiff; Leeds; Liverpool John Moores; Manchester; Nottingham Trent.

ADMISSIONS INFORMATION
Number of applicants per place (approx) Aberystwyth 8; Bangor 3; Bristol 6; Cardiff 8; Leeds 7; Liverpool John Moores 6; London (RH) 6; Newcastle 15; Nottingham 6; Southampton 7; Swansea 6.

Advice to applicants and planning the UCAS personal statement Interests in animals should be described, together with any first-hand experience gained. Visits to zoos, farms, fish farms etc and field courses attended should be described, together with any special points of interest you noted.

Selection interviews Yes Hull, London (RH), Manchester, Newcastle; **Some** Derby, Roehampton, Southampton; **No** Cardiff, Liverpool, Swansea.

Interview advice and questions Past questions have included: Why do you want to study Zoology? What career do you hope to follow on graduation? Specimens may be given to identify. Questions usually asked on the A-level subjects. See also **Chapter 5**.

AFTER-RESULTS ADVICE
Offers to applicants repeating A-levels Higher Bristol, Hull, Leeds, Swansea; **Same** Aberystwyth, Bangor, Cardiff, Derby, Liverpool, Liverpool John Moores, London (RH), Roehampton, Swansea.

GRADUATE DESTINATIONS AND EMPLOYMENT (2013/14 HESA)
Graduates surveyed 1,120 **Employed** 450 **In voluntary employment** 75 **In further study** 245 **Assumed unemployed** 110

Career note See **Biology**.

OTHER DEGREE SUBJECTS FOR CONSIDERATION
Animal Ecology; Animal Sciences; Aquaculture; Biological Sciences; Biology; Ecology; Fisheries Management; Marine Biology; Parasitology; Veterinary Science; Wildlife Management.

8

INFORMATION FOR INTERNATIONAL STUDENTS

The choice of a subject to study (from over 50,000 degree courses) and of a university or college (from more than 150 institutions) is a major task for students living in the UK. For overseas and EU applicants it is even greater, and the decisions that have to be made need much careful planning, preferably beginning two years before the start of the course. **NB** Beware that there are some private institutions offering bogus degrees: check www.ucas.com to ensure your university and college choices are legitimate.

APPLICATIONS AND THE POINTS-BASED IMMIGRATION SYSTEM
In addition to submitting your application through UCAS (see **Chapter 4**) a Points-based Immigration System is now in operation for overseas students. The main features of this system include:

- **Confirmation of Acceptance for Studies (CAS) number** When you accept an offer the institution will send you a CAS number which you will need to include on your visa application.
- **Maintenance** Students will need to show that they are able to pay for the first year's tuition fees, plus £1000–£1300 per month for accommodation and living expenses. Additional funds and regulations apply for those bringing dependants into the UK.
- **Proof of qualifications** Your visa letter will list all the qualifications that you submitted to obtain your university place and original proof will be required of these qualifications when submitting your visa application. These documents will be checked by the Home Office. Any fraudulent documents will result in your visa application being rejected and a possible ban from entering the UK for 10 years.
- **Attendance** Once you have started your course, your attendance will be monitored. Non-attending students will be reported to the UK Border Agency.

Full details can be obtained from www.ukcisa.org.uk.

SELECTION, ADMISSION AND FINANCE
The first reason for making early contact with your preferred institution is to check their requirements for your chosen subject and their selection policies for overseas applicants. For example, for all Art and some Architecture courses you will have to present a portfolio of work or slides. For Music courses your application often will have to be accompanied by a recording you have made of your playing or singing and, in many cases, a personal audition will be necessary. Attendance at an interview in this country is compulsory for some universities and for some courses. At other institutions the interview may take place either in the UK or with a university or college representative in your own country.

The ability to speak and write good English is essential and many institutions require evidence of competence, for example scores from the International English Language Testing System (IELTS) or from the Test of English as a Foreign Language (TOEFL) (see www.ielts.org and www.ets.org/toefl). For some institutions, you may have to send examples of your written work. Each institution provides information about its English language entry requirements and a summary of this is given for each university listed below. International students should note that the recommended threshold for minimum English language requirements is IELTS 6.5–7.0. Recent research indicates that students with a lower score may have difficulty in dealing with their course.

In the next chapter you will find a directory of universities and colleges in the UK, together with their contact details. Most universities and colleges in the UK have an overseas student adviser who can advise you on these and other points you need to consider, such as passports, visas, entry certificates, evidence of financial support, medical certificates, medical insurance, and the numbers of overseas students in the university from your own country. All these details are very important and need to be considered at the same time as choosing your course and institution.

The subject tables in **Chapter 7** provide a comprehensive picture of courses on offer and of comparative entry levels. However, before making an application, other factors should be considered, such as English language entry requirements (see above), the availability of English language teaching, living costs, tuition fees and any scholarships or other awards which might be offered. Detailed information about these can be obtained from the international offices in each university or college, British higher education fairs throughout the world, the British Council offices abroad and from websites: see www.britishcouncil.org; www.education.org.

Below is a brief summary of the arrangements made by each university in the UK for international students aiming to take a full-time degree programme. The information is presented as follows:

- Institution.
- International student numbers.
- English language entry requirements for degree programmes, shown in IELTS scores. These vary between universities and courses, and can range from 5.5 to 7.5. For full details, contact the university or college.
- Arrangements for English tuition courses.
- International Foundation courses.
- Annual tuition fees (approximate) for full-time undergraduate degree courses. Tuition fees also usually include fees for examinations and graduation. These figures are approximate and are subject to change each year. EU students pay 'home student' fees, except for those from the Channel Islands and the Isle of Man; students from an Overseas Territory are eligible to pay home fees at universities and other institutions of higher education, provided that they meet any residence requirements. For a list of British and other EU member states Overseas Territories, see p. 574. More information for international students is available at the UK Council for International Student Affairs, www.ukcisa.org.uk.
- Annual living costs. These are also approximate and represent the costs for a single student over the year. The living costs shown cover university accommodation (usually guaranteed for the first year only), food, books, clothing and travel in the UK, but not travel to or from the UK. (Costs are likely to rise year by year in line with the rate of inflation in the UK.) Overseas students are normally permitted to take part-time work for a period of up to 20 hours per week.
- Scholarships and awards for non-EU students (most universities offer awards for EU students).

UNIVERSITY INFORMATION AND FEES FOR UNDERGRADUATE INTERNATIONAL STUDENTS

Applicants should check university websites before applying. **The fees published below (unless otherwise stated) are those being charged to students in 2016/17 (check websites for 2017/18 fees).**

Aberdeen Approximately 14% of students come from 120 nationalities. *English language entry requirement (or equivalent):* IELTS 6.0; Medicine 7.0. Four-week English course available in August before the start of the academic year. *Fees:* £13,000–£16,200; Clinical Medicine £28,600. *Living costs:* £650–£850 per month.

Abertay About 10% of the student population are international students. *English language entry requirement (or equivalent):* IELTS 6.0 (no band less than 5.5). Pre-sessional English course available, also full-time English course September to May and free English tuition throughout degree course. *Fees:* £13,800–£17,200. *Living costs:* £820 per month.

Aberystwyth International students make up approximately 7% of the undergraduate student population. *English language entry requirement (or equivalent):* IELTS 6.5–7. Full-time tuition in English available. *Fees:* Arts and Social Science subjects £10,500, Science subjects £12,000. *Living costs:* £800 per month. International scholarships available.

Anglia Ruskin Twenty-one per cent of the student population are international students. *English language entry requirement (or equivalent):* IELTS 6.0, with minimum of 5.5 in each element. A one-year International Foundation programme available. *Fees:* Arts subjects £9,800; Science subjects £10,300. Scholarships available. *Living costs:* £8,750.

Arts London A large number of international students. *English language entry requirement (or equivalent):* IELTS 6.0 for practice-based courses, 6.5 for theory-based courses. Language Centre courses in academic English for four to 24 weeks. *Fees:* £15,950. *Living costs:* £1,020 per month. Scholarships and bursaries available.

Aston Over 1,000 international students from over 130 countries, with 15% of the total student population from overseas. *English language entry requirement (or equivalent):* IELTS 6.0–6.5. International Foundation programme offered as a bridge to the degree courses. Pre-sessional English classes also available for four, eight, 12, 16, 20 and 30 weeks. *Fees:* Languages and Social Science courses £13,500; Engineering and Applied Science courses £14,500–£16,500; Life and Health Sciences £13,500–16,500; Aston Business School £13,500. *Living costs:* £820 per month. Scholarships offered, including bursaries for engineering and science subjects.

Bangor Around 20% of the student population come from 115 countries worldwide. *English language entry requirement (or equivalent):* IELTS 5.0–7.0. Pre-study English course available starting September, January or April depending on level of English proficiency, leads to International Foundation course. One-month or two-month courses before commencement of degree course also offered. *Fees:* Arts, Social Sciences and Education £11,500; Bangor Business School courses £12,000; Law £11,500; Science, Engineering and Health Studies £13,000. *Living costs:* £900–£1,100 per month. International entrance scholarships available.

Bath Over 1,500 international students from around 100 countries. *English language entry requirement (or equivalent):* IELTS 6.0–7.0. *Fees:* £10,750–£18,100. *Living costs:* £9,500. Scholarships, bursaries and awards available.

Bath Spa Students from 40 countries. *English language entry requirement (or equivalent):* IELTS 6.0 (minimum of 5.5 in all bands). Pre-sessional English courses for four or five weeks and 11 or 12 weeks. *Fees:* £11,300. *Living costs:* £7,400–£9,840.

Bedfordshire Over 3,000 EU and international students. *English language entry requirement (or equivalent):* IELTS 6.0, with minimum of 5.5 in each element. General English programmes are offered, including a summer school. *Fees:* £9,750. *Living costs:* £6,500–£7,500.

Birmingham Over 4,000 international students from 152 countries. *English language entry requirement (or equivalent):* IELTS 6.0–7.0, depending on programme of study. Pre-sessional English language programmes last between six and 42 weeks depending on language proficiency (IELTS 4.0–5.0). *Fees:* Non-laboratory subjects £12,565–£14,550; Laboratory subjects £17,145; Clinical Medicine £31,000. *Living costs:* £12,140–£16,000; Clinical Medicine £28,100. Awards are offered by some subject departments including all Engineering subjects, Computer Science, Earth Sciences, Law, and Psychology.

Birmingham (UC) There are 1100 students from 65 countries. Specific entry requirements for each country are found on the College website. *English language entry requirement (or equivalent):* IELTS 6.0, with minimum of 5.5 in each band. Pre-sessional English programme for six or 10 weeks depending on language ability. *Fees:* £9,600. *Living costs:* £7,380

Birmingham City Large number of international students. *English language entry requirement (or equivalent):* IELTS 6.0, with minimum of 5.5 in each band. Pre-sessional language courses of six and 10 weeks. Orientation programme for all students. *Fees:* All undergraduate courses £12,000; Conservatoire/ Acting courses £15,500. *Living costs:* £7,380–£8,840 Music bursaries.

Bishop Grosseteste *Fees:* Contact the University.

Bolton There are 623 international students from 79 countries represented. *English language entry requirement (or equivalent):* IELTS 6.0. English Foundation programme for six, 12, 18 and 24 weeks. Foundation programme also available in Business and Management. *Fees:* £11,250. *Living costs:* £6,860.

Bournemouth A large number of international students. *English language entry requirement (or equivalent):* IELTS 6.0, with a minimum of 5.5 in each component. Pre-sessional English programmes from two to 39 weeks. *Fees:* £13,500. *Living costs:* £7,000–£8,000. Some subject awards available.

Bournemouth Arts *Fees:* £13,995. *Living costs:* £6,500–£8,500.

BPP A private university dedicated to business and the professions, based in London. Contact the University for information. *Fees:* Contact the University.

Bradford Over 100 countries represented (22%). *English language entry requirement (or equivalent):* IELTS 6.0, with minimum of 5.5 in each element. Pre-sessional English language courses for 10, 20, 30 and 40 weeks. *Fees:* Science and Engineering courses £15,420; Management and Social Science courses £12,950. *Living costs:* £1,015 per month. Ten scholarships to cover the duration of the course.

Brighton Some 1,400 international students from over 100 countries. *English language entry requirement (or equivalent):* IELTS 6.0, with no less than 5.5 for each component. Pre-sessional English courses for four to 30 weeks. *Fees:* Classroom-based courses £11,780; Laboratory and studio-based courses £13,500. *Living costs:* £800 per month. Merit-based scholarships available

Brighton and Sussex (MS) *English language entry requirement (or equivalent):* IELTS 7.5, with no less than 7.0 in each section. *Fees:* £27,405. *Living costs:* £8,500. Scholarships based on merit and financial need available.

Bristol Approximately 1,500 students from over 100 countries. *English language entry requirement (or equivalent):* IELTS 6.0–7.5 depending on programme of study. Pre-sessional language courses for six and 10 weeks and a year-long International Foundation programme. *Fees:* Arts courses £15,600; Science courses £18,800; Clinical courses £35,000. *Living costs:* £7,400–£11,000. Scholarships and bursaries available.

Brunel More than 2,000 international students from over 110 countries. *English language entry requirement (or equivalent):* IELTS 6.0–7.0. Pre-sessional English language courses available from four to 50 weeks. *Fees:* £13,500–£16,500. *Living costs:* £7,380. International, academic excellence and country-specific scholarships available.

Buckingham Eighty nationalities represented at this small university. *English language entry requirement (or equivalent):* IELTS 6.5, with a minimum of 6.0 in each component. Foundation English courses offered. *Fees:* £12,870–£17,160. *Living costs:* £8,000–£10,000. International higher achiever scholarship available for students from Nigeria and Ghana. Some bursaries also available.

Bucks New Around 7.5% of the student population are international students coming from 50 countries. *English language entry requirement (or equivalent):* IELTS 6.0, with a minimum of of 5.5 in each element. English foundation programme available for one year. *Fees:* £9,500. *Living costs:* £6,000–£7,000. Academic achievement scholarships available.

Cambridge Over 1,000 international undergraduate students. *English language entry requirement (or equivalent):* IELTS 7.5 overall, with minimum of 7.0 in each element. Pre- and in-sessional English support is available. *Fees:* Tuition fees range between £15,816 and £38,283, depending on the course studied. College fees vary between £5,400 and £7,720 per year, depending on the college. *Living costs:* £9,400. Financial awards are offered to international students through the University of Cambridge and by some colleges. Scholarships for students from Canada and Hong Kong are also available.

Canterbury Christ Church International students from over 80 countries. *English language entry requirement (or equivalent):* IELTS 6.0, with a minimum of 5.5 in each section. *Fees:* £11,000. *Living costs:* £9,000. International student scholarship of £1,500 per year for up to three years of study.

Cardiff Over 3,500 international students from 100 countries. *English language entry requirement (or equivalent):* IELTS 6.5. Pre-sessional language courses from eight to 12 weeks. In-sessional support is also available. Induction course for all students. International Foundation courses for Business, Engineering and Health and Life Sciences. *Fees:* Arts-based courses £14,000; Business School courses £14,500; Science-based courses £17,500; Biosciences courses £18,000; Clinical courses £31,000. *Living costs:* £7,380. Law scholarships offered on the basis of academic merit.

Cardiff Met The University has over 800 international students enrolled from 120 different countries. *English language entry requirement (or equivalent):* IELTS 6.0, with a minimum of 5.5 in each section. International Foundation course and pre-sessional English courses available. *Fees:* £10,800. *Living costs:* £5,500–£6,500. Academic and sports scholarships available.

Central Lancashire Over 2,000 international students from over 100 countries. *English language entry requirement (or equivalent):* IELTS 6.0, with a minimum of 5.5 in each element. *Fees:* Non-laboratory courses £11,450; Laboratory courses £12,450. *Living costs:* £820 per month. Scholarships and bursaries available for international students. Scholarships for students from Indonesia and Palestine are also available.

Chester Over 18,000 students from over 130 countries globally. *English language entry requirement (or equivalent):* IELTS 6.0, with a minimum of 5.5 in each element. International Foundation programmes available in business, law and social sciences, engineering and computing, life sciences and creative arts. Pre- and in-sessional English language courses also available. *Fees:* £11,500. *Living costs:* £7,380. International students are automatically considered for the University of Chester International Scholarship upon application.

Chichester International students from several countries. *English language entry requirement (or equivalent):* IELTS 6.0 or 5.5 if taking a joint degree with International English Studies. No component may be less than 5.5. Pre-sessional programme for five and 10 weeks available. International Academic and Language Support (IALS) is offered alongside any degree. *Fees:* Classroom-based courses £10,250; Laboratory/studio/teaching-based courses £11,700. *Living costs:* £9,660.

City A large international community with students from over 160 countries. *English language entry requirement (or equivalent):* IELTS 6.0 (6.5 for Law and Journalism). Pre-sessional English language courses are available as four-, eight- and 12-week programmes. International Foundation programmes in business, humanities and social sciences and engineering, computer science and mathematics. *Fees:* £12,000–£15,000. *Living costs:* £1,200 per month. Academic scholarships available.

Coventry About 2,500 international students. *English language entry requirement (or equivalent):* IELTS 6.0. International Foundation and pre-sessional English programmes available. *Fees:* £11,500. *Living costs:* £6,000–£7,000. Scholarships available.

Creative Arts *Fees:* £12,010. *Living costs:* £7,500–£10,000. Undergraduate creative scholarships available.

Cumbria *English language entry requirement (or equivalent):* IELTS 6.0, with at least 5.5 in each component (6.0 for health courses and Social Work). International Foundation Programme and pre- and in-sessional English language courses available. *Fees:* £10,500. *Living costs:* £5,500. International scholarships available.

De Montfort Over 1,000 international students from more than 100 countries. *English language entry requirement (or equivalent):* IELTS 6.0–7.0. Pre-sessional English language courses and one-year International Foundation Certificate available. *Fees:* Classroom-based £11,750; Laboratory-based £12,250. *Living costs:* £9,000–£11,000. Some scholarships for overseas students.

Derby Students from 70 countries. *English language entry requirement (or equivalent):* IELTS 6.0, with a minimum of 5.5 in all areas. Courses offered to those needing tuition in English language. International Foundation Programme and pre-sessional English courses available. Language development sessions available throughout the course. *Fees:* Classroom-based courses £10,900; Resource-intensive courses £11,190; Occupational Therapy courses £11,725. *Living costs:* £900 per month. International scholarships available.

Dundee Students from 83 countries. *English language entry requirement (or equivalent):* IELTS 6.0. Foundation programme in business, engineering, physics, maths, and life sciences available. Pre-sessional programmes of four, 10 and 24 weeks also available. *Fees:* £12,900–£28,600. *Living costs:* £7,000–£8,000. International scholarships available.

Durham Over 4,500 international students from 156 countries. *English language entry requirement (or equivalent):* IELTS 6.5, with no component under 6.0. Pre- and in-sessional English language programmes available. *Fees:* Classroom-based £14,900; Laboratory-based £18,900. *Living costs:* £5,000–£7,000. University-administered scholarships and bursaries as well as College and Departmental Prizes available.

East Anglia Over 2,000 international students from 120 countries. *English language entry requirement (or equivalent):* IELTS 6.0 (higher for some courses). International Foundation and pre-sessional programmes available. *Fees:* Classroom-based subjects £14,500; Laboratory-based subjects £17,850; Medicine £28,550. *Living costs:* £7,200. International scholarships available.

East London About 3,300 international students from 120 countries. *English language entry requirement (or equivalent):* IELTS 5.5–6.0. Pre-sessional English courses of five, 10 and 15 weeks. *Fees:* £10,700. *Living costs:* £9,000. Range of international scholarships available.

Edge Hill There is a small number of international students. *English language entry requirement (or equivalent):* IELTS 6.0, with a minimum of 5.5 in each element. International Foundation Programme available. *Fees:* £11,150. *Living costs:* £7,000–£8,000. International students will automatically be considered for a scholarship upon application.

Edinburgh Some 4,000 international students from 120 countries. *English language entry requirement (or equivalent):* IELTS 6.5–7.5. English language courses offered throughout the year. *Fees:* £15,850–£20,850. *Living costs:* £605–£1,230 per month. International maths scholarship available.

Edinburgh Napier Approximately 4,000 international students. *English language entry requirement (or equivalent):* IELTS 6.0 overall with no component below 5.5. Pre- and in-sessional language support provided as well as English as a Foreign Language (EFL) modules within the course. *Fees:* Classroom-based and journalism courses £11,250; laboratory-based courses £13,060. *Living costs:* £890 per month. Merit-based scholarships available as well as scholarships for students from Hong Kong and India.

Essex International students from over 135 countries. *English language entry requirement (or equivalent):* IELTS 6.0. Pre-sessional English language programmes from five to 15 weeks and academic English classes provided during the year. *Fees:* Laboratory-based courses in Biological Sciences, Health and Human Sciences and Psychology £14,950; all other full-time undergraduate degrees £12,950. *Living costs:* £7,250–£10,000. A comprehensive package of scholarships and bursaries is available. See www.essex.ac.uk/studentfinance.

Exeter Around 4,000 international students from 140 countries. *English language entry requirement (or equivalent):* IELTS 6.5–7.5. International Foundation and Diploma programmes available as well as pre-sessional English language programmes of six and 10 weeks. *Fees:* Arts, Humanities, Social Science (including Business and Law), Mathematics, Geography £15,500; Accounting £17,500; Science and Engineering (including Psychology and Sport Sciences) £18,000; Combined Honours programmes that combine a science and a non-science subject £16,500; Medicine £27,000. *Living costs:* £7,600–£10,100. A range of scholarships and awards are available. Further information is available at www.exeter.ac.uk/studying/funding/prospective.

Falmouth *English language entry requirement (or equivalent):* IELTS 6.0. Discipline-specific academic English courses available throughout the year. *Fees:* £15,000. *Living costs:* £320–£540 per week. International scholarships available.

Glasgow Over 2,000 international students. *English language entry requirement (or equivalent):* IELTS 6.5 (higher for some courses). Pre- and in-sessional English language courses available. *Fees:* Arts and Social Sciences programmes £15,250; Engineering, Science, College of Medical, Veterinary and Life Sciences programmes £18,900; Clinical courses £33,950; Veterinary Medicine and Surgery £26,250. *Living costs:* £11,500. Fee-waiver scholarships and automatic Fourth Year scholarships available (not for Dentistry, Medicine or Veterinary Science).

Glasgow Caledonian Students from 70 countries. *English language entry requirement (or equivalent):* IELTS 6.0, with minimum 5.5 in each element. English language programmes available. *Fees:* £10,200–£14,500. *Living costs:* £820 per month. Merit-based scholarships as well as a guaranteed scholarship of £1,000 for full-time self-funded students.

Gloucestershire International students from more than 60 countries. *English language entry requirement (or equivalent):* IELTS 5.5. English language support and mentor scheme with other international students. *Fees:* £11,500. *Living costs:* £7,000–£9,000. International scholarships and bursaries available.

Glyndŵr The University welcomes students from Europe and worldwide. *English language entry requirement (or equivalent):* IELTS 6.0, with a minimum of 5.5 in each element. In-sessional and intensive English language courses available. *Fees:* £10,500. *Living costs:* £7,500. Scholarships available.

Greenwich Over 4,900 international students (including those from European countries). *English language entry requirement (or equivalent):* IELTS 6.0, with a minimum of 5.5 in each component. Pre-sessional English courses, Access and International Foundation programmes available. *Fees:* £11,200. *Living costs:* £9,500–£10,500. Scholarships open to applicants from 25 countries.

Harper Adams Students from around 30 different countries. *English language entry requirement (or equivalent):* 6.0, with a minimum of 5.5 in each component. Pre-sessional English language programmes available from six weeks to six months. *Fees:* £10,200. *Living costs:* £9,250. Scholarships available.

Heriot-Watt One third of the student population are from outside of the UK. *English language entry requirement (or equivalent):* IELTS 6.0. Several English language courses are offered; these range in length depending on students' requirements. *Fees:* Laboratory-based Science and Engineering courses £16,420; Non-laboratory-based courses £13,020. *Living costs:* £8,000. Some international scholarships are available.

Hertfordshire Students from over 90 countries are at present studying at the University. *English language entry requirement (or equivalent):* IELTS 6.0. English language tuition is offered in the one-year International Foundation course, in a course for the Foundation Certificate in English for Academic Purposes, and in a pre-sessional intensive English course held during the summer months. *Fees:* Classroom-based courses £11,000; Laboratory-based courses £11,500. *Living costs:* £815–£1,030 per month. International scholarships available.

Huddersfield International students from over 80 countries. *English language entry requirement (or equivalent):* IELTS 6.0, with a minimum of 5.5 in each element. English language courses available and a one-year International Foundation course in English language with options in Business, Computing, Engineering, Mathematics and Music. Students guaranteed entry to Huddersfield courses on completion. *Fees:* Computing, Engineering and Science courses £14,000; all other courses £13,000. *Living costs:* £6,500–£7,500. International students are automatically considered for a scholarship of up to £2,000 per year upon application.

Hull Ten per cent of students are from outside the EU. *English language entry requirement (or equivalent):* IELTS 6.0–7.0. English summer study programmes available. *Fees:* Non-Science programmes £12,500; Science programmes £15,000. *Living costs:* £6,500–£8,500. Excellent overseas scholarship provisions depending on the chosen subject and the student's country of origin.

Hull York (MS) *English language entry requirement (or equivalent):* 7.5, with a minimum of 7.0 in each component. *Fees:* £25,930.

IFS (UC) The University College offers a range of finance courses leading to professional qualifications. Contact the College for details: www.ifslearning.ac.uk. *Fees:* £10,500.

Imperial London Some 5,000 international students from over 110 countries. *English language entry requirement (or equivalent):* IELTS 6.5–7.0. Pre-sessional English course available for five weeks. *Fees:* Engineering and Life Sciences £26,000; Medicine £36,400; Biomedical Sciences £25,750; Chemistry £26,500; Mathematics £23,500; Physics £25,500. *Living costs:* £11,223–£14,838. Scholarships available.

Keele Large number of overseas students. *English language entry requirement (or equivalent):* IELTS 6.0–7.0. English language summer school before the start of degree course. International Foundation year degree programmes (entry IELTS 4.5). *Fees:* £12,325–£15,500; Medicine £27,000–£34,000. *Living costs:* £7,000–£9,500. General, course-specific and country-specific scholarships available for international students. Bursaries also available.

Kent About 25% of the student population are from overseas. English language requirement (or equivalent): IELTS 6.5. Pre-sessional courses and International Foundation programme available. *Fees:* Non-laboratory £12,890; Laboratory £15,380; International Foundation Programme £11,250. *Living costs:*

£7,000–£13,000. International scholarships available as well as for students from China, Hong Kong and Trinidad and Tobago.

Kingston More than 2,000 international students from over 70 countries. *English language entry requirement (or equivalent):* IELTS 6.0–6.5. Foundation level Science and Technology courses. Pre-sessional English language courses and free English support during degree studies. *Fees:* Classroom-based courses £11,700; Art and Design courses £14,100; Laboratory/other studio-based courses £13,000; Pharmacy courses £13,400. *Living costs:* £6,500–£10,000. International scholarship worth £4,000 per year of study.

Lancaster Twenty per cent of student population from over 100 countries. *English language entry requirement (or equivalent):* IELTS 5.5–6.0. Pre-sessional and in-session English language courses cover reading, writing, listening and speaking skills. *Fees:* £14,500–£28,050. *Living costs:* £7,840.

Leeds Approximately 4,000 students from outside the UK. *English language entry requirement (or equivalent):* IELTS 6.0, with a minimum of 5.5 in each component. *Fees:* £15,000–£31,500. *Living costs:* £575–£760 per month. International subject-specific scholarships available.

Leeds Beckett Over 2,500 international students from 110 countries. *English language entry requirement (or equivalent):* IELTS 6.0 (IELTS 4.0 or 5.0 for the International Foundation programme, starting September or February). Also general English courses. *Fees:* £9,700. *Living costs:* £885–£1,400 per week. Scholarships available.

Leeds Trinity *English language entry requirement (or equivalent):* IELTS 6.0 overall, with a minimum of 5.5 in each component (may be higher for some courses). Pre-sessional English course available. *Fees:* £11,000–£12,500. *Living costs:* £820 per month. International scholarship worth £1,000 awarded based on academic and professional merit.

Leicester Fourteen per cent of full-time students are from outside the UK. *English language entry requirement (or equivalent):* IELTS 6.0 (IELTS 6.5 for Law, Medicine, Arts and Social Science programmes, 5.5 for the Foundation year). English language preparatory programmes and on-going support Foundation programme. *Fees:* Non-Science degrees £14,000; Science degrees £17,270; Geography BSc £14,585; Medicine £17,270–£35,170. *Living costs:* £800 per month. International scholarships available.

Lincoln Over 2,000 students from more than 40 countries. *English language entry requirement (or equivalent):* IELTS 6.0. Pre- and in-sessional English language courses available. *Fees:* £12,800–£14,500. *Living costs:* £800 per month. Scholarships for Mathematics and Physics as well as for high-achieving international students. Engineering bursaries also available.

Liverpool Approximately 3800 international (non-EU) students from over 120 countries in the first year for undergraduate and postgraduate programmes. *English language entry requirement (or equivalent):* Science and Engineering: IELTS 6.0, min 5.5 in each component. Humanities and Social Sciences, Health and Life Sciences, Geography, Planning and Carmel College: IELTS 6.5, min 5.5 in each component. *Fees:* £13,850–£17,350; Dentistry, Medicine and Veterinary Science £30,850. *Living costs:* £440–£1,090 per month. Scholarships available, including special awards for students from Hong Kong.

Liverpool Hope Approximately 700 international students. *English language entry requirement (or equivalent):* IELTS 6.0. Language courses available. *Fees:* £10,800. *Living costs:* £7,380. International Excellence bursary and Music scholarship available.

Liverpool John Moores A large number of overseas students. *English language entry requirement (or equivalent):* IELTS 6.0. Pre-sessional and in-session English tuition available. *Fees:* Laboratory-based courses £12,000; Classroom-based courses £11,000–£11,350. *Living costs:* £800 per month. International scholarships available.

London (Birk) Students from over 120 countries *English language entry requirement (or equivalent):* IELTS 6.5; Arts Policy, English Literature, Law and Psychology 7.0. Pre-sessional English courses and free online study skills materials available. *Fees:* £13,000. *Living costs:* £12,000–£13,000. Scholarships available including a merit scholarship for students from Thailand, Vietnam and India.

London (Court) Approximately 25%–30% students are from overseas. *English language entry requirement (or equivalent):* IELTS 7.0. *Fees:* £16,800. *Living costs:* £1,500 per month. Scholarships available.

London (Gold) Students from more than 130 countries. *English language entry requirement (or equivalent):* IELTS 6.5; IELTS 5.5 for Extension degrees and IELTS 5.0 for entry to the one-year Foundation course. Certificate course in Language and Contemporary Culture or pre-sessional programmes available. *Fees:* £13,100–£19,420. *Living costs:* £650–£1,350 per month. Country-specific scholarships available.

London (Inst Educ) Over 1,000 international students from 111 different countries. *English language entry requirement (or equivalent):* IELTS 6.0. Academic English course available. *Fees:* £14,785. *Living costs:* £13,388. Scholarship for students from Vietnam.

London (Inst Paris) *English language entry requirement (or equivalent):* IELTS 6.5, with a minimum of 5.5 in each element. *Fees:* £13,200 (for 2015/16). *Living costs:* £296–£817 per month. Bursaries available.

London (King's) A large number of international students (20%). *English language entry requirement (or equivalent):* IELTS 6.0-7.5. Pre-sessional summer courses and a one-year Foundation course available. *Fees:* Classroom-based £16,250; Laboratory-based £21,750; Pharmacy £19,000. *Living costs:* £1,000–£1,200 per month. Awards available.

London (QM) Students from over 150 countries. *English language entry requirement (or equivalent):* IELTS 6.0-7.0. International Foundation course covering English language tuition and specialist courses in Business, Management, Economics, Mathematics, Spanish, Geography and European Studies. The course guarantees progression to linked degree courses including Law. *Fees:* Classroom-based subjects £14,100; Laboratory-based subjects £16,950; Dentistry and Medicine £30,900. *Living costs:* £1,050 per month. Subject-specific bursaries and scholarships available.

London (RH) Twenty per cent of students from over 120 countries. *English language entry requirement (or equivalent):* IELTS 6.0-7.0. Pre-sessional English course available. Ten-month Foundation course with studies in English language and introduction to specialist studies in a range of degree subjects. *Fees:* £13,500–£15,200. *Living costs:* £6,640–£9,860. Bursaries and scholarships available.

London (RVC) About 110 international students. *English language entry requirement (or equivalent):* IELTS 6.5-7.0. *Fees:* £12,610–£33,000. *Living costs:* £13,388–£20,900. International scholarships available.

London (St George's) There are a variety of courses that international and non-EU students can apply to. Full details on entry requirements for each individual course are available on the University website. *English language entry requirement (or equivalent):* a language level of at least CEFR B1. Pre-sessional English courses available. *Fees:* Physiotherapy £14,500; Biomedical Science £14,730; Diagnostic Radiography £15,970; Medicine £18,990 (years one and two), £33,640 (years three, four and five); International Medicine (six years) £30,760; International Graduate Medicine (four years) £33,640. *Living costs:* £1,200 per month.

London (SOAS) Large number of international students (30%). *English language entry requirement (or equivalent):* IELTS 7.0. A one-year Foundation programme and English language courses available with an entry requirement of IELTS 4.0. Three-day International Students' Orientation programme. *Fees:* £14,590. *Living costs:* £1,000 per month.

London (UCL) Some 7000 students (34% of the total student body) are from countries outside the UK. *English language entry requirement (or equivalent):* Science and Engineering IELTS 6.5; Arts courses 7.0; Speech Science and Law 7.5. *Fees:* Arts £16,130; Social Sciences, Humanities, Science, Engineering £21,320; Medicine £31,720. *Living costs:* £1,380 per month. Scholarships available.

London (UCL Sch Pharm) Approximately 25% of the student body are international students. *English language entry requirement (or equivalent):* IELTS 6.5. *Fees:* £18,670. *Living costs:* £950 per month.

London LSE Approximately 5,500 international students represent 150 countries. *English language entry requirement (or equivalent):* IELTS 7.0. Academic English language courses available. *Fees:* £17,712. *Living costs:* £1,000–£1,200 per month. A limited number of international scholarships available.

London Met Over 4,000 students from 147 countries. *English language entry requirement (or equivalent):* IELTS 6.0. One-year International Foundation programme (IELTS entry requirement 4.5). Full range of English courses. *Fees:* £10,950. *Living costs:* £1,020 per month.

London Regent's *English language entry requirement (or equivalent):* IELTS 6.0. *Fees:* £15,950. *Living costs:* £1,000–1,200 per month. Scholarships available.

London South Bank Approximately 2,500 international students, including 1300 from the EU. *English language entry requirement (or equivalent):* IELTS 6.0. Pre-study English course and a University Foundation course for overseas students. *Fees:* From £11,600. *Living costs:* £820–£2,200 Range of scholarships available including a Nationality scholarship and a Brazilian Scientific Mobility Programme.

Loughborough Some 1,000 undergraduate students from outside the UK. *English language entry requirement (or equivalent):* IELTS 6.5 with a minimum of 6.0 in all sub-tests. Special pre-sessional courses offered by the Student Support Centre. *Fees:* Classroom-based subjects and School of Business £14,950; Laboratory-based subjects £18,950. *Living costs:* £3,600. Self-funded international students are automatically considered for an international scholarship upon application.

Manchester A high proportion of international students from over 154 countries. *English language entry requirement (or equivalent):* IELTS 6.0–7.0. Foundation Year programme available as well as pre- and in-sessional English language courses. *Fees:* Non-laboratory £15,500; Laboratory £20,000; Clinical £35,000. *Living costs:* £9,390. Some scholarships and bursaries are available.

Manchester Met A large number of international students. *English language entry requirement (or equivalent):* IELTS 6.0. General, academic and pre-sessional English language courses available. *Fees:* Classroom-based courses £11,800; Laboratory-based courses £12,650; Physiotherapy £13,650 (for 2015/16); Architecture £19,000. *Living costs:* £7,380. Variety of international scholarships and awards available.

Middlesex International students from 30 countries around the world. *English language entry requirement (or equivalent):* IELTS 6.0. Pre-sessional English course available. *Fees:* £11,200–£11,500 (for 2015/16). *Living costs:* £950–£1,500 per month. Scholarships available.

NCH London *English language entry requirement (or equivalent):* IELTS 7.0, with a minimum of 6.5 in each component. *Fees:* £21,700. *Living costs:* £1,250 per month. International scholarship of £2,000 awarded based on academic ability.

Newcastle Over 2,500 students from outside the UK. *English language entry requirement (or equivalent):* IELTS 6.0–7.5. Pre- and in-sessional English language courses as well as an International Foundation programme. *Fees:* Non-science subjects £13,315; Science subjects £17,080; Medicine/Dentistry £31,610. *Living costs:* £8,600. International scholarships available.

Newman *English language entry requirement (or equivalent):* IELTS 6.0. *Fees:* £11,000. *Living costs:* £600 per month. Scholarships available.

Northampton Over 1,000 international students from over 130 countries. *English language entry requirement (or equivalent):* IELTS 6.0. English language courses available. *Fees:* £10,900 for all BA/BSc courses, except Podiatry and Occupational Therapy (£11,900). *Living costs:* £2,583–£5,586. Scholarships and bursaries are available, please see our website for more details.

Northumbria Students from over 100 countries. *English language entry requirement (or equivalent):* IELTS 5.5–6.5. English language and Foundation courses available. *Fees:* £12,000–£15,500. *Living costs:* £820 per month. Country scholarships for students from over 15 countries; some merit-based course scholarships.

Norwich Arts Approximately 650 international students. *English language entry requirement (or equivalent):* IELTS 6.0 (with a minimum of 5.5 in all sections). English language study and pre-course training offered with the International Foundation course. *Fees:* £13,000.

Nottingham Students from over 150 countries. *English language entry requirement (or equivalent):* IELTS 6.0–6.5 (7.5 for Medicine). Pre- and in-sessional English language courses available. *Fees:* £14,850–

£19,120; Medicine £20,140 (Years 1 and 2), £35,010 (Years 3, 4 and 5). *Living costs:* £820 per month. Scholarships for siblings and Science applicants.

Nottingham Trent Large number of overseas students. *English language entry requirement (or equivalent):* IELTS 6.0–7.0. English language courses (19, 10 and five weeks) available. *Fees:* £12,100–£12,900. *Living costs:* £8,000. International scholarships available.

Open University Courses are open to students throughout the world with study online or with educational partners. Tutorial support is by telephone, fax, computer conferencing or email. *Fees:* Non-EU students' fees vary depending on type of course.

Oxford Students from 140 countries (one third of the student body). *English language entry requirement (or equivalent):* IELTS 7.0. English language courses available. *Fees:* Tuition fee £15,296–£22,515, Clinical Medicine £31,005; College fee £7,135. *Living costs:* £970–£1,433 per month. University and college scholarships and awards are available.

Oxford Brookes Large number of international students. *English language entry requirement (or equivalent):* IELTS scores for Engineering and Construction 5.5; for Business, Social Sciences, Computing and Humanities 6.0; for Law and Psychology 6.5. Large number of English language support courses from two weeks to two years offered by the Centre for English Language Studies. *Fees:* £12,640–£14,500. *Living costs:* £10,850. Engineering scholarship available for students from India as well as family awards.

Plymouth *English language entry requirement (or equivalent):* IELTS 6.0. 'English for University' courses available with IELTS entry requirement of 4.5. *Fees:* Classroom-based courses £12,250; Laboratory-based courses £12,500. *Living costs:* £1,000 per month. International scholarship available.

Portsmouth Students from over 100 countries. *English language entry requirement (or equivalent):* IELTS 6.0 (5.5 for Foundation-level study). Induction, academic skills and language courses available. *Fees:* Classroom-based courses £12,000; Classroom- and laboratory-based courses £12,700; Laboratory-based courses £13,700. *Living costs:* £7,000–£8,000. International scholarships available.

Queen Margaret Around 25% of students are international coming from over 70 countries. *English language entry requirement (or equivalent):* IELTS 6.0. English language support available. *Fees:* Classroom-based courses £11,000; Laboratory/studio-based courses £12,500. *Living costs:* £7,380. Scholarships for students from China, Canada, USA and India as well as other international scholarships.

Queen's Belfast Approximately 1,200 international students from over 80 countries. *English language entry requirement (or equivalent):* IELTS 6.0–7.0. Special English language summer schools and pre-university language courses are provided, also weekly language courses. Three-day orientation programme held before the start of the academic year. *Fees:* Classroom-based courses £13,945; Courses with a substantial workshop or laboratory component or pre-clinical elements of nursing courses £17,885; Pre-clinical elements of medical and dental courses £18,470; Clinical elements of medical and dental courses £34,830. *Living costs:* £5,500–£7,000. International scholarships available.

Reading More than 5,000 students from over 140 countries. *English language entry requirement (or equivalent):* IELTS 6.5–7.0. International Foundation programme offering English language tuition and specialist studies in a choice of 14 subjects. Other pre-sessional English courses offered. *Fees:* Non-laboratory courses £15,300; Laboratory courses £18,400. *Living costs:* £850–£1,500 per month. Some scholarships offered.

Robert Gordon Over 1,000 international students from more than 65 countries. *English language entry requirement (or equivalent):* IELTS 6.0. Pre-sessional English programme available as well as language classes and one-to-one support during the year. *Fees:* £11,400–£14,850. *Living costs:* £7,000–£9,000. Merit scholarships for specific subjects available.

Roehampton Students from more than 140 countries. *English language entry requirement (or equivalent):* IELTS 6.0, with a minimum of 5.5 in each component. International Foundation programme and pre-sessional English courses available. *Fees:* £12,500. *Living costs:* £7,500–£8,500. International scholarships available.

Royal Agricultural Univ Over 1,200 international students from over 40 different countries. *English language entry requirement (or equivalent):* IELTS 6.0. International Foundation Year and English language courses available. *Fees:* £10,000. *Living costs:* £8,000–£10,000. International scholarships available.

St Andrews Over 1,500 international students from more than 120 different countries. *English language entry requirement (or equivalent):* IELTS 6.5–7.0. International Foundation programme available as well as pre- and in-sessional English language courses. *Fees:* £17,890; Medicine £25,200. *Living costs:* £14,000–£16,000. Scholarships available.

St Mark and St John *English language entry requirement (or equivalent):* IELTS 6.0. English Preparation Programme available. *Fees:* £11,000; Speech and Language Therapy £11,750. *Living costs:* £1,000 per month.

St Mary's Qualifications from any country will be considered and measured against British equivalents. 5,000 international students. *English language entry requirement (or equivalent):* IELTS 6.0 (minimum 5.5). In-sessional English language programme available. *Fees:* £11,000. *Living costs:* £7,000–£8,000.

Salford More than 3,000 international students from over 100 countries. *English language entry requirement (or equivalent):* IELTS 6.0–7.0. English study programmes and a very comprehensive International Foundation year. *Fees:* £11,500–£13,300. *Living costs:* £800–£1,000 per month. Scholarships and bursaries available.

Sheffield Over 5,000 international students from 125 countries. *English language entry requirement (or equivalent):* IELTS 6.0. Preparatory English courses (one–nine months) and an international summer school with English classes. *Fees:* £15,250–£19,500; Clinical Medicine £34,750. *Living costs:* £7,380. Faculty scholarships and international merit scholarships available.

Sheffield Hallam Over 80 countries represented by 3,000 international students. *English language entry requirement (or equivalent):* IELTS 6.0–7.0. Pre-sessional and academic English language courses available. *Fees:* £12,250–£12,500. *Living costs:* £800 per month. International scholarships available as well as country-specific scholarships for students from Africa, South Asia and South East Asia.

South Wales *English language entry requirement (or equivalent):* IELTS from 6.0. Pre-sessional course offered in English with course lengths of between five and 10 weeks depending on the applicant's proficiency. An International Foundation Programme is also offered. *Fees:* £11,900. *Living costs:* £4,800–£8,800. International students automatically considered for a scholarship upon application.

Southampton Over 6,500 international students from more than 135 countries. *English language entry requirement (or equivalent):* IELTS 6.0–7.0. English courses offered and also an International Foundation course covering Arts, Humanities, Social Sciences and Law. *Fees:* £15,390–£18,910; Clinical Medicine £40,230. *Living costs:* £7,200–£8,800. International Merit scholarship available.

Southampton Solent Students from over 50 countries. *English language entry requirement (or equivalent):* IELTS 6.0. Induction programme and language tuition available. *Fees:* Engineering and technology-based courses (Band B) £11,475; Courses with a studio, lab or fieldwork element (Band C) £11,000; All other courses (Band D) £10,500. *Living costs:* £8,000.

Staffordshire Students from over 70 countries. *English language entry requirement (or equivalent):* IELTS 6.0. English tuition available. *Fees:* £10,600. *Living costs:* £7,000. International scholarships available.

Stirling Thirteen per cent of the student population are overseas students from 70 nationalities. *English language entry requirement (or equivalent):* IELTS 6.0. English language tuition available as well as an International Foundation in Business, Finance, Economics and Marketing. *Fees:* £11,555–£13,760. *Living costs:* £5,000–£6,000. Some scholarships are available. Please see www.stir.ac.uk/scholarships.

Stranmillis (UC) *Fees:* £13,945. *Living costs:* £7,500.

Strathclyde Students from 100 countries. *English language entry requirement (or equivalent):* IELTS 6.5. Pre-entry and pre-sessional English tuition available. *Fees:* £13,000–£18,600. *Living costs:* £7,700–£9,800.

Sunderland Approximately 17 per cent of students are international and come from over 100 countries. *English language entry requirement (or equivalent):* IELTS 6.0. English language tuition available. *Fees:* £10,500. *Living costs:* £485–£1,164 per month. International students are automatically considered for a £1,500 scholarship upon application.

Surrey Students from over 120 different countries. *English language entry requirement (or equivalent):* IELTS 6.0–7.5. English language courses and summer courses offered. *Fees:* £14,000–£17,500; Veterinary Medicine £27,500. *Living costs:* £6,479. Scholarships and bursaries offered, including awards for students on Civil Engineering courses.

Sussex More than 2,500 international students. *English language entry requirement (or equivalent):* IELTS 6.0–7.0 (7.5 for Medicine). English language and study skills courses available. International Foundation courses offered, covering English language tuition and a choice from Humanities, Law, Media Studies, Social Sciences and Cultural Studies and Science and Technology. *Fees:* £14,800–£18,300; Medicine £27,405. *Living costs:* £550–£1,120 per week. International scholarships available.

Swansea Students from over 100 countries. *English language entry requirement (or equivalent):* IELTS 6.0–6.5. Pre-sessional English language courses available and on-going support during degree courses. *Fees:* £12,900–£16,950. *Living costs:* £6,000–£9,000. Some overseas scholarships and prizes.

Teesside Students from over 100 countries. *English language entry requirement (or equivalent):* IELTS 5.5–7.0. Free English courses available throughout the year while following degree programmes. International summer school available. *Fees:* £10,750. *Living costs:* £1,015 per month. Scholarship available for self-funded students.

Trinity Saint David International students are well represented at the University. *English language entry requirement (or equivalent):* IELTS 6.0. International Foundation programme available. *Fees:* £10,000 (for 2015/16). *Living costs:* £6,500–£7,500. International scholarships available.

UHI *English language entry requirement (or equivalent):* IELTS 6.0; minimum 5.5 in all four components. *Fees:* Art, Humanities, Social Science and Business courses £10,000; Science and Technology courses £11,000. *Living costs:* £610–£850 per month.

Ulster Students from over 40 countries. *English language entry requirement (or equivalent):* IELTS 6.0. Pre- and in-sessional English language courses available. International Foundation Programme in Business is also available. *Fees:* £12,890. *Living costs:* £6,000–£7,000. International scholarships available.

Univ Law More than 1,200 students from over 100 countries. *English language entry requirement (or equivalent):* IELTS 6.5–7.0. *Fees:* £23,000–£28,500. *Living costs:* £8,000. International scholarships available.

UWE Bristol More than 1,750 international students. *English language entry requirement (or equivalent):* IELTS 6.0, with a minimum of 5.5 in each component. Pre- and in-sessional English language courses offered. *Fees:* £11,750. *Living costs:* £7,000–£14,000. Scholarships based on academic, sports and entrepreneurial excellence available as well as country- and programme-specific scholarships.

Warwick Over 3,500 international students. *English language entry requirement (or equivalent):* IELTS 6.0 for Science courses, 6.5 for Arts courses, 6.5 for MORSE courses, and 7.0 for Social Studies and Business courses. English language support available. *Fees:* Classroom-based courses £16,620; Laboratory-based courses £21,200; Medicine £19,400–£33,820. *Living costs:* £6,500–£7,500. More than 20 awards available for overseas students.

West London A large number of international students. *English language entry requirement (or equivalent):* IELTS 5.5. International Foundation programme and English language support available. *Fees:* £10,650. *Living costs:* £13,700. International scholarships available.

West Scotland Over 1,100 international students from around 70 countries. *English language entry requirement (or equivalent):* IELTS 6.0. English language Foundation course available. *Fees:* £11,220. *Living costs:* £600 per month. International scholarships available.

Westminster Students from 150 countries (51% Asian). *English language entry requirement (or equivalent):* IELTS 6.0. Pre- and in-sessional Academic English courses available. *Fees:* £12,250. *Living costs:* £900–£1,800. International scholarships available.

Winchester Some 600 international students from 60 countries. *English language entry requirement (or equivalent):* IELTS 6.0. Language courses available. *Fees:* £11,300. *Living costs:* £7,500–£8,500. International scholarships available.

Wolverhampton Over 2,500 international students from over 100 countries. *English language entry requirement (or equivalent):* IELTS 6.0. English courses available over one or two months or longer. International student programme. *Fees:* £11,250. *Living costs:* £7,200. Scholarships and bursaries available.

Worcester *English language entry requirement (or equivalent):* IELTS 6.0. English language support available. *Fees:* £11,400. *Living costs:* £6,000–7,500. Two international scholarships of up to £3,000 available.

York Fifteen per cent of students from outside the UK. *English language entry requirement (or equivalent):* IELTS 6.5–7.0 (7.5 for Medicine). Six-month and pre-sessional English language courses. Intensive vacation courses. *Fees:* £15,680–£20,100; Medicine £25,930. *Living costs:* £7,420–£10,180. Several scholarships for overseas students.

York St John *English language entry requirement (or equivalent):* IELTS 6.0. Pre-sessional courses and International Foundation Programme available. *Fees:* £10,000; Occupational Therapy/Physiotherapy £11,500. *Living costs:* £820 per month. Self-funded international students are eligible for an International Fee Waiver of £1,000.

BRITISH OVERSEAS TERRITORIES STUDENTS

Students from British Overseas Territories are now treated as home students for fee purposes at universities and other institutions of higher education in the UK. The territories to which this policy applies are:

British Overseas Territories Anguilla, Bermuda, British Antarctic Territory, British Indian Ocean Territory, British Virgin Islands, Cayman Islands, Falkland Islands, Montserrat, Pitcairn, Henderson, Ducie and Oeno Islands, South Georgia and the South Sandwich Islands, St Helena and Dependencies (Ascension Island and Tristan de Cunha), Turks and Caicos Islands.

Overseas Territories of other EU member states Aruba, Faroe Islands, French Polynesia, French Southern and Antarctic Territories, Greenland, Netherland Antilles (Bonaire, Curaçao, Saba, Sint Eustatius and Sint Maarten), the Territory of New Caledonia and Dependencies, St-Barthélemy (St Barth), St Pierre et Miquelon, Wallis and Futuna Islands.

9

DIRECTORY OF UNIVERSITIES AND OTHER INSTITUTIONS OFFERING HIGHER EDUCATION COURSES

SECTION 1: UNIVERSITIES AND UNIVERSITY COLLEGES

Listed below are universities and university colleges in the United Kingdom that offer degree and diploma courses at higher education level. Applications to these institutions are submitted through UCAS except for part-time courses, private universities and colleges, and further education courses. For current information refer to the websites shown and also to www.ucas.com for a comprehensive list of degree and diploma courses (see **Appendix 4**).

Aberdeen University of Aberdeen, Students Admissions and School Leavers, University Office, King's College, Aberdeen, Scotland AB24 3FX. Tel 01224 272000; www.abdn.ac.uk

Abertay Abertay University, Bell Street, Dundee, Scotland DD1 1HG. Tel 01382 308045; www.abertay.ac.uk

Aberystwyth Aberystwyth University, Undergraduate Admissions Office, Cledwyn Building, Penglais Campus, Aberystwyth, Wales SY23 3DD. Tel 01970 622021; www.aber.ac.uk

Anglia Ruskin Anglia Ruskin University, Bishop Hall Lane, Chelmsford, England CM1 1SQ. Tel 01245 493131; www.anglia.ac.uk

Arts London University of the Arts London, University of the Arts London, 272 High Holborn, London, England WC1V 7EY. Tel 020 7514 6000; www.arts.ac.uk

Aston Aston University, The Registry (Admissions), Aston Triangle, Birmingham, England B4 7ET. Tel 0121 204 4444; www.aston.ac.uk

Bangor Bangor University, Admissions Office, Bangor University, Bangor, Wales LL57 2TF. Tel 01248 383717; www.bangor.ac.uk

Bath University of Bath, Claverton Down, Bath, England BA2 7AY. Tel 01225 383019; www.bath.ac.uk

Bath Spa Bath Spa University, Admissions Office, Newton Park, Newton St Loe, Bath, England BA2 9BN. Tel 01225 875875; www.bathspa.ac.uk

Bedfordshire University of Bedfordshire, The Admissions Office, University Square, Luton, England LU1 3JU. Tel 01234 400400; www.beds.ac.uk

Birmingham University of Birmingham, Edgbaston, Birmingham, England B15 2TT. Tel 0121 414 3344; www.birmingham.ac.uk

Birmingham (UC) University College Birmingham, Summer Row, Birmingham, England B3 1JB. Tel 0121 604 1040; www.ucb.ac.uk

Birmingham City Birmingham City University, City North Campus, Birmingham, England B42 2SU. Tel 0121 331 5000; www.bcu.ac.uk

Bishop Grosseteste Bishop Grosseteste University, Longdales Road, Lincoln, England LN1 3DY. Tel 01522 527347; www.bishopg.ac.uk

Bolton University of Bolton, Recruitment and Admissions, Deane Road, Bolton, England BL3 5AB. Tel 01204 900600; www.bolton.ac.uk

Bournemouth Bournemouth University, Talbot Campus, Fern Barrow, Poole, England BH12 5BB. Tel 01202 961916; www.bournemouth.ac.uk

Bournemouth Arts Arts University Bournemouth, Wallisdown, Poole, England BH12 5HH. Tel 01202 533011; www.aub.ac.uk

BPP BPP University, 6th Floor Boulton House, Chorlton Street, Manchester, England M1 3HY. Tel 03331 224359; www.bpp.com

Bradford University of Bradford, Course Enquiries Office, Richmond Road, Bradford, England BD7 1DP. Tel 0800 073 1255; www.bradford.ac.uk

Brighton University of Brighton, The Registry (Admissions), Mithras House, Lewes Road, Brighton, England BN2 4AT. Tel 01273 600900; www.brighton.ac.uk

Brighton and Sussex (MS) Brighton and Sussex Medical School, BSMS Admissions, The Checkland Building, University of Brighton, Brighton, England BN1 9PH. Tel 01273 643529; www.bsms.ac.uk

Bristol University of Bristol, Howard House, Queens Avenue, Bristol, England BS8 1SN. Tel 0117 928 9000; www.bristol.ac.uk

Brunel Brunel University London, Admissions Office, Uxbridge, England UB8 3PH. Tel 01895 265265; www.brunel.ac.uk

Buckingham University of Buckingham, Admissions Office, Hunter Street, Buckingham, England MK18 1EG. Tel 01280 820313; www.buckingham.ac.uk

Bucks New Buckinghamshire New University, Admissions, Queen Alexandra Road, High Wycombe, England HP11 2JZ. Tel 0800 056 5660,; www.bucks.ac.uk

Cambridge University of Cambridge, Cambridge Admissions Office, Fitzwilliam House, 32 Trumpington Street, Cambridge, England CB2 1QY. Tel 01223 333308; www.cam.ac.uk

Canterbury Christ Church Canterbury Christ Church University, Admissions, North Holmes Road, Canterbury, England CT1 1QU. Tel 01227 782900; www.canterbury.ac.uk

Cardiff Cardiff University, Admissions, MacKenzie House, 30–36 Newport Road, Cardiff, Wales CF10 3XQ. Tel 029 2087 4000; www.cardiff.ac.uk

Cardiff Met Cardiff Metropolitan University, Llandaff Campus, Western Avenue, Cardiff, Wales CF5 2YB. Tel 029 2041 6070; Admissions Enquiries 029 2041 6010; www.cardiffmet.ac.uk

Central Lancashire University of Central Lancashire, Course Enquiries, University of Central Lancashire, Preston, England PR1 2HE. Tel 01772 892400; www.uclan.ac.uk

Chester University of Chester, Undergraduate Admissions, Parkgate Road, Chester, England CH1 4BJ. Tel 01244 511000; www.chester.ac.uk

Chichester University of Chichester, Admissions, Bishop Otter Campus, College Lane, Chichester, England PO19 6PE. Tel 01243 816002; www.chi.ac.uk

City City University London, Undergraduate Admissions Office, Northampton Square, London, England EC1V 0HB. Tel 020 7040 5060; www.city.ac.uk

Coventry Coventry University, The Alan Berry Building, Priory Street, Coventry, England CV1 5FB. Tel 024 7765 2222; www.coventry.ac.uk

Creative Arts University for the Creative Arts, Enquiries Service, Falkner Road, Farnham, England GU9 7DS. Tel 01252 892960; www.ucreative.ac.uk

Cumbria University of Cumbria, Fusehill Street, Carlisle, Cumbria, England CA1 2HH. Tel 0845 606 1144; www.cumbria.ac.uk

De Montfort De Montfort University, De Montfort University, The Gateway, Leicester, England LE1 9BH. Tel 0116 250 6070; www.dmu.ac.uk

Derby University of Derby, Admissions, Kedleston Road, Derby, England DE22 1GB. Tel 01332 591167; www.derby.ac.uk

Dundee University of Dundee, Admissions and Student Recruitment, Nethergate, Dundee, Scotland DD1 4HN. Tel 01382 383838; www.dundee.ac.uk

Durham Durham University, The Palatine Centre, Stockton Road, Durham, England DH1 3LE. Tel 0191 334 6128; www.dur.ac.uk

East Anglia University of East Anglia, Admissions Office, Norwich Research Park, Norwich, England NR4 7TJ. Tel 01603 591515; www.uea.ac.uk

East London University of East London, Docklands Campus, 4–6 University Way, London, England E16 2RD. Tel 020 8223 3333; www.uel.ac.uk

Edge Hill Edge Hill University, St Helens Road, Ormskirk, England L39 4QP. Tel 01695 575171; www.edgehill.ac.uk

Edinburgh University of Edinburgh, Old College, South Bridge, Edinburgh, Scotland EH8 9YL. Tel 0131 650 1000; www.ed.ac.uk

Edinburgh Napier Edinburgh Napier University, Student Recruitment Team, Merchiston Campus, Edinburgh, Scotland EH1 05DT. Tel 0333 900 6040; www.napier.ac.uk

Essex University of Essex, Undergraduate Admissions, Wivenhoe Park, Colchester, England CO4 3SQ. Tel 01206 873666; www.essex.ac.uk

Exeter University of Exeter, Admissions Office, 8th Floor, Laver Building, North Park Road, Exeter, England EX4 4QE. Tel 0844 620 0012; www.exeter.ac.uk

Falmouth Falmouth University, Admissions Office, Woodlane, Falmouth, England TR11 4RH. Tel 01326 213730; www.falmouth.ac.uk

Glasgow University of Glasgow, Recruitment and International Office, 71 Southpark Avenue, Glasgow, Scotland G12 8QQ. Tel 0141 330 2000; www.gla.ac.uk

Glasgow Caledonian Glasgow Caledonian University, Cowcaddens Road, Glasgow, Scotland G4 0BA. Tel 0141 331 8630; www.gcu.ac.uk

Gloucestershire University of Gloucestershire, Admissions Office, The Park, Cheltenham, England GL50 2RH. Tel 0844 801 0001; www.glos.ac.uk

Glyndŵr Glyndŵr University, Mold Road, Wrexham, Wales LL11 2AW. Tel 01978 293439; www.glyndwr.ac.uk

Greenwich University of Greenwich, Old Royal Naval College, Park Row, London, England SE10 9LS. Tel 020 8331 9000; www.gre.ac.uk

Harper Adams Harper Adams University, Admissions Office, Newport, England TF10 8NB. Tel 01952 815000; www.harper-adams.ac.uk

Heriot-Watt Heriot-Watt University, Admissions Unit, Edinburgh Campus, Edinburgh, Scotland EH14 4AS. Tel 0131 449 5111; www.hw.ac.uk

Hertfordshire University of Hertfordshire, University Admissions Service, College Lane, Hatfield, England AL10 9AB. Tel 01707 284800; www.herts.ac.uk

Huddersfield University of Huddersfield, Admissions Office, Queensgate, Huddersfield, England HD1 3DH. Tel 01484 473969; www.hud.ac.uk

Hull University of Hull, Admissions Service, Cottingham Road, Hull, England HU6 7RX. Tel 01482 466100; www.hull.ac.uk

Hull York (MS) Hull York Medical School, Admissions Office, University of York, Heslington, York, England YO10 5DD. Tel 0870 124 5500; www.hyms.ac.uk

IFS (UC) IFS University College, 25 Lovat Lane, London, England EC3R 8EB. Tel 0207 337 6293; www.ifslearning.ac.uk

Imperial London Imperial College London, Registry, Level 3 Sherfield Building, South Kensington Campus, London, England SW7 2AZ. Tel 020 7589 5111; www.imperial.ac.uk

Keele   Keele University, Admissions, Directorate of Planning and Academic Administration, Keele University, Keele, England ST5 5BG. Tel 01782 734010; www.keele.ac.uk

Kent   University of Kent, Enrolment Management Services, The Registry, Canterbury, England CT2 7NZ. Tel 01227 827272; www.kent.ac.uk

Kingston   Kingston University, River House, 53–57 High Street, Kingston upon Thames, England KT1 1LQ. Tel 020 8417 9000; www.kingston.ac.uk

Lancaster   Lancaster University, Undergraduate Admissions Office, Bailrigg, Lancaster, England LA1 4YW. Tel 01524 592028; www.lancaster.ac.uk

Leeds   University of Leeds, Undergraduate Admissions Office, Leeds, England LS2 9JT. Tel 0113 343 2336; www.leeds.ac.uk

Leeds Beckett   Leeds Beckett University, City Campus, Leeds, England LS1 3HE. Tel 0113 812 3113; www.leedsbeckett.ac.uk

Leeds Trinity   Leeds Trinity University, Admissions, Brownberrie Lane, Horsforth, Leeds, England LS18 5HD. Tel 0113 283 7123; www.leedstrinity.ac.uk/courses/how-to-apply

Leicester   University of Leicester, Admissions Office, University Road, Leicester, England LE1 7RH. Tel 0116 252 5281; www.le.ac.uk

Lincoln   University of Lincoln, Academic Registry, Brayford Pool, Lincoln, England LN6 7TS. Tel 01522 886644; www.lincoln.ac.uk

Liverpool   University of Liverpool, Marketing and Communications, Foundation Building, Brownlow Hill, Liverpool, England L69 7ZX. Tel 0151 794 5927; www.liv.ac.uk

Liverpool Hope   Liverpool Hope University, Student Recruitment, Hope Park, Liverpool, England L16 9JD. Tel 0151 291 3111; www.hope.ac.uk

Liverpool John Moores   Liverpool John Moores University, Kingsway House, 2nd Floor, Hatton Garden, Liverpool, England L3 2AJ. Tel 0151 231 5090; www.ljmu.ac.uk

London (Birk)   Birkbeck, University of London, Malet Street, London, England WC1E 7HX. Tel 020 7631 6000; www.bbk.ac.uk

London (Court)   Courtauld Institute of Art, University of London, Somerset House, Strand, London, England WC2R 0RN. Tel 020 7848 2645; www.courtauld.ac.uk

London (Gold)   Goldsmiths, University of London, Lewisham Way, London, England SE14 6NW. Tel 020 7919 7171; www.gold.ac.uk

London (Hey)   Heythrop College, University of London, Registry, Kensington Square, London, England W8 5HN. Tel 020 7795 6600; www.heythrop.ac.uk

London (Inst Educ)   Institute of Education, University of London, 20 Bedford Way, London, England WC1H 0AL. Tel 020 7612 6000; www.ioe.ac.uk

London (Inst Paris)   University of London Institute in Paris, 9–11 rue de Constantine, 75340, Paris, France Cedex 07. Tel +33 (0) 1 44 11 73 83/76; www.ulip.lon.ac.uk

London (King's)   King's College London, University of London, Enquiries, Strand, London, England WC2R 2LS. Tel 020 7836 5454; www.kcl.ac.uk

London (QM)   Queen Mary University of London, Queen Mary University of London, Admissions Office, Mile End Road, London, England E1 4NS. Tel 020 7882 5511; www.qmul.ac.uk

London (RH)   Royal Holloway, University of London, Egham Hill, Egham, England TW20 0EX. Tel 01784 434455; www.rhul.ac.uk

London (RVC)   Royal Veterinary College, University of London, Royal Veterinary College, Royal College Street, London, England NW1 0TU. Tel 020 7468 5147; www.rvc.ac.uk

London (St George's) St George's, University of London, Cranmer Terrace, London, England SW17 0RE. Tel 020 8672 9944; www.sgul.ac.uk

London (SOAS) School of Oriental and African Studies, University of London, Thornhaugh Street, Russell Square, London, England WC1H 0XG. Tel 020 7637 2388; www.soas.ac.uk

London (UCL) University College London, University of London, University College London, Gower Street, London, England WC1E 6BT. Tel 020 7679 3000; www.ucl.ac.uk (or www.ucl.ac.uk/prospectus if you want to link directly to the Undergraduate Prospectus)

London (UCL Sch Pharm) UCL School of Pharmacy University College London, University of London, 29–39 Brunswick Square, London, England WC1N 1AX. Tel 020 7753 5831; www.ucl.ac.uk/pharmacy

London LSE London School of Economics and Political Science, Student Recruitment Office, Houghton Street, London, England WC2A 2AE. Tel 020 7955 6133; www.lse.ac.uk

London Met London Metropolitan University, Admissions Office, 166–220 Holloway Road, London, England N7 8DB. Tel 020 7133 4200; www.londonmet.ac.uk

London Regent's Regent's University London, Inner Circle, Regent's Park, London, England NW1 4NS. Tel 020 7487 7700; www.regents.ac.uk

London South Bank London South Bank University, Admissions Office, 90 London Road, London, England SE1 6LN. Tel 0800 923 8888; www.lsbu.ac.uk

Loughborough Loughborough University, Undergraduate Admissions Office, Loughborough, England LE11 3TU. Tel 01509 223522; www.lboro.ac.uk

Manchester University of Manchester, Student Recruitment and Admissions, Rutherford Building, Oxford Road, Manchester, England M13 9PL. Tel 0161 275 2077; www.manchester.ac.uk

Manchester Met Manchester Metropolitan University, Admissions Office, All Saints Building, All Saints, Manchester, England M15 6BH. Tel 0161 247 2000; www.mmu.ac.uk

Medway Sch Pharm Medway School of Pharmacy, Anson Building, Central Avenue, Chatham Maritime, Chatham, England ME4 4TB. Tel 01634 202936; www.msp.ac.uk

Middlesex Middlesex University, Hendon Campus, The Burroughs, London, England NW4 4BT. Tel 020 8411 5555; www.mdx.ac.uk

Mont Rose (Coll) Mont Rose College, 267 Cranbrook Road, Ilford, London, England IG1 4TG. Tel 020 8556 5009; https://mrcollege.ac.uk

NCH London New College of the Humanities, 19 Bedford Square, London, England WC1B 3HH. Tel 020 7637 4550; www.nchlondon.ac.uk

Newcastle Newcastle University, Student Services, King's Gate, Newcastle-upon-Tyne, England NE1 7RU. Tel 0191 208 6000; www.ncl.ac.uk

Newman Newman University, Admissions Registrar, Genners Lane, Bartley Green, Birmingham, England B32 3NT. Tel 0121 476 1181; www.newman.ac.uk

Northampton University of Northampton, Enquiries, Park Campus, Boughton Green Road, Northampton, England NN2 7AL. Tel 0800 358 2232; www.northampton.ac.uk

Northumbria Northumbria University, 2 Ellison Place, Newcastle-upon-Tyne, England NE1 8ST. Tel 0191 349 5600; www.northumbria.ac.uk

Norwich Arts Norwich University of the Arts, Admissions, Francis House, 3–7 Redwell Street, Norwich, England NR2 4SN. Tel 01603 610561; www.nua.ac.uk

Nottingham University of Nottingham, University Park, Nottingham, England NG7 2RD. Tel 0115 951 5559; www.nottingham.ac.uk

Nottingham Trent Nottingham Trent University, Admissions, Nottingham Trent University, Dryden Centre, Burton Street, Nottingham, England NG1 4BU. Tel 0115 848 4200; www.ntu.ac.uk

Open University Open University, Walton Hall, Milton Keynes, England MK7 6AA. Tel 0300 303 5303; www.open.ac.uk

Oxford University of Oxford, Undergraduate Admissions and Outreach, University Offices, Wellington Square, Oxford, UK OX1 2JD. Tel 01865 288000; www.ox.ac.uk

Oxford Brookes Oxford Brookes University, Admissions Office, Headington Campus, Gipsy Lane, Oxford, England OX3 0BP. Tel 01865 484848; www.brookes.ac.uk

Plymouth Plymouth University, Central Admissions, Drake Circus, Plymouth, England PL4 8AA. Tel 01752 585858; www.plymouth.ac.uk

Portsmouth University of Portsmouth, Academic Registry, University House, Winston Churchill Avenue, Portsmouth, England PO1 2UP. Tel 023 9284 8484; www.port.ac.uk

Queen Margaret Queen Margaret University, Edinburgh, The Admissions Office, Queen Margaret University, Queen Margaret University Drive, Musselburgh, Edinburgh, Scotland EH21 6UU. Tel 0131 474 0000; www.qmu.ac.uk

Queen's Belfast Queen's University Belfast, Admissions Service, University Road, Belfast, Northern Ireland BT7 1NN. Tel 028 9024 5133; www.qub.ac.uk

Reading University of Reading, Student Recruitment Office, PO Box 217, Reading, England RG6 6AH. Tel 0118 378 8372; www.reading.ac.uk

Richmond (Am Int Univ) Richmond, The American International University in London, Queen's Road, Richmond-upon-Thames, England TW10 6JP. Tel 020 8332 8200; www.richmond.ac.uk

Robert Gordon Robert Gordon University, Admissions Office, Garthdee House, Garthdee Road, Aberdeen, Scotland AB10 7QB. Tel 01224 262728; www.rgu.ac.uk

Roehampton University of Roehampton, Recruitment, International and Admissions, Lawrence Building, University of Roehampton, Roehampton Lane, London, England SW15 5PJ. Tel 020 8392 3232; www.roehampton.ac.uk

Royal Agricultural Univ Royal Agricultural University, Stroud Road, Cirencester, England GL7 6JS. Tel 01285 652531; www.rau.ac.uk

St Andrews University of St Andrews, Admissions Application Centre, St Katharine's West, 16 The Scores, St Andrews, Scotland KY16 9AX. Tel 01334 462150; www.st-andrews.ac.uk

St Mark and St John University of St Mark and St John, Admissions Office, Derriford Road, Plymouth, England PL6 8BH. Tel 01752 636890; www.marjon.ac.uk

St Mary's St Mary's University, Registry, Waldegrave Road, Strawberry Hill, Twickenham, England TW1 4SX. Tel 020 8240 4029; www.stmarys.ac.uk

Salford University of Salford, Admissions Officer, The Crescent, Salford, England M5 4WT. Tel 0161 295 4545; www.salford.ac.uk

Sheffield University of Sheffield, Western Bank, Sheffield, England S10 2TN. Tel 0114 222 8030; www.sheffield.ac.uk

Sheffield Hallam Sheffield Hallam University, Admissions Office, City Campus, Howard Street, Sheffield, England S1 1WB. Tel 0114 225 5555; www.shu.ac.uk

South Wales University of South Wales, Treforest Campus, Pontypridd, Wales CF37 1DL. Tel 0345 576 0101; www.southwales.ac.uk

Southampton University of Southampton, University Road, Southampton, England SO17 1BJ. Tel 023 8059 5000; www.southampton.ac.uk

Southampton Solent Southampton Solent University, Admissions & Enrolment, East Park Terrace, Southampton, England SO14 0YN. Tel 023 8201 3000; www.solent.ac.uk

Staffordshire Staffordshire University, Admissions & Enquiries, College Road, Stoke-on-Trent, England ST4 2DE. Tel 01782 294400; www.staffs.ac.uk

Stirling University of Stirling, UG Admissions Office, Stirling, Scotland FK9 4LA. Tel 01786 467044; www.stir.ac.uk

Stranmillis (UC) Stranmillis University College, Academic Registry, Stranmillis Road, Belfast, Northern Ireland BT9 5DY. Tel 028 9038 1271; www.stran.ac.uk

Strathclyde University of Strathclyde, 16 Richmond Street, Glasgow, Scotland G1 1XQ. Tel 0141 552 4400; www.strath.ac.uk

Sunderland University of Sunderland, Edinburgh Building, City Campus, Chester Road, Sunderland, England SR1 3SD. Tel 0191 515 3000; www.sunderland.ac.uk

Surrey University of Surrey, Stag Hill, Guildford, England GU2 7XH. Tel 01483 300800; www.surrey.ac.uk

Sussex University of Sussex, Student Recruitment and Marketing, Level 2 North Stand, American Express Community Stadium, Village Way, Brighton, England BN1 9BL. Tel 01273 876787; www.sussex.ac.uk

Swansea Swansea University, Admissions, Singleton Park, Swansea, Wales SA2 8PP. Tel 01792 205678; www.swansea.ac.uk

Teesside Teesside University, Admissions Office, Teesside University, Middlesbrough, England TS1 3BA. Tel 01642 218121; www.tees.ac.uk

Trinity Saint David Trinity Saint David, University of Wales, Academic Registry, Lampeter, Wales SA48 7ED. Tel Carmarthen 01267 676767; Lampeter 01570 422351; Swansea 07192 481000; www.trinitysaintdavid.ac.uk

UHI University of the Highlands and Islands, Course Information Unit, Executive Office, Ness Walk, Inverness, Scotland IV3 5SQ. Tel 01463 279000; www.uhi.ac.uk

Ulster Ulster University, Belfast Campus, York Street, Belfast, Northern Ireland BT15 1ED. Tel 028 701 23456; www.ulster.ac.uk

Univ Law University of Law, Braboeuf Manor, St Catherines, Guildford, England GU3 1HA. Tel 0800 289997; www.law.ac.uk

UWE Bristol University of the West of England, Bristol, Admissions Office, UWE Bristol, Frenchay Campus, Coldharbour Lane, Bristol, England BS16 1QY. Tel 0117 328 3333; www.uwe.ac.uk

Warwick University of Warwick, Student Recruitment, Outreach and Admissions Service, Coventry, England CV4 7AL. Tel 024 7652 3723; www.warwick.ac.uk

West London University of West London, Course Information Centre, St Mary's Road, London, England W5 5RF. Tel 0800 036 8888; www.uwl.ac.uk

West Scotland University of the West of Scotland, Admissions Office, High Street, Paisley, Scotland PA1 2BE. Tel 0141 848 3727; www.uws.ac.uk

Westminster University of Westminster, Head Office at Regent Campus, 309 Regent Street, London, England W1B 2HW. Tel 020 7915 5511; www.westminster.ac.uk

Winchester University of Winchester, Course Enquiries and Applications, University of Winchester, Winchester, England SO22 4NR. Tel 01962 827234; www.winchester.ac.uk

Wolverhampton University of Wolverhampton, Wulfruna Street, Wolverhampton, England WV1 1LY. Tel 01902 321000; www.wlv.ac.uk

Worcester University of Worcester, Admissions Office, Henwick Grove, Worcester, England WR2 6AJ. Tel 01905 855111; www.worcester.ac.uk

York University of York, Student Recruitment and Admissions, The Stables, Heslington, York, England YO10 5DD. Tel 01904 320000; www.york.ac.uk

York St John York St John University, Lord Mayor's Walk, York, England YO31 7EX. Tel 01904 624624; www.yorksj.ac.uk

SECTION 2: SPECIALIST COLLEGES OF AGRICULTURE AND HORTICULTURE, ART, DANCE, DRAMA, FASHION, MUSIC, OSTEOPATHY AND SPEECH

Many colleges and institutes provide undergraduate and postgraduate courses in a wide range of subjects. While many universities and university colleges offer courses in art, design, music, drama, agriculture, horticulture and courses connected to the land-based industries, the specialist colleges listed below provide courses at many levels, often part-time, in these separate fields.

It is important that you read prospectuses and check websites carefully and go to Open Days to find out as much as you can about these colleges and about their courses which interest you. Applications for full-time courses at the institutions listed below are through UCAS.

Abbreviations used below A = Art and Design; **Ag** = Agriculture, Animals and Land-related courses; **C** = Communication; **D** = Drama, Performing and Theatre Arts; **Da** = Dance; **F** = Fashion; **H** = Horticulture and Landscape-related courses; **M** = Music.

Academy of Live and Recorded Arts (ALRA) Also has a northern base in Wigan. Studio 24, Royal Victoria Patriotic Building, John Archer Way, London, England SW18 3SX. Tel 020 8870 6475; www.alra.co.uk [**D**]

Anglo-European College of Chiropractic 13–15 Parkwood Road, Bournemouth, England BH5 2DF. Tel 01202 436200; www.aecc.ac.uk

Architectural Association School of Architecture 36 Bedford Square, London, England WC1B 3ES. Tel 020 7887 4051; www.aaschool.ac.uk

Arts Educational Schools London Cone Ripman House, 14 Bath Road, London, England W4 1LY. Tel 020 8987 6666; www.artsed.co.uk [**A**]

Askham Bryan College Land-based college. Askham Bryan, York, England YO23 3FR. Tel 01904 772277; www.askham-bryan.ac.uk [**Ag**]

Banbury and Bicester College Part of the Activate Learning Group. Banbury Campus, Broughton Road, Banbury, England OX16 9QA. Tel 0808 168 6626; www.banbury-bicester.ac.uk

Belfast Metropolitan College Offers a breadth of vocational and academic courses. Titanic Quarter Campus, 7 Queens Road, Belfast, Northern Ireland BT3 9FQ. Tel 028 9026 5265; www.belfastmet.ac.uk

Berkshire College of Agriculture Hall Place, Burchetts Green, Maidenhead, England SL6 6QR. Tel 01628 824444; www.bca.ac.uk [**Ag**]

Bicton College East Budleigh, Budleigh Salterton, England EX9 7BY. Tel 01395 562400; www.bicton.ac.uk [**Ag**]

Bishop Burton College Land-based college. Learner Services, York Road, Bishop Burton, England HU17 8QG. Tel 01964 553000; www.bishopburton.ac.uk [**Ag**]

Bristol Old Vic Theatre School Bristol Old Vic Theatre School is an affiliate of the Conservatoire for Dance and Drama and is an Associate School of the University of the West of England. 1–2 Downside Road, Clifton, Bristol, England BS8 2XF. Tel 0117 973 3535; www.oldvic.ac.uk [**D**]

British College of Osteopathic Medicine Lief House, 120–122 Finchley Road, London, England NW3 5HR. Tel 020 7435 6464; www.bcom.ac.uk

British Institute of Technology and E-commerce 252–262 Romford Road, London, England E7 9HZ. Tel 020 8552 3071; www.bite.ac.uk

British School of Osteopathy 275 Borough High Street, London, England SE1 1JE. Tel 020 7407 0222; Student Admissions 020 7089 5316; www.bso.ac.uk

Brooksby Melton College Melton Mowbray Campus, Ashfordby Road, Melton Mowbray, England LE13 0HJ. Tel 01664 850850; www.brooksbymelton.ac.uk [**Ag**]

Camberwell College of Art, University of the Arts London Peckham Road, London, England SE5 8UF. Tel 020 7514 6302; www.arts.ac.uk/camberwell [**A**]

Capel Manor College Land-based college. Administrative Office, Bullsmore Lane, Enfield, England EN1 4RQ. Tel 08456 122122; www.capel.ac.uk [**H**]

Central Saint Martins College, University of the Arts London 1 Granary Square, King's Cross, London, England N1C 4AA. Tel 020 7514 7023; www.arts.ac.uk/csm [**A**]

Chelsea College of Arts, University of the Arts London 16 John Islip Street, London, England SW1P 4JU. Tel 020 7514 7751; www.arts.ac.uk/chelsea [**A**]

City and Guilds of London Art School 124 Kennington Park Road, London, England SE11 4DJ. Tel 020 7735 2306; www.cityandguildsartschool.ac.uk [**A**]

Cleveland College of Art and Design Green Lane, Linthorpe, Middlesbrough, England TS5 7RJ. Tel 01642 288000; www.ccad.ac.uk [**A**]

College of Agriculture, Food and Rural Enterprise (CAFRE) Greenmount Campus, 45 Tirgracy Road, Antrim, Northern Ireland BT41 4PS. Tel 0800 028 4291; www.cafre.ac.uk [**Ag**]

College of Estate Management Whiteknights, Reading, England RG6 6AW. Tel 0800 019 9697; www.cem.ac.uk

Drama Centre London, University of the Arts London Saffron House, 10 Back Hill, London, England EC1R 5LQ. Tel 020 7514 8769; www.arts.ac.uk/csm/drama-centre-london [**D**]

Duchy College Land-based college. Rosewarne Campus, Camborne, England TR14 0AB. Tel 01209 722100; www.duchy.ac.uk [**Ag**]

East 15 Acting School Hatfields, Rectory Lane, Loughton, England IG10 3RY. Tel 020 8508 5983; www.east15.ac.uk [**D**]

Easton and Otley College Land-based. Easton, Norwich, England NR9 5DX. Tel 01603 731200; www.eastonotley.ac.uk [**Ag**]

Edinburgh College of Art Academic Registry, Lauriston Place, Edinburgh, Scotland EH3 9DF. Tel 0131 651 5763; www.eca.ed.ac.uk [**A**]

European School of Osteopathy Boxley House, The Street, Boxley, Maidstone, England ME14 3DZ. Tel 01622 671558; www.eso.ac.uk

Fashion Retail Academy 15 Gresse Street, London, England W1T 1QL. Tel 020 7307 2345; www.fashionretailacademy.ac.uk [**F**]

Glasgow Clyde College Mosspark Drive, Glasgow, Scotland G52 3AY. Tel 0141 272 9000; www.glasgowclyde.ac.uk

Glasgow School of Art 167 Renfrew Street, Glasgow, Scotland G3 6RQ. Tel 0141 353 4500; www.gsa.ac.uk [**A**]

Gray's School of Art, Robert Gordon University Garthdee House, Garthdee Road, Aberdeen, Scotland AB10 7QB. Tel 01224 262728; www.rgu.ac.uk/grays [**A**]

Guildford School of Acting Conservatoire, University of Surrey Stag Hill Campus, Guildford, England GU2 7XH. Tel 01483 684040; www.conservatoire.org [**D**]

Guildhall School of Music and Drama Silk Street, London, England EC2Y 8DT. Tel 020 7628 2571; www.gsmd.ac.uk [**M**]

Hadlow College Hadlow, Tonbridge, England TN11 0AL. Tel 01732 850551; www.hadlow.ac.uk [**Ag**]

Hartpury College Land-based college. Hartpury House, Hartpury, England GL19 3BE. Tel 01452 702345; www.hartpury.ac.uk [**Ag**]

Heatherley School of Fine Art 75 Lots Road, London, England SW10 0RN. Tel 020 7351 4190; www.heatherleys.org [**A**]

Hereford College of Arts Folly Lane, Hereford, England HR1 1LT. Tel 01432 273359; www.hca.ac.uk [**A**]

Kingston Maurward College Land-based college. Kingston Maurward, Dorchester, England DT2 8PY. Tel 01305 215000; Course Enquiries 01305 215215; www.kmc.ac.uk [**Ag**]

Leeds College of Art Blenheim Walk, Leeds, England LS2 9AQ. Tel 0113 202 8000; www.leeds-art.ac.uk [**A**]

Leeds College of Music 3 Quarry Hill, Leeds, England LS2 7PD. Tel 0113 222 3416; www.lcm.ac.uk [**M**]

Liverpool Institute for Performing Arts LIPA, Mount Street, Liverpool, England L1 9HF. Tel 0151 330 3000; www.lipa.ac.uk [**D**]

London Academy of Music and Dramatic Art 155 Talgarth Road, London, England W14 9DA. Tel 020 8834 0500; www.lamda.org.uk [**M**]

London College of Communication, University of the Arts London Elephant and Castle, London, England SE1 6SB. Tel 020 7514 6599; www.arts.ac.uk/lcc [**C**]

London College of Fashion, University of the Arts London 20 John Princes Street, London, England W1G 0BJ. Tel 020 7514 7400; www.arts.ac.uk/fashion [**F**]

Metanoia Institute 13 North Common Road, London, England W5 2QB. Tel 020 8579 2505; www.metanoia.ac.uk

Mountview Academy of Theatre Arts Mountview Academy of Theatre Arts, Clarendon Road, London, England N22 6XF. Tel 020 8881 2201; www.mountview.org.uk [**D**]

Myerscough College Land-based college. Myerscough Hall, St Michael's Road, Bilsborrow, Preston, England PR3 0RY. Tel 01995 642222; www.myerscough.ac.uk [**Ag**]

Northern School of Contemporary Dance 98 Chapeltown Road, Leeds, England LS7 4BH. Tel 0113 219 3000; www.nscd.ac.uk [**Da**]

Plumpton College Land-based college. Ditchling Road, Plumpton, England BN7 3AE. Tel 01273 890454; www.plumpton.ac.uk [**Ag**]

Plymouth College of Art Tavistock Place, Plymouth, England PL4 8AT. Tel 01752 203434; www.plymouthart.ac.uk [**A**]

Ravensbourne 6 Penrose Way, Greenwich Peninsula, London, England SE10 0EW. Tel 020 3040 3500; www.ravensbourne.ac.uk [**C**]

Reaseheath College Land-based college. Reaseheath, Nantwich, England CW5 6DF. Tel 01270 625131; HE Enquiries 01270 613284; www.reaseheath.ac.uk [**Ag**]

Rose Bruford College Lamorbey Park Campus, Burnt Oak Lane, Sidcup, England DA15 9DF. Tel 020 8308 2600; www.bruford.ac.uk [**D**]

Royal Academy of Dance 36 Battersea Square, London, England SW11 3RA. Tel 020 7326 8000; www.rad.org.uk [**Da**]

Royal Academy of Dramatic Art (RADA) All Higher Education courses are validated by King's College London. 62–64 Gower Street, London, England WC1E 6ED. Tel 020 7636 7076; www.rada.ac.uk [**D**]

Royal Academy of Music, University of London This is Britain's senior conservatoire, founded in 1822. Marylebone Road, London, England NW1 5HT. Tel 020 7873 7373; www.ram.ac.uk [**M**]

Royal Central School of Speech and Drama Royal Central School of Speech and Drama, Eton Avenue, London, England NW3 3HY. Tel 020 7722 8183; www.cssd.ac.uk [**D**]

Royal College of Music Prince Consort Road, London, England SW7 2BS. Tel 020 7591 4300; www.rcm.ac.uk [**M**]

Royal Conservatoire of Scotland 100 Renfrew Street, Glasgow, Scotland G2 3DB. Tel 0141 332 4101; www.rcs.ac.uk [**M**]

Royal Northern College of Music 124 Oxford Road, Manchester, England M13 9RD. Tel 0161 907 5200; www.rncm.ac.uk [**M**]

Royal Welsh College of Music and Drama Castle Grounds, Cathays Park, Cardiff, Wales CF10 3ER. Tel 029 2039 1361; www.rwcmd.ac.uk [**M**]

Ruskin School of Art 74 High Street, Oxford, England OX1 4BG. Tel 01865 276940; www.rsa.ox.ac.uk [**A**]

Scotland's Rural College Student Recruitment and Admissions Office, SAC Riverside Campus, University Avenue, Ayr, Scotland KA8 0SR. Tel 0800 269453; www.sruc.ac.uk [**Ag**]

Slade School of Fine Art, University College London Part of UCL. The Slade School, Gower Street, London, England WC1E 6BT. Tel 020 7679 2313; www.ucl.ac.uk/slade [**A**]

Sparsholt College Hampshire Westley Lane, Sparsholt, Winchester, England SO21 2NF. Tel 01962 776441; www.sparsholt.ac.uk [**H**]

Trinity Laban Conservatoire of Music and Dance King Charles Court, Old Royal Naval College, London, England SE10 9JF. Tel 020 8305 4444; www.trinitylaban.ac.uk [**M**]

Wimbledon College of Arts, University of the Arts London Merton Hall Road, London, England SW19 3QA. Tel 020 7514 9641; www.wimbledon.arts.ac.uk [**A**]

Winchester School of Art, University of Southampton Park Avenue, Winchester, England SO23 8DL. Tel 023 8059 6900; www.southampton.ac.uk/wsa [**A**]

Writtle College Lordship Road, Chelmsford, England CM1 3RR. Tel 01245 424200; www.writtle.ac.uk [**H**]

SECTION 3: FURTHER EDUCATION AND OTHER COLLEGES OFFERING HIGHER EDUCATION COURSES

Changes are taking place fast in this sector, with the merger of colleges and the introduction of University Centres. These are linked to further education colleges and to one or more universities, and provide Foundation and Honours degree courses (often part-time) and sometimes postgraduate qualifications.

The following institutions appear under various subject headings in the tables in **Chapter 7** and are in UCAS for some of their courses. See prospectuses and websites for application details.

Abingdon and Witney College Abingdon Campus, Wootton Road, Abingdon, England OX14 1GG. Tel 01235 555585; www.abingdon-witney.ac.uk

Accrington and Rossendale College Broad Oak Campus, Broad Oak Road, Accrington, England BB5 2AW. Tel 01254 389933; www.accross.ac.uk

Amersham and Wycombe College Stanley Hill, Amersham, England HP7 9HN. Tel 0800 614016; www.amersham.ac.uk

Andover College Charlton Road, Andover, England SP10 1EJ. Tel 01264 360000; www.andover.ac.uk

Argyll College (UHI partner college – see Section 1) West Bay, Dunoon, Scotland PA23 7HP. Tel 0845 230 9969; www.argyll.uhi.ac.uk

Aylesbury College Oxford Road, Aylesbury, England HP21 8PD. Tel 01296 588588; www.aylesbury.ac.uk

Ayrshire College Formerly Kilmarnock College, Ayr College, and James Watt College (North Ayrshire campuses). Dam Park, Ayr, Scotland KA8 0EU. Tel 0300 303 0303; www.ayrshire.ac.uk

Barking and Dagenham College Rush Green Campus, Dagenham Road, Romford, England RM7 0XU. Tel 020 8090 3020; www.barkingdagenhamcollege.ac.uk

Barnet and Southgate College Wood Street, Barnet, England EN5 4AZ. Tel 020 8266 4000; www.barnetsouthgate.ac.uk

Barnfield College New Bedford Road Campus, New Bedford Road, Luton, England LU2 7BF. Tel 01582 569569; http://college.barnfield.ac.uk

Barnsley College Church Street, Barnsley, England S70 2AN. Tel 01226 216165; www.barnsley.ac.uk

Basingstoke College of Technology Worting Road, Basingstoke, England RG21 8TN. Tel 01256 354141; www.bcot.ac.uk

Bath College Student Advice Centre, Avon St, Bath, England BA1 1UP. Tel 01225 312191; www.bathcollege.ac.uk

Bedford College Cauldwell Street, Bedford, England MK42 9AH. Tel 01234 291000; www.bedford.ac.uk

Bexley College Walnut Tree Road, Erith, England DA8 1RA. Tel 01322 404000; www.bexley.ac.uk

Birmingham Metropolitan College Jennens Road, Birmingham, England B4 7PS. Tel 0845 155 0101; www.bmetc.ac.uk

Bishop Auckland College Woodhouse Lane, Bishop Auckland, England DL14 6JZ. Tel 01388 443000; www.bacoll.ac.uk

Blackburn College Feilden Street, Blackburn, England BB2 1LH. Tel 01254 292929; www.blackburn.ac.uk

Blackpool and The Fylde College Ashfield Road, Bispham, Blackpool, England FY2 0HB. Tel 01253 504343; www.blackpool.ac.uk

Bolton College Deane Road Campus, Deane Road, Bolton, England BL3 5BG. Tel 01204 482000; www.boltoncollege.ac.uk

Boston College Skirbeck Road, Boston, England PE21 6JF. Tel 01205 365701; www.boston.ac.uk

Bournemouth and Poole College Customer Enquiry Centre, North Road, Poole, England BH14 0LS. Tel 01202 205205; www.thecollege.co.uk

Bournville College Longbridge Lane, Longbridge, Birmingham, England B31 2AJ. Tel 0121 477 1300; www.bournville.ac.uk

Bracknell and Wokingham College College Information Centre, Church Road, Bracknell, England RG12 1DJ. Tel 0845 330 3343; www.bracknell.ac.uk

Bradford College Admissions Office, Great Horton Road, Bradford, England BD7 1AY. Tel 01274 433333; www.bradfordcollege.ac.uk

Bridgend College Cowbridge Road, Bridgend, Wales CF31 3DF. Tel 01656 302302; www.bridgend.ac.uk

Bridgwater College Bath Road, Bridgwater, England TA6 4PZ. Tel 01278 455464; www.bridgwater.ac.uk

Brockenhurst College Lyndhurst Road, Brockenhurst, England SO42 7ZE. Tel 01590 625555; www.brock.ac.uk

Bromley College of Further and Higher Education Rookery Lane, Bromley, England BR2 8HE. Tel 020 8295 7000; www.bromley.ac.uk

Brooklands College Weybridge Campus, Heath Road, Weybridge, England KT13 8TT. Tel 01932 797797; www.brooklands.ac.uk

Burnley College Princess Way, Burnley, England BB12 0AN. Tel 01282 733373; www.burnley.ac.uk

Burton and South Derbyshire College Student Services, Lichfield Street, Burton-on-Trent, England DE14 3RL. Tel 01283 494400; www.burton-college.ac.uk

Bury College Woodbury Centre, Market Street, Bury, England BL9 0BG. Tel 0161 280 8280; www.burycollege.ac.uk

Buxton and Leek College Stockwell Street, Leek, England ST13 6DP. Tel 0800 074 0099; www.blc.ac. uk

Calderdale College Francis Street, Halifax, England HX1 3UZ. Tel 01422 399399; www.calderdale. ac.uk

Cambridge Regional College Kings Hedges Road, Cambridge, England CB4 2QT. Tel 01223 418200; www.camre.ac.uk

Canterbury College New Dover Road, Canterbury, England CT1 3AJ. Tel 01227 811111; www.cant-col. ac.uk

Carlisle College Information Unit, Victoria Place, Carlisle, England CA1 1HS. Tel 01228 822700; www. carlisle.ac.uk

Carmel College Prescot Road, St Helens, England WA10 3AG. Tel 01744 452200; www.carmel.ac.uk

Carshalton College Nightingale Road, Carshalton, England SM5 2EJ. Tel 020 8544 4501; www.carshalton. ac.uk

CECOS London College 51A Marlborough Road, London, England E18 1AR. Tel 020 7359 3316; http:// cecos.co.uk

Central Bedfordshire College (formerly Dunstable College) Kingsway, Dunstable, England LU5 4HG. Tel 01582 477776; www.centralbeds.ac.uk

Central Campus, Sandwell College 1 Spon Lane, West Bromwich, England B70 6AW. Tel 0800 622006; www.sandwell.ac.uk

Central College Nottingham High Road, Beeston, Nottingham, England NG9 4AH. Tel 0115 914 6414; www.centralnottingham.ac.uk

Central Film School London 3rd Floor, Universal House, 88–94 Wentworth Street, London, England E1 7SA. Tel 020 7377 6060; www.centralfilmschool.com

Chelmsford College 102 Moulsham Street, Chelmsford, England CM2 0JQ. Tel 01245 293031; www. chelmsford.ac.uk

Chesterfield College Infirmary Road, Chesterfield, England S41 7NG. Tel 01246 500500; www.chesterfield. ac.uk

Chichester College Westgate Fields, Chichester, England PO19 1SB. Tel 01243 786321; www.chichester. ac.uk

City and Islington College The Marlborough Building, 383 Holloway Road, London, England N7 0RN. Tel 020 7700 9200; www.candi.ac.uk

City College Brighton and Hove Pelham Street, Brighton, England BN1 4FA. Tel 01273 667788; www. ccb.ac.uk

City College Coventry Swanswell Centre, 50 Swanswell Street, Coventry, England CV1 5DG. Tel 024 7679 1000; www.covcollege.ac.uk

City College Norwich Ipswich Road, Norwich, England NR2 2LJ. Tel 01603 773311; www.ccn.ac.uk

City College Plymouth (formerly Plymouth College of Further Education) Kings Road, Devonport, Plymouth, England PL1 5QG. Tel 01752 305300; www.cityplym.ac.uk

City of Bristol College Ashley Down Road, Bristol, England BS7 9BU. Tel 0117 312 5000; www.cityofbristol. ac.uk

City of Liverpool College Bankfield Road, Liverpool, England L13 0BQ. Tel 0151 252 3000; www.liv-coll. ac.uk

City of London College 71 Whitechapel High Street, London, England E1 7PL. Tel 020 7247 2177; www. clc-london.ac.uk

City of Oxford College Part of the Activate Learning Group. Oxpens Road, Oxford, England OX1 1SA. Tel 01865 550550; www.cityofoxford.ac.uk

City of Westminster College 25 Paddington Green, London, England W2 1NB. Tel 020 7723 8826; www.cwc.ac.uk

City of Wolverhampton College Paget Road Campus, Paget Road, Wolverhampton, England WV6 0DU. Tel 01902 836000; www.wolvcoll.ac.uk

Cliff College Calver, Hope Valley, Derbyshire, England S32 3XG. Tel 01246 584202; www.cliffcollege.ac.uk

Colchester Institute Course Enquiries, Sheepen Road, Colchester, England CO3 3LL. Tel 01206 712000; www.colchester.ac.uk

Coleg Llandrillo Llandudno Road, Rhos-on-Sea, Wales LL28 4HZ. Tel 01492 546666; www.llandrillo.ac.uk

Coleg Menai Ffriddoedd Road, Bangor, Wales LL57 2TP. Tel 01248 370125; www.gllm.ac.uk/menai

Coleg Sir Gâr Graig Campus, Sandy Road, Pwll, Wales SA15 4DN. Tel 01554 748000; www.colegsirgar.ac.uk

Coleg y Cymoedd Cwmdare Road, Aberdare, Wales CF44 8ST. Tel 01685 887500; www.cymoedd.ac.uk

College of Haringey, Enfield and North East London (formed in 2009 from a merger between Enfield College and the College of North East London) Enfield Centre, 73 Hertford Road, Enfield, England EN3 5HA. Tel 020 8442 3103; www.conel.ac.uk

College of North West London Willesden Centre, Dudden Hill Lane, London, England NW10 2XD. Tel 020 8208 5000; Course Information 020 8208 5050; www.cnwl.ac.uk

College of West Anglia King's Lynn Centre, Tennyson Avenue, King's Lynn, Norfolk, England PE30 2QW. Tel 01553 761144; www.cwa.ac.uk

Cornwall College Camborne Campus, Trevenson Road, Pool, Redruth, England TR15 3RD. Tel 0845 223 2567; www.cornwall.ac.uk

Craven College High Street, Skipton, England BD23 1JY. Tel 01756 708001; www.craven-college.ac.uk

Darlington College Central Park, Haughton Road, Darlington, England DL1 1DR. Tel 01325 503030; www.darlington.ac.uk

Dearne Valley College Manvers Park, Wath-upon-Dearne, Rotherham, England S63 7EW. Tel 01709 513355; www.dearne-coll.ac.uk

Derby College Roundhouse Road, Pride Park, Derby, England DE24 8JE. Tel 0800 028 0289; www.derby-college.ac.uk

Derwentside College Consett Campus, Front Street, Consett, England DH8 5EE. Tel 01207 585900; www.derwentside.ac.uk

Doncaster College High Melton, Doncaster, England DN5 7SZ. Tel 0800 358 7474; www.don.ac.uk

Dudley College The Broadway, Dudley, England DY1 4AS. Tel 01384 363000; www.dudleycol.ac.uk

Ealing, Hammersmith and West London College The Green, London, England W5 5EW. Tel 020 8741 1688; www.wlc.ac.uk

East Berkshire College Langley Campus, Station Road, Langley, England SL3 8BY. Tel 01753 793000; www.eastberks.ac.uk

East Durham College Houghall Campus, Houghall, England DH1 3SG. Tel 0191 518 8222; www.eastdurham.ac.uk

East Kent College Ramsgate Road, Broadstairs, England CT10 1PN. Tel 01843 605040; Admissions 01843 605049; www.eastkent.ac.uk

East Riding College Beverley Campus, Flemingate Centre, Armstrong Way, Beverley, England HU17 0GH. Tel 0345 120 0044; www.eastridingcollege.ac.uk

East Surrey College Gatton Point, London Road, Redhill, England RH1 2JX. Tel 01737 788445; www.esc.ac.uk

Eastleigh College Chestnut Avenue, Eastleigh, England SO50 5FS. Tel 023 8091 1299; www.eastleigh.ac.uk

Edinburgh College (formed from a merger of Edinburgh's Telford College, Jewel and Esk College, and Stevenson College) Granton Campus, 350 West Granton Road, Edinburgh, Scotland EH5 1QE. Tel 0131 660 1010; www.edinburghcollege.ac.uk

European Business School London Admissions Department, Regent's College, Regent's Park, Inner Circle, London, England NW1 4NS. Tel 020 7487 7505; www.regents.ac.uk/about/schools/european-business-school-london

European School of Economics 8-9 Grosvenor Place, London, England SW1X 7SH. Tel 020 7245 6148; www.eselondon.ac.uk

Exeter College Hele Road, Exeter, England EX4 4JS. Tel 01392 400500; www.exe-coll.ac.uk

Fareham College Bishopsfield Road, Fareham, England PO14 1NH. Tel 01329 815200; www.fareham.ac.uk

Farnborough College of Technology Boundary Road, Farnborough, England GU14 6SB. Tel 01252 407040; www.farn-ct.ac.uk

Forth Valley College Falkirk Campus, Grangemouth Road, Falkirk, Scotland FK2 9AD. Tel 0845 634 4444; www.forthvalley.ac.uk

Furness College Channelside, Barrow-in-Furness, England LA14 2PJ. Tel 01229 825017; www.furness.ac.uk

Gateshead College Baltic Campus, Quarryfield Road, Baltic Business Quarter, Gateshead, England NE8 3BE. Tel 0191 490 0300; www.gateshead.ac.uk

Gloucestershire College Gloucester Campus, Llanthony Road, Gloucester, England GL2 5JQ. Tel 0345 155 2020; www.gloscol.ac.uk

Gower College Swansea (Coleg Abertawe is now part of Gower College Swansea.) Tycoch Campus, Tycoch Road, Swansea, Wales SA2 9EB. Tel 01792 284000; www.gowercollegeswansea.ac.uk

Grantham College Stonebridge Road, Grantham, England NG31 9AP. Tel 01476 400200; www.grantham.ac.uk

Great Yarmouth College Suffolk Road, Southtown, Great Yarmouth, England NR31 0ED. Tel 01493 655261; www.gyc.ac.uk

Greenwich School of Management Meridian House, Royal Hill, London, England SE10 8RD. Tel 020 8516 7800; www.gsm.org.uk

Guildford College Stoke Park Campus, Stoke Road, Guildford, England GU1 1EZ. Tel 01483 448500; www.guildford.ac.uk

Hackney Community College Shoreditch Campus, Falkirk Street, London, England N1 6HQ. Tel 020 7613 9123; www.tcch.ac.uk

Halesowen College Whittingham Road, Halesowen, England B63 3NA. Tel 0121 602 7777; www.halesowen.ac.uk

Harlow College Velizy Avenue, Harlow, England CM20 3EZ. Tel 01279 868000; www.harlow-college.ac.uk

Harrogate College Hornbeam Park, Harrogate, England HG2 8QT. Tel 01423 878211; www.harrogate.ac.uk

Harrow College Harrow on the Hill Campus, Lowlands Road, Harrow, England HA1 3AQ. Tel 020 8909 6000; www.harrow.ac.uk

Hartlepool College of Further Education Stockton Street, Hartlepool, England TS24 7NT. Tel 01429 295000; www.hartlepoolfe.ac.uk

Havering College Ardleigh Green Road, Hornchurch, England RM11 2LL. Tel 01708 455011; Course Information 01708 462801; www.havering-college.ac.uk

Heart of Worcestershire College Osprey House, Albert Street, Redditch, England B97 4DE. Tel 01527 570020; www.howcollege.ac.uk

Henley College Coventry Henley Road, Bell Green, Coventry, England CV2 1ED. Tel 024 7662 6300; www.henley-cov.ac.uk

Herefordshire and Ludlow College Folly Lane, Hereford, England HR1 1LS. Tel 0800 032 1986; www.hlcollege.ac.uk

Hertford Regional College Ware Centre, Scotts Road, Ware, England SG12 9JF. Tel 01992 411400; www.hrc.ac.uk

Highbury College Portsmouth Tudor Crescent, Portsmouth, England PO6 2SA. Tel 023 9238 3131; www.highbury.ac.uk

Highland Theological College (UHI partner college – see Section 1) High Street, Dingwall, Scotland IV15 9HA. Tel 01349 780000; www.htc.uhi.ac.uk

Hillcroft College South Bank, Surbiton, England KT6 6DF. Tel 020 8399 2688; www.hillcroft.ac.uk

Hopwood Hall College Rochdale Campus, St Mary's Gate, Rochdale, England OL12 6RY. Tel 01706 345346; www.hopwood.ac.uk

Hugh Baird College Balliol Road, Bootle, England L20 7EW. Tel 0151 353 4444; www.hughbaird.ac.uk

Hull College The Queen's Gardens Centre, Wilberforce Drive, Hull, England HU1 3DG. Tel 01482 598744; www.hull-college.ac.uk

Huntingdonshire Regional College California Road, Huntingdon, England PE29 1BL. Tel 01480 379106; www.huntingdon.ac.uk

Isle of Wight College Medina Way, Newport, Isle of Wight, England PO30 5TA. Tel 01983 526631; www.iwcollege.ac.uk

Kendal College Milnthorpe Road, Kendal, England LA9 5AY. Tel 01539 814700; www.kendal.ac.uk

Kensington and Chelsea College Chelsea Centre, Hortensia Road, London, England SW10 0QS. Tel 020 7573 5333; www.kcc.ac.uk

Kensington College of Business Wesley House, 4 Wild Court, London, England WC2B 4AU. Tel 020 7404 6330; www.kensingtoncoll.ac.uk

Kidderminster College Market Street, Kidderminster, England DY10 1AB. Tel 01562 820811; www.kidderminster.ac.uk

Kingston College Kingston Hall Road, Kingston upon Thames, England KT1 2AQ. Tel 020 8546 2151; www.kingston-college.ac.uk

Kirklees College Information Office, Waterfront Quarter, Manchester Road, Huddersfield, England HD1 3LD. Tel 01484 437070; www.kirkleescollege.ac.uk

Knowsley Community College Rupert Road, Roby, Kirkby, England L36 9TD. Tel 0151 477 5850; www.knowsleycollege.ac.uk

Lakes College, West Cumbria Hallwood Road, Lillyhall Business Park, Workington, England CA14 4JN. Tel 01946 839300; www.lcwc.ac.uk

Lambeth College 45 Clapham Common South Side, London, England SW4 9BL. Tel 020 7501 5010; www.lambethcollege.ac.uk

Lancaster and Morecambe College Morecambe Road, Lancaster, England LA1 2TY. Tel 01524 66215; www.lmc.ac.uk

Lansdowne College 40–44 Bark Place, London, England W2 4AT. Tel 020 7616 4400; www.lansdownecollege.com

Leeds City College Park Lane Campus, Park Lane, Leeds, England LS3 1AA. Tel 0113 386 1997; www.leedscitycollege.ac.uk

Leeds College of Building North Street, Leeds, England LS2 7QT. Tel 0113 222 6000; www.lcb.ac.uk

Leicester College Freemen's Park Campus, Aylestone Road, Leicester, England LE2 7LW. Tel 0116 224 2240; www.leicestercollege.ac.uk

Leo Baeck College The Sternberg Centre, 80 East End Road, London, England N3 2SY. Tel 020 8349 5600; www.lbc.ac.uk

Lewisham Southwark College Lewisham Way, London, England SE4 1UT. Tel 020 3757 3000; Course Enquiries 0800 834545; www.lesoco.ac.uk

Lews Castle College (UHI partner college – see Section 1) Castle Grounds, Stornoway, Isle of Lewis, Scotland HS2 0XR. Tel 01851 770000; www.lews.uhi.ac.uk

Lincoln College Monks Road, Lincoln, England LN2 5HQ. Tel 01522 876000; www.lincolncollege.ac.uk

London School of Advanced Studies Senate House, Malet Street, London, England WC1E 7HU. Tel 020 7862 8653; www.sas.ac.uk

London School of Commerce Chaucer House, White Hart Yard, London, England SE1 1NX. Tel 020 7357 0077; www.lsclondon.co.uk

London School of Science and Technology First Floor, Alperton House, Bridgwater Road, Wembley, England HA0 1EH. Tel 020 8795 3863; www.lsst.ac

Loughborough College Radmoor Road, Loughborough, England LE11 3BT. Tel 01509 618375; www.loucoll.ac.uk

Macclesfield College Park Lane, Macclesfield, England SK11 8LF. Tel 01625 410002; www.macclesfield.ac.uk

Mid-Cheshire College Hartford Campus, Chester Road, Northwich, England CW8 1LJ. Tel 01606 74444; www.midchesh.ac.uk

Middlesbrough College Dock Street, Middlesbrough, England TS2 1AD. Tel 01642 333333; www.mbro.ac.uk

Mid-Kent College Medway Campus, Medway Road, Gillingham, England ME7 1FN. Tel 01634 402020; www.midkent.ac.uk

Milton Keynes College Chaffron Way Campus, Woughton Campus West, Leadenhall, Milton Keynes, England MK6 5LP. Tel 01908 684444; www.mkcollege.ac.uk

Moray College (UHI partner college – see Section 1) Moray Street, Elgin, Scotland IV30 1JJ. Tel 01343 576000; Course Enquiries 0845 272 3600; www.moray.uhi.ac.uk

Moulton College West Street, Moulton, England NN3 7RR. Tel 01604 491131; www.moulton.ac.uk

NAFC Marine Centre, University of the Highlands and Islands (UHI partner college – see Section 1) NAFC Marine Centre, Port Arthur, Scalloway, Scotland ZE1 0UN. Tel 01595 772000; www.nafc.uhi.ac.uk

Nazarene Theological College Dene Road, Didsbury, Manchester, England M20 2GU. Tel 0161 445 3063; www.nazarene.ac.uk

Neath Port Talbot College Neath Campus, Dwr-y-Felin Road, Neath, Wales SA10 7RF. Tel 01639 648000; www.nptcgroup.ac.uk

Nelson and Colne College Reedyford Site, Scotland Road, Nelson, England BB9 7YT. Tel 01282 440272; www.nelson.ac.uk

Nescot, North East Surrey College of Technology Reigate Road, Ewell, Epsom, England KT17 3DS. Tel 020 8394 3038; www.nescot.ac.uk

New College Durham Framwellgate Moor Campus, Durham, England DH1 5ES. Tel 0191 375 4000; www.newcollegedurham.ac.uk

New College Nottingham The Adams Building, Stoney Street, Nottingham, England NG1 1NG. Tel 01159 100100; www.ncn.ac.uk

New College Stamford Drift Road, Stamford, England PE9 1XA. Tel 01780 484300; www.stamford.ac.uk

New College Swindon New College Drive, Swindon, England SN3 1AH. Tel 01793 611470; www.newcollege.ac.uk

New College Telford King Street, Wellington, Telford, England TF1 1NY. Tel 01952 641892; www.nct.ac.uk

Newbury College Monks Lane, Newbury, England RG14 7TD. Tel 01635 845000; www.newbury-college.ac.uk

Newcastle College Rye Hill Campus, Scotswood Road, Newcastle-upon-Tyne, England NE4 7SA. Tel 0191 200 4000; www.ncl-coll.ac.uk

Newcastle-under-Lyme College Knutton Lane, Newcastle-under-Lyme, England ST5 2GB. Tel 01782 254254; www.nulc.ac.uk

Newham College East Ham Campus, High Street South, London, England E6 6ER. Tel 020 8257 4446; www.newham.ac.uk

Norland College York Place, London Road, Bath, England BA1 6AE. Tel 01225 904040; www.norland.co.uk

North East Scotland College Aberdeen City Campus, Gallowgate, Aberdeen, Scotland AB25 1BN. Tel 0300 330 5550; www.abcol.ac.uk

North Hertfordshire College Stevenage Centre, Monkswood Way, Stevenage, England SG1 1LA. Tel 01462 424242; www.nhc.ac.uk

North Highland College (UHI partner college – see Section 1) Ormlie Road, Thurso, Scotland KW14 7EE. Tel 01847 889000; www.northhighland.ac.uk

North Kent College Oakfield Lane, Dartford, England DA1 2JT. Tel 0800 074 1447; www.northkent.ac.uk

North Lindsey College Kingsway, Scunthorpe, England DN17 1AJ. Tel 01724 281111; www.northlindsey.ac.uk

North Nottinghamshire College Carlton Road, Worksop, England S81 7HP. Tel 01909 504504; Student Services 01909 504500; www.nnotts-col.ac.uk

North Shropshire College Oswestry Campus, Shrewsbury Road, Oswestry, England SY11 4QB. Tel 01691 688000; www.nsc.ac.uk

North Warwickshire and Hinckley College Nuneaton Campus, Hinckley Road, Nuneaton, England CV11 6BH. Tel 024 7624 3000; www.nwhc.ac.uk

Northampton College Booth Lane, Northampton, England NN3 3RF. Tel 0300 123 2344; www.northamptoncollege.ac.uk

Northbrook College, Sussex West Durrington Campus, Littlehampton Road, Worthing, England BN12 6NU. Tel 0845 155 6060; www.northbrook.ac.uk

Northern Regional College (formerly North East Institute of Further and Higher Education) Ballymena Campus, Trostan Avenue Building, Ballymena, Northern Ireland BT43 7BN. Tel 028 2563 6221; www. nrc.ac.uk

Northumberland College College Road, Ashington, England NE63 9RG. Tel 01670 841200; www. northumberland.ac.uk

Oaklands College Smallford Campus, Hatfield Road, St Albans, England AL4 0JA. Tel 01727 737000; www.oaklands.ac.uk

Oldham College Rochdale Road, Oldham, England OL9 6AA. Tel 0161 785 4000; www.oldham.ac.uk

Orkney College (UHI partner college – see Section 1) East Road, Kirkwall, Scotland KW15 1LX. Tel 01856 569000; www.orkney.uhi.ac.uk

Pearson College 80 Strand, London, England WC2R 0RL. Tel 020 3441 1301; www.pearsoncollegelondon. ac.uk

Pembrokeshire College (Coleg Sir Benfro) Merlins Bridge, Haverfordwest, Wales SA61 1SZ. Tel 01437 753000; Freephone 0800 977 6788; www.pembrokeshire.ac.uk

Perth College (UHI partner college – see Section 1) Crieff Road, Perth, Scotland PH1 2NX. Tel 0845 270 1177; www.perth.uhi.ac.uk

Peterborough College Park Crescent, Peterborough, England PE1 4DZ. Tel 0345 872 8722; www. peterborough.ac.uk

Peter Symonds College Owens Road, Winchester, England SO22 6RX. Tel 01962 857500; www.psc.ac.uk

Petroc Old Sticklepath Hill, Sticklepath, Barnstaple, England EX31 2BQ. Tel 01271 345291; www.petroc. ac.uk

Portsmouth College Tangier Road, Copnor, Portsmouth, England PO3 6PZ. Tel 023 9266 7521; www. portsmouth-college.ac.uk

Preston's College Fulwood Campus, St Vincent's Road, Preston, England PR2 8UR. Tel 01772 225000; www.preston.ac.uk

Redbridge College Chadwell Heath Campus, Little Heath, Barley Lane, Romford, England RM6 4XT. Tel 020 8548 7400; www.redbridge-college.ac.uk

Redcar and Cleveland College Corporation Road, Redcar, England TS10 1EZ. Tel 01642 473132; www. cleveland.ac.uk

Richmond-upon-Thames College Egerton Road, Twickenham, England TW2 7SJ. Tel 020 8607 8000; www.rutc.ac.uk

Riverside College Kingsway Campus, Kingsway, Widnes, England WA8 7QQ. Tel 0151 257 2800; www. riversidecollege.ac.uk

Rotherham College of Arts and Technology Town Centre Campus, Eastwood Lane, Rotherham, England S65 1EG. Tel 01709 722777; www.rotherham.ac.uk

Royal National College for the Blind Venns Lane, Hereford, England HR1 1DT. Tel 01432 376621; www. rnc.ac.uk

Runshaw College Langdale Road, Leyland, England PR25 3DQ. Tel 01772 622677; www.runshaw.ac.uk

Ruskin College Ruskin Hall, Dunstan Road, Old Headington, Oxford, England OX3 9BZ. Tel 01865 759600; www.ruskin.ac.uk

Sabhal Mòr Ostaig (UHI partner college – see Section 1) ACC, Sleat, Scotland IV44 8RQ. Tel 01471 888000; www.smo.uhi.ac.uk

St Helens College Water Street, St Helens, England WA10 1PP. Tel 0800 996699; www.sthelens.ac.uk

School of Audio Engineering Institute SAE Institute Admissions, Littlemore Park, Armstrong Road, Oxford, England OX4 4FY. Tel 03330 112315; www.sae.edu

Scottish Association for Marine Science (UHI partner college – see Section 1) Scottish Marine Institute, Oban, Argyll, Scotland PA37 1QA. Tel 01631 559000; www.sams.ac.uk

Selby College Abbot's Road, Selby, England YO8 8AT. Tel 01757 211000; www.selby.ac.uk

Sheffield College City Campus, Granville Road, Sheffield, England S2 2RL. Tel 0114 260 2600; www.sheffcol.ac.uk

Shetland College (UHI partner college – see Section 1) Gremista, Lerwick, Scotland ZE1 0PX. Tel 01595 771000; www.shetland.uhi.ac.uk

Shrewsbury College of Arts and Technology London Road, Shrewsbury, England SY2 6PR. Tel 01743 342340; www.shrewsbury.ac.uk

Solihull College Blossomfield Campus, Blossomfield Road, Solihull, England B91 1SB. Tel 0121 678 7000; www.solihull.ac.uk

Somerset College Wellington Road, Taunton, England TA1 5AX. Tel 01823 366331; www.somerset.ac.uk

South and City College Birmingham Digbeth Campus, High Street Deritend, Digbeth, England B5 5SU. Tel 0800 111 6311; www.sccb.ac.uk

South Cheshire College Dane Bank Avenue, Crewe, England CW2 8AB. Tel 01270 654654; www.scc.ac.uk

South Devon College Vantage Point, Long Road, Paignton, England TQ4 7EJ. Tel 01803 540540; www.southdevon.ac.uk

South Downs College College Road, Waterlooville, England PO7 8AA. Tel 023 9279 7979; www.southdowns.ac.uk

South Essex College Nethermayne, Basildon, England SS16 5NN. Tel 0845 521 2345; www.southessex.ac.uk

South Gloucestershire and Stroud College (formerly Filton College) Stroud Campus, Stratford Road, Stroud, England GL5 4AH. Tel 01453 763424; www.sgscol.ac.uk

South Lanarkshire College Scottish Enterprise Technology Park, College Way, East Kilbride, Scotland G75 0NE. Tel 01355 807780; www.south-lanarkshire-college.ac.uk

South Leicestershire College South Wigston Campus, Blaby Road, South Wigston, England LE18 4PH. Tel 0116 264 3535; www.slcollege.ac.uk

South Staffordshire College Cannock Campus, The Green, Cannock, England WS11 1UE. Tel 0300 456 2424; www.southstaffs.ac.uk

South Thames College Wandsworth High Street, London, England SW18 2PP. Tel 020 8918 7777; www.south-thames.ac.uk

South Tyneside College Westoe Campus, St George's Avenue, South Shields, England NE34 6ET. Tel 0191 427 3500; www.stc.ac.uk

Southampton City College St Mary Street, Southampton, England SO14 1AR. Tel 023 8048 4848; www.southampton-city.ac.uk

Southern Regional College (formerly Upper Bann Institute) Portadown Campus, 36 Lurgan Road, Portadown, Northern Ireland BT63 5BL. Tel 0300 123 1223; www.src.ac.uk

Southport College Mornington Road, Southport, England PR9 0TT. Tel 01704 392704; www.southport-college.ac.uk

Stafford College Earl Street, Stafford, England ST16 2QR. Tel 01785 223800; www.staffordcoll.ac.uk

Staffordshire University Regional Federation Partnerships Office, E200 Cadman Building, College Road, Stoke-on-Trent, England ST4 2DE. Tel 01782 353517; www.staffs.ac.uk

Stephenson College Thornborough Road, Coalville, England LE67 3TN. Tel 01530 836136; www.stephensoncoll.ac.uk

Stockport College Town Centre Campus, Wellington Road South, Stockport, England SK1 3UQ. Tel 0161 296 5000; www.stockport.ac.uk

Stockton Riverside College Harvard Avenue, Stockton-on-Tees, England TS17 6FB. Tel 01642 865400; www.stockton.ac.uk

Stoke-on-Trent College Cauldon Campus, Stoke Road, Shelton, Stoke-on-Trent, England ST4 2DG. Tel 01782 208208; www.stokecoll.ac.uk

Stratford-upon-Avon College The Willows North, Alcester Road, Stratford-upon-Avon, England CV37 9QR. Tel 01789 266245; www.stratford.ac.uk

Strode College Church Road, Street, England BA16 0AB. Tel 01458 844400; www.strode-college.ac.uk

Strode's College High Street, Egham, England TW20 9DR. Tel 01784 437506; www.strodes.ac.uk

Sunderland College Bede Campus, Durham Road, Sunderland, England SR3 4AH. Tel 0191 511 6000; www.sunderlandcollege.ac.uk

Sussex Coast College Hastings (formerly Hastings College of Art and Technology) Station Plaza Campus, Station Approach, Hastings, England TN34 1BA. Tel 01424 442222; www.sussexcoast.ac.uk

Sussex Downs College Eastbourne Campus, Cross Levels Way, Eastbourne, England BN21 2UF. Tel 030 3003 9300; www.sussexdowns.ac.uk

Tameside College Beaufort Road, Ashton-under-Lyne, England OL6 6NX. Tel 0161 908 6600; www.tameside.ac.uk

Telford College of Arts and Technology Haybridge Road, Wellington, Telford, England TF1 2NP. Tel 01952 642200; www.tcat.ac.uk

The Islamic College 133 High Road, London, England NW10 2SW. Tel 020 8451 9993; www.islamic-college.ac.uk

The London College UCK Kensington Campus, Victoria Gardens, Notting Hill Gate, London, England W11 3PE. Tel 020 7243 4000; www.lcuck.ac.uk

The Manchester College Ashton Old Road, Openshaw, Manchester, England M11 2WH. Tel 0161 909 6655; www.themanchestercollege.ac.uk

Tottenham Hotspur Foundation Bill Nicholson Way, 748 High Road, London, England N17 0AP. Tel 020 8365 5138; www.tottenhamhotspur.com/foundation

Totton College Water Lane, Totton, Southampton, England SO40 3ZX. Tel 023 8087 4874; www.totton.ac.uk

Trafford College Talbot Road Campus, Talbot Road, Stretford, England M32 0XH. Tel 0161 886 7000; www.trafford.ac.uk

Tresham College of Further and Higher Education Kettering Campus, Windmill Avenue, Kettering, England NN15 6ER. Tel 0345 658 8990; www.tresham.ac.uk

Truro and Penwith College College Road, Truro, England TR1 3XX. Tel 01872 267000; www.truro-penwith.ac.uk

Tyne Metropolitan College Battle Hill Drive, Wallsend, England NE28 9NL. Tel 0191 229 5000; www.tynemet.ac.uk

University Campus Oldham Cromwell Street, Oldham, England OL1 1BB. Tel 0161 334 8800; www.uco.oldham.ac.uk

University Campus Suffolk Admissions Office, Waterfront Building, Neptune Quay, Ipswich, England IP4 1QJ. Tel 01473 338000; www.ucs.ac.uk

University Centre Croydon College Road, Croydon, England CR9 1DX. Tel 020 8760 5934; www.croydon.ac.uk

University Centre Grimsby Nuns Corner, Laceby Road, Grimsby, England DN34 5BQ. Tel 0800 315002; www.grimsby.ac.uk

Uxbridge College Uxbridge Campus, Park Road, Uxbridge, England UB8 1NQ. Tel 01895 853333; www.uxbridge.ac.uk

Wakefield College Margaret Street, Wakefield, England WF1 2DH. Tel 01924 789789; www.wakefield.ac.uk

Walsall College Wisemore Campus, Littleton Street West, Walsall, England WS2 8ES. Tel 01922 657000; www.walsallcollege.ac.uk

Waltham Forest College Forest Road, Walthamstow, London, England E17 4JB. Tel 020 8501 8501; www.waltham.ac.uk

Warrington Collegiate Winwick Road, Warrington, England WA2 8QA. Tel 01925 494494; www.warrington.ac.uk

Warwickshire College Leamington Centre, Warwick New Road, Leamington Spa, England CV32 5JE. Tel 0300 456 0047; www.warwickshire.ac.uk

West Cheshire College Chester Campus, Eaton Road, Handbridge, Chester, England CH4 7ER. Tel 01244 656555; www.west-cheshire.ac.uk

West Herts College Watford Campus, Hempstead Road, Watford, England WD17 3EZ. Tel 01923 812345; www.westherts.ac.uk

West Highland College (formed from a merger between Lochaber and Skye and Wester Ross College; UHI partner college – see Section 1) Carmichael Way, Fort William, Scotland PH33 6FF. Tel 01379 874000; www.whc.uhi.ac.uk

West Kent College Tonbridge Campus, Brook Street, Tonbridge, England TN9 2PW. Tel 0845 207 8220; www.westkent.ac.uk

West Nottinghamshire College Derby Road, Mansfield, England NG18 5BH. Tel 0808 100 3626; www.wnc.ac.uk

West Suffolk College Out Risbygate, Bury St Edmunds, England IP33 3RL. Tel 01284 701301; www.westsuffolkcollege.ac.uk

West Thames College London Road, Isleworth, England TW7 4HS. Tel 020 8326 2000; www.west-thames.ac.uk

Westminster Kingsway College Victoria Centre, Vincent Square, London, England SW1P 2PD. Tel 0870 060 9800; www.westking.ac.uk

Weston College Knightstone Campus, Knightstone Road, Weston-super-Mare, England BS23 2AL. Tel 01934 411411; www.weston.ac.uk

Weymouth College Cranford Avenue, Weymouth, England DT4 7LQ. Tel 01305 761100; www.weymouth.ac.uk

Wigan and Leigh College Parson's Walk, Wigan, England WN1 1RS. Tel 01942 761600; www.wigan-leigh.ac.uk

Wiltshire College Chippenham Campus, Cocklebury Road, Chippenham, England SN15 3QD. Tel 01225 350035; www.wiltshire.ac.uk

Wirral Metropolitan College Conway Park Campus, Europa Boulevard, Conway Park, Birkenhead, England CH41 4NT. Tel 0151 551 7777; www.wmc.ac.uk

Yeovil College Mudford Road, Yeovil, England BA21 4DR. Tel 01935 423921; www.yeovil.ac.uk

Yeovil College University Centre 91 Preston Road, Yeovil, England BA20 2DN. Tel 01935 845454; www.ucy.ac.uk

York College Sim Balk Lane, York, England YO23 2BB. Tel 01904 770400; www.yorkcollege.ac.uk

Yorkshire Coast College Lady Edith's Drive, Scarborough, England YO12 5RN. Tel 01723 372105; www.yorkshirecoastcollege.ac.uk

A-LEVELS AND AS • SCOTTISH HIGHERS/ADVANCED HIGHERS • ADVANCED WELSH BACCALAUREATE – SKILLS CHALLENGE CERTIFICATE • IB INTERNATIONAL BACCALAUREATE DIPLOMA (IB CERTIFICATE IN HIGHER LEVEL; IB CERTIFICATE IN STANDARD LEVEL; IB CERTIFICATE IN EXTENDED ESSAY; IB CERTIFICATE IN THEORY OF KNOWLEDGE) • BTEC • EXTENDED PROJECT • MUSIC EXAMINATIONS • ART AND DESIGN FOUNDATION STUDIES

A-levels and AS

Grade					Tariff points
GCE & AVCE Double Award	A-level with additional AS	GCE A-level and AVCE	GCE AS Double Award	GCE AS & AS VCE	
A*A*					112
A*A					104
AA					96
AB					88
BB					80
	A*A				76
BC					72
	AA				68
CC	AB				64
CD	BB	A*			56
	BC				52
DD		A			48
	CC				44
	CD				42
DE		B	AA		40
			AB		36
	DD				34
EE		C	BB		32
	DE				30
			BC		28
		D	CC		24
	EE		CD		22
			DD	A	20
		E	DE	B	16
			EE	C	12
				D	10
				E	6

Scottish Highers/Advanced Highers

Grade	Higher	Advanced Higher
A	33	56
B	27	48
C	21	40
D	15	32

Advanced Welsh Baccalaureate – Skills Challenge Certificate (first teaching September 2015 and first award 2017)

Grade	Tariff points
A*	56
A	48
B	40
C	32
D	24
E	16

IB International Baccalaureate Diploma

Whilst the IB Diploma does not attract UCAS Tariff points, the constituent qualifications of the IB Diploma do, so the total Tariff points for an IB Diploma can be calculated by adding together each of the following four components:

IB Certificate in Higher Level

Grade	Tariff points
H7	56
H6	48
H5	32
H4	24
H3	12
H2	0
H1	0

Size band: 4
Grade bands: 3–14

IB Certificate in Standard Level

Grade	Tariff points
S7	28
S6	24
S5	16
S4	12
S3	6
S2	0
S1	0

Size band: 2
Grade bands: 3–14

IB Certificate in Extended Essay

Grade	Tariff points
A	12
B	10
C	8
D	6
E	4

Size band: 1
Grade bands 4–12

IB Certificate in Theory of Knowledge

Grade	Tariff points
A	12
B	10
C	8
D	6
E	4

Size band: 1
Grade bands: 4–12

Certificates in Extended Essay and Theory of Knowledge are awarded Tariff points when the certificates have been taken individually.

BTEC

Grade	Tariff points
D*D*D*	168
D*D*D	160
D*DD	152
DDD	144
DDM	128
DMM	112
MMM	96
MMP	80
MPP	64
PPP	48

Size band: 4+4+4 = 12
Grade bands: 4–14

Extended Project – Stand alone

Grade	Tariff points
A*	28
A	24
B	20
C	16
D	12
E	8

Music examinations

Performance			Theory			Tariff points
Grade 8	Grade 7	Grade 6	Grade 8	Grade 7	Grade 6	
D						30
M						24
P						18
	D					16
	M	D				12
	P	M	D			10
			M			9
		P	D			8
			M			7
		P		P	D	6
					M	5
					P	4

Additional points will be awarded for music examinations from the Associated Board of the Royal Schools of Music (ABRSM), University of West London, Rockschool and Trinity Guildhall/Trinity College London (music examinations at grades 6, 7, 8 (D=Distinction; M=Merit; P=Pass)).

Art and Design Foundation Studies

Grade	Tariff points
D	112
M	96
P	80

Size band: 4+4 = 8
Grade bands: 10–14

NB Full acknowledgement is made to UCAS for this information. For further details of all qualifications awarded UCAS Tariff points see www.ucas.com/advisers/guides-and-resources/tariff-2017. Note that the Tariff is constantly updated and new qualifications are introduced each year.

APPENDIX 2
INTERNATIONAL QUALIFICATIONS

Universities in the UK accept a range of international qualifications and those which normally satisfy the minimum general entrance requirements are listed below. However, the specific levels of achievement or grades required for entry to degree courses with international qualifications will vary, depending on the popularity of the university or college and the chosen degree programme. The subject tables in **Chapter 7** provide a guide to the levels of entry to courses although direct comparisons between A-level grades and international qualifications are not always possible except for the three European examinations listed at the end of this Appendix. Students not holding the required qualifications should consider taking an International Foundation course.

International students whose mother tongue is not English and/or who have not studied for their secondary education in English will be required to pass an English test such as IELTS (International English Language Testing System) or TOEFL (the Test of English as a Foreign Language). Entry requirements vary between universities and courses. For the IELTS, scores can range from 5.5 to 7.5, for the TOEFL internet-based test, scores range from 0–120 (see www.ielts.org and www.ets.org/toefl).

Algeria Baccalaureate de l'Enseignement Secondaire
Argentina Completion of Year One of a Bachelor degree
Australia Completion of Year 12 certificates
Austria Reifazeugnis/Maturazeugnis
Bahrain Two-year diploma or associate degree
Bangladesh Bachelor of Arts, Science and Commerce
Belgium Certificat d'Enseignement Secondaire Superieur
Bermuda Diploma of Arts and Science
Bosnia-Herzegovina Secondary School Leaving Diploma
Brazil Completion of Ensino Medio and a good pass in the Vestibular
Brunei Brunei GCE A-level
Bulgaria Diploma za Zavarshino Sredno Obrazovanie (Diploma of Completed Secondary Education)
Canada Completion of Grade 12 secondary/high school certificate or equivalent
Chile Completion of Year one of a Bachelor degree
China Completion of one year of a Bachelor degree from a recognised university with good grades
Croatia Matura (Secondary school leaving diploma)
Cyprus Apolytirion/Lise Bitirme Diploma with good grades
Czech Republic Vysvedceni o Maturitni Zkousce/Maturita
Denmark Studentereksamen (HF), (HHX), (HTX)
Egypt Completion of year one of a Bachelor degree or two-year Diploma
Finland Ylioppilastutkinoto/Studentexamen (Matriculation certificate)
France French Baccalauréat
Gambia West African Senior Secondary Certificate Exam (WASSCE) Advanced Level
Georgia Successful completion of Year One of a Bachelor degree
Germany Abitur
Ghana West African Senior Secondary Certificate Exam (WASSCE)/A-levels
Greece Apolytirion of Eniaio Lykeio (previously Apolytirion of Lykeio)
Hong Kong A-levels/HKALE
Hungary Erettsegi/Matura
Iceland Studentsprof
India High grades from Standard XII School Leaving examinations from certain examination boards

Ireland Irish Leaving Certificate Higher Level
Israel Bagrut
Italy Diploma Conseguito con l'Esame di Stato (formerly the Diploma di Matura) with good grades
Japan Upper Secondary School leaving diploma/Kotogakko Sotsugyo Shomeisho plus Foundation year
Kenya Cambridge Overseas Higher School Certificate
Lebanon Lebanese Baccalaureate plus Foundation year
Malaysia Sijil Tinggi Persekolahan Malaysia (STPM, Malaysia Higher School Certificate)
Mauritius Cambridge Overseas Higher School Certificate or A-levels
Mexico Bachillerato plus Foundation year
Netherlands Voorbereidend Wetenschappelijk Onderwijs (VWO)
Nigeria Successful completion of year one of a Bachelor degree
Norway Diploma of a completed 3-year course of upper secondary education
Pakistan Bachelor degree
Poland Matura
Portugal Diploma de Ensino Secundario
Russian Federation Diploma of completed Specialised Secondary Education or successful completion of first year of Bakalav
Saudi Arabia Successful completion of first year of a Bachelor degree
Serbia and Montenegro Matura
Singapore Polytechnic Diploma or A-levels
South Korea Junior College Diploma
Spain Curso de Orientacion Universitaria (COU) with good grades
Sri Lanka A-levels
Sweden Fullstandigt Slutbetyg fran Gymnasieskolan
Taiwan Senior High school Diploma
Thailand Successful completion of year one of a Bachelor degree
Turkey Devlet Lise Diplomasi (State High School Diploma) with good grades
Uganda Uganda Advanced Certificate of Education (UACE) or East African Advanced Certificate of Education
Ukraine Successful completion of year one of a Bachelor degree
USA Good grades from the High School Graduation Diploma with SAT and/or APT

COMPARISONS BETWEEN A-LEVEL GRADES AND THE FOLLOWING EUROPEAN EXAMINATIONS

A-level grades	AAA	AAB	ABB	BBB	BBC	BCC
European Baccalaureate	85%	80%	77%	75%	73%	70%
French Baccalauréat	14 Bien	13 Assez Bien	13 Assez Bien	12 Assez Bien	12 Assez Bien	11 Passable
German Abitur	1.3–1.5	1.5–1.6	1.7–1.8	1.8–2.0	2.0–2.2	2.2–2.4

APPENDIX 3
PROFESSIONAL ASSOCIATIONS

Professional associations vary in size and function and many offer examinations to provide members with vocational qualifications. However, many of the larger bodies do not conduct examinations but accept evidence provided by the satisfactory completion of appropriate degree and diploma courses. When applying for courses in vocational subjects, therefore, it is important to check whether your chosen course is accredited by a professional association, since membership of such bodies is usually necessary for progression in your chosen career after graduation.

Information about careers, which you can use as background information for your UCAS application, can be obtained from the organisations below listed under the subject table headings used in **Chapter 7**. Full details of professional associations, their examinations and the degree courses accredited by them are published in *British Qualifications* (see **Appendix 4**).

Some additional organisations that can provide useful careers-related information are listed below under the subject table headings and other sources of relevant information are indicated in the subject tables of **Chapter 7** and in **Appendix 4**.

Accountancy/Accounting
Accounting Technicians Ireland www.accountingtechniciansireland.ie
Association of Accounting Technicians www.aat.org.uk
Association of Chartered Certified Accountants www.accaglobal.com
Association of International Accountants www.aiaworldwide.com
Chartered Accountants Ireland www.charteredaccountants.ie
Chartered Institute of Internal Auditors www.iia.org.uk
Chartered Institute of Management Accountants www.cimaglobal.com
Chartered Institute of Public Finance and Accountancy www.cipfa.org
Chartered Institute of Taxation www.tax.org.uk
Institute of Chartered Accountants in England and Wales www.icaew.com
Institute of Chartered Accountants of Scotland www.icas.com
Institute of Financial Accountants www.ifa.org.uk

Actuarial Science/Studies
Institute and Faculty of Actuaries www.actuaries.org.uk

Agricultural Sciences/Agriculture
Innovation for Agriculture www.innovationforagriculture.org.uk

Animal Sciences
British Horse Society www.bhs.org.uk
British Society of Animal Science www.bsas.org.uk

Anthropology
Association of Social Anthropologists of the UK and Commonwealth www.theasa.org
Royal Anthropological Institute www.therai.org.uk

Archaeology
Chartered Institute for Archaeologists www.archaeologists.net
Council for British Archaeology new.archaeologyuk.org

Architecture
Chartered Institute of Architectural Technologists www.ciat.org.uk
Royal Incorporation of Architects in Scotland www.rias.org.uk
Royal Institute of British Architects www.architecture.com

Art and Design
Arts Council England www.artscouncil.org.uk
Association of Illustrators www.theaoi.com
Association of Photographers www.the-aop.org
British Association of Art Therapists www.baat.org
British Association of Paintings Conservator-Restorers www.bapcr.org.uk
British Institute of Professional Photography www.bipp.com
Chartered Society of Designers www.csd.org.uk
Crafts Council www.craftscouncil.org.uk
Creative Scotland www.creativescotland.com
Design Council www.designcouncil.org.uk
Institute of Conservation www.icon.org.uk
Institute of Professional Goldsmiths www.ipgoldsmiths.com
National Society for Education in Art and Design www.nsead.org
Royal British Society of Sculptors www.rbs.org.uk
Textile Institute www.texi.org

Astronomy/Astrophysics
Royal Astronomical Society www.ras.org.uk

Biochemistry (see also Chemistry)
Association for Clinical Biochemistry and Laboratory Medicine www.acb.org.uk
Biochemical Society www.biochemistry.org
British Society for Immunology www.immunology.org

Biological Sciences/Biology
British Society for Genetic Medicine www.bsgm.org.uk
Genetics Society www.genetics.org.uk
Institute of Biomedical Science www.ibms.org
Royal Society of Biology www.rsb.org.uk

Building and Construction
Chartered Institute of Building www.ciob.org
Chartered Institution of Building Services Engineers www.cibse.org
Construction Industry Training Board (CITB) www.citb.co.uk

Business and Management Courses
Chartered Institute of Personnel and Development www.cipd.co.uk
Chartered Institute of Public Relations www.cipr.co.uk
Chartered Management Institute www.managers.org.uk
Communications Advertising and Marketing (CAM) Education Foundation
    www.camfoundation.com
Department for Business, Innovation, and Skills www.bis.gov.uk
Institute of Administrative Management www.instam.org
Institute of Chartered Secretaries and Administrators www.icsa.org.uk
Institute of Consulting www.iconsulting.org.uk
Institute of Export www.export.org.uk
Institute of Practitioners in Advertising www.ipa.co.uk
Institute of Sales and Marketing Management www.ismm.co.uk
Skills CFA www.skillscfa.org

Chemistry
National Nanotechnology Initiative www.nano.gov
Royal Society of Chemistry www.rsc.org

Computer Courses
BCS The Chartered Institute for IT www.bcs.org
Institution of Analysts and Programmers www.iap.org.uk
Learning and Performance Institute www.learningandperformanceinstitute.com

Consumer Studies/Sciences
Chartered Trading Standards Institute www.tradingstandards.uk

Dance
Council for Dance Education and Training www.cdet.org.uk

Dentistry
British Association of Dental Nurses www.badn.org.uk
British Association of Dental Therapists www.badt.org.uk
British Dental Association www.bda.org
British Society of Dental Hygiene and Therapy www.bsdht.org.uk
Dental Laboratories Association www.dla.org.uk
Dental Technologists Association www.dta-uk.org
General Dental Council www.gdc-uk.org

Dietetics
British Dietetic Association www.bda.uk.com

Drama
Equity www.equity.org.uk
Society of British Theatre Designers www.theatredesign.org.uk

Economics
Royal Economic Society www.res.org.uk

Education and Teacher Training
Department for Education www.education.gov.uk
Education Workforce Council www.ewc.wales
General Teaching Council for Northern Ireland www.gtcni.org.uk
General Teaching Council for Scotland www.gtcs.org.uk

Engineering/Engineering Sciences
Energy Institute www.energyinst.org
Engineering Council UK www.engc.org.uk
Institute for Manufacturing www.ifm.eng.cam.ac.uk
Institute of Acoustics www.ioa.org.uk
Institute of Marine Engineering, Science and Technology www.imarest.org
Institution of Agricultural Engineers www.iagre.org
Institution of Civil Engineers www.ice.org.uk
Institution of Engineering Designers www.institution-engineering-designers.org.uk
Institution of Engineering and Technology www.theiet.org
Institution of Mechanical Engineers www.imeche.org
Nuclear Institute www.nuclearinst.com
Royal Aeronautical Society www.aerosociety.com

Environmental Science/Studies
Chartered Institute of Ecology and Environmental Management www.cieem.net
Chartered Institute of Environmental Health www.cieh.org
Chartered Institution of Wastes Management www.ciwm.co.uk
Chartered Institution of Water and Environmental Management www.ciwem.org
Environment Agency www.environment-agency.gov.uk
Institution of Environmental Sciences www.theies-uk.org.uk
Institution of Occupational Safety and Health www.iosh.co.uk
Royal Environmental Health Institute of Scotland www.rehis.com
Society for the Environment www.socenv.org.uk

Film, Radio, Video and TV Studies
British Film Institute www.bfi.org.uk
Creative Skillset (National Training Organisation for broadcast, film, video and multimedia) www.creative
 skillset.org

Finance (including Banking and Insurance)
Chartered Banker www.charteredbanker.com
Chartered Institute of Loss Adjusters www.cila.co.uk
Chartered Insurance Institute www.cii.co.uk
Chartered Institute for Securities and Investment www.cisi.org
Financial Skills Partnership www.financialskillspartnership.org.uk
IFS University College www.ifslearning.ac.uk
Personal Finance Society www.thepfs.org

Food Science/Studies and Technology
Institute of Food Science and Technology www.ifst.org
Society of Food Hygiene and Technology www.sofht.co.uk

Forensic Science
Chartered Society of Forensic Sciences www.csofs.org

Forestry
Institute of Chartered Foresters www.charteredforesters.org
Wood Technology Society www.worldtechnologysociety.org
Royal Forestry Society www.rfs.org.uk

Geography
British Cartographic Society www.cartography.org.uk
Royal Geographical Society www.rgs.org
Royal Meteorological Society www.rmets.org

Geology/Geological Sciences
Geological Society www.geolsoc.org.uk

Health Sciences/Studies
British Academy of Audiology www.baaudiology.org
British and Irish Orthoptic Society www.orthoptics.org.uk
British Association of Prosthetists and Orthotists www.bapo.com
British Chiropractic Association www.chiropractic-uk.co.uk
British Occupational Hygiene Society www.bohs.org
General Osteopathic Council www.osteopathy.org.uk
Institute for Complementary and Natural Medicine www.icnm.org.uk
Institution of Occupational Safety and Health www.iosh.co.uk
Institute of Osteopathy www.osteopathy.org
Society of Homeopaths www.homeopathy-soh.org

History
Royal Historical Society www.royalhistsoc.org

Horticulture
Institute of Horticulture www.horticulture.org.uk

Hospitality and Event Management
Institute of Hospitality www.instituteofhospitality.org
People 1st www.people1st.co.uk

Housing
Chartered Institute of Housing www.cih.org

Human Resource Management and Librarianship
Chartered Institute of Personnel and Development www.cipd.co.uk

Information Management
Association for Information Management www.aslib.co.uk
Chartered Institute of Library and Information Professionals www.cilip.org.uk

Landscape Architecture
Landscape Institute www.landscapeinstitute.org

Languages
Chartered Institute of Linguists www.ciol.org.uk
Institute of Translation and Interpreting www.iti.org.uk

Law
Bar Council www.barcouncil.org.uk
Chartered Institute of Legal Executives www.cilex.org.uk
Faculty of Advocates www.advocates.org.uk
Law Society of England and Wales www.lawsociety.org.uk
Law Society of Northern Ireland www.lawsoc-ni.org
Law Society of Scotland www.lawscot.org.uk

Leisure and Recreation Management/Studies
Chartered Institute for the Management of Sport and Physical Activity www.cimspa.co.uk

Linguistics
British Association for Applied Linguistics www.baal.org.uk
Royal College of Speech and Language Therapists www.rcslt.org

Marine/Maritime Studies
Nautical Institute www.nautinst.org

Marketing (including Public Relations)
Chartered Institute of Marketing www.cim.co.uk
Chartered Institute of Public Relations www.cipr.co.uk
Institute of Sales and Marketing Management www.ismm.co.uk

Materials Science/Metallurgy
Institute of Materials, Minerals and Mining www.iom3.org

Mathematics
Council for the Mathematical Sciences www.cms.ac.uk

Institute of Mathematics and its Applications www.ima.org.uk
London Mathematical Society www.lms.ac.uk
Mathematical Association www.m-a.org.uk

Media Studies
British Broadcasting Corporation www.bbc.co.uk/careers/home
National Council for the Training of Journalists www.nctj.com
Creative Skillset (National training organisation for broadcast, film, video and multimedia) www.creative
    skillset.org
Society for Editors and Proofreaders www.sfep.org.uk
Society of Authors www.societyofauthors.org

Medicine
British Medical Association www.bma.org.uk
General Medical Council www.gmc-uk.org
Institute for Complementary and Natural Medicine www.icnm.org.uk

Microbiology (see also Biological Sciences/Biology)
Microbiology Society www.microbiologysociety.org

Music
Incorporated Society of Musicians www.ism.org
Institute of Musical Instrument Technology www.imit.org.uk

Naval Architecture
Royal Institution of Naval Architects www.rina.org.uk

Neuroscience
InnerBody www.innerbody.com
Instant Anatomy www.instantanatomy.net

Nursing and Midwifery
Community Practitioners' and Health Visitors' Association www.unitetheunion.org/cphva
Health and Social Care in Northern Ireland http://online.hscni.net
Nursing and Midwifery Council www.nmc-uk.org
Royal College of Midwives www.rcm.org.uk
Royal College of Nursing www.rcn.org.uk

Nutrition (see Dietetics)

Occupational Therapy
British Association/College of Occupational Therapists www.cot.co.uk

Optometry
Association of British Dispensing Opticians www.abdo.org.uk
British and Irish Orthoptic Society www.orthoptics.org.uk
College of Optometrists www.college-optometrists.org
General Optical Council www.optical.org

Pharmacology
British Toxicology Society www.thebts.org
Royal Pharmaceutical Society of Great Britain www.rpharms.com

Pharmacy
Royal Pharmaceutical Society of Great Britain www.rpharms.com

Photography
Association of Photographers www.the-aop.org
British Institute of Professional Photography www.bipp.com
Royal Photographic Society www.rps.org

Physical Education (see Education Studies and Teacher Training and Sports Sciences/Studies)

Physics
Institute of Physics www.iop.org
Institute of Physics and Engineering in Medicine www.ipem.ac.uk

Physiotherapy
Association of Chartered Physiotherapists in Animal Therapy www.acpat.org
Chartered Society of Physiotherapy www.csp.org.uk

Plant Sciences (see Biological Sciences/Biology)

Podiatry
Society of Chiropodists and Podiatrists www.scpod.org

Property Management and Surveying
Chartered Institute of Building www.ciob.org
Chartered Surveyors Training Trust www.cstt.org.uk
National Association of Estate Agents www.naea.co.uk
Royal Institution of Chartered Surveyors www.rics.org

Psychology
British Psychological Society www.bps.org.uk

Radiography
Society and College of Radiographers www.sor.org

Social Work
Care Council for Wales www.ccwales.org.uk
Health and Care Professions Council www.hpc-uk.org
Northern Ireland Social Care Council www.niscc.info
Scottish Social Services Council www.sssc.uk.com

Sociology
British Sociological Association www.britsoc.co.uk

Speech Pathology/Sciences/Therapy
Royal College of Speech and Language Therapists www.rcslt.org

Sports Sciences/Studies
British Association of Sport and Exercise Sciences www.bases.org.uk
Chartered Institute for the Management of Sport and Physical Activity www.cimspa.co.uk
English Institute of Sport www.eis2win.co.uk
Society of Sports Therapists www.society-of-sports-therapists.org
Sport England www.sportengland.org
Sportscotland www.sportscotland.org.uk
Sportscotland Institute of Sport www.sportscotland.org.uk/sisport
Sport Wales www.sportwales.org.uk
Sports Institute Northern Ireland www.sini.co.uk
UK Sport www.uksport.gov.uk

Statistics
Royal Statistical Society www.rss.org.uk

Tourism and Travel
Institute of Travel and Tourism www.itt.co.uk

Town and Country Planning
Royal Town Planning Institute www.rtpi.org.uk

Transport Management and Planning
Chartered Institute of Logistics and Transport www.ciltuk.org.uk

Veterinary Science/Medicine/Nursing
Association of Chartered Physiotherapists in Animal Therapy www.acpat.org
British Veterinary Nursing Association www.bvna.org.uk
Royal College of Veterinary Surgeons www.rcvs.org.uk
Royal Veterinary College www.rvc.ac.uk

Zoology
Royal Entomological Society www.royensoc.co.uk
Zoological Society of London www.zsl.org

APPENDIX 4
BOOKLIST AND USEFUL WEBSITES

Unless otherwise stated, the publications in this list are all available from Trotman Publishing.

STANDARD REFERENCE BOOKS
British Qualifications 2016, 46th edition, Kogan Page
British Vocational Qualifications, 12th edition, Kogan Page

OTHER BOOKS AND RESOURCES
Choosing Your Degree Course & University, 14th edition, Brian Heap
Destinations of Leavers from Higher Education 2013/14, Higher Education Statistics Agency Services (available from HESA)
Getting into course guides: Art & Design Courses, Business & Economics Courses, Dental School, Engineering Courses, Law, Medical School, Nursing & Midwifery, Oxford & Cambridge, Pharmacy and Pharmacology Courses, Physiotherapy Courses, Psychology Courses, Veterinary School
A Guide to Uni Life, Lucy Tobin
How to Complete Your UCAS Application: 2017 Entry, Beryl Dixon
How to Write a Winning UCAS Personal Statement, 3rd edition, Ian Stannard
Studying Abroad, 5th edition, Cerys Evans
Studying and Learning at University, Alan Pritchard, SAGE Study Skills Series
The Times Good University Guide 2016, John O'Leary, Times Books
Your Gap Year, 7th edition, Susan Griffith, Crimson Publishing

USEFUL WEBSITES
Education, course and applications information
www.gov.uk/browse/education
www.erasmusplus.org.uk
www.hesa.ac.uk
www.opendays.com (information on university and college Open Days)
http://unistats.direct.gov.uk (official information from UK universities and colleges for comparing courses)
www.ucas.com
www.disabilityrightsuk.org

Careers information
www.army.mod.uk/join
www.aspire-igen.com/aspire-international
www.careerconnect.org.uk
www.insidecareers.co.uk
www.isco.org.uk
www.milkround.com
www.healthcareers.nhs.uk
www.prospects.ac.uk
www.socialworkandcarejobs.com
www.tomorrowsengineers.org.uk
www.trotman.co.uk

Gap Years
www.etrust.org.uk/the-year-in-industry (Year in Industry)
www.gapyear.com
www.gap-year.com

Study overseas
www.acu.ac.uk
www.allaboutcollege.com
www.fulbright.org.uk
www.thirdyearabroad.com

COURSE INDEX

INDEX OF ADVERTISERS